AA

Bed & Breakfast 1999

AA Lifestyle Guides

Produced by AA Publishing

Atlas prepared by the AA's Cartographic Department

Directory generated by the AA Establishment Database,
Information Research and Control, Hotel and Touring Services

Advertisements

Head of Advertisement Sales: Christopher Heard Tel. 01256 491544

Advertisement Production: Karen Weeks Tel. 01256 491545

Typeset/Reprographics by Avonset, Bath
Printed and bound in Italy by Printer Trento srl
Cover photograph: Millbrook Farmhouse, Axminster
Illustrations by Alan Rowe, Alton

The contents of this publication are believed correct at the time of printing. Nevertheless the Publisher cannot be held responsible for any errors or omissions or for changes in the details given in this guide or for the consequences of any reliance on the information provided in the same. Although every effort has been made to ensure accuracy we always welcome any information from readers to assist in such efforts and to keep the book up to date.

Assessments of the establishments in this guide are based on the experience(s) of the AA's professional hotel and restaurant inspectors on the occasion(s) of their visit(s) and therefore the descriptions given in this guide may contain an element of subjective opinion which may not dictate a reader's experience on another occasion.

A CIP catalogue record for this book is available from the British Library

Published by AA Publishing which is a trading name of Automobile Association Developments Limited whose registered office is Norfolk House, Basingstoke, Hampshire RG24 9NY
Registered number: 1878835
AA Ref 10190 **ISBN 0749519320**

CONTENTS

AA QUALITY ASSESSMENT

HOW THE AA APPLIES QUALITY STANDARDS TO GUEST ACCOMMODATION AND WHAT THE Q AWARDS MEAN

Inspection Procedures

Establishments applying for AA quality assessment are visited on a 'mystery guest' basis by one of the AA's team of qualified accommodation inspectors. The inspector will stay overnight to make a thorough test of the accommodation, food, and hospitality offered, and only after settling the bill the following morning will he/she declare identity and ask to be shown round the premises. The inspector will then complete a full report, making a recommendation for the appropriate quality level.

After this first visit, the establishment will receive an annual visit to check that standards are maintained. If it changes hands, the new owners must re-apply for classification, as AA recognition is not transferable.

In the 1990s, a guest can expect to find the following minimum standards in Guest Accommodation at all Q levels:

a pleasant, professional check in and check out, with a properly prepared bill.

clean, comfortable, secure accommodation, with bedrooms equipped to modern standards, large enough to allow guests freedom of movement.

beds, bedding and other bedroom furniture and appointments in good condition. Bedding and towels changed for each new guest, and at least weekly if the room is taken for a long stay. Additional pillows and blankets available on request.

adequate lighting and comfortable seating, a wardrobe or properly fitted hanging alcove, and shelves or drawers.

lined curtains or blinds correctly fitted and functioning.

adequate, clean and comfortable floor covering with bedside rugs, or fitted carpets.

proper attention to hygiene in bathrooms and WCs; adequate provision of toilet tissue and fresh soap.

adequate heating at no extra cost, and extra heating available at no extra cost on request.

a sufficient hot water supply at reasonable times.

well prepared, wholesome meals served at reasonable times, and presented in an appetising manner.

What the Q Awards denote

The Q awards assess guest accommodation at five levels of quality, from one Q at the simplest, to 5 Q s at the luxury end of the spectrum. The awards take into account the level of comfort and degree of style and quality of the furnishings and decor throughout the establishment; the levels of service and hospitality displayed by owners and staff; the friendliness of the atmosphere; last but not least, the quality of the meals.

At all Q levels, cleanliness and good housekeeping are of the highest importance.

At 1 Q level

Clean, secure accommodation, with adequate bathroom facilities, and providing an acceptable standard of comfort and food, including a cooked breakfast

At 2 Q level

Likely to have some bedrooms with en suite or private bathrooms

Greater degree of quality and comfort in the furnishings and decor than at the one Q level

At 3 Q level

A degree of professionalism from the staff, with guests shown to their rooms, and offered help with luggage. Explanation of facilities volunteered.

At least 40 per cent of bedrooms will have en suite or private bathrooms, and other facilities (e.g. tea and coffee making equipment, TVs).

Good quality furnishing and decor, with pleasing colour schemes.

Freshly cooked, carefully prepared food, with a good choice of items at breakfast (e.g. cereals, fruit juices, preserves, tea and coffee).

At 4 Q level

Warm welcome and efficient registration on arrival, with offer of refreshment. Attentive service throughout the stay.

High quality accommodation, in spacious, comfortable rooms, offering a degree of luxury. There will be armchairs, ample wardrobes and drawers, a full length mirror, and well planned lighting. Amenities such as clock radios, televisions, and hair dryers will widely be available. The majority of rooms will be en suite, or have private bathrooms with an ample provision of good quality towels and toiletries.

Comfortable, attractive sitting room with armchairs, sofas, reading material and/or television

A breakfast/dining room with high quality seating and tables, attractively set good quality cutlery and tableware.

A wide choice of high-quality breakfast cereals and fruit juices, with a choice of teas and freshly made coffee and a choice of cooked dishes. Good home cooking and a well planned menu for the evening meal if provided, with an emphasis on fresh ingredients.

At 5 Q level

Here the emphasis is on excellence in every department, starting with the highest standards of hospitality and service.

Guests should be made to feel welcome and completely at home, and shown friendly attention to their wishes; nothing should seem too much trouble.

Furnishings and decor throughout should be of the highest quality, with personal touches such as ornaments, paintings and fresh flowers, especially in sitting and dining rooms, creating a home-like atmosphere. Styles of furniture and decor should be harmonious and pleasing to the eye. Fitted carpets and rugs or other floor surfaces should be of high quality and scrupulously well maintained.

Lighting and heating systems should be designed to maximise guest comfort. Beds and bedding should be of excellent standard. Bedrooms should be equipped with every modern convenience, to the highest standard, and be of generous proportions. Towels and bedding should be of the highest quality and in the case of a long stay, changed every two or three days.

Breakfast should offer a wide range of freshly prepared hot dishes, with excellent bakery and luxury cereals, fresh fruit, cheeses and cold meats. Evening meals should be based on high quality fresh ingredients, locally sourced where possible, skilfully cooked and appetisingly presented.

Check out and billing procedures should be every bit as courteous and efficient as check in procedures.

HINTS FOR BOOKING YOUR STAY

The AA inspects and classifies more than 3000 small private hotels, guest houses, farmhouses and inns for its AA Recommended, AA Selected' and AA Premier Selected categories. The precise number of places in the guide varies slightly from year to year, and we are delighted that each year we have an increase both in the total number of establishments in the guide and – as a result of continuously improving standards – in the top two categories.

Q Quality Awards

All the establishments listed in the directory are given awards of between one and five Q for quality. More details about the Q awards can be found in the section headed *'Quality Assessment'* on page 4. Those places that have gained the two highest ratings - QQQQ and QQQQQ awards - have their entries highlighted in the directory.

For quick reference, you will find a list of the establishments awarded five Q on page 14.

Common to All

Whatever the type of establishment, there are certain requirements common to all, including a well-maintained exterior, clean and hygienic kitchens; good standards of furnishing; friendly and courteous service; access to the premises at reasonable times; the use of a telephone; and a full, cooked breakfast in the British or Irish tradition.

Bedrooms should be equipped with comfortable beds, a wardrobe, a bedside cabinet, a washbasin (unless there is an en suite or private bath/shower room) with soap, towel, mirror and shaver socket and at least a carpet beside the bed. There should not be an extra charge for the use of baths or lavatories, and heating should not be metered.

NB. Where the entry for an establishment shows the central heating abbreviation, it does not necessarily mean that central heating will be available all year round. Some places only use it in winter, and then it will be at at their own discretion.

Staying at a guest house

The term *'guest house'* can lead to some confusion, particularly when many include the word 'hotel' in their name. For AA purposes, small and private hotels are included in this category when they cannot offer all the services required for our hotel star rating system.

The term does not imply that guest houses are inferior to hotels, just that they are different. Many, indeed, offer a very high standard of accommodation. It is not unusual to be offered en suite bathrooms, for instance, or to find a direct-dial telephone and a colour television in your room.

Some guest houses offer bed and breakfast only, so guests must go out for the evening meal. It is also wise to check when booking if there are any restrictions to your access to the house, particularly in the late morning and during the afternoon.

However, many guest houses do provide an evening meal. They may only be able to offer a set meal, but many offer an interesting menu and a standard of service that one would expect in a good restaurant. You may have to arrange dinner in advance, so you should ask about the arrangements for evening meals when booking. Many places have a full licence, or at least a table licence and wine list.

London

Guest houses in the London section of the book are all small hotels. London prices tend to be higher than outside the capital, but those that we list offer cost-conscious accommodation, although normally only bed and breakfast is provided. We have also included a few which provide a full meal service and the charges for these will naturally be higher.

Staying at a farmhouse

Farmhouse accommodation is particularly noted for being inexpensive and cosy, with a high standard of good home-cooking. Those listed in our book are generally working farms, and some farmers are happy to allow visitors to look around, or even to help feed the animals. However, we must stress that the modern farm is a potentially dangerous place, especially where machinery and chemicals are concerned, and visitors must be prepared to exercise care, particularly if they bring children.

Never leave children unsupervised around the farm.

Sometimes, guest accommodation is run as a separate concern from the farm, and visitors are discouraged from venturing on to the working land. In other cases, the land has been sold off and only the house remains. Although the directory entry states the acreage and the type of farming carried out, you should check when booking to make sure that it matches your expectations.

As with guest houses, standards will vary considerably, and are often far above what one would expect. Some of our farmhouses are grand ex-manor houses furnished with antiques and offering a stylish way of life, whereas others offer more simply furnished accommodation, and in others guests may have to share the family bathroom and sitting/dining room.

Off the beaten track

All of the farmhouses are listed under town or village names, but obviously many will be some distance from any other habitation. The owners will, of course, give directions when you book, and we publish a six-figure map reference against the directory entry which can be used in conjunction with Ordnance Survey large-scale maps like the 1:50 000 Landranger series.

Staying at a inn

We all know what we can expect to find in a traditional inn – a cosy bar, a convivial atmosphere, good beer and pub food. Nevertheless, there are a few extra criteria which must be met for the AA classification: breakfast is a must, in a suitable breakfast room, and the inn should also serve at least light meals during licensing hours.

In this guide, a number of small, fully licensed hotels are classified as inns, and the character of the properties will vary according to whether they are traditional country inns or larger establishments in towns. Again it is important to check details before you book, and also remember to ask if you can arrive at any time of the day or only during opening hours.

Booking

Book as early as possible, particularly for the peak holiday period from the beginning of June to the end of September, and bear in mind that Easter and other public holidays may be busy, too. In some parts of Scotland the skiing season is a peak holiday period.

Although it is possible for chance callers to find a night's accommodation, it is by no means a certainty, especially at peak holiday times and in popular areas, so it is always advisable to book as far in advance as possible. Some may only accept weekly bookings from Saturday. Some establishments will require a deposit on booking.

We have tried to provide as much information as possible about the establishments in our directory, but if you require further information, write to or telephone the establishment itself. Do remember to enclose a stamped addressed envelope, or an international reply-paid coupon if writing from overseas, and please quote this publication in any enquiry. Although we try to publish accurate and up to date information, please remember that any details, and particularly prices, are subject to change without notice and this may happen during the currency of the guide.

Smoking Regulations

'No-smoking' when used by itself in the guide indicates a total ban on smoking throughout all main areas of the premises. If only certain areas are designated no-smoking (eg bedrooms, dining room) this is shown.

Although we have tried to get accurate information on this question from the establishments, you must remember that the situation may change during the currency of this edition. If the freedom to smoke or to be in a smoke-free atmosphere is important to you, please make sure about the rules before you book.

Cancellation

If you find that you must cancel a booking, let the proprietor know at once, because if the room you booked cannot be re-let, you may be held legally responsible for partial payment. Whether it is a matter of losing your deposit, or of being liable for compensation, you should seriously consider taking out cancellation insurance, such as AA Travelsure.

Complaints

Readers who have any cause to complain are urged to do so on the spot. This should provide an opportunity for the proprietor to correct matters. If a personal approach fails, readers should inform: AA Hotel Services, Fanum House, Basingstoke, Hants, RG21 4EA.

Fire Precautions

Many of the establishments listed in the Guide are subject to the requirements of the Fire Precautions Act of 1971. As far as we can discover, every establishment in this book has applied for, and not been refused, a fire certificate.

The Fire Precautions Act does not apply to Ireland, the Channel Islands or the Isle of Man, which exercise their own rules regarding fire precautions for hotels.

Food and drink

If you intend to take dinner at an establishment, note that sometimes the meal must be ordered in advance of the actual meal time. In some cases, this may be at breakfast time, or even on the previous evening. If you have booked on bed, breakfast and evening meal terms, you may find that the tariff includes only the set menu, but, if there is one, you can usually order from the à la carte menu and pay a supplement. On Sundays, many establishments serve the main meal at midday, and provide only a cold supper in the evening.

Some establishments provide only a Continental breakfast. A full English breakfast may be available at extra charge.

In some parts of Britain, particularly in Scotland, high tea (i.e. a savoury dish followed by bread and butter, scones, cakes, etc.) is sometimes served instead of dinner, but dinner may be available as an alternative. The last time at which high tea or dinner may be ordered on weekdays is shown, but this may vary at weekends.

Licensed Premises

The directory entry will show whether or not the establishment is licensed to serve alcohol. Many places in the guest house category hold a residential or restaurant licence only, but all inns hold a full licence. Licensed premises are not obliged to remain open throughout the permitted hours, and they may do so only when they expect reasonable trade.

Note that in establishments which have registered clubs, club membership does not come into effect, nor can a drink be bought, until 48 hours after joining.

Payment

Most proprietors will only accept cheques in payment of accounts if notice is given and some form of identification (preferably a cheque card) is produced. If a hotel accepts credit or charge cards, this is shown by the appropriate credit card symbol in its directory entry (see page 13 for details).

Best Budget Bargains

Establishments that offer bed and breakfast for £18 or under are indicated by the symbol against their entry.

Prices

It should be noted that daily terms quoted throughout this publication show minimum and maximum prices for both one (s) and two persons (d) and include a full breakfast. If dinner is also included this will be indicated in parenthesis (incl. dinner). Weekly terms, where available, show minimum and maximum prices per person, which take into account minimum double occupancy and maximum single occupancy, where appropriate, and may include the price of an evening meal (wkly hlf-bd).

VAT is payable in the United Kingdom and in the Isle of Man, on both basic prices and any service. VAT does not apply in the Channel Islands. With this exception, prices quoted in the Guide are inclusive of VAT (and service where applicable).

You should always confirm the current prices before making a booking. Those given in this book have been provided by proprietors in good faith, and must be accepted as indications rather than firm quotations.

Unconfirmed prices

In some cases, proprietors have been unable to provide us with their 1999 charges, but to give you a rough guide we publish the 1998 price, prefixed with an asterisk (*). It is also a good idea to ascertain all that is included in the price. Weekly terms can vary according to the meals that are included. We cannot indicate whether or not you are able to arrive mid-week, so if this is your intention, do check when making your reservation. Where information about 1999 prices is not given, you are requested to make enquiries direct.

The Republic of Ireland

Prices for the Republic of Ireland are shown in Irish punts. At the time of going to press (August 1998), the exchange rate is one Punt = £1.18 Sterling.

USEFUL INFORMATION - IRELAND

Map References

In the Irish Directory, the six-figure map references shown against establishments have been taken from the Irish National Grid.

Prices

In the Republic, prices are quoted in Punts, indicated by the symbol IR£. Please consult your bank or the daily paper for the current exchange rate. Hotels must display tariffs, either in the bedrooms or at reception. Application of VAT and service charges varies, but all prices quoted must be inclusive of VAT.

Telephone Numbers

Area codes shown against the numbers in the Republic of Ireland are applicable only within the Republic. If dialling from outside, you will need to check with the telephone directory. The area codes shown for Britain and Northern Ireland cannot be used directly from the Republic.

Please also see note on telephone numbers in the Republic of Ireland

Fire Precautions

Northern Ireland: The Fire Services (NI) Order 1984 covers establishments accommodating more than 6 persons, and they must have a fire certificate issued by the Northern Ireland Fire Authority. Places accommodating fewer than 6 persons must have adequate exits.

Republic of Ireland:

Safety regulations are a matter for local authority regulations, but AA officials inspect emergency notices, fire-fighting equipment and fire exits.

For your own and others' safety, you must read the emergency notices displayed and be sure you understand them.

Licensing Regulations

Northern Ireland: public houses open from 11.30 - 23.00, and on Sun 12.30 - 14.30 and 19.00 - 22.00. Hotels can serve residents without restriction. Non-residents can be served from 12.30 - 22.00 on Christmas Day. Children under 18 are not allowed in the bar area and may neither buy nor consume liquor in hotels.

Republic of Ireland: general licensing hours at present are 10.30 - 23.00 (23.30 in summer), Mon - Sat. On Sun and St Patrick's Day (17 March) 12.30 - 14.00 and 16.00 - 23.00.

Hotels can serve residents without restriction. There is no service on Christmas or Good Friday.

Codes of Practice

The Hotel Industry Voluntary Code of Booking Practice was revised in 1986, and the AA encourages its use in appropriate establishments. Its prime object is to ensure that the customer is clear about the precise services and facilities s/he is buying and what price will have to be paid, before entering into a contractually binding agreement. If the price has not been previously confirmed in writing, the guest should be handed a card at the time of registration, stipulating the total obligatory charge.

The Tourism (Sleeping Accommodation Price Display) Order 1977 compels hotels, motels, guest houses, farmhouses, inns and self-catering accommodation with four or more letting bedrooms to display in entrance halls the minimum and maximum prices charged for each category of room. This order complements the Voluntary Code of Booking Practice. The tariffs quoted in the directory of this book may be affected in the coming year by inflation, variations in the rate of VAT and many other factors.

SYMBOLS & ABBREVIATIONS

Bed and breakfast for £18 or under	
Quality assessment (see p.4)	Q
Telephone number	☎
Private bath and WC	**bth**
Private shower and WC	**shr**
1998 prices	*
Full central heating	**Cen ht**
On-site parking for cars	**P**
Special facilities for children (see p.13)	**ch fac**
Single room including breakfast per person per night	**s**
Double room (2 persons sharing a room) including breakfast per night	**d**
Member of the Blue Book Consortium	IRELAND'S BLUE BOOK
Children Friendly (see p.25)	

Child Free Zone (see p.25)	
Best British Breakfast Award (see p.28)	
Weekly terms, bed and breakfast, per person	**b&b wkly**
Weekly terms bed, breakfast and evening meal, per person	**wkly hlf-bd**
A la carte	**alc**
Lounge with colour television	**CTV**
Easter	**Etr**
Family bedroom	**fmly**
From	**fr**
Time last dinner can be ordered	**Last d**
Letting bedrooms in main building	**rm**
Restricted service	**rs**
Credit cards (see p.13)	

The example of an entry below is intended to help you find your way through the directory.

SAMPLE ENTRY (fictitious)

1 **CHESTER** Cheshire Map **07** SJ46

2 QQQQ **Mikes Layby** 17 City Wall XY21 1AB (3) (2m W off A30) (4)

5 ☎ 01222 333333 FAX 01222 333334

6 Closed 2 wks Xmas rs Jan

7 A lovely Victorian rectory. There is a sun lounge. Breakfast is hearty. There are also vegetarian dishes at dinner.

8 14 bth/shr (1 fmly) No smoking in 4 bedrooms No smoking area of dining room CTV in all bedrooms No dogs Fishing Golf 18 Last d 6pm

9 ROOMS: s £12.50-£15.50; d £26-£31
MEALS: Lunch £6-£9alc Dinner £8-£10alc*

10 CARDS:

HOW TO USE THIS GUIDE

1) Towns are listed in alphabetical order under each country: England, Channel Islands, Isle of Man, Scotland, Wales, Northern Ireland and the Republic of Ireland.

The town name is followed by the administrative county or region.

The map reference denotes the map page number, followed by the National Grid Reference. To find the location, read the first figure across and the second figure vertically within the lettered square.

2 a) This symbol indicates that the establishment expects to provide bed and breakfast for under £18 per person, per night during 1999, but remember that circumstances and prices can change during the currency of the Guide.

b) Establishments in Britain with no identifying symbol are either guest houses or small hotels. Farmhouses are identified by the symbol, Inns by the symbol. Establishments are lisited in alphabetical order. Guest Houses and Town and Country (Ireland only) are identified by GH and T&C.

c) All establishments are rated for quality on a scale of one to five, denoted by the symbol .See page 4 for a full explanation.

3) Establishment name, address, postal code. When an establishment's name is shown in italics the particulars have not been confirmed by the proprietor. Farmhouse entries only – as they are often in remote areas, we provide a six-figure map reference which can be used with Ordnance Survey maps. This Ordnance Survey map reference is shown in italics in parenthesis after the establishment name, eg (SN191184).

4) Directions are given wherever they have been supplied by the proprietor.

5) Telephone numbers may be changed during the currency of this book in some areas. In case of difficulty, check with the operator.

6) Opening details – unless otherwise stated, the establishments are open all year, but where dates are shown they are inclusive: e.g. 'Apr-Oct' indicates that the establishment is open from the beginning of April to the end of October.

Some places are open all year, but offer a restricted service off season. The abbreviation 'rs' indicates this. It may mean either that evening meals are not served or that other facilities listed are not available. If the text does not say what the restricted services are, you should check before booking.

7) Description of the property.
Note – if there are rooms adapted for or suitable for disabled people reference may be made in the description. Guests with any form of disability should notify proprietors, so that arrangements can be made to minimise difficulties, particularly in the event of an emergency.

8) Accommodation details (For key to symbols and abbreviations, see page 11)

The first figure shows the number of letting

bedrooms. Where rooms have en suite bath or shower, the number precedes the appropriate abbreviation. Other bedrooms may be shown in this number that have a private bathroom facility adjacent.

Annexe – bedrooms available in an annexe are shown. Their standard is acceptable, but facilities may not be the same as in the main building, and it is advisable to check the nature of the accommodation and tariff before making a reservation.

fmly – indicates family bedrooms.

No smoking – if the establishment is only partly no-smoking, the areas where smoking is not permitted are shown

All CTV – means televisions permanently in bedrooms or available on request. Colour television may also be available in the lounge.

No dogs – Establishments which do not normally accept dogs may accept guide dogs. Some establishments that accept dogs may restrict the size and breed of dogs permitted and the rooms into which they may be taken. Generally, dogs are not allowed in the dining room. Check when booking the conditions under which pets are accepted.

No children – indicates that children cannot be accommodated. A minimum age may be specified (e.g. No children 4 yrs = no children under four years old). Although establishments may accept children of all ages they may not necessarily be able to provide special facilities. If you have very young children, check before booking about provisions like cots and high chairs, and any reductions made.

ch fac – indicates establishments with special facilities for children, which will include baby-sitting service or baby intercom system, playroom or playground, laundry facilities, drying and ironing facilities, cots, high chairs and special meals.

No coaches – this information is published in good faith from details supplied by the establishments concerned. Inns, however, have well-defined legal obligations towards travellers, and any member with cause for complaint should take this up with the proprietor or the local licensing authority.

Additional facilities – such as lifts or any leisure activities available are listed.

9) Price Guide: Rooms – these are prices per night. **s** – Bed and breakfast per person; **d** – Bed and breakfast two persons.

wkly b+b – indicates the cost of bed and breakfast for one week;

wkly hlf-bd - means price includes dinner. The price range indicates the minumum and maximum during the year. For a full explanation see page 9.

Prices given have been provided by the owner in good faith, and are indications rather than firm quotations. Some establishments offer free accommodation to children provided they share the parents' room. Check current prices before booking.

10) Payment details (the following cards or discount vouchers may be accepted, but check current details when booking)

Diners
Master Card
Visa
Connect
Switch
Delta
American Express

BEST BED & BREAKFAST - PREMIER SELECTED

A quick reference list in country and county order - England, Channel Islands, Scotland, Wales, Northern Ireland, Republic of Ireland - of all the 1999 PREMIER SELECTED QQQQQ establishments - the AA's highest rating for Guest Houses, Farmhouses, and Inns

ENGLAND

BERKSHIRE

MAIDENHEAD
Beehive Manor
☎ 01628 620980

SULHAMSTEAD
The Old Manor
☎ 01189 832423

BUCKINGHAMSHIRE

BEACONSFIELD
The George Hotel
☎ 01494 673086

NEWPORT PAGNELL
The Limes
☎ 01908 617041

CHESHIRE

CHESTER
Grove House
☎ 01829 740893
Redland Private Hotel
☎ 01244 671024

KNUTSFORD
Laburnum Cottage Guest House
☎ 01565 872464

MACCLESFIELD
Hardingland Farm Country House
☎ 01625 425759

MALPAS
Tilston Lodge
☎ 01829 250223

NANTWICH
Oakland House
☎ 01270 567134
The Limes
☎ 01270 624081

CORNWALL & ISLES OF SCILLY

CRACKINGTON HAVEN
Manor Farm
☎ 01840 230304
Trevigue Farm
☎ 01840 230418

FALMOUTH
Prospect House
☎ 01326 373198

HAYLE
Treglisson
☎ 01736 753141

LAUNCESTON
Hurdon Farm
☎ 01566 772955
Percy's at Coombeshead
☎ 01409 211236

LIZARD
Landewednack House
☎ 01326 290909

PADSTOW
St Petroc's House
☎ 01841 532700

PENZANCE
Chy-an-Mor
☎ 01736 363441
Ennys Farm
☎ 01736 740262

POLPERRO
Trenderway Farm
☎ 01503 272214

ST AUSTELL
Anchorage House Guest Lodge
☎ 01726 814071

ST BLAZEY
Nanscawen House
☎ 01726 814488

TRURO
Arrallas
☎ 01872 510379

CUMBRIA

AMBLESIDE
Grey Friar Lodge Country House Hotel
☎ 015394 33158
Rowanfield Country House
☎ 015394 33686

APPLEBY-IN-WESTMORLAND
Brampton Tower Country House
☎ 017683 53447

BORROWDALE
Hazel Bank
☎ 017687 77248

BRAMPTON
Cracrop Farm
☎ 016977 48245

CARTMEL
Uplands Hotel
☎ 015395 36248

COCKERMOUTH
Low Hall
☎ 01900 826654

CONISTON
Coniston Lodge Hotel
☎ 015394 41201
Wheelgate Country House
☎ 01539 441418

KENDAL
Lane Head Country House Hotel
☎ 01539 731283

Low Jock Scar
☎ 01539 823259

KESWICK
Derwent Cottage
☎ 017687 74838
The Grange Country House
☎ 017687 72500

KIRKBY THORE
Bridge End Farm
☎ 017683 61362

LONGTOWN
Bessiestown Farm Country Guest House
☎ 01228 577219

LORTON
New House Farm
☎ 01900 85404

LORTON
Winder Hall
☎ 01900 85107

NEAR SAWREY
Ees Wyke Country House
☎ 015394 36393

WINDERMERE
Newstead
☎ 015394 44485

DERBYSHIRE

BELPER
Dannah Farm Country Guest House
☎ 01773 550273

BUXTON
Coningsby
☎ 01298 26735

DOVERIDGE
Beeches Farmhouse
☎ 01889 590288

HOPE
Underleigh House
☎ 01433 621372

WESTON UNDERWOOD
Park View Farm
☎ 01335 360352

DEVON

AXMINSTER
Millbrook Farmhouse
☎ 01297 35351

BANTHAM
Widcombe House
☎ 01548 561084

BOVEY TRACEY
Front House Lodge
☎ 01626 832202

CHAGFORD
Parford Well
☎ 01647 433353

CHILLATON
Tor Cottage
☎ 01822 860248

CHULMLEIGH
The Old Bakehouse
☎ 01769 580074

CROYDE
The Whiteleaf
☎ 01271 890266

DARTMOUTH
Broome Court
☎ 01803 834275
Ford House
☎ 01803 834047
Hedley House
☎ 01803 835849
Nonsuch House
☎ 01803 752829

HORN'S CROSS
Lower Waytown
☎ 01237 451787

LYDFORD
Moor View House
☎ 01822 820220

LYNMOUTH
Bonnicott House
☎ 01598 753346

LYNTON
Victoria Lodge
☎ 01598 753203

MORCHARD BISHOP
Wigham
☎ 01363 877350

MORETONHAMPSTEAD
Blackaller Hotel & Restaurant
☎ 01647 440322
Gate House
☎ 01647 440479

PARKHAM
The Old Rectory
☎ 01237 451443

SOUTH MOLTON
Kerscott Farm
☎ 01769 550262

TEIGNMOUTH
Thomas Luny House
☎ 01626 772976

TIVERTON
Hornhill
☎ 01884 253352

TORQUAY
Mulberry House
☎ 01803 213639

TOTNES
The Watermans Arms
☎ 01803 732214

WHIMPLE
Woodhayes
☎ 01404 822237

DORSET

DORCHESTER
Yalbury Cottage Hotel & Restaurant
☎ 01305 262382

EVERSHOT
Rectory House
☎ 01935 83273

SHERBORNE
The Old Vicarage
☎ 01963 251117

WEYMOUTH
Esplanade Hotel
☎ 01305 783129

DURHAM, CO

DARLINGTON
Clow Beck House
☎ 01325 721075

FIR TREE
Greenhead Country House Hotel
☎ 01388 763143

ESSEX

COLCHESTER
Hockley Place
☎ 01206 251703

GLOUCESTERSHIRE

CHELTENHAM
Cleeve Hill Hotel
☎ 01242 672052
Lypiatt House
☎ 01242 224994

CHIPPING CAMPDEN
The Malt House
☎ 01386 840295

FRAMPTON ON SEVERN
The Old School House
☎ 01452 740457

GUITING POWER
Guiting Guest House
☎ 01451 850470

LECHLADE
Cottage-by-the-Church
☎ 01367 860613

OLD SODBURY
The Sodbury House Hotel
☎ 01454 312847

STOW-ON-THE-WOLD
College House
☎ 01451 832351
Crestow House
☎ 01451 830969

TETBURY
Tavern House
☎ 01666 880444

GREATER MANCHESTER

ALTRINCHAM
Ash Farm Country Guest House
☎ 0161 929 9290

HAMPSHIRE

BROCKENHURST
Thatched Cottage Hotel & Restaurant
☎ 01590 623090

FORDINGBRIDGE
The Three Lions
☎ 01425 652489

HAYLING ISLAND
Cockle Warren Cottage Hotel
☎ 01705 464961

LYMINGTON
Efford Cottage
☎ 01590 642315

RINGWOOD
Little Forest Lodge
☎ 01425 478848

ROMSEY
Highfield House
☎ 01794 340727

SWAY
The Nurse's Cottage
☎ 01590 683402

WINCHESTER
The Wykeham Arms
☎ 01962 853834

HEREFORDSHIRE

LEOMINSTER
Hills Farm
☎ 01568 750205

WHITNEY-ON-WYE
The Rhydspence Inn
☎ 01497 831262

KENT

CANTERBURY
Magnolia House
☎ 01227 765121
Thanington Hotel
☎ 01227 453227
The Old Rectory
☎ 01227 730075

PENSHURST
Swale Cottage
☎ 01892 870738

ROYAL TUNBRIDGE WELLS
Danehurst House
☎ 01892 527739
The Old Parsonage
☎ 01892 750773

SITTINGBOURNE
Hempstead House Country Hotel
☎ 01795 428020

LANCASHIRE

CARNFORTH
New Capernwray Farm
☎ 01524 734284

SLAIDBURN
Parrock Head Country Farmhouse Hotel
☎ 01200 446614

YEALAND CONYERS
The Bower
☎ 01524 734585

LONDON

LONDON E11
Lakeside
☎ 0181 989 6100

LONDON N4
Mount View
☎ 0181 340 9222

LONDON N4
Ossian House
☎ 0181 340 4331

LONDON NW3
Sandringham Hotel
☎ 0171 435 1569

LONDON SW7
Gallery Hotel
☎ 0171 915 0000

LONDON W7
Wellmeadow Lodge Hotel
☎ 0181 567 7294

NORTHUMBERLAND

CORBRIDGE
The Courtyard
☎ 01434 606850

OXFORDSHIRE

BURFORD
Burford House
☎ 01993 823151

BURFORD
Elm House
☎ 01993 823611

HENLEY-ON-THAMES
Lenwade
☎ 01491 573468

OXFORD
Chestnuts Guest House
☎ 01865 553375

OXFORD
Cotswold House
☎ 01865 310558

OXFORD
Fallowfields Country House Hotel & Restaurant
☎ 01865 820416

THAME
The Dairy
☎ 01844 214075
Upper Green Farm
☎ 01844 212496

SHROPSHIRE

CHURCH STRETTON
Jinlye Guest House
☎ 01694 723243

LUDLOW
Line Farm
☎ 01568 780400
Number Twenty Eight
☎ 01584 876996

SHREWSBURY
Mytton Hall
☎ 01743 850264

WHITCHURCH
Dearnford Hall
☎ 01948 662319

SOMERSET

BATH
Apsley House Hotel
☎ 01225 336966
Cheriton House
☎ 01225 429862

Dorian House
☎ 01225 426336
Haydon House
☎ 01225 444919
Holly Lodge
☎ 01225 424042
Kennard Hotel
☎ 01225 310472
Leighton House
☎ 01225 314769
Meadowland
☎ 01225 311079
Monkshill Guest House
☎ 01225 833028
Siena Hotel
☎ 01225 425495

BEERCROCOMBE
Frog Street Farm
☎ 01823 480430
Whittles Farm
☎ 01823 480301

BRIDGWATER
Woodlands
☎ 01278 423442

CREWKERNE
Broadview Gardens
☎ 01460 73424

DULVERTON
Dassels Country House
☎ 01398 341203

DUNSTER
Dollons House
☎ 01643 821880

ILMINSTER
Keymer Cottage
☎ 01460 234460

KILVE
Hood Arms
☎ 01278 741210

LANGPORT
Hillards Farm
☎ 01458 251737
Muchelney Ham Farm
☎ 01458 250737

NORTON ST PHILIP
Monmouth Lodge
☎ 01373 834367
The Bath Lodge Hotel
☎ 01225 723040

PORLOCK
The Cottage Hotel
☎ 01643 863300

RODE
Irondale
☎ 01373 830730

SOMERTON
Lydford House
☎ 01963 240217
The Lynch Country House
☎ 01458 272316

TAUNTON
Allerford Farm
☎ 01823 461210
Cutsey House
☎ 01823 421705
Heathfield Lodge
☎ 01823 432286

WELLS
Beaconsfield Farm
☎ 01749 870308
Littlewell Farm
☎ 01749 677914

WEST BAGBOROUGH
Bashfords Farmhouse
☎ 01823 432015
Tilbury Farm
☎ 01823 432391

WHEDDON CROSS
Little Brendon Hill Farm
☎ 01643 841556

WINSFORD
Savery's at Karslake House
☎ 01643 851242

YEOVIL
Holywell House
☎ 01935 862612

STAFFORDSHIRE

CHEDDLETON
Choir Cottage and
Choir House
☎ 01538 360561

OAKAMOOR
Bank House
☎ 01538 702810

STOKE-ON-TRENT
Hanchurch Manor
☎ 01782 643030

TAMWORTH
Oak Tree Farm
☎ 01827 56807

SUFFOLK

BEYTON
Manorhouse
☎ 01359 270960

BURY ST EDMUNDS
Twelve Angel Hill
☎ 01284 704088

FRESSINGFIELD
Chippenhall Hall
☎ 01379 588180

HARTEST
The Hatch
☎ 01284 830226

SUSSEX, EAST

ARLINGTON
Bates Green
☎ 01323 482039

BATTLE
Brakes Coppice Farm
☎ 01424 830347

HARTFIELD
Bolebroke Watermill
☎ 01892 770425

HASTINGS & ST LEONARDS
Bryn-y-Mor
☎ 01424 722744
Parkside House
☎ 01424 433096

RUSHLAKE GREEN
Great Crouch's
☎ 01435 830145

RYE
Benson Hotel
☎ 01797 225131
Cadborough
☎ 01797 225426
Jeake's House
☎ 01797 222828
King Charles II Guest House
☎ 01797 224954
Playden Cottage Guesthouse
☎ 01797 222234
The Old Vicarage
Guest House
☎ 01797 222119

UCKFIELD
Hooke Hall
☎ 01825 761578

SUSSEX, WEST

BOSHAM
Kenwood
☎ 01243 572727

MIDHURST
Park House Hotel
☎ 01730 812880

ROGATE
Mizzards Farm
☎ 01730 821656

SUTTON
The White Horse Inn
☎ 01798 869221

WARWICKSHIRE

STRATFORD-UPON-AVON
Glebe Farm House
☎ 01789 842501

WARWICK
Shrewley House
☎ 01926 842549

WILTSHIRE

BRADFORD ON AVON
Bradford Old Windmill
☎ 01225 866842
Burghope Manor
☎ 01225 723557
Fern Cottage
☎ 01225 859412
Hillcrest
☎ 01225 868677
Widbrook Grange
☎ 01225 863173

CALNE
Fenwicks
☎ 01249 760645

LACOCK
At the Sign of the Angel
☎ 01249 730230

MALMESBURY
Horse & Groom Inn
☎ 01666 823904

MIDDLE WINTERSLOW
The Beadles
☎ 01980 862922

WOODFALLS
The Woodfalls Inn
☎ 01725 513222

WORCESTERSHIRE

BROADWAY
Mill Hay House
☎ 01386 852498
Old Rectory
☎ 01386 853729
The Pond House
☎ 01386 831687

YORKSHIRE, EAST RIDING OF

SLEDMERE
The Old Rectory
☎ 01377 267617

YORKSHIRE, NORTH

BEDALE
Elmfield Country House
☎ 01677 450558

HARROGATE
Ruskin Hotel
☎ 01423 502045

LEYBURN
Park Gate House
☎ 01677 450466

PICKERING
Burr Bank
☎ 01751 417777

REETH
Arkleside Hotel
☎ 01748 884200

RICHMOND
Whashton Springs Farm
☎ 01748 822884

YORK
Arndale Hotel
☎ 01904 702424

CHANNEL ISLANDS

GUERNSEY
ST PETER PORT
Midhurst House
☎ 01481 724391

ISLE OF MAN

ONCHAN
Engelwood Lodge
☎ 01624 616050

SCOTLAND

ABERDEEN CITY

ABERDEEN
Ewood House
☎ 01224 648408

ABERDEENSHIRE

ABOYNE
Arbor Lodge
☎ 01339 886951

ANGUS

ARBROATH
Farmhouse Kitchen
☎ 01241 860202

ARGYLL & BUTE

CARDROSS
Kirkton House
☎ 01389 841951

CONNEL
Ards House
☎ 01631 710255

DUNOON
The Anchorage
Hotel & Restaurant
☎ 01369 705108

TOBERMORY
Fairways Lodge
☎ 01688 302238

AYRSHIRE, EAST

DARVEL
Scoretulloch House
☎ 01560 323331

AYRSHIRE, SOUTH

BALLANTRAE
Cosses Country House
☎ 01465 831363

CITY OF EDINBURGH

EDINBURGH
Elmview
☎ 0131 228 1973

CITY OF GLASGOW

GLASGOW
Drambuie Scottish Chefs Centre Hotel
☎ 0141 427 1106

DUMFRIES & GALLOWAY

DALBEATTIE
Auchenskeoch Lodge
☎ 01387 780277

FIFE

ABERDOUR
Hawkcraig House
☎ 01383 860335

ANSTRUTHER
Hermitage Guest House
☎ 01333 310909

AUCHTERMUCHTY
Ardchoille Farmhouse
☎ 01337 828414

CUPAR
Todhall House
☎ 01334 656344

HIGHLAND

BOAT OF GARTEN
Glenavon House
☎ 01479 831213

DORNOCH
Fourpenny Cottage
☎ 01862 810727

DORNOCH
Highfield
☎ 01862 810909

FORT WILLIAM
Ashburn House
☎ 01397 706000

FORT WILLIAM
The Grange
☎ 01397 705516

GAIRLOCH
Birchwood
☎ 01445 712011

GRANTOWN-ON-SPEY
Ardconnel House
☎ 01479 872104

INVERNESS
Ballifeary House Hotel
☎ 01463 235572

Culduthel Lodge
☎ 01463 240089

Millwood House
☎ 01463 237254

Moyness House Hotel
☎ 01463 233836

KENTALLEN
Ardsheal House
☎ 01631 740227

STRATHPEFFER
Craigvar
☎ 01997 421622

MORAY

ELGIN
The Croft
☎ 01343 546004

The Pines Guest House
☎ 01343 542766

PERTH & KINROSS

ABERFELDY
Fernbank House
☎ 01887 820345

RENFREWSHIRE

LOCHWINNOCH
East Lochhead
☎ 01505 842610

PAISLEY
Myfarrclan Guest House
☎ 0141 884 8285

SCOTTISH BORDERS

GALASHIELS
Maplehurst Guest House
☎ 01896 754700

JEDBURGH
The Spinney
☎ 01835 863525

STIRLING

CALLANDER
Arran Lodge
☎ 01877 330976

WALES

CONWY

LLANDUDNO
Bryn Derwen Hotel
☎ 01492 876804

The Lighthouse
☎ 01492 876819

DENBIGHSHIRE

RUTHIN
Eyarth Station
☎ 01824 703643

GWYNEDD

BONTDDU
Borthwnog Hall Hotel
☎ 01341 430271

CAERNARFON
Pengwern Farm
☎ 01286 831500

DOLGELLAU
Tyddynmawr Farmhouse
☎ 01341 422331

NEATH PORT TALBOT

NEATH
Green Lanterns Guest House
☎ 01639 631884

POWYS

NEWTOWN
Dyffryn Farmhouse
☎ 01686 688817

PENYBONT
Ffaldau Country House & Restaurant
☎ 01597 851421

NORTHERN IRELAND

BELFAST

BELFAST
Rayanne Country House & Restaurant
☎ 01232 425859

DOWN

HOLYWOOD
Beech Hill
☎ 01232 425892

NEWTOWNARDS
Edenvale House
☎ 01247 814881

LONDONDERRY

COLERAINE
Greenhill House
☎ 01265 868241

TYRONE

DUNGANNON
Grange Lodge
☎ 01868 784212

REPUBLIC OF IRELAND

CARLOW

CARLOW
Barrowville Town House
☎ 050 343324

CORK

FERMOY
Ballyvolane House
☎ 025 36349

KANTURK
Assolas Country House
☎ 029 50015

KINSALE
Perryville House
☎ 021 772731

YOUGHAL
Ahernes
☎ 024 92424

DONEGAL

LETTERKENNY
Castle Grove Country House & Restaurant
☎ 074 51118

DUBLIN

DUBLIN
Aberdeen Lodge
☎ 01 2838155

Ariel House
☎ 01 6685512

Butlers Town House
☎ 01 6674022

Cedar Lodge
☎ 01 6684410

Fitzwilliam Park
☎ 01 6628280

Glenogra Guest House
☎ 01 6683661

Merrion Hall
☎ 01 6681426

Morehampton Lodge
☎ 01 2837499

The Grey Door
☎ 01 6763286

DUN LAOGHAIRE
Chestnut Lodge
☎ 01 2807860

GALWAY

CLIFDEN
Maldua Guest House
☎ 095 21171

GALWAY
Killeen House
☎ 091 524179

OUGHTERARD
River Run Lodge
☎ 091 552697

KERRY

CARAGH LAKE
Caragh Lodge
☎ 066 69115

KENMARE
Sallyport House
☎ 064 42066

KILLARNEY
Earls Court House
☎ 064 34009

Kathleen's Country House
☎ 064 32810

KILDARE

ATHY
Coursetown Country House
☎ 0507 31101

KILKENNY

KILKENNY
Newlands Country House
☎ 056 29111

LOUTH

CARLINGFORD
Jordans Townhouse & Restaurant
☎ 042 73223

WESTMEATH

MULLINGAR
Crookedwood House
☎ 044 72165

WEXFORD

ROSSLARE HARBOUR
Churchtown House
☎ 053 32555

ENGLAND • SCOTLAND • WALES • IRELAND

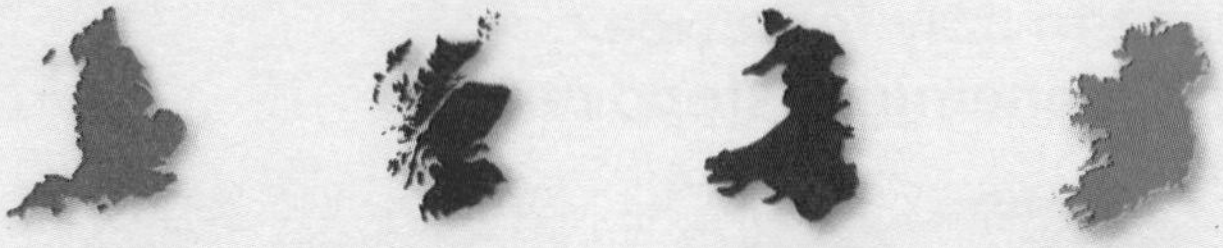

BED & BREAKFAST OF THE YEAR AWARDS

Every year we present our Inspectors with a difficult task - to nominate those establishments which they feel offer exceptionally high standards for our Bed & Breakfast of the Year Awards.

From a shortlist of around twenty, one is selected to represent each country in the Guide - four establishments which we feel are outstanding examples of the very best small hotels, inns, guest houses and farmhouses in Britain. A full page colour photograph of the winning establishment opens each country section in the Guide.

ENGLAND

Bessiestown Lodge, Longtown, Cumbria.

For more than two decades, Margaret and Jack Sissons have been welcoming guests to their charming farmhouse. There are secluded gardens to enjoy, and during the summer months, a heated swimming pool is available just across the courtyard. Margaret's home-cooked meals are worthy of note - no starters are offered, to allow seconds of her very popular puddings!

SCOTLAND

Farmhouse Kitchen, Arbroath, Angus.

A peaceful setting deep in the heart of the Angus countryside, and breakfast at the communal kitchen table help guests soak up the farmhouse atmosphere. Sandra Caldwell's home-baking, and the 'super sun lounge with comfy leather chairs' add the perfect finishing touches to a relaxing break.

WALES

Bryn Derwen Hotel, Llandudno, Conwy

Stuart Langfield's 'intuitive cooking', legacy of his days as a catering lecturer, is just one reason to visit this Victorian gentleman's residence, restored with taste and sympathy by Stuart and his wife, Valerie. A flair for interior design is apparent in the use of rich fabrics and elegant furnishings throughout the house, creating an atmosphere of warmth and relaxation.

IRELAND

Churchtown House, Rosslare Harbour, Co Wexford

'I send my friends here and they love it!' remarked our Inspector of Patricia and Austin Cody's delightful Georgian house. The Codys are convivial hosts and the time and energy which they have expended in restoring the house is matched only by their committment to providing a comfortable and friendly environment for their guests.

CHILDREN FRIENDLY AND CHILD-FREE ZONES

Our theme in the Bed & Breakfast Guide this year is 'Family Welcome'. You will see two symbols denoting whether children are welcome or not:

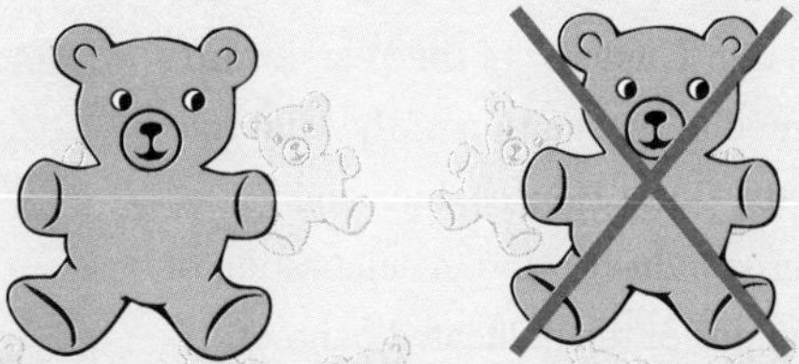

We surveyed all the establishments in the Guide about their facilities for children, including whether there is a safe place for children to play, laundry/ironing facilities, cots, high chairs, a babysitting service etc. If they were able to answer 'yes' to all these questions, we have given them a teddy bear symbol. These are places which go out of their way to welcome children, and consider themselves particularly 'family friendly'. However there are some who, despite qualifying for a symbol, would rather not be highlighted. Therefore, if an establishment does not have a teddy bear, it does not necessarily mean that it does not welcome children.

If an establishment does take children but has an age restriction (*for example, no children under 12*), this will be found in the details at the end of their entry, thus **'no children 12yrs'.**

We also sent out a survey asking for more details on people's views on children. Some places were more emphatic about not welcoming children, and to these we have offered our 'child-free zone' symbol, the crossed through teddy bear. There is also a quick reference list of child-free zones, and some places may appear on this list but did not want a symbol beside their entry.

Our 'child-free zones' are, of course, not intended as a list of places which are 'child-hating'. Some establishments, due to their style, or furnishings, or proximity to dangerous cliffs, perhaps, are more appropriate for families with older children, business people, people who are taking a holiday away from the children, or elderly people wanting a quiet break, in which case they may like to know that 'other people's children' will not be waking them up in the morning or chatting to them at breakfast.

For the list of 'child-free zones' please consult the Contents Page.

Please note that the symbols and list are intended as an indication only, and an establishment's position on children may alter during the currency of the guide, so please check when booking.

LANDLADY OF THE YEAR

1998-9 sees the fifth year of our 'Landlady of the Year' award - a much-coveted title presented in recognition of the vital role played by Bed and Breakfasts, Guest Houses, Inns and Farmhouses in Britain's tourist industry, and in celebration of the hard work and good humour of the dedicated band of people who work so hard to make your holidays successful.

The top twenty finalists were invited to a lunch at the Dorchester, where the winners were announced.

Sally Tompkins, of The Gables, Oxford, was this year's winner, receiving a specially commissioned trophy from Caithness Glass and a weekend for two in Barcelona. Jeanne Martin of Wheal Lodge, St Austell, and Jane Conolly of Hills Farm, Leominster were the runners up, and also received trophies. The other finalists were presented with commemorative bowls, ensuring no one left empty-handed.

John Howard(Director, AA Publishing) and Leigh Baldham(Marketing Director, Caithness Glass) with all twenty finalists.

Every year our Inspectors are asked to nominate those landladies and gentlemen whom they feel offer the most outstanding hospitality to their guests. This year there were 92, the most we've ever had, demonstrating the calibre of AA listed establishments.

The selection process involves written tests, undercover visits, telephone enquiries, and this year spoof radio interviews. We look for friendliness, good humour and an ability to remain calm under pressure!

AWARD

Sally, who was a runner up in last year's final, put her success this year down to her commitment to "maintaining high standards of maintenance, cleanliness, and service, and a warm friendly welcome to every guest." Our undercover judge described her as "a fantastically bubbly, friendly lady who puts everyone at their ease." Her gabled, Victorian house is charming, with a lovely garden and pretty bedrooms with all kinds of extras.

Leigh Baldham, Sally Tompkins, John Howard.

CONGRATULATIONS ALSO TO...

Jeanne Martin, Wheal Lodge, St Austell.

Mrs Martin is an absolute delight, and her comfortable home, perched high above Carlyon Bay, is blessed with beautiful views. Loyal guests return year after year to be plied with excellent home baking and generally spoiled rotten!

Jane Conolly, Hills Farm, Leominster.

An impressive 15th-century building, part of a 120 acre arable farm, Hills Farm overlooks the surrounding countryside and has been home to the Conollys for many years. Jane is an accomplished chef, producing imaginative dishes, and she and husband Peter are chatty and warmly hospitable.

Jeanne Martin, Sally Tompkins and Jane Conolly.

BEST BRITISH BREAKFAST AWARD

Breakfast - the most important meal of the day? And by breakfast, we don't mean half a cup of tea and one slice of toast as you dash out of the house at 7.30, but something much more leisured, traditional and substantial. A major pleasure of staying in a Bed & Breakfast, surely, is the prospect of a delicious, piping hot plateful of crispy bacon and sausages, eggs just how you like them, mountains of toast and shining pots of tea or coffee. All lovingly prepared by someone else and consumed in a gentle glow of goodwill as you anticipate a day exploring a new area, assured in the knowledge that lunch will not be necessary, or even possible, after such a perfect repast. For this reason, we decided to make an award for the Best British Breakfast, as recommended by our dedicated Inspectors.

From the 3000 establishments in the Guide, we received fifty nominations (some of which were extremely enthusiastic...). We then asked those establishments to send us a copy of their breakfast menu, and also their answers to some intriguing questions - what, indeed are the 'Breakfast Philosophies' of the establishments providing the very best in British Breakfasts? Their responses were truly a delight - descriptions of home made breads and preserves, ('two kinds of marmalade, four kinds of jam'), 'honey from our own hives... and sausages from our pigs', 'our own special tea', 'free range duck and hen (and sometimes peafowl!) eggs', 'the most wonderful oak-smoked kippers in the world...' to make you weep with joy.

It was with great difficulty that we were able to reduce the list to these seven regional winners.

South East England - Julia & Paul Masters, The Old Vicarage, Rye, East Sussex

East Anglia - John & Bernie Clarke, Twelve Angel Hill, Bury St Edmunds, Suffolk

Central England - Mrs Elaine Sutcliffe, Choir Cottage & Choir House, Cheddleton, Staffordshire

Northern England - Mrs Enid Davies, Low Hall, Cockermouth, Cumbria

South West England - Mr & Mrs Chilcott, Wigham Farm, Morchard Bishop, Devon

Scotland - Mrs Kornelia Inverarity, Fossil House and Cottage, St Andrews, Fife

NATIONAL WINNER

Northern Ireland - Raymond & Anne McClelland, Rayanne House, Holywood, Belfast

One of the questions we asked was whether they had ever received any 'bizarre' breakfast requests, and it seems that some people have a definite taste for intriguing flavour combinations... for example, kippers with marmalade, the parson's nose of last night's turkey with strawberry jam, 'eggs fried 'easy over', cooked hard, broken up and served with sausage and marmalade', 'kippers with scotch pancakes and smothered with maple syrup', or our particular favourite, '... the guest who asked for peanut butter and raspberry jam and then proceeded to spread both all over their sausages and bacon'! Burnt toast is a common request, as is scrambled eggs made with the white only, which causes puzzlement and wrinkled noses amongst our nominees.

We have nothing but admiration, however, for the 'lady who consumed three portions of Raspberry Pavlova at supper' who requested, and was granted, the remains of it for breakfast!

We asked them to tell us what they think constitutes a 'great' breakfast and received a multitude of detailed replies.

'An immaculately presented meal which offers choice, nourishment, tastes delicious and is satisfying.' said John & Gill Donald, of Todhall House, Dairsie, Fife. 'A meal to be looked forward to and looked back on with satisfaction,' was the opinion of the Campbells of Kippielaw Farmhouse, East Linton, East Lothian, while Julia and Paul Masters of The Old Vicarage in Rye, felt that it meant 'Having a breakfast of your choice at a 'comfortable' time, prepared by someone else; cooked to perfection and served in a relaxed atmosphere...'. We particularly admired the honesty and good sense of Hilary Cumming of Keymer Cottage, Buckland St Mary, who described a great breakfast as including '...sufficient food to allow for 'seconds'. This is also a cunning way for the landlady who claims not to eat a cooked breakfast to clean up the odd sausage or piece of fried bread!'

When it came to the question of a 'Breakfast Philosophy', we had no idea what to expect in response. Did such a thing even exist? But we needn't have worried. Those who prepare breakfast for their guests have indeed considered why they do it and what it is they hope to achieve. Peta and Anthony Lloyd, of Fallowfields, Southmoor, Oxfordshire, neatly sum up what they aim to provide - ***'The finest of breakfasts with the broadest of smiles.'***

Jackie Somerville, of Holywell House, Holywell, Somerset, believes that '...to create the quintessential 'Great British Breakfast', one must combine unique touches with a respect for the tradition associated with this wonderful British institution.'

Mrs Campbell, of Kippielaw Farmhouse, East Linton, East Lothian, says 'I try to look after guests as if they were visiting family members and try to anticipate their needs.'

For Margaret Matysik, of Thatched Cottage Hotel & Restaurant, Brockenhurst, Hampshire, it is important 'To ensure that a guest can come into the dining room feeling grumpy but leave smiling and contented...', while Sally Townend, of New Capernwray Farm, Carnforth, Lancashire, is convinced that 'Breakfast should be as much of an event as a dinner party... the same care and attention to detail should be taken with breakfast for one person as one would take for six.'

The final word comes from Kathy Ritchie, of Tilston Lodge, Malpas, Cheshire. 'Guests may forget the colour of their room and even what I look like, but they will always remember their breakfast!'

So it seems that, although many B&B proprietors are far too busy to eat breakfast themselves, (at least before lunchtime!) they have very decided ideas about what their public require and deserve. They believe in offering the widest choice of the best possible ingredients, of being prepared to attempt special requests, no matter how odd they may think them, and to serve this most vital of meals in a style and at a time to suit their guests, rather than themselves. They like to think that they have 'set you up for the day', and that you will always remember the care they have taken, leaving you dreaming of the smell of fresh home made bread, the freshest eggs imaginable, and sausages which any pig would be proud to be a part of.

THE JOB IN QUEST

Stoic, Sage and Superstar - the Bed and Breakfast Landlady

(Full Breakfast, Taxi Service and Lifelong Friendship Optional).

By Denise Laing

The job profile would surely demand some highly impressive qualifications and experience: the versatility of a Houdini, the high level diplomacy of a Chris Patten (though supervising the handover of Hong Kong to China might not be challenging enough), the counselling/agony aunt skills of Marj Proops, the political expertise and sensitivity of, well, a consummate politician (some imagination required here), the Fixit abilities of Hannibal, the personal resources of a National Rescue Service, and the sense of humour of the laughing policeman. The job in question? Bed and breakfast landlady.

Now, we accept that only la crème de la crème of the UK and Ireland's guesthouses, farmhouses and inns are classified by the AA and listed in this guide, and that the professionals who run them are a pretty magnificent bunch of women (and men!). But quite how talented, dedicated, generous and altogether amazing these people are is, we feel, rarely fully appreciated. Though our poll was only conducted amongst those B & Bs which were selected as being the very best of a marvellous band, we suspect that the characteristics they share and the tales they relate are universal.

The first, and perhaps most astonishing fact our survey revealed was the extent to which landladies - often though not always supported by strong and practical husbands - will exceed all normal calls of duty and decency. The goodwill and simple friendship which they are prepared to offer complete strangers is frankly mind-boggling, and when this is extended to foreign visitors must do more for British tourism than any high-profile advertising campaign by the various tourist boards.

The Australian lady who slipped off her chair and disappeared under the breakfast table at Walnut Cottage, Cadnam in Hampshire hadn't fallen into a stupor after too many Crocodile Dundee jokes, or despaired at the prospect of another plate piled high with a full

IDN...

English breakfast. Apparently unhurt after a car accident the previous evening, she was actually suffering from delayed concussion and spent the next five days in hospital. Charlotte and Eric Osgood happily ferried the shocked husband back and forth to her bedside, and gave him their own bedroom in their fully-booked guesthouse - plus all meals - until his wife was discharged.

There was no hesitation, either, by Marjorie and Euan Aitken of Upper Green Farm, Thame, when an elderly guest fell while climbing over a stile on a pre-breakfast walk and broke his shoulder. First they drove him and his wife to the local cottage hospital for a diagnosis, and then on to Oxford for an X-ray and treatment. They didn't even need to discuss with each other what to do next with their highly distressed guests; after a brief pause to clear away breakfast things, make beds and tidy around, they covered the 200-mile round trip to their guests' home in convoy, carefully depositing them and their car before dashing back with five minutes to spare before the next guests arrived. Sally Tompkins made two trips across Oxford with one guest after his boisterous 3-year-old had locked the keys to their hire car in the boot. The first set they were given didn't fit, and by the time they returned again, hot and bothered, to The Gables Guest House with the right keys, the little boy had smeared most of an ice cream and all of a melted chocolate bar across the back seat of her car. Sally didn't record her reaction to the mess, but one suspects that landladies carry a damp sponge in a special case wherever they go, and she just wiped away the sticky goo without any fuss.

Other B & B owners, like Tony and Joan Flitney, have provided a full unscheduled room service when accidents or illness have forced guests to become bedridden. The couple happily fed, watered and supported the elderly grandparents of a sick 5-year-old whose week's holiday was spent feeling poorly in their guest house at Warwick Court in Weymouth. Unsurprisingly, kindnesses like these create bonds which often turn into lifelong friendships.

Several landladies have good reason to remember their first ever guests, but perhaps few are quite as memorable as Diane Wilson's. She was terrified when confronted by four menacing bikers at Home Farm, Wingfield, dressed from head to foot in leather and tattoos. Fortunately she kept her wits about her, and knew how to disarm them: a pot of tea and a large freshly-baked cream cake quickly had them purring, and the extra-massive full English breakfast the next morning left them

struggling to heave bulging stomachs across their motorbikes. So keen and excited was Margaret Brown to welcome her first guest to The Green Lantern at Neath that she sat in a prominent position at her hillside farmhouse watching for his arrival. When he was spotted driving up the long unsigned lane to the house, she got ready to welcome him, and then, appalled, saw him turn around and drive away.

Margaret's husband was dispatched at high speed to capture the confused guest, and he has returned voluntarily many times to share happy reunions. Health-conscious Heather McQueen was delighted with herself for devising a new way to cook eggs when she first started her B & B at Burness House, St Andrews. She gently fried the eggs in a tiny amount of oil, and then popped the pan under the grill to finish them off. Thrilled with the result, she was horrified to read an entry in the visitors' book from her Dutch guests: 'We loved your rubber eggs; stay as spontaneous as you are!' She fries like everyone else now.

Diplomacy, patience and a poker face, are sometimes called for in a landlady when presented with a tricky situation. Janice Cole of Poland Mill, Odiham got to like both the mistress and the wife of a regular visitor to her guest house, and delicately passed on messages from whichever woman was absent without embarrassing the Lothario, or inflaming the current favourite. The African chief who arrived amidst much publicity at Trafford Bank in Inverness to head-hunt for an ancestor's long-buried skull in order to repatriate it, then asked Peter McKenzie to keep the treasured relic in his safe for the duration of his stay. Certainly one of the more unusual and delicate requests a B & B proprietor might receive. Peter, however, unfazed, rose magnificently to the occasion. A persistently miserable sextet of American psychologists nearly drove Olive O'Gorman crazy when they stayed at Glasha in Ballymacarbry, Co Waterford for four nights. She soon found a way to defuse their unhappiness and constant criticism of everything Irish: whenever they returned to the house she was waiting to intercept them with huge welcoming smiles, exuberant words of comfort, and plenty of Irish coffee. The effort was worth it when these fractious experts in human behaviour warmed to Olive's maternal touch, and quickly became good children.

When Jeanne Martin tried to rescue a pair of young lovers from the wrath of their parents, she nearly trapped herself in her own tangled web. On the first day of their fortnight's holiday in Cornwall, the girl's mother rang up to say she was staying in the area and would like to join them for dinner, and to see their rooms (plural). The couple, who were out for the day, were sharing a double bedroom, and Jeanne decided on the spur of the moment that this woman should not find out. She and her husband had only a short time to empty their own bedroom - the guest house was completely full - and place the young man's belongings in it ready for inspection, though choosing the right toothbrush caused some worry. The unsuspecting pair had to be waylaid when they returned, warned of the situation, and presented to the delighted mum as the innocents they were not! A bottle of champagne was Jeanne's reward the next day, although one suspects she thrives on such excitement.

Double-bookings might be the obvious dreaded nightmare for landladies, but only a few of our heroines reported these as a difficult or memorable situation. Poor water pressure or problems associated with very old properties, on the other hand, often present difficulties, and can be baffling for foreign visitors. The four smart young Italian males who stayed at Higher Park Farm, Dorchester had not reckoned on the dairy being hosed down at a time of reduced water pressure when they decided to take simultaneous showers. Dashing about in bath towels, covered to the eyebrows in soap and with almost no English, they had to be escorted to the dairy before they understood the problem. Marigold King was hugely relieved when they saw the joke and started to laugh, and perhaps offered to hose them down with the herd!

The four Japanese guests who descended unannounced at Higher Cadham Farm, Jacobstowe, on the night of December 21 enjoyed an experience they will never forget. Jenny King had arranged a Christmas dinner celebration for a local organisation in her dining room, but she gallantly welcomed her unexpected guests, and laid a table for them in the corner of the room. They threw themselves into the evening, enjoying turkey, crackers, poppers and the wine presented by the other diners, and were quite overwhelmed when carol singers arrived to make the evening perfect.

Guests often bring, leave behind, and require some unusual baggage, and as usual the intrepid landlady has to take it all in her stride. Aileen Kennedy of Newlands Country House, Co Kilkenny found a tiny baby asleep on a bed after a large, friendly family left one morning. A full ninety minutes later they returned, red-faced and anxious, to retrieve their infant, and admit that everyone thought someone else had got it. An elderly lady booking her extended

family into The Old Rectory, Parkham kept landlady Jean Langton on the phone for half an hour trying to allocate rooms for sharing. The figures could not be made to tally, until grandma remembered that she had included her late husband who wouldn't need a bed, just some space on the mantlepiece. A regular elderly visitor to Playden Cottage Guesthouse outside Rye caused havoc with the mobile phones, radios and remote alarm systems on one visit when he brought a satellite-seeking gadget to play with. Asked what he was doing, he replied proudly that his instrument could tell him precisely where he was located at any given time. Sheelagh Fox didn't have the heart to tell him, unscientifically, that he was actually standing in her garden, and was amused to discover later that he and his wife ended up in Eastbourne whilst trying to find Tunbridge Wells. Sally Arundel spent several days sharing tears and sympathy with one young and solitary foreign guest who was shattered over a broken engagement. The nurturing she provided was cathartic for both of them, and when the girl left Torcroft Country House in Newton Abbot, her vitality and self-esteem had been fully restored.

Squabbling spouses are an occupational hazard for landladies, but they don't often need the law to separate them. Enid Davies listened with terror late one night as two of her guests crashed around in their room at Low Hall, Cockermouth, the sound of breaking glass and screams filling the quiet Cumbrian air. When she banged on the door to request a cessation of hostilities, the woman yelled that her husband was trying to kill her, and Enid dashed off to call the police. Enid's husband's return with two late-arriving guests coincided with the police arrival, much to the amazement of other guests, watching from their windows, and the alarm of the two late arrivals who must have wondered where they were and what they were letting themselves in for. Peace was restored, and the warring couple separated for the night. But when Enid heard the girl trying to creep back to her murderous man, she became very stern, and ordered her back to bed like a naughty schoolgirl.

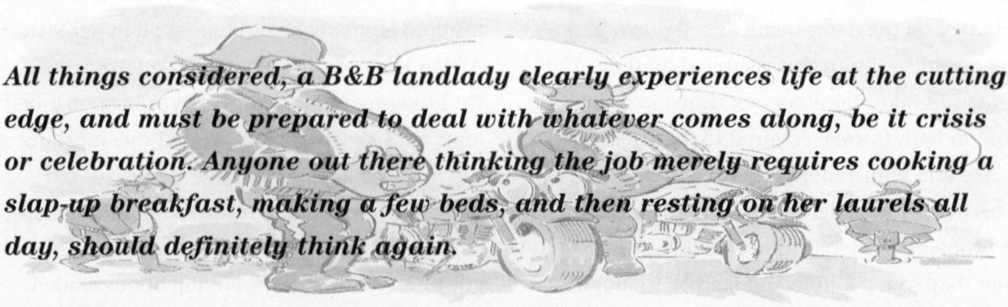

All things considered, a B&B landlady clearly experiences life at the cutting edge, and must be prepared to deal with whatever comes along, be it crisis or celebration. Anyone out there thinking the job merely requires cooking a slap-up breakfast, making a few beds, and then resting on her laurels all day, should definitely think again.

Top twenty landladies 1998

WINNER

Sally Tompkins,
Gables Guest House, Oxford -
winner

RUNNER UP

Jeanne Martin,
Wheal Lodge, St Austell -
runner-up

Jane Conolly,
Hills Farm, Leominster -
runner-up

Euan Aitken,
Upper Green Farm, Thame

Louise Aldridge,
Cranberry House Guest House, Llandudno

Tony Barnfield,
The Nurse's Cottage, Sway

Ruth Cowley,
Channel View, Weymouth

Hilary Cumming,
Keymer Cottage, Ilminster

Margaret Fenwick,
Fenwicks, Calne

Sheelagh Fox,
Playden Cottage, Rye

Jill Hookham-Bassett,
Stourcastle Lodge, Sturminster Newton

Mariette Jelley,
Cottage B&B, Lymington

Jenny King,
Higher Cadham Farm, Jacobstowe, Okehampton

Caroline Lawler,
Tynte House,
Dunlavin

Isabel Marley,
The Roods, Inverkeithing

Peter McKenzie,
Trafford Bank, Inverness

Olive O'Gorman,
Glasha, Ballymacarbry

Rosemary Votier,
Morden House,
Cromer

Diane Wilson,
Home Farm, Bradford-on-Avon

Anne-Marie Yuille-Baddeley,
The Beadles, Salisbury

TOP TWENTY LANDLADIES 1997

WINNER

Jean Manson,
Post Office House, John O'Groats -
winner

RUNNER-UP

Sheila Hawkey,
Ewood House, Aberdeen -
runner-up

Sally Tompkins,
Gables Guest House, Oxford -
runner-up

Sheila Adams,
Orchard Cottage, Langport

Margaret Browne,
Ballymakeigh House, Killeagh, Youghal

Daphne Burgoine,
Fairway Lodge Guest House, Okehampton

Jane Dooley,
Highfield, Dornoch

Jenny Hadfield,
Jeake's House,
Rye

Kornelia Inverarity,
Fossil House Bed & Breakfast,
St Andrews

Alice Jennings,
The Jays, Aberdeen

***Sally Low,* ***
Coombe Farm House, Looe

Margaret Massey,
Dene House, Hexham

Julia Masters,
The Old Vicarage Guest House, Rye

Christine McClement,
Duncraggan, Blairgowrie

Norma McPherson,
Ardent House, Hopeman

***Jenny Richardson-Brown,* •**
Wytchwood, Teignmouth

Teresa Sampson,
Kerscott Farm, South Molton

Margaret Smith,
Hurdon Farm, Launceston

Val Sunter,
Higher House Farm, Kendal

Lynne Tuckett,
Trenderway Farm, Polperro

**** no longer AA appointed***

England

Inspector's selected bed & breakfast of the year:

Bessiestown Lodge, Longtown, Cumbria

ABBERLEY Worcestershire Map **03** SO76

Q Q Q **Whoppets Wood** WR6 6BU (1.3m from 'Shavers End' signpost off A451 between Dunley and Great Witley at Dick Brook Bridge)
☎ 01299 896545
Closed Dec-1 Jan
This late 18th-century farmhouse is quietly situated about a mile south-east of the village. It has panoramic views of the valley and is popular with walkers; the Worcestershire Way can be accessed directly from the extensive grounds. The no-smoking accommodation includes a two bedroom family suite and another room on ground floor level with its own dining area, kitchen and entrance. The third room is the only one without an en suite facility, but it does have an adjacent private bathroom.
3 rms (2 bth/shr) (2 fmly) No smoking CTV in all bedrooms Tea and coffee making facilities No dogs Cen ht No children 4yrs 6P No coaches
ROOMS: s £20-£20; d £35-£40

ABBEY DORE Herefordshire Map **03** SO33

Q Q Q **Tan House Farm** *(SO385305)* HR2 0AA (turn right off A465 at Wormbridge and follow signs for Dore Abbey) ☎ 01981 240204
FAX 01981 240204 Mrs G Powell
rs Nov-Mar (prior booking only)
Parts of this stone built farmhouse are reputed to date back over 300 years. It is quietly located on a working farm, next to the 12th-century Cistercian Dore Abbey in the beautiful Golden Valley. The traditionally furnished accommodation comprises one double and one twin bedded room. All guests share one table in the combined breakfast room and lounge, which has some nice antique furniture.
3 rms (1 shr) No smoking in bedrooms CTV in 1 bedroom Tea and coffee making facilities No dogs (ex guide dogs) CTV 3P 350 acres arable cattle sheep horses
ROOMS: s £16; d £32-£40*

ABBOTS BROMLEY Staffordshire Map **07** SK02

Q Q **Crown** Market Place WS15 3BS (on B5013, in centre of village, opposite Butter Cross) ☎ 01283 840227 FAX 01283 840016
This black and white inn is situated in the centre of the village, with easy access to Alton Towers, the Potteries and other attractions. A wide selection of freshly cooked meals and snacks is offered in the bars, whilst upstairs, well maintained bedrooms sharing two modern shower rooms are comfortably furnished; new for this year are direct dial telephones.
6 rms (1 fmly) No smoking in 3 bedrooms CTV in all bedrooms
Tea and coffee making facilities Direct dial from bedrooms Cen ht 40P
Last d 9.30pm
ROOMS: s fr £25; d £45*
MEALS: Lunch £4.50-£15alc Dinner £7.75-£15alc*
CARDS:

This symbol indicates a 'Child Friendly' establishment - see page 25 for details

Q Q **Marsh** *(SK069261)* WS15 3EJ (1m N on B5013 of Abbots Bromley) ☎ 01283 840323 Mrs M K Hollins
Closed Dec
Part of an actively managed smallholding, where guests are encouraged to walk around the fields, this modernised farmhouse is peacefully situated just north of the village. There are two comfortably furnished bedrooms which are tastefully furnished, mainly with period pieces that compliment the exposed beams. A generous breakfast is served in the spacious dining room, where afternoon teas are also served.
2 rms (1 fmly) No smoking in dining room CTV in all bedrooms
Tea and coffee making facilities Cen ht 8P 64 acres dairy
ROOMS: s £18-£20; d £32-£40; wkly b&b £110-£120*

ABINGDON Oxfordshire Map **04** SU49

Selected

Q Q Q Q **Dinckley Court** Burcot OX14 3DP (from M40junct 7 take A329 then turn right onto A4074 Oxford road then onto A415 to Abingdon) ☎ 01865 407763 FAX 01865 407010
Set in extensive grounds close to the Thames and within easy reach of Oxford, Dinckley Court is a peaceful haven for visitors to the area. Mrs Godfrey has a genuine interest in guests' wellbeing, even offering transport to and from the local station if required. Bedrooms are comfortable, all having en suite bathrooms. Breakfast and dinner take place in the farmhouse style kitchen and fresh and organic ingredients are used to cook meals.
4 bth/shr (1 fmly) No smoking CTV in all bedrooms Tea and coffee making facilities No dogs (ex guide dogs) Cen ht CTV 10P
No coaches Fishing Last d 9pm
ROOMS: s £35-£45; d £45-£55*
CARDS:

Q Q Q **Rafters** Abingdon Rd OX13 6NU (turn off A34 onto A415 towards Whitney, establishment is on the right hand side of the main road in Marcham by the first street light) ☎ 01865 391298 FAX 391173
Close to Abingdon and Oxford, Rafters has the comforts of home and a warm welcome. All bedrooms have en suite facilities, televisions and tea making

equipment. Mrs Grawert provides extra touches such as a fridge in the breakfast room for guests' use. Breakfast is carefully prepared and guests have a choice from the menu. Evening meals can be arranged prior to arrival.
3 bth/shr (1 fmly) No smoking CTV in all bedrooms Tea and coffee making facilities No dogs (ex guide dogs) Cen ht 3P
ROOMS: s £26-£45; d £35-£50

ACASTER MALBIS North Yorkshire Map 08 SE54

QQQ **Ship** YO23 1UH (2m S of A64 bypass, accessible through villages of Copmanthorpe or Bishopthorpe) ☎ 01904 705609 & 703888 FAX 01904 705971
Standing on the banks of the River Ouse, this interesting old inn has its own quay, complete with cruise boat. It offers a good range of food in its bar, while the dining room is used when the bar gets busy, and for breakfast. Bedrooms come in a variety of sizes, all of which are thoughtfully equipped and pleasantly furnished in pine.
8 bth/shr No smoking in bedrooms CTV in all bedrooms Tea and coffee making facilities Cen ht 60P Fishing Last d 9.30pm
CARDS:

ADBASTON Staffordshire Map 07 SJ72

QQ **Offley Grove** *(SJ760270)* ST20 0QB (4m off A519, between Shebdon and Adbaston) ☎ 01785 280205 Mrs M Hiscoe-James
Situated on the borders of Staffordshire and Shropshire, this house, set amidst 45 acres of arable farmland, is ideally located for visiting Ironbridge or the Potteries. Bedrooms are attractively furnished and there are two homely lounges for guests' relaxation. A play area is available for children and two self-catering cottages are available in converted outbuildings.
3 rms (1 shr) No smoking in bedrooms No smoking in dining room Tea and coffee making facilities No dogs (ex guide dogs) Cen ht CTV P Childrens play area 45 acres arable sheep
ROOMS: s £16.50; d £33-£40*

ALBURY Surrey Map 04 TQ04

QQQ **Drummond Arms** The Street GU5 9AG (off main A25 between Guildford and Dorking, take A248 marked Albury, Godalming, establishment 1m on right) ☎ 01483 202039 FAX 01483 202039
This is a charming old inn in the centre of the small village of Albury. Located on the A248 between Godalming and Dorking, it is also within easy reach of Guildford, and is ideal for both the business and leisure traveller. The rooms are well furnished and comfortable and all have modern en-suite facilities. The separate restaurant offers a set price menu, and a good selection of hearty traditional pub food is available in the bar. There is an attractive garden running down to a small river with a weir, and ducks paddle lazily around.
7 bth/shr (1 fmly) CTV in all bedrooms Tea and coffee making facilities No dogs (ex guide dogs) Cen ht No children 14yrs 70P No coaches Last d 9.30pm
ROOMS: s £40-£55; d £55-£66*
CARDS:
See advertisement under GUILDFORD

ALCONBURY Cambridgeshire Map 04 TL17

QQQ ***The Manor House Hotel*** Chapel St PE17 5DY (signposted close to junct of A1/A14 N of Huntingdon) ☎ 01480 890423 FAX 01480 891663
Located in the centre of the village, this 16th-century manor farmhouse now serves as a popular Inn. The proprietors have totally refurbished the accommodation, bedrooms are cheerfully decorated with co-ordinated colour schemes, quality soft furnishings, pine furniture and a good range of facilities, and some four-poster bedrooms are available. Public areas are cosy and inviting with exposed beams and open fires. Diners have a choice of eating options - the more formal setting of the restaurant, or snacks in the character bar.
5 bth/shr (2 fmly) No smoking in area of dining room CTV in all bedrooms Tea and coffee making facilities Direct dial from bedrooms Cen ht 25P Last d 9pm
CARDS:

ALFRETON Derbyshire Map 08 SK45

QQQ **Oaktree Farm** *(SK385566)* Matlock Rd, Oakerthorpe, Wessington DE55 7NA (from M1 N junct 28 onto A38 follow A615 signed Matlock and fork left at Peacock Inn under bridge and past cottages for farmhouse on left) ☎ 01773 832957 & 0411 435285 (mobile) Mrs K Prince
This modern house, faced in local stone, enjoys an outlook over open farmland. Bedrooms are individually furnished, fresh and appealing with co-ordinated decor. Dinner is available by prior arrangement, using fresh vegetables and potatoes from the owners' personal smallholding, whilst free-range eggs are a feature of the breakfast. Coarse fishing is offered to residents in the small private lake within the grounds.
3 bth/shr No smoking CTV in all bedrooms Tea and coffee making facilities No dogs (ex guide dogs) Cen ht CTV 10P Fishing 22 acres mixed Last d 6pm
ROOMS: s £20-£23; d £38-£42; wkly b&b £125-£135; wkly hlf-bd £160-£175*

Q Q Q **The Plough** 20 Nottingham Rd DE55 7HL ☎ 01773 832372 FAX 01773 520434
An original town centre public house which is very popular with the local community for its friendly and enthusiastic proprietors and the comfortable and relaxed environment. The public rooms offer a cosy bar area with beamed ceilings and an open fire, and the rear of the property opens out onto an award-winning courtyard garden. The accommodation is fresh and appealing, with colour co-ordinated decor and soft furnishings, a good range of facilities and en suite bathrooms.
4 shr CTV in all bedrooms Tea and coffee making facilities Cen ht CTV 5P Last d 7.30pm
ROOMS: s fr £39.50; d fr £59*
MEALS: Dinner £8.50-£12*

ALKMONTON Derbyshire Map **07** SK13

Selected

Q Q Q Q **Dairy House** *(SK198367)* DE6 3DG (3m up Woodyard Lane after turning off A50 at Foston) ☎ 01335 330359 FAX 01335 330359 Mr A Harris
Closed 24-26 Dec
An ancient farmhouse full of character where a relaxed and friendly atmosphere is created by the charming owners, Mr and Mrs Harris. Guests can relax in a very comfortable lounge and enjoy freshly cooked farmhouse breakfasts and dinners, which are served communally at a large polished table in a separate dining area.
7 rms (1 bth 3 shr) No smoking Tea and coffee making facilities No dogs (ex guide dogs) Licensed Cen ht CTV No children 14yrs 8P 18 acres stock grazing Last d 7pm
ROOMS: s £17-£24; d £34-£40; wkly b&b £112-£168; wkly hlf-bd £210-£266*

ALMONDSBURY Gloucestershire Map **03** ST68

Selected

Q Q Q Q **Abbotts Way** Gloucester Rd BS12 4JB (on A38, 2m N of junct 16, M5) ☎ 01454 613134 FAX 01454 613134
This large modern house, set in 12 acres of gardens, offers panoramic views of the Severn Vale and the two Severn Bridges from its elevated position. The cities of Bath and Bristol are both easily accessible. Geoff and Pam Watkins extend a warm welcome. Bedrooms are comfortable and well furnished, and the spacious conservatory is a delightful setting in which to enjoy breakfast.
6 rms (5 shr) (2 fmly) No smoking CTV in all bedrooms Tea and coffee making facilities No dogs (ex guide dogs) Cen ht CTV 10P No coaches Indoor swimming pool (heated) Sauna
ROOMS: s £28; d £43; wkly b&b £196*
CARDS:

ALNMOUTH Northumberland Map **12** NU21

Selected

Q Q Q Q ***High Buston Hall*** High Buston NE66 3QH (off A1068 between Alnmouth & Warkworth) ☎ 01665 830341 FAX 01665 830341
Closed Xmas-Jan
This Georgian Grade II listed country house stands in five acres of grounds in an elevated position looking out towards Alnmouth and the Northumberland coastline. The home of John and Alison Edwards, it is lovingly furnished with antiques and period pieces, yet the atmosphere is informal and relaxing - truly a family home. Bedrooms are huge, one has a four-poster bed and its own bathroom opposite; the other two rooms are fully en suite. There is a lovely lounge and an imposing dining room where Alison's home-cooked meals are served dinner party-style around one large table.
3 rms (2 bth/shr) No smoking CTV in all bedrooms Tea and coffee making facilities No dogs (ex guide dogs) Licensed Cen ht 9P No coaches Last d 9am

Selected

Q Q Q Q **Marine House Private Hotel** 1 Marine Dr NE66 2RW (facing golf course and beach) ☎ 01665 830349
Looking out over the golf links and Alnmouth Bay, this 17th-century Listed building started life as a granary and has also served as a vicarage. Now a family-run hotel it offers a variety of attractive bedrooms in different sizes, all individual and stylishly decorated with eye-catching fabrics. There is a comfortable first floor lounge and a little dispense bar half-way up the stairs. Son Ian Inkster, a chef by profession, is winning praise for the standard of his meals, where the emphasis is placed on freshly produced dishes.
10 bth/shr No smoking in bedrooms No smoking in dining room CTV in all bedrooms Tea and coffee making facilities Licensed Cen ht CTV No children 7yrs 12P No coaches Last d 4pm
CARDS:

ALNWICK Northumberland Map **12** NU11

Selected

Q Q Q Q **Bondgate House Hotel** Bondgate Without NE66 1PN (turn off A1 and head for town centre, 200 yds past war memorial on right) ☎ 01665 602025 FAX 01665 602554
This restored Georgian house stands just before the arch which leads to the town centre. Bedrooms are well maintained, furnished with quality pine and good seating, whilst several have attractive window seats. The attractive dining room has a soothing blue colour scheme, and is

licensed for residents to enjoy a drink with their meals. The ground floor lounge has useful tourist information.
8 rms (5 shr) (3 fmly) No smoking in dining room CTV in all bedrooms Tea and coffee making facilities No dogs (ex guide dogs) Licensed Cen ht CTV 8P Last d 4.30pm
ROOMS: s £23-£25; d £42-£44*
CARDS:

ALSAGER Cheshire Map **07** SJ75

Selected

QQQQ **Sappho Cottage** 118 Crewe Rd ST7 2JA (5 mins from M6 J16, follow signs for Alsager turn right at first traffic lights, Sappho Cottage is then exactly one mile on right hand side)
☎ 01270 882033 FAX 01270 883556
This attractive house, dating from the mid 19th century, is just a short drive from the Potteries. It lies on the Crewe side of the town and has a small forecourt car park and pretty rear gardens. Just three bedrooms are provided and these have individual decor to reflect the seasons they are named after. All are equipped with modern facilities and other thoughtful extras. A cosy lounge is provided and this has a large selection of books and magazines. Sheila Clothier is the friendly owner and she offers warm hospitality and serves good home cooking.
3 bth/shr No smoking CTV in all bedrooms Tea and coffee making facilities No dogs Cen ht ch fac 3P No coaches Last d 4pm
ROOMS: s £25-£30; d £40-£45*

ALSTON Cumbria Map **12** NY74

Selected

QQQQ **Ivy Farmhouse** *(NY744414)* Garrigill CA9 3DU (from Penrith turn off A686 2m before Alston signposted, from Alston turn off B6277 after 2m signposted, farmhouse opposite St John's church) ☎ 01434 382501 FAX 01434 382501 Mrs K Wells
This traditional, appealing farmhouse is peacefully situated within the centre of this northern Penine village. The entire house has recently been refurbished and the bedrooms are spacious and comfortable whilst the dining room and television lounge succeed in providing a relaxing environment. Stables are provided for those arriving on horseback.
3 shr (1 fmly) No smoking CTV in all bedrooms Tea and coffee making facilities Cen ht CTV 10P Last d 6pm
ROOMS: s £18.50-£28; d £35-£45; wkly b&b £122.50-£157.50; wkly hlf-bd £192.50-£227.50*

ALTON Hampshire Map **04** SU73

QQ **White Hart** London Rd, Holybourne GU34 4EY
☎ 01420 87654 FAX 01420 543982
This pretty pub in the village of Holybourne is the focus of social life in the village. Games and the occasional disco make for a lively atmosphere. A good selection of handpulled beers is served with a smile. The four bedrooms have been totally refurbished and are smart and attractive.
4 rms No smoking in dining room CTV in all bedrooms Tea and coffee making facilities No dogs (ex guide dogs) Cen ht 40P 6 piste petanque terrain Last d 10pm
ROOMS: s £25-£25; d £40-£40; wkly b&b £175-£175*
MEALS: Lunch £1.75-£11.95alc Dinner £1.75-£11.95alc*
CARDS:

ALTON Staffordshire Map **07** SK04

QQQ ***Bull's Head*** High St ST10 4AQ ☎ 01538 702307 FAX 702065
This old village inn is ideally situated for visitors to Alton Towers and the Staffordshire moorlands. The bar, with its welcoming fire in the inglenook fireplace, is popular with locals, and the light dining room is decorated in country style.
6 shr (2 fmly) CTV in all bedrooms Tea and coffee making facilities No dogs Cen ht 12P Last d 10pm
CARDS:

ALTRINCHAM Greater Manchester Map 07 SJ78

Premier Selected

Q Q Q Q Q **Ash Farm Country** Park Ln, Little Bollington WA14 4TJ (turn off A56 beside Stamford Arms)
☎ 0161 929 9290 FAX 0161 928 5002
Closed 22 Dec-14 Jan
Ash Farm is the delightful home of international snooker star David Taylor and his charming wife, Janice. It is found in a quiet country lane and is very convenient for both the M56 and Manchester airport. The house is very attractively furnished and the building dates back to the 18th century, with the benefit of being surrounded by National Trust land. The bedrooms are very well equipped and one now boasts a huge seven foot bed whilst the furnishings are worthy of a country house. Excellent home cooked dinners and breakfasts are served around a large table and guests can relax afterwards in front of an inviting open fire.
3 rms (2 bth/shr) No smoking in bedrooms CTV in all bedrooms Tea and coffee making facilities Direct dial from bedrooms No dogs (ex guide dogs) Licensed Cen ht No children 9yrs 6P No coaches Snooker Last d 7pm
ROOMS: s £39-£46; d £52-£64*
CARDS:

Selected

Q Q Q Q **The Old Packet House** Navigation Rd, Broadheath WA14 1LW (on A56 Altrincham/Sale road at junct with Navigation Road) ☎ 0161 929 1331 FAX 0161 929 1331
This attractive black and white inn dates back to the early 18th century. It is conveniently situated next to the Bridgwater canal and provides cosy, modern and well equipped bedrooms. An interesting range of food is served in the delightful bar which also has an open fire during the colder weather. Very friendly and attentive service is provided by a full brigade of staff.
4 bth/shr No smoking in area of dining room CTV in all bedrooms Tea and coffee making facilities No dogs (ex guide dogs) Cen ht 10P No coaches Last d 9pm
ROOMS: s £45; d £65*
MEALS: Lunch fr £12.40 Dinner fr £12.40*
CARDS:

AMBLE Northumberland Map 12 NU20

Q Q **The Trap** North Broomhill NE65 9UT (turn off A1068 at Red Row and proceed for 1.5m) ☎ 01670 761672
This friendly B&B takes its name from the pub above which it sits, and presents bright modern accommodation with its own entrance quite separate from the bar. Also upstairs is a combined lounge and breakfast room.
5 rms (1 bth 1 shr) (3 fmly) No smoking in bedrooms Tea and coffee making facilities No dogs (ex guide dogs) Cen ht CTV 50P No coaches Snooker
ROOMS: s £17.50; d £35*
CARDS:

AMBLESIDE Cumbria Map 07 NY30

Selected

Q Q Q Q **Amboseli Lodge** Rothay Rd LA22 0EE (M6junct36, A59 to Ambleside, through traffic lights, past Garden Centre on left, enter one way system keeping right, turn right past Horseshoe Hotel)
☎ 015394 31110 FAX 015394 31111
Closed 1-28 Dec
Situated in the centre of the town, this appealing house has recently undergone refurbishment to offer an improved standard of accommodation. Jean and Ray Fry are experienced hoteliers and offer a warm welcome. The bedrooms are homely, well equipped and provide power showers and baths. Breakfast is served in the conservatory and during the summer months guests can enjoy the garden to the rear.
3 bth/shr No smoking CTV in all bedrooms Tea and coffee making facilities Cen ht No children 3P No coaches
ROOMS: d £40-£52; wkly b&b £140-£182
CARDS:

Q Q Q ***2 Cambridge Villas*** Church St LA22 9DL ☎ 015394 32142
Closed 30 Nov-1 Jan
A relaxed friendly atmosphere prevails at this comfortable and welcoming family run guest house near the centre of town. Throughout, the house is decorated to a high standard and attractive fabrics have been used to good

effect in the compact modern bedrooms. Public areas include an inviting first floor lounge and a smart dining room where hearty breakfasts are served at individual tables.
5 rms (1 fmly) No smoking in bedrooms No smoking in dining room CTV in all bedrooms Tea and coffee making facilities No dogs Cen ht CTV Last d 10.30am

---

Q Q Q **Compston House Hotel** Compston Rd LA22 9DJ
(in centre of village overlooking the park)
☎ 015394 32305
This inviting hotel is ideally situated close to the town centre and continues to offer good value bed and breakfast accommodation. The comfortable bedrooms are nicely proportioned and well maintained, while the stylish lounge has an impressive marble fireplace that is unusually situated beneath a window. The owners, Mr and Mrs Smith are cheerful and provide a warm welcome and plenty of local information.
8 shr (1 fmly) No smoking in 4 bedrooms No smoking in dining room CTV in all bedrooms Tea and coffee making facilities No dogs (ex guide dogs) Licensed Cen ht No children 5yrs 2P No coaches Complimentary membership of private leisure club Last d 10am
ROOMS: d £35-£59✻

Selected

Q Q Q Q **Drunken Duck** Barngates LA22 0NG
(from Ambleside go towards Hawkshead, turn left on B5285 follow for 2.5m, turn right signposted Drunken Duck Inn, 0.5m up hill)
☎ 015394 36347 FAX 015394 36781
This 400 year old former coaching inn stands midway between Ambleside and Tarn Hows offering views of the local peaks. Comfortably furnished with antique pieces, the bedrooms offer modern convenience without spoiling the character of the building. At dinner guests are offered a variety of dishes which are freshly prepared to order. A small but well balanced wine list accompanies the menu. Breakfast has a comprehensive menu and depends essentially on local produce.
8 bth 2 annexe shr No smoking in dining room CTV in all bedrooms Tea and coffee making facilities Direct dial from bedrooms Cen ht 40P Fishing Last d 9pm
CARDS:

Selected

Q Q Q Q **Easedale** Compston Rd LA22 9DJ
(on one way system going north through Ambleside - bottom of Compston Road on corner overlooking bowling & putting greens)
☎ 015394 32112 FAX 32112
Mid Feb-Mid Nov & 27 Dec-4 Jan
This guest house lies in a central position, but looks out onto the local park. The dining room is contained in a new extension, whilst the comfortable guests' lounge features a fine marble fireplace. Bedrooms vary in size but they are smartly furnished in contemporary style making good use of the available space.
7 rms (5 shr) (1 fmly) No smoking CTV in all bedrooms Tea and coffee making facilities No dogs Cen ht CTV 7P No coaches
ROOMS: d £36-£54; wkly b&b £121-£180✻

Selected

Q Q Q Q ***Glen Rothay Hotel*** Rydal LA22 9LR ☎ 015394 34500
This delightful Lakeland inn overlooks Rydal Water and is set against the backdrop of Rydal Mount, the home of Wordsworth for many years. Chris Carss, the new proprietor is certainly ringing the changes and the newly refurbished bedrooms offer high levels of comfort and quality. Dining here is a highlight and the ambitious cooking makes excellent use of local game and fish. The historic public rooms have been sympathetically maintained to reflect the ancient origins of the house.
8 bth/shr

Premier Selected

Q Q Q Q Q **Grey Friar Lodge Country House Hotel** Brathay LA22 9NE (1.5m W off A593) ☎ 015394 33158 FAX 015394 33158
Mar-Oct
This former vicarage is now a delightful country house enthusiastically run by Sheila and Tony Sutton. The house is delightfully furnished with antiques and bric-a-brac to give a warm and relaxing atmosphere. There are two comfortable lounges and a lovely dining room with lace-covered tables. Bedrooms come in a variety of sizes and are all thoughtfully equipped with personal touches including books and home-made sponge cake on arrival. Most of the bedrooms and all the public rooms enjoy magnificent views of the Brathay valley. Sheila's five course dinners and hearty breakfasts are winning deserved praise and Tony will be happy to give advice on the area, his experience of fell walking makes him a wealth of information.
8 bth/shr No smoking in bedrooms No smoking in dining room No smoking in 1 lounge CTV in all bedrooms Tea and coffee making facilities No dogs Licensed Cen ht No children 12yrs 12P No coaches Last d 7.30pm
ROOMS: s £33.50-£36; d £47-£67; wkly b&b £161-£225; wkly hlf-bd £245-£320✻

Q Q Q **Haven Cottage** Rydal Rd LA22 9AY (on A591 opposite health centre, 250yds from the Bridge House)
☎ 015394 33270 FAX 015394 33270

New proprietors, Brian and Lyn Heward are making some changes to this delightful guest house. Hospitality is definitely to the fore and every effort is made to make guests feel at home. The bedrooms, some of which are compact, are all tastefully furnished and offer a good standard of equipment.

8 bth/shr (1 fmly) No smoking CTV in all bedrooms Tea and coffee making facilities No dogs (ex guide dogs) Cen ht 10P

ROOMS: s £23-£30; d £36-£50; wkly b&b £112-£147*

Q Q Q **Kent House** Lake Rd LA22 0AD (from town centre, by post office in one way system 300yds on left on terrace above main road)
☎ 015394 33279 FAX 015394 33279

This traditional Lakeland house enjoys a super location sitting high above the main street overlooking the bustle of the town below. It's best to leave one's car on the main road first and ask Richard Lee for help with luggage and parking. Kent House has lots of stylish touches and those interested in good food will appreciate Richard's creative cooking at both dinner and breakfast. Bedrooms are thoughtfully equipped and include radios, phones and hair dryers.

6 bth/shr (2 fmly) No smoking in dining room No smoking in lounges CTV in all bedrooms Tea and coffee making facilities Direct dial from bedrooms Licensed Cen ht 2P No coaches Last d noon

ROOMS: d £35-£59; wkly b&b £127.50-£173; wkly hlf-bd £236-£281*

CARDS:

Q Q Q ***Lyndhurst Hotel*** Wansfell Rd LA22 0EG (leave M6 at junct 36 onto A591) ☎ 015394 32421 FAX 015394 32421

Helen and Chris Green run a friendly and stylish hotel set on three levels just south of the town centre. Downstairs there is a cosy little lounge and adjoining residents bar, leading to an attractive conservatory dining room adorned with Helen's photographs of the Lakes. Bedrooms vary in size but most are stylishly decorated, have en suite facilities, and include one with a four-poster. The two rooms in an adjacent cottage are ideal as a family unit.

6 shr 2 annexe shr No smoking in 1 bedrooms No smoking in area of dining room No smoking in 1 lounge CTV in all bedrooms Tea and coffee making facilities No dogs Licensed Cen ht No children 5yrs 8P No coaches Last d 4pm

Selected

Q Q Q Q **Riverside Lodge Country House** Rothay Bridge LA22 0EH (follow A593 from Ambleside, turning right after crossing Rothay Bridge) ☎ 015394 34208

Occupying a delightful riverside setting, with a private footbridge connecting the car park to the house, this fine period property is surprisingly secluded, yet within walking distance of the town centre. It has the charm and character of a cottage, with the cosy lounge and pretty dining room having low beamed ceilings; in the lounge there is a stone fireplace. Bedrooms vary in size, with most overlooking the river.

5 bth/shr (1 fmly) No smoking in dining room No smoking in lounges CTV in all bedrooms Tea and coffee making facilities No dogs (ex guide dogs) Cen ht No children 10yrs 6P No coaches Fishing

ROOMS: d £45-£60

CARDS:

Premier Selected

Q Q Q Q Q **Rowanfield Country House** Kirkstone Rd LA22 9ET (off A591 at Bridge House, signed 'Kirkstone') ☎ 015394 33686 FAX 015394 31569

mid Mar-mid Nov, Xmas & New Year

This Lakeland house sits high behind Ambleside and boasts splendid panoramic views across Windermere and the peaks beyond. Proprietors Jane and Phil Butcher have restored the house creating a simple farmhouse style with fine furnishings. Bedrooms are individual in style but all are thoughtfully equipped. A lounge looks out onto the fantastic view, whilst the homely dining room gives comfort and space in which to enjoy Phil's excellent cooking. Dinner is four courses, offering home made soups and an excellent selection of main courses and puddings. Breakfast is the second culinary delight with home made and local produce heavily featured.

7 bth/shr (1 fmly) No smoking CTV in all bedrooms Tea and coffee making facilities No dogs Cen ht No children 8yrs 8P No coaches Last d 5pm

ROOMS: d £58-£72; wkly b&b £203-£238; wkly hlf-bd £309-£315

CARDS:

QQQ *Rydal Lodge Hotel* LA22 9LR (2m NW A591)
☎ 015394 33208
Closed 3 Jan-12 Feb
Situated on the main road in the small village of Rydal, just north of Ambleside, this 16th-century coaching inn offers warm hospitality and tasty home-cooked dinners. Bedrooms have modern appointments and are individually decorated. There is a choice of two lounges, one on the first floor. The dining room overlooks the pretty gardens which run down to the River Rothay.
8 rms (2 shr) (1 fmly) No smoking in dining room Tea and coffee making facilities Licensed CTV ch fac 12P Fishing Last d 7pm
CARDS:

QQQ **Rysdale Hotel** Rothay Rd LA22 0EE (leave M6 junc36 to Ambleside on A591 enter one-way system follow town centre signs, hotel opposite church & bowling green) ☎ 015394 32140 FAX 015394 33999
This private hotel occupies a central position overlooking the park. There is a very smart lounge, a stylish bar and a bright breakfast room. The attractive bedrooms come in two standards, with some rooms having hairdryers and trouser presses.
9 rms (7 bth/shr) (1 fmly) No smoking CTV in all bedrooms Tea and coffee making facilities Licensed Cen ht CTV No children 8yrs 2P No coaches
ROOMS: s £18-£25; d £34-£54*
CARDS:

ANDOVER Hampshire Map 04 SU34

QQQ **Broadwater** Amport SP11 8AY (from A303 take turning for Hawk Conservancy/Amport. At T-junction, turn right, first road right, first cottage on right) ☎ 01264 772240 FAX 01264 772240
Closed 20-31 Dec
Located in the peaceful village of Amport just a short distance west of Andover. This charming cottage with a warm friendly atmosphere is looked after by owner Mrs Mallam. The two en suite bedrooms are of a good size, brightly decorated and comfortably furnished with period pieces. There is a small cosy lounge/dining room, where a generous breakfast is offered, and guests can enjoy a stroll around the attractive garden.
2 bth/shr No smoking in bedrooms No smoking in dining room Tea and coffee making facilities No dogs Cen ht CTV 3P No coaches
ROOMS: s £25-£30; d £45*
CARDS:

Selected

QQQQ **Lains Cottage** Quarley SP11 8PX (from Andover take A303 W, after 5m exit for Quarley and at 'T'-junct turn left. After 200 yds turn right into Cholderton Lane, cottage on right)
☎ 01264 889697 FAX 01264 889227
Closed 22 Dec-6 Jan
Lains Cottage is set in a well maintained garden in the peaceful village of Quarley, a short drive to the west of Andover. The bedrooms are spacious, attractively decorated and comfortably furnished. There is a small cosy lounge in which to relax and breakfast is served in the elegant dining room, where guests share one large table.
3 bth/shr (1 fmly) No smoking CTV in all bedrooms Tea and coffee making facilities No dogs (ex guide dogs) Cen ht No children 8yrs 6P
ROOMS: s £26-£35; d £42-£46

APPLEBY-IN-WESTMORLAND Cumbria Map 12 NY62

QQQ **Bongate House** Bongate CA16 6UE (0.5m from town centre on B6542 signposted Brough) ☎ 017683 51245 FAX 017683 51423
Closed Xmas & New Year
A warm welcome awaits visitors at the home of Ann and Malcolm Dayson, where a separate lounge and cosy bar mean that a stay is most relaxing. Breakfast and other meals are served in the spacious dining room. Bedrooms are comfortable, and the larger rooms have en suite facilities. The grounds are home to two goats and a pot bellied pig! Well tended gardens and a croquet lawn lie behind the traditionally furnished house.
8 rms (1 bth 4 shr) (4 fmly) No smoking in dining room No smoking in 1 lounge CTV in all bedrooms Tea and coffee making facilities Licensed Cen ht No children 7yrs 10P Croquet & putting lawn Last d 6pm
ROOMS: s £18-£20.50; d £36-£41; wkly b&b £120-£135; wkly hlf-bd £180-£200

Premier Selected

QQQQQ *Brampton Tower Country House* Brampton Tower, Croft Ends CA16 6JN (one and a half miles from centre of Appleby on Long Marton road B6542) ☎ 017683 53447 FAX 017683 53447
Brampton Tower sits happily in the Eden Valley with views of the surrounding countryside and moors. This family home is in fact a Victorian folly, locally known as Cuckoo Castle, having its own Pele Tower. Bedrooms are comfortable, offering modern facilities in a traditional setting, one boasting a Georgian four-poster bed. A cosy lounge where guests may quietly relax or read one of the many books is available. Breakfast is a hearty affair taken around a communal table in the dining room, which is decorated with collections of plates. Neat and tidy gardens lead out to stables and grazing land all guarded by this historic sandstone tower.
2 bth/shr No smoking CTV in all bedrooms Tea and coffee making facilities No dogs (ex guide dogs) Licensed Lift Cen ht CTV No children 12yrs 10P No coaches Riding Snooker Last d noon

APPLEDORE Kent Map 05 TQ92

QQQ **The Railway Hotel** Station Rd TN26 2DF
(leave M20 junct 10 follow A2070 for Brenzett at rdbt at Brenzett turn right onto B2080 to Appledore continue for 2m, hotel on left)
☎ 01233 758253 758668 & 758785 FAX 01233 758705
Closed 24 Dec-1 Jan
This small hotel is set in rural surroundings yet conveniently located for all the major routes. The twelve en suite rooms are equipped for business travellers and tourists alike, and situated in a modern building with a railway theme. This theme is continued throughout the public areas which include a well appointed bar and spacious restaurant where good home cooked food is provided. Guests also have use of a bright modern lounge.
12 bth/shr (4 fmly) No smoking in 2 bedrooms No smoking in area of dining room CTV in all bedrooms Tea and coffee making facilities Direct dial from bedrooms Licensed Cen ht 47P Golf Fishing Last d 9.30pm
ROOMS: s £32.50; d £50; wkly b&b £155; wkly hlf-bd fr £215*
CARDS:

ARLINGTON East Sussex Map 05 TQ50

Premier Selected

Q Q Q Q Q ♥ **Bates Green** *(TQ553077)* BN26 6SH (2m W of A22 towards Arlington turn right Old Oak Inn)
☎ 01323 482039 FAX 01323 482039 Mrs C McCutchan
Closed 22-27 Dec

Bates Green is in an idyllic setting along a peaceful country lane in the village of Arlington. Formerly an 18th-Century gamekeeper's cottage the building has been lovingly restored to retain many of the original features. The three bedrooms are individually furnished, decorated in a cottage style and equipped with many thoughtful extras such as mineral water and fresh flowers. Guests have use of a comfortable lounge, with log fire in the winter months, and can relax in the gardens when the weather permits. An extensive choice of breakfast is provided in the cosy dining room.

3 bth/shr No smoking CTV in all bedrooms Tea and coffee making facilities No dogs Cen ht No children 12yrs 3P Tennis (hard) 130 acres sheep turkey
ROOMS: d £48-£56*

ARMSCOTE Warwickshire Map 04 SP24

Q Q Q **Willow Corner** CV37 8DE (from A429 turn left at Armscote sign, at little tree in centre of Armscote turn left)
☎ 01608 682391 FAX 01608 682391

Mrs Power is a friendly host who welcomes guests to her home - a charming Cotswold stone cottage in the quiet hamlet of Armscote. The house is thatched and surrounded by an attractive and colourful English country garden. Guests have the use of a delightful beamed lounge, tastefully furnished and with comfortable seating arranged around a large inglenook fireplace; breakfast is taken communally around a polished table. Bedrooms are cosy, cheerfully decorated and have a thoughtful range of extras and useful facilities; each room has an en suite shower room with power shower.

3 shr CTV in all bedrooms Tea and coffee making facilities Cen ht CTV No children 6yrs 3P Golf 18

ARNSIDE Cumbria Map 07 SD47

Selected

Q Q Q Q **Willowfield Hotel** The Promenade LA5 0AD (turn off A6 at Milnthorpe traffic lights onto B5282, right at T-junction on entering village and right again at Albion public house)
☎ 01524 761354

Arnside is one of the area's best kept secrets. This splendid Victorian house is idyllically set amidst gardens, just off the promenade. Janet and Ian Kerr's family-run hotel has stunning views across the estuary of Morecambe Bay to the Lake District, which is 30 minutes drive away. The atmosphere throughout is friendly and relaxing and the bedrooms are all individually and attractively decorated. The public rooms feature photographs of the area, many taken by Ian.

10 rms (7 shr) (2 fmly) No smoking CTV in all bedrooms Tea and coffee making facilities Licensed Cen ht 8P No coaches Last d 7pm
ROOMS: s £20-£23; d £40-£52; wkly b&b £119.16-£161; wkly hlf-bd £203-£245*
CARDS:

ARUNDEL West Sussex Map 04 TQ00

Q Q Q **Arden** 4 Queens Ln BN18 9JN ☎ 01903 882544

Down a quiet lane just south of the bridge over the river Arun, this early Victorian villa is just a few moments from the town centre. Immaculately well kept by friendly owners Carol and Jeff Short, a couple of the neat bedrooms are on the ground floor where the pine-furnished breakfast room is also to be found. This is a no smoking establishment.

8 rms (3 shr) No smoking CTV in all bedrooms Tea and coffee making facilities No dogs (ex guide dogs) Cen ht No children 5yrs 4P No coaches
ROOMS: s £18-£28; d £34-£40*

Q Q Q **Bridge House** 18 Queen St BN18 9JG (next to river bridge opposite castle) ☎ 01903 882779 & 0500 323224 (free) FAX 01903 883600
Closed 23-30 Dec

Next to the bridge over the River Arun at the centre of town, Bridge House has been run by the Hutchinson family for over 20 years. The dining room, where a good choice of straightforward dishes is offered, enjoys a particularly good view of the castle. Most of the well kept bedrooms are in the main building, dating from the 16th century, but in addition there are three in a separate cottage. A fully equipped laundry room is available to guests.

16 rms (12 bth/shr) 3 annexe bth/shr (6 fmly) No smoking in 4 bedrooms No smoking in dining room No smoking in lounges CTV in all bedrooms Tea and coffee making facilities Licensed Cen ht CTV 12P Last d 7.30pm
ROOMS: s £20-£32; d £38-£46*
CARDS:

ASHBOURNE Derbyshire Map 07 SK14

See also Stanton & Waterhouses

Q ♥ **Air Cottage Farm** *(SK142523)* Ilam DE6 2BD (from Ashbourne take A515 and turn left when signposted Thorpe/Dovedale/Ilam. At Ilam turn right at the Memorial Stone to Alstonfield) ☎ 01335 350475 Mrs J Wain
Mar-Nov

The farm lane leading to this traditional stone-built house commands marvellous views across to Thorpe Cloud and Dovedale down below. Bedrooms are straightforward but pleasant in design. There is a large lounge and a freshly-prepared breakfast is served around one table in the cosy dining room.

3 rms No smoking in dining room No smoking in lounges Tea and coffee making facilities No dogs (ex guide dogs) Cen ht CTV P Resident beauty and holistic therapist available 66 acres beef cattle sheep
ROOMS: s £16-£18; d £32-£36; wkly b&b £112-£126*

Selected

Q Q Q Q **Collycroft** *(SK166434)* DE6 2GN (2.5m S off A515)
☎ 01335 342187 Mrs M Hollingsworth

A warm welcome is assured at this 18th century stone farmhouse surrounded by 250 acres of grazing land. Indeed, visitors are welcome to watch, or even assist, at milking time, but the temptation is great just to linger in the attractive and colourful gardens. Bedrooms are spacious and the en suite double room boasts matching satinwood-veneered mahogany furniture. Typical farmhouse breakfasts are served in the pleasant dining room, whilst the adjacent lounge is comfortable and relaxing.

3 rms (1 shr) No smoking in bedrooms CTV in all bedrooms Tea and coffee making facilities No dogs (ex guide dogs) Cen ht CTV 10P 260 acres dairy beef sheep

Q Q Q **Dog and Partridge** Swinscoe DE6 2HS (from Ashbourne take A52 towards Leek. Establishment is located after 4m on the left hand side) ☎ 01335 343183 FAX 342742

On the Leek road, not far from Alton Towers, is this 17th-century coaching inn. A variety of accommodation is offered; some in the main building, and some in separate blocks. There are also five self catering units, which are very well appointed and used as guest accommodation during quieter periods. The bar and restaurant are welcoming and there are three menus for evening diners. Children are also well catered for with play areas both inside and out.

25 bth/shr No smoking in 3 bedrooms CTV in all bedrooms Tea and coffee making facilities Direct dial from bedrooms ch fac 90P Fishing Last d 11pm

ROOMS: s £30-£60; d £40-£70; wkly b&b £140-£265; wkly hlf-bd £200-£295*

MEALS: Lunch £8.95-£15.95 Dinner £9.95-£10.95&alc*

CARDS:

Q Q Q **Green Man** St Johns St DE6 1GH
☎ 01335 345783 FAX 01335 346613

In the heart of Ashbourne lies this lovely old coaching inn. The new owners have completed a thorough refurbishment of the bedrooms and public areas, which feature a beautiful breakfast room with natural pine furniture. The bars have a lot of character and a varied selection of bar meals is available. A choice of function rooms is available.

18 bth/shr (1 fmly) No smoking in dining room CTV in all bedrooms Tea and coffee making facilities Direct dial from bedrooms No dogs (ex guide dogs) Cen ht 30P Darts Last d 8.30pm

ROOMS: s £35-£40; d £50-£65*

MEALS: Lunch £9-£20 Dinner £9-£20*

CARDS:

Selected

Q Q Q Q **Lichfield** Bridge View, Mayfield DE6 2HN (from town take A52 for Leek, after 1.25m at Queens Arms turn left, 200yds up hill on left) ☎ 01335 344422 FAX 01335 344422

Closed 25 & 26 Dec

This charming detached Georgian house stands high above the River Dove in its own attractive gardens on the edge of the village of

contd.

Mayfield, only one and a half miles from the market town of Ashbourne. Breakfast is served at individual scrubbed pine tables in a pleasant dining room and there is also a comfortable lounge with plenty of books of local interest to browse through. Bedrooms have carefully co-ordinated furnishings and some enjoy fine views over the river below.
3 shr (1 fmly) No smoking CTV in all bedrooms Tea and coffee making facilities No dogs Cen ht CTV 10P No coaches
ROOMS: d £43-£45; wkly b&b £147-£154*

Q Q Q **Stone Cottage** Green Ln, Clifton DE6 2BL ☎ 01335 343377
rs 25 Dec
Stone Cottage is situated in the quiet village of Clifton, just a mile and a half from the centre of Ashbourne. Whilst room sizes vary, each of the bedrooms is attractively appointed and well equipped, with two of the rooms offering four-poster beds. Dinner is available by prior arrangement and breakfast is served in the conservatory dining room, overlooking the attractive gardens.
3 bth/shr (1 fmly) No smoking in bedrooms No smoking in dining room CTV in all bedrooms Tea and coffee making facilities Cen ht CTV 4P No coaches Last d 9.30am
ROOMS: s £25-£32; d £38-£54; wkly b&b £120-£170; wkly hlf-bd £197-£247*
CARDS:

ASHBURTON Devon Map **03** SX76

See also Bickington & Poundsgate

Selected

Q Q Q Q **Gages Mill** Buckfastleigh Rd TQ13 7JW (from Exeter take A38 towards Plymouth, take second exit to Ashburton, cross over A38, first left by Shell Garage, premises is first property on left)
☎ 01364 652391 FAX 01364 652391
Mar-Nov
This 14th-century wool mill is situated in an acre of lawned gardens on the edge of Dartmoor National Park. Bedrooms are tastefully decorated and equipped with modern facilities, and many have attractive countryside views. There are two lounges, one with a small bar for guests' use. Interesting dishes, using local produce, are served in the attractive dining room.
8 bth/shr No smoking in dining room CTV in 4 bedrooms Tea and coffee making facilities No dogs (ex guide dogs) Licensed Cen ht CTV No children 12yrs 10P No coaches Croquet Last d day before
ROOMS: s £20-£24.50; d £40-£49; wkly b&b £133-£140; wkly hlf-bd £220.50-£227.50*

See page 14-20 for a list of Premier Selected establishments

Selected

Q Q Q Q **Greencott** Landscove TQ13 7LZ
☎ 01803 762649
Closed Xmas Day/Boxing Day
Located in a totally secluded spot near Ashburton in the village of Landscove, Greencott has been totally renovated and offers the guest modern facilities in an olde worlde atmosphere. Both bedrooms are en suite, well equipped and carefully decorated and furnished. Traditional country cooking is served around the oak dining table. Friendliness and good service are paramount to the proprietors, Mr & Mrs Townsend.
2 bth/shr No smoking in bedrooms No smoking in dining room No dogs (ex guide dogs) Cen ht ch fac 3P Last d 5pm
ROOMS: s £16-£17; d £32-£34; wkly b&b £112; wkly hlf-bd £161*

Q Q Q **Rosary Mount** Buckfastleigh Rd TQ13 7JL ☎ 01364 653900
FAX 01364 653 901
Closed 23 Dec-2 Jan
Situated mid-way between Ashburton and Buckfastleigh, this country home is peacefully set in its own gardens. Just inside the Dartmoor National Park, Rosary Mount offers comfortable, no-smoking accommodation. There is a spacious TV lounge, and breakfast is served around one large table in an elegant dining room.
3 rms No smoking Tea and coffee making facilities No dogs Cen ht CTV No children 8yrs 6P No coaches
ROOMS: s £25; d £35*

ASHBY-DE-LA-ZOUCH Leicestershire Map **08** SK31

See Coalville

ASHFORD Kent Map **05** TR04

Q Q Q **Croft Hotel** Canterbury Rd, Kennington TN25 4DU (approx 1.5 miles from junction 9 or 10 off the M20 then take A28 road towards Canterbury) (The Independents) ☎ 01233 622140 FAX 01233 635271
A 250 year old building set in two acres of gardens just north of the town. This friendly family run commercial hotel offers comfortable accommodation in the main building, or spacious chalet style rooms in the two outer extensions. The public areas include a cosy lounge, bar and restaurant where a choice of menus is offered at dinner with simple uncomplicated dishes.
15 bth/shr 13 annexe bth/shr (4 fmly) No smoking in 6 bedrooms No smoking in dining room CTV in all bedrooms Tea and coffee making facilities Direct dial from bedrooms Licensed Cen ht CTV 30P Gymnasium Last d 8.30pm
ROOMS: s £42-£48; d £54-£64
CARDS:

Q **Curtis** Waterman Quarter, Headcorn TN27 9JJ (take A274 Maidstone, 1m S of Headcorn take 1st right turn at X-roads for Waterman Quarter, farm is 0.5m on left marked by milk marque sign)
☎ 01622 890393 Miss M A Ray
Located in the heart of the Kent countryside Curtis Farm is just a few miles from pretty Headcorn. A working 59 acre Jersey dairy farm it offers an attractive river walk and coarse fishing on the Hammer stream. Bedrooms are comfortable and simply appointed, a hearty breakfast is served.
2 rms (1 fmly) No smoking Tea and coffee making facilities No dogs (ex guide dogs) Cen ht CTV No children 5yrs 4P Fishing 59 acres dairy
ROOMS: s £23-£25; d £40-£42*

Q Q Q **Warren Cottage** 136 The Street, Willesborough TN24 0NB (exit M20 at junct 10 onto B2164 Kennington Rd towards Canterbury. Turn right into The Street, house on left)
☎ 01233 621905 & 632929 FAX 01233 623400
A warm and friendly welcome awaits guests at this charming 16th-century house. The four bedrooms are comfortably furnished and equipped with

many extras. There is a small cosy lounge with a log fire on cooler evenings and a well appointed dining room where an evening meal is available; guests also have a choice of breakfasts.
4 shr No smoking in bedrooms No smoking in dining room CTV in all bedrooms Tea and coffee making facilities No dogs (ex guide dogs) Licensed Cen ht CTV 20P No coaches Last d 9.30pm
ROOMS: s £34.90-£41.90; d £50-£69.90*
CARDS:

ASHFORD-IN-THE-WATER Derbyshire Map 07 SK16

QQQ **Fieldside** Longstone Ln DE45 1NH (turn off A6 NW of Bakewell into Ashford village, take first right (B6465) signed Monsal Head-Wardlow and first right again, house on left) ☎ 01629 813242 FAX 01629 814589
Closed Xmas
As the name suggests, this detached house sits in a delightful rural location on the edge of this picturesque Derbyshire village. Guests have the use of a spacious lounge, and breakfast is served around one polished table in the dining room. Bedrooms are fresh and appealing, nicely decorated and furnished, and each has an adjacent private bath or shower room; a ground floor bedroom is available.
3 bth/shr (1 fmly) No smoking CTV in all bedrooms Tea and coffee making facilities Cen ht CTV 4P No coaches
ROOMS: s £19.50-£21; d £40-£42; wkly b&b £110-£120

ASTHALL Oxfordshire Map 04 SP21

QQQ *Maytime* OX18 4HW (0.25m N off A40)
☎ 01993 822068 FAX 01993 822635
When driving along the A40 it is worth navigating the narrow country lanes to the pretty hamlet of Asthall, where you will find this charming creeper clad inn. The cosy character bar has a welcoming feel, and the extensive menu is based round fresh produce which is imaginatively prepared. Bedrooms are bright and spacious and have a number of thoughtful extra touches.
6 annexe bth No smoking in area of dining room CTV in all bedrooms Tea and coffee making facilities Direct dial from bedrooms Cen ht 100P Last d 9.30pm
CARDS:

ASTON MUNSLOW Shropshire Map 07 SO58

Selected

QQQQ **Chadstone** SY7 9ER (8m N of Ludlow off the B4368)
☎ 01584 841675
This large modern house stands in the quiet village of Aston Munslow, which is east of Craven Arms on the road to Bridgnorth. To the rear across the large garden, it has pleasant rural views, with the Clee Hills in the background. The bedrooms, which include a room on ground floor level, have modern furnishings, facilities and equipment. There is a sizeable lounge and pleasant dining room, where separate tables can be provided. Hospitality from proprietors Judith and John Lee is warm and friendly.
3 bth/shr No smoking in bedrooms No smoking in dining room CTV in all bedrooms Tea and coffee making facilities No dogs Licensed Cen ht CTV No children 12yrs 6P No coaches Last d 7pm
ROOMS: s £21-£25; d £42-£50; wkly b&b £135-£155; wkly hlf-bd £220-£240

ASWARBY Lincolnshire Map 08 TF03

QQQ **Tally Ho** NG34 8SA (3m S of Sleaford, on A15)
☎ 01529 455205 FAX 01529 455205
This delightful traditional inn is located on the A15. Bedrooms are situated in an adjacent building. Each room is bright and well appointed with modern en suite facilities. A wide range of snacks and meals are available, at lunch and dinner, in the charming bar or within the attractively appointed restaurant; service is friendly and attentive.
6 annexe bth/shr CTV in all bedrooms Tea and coffee making facilities Cen ht 40P No coaches Last d 10pm
ROOMS: s £33; d £48
MEALS: Lunch £10.25-£12.95alc Dinner £13.50-£18.50alc
CARDS:

AUDLEY Staffordshire Map 07 SJ75

Selected

QQQQ **Domvilles** *(SJ776516)* Barthomley Rd ST7 8HT (leave M6, junct 16, follow signs to Barthomley)
☎ 01782 720378 Mrs E E Oulton
Closed 25 Dec
This large 18th-century house is surrounded by a 250 acre dairy farm, and excellent views are afforded over the Cheshire plain to Jodrell Bank and beyond. Bedrooms are not particularly large but all are attractively decorated and equipped with fine antique furniture. Four-poster and other beds are all at least 100 years old. Visitors are welcome to explore the farm and view the twice-daily milking of the livestock.
6 bth/shr (2 fmly) CTV in all bedrooms Tea and coffee making facilities No dogs (ex guide dogs) CTV 8P Table tennis 225 acres dairy mixed Last d 6pm

AVETON GIFFORD Devon Map 03 SX64

Selected

QQQQ **Court Barton** *(SX695478)* TQ7 4LE
(Turn off A379 into Averton Gifford, follow signs for St Andrews church, the guest house is situated just below the church)
☎ 01548 550312 FAX 01548 550312 Mrs J Balkwill
Closed Xmas

contd.

Located next to the parish church and surrounded by well kept gardens, this 16th-century farmhouse enjoys a picturesque setting in the heart of the Devon countryside. Welcoming hosts John and Jill Balkwill have sympathetically renovated the house to provide large bedrooms, traditionally furnished and equipped with lots of thoughtful extras. A comfortable sitting room is available for guests, and farmhouse breakfasts are served in the dining room at English oak tables made by a local craftsman.
7 rms (6 bth/shr) (2 fmly) No smoking in dining room CTV in all bedrooms Tea and coffee making facilities No dogs (ex guide dogs) Cen ht CTV 10P Outdoor swimming pool Table tennis Pool table Croquet 40 acres mixed
ROOMS: s £20-£35; d £40-£56
CARDS:

AXMINSTER Devon Map **03** SY29

Selected

Q Q Q Q **Manor House** Combpyne EX13 6SX
(take A3052, Seaton to Lyme Regis road. Turn N at Rousdon signed Combpyne and after 0.75m house on right facing duck pond)
☎ 01297 445084 FAX 01297 445084
Closed 23 Dec-2 Jan rs Dec-Feb (min 2 nights stay)
This charming former nunnery was mentioned in the Domesday Book and offers perfect peace and tranquillity in the hamlet of Combpyne, a short drive from Lyme Regis. Constructed of local stone it retains much of its original character with leaded windows, an inglenook fireplace and flagstoned floors. The bedrooms have private facilities and are tastefully decorated with thoughtful extra touches. Proprietors Nicky and Donald Campbell serve breakfast in the Nun's Parlour, and guests are encouraged to use the family lounge and the beautiful garden.
3 bth/shr No smoking in dining room CTV in all bedrooms Tea and coffee making facilities No dogs Cen ht CTV 3P No coaches Croquet Badminton
ROOMS: d £48-£54*

Premier Selected

Q Q Q Q Q **Millbrook Farmhouse** *(SY304987)* Chard Rd EX13 5EG (on A358) ☎ 01297 35351 FAX 01297 35739 Mrs S Gay
Closed Xmas, 2wks autumn & 3wks spring
Situated on the outskirts of the town, Millbrook Farm is a delightful thatched longhouse, sympathetically restored and set in an acre of lovely gardens. Sybil and John Gay welcome guests to their charming abode where Mrs Gay serves dinner and breakfast at one large table in the attractive dining room. The sitting room boasts a huge inglenook fireplace and oak panelled walls. The tasteful decoration of the ground floor, with many personal touches and items of interest, is carried through to the bedrooms, which also feature a number of extra facilities.
3 rms (1 bth/shr) (2 fmly) No smoking CTV in all bedrooms Tea and coffee making facilities No dogs (ex guide dogs) Cen ht CTV 5P Putting Croquet Last d 5pm
ROOMS: d £34-£40*

Selected

Q Q Q Q **Tytherleigh Arms** Tytherleigh EX13 7BE (M5 junct 25, follow A358, situated between Chard and Axminster on main road)
☎ 01460 220400 & 220214 FAX 01460 220406
This 17th-Century inn is situated midway between Axminster in Devon and Chard in Somerset. The historical port of Lyme Regis is just 12 miles away and the many attractions of this beautiful area are all within easy reach by car. The bedrooms have their own access from the courtyard, are well equipped and fitted with modern pine furniture. An extensive range of dishes is available from the menu, as well as the daily specials in the restaurant or the heavily beamed bar with its roaring fire on cooler evenings. Resident proprietors Daivd Lawrence and Sally Hiscox extend a friendly welcome to all their guests.
5 shr (1 fmly) No smoking in dining room CTV in all bedrooms Tea and coffee making facilities Direct dial from bedrooms Cen ht 50P Beauty salon Last d 9pm
ROOMS: s fr £36; d fr £60; wkly b&b fr £225*
MEALS: Lunch £10-£20alc Dinner £10-£25alc*
CARDS:

AYLESBURY Buckinghamshire Map **04** SP81

Q Q Q **The Hamlet** 3 Home Close, Weston Turville HP22 5SP
(Aylesbury to Wendover A413, turn left onto B4544 to Weston Turville. In village take 2nd right into Bates Lane and first leftinto Home Close)
☎ 01296 612660 & 422039 FAX 01296 612660 & 01296 392805
rs 15 Dec-7 Jan
The Hamlet is a small private residence tucked away in the pretty village of Weston Turville. All three rooms feature bright fabrics and tasteful attractive decor. There is an airy conservatory which guests are welcome to use. Proprietor Maria Burgess is a welcoming host.
3 rms (1 bth/shr) No smoking in bedrooms No smoking in area of dining room No smoking in lounges CTV in all bedrooms Tea and coffee making facilities Direct dial from bedrooms No dogs Cen ht CTV 6P No coaches
ROOMS: s £20-£23; d £40-£46*
CARDS:

AYLESFORD Kent Map **05** TQ75

Q Q Q *Aylesford* Forstal Rd ME20 7AH ☎ 01622 717208
FAX 01622 717208
This former pub on the edge of the town has been skilfully converted to provide smart comfortable accommodation. Bedrooms are spacious and well equipped for the business guest, and most have en suite facilities. There is a comfortable television lounge and a generous breakfast is served.
6 rms (2 bth/shr) No smoking in bedrooms No smoking in dining room CTV in all bedrooms Tea and coffee making facilities No dogs (ex guide dogs) Cen ht CTV 5P
CARDS:

This symbol indicates a 'Child Friendly' establishment - see page 25 for details

BAKEWELL Derbyshire Map **08** SK26

Q Q Q Avenue House Haddon Rd DE45 1EP (300yds from town centre on A6 towards Matlock) ☎ 01629 812467
Feb-Oct
This large corner house is situated on the edge of the town, with a colourful small garden. Bedrooms are spacious, bright and nicely decorated. The comfortable and cosy lounge area is also used as the breakfast room, where guests are served at individual tables.
3 bth/shr No smoking CTV in all bedrooms Tea and coffee making facilities No dogs Cen ht CTV 4P No coaches
ROOMS: d £40-£44; wkly b&b £126-£140*

Q Q Barleycorn Croft Sheldon DE45 1QS
(from A6 to Buxton, 1.5m form Bakewell take left turn 500yds past Ashford turning. House is last one on left hand side in Sheldon back from green)
☎ 01629 813636
Just three miles from Bakewell in the hamlet of Sheldon, this pleasant barn conversion enjoys fine views over the surrounding countryside. Private access is provided to the accommodation which offers one twin and one double bedroom, sharing a modern bathroom. However, rooms are only let to one party at a time, whether that be two or four people. There is also a comfortable television lounge and breakfast room.
2 rms No smoking Tea and coffee making facilities No dogs (ex guide dogs) Cen ht CTV No children 7yrs 4P No coaches
ROOMS: s £20-£25; d £30-£35; wkly b&b £105-£140

Q Q Q Bene-Dorme The Avenue DE45 1EQ (just off A6 near Rutland Recreation Ground) ☎ 01629 813292 FAX 01629 813292
Closed 21 Dec-1 Jan
Mr & Mrs Twigg offer a warm, friendly welcome to their newly built, small family run guest house, which is situated in a quiet close just a few minuets walk from Bakewell town centre, with its range of shops and amenities. The accommodation is tastefully decorated and soundly appointed, all rooms have beautifully tiled modern en suite facilities. Breakfast is served in the homely dining room, (surrounded by numerous family photographs) which also overlooks the patio with an ornamental fishpond and waterfall.
3 bth/shr No smoking CTV in all bedrooms Tea and coffee making facilities No dogs (ex guide dogs) Cen ht 4P
ROOMS: d £42-£45*

Q Q Q Bourne House Haddon Rd DE45 1AW (200 mtrs from Bakewell Town Centre on A6 towards Matlock. Last house on left before park)
☎ 01629 813274
This former Manse sits beside Bakewell park, just off the Matlock road, and is a short riverside walk from the town centre. Guests have their own entrance to the house. Bedrooms are all fresh and neat, each with either modern en suite shower rooms or sole use of a shower. Breakfast is served at individual tables in a separate dining room which overlooks the adjoining park.
3 rms (2 shr) No smoking CTV in all bedrooms Tea and coffee making facilities No dogs Cen ht No children 7yrs 5P
ROOMS: s £25-£34; d £38-£44

Q Q Q Castle Cliffe Private Hotel Monsal Head DE45 1NL (from Ashford-in-the-Water on A6 take the B6465 to Monsal Head)
☎ 01629 640258 FAX 01629 640258
Perched high above Monsal Dale and with marvellous views from many of the bedrooms, this well maintained guest house offers comfortable and neatly decorated bedrooms, most of which have modern en suites. The spacious dining room features freshly prepared British regional dishes. There is a cosy bar and a comfortable lounge to relax in.
9 rms (7 shr) (2 fmly) No smoking in dining room No smoking in lounges CTV in 2 bedrooms Tea and coffee making facilities No dogs (ex guide dogs) Licensed CTV 15P No coaches Last d 5pm
ROOMS: s £35-£37.50; d £50-£56; wkly b&b £155-£180; wkly hlf-bd £248-£270*
CARDS:

Q Q Q Croft Cottages Coombs Rd DE45 1AQ
(Coombs Rd runs parallel with river on A619 side of Bakewell Bridge)
☎ 01629 814101 FAX 01629 815083
This delightful building, a Derbyshire stone Grade II listed building, sits close to the River Wye and the town centre. Thoughtfully equipped bedrooms, some of which overlook the colourful cottage garden, are available in the main house or in the adjoining barn suite which offers a comfortable ground floor lounge and first floor bedroom. Breakfast is taken in a separate dining room/lounge which has a striking fireplace.
4 bth/shr (1 fmly) No smoking in dining room No smoking in lounges CTV in all bedrooms Tea and coffee making facilities Cen ht
ROOMS: d £42-£54

Q Q Everton Haddon Rd DE45 1AW (on A6, south side of town)
☎ 01629 813725
Etr-Oct
Just a few minutes walk from the town centre, this semi-detached Victorian house overlooks Bakewell park. The bright fresh bedrooms, one of which now has modern en suite facilities, are cheerfully decorated. Breakfast is served in the cosy dining room.
3 rms (1 shr) CTV in all bedrooms Tea and coffee making facilities No dogs (ex guide dogs) Cen ht No children 10yrs 3P No coaches
ROOMS: d £36-£42; wkly b&b £126-£140*

Q Q *George Hotel* Church St, Youlgreave DE45 1UW (Turn off A6 between Matlock & Bakewell onto B5056 Ashbourne road, keep going to Youlgreave, hotel opposite church) ☎ 01629 636292 FAX 01632 636292
A friendly village inn, which dates back to the 17th century, that sits in the village of Youlgreave. With the village sitting roughly in the middle of the Peaks, guests find themselves close to the picturesque Lathkill Dale and Bradford Dale walks. The traditional public bars are popular with both locals and walkers alike, and there is a comprehensive choice of home-cooked bar meals available within these bars. Bedroom styles vary, the two most recently added rooms are both spacious and attractively decorated and each has a good modern shower room; the remaining original bedroom shares a general bathroom, but this is scheduled for upgrading and alterations during the coming year.
3 rms (2 shr) (1 fmly) CTV in all bedrooms Tea and coffee making facilities Cen ht 12P Last d 8.30pm

Q Q Holly House The Avenue DE45 1EQ (take A6 Matlock road and after filling station turn right into The Avenue) ☎ 01629 813207
Closed Xmas
Situated in a quiet cul-de-sac near the town centre, Christine Wright's pleasant home offers two nicely furnished bedrooms, sharing a bathroom. There is a comfortable lounge, with a piano in the corner, and breakfast is served around one highly polished yew table in the attractive dining room.
2 rms No smoking CTV in all bedrooms Tea and coffee making facilities No dogs (ex guide dogs) Cen ht CTV 4P No coaches
ROOMS: d fr £36*

Q Q Q Willow Croft Station Rd, Great Longstone DE45 1TS
(turn off A6 at Ashford onto B6465, after 1.5m turn left under bridge signed Gt Longstone, pass White Lion on left, take next left Station Rd)
☎ 01629 640576
Closed 15 Dec-4 Jan
Willow Croft is situated in a charming Peak District village just five miles from Bakewell. Bedrooms, all of them on the ground floor, are neatly decorated and furnished, whilst there is a spacious combined lounge and breakfast room with patio doors opening onto the well tended front garden.
3 bth/shr No smoking CTV in all bedrooms Tea and coffee making facilities Cen ht 3P No coaches
ROOMS: s £20-£25; d £36-£45; wkly b&b £119-£126*

BAMFORD Derbyshire Map 08 SK28

Q Q Q ***Moorlands*** Shatton Ln S33 0BG (Turn off A625 between Hathersage & Hope, turn off to Shatton, opposite the High Peak Centre)
☎ 01433 651911
Quietly situated in a small cluster of dwellings, this stone faced house offers three attractively decorated bedrooms, sharing an adjacent modern bathroom. There is a very comfortable lounge area and a choice of settings for breakfast, either around one highly polished table in the nicely furnished dining room or in the conservatory, facing the large colourful garden to the rear.
3 rms No smoking in bedrooms CTV in all bedrooms Tea and coffee making facilities Cen ht CTV 3P No coaches

Q Q Q The Outpost Shatton Ln S30 0BG (Turn off A625 over little bridge opposite Proctors Garden Centre) ☎ 01433 651400
Closed 24 Dec-2 Jan
Enjoying a peaceful location, this house displays the owner's skills as a craftsman with wood, including attractive furniture and oak wall panelling. One double room looks out over the garden, and another room can be combined with a single room to create a family suite. Dinner is available by arrangement in the beamed dining room, with breakfast served in the conservatory.
3 rms (1 shr) (1 fmly) No smoking CTV in all bedrooms Tea and coffee making facilities No dogs Cen ht CTV 3P No coaches
ROOMS: s £17.50; d £35-£45; wkly b&b fr £105*

Q Q Q Pioneer House Station Rd S33 0BN (turn off A625 onto A6013, house on right after approx third of a mile) ☎ 01433 650638
Solidly built out of local stone at the turn of the century, this house lies in the Hope Valley, close to Ladybower reservoir and other attractions. Bedrooms are comfortably furnished in keeping with the style of the house whilst, downstairs, breakfast is served around one pine table in the dining room, complete with feature fireplace. There is also a lounge for guests' use.
3 bth/shr No smoking CTV in all bedrooms Tea and coffee making facilities No dogs Cen ht No children 4P
ROOMS: d £37-£44*

Q Q The White House Shatton Ln S33 0BG (A625 Hathersage to Hope, turn left opposite High Peak Garden Centre into Hamlet of Shatton. The White House is 250yds on left) ☎ 01433 651487 FAX 01433 651487
This large detached house is quietly situated amidst large neatly tended gardens. Bedrooms are spacious and laid out in a practical way, and there is also a cosy lounge available for guests' use. Breakfast is served around one table in the nicely furnished dining room which overlooks the garden.
4 rms No smoking in bedrooms No smoking in dining room CTV in all bedrooms Tea and coffee making facilities Cen ht CTV 4P No coaches
ROOMS: s £17-£20; d £34-£37; wkly b&b £112*

Q Q Ye Derwent Hotel Main Rd S33 0AY
☎ 01433 651395 FAX 01433 651943
This village inn, situated close to Ladybower reservoir, remains popular with families and walkers. Facilities have been further upgraded, with additional en suite facilities added, and a full range of meals offered in the cosy dining area or bar lounge, which is also frequented by locals.

12 rms (4 bth 2 shr) (2 fmly) CTV in all bedrooms Tea and coffee making facilities Cen ht 40P Boat for hire Last d 9.15pm
ROOMS: s £25-£38; d £42-£48; wkly b&b £140-£168; wkly hlf-bd fr £185*
MEALS: Lunch fr £6.35&alc Dinner fr £6.35&alc*
CARDS:

BAMPTON Devon Map **03** SS92

Selected

Q Q Q Q **The Old Mill** Shillingford EX16 9BW (on B3227)
☎ 01398 331064 FAX 01398 331064
This stone built corn mill has been carefully restored by its present owners and is surrounded by attractive and well maintained gardens through which runs the original leat. The bedrooms are spacious, well equipped and fitted with modern pine furniture. They are arranged so as allow the formation of family suites, with either a patio or their own private lounge. The lounge in the main house is for the use of guests taking dinner. Proprietor Di Burnell accommodates individual guests' tastes, discussing the menu daily in order to provide a choice of home cooked dishes using fresh local ingredients. Activities such as horseriding, shooting and fishing (in season) can be arranged.
2 bth/shr 2 annexe shr (2 fmly) No smoking CTV in all bedrooms Tea and coffee making facilities No dogs Licensed Cen ht CTV 20P No coaches Fishing Riding Last d noon
ROOMS: d £52-£62*
CARDS:

BANBURY Oxfordshire Map **04** SP44

Q Q Q ***The Blinking Owl*** Main St, North Newington OX15 6AE
☎ 01295 730650
This lovely old ironstone inn is full of character. It is located just a few minutes drive from the town. The owl theme is carried through the establishment in the carpet design and with ornaments. The accommodation is separate from the tap room, ensuring quiet. Throughout, the atmosphere is convivial and the bedrooms are suitably appointed. Guests should make sure to sample some of the real ales.
3 bth/shr CTV in all bedrooms Tea and coffee making facilities No dogs (ex guide dogs) Cen ht 12P Last d 9pm

Q Q Q ***Easington House Hotel*** 50 Oxford Rd OX16 9AN (300yds from Banbury Cross on right, entrance to parking via lane)
☎ 01295 270181 FAX 01295 269527
Closed Xmas/New Year
This pretty house is set back from the old Oxford road. Proprietors Mr and Mrs Hearne take a close interest in their guests' welfare and help to create a warm atmosphere. Well appointed, comfortable bedrooms vary in size. There is a cosy guests' lounge where small meetings can be held. Dinner is sometimes available but on quieter nights staff are happy to recommend a local restaurant.
12 rms (11 bth/shr) (3 fmly) No smoking in dining room CTV in all bedrooms Tea and coffee making facilities Direct dial from bedrooms Licensed Cen ht 27P Last d 8.30pm
CARDS:

Selected

Q Q Q Q **La Madonette Country** North Newington OX15 6AA (from M40 junct 11 follow signs to Banbury Cross. Take B4035 (Shipston-on-Stow) for approx 2.5m then turn left for North Newington) ☎ 01295 730212 FAX 01295 730363
Set in its own grounds in tranquil Cotswold surroundings, this pretty 18th century former miller's house has its own mill stream running by. Bedrooms, one with a four poster and an enormous corner bath, are comfortably furnished with many thoughtful extras provided to ensure guests comfort. A tastefully decorated lounge with its own bar is available for guests. Proprietor Patti Ritter offers a warm welcome and serves a generous breakfast in the intimate French inspired dining room. A small conference room is popular for business meetings, and there are several self-catering cottages on the property.
5 bth/shr (2 fmly) No smoking in dining room CTV in all bedrooms Tea and coffee making facilities Direct dial from bedrooms No dogs (ex guide dogs) Licensed Cen ht CTV 20P No coaches Outdoor swimming pool (heated)
ROOMS: d £37-£45*
CARDS:

Q Q **Roebuck** Stratford Rd, Drayton OX15 6EN (exit M40 at junc 11, premises on A442) ☎ 01295 730542 FAX 01295 730542
Closed Dec
This friendly inn on the outskirts of Banbury in the quiet village of Drayton has a comfortable bar where the beer has won many awards. The smart restaurant serves home cooked meals, and snacks are also available. The two bedrooms are well equipped and comfortable.
2 rms No smoking in bedrooms No smoking in dining room CTV in all bedrooms Tea and coffee making facilities No dogs Cen ht 20P Last d 9.30pm
ROOMS: s £28; d £38*
MEALS: Bar Lunch £2-£9 Dinner £15-£22alc*
CARDS:

BANTHAM Devon Map **03** SX64

Q Q Q **Sloop** TQ7 3AJ (from A379 at mini roundabout at Church Stow take Bantham Rd, 2.5m to village, premises on left)
☎ 01548 560489 & 560215 FAX 01548 561940
Situated in an outstanding part of Devon, well known for its natural beauty, the interior of the Sloop is reminiscent of a 16th-century galleon. Its bedrooms are well equipped and comfortable. Local fresh fish is a special feature of the menu.
5 bth/shr (2 fmly) CTV in all bedrooms Tea and coffee making facilities Cen ht 35P No coaches Last d 10pm
ROOMS: s £32-£64; d £60-£66; wkly hlf-bd £325-£345*
MEALS: Lunch £5-£16alc Dinner £5-£18alc*
CARDS:

Premier Selected

Q Q Q Q Q **Widcombe House** TQ7 3AA (off A379 Totnes to Plymouth. At Bantham Cross take road signed Bantham and Widcombe. House 1.5m on left) ☎ 01548 561084
Feb-Oct
Owners John Paine and Jill Hutcheson have set high standards at this attractive house set in manicured gardens a short drive from *contd.*

the village. The three bedrooms have restful colour schemes and good quality furniture. Jill Hutcheson is Cordon Bleu trained and delicious menus testify to her culinary skills.
3 rms (2 bth/shr) No smoking CTV in all bedrooms Tea and coffee making facilities No dogs Cen ht No children 14yrs 9P No coaches Last d noon
ROOMS: s £30-£40; d £52-£60; wkly b&b £182-£210; wkly hlf-bd £280-£308*
CARDS:

BARNARD CASTLE Co Durham Map 12 NZ01

The Fox and Hounds Country Inn & Restaurant Cotherstone DL12 9PF (4m W on B6277) ☎ 01833 650241 FAX 01833 650241
Closed 25 Dec
The atmosphere is friendly and relaxed at this family run inn which overlooks the sloping village green. Bedrooms are bright, cheery and thoughtfully equipped to include telephones, radios and mineral water. The elegant resident lounge is an added bonus, and the approach to mealtimes is flexible.
3 bth/shr (1 fmly) No smoking in bedrooms No smoking in area of dining room No smoking in 1 lounge CTV in all bedrooms Tea and coffee making facilities Direct dial from bedrooms No dogs (ex guide dogs) Cen ht 15P Fishing Riding Last d 10pm
ROOMS: s £39.50; d £57.50; wkly b&b £200-£300*
MEALS: Lunch £10-£20&alc Dinner £10-£20&alc*
CARDS:

Selected

The Homelands 85 Galgate DL12 8ES (400 metres from Town Centre on A67) ☎ 01833 638757
Situated close to the town centre, this stylish and attractive house continues to appeal to both the business and leisure market. Bedrooms have been thoughtfully decorated with pretty fabrics and a good use of stencils. The public rooms are comfortable and a delicious dinner menu is offered in the pleasant dining room which is also popular with the public. Guests can make use of the well tended garden which is very colourful especially during the summer months.
4 rms (3 shr) No smoking in bedrooms No smoking in dining room CTV in all bedrooms Tea and coffee making facilities Direct dial from bedrooms No dogs (ex guide dogs) Licensed Cen ht No children 5 5P No coaches Last d 8.15pm
ROOMS: s £20-£25; d £40-£44*

West Roods *(NZ022141)* West Roods Working Farm, Boldron DL12 9SW (off A66, 2.5m E of Bowes) ☎ 01833 690116 Mr & Mrs R Lowson
May-Oct
This working hill farm lies on a natural plateau and is conveniently accessed directly off the dual-carriageway, although its long farm drive places it far enough away to give peace and quiet. It provides breathtaking panoramic views to the north and east. Margaret and Ronald Lowson place a lifetime of experience into welcoming their guests to their farm and the history of the area, with both children and adults able to learn about farm life. The house itself is plain and practical, but is a cheery home and bedrooms come well equipped.
3 rms (2 shr) (1 fmly) No smoking CTV in all bedrooms Tea and coffee making facilities No dogs Cen ht 6P Table tennis Badminton 54 acres dairy
ROOMS: s fr £18; d fr £36; wkly b&b fr £100*

Selected

Wilson House *(NZ081124)* Barningham DL11 7EB (turn off A66 at Greta Bridge, follow road to Barningham. Turn at second farm on right) ☎ 01833 621218 Mrs H Lowes
Closed 23-28 Dec
This attractive farmhouse stands in 475 acres amongst superb Pennine scenery and offers a genuine welcome to all guests. The bedrooms are pleasantly decorated, and a family suite is offered. The public rooms include a comfortable lounge and two cosy dining rooms. Good home cooking is provided, which uses the best of local produce.
3 rms (2 shr) (1 fmly) No smoking CTV in all bedrooms Tea and coffee making facilities No dogs (ex guide dogs) Cen ht CTV 5P 475 acres mixed livestock Last d 2pm
ROOMS: s £17-£25; d £37-£40*

BARNEY Norfolk Map 09 TF93

Selected

The Old Brick Kilns Little Barney Ln, Barney NR21 0NL (6m NE of Fakenham turn off A148 towards Barney, then towards Little Barney) ☎ 01328 878305 FAX 01328 878948
Guests can expect a warm, friendly welcome from Pam and Alan Greenhalgh at this small country house which is set in its own peaceful grounds amidst rural surroundings. It was originally three separate cottages and has been converted to provide tastefully decorated and comfortably furnished accommodation with a range of useful facilities and thoughtful extras. The public rooms are soundly appointed, featuring a lovely lounge with a log fire, comfortable sofas, board games and local information. In the dining room guests can enjoy a hearty breakfast seated around a large oval table. Dinner is available and special diets can be catered for by prior arrangement.
3 bth/shr No smoking CTV in all bedrooms Tea and coffee making facilities Direct dial from bedrooms No dogs (ex guide dogs) Licensed Cen ht CTV 15P No coaches Fishing Table tennis Boules Croquet Giant chess Last d 10am
ROOMS: s fr £24; d fr £48; wkly b&b £140; wkly hlf-bd £245
CARDS:

BARNSTAPLE Devon Map 02 SS53

See also Bratton Fleming

Cresta 26 Sticklepath Hill EX31 2BU ☎ 01271 374022
Conveniently located at the top of Sticklepath Hill, on the old road to Bideford, this detached family home offers a relaxed and informal atmosphere. The bedrooms are undergoing a programme of upgrading and offer comfortable accommodation equally suitable for tourists and business guests; two ground floor rooms are available. A good breakfast is served in the brightly decorated dining room.
6 rms (2 shr) (2 fmly) No smoking in dining room No smoking in lounges CTV in all bedrooms Tea and coffee making facilities Cen ht 6P No coaches
ROOMS: s £16-£25; d £32-£36; wkly b&b £112-£126*

Heanton House Kings Heanton, Marwood EX31 4ED (From Barnstaple follow A361, turn left after half mile, follow signs for Marwood Gdns. At Guineford crossrds turn right, guest house is on left) ☎ 01271 346342 FAX 01271 346342
With easy access to the North Devon coast and to Barnstaple itself, this large family home is quietly situated in a picturesque village. Bedrooms are comfortably furnished and there is also a spacious lounge, filled with books, videos and games. Breakfast is served around a pine table in the open plan

kitchen. Available by arrangement, evening meals are served in the charming dining room.
4 rms (1 bth/shr) No smoking in bedrooms No smoking in dining room CTV in 2 bedrooms Tea and coffee making facilities No dogs (ex guide dogs) Cen ht CTV 5P No coaches Last d 5pm

Selected

Q Q Q Q **Home Park** *(SS553360)* Lower Blakewell, Muddiford EX31 4ET (take A39 Lynton road from Barnstaple, fork left on B3230 and take second left to Home Park, carry on to very end of no through road) ☎ 01271 342955 FAX 01271 342955 Mrs M Lethaby
Closed 21-31 Dec
From its peaceful elevated position this small, well modernised farmhouse offers stunning views of rolling countryside. Mrs Lethaby provides cheerful hospitality and an excellent home-cooked dinner using fresh local ingredients. Bedrooms are well equipped, and there is a comfortable lounge with a more recent conservatory extension overlooking the beautiful gardens.
3 bth/shr (1 fmly) No smoking CTV in all bedrooms Tea and coffee making facilities No dogs Cen ht CTV ch fac 3P 70 acres sheep mixed Last d 4pm
ROOMS: s £20-£25; d £35-£50✻

Q Q **Rowden Barton** *(SS538306)* Roundswell EX31 3NP (2m South of Barnstaple on B3232) ☎ 01271 344365 Mrs J Dallyn
This homely and welcoming farmhouse enjoys marvellous views over the surrounding countryside and is only a short distance from the North Devon link road. Comfortable bedrooms are complemented by a spacious lounge. Breakfast is served around one large table in the dining room, and dinner is available by prior arrangement.
2 rms No smoking No dogs (ex guide dogs) Cen ht CTV 4P 90 acres beef sheep
ROOMS: s fr £18; d fr £32; wkly b&b fr £90✻

Q Q **West View** Pilton Causeway EX32 7AA (opposite Pilton Park) ☎ 01271 342079 326960 FAX 342079
Split between two properties in an Edwardian terrace, this guest house offers extensive accommodation, rooms in the adjacent property being more recently refurbished. The comfortable lounge and the pine furnished dining room are also housed in the second building, where a choice of dishes is offered for dinner.
10 rms (2 shr) 13 annexe rms (3 shr) (3 fmly) No smoking in dining room CTV in all bedrooms Tea and coffee making facilities Direct dial from bedrooms Licensed Cen ht CTV 21P No coaches Last d 5.30pm
ROOMS: s £18-£20; d £34-£40✻
CARDS:

Q Q Q ***Yeo Dale Hotel*** Pilton Bridge EX31 1PG (from A361 Barnstaple take A39 Lynton, hotel approx 0.25m from A361/A39 roundabout,on left past small park) ☎ 01271 342954 FAX 01271 342954
This family run hotel is located just a few minutes walk from the town centre, across the river Yeo. Comfortable bedrooms, which vary in size, are attractively decorated. There is a spacious lounge and separate bar. Breakfast is served at individual tables in the 17th-century dining room, complete with inglenook fireplace, and dinner is available by arrangement.
10 rms (6 shr) (2 fmly) No smoking in 1 bedrooms No smoking in dining room No smoking in 1 lounge CTV in all bedrooms Tea and coffee making facilities No dogs (ex guide dogs) Licensed Cen ht CTV Last d 11am
CARDS:

We endeavour to be as accurate as possible but changes in personnel and data can occur in establishments after the Guide has gone to press

BARRASFORD Northumberland Map 12 NY97

Q Q Q **Hillcrest House** NE48 4BY (turn off A68 onto B6079 after approx 1m turn right towards Barrasford, travel 0.5m Hillcrest House on right hand side at next junct) ☎ 01434 681426
Mar-Oct
Built in 1935, this detached house lies in attractive country gardens just outside the picturesque village of Barrasford. Inviting public areas include a delightful lounge and a pine furnished dining room where home cooked meals are enjoyed. There's lots to read and a cat lovers theme runs throughout the house. Bedrooms are well proportioned and thoughtfully equipped.
4 shr (1 fmly) No smoking in dining room No smoking in lounges CTV in all bedrooms Tea and coffee making facilities Licensed Cen ht 5P No coaches Last d breakfast
ROOMS: s £18-£20; d £32-£35; wkly b&b £100-£115; wkly hlf-bd £147.50-£160✻

BARTON-ON-SEA Hampshire Map 04 SZ29

Selected

Q Q Q Q **Cleeve House** 58 Barton Court Av BH25 7HG (off A337) ☎ 01425 615211
Situated on a quiet avenue just a few minutes walk from the sea front, this friendly guest house is run by Mrs Carter, who is a natural host, and benefits from loyal guests who return year after year. Her home offers spacious rooms with smart, bright decor. In addition to a comfortable TV lounge and a sunny breakfast room, there is a large self catering flat in the grounds. No evening meals are served at this no-smoking establishment, but guests will enjoy the home made muesli at breakfast, which wins high praise from visitors.
4 rms (2 bth/shr) (1 fmly) No smoking CTV in all bedrooms Tea and coffee making facilities No dogs Cen ht CTV 8P No coaches
ROOMS: s £18; d £36-£42✻

BASINGSTOKE Hampshire Map 04 SU65

See also Hook

Selected

Q Q Q Q **Fernbank Hotel** 4 Fairfields Rd RG21 3DR ☎ 01256 321191 FAX 01256 321191
Closed 2 wks at Xmas
This small hotel, situated in a quiet residential area close to the town centre and within easy reach of the major road networks, offers attractive accommodation. Bedrooms in the Victorian fronted property are equipped with every modern comfort and there is an attractive conservatory sitting room where guests can enjoy a drink. Richard and Theresa White, the resident proprietors, speak Spanish and French.
contd.

16 bth/shr (1 fmly) No smoking in 3 bedrooms No smoking in dining room No smoking in lounges CTV in all bedrooms Tea and coffee making facilities Direct dial from bedrooms No dogs Licensed Cen ht CTV 16P
ROOMS: s £47-£60; d £55-£65*
CARDS:

Selected

Hatchings Woods Ln, Cliddesden RG25 2JF (M3 exit 6, take Alton road A339 and pass under road bridge. Immediate right turn signed Cliddesden B3046, after 0.75m pass garage take next right) ☎ 01256 465279
This delightful property nestles in the pretty village of Cliddesden, yet is ideally located for the town centre and motorway. Mr and Mrs Hatchman offer a warm welcome to their guests and have sought to provide every comfort. The beautifully furnished bedrooms overlook the garden and have private modern facilities. Good cooked breakfasts, including home-made preserves and local honey, are served in the rooms.
3 rms (2 bth/shr) No smoking CTV in all bedrooms Tea and coffee making facilities Direct dial from bedrooms Cen ht No children 10yrs P No coaches
ROOMS: s £21.50-£27; d £45-£50*

BASLOW Derbyshire Map **08** SK27

Rutland Arms Calver Rd DE45 1RP (from M1 follow A619 to Baslow, take A623 towards Stockport, Rutland Arms 0.5m on left next to church) ☎ 01246 583810
rs Nov-Mar,
This cosy and convivial village inn is owned by the local Mansfield Brewery. The beamed lounge bar is mainly open plan with a dining area and open fire, whilst the bedrooms are very well furnished and of a comfortable size; rooms share adjacent general bathroom facilities.
3 rms (1 fmly) No smoking in area of dining room CTV in all bedrooms Tea and coffee making facilities Cen ht 30P
CARDS:

Wheatsheaf Hotel Netherend DE4 1SR (exit M1 junct 29, through Chesterfield follow signs for Chatsworth House. First house on right on entering Baslow) ☎ 01246 582240 FAX 01246 582240
This attractive stone-built inn, which is located in the centre of the village, is an ideal base for touring the Peak district and visiting nearby Chatsworth House. The public rooms are attractively appointed with cottage-style furnishings and fittings; these areas are dedicated to food and beverage operations. Bedrooms are comfortable and well equipped.
5 rms (1 bth 2 shr) (1 fmly) No smoking in dining room No smoking in lounges CTV in all bedrooms Tea and coffee making facilities No dogs (ex guide dogs) Cen ht 100P Last d 9.30pm
CARDS:

BASSENTHWAITE Cumbria Map **11** NY23

Selected

Link House CA13 9YD (exit M6 at junct 40 and take A66 west pass Keswick, at north end of Bassenthwaite Lake turn right onto B5291. Follow road to left) ☎ 017687 76291 FAX 017687 76670
Feb-Nov
Mike and Marilyn Tuppen are going from strength to strength with this fine Victorian house. It has an inviting atmosphere and public rooms include a cosy lounge, provided with lots of reading material, a conservatory and an attractive dining room. Guests speak highly of Marilyn's four course dinners, and favourite dishes are venison in red wine or salmon fillet with a watercress butter. Breakfasts are also a treat and there is a well judged wine list. Bedrooms vary in size, all being individual, and there are some pleasant single rooms.

8 bth/shr (1 fmly) No smoking in bedrooms No smoking in dining room CTV in all bedrooms Tea and coffee making facilities No dogs (ex guide dogs) Licensed Cen ht No children 7yrs 10P No coaches Last d 5pm
ROOMS: s £20-£26; d £40-£52; wkly hlf-bd £250*
CARDS:

BATH Somerset Map **03** ST76

For other locations surrounding **Bath** see also **Box, Bradford on Avon, Combe Hay, Frome, Hinton Charterhouse, Stanton Prior, Swineford and Timsbury**

Abbey Rise 97 Wells Rd BA2 3AN (situated on the A367 going SW from the city centre) ☎ 01225 316177 FAX 01225 316177
This pleasant little guest house is conveniently located a short walk from the city centre. Two of the four bedrooms have modern en suite facilities and all are attractively decorated and well equipped. A stylish dining room is provided and breakfasts are freshly cooked and wholesome. Hospitality is warm and friendly and, although no car parking is provided, nearby street parking is available.
4 rms (2 shr) (1 fmly) No smoking CTV in all bedrooms Tea and coffee making facilities Cen ht 1P No coaches
ROOMS: s £28-£38; d £37-£47*

Remember to return your Prize Draw card for a chance to win an action-packed family weekend at one of the eleven Family Fun Hotels in the Hilton Hotels Directory. See inside the front cover for the card and competition details. Don't forget to fill in your name and address before posting!

Premier Selected

QQQQQ **Apsley House Hotel** Newbridge Hill BA1 3PT
(On A431 1 mile West of city) ☎ 01225 336966 FAX 01225 425462
Closed 1 wk Xmas

Built for the Duke of Wellington, this elegant Georgian house is located about a mile west of the city centre. Each of the bedrooms has an attractive style of its own, all are beautifully maintained and offer a high level of comfort. The spacious public areas are delightfully decorated and furnished, the elegant lounge is a charming reminder of days gone by. Hospitality is warm, friendly and enthusiastic, with the proprietors and their efficient staff having a good rapport with guests. A delicious variety of breakfast items is offered and freshly prepared dishes are a feature of appetising supper trays.

9 bth/shr (3 fmly) No smoking in 2 bedrooms No smoking in dining room No smoking in 1 lounge CTV in all bedrooms Tea and coffee making facilities Direct dial from bedrooms No dogs (ex guide dogs) Licensed Cen ht No children 5yrs 10P

ROOMS: s £50-£65; d £65-£105; wkly b&b £230-£300✱

CARDS:

QQQ **Aran House Number Ninety Three** 93 Wells Rd BA2 3AN
(A367 Wells road, within 0.25m of centre of Bath) ☎ 01225 317977

This Victorian terraced house is conveniently located near the city centre. It provides pretty and well equipped bedrooms, one of which is suitable for families. A combined dining and sitting room features a large library of books and reference guides. Hospitality from owner Chris Pollard is warm and welcoming and street parking is available nearby.

4 shr (1 fmly) No smoking CTV in all bedrooms Tea and coffee making facilities No dogs Cen ht Last d 10am

ROOMS: s £25-£45; d £40-£55✱

Selected

QQQQ **Armstrong House** 41 Crescent Gardens BA1 2NB
(on A4 in Central Bath, 30yds on right at bottom of Charlotte Street, leaving Queens Square) ☎ 01225 442211 FAX 01225 460665
Closed 24 Dec-1 Jan

This delightful end-of-terrace Victorian property, situated within easy walking distance of the centre, has recently been renovated and tastefully decorated throughout. Resident proprietor Tony Conradi welcomes guests and, in the absence of a dining room, serves a substantial continental breakfast in the bedrooms. Armstrong House is a no-smoking establishment.

4 shr (1 fmly) No smoking CTV in all bedrooms Tea and coffee making facilities No dogs (ex guide dogs) Cen ht No children 6yrs 4P No coaches

ROOMS: d £45-£55✱

Q **Arney** 99 Wells Rd BA2 3AN (on A367) ☎ 01225 310020

Arney guest house offers comfortable accommodation. Situated only a short drive away from the city centre, this is an ideal place for the business person or tourist to stay.

3 rms (1 fmly) No smoking in dining room No smoking in lounges CTV in 1 bedroom Tea and coffee making facilities No dogs (ex guide dogs) Cen ht

ROOMS: s £20-£25; d £40-£45✱

QQQ **Ashley Villa Hotel** 26 Newbridge Rd BA1 3JZ
(leaving Bath on the A4, Upper Bristol Rd West, take the left fork at 2nd set traffic lights into Newbridge Rd, hotel is situated 200yds on the right)
☎ 01225 421683 & 428887 FAX 01225 313604

Conveniently located close to the historic delights of this wonderful city, Ashley Villa is an ideal choice for those seeking comfortable, well presented and carefully equipped accommodation. In addition to a choice of lounges, a bar is available for guests. There is an attractive dining room where a full traditional breakfast is served. Should you need to cool off, then take advantage of the lovely swimming pool in the garden.

See advertisement on p.59.

contd.

14 bth/shr (3 fmly) No smoking in 12 bedrooms No smoking in dining room No smoking in 1 lounge CTV in all bedrooms Tea and coffee making facilities Direct dial from bedrooms No dogs (ex guide dogs) Licensed Cen ht CTV 10P Outdoor swimming pool

ROOMS: s £54-£59; d £69-£79; wkly b&b £210-£413✳

CARDS:

Selected

QQQQ **Badminton Villa** 10 Upper Oldfield Park BA2 3JZ (from city centre take A367 then A37 towards Radstock. Take first right 600yds up hill into Upper Oldfield Park and premises are 300yds on right)

☎ 01225 426347 FAX 01225 420393

Closed 24 Dec-1 Jan

This is a charming Victorian house run by Sue and John Burton who invite guests to relax in the comfort of their home. The four bedrooms are well equipped and beautifully presented, some have splendid views across the city to the countryside beyond. There is a pleasant dining room with conservatory which leads to a well tended garden where guests are welcome to stroll. Badminton Villa lies ten minutes' walk from the city centre.

4 bth/shr (1 fmly) No smoking CTV in all bedrooms Tea and coffee making facilities No dogs (ex guide dogs) Cen ht No children 7yrs 5P No coaches

ROOMS: s £40-£45; d £58-£65✳

CARDS:

Selected

QQQQ **Bailbrook Lodge** 35/37 London Rd West BA1 7HZ (from Bath, take the A4 towards Chippenham, at large intersection with A46, go straight on to Batheaston, hotel is immediately on left) (Minotel) ☎ 01225 859090 FAX 01225 859090 & 852299

Closed 25-26 Dec

Bailbrook Lodge is an impressive Georgian building well located for the sites of Bath but away from the hustle and bustle of city life. Set in its own grounds with gardens and a newly added sun terrace, it provides a relaxing setting. There is a good sized dining room where guests can enjoy dinner by arrangement. The comfortably furnished lounge and honesty bar are an added bonus and a good place to unwind after a day seeing the sites of Bath. The hotel rooms are well appointed and some benefit from four-poster beds and original period features.

12 bth/shr (4 fmly) No smoking in 4 bedrooms No smoking in area of dining room CTV in all bedrooms Tea and coffee making facilities No dogs (ex guide dogs) Licensed Cen ht CTV 12P Last d 9pm

ROOMS: s £36-£46; d £52-£72; wkly b&b £150-£180; wkly hlf-bd £140-£200✳

CARDS:

Premier Selected

QQQQQ **Bath Lodge Hotel** BA3 6NH ☎ 01225 723040 FAX 01225 723737

(For full entry see **Norton St Philip**)

Selected

QQQQ **Blairgowrie House** 55 Wellsway BA2 4RT (leave Bath via A367 towards Exeter, Blairglowrie House is to the left of telephone box where the road forks, approx 1 mile from city centre)

☎ 01225 332266 FAX 01225 484535

This elegant Victorian family home is to be found on the main Wellsway road, just a short drive from the city centre and all its attractions. All the bedrooms are well equipped and pleasantly presented. A full English breakfast is offered in an attractive dining room which has some comfortable armchairs where guests are welcome to relax.

3 rms (2 bth/shr) No smoking in dining room CTV in all bedrooms Tea and coffee making facilities No dogs (ex guide dogs) Cen ht No coaches

ROOMS: s £32-£38; d £45-£52✳

Selected

QQQQ **Brocks** 32 Brock St BA1 2LN (leave M4 junct 18 turn onto A46, Brocks is just off A4 between Circus & Royal Crescent)

☎ 01225 338374 FAX 01225 334245

Closed Xmas & 2 wks Jan

Brocks Guest House is a most delightful Georgian property in a charming area of the city. The visitor here is assured of a personal welcome from Mrs Dodd, who has created a comfortable elegance in

contd. on p.60.

all the rooms, each one displaying a style of its own to compliment the Georgian era. A traditional breakfast is offered in a lovely dining room where guests sit at pretty tables and can enjoy the beautiful pieces of antique furniture. The famous Royal Crescent is just a short walk away.
6 bth/shr (3 fmly) No smoking in bedrooms No smoking in dining room CTV in all bedrooms Tea and coffee making facilities No dogs (ex guide dogs) Cen ht 1P No coaches
ROOMS: s £48-£60; d £57-£70*
CARDS:

Selected

Brompton House St John's Rd BA2 6PT (off M4 at junc 18, A46 to Bath, A4 to city centre, cross Cleveland Bridge, A36 then first right into St.Johns Road) ☎ 01225 420972 FAX 01225 420505
Closed Xmas & New Year
Formerly the Rectory for St Mary's Church this delightful family guest house is set in beautiful and mature tree lined gardens, which display a blaze of colour to be enjoyed by everyone. Rooms are all very comfortable and well equipped, complemented by co-ordinating fabrics. There is a beautifully presented lounge where visitors are welcome to rest and perhaps enjoy a drink from the bar. Guests here are made to feel at ease in warm surroundings. Brompton House has a no-smoking policy.
18 bth/shr (2 fmly) No smoking CTV in all bedrooms Tea and coffee making facilities Direct dial from bedrooms No dogs Licensed Cen ht No children 10yrs 20P No coaches
ROOMS: s £45-£65; d £55-£95*
CARDS:

See advertisement on p.59.

Premier Selected

Burghope Manor Winsley BA15 2LA ☎ 01225 723557 FAX 01225 723113

(For full entry see **Bradford on Avon**)

Cairngorm 3 Gloucester Rd, Lower Swainswick BA1 7BH (from M4 junct 18 take A46 towards Bath, after 7m turn left to Swainswick and left again to Lower Swainswick, after 1m Cairngorm is on left)
☎ 01225 429004
Closed Xmas
The Biggs family work hard to ensure your stay is comfortable and relaxing. A real home from home, this small bed and breakfast provides a good touring base just two miles from the centre of the city. The bedrooms are light and bright, the more compact ones compensated by wonderful views of Bath.
3 shr (1 fmly) No smoking CTV in all bedrooms Tea and coffee making facilities No dogs (ex guide dogs) Cen ht No children 12mths 4P No coaches
ROOMS: s £17-£20; d £32-£38; wkly b&b £102-£124

Carfax Hotel Great Pulteney St BA2 4BS (follow outer circle from A4/A46, turn into Pulteney St at Holbourne Museum before crossing Cleveland Bridge. Hotel opp Bath rugby ground entrance)
☎ 01225 462089 FAX 01225 443257
Conveniently located for the City centre on one of Bath's landmark streets, the Carfax is a warm, well maintained establishment offering traditional accommodation and service. Bedrooms have been particularly well equipped with both the business and leisure guest in mind. You are welcome to relax in the elegance of the newly re-furbished lounge or enjoy a range of dishes from the breakfast and dinner menus in the attractive dining room.

37 rms (36 bth/shr) (3 fmly) No smoking CTV in all bedrooms Tea and coffee making facilities Direct dial from bedrooms No dogs (ex guide dogs) Lift Cen ht ch fac 17P Games room Table tennis/football Air hockey Last d 7pm
ROOMS: s £45.75-£54; d £68-£80; wkly b&b £224-£353.50; wkly hlf-bd £255.50-£350
CARDS:

Premier Selected

Cheriton House 9 Upper Oldfield Park BA2 3JX (south of Bath, 0.5m along the A367) ☎ 01225 429862 FAX 01225 428403
Situated in a quiet residential area to the South of the city, this is a gracious abode built in the 1880s. Wonderful views over beautiful Georgian Bath can be enjoyed. Careful restoration and re-decoration has resulted in superb public rooms and a selection of beautifully presented bedrooms, with engaging individual touches such as stencilled butterflies and dragonflies. A four-poster bed is a recent addition and a ground floor room is also available. Hosts John and Iris make every effort to ensure your stay is comfortable, enjoyable and memorable for all the right reasons. A 10 minute stroll will take you from the doorstep to the very centre of Bath, so why not take advantage of the private parking and stretch your legs!
9 bth/shr (1 fmly) No smoking in 2 bedrooms No smoking in dining room CTV in all bedrooms Tea and coffee making facilities Direct dial from bedrooms No dogs (ex guide dogs) Cen ht No children 12yrs 9P No coaches
ROOMS: s £40-£46; d £60-£74*
CARDS:

Selected

QQQQ **Chesterfield House** 11 Great Pulteney St BA2 4BR ☎ 01225 460953 FAX 01225 448770

Occupying a prime position on the gracious sweep of Great Pulteney Street, this Grade I listed property is conveniently located just a short stroll from the city centre and Henrietta Park. Bedrooms are well decorated and comfortable with some offering fine views across the surrounding Georgian architecture. Guest parking is available by arrangement.

19 bth/shr (3 fmly) No smoking in dining room CTV in all bedrooms Tea and coffee making facilities No dogs (ex guide dogs) Licensed Cen ht CTV 8P No coaches

ROOMS: s £40-£60; d £55-£90*

CARDS:

See advertisement on p.61.

Selected

QQQQ **Cranleigh** 159 Newbridge Hill BA1 3PX (on A431 West side of city,) ☎ 01225 310197 FAX 01225 423143

Cranleigh is a charming Victorian house a short distance from the city centre. The spacious bedrooms offer comfort and quality; each room has been individually decorated and furnished. Some have excellent views of the local countryside, and the original fireplaces give a homely atmosphere. Breakfast is a delight, the menu offers interesting choices and is served in the elegant lounge/dining room. In the summertime, the south facing garden is a good place to relax.

5 shr (2 fmly) No smoking CTV in all bedrooms Tea and coffee making facilities No dogs (ex guide dogs) Cen ht No children 5yrs 5P No coaches

ROOMS: s £48-£55; d £65-£78*

CARDS:

QQQ **Della Rosa** 59 North Rd, Combe Down BA2 5DF (take inner ring road around Bath to Widcombe, turn off onto Prior Park Rd, up hill 1m to top and turn right 200yds on right) ☎ 01225 837193 FAX 01255 835264

Jill and Bunny Harvey extend a warm welcome to their spacious family home. Situated on the outskirts of the city, Della Rosa offers comfortable accommodation and ample parking. Bedrooms are equipped with modern facilities, there is a lounge for guests' use and breakfast is served at separate tables in an attractive dining room.

6 rms (3 shr) (1 fmly) No smoking in 2 bedrooms No smoking in dining room CTV in all bedrooms Tea and coffee making facilities Cen ht 9P No coaches

ROOMS: s £22-£34; d £40-£50*

Selected

QQQQ **Devonshire House** 143 Wellsway BA2 4RZ (1m from city centre on A367 out of Bath) ☎ 01225 312495 FAX 01225 335534

Dating from 1880, this charming little guest house is within comfortable strolling distance of the Georgian delights of Bath. The owners, Albie and Eileen make every effort to ensure your stay is both pleasurable and memorable. Three well equipped and prettily decorated bedroom are provided, and all are very comfortable. Don't miss out on the delicious dinners, served, as is breakfast, in the newly created dining room which was until recently an antiques shop.

3 bth/shr (1 fmly) No smoking CTV in all bedrooms Tea and coffee making facilities No dogs Cen ht No children 6yrs 6P No coaches

ROOMS: s £38-£45; d £55-£65; wkly b&b £175-£200*

CARDS:

Premier Selected

Q Q Q Q Q **Dorian House** 1 Upper Oldfield Park BA2 3JX (off A367 turn into Upper Oldfield Park, third building on left)
☎ 01225 426336 FAX 01225 444699

Dorian House is a fine Victorian building enjoying some magnificent views of Bath and just a ten minute stroll from the city's historic attractions. Each bedroom has been individually designed and attractively decorated to ensure warmth and comfort. There is an attractive sitting room furnished with some fine antiques – an ideal setting in which to relax and unwind. A choice of cooked English or continental breakfast is offered and is served in the elegant dining room. There is an honesty bar from which guests may serve themselves.

8 bth/shr (2 fmly) No smoking in dining room CTV in all bedrooms Tea and coffee making facilities Direct dial from bedrooms No dogs (ex guide dogs) Licensed Cen ht 10P

ROOMS: s £40-£55; d £55-£80

CARDS:

Q Q *Dorset Villa* 14 Newbridge Rd BA1 3JZ (A4 from Queens Sq in city centre, approx 1m to Sportsman pub, stay left, house 100yds on right)
☎ 01225 425975 FAX 01225 425975

Closed 25 Dec-Jan

This attractive property, situated on the Bristol Road out of the city, offers comfortable accommodation. Bedrooms, most of which are en suite, provide modern facilities, and breakfast is served in a good-sized dining room.

8 rms (6 shr) (1 fmly) No smoking in bedrooms No smoking in dining room CTV in all bedrooms Tea and coffee making facilities No dogs (ex guide dogs) Cen ht 5P No coaches

Selected

Q Q Q Q **Eagle House** Church St, Bathford BA1 7RS (from A4 take A363 for 150yds towards Bradford-on-Avon, fork left into Bathford Hill and take first right into Church St. House is 200yds on right) ☎ 01225 859946 FAX 01225 859430

Closed 20 Dec-1 Jan

This fine Georgian country house is located in the pretty conservation village of Bathford and commands lovely views over the city of Bath. It lies in its own beautiful grounds and has walled gardens. Bedrooms are generally spacious and include several suitable for families. All are well equipped and furniture and soft furnishings are in keeping with the nature of the building. Two rooms are located in a cottage within the grounds. A delightful drawing room is provided for guests, this is elegantly furnished and has a cheery log fire for the colder evenings. The atmosphere throughout is peaceful and relaxing.

6 bth/shr 2 annexe bth/shr (2 fmly) No smoking in 1 bedrooms CTV in all bedrooms Tea and coffee making facilities Direct dial from bedrooms Licensed Cen ht 10P Tennis (grass) Croquet lawn Children's play area

ROOMS: s £36-£46; d £45-£76

CARDS:

Q Q Q **Edgar Hotel** 64 Great Pulteney St BA2 4DN (take A46 off m'way 10m, A4 1m. Left at majortraffic lights,over bridge,2nd turning on right. End of rd left onto Gt Pulteney St) ☎ 01225 420619 FAX 01225 466916

rs Xmas

This comfortable Georgian property, situated only a short, level walk from the city centre, caters both for business guests and tourists. Bedrooms are equipped with a range of modern facilities.

16 bth/shr (1 fmly) No smoking in bedrooms No smoking in dining room CTV in all bedrooms Tea and coffee making facilities No dogs (ex guide dogs) Cen ht

ROOMS: s £30-£45; d £40-£65*

CARDS:

Selected

QQQQ **Gainsborough Hotel** Weston Ln BA1 4AB (W from Queens Square on A4 for 1m, turn right into Park Lane by park corner and left at top for 600yds. Hotel approx 0.25m from main hospital gates) (The Independents) ☎ 01225 311380 FAX 01225 447411
Closed 23 Dec-7 Jan approx

The Gainsborough Hotel is an elegant Victorian house located just a short drive from the centre of Bath. Bedrooms are well presented and comfortable, and some ground floor rooms are available. The hotel also has a large lounge and adjacent bar, where guests are welcome to have a drink prior to an evening foray. Alternatively, take a drink onto the patio overlooking the garden, and catch the last rays of sunshine before it sinks below the lofty trees. Full English breakfasts are served in the attractive surroundings of the dining room which is found on the lower ground floor.

17 bth/shr (3 fmly) No smoking in 8 bedrooms No smoking in dining room No smoking in lounges CTV in all bedrooms Tea and coffee making facilities Direct dial from bedrooms No dogs Licensed Cen ht 18P No coaches

ROOMS: s £35-£48; d £52-£85*

CARDS:

Selected

QQQQ **Green Lane House** Green Ln BA3 6BL ☎ 01225 723631 FAX 01225 723773

(For full entry see **Hinton Charterhouse**)

QQQ **Haute Combe Hotel** 174/176 Newbridge Rd BA1 3LE (from city centre take A4 Bristol direction, pass Royal Victoria Park on right, left onto Newbridge Rd hotel on right after passing Hartwells Garage) ☎ 01225 420061 & 339064 FAX 01225 446077
rs 25-26 Dec

Haute Combe is an attractive Edwardian house situated within easy reach of the city centre. Jane and David Carnegie offer comfortable accommodation and a warm friendly atmosphere. The bedrooms are of a good size, and well equipped with many modern amenities. There are two cosy lounges, one of which includes a small bar. A short a la carte menu is offered at dinner and there is a choice at breakfast; meals are served in the light and airy dining room.

12 bth/shr (5 fmly) No smoking in bedrooms No smoking in dining room No smoking in 1 lounge CTV in all bedrooms Tea and coffee making facilities Direct dial from bedrooms Licensed Cen ht CTV 12P No coaches Last d 6pm

ROOMS: s £42-£52; d £55-£75

CARDS:

Premier Selected

QQQQQ **Haydon House** 9 Bloomfield Park BA2 2BY (follow signs marked A367 Exeter. At large rdbt turn left. After 0.75m turn right at shopping centre, fork right then take 2nd right for 200yds) ☎ 01225 444919 & 427351 FAX 01225 444919

Located in a quiet residential area, this charming house offers comfort, elegance and hospitality of the highest standard. The spacious bedrooms are individually and tastefully appointed, soft pleasing colour schemes have been chosen and there are many extra thoughtful touches including mineral water, fresh flowers and a decanter of sherry. The sumptuous sitting room features some fine period furniture and comfortable seating, which makes it the ideal place to relax. An extensive breakfast menu is offered, which includes such delights as Scottish whisky or rum porridge! It is served in the delightful dining room, guests sharing one large table in true family style.

5 bth/shr (1 fmly) No smoking CTV in all bedrooms Tea and coffee making facilities Direct dial from bedrooms No dogs Cen ht 1P No coaches Sun Terrace

ROOMS: s £45-£60; d £65-£85*

CARDS:

Q Q Q Henrietta Hotel Henrietta St BA2 6LR ☎ 01225 447779
FAX 01225 444150
rs Xmas
Henrietta Hotel is located just off the gracious sweep of Great Pulteney Street, a short stroll from the city centre. All bedrooms are simply furnished, warm and comfortable and include many original features. Traditional breakfasts are served in the dining room. A small lounge which overlooks a pretty walled garden is also available to guests.
10 shr (3 fmly) No smoking in 5 bedrooms No smoking in dining room CTV in all bedrooms Tea and coffee making facilities No dogs (ex guide dogs) Cen ht CTV
ROOMS: s £30-£45; d £45-£65*
CARDS:

HAUTE COMBE HOTEL

174/176 Newbridge Road, Bath BA1 3LE
Tel: (01225) 420061/339064
Commended **Fax: (01225) 446077** Q Q Q
E-mail: 101352.42@compuserve.com
Lovely period property with many original features, close to city sights, marina and peaceful country walks along Cotswold Way. Service is our speciality and our large newly refurbished rooms are all ensuite and very well-equipped with remote colour Sky TV, direct dial phone, radio alarm, tea/coffee and biscuits, shampoo and shower cap, hairdrier, iron and board, trouser press, shoe-shine etc. Relax in our sunny lounge, and enjoy an a la carte dinner in the dining room or snack at the bar. The hotel is a non-smoking establishment apart from a separate smoking lounge. Large English breakfast. Our large car park and unrestricted on-road parking make bringing your car to Bath a pleasure. Level walk to the centre or beat the traffic problems with a £1.00 return shuttle bus to the abbey leaving Newbridge every 15 minutes.
Open all year.

Gainsborough Hotel

AA Selected QQQQ

The Gainsborough Country House Hotel is situated in its own large attractive grounds, (with 2 sun terraces) and is close to the lovely Botanical Gardens and Victoria Park. The hotel is both spacious and very comfortable, and provides a relaxed and informal atmosphere for guests. The Abbey, Roman Baths, and Centre are within easy walking distance via the park. All of our 16 tastefully furnished bedrooms are en-suite, with colour TV, satellite TV, tea/coffee facilities, telephones, hairdryers etc. The hotel has a friendly bar overlooking the hotel lawns, and our own private car park. Highly recommended. Warm welcome from the friendly staff.

Single £32-£46, Doubles £52-£80 per night (incl. breakfast & VAT)
Access, Visa, Mastercard, Eurocard, American Express all welcome.
Weston Lane – Bath – Avon – BA1 4AB
Tel: Bath (01225) 311380 Fax: (01225) 447411

Selected

Q Q Q Q Hermitage Bath Rd SN13 8DT BATH ☎ 01225 744187
FAX 01225 743447

(For full entry see **Box**)

Selected

Q Q Q Q Highways House 143 Wells Rd BA2 3AL (on the A367)
☎ 01225 421238 FAX 01225 481169
Closed Xmas
Guests are assured of a warm welcome when arriving at this elegant Victorian Villa situated on the southern side of the city. Just a 10 minute walk from the centre, this is an ideal location from which to explore the Georgian splendour of Bath. Comfortable bedrooms are well equipped and attractive, and a spacious lounge is available for rest and relaxation. Generous breakfasts are served in the bright and cheerful dining room.
7 rms (6 bth/shr) No smoking CTV in all bedrooms Tea and coffee making facilities No dogs (ex guide dogs) Cen ht No children 5yrs 8P
ROOMS: s £35-£42; d £56-£68
CARDS:

Premier Selected

Q Q Q Q Q Holly Lodge 8 Upper Oldfield Park BA2 3JZ
(0.5m SW of city centre off A367)
☎ 01225 424042 01225 339187 FAX 01225 481138
Occupying an enviable elevated location, Holly Lodge offers expansive views across the city of Bath. Rich colours, sumptuous fabrics and engaging personal touches are found throughout the establishment. The gracious lounge offers unparalleled comfort and adjoins a smart and stylish breakfast room. The owner has every right to be proud of the terraced garden, a pleasant environment in which to relax and unwind. Ample parking is available.
7 bth/shr No smoking CTV in all bedrooms Tea and coffee making facilities Direct dial from bedrooms No dogs Cen ht 8P No coaches
ROOMS: s £48-£55; d £75-£89
CARDS:

Q Q Q Holly Villa 14 Pulteney Gardens BA2 4HG
☎ 01225 310331 FAX 01225 339334
Closed Xmas/New Year & Jan/Feb
Holly Villa is a friendly little guest house where guests are made to feel welcome and 'at home'. The bedrooms are pretty and light and and vary in size. There is a cosy lounge with television for guests' use. A full English breakfast is served in an attractive dining room which overlooks the award winning garden, where one may relax on summer afternoons after a busy day in the city.
6 rms (5 shr) (1 fmly) No smoking No dogs Cen ht CTV
No children 8yrs 2P No coaches
ROOMS: d fr £45*

Premier Selected

Q Q Q Q Q Kennard Hotel 11 Henrietta St BA2 6LL
(from A4 London Road turn left onto A36 over river past fire station) ☎ 01225 310472 FAX 01225 460054
Well located for the sights of Bath, this delightful Georgian town house has its own special charm and character. A combination of high standards of accommodation, warm hospitality and gracious surroundings make this a wonderful place to rest and relax. All rooms are equipped with modern facilities and some have lovely views of Bath. Breakfast is served in an attractive and stylish room; guests can choose between a cooked English or Continental breakfast - gooseberry chutney served alongside all hot dishes is a memorable touch. Richard Ambler and Malcolm Wright have a wealth of experience in making guests feel welcome and have perfected the balance of genuine hospitality and professionalism.
13 rms (11 shr) (2 fmly) No smoking CTV in all bedrooms Tea and coffee making facilities Direct dial from bedrooms No dogs (ex guide dogs) Cen ht No children No coaches
ROOMS: s £45-£55; d £78-£95
CARDS:

Q Q Q *Lamp Post Villa* 3 Crescent Gardens, Upper Bristol Rd BA1 2NA
(on A4, Bristol side of city) ☎ 01225 331221 FAX 01225 426783
Closed 24-26 Dec
The Lamp Post Villa is located to the east of the city centre. Bedrooms are neat and brightly decorated and have many modern amenities. A choice of English or continental breakfast is offered, served in the cosy dining room which is on the lower ground floor. Other public areas include a small reception lounge.
4 bth/shr (1 fmly) No smoking in bedrooms No smoking in dining room CTV in all bedrooms Tea and coffee making facilities Direct dial from bedrooms Cen ht CTV 4P No coaches
CARDS:

Selected

Q Q Q Q Laura Place Hotel 3 Laura Place, Great Pulteney St BA2 4BH (turn left off A4 at 1st traffic lights over Cleveland Bridge, past fire station then turn right along Henrietta Rd into Laura Place)
☎ 01225 463815 FAX 01225 310222
Mar-21 Dec

This beautiful Georgian town house is located just a short walk from the city centre. Looking out to the famous Pulteney Street with an elegant fountain in the foreground, the hotel offers warm comfortable rooms furnished to a high standard. Some feature delightful four-poster beds and antique pieces, and some have rooftop views across the city, a delight in an area of such notable architecture. The hospitality here is warm and friendly, this is an ideal base from which to explore the city.
8 rms (7 bth/shr) (1 fmly) No smoking CTV in all bedrooms Tea and coffee making facilities Direct dial from bedrooms No dogs (ex guide dogs) Cen ht No children 11yrs 10P No coaches
ROOMS: d £66-£90; wkly b&b £208-£283*
CARDS:

Premier Selected

QQQQQ **Leighton House** 139 Wells Rd BA2 3AL
(leave A36 at Churchill Bridge in town centre and take A367, house on left after 600 mtrs at junction with Hayesfield Park)
☎ 01225 314769 FAX 01225 443079
rs Jan (limited availability)
Built in the 1870s, Leighton House is a wonderful example of Victorian splendour, close to the city centre. Hospitable owners Marilyn and Colin Humphrey are justly proud of their home and delight in sharing its comforts with guests. Bedrooms are thoughtfully equipped and individually decorated, and two are located at ground floor level. Breakfast is served in the attractive dining room which overlooks the neatly tended gardens.
8 bth/shr (1 fmly) No smoking CTV in all bedrooms Tea and coffee making facilities Direct dial from bedrooms No dogs (ex guide dogs) Cen ht No children 7yrs 8P No coaches
ROOMS: s £40-£64; d £55-£79
CARDS:

The Hermitage B&B

Bath Road, Box,
Wilts SN13 8DT
Tel: 01225 744187 Fax: 01225 743447

16th Century Country House and Lodge in its own grounds. 5 rooms (3 non-smoking) are en-suite with TV, tea and coffee. Superb outdoor pool, heated to 80°+ May-Aug. Private parking. Pubs 2 mins. BATH (5 miles). Visit Stonehenge, Avebury and Cheddar.

Tel: Ruth and Paul Best
Double rooms £45-£55.
Families from £55
Arrival times and deposits requested

English Tourist Board

AA Selected QQQQ

Holly Lodge

8 Upper Oldfield Park,
Bath Avon BA2 3JZ
Tel: 01225 339187 or 424042 Fax: 01225 481138

Holly Lodge is a large Victorian house set in its own grounds and enjoys magnificent views over the City. It is situated only 10 minutes from the centre. Individually interior designed rooms, all with bathrooms and some with four poster beds, have TV and satellite movies, direct dial telephone and hot drink facilities. Imaginative breakfasts are enjoyed in the conservatory type breakfast room. Beautiful lounge and well lit car park. Holly Lodge features in many well known guide books and is graded ETB de-luxe. For the comfort and convenience of our guests Holly Lodge is strictly no smoking. Well worth the extra splurge.

Selected

Q Q Q Q **Marlborough House** 1 Marlborough Ln BA1 2NQ (premises on the corner of A4 and Marlborough Lane, W of Queen Square in city centre) ☎ 01225 318175 & 466127 FAX 01225 466127
Warm hospitality is offered here in this sunny Victorian town house which may be found just five minutes walk from the city centre. The bedrooms are pretty, comfortable and well equipped, with pleasant views. Breakfast is served in an attractive dining room which also has some very comfortable chairs where visitors are welcome to relax.
8 rms (6 shr) (1 fmly) No smoking CTV in all bedrooms Tea and coffee making facilities Direct dial from bedrooms Cen ht 3P No coaches Massage/aromatherapy on request
ROOMS: s £35-£45; d £65-£75
CARDS:

Premier Selected

Q Q Q Q Q **Meadowland** 36 Bloomfield Park BA2 2BX (turn off A367 at Bearflat into Bloomfield Rd, Bloomfield Pk is second on right)
☎ 01225 311079 FAX 01225 31107
A fifteen minute walk will take you from this charming and stylish house to the centre of Bath. Owners Mr and Mrs Andrew take delight in sharing their beautiful home with guests and have created three well-equipped and tastefully decorated bedrooms of real quality. This is somewhere to relax and unwind, perhaps with a book in the elegant drawing room or alternatively, in the attractive and peaceful gardens.
3 bth/shr (1 fmly) No smoking CTV in all bedrooms Tea and coffee making facilities No dogs Cen ht CTV No children 5yrs 4P No coaches
ROOMS: s £50-£55; d £65-£75*
CARDS:

Premier Selected

Q Q Q Q Q **Monkshill** Shaft Rd, Monkton Combe BA2 7HL (from A36 turn left onto A3062(Prior Park Rd), left at top of hill into North Rd, then right into Shaft Rd. Estab 100yds on right past playing fields) ☎ 01225 833028 FAX 01225 833028
Closed 2 wks over Xmas and New York
Monkshill is a delightful Edwardian house set in attractive gardens and with superb views across the Limpley Stoke Valley. The bedrooms are spacious, comfortably furnished in keeping with the house, and equipped with many thoughtful extras. The attractive sitting room with its many personal touches has a real homely feel and invites relaxation. A choice of breakfasts is offered in the elegant dining room where guests share one large table in family style.
3 rms (2 bth/shr) (1 fmly) No smoking CTV in all bedrooms Tea and coffee making facilities Cen ht 8P No coaches Croquet lawn
ROOMS: s £45-£60; d £60-£75*
CARDS:

Premier Selected

Q Q Q Q Q **Monmouth Lodge** BA3 6LH ☎ 01373 834367

(For full entry see **Norton St Philip**)

Q Q Q **North Lodge** Sulis Manor Rd BA2 2AL (from A4 take A367 Exeter road for approx 2m. Turn left at Odd Down Park & Ride, then left again into Sulis Manor Rd and premises are 100yds along)
☎ 01225 837782 FAX 01225 837782
Situated on the southern edge of the city, North Lodge is a recently renovated property run by Gill and Doug Hayward. The bedrooms are light and airy, and one is located on the ground floor, especially suited to the less able. A sitting room is provided for guests, and breakfast is served in the sunny conservatory which overlooks the gardens.
3 shr No smoking CTV in all bedrooms Tea and coffee making facilities No dogs (ex guide dogs) Cen ht CTV No children 12yrs 4P No coaches
ROOMS: d £40-£55; wkly b&b £133-£175

Selected

Q Q Q Q **Oakleigh House** 19 Upper Oldfield Park BA2 3JX (off A367) ☎ 01225 315698 FAX 01225 448223
You are assured of warmth and comfort at Oakleigh House, which has four well presented bedrooms to offer. Being away from the bustle of the city centre makes this a quiet location to stay, yet its attractions are nearby. A full English breakfast is served in a pleasant dining room, and there is a cosy lounge for guests to use.

4 bth/shr No smoking in dining room No smoking in lounges CTV in all bedrooms Tea and coffee making facilities No dogs (ex guide dogs) Cen ht No children 18yrs 4P No coaches
ROOMS: s £35-£45; d £55-£68*
CARDS:

Selected

Q Q Q Q **Oldfields Hotel** 102 Wells Rd BA2 3AL (off A367 from Bath City Centre. 6oomtrs on R.H.S on corner of Upper Oldfield Park)
☎ 01225 317984 FAX 01225 444471
Closed 3-31 Jan
This elegant Victorian house commands fine views across the city, taking in much of the beautiful architecture for which it is so famous. Guests are assured of warm hospitality in the charming and stylish surroundings of this lovely building. Bedrooms are tastefully decorated and comfortable; a range of thoughtful touches include bottled water, reading material and boiled sweets. The public rooms, which have an inviting atmosphere, are beautifully furnished and breakfast is memorable affair. The city centre, with all it's charm, and excellent shopping, is close at hand.
14 bth/shr (2 fmly) No smoking CTV in all bedrooms Tea and coffee making facilities Direct dial from bedrooms No dogs (ex guide dogs) Cen ht 12P
ROOMS: s £45-£60; d £58-£80; wkly b&b £175-£220
CARDS:

Q Q Q **Old Red House** 37 Newbridge Rd BA1 3HE (1 mile W of city centre along Upper Bristol Rd, situated on left just past The Sportsman Pub)
☎ 01225 330464 FAX 01225331661
Formerly a baker's shop, The Old Red House was built at the turn of the century and is well located just a mile from the city centre. This family home is tastefully decorated and sympathetically restored with many period features. Breakfast is served at a large communal table where a wide variety of items is on offer. A delightful conservatory is an added bonus.
3 rms (1 bth 1 shr) (1 fmly) No smoking CTV in all bedrooms Tea and coffee making facilities Cen ht CTV No children 4yrs 4P No coaches
ROOMS: s £28-£45; d £42-£62*
CARDS:

Selected

QQQQ **Orchard Lodge** Warminster Rd (A36), Bathampton BA2 6XG (1m from city centre on A6 Warminster road)
☎ 01225 466115 FAX 01225 446050
This purpose built establishment, situated beside the A36, is but a short distance from the centre. The spotless bedrooms are very well equipped and those at the rear enjoy splendid views across the valley to Salisbury Hill and the surrounding countryside. The attractive dining room provides a relaxing environment in which to enjoy breakfast before exploring the delights of the nearby city of Bath.
14 bth/shr (3 fmly) No smoking in 4 bedrooms No smoking in dining room No smoking in lounges CTV in all bedrooms Tea and coffee making facilities Direct dial from bedrooms Cen ht 16P Sauna Solarium Last d 7.45pm
ROOMS: s £39-£48; d £40-£62
CARDS:

Selected

QQQQ **Owl House** Lower Kingsdown Rd, Kingsdown SN13 8BB ☎ 01225 743883 FAX 01225 744450

(For full entry see **Box**)

Selected

QQQQ **The Parade Park** 8,9,10 North Pde BA2 4AL
☎ 01225 463384 FAX 01225 442322
Located in the centre of Bath, ideal for those wishing to explore the city, this elegant Georgian house has been comfortably appointed and appropriately furnished. Bedrooms, which vary in size, are brightly decorated and equipped with many thoughtful amenities. A varied selection is offered at breakfast which is served in the well presented dining room. Guests may use the attractive lounge where a selection of magazines and tourist information is provided.
23 bth/shr (4 fmly) No smoking CTV in all bedrooms Tea and coffee making facilities No dogs Licensed Cen ht
ROOMS: s £45-£60; d £55-£75✳
CARDS:

Selected

QQQQ **Paradise House Hotel** Holloway BA2 4PX
(A36 Bristol/Warminster road round Bath at Churchill Bridge rdbt, take A367 then take 3rd left, go downhill into cul de sac, house 200 yds on left) ☎ 01225 317723 FAX 01225 482005
Closed 3 days Xmas
This impressive Georgian house dating back to 1720 has been delightfully restored over recent years. Built of the mellow Bath stone it overlooks the city and many rooms have superb views. Bedrooms are individually decorated with striking colour schemes and furnishings are in keeping with the elegance of the house. A comfortable sitting room is provided and this opens onto the pretty gardens.
8 bth/shr (1 fmly) No smoking in bedrooms No smoking in dining room CTV in all bedrooms Tea and coffee making facilities Direct dial from bedrooms No dogs Cen ht 5P No coaches Croquet lawn Boules pitch
ROOMS: s £45-£65; d £65-£100; wkly b&b £230-£320
CARDS:

QQQ **Park Farm Cottage** 2 Park Farm Cottage, Royal Victoria Park BA1 2LZ ☎ 01225 339589
This delightful former farmhouse occupies an enviable position on the edge of Victoria Park, yet only a short level walk from all the attractions of the city centre. Mr and Mrs Jackson welcome their guests and invite them to enjoy the character and charm of their comfortable family home.
2 rms No smoking CTV in 1 bedroom Tea and coffee making facilities Direct dial from bedrooms No dogs (ex guide dogs) Cen ht CTV 2P No coaches
ROOMS: s £25-£35; d £35-£50✳

Selected

QQQQ **The Plaine** BA3 6LE BATH ☎ 01373 834723
FAX 01373 834101

(For full entry see **Norton St Philip**)

QQQ **Hotel St Clair** 1 Crescent Gardens, Upper Bristol Rd BA1 2NA (on main A4, Bristol side of Bath) ☎ 01225 425543 FAX 01225 425543
This friendly hotel lies within easy reach of the city centre. Modern bedrooms include some suitable for families and all are equipped with modern facilities. A small foyer lounge area is provided and, although there is no car park, a large public car park is located at the rear.
10 rms (7 bth/shr) (3 fmly) No smoking in 2 bedrooms No smoking in dining room CTV in all bedrooms Tea and coffee making facilities No dogs Licensed Cen ht Last d 8.30pm
ROOMS: s £28-£48; d £38-£58✳
CARDS:

Q Q Q **St Leonards** Warminster Rd BA2 6SQ (leave M4 at junct 18, turn right at junct with A4 towards Bath. Turn left on A36 Warminster road, climb hill and 200yds on left past Bathampton sign)
☎ 01225 465838 FAX 01225 442800
St Leonards is an elegant Victorian guest house which enjoys superb views across the Bath countryside and the Kennet canal. Mr Pugh and Ms Morgan Griffiths welcome guests, and offer well equipped, comfortable rooms. There is a small lounge and an attractive dining room where a full English breakfast is offered. St Leonards is on a bus route into the city, which is just a 15 minute stroll away.
6 shr No smoking CTV in all bedrooms Tea and coffee making facilities Cen ht 10P No coaches
ROOMS: s £25-£44; d £40-£68; wkly b&b £145-£238*
CARDS:

Selected

Q Q Q Q **Sarnia** 19 Combe Park BA1 3NR (upper Bristol rd A4 from city centre, after 1m fork right at lights, A431, turn right at rdbt into Combe Pk in same road as Royal United Hospital)
☎ 01225 424159 FAX 01225 337689
Closed 24 Dec-2 Jan
Sarnia is an attractive family home, where guests are assured of a warm welcome. The three bedrooms are comfortable and well presented, each enjoying a pleasant outlook. An open fire in the spacious family lounge invites guests to relax. A light supper tray is offered. Sarnia is located just across the road from the Royal United Hospital, and a bus to the centre passes frequently.
3 bth/shr (1 fmly) No smoking CTV in all bedrooms Tea and coffee making facilities No dogs (ex guide dogs) Cen ht CTV 3P No coaches
ROOMS: s £25-£40; d £45-£60
CARDS:

This symbol indicates a 'Child Friendly' establishment - see page 25 for details

Q Q Q **Seven Springs** 4 High St, Woolley BA1 8AR (from M4 junct 18 take A46 to Swainswick, signposted Upper Swainswick/Tadwick/Langridge to signpost for Woolley) ☎ 01225 858001
Closed 23 Dec-3 Jan
Seven Springs, an end of terrace stone cottage, can be found in the hamlet of Woolley, 3 miles north of Bath, and is well worth a small diversion off the beaten track. The welcoming proprietors, Mr and Mrs Little, are friendly and make sure that guests have all they need for a relaxing, leisurely stay. Bedrooms are comfortable and of a good size, with some thoughtful touches, all with en suite bath or shower rooms. Outside, stone terraces and terracotta pots give a very Mediterranean feel but views from the higher ground truly capture the beauty of the English countryside. An enjoyable breakfast is served and this sets guests up for a busy day discovering Bath and the South West.
3 bth/shr (2 fmly) No smoking CTV in all bedrooms Tea and coffee making facilities No dogs Cen ht 14P
ROOMS: d fr £40

Premier Selected

Q Q Q Q Q **Siena Hotel** 24/25 Pulteney Rd BA2 4EZ (from M4, take A46 then the A4 to Bath follow signs for A367 Wells/Exeter, the hotel is located on the right 100metres beyond St Mary's church) ☎ 01225 425495 FAX 01225 469029
A fine example of Victorian architecture, The Siena Hotel is situated within a few minutes level walk of the city centre. Set in a walled garden and with excellent views of the city, the hotel offers a relaxed and friendly atmosphere in which the commitment and involvement of the resident proprietor plays an important role. The building was recently renovated to its former glory, retaining and restoring the many period features. Public areas are comfortable and the bedrooms vary in size; some are elegant and spacious, while others have a more cottagey atmosphere.
15 bth/shr (3 fmly) No smoking in 11 bedrooms No smoking in dining room CTV in all bedrooms Tea and coffee making facilities Direct dial from bedrooms Licensed Cen ht CTV 15P Unlimited free golf at nearby Entry Hill GC Last d 8.30pm
ROOMS: s £52.50-£70; d £70-£95; wkly b&b £235-£297.50*
CARDS:

Selected

Q Q Q Q **Somerset House Hotel & Restaurant** 35 Bathwick Hill BA2 6LD (400yds up Bathwick Hill from St Mary-the-Virgin church, at junct with A36) (The Circle) ☎ 01225 466451 FAX 01225 317188
Benefiting from magnificent views over the city, this elegant Georgian property is located just a short walk from most of the city's main attractions. Bedrooms are comfortable and well equipped. Situated in the original Georgian kitchens, the restaurant continues to gain praise; the short menu is recited and features fresh local produce, the cheeses are particularly noteworthy.
10 bth/shr (5 fmly) No smoking Tea and coffee making facilities Direct dial from bedrooms Licensed Cen ht CTV No children 6yrs 12P No coaches Last d 6.30pm
ROOMS: s £23.50-£35; d £47-£70; wkly b&b fr £224; wkly hlf-bd fr £281
CARDS:

Selected

Q Q Q Q **Sydney Gardens Hotel** Sydney Rd BA2 6NT (behind Holburne Museum, on A36)
☎ 01225 464818 & 445362 FAX 01225 484347
Closed 24 Dec-1 Feb
Sydney Gardens is a charming Victorian house enjoying a beautiful location just across the park from Bath's attractions. The hospitality is friendly and the accommodation is beautifully presented with every comfort in mind. There is a delightful sitting room for guests, and a pleasant dining room with pretty tables, fresh flowers and a happy atmosphere.
6 bth/shr (1 fmly) No smoking CTV in all bedrooms Tea and coffee making facilities Direct dial from bedrooms Cen ht No children 5yrs 8P No coaches
ROOMS: s £45-£59; d £59-£75
CARDS:

Selected

Q Q Q Q **Villa Magdala Hotel** Henrietta Rd BA2 6LX (turn left off A4 following signs for A36 to Warminster. Henrietta Road is 2nd on right) ☎ 01225 466329 FAX 01225 483207
A gracious and stylish Victorian Town House, Villa Magdala is just a short, level walk from the many and varied City sights. Pleasant views can be enjoyed from the sumptuously appointed bedrooms, all of which are equipped to meet the demands of business and leisure visitors. The delightful lounge and dining room overlook one of Bath's mature parks.
17 bth/shr (4 fmly) No smoking CTV in all bedrooms Tea and coffee making facilities Direct dial from bedrooms No dogs (ex guide dogs) Cen ht 19P No coaches
ROOMS: s £60-£80; d £70-£100
CARDS:

Q Q **Waltons** 17-19 Crescent Gardens, Upper Bristol Rd BA1 2NA (on A4) ☎ 01225 426528
Waltons is located within easy reach of the city centre. Bedrooms vary in size, are modestly appointed, but comfortable and adequately equipped. There is a nicely furnished lounge in which guests can relax. Breakfast is taken at individual tables in the brightly decorated dining room.
15 rms (3 fmly) No smoking in dining room CTV in all bedrooms Tea and coffee making facilities Direct dial from bedrooms No dogs (ex guide dogs) Cen ht CTV
ROOMS: s £25-£27; d £43-£47*

Selected

QQQQ **Wentworth House** 106 Bloomfield Rd BA2 2AP (follow A367 signed Exeter then Radstock/Shepton Mallet, continue until shops then just past 'The Bear' public house take right road fork)
☎ 01225 339193 FAX 01225 310460

Situated on the southern side of the city and a fifteen minute walk to the centre, this lovingly maintained Victorian House offers a combination of warm hospitality and comfort. All rooms are well equipped, individually furnished and decorated to a high standard. During the summer guests can soak up the sunshine whilst lazing beside the outdoor swimming pool.

15 shr No smoking in dining room CTV in all bedrooms Tea and coffee making facilities Direct dial from bedrooms No dogs (ex guide dogs) Licensed Cen ht No children 5yrs 20P Outdoor swimming pool

ROOMS: s £40-£60; d £60-£90*

CARDS:

QQ **White** 23 Pulteney Gardens BA2 4HG ☎ 01225 426075

White Guest House is in a Victorian terrace just a short walk from the city centre. The hospitality here is warm and relaxed, and there is a choice of three bedrooms which are pretty and well equipped.

3 rms (2 shr) No smoking CTV in all bedrooms Tea and coffee making facilities No dogs Cen ht No coaches

ROOMS: s £24-£26; d £38-£44*

The AA's professional Inspectors make regular and anonymous visits to all the establishments listed in the Guide. They accept no gifts or favours from proprietors

Premier Selected

QQQQQ *Widbrook Grange* Trowbridge Rd, Widbrook BA15 1UH ☎ 01225 863173 & 864750 FAX 01225 862890

(For full entry see **Bradford on Avon**)

BATTLE East Sussex Map **05** TQ71

Premier Selected

QQQQQ ➤ **Brakes Coppice** *(TQ766134)* Telham Ln TN33 0SJ (off A2100 towards Crowhurst, 1m on left) ☎ 01424 830347 FAX 01424 830347 Mrs F Ramsden

Closed 20 Dec-2 Jan

Found at the end of its own private lane, Michael and Fay Ramsden's farmhouse offers peace and tranquillity. Guests are welcomed on arrival with a pot of tea and some of Fay's delicious home baking, served in a spacious and comfortable lounge. There are wonderful views across rolling fields to the sea in the far distance. Breakfast, which includes free range eggs and home made conserves, is served in a well-appointed dining room. Bedrooms come equipped with every modern amenity including thoughtful extras like mineral water, biscuits and even a pair of binoculars with which to watch the wildlife. This is a no-smoking establishment.

3 bth/shr No smoking CTV in all bedrooms Tea and coffee making facilities Direct dial from bedrooms No dogs Cen ht CTV No children 12yrs 5P 70 acres cattle

ROOMS: s £30-£35; d £45-£50*

Selected

QQQQ ➤ **Farthings Farm** *(TQ734149)* Catsfield TN33 9BA (from Battle on A271-turn left onto B2204 towards Catsfield for 1m. Farm located on left of a sharp S-bend and farmhouse is 0.5m down farm lane) ☎ 01424 773107 Mr & Mrs J Rodgers

An Edwardian farmhouse situated about 20 minutes walk from Battle Abbey along the 1066 country walk which runs adjacent to this small working farm. The house has been furnished and decorated with great style by charming hosts Penny and John Rodgers. There are three bedrooms, two of which have dedicated bathrooms. Guests are invited to join in the house party atmosphere, and dinners can be served round a farmhouse table or, more intimately, in the guest lounge and dining room. Single party bookings enable guests to fully enjoy the peace and tranquillity that this most historic part of England offers.

3 rms (1 bth 1 shr) No smoking in bedrooms No smoking in area of dining room No smoking in 1 lounge Tea and coffee making facilities No dogs (ex guide dogs) Cen ht CTV 3P Outdoor swimming pool 70 acres dairy Last d 6pm

ROOMS: s £23; d £46; wkly b&b £160; wkly hlf-bd £230*

Selected

QQQQ ➤ **Fox Hole Farm** *(TQ694166)* Kane Hythe Rd TN33 9QU (turn off A271 onto B2096 farm three quarters of a mile from junction on right) ☎ 01424 772053 FAX 01424 773771 Mr & Mrs P Collins

Experienced hoteliers Paul and Pauline Collins have moved away from the hubbub of a seaside resort to this charming country retreat. Just outside Battle with its historic abbey, Foxhole Farm is a collection of cottages set in idyllic 40 acre grounds. The three rooms are tastefully decorated in rural style with exposed beams setting the tone. A thoughtful range of extras is much appreciated by guests. Guests seeking peace and quiet could do no better than to choose this lovely farmhouse.

3 bth No smoking CTV in all bedrooms Tea and coffee making facilities No dogs (ex guide dogs) Cen ht No children 10yrs 6P 40 acres beef chickens sheep

ROOMS: s £30-£49; d £40-£59; wkly b&b £140-£205

CARDS:

QQQ ➤ **Little Hemingfold Farmhouse Hotel** *(TQ774149)* Hastings Rd, Telham TN33 0TT (1.5 S of Battle on A2100, blue Hotel sign on left, 0.5m down farm track) ☎ 01424 774338 FAX 01424 775351 Mr & Mrs P Slater

Closed 6 Jan-12 Feb

In an idyllic location, Little Hemingfold is an ideal retreat from the bustle of modern life. The 40 acres of land include a bluebell wood and a trout lake. Day rooms are comfortable and relaxing with a real log fire and good supply of books in the sitting room, a separate bar and an appealing candle-lit dining room where the daily-changing menu often includes home-grown produce. The largely traditionally furnished bedrooms are located in the original farmhouse or adjacent converted Victorian farm buildings. Four rooms have their own log-burning stoves.

4 bth 9 annexe rms (7 bth) No smoking in dining room No smoking in 1 lounge CTV in all bedrooms Tea and coffee making facilities Direct dial from bedrooms Licensed Cen ht 30P Outdoor swimming pool Golf 18 Tennis (grass) Fishing Boules Croquet Riding Stables 40 acres mixed Last d 7pm

ROOMS: s £38-£65; d £76-£90; wkly b&b £252-£280; wkly hlf-bd £350-£378*

CARDS:

QQQ **Netherfield Hall** Netherfield TN33 9PS (from High Street roundabout take A2100 London Road for 100yds to left turn for Netherfield. House on left after 2.5m opposite church) ☎ 01424 774450 FAX 01424 774450

Closed Feb rs Mon Tue

Opposite the church in Netherfield, the Hall was built in the 1980s but incorporates various old beams and stone features from the now demolished Burwash Abbey. The three bedrooms - one with WC, one with shower and one fully en suite - are all on the ground floor, off a picture gallery. Public rooms include a small tea room with verandah and separate breakfast room plus a very comfortable lounge boasting a real fire in winter.

3 rms (2 shr) 1 annexe shr No smoking CTV in 3 bedrooms Tea and coffee making facilities Cen ht CTV No children 12yrs 8P No coaches Golf 9

wkly b&b £120-£150

BEACONSFIELD Buckinghamshire Map **04** SU99

Premier Selected

Q Q Q Q Q **George Hotel** Wycombe End, Old Town HP9 1LZ (off M40 at junc 2, 0.5m into Beaconsfield, Hotel over main roundabout on right) ☎ 01494 673086 FAX 01494 674034
John and Herta Hetherington have skilfully restored this delightful Tudor inn, situated in the picturesque old town. The George has six luxury suites in the main house and three 'cottages' in the converted stable-block, each accommodating up to four people. The rooms have been carefully planned with many home comforts and they are all furnished with beautiful antiques and paintings. The George is ideally located for visiting Windsor, Henley and London's West End. There are now also several charming self-catering cottages in the village available for long and short lets.
9 bth/shr (5 fmly) No smoking CTV in all bedrooms Tea and coffee making facilities Direct dial from bedrooms No dogs (ex guide dogs) Cen ht No coaches
ROOMS: s £92.82-£104.57; d £116.32-£135.12*
CARDS:

BEDALE North Yorkshire Map **08** SE28

See also Hunton

Premier Selected

Q Q Q Q Q **Elmfield Country House** Arrathorne DL8 1NE (from A1 follow A684 through Bedale towards Leyburn. After village of Patrick Brompton turn right towards Richmond. Premises 1.5m on right) ☎ 01677 450558 FAX 01677 450557
Jim and Edith Lillie look forward to welcoming you to this former gamekeeper's cottage, now extended and fully modernised, it is set in its own garden and enjoys a peaceful location with views over open farmland. Bedrooms are both spacious and comfortable, and one room has a four-poster bed. The stylish lounge, with a small corner bar, leads to the dining room where a home-cooked set dinner is offered. There is also a large conservatory lounge and a games room for those with energy to spare.
9 bth/shr (2 fmly) No smoking in 4 bedrooms No smoking in dining room CTV in all bedrooms Tea and coffee making facilities Direct dial from bedrooms No dogs (ex guide dogs) Licensed Cen ht 20P Fishing Solarium Pool table Darts Last d before noon
ROOMS: s fr £31; d £44-£50; wkly b&b £154-£175; wkly hlf-bd £238-£249*
CARDS:

Q Q Q **Southfield** 96 Southend DL8 2DS (A1 Northbound, at Leeming Motel take A684 to Bedale. Turn left at White Bear pub. 400 yds on right, fronted by white stones) ☎ 01677 423510
Marjorie Keighley has been welcoming guests to her 'home from home' guest house for over 21 years. Arriving guests are treated to tea and freshly baked treats from the kitchen. Bedrooms are traditionally furnished with a host of thoughtful extras and a wide range of additional toiletries. An attractive lounge is provided just off the dining room where guests take breakfast round the same table. Vegetarian breakfasts are also provided.
4 rms (2 shr) No smoking Tea and coffee making facilities No dogs (ex guide dogs) 4P
ROOMS: s £20; d £40

BEDFORD Bedfordshire Map **04** TL04

Q Q **Bedford Oak House** 33 Shakespeare Rd MK40 2DX (NW on connecting road between A6/A428) ☎ 01234 266972 FAX 01234 266972
This efficiently run family home offers an attractive wood-panelled breakfast room and a comfortable residents' lounge. Bedrooms are bright and neatly appointed with modern en suite shower rooms.
15 rms (14 shr) No smoking in dining room CTV in all bedrooms Tea and coffee making facilities No dogs (ex guide dogs) Cen ht CTV No children 16yrs 17P No coaches
ROOMS: s £31-£35; d £38-£45*
CARDS:

Q Q ***Hertford House Hotel*** 57 De Parys Av MK40 2TR
☎ 01234 350007 & 354470 FAX 01234 353468
Closed 24 Dec-2 Jan
This family run hotel sits in a tree-lined avenue, between the busy town centre and Bedford park. Guests have the use of a ground-floor reception and lounge, and a first-floor breakfast room which overlooks playing fields. Bedrooms are generally of comfortable proportions and soundly appointed, each has a courtesy beverage tray.
17 rms (13 bth/shr) (4 fmly) No smoking in 4 bedrooms No smoking in dining room CTV in all bedrooms Tea and coffee making facilities Cen ht CTV 14P Indoor swimming pool 2 mins walk away
CARDS:

BEER Devon Map **03** SY28

Q Q Q **Bay View** Fore St EX12 3EE (turn off A3092 & follow signs to Beer, Guest house at bottom of Fore Street on the left) ☎ 01297 20489
Mar-Oct
This popular sea front guest house continues to offer a good standard of budget accommodation. Many of the bedrooms, some of which boast en suite facilities, have been upgraded to a superior level, with attractive fabrics and furnishings. Additional rooms are available in an adjacent cottage. There is a comfortable guest lounge next to the tea room where snacks are available all day.
6 rms (2 bth/shr) 3 annexe rms (1 bth/shr) (1 fmly) CTV in all bedrooms Tea and coffee making facilities Cen ht CTV
ROOMS: s £15.50-£22; d £31-£45; wkly b&b £103-£130*

Q Q Q ***Mullions*** New Rd EX12 3EB (on B3172, Seaton to Beer road) ☎ 01297 21377
Set high above the village of Beer, The Mullions has spacious bedrooms, some with marvellous views to the sea. There is a comfortable lounge in addition to an attractive conservatory where guests can enjoy a drink at the small bar.
5 bth/shr (3 fmly) No smoking in 2 bedrooms No smoking in dining room No smoking in 1 lounge CTV in 3 bedrooms Licensed Cen ht CTV 6P No coaches Last d noon

BEERCROCOMBE Somerset Map 03 ST32

Premier Selected

Q Q Q Q Q **Frog Street Farm** *(ST317197)* Frog St TA3 6AF (from M5 junct 25 follow signs to A358, then for Hatch Beauchamp, at Hatch Inn follow signs to Beercrocombe over bridge and down 'no-through' road) ☎ 01823 480430 FAX 01823 480430 Mrs V Cole
Mar-Oct
Surrounded by tranquil countryside with an abundance of wildlife, this delightful 15th-century farmhouse is home to the Cole Family who extend a warm welcome to their guests. The bedrooms are spacious, individually furnished and decorated in a relaxing, country style. There is a choice of charming sitting rooms, one featuring fine Jacobean panelling dating back to the period of James I of England. Delicious three course, home-cooked dinners are available by prior arrangement; guests are encouraged to bring their own wine. If time allows, Mrs Cole discusses the menu beforehand to ensure any likes and dislikes are catered for.
3 bth/shr No smoking Tea and coffee making facilities No dogs Cen ht CTV No children 11yrs 6P 160 acres racehorse stud, beef Last d 2pm
ROOMS: d fr £50*

Premier Selected

Q Q Q Q Q **Whittles** *(ST324194)* TA3 6AH (turn off A358 follow directions to Hatch Beauchamp, then Beercrocombe. 0.75 miles into village) ☎ 01823 480301 FAX 01823 480 301 Mr & Mrs Mitchem
Feb-Nov
Parts of Claire and John Mitchem's farmhouse date back to the 16th century, while the front part of the house was added in the 19th century. Guests have their own drawing room and cosy sitting room, both very comfortable and spacious. Similarly the bedrooms are individually furnished, attractively decorated and well equipped. Breakfast is taken around a large table in the dining room, with farmhouse fare on offer.
3 bth No smoking in bedrooms No smoking in dining room No smoking in 1 lounge CTV in all bedrooms Tea and coffee making facilities No dogs Licensed Cen ht No children 16yrs 4P 200 acres beef dairy Last d 6.30pm(previous day)
ROOMS: s £30-£32; d £48-£50; wkly b&b £161-£175; wkly hlf-bd £273-£287*

Remember to return your Prize Draw card for a chance to win an action-packed family weekend at one of the eleven Family Fun Hotels in the Hilton Hotels Directory. See inside the front cover for the card and competition details. Don't forget to fill in your name and address before posting!

BELPER Derbyshire Map 08 SK34

Premier Selected

Q Q Q Q Q **Dannah** *(SK314502)* Bowmans Ln, Shottle DE56 2DR (from Belper A517 Ashbourne rd for approx 1.5m Hanging Gate pub on right take next right to Shottle continue 1m to village over x-rds turn rt) ☎ 01773 550273 & 550630 FAX 01773 550590
Mrs J L Slack
Closed 25-26 December
This 18th-century farmhouse is still a working farm, and visitors are encouraged to walk the surrounding footpaths to admire the countryside. Bedrooms are comfortably furnished; two of them are split level, offering a private lounge on the ground floor and a bedroom with a four poster bed. In addition to the lounge bar there are two other lounges, one with an honesty bar.
8 rms (7 bth/shr) (1 fmly) No smoking in bedrooms No smoking in dining room No smoking in 1 lounge CTV in all bedrooms Tea and coffee making facilities No dogs (ex guide dogs) Licensed Cen ht No children 8yrs 20P 128 acres mixed Last d 6.15pm
ROOMS: s £49.50-£55; d £70-£90; wkly b&b £220-£300*
CARDS:
See advertisement under DERBY

Q **The Hollins** 45 Belper Ln DE56 2UQ (at Belper Mill, off A6 onto A517. Proceed for 250m, take next right into Belper Lane. House on left, 250m ahead past Mount Pleasant Dr) ☎ 01773 823955
Located in a quiet residential area, this detached house is conveniently placed for the town and the Midshires walk. Bedrooms, sharing an adjacent bathroom, are simply furnished but well maintained whilst, downstairs, a hearty breakfast is served around one table in the combined dining room and lounge.
2 rms No smoking CTV in all bedrooms Tea and coffee making facilities Cen ht No children 4yrs 2P No coaches
ROOMS: s £19-£22; d £32-£35*

Selected

Q Q Q Q **Shottle Hall** Shottle DE56 2EB (Leave A517 at crossroads with B5023, 200yds towards Wirksworth then turn right & proceed for 0.5m) ☎ 01773 550276 & 550203 FAX 01773 550276
Closed Nov & Xmas
Shottle Hall is set in a very rural location with extensive grounds, Mr and Mrs Matthews are welcoming hosts. Mrs Matthews bakes and cooks all the food herself and serves a choice of main courses which range from freshly caught salmon to free range chicken, and from the simple to the more elaborate sauced dishes. Dinners are taken in an elegant dining room which overlooks the rolling hills of the Ecclestone Valley. The bedrooms have good modern bathroom and shower suites. They are furnished with comfort foremost, but in a style which takes advantage of the rooms' proportions and remaining architectural features.
8 rms (4 bth 2 shr) (3 fmly) No smoking in bedrooms CTV in 3 bedrooms Tea and coffee making facilities Licensed Cen ht CTV 30P No coaches Last d 6pm
ROOMS: s £28-£37.50; d £50-£68; wkly b&b £182-£248.50; wkly hlf-bd £280-£346.50

Prices shown in the directory are meant as a guide only and are subject to change. Please check before you book

BERE ALSTON Devon Map **02** SX46

Q Q Q **Treyard** Weir Quay, Bere Alston PL20 7BS (from Tavistock follow A390 Liskeard, turn left at Gulworthy onto B3267. At Bere Alston follow signs to Weir Quay, Treyard is to right of T-junct) ☎ 01822 840664 FAX 01822 840664
In the tiny hamlet of Weir Quay, Treyard is a historic house surrounded by beautiful gardens with many unusual species such as banana and eucalyptus trees. Parts of the grounds used to contain the Tamar smelting works and their ruins, now containing a lily pond and barbecue, can be seen around the garden. The self contained cottage has been furnished and equipped to a good standard. Dinner is also available, cooked by Mr Pearce who is an enthusiastic cook.
2 bth/shr No smoking CTV in all bedrooms Tea and coffee making facilities No dogs (ex guide dogs) Cen ht CTV No children 13yrs 2P No coaches Last d noon
ROOMS: s fr £22; d fr £44; wkly b&b fr £140; wkly hlf-bd fr £230

BERE REGIS Dorset Map **03** SY89

Q Q Q ***Appletree Cottage*** 12 Shitterton BH20 7HU (From village continue along West St & take 3rd turning left after telephone box, follow lane over bridge; cottage 5th house after bend) ☎ 01929 471686
Rest and relaxation are assured in this peaceful hamlet deep in Hardy country, ideally situated for exploring the area. With thatched roof, beams, inglenook fireplace, white-washed walls and roses around the door, this 17th-century cottage is a little gem! Originally two dwellings, this provides guests with a private lounge and separate staircase leading to two pretty bedrooms.
2 rms No smoking No dogs Cen ht CTV No coaches

BERKELEY Gloucestershire Map **03** ST69

Selected

Q Q Q Q ***Greenacres** (ST613908)* Breadstone GL13 9HF (2m W off A38, turn off A38 to Breadstone, in 0.75m on sharp left hand bend turn right up no through road, farm 300yds on right)
☎ 01453 810348 FAX 01453 810348 Mrs B Evans
Closed 24 Dec-2 Jan
Situated in an elevated position with fine views over the surrounding countryside, this large modern house offers good amenities close to Slimbridge and Berkeley Castle. Bedrooms are comfortable and well equipped with modern en suite facilities and hand crafted furniture, made on site in the family workshops. Public areas include a bright attractive dining room and a comfortable sitting room for guests' use. Barbara Evans is a friendly and caring hostess with a good knowledge of the surrounding area and its attractions.
4 bth/shr CTV in all bedrooms Tea and coffee making facilities No dogs (ex guide dogs) Cen ht CTV No children 10yrs 10P Sauna 17 acres horse breeding

BERWICK-UPON-TWEED Northumberland Map **12** NT95

Selected

Q Q Q Q ***Dervaig Guest House*** 1 North Rd TD15 1PW (turn off A1 at A1167 (North Road) to town, last house on right before railway bridge)
☎ 01289 307378
This detached Victorian house lies off the main road, north of the town centre and is conveniently located near to the railway station. The well proportioned bedrooms are comfortable, prettily decorated and spacious. There is an attractive lounge and the dining room features a fine collection of china plates. The sculptures of Laurel and Hardy on the landing will raise a smile! The house has a beautiful secluded garden both at the front and the rear.

5 bth/shr (3 fmly) No smoking in bedrooms No smoking in dining room CTV in all bedrooms Tea and coffee making facilities Cen ht 8P No coaches

Selected

Q Q Q Q **The Old Vicarage** Church Rd, Tweedmouth TD15 2AN (from S through Tweedmouth, right at Queens Head Pub, first left. From N through Berwick, over bridge to Tweedmouth, left at Angel Inn, first right) ☎ 01289 306909
Closed Xmas & New Year
Lying in well tended gardens, this imposing 19th-century house is found on a quiet street south of the River Tweed. It has been sympathetically furnished to reflect its original character, with antique and period pieces as well as stripped pine. Comfortable bedrooms are well proportioned and contain many thoughtful touches such as sweets and toiletries. There is a cosy lounge with reading material, tourist information and board games, as well as a fridge with soft drinks and snacks. The elegant dining room is spacious and Tina Richardson puts a lot of care into her breakfasts, with local Craster kippers a speciality.
7 rms (4 shr) (1 fmly) No smoking in dining room No smoking in lounges CTV in all bedrooms Tea and coffee making facilities Cen ht CTV 5P
ROOMS: s £15-£17; d £32-£50; wkly b&b £100-£157*

BETLEY Staffordshire Map **07** SJ74

Selected

Q Q Q Q **Betley Court Farm** *(SJ753484)* CW3 9BH (leave M6 junct 16 onto A500 until 2nd rdbt, then A531, farm in two and a half miles on right)
☎ 01270 820229 Mrs J Speed
This impressive farmhouse is very much a working farm and it lies in the heart of a lovely Staffordshire village. It has 200 acres of mixed farmland, and children are especially welcome. Bedrooms are attractively decorated and well equipped. The Speed family are friendly and welcoming and a homely atmosphere prevails.
3 bth/shr (1 fmly) No smoking CTV in all bedrooms Tea and coffee making facilities Cen ht ch fac P Fishing Riding 220 acres mixed
ROOMS: s £25-£28; d £40-£44*

See page 14-20 for a list of Premier Selected establishments

BETTISCOMBE Dorset Map **03** SY39

Q Q Q *Marshwood Manor* DT6 5NS ☎ 01308 868442
Closed Dec-Jan
Nestling in 10 acres of gardens and woodland, this peaceful Victorian manor house offers guests a friendly and relaxed atmosphere. Bedrooms are spacious and bright, and all have modern en suite facilities. Good home-cooked meals are served in the evenings, with delicious home-made bread and preserves, and traditional puddings. Much of the fresh fruit and vegetables comes from the garden.
6 rms (2 bth 3 shr) (3 fmly) No smoking in dining room CTV in all bedrooms Tea and coffee making facilities Licensed Cen ht 15P No coaches Outdoor swimming pool (heated) Croquet Putting
CARDS:

See advertisement under BRIDPORT

BEVERLEY East Riding of Yorkshire Map **08** TA03

See also Leven

Q Q Q **The Eastgate** 7 Eastgate HU17 0DR (200 yards from Beverley Minster) ☎ 01482 868464 FAX 01482 871899
Centrally situated in the delightful town of Beverley, this family owned and run hotel provides modern and well equipped bedrooms together with comfortable public rooms. Very friendly service is provided by the resident owners who are always on hand to meet guests' needs.
18 rms (7 shr) (5 fmly) No smoking in bedrooms No smoking in dining room CTV in all bedrooms Tea and coffee making facilities Cen ht CTV
ROOMS: s £20-£35; d £36-£46

BEXHILL East Sussex Map **05** TQ70

Q Q Q **The Arosa** 6 Albert Rd TN40 1DG (from seafront turn N onto Devonshire Road, first left, first left onto Albert Road, premises on right) ☎ 01424 212574 & 732004 FAX 01424 212574 & 732004
This small hotel is situated in a quiet residential street, yet is close to the sea front, the shops and the De La Warr Pavilion. Bedecked in flowers in the summer months, this Edwardian town house is run in a relaxed and friendly manner by resident proprietors Christine and Tony Bayliss. Well-equipped bedrooms, some suitable for families, have attractive co-ordinating decor and most are en suite. There is a cosy lounge with board games and videos for the odd rainy day and a dining room where substantial breakfasts start the day and dinners are served(order by 12 noon please).A snack menu is also available during the day and a traditional Sunday lunch is offered.
9 rms (6 bth/shr) (2 fmly) No smoking in dining room CTV in all bedrooms Tea and coffee making facilities Direct dial from bedrooms No dogs (ex guide dogs) Cen ht CTV No coaches Last d noon
ROOMS: s £25-£30; d £40-£50; wkly b&b £120-£180; wkly hlf-bd £172-£232
CARDS:

Q Q Q **Bedford Lodge Hotel** Canmtelupe Rd TN40 1PR (from Hastings on A259 (coast road), turn left at lights, then next left after Coombs Garage, then second left. Hotel 100yds on right) ☎ 01424 730097 FAX 01424 217552
Michael and Beryl Gebbie offer a homely atmosphere at their small hotel, located in a quiet residential street close to the seafront and a short walk from the town centre. All the well kept bedrooms have en suite facilities. There is a small lounge with a piano and board games and home-cooked dinners are offered in the pine-furnished dining room.
6 rms (3 shr) (1 fmly) No smoking CTV in all bedrooms Tea and coffee making facilities Licensed Cen ht No children 8yrs No coaches Last d 6pm
ROOMS: s £22-£26; d £44-£52; wkly b&b £125-£150; wkly hlf-bd £155-£200✳
CARDS:

Q Q Q *Park Lodge* 16 Egerton Rd TN39 3HH (turn off A27 to Bexhill seafront, Egerton Rd runs W off the only roundabout on the seafront) ☎ 01424 216547 & 215041 FAX 01424 217460
Conveniently located for the shops, the seafront and the De La Warr Pavilion, this friendly, family run hotel is well kept by owner Mrs Rogers. Individually furnished bedrooms are well equipped and attractively decorated. There is a small lounge with magazines and a good range of tourist information, and a brightly decorated dining room where home-cooked evening meals are offered.
10 rms (9 bth/shr) (2 fmly) No smoking in bedrooms No smoking in dining room CTV in all bedrooms Tea and coffee making facilities Direct dial from bedrooms Licensed Cen ht 4P No coaches Last d 3pm
CARDS:

BEYTON Suffolk Map **05** TL96

Premier Selected

Q Q Q Q Q **Manorhouse** The Green IP30 9AF (Beyton is signposted off A14, 4mE of Bury St. Edmunds) ☎ 01359 270960 FAX 01359 271425
Expect a friendly welcome from Mrs Dewsbury, the charming hostess of this delightful farmhouse, which stands in attractive gardens overlooking the village green. The sitting and dining room has a wealth of exposed beams, is tastefully decorated, and furnished with some lovely period pieces. The accommodation is spacious, and rooms are comfortably appointed. In addition to a hearty breakfast, freshly prepared and interesting dinners are available by prior arrangement.
2 bth/shr 2 annexe shr No smoking CTV in all bedrooms Tea and coffee making facilities No dogs Cen ht No children 4yrs 6P No coaches Last d 10am
ROOMS: s £28-£35; d £40-£50

BIBURY Gloucestershire Map **04** SP10

Selected

Q Q Q Q **Cotteswold House** Arlington GL7 5ND (Bibury is situated on the B4425 between Cirencester/Burford, Enter village from Cirencester, Cotteswold House is on left)
☎ 01285 740609 FAX 740609
Situated in the small village of Bibury, close to the river Coln, this well maintained property offers welcoming accommodation in an area ideal for exploring the Cotswolds. The bedrooms are attractively decorated and have good facilities and comfortable furnishings. There is a self-catering option available.
3 bth/shr (1 fmly) No smoking CTV in all bedrooms Tea and coffee making facilities No dogs (ex guide dogs) Cen ht 5P No coaches
ROOMS: s £25-£30; d £40-£45

BICKINGTON (NEAR ASHBURTON) Devon Map **03** SX77

Selected

Q Q Q Q **East Burne** *(SX799711)* TQ12 6PA (1.5m from A38 off A383) ☎ 01626 821496 FAX 01626 821105 Mrs E A Ross
Closed Xmas & New Year
Situated in a peaceful valley, this Grade II listed medieval house is a real rural retreat. The bedrooms, one of which is on the ground floor, offer comfortable accommodation. There is an attractive guest lounge and a traditional beamed dining room where English breakfasts are served, often with eggs from the farm's own hens. The house is surrounded by extensive farmland, and guests can use the sheltered outdoor pool and picnic area.
3 bth/shr No smoking CTV in 2 bedrooms Tea and coffee making facilities No dogs (ex guide dogs) CTV 8P Outdoor swimming pool (heated) 40 acres horses sheep
ROOMS: s £25-£21; d £50-£42; wkly b&b fr £140*

BICKLEIGH Devon Map **03** SS90

Selected

Q Q Q Q **Fisherman's Cot** EX16 8RW
(M5 junct27, follow signs for Bickleigh)
☎ 01884 855237 FAX 01884 855241
Overlooking the River Exe, beside the 14th-century Bickleigh Bridge, this charming, thatched property has a Waterside bar and restaurant. Bedrooms are well equipped with modern facilities; some are situated in the main building, while others are located in lodges across the car park. An extensive selection of dishes is available from a range of menus, as well as a carvery offering various roasted meats, vegetables and puddings.
21 bth/shr (3 fmly) No smoking in 15 bedrooms No smoking in area of dining room CTV in all bedrooms Tea and coffee making facilities Direct dial from bedrooms Cen ht CTV 100P Fishing Last d 10pm
ROOMS: s £46; d £66
MEALS: Lunch £1.95-£5.95 Dinner £6.95-£11.95
CARDS:

BIDEFORD Devon Map **02** SS42

See also Parkham & Westward Ho!

Q Q Q **Mount Hotel** Northdown Rd EX39 3LP (Bideford turning off A39, right after Rydon garage, premises 600 yards) ☎ 01237 473748
Closed Xmas
This small Georgian townhouse is to be found in a partly walled garden, close to the centre of this historic, riverside town. It was recently taken over by Andrew and Heather Laugharne who have commenced a programme of improvements. A comfortable sitting room is available for guests, while a varied breakfast is served in the spacious dining room. With prior arrangement, light refreshments are provided.
6 shr (1 fmly) No smoking CTV in all bedrooms Tea and coffee making facilities No dogs (ex guide dogs) Licensed Cen ht CTV 4P No coaches Last d noon
ROOMS: s £24-£26; d £43-£49; wkly b&b £140-£175*
CARDS:

Selected

Q Q Q Q **Pines at Eastleigh** Old Barnstaple Rd, Eastleigh EX39 4PA (turn off A39 Barnstaple/Bideford road onto A386 signposted Torrington. After 0.75m turn left signposted Eastleigh, 2m to village, house on right)
☎ 01271 860561 FAX 01271 861248
rs Jan & Nov (no evening meals)
This Grade II Listed Georgian farmhouse is surrounded by open fields, and in the courtyard garden guests will find the gently running water most relaxing. Most of the bedrooms, which vary in size, are situated in converted farm buildings and are comfortable, brightly decorated and well appointed. Freshly prepared evening meals feature local produce wherever possible, including fresh fish from Bideford Bay, and there is a choice of two lounges in which to relax after dinner.
2 bth/shr 4 annexe bth/shr No smoking CTV in all bedrooms Tea and coffee making facilities Direct dial from bedrooms Licensed Cen ht CTV ch fac 12P No coaches Board games Last d 7pm
ROOMS: s £30-£40; d £60-£80; wkly b&b £180-£250; wkly hlf-bd £270-£340
CARDS:

See advertisement on p.81.

Sunset Hotel Landcross EX39 5JA (from Bideford Town take A386, 1.5m to Landcross, Hotel on left) ☎ 01237 472962
Mar-Nov
Overlooking picturesque Devon countryside, this small and friendly country hotel offers comfortable no-smoking accommodation in individually furnished and decorated bedrooms. A cosy lounge adjoins the dining room where home cooked dinners, featuring fresh local produce, are carefully prepared by Mrs Lamb.
4 shr (2 fmly) No smoking CTV in all bedrooms Tea and coffee making facilities Licensed Cen ht CTV 6P No coaches Last d 7pm
ROOMS: s £30-£40; d £49-£59; wkly b&b £170-£200; wkly hlf-bd £222.50-£240*
CARDS:

BILLINGSHURST West Sussex Map 04 TQ02

Newstead Hall Hotel Adversane RH14 9JH (premises at crossroads of A29 and B2133 2m S of Billinghurst)
☎ 01403 783196 FAX 01403 784228
This Tudor-style hotel prides itself on its friendly, welcoming atmosphere. Five bedrooms in the older part of the building have an individual character; one has panelled walls and a four-poster, while the remainder, in a modern extension, are more uniform in style. There is a very comfortable bar and restaurant that attracts outside trade as well as residents, who also have their own bar/lounge overlooking the garden. A meeting room for up to 20 is available.
15 bth/shr No smoking in dining room CTV in all bedrooms Tea and coffee making facilities Direct dial from bedrooms Licensed Cen ht 60P No coaches Last d 9.30pm
CARDS:

BINGHAM Nottinghamshire Map 08 SK73

Selected

Yeung Sing Hotel & Restaurant Market St NG13 8AB (turn off A46/A52 at rdbt-signpost Bingham, follow rd for about 1m, situated on a corner nr zebra crossing on left)
☎ 01949 831831 FAX 01949 838833
Closed 25-26 Dec
This family run hotel is part of the highly successful Yeung Sing restaurant, which is centrally situated in the market town of Bingham. All of the bedrooms are comfortably appointed and well equipped and each room has modern en suite facilities. Also available to guests are two lounges on the first floor and the ground floor restaurant, which serves a fine selection of Cantonese and regional Chinese dishes.
15 bth/shr (2 fmly) No smoking in area of dining room No smoking in 1 lounge CTV in all bedrooms Tea and coffee making facilities Direct dial from bedrooms Licensed Lift Cen ht 30P Last d 8pm
ROOMS: s £43; d £56; wkly b&b £301*
CARDS:

BINGLEY West Yorkshire Map 07 SE13

Selected

Five Rise Locks Beck Ln BD16 4DD (off A650 at Dacre, Son and Hartley turn onto Park rd, at crossrds sign turn left hotel on left) ☎ 01274 565296 FAX 01274 568828
Closed 24-26 & 31 Dec, 1 Jan
Enjoying fine views over the Aire valley and the canal locks from which the hotel draws its name, this imposing house stands in its own grounds and continues to improve under the present ownership. It offers well equipped bedrooms together with a comfortable lounge. Excellent home cooking is provided by Patricia Oxley using local produce where possible.
7 bth/shr 2 annexe bth/shr (2 fmly) No smoking in 2 bedrooms No smoking in dining room No smoking in 1 lounge CTV in all bedrooms Tea and coffee making facilities Direct dial from bedrooms Licensed Cen ht CTV 15P No coaches Pool table Table tennis Last d 8.30pm
ROOMS: s £32.50-£47; d £55-£59*
CARDS:

BIRDWOOD Gloucestershire Map 03 SO71

Kings Head GL19 3EF (on A40 Gloucester to Ross on Wye)
☎ 01452 750348
This popular and busy hostelry stands on the main Gloucester to Ross-on-Wye road. It provides modern furnished and equipped accommodation, which includes a family bedded room and two bedrooms with their own private patios. A good selection of meals is available both at lunch time and in the evening.
6 rms (5 shr) (1 fmly) No smoking in dining room CTV in all bedrooms Tea and coffee making facilities No dogs (ex guide dogs) Cen ht CTV 100P Pool Last d 9pm

BIRMINGHAM West Midlands Map 07 SP08

See also Blackheath

Ashdale House Hotel 39 Broad Rd, Acock's Green B27 7UX (off A41, first on left after Acocks Green Centre towards City Centre)
☎ 0121-706 3598 & 0121-707 2324 FAX 0121-706 3598
Standing in a quiet side road, this large Victorian house offers comfortable accommodation together with friendly and attentive service. There is a comfortable lounge and good hearty breakfasts are served in the cosy dining room.
9 rms (4 shr) (2 fmly) No smoking in dining room No smoking in lounges CTV in all bedrooms Tea and coffee making facilities Cen ht CTV 4P No coaches
ROOMS: s £20-£25; d £34-£40*
CARDS:

Awentsbury Hotel 21 Serpentine Rd, Selly Park B29 7HU (A38 from city centre, after 2m at end of dual carriageway and just after fire stn, take the 1st left, then left again and then 1st right)
☎ 0121 472 1258 FAX 0121 472 1258
This large detached house is situated in a residential suburb, about 2 miles south of the city centre, convenient for people visiting the University. The bedrooms are quite well equipped, and rooms on ground floor level, as well as family bedded rooms are available. Separate tables are provided in the traditionally furnished dining room.
16 rms (6 shr) (1 fmly) No smoking in dining room CTV in all bedrooms Tea and coffee making facilities Direct dial from bedrooms Cen ht 13P Last d 7pm
ROOMS: s £29-£39; d £44-£52*
CARDS:

Selected

QQQQ **Bridge House Hotel** 49 Sherbourne Rd, Acocks Green B27 6DX ☎ 0121 706 5900 FAX 0121 624 5900
Closed Xmas
Situated adjacent to Acocks Green Railway station on the edge of the village, this private hotel offers comfortable accommodation convenient for the city centre and the NEC. Bedrooms are very well equipped and have the benefit of en suite facilities. Public areas include a well stocked lounge bar, a comfortable sitting area and a spacious restaurant. There is also a split level function room. The Hopwood family and their staff are friendly and caring people who are constantly re-investing in the hotel to improve guest comfort and facilities.
46 bth/shr (1 fmly) No smoking in 42 bedrooms No smoking in area of dining room No smoking in 1 lounge CTV in 48 bedrooms Tea and coffee making facilities Direct dial from bedrooms No dogs (ex guide dogs) Licensed Cen ht CTV 55P Last d 8.30pm
CARDS:

QQQ **Cape Race Hotel** 929 Chester Rd, Erdington B24 0HJ (on A452, 2m from juncts 5 and 6 of M6, between A38 & A5127)
☎ 0121 373 3085 FAX 0121 373 3085
This large detached house is located in the North Birmingham suburb of Erdington, where the M6 is within easy reach. Soundly maintained modern bedrooms are well equipped and equally suitable for both tourists and business visitors. There is a cosy lounge and a small dining room where separate tables are provided, and which contains a bar.
9 rms (8 shr) CTV in all bedrooms Tea and coffee making facilities Direct dial from bedrooms No dogs (ex guide dogs) Licensed Cen ht CTV 9P No coaches Outdoor swimming pool (heated) Tennis (hard) Last d 8.30pm
ROOMS: s £26-£32; d £44-£46
CARDS:

QQQ **Central** 1637 Coventry Rd, South Yardley B26 1DD (off M42 at NEC junc, A45, continue past MacDonalds and Harry Ramsden Fish Shop, pull in after the set of houses on left)
☎ 0121 706 7757 FAX 7067757

Situated between the town centre and the airport, this friendly house has been lovingly furnished by the resident owners Mr & Mrs Mousley. The freshly decorated bedrooms have been thoughtfully equipped. Breakfast is served in the cosy dining room.
5 bth/shr (1 fmly) CTV in all bedrooms Tea and coffee making facilities No dogs (ex guide dogs) Cen ht 4P No coaches
ROOMS: s £18.50-£20; d £36-£40; wkly hlf-bd £129-£140*

QQ **Elston** 749-751 Washwood Heath Rd, Ward End B8 2JY (on A47/A4040 crossroads 1.5miles from junct 5/6 of the M6)
☎ 0121 327 3338 FAX 688 0781
rs Fri, Sat & Sun
This privately owned guest house is situated on the A47, near is junction with the A4040, in the northern suburb of Ward End. It provides modern furnished and equipped accommodation, which includes bedrooms on ground floor level. Both the small dining room and the cosy lounge overlook the pleasant rear garden.
12 rms (1 shr) No smoking in dining room No smoking in lounges CTV in all bedrooms Tea and coffee making facilities Cen ht CTV 11P No coaches Last d 8pm
ROOMS: s fr £18.50; d fr £34; wkly b&b fr £92; wkly hlf-bd fr £112*
CARDS:

QQQ **Lyndhurst Hotel** 135 Kingsbury Rd, Erdington B24 8QT (from M6 junct 6 follow A5127 then take right fork, signed Minworth, into Kingsbury Rd for hotel on right) ☎ 0121 373 5695 FAX 0121 373 5695
This large Victorian house is situated in the North Birmingham suburb of Erdington, and is within half a mile of the M6. It provides well equipped accommodation which includes bedrooms on ground floor level and family bedded rooms. Other facilities include a lounge, a conference room for up to 40 delegates, a cocktail bar and an attractive restaurant which overlooks the garden.

See advertisement on p.83.
contd.

14 rms (13 bth/shr) (3 fmly) No smoking in 5 bedrooms No smoking in area of dining room No smoking in 1 lounge CTV in all bedrooms Tea and coffee making facilities No dogs (ex guide dogs) Licensed Cen ht CTV 15P No coaches Last d 8.15pm
ROOMS: s £30-£44; d £42.50-£56; wkly b&b £210-£285
CARDS:

Prince Hotel Station St B5 4DY (off M6 junct 6 onto A38 into city centre to Smallbrook Queens way, turn into Hill St, then into Station St, nr Pallasades shopping centre) ☎ 0121 643 1134 FAX 0121 643 3209
The Prince Hotel is conveniently located close to the Bull Ring Bus station and New Street railway station. The public areas include a ground floor bar and a lower ground floor breakfast room. Although bedrooms are plainly decorated they are all soundly appointed and well equipped, the majority have en suite facilities.
40 rms (39 bth/shr) (2 fmly) CTV in all bedrooms Tea and coffee making facilities Direct dial from bedrooms No dogs (ex guide dogs) Lift Cen ht
ROOMS: s £50-£75; d £65-£85*
MEALS: Bar Lunch £3.75*
CARDS:

Robin Hood Lodge Hotel 142 Robin Hood Ln, Hall Green B28 0JX (on A4040, 5m from city centre)
☎ 0121 778 5307 & 0121 608 6622 FAX 0121 608 6622
This much extended house is about two miles south-east of the city centre. It provides well maintained modern accommodation, which includes family bedded rooms, and bedrooms on ground floor level. A further three bedrooms are located in the house next door. The bright and pleasant dining room overlooks the garden. There is also a comfortable lounge.
9 rms (1 bth 4 shr) (1 fmly) CTV in all bedrooms Tea and coffee making facilities Licensed Cen ht CTV 11P No coaches Last d 8pm
ROOMS: s £24-£33; d £38-£49
CARDS:

Rollason Wood Hotel 130 Wood End Rd, Erdington B24 8BJ (M6 N/S junct 6-exit for Birmingham Rd NE. At island take A5127 to Sutton & Erdington for 1m, at island turn right onto A4040, hotel 0.25m on left) ☎ 0121 373 1230 FAX 0121 382 2578
Owners Mr & Mrs Ingram warmly welcome guests to their hotel, where the atmosphere is relaxed and informal. Bedrooms are modestly furnished but suitably equipped. The public facilities include a bar lounge and a spacious dining room, a carte menu is offered at dinner and there is a choice of breakfasts.
35 rms (1 bth 10 shr) (4 fmly) No smoking in area of dining room CTV in all bedrooms Tea and coffee making facilities Licensed Cen ht CTV 35P Games room Last d 8.30pm
ROOMS: s £18-£36; d £32-£49.50; wkly b&b £123-£212
CARDS:

Tri-Star Hotel Coventry Rd, Elmdon B26 3QR (on A45)
☎ 0121 782 1010 & 021-782 6131
This is a handily placed roadside guesthouse, popular with both business and leisure guests using the NEC and adjacent airport. The bedrooms are well cared for and their modern bathrooms are fully tiled. Public areas extend to a comfortable lounge which opens into the dining room, a separate games room and a small bar.
15 rms (11 shr) (3 fmly) CTV in all bedrooms Tea and coffee making facilities No dogs Licensed Cen ht CTV 25P No coaches Pool table Last d 8pm
CARDS:

BIRMINGHAM (NATIONAL EXHIBITION CENTRE)
West Midlands

See **Hampton-in-Arden**

BISHOP'S CASTLE Shropshire Map 07 SO38

Selected

The Boar's Head Church St SY9 5AE (from A488 follow signs to livestock market, continue past market Inn is on the left at crossroads)
☎ 01588 638521 FAX 630126
This 17th-century inn stands close to the town centre. A lot of the original character has been retained, and is enhanced by features such as the flagstoned floor and exposed timbers in the bar. Set price and a la carte menus offer a choice of home cooked dishes, which are served in the adjacent restaurant. The well equipped bedrooms are all located on the ground floor of a separate building. One of them is furnished for family occupation.
4 bth/shr (1 fmly) No smoking in dining room CTV in all bedrooms Tea and coffee making facilities Direct dial from bedrooms Cen ht CTV ch fac 20P Pool table Last d 9.30pm
ROOMS: s £35-£40; d £55-£65; wkly b&b £165-£195; wkly hlf-bd £210-£245
MEALS: Lunch £4.50-£11.50alc Dinner £4.50-£11.50alc
CARDS:

The Old Brick Guesthouse 7 Church St SY9 5AA (from A488, turn by Community College into Bishops Castle, follow road past church into town, 100yds on left hand side) ☎ 01588 638471
Closed Xmas
Dating from the early 18th century, this house displays much character, with exposed beams and timbers, as well as an inglenook fireplace in the cosy lounge. A home cooked dinner is likely to include fruit and vegetables from the owners' garden. Bedrooms are comfortably furnished, including one on the ground floor and inter-connecting rooms ideal for a family.
4 bth/shr (1 fmly) No smoking in dining room CTV in all bedrooms Tea and coffee making facilities Licensed Cen ht 5P No coaches Last d 3pm
ROOMS: s £27.50; d £45; wkly b&b £141.75-£225.75*
CARDS:

BISHOPSWOOD Somerset Map **03** ST21

Q Q Q **Hawthorne House** TA20 3RS (from Ilminster, turn right off A303 signed Bishopswood, house on right after a mile) ☎ 01460 234482
This delightful cottage, situated in the peaceful hamlet of Bishopswood in the Blackdown Hills, was built in 1879 and offers a relaxed atmosphere and comfortable accommodation. Bedrooms are equipped with modern facilities and there is an elegant sitting room for guests. Breakfast is served in a conservatory overlooking the terraced garden to the hills beyond, and dinner is available by arrangement.
3 bth/shr No smoking Tea and coffee making facilities Cen ht CTV
No children 12yrs 5P No coaches Last d breakfast
ROOMS: s £24.50; d £39; wkly b&b £122.50; wkly hlf-bd £210*

BLACKHEATH West Midlands Map **07** SO98

Q Q ***Highfield House Hotel*** Holly Rd, Rowley Regis B65 0BH
(M5 junct 2, follow signs to Blackheath, up Henderson Way and at next traffic lights left into Holly Rd) ☎ 0121 559 1066 FAX 0121 559 1066
This large building, now a commercial guest house, stands just off Blackheath High Street, within easy reach of the M5. It provides fairly modern accommodation, which includes two bedrooms on the ground floor of an extension. Each of these has its own entrance from the car park. Separate tables are provided in the traditionally furnished breakfast room and there is a homely lounge.
14 rms (2 bth/shr) No smoking in dining room CTV in all bedrooms
Tea and coffee making facilities No dogs (ex guide dogs) Licensed Cen ht
CTV 12P No coaches Last d 6pm
CARDS:

BLACKPOOL Lancashire Map **07** SD33

Q Q ***Arosa Hotel*** 18-20 Empress Dr FY2 9SD
(Empress Drive runs off promenade cliffs and Chequers Hotels)
☎ 01253 352555 FAX 01253 352555
Quietly situated close to the North Shore, this guest house offers good value for money in generally spacious, yet simply furnished bedrooms, including two on the ground floor. In addition to the bar lounge, there is a sun lounge to the front and meals are served in the spacious dining room.
20 rms (3 bth 16 shr) (7 fmly) CTV in all bedrooms Tea and coffee making facilities Licensed Cen ht CTV 5P Last d 5pm

Q Q **Ashcroft Private Hotel** 42 King Edward Av FY2 9TA
(turn off Queen Prom 2nd right after Savoy hotel) ☎ 01253 351538
Bright, cheerfully decorated accommodation is provided at this small, friendly and personally run hotel. There is a spacious, comfortably furnished lounge bar, a sun lounge and a neatly furnished dining room, where dinner is available by prior arrangement.
10 rms (7 shr) (2 fmly) No smoking in dining room CTV in all bedrooms Tea and coffee making facilities No dogs (ex guide dogs) Licensed Cen ht CTV 2P No coaches Last d 2pm
ROOMS: s £15-£21; wkly b&b £98-£118; wkly hlf-bd £154-£174*
CARDS:

Q Q **Berwick Private Hotel** 23 King Edward Av FY2 9TA
☎ 01253 351496 FAX 351496
This pleasant and well cared for guest house is situated on a quiet side road just off the promenade. Good home cooking is provided in the small dining room. A comfortable sun lounge is also available for guests' use.
8 rms (7 bth/shr) (3 fmly) No smoking in bedrooms No smoking in dining room CTV in all bedrooms Tea and coffee making facilities No dogs (ex guide dogs) Licensed Cen ht CTV No children 4P No coaches Last d 3pm
ROOMS: d £36-£44

Selected

Q Q Q Q **Burlees Hotel** 40 Knowle Av FY2 9TQ
(from Queens Promenade right at Uncle Toms Cabin into Knowle Av)
☎ 01253 354535 FAX 01253 354535
Mar- Mid Nov
Mike and Linda Lawrence welcome guests to their double fronted property, situated in a quiet residential area of North Shore. A short walk away from Blackpool's famous promenade and trams, the house offers comfortable lounges and brightly decorated bedrooms which have been thoughtfully equipped. In the light and airy dining room with its pine furniture, guests can enjoy home cooked meals. The main lounge offers a place to relax and looks out onto well tended gardens.
9 shr (2 fmly) No smoking in 7 bedrooms No smoking in dining room CTV in all bedrooms Tea and coffee making facilities No dogs Licensed Cen ht CTV 5P No coaches Last d 4pm
ROOMS: s £23-£25; d £46-£51; wkly b&b £135-£160; wkly hlf-bd £190-£220
CARDS:

Q Q Q **Castlemere Hotel** 13 Shaftesbury Av, North Shore FY2 9QQ
☎ 01253 352430 FAX 01253 352430
Situated in the residential North Shore area, but just five minutes from the main attractions, this tastefully converted house offers a well maintained and modern standard of accommodation. Mr and Mrs Hayward are fine hosts and provide extensive local information. Dinner and breakfast are served in the cheery dining room whilst a tasteful residents bar provides a venue in which to relax.
9 bth/shr (1 fmly) No smoking in dining room CTV in all bedrooms Tea and coffee making facilities No dogs (ex guide dogs) Licensed Cen ht CTV 4P No coaches Last d noon
ROOMS: s £20-£25; d £40-£50; wkly b&b £140-£175; wkly hlf-bd £182-£217*
CARDS:

Q Q ***Claytons*** 28 Northumberland Av, off Queens Promenade FY2 9SA
(off Queens Promenade, nr Uncle Toms Cabin) ☎ 01253 355397
FAX 01253 500142
Just off Queens Promenade, this family run guest house offers a useful suite on the top floor. Other bedrooms, whilst being quite compact, are neatly furnished, all rooms are en suite. A good choice of popular dishes is offered and there is a well stocked adjacent bar, as well as a sun lounge. Margaret and Gerry Clayton are jazz enthusiasts and sometimes organise trips to local jazz clubs.
6 shr (1 fmly) No smoking in 3 bedrooms No smoking in dining room CTV in all bedrooms Tea and coffee making facilities No dogs (ex guide dogs) Licensed Cen ht CTV No children 3yrs No coaches Last d 4pm
CARDS:

Q Q **Cliff Head Hotel** 174 Queens Promenade, Bispham FY2 9JN
(premises on corner of Cavendish Road off promenade) ☎ 01253 591086
FAX 01253 590952
This family run seafront hotel, situated just opposite Bispham tram station, offers good value four course evening meals. There is a cosy visitors lounge and bedrooms, some on the ground floor, are pleasantly furnished.
10 bth/shr (3 fmly) No smoking in dining room CTV in all bedrooms Tea and coffee making facilities Licensed Cen ht CTV 4P Last d 6pm
ROOMS: d £33-£43; wkly hlf-bd £120-£135

Q Q Q ***Cliftonville Hotel*** 14 Empress Dr FY2 9SE (head N past North Pier for 0.75m to Glynn Square, Empress Drive is fourth turning on the right next to Cliffs Hotel) ☎ 01253 351052 FAX 01253 540052
May-7 Nov & Xmas/New Year rs Apr
This modern fronted hotel, situated in a quiet road off the north shore promenade, provides bedrooms which come in a variety of sizes. All are thoughtfully equipped and include a selection of refurbished rooms, one with a four poster bed. Reception rooms extend to a bright and airy sun lounge, separate bar lounge and spacious dining room. It is here that freshly prepared meals are served and breakfast is a most substantial affair.
18 shr (9 fmly) No smoking in dining room CTV in all bedrooms Tea and coffee making facilities No dogs (ex guide dogs) Licensed Lift Cen ht CTV 6P Pool table Last d 5.30pm
CARDS:

Q Q **The Colby Hotel** 297 The Promenade FY1 6AL
(on promenade midway between Blackpool Tower and Pleasure Beach)
☎ 01253 345845 FAX 01253 345845
Etr-Nov rs Apr-May
Further improvements have been made at this small hotel enjoying an enviable location on the promenade. The recently refurbished lounge bar provides the perfect vantage point to watch the world go by, with dinner and breakfast being served in the bright dining room. Bedrooms, including

family rooms and some with four-poster beds, have also been upgraded, offering comfort and such extras as trouser presses and hairdryers.
14 shr (5 fmly) No smoking in dining room CTV in all bedrooms Tea and coffee making facilities Direct dial from bedrooms No dogs Licensed Cen ht 2P No coaches Pool table Last d 6pm
ROOMS: s £16-£24; d £32-£48; wkly b&b £100.80-£151.20; wkly hlf-bd £141.75-£195.30
CARDS:

Q Q Q *Commodore Hotel* 246 Queens Promenade, North Shore FY2 9HA (off M55 at Kirkham exit, follow Chevelys signs, at Chevelys centre left at lights, travel towards Blackpool for 2m, Hotel on left) ☎ 01253 351440
This proprietor run hotel enjoys a quiet location towards the northern end of the promenade, yet within easy reach of all the attractions via the tram system. Bedrooms, a number of which have sea views, are of a reasonable size, well maintained and attractively decorated. Having previously run a restaurant the owners are totally at home in the kitchen and produce substantial freshly prepared meals.
18 annexe bth/shr (4 fmly) No smoking in dining room CTV in all bedrooms Tea and coffee making facilities No dogs (ex guide dogs) Licensed Cen ht 8P
CARDS:

Q Q **Denely Private Hotel** 15 King Edward Av FY2 9TA (approximately 1m north of Blackpool Tower) ☎ 01253 352757
Closed Xmas & New Year
This long established guest house, offering a warm welcome and friendly service, is situated on a side road just off the North Shore Promenade. Well maintained bedrooms are complemented by a spacious lounge and a bright dining room, where freshly prepared evening meals are served.
9 rms (2 shr) (2 fmly) No smoking in dining room Tea and coffee making facilities No dogs Cen ht CTV 6P Last d 3.30pm
ROOMS: s £15.80-£17.80; d £31.60-£35.60; wkly b&b £105.07-£118.37; wkly hlf-bd £142.10-£156.10*

Q Q Q **Derwent Private Hotel** 8 Gynn Av, North Shore FY1 2LD (60 yards from N promenade, 100 yards from Gynn Square) ☎ 01253 355194 FAX 01253 596618
Brenda and Keith Regardsoe continue to improve this small hotel, situated close to Gynn Gardens on the quieter North Shore. En suite facilities have recently been installed. There is a spacious lounge for guests to relax in as well as a small but fully stocked bar, meals are served at individual tables in the panelled dining room.
11 rms (6 shr) (2 fmly) No smoking in dining room Tea and coffee making facilities Licensed Cen ht CTV P Last d 2pm
ROOMS: s £19-£24; d £32-£42; wkly b&b £100-£120; wkly hlf-bd £130-£156*
CARDS:

Q Q **The Garville Hotel** 3 Beaufort Av, North Shore FY2 9HQ (from Tower travel 2.5m N up to Redbank Road, turn right, Beaufort Ave is first on left, Hotel is 30 metres on left) ☎ 01253 351004 FAX 01253 351004
Closed Jan & 2 wks mid-May
Situated at the quieter end of town, just off the promenade, this friendly guest house offers well maintained and brightly furnished accommodation. There is a cosy visitors lounge and a hearty breakfast is served in the recently refurbished dining room.
7 shr (3 fmly) No smoking in bedrooms No smoking in dining room CTV in all bedrooms Tea and coffee making facilities No dogs (ex guide dogs) Cen ht CTV No children 3yrs 5P No coaches
ROOMS: s £18-£22; d £32-£42; wkly b&b £90-£125*

Q Q Q **Hartshead Hotel** 17 King Edward Av FY2 9TA (off Promenade at Cliffs Hotel) ☎ 01253 353133 & 357111
Closed 7 Nov-Feb rs Mar-Etr
Margaret and Michael Dowling offer home from home hospitality and comfort at their private hotel which is conveniently situated in the quieter

---

North Shore area, just 200 yards from the Promenade and within walking distance of the town centre. Bedrooms are neatly decorated and have been thoughtfully equipped. There is a pleasant sun lounge in addition to the spacious and comfortable lounge bar. Freshly prepared meals are served in the attractive dining room with good home cooking the order of the day.
10 bth/shr (3 fmly) No smoking in bedrooms No smoking in dining room CTV in all bedrooms Tea and coffee making facilities Direct dial from bedrooms Licensed Cen ht CTV 6P No coaches Last d 4pm
ROOMS: s £15-£21; d £30-£42; wkly b&b £107-£126; wkly hlf-bd £119-£140*
CARDS:

Q Q Q **Lynstead Private Hotel** 40 King Edward Av FY2 9TA (adjacent to Queens Promenade) ☎ 01253 351050
Closed last wk Dec & 1st 2 wks Jan rs mid Nov-Dec & mid Jan-Etr
This well established and personally run guest house features interestingly furnished public areas. A collection of teapots adorns the dining room, the bar has transport models, including of course, the tram-cars, and calendar plates are displayed in the spacious and comfortable lounge. There is a chair lift between the first and second floors.
10 shr (4 fmly) No smoking Tea and coffee making facilities No dogs (ex guide dogs) Licensed Lift Cen ht CTV No children 3yrs No coaches Last d noon
ROOMS: s £18-£21; d £36-£42; wkly b&b £126-£133; wkly hlf-bd £130-£168*

Q Q Q **Lynwood** 38 Osborne Rd FY4 1HQ (adjoining promenade, opposite Sandcastle Centre) ☎ 01253 344628
Closed Xmas & New Year
This friendly guest house is situated on the south shore, close to the Pleasure Beach and Sandcastle Centre. Bedrooms are comfortable and attractively decorated, and there is also an inviting lounge available for guest use. Breakfast is served in the bright dining room.

contd

8 rms (1 bth 5 shr) (1 fmly) No smoking in dining room CTV in all bedrooms Tea and coffee making facilities No dogs Cen ht CTV 1P No coaches Last d breakfast
ROOMS: s £15-£24; d £30-£48; wkly b&b £105-£156

Selected

QQQQ **Mains Hall** Mains Ln, Little Singleton FY6 7LE (exit M55 at junct 3 and take A585 signed Fleetwood for 5 miles. Mains Hall is half a mile past the second set of traffic lights on the right) ☎ 01253 885130 FAX 01253 894132
Dating back to 1536 in parts, this Grade II Listed building enjoys a quiet location overlooking the river Wyre. Generally spacious bedrooms, including one with a fine carved four poster bed, are attractively furnished and thoughtfully equipped. Carved wood panelling is also a feature of the entrance hall, leading into a cosy bar and two dining rooms, popular with locals and visitors alike. There is also a conservatory function room to the side of the main building.
10 bth/shr No smoking in bedrooms No smoking in area of dining room CTV in all bedrooms Tea and coffee making facilities Direct dial from bedrooms Licensed Cen ht CTV 60P No coaches Fishing Last d 10pm
ROOMS: s £50-£70; d £50-£120*
CARDS:

QQQ **North Crest Private Hotel** 22 King Edward Av FY2 9TD (off Queens Promenade, 1m N of North Pier) ☎ 01253 355937
The North Crest is a very well kept small hotel in a quieter area of the town, just off the north promenade. The friendly Mr and Mrs Hill are continually making improvements to the hotel and all rooms are now en suite. There is also a comfortable lounge and a cheerful dining room with a small bar.
7 bth/shr (3 fmly) No smoking in bedrooms No smoking in dining room CTV in all bedrooms Tea and coffee making facilities Licensed Cen ht CTV 3P Last d 3pm
ROOMS: s £16-£25; d £32-£50; wkly b&b fr £100; wkly hlf-bd fr £135*
CARDS:

Selected

QQQQ **The Old Coach House** 50 Dean St FY4 1BP (at end of M55 follow signs for main car park, at Go-Karts turn right, at traffic lights turn left, next traffic lights left, Dean St second on right) ☎ 01253 349195 FAX 01253 344330
Claire and Mark Smith are super hosts, offering a warm and friendly welcome to their historic home, just minutes walk from Blackpool's famous Pleasure Beach and South Pier. Rooms are tastefully appointed with thoughtful accessories and two boast four-poster beds. Meals are served in the period decorated dining room which is a popular venue, whilst a delightful conservatory offers comfort and a place in which one can relax.
7 bth/shr (2 fmly) No smoking in 2 bedrooms No smoking in dining room CTV in all bedrooms Tea and coffee making facilities Direct dial from bedrooms No dogs (ex guide dogs) Licensed Cen ht 10P No coaches Last d 9pm
ROOMS: s £27.50-£60; d £48.18-£65; wkly b&b fr £168.63; wkly hlf-bd fr £231.28*
CARDS:

QQQ **Sunny Cliff** 98 Queens Promenade, Northshore FY2 9NS (1.5m N of Tower on A584, just past Uncle Toms Cabin) ☎ 01253 351155
Etr-8 Nov
After four decades under the same ownership, this friendly guest house overlooking the seafront, enjoys a loyal following of happy guests. Spacious bedrooms are brightly furnished and well maintained whilst downstairs, the bar is discreetly tucked away behind the restaurant where a range of homemade dishes is offered. In addition to the comfortable sitting room, there is also a sun lounge where visitors can watch the world pass by.
9 shr (3 fmly) No smoking in dining room CTV in all bedrooms Tea and coffee making facilities Licensed CTV 8P No coaches Last d 5pm
ROOMS: s £19-£22; d £36-£44; wkly b&b £110-£125; wkly hlf-bd £145-£160*

Selected

QQQQ **Sunray** 42 Knowle Av, Queens Promenade FY2 9TQ (from Tower, head N along Prom turning right at Uncle Toms Cabin, hotel 300yds on left) ☎ 01253 351937 FAX 01253 593307
Closed mid Dec-mid Jan
Jean and John Dodgson have been welcoming visitors to this attractive guest house, set in colourful gardens just off Queens Promenade, for well over a quarter of a century. Their success is shown in the numbers who return. The nicely furnished bedrooms have a number of thoughtful extras to add to guests' comfort. Downstairs there is a comfortable lounge with books, toys and games, and a home cooked meal is offered at 5.30pm allowing plenty of time to enjoy a show in one of the town's theatres.
9 bth/shr (2 fmly) CTV in all bedrooms Tea and coffee making facilities Direct dial from bedrooms Cen ht CTV 6P No coaches Last d 3pm
ROOMS: s £25-£30; d £50-£60; wkly b&b £150-£180; wkly hlf-bd £222-£252
CARDS:

QQ **Surrey House Hotel** 9 Northumberland Av FY2 9SB (continue along Prom to Gynn Sq roundabout leading to Queens Prom, hotel is on fifth rd after roundabout) ☎ 01253 351743
Bedrooms are furnished in a straightforward way at this small hotel which is situated just 100 yards from the promenade, to the north of the town centre. There is a spacious sitting room, a separate sun lounge and a bright dining room where meals, including a home cooked dinner, are served.
12 rms (2 bth 9 shr) (2 fmly) No smoking in dining room CTV in 2 bedrooms Tea and coffee making facilities Cen ht CTV 7P Table tennis Pool table Last d 4.30pm
ROOMS: s £20-£23; d £40-£46; wkly b&b £140-£161; wkly hlf-bd £182-£203*

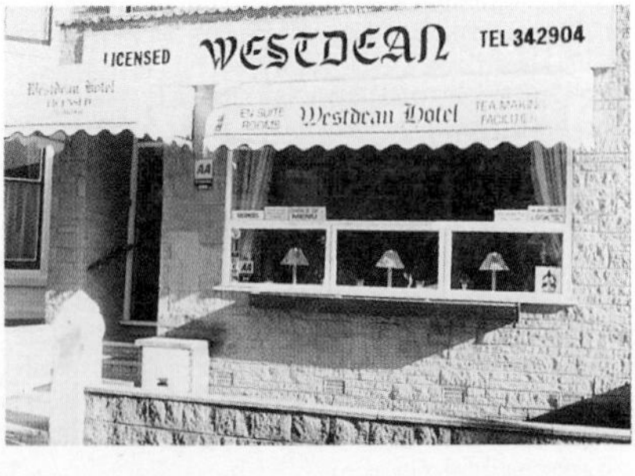

QQQ **Westdean Hotel** 59 Dean St FY4 1BP (Along Promenade from Pleasure Beach towards Blackpool Tower, first right after South PIer into Dean Street) ☎ 01253 342904 FAX 342904
Ideally located for the Pleasure Beach, Sandcastle and South Pier, this private hotel has a friendly and welcoming atmosphere. Bedrooms vary in size, some being quite spacious, but all are attractively decorated and furnished. The recently refurbished dining room is a pleasant area in which to enjoy dinner, and a sun lounge and bar are also available.

11 rms (10 shr) (3 fmly) No smoking in dining room CTV in all bedrooms Tea and coffee making facilities No dogs Licensed Cen ht CTV 2P Games room Pool table Dart board Last d 3pm
ROOMS: s £18-£25; d £36-£50; wkly b&b £109-£125; wkly hlf-bd £145-£159✻
CARDS:

Q Q Q Wilmar 42 Osborne Rd FY4 1HQ ☎ 01253 346229
Closed 23-27 Dec
This friendly guest house is situated within easy walking distance of the Pleasure Beach. Comfortable bedrooms are brightly decorated and the lounge is attractively furnished. A set evening meal is served at 5pm, allowing plenty of time to attend the shows.
7 shr No smoking in dining room CTV in all bedrooms Tea and coffee making facilities No dogs (ex guide dogs) Licensed Cen ht CTV No children 13yrs No coaches Last d 10am
ROOMS: s £16-£25; d £32-£50; wkly b&b £105-£120; wkly hlf-bd £135-£160✻

Q Q Q Windsor Hotel 53 Dean St FY4 1BP
☎ 01253 400232 FAX 01253 346886
Conveniently located close to the South Pier and Pleasure Beach, this privately owned hotel offers comfortably furnished bedrooms, some with four-poster beds. Dinner is served at separate tables in the traditional dining room and bar, and a sun lounge is provided for guests.
12 shr (3 fmly) No smoking in 6 bedrooms No smoking in dining room CTV in all bedrooms Tea and coffee making facilities No dogs (ex guide dogs) Licensed Cen ht CTV 8P Last d 7pm
ROOMS: s £20-£25; d £34-£46; wkly b&b £102-£114; wkly hlf-bd £138-£150✻
CARDS:

Q Q Q *Windsor Park Hotel* 96 Queens Promenade FY2 9NS (Queens Promenade, main road North shore) ☎ 01253 357025
24 Mar-5 Nov, 24 Dec-2 Jan
This attractive seafront hotel is found on the North Shore and offers all round comforts. Pleasant public rooms extend to a sun lounge and lounge bar. Meals can be enjoyed in the attractive dining room, and the breakfast is substantial. Bedrooms are thoughtfully equipped and offer modern amenities.
11 shr (1 fmly) No smoking CTV in all bedrooms Tea and coffee making facilities No dogs (ex guide dogs) Licensed Cen ht CTV 9P No coaches Last d 7pm
CARDS:

Q Q Q *Woodleigh Private Hotel* 32 King Edward Av, North Shore FY2 9TA (head North to Queens promenade to Gynne rdbt, turn right at Cliffs Hotel) ☎ 01253 593624
Enthusiastic new owners are making further improvements to the already good standards at this family run small hotel. Attractively decorated bedrooms, which vary in size, are comfortable, as is the inviting lounge. Home cooking is served in the dining room, with portions to satisfy the heartiest of appetites.
10 shr (2 fmly) No smoking in dining room CTV in all bedrooms Tea and coffee making facilities Cen ht CTV No coaches Last d 3pm

BLAKENEY Gloucestershire Map 03 SO60

Q Q Q Viney Hill Country Viney Hill GL15 4LT (2.5m from Lydney off A48 on unclassed road signposted "Viney Hill") ☎ 01594 516000 FAX 01594 516018
A delightful farmhouse built in 1741 and tastefully extended, Viney Hill is set in half an acre of lawns and gardens and adjacent to the Royal Forest of Dean and Wye Valley. Bedrooms are comfortably furnished, brightly decorated, and have good views of the countryside. The two lounges are cosy and there is an attractive dining room where evening meals are available by arrangement.
6 bth/shr No smoking CTV in all bedrooms Tea and coffee making facilities No dogs (ex guide dogs) Licensed Cen ht CTV 10P No coaches Last d 1pm
ROOMS: s fr £32; d fr £48
CARDS:

See advertisement under GLOUCESTER

BLAKENEY Norfolk Map 09 TG04

Q Q Q Flintstones Wiveton, Blakeney Rd NR25 7TL (from A148 at Letheringsett, follow signs to Wildflower Centre then to Glanford/Wiverton. Hotel is on right on the Blakeney Road past the Bell Pub) ☎ 01263 740337
Closed 24-26 Dec
Sitting in the quiet village of Wiveton, one mile inland from Cley-next-the-Sea and Titchwell, this small family guest house is popular with bird watchers. Bedrooms have colour co-ordinated decor and soft furnishings, and most have en suite shower rooms. There is also a combined breakfast-room and lounge area. It should be noted that the establishment is no-smoking.
5 shr (3 fmly) No smoking CTV in all bedrooms Tea and coffee making facilities Cen ht 5P No coaches
ROOMS: s £22.50; d £35-£39; wkly b&b £122.50✻

BLANDFORD FORUM Dorset Map 03 ST80

Selected

Q Q Q Q ♈ Home Farm *(ST868069)* Bryanston DT11 0PR (1.5m NW, opposite village shop) ☎ 01258 452919 Mr & Mrs J Tory
Situated in the centre of this pretty village, a short distance from historic Blandford Forum, 200-year-old Home Farm is beautifully appointed. The bedrooms are comfortable, tastefully decorated and furnished with antique and other pieces in keeping with the character of the house. The first floor lounge is a listed room and boasts marvellous oak panelled walls and an open fire. Breakfast is taken around a large pine table in a farmhouse kitchen atmosphere.
3 rms (2 bth/shr) No smoking Tea and coffee making facilities Cen ht CTV 10P 800 acres dairy arable
ROOMS: s £22.50; d £45✻

Q Q Q **Restharrow** North St, Winterborne Stickland DT11 0NH (head N off A354 at Winterbourne Whitechurch towards Winterbourne Stickland. Establishment is located 150yds beyond "Shire Horse Inn") ☎ 01258 880936 FAX 01258 880936
Attractive accommodation with modern facilities is on offer at this well presented property. Rooms are well equipped, with thoughtful extras, and there is a comfortable lounge. Breakfast is served at one large pine table overlooking the flower-filled garden - a riot of colour in summer. Home produced eggs and honey, and home-made preserves are included with the enjoyable meals.
2 shr No smoking CTV in all bedrooms Tea and coffee making facilities No dogs Cen ht CTV 3P No coaches
ROOMS: s £25-£30; d £35-£40; wkly b&b £123-£140

BLEDLOW Buckinghamshire Map 04 SP70

Selected

Q Q Q Q **Cross Lanes** Cross Lanes Cottage HP27 9PF (leave M40 junc 6, B4009 continue on this road after passing Beldlow village sign Cross Lanes 1st property on right, behind gates) ☎ 01844 345339
Situated in the conservation village of Bledlow, Cross Lanes, personally run by Mr and Mrs Coulter, is a delightful cottage, partly dating back to the 16th century. Pretty hanging baskets decorate the outside of this immaculately maintained home, where good hospitality and comfort are assured. Breakfast is served in the cosy dining room, and local pubs and restaurants can be recommended for dinner. The bedrooms, all with showers, are in the newer part of the cottage and offer good quality furnishings and pretty co-ordinated fabrics.
3 shr No smoking CTV in all bedrooms Tea and coffee making facilities No dogs (ex guide dogs) Cen ht CTV No children 14yrs 6P No coaches
ROOMS: d £50; wkly b&b £157*

BLOCKLEY Gloucestershire Map 04 SP13

Selected

Q Q Q Q **Lower Brook House** Lower St GL56 9DS (from Moreton-in Marsh A44 (to Broadway) through Bourton-on-Hill,past garage on left. Take next turn right to Blockley Road leading to the car park) ☎ 01386 700286 FAX 01386 700286
Situated on the edge of this tranquil Cotswold village, Lower Brook House dates back to the 17th century and retains many of its original features. Recently re-arranged, the public areas include a brighter more spacious dining area and two charming lounges. Flagstone floors and a huge inglenook fireplace are just a couple of the outstanding features. Bedrooms too have been refurbished, with bright decoration and many thoughtful extras such as fresh flowers, fruit and mineral water. Breakfasts are special, with bowls of fresh fruit salad and home-made bread as well as traditional English fare.
5 bth/shr No smoking in bedrooms No smoking in dining room No smoking in 1 lounge CTV in all bedrooms Tea and coffee making facilities No dogs (ex guide dogs) Cen ht 10P No coaches Gardens with Koi carp pool
ROOMS: s £30-£50; d £50-£85*
CARDS:

BODMIN Cornwall & Isles of Scilly Map 02 SX06

Q Q Q **Mount Pleasant Moorland Hotel** Mount PL30 4EX (from Bodmin follow A30 signed Launceston for 4m, then turn right signed Millpool, continue for 3m) ☎ 01208 821342
Apr-Sep
Jeremy and Colette Capper's charming period property lies on the edge of the rugged Bodmin Moor. Except on the warmest of days, a log fire burns in the old stone inglenook. In addition to the cosy bar, there is a sun lounge and separate TV lounge. Colette's home cooked dinners are available by prior arrangement. Breakfasts include hand made sausages and Cornish hog's pudding from the local butcher, and eggs from their own hens. Bedrooms are neatly furnished and decorated.
7 bth/shr (1 fmly) No smoking in bedrooms No smoking in dining room No smoking in 1 lounge Tea and coffee making facilities No dogs Licensed Cen ht CTV No children 5yrs 10P No coaches Outdoor swimming pool (heated) Last d 5pm
ROOMS: s £24-£27.50; d £48-£55; wkly hlf-bd £240*
CARDS:

BOLTON Greater Manchester Map 07 SD70

Q Q Q **Broomfield Hotel** 33-35 Wigan Rd, Deane BL3 5PX (exit M61 at junc 5, take A58 for 2 miles, hotel on right) ☎ 01204 61570 FAX 01204 650932
New owners are continuing to improve this small hotel, conveniently situated alongside the A58 on the outskirts of the town. Bedrooms, although compact in some cases, are brightly decorated and modern in design. There is a cosy lounge bar, and home cooked food features in the dining room.
15 bth/shr (2 fmly) No smoking in 4 bedrooms No smoking in dining room CTV in all bedrooms Tea and coffee making facilities Licensed Cen ht CTV 12P Last d 8.30pm
ROOMS: s £32; d £44-£46*
CARDS:

Selected

Q Q Q Q **Heron Lodge** 8 Bolton Rd, Turton Bottoms, Edgworth BL7 0DS (from M65 junct 5 take B623 Haslington Rd for 1m. Turn right at Grey Mare signposted Edgworth. Lodge is on the left at bottom of Edgeworth village) ☎ 01204 852262 FAX 01204 852262
Standing in the centre of the village of Edgworth and next to a delightful pub, this charming stone built house offers very well furnished and comfortable bedrooms together with a pleasant lounge. Good breakfasts are served in the attractive dining room and very friendly service is provided.
3 bth/shr No smoking Tea and coffee making facilities No dogs (ex guide dogs) Cen ht CTV 6P
ROOMS: s £26-£32; d £45-£50*

BOLTON-BY-BOWLAND Lancashire Map 07 SD74

Q Q Q **Middle Flass Lodge** Settle Rd BB7 4NY (A59 Skipton to Clitheroe Rd, take turning for Sawley. Follow signpost for Bolton-by-Bowland at Copynook, second left signed Settle. 3m on right) ☎ 01200 447259 FAX 01200 447300
Situated between Clitheroe and Gisburn, in the Forest of Bowland, this friendly guest house has been created out of redundant farm buildings.

Bedrooms are modern in style, but retain the original exposed timbers which are also found in the spacious restaurant. A separate visitors' sitting room is provided. It should be noted that the house is no-smoking throughout.

5 bth/shr (1 fmly) No smoking CTV in all bedrooms Tea and coffee making facilities No dogs Licensed Cen ht CTV 24P No coaches Last d 6.30pm
ROOMS: s £25-£37.50; d £40-£55; wkly b&b £140-£185; wkly hlf-bd £245-£290
CARDS:

BONSALL Derbyshire Map **08** SK25

QQQ **Sycamore** 76 High St DE4 2AR (leave A6 at Cromford onto B5036 then A5012. At Pig of Lead pub turn right into Bonsall) ☎ 01629 823903 FAX 823903
Sycamore House, a Grade II listed building, is situated at the top of the village and is conveniently located for Matlock and the surrounding Peak District. Bedrooms vary in size, but all are nicely decorated, comfortably furnished and well equipped. A carefully prepared home cooked meal is served in the beamed dining room and there is a cosy lounge with a welcoming open fire in the colder months.
5 bth/shr (1 fmly) No smoking in bedrooms No smoking in dining room CTV in all bedrooms Tea and coffee making facilities No dogs (ex guide dogs) Licensed Cen ht CTV 7P No coaches
ROOMS: s £30-£35; d £44-£48; wkly b&b £149-£163; wkly hlf-bd £245-£270

See advertisement under MATLOCK

BOROUGHBRIDGE North Yorkshire Map **08** SE36

Selected

QQQQ **The Crown** Roecliffe YO51 9LY (turn off A1 at Boroughbridge and follow signs for Ripon. At Roecliffe sign on rdbt follow road into Roecliffe village and The Crown is on right) ☎ 01423 322578 FAX 01423 324060
Lying in a quiet village just a mile off the A1, this old inn boasts modern, well appointed bedrooms which will appeal to the business traveller as well as the tourist. Of even greater attraction however, is the quality of food and the imaginative menus served in both the bar and restaurant.
12 bth/shr CTV in all bedrooms Tea and coffee making facilities Direct dial from bedrooms Cen ht ch fac 70P Fishing Last d 9.30pm
ROOMS: s £35-£45; d £60-£90; wkly b&b £130-£160; wkly hlf-bd £180-£220✱
MEALS: Lunch £15-£40alc Dinner £15-£40alc✱
CARDS:

BORROWDALE Cumbria Map **11** NY21

Selected

QQQQ **Greenbank** CA12 5UY (3m S of Keswick on B5289) ☎ 017687 77215 FAX 017687 77215
Feb-Dec
This Victorian house sits in its own grounds in the heart of Borrowdale, enjoying breathtaking views across the valley to Derwentwater and northwards towards Skiddaw. Jean Wood offers a warm welcome to all her guests who can enjoy comfortable bedrooms which have been thoughtfully equipped. Two lounges are available, one with an honesty bar, offering panoramic views. Dinner can be enjoyed in the tastefully appointed dining room and here too a substantial breakfast is served. Gardens are mature and well maintained with a small trail through them from the house.
10 bth/shr (1 fmly) No smoking in bedrooms No smoking in dining room No smoking in 1 lounge Tea and coffee making facilities No dogs Licensed Cen ht CTV 15P No coaches Last d 5pm
ROOMS: s £24; wkly b&b £154-£245; wkly hlf-bd £231-£308
CARDS:

Premier Selected

QQQQQ **Hazel Bank** Rosthwaite CA12 5XB (6m from Keswick on B5289 Seatoller road, turn left at sign just before Rosthwaite village) ☎ 017687 77248 FAX 017687 77373
Apr-Oct rs Mar & Nov
This imposing Victorian residence, set in four acres of lawns and woodland, commands magnificent views of the Borrowdale valley and rugged fells from its elevated position in the village of Rosthwaite. Bedrooms, including one with a four-poster, are well proportioned, individually furnished and thoughtfully equipped. The attractive public areas feature an inviting lounge and a stylish dining room. John and Gwen Nuttall are enthusiastic hosts who make their guests feel very much at home. John's first class home cooking deservedly earns praise.
6 bth/shr No smoking CTV in all bedrooms Tea and coffee making facilities Licensed Cen ht No children 6yrs 12P No coaches Last d 7pm
ROOMS: (incl. dinner) s £47.50; d £95; wkly hlf-bd £297✱
CARDS:

BOSCASTLE Cornwall & Isles of Scilly Map **02** SX09

QQQ **Old Coach House** Tintagel Rd PL35 0AS (at junct of B3266 and B3263) ☎ 01840 250398 FAX 01840 250346
Located in the upper area of the village, with glorious views over the surrounding countryside, The Old Coach House dates back about three hundred years. Bedrooms are well equipped and the majority have recently been upgraded. Two rooms are situated on the ground floor and are suitable for the less able. Breakfast is taken at separate tables in the conservatory, overlooking the garden to the rear of the property.
8 bth/shr (3 fmly) No smoking in 6 bedrooms No smoking in dining room No smoking in lounges CTV in all bedrooms Tea and coffee making facilities Cen ht CTV 9P No coaches
ROOMS: s £17-£35; d £34-£40; wkly b&b £115-£126
CARDS:

St Christophers Hotel High St PL35 0BD (from A39 at Camelford take B3266, first left past 30mph signs, first right) ☎ 01840 250412
mid Feb-mid Dec
Dating from Georgian times, St Christopher's stands in one of the quieter areas of the village. The restaurant is the main focus, serving a short, imaginative fixed-price menu each evening. Well equipped bedrooms are neatly furnished and decorated, varying in size and style. A warm and friendly welcome awaits guests.
9 rms (8 shr) (1 fmly) No smoking CTV in all bedrooms Tea and coffee making facilities Licensed Cen ht CTV 8P No coaches Last d 8pm
CARDS:

Selected

Tolcarne House Hotel & Restaurant Tintagel Rd PL35 0AS (at junct of B3266/B3263 in Boscastle) ☎ 01840 250654 FAX 01840 250654
Apr-Oct rs Feb-Mar & Nov (prior booking only)
This charming Victorian residence has been enthusiastically improved by Margaret and Graham Crown over the last five years. Set in mature gardens with splendid views over the surrounding countryside, Tolcarne House is the ideal centre for touring the area. The very well equipped bedrooms vary in size and are priced accordingly. An open fire burns in the lounge on cooler evenings and there is a separate cosy bar/lounge. A fixed-price menu, including a variety of local dishes is offered each evening, with a carte available for those guests wishing to dine later.
8 bth/shr (1 fmly) No smoking in 4 bedrooms No smoking in dining room No smoking in 1 lounge CTV in all bedrooms Tea and coffee making facilities Licensed Cen ht No children 7yrs 15P No coaches Croquet Last d 8.45pm
ROOMS: s £28-£30; d £46-£64; wkly b&b £165-£215; wkly hlf-bd £250-£310*
CARDS:

BOSHAM West Sussex Map 04 SU80

Premier Selected

Kenwood Off A259 PO18 8PH (400m W of Bosham roundabout on A259) ☎ 01243 572727 FAX 01243 572738
With the Godden family providing a warm and caring welcome, guests feel immediately at ease on entering this large creeper-clad Victorian house, which is set in several acres of mature grounds with extensive views over the harbour. Inside, the decor and furnishings retain period charm with numerous 'collections' adorning every ledge and mantelpiece. Breakfast is taken in one of the conservatories, which also contains a fridge and microwave oven, for guests who wish to stay in during the evenings and cater for themselves, rather than venturing out. The other conservatory has a pool table, whilst the central lounge features a splendid grand piano. Bedrooms are spacious and traditionally furnished but with modern conveniences. The gardens are home to peacocks and rabbits, and there is a slide, swing and sandpit for children.
3 bth/shr (1 fmly) No smoking in dining room CTV in all bedrooms Tea and coffee making facilities Direct dial from bedrooms No dogs (ex guide dogs) Cen ht CTV 14P No coaches Outdoor swimming pool (heated) Fitness equipment Pool table
ROOMS: d £50; wkly b&b £168*

BOURNEMOUTH Dorset Map 04 SZ09

Alum Grange Hotel 1 Burnaby Rd, Alum Chine BH4 8JF (M27 to A31, at Ringwood turn left onto A338, 2nd exit at Frizzel House rdbt, left at lights, right at next rdbt and left as sea comes into view) ☎ 01202 761195 FAX 760973
Ideally located for Alum Chine beach, this small hotel is set in a quiet area of the town. The hotel has been decorated along a nautical theme. Bedrooms are neatly furbished and the 'Celebration Room' offers a four-poster bed and private balcony with panoramic views of the bay. The cosy bar is an ideal place to relax before enjoying evening meals which are served in the adjoining dining area.
14 rms (5 bth 7 shr) (7 fmly) No smoking in 4 bedrooms No smoking in dining room No smoking in 1 lounge CTV in all bedrooms Tea and coffee making facilities Licensed Cen ht CTV 10P Small snooker/pool table
ROOMS: s £20-£25; d £40-£50; wkly b&b £121-£175; wkly hlf-bd £175-£231
CARDS:

Amitie 1247 Christchurch Rd, Boscombe East BH7 6BP (on A35 near junct with A3060 at Iford, mid-way between Bournemouth and Christchurch) ☎ 01202 427255
Personally run by owners Anne and Norm Pickering, business and leisure guests alike are assured of a warm welcome and value for money. Bedrooms are attractively decorated and equipped with lots of extra touches such as shoe cleaning kits and ceiling fans. Breakfast is served in the well appointed dining room, which displays an interesting collection of wall plates and travel memorabilia.
7 bth/shr (1 fmly) No smoking in 3 bedrooms No smoking in dining room No smoking in lounges CTV in all bedrooms Tea and coffee making facilities No dogs (ex guide dogs) Cen ht No children 12yrs 8P No coaches
ROOMS: s £18-£22; d £36-£44

Selected

The Boltons Hotel 9 Durley Chine Rd South, West Cliff BH2 5JT (from Wessex Way turn off for West Cliff, second roundabout right onto West Cliff Road, second right Durley Chine Road South) (The Circle) ☎ 01202 751517 FAX 01202 751629
Closed Nov
This fine Victorian property has been tastefully refurbished to offer appealing public rooms that include a lounge, a well proportioned dining room and a cosy residents' bar that opens onto the patio. The swimming pool is situated in the secluded gardens. Bedrooms are well equipped, but vary in size.
12 bth/shr (2 fmly) CTV in all bedrooms Tea and coffee making facilities Direct dial from bedrooms Licensed Cen ht CTV 12P Outdoor swimming pool (heated) Last d 5pm
CARDS:

Q Q Q **Carisbrooke Hotel** 42 Tregonwell Rd BH2 5NT (from direction of Ringwood, follow signs for BIC, past Wessex hotel then 3rd left) ☎ 01202 290432 FAX 01202 310499
Situated close to the town centre and beach, the Carisbrooke has new owners. Plans are in hand to update the hotel and its facilities. Bedrooms are brightly decorated, comfortably furnished and well equipped, the majority of rooms having en suite bathrooms. The public rooms are a strong feature of the hotel, with a well appointed lounge, snug bar and an attractive dining room. A choice of menus is offered at dinner and breakfast.
22 rms (19 bth/shr) (6 fmly) No smoking in dining room CTV in all bedrooms Tea and coffee making facilities Direct dial from bedrooms Licensed Cen ht CTV 18P Last d 7pm
ROOMS: s £18-£30; d £36-£60; wkly b&b £120-£180; wkly hlf-bd £160-£325*
CARDS:

Q Q Q **Cherry View Hotel** 66 Alum Chine Rd BH4 8DZ (at junct A35/A338 follow B3065 towards Alum Chine, 0.25m left at traffic lights into Western Road, Hotel across next rdbt) ☎ 01202 760910 FAX 01202-768009
Apr-Oct rs Nov, Dec, March
This friendly, family run hotel is situated close to Alum Chine. The accommodation has been upgraded and provides comfortably furnished en-suite rooms. A daily changing set price menu is provided at dinner and served in the brightly decorated dining room. There is a cosy bar in which to enjoy a pre-dinner drink. Further public rooms include a small lounge.
11 bth/shr (1 fmly) No smoking in 6 bedrooms No smoking in dining room No smoking in 1 lounge CTV in all bedrooms Tea and coffee making facilities No dogs Licensed Cen ht CTV No children 7yrs 11P Last d 4pm
ROOMS: s £28-£31; d £40-£44; wkly b&b £130-£145; wkly hlf-bd £180-£200
CARDS:

Q Q Q **Cransley Hotel** 11 Knyveton Rd, East Cliff BH1 3QG (turn off A338 at St Paul's roundabout by ASDA Store, continue over next roundabout keeping Abbey Life building on right. Knyveton Rd 1st on left) ☎ 01202 290067 FAX 01202 294368
This hotel is located in a quiet residential area at East Cliff. Bedrooms are decorated with rich papers and matching fabrics. The one room without en suite facilities has its own private bathroom; ground floor rooms are provided, which are popular with less mobile guests. A comfortable lounge is available and this, like the separate dining room, opens out onto pretty lawns and gardens.
12 bth/shr No smoking CTV in all bedrooms Tea and coffee making facilities No dogs (ex guide dogs) Licensed CTV No children 5yrs 8P No coaches Last d 5pm
ROOMS: s £20-£22; d £40-£44*

Q Q Q **Dene Court** 19 Boscombe Spa Rd BH5 1AR (Off A338 at Bournemouth Stn rdbt, take A35 to Boscombe. Boscombe Spa Rd is 1st right after Boscombe gdns which are approx 0.5m along Christchurch Rd) ☎ 01202 394874
Conveniently located for the centre of Boscombe and the pier, this friendly family owned guest house offers good value accommodation, and is popular for bargain breaks. The house is well maintained and has a spacious dining room in addition to a comfortable basement lounge and an attractive bar and games room. The modern rooms are bright and attractive.
17 rms (15 bth/shr) (9 fmly) No smoking in dining room CTV in all bedrooms Tea and coffee making facilities No dogs Licensed Cen ht CTV 15P Snooker Last d 4.30pm
ROOMS: s £16.50-£26; d £33-£52*
CARDS:

Q Q Q **Dorset House** 225 Holdenhurst Rd BH8 8DD (from A338/A35 onto St Pauls rdbt into St Paul's Rd, left over Holdenhurst Rd past travel interchange, straight over mini rdbt on left) ☎ 01202 397908

Closed 21 Dec-7 Jan
Conveniently situated close to local amenities, this friendly guest house offers well appointed and comfortable accommodation. The attractively decorated bedrooms are furnished in modern style and equipped with many useful facilities. An evening meal is available and there is a choice at breakfast, which is served in the bright cosy dining room.
4 rms (3 shr) No smoking CTV in all bedrooms Tea and coffee making facilities No dogs Cen ht CTV No children 15yrs 6P No coaches Last d 5.30pm
ROOMS: s £23-£25; d £38-£42; wkly b&b £133-£161; wkly hlf-bd £192.50-£220.50

Q Q Q **East Cliff Cottage Hotel** 57 Grove Rd BH1 3AT (Wessex Way into Bournemouth, left at East Cliff Rd sign, next roundabout turn right, left into Meyrick Rd, left into Grove Rd) ☎ 01202 552788 FAX 01202 556400
Just three hundred yards from the sea front in a quiet area, this private hotel is the former home of the actor Stewart Grainger and is just a short walk from the East Cliff Lift. Good size family accommodation is available and the bedrooms are comfortable and decorated in period style. Drinks can be enjoyed in a cosy lounge adjoining a spacious dining room where home cooking is offered.
10 rms (6 bth/shr) (4 fmly) CTV in all bedrooms Tea and coffee making facilities Direct dial from bedrooms Licensed Cen ht CTV 10P No coaches Last d 7.30pm
ROOMS: s £19.50-£28; d £39-£56; wkly b&b £130-£185; wkly hlf-bd £179-£215*
CARDS:

Selected

Q Q Q Q **Farthings** St Peters Roundabout, Top of Hill, Bath Rd, 5/7 Grove Rd BH1 3AS (On rdbt at top of hill on Bath Rd going from Pier to Lansdowne) ☎ 01202 558660 FAX 01202 293766
This restaurant with rooms offers a selection of accommodation to suit all pockets, ranging from a superior room with whirlpool bath and multi-headed shower to a standard room with a bathroom across the corridor. The restaurant, popular with locals and residents alike, serves an interesting range of dishes at both lunch and dinner. During the summer months guests can dine in the attractive gardens to the rear of the property.
5 rms (3 bth/shr) No smoking in area of dining room CTV in all bedrooms Tea and coffee making facilities Direct dial from bedrooms No dogs (ex guide dogs) Licensed Cen ht 25P No coaches Last d 10pm
ROOMS: s £30-£41; d £58-£88*
CARDS:

Highclere Hotel 15 Burnaby Rd, Alum Chine BH4 8JF
(on A338 to Westbourne follow signs for Alum Chine, turn left 0.75m down Alunhurst Rd into Crosby Rd, Burnby Rd is at T-junct, hotel is 50yds on left) ☎ 01202 761350 FAX 767110
Apr-Sep
The quiet residential area of Alum Chine is close to the sea, and some rooms in this pretty guest house have the benefit of seaviews. All are well furnished and spacious with en suite bathrooms or showers. The house is tastefully furnished throughout. A home cooked evening meal is offered.
9 bth/shr (5 fmly) No smoking in dining room CTV in all bedrooms Tea and coffee making facilities Direct dial from bedrooms Licensed Cen ht CTV No children 3yrs 6P No coaches Last d 4pm
ROOMS: s £20-£25; d £40-£50; wkly b&b £130-£165; wkly hlf-bd £160-£175*
CARDS:

Holmcroft Hotel 5 Earle Rd, Alum Chine BH4 8JQ
(off A338 at Westbourne sign, straight over County Gates roundabout, left at first traffic lights, at mini roundabout right, Earle Rd seventh on left)
☎ 01202 761289 & 761395 FAX 761289
This personally run hotel is located in a quiet residential area between Bournemouth and Poole, just a few minutes stroll away from the wooded chines and sandy beaches. The smartly appointed dining room offers a choice of home cooked meals, and a cosy residents bar is also available.
19 bth/shr (2 fmly) No smoking CTV in all bedrooms Tea and coffee making facilities Direct dial from bedrooms No dogs (ex guide dogs) Licensed Cen ht CTV No children 8yrs 13P No coaches Last d 5pm
CARDS:

Linwood House Hotel 11 Wilfred Rd BH5 1ND
(Wessex Way to Boscombe, follow signs to Shelley Museum)
☎ 01202 397818 FAX 01202 397818
Mar-Oct
Situated in a peaceful residential area and close to the local attractions. Linwood house is the home of Thelma and Gerry Witham and has been furnished throughout to a very comfortable standard. Bedrooms are equipped with many modern amenities and are attractively decorated. The spacious well appointed lounge opens onto the well maintained garden where guests can relax in the tranquil setting. Sound traditional cooking is offered at dinner and a generous English breakfast, this is served in the cosy dining room.
10 rms (1 bth 7 shr) (2 fmly) No smoking in dining room CTV in all bedrooms Tea and coffee making facilities Licensed Cen ht CTV No children 6yrs 7P No coaches Last d 9am
ROOMS: s £24-£30; d £48-£60; wkly b&b £109-£142; wkly hlf-bd £151-£184

Newfield Private Hotel 29 Burnaby Rd, Alum Chine BH4 8JF
☎ 01202 762724 & 760938
This late Victorian house is located in a quiet residential area and benefits from being within easy walking distance of the sea. The bedrooms continue to be upgraded to meet present day needs. A set menu is offered at dinner and Elizabeth Tovey provides honest English dishes. Further facilities include a comfortably appointed lounge and small bar.
10 rms (1 bth 7 shr) (4 fmly) No smoking in dining room CTV in all bedrooms Tea and coffee making facilities Licensed Cen ht CTV 4P Last d 2pm
ROOMS: s £20-£25; d £40-£50; wkly b&b £130-£160; wkly hlf-bd £185-£230
CARDS:

Northover Private Hotel 10 Earle Rd, Alum Chine BH4 8JQ
(situated 400yds fron seafront) ☎ 01202 767349
The Northover Private Hotel enjoys a peaceful but accessible position, and is well located for the beach. Several of the rooms are suitable for family occupancy and the majority have en suite facilities. Mr and Mrs Habgood's attentive service will ensure your stay is enjoyable. A four course evening meal is provided by prior arrangement.
10 rms (7 bth/shr) (4 fmly) No smoking Tea and coffee making facilities Licensed Cen ht CTV 11P No coaches Last d 5pm

Sea Dene Hotel 10 Burnaby Rd, Alum Chine BH4 8JF
(from Country Gates gyratory rdbt take Alum Chine exit into The Avenue, left at lights, right at next rdbt, 7th left is Crosby Rd, hotel at bottom)
☎ 01202 761372 FAX 01202 761372
Only three minutes' walk along a rhododendron-lined chine to the beautiful sandy beaches, Sea Dene is personally run by Elizabeth Jones. By prior arrangement, a home cooked evening meal is available; catering for vegetarians and vegans is a speciality, without forgetting the carnivores! Alum Chine is conveniently located for Bournemouth and Poole.
6 shr (1 fmly) CTV in all bedrooms Tea and coffee making facilities Licensed Cen ht No children 3yrs 4P No coaches

Selected

Silver Trees 57 Wimborne Rd BH3 7AL (follow A338 into Bournemouth then A347 to Bournemouth University, Silvertrees is 1m from A338/A347 junct) ☎ 01202 556040 FAX 01202 556040
An attractive, detached Victorian property, set in well tended gardens on the edge of town. The house retains much of its original character and the stained glass windows are a fine feature. A warm welcome awaits guests along with a good standard of accommodation, particularly in the public areas, where a cosy lounge is provided in addition to the traditionally furnished dining room.
5 shr (1 fmly) No smoking in 3 bedrooms No smoking in dining room No smoking in 1 lounge CTV in all bedrooms Tea and coffee making facilities No dogs Cen ht No children 5yrs 10P No coaches
ROOMS: s £26-£28; d £44-£46
CARDS:

Hotel Sorrento 16 Owls Rd, Boscombe BH5 1AG
(turn left off A35 at St Johns Church then turn left at crossroads)
☎ 01202 394019
mid Feb-early Jan rs Xmas
Midway between the Pier and the Chine Gardens, and within a few minutes walk of the Sovereign Shopping Centre, Hotel Sorrento is personally run by Myra and Richard Titcumb and their daughter. A four course dinner menu is available, with a choice of starters and desserts. In addition to the comfortable lounge a spacious bar/lounge is provided, with a dartboard, games and selection of books.
19 rms (17 bth/shr) (5 fmly) No smoking in dining room CTV in all bedrooms Tea and coffee making facilities Licensed Cen ht CTV No children 2yrs 17P No coaches Solarium Mini-gym Last d 4pm
ROOMS: s £20-£24; d £40-£48; wkly b&b £126-£160; wkly hlf-bd £140-£195
CARDS:

Q Q Q **Thanet Private Hotel** 2 Drury Rd, Alum Chine BH4 8HA (follow signs for Alum Chine Beach hotel is on corner of Alumhurst Rd & Drury Rd) ☎ 01202 761135 FAX 01202 761135

Apr-Oct

This well maintained, private hotel is in a quiet residential location, close to the Chine and within easy reach of the town's amenities. Bedrooms which are equipped with thoughtful extras, are comfortable, and neatly furnished and decorated. Home cooked meals are served in the attractive dining room and a well appointed lounge is available to guests.

8 rms (5 shr) (1 fmly) No smoking CTV in all bedrooms Tea and coffee making facilities No dogs (ex guide dogs) Licensed Cen ht No children 7yrs 6P Last d 5pm

ROOMS: s £17-£20.75; d £34-£41.50; wkly b&b £102-£147; wkly hlf-bd £138-£177.50*

CARDS: MasterCard, Barclaycard Visa

Selected

Q Q Q Q **Tudor Grange Hotel** 31 Gervis Rd BH1 3EE (follow signs for East Cliff) ☎ 01202 291472 & 291463

Tudor Grange, just five minutes from the East Chair Lift, is a unique, period-style house in a quiet residential area. The oak-panelled lounge and dining room look out over the lovingly tended garden. Many original features have been retained, such as the 300-year-old main stairway. Dinner is available by arrangement.

12 rms (11 bth/shr) (4 fmly) No smoking in dining room CTV in all bedrooms Tea and coffee making facilities Direct dial from bedrooms Licensed Cen ht CTV 11P No coaches Use of indoor pool at neighbouring hotel Last d 7pm

ROOMS: s £27-£32; d £50-£64*

CARDS: MasterCard, Barclaycard Visa

Q Q Q **Valberg Hotel** 1a Wollstonecraft Rd, Boscombe BH5 1JQ (from Christchurch Rd to Boscombe Pier turn left onto Marina Drive, first right, first left) ☎ 01202 394644/394426

Situated between the seafront and Boscombe town centre, this large detached villa is delightful during the summer with its colourful array of plants and hanging baskets. Two of the bedrooms are on the ground floor and others benefit from having their own balconies. Evening meals are provided by prior arrangement in a pleasant dining room. From the guests' lounge, patio doors open onto attractive gardens.

10 shr (2 fmly) No smoking in dining room CTV in all bedrooms Tea and coffee making facilities No dogs Licensed Cen ht CTV No children 4yrs 9P No coaches Last d noon

Q Q Q **West Dene Private Hotel** 117 Alumhurst Rd, Alum Chine BH4 8HS (A338 from Ringwood, through Poole to Bournemouth) ☎ 01202 764843 FAX 01202 764843

Mar-Oct rs Nov-Feb (room only service)

Superb views of the sparkling sea can be enjoyed from this friendly hotel, just a short walk from Alum Chine and the golden sands. Public areas include a spacious dining room, comfortable lounge and cosy bar. Bedrooms are light and airy with seaward facing rooms being in great demand.

17 rms (5 bth 7 shr) (4 fmly) No smoking in bedrooms No smoking in dining room CTV in 15 bedrooms Tea and coffee making facilities No dogs Licensed Cen ht CTV No children 4yrs 17P Last d 5pm

ROOMS: s £25.50-£32.50; d £51-£57; wkly b&b £157.50-£164.50; wkly hlf-bd £210-£259*

CARDS: MasterCard, American Express, Barclaycard Visa, Diners Club

Q Q **Woodford Court Hotel** 19-21 Studland Rd, Alum Chine BH4 8HZ (1m from A35, turn-off at Liverpool-Victoria roundabout in Westbourne. Follow signs for Alum Chine) ☎ 01202 764907 FAX 01202 761214

Located in a quiet residential area close to the wooded chines and sandy beaches, this hotel is personally run by the Peters family. A huge collection of hippos in all shapes and sizes adorns the public areas which include a bar and restaurant. Twice weekly entertainment is provided during the season. The accommodation is comfortable and benefits from a range of thoughtful extras.

35 bth/shr (11 fmly) No smoking in dining room No smoking in 1 lounge CTV in all bedrooms Tea and coffee making facilities Direct dial from bedrooms Licensed Cen ht CTV No children 2yrs 18P No coaches Golf holidays arranged Last d 6.15pm

ROOMS: (incl. dinner) s £24.50-£33; d £49-£66; wkly b&b £129-£185; wkly hlf-bd £171-£231

CARDS: MasterCard, American Express, Barclaycard Visa, Diners Club, Barclays Connect, Delta, Switch

Selected

Q Q Q Q **Wood Lodge Hotel** 10 Manor Rd, East Cliff BH1 3EY (leave A338 at St Pauls roundabout by Bournemouth Railway station, follow signs to East Cliff) ☎ 01202 290891 FAX 290892

Mar-Nov

Wood Lodge is located in one of the most pleasant tree-lined areas of the town. The well appointed bedrooms offer comfort and good modern facilities. Diners can look out onto award winning gardens whilst enjoying a relaxing meal. Honest English cooking is offered with a good choice of menus. Other public areas include a choice of lounges and a small cosy bar. Paul and Catherine Adcock are charming hosts and a warm welcome is assured.

15 rms (14 bth/shr) (4 fmly) No smoking in dining room CTV in all bedrooms Tea and coffee making facilities Licensed Cen ht CTV 12P 9 hole putting green 2 bowls rinks Last d 7.30pm

ROOMS: s £23.50-£31; d £47-£62*

CARDS: MasterCard, Barclaycard Visa

BOURTON Dorset Map **03** ST73

Selected

Q Q Q Q 🍺 ***White Lion Inn & Bush Restaurant*** High St SP8 5AT (off A303, opposite B3092 to Gillingham) ☎ 01747 840866 FAX 01747 840799

Set in the heart of the West Country, this traditional village inn dates back to 1723 and is located within a five minute drive of Stourhead House. The bar retains its original character and charm, with flagstone floors and a log fire; a range of bar meals is available. In the spacious beamed restaurant an a la carte menu together with special dishes advertised on blackboards are offered. The two cosy bedrooms are attractively furnished and decorated.

2 annexe bth/shr No smoking in bedrooms No smoking in area of dining room No smoking in lounges CTV in all bedrooms Tea and coffee making facilities No dogs (ex guide dogs) Cen ht 36P Last d 9.30pm

CARDS: MasterCard, Barclaycard Visa

BOURTON-ON-THE-WATER Gloucestershire Map **04** SP12

Selected

QQQQ **Coombe House** Rissington Rd GL54 2DT (exit A429, through village, Hotel past model village on left; or exit A424 at Burford on Stow, continue into Bourton on the Water, 0.5m on right)
☎ 01451 821966 FAX 01451 810477
Closed 24, 25 & 31 Dec
Situated on the outskirts of this pretty village, Coombe House is a large detached building of mellow stone set in beautifully tended gardens. Bedrooms are comfortable and well equipped with lots of homely touches to enhance guest comfort. Public areas include a dining room and a comfortable lounge.
7 bth/shr (2 fmly) No smoking CTV in all bedrooms Tea and coffee making facilities No dogs Licensed Cen ht 10P No coaches
ROOMS: s £48; d £65-£75; wkly b&b £205-£230
CARDS:

Selected

QQQQ **The Cotswold House** Lansdowne GL54 2AR (turn off A429 into Landsdown and continue for 0.5m to Cotswold House on right opposite UK Garage) ☎ 01451 822373
Situated on the edge of this pretty Cotswold village, the house, build of mellow sand stone, offers comfortable accommodation close to the local attractions. Bedrooms are well equipped and extras include modern en-suite or private facilities. A garden bungalow, converted from the original village telephone exchange, is an ideal family complex where a sitting room is available in addition to the spacious bedroom. The comfortable sitting area, overlooking the pretty garden, with its open fire adjoins the dining room, where tasty English breakfasts are served. John and Jean Meadows are friendly and attentive hosts.
3 bth/shr 1 annexe bth/shr (1 fmly) No smoking in dining room No smoking in 1 lounge CTV in all bedrooms Tea and coffee making facilities No dogs Cen ht 5P No coaches
ROOMS: s £25-£40; d £40-£50; wkly b&b £140-£175✻

Selected

QQQQ *Kingsbridge* Riverside GL54 2BP (Turn off A436 towards Bourton-on-the-Water, inn in centre of village opposite Lloyds Bank)
☎ 01451 820371 FAX 01451 810179
Beside the river in the centre of this much visited Cotswold village, the Kingsbridge Inn offers a friendly atmosphere, appealing to locals and visitors alike. The front facing bedrooms are attractively furnished and decorated, each being well equipped. An extensive range of traditional bar meals are on offer at the popular bar. During the summer months drinks and meals can be enjoyed in the garden, younger visitors making full use of the children's play area.

3 shr No smoking in bedrooms No smoking in area of dining room CTV in all bedrooms Tea and coffee making facilities No dogs (ex guide dogs) Cen ht 5P Last d 10pm
CARDS:

Selected

QQQQ *Lansdowne Villa* Lansdowne GL54 2AT (in village centre, 400yds from church) ☎ 01451 820673 FAX 01451 822099
Closed 2 Dec-Jan
Situated at the edge of a famous Cotswold village, close to the church, Lansdowne Villa is an impressive modern house offering comfortable, well equipped accommodation for both the business and leisure traveller. Bedrooms are modern and have many extras including modern en suite facilities. Public areas include a bright attractive dining room and a comfortable guest lounge. Marie-Anne and Tony Baker are friendly, attentive hosts and ensure that a visit here is enjoyable.
12 bth/shr (1 fmly) No smoking in bedrooms No smoking in dining room CTV in all bedrooms Tea and coffee making facilities Licensed Cen ht CTV 14P Last d 5.30pm
CARDS:

Selected

QQQQ **Lawns** Station Rd GL54 2ER (turn off A429 into Bourton-on-Water, first house on right hand side) ☎ 01451 821195 FAX 821195
Closed 25 & 26 Dec
The Lawns is a Cotswold stone house with some fine rural views. Bedrooms are spacious and well equipped and all have modern en suite facilities. Breakfast is taken in the dining room, overlooking the garden, and there is also a cosy lounge for guest use. The Davanzo family are friendly and attentive hosts.

2 bth/shr 3 annexe bth/shr (1 fmly) No smoking in bedrooms No smoking in dining room CTV in all bedrooms Tea and coffee making facilities No dogs (ex guide dogs) Cen ht CTV 6P
ROOMS: d £45-£55*

QQQ ***Polly Perkins*** 1 The Chestnuts, High St GL54 2AN (off A429, enter village and turn right into Moore Rd, continue to T-junction with High St. Turn left, house on right opposite bridge over river) ☎ 01451 820244 FAX 01451 820558
This personally run establishment, which dates back 300 years, combines guest house accommodation with a restaurant and tea-rooms. The owners have made many recent improvements; bedrooms, which include a family room, have modern equipment and facilities. A quiet lounge is available to guests.
8 bth/shr (1 fmly) CTV in all bedrooms Tea and coffee making facilities Licensed Cen ht 15P
CARDS:

Selected

QQQQ **The Ridge** Whiteshoots Hill GL54 2LE (0.5m S on A429) ☎ 01451 820660 FAX 01451 822448
This large house, which is set in extensive and delightful gardens, is situated just south of Bourton-on-the-Water. The bedrooms, which are all located in an adjoining house, have modern equipment and facilities. Rooms on ground floor level and a family room are available. Separate tables are provided in the traditionally furnished breakfast room, which has an adjacent small lounge area.
1 bth 4 annexe bth/shr (1 fmly) No smoking CTV in all bedrooms Tea and coffee making facilities No dogs Cen ht CTV No children 6yrs 12P No coaches

BOVEY TRACEY Devon Map 03 SX87

QQ **Blenheim Hotel** Brimley Rd TQ13 9DH (A382 to Bovey Tracy, after 1m take first left on roundabout to Brimley. Follow road to end and turn left at T-junct. Hotel 100yds on right) ☎ 01626 832422
rs 25 & 26 Dec
Set in its own secluded gardens, this large and attractive Victorian house backs onto open moorland. Bedrooms are spacious and there are comfortable lounges and a dining area with separate tables for guests.
4 rms (1 shr) (1 fmly) No smoking in dining room No smoking in 1 lounge CTV in all bedrooms Tea and coffee making facilities Cen ht CTV 8P No coaches
ROOMS: s £28-£30; d £56-£60

Premier Selected

QQQQQ **Front House Lodge** East St TQ13 9EL (turn off A38 onto A382 into Bovey Tracey, go through town centre, Front House Lodge is situated past the Town Hall on the right hand side) ☎ 01626 832202 FAX 832202
Ideally situated in the centre of old Bovey Tracey, is this charming 16th-century property. Friendly hosts Gail and Ian Campbell offer guests refreshments in the comfortable lounge on arrival, and aim to create an enjoyable and relaxing atmosphere. The pretty bedrooms are individually decorated in floral themes, and each is provided with a tea tray. Personal touches abound in the form of dried flower decorations, scatter cushions on the beds and chairs, and a wide range of toiletries in the bathrooms. Home cooked dinners are available by prior arrangement.
6 rms (3 bth 2 shr) (2 fmly) No smoking CTV in all bedrooms Tea and coffee making facilities No dogs Licensed Cen ht CTV 6P Last d 10am
ROOMS: s £25-£30; d £45-£48*
CARDS:

BOWNESS-ON-WINDERMERE Cumbria

See **Windermere**

BOX Wiltshire Map **03** ST86

Q Q Q **Cheney Cottage** Ditteridge SN13 8QF (take A4 Bath-Chippenham road and just before Box turn left signposted Ditteridge. Continue to T-junct and turn left, house 0.5m on left) ☎ 01225 742346 FAX 742346
Closed 21 Dec-5 Jan
Warm hospitality awaits guests at this charming thatched house, set in the Wiltshire countryside in extensive well tended gardens with beautiful views of the Box Valley. The rooms are all attractively decorated and equipped with such thoughtful extras as shoe cleaning kits, biscuits and fresh flowers. In the old stable block, there are three well furnished en suite rooms, one of which is particularly spacious.
3 rms (2 shr) 3 annexe bth/shr (1 fmly) No smoking CTV in 3 bedrooms Tea and coffee making facilities No dogs (ex guide dogs) Cen ht CTV 8P No coaches Tennis (hard)
ROOMS: s £25; d £42-£48; wkly b&b £168

See advertisement under BATH

Selected

Q Q Q Q **Hermitage** Bath Rd SN13 8DT (5m from Bath on A4 towards Chippenham, Hermitage is first drive on left after 30mph signs) ☎ 01225 744187 FAX 01225 743447
Closed 22 Dec-6 Jan
This fine old stone house is only six miles from Bath and is set in gardens which feature an outdoor heated swimming pool. Two bedrooms are in small cottages in the garden, and three more are in the main house. Hearty breakfasts are served in the spacious breakfast room.
3 shr 2 annexe shr (2 fmly) No smoking in 3 bedrooms No smoking in dining room No smoking in lounges CTV in all bedrooms Tea and coffee making facilities No dogs (ex guide dogs) Cen ht 6P No coaches Outdoor swimming pool (heated)
ROOMS: s £30-£40; d £42-£50✳ **See advertisement under BATH**

Selected

Q Q Q Q **Owl House** Lower Kingsdown Rd, Kingsdown SN13 8BB ☎ 01225 743883 FAX 01225 744450
Only five miles from the city centre with views over the valleys to Bath, the Owl House has an idyllic location for those wanting peace and quiet. Rooms, all with en suite facilities, are comfortable and well furnished. In summer breakfast is served on the patio.
3 bth/shr (1 fmly) No smoking CTV in all bedrooms Tea and coffee making facilities No dogs (ex guide dogs) Cen ht CTV 4P No coaches
ROOMS: s £25-£35; d £45-£55✳
CARDS:

BOXFORD Suffolk Map **05** TL94

Q Q Q **Cox Hill House** CO10 5JG (off A134 onto A1071, take second sign left to Boxford, next right to Kersey. House 0.5m at top of Cox Hill.) ☎ 01787 210449
Closed 24-26 Dec
Cox Hill House sits amid delightful grounds and gardens in a peaceful and rural location overlooking the old wool village of Boxford. Accomodation is attractively decorated and comfortably furnished and the bedrooms are well equipped. Breakfast is served around one table and guests are welcome to enjoy the lovely garden.
3 bth/shr No smoking CTV in all bedrooms Tea and coffee making facilities No dogs (ex guide dogs) No children 12yrs 20P No coaches Golf arrangement with two courses
ROOMS: s £30-£35; d £38-£45✳

BRADFIELD Essex Map **05** TM13

Q Q Q ***Emsworth House*** Ship Hill CO11 2UP (off A120/B1352 from Colchester or Harwich, A137/B1352 coming from Ipswich) ☎ 01255 870860 & 0467 477771 (mobile)
This charming house enjoys stunning views of the River Stour and surrounding countryside. The bedrooms, which all have river views, are traditionally furnished and have some lovely extra touches. Proprietor Penny Linton also runs art courses by arrangement.
3 rms (1 bth) No smoking in 1 bedrooms No smoking in area of dining room No smoking in 1 lounge CTV in all bedrooms Tea and coffee making facilities Cen ht CTV 11P No coaches Croquet Badminton
Last d 11pm

BRADFORD West Yorkshire Map **07** SE13

See also **Thornton**

Q Q Q **Ann's Manor House** Wellfield House, 852 Thronton Rd, Thornton BD13 3QB (M606 Bradford-follow Ring Road, left at lights(B6145) through Thornton village, past church and estab. is on the right 50yds after Landrover garage) ☎ 01274 830925

Situated just to the east of Bradford, as the land rises to the Pennines, this stone built detached house offers three comfortable bedrooms, all recently refurbished. Breakfast is served around one table by the friendly owners.
3 shr (1 fmly) No smoking CTV in all bedrooms Tea and coffee making facilities Cen ht
ROOMS: s fr £20; d fr £40

BRADFORD ON AVON Wiltshire Map **03** ST86

Premier Selected

QQQQQ **Bradford Old Windmill** 4 Masons Ln BA15 1QN (enter Bradford on A363, at mini roundabout at Castle Pub turn to town centre, 50 yards on left look for first roadside house, driveway before house) ☎ 01225 866842 FAX 01225 866648
Mar-Oct
Guests will be enchanted by this unusual property, which has been sympathetically restored yet still retains many of its original features. The circular lounge is the perfect place to unwind after a day exploring this beautiful area. Each of the three bedrooms is individually decorated and guests may choose from a round room, complete with water bed, or a suite with its own minstrels' gallery. The owners are renowned for their vegetarian feasts, served on three evenings a week at one large refectory table, there is an extensive breakfast menu, which includes a variety of vegetarian delights as well as a conventional English choice.
3 bth/shr No smoking CTV in all bedrooms Tea and coffee making facilities No dogs Cen ht No children 6yrs 3P No coaches
Last d previous day
ROOMS: s £65-£89; d £75-£99
CARDS:

Premier Selected

QQQQQ **Burghope Manor** Winsley BA15 2LA (from A36 Bath-Warminster rd take B3108 Winsley rd, on entering Winsley take 1st right off by-pass, first left at cross-roads, gates at top of lane)
☎ 01225 723557 FAX 01225 723113
Closed Xmas/New Year
Burghope Manor is a beautiful 13th-century Manor House. Whilst the public rooms reflect the grandeur and elegance of days gone by, they also have a very pleasing and homely feel; further enhanced by the display of many family treasures. Bedrooms, some of which are located in the Dower House across the garden, have been equipped with modern facilities. Rooms in the main house tend to be more spacious.
3 bth/shr 3 annexe bth/shr (1 fmly) No smoking in bedrooms No smoking in dining room No smoking in lounges CTV in 4 bedrooms Tea and coffee making facilities No dogs Cen ht CTV No children 10yrs 20P Shooting and fishing by arrangement
ROOMS: s £60-£70; d £70-£80*
CARDS:

Premier Selected

QQQQQ **Fern Cottage** Monkton Farleigh BA15 2QJ (Turn off A363 at sign for Monkton Farleigh. After 1m turn right at T-junct by Manor House gates, first cottage on left)
☎ 01225 859412 FAX 01225 859018
This 17th-century stone cottage lies in a pretty conservation village on the edge of Bradford-on-Avon. There are three delightful bedrooms, one of which is in the adjacent Coach House, and available for self-catering holidays. All rooms are beautifully decorated, furnished with quality pieces and well equipped. Home cooked breakfasts are served at one large table in the dining room.
2 bth/shr 1 annexe bth/shr No smoking CTV in all bedrooms Tea and coffee making facilities No dogs (ex guide dogs) Cen ht 5P No coaches
ROOMS: s £30-£36; d £50-£58*

Premier Selected

QQQQQ **Hillcrest** 6 Bradford Rd, Winsley BA15 2HN (from Bath-A36 Warminster for 4m, left at lights onto B3108, continue up hill, ignoring Winsley sign, at t-junct turn right, estab on left at bend)
☎ 01225 868677 FAX 01225 868655
Closed Xmas & New Year
Guests can be sure of a lovely stay at this splendid property, designed and built to owner Elizabeth Litherland's specifications. The beautifully

contd.

landscaped gardens overlook open countryside. Bedrooms offer high quality accommodation, stylishly decorated with dark wood furniture and classic fabrics. The lounge is spacious and the dining room is the attractive setting for meals, which are served around one large table.
2 shr No smoking CTV in all bedrooms Tea and coffee making facilities No dogs Cen ht No children 7yrs 5P No coaches South-facing terrace for sun bathing Last d Day before
ROOMS: s £45; d £45-£50*

Selected

Q Q Q Q **Home Farm** Farleigh Rd, Wingfield BA14 9LG (exit A36 onto A366 to Fairleigh Hungerford, pass castle into Wingfield, gate to premises after three cottages)
☎ 01225 764492 FAX 01225 764492
Closed Xmas & New Year
Conveniently located within a few miles of the city of Bath, Home Farm stands in two acres of immaculately kept gardens and overlooks farmland. A friendly and relaxed atmosphere prevails. The well equipped bedrooms are comfortable and traditionally decorated with tastefully co-ordinating fabrics. Breakfast is served around one large table in the elegant dining room.
3 shr (1 fmly) No smoking CTV in all bedrooms Tea and coffee making facilities No dogs (ex guide dogs) Cen ht CTV 12P No coaches
ROOMS: d £50; wkly b&b £150*
CARDS:

Premier Selected

Q Q Q Q Q **Irondale** 67 High St BA3 6PB ☎ 01373 830730 FAX 01373 830730

(For full entry see **Rode**)

Q Q Q **Midway Cottage** Farleigh Wick BA15 2PU (situated on A363 midway between Bathford and Bradford on Avon next to Fox & Hounds public house) ☎ 01225 863932
This delightful Victorian country cottage lies midway between Bath and Bradford upon Avon. It is well maintained and has pretty rear gardens. Smart, modern and well equipped bedrooms are provided and there is an attractive breakfast room.
3 shr No smoking in bedrooms No smoking in dining room CTV in all bedrooms Tea and coffee making facilities Direct dial from bedrooms 3P No coaches Golf 18
ROOMS: d £38-£40

Q Q Q **Serendipity** 19f Bradford Rd, Winsley BA15 2HW (turn off A36 Bath/Warminster road onto B3108turn right after 1.5m into village of Winsleyand establishment on right on main road) ☎ 01225 722380
rs Xmas
The Shepherd family offers a warm welcome and guests are made to feel very much at home. Just two bedrooms are provided and these are both are equipped with modern facilities. There is a delightful rear garden and beyond this lies a protected wild flower meadow.
3 shr (1 fmly) No smoking CTV in all bedrooms Tea and coffee making facilities No dogs (ex guide dogs) Cen ht 5P No coaches beautiful gdns, walks, croquet

Premier Selected

Q Q Q Q Q ***Widbrook Grange*** Trowbridge Rd, Widbrook BA15 1UH (1m from town centre beyond the canal bridge on A363)
☎ 01225 863173 & 864750 FAX 01225 862890
Lovely Wiltshire countryside surrounds this beautiful former farmhouse which has been tastefully renovated by owners Pauline and John Price. Spacious bedrooms, some with four-poster or half-tester beds, offer genuine quality both within the main house and adjacent courtyard buildings. Guests can enjoy an aperitif in one of two elegant drawing rooms prior to dinner in the gracious dining room.
4 rms (3 bth/shr) 15 annexe bth (2 fmly) No smoking in 3 bedrooms No smoking in dining room No smoking in 1 lounge CTV in all bedrooms Tea and coffee making facilities Direct dial from bedrooms No dogs Licensed Cen ht 50P Indoor swimming pool (heated) Gymnasium Last d 6.30pm
CARDS:

BRAINTREE Essex Map 05 TL72

Q Q Q **Park Farmhouse** *(TL812223)* Church Rd, Bradwell CM7 8EP (turn off A120 beside The Swan PH signposted Bradwell Village continue for half a mile farmhouse stands back from the road on right)
☎ 01376 563584 Mrs J Reddington
Closed Xmas
A friendly welcome awaits guests at this delightful 17th-century farmhouse. In the dining room, which overlooks the pretty garden, a hearty breakfast is served, including home made bread and marmalade. One bedroom has a four-poster and visitors may use the cosy lounge.
2 rms No smoking Tea and coffee making facilities No dogs (ex guide dogs) Cen ht CTV No children 12yrs 3P 1 acres arable
ROOMS: s £17.50-£21; d £34-£36*

Q Q Q ***Spicers** (TL730293)* Rotten End, Wethersfield CM7 4AL (take B1053 from Braintree to Shalford, at Shalford turn right signed Rotten End, farm is second house on right over the river)
☎ 01371 851021 Mrs D A Douse
Spicers Farm looks out over tranquil countryside. There is a cheerfully decorated conservatory breakfast room and a comfortable guest sitting room

full of local information. En suite bedrooms have lovely views and are all comfortably appointed and thoughtfully equipped.
3 bth/shr No smoking in bedrooms No smoking in dining room CTV in all bedrooms Tea and coffee making facilities No dogs (ex guide dogs) Cen ht 5P 72 acres arable

BRAITHWAITE Cumbria Map **11** NY22

Q Q Q **Maple Bank** CA12 5RY (off A66, take Thornwaite turning just after Braithwaite (approx 30mtrs) ☎ 01768 778229 FAX 017687 78229
This Edwardian residence stands in its own well tended garden and enjoys views across the Derwent valley towards Skiddaw. Bedrooms are comfortably furnished. There is a pleasant lounge, and enjoyable home cooking is served at individual tables in the dining room.
7 shr (1 fmly) No smoking in 3 bedrooms No smoking in dining room CTV in all bedrooms Tea and coffee making facilities No dogs Licensed Cen ht CTV No children 12yrs 10P No coaches Free access to lawn tennis/bowling club Last d 4pm
ROOMS: d £48-£52; wkly b&b fr £168; wkly hlf-bd fr £238
CARDS:

BRAMPTON Cumbria Map **12** NY56

See also Castle Carrock

Q Q Q **The Blacksmiths Arms** Talkin Village CA8 1LE (A69 to Brampton, take B6413 to Castle Carrock, after railway level crossing take second left signposted Talkin) ☎ 016977 3452 FAX 016977 3396
This inn offers comfortable bedrooms which have been thoughtfully equipped and furnished. Evening meals can be taken in either the bar-lounge or wood panelled restaurant and range from bar meals to a la carte dishes. A substantial freshly prepared breakfast is also on offer.
5 bth/shr (2 fmly) CTV in all bedrooms Tea and coffee making facilities No dogs (ex guide dogs) Cen ht 20P Last d 9pm
ROOMS: s £30; d £45*
MEALS: Lunch £5.25-£16.55alc Dinner £5.25-£16.55alc*
CARDS:

Premier Selected

Q Q Q Q Q **Cracrop** *(NY521697)* Kirkcambeck CA8 2BW (off B6318, 7m N of town) ☎ 016977 48245 FAX 016977 48333
Mrs M Stobart
Jan-Nov
Dating from 1847, this charming period farmhouse sits in landscaped gardens amidst attractive open countryside. Bedrooms - two large doubles and a twin, plus a cosy single - are most inviting and Marjorie Stobart has equipped them with a host of thoughtful extras. Downstairs there is a traditionally furnished, comfortable lounge and the dining room is tastefully decorated. It is here that Marjorie provides a substantial breakfast, taken around a communal table. Guests can relax by the pond in the neatly tended garden, or take the farm's sign-posted country trail and other local walks. Additionally, there is a well equipped fitness room, sauna and spa bath for those seeking to keep fit.
4 shr No smoking CTV in all bedrooms Tea and coffee making facilities No dogs (ex guide dogs) Cen ht CTV No children 10yrs 5P Fishing Sauna Gymnasium Marked farm trail 485 acres arable beef sheep Last d 1pm
ROOMS: s £25-£30; d £50-£50*
CARDS:

Q Q Q **Denton House** Low Row CA8 2LQ (4m E on A69) ☎ 016977 46278 FAX 016977 46278
Denton house is a fine Victorian property which offers views toward Hadrian's Wall from it's position on the main road east of Brampton. Period

features have been retained in this attractively decorated home and the two spacious bedrooms are tastefully furnished. A friendly and warm atmosphere prevails and host, Hazel Hamilton, also provides a substantial breakfast, offered at a communal table in the lounge.
2 rms No smoking in bedrooms No smoking in dining room Tea and coffee making facilities Cen ht CTV 4P
ROOMS: d £32*

Q Q *Weary Sportsman* Castle Carrock CA4 9LU (on B6413) ☎ 01228 70230
This traditional country inn with oak beams and fireplace lies in the heart of the village. Many bedrooms overlook the pretty garden. A cosy residents' lounge is located away from the public rooms. The spacious lounge bar offers a wide ranging menu.
3 rms (2 fmly) No dogs (ex guide dogs) Cen ht CTV No children 8yrs 18P Last d 8.45pm

BRANDON Suffolk Map **05** TL78

Q Q **Riverside Lodge** 78 High St IP27 0AU (from A11 at Barton Mills roundabout junction, take B1065 to Brandon. Establishment situated by river bridge in High St, parking at rear) ☎ 01842 811236
This 16th-century Grade II listed merchant's house offers two comfortable bedrooms with modern facilities. There is a relaxing lounge on the first floor, and the amenities in the grounds include a grass tennis court. Breakfast is served a short walk away at the owners' hotel.
3 bth/shr (1 fmly) No smoking in bedrooms No smoking in dining room No smoking in 1 lounge CTV in all bedrooms Tea and coffee making facilities No dogs (ex guide dogs) Cen ht CTV 12P Tennis (grass) Fishing
ROOMS: s fr £25; d fr £40*
CARDS:

BRANSFORD Worcestershire Map **03** SO75

Q Q *Croft* WR6 5JD (on A4103, 4m from Worcester) ☎ 01886 832227
Parts of this detached property date back to the 16th and 18th centuries. The accommodation includes a family bedded room. A cosy lounge and a traditionally furnished dining room are on offer to guests here.
5 rms (3 shr) (1 fmly) No smoking in bedrooms Tea and coffee making facilities Licensed Cen ht CTV 5P No coaches Sauna Jacuzzi Arrangement with golf course Last d 5.30pm
CARDS:

BRANSGORE Hampshire Map **04** SZ19

Selected

Q Q Q Q ***Tothill House*** Black Ln, off Forest Rd BH23 8DZ (from A35, turn right into Forest Road, left into Black Lane and house is third gate on the right) ☎ 01425 674414 FAX 01425 672235
Set in peaceful woodlands in the heart of the New Forest, this charming Victorian cottage offers comfortable accommodation of a very high standard. The attractively decorated bedrooms are spacious and individually furnished to reflect the character of the house. Guests have use of the small library lounge with its selection of books and magazines. A generous English breakfast is served in the well appointed dining room.
3 rms (2 shr) No smoking CTV in all bedrooms Tea and coffee making facilities No dogs (ex guide dogs) Cen ht CTV No children 16yrs 10P No coaches

Selected

Q Q Q Q **Wiltshire House** West Rd BH23 8BD (off A31 towards Burley, right fork towards Christchurch, at Bransgore turn right at Carpenters Arms, down hill) ☎ 01425 672450 FAX 01425 672450
Wiltshire House is set in a large secluded garden. Owners Pam & Gerald Hooper offer a warm and friendly welcome to their guests. The house has been tastefully furnished and decorated to reflect the style of the building. Bedrooms are bright, comfortable and with many extra touches. The sitting/dining room has a relaxing, homely atmosphere. To start the day, a generous breakfast is offered.
3 rms (2 bth/shr) (2 fmly) No smoking CTV in 2 bedrooms Tea and coffee making facilities No dogs (ex guide dogs) Cen ht CTV 4P No coaches
ROOMS: s £20-£26; d £36-£44; wkly b&b £125-£150*

BRATTON FLEMING Devon Map **03** SS63

Selected

Q Q Q Q **Bracken House** EX31 4TG (off A399, signposted Bratton Fleming, left hand side, just after Post Office) ☎ 01598 710320
late Mar-early Nov
Bracken House stands in eight acres of gardens and woodland with a lake. Converted to a small hotel from a rectory, it offers a drawing room with well stocked bar, and a library with a wide range of books. Each evening an interesting choice is offered at dinner, including a vegetarian option, complemented by a good selection of wines. Bedrooms are light and airy, varying in size, but all are well equipped.
8 bth/shr No smoking in dining room No smoking in 1 lounge CTV in all bedrooms Tea and coffee making facilities Licensed Cen ht No children 12yrs 12P No coaches Last d 6pm
ROOMS: d £56-£76; wkly b&b £175-£231; wkly hlf-bd £287-£343
CARDS:

BREDWARDINE Herefordshire Map **03** SO34

Selected

Q Q Q Q **Bredwardine Hall** HR3 6DB (from Hereford take A438 for 10m and turn left signposted Hay-on-Wye B4352, cont over bridge into village centre) ☎ 01981 500596
Closed 15 Dec-10 Jan
This stone built, mid-Victorian manor house is set in extensive and mature gardens, to the east of Hay-On-Wye. It provides well equipped accommodation, which includes family rooms. There is a comfortably furnished lounge and separate tables are provided in the dining room, which also contains an honesty bar.
5 rms (3 bth 1 shr) No smoking in bedrooms No smoking in dining room CTV in all bedrooms Tea and coffee making facilities No dogs (ex guide dogs) Licensed Cen ht No children 10yrs 7P No coaches Last d 6pm
ROOMS: s £27-£31; d £44-£52; wkly b&b £140-£175; wkly hlf-bd £245-£280*

BRIDESTOWE Devon Map **02** SX58

Q Q Q **Week** *(SX519913)* EX20 4HZ (exit A30 at Sourton junc, turn right, turn left signposted Bridestowe, second right, cross duel carriageway, left at crossroads, house 0.5m on right) ☎ 01837 861221 FAX 861221
Mrs Margaret Hockridge
Closed Xmas
Margaret Hockridge provides a traditional farmhouse atmosphere and real home cooking combined with modern facilities and comforts. Bedrooms vary in size and style and one room is located on the ground floor. Dinner is served by arrangement and a comfortable lounge is available for guests. Self catering cottages are also available, recently converted from former farm buildings.
5 bth/shr (2 fmly) No smoking CTV in all bedrooms Tea and coffee making facilities Cen ht CTV 10P Outdoor swimming pool (heated) Golf 18 180 acres dairy mixed sheep Last d 5pm
ROOMS: s £23-£24; d £46-£48; wkly b&b £160-£168; wkly hlf-bd £231-£248*
CARDS:

BRIDGNORTH Shropshire Map **07** SO79

Q Q Q **Bearwood Lodge Hotel** 10 Kidderminster Rd WV15 6BW (on A442, 50yds S of Bridgnorth bypass island) ☎ 01746 762159
This is a small guest house owned and run by the friendly Lloyd family; it offers bright, well equipped bedrooms. An attractive breakfast room is provided as well as a cosy lounge and, for the summer months, there is also a large conservatory overlooking the rear gardens.
7 rms (6 shr) (2 fmly) No smoking CTV in all bedrooms Tea and coffee making facilities Licensed Cen ht No children 5yrs 9P No coaches
ROOMS: s £25-£39; d £36-£40*

Q Q Q **Bulls Head** Chelmarsh WV16 6BA (S on B4555, 200 yds pass Chelmarsh church on right hand side) ☎ 01746 861469 FAX 862646
rs 25 Dec
This well established inn enjoys fine views across the Severn valley and Chelmarsh reservoir. The comfortable modern accommodation includes two new bedrooms in converted outbuildings. Self-catering cottages are also available. A wide range of meals and snacks is served, either in one of the bars or in the dining room.
9 bth/shr 1 annexe bth/shr (2 fmly) No smoking in area of dining room CTV in all bedrooms Tea and coffee making facilities Cen ht 50P Jacuzzi Last d 9.30pm
ROOMS: s £25-£28; d £36-£43; wkly b&b £126-£150; wkly hlf-bd £196-£220*
MEALS: Lunch £10.60-£18&alc Dinner £10.60-£18&alc*
CARDS:

Q Q Q **Fodder House** Oldfield WV16 6AQ (take B4364 Ludlow/Bridgnorth road, 3m from Bridgnorth turn for Oldfield on the left, in 0.5m 3rd house on left) ☎ 01746 789509 FAX 01746 789509
Set amidst 30 acres of farmland, this barn conversion lies deep in the Shropshire countryside. Attractively furnished bedrooms include one with en suite facilities and another with a private bathroom. There is a spacious lounge, with some fine antique pieces, and breakfast is served around one table in the dining room.
2 rms (1 bth/shr) No smoking CTV in all bedrooms Tea and coffee making facilities No dogs (ex guide dogs) Cen ht CTV 2P
ROOMS: s £22-£24; d £40; wkly b&b £120-£140*

Q ***Kings Head Hotel*** Whitburn St WV16 4QN (off main street of High Town down narrow road) ☎ 01746 762141
This former coaching inn dates back to the 17th century. It provides traditionally furnished accommodation, including family bedded rooms, and is popular with fishermen. Public areas have much character and provide a choice of quaint bars.
5 rms (3 fmly) CTV in all bedrooms Tea and coffee making facilities No dogs (ex guide dogs) Cen ht 7P No coaches Snooker Last d 9pm

Q Q Q **Oldfield Cottage** Oldfield WV16 6AQ (B4364 from Bridgnorth, after 3 miles pass Down Inn, take second turn left signposted Oldfield, 0.25 mile on right) ☎ 01746 789257
Closed 24-25 Dec
Set well back from a country lane, this is a welcoming cottage. The beamed lounge has a large mellow brick fireplace and doubles as a breakfast room. Both bedrooms, with modern en suite shower rooms, are located in an adjacent converted stable block and enjoy views over open farmland.
2 annexe shr No smoking CTV in all bedrooms Tea and coffee making facilities Cen ht CTV 3P No coaches Last d 10am
ROOMS: d £40-£45

Q Q Q **Severn Arms Hotel** Underhill St, Low Town WV16 4BB (turn off A442, onto B4363 and establishment facing river bridge crossing) ☎ 01746 764616 FAX 01746 761750
Closed 1 Jan-28 Feb
This private hotel started life in 1690 as a pub. Bedrooms include some suitable for families and all are equipped with modern facilities. A comfortable lounge is provided for residents and good value evening meals are available.
10 rms (2 bth 4 shr) (5 fmly) CTV in 8 bedrooms Tea and coffee making facilities Direct dial from bedrooms Licensed Cen ht CTV Fishing Last d 4pm
ROOMS: s £26-£38; d £52; wkly b&b £172-£256; wkly hlf-bd £259-£343*
CARDS:

BRIDGWATER Somerset Map **03** ST33

Q Q Q **Admirals Rest** 5 Taunton Rd TA6 3LW (exit M5 junct24, turn right onto A38 towards Bridgwater. After 1.5m reach junct A38/A39, straight ahead, house immediately on right) ☎ 01278 458580 FAX 01278 458580
Centrally located, Admiral's Rest is personally supervised by Mrs Parker. Bedrooms are spacious and each is well equipped. One room on the second floor is especially suitable as a family room. Home cooked evening meals are available by prior arrangement.
4 shr (2 fmly) No smoking in dining room No smoking in lounges CTV in all bedrooms Tea and coffee making facilities No dogs Cen ht 5P No coaches Last d breakfast same day
ROOMS: s £16-£20; d £32-£36; wkly b&b fr £100*

Q Q Q **Chinar** 17 Oakfield Rd TA6 7LX (exit M5 junc 23, follow signs for Minehead, left at lights past Safeways onto West Street, past Haygrove School, Oakfields Rd next on right) ☎ 01278 458639
Located in a quiet residential area on the edge of Bridgwater, Chinar is ideal for visiting the many local attractions. The bedrooms are well equipped and both are en suite. There is a comfortable lounge for guests. A really good choice is available at breakfast, including muffins, waffles and scrambled eggs with smoked salmon, as well as traditional English Breakfasts.
2 shr No smoking in bedrooms CTV in all bedrooms Tea and coffee making facilities Cen ht CTV No children 6yrs 2P No coaches
ROOMS: s fr £23; d fr £45*

Q Q Q ***Moxhill Farmhouse (ST254417)*** Combwich TA5 2PN (follow A39 into Bridgwater/Minehead road into Cannington (three and a half miles). Take right turning onto Hinckley Point Rd, farmhouse on left) ☎ 01278 652285 FAX 01278 653942 Mrs C L Venner
This 17th-century farmhouse is part of a working dairy farm. The Venner family offer guests comfortable well equipped bedrooms with en suite facilities. There is a cosy lounge, and a well laid out dining room where freshly cooked and appetising dinners are available by prior arrangement.
3 bth/shr (2 fmly) No smoking CTV in all bedrooms Tea and coffee making facilities Licensed Cen ht ch fac 4P 135 acres dairy Last d 6pm

Q Q ***Rockfield House*** Puriton Hill, Puriton TA7 8AG (Just off M5 junct 23 on the A39 at top of hill on right) ☎ 01278 683561 FAX 01278 683561
Closed 25-31 Dec
A warm welcome awaits visitors to this large family house. The comfortable bedrooms are well equipped, and hearty breakfasts are served in the attractive dining room, where freshly cooked dinners are available by prior arrangement.
2 rms (1 shr) 1 annexe shr (1 fmly) No smoking CTV in all bedrooms Tea and coffee making facilities No dogs Cen ht CTV 5P No coaches Last d 4pm

Premier Selected

QQQQQ **Woodlands** 35 Durleigh Rd TA6 7HX (M5 junc 24 towards Bridgwater, left at lights by Safeway, left at next major lights into West St, 0.75m left into narrow drive before school sign)
☎ 01278 423442
This attractive, Victorian, Gothic style listed property, peacefully set in two acres of delightful gardens, is situated down a narrow drive within walking distance of the town centre. Resident proprietors Richard and Diane Palmer have lovingly restored Woodlands to its former elegance and charm. The bedrooms, whilst equipped with modern comforts and thoughtful touches like reading materials and fresh flowers, still retain original fireplaces and gothic window frames. The drawing and dining rooms both have access to the wonderful garden, a lovely place to sit and enjoy the summer sunshine. Dinner is available by arrangement and takes the form of a set three course meal. Diane Palmer is a Cordon Bleu cook and takes care to check the likes and dislikes of her guests before deciding on a menu each day. Most evenings badgers can be seen eating on the terrace, a sight which will remain long in the memory.
4 rms (3 bth/shr) No smoking in bedrooms No smoking in dining room CTV in all bedrooms Tea and coffee making facilities No dogs (ex guide dogs) Cen ht CTV 4P No coaches Last d 3pm
ROOMS: s £22-£32; d £44-£50*
CARDS:

BRIDLINGTON East Riding of Yorkshire Map **08** TA16

QQQ **Bay Court Hotel** 35a Sands Ln YO15 2JG
(head N through town centre Flanborough Rd, turn right onto Sands Ln (signed North Beach) hotel on left at the end of lane opposite sea front)
☎ 01262 676288
Delightfully located with excellent views, this small hotel caters for the discerning guest throughout the year. The bedrooms are individually decorated and there is a comfortable lounge with a log fire. A home cooked dinner is provided in the small candlelit dining room, which also doubles as a tea room during the day.
7 rms (3 bth/shr) No smoking in bedrooms No smoking in dining room CTV in all bedrooms Tea and coffee making facilities Licensed Cen ht CTV 5P No coaches Last d 6.45pm
ROOMS: s £19; d £39-£52; wkly b&b £114-£156;
wkly hlf-bd £170-£206*
CARDS:

QQQ **Bay Ridge Hotel** Summerfield Rd YO15 3LF (head towards Bridlington south side seafront, premises are down Summerfield Rd which is off South Marine Drive) ☎ 01262 673425
Standing in a quiet side road just off the seafront, this family owned and run hotel offers very good value for money. The modern bedrooms are bright and fresh and the public rooms are comfortable and inviting. Throughout, the service is friendly and attentive.
14 rms (6 bth 6 shr) (5 fmly) No smoking in dining room CTV in all bedrooms Tea and coffee making facilities Licensed Cen ht CTV 7P Bar billiards Darts Library Last d 5.45pm
ROOMS: s £20-£21.50; d £40-£43; wkly b&b £135-£140;
wkly hlf-bd £150-£160*
CARDS:

QQQ **Langdon Hotel** Pembroke Ter YO15 3BX (Near the harbour and shops overlooking the sea) ☎ 01262 400124 FAX 01262 400124
This family-owned hotel, situated close to the sea-front and the Spa Theatre, offers pleasantly furnished and comfortable bedrooms. All are tastefully decorated and offer thoughtful facilities. The reception rooms extend to a small garden porch, lounge and cosy bar. The dining room is bright and cheerful and it is here that home cooked meals are served.
20 rms (17 bth/shr) (8 fmly) No smoking in bedrooms No smoking in dining room CTV in all bedrooms Tea and coffee making facilities No dogs (ex guide dogs) Licensed Lift Cen ht 3P Last d noon

QQQ **Marton Grange** Flamborough Rd, Marton cum Sewerby YO15 1DU (on B1255, 600yds from Links golf club)
☎ 01262 602034 FAX 01262 602034
This detached Georgian house is surrounded by a three-acre garden. The public rooms include a comfortable lounge with a pleasant garden extension. Meals are home-cooked, and served in one of the two dining rooms. Bedrooms are well equipped, several are suitable for the less able.
10 bth/shr (1 fmly) No smoking in 1 bedrooms No smoking in dining room No smoking in lounges CTV in all bedrooms Tea and coffee making facilities Lift Cen ht No children 2yrs 12P No coaches Small pool table Books Games Last d 3pm
ROOMS: s £16-£18; d £30-£34*

QQQ ***Southdowne Hotel*** 78 South Marine Dr YO15 3NS
☎ 01262 673270
A well furnished and comfortable hotel standing on the seafront with fine coastal views. The bedrooms are bright and fresh and the lounge is very inviting.
12 rms (8 shr) (2 fmly) No smoking CTV in 8 bedrooms Tea and coffee making facilities No dogs Licensed Cen ht CTV 10P No coaches Last d 5.30pm

BRIDPORT Dorset Map **03** SY49

See also Bettiscombe & Chideock

Selected

QQQQ **Britmead House** West Bay Rd DT6 4EG
(approaching Bridport on A35 follow signs for West Bay,Britmead House is 800yds S of the A35) ☎ 01308 422941 FAX 422516
This small hotel is located between the pretty harbour of West Bay and the market town of Bridport, providing a good base for touring the local area. Bedrooms are well maintained and offer good facilities with thoughtful extra touches. The guest lounge and dining room overlook

the garden towards the Dorset Coastal Path and the emphasis is on traditional, home cooked produce.

7 bth/shr (1 fmly) No smoking in dining room CTV in all bedrooms Tea and coffee making facilities Licensed Cen ht No children 5yrs 8P Last d 5pm
ROOMS: s £26-£37; d £42-£60; wkly b&b £119-£154; wkly hlf-bd £217-£252*
CARDS:

BRIGG Lincolnshire Map **08** TA00

Q Q ***Hamsden Garth*** Cadney Rd, Howsham LN7 6LA (from Brigg take A1084 for 2m then B1434, at Howsham turn right into Cadney Rd, 400yds on right) ☎ 01652 678703 FAX 01652 678703
This modern, comfortably appointed family home sits in a quiet rural location on the edge of the village of Howsham, just 4 miles from Brigg and the M180 motorway. Friendly proprietors welcome guests to their home, offering contemporary bedrooms which share a modern general bathroom with separate shower and bath. Guests are welcome to use the lounge, whilst a hearty breakfast is taken around a large polished wooden table in a separate dining room, overlooking the rear garden; ample off road parking is provided and a courier service can be arranged, to and from, Humberside airport which is 8 miles away.
2 rms (2 fmly) No smoking CTV in all bedrooms Tea and coffee making facilities Cen ht CTV 10P No coaches

BRIGHTON & HOVE East Sussex Map **04** TQ30

See also Rottingdean

Selected

Q Q Q Q **Adelaide Hotel** 51 Regency Square BN1 2FF (on sea front square opposite West Pier) (The Circle)
☎ 01273 205286 FAX 01273 220904
This Regency house overlooks a garden square near the centre of the town. The en suite bedrooms vary in size and all are individually decorated in attractive colour schemes. A good range of extras is provided in the rooms. An elegant residents' lounge is provided, decorated in period style. In the bright and airy dining room a good choice is offered at breakfast. Room service is available during the day and evening.
12 bth/shr (1 fmly) No smoking in dining room CTV in all bedrooms Tea and coffee making facilities Direct dial from bedrooms No dogs Licensed Cen ht No coaches
ROOMS: s £41-£60; d £65-£82*
CARDS:

Selected

Q Q Q Q **Ainsley House Hotel** 28 New Steine BN2 1PD
☎ 01273 605310 FAX 01273 688604
Closed 24-27 Dec
Happy to help with advice on where to eat locally and places of interest in the area, the resident proprietors are keen to make guests feel relaxed and at home. All rooms have been comfortably furnished and have extras such as sweets and bottled water. A good choice of breakfast is offered and dinner is available by arrangement. Guests can take advantage of a comfy lounge.
11 rms (8 shr) (3 fmly) No smoking in 2 bedrooms No smoking in dining room CTV in all bedrooms Tea and coffee making facilities Direct dial from bedrooms No dogs (ex guide dogs) Cen ht CTV Last d 4pm
ROOMS: s £23-£30; d £42-£68*
CARDS:

Q Q Q **Allendale Hotel** 3 New Steine BN2 1PB ☎ 01273 675436 FAX 01273 602603
Closed 24-25 Dec
A period townhouse on one side of a sea-facing Regency Square, the Allendale is just a short walk from the town centre. Bedrooms vary in size but all are well equipped. The day rooms, comprising an open-plan lounge and dining room, have crystal chandeliers and velvet curtains.
12 rms (7 shr) (3 fmly) No smoking in 2 bedrooms No smoking in dining room CTV in all bedrooms Tea and coffee making facilities Direct dial from bedrooms No dogs (ex guide dogs) Licensed Cen ht No children 5yrs No coaches Last d 4pm
ROOMS: s £20-£35; d £44-£70; wkly b&b £160-£245; wkly hlf-bd £244-£329*
CARDS:

QQQ **Alvia Hotel** 36 Upper Rock Gardens BN2 1QF
(from Palace Pier rdbt turn left, approx 500yds on left is set traffic lights, turn left into Lower Rock Gdns cont along rd to Upper Rock Gdns)
☎ 01273 682939 FAX 01273 682939
Friendly owners David and Gina Scourfield keep everything in perfect order at their Victorian house, just a short walk from the seafront. Bedrooms are bright and well equipped and breakfasts, served in an attractive dining room, include cooked options for vegetarians.
10 rms (7 bth/shr) (2 fmly) No smoking in 8 bedrooms No smoking in dining room No smoking in lounges CTV in all bedrooms Tea and coffee making facilities No dogs (ex guide dogs) Cen ht 5P
ROOMS: s fr £18; d £40-£60; wkly b&b £108-£180*
CARDS:

QQQ **Ambassador Hotel** 22 New Steine, Marine Pde BN2 1PD
(from M23 to Brighton-at the rdbt opposite Palace Pier, turn left into Marine Parade. New Steine is located down this road on the left)
☎ 01273 676869 FAX 01273 689988
A friendly, relaxing atmosphere characterises this elegant Regency house, located on a seafront square close to the town centre. Attractively decorated and comfortably furnished rooms are mostly en suite. There is a small lounge and a spacious, bright dining room.
21 bth/shr (8 fmly) No smoking in 1 bedrooms No smoking in dining room CTV in all bedrooms Tea and coffee making facilities Direct dial from bedrooms No dogs Licensed Cen ht CTV
ROOMS: s £24-£36; d £42-£70; wkly b&b £140-£200*
CARDS:

Selected

QQQQ **Amblecliff Hotel** 35 Upper Rock Gardens BN2 1QF
(where A23 ends opposite the Palace Pier turn left along Marine Parade, left at second traffic lights into Lower Rock, cross traffic lights)
☎ 01273 681161 & 676945 FAX 01273 676945
Close to the seafront, this Victorian building is just a short walk from the town centre. Expect a warm and friendly welcome and very stylish bedrooms complete with particularly comfortable, high quality beds. Fresh flowers in the small lounge are a feature and the breakfast area is well appointed.
8 bth/shr (3 fmly) No smoking CTV in all bedrooms Tea and coffee making facilities Direct dial from bedrooms No dogs (ex guide dogs) Licensed Cen ht CTV No children 4yrs 3P
ROOMS: d £45-£68; wkly b&b £135-£204*
CARDS:

Selected

QQQQ **Arlanda Hotel** 20 New Steine BN2 1PD
(from Palace Pier travel 400 yards E along Marine Parade, New Steine is on the left)
☎ 01273 699300 FAX 01273 600930
This late Georgian town house lies near the seafront and just a short walk from the town centre. The hotel provides attractively decorated and well equipped accommodation. A good choice of dishes is offered in the pleasant dining room, and the comfortable lounge boasts a pair of fine period fireplaces and a cabinet full of the trophies won by the owners during their careers as international table tennis players. Light refreshments can be provided throughout the day.
12 bth/shr (4 fmly) No smoking in dining room CTV in all bedrooms Tea and coffee making facilities Direct dial from bedrooms No dogs (ex guide dogs) Licensed Cen ht Last d 4pm
ROOMS: s £25-£36; d £48-£80*
CARDS:

Selected

QQQQ **Ascott House Hotel** 21 New Steine, Marine Pde BN2 1PD (from Palace Pier go East along Marine Parade for 400yds and New Steine can be found on the left hand side)
☎ 01273 688085 FAX 01273 623733
Set just off the seafront, this well kept hotel is within easy walk of the town centre. Bedrooms are equipped with every modern facility including good work space for business guests. Breakfast and a good selection of home cooked dinners are served in a well appointed dining room. A comfortable lounge is also available for guests' use. Light refreshments are available throughout the day.
12 rms (10 shr) (8 fmly) No smoking in bedrooms No smoking in dining room No smoking in 1 lounge CTV in all bedrooms Tea and coffee making facilities Direct dial from bedrooms No dogs Licensed Cen ht No children 3yrs No coaches Last d 4.30pm
ROOMS: s £20-£36; d £40-£80
CARDS:

QQQ **Brighton Marina House Hotel** 8 Charlotte St, Marine Pde BN2 1AG ☎ 01273 605349 & 679484 FAX 01273 605349/679484
Situated just off the seafront, yet close to the town centre, this hotel offers a variety of well equipped bedrooms. There is a small downstairs dining room where guests breakfast and can also have a home-cooked dinner, perhaps sampling Mrs Jung's authentic Indian cuisine.
10 rms (7 shr) (3 fmly) CTV in all bedrooms Tea and coffee making facilities No dogs Licensed Cen ht No coaches Exercise Cycle Last d 4pm
ROOMS: s £15-£39; d £35-£69; wkly b&b £114-£234; wkly hlf-bd £195-£381*
CARDS:

Cavalaire House 34 Upper Rock Gardens BN2 1QF (follow A259 towards Newhaven, turn left at second set of traffic lights) ☎ 01273 696899 FAX 01273 600504

This Victorian town house is just a short walk from the Royal Pavilion and the centre of town. Bedrooms vary in size but all are comfortably appointed. There is a little library of books for guests' use in the open-plan lounge/breakfast room, which also features a marble fireplace.

9 rms (6 bth/shr) (2 fmly) No smoking in 2 bedrooms No smoking in dining room No smoking in lounges CTV in all bedrooms Tea and coffee making facilities No dogs (ex guide dogs) Licensed Cen ht CTV No children 5yrs No coaches

ROOMS: s £19-£25; d £38-£55

CARDS:

Cornerways Private Hotel 18-20 Caburn Rd BN3 6EF (A270 Old Shoreham Road, adjacent to crossroads at junct with Dyke Road) ☎ 01273 731882

This is a small Victorian hotel situated to the north of the town centre. Bedrooms are bright and well maintained and there is a homely resident's lounge. Snacks are available during the day, and dinners by prior arrangement.

10 rms (1 shr) (2 fmly) No smoking in dining room CTV in 7 bedrooms Tea and coffee making facilities Licensed Cen ht CTV Last d 2pm

---

Gullivers 10 New Steine BN2 1PB (A23 to Brighton leads directly to Sea Front and Palace Pier. Turn left onto Marine Parade towards the Marina. New Steine on left after BP garage) ☎ 01273 695415

Closed Xmas

A bright and attractive establishment situated close to the seafront in one of Brighton's Regency squares. Proprietor Sylvia Harrison offers a warm welcome to guests, who enjoy the spacious well equipped bedrooms. An airy dining room doubles as a lounge and is available to guests throughout the day.

8 rms (4 shr) No smoking in dining room No smoking in lounges CTV in all bedrooms Tea and coffee making facilities Direct dial from bedrooms No dogs (ex guide dogs) Cen ht No children 5yrs

ROOMS: s £20-£22; d £38-£54; wkly b&b £110-£138*

CARDS:

Kempton House Hotel 33/34 Marine Pde BN2 1TR (A23, London direction, to roundabout in front of Palace Pier, left onto Marine Parade, A259, premises 250 yards on left) ☎ 01273 570248 FAX 01273 570248

This appealing hotel enjoys a good location opposite Brighton Pier. The bedrooms, though not large, are attractively furnished, and equipped with every modern amenity. Public rooms comprise a combined dining room, bar and reception area. A fixed-price evening meal can be arranged.

12 shr (4 fmly) CTV in all bedrooms Tea and coffee making facilities Direct dial from bedrooms Licensed Cen ht No coaches Last d 9am

ROOMS: s £32-£56; d £42-£68*

CARDS:

Kimberley Hotel 17 Atlingworth St BN2 1PL ☎ 01273 603504 FAX 01273 603504

Occupying a quiet location close to the seafront, this friendly guest house has been run by Bernard and Marianne Roland for over 31 years. The accommodation has been comfortably furnished in the traditional style and there is a well furnished TV lounge, an adjoining bar and a spacious breakfast room.

15 rms (6 bth/shr) (3 fmly) No smoking in dining room CTV in all bedrooms Tea and coffee making facilities No dogs (ex guide dogs) Licensed Cen ht CTV No coaches

ROOMS: s £22-£25; d £40-£50; wkly b&b £140-£160*

CARDS:

Malvern Hotel 33 Regency Square BN1 2GG (The Malvern Hotel is situated in Regency Sq which is directly opposite West Pier) ☎ 01273 324302 FAX 01273 324285

At the head of Regency Square, the Malvern Hotel offers well equipped bedrooms with extras such as biscuits, fresh flowers and pot-pourri. Downstairs there is a well appointed lounge with lots of magazines, tourist information and more fresh flowers. There is a separate bar and breakfast room.

13 shr No smoking in dining room CTV in all bedrooms Tea and coffee making facilities Direct dial from bedrooms No dogs (ex guide dogs) Licensed Cen ht

Melford Hall Hotel 41 Marine Pde BN2 1PE ☎ 01273 681435 FAX 01273 624186

Closed 24-26 Dec

Grade II listed and built around 250 years ago, this popular hotel has been run by the Dixon family for over 20 years. Overlooking Brighton Pier, the Hotel offers a range of well equipped bedrooms, most with sea views, furnished in the traditional style. Public rooms include a comfortable lounge, and an attractive breakfast room.

25 rms (23 bth/shr) (4 fmly) No smoking in dining room CTV in all bedrooms Tea and coffee making facilities Direct dial from bedrooms No dogs (ex guide dogs) Cen ht CTV No children 2yrs 12P No coaches

ROOMS: s £30-£34; d £50-£60*

CARDS:

See advertisement on p.107.

Selected

New Steine Hotel 12a New Steine, Marine Pde BN2 1PB (A27 ends opposite Palace Pier, turn left along Marine Parade. Approx 300 yards along on the left is the New Steine) ☎ 01273 681546 FAX 681546

1 Mar-18 Dec

Situated in a fine Regency Square close to the town and seafront, the New Steine Hotel retains much of its original character. Rooms are individually decorated and comfortably furnished, and those that are en suite offer good shower rooms. Day rooms include a well appointed lounge, and breakfast is served in the dining room.

contd.

10 rms (6 shr) No smoking in dining room CTV in all bedrooms Tea and coffee making facilities No dogs (ex guide dogs) Cen ht CTV No children 12yrs No coaches
ROOMS: s £25; d £45-£59*
CARDS:

Q Q Q Paskins Town House 18/19 Charlotte St BN2 1AG (A23 to pier, turn left, Charlotte Street on left) (The Independents)
☎ 01273 601203 FAX 01273 621973
You can be sure of a friendly welcome at this small hotel. Bedrooms vary in size but are all bright, welcoming and well equipped. Two feature four-poster beds. The breakfasts are well worth getting up for, with their organic ingredients including free range eggs and bacon. There is a good cooked option for vegetarians.
19 rms (16 bth/shr) (2 fmly) No smoking in area of dining room CTV in all bedrooms Tea and coffee making facilities Direct dial from bedrooms Licensed Cen ht Last d 5.30pm
ROOMS: s £20-£35; d £40-£80; wkly b&b £120-£240*
CARDS:

Q Q *Queensbury Hotel* 58 Regency Square BN1 2GB ☎ 01273 325558 FAX 01273 324800
Closed 24-28 Dec
The Queensbury is conveniently located for the seafront, the shops and the conference centre. Five of the bedrooms are fully en suite whilst all but one of the others benefit from having a shower in the room. There is a comfortable lounge and bright breakfast room.
16 rms (7 bth/shr) (8 fmly) No smoking in dining room CTV in all bedrooms Tea and coffee making facilities Cen ht CTV
CARDS:

Selected

Q Q Q Q Regency Hotel 28 Regency Square BN1 2FH (opposite West Pier) ☎ 01273 202690 FAX 01273 220438
This Regency town house is set in an open square opposite the West Pier with views of the sea. The dining room and lounge are decorated and furnished in period style and boast a crystal chandelier and wall-lights. Bedrooms vary in size and style, with the best having an antique half-tester bed and balconied bow window. All are very well equipped with modern comforts.
13 rms (10 bth/shr) (1 fmly) No smoking in 6 bedrooms No smoking in dining room CTV in all bedrooms Tea and coffee making facilities Direct dial from bedrooms No dogs (ex guide dogs) Licensed Cen ht CTV No coaches Golf riding & tennis can be arranged Last d 4pm
ROOMS: s £40-£50; d £64-£75
CARDS:

Q Q Ship Hotel Hove St BN3 2TR ☎ 01273 734936
This friendly hostelry is close to the Hove seafront and offers modest good value accommodation over two floors of this long established property. Freshly prepared lunches and dinners are served in one of two bars and guest rooms are all comfortable and have colour TV.
12 rms (3 bth/shr) (1 fmly) CTV in all bedrooms Tea and coffee making facilities No dogs (ex guide dogs) Cen ht No coaches 3 pool tables Last d 9.15pm
ROOMS: s £22-£35; d £40-£55
MEALS: Lunch £10.50-£16 Dinner £10.50-£16
CARDS:

Selected

Q Q Q Q Topps Hotel 17 Regency Square BN1 2FG (opposite West Pier) ☎ 01273 729334 FAX 01273 203679
An attractive Regency property located on one of Brighton's seafront squares. The hotel is only a short stroll from Western Road and its shops. Bedrooms here are very generously sized, have comfortable seating and a wealth of quality extras; chocolates and bathrobes to name but a couple. Staff are friendly and charming.
15 bth/shr (3 fmly) No smoking in dining room CTV in all bedrooms Tea and coffee making facilities Direct dial from bedrooms No dogs (ex guide dogs) Licensed Lift Cen ht
ROOMS: s £49-£79; d £84-£129*
CARDS:

Q Q Q Trouville Hotel 11 New Steine, Marine Pde BN2 1PB (A259 approx 300 yards from the Palace Pier situated in a seafront square)
☎ 01273 697384
Closed Xmas & Jan
The Trouville is an attractive Grade II listed building situated in a Regency seafront square. The bedrooms have been thoughtfully decorated and furnished to provide comfortable and well appointed accommodation. Guests are offered a choice of cooked breakfast in the open-plan lounge and dining room.
8 rms (6 shr) (2 fmly) No smoking in dining room CTV in all bedrooms Tea and coffee making facilities No dogs Licensed Cen ht CTV No coaches
ROOMS: s £25-£35; d £49-£57; wkly b&b £165-£190*
CARDS:

Selected

QQQQ **The Twenty One** 21 Charlotte St BN2 1AG (turn off A23 onto A259 towards Newhaven proceed for 0.5m, Charlotte Street on the left)
☎ 01273 686450 & 681617 FAX 01273 695560
Bedrooms here each have their own character: the Victorian Room with antique furniture and canopied bed, the Green Room with twin four-poster beds and the Honeymoon Suite with its own rattan-furnished conservatory seating area. All are well equipped and come with extras that range from biscuits and sweets to bathrobes and a fridge with complimentary mineral water. There is a comfortable residents' lounge and a dining room where evening meals are served by prior arrangement.
6 shr No smoking in dining room No smoking in lounges CTV in all bedrooms Tea and coffee making facilities Direct dial from bedrooms No dogs Cen ht CTV Last d 4pm
ROOMS: s £45-£70; d £50-£99; wkly b&b £136.50-£434; wkly hlf-bd £276.50-£574*
CARDS:

Melford Hall Hotel

41 MARINE PARADE,
BRIGHTON,
SUSSEX BN2 1PE
TELEPHONE: 01273 681435
On the corner of Garden Square

A seafront hotel with all rooms en suite. Ground floor and four posters rooms available. Most enjoying panoramic views of the sea and Palace pier. All rooms have colour TV, tea & coffee tray, hair dryer, radio/alarm, direct dial telephone and central heating. Close to Brighton's famous Lanes, Royal Pavilion and shopping centre.

21 The Twenty One HOTEL IN A CLASS OF ITS OWN

The Twenty One

21 Charlotte Street, Brighton BN2 1AG
Telephone: 01273 686450/681617
Fax: 01273 695560/681617
E-mail: rooms@the21.co.uk
http://www.s-h-systems.co.uk/hotels/21

Victorian Room with balcony

Celebrating 21 years as Brighton's premiere B&B

SPECIAL OFFER: 10% DISCOUNT ON 2 OR MORE NIGHTS.

Ideally placed for all major attractions and conferences. All rooms fully en-suite and luxuriously appointed and contain biscuits, chocolates, sweets and toiletries. Enjoy the ultimate Breakfast in our Bon Appetit room catering for Vegans, Vegetarians, Continental and of course the full English.

SPECIALLY HIGHLIGHTED BY
TimeOut – Daily Telegraph – Sunday Independent

Bridal Suite with conservatory and patio

Q Q Q **Westbourne Hotel** 46 Upper Rock Gardens BN2 1QF
(A23 to Brighton, turn left at rdbt by Palace Pier to Marine Parade going towards Marina, 100yds turn left at lights, hotel is up rd on right)
☎ 01273 686920 FAX 01273 686920
Just a short walk from the seafront, this Victorian house is kept in good order by friendly owners Luis and Sue Esteves. Bedrooms are attractively decorated and well furnished while the day rooms include a comfortable lounge and a bright breakfast room which also houses a small bar.
10 rms (6 shr) (4 fmly) No smoking in 3 bedrooms No smoking in dining room CTV in all bedrooms Tea and coffee making facilities No dogs Licensed Cen ht Last d 6pm
ROOMS: s £20-£30; d £38-£50; wkly b&b £133-£196*
CARDS:

BRIGSTEER (NEAR KENDAL) Cumbria Map **07** SD48

Q Q Q **Barrowfield** *(SD484908)* LA8 8BJ (4m on dual-carriageway, left after tourist info sign to T junct, left to Brigsteer. Half way down hill on S bend go right. Over 4 cattlegrids) ☎ 015395 68336 Mrs B Gardner
Apr-Oct
Reached by a mile-long private track which meanders through forest and farmland, this traditional and inviting farmhouse offers peace and seclusion, only ten minutes' drive from Kendal. There is a comfortable lounge where breakfast is served. Several walks are in the area.
3 rms (1 fmly) No smoking No dogs Cen ht CTV 6P 180 acres dairy sheep
ROOMS: d fr £34*

Q Q Q **Low Plain Farmhouse** *(SD474900)* Brigsteer LA8 8AX
(M6 junct36, take A591 signed Kendal, across A590 junction and take next left signed Brigsteer. Left at T junction, downhill passed pub, 0.5m on left)
☎ 015395 68464 Mrs J Macbeth
Etr-Oct
This very smart and traditionally styled farmhouse lies within the idyllic Lyth Valley and enjoys rural peace and quiet, just five minutes from Kendal. The bedrooms are richly furnished, enhanced by a host of thoughtful extras. A hearty Cumbrian breakfast is served in the cosy dining room
3 shr No smoking CTV in all bedrooms Tea and coffee making facilities No dogs (ex guide dogs) Cen ht P 13 acres non-working
ROOMS: d fr £45*

BRIMFIELD Shropshire Map **03** SO56

Selected

Q Q Q Q **Roebuck** SY8 4NE (located in the centre of the village of Brimfield just A49 between Leominster & Ludlow)
☎ 01584 711230 FAX 711654
This 15th-century inn provides three well equipped bedrooms and has a fine reputation for its food. A well chosen carte menu is complemented by blackboard choices and many fish specialities. Diners may use the attractive pine furnished restaurant or the bar areas. A peaceful and relaxing atmosphere prevails with staff friendly and welcoming.

3 bth/shr No smoking in bedrooms No smoking in dining room Tea and coffee making facilities Direct dial from bedrooms Cen ht 18P Last d 9.30pm
ROOMS: s £45; d £60
MEALS: Lunch £10.40-£28.50alc Dinner £12-£28.95alc
CARDS:

BRISTOL Bristol Map **03** ST57

Q Q **Alcove** 508-510 Fishponds Rd, Fishponds BS16 3DT
(leave M32 junct 2 follow signs to Fishponds & turn left into Fishponds Rd)
☎ 0117 965 3886 & 965 2436 FAX 0117 965 3886
This well run guest house is managed by the resident proprietors. Bedrooms offer modern comforts and there is a cosy little breakfast room where a traditional breakfast is served.
9 rms (5 bth/shr) (2 fmly) No smoking in dining room CTV in all bedrooms Tea and coffee making facilities No dogs (ex guide dogs) Cen ht CTV 9P No coaches
ROOMS: s £32-£35; d £40-£48*

Q Q Q **Downlands House** 33 Henleaze Gardens, Henleaze BS9 4HH
(from M32, follow Westbury on Trym signs, left into Henleaze Gardens opposite Badminton School) ☎ 0117 962 1639 FAX 0117 962 1639
This elegant Victorian property, situated close to the Downs, Clifton village and Bristol Zoo, offers well appointed accommodation. The bedrooms are equipped with modern comforts and thoughtful touches like reading material and quality toiletries. Breakfast is served in a bright conservatory style room.
9 rms (6 shr) (1 fmly) No smoking in dining room CTV in all bedrooms Tea and coffee making facilities Cen ht No coaches
ROOMS: s £34-£45; d £47-£55
CARDS:

Q Q Q **Mayfair Hotel** 5 Henleaze Rd, Westbury on Trym BS9 4EX
(exit M5 at junc 17, A4018, before third roundabout turn into Henleaze Road, Hotel 50 yds on left) ☎ 0117 962 2008
This elegant semi-detached Victorian property is situated in a smart residential area close to Bristol Zoo and Clifton village. The Mayfair offers comfortable bedrooms and a friendly, relaxed atmosphere. There is an attractive lounge for guests' use and breakfast is served at separate tables is an airy dining room.

9 rms (3 shr) (1 fmly) No smoking in dining room No smoking in lounges CTV in all bedrooms Tea and coffee making facilities Cen ht CTV 9P No coaches
ROOMS: s £25-£38; d £44-£48✻
CARDS:

QQ **Oakfield Hotel** 52-54 Oakfield Rd, Clifton BS8 2BG (1.25m from city centre, nr BBC Whiteladies Rd, 1st left after passing BBC, 100 yds up Oakfield Rd on left hand side) ☎ 0117 973 5556 FAX 0117 974 4141
Closed 24 Dec-1 Jan
The Hurley family have been providing traditional standards of comfort and hospitality for over 50 years. The bedrooms are well equipped and the beds are all of a good quality. Dinner is available by arrangement and usually a home cooked roast is served in the hotel's spacious dining room.
27 rms (4 fmly) No smoking in dining room No smoking in 1 lounge CTV in all bedrooms Tea and coffee making facilities Cen ht CTV 9P Last d 7pm
ROOMS: s £27-£30; d £37-£40; wkly b&b fr £189; wkly hlf-bd fr £234.50✻

QQ **Rowan Lodge** 41 Gloucester Rd North, Filton Park BS7 0SN (from M5 junct 16 to Filton/Bristol for approx 3.25m and Rowan Lodge is on junct of A38 and Bronksea Rd) ☎ 0117 931 2170 FAX 975601
Closed Xmas & New Year
This small private hotel is located at Filton and is convenient for the many industrial areas nearby. Bedrooms are equipped with modern amenities and some are suitable for families. A comfortable lounge/ breakfast room is provided.
6 rms (3 shr) (2 fmly) No smoking in dining room No smoking in lounges CTV in all bedrooms Tea and coffee making facilities Cen ht 8P No coaches
ROOMS: s £24-£33; d £38-£44; wkly b&b £112-£168✻
CARDS:

QQ ***Washington Hotel*** 11-15 St Pauls Rd, Clifton BS8 1LX (follow A4018 into city, turn right at lights opposite BBC buildings, hotel is 200yds on left) (The Independents) ☎ 0117 973 3980 FAX 0117 9734740
Closed 23 Dec-3 Jan
This terraced property, close to the village of Clifton and within walking distance of the centre of the city, offers secure parking. The bedrooms, which vary in style, are equipped with modern comforts to meet the needs of business and leisure guests alike.
46 rms (40 bth/shr) (4 fmly) No smoking in 13 bedrooms No smoking in dining room CTV in all bedrooms Tea and coffee making facilities Direct dial from bedrooms Licensed Cen ht 20P Last d 11pm
CARDS:

Selected

QQQQ **Westbury Park Hotel** 37 Westbury Rd, Westbury-on-Trym BS9 3AU (on A4018) ☎ 0117 962 0465 FAX 0117 962 8607
Situated on the famous Durdham Downs, this attractive Victorian property offers accommodation ideal for tourists and business guests. Bedrooms have been tastefully decorated and equipped, with modern comforts and thoughtful extra touches. There is a restful lounge adorned with fresh flowers, a bar where snacks are available and an elegant dining room where breakfast is served.
8 bth/shr (2 fmly) No smoking in dining room CTV in all bedrooms Tea and coffee making facilities Direct dial from bedrooms Licensed Cen ht CTV 4P No coaches
CARDS:

BRIXHAM Devon Map **03** SX95

QQQ **Harbour View Hotel** 65 King St TQ5 9TH (follow A380 onto A3022 Brixham Rd to town centre/harbour, left at lights, right at T junct, hotel is on right of inner harbour) ☎ 01803 853052
Mr and Mrs James offer guests a warm welcome at their harbour-front guest house. The bedrooms are all well equipped, several are now en suite, and some benefit from delightful views over the busy fishing harbour. A traditional English breakfast is served in the dining room, which also has a cosy lounge area for guests' use.
9 rms (5 bth/shr) (1 fmly) CTV in all bedrooms Tea and coffee making facilities No dogs Cen ht 4P No coaches
ROOMS: s £19-£25; d £35-£39✻
CARDS:

QQQ ***Ranscombe House Hotel*** Ranscombe Rd TQ5 9UP ☎ 01803 882337 FAX 01803 882337
Bedrooms here are comfortable and well-equipped, and two are suitable for families. Evening meals are served in the dining room, and there is a separate lounge with comfortable seating. The cellar bar, which opens out onto the gardens, is a good place to relax with a pre-dinner drink.
9 bth/shr (2 fmly) No smoking in dining room No smoking in lounges CTV in all bedrooms Tea and coffee making facilities Direct dial from bedrooms No dogs (ex guide dogs) Licensed Cen ht CTV 16P No coaches Last d 4pm
CARDS:

QQQ **Sea Tang** 67 Berry Head Rd TQ5 9AA (take A3022 to outskirts of Brixham, follow signs to 'Harbour East Car Park' Sea Tang is on right, opposite Marina, 100 metres before car park) ☎ 01803 854651 FAX 01803 854651
This Victorian terraced house is situated opposite the Marina and is only a short walk from the town and Berry Head Country Park. The bedrooms are

contd.

all tastefully decorated and have every modern convenience. Several rooms have stunning views over the harbour and across Torbay.
7 shr (1 fmly) No smoking CTV in all bedrooms Tea and coffee making facilities No dogs Cen ht CTV No children 8yrs No coaches
ROOMS: s £21-£23; d £34-£40; wkly b&b £105-£133

BROADSTAIRS Kent Map **05** TR36

Q Q Q **Bay Tree Hotel** 12 Eastern Esplanade CT10 1DR ☎ 01843 862502 FAX 01843 860589
The Bay Tree, a family run private hotel, enjoys a prime sea-facing position on the East Cliff. It offers a good range of neat, well equipped bedrooms, the best with a balcony and sea view. There is a comfortable bar lounge and a separate front dining room that offers a good choice of menu at both breakfast and dinner.
11 bth/shr No smoking in dining room CTV in all bedrooms Tea and coffee making facilities No dogs (ex guide dogs) Licensed Cen ht CTV No children 10yrs 12P No coaches Last d 4pm
ROOMS: s £24-£27; d £48-£54; wkly b&b £144-£162; wkly hlf-bd £204-£222*
CARDS:

Q Q Q **Devonhurst Hotel** Eastern Esplanade CT10 1DR (proceed down Broadstairs High Street, pass Barclays Bank take the third or fourth turning on the right into Rectory Road or Dickens Road) ☎ 01843 863010 FAX 01843 868940
A warm welcome is assured at this small family run hotel, overlooking the sea and close to the town centre. Bedrooms are brightly decorated and comfortably furnished. There is a small cosy lounge linked to the attractive dining room. Guests are offered a choice of dishes at dinner and breakfast.
9 shr (1 fmly) No smoking in 4 bedrooms No smoking in dining room CTV in all bedrooms Tea and coffee making facilities No dogs (ex guide dogs) Licensed Cen ht CTV No children 5yrs No coaches Last d 5.30pm
ROOMS: d £47-£53; wkly b&b £132-£154; wkly hlf-bd £184-£208*
CARDS:

Q **East Horndon Private Hotel** 4 Eastern Esplanade CT10 1DP ☎ 01843 868306
Mar-Nov
This Victorian building is a long-established guest house, personally run by Mrs Margaret Miller. The range of bedrooms includes spacious family rooms with en suite facilities. Public areas comprise a cosy bar lounge and a front dining room, evening meals can be provided by arrangement.
10 rms (4 bth/shr) (6 fmly) No smoking in bedrooms No smoking in dining room CTV in all bedrooms Tea and coffee making facilities Licensed Cen ht No coaches Last d noon
CARDS:

Q Q Q ***Gull Cottage*** 5 Eastern Esplanade CT10 1DP (at bottom of High Street turn left into Albion Street, take third right into Eastern Esplande) ☎ 01843 861936
Closed Nov-Mar
Lovingly restored and retaining much of its Victorian charm and character, this comfortable no-smoking guest house is the home of Joan and David Watling. The accommodation has been completely refurbished to a high standard and some rooms have sea views. There is a spacious lounge and sunny front dining room, where evening meals can be served by arrangement.
8 rms (6 shr) (3 fmly) No smoking CTV in 7 bedrooms Tea and coffee making facilities No dogs (ex guide dogs) Licensed Cen ht CTV No children 6yrs 6P

Q Q Q **Oakfield Private Hotel** 11 The Vale CT10 1RB (half way down Broadstairs High Street turn right into Queens Road, third right into the Vale, Hotel is 50 yards on the right) ☎ 01843 862506 FAX 01843 600659
This popular licensed guest house is located close to the shops and the seafront. The well equipped and attractive bedrooms all have modern en suite facilities. There is a well stocked bar and a games room with a pool table. Home-cooked evening meals are served in the dining room.
11 rms (10 shr) No smoking in 4 bedrooms No smoking in dining room No smoking in 1 lounge CTV in all bedrooms Tea and coffee making facilities No dogs (ex guide dogs) Licensed Cen ht CTV 11P No coaches Golf Games room Pool table Darts Last d 6pm
ROOMS: s £23.50-£25.50; d £47-£51; wkly b&b £164.50-£178.50; wkly hlf-bd £185-£210*
CARDS:

BROADWAY Worcestershire Map **04** SP03

Q Q Q **Bourne House** Leamington Rd WR12 7DZ (off High Street onto B4632, 3rd house on left after library) ☎ 01386 853486 FAX 01386 853793
Closed 24-31 Dec
This attractive stone built house, fronted by a neat garden, is a short distance from the High Street. The twin-bedded room and the double with four-poster are compact, soundly maintained and well equipped. There is a cosy lounge and a homely breakfast room with separate tables.
2 shr (2 fmly) No smoking CTV in all bedrooms Tea and coffee making facilities No dogs Cen ht CTV No children 11yrs 2P No coaches
ROOMS: s fr £35; d £45; wkly b&b £120*

Selected

Q Q Q Q **Cowley House** Church St WR12 7AE (off Village Green into Snowhill Rd) ☎ 01386 853262
This lovely old house and converted granary is situated close to the village centre. It is built of mellow Cotswold stone with its character enhanced by original features such as exposed beams and stone flagged floors. The bedrooms, one with an ornately carved antique four-poster bed, have modern equipment and facilities. There is an attractive and comfortable lounge and a pleasant breakfast room.
3 bth/shr No smoking CTV in all bedrooms No dogs Cen ht CTV No children 10yrs 3P No coaches
ROOMS: s £30-£35; d £45-£65*

Selected

Q Q Q Q **Leasow House** Laverton Meadows WR12 7NA BROADWAY ☎ 01386 584526 FAX 01386 584596

(For full entry see **Laverton**)

Selected

Q Q Q Q ***Milestone House*** 122 Upper High St WR12 7AJ (From the Broadway by-pass(A44) follow signs to Broadway, house located on left at Upper High St) ☎ 01386 853432 FAX 01386 853432
This lovely old house is built of mellow Cotswold stone and stands just a short walk from the village centre. To the rear is a neat and pleasant

garden, as well as a private car park. The no smoking accommodation has modern facilities and equipment and includes one room in a separate wing at the back of the main house. There are two attractively appointed sitting rooms, one of which has an inglenook fireplace. Separate tables are provided in the pleasant conservatory breakfast room.

4 bth/shr No smoking CTV in all bedrooms Tea and coffee making facilities No dogs Licensed Cen ht No children 15yrs 5P No coaches
CARDS:

Premier Selected

QQQQQ **Mill Hay House** Snowshill Rd WR12 7JS (turn off A44 (at Broadway Main Green) towards Snowshill. House 0.75 mile on right) ☎ 01386 852498 FAX 01386 858038
Mill Hay is a Queen Anne country house set in three acres of landscaped gardens. It stands adjacent to the site of a watermill dating from the 12th century. The house, built of red brick and mellow Cotswold stone, has been lovingly restored to provide quality accommodation in a peaceful rural location. Bedrooms are comfortable, with thoughtful extras. Public areas retain many original features including floors and panelling, and are furnished with some fine period pieces.
3 bth/shr No smoking in bedrooms No smoking in dining room No smoking in 1 lounge CTV in all bedrooms Tea and coffee making facilities Direct dial from bedrooms No dogs (ex guide dogs) Cen ht CTV No children 12yrs 15P No coaches 3 acre garden with medieval pond & moat
ROOMS: s £63-£90; d £70-£100; wkly b&b £220-£315*
CARDS:

Premier Selected

Q Q Q Q Q **Old Rectory** Church St WR12 7PN (from Broadway take B4632 Stratford Rd for one and a half miles turn right into Church St at Bell Inn) ☎ 01386 853729 FAX 01386 858061
Closed 23-27 Dec
Situated at the end of a quiet lane opposite the 11th-century village church, this mellow Cotswold stone house has been lovingly restored to provide guest accommodation. Bedrooms have modern en suite facilities and several homely extras. The breakfast room contains period furniture and has a small sitting area in front of the log fire. The walled garden contains fruit trees, some of which are centuries old and produce fruit which is used to prepare breakfast.
6 bth/shr 2 annexe bth/shr (2 fmly) No smoking CTV in all bedrooms Tea and coffee making facilities Direct dial from bedrooms No dogs (ex guide dogs) Cen ht No children 8yrs 10P No coaches
ROOMS: s £55-£85; d £65-£105; wkly b&b £210-£345*
CARDS:

Q Q Q **Olive Branch Guest House** 78 High St WR12 7AJ (on A44, close to junction with Stratford Road) ☎ 01386 853440 FAX 01386 853440
Situated at the end of the High Street, this Cotswold stone property dates back to the 16th century and retains many original features. Bedrooms are comfortable, well equipped and all have modern en suite or private bathrooms. The dining room with its flagstone floor and exposed beams is the cosy setting for one of Wendy Riley's tasty breakfasts.
8 rms (6 bth/shr) (1 fmly) No smoking in dining room CTV in all bedrooms Tea and coffee making facilities No dogs (ex guide dogs) Cen ht 9P No coaches Last d 7.30pm
ROOMS: s £20-£22; d £44-£56*
CARDS:

Q Q Q **Pathlow** 82 High St WR12 7AJ (from A44 take Evesham road at new rdbt until reaching by-pass, road then becomes Broadway High Street) ☎ 01386 853444 FAX 01386 853444
Modern-equipped and nicely appointed accommodation is on offer at this 18th-century Cotswold stone house. The attractively decorated dining room doubles as a tea shop during the day. There is a cosy lounge and a pleasant cottage style garden.
6 rms (3 shr) 1 annexe shr (2 fmly) No smoking CTV in all bedrooms Tea and coffee making facilities Cen ht CTV 8P Last d 6pm
ROOMS: s £25-£35; d £35-£50; wkly b&b £122.50-£157.50; wkly hlf-bd £192.50-£262.50*

Premier Selected

Q Q Q Q Q **Pond House** Lower Fields, Weston Rd, Bretforton WR11 5QA (B4632 to Broadway, turn onto B4035 at Weston-sub-Edge. House 0.5m on left after crossing old railway bridge) ☎ 01386 831687
rs Dec-Feb
Set at the foot of the North Cotswolds escarpment and enjoying magnificent views of all the hills, this extended farm cottage offers comfortable accommodation in a superb setting. Bedrooms are very well equipped and the house has a homely sitting room. The conservatory breakfast room overlooks the pretty gardens. Friendly hospitality is extended by hosts Ray and Anne Payne.
4 bth/shr (1 fmly) No smoking CTV in all bedrooms Tea and coffee making facilities No dogs Cen ht No children 5yrs 10P No coaches
ROOMS: s £38-£46; d £48-£52; wkly b&b £154-£238*
See advertisement under Chipping Campden

Selected

Q Q Q Q **Southwold House** Station Rd WR12 7DE (located on B4632 opposite turning signposted to Winchcombe) ☎ 01386 853681 FAX 01386 854610
Southwold House is an impressive Edwardian building offering well equipped and comfortable accommodation, close to major attractions. Bedrooms are homely and most have the benefit of modern en suite facilities. A comprehensive breakfast selection is served in the attractive dining room, which overlooks the pretty garden. A comfortable sitting room is available for guests' use.
8 rms (6 shr) No smoking CTV in all bedrooms Tea and coffee making facilities Cen ht CTV 8P
ROOMS: s £20-£21; d £40-£44*
CARDS:

Selected

Tudor Cottage 56 High St WR12 7DT (town centre, next to Horse & Hound public house) ☎ 01386 852674
Closed 24-26 Dec
Tudor Cottage dates from the 17th century and has been carefully refurbished to provide comfortable accommodation close to the major attractions. Bedrooms are very individual and homely with quality decor and soft fabrics in addition to modern en suite shower rooms. The cosy dining room is used for the delicious home cooked breakfasts and afternoon cream teas during the summer months.
4 bth/shr (1 fmly) No smoking CTV in all bedrooms Tea and coffee making facilities Cen ht 4P
ROOMS: d £50-£65

Selected

Windrush House Station Rd WR12 7DE (from A44 take B4632) ☎ 01386 853577
Closed Xmas
This well maintained, large Edwardian house stands just a couple of minutes walk west of the village centre. It has a large and pleasant garden at the rear, and provides modern equipped bedrooms. There is a pleasant combined lounge and breakfast room, which is traditionally furnished.
4 shr No smoking in bedrooms No smoking in dining room Tea and coffee making facilities Cen ht 55P No coaches
ROOMS: s £25-£30; d £40-£50

BROCKENHURST Hampshire Map 04 SU30

Selected

The Cottage Sway Rd SO42 7SH (from Lyndhurst on A337, turn right at Careys Manor into Grigg Lane. Continue 0.5m to crossroads, straight over and cottage next to war memorial)
☎ 01590 622296 FAX 01590 623014
Closed Dec-Jan
A former forester's cottage that has been lovingly restored to retain its character. Terry and Barbara Eisner offer warm hospitality and a relaxed atmosphere. Bedrooms are brightly decorated and comfortably appointed, with many thoughtful extras. For guests' further enjoyment, a drinks cabinet is provided in the cosy lounge. Breakfast is served in the attractive dining room.
7 bth/shr No smoking in bedrooms No smoking in dining room CTV in all bedrooms Tea and coffee making facilities Licensed Cen ht CTV No children 10yrs 12P No coaches
ROOMS: s £49-£70; d £69-£85; wkly b&b £241.50-£297.50*
CARDS:

Premier Selected

Thatched Cottage Hotel & Restaurant 16 Brookley Rd SO42 7RR (from M27 junct 1, drive south on A337 through Lyndhurst to Brockenhurst and turn right just before level crossing)
☎ 01590 623090 FAX 01590 623479
Closed 4-31 Jan
This delightful 17th-century thatched cottage has been converted into a small hotel of some quality. It has been furnished with thought and care that combines all modern essentials with old world charm. The bedrooms vary in size but the lack of space in some is compensated for in the quality of the appointments and the many useful extras that are provided. The stylishly furnished restaurant with its open kitchen offers interesting and well prepared dishes at dinner. The breakfast menu is of equal interest and includes American pancakes and eggs benedictine.
5 bth/shr No smoking in dining room CTV in all bedrooms Tea and coffee making facilities Direct dial from bedrooms Licensed Cen ht No children 10yrs 10P No coaches Last d 9.30pm
ROOMS: d £90-£135; wkly b&b £290-£420*
CARDS:

BROMPTON REGIS Somerset Map 03 SS93

Lower Holworthy *(SS978308)* TA22 9NY (on edge of Wimbleball Lake) ☎ 01398 371244 Mrs G Payne
This 200-year-old working livestock farm overlooks, and has access to, Wimbleball Lake, an ideal spot for fishing. The rooms are

contd.

comfortable and the attractive dining room is a pleasant setting for the hearty breakfast provided. Appetising dinners are also available by prior arrangement.
3 rms (1 bth 1 shr) CTV in 1 bedroom Tea and coffee making facilities No dogs (ex guide dogs) Cen ht CTV ch fac 6P Fishing
200 acres beef sheep
ROOMS: s £21; d £42*

BROMSGROVE Worcestershire Map **07** SO97

Q Q Q **Lower Bentley** *(SO962679)* Lower Bentley B60 4JB
(off A38 onto B4091, under bridge at crossroads, left into Moregate Rd, first right, third left into Lower Bentley Lane, farm is on left)
☎ 01527 821286 FAX 01527 821286 Mr & Mrs A Gibbs
This large Victorian house, located on a dairy farm, is fronted by a pleasant garden and ornamental pond. The accommodation is spacious and has traditional furnishings. All guests share one table in the breakfast room. There is an attractive and comfortably furnished lounge.
3 rms (2 bth) CTV in all bedrooms Tea and coffee making facilities Cen ht CTV 5P 346 acres dairy beef

Selected

Q Q Q Q **Rosa Lodge** 38 Station Rd B60 1PZ (take B4096 off A38 at junct with M42, after 1.25 miles turn left up Green Hill. First right into Station Rd, take drive on right before rail bridge)
☎ 0121 445 5440 FAX 0121 445 5440
Situated in a quiet residential area, this red brick house offers value for money accommodation close to motorway networks and places of interest. Bedrooms are comfortable, tastefully decorated and equipped with lots of homely extras. The spacious lounge has a conservatory overlooking the garden, and dinner is available by prior arrangement.
3 bth/shr No smoking in bedrooms No smoking in dining room No smoking in 1 lounge CTV in all bedrooms Tea and coffee making facilities No dogs (ex guide dogs) Cen ht CTV No children 12yrs 4P No coaches Games room Last d 8.45pm
ROOMS: s £26; d £52*
CARDS:

See advertisement under
BIRMINGHAM (NATIONAL EXHIBITION CENTRE)

BROMYARD Herefordshire Map **03** SO65

Q Q Q ***Chase*** Bishops Frome WR6 5BP (centre of village, 1m from foot of Frome's Hill on A4103) ☎ 01885 490234 FAX 01885 490547
This pleasant hostelry which is popular for its food, is located in the centre of the village of Bishop's Frome, which is just south of Bromyard. Personally run, it provides modern equipped, no-smoking accommodation and has a lounge bar of some character
5 rms (3 shr) No smoking in bedrooms CTV in all bedrooms Tea and coffee making facilities Cen ht 15P Last d 9.30pm
CARDS:

BROUGH Cumbria Map **12** NY71

Selected

Q Q Q Q **Augill Castle** CA17 4DE
(M6 junct38, A685 through Kirkby Stephen. Continue through Brough Sowerrby and take left turn to South Stainmore. Castle 1m on left)
☎ 017683 41937 FAX 017683 341936
This splendid Victorian, neo-gothic Castle nestles in delightful pastoral farmland just off the A685 heading towards South Stainmore.
Having been left derelict, Simon and Wendy Bennet have sympathetically restored the house to its original beauty whilst adding a plethora of stylish, cosmopolitan touches throughout. The bedrooms - all south facing - enjoy stunning views of the Pennines and Cumbrian mountains and are furnished to a high standard with period furniture; and in some, walk in wardrobes converted from the castles' original grand turrets! The flamboyance of the house is best found in the opulent lounges and dining room were a 'House Party' style dinner is served around a huge oak table. Having owned a restaurant in London, Simon ensures that the traditional set menu include treats such as roasted rack of minted Dales Lamb or perhaps a baked chocolate custard. A full residential licence allows for a modest selection of wines.

6 bth/shr (3 fmly) No smoking in bedrooms No smoking in 1 lounge Tea and coffee making facilities No dogs (ex guide dogs) Licensed Cen ht CTV 8P No coaches Last d by arrangement
ROOMS: s £40-£50; d £60-£80*
CARDS:

Selected

Q Q Q Q **Augill House** *(NY814148)* CA17 4DX (400yds off A66) ☎ 017683 41305 Mrs J M Atkinson
This impressive Georgian farmhouse nestles in gardens east of the town. Each tastefully decorated bedroom is individually furnished and thoughtfully equipped including little touches such as biscuits and toiletries. Downstairs there is an inviting lounge with a small dining room adjacent, but in summer Jeanette's home-cooked meals are taken in the stylish conservatory, looking out onto the front garden dominated by a magnificent copper beech.
3 bth/shr No smoking CTV in all bedrooms Tea and coffee making facilities Direct dial from bedrooms No dogs (ex guide dogs) Cen ht CTV No children 12yrs 6P 40 acres mixed Last d 4pm
ROOMS: s £25-£30; d £40-£44; wkly b&b £140*

Q Q Q **The Castle Hotel** Main St CA17 4AX (on Main Street of Brough just off the A66 Penrith to Scotch Corner road)
☎ 017683 41252 FAX 41775
Set in the centre of the village, this hotel offers well equipped, decent sized bedrooms, two bars and an attractive dining room which has striking murals depicting the age of chivalry. A comfortable lounge is also provided for guests who seek to relax.
14 bth/shr (2 fmly) No smoking in dining room CTV in all bedrooms Tea and coffee making facilities Direct dial from bedrooms Cen ht CTV 100P Last d 9pm
ROOMS: s £30-£35; d £40-£45; wkly b&b £140-£175; wkly hlf-bd £245-£245*
CARDS:

BRUNTINGTHORPE Leicestershire Map **04** SP68

Selected

Q Q Q Q ❦ Knaptoft House Farm & The Greenway *(SP619894)* Bruntingthorpe Rd, Bruntingthorpe LE17 6PR (at Bruntingthorpe/ Saddington crossroads turn off A5199 (former A50) for Bruntingthorpe, premises located on the left after 1m beyond Shearsby Hotel) ☎ 0116 247 8388 FAX 0116 247 8388 Mrs A T Hutchinson

Closed Xmas

This farmhouse and adjoining modern bungalow stand in its own secluded location and is family run by mother and daughter. The accommodation offers soundly appointed bedrooms, (three on the ground floor) which are attractively decorated, thoughtfully furnished and maintained in pristine condition. Each building has its own comfortable lounge with a wood burning stove and guests can enjoy a freshly cooked breakfast in the bright, cheerful dining room. Another feature worthy of a mention is the restored medieval fishponds in the grounds, where guests are welcome to fish, by arrangement.

3 rms (2 shr) 3 annexe shr No smoking in 4 bedrooms No smoking in dining room No smoking in lounges CTV in all bedrooms Tea and coffee making facilities No dogs Cen ht No children 5yrs 10P Fishing 145 acres mixed

ROOMS: s fr £25; d £38-£42*

CARDS:

BUCKFAST Devon Map **03** SX76

Q Q Q ***Furzeleigh Mill Country Hotel*** Dart Bridge TQ11 0JR (beside A38 between Buckfast & Dartmoor) ☎ 01364 643476 FAX 01364 643476

This carefully converted 16th-century corn mill lies on the edge of Dartmoor. The bedrooms are small but well equipped. There are extensive public areas which include two dining rooms where a wide selection is offered. A small comfortable lounge with a separate bar is provided.

15 rms (13 bth/shr) (2 fmly) No smoking in dining room CTV in all bedrooms Tea and coffee making facilities Licensed Cen ht CTV 32P Last d 8.30pm

CARDS:

BUCKFASTLEIGH Devon Map **03** SX76

Selected

Q Q Q Q ***Dartbridge*** Totnes Rd TQ11 0JR (turn off A38 onto A384, The Dartbridge Inn is 150 yds on the left) ☎ 01364 642214 FAX 01364 643977

Close to the banks of the River Dart, this inn is not far from Dartmoor National Park. The bedrooms are attractively decorated and well equipped with modern comforts. An extensive choice of dishes is offered on the daily specials board and, together with an a la carte menu, is available in the large panelled bar with its open fires.

11 bth/shr (1 fmly) No smoking in dining room CTV in all bedrooms Tea and coffee making facilities Direct dial from bedrooms No dogs (ex guide dogs) Cen ht 100P Last d 9.30pm

CARDS:

Q Q Q Kilbury Manor Farm Colston Rd TQ11 0LN (turn off A38 at Dart Bridge junct onto B3380 to Buckfastleigh, left turn after 0.5m into Old Totnes Rd, at bottom turn right, farm on right) ☎ 01364 644079 FAX 01364 644059

Closed 25 Dec-Jan

Located in an idyllic spot near to the historic village of Buckfastleigh and Buckfast Abbey, this early 18th-century house surrounded by six acres of gardens, orchard and pasture, offers guests comfortable accommodation, with modern facilities. Owned by Graham Rice with his partner Suzanne Lewis, who is an accomplished cook, guests will be pleasantly surprised at the innovative and extensive menu offered at dinner, not to mention the imaginative breakfast also available.

3 bth/shr No smoking in 2 bedrooms No smoking in dining room No smoking in lounges CTV in all bedrooms Tea and coffee making facilities 6P No coaches Last d 6pm

ROOMS: s £23-£25; d £38-£44; wkly b&b £145-£158*

BUDE Cornwall & Isles of Scilly Map **02** SS20

Selected

Q Q Q Q Cliff Hotel Maer Down, Crooklets Beach EX23 8NG (from A39 continue through Bude town towards Crooklets beach, turn first right, at crossroads go straight over, premises at end of road) ☎ 01288 353110 FAX 01288 353110

Apr-Oct

Many guests regularly return to this family run hotel. The spacious bedrooms are attractive, and exceptionally well equipped. Public areas are spacious, and there are superb leisure facilities. The new, sheltered patio area at the rear of the hotel has proven extremely popular. A fine reputation has been gained for the cuisine, which uses fresh fish caught from the hotel's own boat, herbs and vegetables taken from the garden and free range eggs from their own hens.

contd.

Cliffe Hotel

15 bth/shr (12 fmly) No smoking in area of dining room No smoking in 1 lounge CTV in all bedrooms Tea and coffee making facilities Direct dial from bedrooms Licensed CTV 16P Indoor swimming pool (heated) Tennis (hard) Putting All weather bowling green Gym Last d 6pm
ROOMS: s £28-£38; d £50-£70; wkly b&b £160-£210; wkly hlf-bd £230-£280*
CARDS:

Selected

QQQQ **Court Farm** *(SS224037)* Marhamchurch EX23 0EN (Turn off A39 just south of Bude into the village of Marhamchurch. Premises located opposite the village store)
☎ 01288 361494 FAX 01288 361494 Mrs M Trewin
Closed 20-28 Dec
Court Farm stands opposite the village shop and the church, in an unusually central location. Mary Trewin welcomes guests to her farmhouse home, where a range of self catering cottages are also available, converted from former farm buildings. Bedrooms are comfortably furnished and attractively co-ordinated, the majority having en suite facilities. A hearty breakfast is served in the dining room. It is possible to use the swimming pool whatever the weather.
5 bth/shr (2 fmly) No smoking in dining room No smoking in lounges CTV in all bedrooms Tea and coffee making facilities No dogs CTV 5P Indoor swimming pool (heated) Tennis (hard) Table tennis 180 acres mixed
ROOMS: s £18-£21; d £36-£44*

Selected

QQQQ **Downlands** 1 Flexbury Av EX23 8RE
(turn right off A39 take road to Bude, through one-way system, past P.O., road forks, take right fork but left hand lane, Downlands is approx 200yds) ☎ 01288 355545
Closed Jan
Yvonne Phillips welcomes guests to her attractive, detached property. Bedrooms are neatly furnished and decorated; two rooms are available on the ground floor. A comfortable, spacious sitting room is provided for guests. In the well appointed dining room, an interesting choice is offered at breakfast, all freshly cooked, with plenty of fruit for those wanting a lighter start to the day.
7 bth/shr (3 fmly) No smoking in 2 bedrooms No smoking in dining room CTV in all bedrooms Tea and coffee making facilities No dogs (ex guide dogs) Cen ht 10P No coaches
ROOMS: s £22-£28; d £40-£52*

QQ **Links View** 13 Morwenna Ter EX23 8BU (premises situated in the centre of Bude adjacent to the Golf Club) ☎ 01288 352561
Closed Dec
Naturally popular with golfers due to its location adjacent to the golf course, this small guest house is also ideally suited to tourists. Bedrooms are neatly furnished and decorated; three rooms having their own showers. Breakfast is served in the dining room. A cosy lounge is also available to guests.
11 rms (2 fmly) No smoking in dining room CTV in 7 bedrooms Tea and coffee making facilities No dogs (ex guide dogs) Licensed Cen ht CTV 3P
ROOMS: s £15-£17; d £30-£34; wkly b&b £90-£105*

QQQ **Lower Northcott** *(SS215087)* Poughill EX23 7EL
(from Bude town centre take Poughill road, in Poughill at post office turn left into Northcott Mouth Rd, turn right at B&B notice)
☎ 01288 352350 FAX 01288 352350 Mrs S Trewin
This Georgian house lies in a secluded valley. Families are particularly welcome, many returning on a regular basis. Farmhouse cuisine is a speciality, with vegetarians catered for and traditional 'nursery' puddings especially popular.
5 rms (1 bth 3 shr) (3 fmly) No smoking in bedrooms No smoking in dining room CTV in all bedrooms Tea and coffee making facilities No dogs (ex guide dogs) Cen ht CTV 4P Indoor playroom 470 acres arable beef dairy Last d 6.30pm
ROOMS: s fr £18; d fr £36; wkly hlf-bd fr £175*

QQQ **Pencarrol** 21 Downs View EX23 8RF (turn off A39 to town centre follow signs to Crooklets Beach, Downs View Road is ahead at beach car park exit) ☎ 01288 352478
Closed Dec rs Jan-Mar & Oct-Nov (b & b only)
Crooklets Beach and the town centre are just a short walk away from this friendly guest house, which overlooks the golf course. Bedrooms are neatly furnished and decorated, and from the windows of the first floor lounge there are glorious open views. A set evening meal is served each evening by arrangement.
7 rms (4 shr) (1 fmly) No smoking CTV in all bedrooms Tea and coffee making facilities No dogs (ex guide dogs) Cen ht CTV No coaches
ROOMS: s £15-£18; d £30-£36; wkly b&b £94.50-£130.40

BUDLEIGH SALTERTON Devon Map 03 SY08

Selected

QQQQ ***Long Range Hotel*** 5 Vales Rd EX9 6HS ☎ 01395 443321
Etr-Dec
This family run hotel has a relaxed and friendly atmosphere. It is set in quiet surroundings within easy walking distance of the town centre and the beach, where there is a beach hut for the use of guests. The bedrooms are comfortable, and equipped with modern facilities. There is a lounge and a conservatory where guests can enjoy a pre-dinner drink. Delightful six course home cooked meals, using fresh local ingredients, are offered from the daily changing menu.
7 rms (2 bth 4 shr) (1 fmly) No smoking in bedrooms CTV in all bedrooms Tea and coffee making facilities No dogs Licensed Cen ht 6P Last d 8pm

QQQ **Lufflands** Yettington EX9 7BP (M5 junct 30, A376 for Exmouth, turn left onto B3179 at Clyst St George through Woodbury, straight across Fourfirs X-roads to Yettington, on left) ☎ 01395 568422 FAX 01395 568810
Dating back to the late 1600s, Lufflands is situated in the pretty, unspoilt village of Yettington. Bedrooms are comfortably furnished, some with views over the pretty gardens. The former kitchens now house the TV lounge and the dining room, where guests may enjoy a traditional breakfast.
3 bth/shr (1 fmly) Tea and coffee making facilities No dogs (ex guide dogs) Cen ht 10P No coaches
ROOMS: s £18; d £38; wkly b&b £108-£114*

Q Q Q *Willowmead* 12 Little Knowle EX9 6QS ☎ 01395 443115
A delightful family home with a colourful garden, Willowmead is tucked away in a quiet residential area close to the town centre and the sea. Bedrooms are bright and comfortable and there is a most attractive first-floor lounge. A choice of dishes is offered in the dining room.
4 rms (3 shr) No smoking in bedrooms No smoking in dining room Tea and coffee making facilities Cen ht CTV No children 5yrs 6P No coaches

BUNGAY Suffolk Map **05** TM38

Selected

Q Q Q Q **Earsham Park Farm** *(TM304883)* Harleston Rd, Earsham NR35 2AQ (3m SW of Bungay on A143, on right hand side of road going SW) ☎ 01986 892180 FAX 01986 892180 Mrs B Watchorn
This delightful Victorian house, part of a working 600-acre farm, was originally part of the Duke of Norfolk's deer park. There is a cosy lounge for guests, and breakfast, which consists of farm produced eggs, local bacon and home made muesli, is served in the sunny dining room. Bedrooms are spacious and have smart en suite facilities and many extra touches.
3 bth/shr No smoking CTV in all bedrooms Tea and coffee making facilities No dogs (ex guide dogs) Cen ht 11P Farm walks 589 acres arable pigs poultry Last d 24hrs prior
ROOMS: s £28-£32; d £40-£46*
CARDS:

BUNTINGFORD Hertfordshire Map **05** TL32

Q Q Q **Buckland Bury Farm** *(TL357336)* Buckland Bury SG9 0PY (On A10) ☎ 01763 272958 FAX 01763 272958 Mrs P Hodge
Public rooms at this 300-year old farmhouse retain much original character, the dining room in particular is impressive with its large communal table, exposed beams and fireplace; there is also a comfortable lounge for guests' use. The traditionally furnished bedrooms are well equipped and have a range of thoughtful extras.
3 rms (1 shr) No smoking in bedrooms CTV in all bedrooms Tea and coffee making facilities No dogs (ex guide dogs) Lift Cen ht CTV 12P 550 acres arable
ROOMS: s £20-£30; d £40-£45; wkly b&b £136-£140*

BURFORD Oxfordshire Map **04** SP21

Premier Selected

Q Q Q Q Q **Burford House Hotel** 99 High St OX18 4QA (Turn off A40 between Cheltenham and Oxford following signs for Burford. Burford House is on the High Street)
☎ 01993 823151 FAX 01993 823240

To call it 'A town house hotel in the country' would best describe this super property. The beautifully appointed en suite bedrooms offer a very high level of comfort, with good quality bed linens in addition to a host of extra touches. A number of rooms benefit from four-poster beds, and several have spacious bathrooms with old fashioned tubs. Guests may take advantage of two attractively furnished sitting rooms, or in fine weather, the enclosed garden. In keeping with the high level of service provided, tea and coffee are available on request. Breakfast is served in the front facing dining room, where guests may also enjoy lunch or tea with a tempting array of homemade cakes.
7 bth/shr No smoking in bedrooms No smoking in dining room CTV in all bedrooms Direct dial from bedrooms No dogs (ex guide dogs) Licensed Cen ht CTV
ROOMS: s £75-£115; d £85-£125; wkly b&b fr £275*
CARDS:

Premier Selected

Q Q Q Q Q **Cottage-by-the-Church** Chapel Ln, Filkins GL7 3JG ☎ 01367 860613 FAX 01367 860613

(For full entry see **Lechlade**)

Premier Selected

Q Q Q Q Q **Elm House** Meadow Ln, Fulbrook OX18 4BW (from Burford take A361 towards Chipping Norton for 0.5m, turn right by War Memorial into Meadow Lane. Hotel is behind Memorial 30yds on left)
☎ 01993 823611 FAX 01993 823937
Elm House is tucked away down a narrow lane behind the war memorial in this sleepy village just one mile from the historic town of

contd.

Burford. Exceptional hospitality is provided by David Brewster and Andy Pugh in their spacious Victorian home, which retains many of its original features such as mullioned windows and roaring log fires. The bedrooms are attractively decorated with an individual sense of style, and are all equipped with such welcoming extra touches as fresh flowers. The house is spacious and provides guests with a choice of comfortable seating areas in which to relax. Evening meals, from a daily changing set menu, are prepared by Andy with care and skill, using fresh local ingredients. The beautiful walled garden is well kept, and during the summer months guests can play croquet or enjoy an aperitif prior to dinner.
7 rms (6 bth/shr) No smoking in bedrooms No smoking in dining room No smoking in 1 lounge CTV in all bedrooms Tea and coffee making facilities Direct dial from bedrooms Licensed Cen ht CTV No children 16yrs 10P No coaches Croquet lawn Last d 8pm
ROOMS: s £45-£70; d £50-£75*
CARDS:

BURLEY Hampshire Map **04** SU20

Selected

Q Q Q Q ***Croftland*** 28 Garden Rd BH24 4EA
(at top of High St turn right towards Bransgore and Christchurch, after 200yds garage on right Garden Rd is alongside, Drive 25 yds on left)
☎ 01425 403727 FAX 01425 403727
This pretty country house comes complete with a super outdoor swimming pool in the well tended garden. The three rooms are particularly spacious, well furnished and attractive. The smart lounge has many books and adjoins the conservatory style breakfast room. Proprietors Tony and Sue take real pleasure in having guests to stay and offer a warm welcome to this idyllic part of the New Forest.
4 bth/shr (2 fmly) No smoking in bedrooms No smoking in lounges CTV in all bedrooms Tea and coffee making facilities No dogs (ex guide dogs) Cen ht CTV 5P Outdoor swimming pool

Selected

Q Q Q Q **Pikes Post** Chapel Ln BH24 4DJ (turn off A31 at Picket Post, follow sign posts to Burley village, pass Queens Head pub, turn into Chapel Lane in approx 0.5m Pikes Post on left)
☎ 01425 402285 FAX 01425 402285
Closed Dec-Jan
Set in half an acre of gardens, Pikes Post is an attractive bungalow in the heart of the New Forest. The bedrooms are brightly decorated and comfortably furnished. Public rooms offer a fine dining room and a small cosy lounge. A generous cooked breakfast is served, and other choices are available.
3 bth/shr No smoking CTV in all bedrooms Tea and coffee making facilities No dogs Cen ht No children 4P No coaches
ROOMS: d £40-£44; wkly b&b fr £140*

BURNLEY Lancashire Map **07** SD83

Q Q Q **Ormerod Hotel** 121/123 Ormerod Rd BB11 3QW
(from Burnley centre take A682, turn right 200mtrs after Sainsburys up Ormerod Rd, past Burnley College on left and hotel is 300mtrs on right)
☎ 01282 423255
This friendly and welcoming hotel is situated opposite a park and within easy walking distance of the town centre. Freshly decorated bedrooms are attractively furnished. Public areas are comfortable, and breakfast is served in the wood panelled dining room.

9 bth/shr (2 fmly) CTV in all bedrooms Tea and coffee making facilities Cen ht CTV 8P
ROOMS: s £22-£25; d £38*

BURNSALL North Yorkshire Map **07** SE06

Q Q **Manor House** BD23 6BW (on B6160, approaching from Grassington) ☎ 01756 720231 FAX 720231
Closed Jan 9-25
Enthusiastic new owners have started to make improvements at this guest house situated on the edge of the village. Bedrooms are nicely furnished, and downstairs there is a cosy bar and a comfortable lounge as well as a traditional dining room.
7 rms (6 bth/shr) No smoking Tea and coffee making facilities Licensed Cen ht CTV 9P No coaches Fishing Last d 5pm
ROOMS: d £45-£53; wkly b&b £157.50-£185.50; wkly hlf-bd £205.50-£230.50*

BURROWBRIDGE Somerset Map **03** ST32

Selected

Q Q Q Q ***Saltmoor House*** Saltmoor TA7 0RL
(take A361 through Durston to Burrow Bridge, left at traffic light junct before Burrowbridge into West Yeo Rd, follow for 0.25m)
☎ 01823 698092
Closed 22 Dec-5 Jan
Surrounded by the rural splendour of Somerset, Saltmoor House is a Grade II listed property dating from the 18th century. To step inside is to experience an eloquent expression of sophisticated taste and understated elegance. The owners are justifiably proud of their achievements and are now keen to share their home with appreciative guests. Space is an abundant commodity which enhances comfort within the stylishly simple bedrooms and public areas. Breakfast can be taken in a choice of rooms, one of which has French doors opening on to the walled garden. Close to a wealth of varied attractions, this is an ideal choice for those seeking a base from which to explore the area. Dinner is available by prior arrangement.
4 rms (1 shr) (1 fmly) No smoking No dogs Cen ht No children 18yrs 6P No coaches
CARDS:

BURTON UPON TRENT Staffordshire Map **08** SK22

Q Q Q **Delter Hotel** 5 Derby Rd DE14 1RU
(from A511 turn into Derby Rd at roundabout, Hotel 50 yards on left; from A38, A5121, at Stretton straight over roundabout, hotel 0.5m from rdbt)
☎ 01283 535115 FAX 01283 535115
Closed 25-26 Dec
Conveniently located on the A5121 leading into the town of Burton on Trent, is this well maintained small family run guest house. The present owners, have only been here for fourteen months but since arriving, have

made many improvements. The bedrooms are spacious and attractively decorated. There is also a cosy cellar bar and dining room where evening meals are available by prior arrangement.
6 bth/shr No smoking in lounges CTV in all bedrooms Tea and coffee making facilities No dogs (ex guide dogs) Licensed Cen ht 8P No coaches Last d breakfast
ROOMS: s £29; d £39-£42.50*
CARDS:

Selected

QQQQ **Edgecote Hotel** 179 Ashby Rd DE15 OLB (on A511, Leicester side of town) ☎ 01283 568966 FAX 01283 740118
Edwardian in style, this small hotel has modern facilities carefully blended in. Bedrooms, which vary in size and layout, have all been recently decorated and are well equipped. Downstairs, stained glass is a particular feature of the comfortable sitting room, whilst the airy dining room is oak panelled, in keeping with the style of the house.
11 rms (5 shr) (1 fmly) No smoking in bedrooms No smoking in dining room CTV in all bedrooms Tea and coffee making facilities No dogs (ex guide dogs) Licensed Cen ht CTV 6P Last d 6pm
ROOMS: s £29-£39; d £46-£56
CARDS:

BURWASH East Sussex Map 05 TQ62

QQ **Woodlands** *(TQ656242)* Heathfield Rd TN19 7LA (1m W of Burwash on A265, on right side of road, house set back one third of a mile off road) ☎ 01435 882794 Mrs E Sirrell
Surrounded by sheep pasture, this farmhouse offers six well-kept bedrooms that are reached via timbered corridors. The cosy dining room (dinners are by arrangement) also serves as a TV lounge although guests often join Liz and John Sirrell in their own sitting room with its inglenook fireplace. This is a no-smoking establishment.
3 rms (1 shr) No smoking No dogs Cen ht CTV 4P 100 acres mixed Last d am
ROOMS: s £18-£25; d £38-£42

BURY ST EDMUNDS Suffolk Map 05 TL86

QQQ **Abbey Hotel** 35 Southgate St IP33 2AZ (turn off A14 exit E and take last exit of second rdbt signposted "hotels" for Southgate Street)
☎ 01284 762020 FAX 01284 724770
Accommodation at the Abbey Hotel is in four historic buildings which date from 1150 to 1680. The public rooms are situated within the Tudor Inn section and feature a comfortable lounge and an informal dining area where guests can enjoy a cooked breakfast.
10 bth/shr (2 fmly) No smoking in 5 bedrooms No smoking in dining room CTV in all bedrooms Tea and coffee making facilities Direct dial from bedrooms No dogs (ex guide dogs) Licensed Cen ht 14P No coaches
ROOMS: s £48-£54.50; d £65-£68*
CARDS:

QQQ ***The Chantry Hotel*** 8 Sparhawk St IP33 1RY
(from Cathedral (on your left) proceed South, take next left, get into right hand lane turn right and hotel is on right)
☎ 01284 767427 FAX 01284 760946
At this large Georgian house, on the site of a 12th-century chapel, a cosy lounge bar is available, and meals are served within the spacious dining room. The accommodation is in the main house and an adjacent Tudor annexe, offering a pleasant combination of period furniture and good facilities.
13 bth/shr 3 annexe bth/shr (1 fmly) No smoking in dining room CTV in all bedrooms Tea and coffee making facilities Direct dial from bedrooms Licensed Cen ht 16P No coaches Last d 7pm
CARDS:

QQQ **Dunston Guest House/Hotel** 8 Springfield Rd IP33 3AN
(A14 from London, take A1302, continue on this road and turn left just after pedestrian crossing, guest house is down on left hand side)
☎ 01284 767981
In a peaceful sidestreet setting, Mrs Dakin provides cheerful and welcoming accommodation. Bedrooms are light, with co-ordinated soft furnishings and decor. Guests may use the comfortable lounge and an adjacent conservatory, which opens onto a guests' garden.
10 rms (8 shr) 6 annexe rms (2 shr) (3 fmly) No smoking in 6 bedrooms No smoking in dining room No smoking in lounges CTV in 17 bedrooms Tea and coffee making facilities No dogs Licensed Cen ht CTV 12P
ROOMS: s £20-£30; d £40-£50; wkly b&b £140-£210*

Selected

QQQQ **The Six Bells Country Inn** The Green, Bardwell IP31 1AW (from A143 take turning marked Bardwell Windmill, premises 1m on left just before village green)
☎ 01359 250820 FAX 01359 250820
Closed 25 & 26 Dec rs Mondays
This charming country inn offers accommodation that has a cottagey feel, and forms part of a converted barn. Rooms are bright and cheerful, with pine furniture, en suite showers and lovely views of the surrounding countryside. The restaurant, open for lunch and dinner, offers dishes prepared from local fresh produce and cooked to order.
9 shr (1 fmly) No smoking in dining room CTV in all bedrooms Tea and coffee making facilities Direct dial from bedrooms Cen ht 40P Last d 9.30pm
ROOMS: s £40-£50; d £50-£75; wkly b&b £175-£200; wkly hlf-bd £190.75-£255*
MEALS: Lunch £9.95 Dinner £12.50&alc*
CARDS:

Premier Selected

QQQQQ Twelve Angel Hill 12 Angel Hill IP33 1UZ (in town centre by Abbey ruins and Cathedral)
☎ 01284 704088 FAX 01284 725549
Closed Jan
Bernie and John Clarke offer warm and friendly hospitality at this elegant Georgian town house, close to the cathedral. There are six rooms and all have been tastefully furnished with period furniture. Each has its own individual style and a high level of extra facilities, such as trouser press, books, magazines and mineral water. Public rooms include a dining room where a wide range is offered at breakfast. The Tudor style bar has a fireplace and there is a comfortable lounge.
6 bth/shr No smoking CTV in all bedrooms Tea and coffee making facilities Direct dial from bedrooms No dogs Licensed Cen ht No children 16yrs 3P No coaches
ROOMS: s £50; d £75-£80*
CARDS:

QQ York 32 Springfield Rd IP33 3AR ☎ 01284 753091
Closed Feb
In a quiet suburban setting, York Guest House is a large red brick building, enthusiastically run by the cheerful proprietor, Mrs Reeve. The thoughtfully appointed bedrooms provide comfortable and generally well proportioned accommodation with a pretty, airy decor.
7 rms (1 bth 1 shr) No smoking in 2 bedrooms No smoking in dining room No smoking in lounges CTV in all bedrooms Tea and coffee making facilities Cen ht No children 8yrs 3P No coaches

BUXTON Derbyshire Map 07 SK07

QQQ Buxton View 74 Corbar Rd SK17 6RJ (from Buxton town centre follow A5004 Whaley Bridge Road up Long Hill, 2nd turning on right)
☎ 01298 79222
Situated in a quiet residential area, overlooking the town and surrounding hills, this friendly guest house offers well appointed bedrooms. The lounge is comfortable and homely, and meals are served in the conservatory, facing out on to the garden.
5 bth/shr (1 fmly) No smoking in bedrooms No smoking in dining room CTV in all bedrooms Tea and coffee making facilities Cen ht 7P No coaches Last d 4pm
ROOMS: s £20-£22; d £40-£42; wkly b&b £133-£140; wkly hlf-bd £203-£210

Selected

QQQQ Buxton Wheel House Hotel 19 College Rd SK17 9DZ (A515 into Buxton. 1st left at lights onto Green Ln, 3rd on right onto College Rd.) ☎ 01298 24869 FAX 01298 24869
Closed 24 Dec-2 Jan
This very well maintained private hotel occupies an elevated position in a quiet residential area of the town. Stone built, it lies in attractive grounds and provides smart modern accommodation. Bedrooms are all well equipped and have comfortable beds and chairs. There is a choice of sitting areas for guests, and an attractive dining room.
9 bth/shr (2 fmly) No smoking CTV in all bedrooms Tea and coffee making facilities No dogs Licensed Cen ht CTV 10P Last d noon
ROOMS: s £25-£28; d £43-£48; wkly b&b £148-£180; wkly hlf-bd £225-£252*
CARDS:

Premier Selected

QQQQQ Coningsby 6 Macclesfield Rd SK17 9AH (between A515 and A53 on B5059) ☎ 01298 26735 FAX 01298 26735
This impressive Victorian house stands in immaculate gardens and has been lovingly restored over the years, retaining many original features. The house is just a short walk from the town centre and the Pavilion gardens. Bedrooms are very tastefully decorated and have been furnished and equipped with much care and attention. Downstairs there is a very comfortable guests' lounge and an elegant dining room. Friendly and caring hospitality is provided and the home cooking is of a very good standard.
3 shr No smoking CTV in all bedrooms Tea and coffee making facilities No dogs Licensed Cen ht No children 6P No coaches Last d 4pm
ROOMS: d £55-£70; wkly hlf-bd £274.75-£322*

Selected

QQQQ Grendon Bishops Ln SK17 6UN (0.5m from Buxton centre, just off behind Burbage Parish Church)
☎ 01298 78831
Grendon is a spacious Edwardian house standing in an acre of well tended grounds, overlooking beautiful countryside. The bedrooms are spacious and have been thoughtfully equipped and with one room having a four-poster bed. Public rooms are comfortable, and good home cooking is provided. The breakfast menu offers a wide variety. Friendly and personal service from the resident owners is guaranteed.
3 bth/shr No smoking CTV in all bedrooms Tea and coffee making facilities Cen ht CTV No children 10yrs 8P No coaches Croquet lawn Table tennis Last d 10am
ROOMS: s £28-£36; d £38-£46; wkly b&b £133-£160; wkly hlf-bd £200-£230*
CARDS:

Q Q *Griff* 2 Compton House SK17 9DN ☎ 01298 23628
Situated in a quiet residential area, just a short walk from the refurbished Pavilion Gardens, this large stone built property offers pine furnished bedrooms with modern en suite facilities. A hearty breakfast is served in the traditional dining room.
5 shr No smoking CTV in all bedrooms Tea and coffee making facilities No dogs Cen ht CTV No children 5P No coaches Last d noon

Selected

Q Q Q Q **The Grosvenor House Hotel** 1 Broad Walk SK17 6JE (near Opera House overlooking Pavilion Gardens and the Crescent) ☎ 01298 72439 FAX 01298 72439
Centrally located, overlooking Pavilion Gardens and the Opera House, this large Victorian hotel is also a coffee shop during the summer months. Anne and Graham Fairbairn have created comfortable and tastefully furnished bedrooms, with the larger rooms having fine views. Freshly prepared evening meals are available and there is a welcoming, spacious lounge.
8 bth/shr (2 fmly) No smoking in bedrooms No smoking in dining room CTV in all bedrooms Tea and coffee making facilities No dogs (ex guide dogs) Licensed No children 8yrs No coaches
ROOMS: s £42.50-£50; d £50-£70; wkly b&b £168-£224*

Q Q **Hawthorn Farm** Fairfield Rd SK17 7ED (on A6 Manchester/ Stockport rd) ☎ 01298 23230
Apr-Oct
This delightful Tudor farmhouse, set back from the Manchester road in attractive gardens, has been in the same family for over 300 years and has operated as a guest house since the 1950s. The lounge boasts a feature stone fireplace and many rooms display original beams. Bedrooms, half of which are in converted farm buildings, are well maintained and comfortably furnished.
6 rms (1 shr) 6 annexe rms (4 shr) (1 fmly) No smoking in dining room CTV in 8 bedrooms Tea and coffee making facilities Cen ht CTV 12P No coaches
ROOMS: s £22-£24; d £44-£50*

Selected

Q Q Q Q **Lakenham** 11 Burlington Rd SK17 9AL (Burlington Road runs betwen the B515 Macclesfield rd and the A53 St Johns Rd) ☎ 01298 79209
Enjoying a quiet location, set back from a tree-lined avenue opposite the Pavilion Gardens, this Victorian house retains much of its original character. Bedrooms, including one on the ground floor, are generally spacious and, whilst having the usual modern conveniences, are furnished in period fashion. A hearty breakfast is served in the airy dining room and there is a sitting room for guests' use.
6 bth/shr (3 fmly) No smoking in dining room CTV in all bedrooms Tea and coffee making facilities Licensed Cen ht 9P No coaches Last d 9am
ROOMS: d £50-£55; wkly b&b fr £175

Q Q Q **The Old Manse Private Hotel** 6 Clifton Rd, Silverlands SK17 6QL (from A6 approach Buxton via Safeway rdbt into Dale Rd B5059 200yds before bridge turn right along Peveril Rd into Clifton Rd) ☎ 01298 25638
Closed Xmas & New Year
Situated in a residential area within easy walking distance of the town centre, this large semi-detached Derbyshire stone fronted house offers comfortable value-for-money accommodation. Bedrooms are well equipped and many have modern en suite shower rooms. Public areas include a cosy sitting room with television and a combined bar and dining room where tasty set dinners and English breakfasts are served. Friendly and attentive service is offered by hosts Mr & Mrs Whitaker.
8 rms (4 shr) (2 fmly) No smoking in dining room Tea and coffee making facilities Licensed Cen ht CTV No children 5yrs 4P No coaches Last d 5pm
ROOMS: s fr £21; d £42-£48; wkly hlf-bd £202-£223*

Q Q Q **Roseleigh Hotel** 19 Broad Walk SK17 6JR (A6 to rdbt outside Safeway turn onto London Rd, at lights turn right, 100yds turn left by Swan pub, go down hill and turn right into Hartington Rd) ☎ 01298 24904
Situated opposite the Pavillion Gardens, new owners are returning this hotel to its former glory. Bedrooms, most of them with en suite facilities, are spacious and there is also a comfortable visitors' lounge. Freshly prepared meals are presented in the dining room and vegetarian options are always available.
13 rms (10 bth/shr) (2 fmly) No smoking CTV in all bedrooms Tea and coffee making facilities Licensed Cen ht 12P No coaches Last d 3pm
ROOMS: s £22-£32; d £48-£52; wkly b&b £160-£173; wkly hlf-bd £230-£264*
CARDS:

Q Q *Templeton* 13 Compton Rd SK17 9DN (A515 into Buxton, turn left into Green Lane, 50 yards on left into Compton Road) ☎ 01298 25275 FAX 01298 25275
This family run guest house is situated in a quiet residential area, within easy walking distance of the town centre. Modestly furnished bedrooms offer good value for money, whilst downstairs, there is a cosy lounge and dinner is available by arrangement.
6 rms (4 bth/shr) No smoking in dining room CTV in all bedrooms Tea and coffee making facilities No dogs Licensed Cen ht CTV No children 3yrs 6P No coaches Last d noon

Selected

Q Q Q Q **Westminster Hotel** 21 Broadwalk SK17 6JT (from A6, take 1st exit at rdbt for Bakewell,at 2nd rdbt take 3rd exit into Dale Road, through lights, turn right after 300yds, then 2nd left) ☎ 01298 23929 FAX 01298 71121
Norma and Derek Stephens provide a warm welcome at this small hotel, well situated for the town centre, yet enjoying the peace of the gardens and lake. Bedrooms are spacious, particularly at the front of the building, and all are attractively decorated. Public areas include a visitors' lounge and a dining room, both having pleasant views.

contd.

12 bth/shr No smoking in bedrooms No smoking in dining room CTV in all bedrooms Tea and coffee making facilities No dogs (ex guide dogs) Licensed Cen ht CTV No children 5yrs 14P Last d 3pm
ROOMS: s £32; d £50-£56; wkly b&b £150-£175*
CARDS:

CADNAM Hampshire Map 04 SU31

Selected

Q Q Q Q **Budds** *(SU310139)* Winsor Rd, Winsor SO40 2HN (M27 junct 1 follow A336 signed Totton, at Hayway pub turn left, Budds Farm is 1/3 mile on right hand side)
☎ 01703 812381 Mrs A M Dawe
Apr-Oct
There is a warm, homely atmosphere at this charming thatched farmhouse on the edge of the New Forest. The spacious bedrooms are comfortably appointed and suitably equipped. Guests have use of the cosy lounge. A generous English breakfast is served in the traditional dining room overlooking the pretty cottage garden.
2 rms (1 bth) (1 fmly) No smoking Tea and coffee making facilities No dogs (ex guide dogs) Cen ht CTV 3P 200 acres beef dairy
ROOMS: s £20; d £37-£38*

Selected

Q Q Q Q **Kents** *(SU315139)* Winsor Rd, Winsor SO40 2HN
☎ 01703 813497 Mrs A Dawe
Apr-Oct
This attractive thatched farmhouse belongs to a working dairy farm in the heart of the New Forest. Exposed beams are a feature throughout. The bedrooms overlook the pretty garden, and have quality furnishings and private facilities. A hearty breakfast is served in the traditional dining room, and guests are welcome to use the lounge which features an inglenook fireplace.
2 bth/shr (1 fmly) No smoking No dogs Cen ht CTV No children 8yrs 4P 200 acres beef dairy
ROOMS: d fr £37*

Q Q **The Old Well Restaurant** Romsey Rd, Copythorne SO40 2PE (On A31 between Cadnam and Ower, parallel to M27 between juncts 1 and 2)
☎ 01703 812321 & 812700 FAX 814464
This popular restaurant is located on the edge of the New Forest, offering three attractive rooms which are spacious and have modern bathrooms en suite, and three more simply furnished rooms in the older part of the house. Guests take their breakfast in the main dining room, and evening meals are served.
6 rms (3 bth) (2 fmly) No smoking in area of dining room CTV in all bedrooms Tea and coffee making facilities No dogs (ex guide dogs) Licensed Cen ht CTV No children 3yrs 40P
ROOMS: s £24-£40; d £38-£50*
CARDS:

Selected

Q Q Q Q **Walnut Cottage** Old Romsey Rd SO40 2NP (at Cadnam rdbt take A3090, Old Romsey rd is first on left)
☎ 01703 812275 FAX 01703 812275
Closed 24-26 Dec
This charming cottage is over 150 years old and located on the edge of the New Forest. Charming proprietors Eric and Charlotte Osgood provide a warm welcome and are happy to give guests information on the local area. The bedrooms all have en suite facilities and are attractively furnished; there is a comfortable lounge and guests may enjoy the lovely cottage garden.
3 bth/shr No smoking CTV in all bedrooms Tea and coffee making facilities No dogs (ex guide dogs) Cen ht CTV No children 14yrs 4P No coaches Free loan of bikes
ROOMS: s £28-£30; d £43-£44; wkly b&b £147*

CALDBECK Cumbria Map 11 NY34

Selected

Q Q Q Q ***Swaledale Watch Farm*** *(NY308398)* Whelpo CA7 8HQ (1m SW on B5299) ☎ 016974 78409 FAX 016974 78409
Mr & Mrs Savage
Closed Xmas
This modern farmhouse lies in a picturesque setting by the local stream. Nan and Arnold Savage have transformed their home into an attractive guest house with beautiful stonework and open fires in the comfortable public rooms and in the converted 'cowshed'. This contains two bedrooms and has its own lounge - an ideal unit for a party of four. While it is possible to dine out in the village, Nan's home cooked dinners, not to mention her hearty breakfasts, are as popular as ever.
2 bth/shr 2 annexe bth/shr (2 fmly) No smoking CTV in all bedrooms Tea and coffee making facilities No dogs (ex guide dogs) Cen ht CTV 8P Membership of local leisure centre 300 acres sheep Last d 2pm

CALLINGTON Cornwall & Isles of Scilly Map 02 SX36

Q Q Q **Dozmary** Tors View Close, Tavistock Rd PL17 7DY (from Callington town centre traffic lights, take A390 Tavistock Rd, left turning after 300yds into Tors View Close by 40mph sign)
☎ 01579 383677
Dozmary is a deceptively spacious dormer bungalow offering well presented accommodation. Two of the bedrooms are located on the ground floor. A combined lounge/dining room is available for guests.
3 bth/shr (1 fmly) No smoking CTV in all bedrooms Tea and coffee making facilities No dogs (ex guide dogs) Cen ht 4P No coaches
ROOMS: s £18; d £32; wkly b&b £105*

Q Q Q ***Manor House*** Rilla Mill PL17 7NT ☎ 01579 362354
Set by the River Lynher, these six stone-built cottages have extensive grounds to enjoy. Each cottage contains two bedrooms, a bathroom and an open-plan lounge and dining room.
Breakfast is served in the restaurant. Guests can cater for themselves or dine at the Inn.
6 annexe bth/shr (6 fmly) CTV in all bedrooms Tea and coffee making facilities Cen ht CTV ch fac 50P Last d 9.30pm
CARDS:

CALNE Wiltshire Map **03** ST97

Premier Selected

QQQQQ **Fenwicks** Lower Goatacre SN11 9HY (from Lyneham take A3102 towards Calne, after 0.75m turn left at bus shelter down Goatacre Lane, bear right at Harts Close, fork right at hill bottom) ☎ 01249 760645 FAX 01249 760645
Fenwicks is situated in the quiet and peaceful hamlet of Goatacre, with its attractive well kept gardens enjoying views over the open countryside. There are many places to visit within easy driving distance. Tastefully furnished well equipped bedrooms, with numerous modern comforts, and many thoughtful extras such as fresh fruit, flowers and electric blankets deomnstrate the care taken to guarantee guests a comfortable stay. There is an attractive sitting room where delicious meals are served around one large table. Certainly a place to come and be pampered.
3 bth/shr (1 fmly) No smoking CTV in all bedrooms Tea and coffee making facilities Direct dial from bedrooms No dogs Cen ht No children 8yrs 6P No coaches Last d by arrangement
ROOMS: s £28; d £45; wkly b&b £142-£176.40; wkly hlf-bd £198-£270*
CARDS:

Selected

QQQQ **Maundrell House** Horsebrook, The Green SN11 8DL (from A4 Calne to Marlborough road, turn left at White Hart Inn into The Green, straight ahead to Horsebrook. First house on left) ☎ 01249 821267 FAX 01249 821267
Closed 23 Dec-3 Jan
Situated in historic Calne, this lovely, wysteria clad, Grade II listed house was built in the 17th century. It is furnished and decorated in a comfortable style, suited to this elegant old house. The bedrooms are well equipped and the en suite bathrooms very modern. There are many thoughtful extras for guests' comfort such as biscuits, complimentary wine, fresh flowers and plants. The spacious sitting room has a large fireplace. Breakfast is served around one large table in the elegant dining room.
2 bth/shr No smoking CTV in all bedrooms Tea and coffee making facilities No dogs (ex guide dogs) Cen ht CTV No children 15yrs No coaches
ROOMS: s £28; d £46*

CAMBRIDGE Cambridgeshire Map **05** TL45

See also Little Gransden

QQQ ***Acorn*** 154 Chesterton Rd CB4 1DA ☎ 01223 353888 FAX 01223 350527
This small family run guest house offers bright and cheerful accomodation, all bedrooms are soundly appointed and equipped with a range of extras, and most have en suite facilities. The public areas feature a cosy dining room, and a lounge which guests can share with the family. Dinner is available by prior arrangement.
5 rms (4 shr) (1 fmly) No smoking in 2 bedrooms No smoking in dining room No smoking in lounges CTV in all bedrooms Tea and coffee making facilities No dogs (ex guide dogs) Cen ht CTV 7P Last d 6pm
CARDS:

QQQ **Arbury Lodge** 82 Arbury Rd CB4 2JE (turn off A14 onto A1309 (Milton Road) at 4th set of traffic lights, turn right into Arbury Road) ☎ 01223 364319 01233 566988 FAX 01223 566988
Closed 24-26 Dec
Visitors can expect a friendly welcome from Mrs Celentano at this well maintained family run guest house, which is situated in a relatively quiet residential area just on the outskirts of Cambridge city centre. The bedrooms are soundly appointed, cheerfully decorated and have attractive, well

contd.

co-ordinated soft furnishings and fabrics, some of the rooms have modern en-suite facilities and there are additional bath and shower rooms available for those without. Guests can enjoy a freshly cooked breakfast which is served at individual tables in the cosy dining room.
5 rms (2 shr) (2 fmly) No smoking CTV in all bedrooms Tea and coffee making facilities No dogs (ex guide dogs) Cen ht 8P
ROOMS: s £22-£25; d £38-£49*

Q Q Q **Assisi** 193 Cherry Hinton Rd CB1 4BX ☎ 01223 211466 & 246648 FAX 01223 412900
Closed 16 Dec-7 Jan
This guest house, situated to the south-east of Cambridge city centre, offers comfortable, modern accommodation. The public areas feature a small, pleasantly furnished lounge and a separate breakfast room. Bedrooms are well equipped and most have en suite facilities.
17 bth/shr (1 fmly) No smoking in 5 bedrooms No smoking in dining room No smoking in lounges CTV in all bedrooms Direct dial from bedrooms No dogs Cen ht CTV 15P
ROOMS: s £30-£33; d £43-£45*
CARDS:

Q Q Q **Avimore** 310 Cherry Hinton Rd CB1 4AU (1.75m S of city centre just inside Cambridge Ring Rd) ☎ 01223 410956 FAX 01223 410956
Visitors to this comfortable guest house are assured a warm welcome. Additional bedrooms are planned for the Millennium. Some of the rooms are en suite, though all offer modern facilities and a range of thoughtful extras. A good choice is served at breakfast in the bright and airy dining room.
6 rms (3 shr) (1 fmly) No smoking in bedrooms No smoking in dining room CTV in all bedrooms Tea and coffee making facilities Direct dial from bedrooms No dogs (ex guide dogs) Cen ht 9P No coaches
ROOMS: s £25; d £40-£45*
CARDS:

Q Q Q **Aylesbray Lodge** 5 Mowbray Rd CB1 4SR
(M11 junct 11 towards Cambridge, turn right at 2nd set of lights, go through lights and left at rdbt, Aylesbray Lodge is 50yds on right hand side)
☎ 01223 240089 FAX 01223 240089
This lovely house offers smart accommodation in tasteful, decorative bedrooms. Maximum guest comfort is assured as all rooms have been provided with a wide range of thoughtful facilities and modern en suite shower rooms. Two four-poster beds are available and are well worth requesting. Smoking is restricted to the well appointed lounge. Tasty breakfasts are served in the pleasant dining room.
6 shr (1 fmly) No smoking in bedrooms No smoking in dining room CTV in all bedrooms Tea and coffee making facilities Direct dial from bedrooms No dogs (ex guide dogs) Cen ht 6P
ROOMS: s £30-£35; d £42-£50*
CARDS:

Q Q **Benson House** 24 Huntingdon Rd CB3 0HH (on A604 near New Hall & Fitzwilliam College) ☎ 01223 311594 FAX 01223 510744
Popular with university visitors and tourists, Benson House is located close to the city centre and to New Hall and Fitzwilliam Colleges. Bedrooms come in various shapes and sizes, a few are slightly compact; nevertheless all are pleasant in appearance and soundly appointed.
5 rms (2 shr) (3 fmly) No smoking in dining room CTV in all bedrooms Tea and coffee making facilities Cen ht 5P
ROOMS: s £20-£40; d £36-£50*
CARDS:

Q Q Q **Brooklands** 95 Cherry Hinton Rd CB1 4BS ☎ 01223 242035 FAX 01223 242035
A warm welcome awaits at this small guest house, where the rooms are individually decorated, well equipped and tastefully appointed; one room has a four-poster bed. Guests have the use of a comfortable lounge, and home cooked evening meals are available (by prior arrangement) in the cheerful dining room.
5 bth/shr No smoking in bedrooms No smoking in dining room CTV in all bedrooms Tea and coffee making facilities Direct dial from bedrooms No dogs (ex guide dogs) Cen ht CTV 5P No coaches Snooker Sauna Gymnasium Last d noon
ROOMS: s £30-£35; d £40-£50*
CARDS:

Q Q **City Haven** 20 St Margarets Square CB1 4AP (in cul-de-sac just off Cherry Hinton road) ☎ 01223 411188
A well established and friendly guest house in a quiet cul-de-sac south of the city centre. This no-smoking house offers soundly appointed bedrooms of varying sizes. Breakfast is taken in a separate dining room.
14 rms (3 shr) No smoking CTV in all bedrooms Tea and coffee making facilities No dogs (ex guide dogs) Cen ht 12P
ROOMS: s £23-£30; d £38-£45*
CARDS:

Q Q Q **Cristina's** 47 St Andrews Rd CB4 1DH
☎ 01223 365855 & 327700 FAX 01223 365855
Closed 25-27 Dec
Standards of housekeeping and maintenance are very good throughout this no-smoking establishment, just 15 minutes walk from the city centre. The public areas include a comfortable lounge and an informal dining room. Accommodation is bright and cheerful in appearance, and the majority of rooms have modern en suite showers.
9 rms (7 shr) (1 fmly) No smoking CTV in all bedrooms Tea and coffee making facilities No dogs Cen ht CTV 8P
ROOMS: s £35-£42; d £42-£49*

Q Q Dykelands 157 Mowbray Rd CB1 4SP (A10/M11 junct 11, follow A1309, at 5th set of traffic lights turn right, carry on to the 1st rdbt, 1st exit, Mowbray Rd, last house on right) ☎ 01223 244300 FAX 01223 566746

This family run guest house offers modern comfortable accommodation, generally of good proportions; all the bedrooms are soundly furnished and decorated in a bright, smart colour scheme. A new extension includes a cosy residents' lounge and guests are welcome to use the garden to the rear.

9 rms (6 shr) (3 fmly) No smoking in bedrooms No smoking in dining room No smoking in lounges CTV in all bedrooms Tea and coffee making facilities Cen ht 7P

ROOMS: s £23-£42; d £35-£42*

CARDS:

Q Q Q Fairways 141-143 Cherry Hinton Rd CB1 4BX (from city centre towards Addenbrookes Hospital turn off A1307 (after bridge) then left into Cherry Hinton Rd) ☎ 01223 246063 FAX 01223 212093

Closed 22 Dec-1 Jan

Mr and Mrs Slatter have recently upgraded the bedrooms with hand-made pine furniture, cheerful wall coverings and co-ordinated borders. The public rooms are smartly decorated and include a breakfast room and a pleasant airy lounge which incorporates a well stocked bar. All of the rooms have a range of extra facilities.

15 rms (8 shr) (3 fmly) No smoking in dining room CTV in all bedrooms Tea and coffee making facilities Direct dial from bedrooms No dogs (ex guide dogs) Licensed Cen ht CTV 20P Pool table

ROOMS: s £22-£30; d £37-£48*

CARDS:

Selected

Q Q Q Q **De Freville House** 166 Chesterton Rd CB4 1DA (on ring road at junct of Chesterton Rd and Elizabeth Way) ☎ 01223 354993

The Hunters are enthusiastic and friendly hosts who have tastefully restored and furnished this Victorian house. The lower ground floor breakfast room is particularly cheerful and inviting and guests have the use of a comfortable lounge; Mr Hunter's collection of large clocks and grandfather clocks can be seen throughout the house. Bedrooms are all individually decorated, and light and attractive in appearance, a high proportion have modern en suite or private bathrooms.

8 rms (6 bth/shr) No smoking CTV in all bedrooms Tea and coffee making facilities No dogs Cen ht CTV No children 10yrs 2P No coaches

ROOMS: s £35-£45; d £48-£58

Q Q Q **Hamden** 89 High St, Cherry Hinton CB1 4LU (M11 junct 11 for Cambridge via Trumpington, 2nd set of lights turn right into Long Rd, Queen Ediths Way and Cherry Hinton High Street) ☎ 01223 413263 FAX 01223 245960

Guests receive a warm welcome from Mr and Mrs Casciano at their charming guest house, located in the centre of the village of Cherry Hinton. Bedrooms are light and comfortably appointed, each has a good modern shower room. The public areas are limited to a light and airy open-plan kitchen/breakfast room.

5 shr (1 fmly) No smoking CTV in all bedrooms Tea and coffee making facilities Direct dial from bedrooms No dogs (ex guide dogs) Cen ht No children 10yrs 6P No coaches

ROOMS: s £25-£28; d £40-£45*

CARDS:

Q Q Q ***Hamilton Hotel*** 156 Chesterton Rd CB4 1DA (1m NE of city centre, off ring road A1134) ☎ 01223 365664 FAX 01223 314866

Closed 25 & 26 Dec

Situated close to the city centre this hotel offers warm, comfortable and soundly appointed accommodation. All rooms have a range of extra facilities. The smart public areas include a restaurant with a small dispensing bar, where a selection of evening meals and snacks is served.

18 rms (13 shr) (3 fmly) No smoking in dining room CTV in all bedrooms Tea and coffee making facilities Direct dial from bedrooms No dogs (ex guide dogs) Licensed Cen ht No children 4yrs 18P No coaches Last d noon

CARDS:

Q Q Q **Helen Hotel** 167 Hills Rd CB2 2RJ (1m E, follow signs to A604 Colchester) ☎ 01223 246465 FAX 01223 214406

Closed Xmas

In the south-east of the city, the Papsons' well run guest house is popular with business and leisure guests alike. The public areas have undergone a major refurbishment programme, and further plans are afoot to upgrade the well equipped and relaxing accommodation too.

22 bth/shr (2 fmly) No smoking in dining room No smoking in 1 lounge CTV in all bedrooms Tea and coffee making facilities Direct dial from bedrooms No dogs (ex guide dogs) Licensed Cen ht 12P

ROOMS: s £38-£50; d £55-£65*

CARDS:

Q Q Q ***Lensfield Hotel*** 53 Lensfield Rd CB2 1EN (on SW side of city centre) ☎ 01223 355017 Telex no 818183 FAX 01223 312022

Closed 2wks Xmas

Though accomodation at the Lensfield varies in size and style, it is comfortable and well maintained; the most recently refurbished rooms are of a particularly good standard. On the lower ground floor there is a small bar with a smart restaurant and conservatory adjacent. An extensive a la carte or fixed price menu is offered and due to the proud traditions of the Greek owners, there is always an authentic dish available.

36 rms (2 bth 18 shr) (4 fmly) No smoking in 4 bedrooms No smoking in area of dining room No smoking in lounges CTV in all bedrooms Tea and coffee making facilities Direct dial from bedrooms No dogs Licensed Cen ht CTV 7P Last d 8.45pm

CARDS:

Q Q **Milton** 61-63 Milton Rd CB4 1XA ☎ 01223 311625 FAX 01223 565100

The Milton is found on the northern side of the city and offers soundly appointed accommodation. Soft furnishings and decor are colour co-ordinated and bedrooms have en suite showers. The public rooms include an open-plan dining room and lounge, which overlook the patio and rear garden. Evening meals can be arranged with prior notice.

6 rms (4 shr) No smoking in dining room No smoking in lounges CTV in all bedrooms Tea and coffee making facilities No dogs Cen ht CTV 6P

Selected

Q Q Q Q **Old School Hotel & Guest House** 9 Greenside, Waterbeach CB5 9HW (0.50m from A10 in centre of Waterbeach village overlooking green) ☎ 01223 861609 FAX 01223 441683

Closed Xmas wk

This converted school overlooks the green in the small village of Waterbeach. Mary and Gerry Taylor are enthusiastic hosts who create a relaxed and friendly environment for their guests. The modern

bedrooms are pleasantly decorated and well maintained; each room is thoughtfully equipped and has modern en suite facilities; however, room sizes do vary. Refreshments are readily available in the pleasant conservatory lounge.
8 shr No smoking in dining room CTV in all bedrooms Tea and coffee making facilities Direct dial from bedrooms No dogs (ex guide dogs) Licensed Cen ht CTV 8P No coaches Indoor swimming pool (heated) Sauna Last d 7.45pm
ROOMS: s fr £38.50; d fr £55*
CARDS:

Selected

Q Q Q Q *Sorrento Hotel* 196 Cherry Hinton Rd CB1 4AN
☎ 01223 243533 FAX 01223 213463
The Ruggiero's family run establishment is popular with business and leisure guests who appreciate modern conveniences combined with the warm hospitality offered. Diners have a good choice of traditional dishes from European menus. Most of the well equipped bedrooms have been recently upgraded and are attractive and soundly appointed.
24 bth/shr (5 fmly) No smoking in 4 bedrooms No smoking in area of dining room No smoking in 1 lounge CTV in all bedrooms Tea and coffee making facilities Direct dial from bedrooms Licensed Cen ht CTV 27P Petanque Last d 8.30pm
CARDS:

Q Q Q ***Southampton*** 7 Elizabeth Way CB4 1DE ☎ 01223 357780 FAX 01223 314297
This family run guest house is located in the centre of the city. The property is well presented and features a neat dining room where guests can enjoy a hearty breakfast. The bedrooms are bright and fresh, have modern en suite facilities, and are well equipped.
6 bth/shr (3 fmly) No smoking in dining room CTV in 5 bedrooms Tea and coffee making facilities Direct dial from bedrooms No dogs Cen ht 8P

Q Q Q **Suffolk House** 69 Milton Rd CB4 1XA (1.25m from A10/A14/A1309 junction) ☎ 01223 352016 FAX 01223 566816
A warm welcome can be expected at this family run guest house, situated near the city centre. Most bedrooms are of comfortable proportions, bright and cheerful, thoughtfully laid out, and have en suite facilities. Guests can enjoy a hearty breakfast in the light and airy dining room, which has pleasant views of the garden.
8 bth/shr (4 fmly) No smoking in dining room No smoking in lounges CTV in all bedrooms Tea and coffee making facilities Direct dial from bedrooms No dogs Cen ht No children 10yrs 9P No coaches
ROOMS: s £52-£70; d £58-£72*
CARDS:

CAMELFORD Cornwall & Isles of Scilly Map 02 SX18

Selected

Q Q Q Q **Pendragon House** Davidstow PL32 9XR (located on A395 between A30 Launceston and A39 Camelford. 0.5m beyond St David's Church. Davidstow) ☎ 01840 261131 FAX 01840 261131
With views across Bodmin Moor and Dartmoor, this Victorian former rectory is truly a family home, where guests are welcomed as friends. Ideally located for visiting the many attractions of the area, Pendragon House is set in one and a half acres of well tended, gardens and grounds. The individually furnished and decorated bedrooms vary in size and are comfortable and well equipped. Evening meals are available on request and provide excellent value for money, using fresh local produce where ever possible. Light lunches and cream teas are also served – in the garden on sunny days.
3 bth/shr No smoking CTV in all bedrooms Tea and coffee making facilities No dogs (ex guide dogs) Cen ht No children 7yrs 6P No coaches Last d 9pm
ROOMS: s £20-£21; d £40-£42; wkly b&b £130-£137; wkly hlf-bd £180-£187

CANTERBURY Kent Map 05 TR15

See also Womenswold

Q Q Q **Beech Bank** Duckpit Ln, Waltham CT4 5QA (B2068 from Canterbury for approx 4m, turn right into Petham village and left into Duckpit Lane after The Duke public house. House 2m on left)
☎ 01227 700302 FAX 01227 700302
Closed 20 Dec-5 Jan
A 15th-century Tudor coach house offering three bedrooms, two of which are en suite. The rooms are individually furnished and decorated to maintain the character of the house; they are also equipped with a number of modern facilities. A good choice is served at breakfast, taken in the elegant Victorian conservatory which overlooks the pretty garden, and doubles as a sun lounge.
3 bth/shr (1 fmly) No smoking CTV in 2 bedrooms Tea and coffee making facilities Direct dial from bedrooms No dogs Cen ht No children 4yrs 8P No coaches Badminton Volleyball
ROOMS: s £30-£40; d £40-£45; wkly b&b £210-£280*

Q **Castle Court** 8 Castle St CT1 2QF (at Norman castle turn left into Castle St, house 200 metres on right) ☎ 01227 463441 FAX 01227 463441
This well maintained house offers a good central location in an attractive street near the castle. The bedrooms are bright and well appointed with modest furnishings. A traditional breakfast is served in the lower ground-floor dining room.
10 rms (4 shr) (2 fmly) No smoking in dining room CTV in all bedrooms Cen ht CTV 3P
ROOMS: s £19-£23; d £36-£44*
CARDS:

Q Q **Cathedral Gate Hotel** 36 Burgate CT1 2HA (next to main gateway into cathedral precincts) ☎ 01227 464381 FAX 01227 462800
Built in 1438 this private hotel is centrally located between the tranquillity of the cathedral and the bustle of the shopping precinct. The sloping floors, large oak beams and winding corridors show their mediaeval origins. Bedrooms are attractively furnished and are well equipped. A comfortable lounge is available to guests. Breakfast can be served in the bedroom or the small breakfast room.
12 rms (2 bth) 12 annexe rms (10 bth/shr) (5 fmly) No smoking in dining room CTV in all bedrooms Tea and coffee making facilities Direct dial from bedrooms Licensed Cen ht CTV Last d 9pm
ROOMS: s £22-£51.50; d £40-£76.50*
CARDS:

QQQ **Chaucer Lodge** 62 New Dover Rd CT1 3DT (on A2 out of city centre to Dover, 0.25m S) ☎ 01227 459141 FAX 01227 459141
This well maintained guest house is within a 10 minute walk of the city centre, and provides particularly good amenities, with attractively decorated bedrooms furnished in modern style, and a well appointed dining room. Personally run by the proprietor Mrs M Wilson, the atmosphere is very friendly.
6 bth/shr (2 fmly) No smoking CTV in all bedrooms Tea and coffee making facilities No dogs Cen ht 14P No coaches Last d 6.30pm
ROOMS: s £25-£40; d £40-£50; wkly b&b £175-£285; wkly hlf-bd £240-£380*
CARDS:

Selected

Q Q Q Q **Ersham Lodge Hotel** 12 New Dover Rd CT1 3AP
☎ 01227 463174 FAX 01227 455482
1 Jan-15 Dec
This twin-gabled and galleried Victorian house has been run by the Pellay family for over 18 years, it is located close to the town and cathedral. The bedrooms vary in size and shape, but all are well presented and comfortable, some are situated on the ground floor. There is a cosy lounge bar and a spacious breakfast room which looks out onto the patio and garden.
13 rms (2 bth 10 shr) (3 fmly) No smoking in 6 bedrooms No smoking in dining room CTV in all bedrooms Tea and coffee making facilities Direct dial from bedrooms No dogs (ex guide dogs) Licensed Cen ht 12P
ROOMS: s £38-£47; d £53-£61*
CARDS:

Premier Selected

Q Q Q Q Q **Magnolia House** 36 St Dunstan's Ter CT2 8AX
(from A2 take turning for Canterbury. turn left at first roundabout approaching the city (signposted university). Third turning on right)
☎ 01227 765121 & 0585 595970 FAX 01227 765121
Magnolia House is personally run by Ann and John Davies who welcome guests into their home. Bedrooms are attractive and neatly co-ordinated, with small extra touches. A cosy lounge looks out onto the small front garden, and contains various books and magazines. Herbs from the garden become ingredients for Ann Davies' evening meals, which are a delight and can be sampled from November to February by prior arrangement.
7 bth/shr No smoking CTV in all bedrooms Tea and coffee making facilities No dogs Cen ht No children 12yrs 5P No coaches
ROOMS: s £36-£55; d £68-£110*
CARDS:

See advertisement on p.129.

Premier Selected

Q Q Q Q Q **The Old Rectory** Ashford Rd, Chartham CT4 7HS
(take A28 towards Ashford, follow road for apprx 2.50 miles, Old Rectory on right just before x-roads signed Chartham)
☎ 01227 730075 FAX 01227 731929
Closed 17 Dec-10 Jan
This charming Georgian house is located on the outskirts of Canterbury and offers peaceful well presented accommodation. The bedrooms overlook the garden; they are comfortably furnished and have attractive co-ordinated decor and modern en suite bathrooms. Proprietor Mrs Creasy provides a friendly relaxed atmosphere, and a traditional English breakfast which is served in the dining room.
3 bth/shr No smoking CTV in 1 bedroom Tea and coffee making facilities No dogs (ex guide dogs) Cen ht CTV No children 14yrs 5P No coaches Last d noon
ROOMS: s £30-£45; d £47-£60*
CARDS:

CLOSED

Q Q Q **Oriel Lodge** 3 Queens Av CT2 8AY (entering town on A2 from London, 400yds after first roundabout (Victoria Hotel) turn left into Queens Avenue) ☎ 01227 462845 FAX 01227 462845
A detached Edwardian family house, Oriel Lodge is located near the city centre. The bedrooms are bright and attractively decorated and have been comfortably furnished. Guests are welcomed with afternoon tea and cake in the lounge, where a log fire burns in the winter months. A choice of breakfast is offered and served in the well appointed dining room.
6 rms (2 shr) (1 fmly) No smoking in bedrooms No smoking in dining room CTV in all bedrooms Tea and coffee making facilities No dogs Cen ht No children 6yrs 6P No coaches
ROOMS: s £24-£30; d £40-£60; wkly b&b £126-£189*
CARDS:

Selected

Q Q Q Q **The Pilgrims Hotel** 18 The Friars CT1 2AS
(to Canterbury follow signs for Marlowe Theatre, establishment situated opposite) ☎ 01227 464531 FAX 01227 762514
Located in the centre of historic Canterbury opposite the Marlowe Theatre, the Pilgrims Hotel has parts that date back some 350 years. Bedrooms are all en suite, comfortably appointed and well equipped. Public areas include a spacious bar and an attractive restaurant. A good selection of dishes is available from the bar or restaurant menu and a few daily specials are offered, including fresh fish.
15 bth (1 fmly) CTV in all bedrooms Tea and coffee making facilities Direct dial from bedrooms No dogs (ex guide dogs) Cen ht
Last d 9.30pm
ROOMS: s fr £45; d fr £60*
CARDS:

Premier Selected

QQQQQ **Thanington Hotel** 140 Wincheap CT1 3RY (on A28, just outside City Walls) ☎ 01227 453227 FAX 01227 453225
Personally run by Jill and David Jenkins this Georgian hotel is located close to the town centre and cathedral. The accommodation is divided between a smart modern extension and four superior rooms in the main house, three with four-poster beds. Each room is well equipped, including a trouser press, safe and lots of thoughtful extras. Public rooms comprise a small lounge, and a well appointed dining room.
16 rms (15 bth) (2 fmly) No smoking in 5 bedrooms No smoking in dining room CTV in all bedrooms Tea and coffee making facilities Direct dial from bedrooms Licensed Cen ht CTV 12P No coaches Indoor swimming pool (heated) Threequarter size snooker table
ROOMS: s £48-£52; d £68-£88*
CARDS:

Q Q Q **Upper Ansdore** *(TR118498)* Duckpit Ln, Petham CT4 5QB (from Canterbury take B2068 and turn right through village. Take left hand fork and after 1.5m turn right to Upper Ansdore)
☎ 01227 700672 FAX 01227 700672 Mr & Mrs R D Linch
Closed Xmas & New Year
Parts of Upper Ansdore Farmhouse date back to the 14th century and the house once belonged to a former Lord Mayor of London. Found in a peaceful rural setting, the farmhouse offers far reaching views across the valley. All rooms are en suite and have been comfortably furnished. A full cooked breakfast is served in the dining room.
3 shr (1 fmly) No smoking Tea and coffee making facilities No dogs (ex guide dogs) Cen ht 5P Riding 4 acres mixed smallholding
ROOMS: d £42*

Selected

Q Q Q Q **Waltham Court Hotel** Kake St, Petham CT4 5SB (1.5m through village towards Waltham)
☎ 01227 700413 FAX 01227 700127
This attractive Georgian house is in a quiet rural location between Petham and Waltham. Chives restaurant is the hub of the building and has a good local following. The bedrooms are prettily decorated with pastel fabrics and pine furniture; all four rooms have modern en suite facilities. There is also a bar and comfortable lounge area.
4 bth/shr (1 fmly) No smoking in area of dining room CTV in all bedrooms Tea and coffee making facilities No dogs (ex guide dogs) Licensed Cen ht ch fac 45P Sauna Last d 9.45pm
ROOMS: s £40-£48; d £58-£68; wkly b&b £200-£336; wkly hlf-bd £305-£490*
CARDS:

Selected

Q Q Q Q **The White House** 6 St Peters Ln CT1 2BP (20yds off main shopping area inside old city walls) ☎ 01227 761836
This attractive Regency house is situated in a quiet road close to the shops, and offers comfortable and well maintained accommodation. The bedrooms all have modern en suite facilities and attractive co-ordinated decor. Guests may relax in the lounge where a fire burns in the winter months. A traditional breakfast is served in the smart dining room.
9 bth/shr (2 fmly) No smoking in dining room No smoking in lounges CTV in all bedrooms Tea and coffee making facilities No dogs Cen ht CTV 2P
ROOMS: s £25-£30; d £40-£50*

CARLISLE Cumbria Map 11 NY45

See also Brampton, Castle Carrock & Longtown

Selected

Q Q Q Q **Acer House** 146 Warwick Rd CA1 1LG (M6 junct43, through 4 sets of traffic lights, Acer House is on left opposite St Aidans church) ☎ 01228 531562
This smart, recently refurbished Victorian house is situated in a quiet residential area close to the city centre, handy for the railway station. The bright and well maintained bedrooms benefit from powerful modern showers. A hearty Cumbrian breakfast is served in the traditionally styled dining room.
3 shr No smoking CTV in all bedrooms Tea and coffee making facilities Direct dial from bedrooms No dogs Cen ht No coaches
ROOMS: d £40; wkly b&b £140

Selected

Q Q Q Q **Angus Hotel & Almonds Bistro** 14 Scotland Rd CA3 9DG (exit M6 at junct 44, on A7 after 6th set of traffic lights)
☎ 01228 523546 FAX 01228 531895
rs 24 Dec-6 Jan (b & b only)
Geoff and Elaine Webster offer a warm welcome to guests at their family-run hotel, which lies on the main road north of the city centre. Bedrooms are well equipped and quiet, most are en suite. Almonds Bistro, alongside the hotel, is run by the Websters and offers diners good food and home baking every day except Sunday. A comfortable lounge where drinks can be served is available for use by guests.
14 rms (11 bth/shr) (4 fmly) No smoking in 8 bedrooms No smoking in area of dining room CTV in all bedrooms Tea and coffee making facilities Licensed Cen ht CTV 8P Last d 9.30pm
ROOMS: s £30-£42; d £40-£54; wkly b&b fr £170; wkly hlf-bd fr £227.50
CARDS:

Q Q **Blackwell Farm** *(NY401530)* Blackwell, Durdar CA2 4SH (exit M6 at junct 42 in direction of Dalston. At Black Lion public house crossroads turn right for Carlisle. After 1.5m turn left at White Ox)
☎ 01228 524073 Mrs A Westmorland
A cobbled yard with traditional stables provides a quaint and natural setting for this old farmhouse set close to the racecourse on the edge of the city. Bedrooms are nicely decorated and although lacking washbasins, the bathroom is close by. There is a cosy lounge where breakfast is also taken, around one table.
2 rms (1 fmly) No smoking in bedrooms Tea and coffee making facilities Cen ht CTV 4P 120 acres
ROOMS: s £17; d £32; wkly b&b £119*

Q Q Q **Cambro House** 173 Warwick Rd CA1 1LP (turn off M6 junct 43, straight down Warwick Rd, approx 1m on right hand side before St Adins Church) ☎ 01228 543094
David and Alice Mawson are carefully refurbishing their period Victorian home. Spacious bedrooms are stylish in decor and thoughtfully equipped. An attractive morning room provides the venue for a freshly prepared, hearty Cumbrian breakfast which makes excellent use of local produce.
3 shr No smoking CTV in all bedrooms Tea and coffee making facilities No dogs (ex guide dogs) Cen ht No children 5yrs 2P No coaches
ROOMS: s £20-£25; d £30-£35*

Q Q Q **Cherry Grove** 87 Petteril St CA1 2AW (M6 junct 43, 4th set of traffic lights, Corner House is on left hand side looking up towards M6)
☎ 01228 541942 FAX 541942
In the summer, colourful plants help to pinpoint this red brick house which offers bright cheery bedrooms and a cosy dining room which doubles as a lounge. Recent refurbishment has further increased overall standards and now all bedrooms are smartly en suite.
5 rms (4 shr) (2 fmly) No smoking in 2 bedrooms No smoking in dining room No smoking in lounges CTV in all bedrooms Tea and coffee making facilities Cen ht 2P No coaches Last d 24hrs
ROOMS: s £25-£30; d £35-£40*

Q Q Q **Craighead** 6 Hartington Place CA1 1HL (M6 junct 43 through 4 sets of traffic lights, then take the 4th turning on right hand side)
☎ 01228 596767
rs 25-26 Dec & 1 Jan
Set in a quiet terrace, this deceptively spacious Grade II listed Georgian town house offers individually styled and thoughtfully equipped bedrooms, including one massive family room. John and Pam Smith provide expert customer care. Breakfast is taken at two tables in a fine period sitting room.
5 rms (1 shr) (1 fmly) No smoking in dining room CTV in all bedrooms Tea and coffee making facilities Cen ht CTV No coaches
ROOMS: s £16-£18; d £31-£34; wkly b&b £100-£120*

Q Q Q East View 110 Warwick Rd CA1 1JU
(on main rd into city from junct 43 of M6)
☎ 01228 522112 FAX 522112
An attractively decorated end-of-terrace house with inviting bedrooms in a variety of sizes, most furnished in attractive pine. Breakfast is taken in a stylish little dining room. There is no lounge.
8 shr (3 fmly) No smoking in dining room CTV in all bedrooms Tea and coffee making facilities No dogs (ex guide dogs) Cen ht 4P
ROOMS: s £18-£25; d £32-£35*

Selected

Q Q Q Q Fern Lee 9 St Aidans Rd CA1 1LT (M6 exit junct 43 along Warwick Road. Turn right at 4th set of traffic lights onto Victoria Place. House first on left behind St Aidan's church) ☎ 01228 511930
An impressive programme of upgrading has seen this detached house transformed into a very stylish guest house. The public rooms are attractively decorated and include a comfortable lounge and a cosy dining room; evening meals are available by prior arrangement. Bedrooms are well equipped and contemporary in style, and each room is individually decorated, with quality soft furnishings and cheerful colour schemes.
8 bth/shr (2 fmly) No smoking in bedrooms No smoking in dining room No smoking in 1 lounge CTV in all bedrooms Tea and coffee making facilities No dogs (ex guide dogs) Cen ht CTV 7P
No coaches Last d 7pm
ROOMS: s £22-£25; d £40-£44*

Selected

Q Q Q Q *Howard House* 27 Howard Place CA1 1HR
☎ 01228 29159 & 512550 FAX 01228 512550
Lawrence and Sandra Fisher's late-Victorian town house occupies a discreet position in a residential terrace. Decorated and furnished in period style, with an abundance of pictures, prints and personal items, it has the ambience of a cosy lived-in private home, which it is. One can relax in the lounge or indeed in the bedrooms, all of which are thoughtfully equipped and have seating areas, games and reading material. Breakfast is normally taken round the one table in the dining room.
5 rms (2 shr) (2 fmly) No smoking in dining room CTV in all bedrooms Tea and coffee making facilities No dogs (ex guide dogs) Cen ht CTV Last d 2.30pm
CARDS:

Q Q Q Howard Lodge 90 Warwick Rd CA1 1JU (M6 junct 43 turn into Carlisle, cont along Warwick Rd for approx 1m going thro 5 sets of lights, Howard lodge is on left towards town centre) ☎ 01228 529842
Lying close to the town centre, this red-brick, end-of-terrace house offers individually-styled bedrooms that are decoratively appealing and have modern en suite facilities; each bedroom is well equipped and includes a hair dryer and clock-radio.
6 bth/shr (2 fmly) No smoking in dining room No smoking in lounges CTV in all bedrooms Tea and coffee making facilities Cen ht CTV 7P
Last d 6pm
ROOMS: s £15-£25; d £30-£40; wkly b&b £105-£175; wkly hlf-bd £140-£210*

Selected

Q Q Q Q Ivy House 101 Warwick Rd CA1 1EA (M6 junct 43, road towards Carlisle is Warwick Rd, 1m on right opposite RC church)
☎ 01228 530432
Closed 23-26 Dec
Situated close to the city centre, this ivy clad house provides an ideal location from which to explore local attractions including Hadrian's Wall. The comfortable open plan lounge boasts an imposing Georgian fireplace as well fine period pieces. Bedrooms are attractively decorated and come in a variety of sizes. Breakfast is taken at an antique banqueting table just off the lounge.
3 rms (1 bth/shr) No smoking in dining room No smoking in lounges CTV in all bedrooms Tea and coffee making facilities Cen ht 2P
No coaches
ROOMS: d £28-£36*

Q Q Q Kingstown Hotel 246 Kingstown Rd CA3 0DE
(exit M6 at junct 44, take A7 towards city centre. Hotel 0.25m on left hand side) ☎ 01228 515292 FAX 01228 515292
Situated on the northern side of the city, this small family run hotel has a cosy and inviting atmosphere. Bedrooms are thoughtfully equipped. It has a small residents' bar, attractive adjoining lounge and a bright and cheerful dining room, where freshly prepared home-cooked meals are served.
8 bth/shr (1 fmly) No smoking in dining room CTV in all bedrooms Tea and coffee making facilities Licensed Cen ht 12P No coaches
Last d 9pm
ROOMS: s £28-£37; d fr £45
CARDS:

Q Q Q **The Warren** 368 Warwick Rd CA1 2RU (exit M6 junct 43 and proceed 0.5m down main road. Opposite Esso petrol station)
☎ 01228 533663 & 512916 FAX 01228 533663
This guest house was built in 1938 and once was known as the Star Inn. The comfortable lounge doubles as the breakfast room, although diners can eat in the conservatory. Bedrooms come in a variety of sizes, all adorned with colourful fabrics and equipped with every conceivable extra.
6 rms (5 shr) (1 fmly) No smoking in bedrooms No smoking in area of dining room CTV in all bedrooms Tea and coffee making facilities Direct dial from bedrooms Cen ht CTV 6P No coaches Last d early am
ROOMS: s £16.50-£24; d £40*

CARNFORTH Lancashire Map **07** SD47

Q Q ***Marwin House*** Duke St LA6 1PY ☎ 01524 781144 & 0378 135659
Situated in the unspoilt village of Holme, this attractive white cottage is close to the Yorkshire Dales and South Lakes. Bedrooms are bright and welcoming; a family room is available. A hearty breakfast is served around one table in the comfortable lounge dining room.
2 rms No smoking CTV in all bedrooms Tea and coffee making facilities No dogs Cen ht CTV 4P Last d on request

Premier Selected

Q Q Q Q Q **New Capernwray Farm** Capernwray LA6 1AD (from M6 exit 35 take signs for Over Kellet/Kirkby Lonsdale. Left at village green in Over Kellett, house on left after 2m)
☎ 01524 734284 FAX 01524 734284
Mar-Oct
Peter and Sally Townend offer warm hospitality at their neat white walled farmhouse which is within easy reach of main road routes. Bedrooms are individual, and well equipped with thoughtful little extras. Sally and Peter offer freshly prepared four course dinners in the tastefully decorated dining room. Breakfasts, which depend much on local produce, are an ideal way to start the day. The drawing room is a quiet place to relax with views of the garden and countryside.
3 bth/shr No smoking CTV in all bedrooms Tea and coffee making facilities Cen ht No children 10yrs 4P No coaches Last d 5pm
ROOMS: d £62-£68
CARDS:

CARSINGTON Derbyshire Map **08** SK25

Selected

Q Q Q Q **Henmore Grange** Hopton DE4 4DF (turn into Hopton from B5035 and take first left at Wirksworth end of bypass)
☎ 01629 540420 FAX 01629 540720
Henmore Grange has been created from a stone farmhouse and disused farm buildings, resulting in a property of great character, with many original beams and other features of interest. Some bedrooms overlook Carsington Water whilst others have a view of the carefully tended gardens. The lounge, with its marvellous stone fireplace and wood stove, is a comfortable and relaxing area, whilst the family photographs around the breakfast room add to the welcoming feel of the house.
12 rms (7 bth 3 shr) No smoking in bedrooms No smoking in dining room CTV in 6 bedrooms Tea and coffee making facilities No dogs (ex guide dogs) Licensed Cen ht CTV 14P Last d 6pm
ROOMS: s £19-£31; d £38-£55
CARDS:

CARTMEL Cumbria Map **07** SD37

Premier Selected

Q Q Q Q Q **Uplands Hotel** Haggs Ln LA11 6HD ☎ 015395 36248 FAX 015395 36848
Mar-Dec
Situated just outside the village of Cartmel, this fine country house enjoys super views over to the Morecambe estuary. The lounge is delightful, while the bright and cheery restaurant is an ideal setting for Tom's ambitious cooking. Bedrooms are traditional by design and provide good levels of comfort. Staff are thoughtful and attentive.
5 bth/shr No smoking in dining room CTV in all bedrooms Licensed Cen ht No children 8 yrs 18P No coaches Last d 7.30pm
ROOMS: d fr £88
CARDS:

CARY FITZPAINE Somerset Map **03** ST52

Selected

Q Q Q Q **Cary Fitzpaine** *(ST549270)* BA22 8JB (from A303/A37 junct at Podimore take A37 signed Bristol/Shepton Mallet for 1m. Take 1st right signed Cary Fitzpaine and follow road to farm)
☎ 01458 223250 FAX 01458 223372 Mrs S Crang
Closed 23-26 Dec
This gracious farmhouse, set within a 600 acre mixed farm, serves as an ideal base for exploring the Somerset countryside and offers spacious and elegant accommodation. Owners Andrew and Susie Crang warmly welcome guests to their home and encourage them to make the most of its surroundings. Many attractions are within a short drive including Yeovilton Air Museum, Cricket St Thomas and the Cheddar Caves.
3 bth/shr (1 fmly) No smoking CTV in all bedrooms Tea and coffee making facilities Cen ht CTV 6P Fishing 600 acres arable beef horses sheep
ROOMS: s £20-£22; d £38-£44; wkly b&b £120-£140*
CARDS:

CASTLE ACRE Norfolk Map **09** TF81

Q Q **Lodge Farm** *(TF824170)* Castle Acre PE32 2BS (turn off A1065 5m N of Swaffham, take Rougham Rd out of Castle Acre, after about 1.5m turn right into Lodge Farm, follow signs to Lodge Farm House)
☎ 01760 755506 FAX 01760 755103 Mrs E Coghill
Closed Xmas
This large old farmhouse sits in peaceful rural surroundings and is surrounded by 20 acres of paddocks and gardens. Breakfast is taken around a large communal dining table in an elegant dining room. Bedrooms are spacious and traditionally furnished, providing mineral water and a range of books for guests' use. Please note that this is a no-smoking house, which is also not suitable for pets or very young children.

3 rms (1 bth) No smoking CTV in 1 bedroom Tea and coffee making facilities No dogs Cen ht No children 2yrs 6P 20 acres sheep horses
ROOMS: d £40-£50

CASTLE CARROCK Cumbria Map 12 NY55

Q ❦ **Gelt Hall** *(NY542554)* CA4 9LT (B6413 to Castle Carrock) ☎ 01228 70260 Mr B W Robinson

Overlooking its own working farmyard in the centre of the village, this cosy house dates from the early 17th century and has beams and low ceilings. Bedrooms are traditionally furnished with period pieces and there is a comfortable guests' lounge, where breakfast is served round one table.

3 rms (1 bth) (1 fmly) No dogs Cen ht CTV 7P 250 acres beef dairy sheep Last d 5pm

CASTLE CARY Somerset Map 03 ST63

Selected

Q Q Q Q ❦ ***Clanville Manor** (ST618331)* BA7 7PJ (Turn off A371 onto B3153, entrance to Clanville Manor is via white gate & cattle grid under bridge 0.75m along B3153)
☎ 01963 350124 FAX 01963 350313 Mrs S Snook

Originally built in 1743, Clanville Manor is a proud Georgian farmhouse, set in 200 acres of Somerset countryside. Just a couple of miles outside Castle Cary, the location is perfect for exploring this delightful area with Wells, Glastonbury, Stonehenge and The Mendip Hills, all in easy reach. The age-darkened oak staircase leads to three attractive bedrooms which combine period furniture with contemporary comforts. Breakfast features eggs courtesy of contented hens who wander freely around the fields. The lush grass is also home to the cows, visible from the dining room as they meander back after morning milking! Should the heat of the summer sun prove too intense, the outdoor swimming pool provides welcome relief.

3 rms (1 shr) (1 fmly) No smoking CTV in all bedrooms Tea and coffee making facilities No dogs Cen ht CTV 6P Outdoor swimming pool (heated) 200 acres dairy
CARDS:

Q Q Q **The Horse Pond Inn & Motel** The Triangle BA7 7BD (turn off A303, at Wincanton from E, or Sparkford from W. Inn is at the bottom of main road) ☎ 01963 350318 & 351762 FAX 01963 351764

The four spacious bedrooms here are located in a converted outbuilding, they are comfortably appointed and equipped with many modern amenities. The large bar offers a good selection of ales and traditional pub food is available, served either in the attractive restaurant or bar.

4 bth/shr (2 fmly) No smoking in lounges CTV in all bedrooms Tea and coffee making facilities Direct dial from bedrooms Cen ht 24P No coaches Last d 9pm
ROOMS: s £30-£35; d £40-£45; (room only) wkly b&b £230-£330; wkly hlf-bd £300-£400; ✳
MEALS: Lunch £3-£6&alc Dinner £4.50-£11✳
CARDS:

CASTLE DONINGTON Leicestershire Map 08 SK42

For accommodation details see under **East Midlands Airport, Leicestershire**

CASTLETON Derbyshire Map 07 SK18

Q Q Q **Willow Croft** Pindale Rd S33 8WU (on entering village from E, bear left off A625 at Nag's Head Hotel, keep left through Market Place onto Pindale Rd. Carry up hill, house on left) ☎ 01433 620400
Closed Xmas & New Year

This stone built cottage is situated above the village, enjoying fine views over open farmland and the hills beyond. Freshly decorated bedrooms are attractively furnished, whilst breakfast is served around one table in the homely dining room and there is also a conservatory facing out to the colourful and neatly tended garden.

2 shr No smoking CTV in all bedrooms Tea and coffee making facilities No dogs (ex guide dogs) Cen ht 4P No coaches
ROOMS: d £40-£50✳

CATCOTT Somerset Map 03 ST33

Q Q Q **Honeysuckle** King William Rd TA7 9HU (from Glastonbury take A39 to Bridgwater, after 8 miles turn right to Catcott, proceed past King William pub. House 200yds on right) ☎ 01278 722890
Closed Xmas/New Year

This modern property has a small garden at the rear and is set within the peaceful village of Catcott. A relaxed atmosphere and comfortable accomodation are on offer. Two bedrooms are available, both tastefully decorated, an attractive lounge is also provided for guests. Hearty English breakfasts ensure a perfect start to the day.

2 rms (1 bth/shr) No smoking CTV in all bedrooms Tea and coffee making facilities No dogs (ex guide dogs) Cen ht No children 5yrs 3P
ROOMS: d £30-£36✳

CHADLINGTON Oxfordshire Map 04 SP32

Q Q Q ***Chadlington House Hotel*** OX7 3LZ ☎ 01608 676437 FAX 01608 676503
Closed Jan

This friendly hotel in the quiet village of Chadlington offers spacious, well equipped rooms which have a variety of styles. The ground floor lounge and bar are smart and comfortable and breakfast is served in an attractive dining room.

10 bth/shr (1 fmly) No smoking CTV in all bedrooms Tea and coffee making facilities Direct dial from bedrooms Licensed Cen ht CTV 20P No coaches Last d 7pm
CARDS:

CHAGFORD Devon Map 03 SX78

Selected

Q Q Q Q **Glendarah House** TQ13 8BZ (A30 onto A382 17m W of Exeter, after 4m turnright at Easton Court, signed Chagford, on the left entering village OS: 703 879) ☎ 01647 433270 FAX 01647 433483
Closed Xmas

This Victorian house is run by Julia and Raymond Bellenger who assure guests of a warm and friendly welcome. It is situated on the edge of the delightful Stannary Town of Chagford. Refurbished to a high standard, it offers rural views beyond the well tended gardens to the fields and woodland of Dartmoor. In the tastefully decorated bedrooms, a range of modern comforts is provided. The sitting and dining room, where breakfast is served, is an ideal place to relax and enjoy the tranquility of the surrounding countryside.

5 bth 1 annexe bth No smoking CTV in all bedrooms Tea and coffee making facilities Licensed Cen ht No children 10yrs 7P No coaches
ROOMS: s £25-£35; d £45-£55
CARDS:

All AA listed accommodation can also be found at the AA's Internet site, whose address is: http://www.theaa.co.uk/hotels

Premier Selected

Q Q Q Q Q **Parford Wells** Sandy Park TQ13 8JW (A30 onto A382, after 3 miles turn left at Sandy Park towards Drewsteignton, house 50yds on left) ☎ 01647 433353
This delightful property is set in a lovingly tended walled garden, less than two miles from Chagford. The house, which takes its name from a well in the grounds, is run by Tim Daniel. Bedrooms have been attractively decorated, with thoughtful little extras like fresh flowers and magazines. The sitting room leads to the secluded garden, and is warmed by a wood-burning stove. Breakfast, served around one antique table, includes a range of local produce, carefully prepared English dishes and homebaked bread.
3 bth/shr No smoking No dogs (ex guide dogs) Cen ht CTV 4P No coaches
ROOMS: s £24.50-£49; d £42-£49; wkly b&b £147-£171.50*

Selected

Q Q Q Q **Thornworthy House** TQ13 8EY
(from Chagford Square take the Fernworthy Road and follow signs to Thornworthy. House at end of road)
☎ 01647 433297 FAX 01647 433297
rs 3-31 Jan
Ask for directions and take care negotiating the narrow lanes to Thornworthy House. This impressive stone built property, 1100 feet up on Dartmoor with stunning views, yet only three miles from Chagford is the family home of Hugh and Sheila Rogers. The two double bedrooms are delightfully furnished and benefit from en suite facilities, while the single rooms have shared facilities. In the spacious drawing room a log fire blazes during cooler weather and an honesty bar is provided. Breakfast is served in the dining room and dinner, prepared from fresh local produce, is available by arrangement. Self catering cottages are also available.
3 rms (2 bth) No smoking in bedrooms No smoking in dining room CTV in 2 bedrooms Tea and coffee making facilities Licensed Cen ht CTV 8P No coaches Tennis (hard) Croquet Last d 10.30am
ROOMS: s £30-£35; d £50-£65; wkly b&b £248.50-£283.50; wkly hlf-bd £374.50-£409.50*

CHALFONT ST GILES Buckinghamshire Map **04** SU99

Q Q Q **The Shieling** 81 Bottrells Ln HP8 4EH
(from M40 junct 2, take A355 N for Amersham. After 1.5m N turn right by Magpies pub into Bottrells Lane, follow lane for establishment)
☎ 01494 872147 FAX 871431
This attractive house is set on the edge of the village in a peaceful location. Bedrooms are comfortable and attractively decorated, all have modern en-suite facilities. In the summer months breakfast is served in the delightful garden and in the winter guests may enjoy the log fire in the lounge.
3 bth/shr No smoking in dining room CTV in all bedrooms Tea and coffee making facilities No dogs Cen ht 6P No coaches
ROOMS: s £30; d £45; wkly b&b fr £210*

CHAPEL-EN-LE-FRITH Derbyshire Map **07** SK08

Q Q Q **Squirrels Hotel** 1 Green Ln, Chinley SK12 6AA
(on the B6062 between Whaley Bridge/Chapel en le Frith)
☎ 01663 751200 FAX 01663 750210
This stone built inn is situated in the centre of the village, within the High Peak area, and offers well equipped accommodation. There is a residents' lounge on the first floor and an extensive range of meals and snacks is offered, served in the bar or the separate dining room.

7 bth/shr (2 fmly) CTV in all bedrooms Tea and coffee making facilities Cen ht 20P Snooker Last d 10pm
ROOMS: s £28; d £40*
MEALS: Lunch £9.65-£14.95alc Dinner £9.65-£14.95alc*
CARDS:

CHARD Somerset Map **03** ST30

Q Q Q **Bere** *(ST377058)* Winsham TA20 4JQ (halfway between Crewkerne and Chard on A30 turn left to Winsham. At centre of village turn left past church and under bridge Bere Farm is on right)
☎ 01460 30207 FAX 30207 Mr & Mrs J Jeffery
This fine Georgian property stands in beautiful rural surroundings, just a few miles from the town of Chard. Originally part of the Ford Abbey Estate, the house is set in eight acres of parkland with a stream, meadows, lawns and gardens. Bedrooms are spacious and well equipped and breakfast is served at a large refectory table.
2 bth/shr (2 fmly) No smoking in area of dining room CTV in all bedrooms Tea and coffee making facilities CTV 6P 8 acres non working
ROOMS: s £25-£35; d fr £45; wkly b&b fr £135

Q Q Q **Watermead** 83 High St TA20 1QT
(on A30 through the High St continue up the hill from shopping centre)
☎ 01460 62834 FAX 01460 67448
Trudy and David Cole have been constantly improving the standard of accommodation at this friendly guest house, and rooms are well equipped and comfortable. There is a homely lounge and a spacious dining room where meals are available by arrangement and freshly cooked breakfasts are served.
9 rms (6 shr) (1 fmly) No smoking in dining room No smoking in lounges CTV in all bedrooms Tea and coffee making facilities Cen ht CTV 9P No coaches
ROOMS: s £19-£29; d £41

Selected

Q Q Q Q **Yew Tree Cottage** Hornsbury Hill TA20 3DB
(from Chard (A30) or Ilminster (A303) take the A358 situated 1 mile from Chard centre near Hornsbury Mill)
☎ 01460 64735 FAX 01460 68029
Closed 23 Dec-29 Dec
Yew Tree Cottage, the family home of Jenny and John Wright, is set within easy reach of the major routes, and many local attractions like Chard, Lyme Regis, Cricket St Thomas, Forde Abbey and many National Trust houses and public gardens. The three bedrooms have been tastefully furnished and equipped with modern facilities, and there is a cosy lounge with a log fire. Breakfast, and dinner by arrangement only, is served in an attractive and sunny garden room with access to an acre of lovely grounds.
3 bth/shr No smoking Tea and coffee making facilities No dogs Cen ht No children 10yrs 5P No coaches Last d day before
ROOMS: s fr £36; d £42-£45; wkly b&b £130; wkly hlf-bd £214*

CHARING Kent Map 05 TQ94

QQQ **Barnfield** *(TQ923484)* TN27 0BN
(leave Charing rdbt by A20 exit to Lenham, go 400yds and take 1st left down Hook Lane, straight on for 2.5m, house is on left with metal fence)
☎ 01233 712421 FAX 01233 712421 Mrs P Pym
Closed Xmas
This gracious old farmhouse is peacefully situated a few miles from Ashford. The bedrooms are spacious and traditionally furnished with antique pieces, paintings, books and family mementoes. A farmhouse breakfast is served around one table, and evening meals are provided by arrangement. There is comfortable lounge well stocked with books and games.
5 rms No smoking Tea and coffee making facilities No dogs Cen ht CTV 101P Tennis (hard) 30 acres sheep
ROOMS: s £22-£27; d £40-£44*
CARDS:

CHARLWOOD Surrey

For accommodation details see under **Gatwick Airport, London**

CHARMOUTH Dorset Map 03 SY39

Selected

QQQQ **Hensleigh Hotel** Lower Sea Ln DT6 6LW (turn off A35 into village & at lights turn into Lower Sea Lane, road to the beach, hotel is 300m on left) ☎ 01297 560830 FAX 01297 560830
mid Mar-Oct
Step outside this friendly, family run guest house and breathe in the refreshing sea air. Just a short stroll from the fossil collecting mecca of Charmouth beach, this is an ideal choice for those seeking a relaxing break. Owners Malcolm and Mary take delight in welcoming guests and are happy to share their knowledge of the local area. All bedrooms are crisply maintained and attractively presented, many featuring floral fabrics. A bar and lounge are available and the sun-filled conservatory is a lovely setting for scrumptious breakfasts.
11 bth/shr (1 fmly) No smoking in bedrooms No smoking in dining room CTV in all bedrooms Tea and coffee making facilities Licensed Cen ht 24P
ROOMS: s £25-£27; d £50-£54; wkly b&b £161-£175

Selected

QQQQ **Newlands House** Stonebarrow Ln DT6 6RA
(take eastern slip road from Charmouth Bypass towards village and at bottom of hill at bend turn left into Stonebarrow Lane. House 25yds on left) ☎ 01297 560212
Mar-Oct
This delightful 16th-century house is set in two acres of gardens and orchard on the edge of Charmouth. The bedrooms have en suite facilities and are attractively decorated. There is a cosy bar and comfortable lounge, with a relaxed and friendly atmosphere. Good home cooked evening meals are served in the charming dining room.
12 rms (11 bth/shr) (2 fmly) No smoking CTV in all bedrooms Tea and coffee making facilities No dogs (ex guide dogs) Licensed Cen ht CTV No children 6yrs 15P No coaches Last d noon

All AA listed accommodation can also be found at the AA's Internet site, whose address is: http://www.theaa.co.uk/hotels

CHEADLE Staffordshire Map 07 SK04

QQQ **Mucelli's** 2 Charles St, Cheadle ST10 1ED
(next to St Giles RC church) ☎ 01538 753836 FAX 01538 754650
Two bright and attractively decorated bedrooms are offered at this establishment, which also houses a friendly Italian restaurant. The bedrooms are reached via a pleasant rear courtyard, through the small combined breakfast room and lounge.
2 bth/shr No smoking in bedrooms CTV in all bedrooms Tea and coffee making facilities No dogs Licensed Cen ht No children 16yrs No coaches Last d 8.30pm
ROOMS: s fr £30; d fr £40*
CARDS:

CHEDDAR Somerset Map 03 ST45

See also Draycott

QQ **Market Cross Hotel** Church St BS27 3RA
(in village centre) ☎ 01934 742264
This attractive Regency property is personally run by the owner, Miss Fieldhouse. There is a cosy lounge bar, and a dining room where home cooked meals are available; dinner is by prior arrangement. Bedrooms are comfortable (though some are small) and individually furnished and decorated.
6 rms (3 shr) (2 fmly) No smoking in bedrooms No smoking in dining room CTV in all bedrooms Tea and coffee making facilities Direct dial from bedrooms No dogs (ex guide dogs) Licensed Cen ht CTV ch fac 6P No coaches Last d 6pm
ROOMS: s £21.50-£23.50; d £50-£56*
CARDS:

Selected

Q Q Q Q **Tor Farm** *(ST455534)* Nyland BS27 3UD (take A371 from Cheddar towards Wells, after 2m turn right towards Nyland, Tor Farm 1.5m on right) ☎ 01934 743710 FAX 01934 743710 Mrs C Ladd

Situated right in the heart of the Somerset countryside, only three miles from Cheddar Gorge, this guest house has all the modern comforts and facilities imaginable! There are marvellous views from all rooms, and a new heated swimming pool and barbecue have just been added. Owner Mrs Ladd provides home made food using produce grown on the farm. All the bedrooms are prettily co-ordinated and most have en suite facilities.

7 rms (5 bth/shr) (1 fmly) No smoking in bedrooms No smoking in dining room CTV in 3 bedrooms Tea and coffee making facilities No dogs Licensed Cen ht CTV 12P Outdoor swimming pool (heated) 33 acres beef

ROOMS: s £21-£27; d £35-£46*

CARDS:

CHEDDLETON Staffordshire Map 07 SJ95

Premier Selected

Q Q Q Q Q **Choir Cottage and Choir House** Ostlers Ln ST13 7HS (turn off A520 opposite Red Lion into Hollow Lane pass church and turn left into Ostlers Lane. Cottage is on the right at the top of the hill)) ☎ 01538 360561

This delightful property lies in a quiet village near Leek, conveniently located for Alton Towers and the Potteries. The main house contains the dining room and a choice of lounges. Both bedrooms are situated in an adjacent 300-year-old cottage. The larger Pine Suite also has a small sitting room and two further single bedded rooms. Guests may opt for a cooked or continental breakfast and evening meals are available by prior arrangement. Hospitality from the Sutcliffe family is warm and friendly.

2 annexe bth/shr (1 fmly) No smoking CTV in all bedrooms Tea and coffee making facilities Direct dial from bedrooms No dogs Cen ht No children 4yrs 5P No coaches Last d 4pm

ROOMS: s £30-£39; d £53-£59*

CHELMSFORD Essex Map 05 TL70

Q Q **Beechcroft Private Hotel** 211 New London Rd CM2 0AJ (turn off A12 onto B1007 follow through Galleywood for 3m) ☎ 01245 352462 FAX 01245 347833

Closed 24 Dec-1 Jan

The caring proprietors of this small family run hotel offer well maintained accommodation in bright, soundly appointed rooms. There are two lounges - one a quiet reading room, and the other a TV lounge. Breakfasts are taken in a bright dining room that looks out over the gardens.

20 annexe rms (10 shr) (2 fmly) No smoking in 5 bedrooms No smoking in dining room CTV in 19 bedrooms Tea and coffee making facilities Cen ht CTV 15P No coaches

ROOMS: s £29-£45; d £47-£59*

CARDS:

Q Q Q **Boswell House Hotel** 118/120 Springfield Rd CM2 6LF (follow directions to Riverside Ice and Leisure Centre, over river, premises at junction with Victoria/Springfield Rd) ☎ 01245 287587 FAX 01245 287587

Closed 24 Dec-4 Jan

Guests are assured of a warm welcome here; the conscientious owners have previously been selected for the finals of our Landlady of the Year award. The accommodation provides comfortably proportioned bedrooms that have a good range of amenities and modern en suite bathrooms. Guests also have the use of a comfortably furnished lounge-bar area and a dining room.

13 bth/shr (2 fmly) No smoking in 9 bedrooms No smoking in dining room No smoking in 1 lounge CTV in all bedrooms Tea and coffee making facilities Direct dial from bedrooms No dogs (ex guide dogs) Licensed Cen ht CTV ch fac 15P Last d 8.30pm

ROOMS: s £45-£48; d £60-£65*

CARDS:

Q Q **Tanunda Hotel** 217/219 New London Rd CM2 0AJ ☎ 01245 354295 FAX 01245 345503

Closed Xmas & New Year for 3 wks

Bedrooms here are of various sizes and styles, generally light in appearance and with modest appointments. The room service menu offers a small selection of snacks during the early evening, and breakfast is taken in the ground floor dining room. There are now two lounge areas - one with a piano and a selection of board games.

20 rms (2 bth 9 shr) CTV in all bedrooms Tea and coffee making facilities Direct dial from bedrooms No dogs (ex guide dogs) Licensed Cen ht CTV 20P

ROOMS: s £31-£48; d £46-£58*

CARDS:

Q Q ■ **Windmill Motor Inn** Chatham Green, Little Waltham CM3 3LE (junct A130/A131, take A131 to Braintree and after a mile turn left to Chatham Green. Inn 400 yds on left marked by a brown sign)
☎ 01245 361188 FAX 362996
Although the working days of the Windmill are long gone, much of its 19th century character remains. The bar features open fireplaces, a piano and exposed beams, and offers a good range of simple meals. The modern accommodation is split between the courtyard rooms and the four circular mill rooms. Continental breakfasts are delivered to the bedrooms.
7 shr No smoking in 1 bedrooms CTV in all bedrooms Tea and coffee making facilities No dogs (ex guide dogs) Cen ht 20P Last d 9pm
ROOMS: s £40; d £58✻
MEALS: Lunch £15-£20alc Dinner £15-£20alc✻
CARDS: MasterCard Visa Delta Switch

CHELTENHAM Gloucestershire Map **03** SO92

Q Q Q **Battledown Hotel** 125 Hales Rd GL52 6ST
(turn off A40 onto B4075, hotel is 0.5m on right)
☎ 01242 233881 & 0374 899734 FAX 01242 524198
This attractive Grade II listed villa is close to the town centre. Mr and Mrs Smurthwaite offer brightly decorated rooms which are equipped with modern facilities. The public areas comprise a restaurant with separate tables and a comfortable lounge. At the rear there is an attractive garden.
8 rms (6 shr) No smoking in 6 bedrooms No smoking in dining room No smoking in lounges CTV in all bedrooms Tea and coffee making facilities No dogs Cen ht 7P No coaches Last d 6pm
ROOMS: s £22.50; d £45-£49.50✻
CARDS: MasterCard Visa Delta

Selected

Q Q Q Q **Beaumont House Hotel** Shurdington Rd GL53 0JE
(SW side of town, on A46) ☎ 01242 245986 FAX 01242 520044
Built in the 1850s, Beaumont House has been home to the O'Byrne family for many years and their commitment to their guests is obvious. Bedrooms are equipped with modern comforts and the public areas include an elegant drawing room, where guests can enjoy a drink before dinner, and an attractive dining room. Dinners, by arrangement, are home-cooked and prepared from the best of fresh ingredients and, on warmer days, the garden is the perfect place to unwind.
15 bth/shr No smoking in dining room No smoking in lounges CTV in all bedrooms Tea and coffee making facilities Direct dial from bedrooms No dogs (ex guide dogs) Licensed Cen ht No children 10yrs 20P No coaches Last d 8pm
ROOMS: s £39-£46; d £48-£68✻
CARDS: MasterCard American Express Visa Delta

Selected

Q Q Q Q **Beechworth Lawn Hotel** 133 Hales Rd GL52 6ST
(off the A40 London Rd) ☎ 01242 522583 FAX 01242 522583
Located close to the town centre, this impressive Victorian house offers well equipped and comfortable accommodation with two bedrooms situated at ground floor level. The dining room provides breakfasts, and dinner by arrangement. There is also a comfortable lounge for guest use.
8 rms (6 shr) (2 fmly) CTV in all bedrooms Tea and coffee making facilities Cen ht 10P No coaches Last d 7pm
ROOMS: s £27-£36; d £46-£55✻

Selected

Q Q Q Q ***Charlton House*** 18 Greenhills Rd, Carlton Kings GL53 9EB ☎ 01242 238997 FAX 01242 238997
Closed 22 Dec-3 Jan
Situated in a quiet residential area this non-smoking establishment offers comfortable accommodation within easy reach of the main attractions. Bedrooms are well equipped and a modern en suite shower room is also available. The spacious combined living room contains a sitting area and a dining section where breakfast is taken. Dinner is available by prior arrangement.
3 rms (1 shr) No smoking CTV in all bedrooms Tea and coffee making facilities No dogs Cen ht CTV No children 10yrs 5P No coaches Last d early am
CARDS: MasterCard Visa

Premier Selected

Q Q Q Q Q **Cleeve Hill Hotel** Cleeve Hill GL52 3PR
(on B4632 2.5m from Cheltenham between Prestbury and Winchcome)
☎ 01242 672052 FAX 679969
Situated in a commanding position overlooking the Malvern Hills, this hotel offers spacious and very comfortable public rooms including a conservatory dining area where guests can enjoy breakfast. Bedrooms are well equipped with lots of thoughtful extras in addition to excellent facilities.
10 bth/shr (1 fmly) No smoking CTV in all bedrooms Tea and coffee making facilities Direct dial from bedrooms No dogs (ex guide dogs) Licensed Cen ht No children 8yrs 12P No coaches
ROOMS: s £50; d £56-£80✻
CARDS: MasterCard Visa

QQQ **Hannaford's** 20 Evesham Rd GL52 2AB (N on A435 Evesham road) ☎ 01242 515181 & 524190 FAX 01242 257571
Closed 23-31 Dec
This attractive Regency townhouse is a short walk from the centre of Cheltenham. On the ground floor there is a bright and pleasantly appointed dining room together with a conservatory bar area and lounge. The bedrooms vary in size but all are comfortable and well equipped. A good home-cooked dinner is available by arrangement.
8 bth/shr (1 fmly) No smoking in dining room CTV in all bedrooms Tea and coffee making facilities Direct dial from bedrooms No dogs (ex guide dogs) Licensed Cen ht CTV Last d breakfast
ROOMS: s £35-£45; d £55-£65*
CARDS:

Selected

QQQQ **Hollington House Hotel** 115 Hales Rd GL52 6ST (situated 700yds off the London Rd A40 on the Oxford side of town and 1 mile from town centre and just 1.5 miles from race course) (The Independents) ☎ 01242 256652 FAX 01242 570280
Situated close to the eastern end of this Regency Spa town, Hollington House is a large Victorian villa not far from the major attractions. Bedrooms are comfortable and well equipped, while public areas include a cosy bar lounge. Jurgen and Annette Berg are friendly and attentive hosts.
9 rms (8 shr) (3 fmly) No smoking in bedrooms No smoking in dining room CTV in all bedrooms Tea and coffee making facilities No dogs Licensed Cen ht No children 3yrs 16P Special interest excursions by prior arrangement Last d 5pm
ROOMS: s £30-£45; d £45-£65*
CARDS:

QQ **Ivy Dene House Hotel** 145 Hewlett Rd GL52 6TS
☎ 01242 521726 & 521776
Mr and Mrs O'Connor offer guests a warm welcome at their Victorian guest house situated close to the town centre. The bedrooms are bright with good facilities and are consistently well maintained. A full English breakfast is served in the traditionally decorated dining room.
9 rms (5 shr) (2 fmly) No smoking in dining room CTV in all bedrooms Tea and coffee making facilities Cen ht CTV
ROOMS: s £22.50-£25; d £45-£50*

QQQ **Kielder** 222 London Rd, Charlton Kings GL52 6HW (1 mile from Cheltenham on A40 opposite Holy Apostles Church) ☎ 01242 237138
Just a short walk from the centre of town, this attractive Victorian town house is owned and run by the very friendly Mrs Sekulic. The comfortable and attractive bedrooms are being redecorated, making use of rich Laura Ashley fabrics. The small dining room/lounge on the ground floor is the setting for a hearty breakfast.
3 rms (1 shr) (1 fmly) No smoking CTV in all bedrooms Tea and coffee making facilities No dogs Cen ht 5P No coaches
ROOMS: s fr £24; d £34-£42*

Selected

QQQQ **Lawn House** 11 London Rd GL52 6EX (on A40, follow signs for General Hospital (in next road))
☎ 01242 578486 FAX 01242 578486
This majestic Regency townhouse is a Grade II listed building with many of its original features retained. The elegant and tastefully appointed breakfast room overlooks the spacious garden at the rear. All the bedrooms are well equipped and immaculately maintained throughout.
8 rms (1 bth 2 shr) (1 fmly) No smoking CTV in all bedrooms Tea and coffee making facilities No dogs (ex guide dogs) Cen ht CTV No children 2yrs 8P No coaches
ROOMS: s £25-£28; d £37.50-£47.50*
CARDS:

QQ **Lonsdale House** Montpellier Dr GL50 1TX (turn off A46 towards Stroud 0.25m from town centre by Eagle Star building)
☎ 01242 232379 FAX 01242 232379
This impressive Regency property is just a short walk from the town centre shops and other amenities. Privately owned and personally run, it provides modern accommodation, which includes family bedded rooms. There is a comfortable lounge, and a breakfast room, where separate tables are provided.
10 rms (3 shr) (3 fmly) No smoking in dining room No smoking in lounges CTV in all bedrooms Tea and coffee making facilities No dogs Cen ht 6P No coaches
ROOMS: s £20-£30; d £40-£52*
CARDS:

Premier Selected

QQQQQ **Lypiatt House** Lypiatt Rd GL50 2QW (on A40)
☎ 01242 224994 FAX 01242 224996
Set in the Tivoli area, close to fashionable Montpellier, this early Victorian house offers quality accommodation. Bedrooms are spacious, and all have a modern en suite bath or shower room. Public areas retain

many original features, and the comfortable sitting room has a conservatory extension with an honesty bar.
10 bth/shr No smoking in dining room CTV in all bedrooms Tea and coffee making facilities Direct dial from bedrooms No dogs (ex guide dogs) Licensed Cen ht 14P Last d 9am
ROOMS: s £50-£56; d £60-£75✻
CARDS:

Selected

QQQQ **Malvern View** Cleeve Hill GL52 3PR (exit A40 onto B4075, signposted to Broadway,pass through Prestbury on B4632, follow signs to Broadway up Cleeve Hill, house near top on right) ☎ 01242 672017 FAX 01242 676207
Overlooking the Malvern Hills, on the outskirts of the town, this house is popular with racing enthusiasts who come for the nearby National Hunt course. Bedrooms are well equipped and comfortable, and all have en suite facilities. The public areas include a spacious dining room with fine views over the surrounding countryside, and a comfortable lounge. Valerie Choak is a friendly hostess with a good knowledge of local attractions.
3 bth/shr No smoking in 1 bedrooms No smoking in dining room No smoking in lounges CTV in all bedrooms Tea and coffee making facilities No dogs (ex guide dogs) Cen ht No children 12P No coaches
ROOMS: s £30-£35; d £45-£50✻

Selected

QQQQ **Manor Barn** Cowley GL53 9NN (6m S, off A435 Cheltenham/Cirencester road, at phone box follow rd for 100 metres, fork right at minor junct, Manor Barn is 25 metres ahead on left)
☎ 01242 870229
Situated in a delightful rural location a short distance from the famous spa town of Cheltenham, this sympathetic conversion of a granary and stables is ideal for those seeking a peaceful break. The bedrooms are decorated in keeping with the character of the building and are supplemented by a lounge and dining area that has a log fire for the winter evenings.
3 shr No smoking No dogs Cen ht CTV No children 7yrs 6P No coaches Last d by arrangement
ROOMS: s £19-£25; d £38-£40✻

Selected

QQQQ **Milton House** 12 Royal Pde, Bayshill Rd GL50 3AY (exit M5 junc 11, head to town centre, at Montpellier area turn left at old lamp post in centre of road, road bears left, Bayshill Rd second on right) ☎ 01242 582601 FAX 01242 222326
Closed 24 Dec-1 Jan
Situated on a Regency terrace in fashionable Montpellier, Milton House has been sympathetically restored by Alex and Penny Gamez to provide modern facilities, while still retaining the style of a bygone age. Bedrooms vary in size but all are equipped with modern en suite facilities and lots of homely extras. Public areas include an elegant dining room and a choice of comfortable lounges, one of which is in the conservatory overlooking the garden.
8 bth/shr (2 fmly) No smoking in bedrooms No smoking in dining room No smoking in 1 lounge CTV in all bedrooms Tea and coffee making facilities Direct dial from bedrooms Licensed Cen ht CTV No children 8yrs 6P No coaches
ROOMS: s £40; d £55-£68
CARDS:

Selected

QQQQ **Moorend Park Hotel** Moorend Park Rd GL53 0LA (exit M5 junc 11A, take A417 for Cheltenham, after 3.4m turn left at first traffic lights, premises are the corner house)
☎ 01242 224441 FAX 01242 572413
Closed Xmas/New Year
Between Shurdington and Leckhampton, this spacious Victorian villa retains many original features including fine mouldings in the public rooms. Bedrooms are spacious and well equipped, and all benefit from modern en suite facilities. Home-cooked breakfasts are taken in the dining room and light meals and continental breakfasts are available by room service. There is a choice of lounges, one with a bar, the other allocated to non-smokers.
10 bth/shr (3 fmly) No smoking in 4 bedrooms No smoking in dining room CTV in all bedrooms Tea and coffee making facilities Direct dial from bedrooms Licensed Cen ht 25P No coaches Last d 6pm
ROOMS: s £39-£44; d £49-£56✻
CARDS:

QQ **North Hall Hotel** Pittville Circus Rd GL52 2PZ (1m NE of town centre) ☎ 01242 520589 FAX 01242 216953
Closed 20 Dec-6 Jan
This fine Victorian house offers its guests spacious comfort and modern facilities. Most of its 20 bedrooms are en suite. In addition to its bar there is also a comfortable lounge overlooking the gardens.
20 rms (16 bth/shr) No smoking in dining room CTV in all bedrooms Tea and coffee making facilities Direct dial from bedrooms Licensed Cen ht 20P Last d 7.15pm
ROOMS: s £27.50-£55; d £60.50-£90✻
CARDS:

See advertisement on p.143.

Q Q Q ♥ **Pardon Hill** *(SO983298)* Prescott, Gotherington GL52 4RD (turn off A435 Cheltenham to Evesham road towards Gotherington, go through the village & under old railway bridge, farm half a mile on right) ☎ 01242 672468 FAX 01242 672468 Mrs J Newman

Taking its name from the nearby Pardon Hill, this delightful farmhouse enjoys views of the Oxenton and Dixton Hills. The three bedrooms are well furnished in pine and decorated with smart fabrics. Breakfast is served around a communal wooden dining table in the dining room adjoining the newly built conservatory.

3 bth/shr No smoking in bedrooms CTV in all bedrooms Tea and coffee making facilities Cen ht 6P Riding 300 acres mixed

ROOMS: s fr £25; d fr £40*

Selected

Q Q Q Q **Stretton Lodge Hotel** Western Rd GL50 3RN (M5 junct 11 thro 2 rdbts into Landsdown Rd, left at lights into Christchurch Rd, turn at end into Malvern Rd, then Western Rd, 2nd on right) (The Circle) ☎ 01242 570771 FAX 01242 528724

This elegant Victorian house retains many of its original features. Bedrooms are comfortable and very well equipped including quality decor, fabrics and lots of homely extras. Public areas are spacious and include an elegant sitting room and a dining room where breakfast is served. A daily changing a la carte dinner menu is available by prior arrangement.

4 bth/shr (1 fmly) No smoking CTV in all bedrooms Tea and coffee making facilities Direct dial from bedrooms Licensed Cen ht CTV 7P No coaches Last d 7pm

ROOMS: s £35-£48; d £52-£78; wkly b&b £160-£195; wkly hlf-bd £215-£280

CARDS: MasterCard AMERICAN EXPRESS BARCLAYCARD VISA Barclays CONNECT DELTA S

Q Q Q **Wishmoor House** 147 Hales Rd GL52 6TD (just off A40 on the B4075) ☎ 01242 238504 FAX 01242 226090

A late Victorian semi-detached property, Wishmoor is owned and run by Mr and Mrs Risborough. Bedrooms are well equipped, fresh and airy, some having views over the nearby hills. Family rooms are available.

11 rms (7 shr) (1 fmly) No smoking in 3 bedrooms No smoking in dining room CTV in all bedrooms Tea and coffee making facilities No dogs (ex guide dogs) Cen ht 11P No coaches Last d noon

ROOMS: s £20-£32; d £38-£46; wkly b&b £140-£224; wkly hlf-bd £224-£308*

CARDS: MasterCard AMERICAN EXPRESS BARCLAYCARD VISA

CHERITON BISHOP Devon Map 03 SX79

Q Q ♥ **Holly Farm** *(SX767943)* EX6 6JD (turn off A30 at Cheriton Bishop, 0.5m into village, second turning right signed for Yeofold, farm 1m on left) ☎ 01647 24616 & 0378 917409 Mr G Sears

Located in the heart of beautiful mid-Devon countryside, this farm, set in forty acres, rears sheep and has livery stables. Accommodation is comfortable and practical, with a spacious lounge offering colour TV, Hi-Fi and reading material. Riding, golf and shooting can all be arranged.

3 rms No smoking in 2 bedrooms No smoking in dining room Tea and coffee making facilities No dogs (ex guide dogs) Cen ht CTV No children 2yrs 6P Outdoor swimming pool (heated) Riding can be arranged 40 acres sheep horses

ROOMS: s £18; d £32-£35*

See page 14-20 for a list of Premier Selected establishments

CHESTER Cheshire Map 07 SJ46

See also Malpas

Q Q Q ***Bawn Park Hotel*** 10 Hoole Rd, Hoole CH2 3NH (turn off M53 onto A56 towards Chester, straight across rdbt, 1 mile on right) ☎ 01244 324971 FAX 01244 310951

This large detached corner house is conveniently located for both the city centre and motorway network. Spacious bedrooms are freshly decorated and well equipped. Breakfast is served in the spacious dining room, and there is also a comfortable sitting room.

7 rms (5 bth/shr) (2 fmly) No smoking in dining room No smoking in 1 lounge CTV in all bedrooms Tea and coffee making facilities Cen ht CTV 12P

CARDS: MasterCard AMERICAN EXPRESS BARCLAYCARD VISA

Q Q Q ***Egerton Lodge*** 57 Hoole Rd, Hoole CH2 3NJ (on A56) ☎ 01244 320712

This Victorian house is run by Susan Denham and is close to the city centre. Recently refurbished and tastefully decorated offering bright fresh bedrooms, two of which have four poster beds. There is a well furnished dining room where breakfast is served.

4 shr (1 fmly) No smoking CTV in all bedrooms Tea and coffee making facilities No dogs (ex guide dogs) Cen ht No children 7yrs 5P No coaches

Q Q ***Eversley Hotel*** 9 Eversley Park CH2 2AJ (off A5116 signed to Ellesmere Port) ☎ 01244 373744

Closed 24 Dec-2 Jan

Situated one mile from the City centre, this late Victorian semi-detached house offers simply appointed accommodation. Bedrooms are well equipped, and there is a combined bar and dining room where friendly service is provided by the resident owner, Bryn Povey.

11 rms (4 bth 5 shr) (3 fmly) CTV in all bedrooms Tea and coffee making facilities No dogs Licensed Cen ht CTV 17P Last d 6pm

See advertisement on page 145.

Q Q ***Gables*** 5 Vicarage Rd, Hoole CH2 3HZ (exit M53 at junc 12, cross A41 towards Chester, 1m turn left at Church) ☎ 01244 323969

Closed 25 Dec-2 Jan

This small family-run guest house in a quiet residential area of the city provides good-value accommodation. Bedrooms are well maintained and equipped with televisions and tea trays. The smart breakfast room also has a small sitting area.

6 rms (4 fmly) No smoking in 3 bedrooms No smoking in lounges CTV in all bedrooms Tea and coffee making facilities No dogs CTV 6P

Q Q Q **Gloster Lodge Hotel** 44 Hoole Rd, Hoole CH2 3NL (on A56.Hotel on main 'hotel' rd going into Chester straight from M56 & joining A56. Est. is 1/2m down A56 on right opposite All Saints Church) ☎ 01244 348410 & 320231

Closed 24-31 Dec

This small private hotel is conveniently placed for local amenities. It provides well equipped, en suite modern bedrooms, three of which are in a separate building, and a pretty breakfast room.

5 bth/shr 3 annexe bth/shr (2 fmly) No smoking in 1 bedrooms CTV in all bedrooms Tea and coffee making facilities Direct dial from bedrooms Licensed Cen ht 9P No coaches Last d 8pm

CARDS: MasterCard AMERICAN EXPRESS BARCLAYCARD VISA

Selected

Q Q Q Q **Golborne Manor** Platts Ln, Hatton Heath CH3 9AN (5m S of A41 Whitchurch rd. Turn right after DP Motors & Demon Tyres into Platts Lane, then 400yds on left) ☎ 01829 770310 & 0374 695268 FAX 01829 770370

This beautiful mid-Victorian Manor House, set in glorious countryside with views of open fields and hills, offers spacious and comfortable accommodation. One bedroom has a four-poster and all are en suite.

Breakfast is served around one large table in a well furnished dining room and there is a lounge which also enjoys the fine views.

3 bth/shr (1 fmly) No smoking CTV in all bedrooms Tea and coffee making facilities No dogs Cen ht 6P No coaches Table tennis Three-quarter snooker table
ROOMS: s £28-£35; d £55-£68*

Selected

Q Q Q Q **Green Gables** 11 Eversley Park CH2 2AJ
(off A5116 signed 'Countess of Chester Hospital')
☎ 01244 372243 FAX 01244 376352
This Victorian house is surrounded by lawns and gardens in a quiet area of the city. Four bedrooms are provided and these are equipped with trouser presses, telephones and other modern facilities. All are well maintained and some are suitable for families. A sitting room is provided and the breakfast room is light and strikingly decorated.
4 shr (1 fmly) No smoking CTV in all bedrooms Tea and coffee making facilities Direct dial from bedrooms No dogs (ex guide dogs) Cen ht CTV 11P Last d 8pm
ROOMS: s £23-£36; d fr £36*

Premier Selected

Q Q Q Q Q **Grove House** Holme St, Tarvin CH3 8EQ (5m E of Chester, take A51 from Chester to roundabout with A54, continue on A54 and house is on brow of hill before turning for Tarvin village)
☎ 01829 740893 FAX 01829 741769
Closed 20 Dec-5 Jan
Just 5 miles east of Chester, this impressive red brick late Victorian house is surrounded by pretty gardens and mature trees. Bedrooms are spacious, comfortable and furnished with period pieces. Thoughtful extras create a 'home from home' feeling. The elegant dining room has a large polished table, and the spacious drawing room is both comfortable and inviting with an open log fire during cooler months. Helen Spiegelberg is a natural and welcoming hostess for whom nothing is too much trouble.

Grove House

3 bth/shr No smoking in bedrooms No smoking in dining room CTV in all bedrooms Tea and coffee making facilities No dogs Cen ht CTV No children 12yrs 6P No coaches Croquet
ROOMS: s £23-£35; d £40-£56*

Q Q **Pear Tree** 69 Hoole Rd CH2 3NJ ☎ 01244 323260
This is a small family-run guest house conveniently located for the city centre. Bedrooms are modern and include some suitable for families. Two are located in a building at the rear and all are equipped with televisions and other modern facilities. The breakfast room is bright and airy and includes a small sitting area.

contd. on p.144.

9 rms (6 shr) (2 fmly) No smoking in 3 bedrooms No smoking in dining room No smoking in lounges CTV in all bedrooms Tea and coffee making facilities No dogs (ex guide dogs) Cen ht 11P No coaches
wkly b&b £98-£119

Premier Selected

QQQQQ **Redland Private Hotel** 64 Hough Green CH4 8JY
(1m from town leaving on A483 Wrexham rd, then take A5104 Saltney rd for 200yds, opposite Westminster Park)
☎ 01244 671024 FAX 01244 681309
Only one mile from the city centre, this elegant Victorian villa has been beautifully restored by the resident proprietors. Rich wood panelling, suits of armour and antique four poster beds all contribute to the general atmosphere of period splendour. All rooms have modern facilities and have been equipped with thoughtful extras. In addition to the delightful drawing room, a solarium, a sauna and an honesty bar have been provided for added comfort.
13 bth/shr (3 fmly) No smoking in 6 bedrooms No smoking in dining room CTV in all bedrooms Tea and coffee making facilities
Direct dial from bedrooms Licensed Cen ht 12P No coaches
Sauna Solarium
CARDS:

CHESTER-LE-STREET Co Durham Map **12** NZ25

QQQ **Waldridge Fell** Waldridge DH2 3RY (turn off A167 at Waldridge sign, house on left 1.5m up lane) ☎ 0191 389 1908
Standing on the edge of Waldridge village, this former chapel has been tastefully converted into a smart, modern guest house. Bedrooms are well equipped and attractively decorated. The one public room conveniently provides the dining area on one side and a lounge on the other.
5 rms (1 shr) (5 fmly) No smoking in dining room No smoking in lounges CTV in all bedrooms Tea and coffee making facilities Cen ht CTV 8P
ROOMS: s £24-£30; d £39-£43*

CHICHESTER West Sussex Map **04** SU80

QQQ **Red House** Lock Ln, Birdham PO20 7BB
☎ 01243 512488 FAX 01243 514563
Mar-Nov
Friendly owners Mr and Mrs Groom provide a warm welcome to their delightful, listed period cottage which enjoys stunning views over Birdham Pool. Enjoying a most peaceful location, The Red House is an ideal base for touring the surrounding area and visiting both Chichester Theatre and Goodwood racecourse. The two rooms are split between the main house and a converted boathouse, and are tastefully decorated and comfortably furnished. A traditional breakfast is served around one large table in the dining room and dinner is available by prior arrangement.

1 bth/shr 1 annexe bth/shr No smoking CTV in all bedrooms Tea and coffee making facilities No dogs Cen ht 2P No coaches Last d am
ROOMS: s £35; d £60; wkly b&b £200; wkly hlf-bd £300*

CHIDEOCK Dorset Map **03** SY49

QQQ **Betchworth House** Chideock DT6 6JW
(on A35, approx half way between Bridport and Lyme Regis)
☎ 01297 489478
A warm and friendly welcome awaits guests at this charming guest house. Bedrooms are comfortable, well equipped and attractively decorated. They are also provided with many thoughtful extras such as flowers and a selection of toiletries. The Harvey's Dorset cream teas are definitely a must, and can be enjoyed in the dining room or the pretty garden.
6 rms (5 bth/shr) (1 fmly) No smoking CTV in 5 bedrooms Tea and coffee making facilities No dogs Cen ht No children 6 months 12P No coaches cream teas served in pretty gdn/dining room
ROOMS: s £22; d £36-£40*

Selected

QQQQ **Park Farmhouse** Main St DT6 6JD
(on A35 3miles west of Bridport) ☎ 01297 489157
Closed 22-29 Dec
Formerly a working farm, this 16th-century partially-thatched property has retained much of its original character and charm. The bedrooms have been attractively furnished, and have many thoughtful extras. Two of the rooms are located at the rear of the house, a skilfully converted former creamery.
4 bth/shr 2 annexe bth/shr (1 fmly) No smoking in dining room CTV in 2 bedrooms Tea and coffee making facilities Licensed Cen ht CTV ch fac 12P No coaches Last d 7pm
CARDS:

Selected

Warren House

Q Q Q Q **Warren House** DT6 6JW (W of Chideock on main A35 trunk rd between Dorchester & Honiton 4m W of Bridport) ☎ 01297 489704 FAX 01297 489704

This 16th-century thatched house, built with local Dorset stone, has been sympathetically restored yet still retains many of its original features. Bedrooms are spacious, comfortable and well equipped with modern en suite facilities. There is an attractive dining room with separate tables where a full breakfast is served. Other dietary needs can be catered for by prior arrangement, and packed lunches can be provided on request.

4 bth/shr (2 fmly) No smoking CTV in all bedrooms Tea and coffee making facilities No dogs (ex guide dogs) Cen ht CTV ch fac 7P No coaches

ROOMS: s £25-£28; wkly b&b £126-£147*

CHILHAM Kent Map **05** TR05

Q Q Q **Woolpack** High St CT4 8DL (off A28 between Canterbury and Ashford) (Shepherd Neame) ☎ 01227 730208 & 730351 FAX 01227 731053

This historic inn dates back over 600 years and is located near the village square and castle. Bedrooms vary in size and style and are located in the main building as well as in converted stables and cottages. There is a cosy bar which serves a wide range of snacks and blackboard specials. There is also an attractive beamed and panelled restaurant offering a more formal setting.

3 bth 10 annexe shr (3 fmly) CTV in all bedrooms Tea and coffee making facilities Direct dial from bedrooms Cen ht CTV 30P Last d 9.30pm

ROOMS: s fr £42.50; d fr £52.50

MEALS: Lunch £10-£15alc Dinner £15-£20alc

CARDS:

CHILLATON Devon Map **02** SX48

Premier Selected

Q Q Q Q Q **Tor Cottage** Chillaton PL16 0JE (from A30 exit Lewdown thro' Chillaton towards Tavistock, 300mtrs after Post Office take right signed 'Bridlepath No Public Vehicular access' to end) ☎ 01822 860248 FAX 01822 860126

Closed 21 Dec-9 Jan

Maureen Rowlatt's charming home is hidden in its own private valley with 18 acres of grounds and a profusion of wildlife. The interesting gardens are a feature in their own right, with many private little corners. The cottage wing bedroom is beautifully appointed, with many thoughtful extras. There are three other rooms a few steps from the Cottage which have recently been lovingly restored. Celebration dinners and tray suppers are provided by prior arrangement. Mrs Rowlatt is an accomplished vegetarian cook, but is of course only too happy to cater for meat eaters.

1 bth/shr 3 annexe bth/shr No smoking CTV in all bedrooms Tea and coffee making facilities No dogs (ex guide dogs) Cen ht CTV No children 16yrs 8P No coaches Outdoor swimming pool (heated) Jacuzzi Last d 10am

ROOMS: s £38; d £76; wkly b&b £266; wkly hlf-bd £318.50-£441*

CARDS:

CHINNOR Oxfordshire

See **Bledlow (Bucks)**

CHIPPENHAM Wiltshire Map **03** ST97

See also Calne

Q Q Q **Home Farm** *(ST860720)* Home Farm, Harts Ln, Biddestone SN14 7DQ (from A4 between Bath & Chippenham, at Corsham turn off to Biddestone at lights. In village take first right off village green, farm signposted)

☎ 01249 714475 FAX 01249 714475 Mr & Mrs I Smith

Home Farm dates back to the 17th century and, set in 200 acres of mixed farm land, enjoys a peaceful village situation. The cities of Bath and Bristol are within easy driving distance. Bedrooms are well equipped with many extra touches. There is a spacious sitting room and a dining room with a flag stone floor where breakfast is served at one large table.

3 shr (1 fmly) No smoking in bedrooms CTV in all bedrooms Tea and coffee making facilities No dogs (ex guide dogs) Cen ht CTV ch fac 4P 200 acres mixed

ROOMS: s £25-£30; d £40-£45

Q Q *Oxford Hotel* 32/36 Langley Rd SN15 1BX ☎ 01249 652542
This small family-run hotel, set on the edge of the town, offers well equipped bedrooms which vary in style and quality. Dinner is available by arrangement and there is a choice of places to eat within walking distance. A choice of comfortable sitting areas is provided.
13 rms (7 shr) (1 fmly) CTV in all bedrooms Tea and coffee making facilities Licensed Cen ht 9P Last d 5.30pm
CARDS:

Selected

Q Q Q Q **Stanton Manor Hotel** Stanton St Quintin SN14 6DQ (M4 junct 17, take exit for A429 at 1st rdbt then take 1st left turn signposted Stanton St Quintin into the village, estab is on left after the church ☎ 01666 837552 FAX 01666 837022
Closed wknds,Xmas,New Year & first 2 wks of Aug
A delightful manor house, mentioned in the Domesday Book, and set in five acres of gardens and woodland. Resident proprietors Elizabeth and Philip Bullock are friendly hosts, and Stanton Manor offers a relaxed atmosphere. Spacious bedrooms have been attractively co-ordinated and are equipped with every modern facility. The public areas include a comfortable lounge, with a welcoming log burning fire in winter, and a separate bar. In the restaurant, the daily changing menu provides an interesting selection of dishes, carefully prepared using local produce where possible.
10 bth/shr No smoking in dining room CTV in all bedrooms Tea and coffee making facilities Direct dial from bedrooms No dogs (ex guide dogs) Licensed Cen ht 40P No coaches Last d 9pm
ROOMS: s £75; d £95*
CARDS:

CHIPPING CAMPDEN Gloucestershire Map **04** SP13

See also Shipston on Stour

Selected

Q Q Q Q **Holly House** Ebrington GL55 6NL (from Chipping Campden take B4035 towards Shipston on Stour. After half a mile turn left to Ebrington and follow signs) ☎ 01386 593213
Closed Xmas
Situated in a quiet village this late Victorian house has been carefully and tastefully restored by hosts Mr & Mrs J Hutsby to provide comfortable, value for money accommodation. Bedrooms, in converted former outbuildings, are comfortable, well equipped and all have modern en suite facilities. A former garage has also been converted into a spacious lounge with lots of tourist information and a table for planning the day's journey. Breakfast is taken in the original house at one large family table, and dinner is available on Sunday.
3 rms (2 shr) (1 fmly) No smoking CTV in all bedrooms Tea and coffee making facilities No dogs (ex guide dogs) Cen ht 6P No coaches
ROOMS: s £25-£40; d £38-£42; wkly b&b £133-£147*

Premier Selected

Q Q Q Q Q **The Malt House** Broad Campden GL55 6UU (1m S, signposted from B4081) ☎ 01386 840295 FAX 01386 841334
Closed 25-26 Dec
In the heart of the delightful hamlet of Broad Campden, this fine period house retains much of its original charm and character including exposed beams and fireplaces. Bedrooms are furnished with some fine period pieces and all have the benefit of en suite facilities and lots of homely extras. Public areas include two comfortable lounges, furnished with fine antiques, and an inviting restaurant, where imaginative dishes are offered by Julian Brown. The Brown family are very friendly and attentive hosts.
8 rms (5 bth) (2 fmly) No smoking in dining room No smoking in lounges CTV in all bedrooms Tea and coffee making facilities Licensed Cen ht 10P No coaches Croquet Last d noon
ROOMS: s £49.50-£69.50; d £75-£97.50; wkly hlf-bd £350-£400*
CARDS:

Selected

Q Q Q Q **Manor Farm** *(SP124412)* Weston sub Edge GL55 6QH (on B4632 Stratford to Cheltenham Rd and is on the left as you drive through the village of Weston sub Edge)
☎ 01386 840390 & 0589 108812 (mobile) FAX 0870 1640638
Ms L Robbins
Situated at the edge of the village of Weston sub Edge, this lovely Cotswold stone house dates from the 17th century and is ideally situated for major tourist attractions. Bedrooms are comfortable with good beds, period furniture and pretty co-ordinating fabrics. Breakfast is taken in the cosy dining room at one family table and there is an additional lounge with original beams and a wood-burning fire. Lucy Robbins is a friendly hostess who combines good guest care with her Point to Point eventing.
3 bth/shr No smoking CTV in all bedrooms Tea and coffee making facilities Cen ht CTV 8P Riding 600 acres sheep cattle arable horses
ROOMS: s £30; d £40-£45

Selected

Q Q Q Q **Marnic House** Broad Campden GL55 6UR (take B4081 to Chipping Campden straight over t-junct for Broad Campden continue 0.75m Marnic on left entering the village)
☎ 01386 840014 FAX 01386 840441
Closed 21 Dec-1 Jan
Situated on the outskirts of the town in the pretty hamlet of Broad Campden, this house offers comfortable accommodation close to major attractions. Bedrooms include antique pine furniture, pretty decor and lots of extras, as well as modern en suite facilities. Public areas include a cosy dining room with an impressive antique oak table and an adjoining comfortable sitting room overlooking the immaculately tended gardens.
3 bth/shr No smoking CTV in all bedrooms Tea and coffee making facilities No dogs Cen ht CTV No children 13yrs 4P No coaches
ROOMS: s £25-£36; d £40-£46; wkly b&b fr £175*

Q Q Q **Wyldlands** Broad Campden, CHIPPING CAMPDEN GL55 6UR (centre Chipping Campden opposite 'phone box, turn into Sheep St, bear left at top of rd for Broad Campden, hotel is 3rd house on right in village)
☎ 01386 840478
This attractive property is situated in the small village of Broad Campden, a perfect location for touring the Cotswolds. Views over the countryside to the rear are attractive and the garden is a sight to behold. The welcoming Mrs Wadey invites guests to enjoy her garden in the summer months. The well maintained and comfortable bedrooms all have their own bathrooms.
3 bth/shr No smoking CTV in all bedrooms Tea and coffee making facilities No dogs (ex guide dogs) Cen ht 3P No coaches
ROOMS: s £26-£30; d fr £42; wkly b&b fr £147

CHIPPING NORTON Oxfordshire Map **04** SP32

QQQ **The Falkland Arms** Great Tew OX7 4DB (off A361 1.25m, signposted Great Tew)
☎ 01608 683653 FAX 01608 683656
Closed 24-25 Dec
Tucked away in a sleepy Cotswold village, this 500 year-old inn has low-beamed ceilings with over 300 jugs hanging from above, flag stone floors, and an inglenook fireplace. The cosy bedrooms, which include two four posters, are all well equipped and decorated with co-ordinated fabrics and antique furnishings. Downstairs in the bar a wide range of local beers, cask malt whiskies and clay pipes are on offer in addition to 50 different snuffs! Guests may order dinner by prior arrangement, or sample the home cooked bar food at lunch.
6 bth/shr No smoking in bedrooms No smoking in dining room CTV in all bedrooms Tea and coffee making facilities No dogs Cen ht No children 14yrs P Last d 8pm
ROOMS: s £40; d £65
MEALS: Lunch £2.50-£8&alc Dinner £4.95-£12.95alc
CARDS:

QQQ **The Forge House** Church Rd, Churchill OX7 6NJ (exit M40 at junc 11, A361 to Chipping Norton, B4450 to Churchill, premises opposite pub) ☎ 01608 658173 FAX 01608 659262
Situated on the outskirts of Chipping Norton, this former forge is centrally located and personally run by new proprietors Jon and Lin Price. The bedrooms have en suite facilities and are thoughtfully appointed with lots of extra touches. There is a large comfortable lounge where a log fire burns in the winter months; and breakfast is served in the pretty dining room.
6 bth/shr No smoking CTV in all bedrooms Tea and coffee making facilities No dogs (ex guide dogs) Cen ht CTV No children 12yrs 6P One bedroom with jacuzzi
ROOMS: s £35-£45; d £50-£60*
CARDS:

CHISLEHAMPTON Oxfordshire Map **04** SU59

Selected

QQQQ **Coach & Horses** Stadhampton Rd OX44 7UX (beside B480) ☎ 01865 890255 FAX 01865 891995
Closed 26-30 Dec
The spacious bedrooms in this charming 16th-century inn are attractively decorated and located around a pretty courtyard. The low beam ceilings in the bar add to the cosy atmosphere. For those wishing to dine in more formal surroundings, there is an intimate restaurant offering an a la carte menu and daily specials.
9 bth/shr CTV in all bedrooms Tea and coffee making facilities Direct dial from bedrooms Cen ht Last d 10pm
ROOMS: s £47; d £53-£58*
MEALS: Lunch £14.95&alc Dinner £14.95&alc*
CARDS:

CHOLDERTON Wiltshire Map **04** SU24

QQQ **Park House Motel** SP4 0EG (situated at intersection of A303/A338) ☎ 01980 629256 FAX 01980 629256
A 17th-century coaching house with a motel-style extension. Some rooms are located in the main house, the remainder in the courtyard area. The bedrooms are comfortably furnished and equipped with modern amenities. Dinner is served during the week in the comfortably appointed dining room/bar.
33 rms (23 shr) (5 fmly) No smoking in 5 bedrooms No smoking in dining room No smoking in lounges CTV in all bedrooms Tea and coffee making facilities Licensed Cen ht CTV 40P Last d 8.30pm
ROOMS: s £25-£37; d £46-£50*
CARDS:

CHOLMONDELEY Cheshire Map **07** SJ55

QQQ **Cholmondeley Arms** The Cholmondeley Arms SY14 8BT (on A49 6m N of Whitchurch)
☎ 01829 720300 FAX 01829 720123
This former village school was still used to educate local children until 1982. In 1988 the ground floor of the school building was converted into an inn, the character of which is enhanced by period furniture, an abundance of bric-a-brac and a welcoming real fire. Across the former playground, now the car park, the house which was once the headmaster's residence, has been converted into six well equipped bedrooms.
6 bth/shr (1 fmly) CTV in all bedrooms Tea and coffee making facilities Direct dial from bedrooms Cen ht 60P No coaches Last d 10pm
ROOMS: s fr £50; d fr £65*
MEALS: Lunch £3.50-£20alc*
CARDS:

CHORLEY Lancashire Map 07 SD51

See also Eccleston

Q Q Q **Astley House Hotel** 3 Southport Rd PR7 1LB (M6 junct 28, turn right, then right at lights onto A49, 2m to A581, turn left at rdbt, guest house on right after a mile) ☎ 01257 272315
Close to the town centre, this Victorian house offers a choice between the more compact standard rooms and larger en suite rooms. Original plasterwork is an attractive feature and furniture is also in keeping with the style of the house. Breakfast is served at individual pine tables in the brightly furnished dining room.
6 rms (3 bth/shr) No smoking in dining room CTV in all bedrooms Tea and coffee making facilities No dogs (ex guide dogs) Cen ht 6P No coaches
ROOMS: s £20-£22; d £40*
CARDS:

CHRISTCHURCH Dorset Map 04 SZ19

Q Q Q **The Beech Tree** 2 Stuart Rd, Highcliffe on Sea BH23 5JS (from Christchurch take A337 to New Milton, after 2m take 1st turning right past traffic lights in Highcliffe Village) ☎ 01425 272038
New proprietors, Peter and Diana Bevis, have built up a loyal following at this small guest house. Conveniently located close to the seafront and local shops, the property has smart well equipped bedrooms with en suite facilities and pretty co-ordinated decor. There is a comfortable lounge for guest use, and a traditional dining room.
6 shr No smoking in bedrooms No smoking in dining room CTV in all bedrooms Tea and coffee making facilities No dogs (ex guide dogs) Cen ht CTV No children 9P No coaches Last d 9am
ROOMS: d £36-£45*

Q Q Q **The Firs** West Rd, Bransgore BH23 8BE
(M27 junct1, A31 Ringwood, take B3347 Christchurch road, turn left at Sopley into Derritt Lane, 2m past P.Y.O., turn right into West Rd, on left)
☎ 01425 674543
Feb-Oct
Situated in the pretty village of Bransgore, The Firs is a delightful house. Breakfast is served around the communal table in the dining room. Bedrooms are spacious, well equipped and cheery, and one is in a self-contained annexe complete with lounge. With the New Forest on the doorstep and the coast within a short drive, this is a superb location for a relaxing break.
2 bth/shr (2 fmly) No smoking CTV in all bedrooms Tea and coffee making facilities No dogs Cen ht 3P No coaches
ROOMS: d £40-£44; wkly b&b £120-£154*

Q Q **Lyndhurst Lodge** Lyndhurst Rd BH23 4SD
(from M27 follow signs to Lyndhurst, then take A35 for Christchurch past Cat & Fiddle pub, down hill, **GH on left 50yds past Roeshot pub)**
☎ 01425 276796 FAX 01425 276499
Located close to beaches and the New Forest this friendly guest house offers guests a good base for touring. Mr and Mrs Green have just taken over and have refurbished all rooms with new beds and decor. Some rooms have private facilities. The garden and lounge with patio doors is a quiet haven to relax in. Dinner is available on request.
5 rms (3 shr) (1 fmly) No smoking CTV in all bedrooms Tea and coffee making facilities No dogs (ex guide dogs) Cen ht CTV 7P No coaches Last d noon
ROOMS: s £19-£22; d £34-£54*

Prices shown in the directory are meant as a guide only and are subject to change. Please check before you book

CHULMLEIGH Devon Map 03 SS61

Premier Selected

Q Q Q Q Q **Old Bakehouse** South Molton St EX18 7BW (off A377, onto B3096, proceed 2m to village, turn left into S Molton St, guest house is 100yds on left)
☎ 01769 580074 & 580137
rs 2 weeks in Feb
Four thoughtfully decorated bedrooms are available. One is in the thatched former merchant's house which now doubles as a tea-room, while the others are across a flower-bedecked courtyard in the old village bakehouse. For those searching for both the tastes and sights of the real Devon, this is an ideal choice.
3 shr 1 annexe bth (1 fmly) No smoking CTV in all bedrooms Tea and coffee making facilities No dogs (ex guide dogs) Licensed Cen ht No children 5yrs ch fac No coaches Painting holidays arranged on request Last d 10am
ROOMS: s £24-£26; d £44-£48; wkly b&b £154-£168; wkly hlf-bd £266-£280*
CARDS:

CHURCHINFORD Somerset Map 03 ST21

Q Q Q ***The York Inn*** Honiton Rd TA3 7RF
(exit M5 at junc 26, towards Wellington for 0.5m, first left at roundabout, 1m left into Ford St, 2m at top of hill left, 4m phonebox, right to Inn)
☎ 01823 601333
Situated in the village of Churchinford, surrounded by the Blackdown Hills, the York Inn is only a few miles away from Taunton. The bedrooms, one of which is in the converted stable, are very well equipped and comfortably furnished. The bar and dining areas inter-connect in a traditional inn with low ceilings, oak beams and an impressive inglenook fireplace. The dining room offers an extensive choice from a blackboard menu.
3 bth/shr (1 fmly) CTV in all bedrooms Tea and coffee making facilities Cen ht 15P Last d 9.30pm
CARDS:

CHURCH STRETTON Shropshire Map 07 SO49

Selected

Q Q Q Q **Belvedere** Burway Rd SY6 6DP (turn W off A49 at Church Stretton and continue for 0.25miles past war memorial) ☎ 01694 722232 FAX 01694 722232
Situated on the lower slopes of the Long Mynd, this guest house offers well maintained and comfortable accommodation. Bedrooms are thoughtfully equipped and many enjoy fine views over the surrounding countryside and the carefully tended gardens. A freshly cooked dinner is served and there are two lounges, one with TV.

12 rms (6 shr) (2 fmly) No smoking in dining room Tea and coffee making facilities Licensed Cen ht CTV ch fac 10P No coaches Last d 6pm
ROOMS: s £24-£29; d £48-£52; wkly b&b £151.25-£182.70; wkly hlf-bd £224.70-£256.20*
CARDS:

Selected

Q Q Q Q **Gilberries Hall Farm** *(SO514938)* Gilberries Ln SY6 7HZ (turn at traffic light on A49 in village onto B4371 for Much Wenlock, after 4 miles pass Plough Inn on right. Turn left after sign for Cardington) ☎ 01694 771253 Mrs C J Hotchkiss
Feb-Nov
Part of a working farm, this modern farmhouse is located in open countryside close to Wenlock Edge. Well equipped bedrooms are provided and one located at ground floor level is suitable for less mobile guests. A comfortable lounge is available for residents and a heated indoor swimming pool is an extra bonus. Pretty gardens surround the property and hospitality from the Hotchkiss family is warm and friendly.
3 bth/shr (1 fmly) No smoking CTV in all bedrooms Tea and coffee making facilities No dogs (ex guide dogs) Cen ht CTV 6P Indoor swimming pool (heated) 275 acres dairy arable
ROOMS: s £26; d £42-£46; wkly b&b £140*

Premier Selected

Q Q Q Q Q **Jinlye** Castle Hill, All Stretton SY6 6JP (from A49 from Shrewsbury turn onto B4370 to All Stretton. Once in village, turn by red telephone box onto Castle Hill and proceed 1m to top)
☎ 01694 723243 FAX 01694 723243
Situated in an elevated position adjoining the Longmynd and 6,000 acres of National Trust land, this 16th-century stone house has been lovingly restored to offer an excellent combination of quality and character. Most of the spacious bedrooms are furnished with antiques including a notable 17th-century French wedding bed. All bedrooms have modern en suite or private bathrooms and lots of homely extras. Public areas are spacious and retain many original features including exposed beams and open fireplaces. Breakfast and dinner are taken in the dining room around two antique tables.
8 rms (7 bth/shr) No smoking in bedrooms No smoking in dining room No smoking in 1 lounge CTV in all bedrooms Tea and coffee making facilities No dogs Licensed Cen ht CTV No children 12yrs 8P No coaches Mountain bikes for hire Riding stables Last d 2pm
ROOMS: s £42-£51; d £54-£72; wkly b&b £170-£230; wkly hlf-bd £285-£345
CARDS:

CIRENCESTER Gloucestershire Map 04 SP00

Q Q Q **The Bungalow** 93 Victoria Rd GL7 1ES
☎ 01285 654179 & 03789 85975 FAX 01285 656159
This pleasant, well maintained guest house is close to the town centre. It provides well equipped accommodation, including family bedded rooms, and bedrooms on ground floor level. Separate tables are provided in the dining room, which also contains a lounge area. Dinner is served by prior arrangement.
6 bth/shr (2 fmly) No smoking in 1 bedrooms No smoking in dining room CTV in all bedrooms Tea and coffee making facilities No dogs (ex guide dogs) Cen ht CTV 10P No coaches Last d noon
ROOMS: s £25-£30; d £35-£40*

Selected

Q Q Q Q **Eliot Arms** Clark's Hay, South Cerney GL7 5UA (2.5 miles from Cirencester, off the A419 Swindon Rd, in the centre of the village)
☎ 01285 860215 FAX 01285 861121
Situated in the village of South Cerney, south of Roman Cirencester, this Inn dates from the 16th century and many original features remain, including exposed beams and open log fires. The bars are spacious and comfortable with lots of brasses and memorabilia. An elegant no-smoking restaurant is available in addition to tables in the main areas where guests can sample the comprehensive and imaginative menu. Bedrooms are well equipped and all have the benefit of modern en suite facilities.
12 bth/shr (2 fmly) No smoking in 2 bedrooms No smoking in area of dining room No smoking in 1 lounge CTV in all bedrooms Tea and coffee making facilities Direct dial from bedrooms Cen ht ch fac 34P Last d 10pm
ROOMS: s £39.95-£45; d £52.50-£75*
MEALS: Lunch £10-£17alc Dinner £10-£17alc*
CARDS:

Q Q Q **Masons Arms** Meysey Hampton GL7 5JT (off A417 between Poulton and Fairford) ☎ 01285 850164 FAX 01285 850164
Flowering baskets adorn the front of this delightful 17th-century inn situated in the picturesque village of Meysey Hampton. Although compact, bedrooms are all en suite and furnished in traditional style. The bar, with its exposed beams and welcoming open fire is full of character. There is also a separate dining room. A good range of home cooked fare is available in both areas.
8 shr (1 fmly) No smoking in dining room CTV in all bedrooms Tea and coffee making facilities Cen ht 8P No coaches Last d 9.30pm
ROOMS: s £36-£42; d £48-£58
MEALS: Lunch fr £6.50&alc Dinner £4.95-£18.50alc
CARDS:

Selected

Q Q Q Q **Smerrill Barns** Kemble GL7 6BW (off A429 from Cirencester, head towards Kemble and Malmesbury, approx 3m SW of Cirencester)
☎ 01285 770907 FAX 01285 770706
Smerrill Barns is an 18th-century farm building sympathetically converted to provide well equipped accommodation with modern facilities. Compact bedrooms benefit from modern en suite facilities, and public areas include an attractive dining area and occasional comfortable lounge seating, all enhanced by lovely tropical plants. Chris and Valerie Benson are welcoming hosts.
7 bth/shr (1 fmly) No smoking CTV in all bedrooms Tea and coffee making facilities No dogs (ex guide dogs) Licensed Cen ht No children 10yrs 8P No coaches
ROOMS: s £38-£42; d £48-£55*
CARDS:

Q Q Q **Wimborne House** 91 Victoria Rd GL7 1ES (with church in market place on the left, head towards traffic lights, turn right into Victoria Rd, premises on left) ☎ 01285 653890 FAX 01285 653890
Wimborne House is on the edge of Cirencester town centre and is a good base from which to explore the Cotswolds. The well maintained accommodation is comfortable and has good facilities. Separate tables are provided in the dining room and there is a small first floor lounge for residents use.
5 bth/shr No smoking CTV in all bedrooms Tea and coffee making facilities No dogs Cen ht No children 8yrs 8P No coaches Last d 4pm
ROOMS: d £30-£40*

CLACTON-ON-SEA Essex Map 05 TM11

QQQ **Sandrock Hotel** 1 Penfold Rd, Marine Pde West CO15 1JN (follow A12 to A120 and then to town and sea-front, turn right at pier signed Sandrock, in second road on the right)
☎ 01255 428215 FAX 01255 428215
Just off the main parade, this large Victorian house is close to the beach, pier and town centre. The accommodation is well maintained and smart, offering soundly proportioned bedrooms with co-ordinated soft furnishings. Public areas include a comfortable lounge, and a pleasant dining room, with evening meals by arrangement.
8 bth/shr (3 fmly) No smoking in 2 bedrooms No smoking in dining room CTV in all bedrooms Tea and coffee making facilities Licensed Cen ht 6P Last d 7pm
ROOMS: s £23.50-£28; d £47-£50; wkly b&b £158-£160; wkly hlf-bd £208-£212*
CARDS:

CLAPHAM North Yorkshire Map 07 SD76

Selected

QQQQ **Arbutus House** Riverside LA2 8DS (Turn off A65 into village follow riverside almost to the church. Arbutus House is adjacent to bridge on the left)
☎ 015242 51240 FAX 015242 51197
Built in 1820 as the village vicarage, Arbutus House overlooks the river which flows through the centre of this leafy village, by-passed by the main road. The delightful lounge is relaxing and has plenty to read. Bedrooms have a welcoming ambience and are thoughtfully equipped to include bath robes, tissues and toiletries.
6 rms (1 bth 2 shr) (3 fmly) No smoking CTV in all bedrooms Tea and coffee making facilities Cen ht ch fac 7P No coaches Tennis (hard) Fishing by arrangement Last d 2pm
ROOMS: s £16; d £40-£49; wkly b&b £140-£161; wkly hlf-bd £245-£266

CLEY NEXT THE SEA Norfolk Map 09 TG04

QQQ **Marshland** Marshland High St NR25 7RB (Situated on the A149 in High St opposite old telephone box)
☎ 01263 740284
rs Xmas New Year
Marshland has been owned and run by Mr and Mrs Kinsella for a number of years, and is situated in Cley next the Sea, overlooking the world famous bird reserve of Cley marshes. Offering comfortable well maintained accommodation throughout, this establishment also has a heartbeat certificate, so guests can enjoy a healthy home-cooked breakfast.
3 bth/shr No smoking CTV in all bedrooms Cen ht No children 5yrs
ROOMS: s £25-£32; d £28-£36; wkly b&b £98-£126*

CLIFTON UPON TEME Worcestershire Map 03 SO76

QQ **Lion** 1 The Village WR6 6DH (on B4204 between Worcester & Tenbury Wells, in Teme Valley, 3 mils from Martley)
☎ 01886 812617 FAX 01886 812332
This former coaching inn dates back to the 15th century. There are two letting bedrooms, both family bedded and en suite. Both have exposed ceiling beams and wall timbers. There is also a charming lounge bar and a separate restaurant, where a wide range of home cooked dishes is available.
2 bth/shr (1 fmly) No smoking in dining room CTV in all bedrooms Tea and coffee making facilities Cen ht 20P Pool table Last d 9pm
ROOMS: s £40-£55; d £40-£55
MEALS: Lunch £3-£12.50 Dinner £4.50-£16alc
CARDS:

CLIFTONVILLE Kent

See **Margate**

CLITHEROE Lancashire Map 07 SD74

Selected

QQQQ **Brooklyn** 32 Pimlico Rd BB7 2AH (M6, A59 to Clitheroe, take Clitheroe North turning, across roundabout, turn next left, 0.5m premises on left) ☎ 01200 428268
A very well maintained guest house a short walk from the town centre. Bedrooms are fresh and well equipped and the lounge and dining room, which are open plan, are both comfortably furnished. Good home cooking is provided and the friendly Glendinning family offer a warm welcome to their guests.
4 bth/shr No smoking CTV in all bedrooms Tea and coffee making facilities No dogs (ex guide dogs) Licensed Cen ht No coaches Last d 5pm
ROOMS: s £25-£27.50; d £40-£43; wkly b&b £161-£175; wkly hlf-bd £231-£245*
CARDS:

CLOUGHTON North Yorkshire Map 08 TA09

QQQ ***Blacksmiths Arms*** High St YO13 0AE (6m N of Scarborough on the A171 towards Whitby) ☎ 01723 870244
This charming stone-built village inn offers a wide range of well produced food together with delightfully furnished bedrooms, all of which are fully en suite. The bars are full of character and a cosy dining room is also provided.
6 bth/shr (1 fmly) No smoking in bedrooms CTV in all bedrooms Tea and coffee making facilities No dogs (ex guide dogs) Cen ht 35P No coaches Last d 9.45pm
CARDS:

CLOVELLY Devon Map 02 SS32

QQQ ***Burnstone*** *(SS325233)* Higher Clovelly EX39 5RX
☎ 01237 431219 Mrs E Symons
Burnstone Farm is an attractive Devon 'Longhouse' situated off the A39 between Bideford and Bude. The pretty bedrooms share a bathroom, and guests are offered wrapped toiletries and sweets in their rooms. The spacious lounge/dining room has very attractive antique-style Spanish furniture and interesting ornaments.
2 rms (2 fmly) CTV in all bedrooms Tea and coffee making facilities Cen ht CTV 3P Fishing 5 private lakes 500 acres arable mixed

QQQ **Fuchsia Cottage** Burscott, Higher Clovelly EX39 5RR (turn onto B3237 from Clovelly Cross Rdbt after approx 0.75m turn right into Burscott (signposted) establishment approx 300yds on right)
☎ 01237 431398

Situated down a quiet lane, Fuchsia Cottage is a modern house, close to the picturesque village of Clovelly. The bedrooms are bright and cheerful and breakfast is served in the spacious lounge/dining room, with views over the pretty garden.
3 rms (2 shr) (1 fmly) No smoking CTV in 2 bedrooms Tea and coffee making facilities Cen ht 3P
ROOMS: s £15; d £36*

CLUN Shropshire Map 07 SO38

Q Q Q **Hurst Mill** *(SO318811)* SY7 0JA (1m E just off B4368) ☎ 01588 640224 Mrs J Williams
The friendly Williams family have welcomed guests to their pretty farmhouse for over 40 years. Accommodation consists of a double bedded room with en suite facilities, plus a twin and a family room. In addition to the comfortable lounge there is a conservatory overlooking the garden. All share one table in the pleasant dining room, although separate tables can be provided if preferred.
3 rms (1 shr) (1 fmly) No smoking in bedrooms No smoking in dining room No smoking in 1 lounge CTV in 1 bedroom Tea and coffee making facilities Cen ht CTV ch fac 6P Fishing Clay pigeon shooting 100 acres mixed Last d 6.30pm
ROOMS: s £20-£25; d £38-£40; wkly b&b £130*

Selected

Q Q Q Q **New House Farm** *(SO280820)* SY7 8NJ
(take A488 Bishops Castle rd then left at x-rds in Colebatch and follow rd through Cefn Einion and at next X-rds turn right)
☎ 01588 638314 Mrs J Ellison
Mar-Oct
This lovely old house dates back at least 250 years. Fronted by lovely gardens, with panoramic views of the surrounding hills, it is remotely located on a sheep and cattle farm, four miles north of Clun. Offa's Dyke is nearby and the area is popular with walkers. There are two spacious and comfortable bedrooms, both with quality antique furnishings. The one without en suite facilities has its own private bathroom nearby. There is a comfortable and homely lounge and a cosy breakfast room, where all guests share one table.
2 bth/shr (1 fmly) No smoking CTV in all bedrooms Tea and coffee making facilities Cen ht CTV No children 5yrs 6P 315 acres
ROOMS: d £40-£50; wkly b&b £140-£145*

COALVILLE Leicestershire Map 08 SK41

Selected

Q Q Q Q **Church Lane Farm** Ravenstone LE67 2AE
(at A511/A447 junct, take direction Ibstock and Church Lane first on right) ☎ 01530 810536 FAX 01530 810536
A warm welcome awaits at Church Lane Farm House, set in Ravenstone village. The accommodation is tastefully furnished with well chosen period furniture, and the rooms are enhanced by the proprietors artistic flair. The sitting room has an inglenook fireplace, complete with a log burning stove, as well as a collection of glassware. Meals are served around the mahogany table in the beamed dining room. There is also an art studio to the rear of the house, which is run by Mr Thorne who exhibits world-wide.
3 bth/shr No smoking CTV in 4 bedrooms Tea and coffee making facilities Licensed Cen ht CTV No children 18yrs 6P No coaches Painting tuition Photographic weekends Last d noon
ROOMS: s £21.50-£27; d £38-£45*
CARDS:

COCKERMOUTH Cumbria Map 11 NY13

See also Embleton

Premier Selected

Q Q Q Q Q **Low Hall** Brandlingill CA13 0RE
(turn off A66 at Cockermouth junct onto A5086, at 1st crossrds turn left, take 2nd right, guest house is 0.5 mile down the lane) ☎ 01900 826654
Closed Dec 21-Jan 5
Enid and Hugh Davies' warmly welcome guests to their charming 17th-century farmhouse set at the foot of Fellbarrow with lovely views of the Lorton Fells. The variably sized bedrooms are decorated to a high standard and are quite individual in style and character. The reception rooms extend to a cosy lounge where one can join the hosts, a dining room with the grand piano, and the guest lounge with views of the surrounding fells. Breakfasts are substantial with freshly prepared local produce and Enid's home-made preserves.
3 bth/shr No smoking CTV in 1 bedroom Tea and coffee making facilities No dogs (ex guide dogs) Licensed Cen ht CTV No children 10yrs 10P No coaches Boules Croquet
ROOMS: s £25-£30; d £50-£60; wkly b&b £175-£210
CARDS:

Q Q Q **Rose Cottage** Lorton Rd CA13 9DX (leave A66 at Cockermouth and follow signs to Lorton and Buttermere. Rose Cottage on right)
☎ 01900 822189 FAX 01900 822189
Closed 24-27 Dec
Rose Cottage is home to the Graham family who have gradually transformed this former inn to the house it is today. Dinner and breakfast are enjoyed in the spacious dining room which looks onto the front garden. The modern bedrooms offer thoughtful facilities and are all en suite. A small, but comfortable lounge is on the ground floor.
7 bth/shr (2 fmly) No smoking in bedrooms No smoking in dining room CTV in all bedrooms Tea and coffee making facilities Licensed Cen ht 12P Last d 8pm
ROOMS: s £28-£32; d £45-£50; wkly b&b £155-£175; wkly hlf-bd £240-£255
CARDS:

Q Q Q **Sundawn** Carlisle Rd, Bridekirk CA13 0PA
(1.5miles from Cockermouth North on A595 towards Carlisle)
☎ 01900 822384
Closed 20 Dec-5 Jan
Hospitality is assured at this detached Victorian villa two miles north of Cockermouth. There is a pleasant combined lounge/dining room, as well as a separate sun lounge which enjoys panoramic views towards Skiddaw and the Lorton valley. The variously sized bedrooms are comfortably furnished in both period and traditional styles.
3 rms (2 bth/shr) (1 fmly) No smoking CTV in all bedrooms Tea and coffee making facilities No dogs (ex guide dogs) Cen ht CTV 6P No coaches
ROOMS: d £32-£39

Selected

Toddell Cottage Brandlingill CA13 0RB
(from A66 take A5086 towards Egremont. Turn left at Paddle School towards Lorton & Embleton then first right for 0.75m)
☎ 01900 828696 FAX 01900 828696
This charming Jacobean cottage has recently benefited from a sympathetic refurbishment. Public rooms have shelves of interesting reading and open fires. The inviting dining room is the scene for both the ambitious dinner and the creative breakfast that boasts a wide range of freshly prepared dishes. Accommodation provides rural comfort finely balanced with contemporary sophistication and includes a spacious family room.
3 rms (2 bth/shr) (1 fmly) No smoking CTV in 2 bedrooms Tea and coffee making facilities No dogs (ex guide dogs) Licensed Cen ht CTV No children 5yrs 6P No coaches
ROOMS: s £18.50-£25; d £37-£50; wkly b&b £116.55-£157.50; wkly hlf-bd £176.05-£217*

CODSALL Staffordshire Map **07** SJ80

Moors Farm & Country Restaurant *(SJ859048)*
Chillington Ln WV8 1QF (between village of Codsall & Codsall Wood)
☎ 01902 842330 FAX 01902 847878 Mrs D E Moreton
This quietly located farmhouse is situated on a 100-acre mixed holding, which lies to the north of Codsall village. It provides soundly maintained, modern equipped accommodation. Evening meals are available by prior arrangement and are served in the spacious, traditionally furnished dining room, where separate tables are provided. There is also a cosy lounge and a small bar.
7 rms (4 shr) (1 fmly) No smoking CTV in all bedrooms Tea and coffee making facilities No dogs Licensed Cen ht No children 4yrs 20P 100 acres mixed Last d 2pm
ROOMS: s £25-£35; d £40-£50; wkly b&b £175-£245; wkly hlf-bd £250-£320*
CARDS:

COLCHESTER Essex Map **05** TL92

See also Nayland

Four Sevens 28 Inglis Rd CO3 3HU (take B1022 Maldon rd the 2nd on rt) ☎ 01206 546093 FAX 01206 546093
The house is within easy walking distance of the town centre but nevertheless in a tranquil situation. The well appointed bedrooms offer a good standard of decor and very hearty breakfasts are on offer to hungry guests.
6 rms (2 shr) (1 fmly) No smoking in 3 bedrooms No smoking in dining room No smoking in lounges CTV in all bedrooms Tea and coffee making facilities No dogs Cen ht No children 2yrs 2P No coaches Last d 8.30pm
ROOMS: s £35-£40; d £40-£50*

Premier Selected

Hockley Place Church Rd, Frating CO7 7HG (at major junct A12/A120 take 1st exit A120, 2nd exit at rdbt, A133 Elmstead Mkt, 1st left B1029, 1st right, then left at junct Rectory Rd/Church Rd) ☎ 01206 251703 FAX 01206 251578
Closed 15 Dec-Jan
Renowned for its own rhododendron walk, Hockley Place is a tranquil haven for budding horticulturists visiting the famous Beth Chatto gardens nearby. This elegant house stands in five secluded acres of parkland, orchards and farmlands.The spacious public rooms include a beamed dining room and a separate leisure room. The landscaped grounds include a heated outdoor pool and croquet lawn. Also a Wolsey Lodge offering 'en famille' style accommodation. The large and airy bedrooms are pleasantly furnished, with well chosen interior design and a wide range of useful extras. Most dietary needs can be catered for.
4 bth/shr No smoking CTV in all bedrooms Tea and coffee making facilities No dogs (ex guide dogs) Licensed Cen ht CTV No children 12yrs 12P Outdoor swimming pool (heated) Gymnasium Croquet Last d by arrangement
ROOMS: s £40; d £60*
CARDS:

Old Manse 15 Roman Rd CO1 1UR (from High Street into East Hill, Roman Rd is 1st left after Castle, opposite St James' church)
☎ 01206 545154
Closed 23-31 Dec
The Old Manse is conveniently situated just a few minutes walk from the High Street, very close to the Roman walls of Colchester town centre. Bedrooms are well appointed with neat decoration and feature some delightful paintings. Breakfast is served in the downstairs dining room, dotted with wonderful pottery and glass.
3 rms (2 bth/shr) No smoking CTV in all bedrooms Tea and coffee making facilities No dogs (ex guide dogs) Cen ht No children 6yrs 1P No coaches
ROOMS: s £26-£28; d £36-£44*

COLESBOURNE Gloucestershire Map **04** SP01

Selected

Colesbourne GL53 9NP
(on A435 Cirencester to Cheltenham road)
☎ 01242 870376 FAX 01242 870397
Closed 24-26 Dec
This Cotswold stone inn retains much of its original character, with spacious comfortable lounge and bar areas, where welcoming log fires burn during the cooler months. Bedrooms, converted from the former stable block, are comfortably furnished and well equipped with modern en suite facilities. Friendly and attentive service is offered by resident hosts Robert and Elaine Flaxman.

9 annexe bth/shr No smoking in dining room CTV in all bedrooms Tea and coffee making facilities Direct dial from bedrooms No dogs (ex guide dogs) 40P Last d 10pm
ROOMS: s £38-£42; d £56-£62✳
CARDS:

COLLINGBOURNE KINGSTON Wiltshire Map **04** SU25

Selected

Q Q Q Q ***Old School House*** High St SN8 3SD (take A346 from Marlborough and join A338 at Burbage) ☎ 01264 850799
A warm welcome awaits guests at this charming restaurant with rooms. Located just outside Marlborough, Livio's traditional Italian food is a definite treat. This converted school, built in 1845, is still visited by many former pupils, and has a number of interesting architectural features. The en suite bedrooms are well equipped and have many thoughtful touches. One room has disabled access.
3 bth/shr (1 fmly) CTV in all bedrooms No dogs (ex guide dogs) Licensed P
CARDS:

COLNE Lancashire Map **07** SD84

Selected

Q Q Q Q **Higher Wanless** *(SD873413)* Red Ln BB8 7JP (Exit M65 at junc 13, follow signs to Barrewford, right fork past Old Bridge Inn, follow road fro 0.25m to Red Lane, farm first left) ☎ 01282 865301 Mrs C Mitson
Closed Dec & 1st wk in Jan
This 250-year old farmhouse stands close to the Leeds/Liverpool canal and the Pendle Way. There are two spacious bedrooms; one is fully en suite, and both rooms have been very pleasantly furnished and thoughtfully equipped. Guests have the use of a beamed lounge with an open fire. Breakfasts and dinners are served around a large table.
2 rms (1 shr) (2 fmly) No smoking in bedrooms No smoking in area of dining room No smoking in 1 lounge CTV in 1 bedroom Tea and coffee making facilities No dogs Cen ht CTV No children 3yrs 4P 25 acres shire horses sheep Last d 9am
ROOMS: s £20-£24; d £40-£46; wkly b&b £136-£165; wkly hlf-bd £212-£247✳

COLTISHALL Norfolk Map **09** TG21

Selected

Q Q Q Q **The Hedges** Tunstead Rd NR12 7AL (B1150 from Norwich, through Horstead over hump-back bridge, right onto B1354, opposite river turn left into White Lion Rd at top take right fork) ☎ 01603 738361 FAX 01603 738983
Closed 24 Dec-1 Jan
Mr and Mrs Bruce offer a warm, friendly welcome here at this well maintained guest house in a peaceful country lane. Just a short walk away are the River Bure on the Norfolk Broads, the Bure Valley Railway and Wroxham. The bedrooms are warm and comfortable, well equipped with a good range of facilities, and modern en suite bathrooms. Guests can enjoy breakfast in the bright dining room.
6 bth/shr (2 fmly) CTV in all bedrooms Tea and coffee making facilities Licensed Cen ht CTV ch fac 14P No coaches
ROOMS: s £25-£27; d £40-£44; wkly b&b fr £132✳
CARDS:

COLYFORD Devon Map **03** SY29

Selected

Q Q Q Q **Lower Orchard** Swan Hill Rd EX13 6QQ (On the main A3052 in the village of Colyford between Lyme Regis and Sidmouth) ☎ 01297 553615
Conveniently situated near Seaton, this modern 'ranch style' family house offers superior accommodation with both bedrooms enjoying fine views over the Axe Valley. The spacious bedrooms are bright and decorated in a modern style with private facilities and many personal touches. Breakfast is served in the lounge/dining room.
2 bth/shr (1 fmly) CTV in all bedrooms Tea and coffee making facilities Cen ht CTV 10P Outdoor swimming pool
ROOMS: s £30; d £40✳

COLYTON Devon Map **03** SY29

Q Q Q ***Smallicombe Farm*** *(SY196960)* Northleigh EX13 6BU ☎ 01404 831310 FAX 01404 831431 Mrs M Todd
Situated in a peaceful valley Smallicombe Farm, home to the Todd Family, dates back to the Domesday Book. The town of Honiton, famous for its lace and antiques, is but a short drive and the East Devon coast is only six miles away. For those seeking to just enjoy the rural and rustic surroundings, Smallicombe has a range of "rare breeds" farm animals including Berkshire Pigs and Golden Guernsey Goats. There are two comfortable bedrooms with their own sitting and dining areas and modern bathroom facilities. Breakfast is a hearty affair featuring home produced bacon and sausages, and all the meat used for dinner, when required, is from the farm. The warm welcome offered by Maggie Todd also plays an important role in the relaxed and friendly atmosphere of this delightful farm.
2 bth/shr (1 fmly) No smoking CTV in all bedrooms Tea and coffee making facilities No dogs (ex guide dogs) Cen ht CTV Golf 18 30 acres rare breed pigs Last d previous evening

COMBE HAY Somerset Map **03** ST75

Selected

Q Q Q Q ***Wheatsheaf Inn*** BA2 7EG (take A369 Exeter road from Bath to Odd Down and turn left at park and ride for Combe Hay. Follow lane for approx 2m to thatched cottage and turn left) ☎ 01225 833504 FAX 01225 833504
Closed Xmas
Originally built in 1576, The Wheatsheaf is the perfect embodiment of an English country inn with local characters, local flavours, wooden beams, log fire and cheery host. Sensitive conversion of the former stable block has resulted in three lovely bedrooms offering both quality and comfort. Local fish and game feature extensively on the menu, supplemented by a choice of vegetarian meals.

contd.

Wheatsheaf Inn

3 shr (1 fmly) No smoking in bedrooms CTV in all bedrooms Tea and coffee making facilities No dogs Cen ht No children 100P Last d 9.30pm
CARDS:

COMBE MARTIN Devon Map **03** SS54

Selected

QQQQ ***Ashelford*** East Down EX31 4LU ☎ 01271 850469 FAX 01271 850862
Facing south, at the head of its own valley, Ashelford has unrivalled views beyond the National Trust's Arlington Court, to Exmoor in the distance. Erica and Tom McClenaghan welcome guests to their charming home. Dinner is served by prior arrangement, Erica discusses the menu with guests and ensures the very best of home cooking. At breakfast a wide choice is offered, with local produce being used. Two sitting rooms are available, both have fires which are used during cooler months. Each of the charming bedrooms is individually furnished and decorated, with all the rooms being very well equipped.
3 bth/shr No smoking in bedrooms CTV in all bedrooms Tea and coffee making facilities Licensed Cen ht CTV No children 15yrs 9P No coaches Last d by arrangement
CARDS:

CONGLETON Cheshire Map **07** SJ86

Q **Egerton Arms Hotel** Astbury Village CW12 4RQ (1.5m S of Congleton just off A34 next to St Marys Church) ☎ 01260 273946 FAX 01260 277273
A popular inn, situated just opposite the church in the pretty village of Astbury. As well as having a brightly decorated restaurant, the lounge bar is comfortable, with a wide range of bar snacks offered. There is also a garden area.
6 rms No smoking in 2 bedrooms No smoking in area of dining room No smoking in 1 lounge CTV in all bedrooms Tea and coffee making facilities No dogs (ex guide dogs) Cen ht 100P No coaches Golf 18 Fishing can be arranged Last d 9.30pm
ROOMS: s £24; d £32.50*
MEALS: Bar Lunch fr £4.99alc*
CARDS:

CONISTON Cumbria Map **07** SD39

Selected

QQQQ **Arrowfield** Little Arrow, Torver LA21 8AU (1.5m from Coniston village on the A593) ☎ 015394 41741
Mar-Nov
This Victorian house is set in an idyllic spot between Coniston and Torver. Brightly co-ordinated bedrooms offer comfort and are thoughtfully well equipped. The lounge is stylishly elegant with deep comfortable sofas and period features. A substantial breakfast can be enjoyed in the light and airy dining room. Guests can sample the home-made preserves and honey, which are available to buy and take home.
5 shr No smoking CTV in all bedrooms Tea and coffee making facilities No dogs (ex guide dogs) Licensed Cen ht CTV 6P No coaches
ROOMS: s £21-£24; d £42-£48; wkly b&b £147*

Premier Selected

QQQQQ **Coniston Lodge Hotel** Station Rd LA21 8HH (at crossroads on A593 close to filling station, turn up the hill at the crossroads called Station Rd) ☎ 015394 41201
rs Sun & Mon pm
Anthony and Elizabeth Robinson offer a friendly welcome to their private hotel which is reminiscent of a Swiss chalet. Bedrooms are furnished in a modern style and are well equipped. Meals are served in the tastefully co-ordinated dining room. The lounge features a commissioned relief in local slate stone depicting an earlier guest of the Robinsons: Donald Campbell, with his famous Campbell Bluebird.
6 bth/shr No smoking CTV in all bedrooms Tea and coffee making facilities Direct dial from bedrooms No dogs (ex guide dogs) Licensed Cen ht No children 10yrs 9P No coaches Last d 7.30pm
ROOMS: s £29.50-£46.50; d £59-£79; wkly b&b £206.50-£248.50*
CARDS:

Premier Selected

QQQQQ **Wheelgate Country House Hotel** Little Arrow LA21 8AU (1.5m S of Coniston village on W side of the road) ☎ 015394 41418
Early Mar- End Nov
Situated between the villages of Coniston and Torver, Joan and Roger Lupton offer guests a friendly welcome to their home. Dating from 1640, the house offers thoughtfully furnished bedrooms, one boasting an opulent four-poster bed. Lounges are comfortable with deep sofas and antique furniture. A substantial breakfast can be taken in the light dining room preparing Lakeland walkers for their daily adventures.
4 shr 2 annexe bth/shr (2 fmly) No smoking in bedrooms No smoking in dining room No smoking in lounges CTV in all bedrooms Tea and coffee making facilities No dogs (ex guide dogs) Licensed Cen ht 10P No coaches Free membership of Health Club
ROOMS: s £27.50-£31; d £45-£62; wkly b&b £157-£195
CARDS:

COOKHAM DEAN Berkshire Map **04** SU88

Selected

QQQQ **Inn on the Green** The Old Cricket Common SL6 9NZ (A404 towards Marlow High St. Cross suspension bridge towards Bisham. First left into Quarry Wood Rd, right Hills Lane, right at Memorial Cross) ☎ 01628 482638 FAX 01628 487474
Set in a peaceful location overlooking the village green, this fine old inn has been modernised but retains many traditional features. The well-appointed bedrooms are housed in two out-buildings. These are spacious, attractively decorated and furnished with antique style pine furniture. There is an opportunity to sample the cooking of chef Adrian Hutchinson, who offers a set price and carte menu complemented by an interesting wine list.
8 bth/shr (2 fmly) CTV in all bedrooms Cen ht 50P Last d 10pm
ROOMS: s £50-£70; d £80-£90*
MEALS: Lunch £15.95-£21&alc Dinner £15.95-£21&alc*
CARDS:

CORBRIDGE Northumberland Map **12** NY96

Premier Selected

QQQQQ **The Courtyard** Mount Pleasant, Sandhoe NE46 4LX (turn off A68 at signpost for Sandhoe,1m N ofA68/A69 junc at Corbridge,straight over crossrds,up narrow ln to T junct,turn right.Est 1/4m on left) ☎ 01434 606850 FAX 01434 607962
Bill and Margaret Weightman's delightful home, a truly magnificent transformation from old farm building to a stylish country house, enjoys breathtaking panoramic views from its position overlooking the Upper Tyne valley. Margaret's flair for interior design blends with beams and flagstone floors to add an eye-catching dimension to the spacious lounge and dining room. Bedrooms all have luxury bathrooms and two rooms are particularly well proportioned, one with a fine four-poster.
3 bth/shr (1 fmly) No smoking CTV in all bedrooms Tea and coffee making facilities No dogs Licensed Cen ht No children 14yrs 3P No coaches
ROOMS: s £50-£65; d £55-£75; *

QQQ **Priorfield** Hippingstones Ln NE45 5JA (from village centre through market place along Watling St past Wheatsheaf pub and 2nd right into St Helens Lane then 1st rt) ☎ 01434 633179
Mar-Nov
Jill and Nick Steenberg's Edwardian family home lies secluded in its own gardens in a quiet residential lane close to the town centre. The house is a showpiece for Jill's flair for interior design which is prominent in the stylishly decorated bedrooms. The double room's en suite features a whirlpool bath. Breakfast is taken around one large table in the dining room.
2 bth/shr (1 fmly) No smoking in bedrooms CTV in all bedrooms Tea and coffee making facilities No dogs Cen ht No children 4yrs 2P No coaches
ROOMS: d £40-£46*

CORBY Northamptonshire Map **04** SP88

QQ **Raven Hotel** Rockingham Rd NN17 1AG ☎ 01536 202313 FAX 01536 402439
The "rooms above" are located on the first floor of a modern pub which is smart and offers a range of modern popular meals and drinks. The rooms are spacious and bright and are simply furnished but comfortable.
17 rms (6 shr) (3 fmly) No smoking in 2 bedrooms No smoking in area of dining room CTV in all bedrooms Tea and coffee making facilities No dogs (ex guide dogs) Cen ht CTV 40P Free access to local health club Last d 10pm
ROOMS: s £25-£29.50; d £29.50-£34.50*
MEALS: Dinner £5-£7.50*
CARDS:

CORSHAM Wiltshire Map **03** ST87

Selected

QQQQ **Manor Farm** *(ST846679)* Wadswick SN13 8JB (take B3109 from Corsham, past mini-roundabout and turn left at Wadswick signpost. Second farmhouse on left)
☎ 01225 810700 FAX 01225 810307 Mrs C Barton
Feb-Nov
Situated 6 miles East of Bath and close to the villages of Lacock and Castle Combe, this delightful 17th-century farmhouse enjoys a quiet rural setting surrounded by its own farmland. Accommodation is offered in three spacious bedrooms which have been equipped with modern facilities. Breakfast, the only meal served, is taken around one large table in the elegant dining room.
3 shr (1 fmly) No smoking CTV in all bedrooms Tea and coffee making facilities No dogs (ex guide dogs) Cen ht No children 10yrs 3P Riding arranged 500 acres arable sheep
ROOMS: s £25-£30; d £45-£50*
CARDS:

The AA's professional Inspectors make regular and anonymous visits to all the establishments listed in the Guide. They accept no gifts or favours from proprietors

Selected

Q Q Q Q ❦ **Pickwick Lodge Farm** *(ST857708)* Guyers Ln SN13 0PS (turn off A4, Bath side of Corsham, into Guyers Lane. Follow lane to end, farmhouse on right at end)
☎ 01249 712207 FAX 01249 701904 Mrs G Stafford
Closed Xmas/New Year
A warm welcome awaits guests at this picturesque farmhouse built in 1650 and extended in Victorian times. The 300-acre beef and arable farm has many beautiful walks nearby and is within easy reach of Bath. The spacious bedrooms are well equipped with modern facilities and many other thoughtful extras. Breakfast is served at one big table in the attractive dining room.
2 bth/shr (1 fmly) No smoking CTV in all bedrooms Tea and coffee making facilities No dogs (ex guide dogs) Cen ht CTV 6P
300 acres arable beef
ROOMS: d £40-£45; wkly b&b £126-£140*

COTGRAVE Nottinghamshire Map **08** SK63

Selected

Q Q Q Q ❦ **Jerico Farm** *(SK654316)* Fosse Way NG12 3HG (located down a farm drive on A46 1m N of the intersection where the A606 crosses the A46) ☎ 01949 81733 FAX 01949 81733
Mrs S Herrick
Closed Xmas week
This modern brick farmhouse is surrounded by 150 acres of farmland, used for beef cattle, sheep and arable crops. Brightly furnished bedrooms are equipped with many thoughtful extras, including bathrobes. A hearty breakfast is served around one table in the conservatory, while the comfortable lounge, heated by a wood stove in cooler weather, is the ideal place to relax in.
3 rms (1 shr) No smoking CTV in all bedrooms Tea and coffee making facilities No dogs Cen ht CTV No children 5yrs 4P Fishing
150 acres mixed
ROOMS: s £22-£28; d £36-£42*
CARDS:

COVENTRY West Midlands Map **04** SP37

Q Q **Ashleigh House** 17 Park Rd CV1 2LH ☎ 01203 223804
Closed 23 Dec-1 Jan
Ashleigh House is located in a pleasant residential street a short walk from the city centre. Rooms are furnished in a straightforward style, and most have en suite shower rooms. Guests have the use of a small cheerfully appointed lounge and cosy bar; evening meals are readily available.
10 rms (8 shr) (5 fmly) CTV in all bedrooms Tea and coffee making facilities No dogs Licensed Cen ht CTV 12P No coaches Last d 8.45pm
ROOMS: s £20-£25.50; d £36-£40*

Q Q **Croft Hotel** 23 Stoke Green, off Binley Rd CV3 1FP (from Coventry, second turning on right after Humber Road roundabout on A427/428)
☎ 01203 457846 FAX 01203 457846
The Croft is situated in a residential area overlooking the green. Simple, bright bedrooms are offered along with varied public areas. A bar, complete with pool table, serves draught ales and lager, and there are set-price menus with grills and a range of bar snacks.
11 rms (5 shr) (1 fmly) CTV in 6 bedrooms Tea and coffee making facilities Licensed Cen ht CTV 12P No coaches Pool table
Last d 8.30pm
ROOMS: s £24.75-£34.75; d £42-£57.75*
CARDS:

Q Q ***Hearsall Lodge Hotel*** 1 Broad Ln CV5 7AA
☎ 01203 674543 & 678749
A comfortable well established hotel on the fringe of the city. Owner Mrs Entwistle offers comfortable accommodation in a relaxed friendly atmosphere. Bedrooms are attractively decorated, nicely furnished and well equipped. There is a large well appointed lounge and dining room.
12 rms (9 shr) (1 fmly) CTV in all bedrooms Tea and coffee making facilities Licensed Cen ht CTV No coaches
CARDS:

COWES See **WIGHT, ISLE OF**

COWSHILL Co Durham Map **12** NY84

Selected

Q Q Q Q ❦ **Alston & Killhope Riding Centre** *(NY845413)*
Low Cornriggs Farm, Cowshill-in-Weardale DL13 1AQ
(situated at the head of Weardale, A689 on the main road between villages of Cowshill and Lanehead)
☎ 01388 537600 FAX 01388 537600 Mrs J Ellis
Set against the stunning backdrop of the North Pennines, this delightful old farmhouse is stylishly furnished and offers very pleasant bedrooms. The lounges are inviting and include a spacious sun lounge. Good home cooking is provided in the cosy dining room. There is a riding stable on the farm and guests are offered riding activities.
3 bth/shr (1 fmly) No smoking in bedrooms No smoking in dining room No smoking in 1 lounge CTV in 2 bedrooms Tea and coffee making facilities No dogs Licensed Cen ht CTV No children 5yrs 10P Golf 9 Riding 60 acres cattle sheep ponies Last d 8.30pm
ROOMS: s £25-£28; d £40-£42; wkly b&b £130-£175;
wkly hlf-bd £200-£245*
CARDS:

CRACKINGTON HAVEN Cornwall & Isles of Scilly Map **02** SX19

Coombe Barton EX23 0JG (Turn off A39 at Wainhouse corner continue down lane until you reach beach) ☎ 01840 230345 FAX 01840 230788

Mar-Oct rs Nov-Feb

Originally built as the house for the 'Captain' of the slate quarry, some 200 years ago, Coombe Barton has an enviable position by the beach. In addition to the bar and restaurant, a spacious children's room is also provided. A wide range of meals is provided, plus a list of daily special dishes displayed on blackboards.

7 rms (3 bth) (1 fmly) No smoking in area of dining room CTV in 3 bedrooms Tea and coffee making facilities Cen ht CTV 40P Last d 9.30pm

ROOMS: s £19-£25; d £37-£65; wkly b&b £165-£195*

MEALS: Lunch £11.50-£24alc Dinner £11.50-£24alc*

CARDS:

Premier Selected

Manor *(SX159962)* EX23 0JW ☎ 01840 230304 Mrs M Knight

Set in beautifully manicured gardens and grounds, this charming manor house dates back to the The Domesday Book. Located about a mile from the sea, with splendid views over the surrounding countryside, Manor Farm continues to gather a loyal following. Each bedroom is individually furnished and elegantly decorated, with most rooms being en suite. Dinner is served by prior arrangement. Guests eat dinner-party style around a magnificent table in the dining room. An honesty bar is available for drinks. Breakfast is served in the sunny breakfast room in the front of the house, generally at individual tables. Smoking is prohibited in the house.

2 bth 2 annexe shr No smoking No dogs Licensed Cen ht CTV No children 18yrs 6P Table tennis 30 acres Non working Last d 5pm

Premier Selected

Trevigue *(SX136951)* EX23 0LQ ☎ 01840 230418 FAX 01840 230418 Mrs J Crocker

Closed Xmas 3 days rs Nov-Feb (no dinner)

Dating back to the 16th century, Trevigue is a National Trust farmhouse built of local granite. Accommodation is attractively decorated and elegantly furnished, guests having the choice of rooms in the historic main building or the modern, Mediterranean-style house a few hundred yards away. Rugs are scattered over the flag stone floors of the ground floor and log burning fires create a cosy atmosphere. Interesting meals are served in the evenings, and tea, coffee and light lunches are served in a converted barn which also houses an information room.

contd. on p.158.

Trevigue Farm

3 bth/shr 3 annexe bth No smoking CTV in 2 bedrooms Tea and coffee making facilities No dogs Licensed CTV No children 12yrs 20P 500 acres dairy mixed Last d 5pm
ROOMS: s £40-£48; d £48-£58*
CARDS:

CRANBROOK Kent Map **05** TQ73

Selected

Q Q Q Q **Folly Hill Cottage** Friezley Ln, Hocker Edge TN17 2LL (turn off A21 onto A262, through Goudhurst village, past Kennel Holt Hotel sign on right, take 2nd left, Cottage on left at end of lane) ☎ 01580 714299 FAX 01580 714299
Closed Christmas week
Built in the 19th century, this pretty farm cottage can be found at the end of a winding lane in a wonderfully peaceful part of the Kent countryside. The accommodation is modern and very well presented, each has its own private bathroom and lots of thoughtful extra touches. Guests have use of a small lounge adjoining the bedrooms. Both rooms overlook the pretty garden and outdoor pool as well as the fields beyond. Breakfast is served around a communal table in the sunny dining room.
2 bth/shr No smoking CTV in 1 bedroom Tea and coffee making facilities No dogs Cen ht CTV No children 10yrs 5P No coaches Outdoor swimming pool Last d 24 hrs notice
ROOMS: s £26-£30; d £40-£46; wkly b&b £126-£140*

Selected

Q Q Q Q **The Oast** *(TQ755345)* Hallwood Farm TN17 2SP (A229 from Cranbrook, 1m past Duke of Kent pub on left. Farm turning is 400yds on the right) ☎ 01580 712416 FAX 01580 712416 Mrs S Wickham
Mar-Oct rs Nov-Feb
Converted from a 17th-century building originally used for drying hops, The Oast is situated on the edge of the village of Cranbrook. The building forms part of a 200 acre arable and sheep farm. Both rooms are tastefully decorated in keeping with the style of the building, retaining many of the original beams. Rooms are equipped with a host of thoughtful extras and benefit from modern en suite facilities. A traditional farmhouse breakfast is served in the comfortable dining room.
2 bth/shr No smoking CTV in all bedrooms Tea and coffee making facilities No dogs (ex guide dogs) Cen ht No children 5yrs 6P 230 acres arable fruit sheep
ROOMS: d £40-£45*

CRANFORD Greater London

For accommodation details see **Heathrow Airport**

CRASTER Northumberland Map **12** NU22

Q Q Q **Cottage** Dunstan Village NE66 3SZ (NW, off Howick to Embleton road) ☎ 01665 576658 FAX 01665
Located in the village of Dunstan, this family-run inn is a few minutes drive from the fishing village of Craster. Modern ground floor accommodation overlooks secluded gardens to the rear. Guests can make use of a games room, well stocked bar, conservatory and medieval-themed restaurant. The evening menu offers a mouthwatering selection including locally caught fish.
10 bth/shr No smoking in area of dining room CTV in all bedrooms Tea and coffee making facilities Direct dial from bedrooms No dogs (ex guide dogs) Cen ht 35P Last d 9.30pm
ROOMS: s £35; d £63*
MEALS: Bar Lunch £8-£10alc Dinner £16-£20alc*
CARDS:

CRAVEN ARMS Shropshire Map **07** SO48

Selected

Q Q Q Q **Strefford Hall Farm** *(SO444856)* Strefford SY7 8DE (1/4m off A49. 1st house on right) ☎ 01588 672383 FAX 01588 672383 Mrs C Morgan
Closed Xmas & New Year
Part of a large livestock and cereal farm, Strefford Hall sits at the foot of Wenlock Edge. There are fine views from many of the rooms and leaflets are available to describe the many walks through the surrounding area. Bedrooms are comfortable and feature some fine wood panelling to match the central pine staircase. There is a welcoming lounge, and dinner is available by prior arrangement.
3 bth/shr No smoking CTV in all bedrooms Tea and coffee making facilities No dogs (ex guide dogs) Cen ht CTV 3P 350 acres arable beef sheep Last d noon
ROOMS: s fr £25; d £40-£42; wkly b&b fr £140; wkly hlf-bd fr £217*

CRAWLEY West Sussex

For accommodation details see **Gatwick Airport**

CRESSAGE Shropshire Map **07** SJ50

Selected

Q Q Q Q **Cholmondeley Riverside** SY5 6AF (Shrewsbury by-pass: A49 follow to Bridgnorth turn off A458 6m S of Shrewsbury on left hand side) ☎ 01952 510900 FAX 01952 510980
Closed 25 Dec

This fine 17th-century inn lies just a few miles east of Shrewsbury on a bend of the River Severn. It has been completely refurbished over recent years and now provides sound modern accommodation. Public areas make good use of the superb location, with a garden leading down to the river. The conservatory dining room also overlooks the river and offers a wide range of freshly prepared meals. Bedrooms are mostly spacious and all are comfortably furnished. Some have exposed timbers, one has a four-poster bed and all are individually decorated.
6 bth/shr CTV in all bedrooms Tea and coffee making facilities Direct dial from bedrooms Cen ht 60P No coaches Fishing Last d 10pm
ROOMS: s £50-£55; d £65-£90*
MEALS: Lunch £5.95-£15.50alc Dinner £10-£18.50alc*
CARDS:

CREWE Cheshire Map **07** SJ75

Selected

Balterley Hall *(SJ765499)* Balterley CW2 5QG
(exit M6 at junc 16, A500 to Stoke, exit for Audley, at Audley turn right B5500/A52 for Balterley, 2.5m turn left opposite church, 500 yards on left)
☎ 01270 820206 Mrs D Edwards
Closed 24 Dec-1 Jan
Balterley Hall is a fine 17th-century hall surrounded by pleasant grounds and 240 acres of arable farmland. The lounge is comfortably furnished and also contains the dining room where breakfast is served. Of the three bedrooms provided, two are spacious and comfortably equipped. The other is more compact in size but still contains many modern facilities.
3 rms (2 shr) (1 fmly) No smoking in 1 bedrooms No smoking in dining room No smoking in lounges CTV in all bedrooms Tea and coffee making facilities No dogs (ex guide dogs) Cen ht CTV 6P 240 acres arable mixed pigs sheep
ROOMS: s £18-£26; d £34-£40*

CREWKERNE Somerset Map **03** ST40

Premier Selected

Broadview Gardens East Crewkerne TA18 7AG
(on the Yeovil road out of Crewkerne, premises 200 yards on left)
☎ 01460 73424 FAX 73424
The delightful tiered gardens of Broadview are open to the general public on occasion through the National Gardens Scheme. A colonial-style bungalow set in an elevated position close to the town, it is filled with Gillian and Robert Swan's collection of furnishings, porcelain, rugs and pictures. Each of the attractive bedrooms is individually furnished and decorated with every thoughtful extra. By prior arrangement a set home-cooked dinner is available and features fresh produce prepared in a traditional manner.
3 bth/shr No smoking CTV in all bedrooms Tea and coffee making facilities Cen ht 4P No coaches Last d 9am
ROOMS: s £25-£46; d £50-£56; wkly b&b £175-£196; wkly hlf-bd £273-£294
CARDS:

See advertisement under LYME REGIS

Manor Arms North Perrott TA18 7SG (from the A30 take the A3066, signposted Bridport, the premises are situated in the village of North Perrott 1m down this road) ☎ 01460 72901 FAX 01460 72901
This 16th-century inn, a Grade II listed building, is located opposite the village green in the village of North Perrot. In the old world bars with exposed stone walls and an inglenook fireplace, there is a wide selection of freshly cooked dishes to suit all tastes. Meals can be enjoyed in the restaurant, by the fire in the bar, or in the pretty flower-filled garden. Some of the en suite bedrooms are located in the converted coach house at the rear of the property, while others are situated in the inn.
8 shr (1 fmly) No smoking in bedrooms No smoking in dining room No smoking in 1 lounge CTV in all bedrooms Tea and coffee making facilities No dogs (ex guide dogs) Cen ht 22P No coaches Last d 9pm
ROOMS: s £35; d £42-£52
MEALS: Lunch £9-£12&alc Dinner £9-£12&alc
CARDS:

Selected

Manor Farm *(ST409071)* Wayford TA18 8QL
(from Crewkerne take B3165 to Lyme Regis,after 3m at Clapton village turn right into Dunsham Lane,0.5m up hill Manor Farm on right)
☎ 01460 78865 Mr & Mrs A Emery
This delightful Victorian farmhouse is set in a peaceful location and benefits from glorious views over Clapton towards the Axe Valley. The comfortable bedrooms are soundly furnished and a spacious, well appointed sitting room is available to guests. Breakfast is served in the dining room. Guests can enjoy fishing on the lakes or just the peace, tranquillity and wildlife of the area. A self-catering apartment is also available.
3 shr 1 annexe shr No smoking CTV in all bedrooms Tea and coffee making facilities No dogs Cen ht CTV 14P Fishing Riding 20 acres breeding beef

CRICKLADE Wiltshire Map **04** SU09

Upper Chelworth Farm Upper Chelworth SN6 6HD
(From junct 15 take A419 to Crickdale, left at T junct next right and turn into B4040 for 1.5 miles to Ashton Keynes/Chelworth crossroads turn left)
☎ 01793 750440
Closed mid Dec-mid Jan
This Cotswold-stone house offers comfortable bedrooms of various sizes. The gardens tended by Mr Hopkins are particularly noteworthy, and are open to the public, in aid of charity, five times a year. There is a large lounge with a wood burning stove where guests can relax, and an elegant dining room where breakfast is served.
7 rms (6 shr) (1 fmly) No smoking in 2 bedrooms No smoking in dining room CTV in 6 bedrooms Tea and coffee making facilities No dogs (ex guide dogs) Licensed Cen ht CTV 10P No coaches
ROOMS: s £18-£25; d £35-£45; wkly b&b £110-£150*

Prices shown in the directory are meant as a guide only and are subject to change. Please check before you book

CROMER Norfolk Map 09 TG24

Q Q Birch House 34 Cabbell Rd NR27 9HX
☎ 01263 512521 FAX 01263 512521
Guests can expect a friendly welcome at this well maintained guest house, which is situated in a relatively quiet residential road, just off the sea front at the west end of the town centre. The bedrooms have a bright fresh appearance and are kept spotlessly clean although, they do vary in size. The public rooms feature a comfortably furnished reading lounge on the first floor and a neatly appointed dining room, where guests can enjoy a freshly cooked breakfast or a traditional home cooked dinner. Vegetarian choices also supplement the daily changing blackboard specials.
8 rms (1 bth 2 shr) No smoking CTV in all bedrooms Tea and coffee making facilities No dogs (ex guide dogs) Licensed Last d 2pm
ROOMS: s fr £18; d £36-£42; wkly b&b £105-£126; wkly hlf-bd £161-£182*
CARDS:

Q Q Q Brightside 19 Macdonald Rd NR27 9AP (premises situated off the seafront on the Runton Rd (A149) first left after the Cliftonville Hotel)
☎ 01263 513408
Mr and Mrs Bright are the enthusiastic and friendly owners of this well kept guest house, close to the seafront. A warm welcome is assured and guests have plenty of lounge space in which to relax. The attractive bedrooms come in a variety of sizes and styles, but all are prettily decorated and suitably furnished.
6 bth/shr (3 fmly) No smoking CTV in all bedrooms Tea and coffee making facilities No dogs Licensed Cen ht CTV No children 4yrs No coaches Last d 4pm
ROOMS: s £35-£38; d £35-£38; wkly b&b £120-£130*

Q Q Q Chellow Dene 23 MacDonald Rd NR27 9AP (turn off main coastal road between Cromer and Sheringham opposite putting green, Sandcliff Hotel on corner of A140) ☎ 01263 513251
The atmosphere at this family-run guesthouse is friendly and offers a high standard of accommodation. A set dinner and choice of breakfast is readily available and served in the pleasant dining room. Guests also have use of a small lounge. The individually decorated bedrooms are nicely equipped.
7 rms (4 shr) (1 fmly) No smoking in dining room CTV in all bedrooms Tea and coffee making facilities Licensed Cen ht CTV 6P No coaches Last d 5pm
ROOMS: s £18-£19; d £36-£38*

Q Q Q Morden House 20 Cliff Av NR27 0AN
(last road on the right before the traffic lights on the A140 Norwich to Cromer) ☎ 01263 513396
This Victorian guest house is a short distance from the town centre. The public rooms are comfortable and feature a large hall with an open fire place, a beautiful stairwell and leaded light windows. Bedrooms are furnished with period appointments and matching soft furnishings. Vegetarian meals and special diets can easily be accommodated by prior arrangement.
6 rms (4 bth/shr) (1 fmly) No smoking in bedrooms No smoking in dining room No smoking in lounges CTV in all bedrooms Tea and coffee making facilities Licensed Cen ht CTV 3P No coaches Last d 6pm
ROOMS: s £22.50-£25; d £45-£50; wkly b&b £154-£161; wkly hlf-bd £203-£210*
CARDS:

Q Q Sandcliff Private Hotel Runton Rd NR27 9AS
(on seafront towards Sherringham)
☎ 01263 512888 FAX 01263 512888
Closed 21 Dec-4 Jan
Situated on the sea front in Cromer is this family run private hotel which provides cheerfully decorated, well maintained accommodation, some of the bedrooms have unrestricted sea views. The public rooms feature a smart well stocked bar area and a comfortable dining room where guests can enjoy a freshly cooked breakfast or evening meal.
22 rms (3 bth 13 shr) (10 fmly) No smoking in dining room CTV in all bedrooms Tea and coffee making facilities Licensed 10P Golf 18 Last d 6pm
ROOMS: s £21-£26; d £42-£52; wkly hlf-bd £170-£200

Q Q Q Westgate Lodge Private Hotel 10 MacDonald Rd NR27 9AP
☎ 01263 512840
Mr and Mrs Robson offer a friendly welcome to their immaculately maintained small hotel, which provides a high standard of accommodation; each room is attractively decorated and well equipped, is double glazed and has an en-suite shower. The public rooms are also attractively decorated, offering a comfortable lounge and a small bar, and a pleasantly appointed dining room; a five course dinner menu offers a good choice. The adjacent private car park is an added bonus.
11 shr (4 fmly) No smoking in dining room CTV in all bedrooms Tea and coffee making facilities No dogs (ex guide dogs) Licensed Cen ht No children 3yrs 13P Last d 6.30pm
ROOMS: d £40-£50; wkly hlf-bd £210-£215
CARDS:

CROSTHWAITE Cumbria Map 07 SD49

Selected

Q Q Q Q Crosthwaite House LA8 8BP
(exit M6 at junc36, A591 towards Kendal, A590, right onto the A5074, after 4m take small through road for Crosthwaite, 0.5m turn left)
☎ 01539 568264
mid Mar-mid Nov rs Jan-Mar
This idyllic Georgian house is situated at the northern end of the Lyth Valley midway between Kendal and Windermere. Bedrooms are spacious and comfortably furnished with thoughtful extras. The reception rooms offer views over the valley and extend to a light, airy dining room and a lounge. Meals are freshly prepared from carefully devised menus.
6 shr No smoking CTV in all bedrooms Tea and coffee making facilities Licensed Cen ht CTV 12P No coaches Last d 5pm
ROOMS: s £20-£22; d £40-£44; wkly b&b £140-£150; wkly hlf-bd £210-£220*

The AA's professional Inspectors make regular and anonymous visits to all the establishments listed in the Guide. They accept no gifts or favours from proprietors

CROWBOROUGH East Sussex Map **05** TQ53

Q Q Q **The Cottage** Chillies Ln, High Hurstwood TN22 4AA (Leave A26 to High Hurstwood into Chillies Ln downhill approx 1.25m, through wood pass two larger properties next stone house on right)
☎ 01825 732804 FAX 01825 732804
A charming rural retreat in the hamlet of High Hurstwood between Crowborough and Uckfield. The Cottage stands amidst some beautiful countryside and owner Mrs Brown is justly proud of her lovely garden. This is a welcoming place to stay with pets aplenty including the magnificent Macaw, Groucho, who presides over the kitchen. Breakfast is served in an airy conservatory and all four bedrooms are attractively appointed and comfortable.
4 rms (2 shr) (1 fmly) No smoking CTV in all bedrooms Tea and coffee making facilities No dogs (ex guide dogs) Cen ht 4P
ROOMS: s £18-£24; d £40; wkly b&b £120-£130

Q Q Q ***Plough & Horses*** Walshes Rd TN6 3RE ☎ 01892 652614
Closed 24-25 Dec
Situated on the edge of town, near the railway station, this well-kept free house has been run by the Newtons for many years. The pine-furnished bedrooms are all smart and modern, with well co-ordinated soft fabrics and sparkling en suite bathrooms. The extensive bars are traditional in style and offer a good range of bar food plus a restaurant menu with a special selection for children.
8 bth/shr No smoking in bedrooms No smoking in area of dining room No smoking in 1 lounge CTV in all bedrooms Tea and coffee making facilities No dogs (ex guide dogs) Cen ht CTV 40P Last d 10pm
CARDS:

CROYDE Devon Map **02** SS43

Selected

Q Q Q Q **Denham Farm & Country House** *(SS480404)*
North Buckland EX33 1HY (from Braunton on A361 take second left after Knowle signposted North Buckland at Heddon Mill. Continue for 1m to Denham Farm in centre of hamlet)
☎ 01271 890297 FAX 01271 890297 Mr & Mrs Barnes
Closed 18-28 Dec rs Nov-Mar

For generations the Barnes family have been farming in the area, and Jean and Tony have a wealth of local knowledge. Built in the early 1700s, the farmhouse retains much of its character and charm, with modern facilities being sympathetically installed. Each of the attractively decorated bedrooms is well equipped. Wholesome meals are cooked by Jean and served in the sunny dining room.
10 bth/shr (2 fmly) No smoking in dining room No smoking in 1 lounge CTV in all bedrooms Tea and coffee making facilities No dogs Licensed Cen ht CTV 11P Games room Table tennis Skittle alley 160 acres beef sheep Last d prior arrangement
ROOMS: s £25-£28; wkly b&b £168-£175; wkly hlf-bd £252-£259*
CARDS:

Selected

Q Q Q Q **Shuna** Downend EX33 1QE (turn off A361 at Braunton onto B3231 to Croyde, on entering village, guest house is situated 300metres on right hand side) ☎ 01271 890537 FAX 01271 890537 *contd.*

This small establishment has been totally renovated, to provide well equipped accommodation. With views over the dunes, to Baggy Point and Lundy in the distance, the beach is only a two minute walk away. Dee and Stewart Butler are welcoming hosts. There are several small restaurants, pubs and bistros in Croyde where guests may dine.
5 shr (2 fmly) No smoking in dining room No smoking in lounges CTV in all bedrooms Tea and coffee making facilities No dogs (ex guide dogs) Cen ht 8P No coaches
ROOMS: d £40-£50; wkly b&b £140-£157.50
CARDS:

Q Q Q West Winds Moor Ln EX33 1PA
(at village centre turn left and first left again following signs to Croyde Bay)
☎ 01271 890489 FAX 01271 890489
Mar-Nov
Overlooking the golden sands of Croyde Beach, West Winds is conveniently positioned for coastal walks on the beautiful National Trust headland of Baggy Point. The bedrooms are attractively furnished and decorated. In the dining room, evening meals are available by arrangement.
5 bth/shr No smoking in bedrooms No smoking in dining room No smoking in 1 lounge CTV in all bedrooms Tea and coffee making facilities Licensed Cen ht 6P No coaches Last d 7.30pm
ROOMS: s £23-£28*
CARDS:

Premier Selected

Q Q Q Q Q Whiteleaf Croyde Rd EX33 1PN (turn off A361 at Braunton for Croyde, Whiteleaf is on left at 'Road Narrows' sign)
☎ 01271 890266
Conveniently located for easy access to Croyde's sandy beach and the pretty village of Croyde in the other direction, a warm welcome is ensured at this attractive house. Each of the bedrooms has its own character and charm, all are exceptionally well equipped and several have recently been upgraded.

4 bth/shr (2 fmly) No smoking in 2 bedrooms No smoking in dining room No smoking in 1 lounge CTV in all bedrooms Tea and coffee making facilities Direct dial from bedrooms Licensed Cen ht CTV 10P No coaches
ROOMS: s £32-£37; d £54-£60; wkly b&b £165-£186
CARDS:

CROYDON Greater London Map **04** TQ36

Selected

Q Q Q Q Hayesthorpe Hotel 48/52 St Augustines Av CR2 6JJ (W of main Brighton Rd in S Croydon) ☎ 0181 688 8120
FAX 0181 680 1099
Run in hospitable fashion by Michael Culley and Bruno Inzani, this appealing hotel enjoys a peaceful location in a residential area. Bedrooms are well equipped and all have modern en suite facilities. A number of family rooms are available, and one ground floor room has its own conservatory overlooking the garden. There is a well appointed, open-plan bar and dining room where Bruno offers a good choice of meals sometimes featuring dishes from his native Italy.
25 bth/shr (5 fmly) No smoking in 5 bedrooms No smoking in area of dining room CTV in all bedrooms Tea and coffee making facilities Direct dial from bedrooms No dogs (ex guide dogs) Licensed Cen ht 8P
ROOMS: s £45-£60; d £55-£70*
CARDS:

Selected

Q Q Q Q Kirkdale Hotel 22 St Peter's Rd CR0 1HD
(from M25 junct 7 take A23 to Purley then A235 signed Croydon and at Blue Anchor pub turn rt into Aberdeen Rd)
☎ 0181 688 5898 FAX 0181 680 6001
Closed Xmas/New Year
Close to the town centre, this late Victorian Hotel is constantly being improved and restored with many original features still visible. Public areas include a lounge and bar as well as an appealing breakfast room. Bedrooms are well equipped with many modern facilities, and there is a sheltered patio for the summer months.
19 bth/shr (4 fmly) No smoking in bedrooms No smoking in dining room CTV in all bedrooms Tea and coffee making facilities Direct dial from bedrooms No dogs Licensed Cen ht CTV 12P No coaches
ROOMS: s £50-£46; d £62-£70*
CARDS:

CULLOMPTON Devon Map **03** ST00

See also Uffculme

Selected

Q Q Q Q Rullands Rull Ln EX15 1NQ (exit M5 at junc 28, B3181 to Willand, premises 0.5m from centre of Cullompton) ☎ 01884 33356
FAX 01884 35890
This 15th-century country house is surrounded by glorious Devon countryside. Bedrooms are well equipped, offering all modern facilities, and are tastefully furnished in keeping with the character of the building. A family room is reached by a separate outside staircase and one room has a four-poster bed. There are several spacious and comfortable lounges, one with a bar. A limited menu is available at dinner, which demonstrates good use of seasonal and local ingredients.

3 bth/shr 1 annexe bth/shr (1 fmly) No smoking in bedrooms No smoking in dining room No smoking in 1 lounge CTV in all bedrooms Tea and coffee making facilities Licensed Cen ht 20P No coaches Tennis (hard) Last d 9pm
ROOMS: s £25-£35; d £50-£55*
CARDS:

DARLINGTON Co Durham Map **08** NZ21

Q Q Q **Balmoral** 63 Woodland Rd DL3 7BQ (exit A1M at junc 58, premises on A68, opposite the Memorial Hospital) ☎ 01325 461908 FAX 01325 461908
Part of an attractive Victorian terrace, this guest house attracts both leisure and business guests, and has retained much of its fine character, with stripped pine doors, marble fireplaces and period furniture. Bedrooms are individual in both size and style and beautifully decorated. The downstairs dining room also incorporates a small lounge area.
9 rms (4 bth/shr) (2 fmly) No smoking CTV in all bedrooms Tea and coffee making facilities No dogs (ex guide dogs) Cen ht
ROOMS: s £22-£35; d £35-£45; wkly b&b £130-£147*

Premier Selected

Q Q Q Q Q **Clow Beck House** *(NZ281100)* Monk End Farm, Croft on Tees DL2 2SW (take A167 from Darlington for 2m over bridge and follow 3 brown directional signs) ☎ 01325 721075 FAX 01325 720419 Mr & Mrs D Armstrong
Clow Beck House lies in extensive landscaped gardens and is part of a working farm. Owners Heather and David Armstrong are dedicated to the welfare of their guests and provide warm hospitality. Most bedrooms are contained in separate buildings in the gardens, - some are chalet style, each with their own front door - while others are in a newly purpose-built cottage. All rooms are individually decorated and furnished mainly with period pieces and include a wide range of amenities. There is a luxurious lounge in the house, while meals are taken in the new dining room in an impressive extension.
2 rms (1 shr) 12 annexe bth/shr No smoking in dining room CTV in all bedrooms Tea and coffee making facilities Direct dial from bedrooms No dogs (ex guide dogs) Licensed Cen ht CTV 15P Fishing 90 acres mixed
ROOMS: s £40; d £60*
CARDS:

DARTMOUTH Devon Map **03** SX85

Premier Selected

Q Q Q Q Q **Broome Court** Broomhill TQ6 0LD (along A38 to A384, at Totnes turn right onto A381, turn left at Halwell onto A3122 to Dartmouth, at Sportsman Arms turn right and take 3rd right) ☎ 01803 834275 FAX 833260
Located in a designated area of outstanding beauty, Broome Court is tucked away at the end of a quiet lane. Home to Jan Bird and Tom Boughton the atmosphere is very welcoming. Accommodation has been individually furnished in the modern style with lots of extras. There are two lounges and the freshly prepared, traditional breakfast is taken in the old farmhouse kitchen. The self-catering Granary is also available.

3 bth/shr No smoking in bedrooms No smoking in dining room CTV in all bedrooms Tea and coffee making facilities Cen ht CTV No children 12yrs 6P No coaches Golf 27 Golf, tennis and riding available nearby Last d 12 noon
ROOMS: s £35-£45; d £60-£80; wkly b&b £210-£280*

Selected

Q Q Q Q **Captain's House** 18 Clarence St TQ6 9NW (take B3122 Totnes to Dartmouth. Clarence Street is parallel with the river, one block removed) ☎ 01803 832133
This delightful Grade II listed building, which dates from 1730, is situated only a few minutes walk from the town centre and harbour. The bedrooms retain their original character and are individually decorated. All have modern en suite facilities and are well equipped with many extras and personal touches. An extensive choice is offered at breakfast, including home-made bread and preserves, which can be served in the bedrooms.
5 bth/shr No smoking in 1 bedrooms No smoking in dining room CTV in all bedrooms Tea and coffee making facilities Cen ht No children 5yrs No coaches
ROOMS: s £35; d £55-£60; wkly b&b £140-£157.50*

Premier Selected

Q Q Q Q Q **Ford House** 44 Victoria Rd TQ6 9DX (Turn right off A3122 into Townstal Rd leading to Victoria Rd, last house at the bottom of the hill)
☎ 01803 834047 FAX 01803 834047
Mar-Oct
A Regency house, just a short walk from the quayside and town centre. All rooms are well equipped, and individually furnished with many thoughtful extras. Dinner may be taken around a large mahogany table, and the creative set menu features the best of fresh local produce. The lounge has a vast selection of books and an open fire. At quiet periods it is possible to book the whole house for private dinner party weekends.
3 bth/shr No smoking in dining room CTV in all bedrooms Tea and coffee making facilities Direct dial from bedrooms Cen ht 4P No coaches Last d noon
ROOMS: s £45-£80; d £45-£80; wkly b&b £192.50; wkly hlf-bd £367.50*
CARDS:

Premier Selected

QQQQQ **Hedley House** Newcomen Rd TQ6 9BN (from Embankment turn right into Hauley Rd. Opposite Harbour bookshop turn left into Newcomen Rd, premises 300 yards on right) ☎ 01803 835849

From its elevated position near the town centre, Hedley House enjoys glorious views of the River Dart, the Lower Ferry and steam railway in Kingswear on the other side of the estuary. Resident owners, Rob and Marilyn Bird have lovingly restored this terraced property, and accommodation has been individually furnished and decorated to offer expected modern comforts. There is also a cosy sitting room, and a wide ranging breakfast menu. For dinner, Dartmouth offers a good choice of restaurants, including the famous Carved Angel, where special deals can be arranged.

3 bth/shr No smoking Tea and coffee making facilities No dogs (ex guide dogs) Cen ht CTV No children No coaches Last d noon

ROOMS: d £60-£80*

Premier Selected

QQQQQ **Nonsuch House** Church Hill, Kingswear TQ6 0BX (A3022/A379 and turn left onto B3205. After 2m turn left up Higher Contour Rd. House 0.75m on seaward side of hairpin bend)

☎ 01803 752829 FAX 01803 752829

Built in Edwardian times with stunning views across the River Dart to Dartmouth, this spacious house has large bedrooms, all with their own luxuriously appointed bathrooms. A tastefully furnished lounge is situated on the ground floor, while the elegant dining room on the lower ground floor leads into the conservatory overlooking the river. A short menu offering fine home made cuisine, all prepared from fresh produce, is offered. A friendly welcome is assured from the Noble Family.

3 bth/shr No smoking in bedrooms No smoking in dining room CTV in all bedrooms Tea and coffee making facilities No dogs (ex guide dogs) Cen ht No children 12yrs Last d 8pm

ROOMS: s £40-£50; d £60-£80*

Selected

QQQQ **Seale Arms** Victoria Rd TQ6 9SA

(turn off A38 at Buckfastleigh and take A384 to Totnes. At Totes take A381 as far as Halwell and at Halwell take A3122 to Dartmouth)

☎ 01803 832719 FAX 01803 834021

Situated on the edge of the shopping centre and within easy level walking distance of the quay, the Seale Arms offers a lively atmosphere. All the bedrooms are individually decorated and well equipped. Breakfast is taken around a large communal table in the first floor dining room, and a variety of bar meals is available in the comfortable, spacious and well stocked bar.

4 shr (2 fmly) No smoking in 2 bedrooms No smoking in dining room CTV in all bedrooms Tea and coffee making facilities Cen ht No coaches Last d 8.30pm

ROOMS: s £32.50-£35; d £45-£50; wkly b&b £137.81*

MEALS: Bar Lunch fr £1&alc*

Selected

QQQQ **Slide House** Hynetown Rd, Strete TQ6 0RS

☎ 01803 770378 FAX 01803 770197

Feb-Nov

Brian and Colin make their guests feel at home in their tastefully furnished bungalow, where guests can enjoy the comfortable lounge and well tended gardens with a patio facing the sea. The well co-ordinated en suite bedrooms include modern facilities with many personal touches. Breakfast, with home made jams and marmalade, is served in the attractive dining room and dinner can be served by prior arrangement.

3 bth/shr No smoking in bedrooms No smoking in dining room CTV in all bedrooms Tea and coffee making facilities No dogs Cen ht No children 12yrs 6P No coaches Last d previous night

DAWLISH Devon Map **03** SX97

Selected

QQQQ **Walton House** Plantation Ter EX7 9DR

(Plantation Terrace is located off the A379 in the town centre, premises lie to the rear of the Shaftsbury Theatre)

☎ 01626 862760

Situated in a quiet location within easy walking distance of both the town centre and beach, Walton House is a John Nash-designed, Grade II listed Georgian property. Guests are assured of a friendly welcome by John and Doreen Newton to their family home. The bedrooms are all en suite, comfortable and well equipped with modern facilities.

6 bth/shr No smoking in dining room CTV in all bedrooms Tea and coffee making facilities No dogs (ex guide dogs) Cen ht No children 6P

ROOMS: d £34-£42*

Selected

QQQQ **West Hatch Hotel** 34 West Cliff EX7 9DN

(exit M5 at junc 30, A379 towards Dawlish, West Hatch situated 0.25m from centre of Dawlish on road to Teignmouth)

☎ 01626 864211 & 862948 FAX 01626 864211

David and Pat Badcock have welcomed guests to this attractive detached hotel for over ten years. It is well situated for easy access to the beaches, shops, and other amenities and offers a high standard of accommodation. There is a sitting room with satellite TV, a lounge bar, and a dining room where breakfast is served. The comfortable bedrooms are well equipped with a number of extra touches, and beautifully decorated in co-ordinated colours. Ground floor rooms are available and some have the benefit of sea views.
10 bth/shr (2 fmly) No smoking in bedrooms No smoking in dining room CTV in all bedrooms Tea and coffee making facilities No dogs Licensed Cen ht CTV 11P No coaches Spa bath
ROOMS: s £33-£40; d £46-£68; wkly b&b £147-£224*
CARDS:

DEAL Kent Map **05** TR35

QQQ **Blencathra Country** Kingsdown Hill CT14 8EA ☎ 01304 373725
Surrounded by a pleasant garden, this attractive period house is personally run by Peter and Maureen Jailler. Bedrooms are spacious and traditionally furnished, with modern en suite facilities. There is a TV lounge and a smart separate dining room. Evening meals can be provided by arrangement, with vegetarians catered for, along with a choice of hearty and continental breakfast.
7 rms (4 shr) (3 fmly) No smoking CTV in all bedrooms Tea and coffee making facilities No dogs (ex guide dogs) Licensed CTV 7P No coaches Croquet
ROOMS: s £17-£25; d £36-£40*

Selected

QQQQ **Dunkerleys Restaurant** 19 Beach St CT14 7AH (main Canterbury to Dover Rd turn off at rdbt at Deal A258, follow road to Deal Pier, house opposite)
☎ 01304 375016 FAX 01304 380187
Situated overlooking the sea, this is a restaurant with smart comfortably appointed bedrooms. The rooms vary in size but have modern en suite facilities and many useful facilities. There is a new bar/brasserie serving snacks all day. The restaurant has a set-price two or three-course menu at lunch, and a short carte menu for dinner. Chef Stephen Harvey's cooking continues to improve, and a generous English breakfast is served; continental is also available.
16 bth/shr (4 fmly) No smoking in area of dining room CTV in all bedrooms Tea and coffee making facilities Direct dial from bedrooms No dogs (ex guide dogs) Licensed Cen ht No coaches Last d 10pm
ROOMS: s fr £40; d fr £60; wkly b&b £180-£360; wkly hlf-bd £288-£468*
CARDS:

QQQ **Kingsdown Country Hotel & Captains Table** Cliffe Rd CT14 8AJ (from the A2 Canterbury/Dover road take the A258 towards Deal. After 2 miles enter Ringwould and turn right at far end signed Kingsdown)
☎ 01304 373755 FAX 01304 373755
This is a charming house, situated in a quiet fishing village close to Dover and Deal. It offers a high standard of accommodation, with well equipped and comfortable bedrooms. There is a cosy lounge with bar and a dining room, where a choice of home-cooked meals is available.
4 shr No smoking in bedrooms No smoking in dining room CTV in all bedrooms Tea and coffee making facilities No dogs (ex guide dogs) Licensed Cen ht CTV 8P Wind surfing
Last d 1pm

Selected

QQQQ **Sondes Lodge** 14 Sondes Rd CT14 7BW (A258 from Dover, along the Strand past Deal Castle, last one-way street on the right heading to the seafront 2nd guest house on the right) ☎ 01304 368741
This attractive Victorian property, close to the shops and the sea-front, is continually being improved, and proprietors Jayne and Tony Hulme offer a warm welcome. The bedrooms are bright, pretty and well equipped with shower cubicles and remote controlled TV; thoughtful extras are provided such as bathrobes and toiletries.
3 shr (1 fmly) No smoking in dining room CTV in all bedrooms Tea and coffee making facilities No dogs (ex guide dogs) Cen ht No coaches
ROOMS: s £30-£40; d £44-£50*
CARDS:

DELPH Greater Manchester Map **07** SD90

QQQ **Globe Farm** Huddersfield Rd, Standedge, Delph OL3 5LU (on A62 between Oldham and Huddersfield, 0.75m after junct with A670 from Uppermill) ☎ 01457 873040 FAX 01457 873040
Closed Xmas & New Year
This solidly built stone house is located alongside the A62 and enjoys fine views of the hills and dales of the Saddleworth Moors, with the Pennine Way nearby. Attractively furnished bedrooms are offered as well as a comfortable lounge. A hearty breakfast is served, together with a freshly prepared set evening meal by arrangement.
12 shr (1 fmly) No smoking in 4 bedrooms No smoking in dining room CTV in all bedrooms Tea and coffee making facilities No dogs (ex guide dogs) Licensed Cen ht CTV 25P No coaches Last d 5pm
ROOMS: s fr £23; d fr £39.50*
CARDS:

DERBY Derbyshire Map **08** SK33

See also Belper & Melbourne

QQ ***Dalby House Hotel*** 100 Radbourne St, off Windmill Hill Ln DE22 3BU (turn off A52 into Windmill Hill Lane near A52/A38 junct)
☎ 01332 342353
Situated just off the junction of the A38 and A52, this guest house offers modest but good value accommodation in neatly decorated bedrooms. There is a comfortable lounge, and breakfast is served in the spacious dining room overlooking the colourful garden.
9 rms (2 fmly) No smoking in dining room CTV in all bedrooms Tea and coffee making facilities Cen ht CTV 10P No coaches
Last d 7pm

QQQ **Georgian House Hotel** 32/36 Ashbourne Rd DE22 3AD (A52 to Derby, follow signs A52 towards Ashbourne past Friargate 500yds on the right)
☎ 01332 349806 FAX 01332 349959
Set in a conservation area, within walking distance of the city centre, this Grade II listed building dates back to 1765. Public areas include a restaurant, cocktail bar and adjacent public bar where a range of bar meals and cask ales is offered. Bedrooms, a number of which are on the ground floor, are furnished in keeping with the style of the building and are well equipped.
20 bth/shr (2 fmly) No smoking in dining room CTV in all bedrooms Tea and coffee making facilities Direct dial from bedrooms Cen ht CTV ch fac 40P Last d 9.30pm
ROOMS: s £40-£47; d £52-£60
CARDS:

Q Q Q **Rangemoor Park Hotel** 67 Macklin St DE1 1LF
☎ 01332 347252 FAX 01332 369319
A city centre hotel which has been family-owned and run for over 19 years by John and Val Richardson. There are two types of accommodation, those with en suite facilities being larger, while standard rooms, though somewhat smaller, are equally well presented. Just off the entrance lobby is a lounge as well as a spacious breakfast room.
24 rms (13 bth/shr) (3 fmly) No smoking in dining room CTV in all bedrooms Tea and coffee making facilities Direct dial from bedrooms Cen ht CTV 37P
CARDS:

Q Q ***Victoria Park Hotel*** 312 Burton Rd DE23 6AD
(on A5250, 1m from city centre) ☎ 01332 341551
Good value for money is provided at this splendid Victorian property, set back from the main road to the south of the city centre. Bedrooms are simply furnished and well maintained, while breakfast is served in the bright dining room.
11 rms (3 fmly) No smoking in 3 bedrooms No smoking in dining room No smoking in lounges CTV in all bedrooms Tea and coffee making facilities Direct dial from bedrooms Cen ht CTV 15P No coaches

DEVIZES Wiltshire Map **04** SU06

Selected

Q Q Q Q **Blounts Court Farm** *(SU996583)* Coxhill Ln, Potterne SN10 5NQ (A360 to Potterne turn into Coxhill Lane opposite George & Dragon, at fork turn left and follow drive righthanded up to farmhouse) ☎ 01380 727180 Mr & Mrs C Cary
On the top of a wooded hillside with country views, this is an ideal get-away-from-it-all location. The recently converted stable block is now two beautifully decorated rooms with en suite facilities and many personal touches. There is a private lounge and breakfast is served in the farmhouse dining room.
2 shr CTV in all bedrooms Tea and coffee making facilities No dogs (ex guide dogs) Cen ht CTV No children 8yrs P 200 acres Arable
ROOMS: s £30; d £45

Q Q **Eastcott Manor** Easterton SN10 4PL (on B3098 between Urchfoot & Easterton, S of Devizes between A360 Salisbury & A342 Andover)
☎ 01380 813313
Closed 23-31 Dec
This charming 16th-century farmhouse has a relaxed feel about it. Bedrooms are functional, all with private facilities. Farmhouse breakfast, and dinners by arrangement, are served in the dining room at a 400-year old refectory table. There is also a lounge and sunny conservatory where open countryside views can be enjoyed. Stabling is available.
4 bth/shr CTV in all bedrooms Tea and coffee making facilities CTV 7P No coaches Stabling Chair lift Last d 24hrs in advance
ROOMS: s fr £20; d fr £44; wkly b&b £114-£154*

Selected

Q Q Q Q **Greenfields** Bath Rd SN10 1QG (Greenfields is on the left just after entering town limits, from other directons take the A361 Trowbridge road from the town centre)
☎ 01380 729315 FAX 01380 720033
Dave and Dot Churchill make guests welcome to their Edwardian home. With private access to the Kennet and Avon canal at the top of the world famous Caen Hill flight of locks, it is popular with walkers and cyclists. Bedrooms are well equipped with quality furniture and there are many thoughtful extras. There is a cosy lounge for guests use, and a smartly furnished dining room where breakfast is served at one large table.
3 shr (1 fmly) No smoking CTV in all bedrooms Tea and coffee making facilities No dogs (ex guide dogs) Cen ht 4P No coaches
ROOMS: s £22.50-£25; d £38-£40; wkly b&b £105-£115*

A farmhouse hotel & award winning restaurant – in the beautiful Derbyshire Dales

Dine in our eighteenth century licensed farmhouse restaurant on fresh food and homemade desserts after exploring the Derbyshire dales and the thrills of Alton Towers. Excellent ensuite rooms for the family, friends and business makes your stay in the Derbyshire Countryside an experience to remember.

Telephone or Fax Barbara Tunnicliffe on 01889 590288

Beeches, Waldley, Doveridge, Near Ashbourne, Derby DE6 5LR

See gazeteer entry under Doveridge

AAQQQQQ Premier Selected AA 2 Rosettes

ETB 3 Crown Highly Commended

Beeches

To wine & dine, for business, for family, friends and all those special occasions

Dannah Farm

Country Guest House

Relax and unwind in our lovely Georgian farmhouse set amidst beautiful countryside, perfect for walking, touring and discovering the myriad beauties of Derbyshire. Superb, award winning, licensed dining room where we aim to serve the very best in farmhouse cooking. All rooms en-suite. 4 poster available. SAE brochure.

AA QQQQQ Premier Selected

ETB 3 Crown Highly Commended.

Awarded Derbyshire Life Golden Goblet for our food. Winners top national award for excellence and innovation.

1994 Best of Tourism Award

See Gazeteer entry under Shottle

Dannah Farm, Bowmans Lane, Shottle, Nr Belper, Derbyshire DE56 2DR

Telephone: (01773) 550273

Fax: (01773) 550590

Selected

Q Q Q Q **Littleton Lodge** Littleton Panell (A360) SN10 4ES
(4m S of Devizes on A360, 500metres on left after railway bridge)
☎ 01380 813131 FAX 01380 813131
Littleton Lodge has just been totally refurbished by proprietors, Mr and Mrs Linton. All rooms have en suite facilities, TVs and tea trays. The large garden has plenty of space for relaxation. Breakfasts are noted for their originality, guests have the choice of a variety of national styles including English.
3 shr No smoking CTV in all bedrooms Tea and coffee making facilities No dogs Cen ht 4P No coaches Badminton
ROOMS: s £30-£35; d £45-£50
CARDS:

DIBDEN Hampshire Map 04 SU40

Q Q *Dale Farm* Manor Rd, Applemore Hill SO45 5TJ
(A326 towards Fawley, straight across at Dibden roundabout, then 1st right into Manor Rd. After 200yds turn right and then left behind hay barn)
☎ 01703 849632 FAX 01703 840285
This attractive 18th-century farmhouse is conveniently located for Beaulieu and the New Forest. The modern bedrooms are bright and overlook the garden and forest. Breakfast is served in the pine-furnished lounge/dining room.
6 rms (2 shr) (2 fmly) CTV in all bedrooms Tea and coffee making facilities No dogs (ex guide dogs) Cen ht CTV 20P No coaches Fishing Riding Last d 11am

DINTON Buckinghamshire Map 04 SP71

Q Q Q *Wallace (SP770110)* HP17 8UF (from A418 take the turning marked Dinton/Ford, then 1st left signed Upton, where farm can be found on the right) ☎ 01296 748660 FAX 01296 748851 Mrs J M W Cook
Set in the Vale of Aylesbury, this 16th-century farmhouse has a homely atmosphere. The property and surrounding fields abound with dogs, rare breed sheep, ducks and chickens. Guests have use of an attractive sitting room with open fire, and an extensive library. Breakfast is served around a large farmhouse kitchen table.
3 bth/shr (1 fmly) No smoking in bedrooms No smoking in dining room Tea and coffee making facilities No dogs (ex guide dogs) Cen ht CTV 6P Fishing 24 acres beef cattle sheep
CARDS:

DISS Norfolk

See **Fressingfield**

DODDISCOMBSLEIGH Devon Map 03 SX88

Q Q *Whitemoor (SX861866)* EX6 7PU (7m SW of Exeter, continue from M5 onto A38 (direction Plymouth) and take first left after A38/A380 intersection for Dunchideock/Doddiscombsleigh)
☎ 01647 252423 Mrs B Lacey
Situated in a pretty village not far from Exeter, Mrs Lacey offers basic, but comfortable accommodation, in a farmhouse setting. Breakfast is served around a communal table, and dinner can be obtained from a nearby hostelry.
4 rms No smoking Tea and coffee making facilities Cen ht CTV 5P Outdoor swimming pool 284 acres arable mixed

See page 14-20 for a list of Premier Selected establishments

DONCASTER South Yorkshire Map 08 SE50

Q Q *Almel Hotel* 20 Christchurch Rd DN1 2QL
(at rear of Odeon cinema over rbt then next rt and left into Christchurch Rd)
☎ 01302 365230 FAX 01302 341434
Situated close to the town centre and in a quiet side road, this family owned and run hotel offers good value. The bedrooms are modern and mixed in size. There is a separate lounge and bar and home cooking is served in the rear dining room.
30 rms (24 bth/shr) (1 fmly) CTV in all bedrooms Tea and coffee making facilities Licensed Cen ht CTV 8P Last d 8pm
CARDS:

Q Q Q **Balmoral Hotel** 129 Thorne Rd DN2 5BH
(M18 jct 3,towards racecourse,straight over rcecrse rdbt,2nd left (Leicester Ave),straight through traffc lights,reach Thorne rd,turn left,Est on right)
☎ 01302 364385 FAX 364385
This spacious Edwardian house offers modern and well equipped bedrooms. The comfortable public rooms retain many original features including delightful wood-panelling in the hall. Very friendly and attentive service is provided by the resident owners, Nadia & Paul Race. Convenient for the town centre and the racecourse.
11 rms (2 shr) (2 fmly) No smoking in 6 bedrooms No smoking in dining room CTV in all bedrooms Tea and coffee making facilities Cen ht CTV 14P Golf 18 Most things available nearby Last d noon
ROOMS: s £18-£30; d £36-£44*
CARDS:

Selected

Q Q Q Q **Canda Lodge** Hampolebalk Ln, Skellow DN6 8LF
(adjacent to A1 South, 6 miles south off M62 interchange with A1 5 miles north of interchange of M18)
☎ 01302 724028 FAX 01302 728484
This delightful stone built house with its well tended gardens is convenient for the town and racecourse. A courtesy car service is available. Bedrooms are well equipped and delightfully furnished while the public rooms include a lounge and dining room where guests take meals around a large table. Dinner can be pre-arranged.
8 rms (5 bth/shr) (2 fmly) No smoking in 2 bedrooms No smoking in dining room No smoking in lounges CTV in all bedrooms Tea and coffee making facilities Direct dial from bedrooms Cen ht ch fac 12P Golf 36 Sauna
wkly b&b £150-£164
CARDS:

DORCHESTER Dorset Map 03 SY69

See also **Evershot, Sydling St Nicholas and Winterbourne Abbas**

Q Q *Lower Lewell (SY744897)* West Stafford DT2 8AP
(3.5m E of Dorchester, midway between West Stafford and Crossways)
☎ 01305 267169 Mrs M Tomblin
Located in the heart of Hardy country, this charming farmhouse offers a warm and friendly welcome. The spacious bedrooms are suitably furnished and brightly decorated. Breakfast is served in the cosy dining room beside the Inglenook fireplace. The lounge has a homely atmosphere and is the ideal place to relax in.
3 rms (2 fmly) No smoking in dining room Tea and coffee making facilities No dogs Cen ht CTV 8P

Selected

QQQQ **Westwood House Hotel** 29 High West St DT1 1UP (From A35 drive straight into town, hotel is situated within 100yds of 'Top o' Town' rdbt and car park) ☎ 01305 268018 FAX 01305 250282 This smart, town-centre property, was built for Lord Ilchester in 1815. Bedrooms are stylishly simple in design, with bold use of colours. All are well equipped with such personal extra touches as fresh flowers, phone, clock radio, and hair dryer. There is a comfortable lounge for guests and breakfast is taken in the rear conservatory.

6 bth/shr (1 fmly) No smoking in dining room CTV in all bedrooms Tea and coffee making facilities Direct dial from bedrooms Cen ht CTV No coaches

ROOMS: s £35-£85; d £45-£85.50; wkly b&b £200-£280*

CARDS:

The Poachers Inn

Piddletrenthide, Dorset DT2 7QX

Tel: 01300 348358 Fax: 01300 348153

Country in, set in the heart of the lovely Piddle Valley. 6 miles from Dorchester and within easy reach of all Dorset's attractions. All rooms en-suite and have Colour TV, tea and coffee, telephone, swimming pool (May to September). Riverside Garden. Restaurant where half board guests choose from à la carte menu at no extra cost.

AA QQQ

English Tourist Board COMMENDED

BB £26 per person per night

DBB £38 per person per night

Special breaks: Stay Two nights DBB £76 per person, Third night DBB Free from 1st October to 30th April

English Tourist Board COMMENDED

AA QQQ

CHURCHVIEW GUEST HOUSE

WINTERBOURNE ABBAS, DORCHESTER, DORSET DT2 9LS

Telephone: 01305 889296

Our 17th Century Guest House noted for hospitality, traditional breakfasts and delicious evening meals, makes an ideal base for exploring beautiful West Dorset. All character bedrooms are comfortable and well appointed. Meals feature local produce, cream and cheeses. Relaxation is provided by two attractive lounges and licensed bar. Your hosts will give every assistance with local information on attractions, walks and touring to ensure you of a memorable stay. Non-smoking. ***Terms: B&B £21.00-£27.00pp. Dinner, B&B £34.00-£40.00pp.***

For further details please contact Jane and Michael Deller.

Short breaks available.

CHIPPENHALL HALL

Listed Tudor Manor, a period film location and of Saxon origin, with recordings in Domesday Book. Set in 7 acres of gardens and ponds giving total rural tranquillity. Unique atmosphere with beams and inglenook log fires. Fine food and wines. Heated outdoor pool set in rose covered courtyard. All rooms en-suite. We are ETB 3 Crowns, Highly Commended. Winner of 1998 Johansen Award to Country Houses in all Great Britain and Ireland. One mile south of Fressingfield on B1116.

Fressingfield, Eye, Suffolk IP21 5TD

Tel: (01379) 588180 and 586733

Fax: (01379) 586272

Premier Selected

QQQQQ **Yalbury Cottage** Lower Bockhampton DT2 8PZ (turn off A35 past Thomas Hardy's cottage, straight over crossrds, 400yds on left, just past red telephone box and opposite village pump) ☎ 01305 262382 FAX 01305 266412
Closed 28 Dec-28 Jan
Yalbury Cottage is set in the beautiful rural hamlet of Lower Bockhampton, and was originally the home of the local shepherd and keeper of the water meadows. The oak beamed ceilings, inglenook fireplaces and stone walls remain as features in both the lounge and restaurant. This is an ideal venue in which to enjoy the hotel's award-winning cuisine. Bedrooms overlook either the colourful gardens or adjacent fields.
8 bth/shr (1 fmly) No smoking in 6 bedrooms No smoking in dining room CTV in all bedrooms Tea and coffee making facilities Direct dial from bedrooms Licensed Cen ht 20P Last d 8.30pm
ROOMS: s £49; d £74; wkly b&b £259-£343; wkly hlf-bd £336-£448
CARDS:

DORRINGTON Shropshire Map **07** SJ40

Selected

QQQQ **Ashton Lees** Ashton Lees SY5 7JW (establishment is on right hand of A49 just entering village of Dorrington, from Shrewsbury) ☎ 01743 718378
Closed Xmas
This large detached house is set back off the A49 on the northern outskirts of Dorrington village and just 6 miles south of Shrewsbury. The traditionally furnished, comfortable bedrooms are all non smoking. Separate tables are provided in the dining room and dinner is available by prior arrangement. The guest house is licensed with a small bar and welcoming real fires burn during colder weather. The delightful rear garden is quite large and hospitality from the Woodall family is warm and friendly.
3 rms (2 bth/shr) No smoking CTV in all bedrooms Tea and coffee making facilities No dogs (ex guide dogs) Licensed Cen ht CTV 6P No coaches Last d 9am
ROOMS: s £19-£22; d £38-£44; wkly b&b £119.70-£138.60; wkly hlf-bd £192.50-£213.50

DOVER Kent Map **05** TR34

QQQ **Ardmore Private Hotel** 18 Castle Hill Rd CT16 1QW (on A258 next to Dover Castle) ☎ 01304 205895 FAX 01304 208229
Closed Xmas
This delightful non-smoking period house is located close to the castle, town centre and the eastern docks car ferry terminal. Personally run by the proprietor Mr Len Morriss, the atmosphere is very friendly and the accommodation has been well furnished to retain its Victorian elegance, including a sumptuous lounge and well appointed breakfast room.
4 shr (1 fmly) No smoking CTV in all bedrooms Tea and coffee making facilities No dogs Cen ht
ROOMS: d £38-£48*
CARDS:

Selected

QQQQ **Beulah House** 94 Crabble Hill, London Rd CT17 0SA (on A256) ☎ 01304 824615 FAX 828850
This elegant Victorian house is just a short distance from the ports and town centre. Award winning proprietor Anita Owen offers a warm welcome. The en suite bedrooms are well appointed and one room has a four-poster bed. There is an attractive TV lounge, and a generous traditional breakfast is served in the dining room. The three-quarter acre topiary gardens surrounded by trees and shrubs are an outstanding feature.
6 shr (2 fmly) No smoking CTV in all bedrooms Tea and coffee making facilities No dogs Cen ht CTV 11P
ROOMS: s £30-£35; d £46-£48*
CARDS:

QQ **Bleriot's** Belper House, 47 Park Av CT16 1HE (M2/A2 for Dover, right at 2nd rdbt by Duke of York pub, 2nd right after 1m into Connaught Rd(opp castle entrance) and first left into Park Avenue) ☎ 01304 211394
This attractive Victorian house is run by Martin and Mandy Casey who are continually upgrading. Bedrooms are attractively decorated and have modern en suite facilities. There is comfortable guest lounge, and evening meals and snacks are served until 8pm.
8 shr (5 fmly) No smoking in dining room No smoking in lounges CTV in all bedrooms Tea and coffee making facilities No dogs Licensed Cen ht 11P No coaches
ROOMS: s £20-£42; d £38-£42*
CARDS:

QQQ **Castle House** 10 Castle Hill Rd CT16 1QW (A20 for Dover-over 4 rdbts, turn left at lights past BP petrol station, 1st right into Castle Hill Rd and premises are just below Dover Castle) ☎ 01304 201656 FAX 01304 210197
Personally run by proprietors Elizabeth and Rodney Dimech this attractive guest house offers non-smoking accommodation which is bright and comfortably furnished. A small guest lounge is well equipped with books and games. A choice of English or Continental breakfast is offered in the dining room.
6 shr (1 fmly) No smoking CTV in all bedrooms Tea and coffee making facilities No dogs (ex guide dogs) Licensed Cen ht CTV No coaches Last d 6pm
ROOMS: s £25-£28; d £36-£44*
CARDS:

QQQ ***Chrislyn's*** 15 Park Av CT16 1ES (A258, at castle turn right into Connaught Rd, then 1st left into Park Avenue) ☎ 01304 202302
Closed 25 December
Recently refurbished and upgraded, this attractive property is personally run by Mrs Lynn Heynen, who offers a warm welcome. The pretty bedrooms are bright and comfortably furnished, and most have en suite showers. There is a well appointed breakfast room and guests are welcome to use the garden and lounge.
5 rms (4 shr) (2 fmly) No smoking in dining room No smoking in lounges CTV in all bedrooms Tea and coffee making facilities No dogs Cen ht 3P No coaches

Q Q Q ***Cleveland*** 2 Laureston Place, off Castle Hill Rd CT16 1QX (between Dover town centre and Dover Castle, off the A258)
☎ 01304 204622 FAX 01304 211598
This early Victorian guest house is run by proprietors Betty and Alistair Dimech who offer a warm welcome and continue to upgrade the rooms. Bedrooms have modern en suite facilities. There is a cosy dining room downstairs, light refreshments are available and an evening meal can be provided by prior arrangement.
5 shr No smoking in dining room No smoking in lounges CTV in all bedrooms Tea and coffee making facilities Cen ht CTV Last d 7.30pm
CARDS:

Q Q **Cliffe Tavern** High St, St Margarets at Cliffe CT15 6AT (follow M20/A20 to Dover then A2 towards London,1st rdbt turn right towards Deal then 1st right to village, Inn is opposite village church)
☎ 01304 852400 FAX 01304 852749
This attractive local inn in this small village just outside Dover offers 12 attractive well furnished rooms. The two bars stock an interesting range of quality beers and staff have a ready smile for guests. There is also a boldly decorated restaurant Beef and Reef which as the name suggests specialises in steaks and seafood and is appropriately nautically themed.
12 bth/shr (2 fmly) CTV in all bedrooms Tea and coffee making facilities Direct dial from bedrooms Cen ht 35P Riding Last d 9.30pm
ROOMS: s £39.95-£49.95; d £49.95-£65
MEALS: Lunch £15-£22alc Dinner £15-£22alc
CARDS:

Q Q **Dell** 233 Folkestone Rd CT17 9SL (turn off A20 onto B2011, Capel le Ferne turnoff, onto small rdbt, follow sign for Dover West. Est. 3.5m on right) ☎ 01304 202422 FAX 204816
This friendly family-run guest house is well presented and ideally situated for access to the town centre, road links and the ports. The bedrooms are attractively decorated and comfortably furnished, all have TV and some have en suite facilities.
7 rms (2 shr) (3 fmly) No smoking in dining room No smoking in lounges CTV in all bedrooms Tea and coffee making facilities No dogs (ex guide dogs) Cen ht 4P No coaches
ROOMS: s £16-£22; d £32-£48✱
CARDS:

Q Q **Dovers Restover** 69 Folkestone Rd CT17 9RZ (on B2011 opposite Dover Priory Railway Station approx 300mtrs from town centre)
☎ 01304 206031
Located five minutes from the port this well presented guest house offers bright comfortable accommodation. The bedrooms have been attractively decorated and offer colour television and radio alarm. There is a cosy dining room where a traditional breakfast is served.
6 rms (2 shr) No smoking in 3 bedrooms No smoking in dining room CTV in all bedrooms Tea and coffee making facilities No dogs Cen ht 7P No coaches
ROOMS: s £17-£20; d £28-£44✱
CARDS:

Selected

Q Q Q Q **East Lee** 108 Maison Dieu Rd CT16 1RT
☎ 01304 210176 FAX 01304 210176
East Lee is an attractive house located just a few minutes from the port. Personally run by Mr and Mrs Knight, the house has been sympathetically restored and decorated to preserve its Victorian character. The bedrooms are comfortably furnished and have many thoughtful extras. All rooms have modern en suite facilities. A traditional breakfast is served in the delightful dining room and Mrs Knight is happy to cater for any specialist diets by prior arrangement.

4 shr No smoking CTV in all bedrooms Tea and coffee making facilities Direct dial from bedrooms No dogs Cen ht 4P No coaches
ROOMS: d £40-£48✱
CARDS:

Q Q Q ***Gateway Hovertel*** 149-156 Snargate St CT17 9BZ (opposite Dover Marina, beside A20 approach road into Dover, 2mins from Hovercraft & ferry terminal) ☎ 01304 205479 FAX 01304 211504
Closed 23 Dec-6 Jan
This modern hotel overlooks the marina and is conveniently located on the new A20, very close to the ferry terminal, hoverport and the new cruise terminal. Personally run by Mr and Mrs Peters and their team the hotel is open around the clock, the en suite bedrooms are bright and well presented, all have televisions. Public areas include a small lounge, a bar and a pine furnished dining room where a buffet style continental breakfast is served from 3am and full English breakfast from 8-9am. Security-locked parking is available at the hotel.
27 bth/shr (7 fmly) No smoking in dining room CTV in all bedrooms Tea and coffee making facilities No dogs (ex guide dogs) Licensed Cen ht CTV 26P Last d 7pm
CARDS: See advertisement on p.173.

Q Q Q **Hubert House** 9 Castle Hill Rd CT16 1QW (premises located at bottom of Castle Hill Road leading to Dover Castle on the A258)
☎ 01304 202253
This charming Georgian guest house is within walking distance of the ferry port. Bedrooms are furnished in the modern style and all have remote control TV, clock radio alarm and tea tray. There is a small lounge and a well appointed breakfast room. A choice of breakfasts is available and the atmosphere is very friendly. Most rooms have en suite showers.
8 bth/shr (4 fmly) CTV in all bedrooms Tea and coffee making facilities No dogs (ex guide dogs) Cen ht 7P No coaches
ROOMS: s £28-£32; d £40-£46✱
CARDS:

Q Q **Kernow** 189 Folkestone Rd CT17 9SJ (turn off A20 onto B2011 following signs for Local Services. Establishment is located 3m from slip road on the right) ☎ 01304 207797
Conveniently located for the ferries and trains this personally run B&B offers neat comfortable accommodation. There is a bright breakfast room where early breakfast can be arranged.
3 rms CTV in all bedrooms Tea and coffee making facilities No dogs (ex guide dogs) Cen ht CTV 5P
ROOMS: d £28-£34*

Q Q Q **Linden** 231 Folkestone Rd CT17 9SL (travelling S on M20 take second exit after tunnel at Folkestone, first exit at roundabout, B2011, premises 3.5m on right) ☎ 01304 205449 FAX 01304 212499
Closed 24-26 Dec
This charming Victorian terraced house is run by resident proprietors Jean and Roger Walkden. Bedrooms are bright and comfortably furnished with modern facilities. There is a comfortably furnished lounge and open plan dining room, and a free courtesy service will take you to and from the ferries, station and cruise liner terminal.
5 rms (3 shr) (1 fmly) No smoking in dining room No smoking in lounges CTV in all bedrooms Tea and coffee making facilities Cen ht CTV 4P No coaches
ROOMS: s £17-£24; d £34-£50; wkly b&b £110-£160
CARDS:

Selected

Q Q Q Q **Number One** 1 Castle St CT16 1QH (exit A20 to castle, premises at bottom of Castle Hill or exit A2 at A258 into town and premises are on right hand corner before the traffic lights)
☎ 01304 202007 FAX 01304 214078
Closed 25-27 Dec
Situated within walking distance of the seafront and town centre, this delightful Georgian town house has been run by the Reidy family for 22 years. Cosy, comfortable accommodation is provided along with old fashioned hospitality and service. The attractive en suite rooms are equipped with a nice range of thoughtful extras and furnishings and decorations are from the Victorian period. A good choice of breakfast is served to the bedrooms and guests have use of a pretty lounge that opens out onto the well kept walled garden. Garage parking is available for a charge of £2 per night.
5 shr (3 fmly) No smoking in dining room No smoking in lounges CTV in all bedrooms Tea and coffee making facilities No dogs Cen ht 6P No coaches
ROOMS: d £40-£46*

All AA listed accommodation can also be found at the AA's Internet site, whose address is: http://www.theaa.co.uk/hotels

Selected

Q Q Q Q **Owler Lodge** Alkham Valley Rd, Alkham CT15 7DF (from A260 Canterbury road follow signs for Alkham approx 3m, Owler Lodge next to phone box in Alkham) ☎ 01304 826375 FAX 01304
Closed Xmas
Set in the heart of the Alkham valley, this attractive modern property is owned and run by Mr and Mrs Owler. Bedrooms have been tastefully decorated and furnished. All have TVs and modern en suite bathrooms with power showers and a range of thoughtful extras. There is a comfortable lounge and the dining room overlooks the illuminated garden and Koi pond.
3 bth/shr (1 fmly) No smoking CTV in all bedrooms Tea and coffee making facilities No dogs Cen ht CTV No children 5yrs 6P No coaches Last d 8.30pm
ROOMS: s £32-£36; d £42-£46*

Q Q Q **Penny Farthing** 109 Maison Dieu Rd CT16 1RT
☎ 01304 205563 FAX 01304 205563
This well presented Victorian guest house is well situated, just a few minutes away from the ports and station. The bedrooms are spacious and comfortably furnished, all have colour TV and full en suite or private shower. There is a cosy guest lounge and early breakfasts can be arranged.
6 bth/shr (2 fmly) No smoking in dining room No smoking in lounges CTV in all bedrooms Tea and coffee making facilities No dogs Cen ht 6P No coaches
ROOMS: s £22-£24; d £40-£46*

Q Q Q ***Peverall House Hotel*** 28 Park Av CT16 1HD
☎ 01304 202573 & 205088
This impressive Victorian house is close to Connaught Park and has an attractive garden. The accommodation is furnished in pine and is complemented by a cosy, wood-panelled lounge and a well appointed breakfast room. Most of the rooms have a sunny aspect with top floor bedrooms having views of the castle and the town.
6 rms (2 bth) (2 fmly) No smoking in dining room CTV in all bedrooms Tea and coffee making facilities No dogs Licensed Cen ht CTV 8P No coaches Last d noon

Q Q St Albans Bed & Breakfast 71 Folkestone Rd CT17 9RZ (on the Old Dover/London road the B2011, opposite Priory railway station)
☎ 01304 206308

This neatly presented guest house continues to improve and is situated just a short drive from the ports. A family run property, with a welcoming atmosphere. Bedrooms are all equipped with colour TV.

6 rms (3 shr) (1 fmly) No smoking in 3 bedrooms No smoking in dining room No smoking in lounges CTV in all bedrooms Tea and coffee making facilities No dogs Cen ht No coaches

ROOMS: d £32-£50*

CARDS:

Q Q Q St Brelades 80/82 Buckland Av CT16 2NW (to Dover on M2, at last roundabout take last exit to town centre, down hill to mini roundabout, turn left, cont to Buckland Ave, premises on right)
☎ 01304 206126 FAX 01304 211486

This friendly licensed guest house offers a good range of neat, comfortable bedrooms. The open-plan dining room features a dispense bar and reception facilities. There is also a separate lounge. Evening meals are provided each day between 5pm and 8pm; vegetarians are catered for and a choice of breakfast is offered.

6 shr (2 fmly) No smoking in 2 bedrooms No smoking in dining room No smoking in lounges CTV in all bedrooms Tea and coffee making facilities No dogs Licensed Cen ht CTV 6P No coaches Last d 7.30pm

ROOMS: s £30-£38; d £38-£50*

CARDS:

Q Q Q St Martins 17 Castle Hill Rd CT16 1QW (situated on the A258 lee of Dover Castle) ☎ 01304 205938 FAX 01304 208229

Closed Xmas

Close to the castle, town centre and ferry terminal, this period house offers comfortable, well presented accommodation and a friendly atmosphere. Proprietor Mrs Carmen Morriss extends a warm welcome. The bedrooms have pretty fabrics and dècor; most enjoy a sunny aspect and are thoughtfully well equipped with an additional table and chairs. Other facilities include reception, an attractive pine-furnished breakfast room and a very comfortable lounge.

6 shr (3 fmly) No smoking CTV in all bedrooms Tea and coffee making facilities No dogs Cen ht

ROOMS: s £30-£35; d £35-£45*

CARDS:

DOVERIDGE Derbyshire Map 07 SK13

Premier Selected

Q Q Q Q Q Beeches *(SK125370)* Waldley DE6 5LR (A50 in westerly direction, turn right at Doveridge and N down Marston Lane signposted to Waldley. At Waldley take first right then first left)
☎ 01889 590288 FAX 01889 590559 Mrs B Tunnicliffe

Closed 24-30 Dec

This 18th-century farmhouse offers a genuine taste of the country not only in its location, but also in the food that is served. Bedrooms are comfortable and attractively furnished with many thoughtful extras, including fruit, flowers and delicious homemade biscuits. Beyond the small bar, with its roaring open fire and rough hewn tables, there is a range of intimate dining areas. Barbara Tunnicliffe spends much of her time researching old country recipes to make the most of the fresh produce available.

4 bth/shr 6 annexe bth/shr (7 fmly) No smoking in dining room No smoking in lounges CTV in all bedrooms Tea and coffee making facilities Direct dial from bedrooms No dogs (ex guide dogs) Licensed Cen ht 30P 60 acres special animals for guests Last d 9pm

ROOMS: s £42-£42; d £56-£66*

CARDS:

See advertisement under DERBY

DOWNHAM MARKET Norfolk Map 05 TF60

Q Q Q *The Dial House* 12 Railway Rd PE38 9EB ☎ 01366 388358 FAX 01366 382198

rs 24-31 Dec

A delightful 17th-century house located just on the fringe of the town centre, near the train station. Bedrooms are attractively decorated and guests also have the use of a spacious comfortable ground floor lounge. Appealing and imaginative meals are served in a separate dining room around a large communal table - home made breads and preserves are a house speciality.

3 rms (2 bth/shr) No smoking Tea and coffee making facilities Cen ht CTV 5P Last d noon

Q Q The Old Shop 24 London Rd PE38 9AW (turn off A10 at Downham Market sign. Left at traffic lights house at bottom of hill on left)
☎ 01366 382051 FAX 01366 382051

The Old Shop has been created from three cottages with its original style retained throughout. Bedrooms come in varying sizes, and some have en suite showers. Smoking is only permitted in the comfortable residents'

contd.

lounge which has a television and video recorder. Traditional home-cooked evening meals are available on request, and all diets can be catered for by prior arrangement
4 bth/shr (1 fmly) No smoking in bedrooms No smoking in dining room CTV in all bedrooms Tea and coffee making facilities Cen ht CTV Last d noon
ROOMS: s fr £20; d fr £32; wkly b&b £112-£140; wkly hlf-bd £175-£203

DOWNTON Wiltshire Map **04** SU12

Q Q Q ***Warren*** 15 High St SP5 3PG (take A338 signposted to Ringwood and after 5m turn left at traffic lights. Guest house on left opposite Post Office) ☎ 01725 510263
Closed 20 Dec-6 Jan
This charming 15th-century house located in the centre of the village, retains much of its original character. The spacious bedrooms are individually furnished with some fine period furniture. Breakfast is taken in the delightful dining room and there are two comfortable lounges.
6 rms (2 bth/shr) (1 fmly) No smoking in dining room Tea and coffee making facilities Cen ht CTV No children 5yrs 8P No coaches

DRAYCOTT Somerset Map **03** ST45

Selected

Q Q Q Q **Oakland House** Wells Rd BS27 3SU (M5 junct 22, follow signs into Cheddar on A371. Draycott village is 2.5m further and house last on right before market gdn) ☎ 01934 744195
Closed late Dec-mid Jan
A warm, friendly family home on the Mendip Hills with views over the Somerset Moors. Located only 10 miles from Glastonbury, it is ideal for both leisure and business visitors. There are three well furnished bedrooms with modern en suite bathrooms. Guests can relax in the bright and airy sun lounge, and enjoy good home cooked food in the cosy dining room.
3 bth/shr (1 fmly) No smoking in bedrooms No smoking in dining room No smoking in 1 lounge CTV in all bedrooms Tea and coffee making facilities No dogs (ex guide dogs) Cen ht 6P No coaches Large garden for relaxing, 2 acre field for walks Last d by arrangement
ROOMS: s £25-£26; d £38-£40; wkly b&b £115-£140*

DRIFFIELD (GREAT) East Riding of Yorkshire Map **08** TA05

Q Q Q **White Horse** Main St, Hutton Cranswick YO25 9QN (off A164 from Great Driffield, signposted Hutton Cranswick, next to village green) ☎ 01377 270383 271036 FAX 01377 270383
Overlooking the village green, opposite the duck pond, this 16th-century inn is mid-way between Beverley and Driffield. The bars are full of character and have been completely renovated. The recently-added bedroom wing has been designed to offer good facilities for the business traveller. To the rear there is a lounge-bar serving a good range of bar meals.

8 shr (2 fmly) No smoking in area of dining room CTV in all bedrooms Tea and coffee making facilities Cen ht 100P Last d 8pm
ROOMS: s £25-£29.50; d £40-£45*
MEALS: Bar Lunch £6.50-£17.50*
CARDS:

DUDDINGTON Northamptonshire Map **04** SK90

Q Q Q **Royal Oak Hotel** High St PE9 3QE (premises on the A43 0.5m from junc with A47) ☎ 01780 444267 FAX 01780 444369
With pretty views of Welland Valley, the Royal Oak is situated on the cross-roads of two main roads and is the natural focus for the local community. The Inn dates back to the 17th century and is built of local stone. The Morgado family now run this pleasant country inn establishment. All five rooms are prettily decorated, featuring some thoughtful extra touches.
6 bth/shr (2 fmly) No smoking in area of dining room CTV in all bedrooms Tea and coffee making facilities Direct dial from bedrooms Cen ht 75P Last d 9.30pm
ROOMS: s £30-£35; d £40-£45*
MEALS: Lunch £2.10-£6.95&alc Dinner £2.10-£6.95&alc*
CARDS:

DULVERTON Somerset Map **03** SS92

See also East Anstey Oakford & Winsford

Premier Selected

Q Q Q Q Q ***Dassels Country House*** TA22 9RZ (follow signs to East Anstey from B3227, approximately 2 miles) ☎ 01398 341203 FAX 01398 341561
Dassels is an imposing Georgian house in nine acres of beautifully tended gardens, and is home to the Spencer family. The accommodation here is well equipped, some rooms enjoying fabulous views across the rolling countryside. Dassels is noted for good home cooking, including delicious soups, fresh farm turkey, beef and lamb. The dining room also serves a full English breakfast.
9 bth/shr 3 annexe shr (4 fmly) No smoking in 2 bedrooms No smoking in dining room No smoking in lounges CTV in all bedrooms Tea and coffee making facilities Licensed Cen ht CTV 14P No coaches Last d 7pm
CARDS:

We endeavour to be as accurate as possible but changes in personnel and data can occur in establishments after the Guide has gone to press

Selected

QQQQ **Town Mills** High St TA22 9HB
(Dulverton is on B3222, Town Mills is 200 yds on left after crossing the River Barle next to the Mill Leat) ☎ 01398 323124
Closed Xmas
This attractive Georgian mill house is tucked away in the famous Exmoor village of Dulverton. The bedrooms are spacious and well-equipped with one located on the ground floor. An unusual trait of this delightful guest house, is that each bedroom is large enough to take large easy chairs and a dining table, where at a pre-arranged time guests enjoy their cooked breakfast in the privacy of their own room!
5 rms (3 shr) CTV in all bedrooms Tea and coffee making facilities No dogs (ex guide dogs) Cen ht 5P No coaches
ROOMS: d £36-£48

DUNSTER Somerset Map **03** SS94

See also Roadwater

Premier Selected

QQQQQ **Dollons House** Church St TA24 6SH (exit A39 at traffic lights, follow A396 through High Street into Church Street) ☎ 01643 821880 FAX 01643 822016
Closed 25-26 Dec
Parts of the property believed to date back over four hundred years, this listed Grade II property is located in the heart of a medieval village. The two street-facing rooms are successfully run as a craft and flower shop. Each of the bedrooms is individually furnished and decorated with style and flair; two with views of the castle, the other overlooking the lovely, walled gardens at the rear of the property. The sitting room opens onto a large veranda and the garden. An interesting choice is offered at breakfast.
3 bth/shr No smoking CTV in all bedrooms Tea and coffee making facilities No dogs Cen ht CTV No children 16yrs No coaches
ROOMS: s £35-£40; d £50-£55; wkly b&b £175-£192
CARDS:

Selected

QQQQ **The Old Priory** TA24 6RY
(turn off A39 into Dunster. Pass information centre on left, take right fork marked 'unsuitable for heavy goods vehicles'. House adjoining church) ☎ 01643 821540
Dating back to the 12th century, The Old Priory was built by Benedictine monks. Each bedroom is individually furnished and strikingly decorated, yet retains the medieval character of the building. Although the ground-floor bedroom does not have the benefit of an en suite bathroom, it has exclusive use of an adjacent shower room. A comfortable sitting room is provided for guests, who take breakfast around a large refectory table in the dining room.
3 bth/shr Tea and coffee making facilities No dogs (ex guide dogs) Cen ht No children 12yrs 1P No coaches
ROOMS: s £25-£35; d £45-£55*

DURHAM Co Durham Map 12 NZ24

Bay Horse Brandon Village DH7 8ST (take A690 2.5m W)
☎ 0191 378 0498
Popular for its good value home-cooked meals both in its cosy bars and attractive restaurant, this pub also has a block of hotel-standard bedrooms. Annexed and arranged chalet style around the rear courtyard, they are spacious, comfortable and well equipped.
10 annexe bth/shr (1 fmly) CTV in all bedrooms Tea and coffee making facilities Direct dial from bedrooms Cen ht 15P No coaches
Last d 9.30pm
ROOMS: s £31; d £40*
CARDS:

T&C Castle View 4 Crossgate DH1 4PS (adjacent to St Margarets Church in city centre) ☎ 0191 3868852 FAX 0191 3868852
Closed 21 Dec-7 Jan
A warm and friendly atmosphere is assured at this listed building which is over 250 years old and lies in a quiet cobble-stoned street close to the town centre. A charming house, it is stylishly decorated and includes a comfortable lounge/dining room. The en suite bedrooms are full of character.
6 bth/shr No smoking CTV in all bedrooms Tea and coffee making facilities No dogs (ex guide dogs) Cen ht CTV
ROOMS: s fr £38; d fr £50*
CARDS:

Selected

Hillrise 13 Durham Rd West, Bowburn DH6 5AU (junct 61 A1, Hillrise approx 200yds down on left from motorway)
☎ 0191 377 0302 FAX 0191 377 0302
A warm welcome awaits at this well kept guest house. Bedrooms come in a variety of sizes and offer comfortable accommodation. Attractive public areas include a lounge with chunky leather chairs and a bright, spacious dining room where guests can enjoy good home-cooked evening meals and tasty breakfasts.
5 rms (4 shr) (3 fmly) No smoking CTV in all bedrooms Tea and coffee making facilities No dogs (ex guide dogs) Cen ht CTV 4P
Last d 4pm
ROOMS: s £18-£30; d £40-£50*

Lothlorien 48/49 Front St, Witton Gilbert DH7 6SY (3m on A691 Consett rd, opposite Glendenning Arms) ☎ 0191 371 0067
There is a friendly welcome and a home-from-home atmosphere to be found at Mrs Milne's cosy cottage set in the centre of the village. There is an inviting lounge and although bedrooms lack en suite facilities, they are served by two bathrooms close by.
3 rms No smoking in dining room Tea and coffee making facilities
No dogs Cen ht CTV 3P No coaches
ROOMS: s £18-£19; d £36-£38; wkly b&b £126-£133*

Victoria Inn 86 Hallgarth St DH1 3AS (turn off A1 for Bowburn onto the A177 carry on for 2.5m the rdbt is at the top end of Hallgarth St)
☎ 0191 386 5269
This is ostensibly a traditional Victorian pub, but the bed and breakfast operation is quite separate, with its own entrance. Bedrooms are compact but bright and cheery with modern en suites. There is a breakfast room adjacent. No food is served in the bar, but there is an authentic atmosphere and good real ale.
3 bth/shr (1 fmly) No smoking in 1 bedrooms CTV in all bedrooms
Tea and coffee making facilities Licensed Cen ht P

DYMCHURCH Kent Map 05 TR12

Chantry Hotel Sycamore Gardens TN29 0LA (200yds E of Dymchurch village on coast side of A259) ☎ 01303 873137
Tucked well away from the main road this established timber-framed hotel offers easy access to the beach. The bedrooms are simply furnished and neatly presented, most with en suite facilities. There is a cosy beamed bar, restaurant, lounge and furnished front terrace.
7 rms (6 bth/shr) (2 fmly) No smoking in dining room CTV in all bedrooms Tea and coffee making facilities Licensed Cen ht CTV 9P
Table tennis Boules
ROOMS: s £20-£25; d £30-£45; wkly b&b £105-£157.50*
CARDS:

Waterside 15 Hythe Roaf TN29 0LN (on A259 5m W of Hythe) ☎ 01303 872253
Overlooking Romney Marsh and with the Romney, Hythe and Dymchurch Railway to the rear, this guest house is run by Sharon Tinklin. The accommodation comprises bright and modern bedrooms with private facilities. There is a comfortable lounge with licensed bar and the smart dining room offers good wholesome meals using homegrown vegetables.
6 rms (3 shr) (1 fmly) No smoking in dining room CTV in all bedrooms
Tea and coffee making facilities No dogs Licensed Cen ht CTV 7P
No coaches Last d 8pm
ROOMS: s £16-£20; d £30-£38; wkly b&b £101-£126;
wkly hlf-bd £145-£170

EARLS COLNE Essex Map 05 TL82

Riverside Motel 40/42 Lower Holt St CO6 2PH
(on A1124 (formally A604) 8m W of Colchester signed to Halstead)
☎ 01787 223487 FAX 01787 223487
The Riverside Motel sits on the banks of the River Colne, set back from the main road. The purpose built accommodation comprises modern chalet-style annexe bedrooms that are soundly appointed and suitably well equipped; each has a modern en suite shower room. Breakfast is provided in a small breakfast room.
5 shr No smoking in dining room No smoking in lounges CTV in all bedrooms Tea and coffee making facilities Cen ht 30P
ROOMS: s fr £30; d fr £38*
CARDS:

EASINGWOLD North Yorkshire Map 08 SE56

Stillington Mill Mill Ln, Stillington YO61 1NG
☎ 01347 810161 FAX 01347 810265
Set on the edge of the village and in ample grounds, this stone built house is still in the process of change with more bedrooms to be added. Guests have the use of an indoor pool and a tennis court and the breakfast room overlooks a mill pond.
5 rms (3 shr) No smoking CTV in all bedrooms Tea and coffee making facilities No dogs Cen ht CTV 5P No coaches Indoor swimming pool (heated) Tennis (hard) Snooker Half size snooker table
ROOMS: s £18.50-£25; d £37-£50; wkly b&b £95.20-£130.90*

EAST ANSTEY Devon Map 03 SS82

Threadneedle EX16 9JH (located on the Devon/Somerset border just off B3227 between the villages of Oldways end and East Anstey)
☎ 01398 341598
Situated in a pretty village just off the old road to South Molton, Threadneedle is a modern looking house with stables adjoining. Both en suite bedrooms are spacious and have colour TV, magazines and coffee and tea making facilities. Meals are taken in the very spacious dining room with views over the open countryside.
2 shr (1 fmly) No smoking in bedrooms CTV in all bedrooms Tea and coffee making facilities Cen ht 12P No coaches Last d 7.30pm
ROOMS: s £19; d £38*

EASTBOURNE East Sussex Map **05** TV69

See also Wilmington

Q Q Q ***Bay Lodge Hotel*** 61-62 Royal Pde BN22 7AQ (A22, A2021 until joins the B2103 seafront road, right, pedestrian crossing 300 yards along road directly outside premises) ☎ 01323 732515 FAX 01323 735009
Mar-Oct
On the seafront, opposite the Redoubt, the Edwardian Bay Lodge enjoys fine sea views from its conservatory lounge and some of the bedrooms. The lounge boasts rattan seating and lots of green plants. There is also a cosy bar for residents, and dinner is available in the neat restaurant. Bedrooms are equipped with extras like hairdryers and radio alarms.
12 rms (9 bth/shr) No smoking in dining room No smoking in 1 lounge CTV in all bedrooms Tea and coffee making facilities No dogs (ex guide dogs) Licensed Cen ht CTV No children 7yrs 2P No coaches Last d 6pm
CARDS:

Q Q Q **Camelot Lodge** 35 Lewes Rd BN21 2BU (exit A22 onto A2021, premises approx 0.5m after General Hospital) ☎ 01323 725207
Very well kept and in first-rate decorative order, the Smart's Edwardian house offers comfortable en suite bedrooms and appealing public areas. The latter boast a large collection of plates and pictures and other collectibles (there's even a suit of armour in the spacious entrance hall) and include a roomy lounge, cosy bar and plant-filled conservatory dining room that looks out onto an ornamental pond in the garden. Home-cooked dinners, that are available by arrangement, include their own home-grown vegetables. Own parking.
8 bth/shr (2 fmly) No smoking in dining room CTV in all bedrooms Tea and coffee making facilities No dogs (ex guide dogs) Licensed Cen ht No children 5yrs 10P No coaches Last d 4pm
ROOMS: s £23.50-£30; d £47; wkly b&b £147; wkly hlf-bd £196*
CARDS:

Q Q **Chalk Farm Hotel & Restaurant** Coopers Hill, Willingdon BN20 9JD (1m S of Polegate crossroads turn right off A22, immediately after traffic lights) ☎ 01323 503800 FAX 01323 520331
Chalk Farm is a Grade II listed 17th-century farmhouse. Today it is run as a small hotel and restaurant by a local charity giving work experience to

trainees with a learning disability. Bedrooms are being refurbished and have numerous amenities. Public rooms include a red plush bar, lounge and restaurant. There is also a garden centre attached to the hotel.
9 rms (2 bth 4 shr) (2 fmly) No smoking in bedrooms No smoking in dining room No smoking in 1 lounge CTV in all bedrooms Tea and coffee making facilities Direct dial from bedrooms Licensed Cen ht 15P No coaches Cycle hire Last d 8.45pm
ROOMS: s £30-£43; d £43-£58.50*
CARDS:

Q Q Q **Far End Hotel** 139 Royal Pde BN22 7LH (1m E of the Pier on the Seafront) ☎ 01323 725666
Apr-Oct rs 16 Dec-Mar
Fronted by a small patio with pretty flower beds, the Far End has a good position facing the sea and next to Princes Park. Fresh flowers grace the entrance hall and bedrooms have been prettily redecorated by owners Tony and Trish Callaghan. The comfortably furnished first floor lounge enjoys sea views and there is a small separate bar available to diners (dinner is by arrangement). Own parking plus unrestricted street parking.
10 rms (4 shr) No smoking in dining room No smoking in lounges CTV in all bedrooms Tea and coffee making facilities Licensed Cen ht No children 4yrs 8P No coaches Last d 1pm
ROOMS: s £17-£24; d £34-£56; wkly b&b £119-£147; wkly hlf-bd £150-£180*

Q Q **Mowbray Hotel** 2 Lascelles Ter BN21 4BJ (opposite Devonshire Park Theatre) ☎ 01323 720012 FAX 01323 720253
mid Mar-mid Dec
Close to the sea front, this well kept small hotel is run in friendly fashion by the Sharp family. Day rooms include a comfortably furnished lounge and bright dining room, while a lift gives access to the bedroom floors. Apart from one room that has its bathroom next door, all the rooms now have en suite shower rooms.

contd.

15 rms (12 shr) No smoking in dining room CTV in all bedrooms Tea and coffee making facilities Lift Cen ht CTV Last d 4pm
ROOMS: s £15-£23; d £30-£46; wkly b&b £100-£140; wkly hlf-bd £130-£175
CARDS:

Selected

Q Q Q Q **Queens Cliff Hotel** 24 Carew Rd BN21 2JG (take 1st exit off Willingdon rdbt and pass college and hospital until zebra crossing, turn right at Mill Gap Rd, hotel on left at next junction)
☎ 01323 726723 FAX 01323 726723
The generously sized bedrooms at this guest house are prettily decorated and comfortably furnished. Public areas include a well-appointed restaurant where guests can enjoy a traditional dinner. There is also a most appealing bar and lounge as well as a landscaped garden with a furnished patio, ornamental Koi pond and wishing well.
8 bth/shr (1 fmly) No smoking in dining room CTV in all bedrooms Tea and coffee making facilities Licensed Cen ht CTV 8P Last d 6pm
ROOMS: s £25-£34; d £45-£49; wkly b&b £155-£165; wkly hlf-bd £199-£215*
CARDS:

Q Q Q **St Omer Hotel** 13 Royal Pde BN22 7AR ☎ 01323 722152 FAX 726756
Apr-Sep rs Oct-Nov & Mar
A small patio and a conservatory sun lounge make the most of this small hotel's sea front position. Run in friendly fashion by Andrew and Glynis Garman, the other public rooms are a comfortable lounge with a bar and a well-appointed, panelled dining room where Glynis offers traditional English cooking. Bedrooms are well equipped and most are fully en suite with shower.
13 rms (11 shr) No smoking in dining room No smoking in lounges CTV in all bedrooms Tea and coffee making facilities No dogs (ex guide dogs) Licensed Cen ht CTV No children 12yrs Last d 5pm
ROOMS: s £22.50-£27.50; d £45-£55; wkly b&b £143-£175; wkly hlf-bd £188-£219
CARDS:

Q Q Q **Sheldon Hotel** 9-11 Burlington Place BN21 4AS (100yds from Eastbourne seafront, 500yds West of pier)
☎ 01323 724120 FAX 01323 430406
Closed 2 Jan-28 Feb
Close to the sea front this privately owned hotel continues to improve with all rooms now en suite, and new furniture in the bedrooms. Dinners are served in the well-appointed dining room and there is a comfortable residents lounge. Other facilities include a passenger lift to the higher floors.
25 bth/shr (4 fmly) No smoking in bedrooms CTV in all bedrooms Tea and coffee making facilities Direct dial from bedrooms Lift Cen ht CTV 16P Last d 6pm
ROOMS: s £22-£26; d £44-£52; wkly b&b £140-£160; wkly hlf-bd £160-£190*
CARDS:

Q Q ***Stirling House Hotel*** 5-7 Cavendish Place BN21 3EJ
☎ 01323 732263 FAX 01323 732263
Mar-Oct
With a prime position just a few yards from the pier and the sea front, this well-cared for guest house is run by Eric and Elsa Norris. Bedrooms are neat, bright and clean. Public areas include a cosy bar, comfortable TV lounge and a dining room where Elsa offers home-cooked evening meals.
20 rms (11 shr) No smoking in dining room CTV in all bedrooms Tea and coffee making facilities No dogs (ex guide dogs) Licensed CTV No children 10yrs Last d 9am

EAST LAYTON North Yorkshire Map 12 NZ10

Q Q **Mains Gill Farm** DL11 7PN (from Scotch Corner, 4m on A66 towards Penrith opposite junction for East Layton, drive on left)
☎ 01325 718385 Mrs M Henshaw
Etr-Nov
Set well back from the A66, just four miles from Scotch Corner, this farmhouse is surrounded by open fields and grazing animals. Quite spacious bedrooms, all offering fine views to the hills beyond, are traditionally furnished, whilst there is also a comfortable lounge. Breakfast is served around one table and dinner can be available by arrangement.
3 rms No smoking CTV in all bedrooms Tea and coffee making facilities Cen ht CTV 7P 60 acres livestock Last d 5.30pm
ROOMS: s £18-£20; d £32-£36*

EAST MIDLANDS AIRPORT Leicestershire Map 08 SK42

Q Q Q **Donington Park Farmhouse Hotel** Melbourne Rd, Isley Walton DE74 2RN (at the A453 at Isley Walton take Melbourne turn, premises 0.5m on right) (The Circle) ☎ 01332 862409 FAX 01332 862364
Closed Xmas
This 17th-century farmhouse is very close to the racetrack, and offers comfortably appointed and well equipped bedrooms, including a ground floor room adapted for disabled guests. The public areas include a lounge, bar, and a dining room which has a large pine table in front of a huge open fireplace.
9 bth/shr 2 annexe bth/shr (2 fmly) No smoking in 2 bedrooms No smoking in dining room CTV in all bedrooms Tea and coffee making facilities Direct dial from bedrooms Licensed Cen ht 20P Caravan site Last d 8.30pm
ROOMS: s £52-£55; d £66-£76*
CARDS:

EAST PENNARD Somerset Map 03 ST53

Selected

Q Q Q Q ***Pennard Hill Farm*** *(ST576386)* Stickleball Hill BA4 6UG ☎ 01749 890221 Mrs P Judah
This large farmhouse overlooks rolling countryside towards Glastonbury Tor. One of the suites is situated in a converted barn, with

an adjacent indoor swimming pool. The second suite, with a private sitting room, is in the main house and can be let in conjunction with three nearby single rooms. Phoebe Judah offers freshly prepared meals in the spacious dining room.
5 rms

EAST TYTHERLEY Hampshire Map **04** SU22

Selected

QQQQ **Star** SO51 0LW ☎ 01794 340225 FAX 01794 340225
This charming old coaching inn is slightly off the beaten track, in beautiful Hampshire countryside. The comfortable and well equipped rooms have modern en suite facilities. Guests can sit on deckchairs and watch the cricket being played at the club next door. The inn is full of character and is popular with both locals and tourists.
3 shr No smoking CTV in all bedrooms Tea and coffee making facilities No dogs Cen ht 50P Last d 9pm
ROOMS: s £35-£40; d fr £50*
MEALS: Lunch £5.95-£11.95 Dinner £5.95-£12.95*
CARDS:

ECCLESHALL Staffordshire Map **07** SJ82

QQQ **Slindon House Farm** *(SJ826324)* Slindon ST21 6LX
(on A519, 2m N of Eccleshall)
☎ 01782 791237 FAX 01782 791237 Mrs H Bonsall
This large pre-Victorian farmhouse stands on a 170 acre mixed farm. The bedrooms are comfortable and traditionally furnished. Separate tables are available in the combined breakfast room and lounge.
2 rms (1 shr) No smoking Tea and coffee making facilities No dogs (ex guide dogs) Cen ht CTV 6P 170 acres arable, dairy, sheep
ROOMS: s £17.50-£20; d £32-£40; wkly b&b £122.50-£140*

QQ **Wincote Farm** *(SJ823273)* Wincote Ln ST21 6JE
(off A519, Eccleshall to Newport road. 1m on from mini-rdbt turn right into Wincote Lane and the establishment is the first farm on the left)
☎ 01785 850337 Mrs S Norbury
Wincote Farm is a 100 acre mixed holding which was once the home of Lord Nelson of Stafford. The house is set in 3 acres of gardens and provides accommodation which takes the form of one double, one twin and one single bedded room. There is a spacious lounge with an inglenook fireplace and a traditionally furnished dining room.
3 rms (1 bth/shr) (1 fmly) No smoking Tea and coffee making facilities No dogs Cen ht CTV 4P Tennis (hard) Fishing Boating 100 acres arable cows
ROOMS: s £15-£25; d £30-£40; wkly b&b fr £105*

ECCLESTON Lancashire Map **07** SD51

QQQ **Parr Hall Farm** *(SD522173)* Parr Ln PR7 5SL (from M6 junct 27 take A5209 for Parbold, then immediately take B5250 right turn for Eccleston. After 5 miles Parr Lane on right, house on left)
☎ 01257 451917 FAX 01257 453749 Mrs K Motley
This well furnished 17th-century farmhouse is centrally located within a quiet corner of the village. It provides well equipped and comfortable bedrooms which have all been newly furnished. A good breakfast is provided by the resident owner, Kate Motley who is a friendly host. There are ample pubs and restaurants nearby where dinner may be obtained.
4 bth/shr No smoking CTV in all bedrooms Tea and coffee making facilities No dogs Cen ht 20P Croquet 15 acres arable
ROOMS: s £25-£35; d £40-£50; wkly b&b £150-£175*
CARDS:

EDALE Derbyshire Map **07** SK18

QQQ **Edale House** Hope Rd S33 7ZE ☎ 01433 670399 FAX 01433 670128
This Grade II listed, 18th-century house lies on the edge of the village, enjoying fine views of the surrounding countryside from most of the rooms. Bedrooms are spacious, particularly the one with an en suite bathroom. Breakfast is served around one large pine table in the attractive dining room, looking out over the neatly tended garden.
3 rms (2 bth) No smoking CTV in 2 bedrooms Tea and coffee making facilities Cen ht 5P

EDENBRIDGE Kent Map **05** TQ44

QQQ **Knowlands** Five Fields Ln, Four Elms TN8 6NA
(from Four Elms cross roads take Tonbridge road and turn right after 1m into Five Fields Lane. House on right)
☎ 01732 700314 FAX 01732 700314
Closed 20-30 Dec
This attractive Edwardian house is peacefully situated in 3.5 acres with a croquet lawn, rose garden and orchard. Bedrooms have been nicely decorated and provided with lots of thoughtful extras. There is a comfortable drawing room and in the summer months guests may enjoy the terrace and tennis court. A full English breakfast is served around one table in the sunny dining room.
2 rms No smoking CTV in all bedrooms Tea and coffee making facilities Cen ht No children 3P No coaches Tennis (hard)
ROOMS: d £55

Selected

QQQQ **Ye Ole Crown** 74/76 The High St TN8 5AR (M25 junct 6, bear right onto A22 and turn off onto A25, then onto B269 and B2026. Follow signs thereafter) ☎ 01732 867896
LIONHEART *Inns*
Situated in the centre of the town, parts of this period property date back to the 13th century. The bedrooms are a recent addition to the charming old inn and are furnished to a very good and comfortable standard. An extensive range of meals is served in both the bar and restaurant, which are full of character and sympathetically decorated and furnished.
6 bth/shr No smoking in 2 bedrooms No smoking in area of dining room CTV in all bedrooms Tea and coffee making facilities Direct dial from bedrooms Cen ht 12P Last d 10pm
CARDS:

ELTERWATER Cumbria Map **07** NY30

Q Q Q **Britannia** LA22 9HP (A593 from Ambleside, then B5343 to Elterwater) ☎ 015394 37210 FAX 015394 37311
Closed 25 & 26 Dec
Occupying centre stage in this delightful lakeland hamlet, this traditional inn is renowned for its good food and extensive menus which are presented in the two snug bars, the dining room, or outside, weather permitting. Due to the inns' popularity at meal times, residents may reserve a table from 6.30 to 7pm or from 8.30 to 9.30pm in the dining room only. Bedrooms make good use of available space, being nicely furnished and very well equipped. Staff throughout are friendly and nothing is too much trouble.
9 rms (8 shr) 4 annexe rms (1 shr) No smoking in dining room CTV in all bedrooms Tea and coffee making facilities Direct dial from bedrooms Cen ht 8P No coaches Last d 9.30pm
ROOMS: s £20-£29; d £48-£64; wkly b&b £115.50-£217*
CARDS:

ELY Cambridgeshire Map **05** TL58

Selected

Q Q Q Q **Anchor** Sutton Gault CB6 2BD (Sutton Gault signposted off B1381 at southern end of Sutton village (6m W of Ely)) ☎ 01353 778537 FAX 01353 776180
Closed 25-26 Dec
The Anchor is a delightful 350 year old character Inn which is well known for its food, it is situated in quiet rural surroundings beside the New Bedford River, known locally as the Hundred Foot Drain. The menu has a strong British influence and is supplemented with French regional cooking as well as other international dishes. The accommodation comprises of two nicely proportioned bedrooms, one of which is a suite, they are both tastefully decorated, soundly appointed and equipped with a range of useful extras. The public rooms feature delightful gas lamps, undulating floors, a wealth of beams and log fireplaces; guests can also enjoy dinner and breakfast seated around the scrubbed pine tables.
2 bth/shr (1 fmly) No smoking in bedrooms No smoking in area of dining room No smoking in lounges CTV in all bedrooms Tea and coffee making facilities Direct dial from bedrooms No dogs (ex guide dogs) Cen ht No children 7yrs 16P No coaches Fishing Last d 9pm
ROOMS: s £50-£65; d £62-£82.50*
MEALS: Lunch £7.50-£15.50&alc Dinner £20-£26alc*
CARDS:

Q Q **Castle Lodge Hotel** 50 New Barns Rd CB7 4PW (turn off A10 at 1st rdbt N of Cambridge, at lights turn left, over next lights and take next right turn. At top of rd turn left-hotel is on right) ☎ 01353 662276 FAX 01353 666606
Closed 23-27 Dec
Situated close to the cathedral and town centre, parts of this small hotel date back to 1848. Public rooms including a cosy bar, separate lounge, and an extensive functions suite. The dining room offers traditional British cooking. Bedrooms are undergoing a gradual programme of full refurbishment, and though they may vary in size and space, they are all soundly furnished and suitably equipped.
12 rms (2 bth 2 shr) (2 fmly) No smoking in bedrooms No smoking in lounges CTV in all bedrooms Tea and coffee making facilities Direct dial from bedrooms No dogs (ex guide dogs) Licensed Cen ht CTV 6P No coaches Last d 9pm
ROOMS: s £25-£35; d £47.50-£60*
CARDS:

Selected

Q Q Q Q **Hill House** *(TL589817)* 9 Main St, Coveney CB6 2DJ (off A142 3m W of Ely) ☎ 01353 778369 Mrs H Nix
Closed Xmas
This charming Victorian farmhouse is situated in the delightful village of Coveney. Although the bedrooms are part of the main house each room has its own separate entrance. Each has a bright, fresh appearance, and is nicely decorated. Each room is thoughtfully equipped, with a range of useful extras and modern en suite facilities. The public rooms feature a comfortably furnished sitting room and a separate dining room where guests can enjoy breakfast around the communal table. Please note that this is a no-smoking house which is also not suitable for very young children or pets.
3 shr No smoking CTV in all bedrooms Tea and coffee making facilities No dogs Cen ht No children 12yrs 6P 240 acres arable
ROOMS: d £40-£50*

Q Q Q ***Quarterway House*** Ely Rd, Little Thetford CB6 3HP (20miles South of Ely on East side of A10 between Stretham and Little Thetford, 150 yds after layby)
☎ 01353 648964 FAX 01353 648964
Closed 2-21 January
Quarterway House is a traditional house in 4 acres of smallholding. The property has been furnished with restored period furniture in the bedrooms and public rooms. Bedrooms are light and appealing, (although space can be slightly restrictive) and all are equipped with a range of thoughtful extras. Guests have the use of a lounge, with a conservatory. Breakfast is taken communally in the farmhouse kitchen.
3 bth/shr (1 fmly) No smoking CTV in all bedrooms Tea and coffee making facilities Cen ht CTV No children 7yrs 9P No coaches
CARDS:

EMBLETON Cumbria Map **11** NY12

Selected

Q Q Q Q **High Side Farm** *(NY163292)* CA13 9TN (A66 Keswick-Cockermouth, turn left at sign to Lorton/Buttermere, left at T-junction. After 300 mtrs turn right opposite church, Farm at top of hill) ☎ 017687 76893 Mr & Mrs N Marshall
Closed 24 Dec-1 Jan
This 17th-century farmhouse is sedately perched over 600ft up the Ling Fell and commands striking views over the Embleton Valley and Solway Firth to the Scottish peaks. The spacious open plan lounge and dining room are elegantly furnished with deep sofas and fine antique furniture. One piece is a ten foot oak table at which a substantial breakfast can be enjoyed. The bedrooms are both thoughtfully furnished and equipped.
2 shr No smoking in bedrooms CTV in all bedrooms Tea and coffee making facilities Cen ht 2P 2 acres non working
ROOMS: d £40-£45

Selected

Q Q Q Q **Lambfoot House** CA13 9XL (from A66 turn towards Embleton at crossroads signed Lorton/Buttermere/Embleton. Guest house is 200yds on right)
☎ 017687 76424 FAX 017687 76424
Built in 1911, this three storey Edwardian house offers stylish and well equipped accommodation. Ruth and Howard Holden are very welcoming and ensure that guests arrive as customers and leave as friends. The bedrooms include leather loungers, two metre long

'Sultan' beds and top quality quilts. The bright breakfast room maintains the vein of quality with china crockery and fine ornaments.
3 bth/shr No smoking CTV in all bedrooms Tea and coffee making facilities No dogs Cen ht No children 14yrs 5P No coaches
ROOMS: s £16.50-£20; d £36-£46; wkly b&b £115.50-£150

EMSWORTH Hampshire Map 04 SU70

Jingles Hotel 77 Horndean Rd PO10 7PU
(turn off A259 towards Rowlands Castle and continue for approx 1m)
☎ 01243 373755 FAX 01243 373755
Located to the north of the village this family run hotel backs on to surrounding fields. The bedrooms are well presented and comfortably furnished. Guests can enjoy both lounge and cosy bar. The dining room offers good home-cooked food and in the summer months the patio garden and pool are available.
13 rms (8 bth/shr) No smoking in 3 bedrooms No smoking in dining room CTV in all bedrooms Tea and coffee making facilities Licensed Cen ht CTV 14P Outdoor swimming pool (heated) Last d 7pm
ROOMS: s £27-£37; d £44-£60*
CARDS:

EPSOM Surrey Map 04 TQ26

Epsom Downs Hotel 9 Longdown Rd KT17 3PT
(M25 junct 9, at rdbt take A243 to BP Garage on right, turn right at lights, and cont into rd signed Upper High St for 1.5m, then 4th left)
☎ 01372 740643 FAX 01372 723259
5 Jan-20 Dec Closed 20 Dec-4 Jan
A good deal of refurbishment has taken place at this friendly hotel located in a residential street not far from Epsom College. Public areas include a comfortable bar, which is open-plan to the restaurant, and a leather-furnished lounge area by the reception desk. Bright bedrooms are en suite and have direct dial phones.
15 rms (13 bth/shr) (1 fmly) No smoking in dining room CTV in all bedrooms Tea and coffee making facilities Direct dial from bedrooms Licensed Cen ht CTV 11P Last d 8.15pm
CARDS:

The White House Downs Hill Rd KT18 5HW
(0.25 mile from A24) ☎ 01372 722472 FAX 01372 744447
This substantial Edwardian house is set well back from the road behind lawns that sport tables and chairs in summer. Inside there is a spacious bar/dining room with parquet floor and beamed ceiling plus a separate lounge. Bedrooms vary in size, and are well equipped with tea trays, TVs and telephones.
15 rms (4 bth 3 shr) (1 fmly) No smoking in area of dining room CTV in all bedrooms Tea and coffee making facilities No dogs (ex guide dogs) Licensed Cen ht CTV 15P Last d 8.30pm
ROOMS: s £42.50-£57.50; d £55.50-£75.50*
CARDS:

EPWORTH Lincolnshire Map 08 SE70

Epworth Old Rectory 1 Rectory St DN9 1HX
(exit M180 junct 2 onto A161 and signs for Epworth. In town follow brown tourist signs for 'Old Rectory') ☎ 01427 872268
Mar-Oct
Epworth Old Rectory offers guests a chance to stay in the one-time home of John and Charles Wesley. The house has a lot of history and there are two pleasant bedrooms while a combined lounge and dining room is also provided. The house which was built in 1709, is within easy walking distance of the village centre.
2 rms No smoking Tea and coffee making facilities No dogs (ex guide dogs) Cen ht CTV 12P No coaches croquet
ROOMS: s £27.50-£30; d £40-£45*
CARDS:

ESCRICK North Yorkshire Map **08** SE64

Q Q Q **Black Bull Inn** Main St YO19 6JP (from York follow the A19 S for 5m, enter Escrick, take second left up main street, premises located on the left) ☎ 01904 728245 FAX 01904 728154
Only a few miles from York, Escrick is the home of the Black Bull Inn. The public bar, where dinner can be taken, has been sympathetically decorated with antique pieces of furniture throughout. All bedrooms are well equipped. One has a sunken bath, while another boasts a superb four-poster bed.
10 bth/shr No smoking in bedrooms No smoking in dining room CTV in all bedrooms Tea and coffee making facilities No dogs (ex guide dogs) Cen ht 20P Last d 9.30pm
ROOMS: s £30-£35; d £48-£55*
CARDS:

Q Q Q *Church Cottage* YO4 6EX (A19 south of York 5miles from A64 York ringroad. First property on right upon entering Escrick)
☎ 01904 728462 FAX 01904 728896
This sympathetically extended property, lies next to the church from which it takes its name. Here, a warm welcome by the Robinson family is offered to all their guests. Bedrooms are spacious, traditionally furnished and well suited for family use. Public areas extend to a comfortable lounge, with an honesty bar, and a light, airy dining room.
8 bth/shr (3 fmly) No smoking in bedrooms No smoking in dining room CTV in all bedrooms Tea and coffee making facilities No dogs (ex guide dogs) Licensed Cen ht 20P Walking Nearby golf Last d 8pm
CARDS:

See advertisement under YORK

ETTINGTON Warwickshire Map **04** SP24

Q Q **Whitfield** *(SP265506)* CV37 7PN (on A429, 1m N of Ettington)
☎ 01789 740260 Mrs B J Wakeham
Closed Dec
Whitfield Farm is set amongst 220 acres of attractive arable land, seven miles from Stratford-upon-Avon. This friendly family farmhouse offers a spacious comfortable lounge, and quiet, well maintained and cheerfully decorated accommodation; one bedroom is located on the ground floor.
3 rms (2 shr) (1 fmly) No smoking in dining room Tea and coffee making facilities No dogs (ex guide dogs) Cen ht CTV 3P 220 acres mixed
ROOMS: s £17.50-£28; d £31-£35*

EVERSHOT Dorset Map **03** ST50

Premier Selected

Q Q Q Q Q **Rectory House** Fore St DT2 0JW (1.5m off A37 Yeovil to Dorchester road) ☎ 01935 83273 FAX 01935 83273
Closed Dec/Jan
Rectory House, an 18th century listed building, situated at the centre of the unspoilt village of Evershot in Dorset. Angela and Dennis Carpenter warmly welcome guests to their family home that is furnished with period furnishings, rich fabrics and an elegant comfort. Fresh flowers are lovingly arranged throughout the public rooms and the bedrooms. Three of the five bedrooms are situated in a converted stable block, and have views over the beautifully cared-for garden. All the rooms are furnished with the elegance of a bygone era but with the modern comforts of today. Dinner is available in an attractive dining room where Angela's cooking uses the best of fresh local ingredients, and breakfasts are hearty and also offer fresh fruit and freshly squeezed orange juice.

5 rms (2 bth/shr) No smoking CTV in all bedrooms Tea and coffee making facilities No dogs (ex guide dogs) Licensed Cen ht No children 12yrs 7P No coaches Last d 7pm
ROOMS: s £38.50-£55; d £77-£99; wkly b&b £185-£264; wkly hlf-bd £275-£365
CARDS:

See advertisement under DORCHESTER

EVESHAM Worcestershire Map **04** SP04

Q Q Q **Fircroft** 84 Greenhill WR11 4NH (on right, 0.5m N of railway stn) ☎ 01386 45828
Easter-Oct
Situated on the northern outskirts of this historic town, Fircroft is an elegant Victorian house offering value for money accommodation. Bedrooms are well equipped and one has a modern en suite shower room. The dining room has attractive pine tables and the adjacent conservatory lounge opens onto the well tended gardens.
3 rms (1 shr) (1 fmly) No smoking CTV in all bedrooms Tea and coffee making facilities Cen ht 6P attractive gardens
ROOMS: s fr £25; d £36-£42

Q Q *Park View Hotel* Waterside WR11 6BS (0.25m SE on B4035)
☎ 01386 442639
Closed 22 Dec-6 Jan
This large privately owned and personally run guest house is close to the River Avon. It provides modestly appointed accommodation, which represents good value for money. Many of the bedrooms overlook views of the river. Facilities include a TV lounge, a large lounge bar and a traditionally furnished dining room where separate tables are provided.
26 rms (2 fmly) No smoking in dining room Licensed CTV 40P
CARDS:

EWELL Surrey Map **04** TQ26

Q Q Q **Nonsuch Park Hotel** 355/357 London Rd KT17 2DE (on A24)
☎ 0181 393 0771 FAX 0181 393 1415
There is a friendly welcome at this well-kept small hotel opposite the historic Nonesuch Park. Public areas include an attractive, well-stocked bar (with satellite TV), and separate lounge looking out to a furnished patio and garden. A choice of menu is offered in the dining room in the evening.

11 rms (2 bth 4 shr) (1 fmly) No smoking in 4 bedrooms No smoking in dining room No smoking in lounges CTV in all bedrooms Tea and coffee making facilities Direct dial from bedrooms No dogs (ex guide dogs) Licensed Cen ht CTV 11P Last d 8.30pm
ROOMS: s £45-£55; d £62.50-£69.50✳
CARDS:

EXETER Devon Map 03 SX99

See also Tedburn St Mary & Whimple

Q ***Braeside*** 21 New North Rd EX4 4HF ☎ 01392 56875
Conveniently situated close to the university and stations, this friendly family run guest house offers simple, comfortable accommodation and a hearty full English breakfast.
7 rms (3 shr) (1 fmly) No smoking in dining room CTV in all bedrooms Tea and coffee making facilities Cen ht No coaches Last d 4pm
CARDS:

Q Q **Dunmore Hotel** 22 Blackall Rd EX4 4HE (M5 junct 30 follow signs for City Centre, go through centre at mini rbut turn right, house on left)
☎ 01392 431643
This family run guest house is conveniently situated close to the city centre and railway station. Bedrooms are comfortable, some recently upgraded, and dinner is available by prior arrangement.
7 rms (3 shr) (3 fmly) No smoking in dining room CTV in all bedrooms Tea and coffee making facilities Cen ht CTV
ROOMS: s £17-£25; d £30-£40; wkly b&b £90-£125✳
CARDS:

Selected

Q Q Q Q **The Edwardian** 30/32 Heavitree Rd EX1 2LQ
(M5 junct 30 to Middlemoor rbut 2nd exit to Heavitree, Edwardian on Heavitree Rd after St Lukes School)
☎ 01392 276102 & 254699 FAX 01392 276102 & 254699
Closed Xmas
This Edwardian terraced property is close to the city centre. Bedrooms are well equipped and some are furnished in period style with four-posters. Books and local tourist information are provided in the comfortable lounge, and breakfast is served in two adjoining dining rooms.
13 rms (12 bth/shr) (2 fmly) No smoking in 2 bedrooms No smoking in dining room CTV in all bedrooms Tea and coffee making facilities Direct dial from bedrooms Cen ht CTV 5P No coaches
ROOMS: s £26-£36; d £44-£52✳
CARDS:

Selected

Q Q Q Q ***Gissons Arms*** Kennford EX6 7UD (Along A38 towards Torquay, before fork in road, go up slip road on left hand side)
☎ 01392 832444
rs Xmas day/Boxing day
This delightful inn, situated close to the A38 and within easy reach of Exeter, offers comfortable, well equipped accommodation. The bars, open all day, have wooden beams and other features of 15th-century architecture. The inn has a relaxed atmosphere and a good choice is available from the carvery, along with daily specials. For more special occasions, the a la carte menu makes an interesting alternative.
6 shr No smoking in area of dining room CTV in all bedrooms Tea and coffee making facilities Direct dial from bedrooms Cen ht 100P Golf 9 Last d 10pm
CARDS:

Q Q Q **Hotel Gledhills** 32 Alphington Rd EX2 8HN
(M5 junct 31 onto A30 signed Okehampton, after approx 1m take slip rd off to Exeter, follow town centre signs, guest house is along rd on left)
☎ 01392 430469 & 271439 FAX 01392 430469
Closed 2 wks Xmas/New Year
This attractive red brick property is just a short walk from the city centre. Bedrooms are tastefully decorated and equipped. The sitting room, where many of the proprietor's personal pictures and ornaments are on display, has a homely atmosphere, and there is a bar lounge adjacent.
12 rms (10 shr) (4 fmly) No smoking in dining room CTV in all bedrooms Tea and coffee making facilities No dogs Licensed Cen ht CTV 13P No coaches
ROOMS: s £24-£34; d £42-£46
CARDS:

Selected

Q Q Q Q **Holbrook Farm** *(SX991927)* Clyst Honiton EX5 2HR (1m off the A3052 Sidmouth Road near Clyst St Mary)
☎ 01392 367000 Mrs H Glanvill
This modern bungalow is the hub of a 150-acre dairy farm, which enjoys views over rolling countryside. The spacious and attractive bedrooms are well equipped with all modern facilities and have their own separate entrance. Set in a rural location, yet within easy reach of the M5, the City of Exeter and the A30, this is an ideal place from which to explore the delights of the beautiful county of Devon.
3 shr (1 fmly) No smoking CTV in all bedrooms Tea and coffee making facilities No dogs Cen ht 4P 150 acres dairy
ROOMS: s £20-£25; d £39-£40; wkly b&b £136.50

Q Q Q **Mill Farm** *(SX959839)* Kenton EX6 8JR (from Exeter take A379 towards Dawlish and bypassing Exminster go across mini roundabout by Swans Nest. Farm 1.5m on right) ☎ 01392 832471 Mrs D Lambert
Closed Xmas
Delia Lambert presides over this imposing farmhouse, set well back from the Exeter to Dawlish Road. Each of the spacious bedrooms is comfortably

contd.

furnished and has carefully co-ordinated dècor. There is a sunny breakfast room where a choice of dishes is offered, and a cosy lounge.
5 bth/shr (3 fmly) No smoking in dining room No smoking in lounges CTV in all bedrooms Tea and coffee making facilities No dogs Cen ht 12P 60 acres beef
ROOMS: s £24; d £38*

QQQ **Park View Hotel** 8 Howell Rd EX4 4LG
(from M5 follow signs B3183 City Centre until you reach the clock tower roundabout, 3rd exit Elm Grove at end of road T junct, turn left Howell Road) ☎ 01392 271772 FAX 01392 253047
This small family-owned and managed hotel enjoys a peaceful situation overlooking Bury Meadow Park close to the city centre. All the bedrooms in this Grade II Georgian building have been equipped with modern facilities, and there is a spacious and comfortable sitting room for guests' use.
15 rms (2 bth 8 shr) (2 fmly) No smoking in 1 bedrooms No smoking in dining room CTV in all bedrooms Tea and coffee making facilities Direct dial from bedrooms Cen ht CTV 6P Swings Slide
ROOMS: s £22-£32; d £36-£47; wkly b&b £119-£154*
CARDS:

QQ **Rowhorne House** *(SX880948)* Whitestone EX4 2LQ
(A30 to Tedburn-St-Mary follow sign to Whitestone after 2m pass Royal Oak pub go to top of hill, sharp left continue for 2m house on left)
☎ 01392 274675 Mrs S K Lee
Mar-Oct
Shirley and Frank Lee farm one hundred acres, and yet their house is only about four miles from Exeter. A natural warmth and friendliness awaits their guests, and spacious bedrooms and comfortable lounges benefit from marvellous views over the open countryside.
3 rms (2 fmly) No smoking CTV in all bedrooms Tea and coffee making facilities No dogs CTV 6P 103 acres dairy
ROOMS: s £16; d £32; wkly b&b £112*

Selected

QQQQ **Rydon** *(SX999871)* Woodbury EX5 1LB
(B3179 to village and on entering village turn right 10 yds before 30mph sign. Signposted)
☎ 01395 232341 FAX 01395 232341 Mrs S Glanvill
Peacefully located between Exeter and Exmouth, this Devon Longhouse dates back to 1525 and is surrounded by its own farmland which the Glanvill Family have farmed for over 170 years. Each bedroom is individually furnished and decorated. Breakfast is taken in the dining room at separate tables and there is a homely lounge for guests. There are several excellent pubs and restaurants locally, serving a range of meals.
3 bth/shr (1 fmly) No smoking in bedrooms No smoking in dining room Tea and coffee making facilities Cen ht CTV 3P 280 acres dairy
ROOMS: s £25-£29; d £44-£50*

QQ **Sunnymede** 24 New North Rd EX4 4HF ☎ 01392 273844
Closed 21 Dec-5 Jan
This clean, compact guest house is situated close to the centre and offers the guest comfortable accommodation. Breakfast is taken in the attractive conservatory-style dining room.
9 rms (5 shr) (1 fmly) No smoking CTV in all bedrooms Tea and coffee making facilities No dogs (ex guide dogs) Cen ht No children 3yrs No coaches
ROOMS: s £18-£23; d £35-£38*

Q **Telstar Hotel** 77 St Davids Hill EX4 4DW
(Between city centre and St Davids railway stn) ☎ 01392 272466
Closed 23-31 December
This family-run hotel occupies two adjacent houses located within walking distance of the city centre and the railway station. Bedrooms offer the expected level of amenity, and there is a comfortable lounge for guests' use.
18 rms (4 shr) (5 fmly) No smoking in dining room CTV in all bedrooms Tea and coffee making facilities Cen ht CTV 8P
ROOMS: s £15-£25; d £28-£45; wkly b&b £100-£150*
CARDS:

QQ **Trees Mini Hotel** 2 Queen's Crescent, York Rd EX4 6AY
(in the city centre close to the university cathedral and bus station)
☎ 01392 59531
Situated within a short walking distance of the city centre, this small family run guest house is furnished in a comfortable and simple style. The friendly owners offer guests a warm welcome.
10 rms (1 bth) 2 annexe rms (1 fmly) No smoking in 6 bedrooms No smoking in dining room CTV in all bedrooms Tea and coffee making facilities No dogs Cen ht CTV 1P No coaches Last d 7.30pm
ROOMS: s fr £16; d fr £30*

EYE Suffolk Map 05 TM17

QQQ ***White Horse*** Stoke Ash IP23 7ET (on the A140 between Ipswich/Norwich) ☎ 01379 678222 FAX 01379 678557
Situated in the countryside, this 17th-century coaching inn provides a sedate base from which to explore Suffolk. Accommodation takes the shape of spacious, comfortable modern chalets. Two traditionally decorated restaurants promote the extensive menu which is served throughout the Inn. The atmospheric bar area boasts low-beamed ceilings and inglenook fires.
7 annexe bth CTV in all bedrooms Tea and coffee making facilities Direct dial from bedrooms No dogs (ex guide dogs) Cen ht 60P Last d 9.30pm
CARDS:

EYNSHAM Oxfordshire Map 04 SP40

QQQ **All Views** Old Witney Road/Main A40 OX8 1PU
☎ 01865 880891
A modern house with a very attractive garden, and a warm, friendly atmosphere. The smart bedrooms are particularly well equipped with satellite TV, telephone and stylish en suite facilities. The bright dining room with separate tables, is open plan with the kitchen. There is also a cosy lounge with a wood burning stove.
4 bth/shr No smoking in dining room No smoking in lounges CTV in all bedrooms Tea and coffee making facilities Direct dial from bedrooms No dogs (ex guide dogs) Cen ht CTV No children 8yrs 10P No coaches
ROOMS: s £39.95; d £45-£49*
CARDS:

FAIRFORD Gloucestershire Map **04** SP10

Selected

QQQQ **East End House** East End GL7 4AP
(at East End by Eight Bells public house, turn off A417 and take immediate right turn into driveway)
☎ 01285 713715 FAX 01285 713505
Situated in the heart of the village, this impressive Georgian house with beautifully tended walled gardens has a relaxed atmosphere. Bedrooms are spacious, well furnished and comfortable, with lots of thoughtful homely extras and modern private bathrooms. The public rooms are tastefully decorated and furnished with some good period pieces. Diana Ewart is a relaxed and charming hostess who delights in welcoming guests to her home.
2 bth/shr (2 fmly) No smoking in bedrooms No smoking in area of dining room No smoking in lounges CTV in all bedrooms Tea and coffee making facilities No dogs (ex guide dogs) Cen ht CTV 8P No coaches Tennis (hard) Ski machine Last d noon
ROOMS: s £30-£35; d £50-£55; wkly b&b £182-£245*

FAKENHAM Norfolk Map **09** TF92

See **Barney**

FALMOUTH Cornwall & Isles of Scilly Map **02** SW83

Selected

QQQQ **Cotswold House Hotel** Melvill Rd TR11 4DF
(A39 into Falmouth, follow signs for docks, beaches and Princess Pavillion, premises located on the right)
☎ 01326 312077 FAX 01326 319181
Mar-Nov
Pamela and Graham Cain offer a warm welcome to their small, friendly guest house, which is situated close to the town centre and sea front. Bedrooms are attractively furnished with modern facilities. Guests can enjoy the comfortable lounge and cosy bar, adjacent to the dining room where dinner is served.
10 bth/shr (2 fmly) No smoking in dining room CTV in all bedrooms Tea and coffee making facilities No dogs Licensed No children 4yrs 10P Last d 7pm
ROOMS: s £22-£24; d £44-£48; wkly b&b £140-£155; wkly hlf-bd £180-£200*

Selected

QQQQ **Dolvean Hotel** 50 Melvill Rd TR11 4DQ
(premises on the main road to Pendennis Castle and docks)
☎ 01326 313658 FAX 01326 313995
Paul and Carol Crocker have succeeded over the past four years in totally upgrading and re-furbishing this delightful Victorian house. The spotless bedrooms are carefully co-ordinated and furnished comfortably and with care. All the en-suite rooms have many modern facilities and some have lovely harbour views. A comfortable lounge is available for guests to relax in, whilst breakfast is served in the bright and airy dining room.
12 bth/shr (1 fmly) No smoking CTV in all bedrooms Tea and coffee making facilities No dogs (ex guide dogs) Licensed Cen ht CTV No children 5yrs 8P No coaches
ROOMS: s £25; d £40-£46*
CARDS:

Selected

QQQQ Gayhurst 10 Pennance Rd TR11 4EA
(Follow signs to beaches. At the end of Western Terrace turn right at mini rbut onto Pennance Rd, situated 100yds on the right)
☎ 01326 315161
Etr-Oct
Situated in a quiet residential area, with distant coastal views, this detached property is within walking distance of both the town centre and the beach. The bedrooms are well presented and maintained, those with sea views being most popular. Some ground floor bedrooms are available. In addition to the breakfast room, a comfortable lounge is provided.
8 bth/shr (1 fmly) No smoking in dining room No smoking in lounges CTV in all bedrooms Tea and coffee making facilities No dogs (ex guide dogs) No children 5yrs 8P
ROOMS: s £20-£24; d £36-£44; wkly b&b £112-£147

QQQ Harbour House 1 Harbour Ter TR11 2AN
(head to town centre via Dracaena Ave,left onto Kimberley Park Rd, bottom of hill turn left up Quarry Hill,right into Erisey Terrace,continue on road)
☎ 01326 311344
Closed Jan-Feb
Stunning views over Carrick Roads and the Harbour are to be seen from front facing rooms at this cosy, conveniently located guest house. Each of the bedrooms is pleasantly decorated and furnished and there is a family suite located on the ground floor. The breakfast room is light and airy.
6 rms (3 shr) (1 fmly) No smoking in bedrooms No smoking in dining room CTV in all bedrooms Tea and coffee making facilities No dogs Cen ht 4P No coaches
ROOMS: s £15-£18; d £30-£40

Selected

QQQQ Ivanhoe 7 Melvill Rd TR11 4AS
(follow signs Docks & Beach) ☎ 01326 319083 FAX 01326 319083
Mike and Betty Berman are the friendly owners of this pleasant little guest house close to the local beaches and town centre. Pretty wallpapers and fabrics are used to good effect and bedrooms are equipped with many thoughtful personal touches. Many rooms have views of the castle and the bay beyond. Breakfast is served in the pretty cottage-style dining room and a photograph album of dishes is available to help any foreign guests with their choice.
7 rms (4 shr) (1 fmly) No smoking in dining room CTV in all bedrooms Tea and coffee making facilities No dogs Cen ht CTV 4P No coaches
ROOMS: s £18-£25; d £36-£50*
CARDS:

Selected

QQQQ Melvill House Hotel 52 Melvill Rd TR11 4DQ
☎ 01326 316645 FAX 01326 211608
Closed 23-27 Dec
Located close to the town centre and beach, this friendly guest house offers comfortable en suite accommodation, with modern facilities and some personal touches, such as magazines, tissues and pot pourri. Many rooms have harbour and sea views. Guests can relax in the cosy lounge and enjoy Mrs Crawford's cooking in the attractive dining room.
7 bth/shr (3 fmly) No smoking in bedrooms No smoking in dining room CTV in all bedrooms Tea and coffee making facilities No dogs Licensed Cen ht CTV No children 9P
ROOMS: d £40-£50; wkly b&b £125-£155; wkly hlf-bd £173-£206*

Selected

QQQQ Penmere 'Rosehill', Mylor Bridge TR11 5LZ
01326 374470 FAX 01326 378828
Closed 15 Dec-16 Jan
Dating from the middle of the last century this delightful guest house lies in pretty lawns and gardens and commands stunning views over Mylor Creek. Bedrooms are spacious and individually decorated and some are suitable for families. There is a combined lounge and breakfast room, where a log fire burns in colder weather.
6 rms (4 bth/shr) (1 fmly) No smoking CTV in all bedrooms Tea and coffee making facilities No dogs (ex guide dogs) Cen ht 6P No coaches
ROOMS: s £28-£32; d £46-£54

Premier Selected

QQQQQ Prospect House 1 Church Rd, Penryn TR10 8DA
(turn off A39 at Treluswell rbut onto B3292. After 1.5 miles turn right through white gates next to telephone box)
☎ 01326 373198 FAX 01326 373198
Convenient for the town centre and quay, this delightful Grade II listed Georgian Town House, was built for a wealthy ship owner around 1830, and is surrounded by a well tended Cornish walled garden. The bedrooms are tastefully decorated and furnished in keeping with the building. A comfortable and spacious drawing-room is provided and has an open log fire on cold evenings. A traditional English breakfast is served in the dining room, around a large communal table.
4 rms (3 bth/shr) No smoking in bedrooms No smoking in dining room CTV in all bedrooms Cen ht CTV No children 12yrs 4P No coaches
ROOMS: s £35; d £50-£55
CARDS:

Q Q Q ***Red House*** 24 Melvill Rd TR11 4AR (150yds past Princess Pavilion) ☎ 01326 311172
Etr-Oct
Close to the seafront and the town centre, this attractive Victorian property is personally run by Margaret and Ray Grout. The bedrooms are soundly furnished and decorated, all are well equipped, and some rooms are available on the ground floor. A traditional breakfast is served in the dining room, and guests have the use of a sitting room.
8 rms (6 shr) (1 fmly) No smoking in bedrooms No smoking in dining room CTV in all bedrooms Tea and coffee making facilities No dogs (ex guide dogs) Cen ht CTV No children 6yrs 8P

Selected

Q Q Q Q **Rosemary Private Hotel** 22 Gyllyngvase Ter TR11 4DL (A39 Melvill Rd signposted to beaches and seafront)
☎ 01326 314669
Apr-Oct
This private hotel is a short walk from the town centre and the sandy Gyllyngvase Beach. It has pleasant and well maintained gardens and fine views of Falmouth Bay. Bedrooms are well equipped and comfortably furnished and there are some two-bedroom units that are popular with families. A cosy bar and a relaxing lounge are provided.
10 bth/shr (2 fmly) No smoking in dining room CTV in all bedrooms Tea and coffee making facilities No dogs Licensed Cen ht CTV 8P No coaches
ROOMS: s £20-£25; d £40-£50; wkly b&b fr £122; wkly hlf-bd £160-£190

Selected

Q Q Q Q ***Rosemullion Private Hotel*** Gyllyngvase Hill TR11 4DF
☎ 01326 314690
14 May-30 Sep
Terry and Jeanette Chambers have been the friendly and welcoming owners of this 19th-century private hotel for 35 years. Bedrooms are well-maintained and are constantly being upgraded. Many rooms are located at ground-floor level and there are good sea views.
13 rms (3 bth 8 shr) No smoking CTV in all bedrooms Tea and coffee making facilities No dogs No children 18P No coaches

Q Q Q **San Remo Hotel** Gyllyngvase Hill TR11 4DN (from Melville Rd turn rt down Gyllyngvase Hill, San Remo is on left near bottom of the hill) ☎ 01326 312076
Etr-Oct
The San Remo is just fifty yards from the golden sands of Gyllngvase Beach and within walking distance of the town centre. Sheila and Keith Withers are cheerful hosts who offer a home cooked three course meal each evening. The bedrooms are pleasantly decorated and furnished, several are located on the ground floor and some have sea views.
10 rms (8 bth/shr) (1 fmly) No smoking in dining room CTV in all bedrooms Tea and coffee making facilities No dogs (ex guide dogs) No children 5yrs 10P No coaches Last d 5pm
ROOMS: s £21-£23; d £42-£46; wkly b&b £139-£150; wkly hlf-bd £167-£189

Q Q Q ***Springfield*** 69 Melville Rd TR11 4DE (oppposite Fox Rosehill Gardens) ☎ 01326 311768
Mar-Oct
Quietly set in delightful gardens, this secluded detached bungalow is the family home of Mr and Mrs Costin. Ground floor bedrooms are neatly furnished and decorated. The annexe suite with its own sitting room, has french windows which open onto the terraced gardens at the rear. Breakfast is served at separate tables in the new conservatory-styled dining room.
2 bth/shr (1 fmly) No smoking CTV in all bedrooms Tea and coffee making facilities No dogs (ex guide dogs) No children 5yrs 3P No coaches

Q Q Q **Tregenna** 28 Melvill Rd TR11 4AR (A39 for Falmouth and the docks, 50 metres from the Princess Pavilion on right) ☎ 01326 313881
Within easy walking distance of the town centre and local beaches, this friendly guest house is run by the Stone family. The dining room/lounge is comfortably furnished, while bedrooms are smart with modern facilities. A family suite of two rooms is also available.
7 rms (5 shr) (3 fmly) No smoking in 3 bedrooms No smoking in dining room No smoking in 1 lounge CTV in all bedrooms Tea and coffee making facilities Licensed Cen ht CTV 8P No coaches Last d 10am
ROOMS: s £18-£19; d £36-£38; wkly b&b £120-£125; wkly hlf-bd £170-£180✻

Selected

Q Q Q Q **Westcott Hotel** Gyllyngvase Hill TR11 4DN (follow signs to beach) ☎ 01326 311309 FAX 01326 311124
Mar-Oct
This delightful detached property is situated in an elevated position, with views overlooking Falmouth Bay and the lovely sandy Gyllngvase Beach, and is within walking distance of the town centre. Bedrooms are nicely decorated and comfortably furnished, many having sea views. There is a comfortable and spacious lounge and an attractive dining room, where delightful four course meals are served.
10 bth/shr 1 annexe bth No smoking CTV in all bedrooms Tea and coffee making facilities Licensed Cen ht No children 15yrs 11P No coaches Last d 6pm
ROOMS: s £23-£34; d £46-£68; wkly b&b £154-£210; wkly hlf-bd £210-£260
CARDS:

FALSTONE Northumberland Map **12** NY78

Q Q Q **Pheasant** Stannersburn NE48 1DD (from A68 turn onto B6320, follow signs for Kielder Water; from A69, B6079, B6320, follow signs to Kielder Water) (The Circle) ☎ 01434 240382 FAX 01434 240382
Closed 25-26 Dec rs Jan-Feb (closed Mon/Tue)
This charming inn retains the character of a country pub whilst providing comfortable, modern accommodation. Originally a farm house, it features stone walls and low beamed ceilings in the bars. Five of the bedrooms are at ground level and three are upstairs. Delicious home-cooked meals are served in the bar or in the pine furnished dining room.
8 annexe shr (1 fmly) No smoking CTV in all bedrooms Tea and coffee making facilities Cen ht ch fac 40P No coaches Pool room Darts Last d 8.50pm
ROOMS: s £40-£45; d fr £58
MEALS: Bar Lunch £3.75-£7.25 Dinner fr £15alc
CARDS:

FAREHAM Hampshire Map **04** SU50

Selected

Q Q Q Q **Avenue House Hotel** 22 The Avenue PO14 1NS (exit M27 at junc 9, A27 until Tertiary College on right, premises located approx 300 yards on left before traffic lights)
☎ 01329 232175 FAX 01329 232196
This friendly hotel, set back from the road, is conveniently located on the A27 west of the town centre. The bedrooms are well equipped and comfortable with colour TV and modern en suite bathrooms. Drinks can be served in the spacious guest lounge overlooking the garden.
17 bth/shr (3 fmly) No smoking in 5 bedrooms No smoking in dining room CTV in all bedrooms Tea and coffee making facilities Direct dial from bedrooms Licensed Cen ht 25P No coaches
ROOMS: s £46; d £53-£70
CARDS:

FARMBOROUGH Somerset Map **03** ST66

Selected

Q Q Q Q ***Streets Hotel*** The Street BA3 1AR ☎ 01761 471452 FAX 01761 471452
Closed 20 Dec-1 Jan
This is a charming private hotel set in the picturesque village of Farmborough. Bedrooms in both the main house and adjacent coach house are spacious, well equipped and tastefully decorated. Guests can relax in the lounges or the beamed sitting room. Breakfast, and dinner by prior arrangement, are served in the intimate dining room.
3 bth/shr 5 annexe bth/shr CTV in all bedrooms Tea and coffee making facilities Direct dial from bedrooms No dogs Licensed Cen ht CTV No children 6yrs 10P No coaches Outdoor swimming pool (heated) Solarium Last d 8.50pm
CARDS:

FARNBOROUGH Hampshire Map **04** SU85

Selected

Q Q Q Q ***The White Residence*** Farnborough Park, 76 Avenue Rd GU14 7BG (from A325 (Farnborough road) turn at Clockhouse roundabout into Rectory Road, Avenue Road is 4th turning on right)
☎ 01252 375510 FAX 01252 375510
The White Residence is run with flair by proprietor Mrs Allen. The four rooms are named and themed according to the colours featured in the bold decor. All rooms are very well equipped featuring hairdryers, telephones and satellite TV. Although evening meals are not available, the Allens have negotiated a discount at a local restaurant and are happy to recommend others.
4 bth/shr No smoking CTV in all bedrooms Tea and coffee making facilities Direct dial from bedrooms No dogs Cen ht CTV No children 12yrs 4P No coaches
CARDS:

FARNSFIELD Nottinghamshire Map **08** SK65

Q Q **Grange Cottage** Main St NG22 8EA
(turn off A614 (Ollerton/Doncaster) at White Post roundabout, taking 3rd exit to Farnsfield. Through village to Plough Inn, house opposite)
☎ 01623 882259 & 883300 FAX 01623 883435
Grange Cottage is an 18th-century Georgian building which has retained many of its original features. Guests are encouraged to enjoy the delightful quiet garden. Bedrooms are individually furnished and homely, and breakfast is taken around one large table in a separate dining room.
3 rms (1 fmly) CTV in all bedrooms Tea and coffee making facilities Cen ht 6P No coaches
ROOMS: s £20; d £40; wkly b&b £140*

FARRINGTON GURNEY Somerset Map **03** ST65

Selected

Q Q Q Q ***The Parsonage*** Main St BS18 5UB (on A37, at bottom of Rush Hill on edge of village) ☎ 01761 453553
Closed 25-26 Dec
This fine 17th-century Grade II listed building offers comfortable accommodation. Many original features have been retained such as cast iron fireplaces, flag stones and ornate arches. The house was once part of the Duchy of Cornwall Estate and has had visits from members of the Royal Household. The spacious bedrooms have been furnished to a high standard and are well equipped with thoughtful extras including electric blankets. The large lounge leads into the dining room where dinner is available by prior arrangement.
3 rms (3 fmly) No smoking CTV in all bedrooms Tea and coffee making facilities No dogs Cen ht CTV 32P Last d 5.30pm
CARDS:

The AA's professional Inspectors make regular and anonymous visits to all the establishments listed in the Guide. They accept no gifts or favours from proprietors

FAVERSHAM Kent Map 05 TR06

QQQ **White Horse** The Street, Boughton ME13 9AX
(at end of M2 follow signs for A2, immediately after roundabout take slip road to Boughton, 1m to village) (Shepherd Neame)
☎ 01227 751343 FAX 01227 751090
Located in the village of Boughton, this 15th-century inn retains its character with beamed ceilings and exposed brickwork throughout the restaurant and two bars. Diners have the choice of bar snacks, daily blackboard specials and an à la carte menu, plus a carvery at the weekends. Bedrooms are generally spacious, and have a good range of facilities.
13 bth/shr (2 fmly) No smoking in 4 bedrooms CTV in all bedrooms Tea and coffee making facilities Direct dial from bedrooms Cen ht CTV 35P Last d 9.30pm
ROOMS: s fr £42.50; d fr £52.50
MEALS: Lunch £10-£15alc Dinner £15-£20alc
CARDS:

FELIXSTOWE Suffolk Map 05 TM33

QQQ **Fludyer Arms Hotel** Undercliff Rd East IP11 7LU
☎ 01394 283279 FAX 01394 670754
Mr and Mrs Nash are the jovial hosts of this popular haunt, situated close to the sea in a quiet roadside setting. The bedrooms are spacious and well maintained, and most have modern en suite facilities. There are two large bars, one public and the other a lounge saloon, with a separate children's/breakfast room and non-smoking area. The menu concentrates on traditional and fish dishes.
8 rms (6 bth/shr) (1 fmly) No smoking in area of dining room No smoking in 1 lounge CTV in all bedrooms Tea and coffee making facilities 8P Childrens playroom Last d 9pm
ROOMS: s £18-£26; d £32-£40*
MEALS: Bar Lunch £3-£6*
CARDS:

FELSTED Essex Map 05 TL62

Selected

QQQQ ***Potash Farmhouse*** *(TL686196)* Cobblers Green, Causeway End Rd CM6 3LX (from A120, take B1417 to village centre and turn into Chelmsford road, proceed 0.5m to sign for Cobblers Green. Farm signed 400 yds on left)
☎ 01371 820510 FAX 01371 820510 Mr & Mrs R Smith
This charming 15th-century half-moated farmhouse sits in its own quiet grounds and gardens. The public rooms are well cared for and tastefully furnished with some well chosen pieces. Guests have the use of a comfortable lounge, a conservatory with access to the gardens and a beamed breakfast room with a large inglenook fireplace. Bedrooms are of varying sizes, and have a good range of facilities and thoughtful extras.
3 rms No smoking CTV in all bedrooms Tea and coffee making facilities No dogs Cen ht CTV No children 12yrs 6P
160 acres arable

FELTHAM Greater London

For accommodation details see **Heathrow Airport**

FILEY North Yorkshire Map **08** TA18

Q Q Q ***Abbots Leigh*** 7 Rutland St YO14 9JA (from A165 follow signs for town centre, then turn right at church clock tower, then second left)
☎ 01723 513334
This cosy and comfortable guest house provides good value together with very friendly and hospitable service from the resident owners. The modern bedrooms are well furnished and comfortable and there is a lounge available for guest use.
6 bth/shr (3 fmly) No smoking in bedrooms No smoking in dining room CTV in all bedrooms Tea and coffee making facilities No dogs (ex guide dogs) Licensed Cen ht No children 3yrs 4P No coaches Last d 4pm
CARDS:

Q Q Q **Seafield Hotel** 9/11 Rutland St YO14 9JA (exit A64 signposted to Filey, at crossroads in town centre turn right, second left into Rutland Street)
☎ 01723 513715
This attractive mid-terraced hotel lies between the town centre and the beach, and is family owned and run. It offers bright and freshly decorated bedrooms, a residents' bar lounge and a second lounge, as well as a dining room adorned with a number of paintings and photographs.
13 bth/shr (7 fmly) No smoking in bedrooms No smoking in dining room No smoking in 1 lounge CTV in all bedrooms Tea and coffee making facilities No dogs Licensed Cen ht CTV 8P No coaches Last d 4pm
ROOMS: s £18.50-£20.50; d £37-£41; wkly b&b £124-£138; wkly hlf-bd £160-£174
CARDS:

FIR TREE Co Durham Map **12** NZ13

Premier Selected

Q Q Q Q Q **Greenhead Country House Hotel** DL15 8BL (on A68, turn right at Fir Tree Inn)
☎ 01388 763143 FAX 01388 763143
Greenhead is situated at the foot of the Weardale Valley in well tended gardens. Bedrooms are spacious and modern. All have been carefully equipped and comfortably furnished. Public rooms are delightful and include a 50-foot long beamed and stone-arched lounge. There is also a well stocked bar.
8 bth/shr (1 fmly) No smoking in 2 bedrooms No smoking in dining room No smoking in 1 lounge CTV in 7 bedrooms Tea and coffee making facilities No dogs (ex guide dogs) Licensed Cen ht CTV No children 13yrs 20P No coaches Last d 5pm
ROOMS: s £40-£45; d £50-£60
CARDS:

FORD Wiltshire Map **03** ST87

Selected

Q Q Q Q **The White Hart** SN14 8RP (from M4 junct 17 take A429 then A420. Ford is situated alongside A420) ☎ 01249 782213 FAX 01249 783075
An attractive and interesting Cotswold stone inn – the exterior was used for one of the scenes in the film 'Dr Doolittle'. The White Hart is conveniently located for easy access to several centres and many tourist attractions, making the inn an ideal base for exploring. The rooms, most of which are located in former, converted stables are well equipped and comfortable. But it is for the food and ale that the inn has gained an enviable reputation. A specials menu is served at lunch time, while an extensive à la carte menu is served each evening, featuring local game dishes, fresh fish, steaks and poultry. In addition to a comprehensive wine list, a range of traditional beers is available.
3 bth/shr 8 annexe bth/shr No smoking in area of dining room CTV in all bedrooms Tea and coffee making facilities Direct dial from bedrooms Cen ht 150P Outdoor swimming pool (heated) Fishing Last d 10pm
ROOMS: s £50; d £75; wkly b&b £350*
MEALS: Lunch £4.95-£12alc Dinner £9.95-£14alc*
CARDS:

FORDINGBRIDGE Hampshire Map **04** SU11

Selected

Q Q Q Q **Alderholt Mill** Sandleheath SP6 1PU (M27 junct1, B3078 through Fordingbridge in direction of Damerham and Cranbourne. Turn left at crossroads in Sandleheath, 0.5m over bridge, on right)
☎ 01425 653130 FAX 01425 652868
Alderholt Mill is a working water mill, home to Sandra and Richard Harte. The mill is surrounded by cottage gardens and has its own fishing. The cosy bedrooms offer comfortable accommodation, all enjoying country views. Evening meals are available by prior

arrangement. The mill machinery is still intact and can be seen working and producing flour. A speciality of the house is to offer bread made with their own freshly milled flour.
4 shr No smoking CTV in all bedrooms Tea and coffee making facilities Cen ht No children 8yrs 10P No coaches Fishing Last d noon
ROOMS: d £45; wkly b&b fr £142; wkly hlf-bd fr £215
CARDS:

Selected

QQQQ Colt Green North End, Damerham SP6 3HA (A338 to Fordingbridge, follow signs for Sandelheath through to Damerham. Past garage and pub on left, over white bridge, turn right for Martin)
☎ 01725 518240
In the pretty village of Damerham a few miles from Fordingbridge, Colt Green is a single storey property, peacefully located in attractive gardens by a stream. Amanda and Ginge Eames welcome guests to their charming home. Bedrooms are comfortably furnished, each enjoying views over the garden. The cosy lounge/dining room is the venue for breakfast, and light suppers and two course dinners are available by prior arrangement.
3 rms (1 shr) (1 fmly) No smoking CTV in 1 bedroom Tea and coffee making facilities CTV 3P No coaches Last d 10am
ROOMS: s £30-£32.50; d £35-£45; wkly b&b £180-£195; wkly hlf-bd £225-£270*

Premier Selected

QQQQQ The Three Lions Stuckton SP6 2HF (0.5 mile East of Fordingbridge from A338 or B3078. Locate Q8 garage and follow Three Lions tourist signs)
☎ 01425 652489 FAX 01425 656144
Closed 18 Jan-12 Feb rs Sun evening/Mon (no meals)
The Three Lions is perhaps best known for its outstanding cuisine from Chef Mike Womersley. The rooms are airy and attractive and look out over the well manicured garden. Mike's wife Jayne has added lots of charming extra touches and has a keen eye for detail. She has selected some super fabrics and furnishings, and to complement these there are lots of high quality extras. Mike's unpretentious cuisine makes great use of only the freshest local produce.
3 bth/shr No smoking in bedrooms No smoking in dining room CTV in all bedrooms Tea and coffee making facilities No dogs (ex guide dogs) Cen ht 50P No coaches Whirlpool spa in garden Last d 9.45pm
ROOMS: s £65-£75; d £75-£85*
MEALS: Lunch £13.50&alc Dinner £16.50&alc*
CARDS:

FOWEY Cornwall & Isles of Scilly Map **02** SX15

Selected

QQQQ Carnethic House Lambs Barn PL23 1HQ (off A3082, directly opposite "Welcome to Fowey" sign)
☎ 01726 833336 FAX 01726 833336
Closed Dec-Jan
This attractive Regency family house, home to the enthusiastic and friendly owners, David & Trisha Hogg, is set in grounds which include an outdoor heated swimming pool, putting green, golf practice net and a soft tennis court. The dining room, overlooking the gardens, is where a choice is offered from the daily changing dinner menus. The spacious bedrooms are furnished in a variety of styles.
8 rms (5 shr) (2 fmly) No smoking in 2 bedrooms No smoking in dining room CTV in all bedrooms Tea and coffee making facilities Licensed Cen ht ch fac 20P No coaches Outdoor swimming pool (heated) Tennis (grass) Badminton Putting Bowls Golf practice net Last d 8pm
ROOMS: s £30-£40; d £50-£65; wkly b&b £170-£220; wkly hlf-bd £270-£320
CARDS:

QQQ *King of Prussia* Town Quay PL23 1AT (St Austell Brewery)
☎ 01726 832450
This attractive quayside inn is named after an infamous local smuggler who operated around Prussia Cove. All six of the cosy bedrooms enjoy estuary views, and have been recently refurbished with tasteful co-ordinating decor. Home-cooked meals and snacks are available in the convivial first floor public bar.
6 bth/shr (4 fmly) CTV in all bedrooms Tea and coffee making facilities No dogs (ex guide dogs) Cen ht Last d 9.30pm
CARDS:

QQQ Trevanion 70 Lostwithiel St PL23 1BQ (exit A390 onto B3269 signposted for Fowey, on descending the hill premises situated on left 200 mtrs past turning for main car park)
☎ 01726 832602
Mar-Oct
Within easy walking distance of all parts of this historic town, Trevanion Guest House is run by owners Jill and Bob Bullock. The well equipped, comfortable bedrooms are decorated with pretty co-ordinated fabrics. The charming dining room retains many original features. In addition to the hearty cooked breakfast a good selection of alternative choices is offered.
5 rms (2 bth/shr) (1 fmly) No smoking CTV in all bedrooms Tea and coffee making facilities No dogs (ex guide dogs) Cen ht No children 4yrs 3P No coaches
ROOMS: s £22.50; d £40-£45; wkly b&b £135-£152

FOWNHOPE Herefordshire Map **03** SO53

Selected

QQQQ **Bowens Country House** HR1 4PS
(6m SE of Hereford on B4224 in village of Fownhope, opposite the church) ☎ 01432 860430 FAX 01432 860430
Situated in two acres of grounds, which include a putting green and tennis court, this former 17th-century farmhouse retains many original features. Bedrooms are comfortable, well equipped and homely and all have the benefit of modern en suite facilities; some include power showers. Public areas include a sitting room with honesty bar and a cosy dining room.
6 bth/shr 4 annexe bth/shr (4 fmly) No smoking in 4 bedrooms No smoking in dining room CTV in all bedrooms Tea and coffee making facilities Direct dial from bedrooms Licensed Cen ht 15P No coaches Tennis (grass) 9 hole putting green Last d 9pm
ROOMS: s £25-£33.50; d £50-£67; wkly b&b £175-£266; wkly hlf-bd £270-£325*
CARDS:

FRAMLINGHAM Suffolk Map **05** TM26

QQQ **Church Farm** *(TM605267)* Church Rd, Kettleburgh IP13 7LF (from A12, northbound take 2nd left to Wickham market, follow all signs to Easton Farm Park then to Kettleburgh 1.25m, house behind church)
☎ 01728 723532 Mrs A Bater
In a wonderful country setting, next to the village church, this spacious house offers large, well equipped bedrooms. With a large fireplace and woodburning stove, lots of beams and little personal touches, the lounge is very attractive and cosy. Mrs Bater prepares hearty home-cooked farethat is served in the separate dining room.
3 rms (1 shr) No smoking in bedrooms No smoking in dining room Tea and coffee making facilities No dogs Cen ht CTV 10P Clay pigeon shooting 70 acres arable mixed Last d 6.30pm
ROOMS: s £19-£20; d £38-£40; wkly b&b £133-£140; wkly hlf-bd £210-£224

Selected

QQQQ **Woodlands Farm** Brundish IP13 8BP (from A1120 at Dennington, take B116 towards Laxfield, then 4th turning on left. Follow lane for 0.5m and turn left down No Through Road signs)
☎ 01379 384444
Closed 24 Dec-2 Jan
John and Jill Graham offer guests a warm family welcome at this 16th-century farmhouse, which is situated in the heart of the countryside and built in the traditional Suffolk style. Comfortable accommodation is offered throughout, and has been sympathetically decorated to enhance the original exposed beams and low ceilings.
3 bth/shr No smoking Tea and coffee making facilities No dogs Cen ht CTV No children 10yrs 6P No coaches Last d 8.30am
ROOMS: s £25-£30; d £36-£40; wkly b&b £120*

Win a Family Fun Weekend with AA Lifestyle Guides in association with Hilton Hotels. 3 winners will be drawn every 2 months: December 1998; February 1999; April 1999; June 1999; August 1999; October 1999

FRAMPTON ON SEVERN Gloucestershire Map **03** SO70

Premier Selected

QQQQQ ***Old School House*** Whittles Ln GL2 7EB
(in village, take left turning through middle of green. 300yds from end of green turn right into Whittles Lane) ☎ 01452 740457
Closed 21-31 Dec
The Old School House is situated in a picturesque village that boasts the longest village green in England. Many of the building's original features have been retained, and the decor and furniture enhance its character. Bedrooms are spacious and comfortable with lots of homely extras, and modern en suite facilities. The dining room with its large family table is the venure for breakfast. The spacious sitting room contains many fine period pieces and an open fire for the cooler months.
2 bth/shr No smoking in bedrooms Tea and coffee making facilities Cen ht CTV No children 10yrs 10P

FRESSINGFIELD Suffolk Map **05** TM27

Premier Selected

QQQQQ **Chippenhall Hall** IP21 5TD (8m E of Diss 1 mile outside Fressingfield on B1116 to Framlingham)
☎ 01379 588180 & 586733 FAX 01379 586272
This listed Tudor manor house is steeped in history, and there are several references to Chippenhall in the Domesday Book. The building features exposed beams throughout and has been superbly decorated and furnished in period style. During the winter months guests can enjoy a roaring log fire in the sitting room. The bedrooms are spacious and sumptuously furnished, whilst retaining all their original character; they all have modern facilities.
3 bth/shr No smoking in bedrooms No smoking in dining room No smoking in 1 lounge Tea and coffee making facilities No dogs (ex guide dogs) Licensed Cen ht CTV No children 16yrs 20P No coaches Outdoor swimming pool (heated) Croquet lawn Clay pigeon shooting Last d 6pm
ROOMS: d £68-£72; wkly b&b £214-£227; wkly hlf-bd £389-£402*
CARDS:

See advertisement under DISS

FRINTON-ON-SEA Essex Map **05** TM21

Q **Forde** 18 Queens Rd CO13 9BL (over railway crossing into Frinton on Sea, 100mtrs branch left into Queens Rd, premises 100mtrs on left) ☎ 01255 674758
Closed mid Dec-mid Jan

Guests are assured of a warm welcome at this long established, family-run guest house. In addition to the modest bedrooms that are traditionally appointed, there is a cosy television lounge and a breakfast room. Parking outside the house is unrestricted, and the road leads directly to the esplanade and the seafront.
3 rms (1 fmly) No smoking in dining room Cen ht CTV No children 5yrs 1P No coaches
ROOMS: s £22; d £34; wkly b&b £119*

FRITHAM Hampshire Map 04 SU21

Selected

Fritham Farm *(SU243144)* Fritham SO43 7HH (leave M27 at junct 1 and follow signs to Fritham)
01703 812333 FAX 01703 812333 Mrs P Hankinson
Feb-Oct Closed Nov-Mid Feb
Mrs Hankinson welcomes guests to this delightful farmhouse set in the New Forest. The attractive bedrooms are traditionally furnished, have particularly comfortable beds and modern en suite facilities. A farmhouse breakfast is served in the cosy dining room around one table overlooking the garden. There are no televisions in the rooms but there is a very large and comfortable lounge with a television where guests can relax.
3 bth/shr No smoking Tea and coffee making facilities No dogs (ex guide dogs) Cen ht CTV No children 10yrs 4P 51 acres mixed grass
ROOMS: d £37-£42*

FROGMORE Devon Map 03 SX74

Globe TQ7 2NR (3.75m E of Kingsbridge on A379)
01548 531351 FAX 01548 531351
Located in the pretty village of Frogmore in the lovely South Hams countryside of South Devon. Bedrooms are smart and modern and a wide range of food is available in the bars, which also serve real ale and farmhouse cider, and feature exposed timbers and flagged floors. There is a popular beer garden which overlooks Frogmore Creek.
6 rms (3 shr) (2 fmly) No smoking in dining room CTV in all bedrooms Tea and coffee making facilities Cen ht CTV 20P Pool Darts Cycle hire Canoe hire Last d 10pm
ROOMS: s £20-£30; d £30-£40; wkly b&b £110-£120
MEALS: Lunch £4-£11alc Dinner £6-£20alc
CARDS:

FROME Somerset Map 03 ST74

Fourwinds Bath Rd BA11 2HJ (premises on B3090 N of Frome town centre near to sports centre and college)
01373 462618 FAX 01373 453029
This attractive chalet bungalow set in a well maintained garden, is set back from the main road, and is personally run by the proprietors, Mr and Mrs King. Bedrooms are comfortable and well appointed. Mrs King provides an imaginative menu for dinner. The public rooms are open plan, with a small bar area, lounge and cosy dining room.

6 rms (1 bth 3 shr) (1 fmly) No smoking in dining room No smoking in lounges CTV in all bedrooms Tea and coffee making facilities Direct dial from bedrooms No dogs Licensed Cen ht CTV 10P No coaches Last d 7pm
ROOMS: s £30-£40; d £50-£55*
CARDS:

Talbot Inn Mells BA11 3PN (A36 Bath to Warminster Rd turn right into Frome and take A362 to Radstock then follow signs for Mells)
01373 812254 FAX 01373 813599
This coaching inn, run by the jovial Roger Elliott, is situated in the picturesque village of Mells. Set around a courtyard, there are cosy bars serving fine ales and food, for which the inn has earned an AA rosette award. The bedrooms are comfortably furnished and have managed to retain the same character as the inn.
7 bth/shr No smoking in area of dining room CTV in all bedrooms Tea and coffee making facilities Direct dial from bedrooms 10P Last d 9.15pm
ROOMS: s £29.50-£39.50; d £49.50-£59.50*
MEALS: Lunch £5.75-£9alc Dinner £11.30-£19.95alc*
CARDS:

FYLINGDALES North Yorkshire Map **08** NZ90

QQQ **Flask** Robin Hoods Bay YO22 4QH (on A171 11m from Scarborough, 7m from Whitby) ☎ 01947 880305 FAX 01947 880592
The Flask was originally a 16th-century monks' hostel, and is now a comfortable inn offering a good range of well produced food. The bedrooms are well furnished, and thoughtfully equipped while the bar is spacious and has a friendly atmosphere. A good choice of home cooked food is provided including locally caught fish.
6 bth/shr (2 fmly) No smoking in dining room CTV in all bedrooms Tea and coffee making facilities No dogs Cen ht CTV 20P No coaches Last d 9.30pm
ROOMS: s £28; d £44; wkly b&b £140*
MEALS: Bar Lunch £4-£9 Dinner £4-£9*
CARDS:

GAINSBOROUGH Lincolnshire

See **Marton & Sturton by Stow**

GARBOLDISHAM Norfolk Map **05** TM08

QQQ **Ingleneuk Lodge** Hopton Rd IP22 2RQ (turn S off A1066 on to B1111. 1m on right) ☎ 01953 681541 FAX 01953 681633
rs Xmas & New Year
Located just south of the village in a quiet rural location, this bungalow offers spacious public areas overlooking the gardens. The bedrooms are neat and well appointed with modern en suite facilities, one is equipped for disabled guests.
4 bth/shr (1 fmly) No smoking in bedrooms No smoking in dining room CTV in all bedrooms Tea and coffee making facilities Direct dial from bedrooms Licensed Cen ht 20P No coaches
ROOMS: s £33; d £51*
CARDS:

GATWICK AIRPORT (LONDON) West Sussex Map **04** TQ24

QQQ ***Barnwood Hotel*** Balcombe Rd, Pound Hill RH10 7RU (The Independents) ☎ 01293 425800 FAX 01293 425808
Closed Xmas-1 Jan
The owner-run Barnwood Hotel is a fully-fledged hotel with all the services one would expect, including room service during restaurant hours (except for breakfast). The main bar-lounge has benefited from recent refurbishment as have other public areas and some of the well kept bedrooms. The restaurant offers an interesting menu with a range of Indonesian cuisine, as well as more traditional British dishes.
35 bth/shr (3 fmly) No smoking in area of dining room CTV in all bedrooms Tea and coffee making facilities Direct dial from bedrooms No dogs (ex guide dogs) Licensed Cen ht 50P Last d 9pm
CARDS:

QQQ **Copperwood** Russells Crescent, Massetts Rd RH6 7DJ (from M23 junc 9 pass airport onto A23 towards Redhill after 2nd roundabout, Massetts Rd is on right)
☎ 01293 783388 FAX 01293 420156
Closed Xmas
A warm and friendly welcome is guaranteed from resident proprietors Paul and Caroline Hooks. The prettily decorated rooms have been upgraded to feature en suite shower facilities. Full English breakfast is included in the room tariff and served in an attractive breakfast room. Courtesy transport to and from the airport can also be arranged.
5 shr (1 fmly) No smoking CTV in all bedrooms Tea and coffee making facilities Cen ht 5P No coaches
ROOMS: s £30-£32; d fr £45*
CARDS:

QQQ **Corner House** 72 Massetts Rd RH6 7ED
(M25 junct 7 M23 junct 9 over 1st rbut 4th exit on 2nd to Crawley/Redhill 3rd exit at next rbut 2nd turning on left)
☎ 01293 784574 FAX 01293 784620
Closed 24/25/31 Dec
Guests will find a warm welcome at this cheerful family-run budget hotel. Convenient for Gatwick Airport, free transport is available 24 hours a day, with reduced rates for long term car parking on site. The individually decorated bedrooms are clean and bright, and include several on the ground floor, in addition to those in a separate self-contained building across the road from the main property.
13 shr 12 annexe rms (10 bth/shr) (6 fmly) No smoking in bedrooms No smoking in dining room No smoking in 1 lounge CTV in all bedrooms Tea and coffee making facilities Direct dial from bedrooms Licensed Cen ht CTV 40P Last d 10pm
ROOMS: s £31-£37; d £49-£53*
CARDS:

Selected

QQQQ **Gainsborough Lodge** 39 Massetts Rd RH6 7DT (2m NE of airport adjacent A23) ☎ 01293 783982 FAX 01293 785365
rs 22 Dec-4 Jan
Graham and Rosina Everett offer warm and friendly service at this Edwardian house. The accommodation, which is constantly being improved, is split between the main house and the bungalow next door where the rooms are for non-smoking guests. Day rooms include a comfortable lounge with satellite TV plus a selection of books and board games. A particularly wide choice of freshly-prepared breakfasts (including special vegetarian options) are served in the conservatory breakfast room.
18 rms (16 bth/shr) (5 fmly) No smoking in dining room CTV in all bedrooms Tea and coffee making facilities Direct dial from bedrooms No dogs Cen ht CTV 20P No coaches
ROOMS: s £36.50-£38; d £47.50-£50
CARDS:

Selected

Q Q Q Q **The Lawn** 30 Massetts Rd RH6 7DE
(exit M23 at junc 9, follow signs to A23 Redhill, at roundabout by Esso garage take third exit, Massetts Rd 200 yards on right)
☎ 01293 775751 FAX 01293 821803
Located close to Gatwick Airport, this fine Victorian house continues to be upgraded with all bedrooms now en suite. They are brightly decorated, furnished in modern pine and equipped with many thoughtful extras. A choice of breakfast is offered and served in the very attractive dining room.
7 bth/shr (3 fmly) No smoking CTV in all bedrooms Tea and coffee making facilities Direct dial from bedrooms Cen ht 15P No coaches
ROOMS: d £45*
CARDS:

Q Q Q **Prinsted** Oldfield Rd RH6 7EP
(M23 junct 9, follow signs for airport. At airport roundabout take A23 and continue to Texaco Garage, turn right immediately into Woodroyd Av,on left) ☎ 01293 785233 FAX 01293 820624
Closed 23-26 Dec
Set in a quiet residential road within easy reach of Gatwick Airport, owners Stephanie and Bernard Kendall offer a warm welcome at their spacious Victorian guest house. Rooms, which are divided between the main house and adjoining annexe, are neatly decorated and furnished, with the majority offering smart en suite showers.
8 rms (6 shr) No smoking CTV in all bedrooms Tea and coffee making facilities No dogs (ex guide dogs) Cen ht 12P No coaches
ROOMS: s £32; d £37-£45
CARDS:

Q Q Q **Rosemead** 19 Church Rd RH6 7EY
(exit M23 at junc 9, follow A23 Redhill signs through three roundabouts, Church Rd is fourth turning on the right, premises third house on right)
☎ 01293 784965 & 430546 FAX 01293 430547
Ideally placed for Gatwick Airport, new owner Fiona Stimpson offers a warm welcome at this non-smoking Edwardian guest house. The bedrooms are brightly decorated and include remote control TVs, portable fans and beverage facilities. Breakfast is taken in the smart dining room and secure parking is available for guests who want to leave their cars behind when they go abroad.
6 rms (2 shr) (2 fmly) No smoking CTV in all bedrooms Tea and coffee making facilities Cen ht 40P No coaches
ROOMS: s £25-£32; d £38-£47*
CARDS:

Selected

Q Q Q Q ***Vulcan Lodge*** 27 Massetts Rd RH6 7DQ
(exit M25/23 at junc 9, take right exit at third roundabout, Massetts Rd second on the right, premises 0.25m on the right) ☎ 01293 771522

Vulcan Lodge is a charming period house set back from the main road, well located for Gatwick Airport. The bedrooms are all individually decorated and offer a range of thoughtful extras. There is a comfortable lounge available for guest use and breakfast is served in a delightful dining room.
4 rms (3 shr) No smoking in dining room CTV in all bedrooms Tea and coffee making facilities No dogs Cen ht 10P No coaches
CARDS:

Selected

Q Q Q Q **Wayside Manor Farm** Norwood Hill RH6 0EA
(M25 junct 8 go south on A217 through Reigate following Gatwick signs. 2m S of Reigate right onto Norwood Hill 2nd right Collendean Lane) ☎ 01293 862692 FAX 01293 863417
Just ten minutes from Gatwick Airport, this peaceful Edwardian farmhouse has spacious bedrooms that are decorated with many thoughtful extras. Although dinner is not available, there is a *contd.*

good country pub nearby. Overseas visitors or guests without a car can be collected from Gatwick for a nominal charge.
3 bth/shr No smoking in bedrooms CTV in all bedrooms Tea and coffee making facilities No dogs Cen ht CTV 20P No coaches
ROOMS: s £30-£40; d £40-£50*

GAYHURST Buckinghamshire Map **04** SP84

QQQ **Mill** *(SP852454)* MK16 8LT (Take B526 from Newport Pagnell, after 2.5m turn left into Haversham Rd, Mill Farm is 1m on left) ☎ 01908 611489 FAX 01908 611489 Mrs K Adams
Fresh air pursuits such as tennis, fishing and riding are encouraged by the rural setting of this popular 17th-century farm house. It offers attractive bedrooms in keeping with the original character of the building, and an inviting open lounge/breakfast room which features some lovely pieces of furniture and family memorabilia.
3 rms (1 bth 1 shr) 1 annexe bth/shr (1 fmly) No smoking in 2 bedrooms No smoking in dining room No smoking in 1 lounge CTV in all bedrooms Tea and coffee making facilities Cen ht CTV 13P Tennis (hard) Fishing Riding Rough shooting Trout fishing 550 acres mixed
ROOMS: s £15-£20; d £30-£40; wkly b&b £105

GIGGLESWICK North Yorkshire Map **07** SD86

QQQ ***Black Horse Hotel*** Church St BD24 0BE (off A65 Giggleswick to Settle. Inn situated next to St Alkelda church in centre of village) ☎ 01729 822506
Quietly tucked away in the centre of the village beside the church, this inn offers three comfortable bedrooms, all of which are en suite. A roaring log fire provides a welcome focal point to the bar during the winter months and there is a wood panelled dining room, popular with locals as well as visitors.
3 bth/shr (1 fmly) No smoking in bedrooms CTV in all bedrooms Tea and coffee making facilities Cen ht 20P No coaches Last d 8.45pm
CARDS:

GISLINGHAM Suffolk Map **05** TM07

Selected

QQQQ **The Old Guildhall** Mill St IP23 8JT (off A140)
☎ 01379 783361
Closed Jan
Guests are ensured a warm welcome from Ray and Ethel Tranter at this immaculately preserved 15th-century Guildhall, sitting in its own well maintained gardens in the centre of the tranquil village of Gislingham. The building has some striking features and offers wonderful en suite accommodation, which is full of character. The public rooms are open plan and include a comfortable lounge and a small bar cum dining area.
4 bth No smoking CTV in all bedrooms Tea and coffee making facilities Licensed Cen ht 5P No coaches Last d 4pm
ROOMS: s £37.50; d £55; wkly b&b £165; wkly hlf-bd £220*

GLASTONBURY Somerset Map **03** ST53

See also East Pennard, North Wootton, Somerton & West Pennard

QQQ **Cradlebridge** *(ST477385)* BA16 9SD
(take A39 from Glastonbury heading south, after Morlands factory take 2nd right signposted Meare/Wedmore farm is signposted on left after 1m)
☎ 01458 831827 Mrs J Tinney
Closed Xmas
This 200 acre dairy farm, situated one mile west of Glastonbury on the fringe of the Somerset Levels, enjoys views over unspoilt pastures to the Mendip Hills. Two spacious bedrooms have their own front door, and breakfast is served in a cosy dining area. For evening meals the Tinneys will happily recommend one of the fine hostelries in the area.
2 annexe shr (2 fmly) No smoking CTV in all bedrooms Tea and coffee making facilities No dogs Cen ht No children 3yrs 6P 200 acres dairy
ROOMS: s £30; d £45; wkly b&b £135

Selected

QQQQ ***Manor Farm*** Sticklynch, West Pennard BA6 8NA (Turn off A361 just E of Appletree Inn & follow lane & Manor Farm signs)
☎ 01749 890603 FAX 01749 890603
Closed 21-31 Dec
18th-century farmhouse, constructed of grey stone, that enjoys fabulous country views from an elevated position. The letting end of the house has its own front door and consists of three bedrooms, each with its own modern bathroom facility. There is a comfortable sitting room with a television and adjacent kitchen should guests prefer to prepare their own food. Breakfast is served in the conservatory overlooking the garden. The Rowntrees keep dogs and horses.
3 rms (2 bth/shr) No smoking in bedrooms CTV in 1 bedroom Tea and coffee making facilities No dogs (ex guide dogs) Cen ht CTV 6P

QQQ **Wood Lane House** Butleigh BA6 8TG
(A37 to Bristol, turn to Keinton Mandeville at traffic lights at Lydford on Fosse, right to Barton St David, Wood Lane opposite Rose & Portcullis pub)
☎ 01458 850354
Closed Xmas/New Year
This attractive stone-built property, sympathetically converted from stables, is set in a pretty garden and surrounded by open countryside. Bedrooms have been comfortably furnished and equipped with modern facilities. There is a village pub within 200 yards serving excellent food, although light suppers can be provided by prior arrangement.
3 shr No smoking in bedrooms No smoking in dining room CTV in 2 bedrooms Tea and coffee making facilities No dogs (ex guide dogs) Cen ht CTV 3P No coaches
ROOMS: s £23; d £38*

GLOSSOP Derbyshire Map **07** SK09

QQ **Bridge End** 1 Manor Park Rd, Old Glossop SK13 7SQ
(turn left off A57 to Sheffield 0.5m from town centre traffic lights signposted Old Glossop/Glossop Parish Church. House 0.5m on right before pub)
☎ 01457 852559 FAX 01457 852559
Situated in Old Glossop, this neatly decorated guest house offers nicely furnished bedrooms. Breakfast is served around one table and there is a comfortable lounge available for visitors. Cars can be parked at the side of the house by the colourful and attractive small garden.
3 rms (1 shr) No smoking CTV in 2 bedrooms Tea and coffee making facilities CTV 2P No coaches
ROOMS: s £16-£25; d £32-£40*

GLOUCESTER Gloucestershire

See Blakeney (Gloucestershire)

GOATHLAND North Yorkshire Map 08 NZ80

QQQ **Fairhaven Country Hotel** The Common YO22 5AN
(from A169 follw signs for Goathland, at parish church bear right hotel half a mile on right) ☎ 01947 896361
Closed 24-26 Dec, 2wks Jan-Feb
This family-run, detached hotel stands in the village of Goathland and offers many comforts as well as friendly hospitality. There is a comfortable lounge and an attractive dining room. Bedrooms have been steadily upgraded by Mr and Mrs Laflin, the resident owners.
9 rms (4 bth/shr) (3 fmly) No smoking in bedrooms No smoking in dining room CTV in 7 bedrooms Tea and coffee making facilities Licensed Cen ht CTV 9P No coaches Putting green Games room Last d 5pm
ROOMS: s £20-£33; d £40-£52; wkly b&b £140-£182; wkly hlf-bd £210-£245
CARDS:

GODALMING Surrey Map 04 SU94

QQQ **Fairfields** The Green, Elstead GU8 6DF (off A3 5m south of Guildford to Elstead, bear left at Woolpack Inn then 200yds on left)
☎ 01252 702345 FAX 01252 702345
Closed 21-29 Dec
This detached house overlooks the village green and has a delightful sloping rear garden. The pleasantly furnished bedrooms are bright and attractive and have been well equipped. A neat conservatory lounge leads off the breakfast room. No dinners are offered but there is good pub food to be had just across The Green.
3 bth/shr No smoking CTV in all bedrooms Tea and coffee making facilities No dogs Cen ht No children 3P No coaches
ROOMS: s £24.50-£27.50; d £34.50-£37.50

GRAMPOUND Cornwall & Isles of Scilly Map 02 SW94

QQ **Perran House** Fore St TR2 4RS
(on the A390 between St Austell and Truro) ☎ 01726 882066
Situated on the main St Austell road, Perran House, dating back to the 17th century is now under the ownership of Mr & Mrs Diboll, who plan to upgrade the simply furnished but cosy bedrooms. An ideal base for those wishing to visit the historic gardens in the area.
6 rms (3 bth/shr) No smoking CTV in all bedrooms Tea and coffee making facilities No dogs (ex guide dogs) Cen ht 8P No coaches
ROOMS: s £15-£16; d £34-£36; wkly b&b £102-£116*
CARDS:

GRANTHAM Lincolnshire Map 08 SK93

QQ **Roberts Roost** 82 Harrowby Rd NG31 9DS (on A52)
☎ 01476 560719
Closed 1 wk Dec & 1st wk Jan
Pat and Bruce Roberts provide a very homely atmosphere at their cosy guest house, which is located in a quiet residential area of the town. There are three bright, well equipped bedrooms, one of which has a modern en suite shower room. Breakfast is served in a separate dining room.
3 rms (1 bth/shr) (1 fmly) No smoking in 1 bedrooms No smoking in dining room CTV in all bedrooms Tea and coffee making facilities Cen ht CTV 2P No coaches Last d breakfast
ROOMS: s £16-£18; d £30-£34*

The AA's professional Inspectors make regular and anonymous visits to all the establishments listed in the Guide. They accept no gifts or favours from proprietors

GRASMERE Cumbria Map 11 NY30

QQQ **Lake View Country House** Lake View Dr LA22 9TD
(turn off A591 after Prince of Wales then left at Wild Daffodil Tea Shop)
☎ 015394 35384
Mar-Nov rs Dec-Feb
Popular with walkers and tourists alike, this Victorian stone house sits in its own attractive gardens and offers unrestricted views across meadowland to the lake. Bedrooms are furnished in contemporary style and the ground-floor room is spacious, while others make good use of available space. There is a cosy dining room and comfortable sun lounge.
5 rms (3 shr) No smoking in dining room CTV in all bedrooms Tea and coffee making facilities Cen ht No children 12yrs 11P No coaches Fishing permit for guests use Last d noon
ROOMS: s £25.50-£29.50; d £51-£59; wkly b&b £166-£196; wkly hlf-bd £238-£266*

QQQ **Raise View** White Bridge LA22 9RQ
(turn off A591 opposite Swan Hotel and go to the corner of Swan Lane and Pye Lane) ☎ 015394 35215 FAX 015394 35126
Closed Dec-Jan
Proprietors John and Lesley Swift are accomplished hosts and continue to offer a warm welcome. Their well maintained property is attractively decorated throughout. The house backs on to farm fields and gives delightful views of the surrounding fells. The bedrooms vary in size but all are thoughtfully equipped.
6 bth/shr No smoking CTV in all bedrooms Tea and coffee making facilities No dogs Cen ht No children 5yrs 6P No coaches
ROOMS: d £46-£54; wkly b&b £148-£174*

See page 14-20 for a list of Premier Selected establishments

Selected

Q Q Q Q **Rothay Lodge** LA22 9RH (turn left off A591 opposite Swan Hotel, into Swan Lane, at bottom of hill turn sharp left before bridge, car park at end of drive) ☎ 015394 35341
14 Feb-Oct
Situated next to the tumbling waters of Greenhead Ghyll and only a minutes walk from the centre of the village, is this attractive Victorian house where proprietors Jean and Bill Allan extend a genuine welcome to all. The spacious comfortable bedrooms all have modern facilities. The reposing lounge and breakfast room are attractively decorated.
5 bth/shr (1 fmly) No smoking CTV in all bedrooms Tea and coffee making facilities No dogs (ex guide dogs) Cen ht No children 10yrs 5P No coaches
ROOMS: d £40-£52; wkly b&b £155-£170*

GRASSINGTON North Yorkshire Map 07 SE06

Selected

Q Q Q Q **Ashfield House Hotel** Summers Fold BD23 5AE (take B6265 to village centre then turn off Main St into Summers Fold) ☎ 01756 752584 FAX 01756 752584
Closed Jan & early Feb rs Nov-Dec
Linda and Keith Harrison offer friendly hospitality at Ashfield House. Many period features can be seen inside the house including window seats and feature fireplaces. Local produce is used as much as possible in meals which can be enjoyed in the dining room. There are also two cosy lounges. Bedrooms are individual in design and well equipped.
7 bth/shr No smoking CTV in all bedrooms Tea and coffee making facilities No dogs (ex guide dogs) Licensed Cen ht No children 5yrs 7P No coaches Last d 7pm
ROOMS: s £28-£43; d £56-£66; wkly b&b £200-£220; wkly hlf-bd £250-£280
CARDS:

Q Q Q **Grassington Lodge** 8 Wood Ln BD23 5LU (B6265 Grassington after 8 miles turn right in Threshfield continue for 1 mile then turn left at garages, lodge 100yds on right)
☎ 01756 752518 FAX 01756 752518
New owners Sandra and Mike Wade have made a number of improvements to this welcoming guest house, situated on the edge of the village. More en suite facilities have been added and general refurbishment is continuing. The lounge is attractively furnished and breakfast is served in the comfortable dining room.
8 rms (1 bth 5 shr) No smoking CTV in all bedrooms Tea and coffee making facilities No dogs Cen ht 7P No coaches
ROOMS: s fr £39; d £58; wkly b&b £136.50-£196*

GREAT AYTON North Yorkshire Map 08 NZ51

Q Q Q **Royal Oak Hotel** 123 High St TS9 6BW
☎ 01642 722361 & 723270 FAX 01642 724047
rs Sun (closed 3pm-7pm)
Well equipped and delightfully furnished bedrooms are on offer at this 18th-century former coaching inn. There is an extensive range of food available which is served either in the bar or the rear dining room.
5 rms (4 bth/shr) CTV in all bedrooms Tea and coffee making facilities Direct dial from bedrooms Cen ht Last d 9.30pm
ROOMS: s £25-£35; d £50*
MEALS: Lunch £10.75 Dinner £16.75&alc*
CARDS:

GREAT DUNMOW Essex Map 05 TL62

Q Q ***Cowels Cottage*** Cowels Farm Ln, Lindsell CM6 3QG (B184 Dunmow to Thaxted Rd, then via Richmonds Green to Lindsell, follow art gallery signs,past gallery,Cowels Fm lne on left) ☎ 01371 870454
This attractive cottage is located in a peaceful rural setting and offers comfortably appointed bedrooms of a good size. The cosy lounge has a log fire for the colder days and guests share a large table at breakfast in a traditional family style.
3 rms (1 bth/shr) (1 fmly) No smoking in bedrooms No smoking in dining room Tea and coffee making facilities No dogs Cen ht CTV 4P No coaches

Selected

Q Q Q Q **The Starr Restaurant with Rooms** Market Place CM6 1AX (M11 junct 8, E along A120 towards Colchester, in Dunmow town centre turn left into Market Place off High St)
☎ 01371 874321 FAX 01371 876337
Closed 2-8 Jan
This delightful guest house is situated right in the heart of Great Dunmow and features a charming old English restaurant, which has a loyal local following. The accommodation is situated in a tastefully converted stable block, adjacent to the main building. Bedrooms are bright and spacious, attractively decorated, and equipped with well chosen pieces of furniture and many thoughtful extras.
8 annexe bth/shr No smoking in bedrooms No smoking in dining room CTV in all bedrooms Tea and coffee making facilities Direct dial from bedrooms Licensed Cen ht 16P No coaches Last d 9.30pm
ROOMS: s £60; d £90-£110*
CARDS:

GREAT YARMOUTH Norfolk Map 05 TG50

Q Q **Avalon Private Hotel** 54 Clarence Rd, Gorleston-on-Sea NR31 6DR (from A12 follow seafront signs, Clarence Rd is at right-angles to Marine Parade) ☎ 01493 662114 FAX 01493 661521
rs Oct-May
This small family-run guest house is close to the beach and not far from the centre of Gorleston. Bedrooms are well decorated and soundly appointed. Some have en suite shower rooms and there are two family rooms. The public rooms include a breakfast room and a separate bar area as well as a cosy lounge.
9 rms (4 shr) (3 fmly) No smoking in dining room CTV in all bedrooms Tea and coffee making facilities No dogs (ex guide dogs) Licensed Cen ht CTV Last d 10.30am
ROOMS: s £14-£21; d £28-£40; wkly b&b £91-£114; wkly hlf-bd £140-£158*
CARDS:

Q Q Q **Georgian House** 16-17 North Dr NR30 4EW (on seafront, N of Britannia Pier opposite entrance to Venetian Waterways)
☎ 01493 842623
Etr-Nov rs Nov-Etr
The Georgian House sits in the northern end of the resort. Guests have the use of two comfortable lounges and an attractive dining room for breakfast. There are a variety of well kept bedrooms, all different styles and sizes; the delightful four poster room is often asked for.
19 rms (11 bth 6 shr) (1 fmly) No smoking in dining room CTV in all bedrooms Tea and coffee making facilities No dogs Licensed Cen ht No children 5yrs 18P No coaches
ROOMS: d £30-£50; wkly b&b £105-£150*

QQ **Jennis Lodge** 63 Avondale Rd, Gorleston-on-Sea NR31 6DJ (2m S off A12) ☎ 01493 662840

Mr and Mrs Alexander own this friendly guest house, which is close to a sandy beach and the centre of Gorleston. Public rooms include a comfortable lounge and a separate dining room with a corner bar. Bedrooms are variable in size and light in appearance, and are undergoing a programme of redecoration. Two family rooms are also available.

10 rms (2 shr) (4 fmly) CTV in all bedrooms Tea and coffee making facilities Licensed Cen ht CTV Last d 4pm

QQ ***The Malcolm Hotel*** 6 Norfolk Square, Abemarle Rd NR30 1EE ☎ 01493 842381

The public rooms at this small hotel include a well stocked bar-cum-lounge area with games, and a spacious dining room. The accommodation is bright and well maintained, and most rooms have en suite facilities. Home cooked food is readily available from a set dinner menu and vegetarian meals can be provided by prior arrangement.

15 rms (12 shr) (3 fmly) No smoking in dining room CTV in all bedrooms Tea and coffee making facilities Licensed Cen ht CTV 12P

QQQ **Spindrift Private Hotel** 36 Wellesley Rd NR30 1EU (follow signs for seafront continue along St Nicholas Rd & Euston Rd then first left into Wellesley Rd)

☎ 01493 858674 FAX 01493 858674

Closed Xmas

The Spindrift is an inviting and well maintained guest house, set in a tree-lined avenue running parallel to the seafront. Bedrooms are soundly appointed and, although one or two are a little compact, they are all pleasant and comfortable. There are also three family rooms available. The downstairs rooms include a cosy dining room and a residents lounge.

7 bth/shr (3 fmly) No smoking in dining room CTV in all bedrooms Tea and coffee making facilities No dogs (ex guide dogs) Licensed Cen ht CTV No children 3yrs No coaches

wkly b&b £105-£130

CARDS:

QQQ **Squirrels Nest** 71 Avondale Rd, Gorleston-on-sea NR31 6DJ (A47, pass Vauxhall holiday camp, fourth turning off roundabout, A12 to Lowestoft, third roundabout turn left, left on slip road, 2nd right, left)

☎ 01493 662746 FAX 01493 662746

Closed Annual Holidays

Close to the beach and Gorleston town centre, this spacious guest house offers a good range of well appointed accommodation. The public areas offer a well furnished restaurant and adjacent bar, as well as a comfortable lounge. Mrs Squirrell offers an extensive choice from the daily or a la carte menus, as well as a hearty breakfast.

9 bth/shr (1 fmly) No smoking in 4 bedrooms No smoking in dining room CTV in all bedrooms Tea and coffee making facilities Licensed Cen ht CTV 5P Last d 8.30pm

ROOMS: s £18-£35; d £36-£70; wkly b&b £140-£200; wkly hlf-bd £145-£240

CARDS:

QQQ **Winchester Private Hotel** 12 Euston Rd NR30 1DY (follow A12 to main A47 follow signs for sea front left at Sainsburys through lights hotel 400 metres on right)

☎ 01493 843950 FAX 01493 843950

Mar-Nov

The Winchester is conveniently located for all the central attractions, and there is floodlit secure parking to the rear. Bedrooms are light and inviting, with cheerful soft furnishings. Guests have the use of comfortable seating in the entrance hall, where evening drinks and snacks are served upon request, and breakfast and dinner are served at separate tables in the dining room.

14 shr (2 fmly) No smoking in dining room CTV in all bedrooms Tea and coffee making facilities No dogs Cen ht CTV No children 12yrs 14P No coaches Last d 5pm

ROOMS: s £17.50-£21.50; d £33-£40*

GREEN HAMMERTON North Yorkshire Map 08 SE45

QQQ ***Bay Horse*** York Rd YO5 8BN (Turn off A59 located in centre of village) ☎ 01423 330338 & 331113 FAX 01423 331279

An attractive village inn offering a good range of well produced food which is served in the cosy bar. Modern bedrooms are located in a converted stables to the rear and have been well equipped. Friendly service is also provided by the pleasant owners.

10 annexe bth/shr (1 fmly) CTV in all bedrooms Tea and coffee making facilities Direct dial from bedrooms Cen ht 40P Last d 9.30pm

CARDS:

See advertisement under YORK

GREENHEAD Northumberland Map 12 NY66

QQQ **Holmhead** *(NY659661)* Hadrians Wall CA6 7HY (from B6318 turn between Ye Olde Forge Tea Rooms & Youth Hostel beside phonebox, drive over bridge, premises 0.25m off Farm Road) (The Circle)

☎ 016977 47402 FAX 016977 47402 Mr & Mrs B Staff

Closed 19 Dec-9 Jan

Set in some lovely countryside Holmhead Farmhouse is run by Pauline Staff who is a fountain of knowledge regarding nearby Hadrian's Wall. The first floor lounge offers comfortable seating, books and a small honesty bar. While bedrooms are not large they are bright and airy. A ground floor annex offering two bedrooms and a lounge makes an ideal family apartment.

4 shr 1 annexe bth/shr (1 fmly) No smoking Tea and coffee making facilities No dogs Licensed Cen ht CTV 6P Fishing Table tennis Badminton Riding Cycling 300 acres breeding sheep cattle Last d 3pm

ROOMS: s £36-£37; d £50-£52*

CARDS:

GRINDON Staffordshire Map 07 SK05

QQQ ***Summerhill Farm*** *(SJ983532)* ST13 7TT

☎ 01538 304264 Mrs P Simpson

This stone-built farmhouse is quietly located on the outskirts of Grindon village, and overlooks the Dovedale and Manifold valleys. The no-smoking accommodation has modern facilities and equipment, and consists of two doubles and one twin bedded room. There is a homely lounge and a conservatory dining room, where separate tables can be provided.

3 rms (2 shr) No smoking CTV in 2 bedrooms Tea and coffee making facilities Cen ht CTV 6P 52 acres dairy

GUILDFORD Surrey Map 04 SU94

See also Shackleford and advertisement on page 201

QQQ **Blanes Court Hotel** Albury Rd GU1 2BT ☎ 01483 573171 FAX 01483 532780

Closed 1wk Xmas

In a quiet residential street near the Epsom and Dorking roads, this substantial Edwardian house offers variously-sized bedrooms that are individually decorated and furnished. Day rooms include a bar and a vine-

See advertisement on p.201. *contd.*

decked conservatory with Lloyd Loom seating where breakfast is served looking out onto the garden. Sandwiches are available in the evening.
18 rms (3 bth 12 shr) (3 fmly) No smoking in dining room CTV in all bedrooms Tea and coffee making facilities Licensed Cen ht CTV 22P No coaches Outdoor swimming pool (heated)
ROOMS: s £30-£58.50; d £65-£68.50*
CARDS:

GUISBOROUGH North Yorkshire Map 08 NZ61

Q Q ***Fox & Hounds*** Slapewath TS14 6PX (2m on A171)
☎ 01287 632964 FAX 01287 610778
Friendly and attentive service is provided at this charming inn, which offers a range of bar meals as well as a restaurant and carvery in the evening. It is worth asking for one of the more spacious bedrooms, but irrespective of size, all are well equipped. Some have hip baths.
15 bth/shr (2 fmly) CTV in all bedrooms Tea and coffee making facilities Direct dial from bedrooms Cen ht 150P Last d 9.30pm
CARDS:

GUISELEY West Yorkshire Map 07 SE14

Q Q Q **Moor Valley Park Motel** Moor Valley Park, Mill Ln, Hawksworth LS20 8PG (from A65 near Harry Ramsdens take 2nd left exit into Thorpe Ln right at golf club through Hawksworth then left into Mill Ln)
☎ 01943 876083 FAX 01943 870335
Bedrooms here are along motel style lines, very well furnished and thoughtfully equipped, containing lots of pine features and furniture. The main building houses the bar and dining area and the complex is within easy reach of several major towns.
11 annexe bth/shr (3 fmly) CTV in all bedrooms Tea and coffee making facilities Direct dial from bedrooms No dogs (ex guide dogs) Licensed Cen ht P Last d 9.30pm
ROOMS: s fr £35; d fr £42.50*
CARDS:

GUITING POWER Gloucestershire Map 04 SP02

Premier Selected

Q Q Q Q Q **Guiting** GL54 5TZ (A40 Andoversford lights R to Stow-on-the-Wold 4 miles L to Lower Swell B4068 1 mile L to Guiting Power L into village house in centre of village)
☎ 01451 850470 FAX 01451 850034
Situated in the unspoilt village of Guiting Power, this mellow Cotswold stone 16th-century farmhouse retains many of its original features, including exposed beams, inglenook fireplaces and polished wooden floors. Public areas have a comfortable and cosy atmosphere, enhanced by open fires, decorative pottery and family memorabilia. Bedrooms are homely with lots of thoughtful extras including fresh flowers, fruit and even a teddy to cuddle at night. Food is imaginative, cooked on the family Aga and well worth experiencing.
3 shr 1 annexe bth/shr No smoking in bedrooms No smoking in dining room CTV in all bedrooms Tea and coffee making facilities No dogs Cen ht CTV 2P No coaches Last d breakfast
ROOMS: s £30; d £50-£52*
CARDS:

HALFORD Warwickshire Map 04 SP24

Q Q **Halford Bridge** Fosseway CV36 5BN
(premises located on A429 to Fosse way 8m from Stratford on Avon)
☎ 01789 740382 FAX 01789 740382
This listed Cotswold stone coaching inn offers a character lounge bar and a separate restaurant; a good range of bar meals are available and the cottage-style dining room is popular for its game dishes. Bedrooms are modestly appointed; there are plans to create en suite facilities and a character four-poster bedroom.
6 rms (2 bth 3 shr) (1 fmly) No smoking in area of dining room No smoking in 1 lounge CTV in all bedrooms Tea and coffee making facilities No dogs (ex guide dogs) CTV 40P Last d 9.30pm
ROOMS: s £28; d £50; wkly b&b £150; wkly hlf-bd fr £180*
MEALS: Lunch fr £11 Dinner fr £14&alc*
CARDS:

HALTWHISTLE Northumberland Map 12 NY76

Q Q Q **Vallum Lodge** Military Rd, Twice Brewed, nr Bardon Mill NE47 7AN (premises on B6318 400 yards W of Once Brewed National Park visitors centre) ☎ 01434 344248 FAX 01434 344488
Mar-Oct
Located right in the heart of the Northumberland National Park, this lovely house provides comfortable cottage-style accommodation with easy access to Hadrian's Wall and Roman excavations. All rooms are situated on the ground floor and enjoy views of the surrounding countryside. Good-value home-cooked meals are provided in the dining room at individual tables.
7 rms (4 bth/shr) (1 fmly) No smoking in bedrooms No smoking in dining room Tea and coffee making facilities Licensed Cen ht CTV No children 3yrs 25P No coaches Last d 6.30pm
ROOMS: s fr £22; d £42-£52; wkly b&b £143.50-£171.50; wkly hlf-bd £227.50-£248.50
CARDS:

HAMPSTHWAITE North Yorkshire Map 08 SE25

Q Q Q ***Lonsdale House*** Village Green, Hampsthwaite HG3 2ET (4m W)
☎ 01423 771311
Situated about 5 miles from Harrogate, by the village green of Hampsthwaite, is this attractive small double-fronted house. The bedrooms are bright and modern with good facilities, and guests can relax in the cosy lounge bar adjacent to the popular restaurant which is also open to the public. An extensive range of food is available.
4 rms (1 bth 2 shr) (2 fmly) No smoking in bedrooms No smoking in dining room CTV in all bedrooms Tea and coffee making facilities Licensed Cen ht 6P Last d 9pm
CARDS:

HAMPTON-IN-ARDEN West Midlands Map 04 SP28

Q Q Q **The Cottage** Kenilworth Rd B92 0LW (on A452, 2m from M42, 4m from M6) ☎ 01675 442323 FAX 01675 443323
This very pleasant guest house is convenient for the NEC, Birmingham Airport and the International Railway Station. The attractively decorated modern bedrooms are all individually styled. Two rooms are conveniently located on ground floor level and others are suitable for families. There is a cosy lounge and a cottage style breakfast room where individual tables are provided.
9 rms (7 shr) (2 fmly) No smoking in dining room CTV in all bedrooms Tea and coffee making facilities Cen ht CTV 14P
ROOMS: s £25-£28; d £40-£44*

Q Q Q Hollies Kenilworth Rd B92 0LW (on A452, next to Jardenerie Garden Centre) ☎ 01675 442941 & 442681 FAX 01675 442941
This well maintained detached house is personally run, and provides friendly hospitality and well equipped modern accommodation. Some bedrooms are on ground floor level and there is a family bedded room. Separate tables are provided in the combined breakfast room and lounge.
6 shr 2 annexe rms (2 fmly) No smoking in 4 bedrooms No smoking in lounges CTV in all bedrooms Tea and coffee making facilities Cen ht CTV 12P
ROOMS: s £20-£25; d £36-£40

HANLEY CASTLE Worcestershire Map **03** SO84

Selected

Q Q Q Q ***Old Parsonage Farm*** WR8 0BU
(turn off B4211 onto B4209, 150yds on right) ☎ 01684 310124
Closed 2nd wk Dec-2nd wk Jan
This large 18th-century house stands in spacious and attractive gardens on the edge of the village. The accommodation consists of three spacious double bedded rooms. There are two comfortable lounges, one of which has a television, and both have real fires during cold weather. There is also a very pleasant dining room, with period furniture and an inglenook fireplace. Ann Addison is an accomplished cook and her husband Tony is a wine connoisseur.
3 bth (1 fmly) No smoking No dogs Licensed Cen ht CTV
No children 10yrs 6P No coaches Last d day before

HARLESTON Norfolk Map **05** TM28

Selected

Q Q Q Q Heath Farmhouse Homersfield IP20 0EX
☎ 01986 788417
Guests are assured of a warm, friendly welcome from Mrs Hunt at this charming farmhouse which dates back to the 16th century. It is situated on the outskirts of Homersfield not far from Harleston and the market town of Bungay. An ideal place for walkers and keen fishermen alike, as the River Wensum is close by. The accommodation is cosy, comfortable, nicely appointed and spotlessly clean. The public rooms feature two comfortable lounges with wood burners and a dining room with a large polished wood table, where guests can enjoy a hearty breakfast or a lovely home cooked dinner by prior arrangement.
2 rms (1 fmly) No smoking in bedrooms No smoking in dining room Tea and coffee making facilities No dogs (ex guide dogs) Cen ht CTV 8P No coaches Table tennis Last d 10am
ROOMS: s £22; d £38*

HARPFORD Devon Map **03** SY09

Selected

Q Q Q Q Peeks House EX10 0NH
(off A3052, towards Sidmouth turn first left after crossing River Otter)
☎ 01395 567664
Just three miles from the centre of Sidmouth, guests will enjoy the peace and tranquillity of this elegant Grade II listed building, which dates back to the 16th century. Each bedroom is decorated with attractive co-ordinated fabrics and well equipped with useful extras. The elegant dining room looks out over the sun terrace and guests may enjoy five-course evening meals from the fixed-price menu, or choose from a short carte. There is also a comfortable lounge with an open fire.
5 bth/shr No smoking in bedrooms No smoking in dining room CTV in all bedrooms Tea and coffee making facilities No dogs (ex guide dogs) Licensed Cen ht CTV No children 5yrs 6P No coaches Last d 1pm
ROOMS: s £27-£32; d £44-£54; wkly b&b £154-£175; wkly hlf-bd £259-£280*

HARROGATE North Yorkshire Map **08** SE35

Selected

Q Q Q Q **Acacia Lodge** 21 Ripon Rd HG1 2JL
(on A61 600yds N town centre) ☎ 01423 560752 FAX 01423 503725
This mellow stone Victorian House is situated on the Ripon Road and is convenient for both the conference and town centres. Many of the original features such as ornate ceilings and leaded lights have been retained and these along with many other points of interest indicate the care and enthusiasm of the owners Dee and Peter Bateson. The lounge is comfortable and the pretty dining room is the place to enjoy a hearty Yorkshire breakfast.
6 bth/shr (3 fmly) No smoking CTV in all bedrooms Tea and coffee making facilities Direct dial from bedrooms No dogs (ex guide dogs) Cen ht CTV No children 10yrs 7P No coaches
ROOMS: s £45-£58; d £55-£68; wkly b&b £189-£406*

Q Q Q **The Albany Hotel** 22-23 Harlow Moor Dr HG2 0JY
(follow signs for 'Valley Gardens' take road up left side of Gardens this is Valley Drive, Harlow Moor Drive is a continuation of this road)
☎ 01423 565890 FAX 01423 565890
Overlooking the Valley Gardens and within easy walking distance of the town centre, this hotel provides modern and well equipped bedrooms and a spacious bar lounge. Breakfast is served in the pleasant dining room and very friendly service is provided by Mrs Johnson the resident owner.
14 shr (3 fmly) No smoking in dining room CTV in all bedrooms Tea and coffee making facilities No dogs (ex guide dogs) Licensed Cen ht
ROOMS: s £26-£35; d £50-£66; wkly b&b £168-£245*
CARDS:

Selected

Q Q Q Q **Alexa House & Stable Cottages** 26 Ripon Rd HG1 2JJ
(on A61) ☎ 01423 501988 FAX 01423 504086
Dating back to the early 1800s, this centrally located Georgian house welcomes both tourists and business guests. The bedrooms are comfortably furnished and prettily decorated, some with four poster beds. The converted stable cottage bedrooms are on ground level. After taking advantage of the corporate membership to the local health club, guests can relax in the inviting lounge whilst enjoying a drink from the well stocked bar. Delicious breakfasts are served in the spacious dining room.
9 bth/shr 4 annexe bth/shr (2 fmly) No smoking in bedrooms No smoking in dining room CTV in all bedrooms Tea and coffee making facilities Direct dial from bedrooms No dogs (ex guide dogs) Licensed Cen ht CTV 14P Membership of local health/fitness club Last d 6.30pm
ROOMS: s fr £45; d fr £60*
CARDS:

Q Q Q **Anro** 90 Kings Rd HG1 5JX
(follow signs to Conference Centre. House a short distance past on opposite side of road) ☎ 01423 503087 FAX 01423 561719
Closed 22-28 Dec
This friendly guest house is very close to the conference centre and offers bright fresh accommodation together with a homely lounge, as well as a spacious pleasant dining room.
7 rms (4 shr) (1 fmly) No smoking in dining room CTV in all bedrooms Tea and coffee making facilities No dogs Cen ht CTV No children 7yrs No coaches Last d mid-day
ROOMS: s fr £22; d fr £44
CARDS:

Q Q Q **April House** 3 Studley Rd HG1 5JU (find Conference Centre on King's Rd, Moat House Hotel adjoins-turn right opposite along Alexandra Rd, hotel at top on right) ☎ 01423 561879 FAX 01423 504390
This attractive Victorian house has been pleasantly furnished and provides comfortable and well equipped bedrooms. There is a cosy lounge which also doubles as a breakfast room and there is a library available to guests. Friendly service is provided by the resident owners David and Ruth Hayes.
5 rms (1 bth 3 shr) (3 fmly) No smoking CTV in all bedrooms Tea and coffee making facilities No dogs (ex guide dogs) CTV
ROOMS: s £20-£25; d £40-£55; wkly b&b £100-£150

Selected

Q Q Q Q **Ashley House Hotel** 36-40 Franklin Rd HG1 5EE
(on entering Harrogate follow signs for conference centre, opposite centre turn into Strawberry Dale Ave, left into Franklin Rd, premises on right) ☎ 01423 507474 FAX 01423 560858
rs Dec (B & B only)
Conveniently located minutes from the Conference Centre and town centre, this charming hotel consists of three converted Victorian Townhouses set in a quiet tree-lined street. The bedrooms are well furnished in a modern style and thoughtfully equipped. The public rooms include a lounge area and a welcoming "Snug Bar", where guests can choose from a choice of over 75 whiskies.
18 bth/shr (2 fmly) No smoking in 4 bedrooms No smoking in dining room No smoking in lounges CTV in all bedrooms Tea and coffee making facilities Direct dial from bedrooms Licensed Cen ht CTV 6P Last d 4pm
ROOMS: s £35-£60; d £55-£80; wkly b&b £190-£280; wkly hlf-bd £280-£350*
CARDS:

Q Q Q **Ashwood House** 7 Spring Grove HG1 2HS
(off A61, from Ripon Rd turn off into Springfield Ave, turn third left into Spring Grove, premises on left)
☎ 01423 560081 FAX 01423 527928
Closed 24-31 Dec
An impressive Edwardian house situated in a quiet cul-de-sac just a few minutes walk from the conference centre. The public rooms are attractively decorated and comfortably furnished with the pretty bedrooms being mostly spacious and having all the expected facilities.
9 bth/shr (1 fmly) No smoking in 6 bedrooms No smoking in dining room CTV in all bedrooms Tea and coffee making facilities No dogs Licensed Cen ht CTV No children 7yrs 5P No coaches
ROOMS: s £27-£30; d £45-£50; wkly b&b £157.50-£210*

Q Q Q **The Beeches Hotel** 103-105 Valley Dr HG2 0JP
(opposite the Valley Gardens) ☎ 01423 522246 FAX 01423 531940
Closed 23 Dec-3 Jan
Under the same ownership as the nearby Valley Hotel, the Beeches overlooks the Valley Gardens, and is within easy walking distance of the town centre. Bedrooms are generally spacious and comfortably furnished.

Downstairs there is a lounge, with an honesty bar in the corner, and breakfast is served in the traditional dining room.

20 bth/shr (4 fmly) No smoking in dining room CTV in all bedrooms Tea and coffee making facilities Direct dial from bedrooms Licensed Cen ht 4P
ROOMS: s £35-£45; d £55-£65*
CARDS:

Q Q Q **Brooklands** 5 Valley Dr HG2 0JJ ☎ 01423 564609
This friendly family-owned and run hotel overlooks the Valley Gardens and offers comfortable accommodation. Bedrooms have been furnished with lovely old-style pine furniture. A good hearty Yorkshire breakfast is served, and friendly service is provided by Mr and Mrs Curry, the resident owners.
4 bth/shr No smoking in dining room CTV in all bedrooms Tea and coffee making facilities Cen ht No coaches
ROOMS: s £25; d £44*
CARDS:

Selected

Q Q Q Q **Cavendish Hotel** 3 Valley Dr HG2 0JJ (Hotel is situated in centre of Harrogate beside The Valley Gardens) ☎ 01423 509637
The Cavendish is attractively situated opposite the Valley Gardens and only a short walk from the town and the conference centre. Hosts Julian and Helen Dibbs provide a warm and friendly service. The bedrooms are pleasant and well equipped, and include direct-dial telephones. Public rooms are comfortable with drinks being available as required.
9 bth/shr No smoking in 2 bedrooms No smoking in dining room CTV in all bedrooms Tea and coffee making facilities Direct dial from bedrooms Licensed Cen ht No coaches
ROOMS: s £32-£45; d £50-£65*
CARDS:

Selected

Q Q Q Q **The Dales Hotel** 101 Valley Dr HG2 0JP ☎ 01423 507248 FAX 01423 507248
rs 10 Dec-10 Jan (b & b only)
Enjoying a fine view over the Valley Gardens, this well furnished hotel is only a short walk from both the town and the Conference Centre. The house has been delightfully decorated and includes well equipped bedrooms all with either en suite or private facilities. The lounge contains an honesty bar. Good home-cooking can be enjoyed and service is both friendly and attentive. The front garden is well tended and very colourful, especially during the summer time.
8 rms (6 bth/shr) (2 fmly) No smoking in dining room CTV in all bedrooms Tea and coffee making facilities Licensed Cen ht CTV 1P Last d 9am
ROOMS: s £30-£50; d £56-£64*
CARDS:

Selected

Q Q Q Q **Delaine Hotel** 17 Ripon Rd HG1 2JL
☎ 01423 567974 & 529034 FAX 01423 561723
Closed Xmas
The Delaine Hotel is an attractive property surrounded by award-winning gardens, which are a glorious riot of colour during the summer. A warm welcome is assured from Rupert and Marian Viner who have thoughtfully furnished and equipped all bedrooms. Guests can relax in the attractive lounge or enjoy a beverage in the fully licensed bar. Comfortable family accommodation is available in a converted coach house to the rear of the hotel.
9 bth/shr 1 annexe bth (2 fmly) No smoking in bedrooms No smoking in dining room CTV in all bedrooms Tea and coffee making facilities Direct dial from bedrooms No dogs Licensed Cen ht CTV No children 10yrs 12P No coaches
ROOMS: s fr £45; d £58-£62*
CARDS:

Q Q ***Gillmore Hotel*** 98 Kings Rd HG1 5HH (from town centre turn into Kings Rd pass conference centre hotel approx 200yds on right)
☎ 01423 503699 FAX 01423 503699
This large guest house is family run and provides good value for money. The bedrooms are modern and adequately furnished, and public rooms include a comfortable lounge with a large screen TV and an externally accessed bar with a pool table.
22 rms (2 bth 4 shr) (8 fmly) CTV in 9 bedrooms Tea and coffee making facilities Licensed Cen ht CTV 20P Snooker Last d 4pm

This symbol indicates a 'Child Friendly' establishment - see page 25 for details

Q Q Q *Glenayr* 19 Franklin Mount HG1 5EJ (from A61, right into Kings Rd, pass conference centre, proceed through traffic lights, second road on right) ☎ 01423 504259 FAX 504259
This well furnished house is found in a quiet side road close to the Conference Centre. The bedrooms are delightfully decorated and have been thoughtfully equipped. There is a cosy lounge and a good Yorkshire breakfast is served in the attractive dining room.
6 rms (5 shr) No smoking in dining room CTV in all bedrooms Tea and coffee making facilities No dogs (ex guide dogs) Licensed Cen ht 3P No coaches Last d 4.30pm
CARDS:

Q Q Q **Prince's Hotel** 7 Granby Rd HG1 4ST
(off A59 at Empress roundabout) ☎ 01423 883469 FAX 01423 881417
This small hotel is set in the centre of an imposing Victorian terrace of town houses and is within reasonable walking distance of the town centre. There is a delightful lounge and a very attractive dining room where breakfast and pre-arranged dinners are served. The bedrooms, which are all en suite, are pleasantly furnished with good facilities.
6 bth/shr (2 fmly) No smoking in 1 bedrooms No smoking in dining room CTV in all bedrooms Tea and coffee making facilities Direct dial from bedrooms Cen ht CTV No children 3yrs No coaches
ROOMS: s £20-£29; d £40-£50; wkly b&b £140-£280*

Selected

Q Q Q Q **Quality Kimberley Hotel** 11-19 Kings Rd HG1 5JY
(follow signs for Harrogate International Centre or Kings Rd, premises on left approx 150yds past the centre)
☎ 01423 505613 FAX 01423 530270
Closed 24 Dec-03 Jan
This large, completely refurbished hotel is conveniently located for both the town and Conference Centre and many of the best local restaurants. Modern bedrooms boast an impressive range of accessories including trouser presses, fax machines and cable and satellite TV. A full laundry service and good conference facilities are available, and an extensive range of tasty dishes can be enjoyed for breakfast.
48 bth/shr (3 fmly) No smoking in dining room CTV in all bedrooms Tea and coffee making facilities Direct dial from bedrooms No dogs (ex guide dogs) Licensed Lift Cen ht 45P
ROOMS: s £58-£69.50; d £74.50-£89.50; (room only) *
CARDS:

Q Q **Roxanne** 12 Franklin Mount HG1 5EJ
(A661 towards Harrogate, over rdbt onto Skipton Rd for 1m turn left onto King's Rd for 0.5m turn left into Franklin Mount)
☎ 01423 569930 FAX 01423
Closed Xmas week
Situated in a quiet side road close to both the town and the Conference Centre, this family-owned guest house with a pretty front garden, offers pleasant and interesting bedrooms and has a combined dining room and lounge.
5 rms (1 fmly) No smoking in 2 bedrooms No smoking in dining room No smoking in lounges CTV in all bedrooms Tea and coffee making facilities No dogs (ex guide dogs) Cen ht CTV 2P Last d 9pm
ROOMS: s £21.50-£23; d £40-£42; wkly b&b £140-£154; wkly hlf-bd £175-£189*

We endeavour to be as accurate as possible but changes in personnel and data can occur in establishments after the Guide has gone to press

Premier Selected

Q Q Q Q Q **Ruskin Hotel** 1 Swan Rd HG1 2SS
(off A61, Ripon road) ☎ 01423 502045 FAX 01423 506131
Close to the town centre and Conference Centre, this exclusive small hotel is surrounded by well tended gardens and offers individually designed bedrooms with many useful facilities. The lounge is elegantly furnished and the dining room is inviting. Excellent service is provided by Denise and Eric, the resident owners.
6 bth/shr (1 fmly) No smoking in bedrooms No smoking in dining room CTV in all bedrooms Tea and coffee making facilities Direct dial from bedrooms No dogs (ex guide dogs) Licensed Cen ht No children 5yrs 9P No coaches Last d 8.15pm
ROOMS: s £55-£69; d £75-£110; wkly b&b £259-£340; wkly hlf-bd £343-£420*
CARDS:

Q Q Q *Shelbourne* 78 Kings Rd HG1 5JX (on entering Harrogate follow signs for Conference Centre, through traffic lights by Moat House Hotel, premises on right) ☎ 01423 504390 FAX 01423 504390
Opposite the Conference Centre and a short walk from the town, this small family-owned and run guest house has recently added en suite facilities to its rooms. There is a comfortable TV lounge available and hearty breakfasts are served in the rear dining room.
8 rms (3 shr) (3 fmly) No smoking in 3 bedrooms No smoking in dining room CTV in all bedrooms Tea and coffee making facilities Licensed Cen ht CTV 1P No coaches Last d day before
CARDS:

Selected

Q Q Q Q **Valley Hotel** 93-95 Valley Dr HG2 0JP
(Close to the exhibition/conference site over looking and opposite the Valley Gardens) ☎ 01423 504868 FAX 01423 531940
Ideally situated for the Conference Centre, the town and also the Valley Gardens, this family-owned and run hotel offers well furnished and

comfortable accommodation. There is a comfortable lounge and attractive dining room, and service is friendly and attentive.
16 bth/shr (4 fmly) No smoking in dining room CTV in all bedrooms Tea and coffee making facilities Direct dial from bedrooms Licensed Lift Cen ht
ROOMS: s £35-£45; d £55-£65*
CARDS:

Q Q Q **Wharfedale House** 28 Harlow Moor Dr HG2 0JY
(alongside the Valley Gardens in central Harrogate)
☎ 01423 522233
Standing next to the delightful Valley Gardens and convenient for both the town and the Conference Centre, this family-owned and run small hotel provides well equipped bedrooms together with a comfortable and inviting lounge. Good home cooking is served by the enthusiastic owners and vegetarian breakfasts are available
8 bth/shr (2 fmly) No smoking in bedrooms No smoking in dining room CTV in all bedrooms Tea and coffee making facilities Direct dial from bedrooms Licensed Cen ht 3P Last d 4pm
ROOMS: s £29; d £50; wkly b&b £150-£174; wkly hlf-bd fr £203

Q Q Q **Wynnstay House** 60 Franklin Rd HG1 5EE
(in town centre turn into Strawberry Dale opposite the Conference Centre left at the end of the road, last house on right)
☎ 01423 560476 FAX 01423 562539
Guests to this friendly guest house, which is set in a residential road not far from the town's attractions, are very well cared for by the resident owners. The bedrooms are thoughtfully equipped and there is a comfortable lounge with lots of books, magazines and games. Breakfast is served in the pleasant dining room.
6 shr (2 fmly) No smoking in dining room CTV in all bedrooms Tea and coffee making facilities Cen ht CTV No coaches Last d 2pm
ROOMS: s £25; d £46-£50; wkly b&b £140; wkly hlf-bd £189*
CARDS:

HARROW Greater London Map 04 TQ18

Q **Central Hotel** 6 Hindes Rd HA1 1SJ (off A409, opposite Tesco supermarket) ☎ 0181 427 0893 FAX 0181 427 0893
Its own car park is a big plus at this modest establishment located, as its name suggests, near the centre of Harrow. Guests are looked after by chatty resident owner John Ryan who has been here for more than ten years.
11 rms (4 shr) (3 fmly) CTV in 14 bedrooms Tea and coffee making facilities No dogs Cen ht CTV 12P
ROOMS: s £35-£45; d £45-£55*
CARDS:

Q Q **Hindes Hotel** 8 Hindes Rd HA1 1SJ (15 min from M1 on the A409)
☎ 0181 427 7468 FAX 0181 424 0673
This established family-run property continues to improve, and offers bright well-appointed accommodation. Bedrooms are smart and well equipped, while the residents' lounge is most comfortable and the breakfast room light and airy.
14 rms (7 shr) (2 fmly) No smoking in dining room CTV in all bedrooms Tea and coffee making facilities No dogs (ex guide dogs) Cen ht CTV 30P Last d 4.30pm
ROOMS: s £35-£45; d £49-£55*
CARDS:

HARTEST Suffolk Map 05 TL85

Premier Selected

Q Q Q Q Q **The Hatch** Pilgrims Ln, Cross Green IP29 4ED
(6 miles from Bury St Edmunds, take A143 towards Haverhill, then B1066 to Glemsford. First road on left on entering village)
☎ 01284 830226 FAX 01284 830226
Looking over open rolling countryside, this delightful timbered and thatched medieval Suffolk house sits in a sleepy dead end lane. Mr and Mrs Oaten are charming hosts, and from a cup of tea and home-made cakes on arrival, guests are assured of a relaxing stay. The acre of well tended grounds feature a wildflower meadow, and a wonderful array of rosebushes, while inside antiques and fine fabrics complement the wealth of architecture and original features. Accommodation consists of one ground floor en suite room, well suited for the disabled with its separate access, nearby parking and sunny terrace, and a family unit of a cosy single and double bedroom upstairs. *contd.*

3 rms (2 bth/shr) (1 fmly) No smoking TV available Tea and coffee making facilities Cen ht CTV No children 9yrs 3P No coaches Riding Last d 10.30am
ROOMS: s £25-£30; d £45-£55; wkly b&b £160-£175

HARTFIELD East Sussex Map **05** TQ43

Premier Selected

QQQQQ ✔ ***Bolebroke Watermill*** *(TQ481373)* Perry Hill, Edenbridge Rd TN7 4JP (off B2026 1m N of Hartfield)
☎ 01892 770425 FAX 01892 770425 Mrs C Cooper
Feb-Mid Dec
Bolebroke Watermill, parts of which date back to the 11th century, has been sympathetically converted by David and Christine Cooper. Two rooms are in the original mill at the top of steep stairs through trap doors, and have a shared lounge on the ground floor (with much of the original mill machinery still showing). The other bedrooms (two with four-posters) are in the Barn. All are comfortable with thoughtful extras such as magazines, fresh flowers and decanters of sherry. Breakfast includes home-made bread and preserves. Guests can explore the nearby Winnie the Pooh walk which takes in all the sites of famous A A Milne's famous books.
2 bth/shr 3 annexe bth/shr No smoking CTV in all bedrooms Tea and coffee making facilities No dogs (ex guide dogs) Cen ht No children 7yrs 8P 5 acres smallholding
CARDS:

HARTLAND Devon Map **02** SS22

QQ **Fosfelle** EX39 6EF (off A39 onto B3248 for 2m entrance on right)
☎ 01237 441273
Set in five acres of well tended grounds, Fosfelle boasts two fishing lakes and a caravan park. Its restaurant and public bar are popular with holidaymakers and the local farming community alike. Its bedrooms are traditionally furnished and have benefited from recent refurbishment.
7 rms (1 bth 3 shr) (2 fmly) No smoking in bedrooms CTV in 4 bedrooms Tea and coffee making facilities No dogs (ex guide dogs) Licensed Cen ht CTV 20P Fishing Snooker Last d 9pm
ROOMS: s £22-£24; d £44-£48; wkly b&b £135-£140; wkly hlf-bd £190-£200
CARDS:

HARWICH Essex Map **05** TM23

See also Manningtree

QQQ ***Emsworth House*** Ship Hill CO11 2UP
☎ 01255 870860 & 0467 477771 (mobile)

(For full entry see **Bradfield**)

QQQ ✔ **New Farm House** *(TM165289)* Spinnel's Ln CO11 2UJ
☎ 01255 870365 FAX 01255 870837 Mr & Mrs B R Winch

(For full entry see **Wix**)

QQQ ***Una House*** 1 Una Rd, Parkeston CO12 4PP
(A120/A136, first house on left past golf course)
☎ 01255 551390 FAX 01255 551390
Ursula Byrd's small and friendly guest house is ideally located for the port, and is an excellent stopping point for those crossing to the Continent. The comfortable accommodation offers modern en suite facilities in attractively decorated bedrooms. A hearty breakfast sets guests up for the day, and is served in the elegant dining cum sitting room. Though no evening meals are offered, there is no shortage of eating places in the neighbourhood.
3 bth/shr (1 fmly) No smoking in bedrooms No smoking in dining room CTV in all bedrooms Tea and coffee making facilities No dogs (ex guide dogs) Cen ht 4P No coaches

HASTINGS & ST LEONARDS East Sussex Map **05** TQ80

QQ **Argyle** 32 Cambridge Gardens TN34 1EN (from the A21 turn into Bohemia Rd, then turn into Cambridge Rd, turn into Cambridge Gardens)
☎ 01424 421294 FAX 421294
High standards of housekeeping are a feature of this guest house conveniently located for the town centre and the railway station. Bedrooms vary somewhat in size but all have double glazing and controllable central heating. The small TV lounge offers a wide selection of tourist information.
8 rms (3 shr) (3 fmly) No smoking in dining room CTV in all bedrooms Tea and coffee making facilities No dogs Cen ht CTV No children 4yrs
ROOMS: s £16-£20; d £28-£36; wkly b&b fr £91*

Premier Selected

QQQQQ **Bryn-y-Mor** 12 Godwin Rd TN35 5JR
(A259 coast road keeping sea on right bear left at Old Town & follow road up hill, at the Convent turn right into Ashburham Rd then 2nd right) ☎ 01424 722744 FAX 01424 445933
Built as a Victorian gentleman's residence, the interior of this small licensed hotel has been restored in keeping with the period. Original light fittings and stained glass windows are supplemented by many pictures and ornaments which create a nostalgic atmosphere. The main day room is spacious and full of interesting objets d'art. Guests can enjoy a drink from the honesty bar whilst taking in the rooftop views of Old Hastings and the sea beyond. From this lounge, which doubles as the breakfast room, there is a doorway leading to the extensive terraced gardens and swimming pool. Bedrooms combine antique furniture and four-poster beds with modern amenities and smart en suite facilities that feature particularly roomy walk-in showers.
4 shr (2 fmly) No smoking in bedrooms No smoking in dining room No smoking in 1 lounge CTV in all bedrooms Tea and coffee making facilities No dogs (ex guide dogs) Licensed Cen ht CTV 4P No coaches Outdoor swimming pool (heated)
ROOMS: s £35-£45; d £60-£80*
CARDS:

QQQ ***Eagle House*** Pevensey Rd TN38 0JZ (turn off seafront onto London Rd, premises adjacent to St Leonalds Shopping Centre)
☎ 01424 430535 & 441273 FAX 01424 437771
Look for the pair of golden eagles above the door in order to find this peacefully located Victorian hotel. The period of the building is reflected in the interior with parlour plants and some fine chandeliers in the day rooms that include a well-furnished bar, separate sitting room, and fine dining room. Proprietor Cameron Mathesons provides stylish home-cooked dinners.

Comfortable bedrooms, that are traditionally furnished and decorated with flock wallpaper, are provided with all the modern amenities.

20 bth/shr (2 fmly) No smoking in dining room CTV in 23 bedrooms Tea and coffee making facilities Direct dial from bedrooms No dogs (ex guide dogs) Licensed Cen ht 13P No coaches Last d 8.30pm
CARDS:

Selected

QQQQ **Filsham Farmhouse** *(TQ784096)* 111 Harley Shute Rd TN38 8BY (turn off A21 at speed limit sign into Old Harrow Road, house 1.5m on right after railway bridge)
☎ 01424 433109 FAX 01424 461061 Mrs B Yorke
Closed Xmas & New Year
Although no longer part of a working farm, this mellow, red-brick, 17th-century farmhouse retains its historic charm. Furnished with antiques (the friendly proprietors, John and Barbara Yorke, run an antique business next door), the no smoking bedrooms have lots of homely touches like plants, books and magazines. One particularly spacious bedroom has a four-poster and its own private, but not en suite, shower room while the other two rooms share a particularly splendid bathroom with bidet and separate shower. Downstairs in the very comfortable beamed lounge-cum-dining room where winter breakfasts are served in front of a real log fire set in an old inglenook fireplace. Dinners are by arrangement.
3 rms (1 shr) No smoking CTV in all bedrooms Tea and coffee making facilities Cen ht CTV No children 5yrs 4P
1 acres non-working Last d am
ROOMS: s £20-£30; d £35-£50*

Selected

QQQQ ***Greensleeves*** Vicarage Ln, Westfield TN35 4SD (Turn off A21 onto A28, Westfield approx 2m. Turn left into Vicarage Ln, immediately before church. Greensleeves 200yds on left) ☎ 01424 753196 FAX 01424 753196
Closed 19 Dec-2 Jan
This delightful house is located in the small village of Westfield just north of Hastings on the A28. The house is set in its own extensive carefully tended gardens, a passion of owners Mr and Mrs English. All three rooms are stylishly decorated with discreet taste. Linens and soft furnishings are particularly attractive. Breakfasts are enjoyed in a spacious dining room which overlooks the garden round a large wooden table.
3 shr No smoking CTV in all bedrooms Tea and coffee making facilities No dogs (ex guide dogs) Cen ht 6P No coaches

Premier Selected

QQQQQ **Parkside House** 59 Lower Park Rd TN34 2LD (follow town centre signs turn right off A21 at rdbt then first right into Lower Park Rd) ☎ 01424 433096 FAX 01424 421431
Overlooking Alexandra Park, this Victorian house is run by resident proprietor, Brian Kent. Bedrooms are individually decorated and benefit from some beautiful antique furniture. Ornaments and objet d'art add to the appeal, and a wide range of extras, from video players to towelling bathrobes, is offered. A comfortable lounge is open plan to the breakfast room with its honesty bar. There is also a tuck shop to satisfy those hunger pangs. The house is no-smoking throughout and unrestricted street parking is available.
5 rms (4 shr) (1 fmly) No smoking CTV in all bedrooms Tea and coffee making facilities Direct dial from bedrooms No dogs (ex guide dogs) Licensed Cen ht CTV Last d 3pm
ROOMS: s £26-£35; d £50-£56; wkly b&b £165-£175
CARDS:

QQ ***The Ridge Guest House*** 361 The Ridge TN34 2RD
☎ 01424 754240
This family-run, bed and breakfast establishment on the outskirts of town offers generally good-sized, practical en suite bedrooms of which several are on the ground floor. There is a small cosy sitting room with a selection of board games and a spacious breakfast room with a bar for evening drinks.
11 shr (2 fmly) CTV in all bedrooms Tea and coffee making facilities No dogs Licensed Cen ht CTV 40P Last d 9.15pm
CARDS:

Selected

QQQQ **Tower House Hotel** 26-28 Tower Rd West TN38 0RG (A21, follow signs to St Leonards via London Rd, after passing Natwest Bank take first main right into Tower Rd West) ☎ 01424 427217 & 421217
Fronted by hanging baskets that are a riot of colour in summer, Tower House creates a good first impression that is maintained throughout this delightful establishment. Breakfast is taken in a pretty conservatory beyond which is a terrace and well-kept garden. Other day rooms include a dining room, small bar and comfortable lounge. Bedrooms are individually decorated with style and flair and boast a host of comforting extras along with all modern amenities. Joan and Roy Richards are the friendly hosts.
11 bth/shr (2 fmly) No smoking in bedrooms No smoking in dining room CTV in all bedrooms Tea and coffee making facilities Direct dial from bedrooms No dogs Licensed Cen ht CTV No coaches Last d 4pm
ROOMS: s £34-£39; d £48-£65; wkly b&b £204-£234; wkly hlf-bd £295-£325*
CARDS:

HATCH BEAUCHAMP Somerset Map 03 ST32

QQQ **Close House** Hatch Beauchamp TA3 6AE
(exit M5 at junc 25, A358 towards Ilminster, 4m left to Hatch Beauchamp, at Hatch Inn turn into Station Rd, follow road, premises 200 yards on left)
☎ 01823 480424 FAX 01823 480424
Closed Xmas/New Year
This fine 17th Century Manor House tucked away at the end of a private drive behind the quiet village of Hatch Beauchamp. Close House was the home of Col. John Chard VC, hero of Rork's Drift of the Zulu Wars. This solidly built stone property with its own garden and a rural outlook is now the home of Peter and Rosemary Rollason who welcome guests to their home to enjoy its peace and tranquillity. The character of the house has remained largely unaltered, although modern equipment is provided in the bedrooms. Dinner is available by prior arrangement in the large elegant dining room, and there is a choice of traditional, vegetarian or wholefood meals. Mrs Rollason, is also a spiritual healer.
5 rms (1 shr) (1 fmly) No smoking in bedrooms No smoking in dining room CTV in all bedrooms Tea and coffee making facilities No dogs (ex guide dogs) Cen ht CTV 10P No coaches Last d 7.30pm
ROOMS: s fr £20; d £36-£40; wkly b&b £126-£140; wkly hlf-bd £210-£224*

See advertisement under TAUNTON

HATHERSAGE Derbyshire Map 08 SK28

Selected

QQQQ ❦ **Highlow Hall** *(SK218801)* S32 1AX
(take B6001 from Hathersage (signposted Bakewell), after 0.5m turn right opposite Plough Inn signposted Abney, house a mile on left)
☎ 01433 650393 FAX 01433 650393 Mr M B Walker
Closed Dec
This castellated 16th-century manor house is situated above the village of Hathersage and enjoys fine views over the valley and moors beyond. Bedrooms, including one with an antique four poster bed, are comfortably furnished and attractively decorated. Breakfast is served at individual tables in the wood-panelled dining room, and there is a cosy sitting room, warmed by a log fire during the cooler months. There is also a magnificent Great Hall with an inglenook fireplace and the building is surrounded by neatly tended gardens.
3 bth/shr (1 fmly) No smoking in bedrooms Tea and coffee making facilities No dogs Licensed Cen ht CTV No children 12yrs 5P Fishing Riding Last d 7pm
ROOMS: s £40; d £60-£65; wkly b&b £183-£215; wkly hlf-bd £302-£334
CARDS:

QQQ ❦ **Hillfort Farm** *(SK226815)* Castleton Rd S32 1EG
(farm is situatd 0.5m from the village of Hathersage on the right off A625 between Hathersage & Bamford) ☎ 01433 651673 Mrs J Wilcockson
At one time a toll house and then an inn, this 16th-century house, built of mellow local stone, has been extended to offer four spacious and comfortable bedrooms. There is a cosy lounge, with a feature stone fireplace, and dinner can be served, by prior arrangement, in the adjacent beamed dining room. The house is non smoking throughout.
4 shr No smoking CTV in all bedrooms Tea and coffee making facilities No dogs Cen ht No children 12yrs 12P Last d day before
ROOMS: s £25-£50; d £38-£50; wkly b&b £140-£175; wkly hlf-bd £224-£259*

QQQ ❦ **Lane End** *(SK203791)* Abney S32 1AH
(Take B6001 from Hathersage for 0.5m. Turn right opposite Plough Inn and travel 2.5m. House first on right after village sign)
☎ 01433 650371 FAX 01433 650371 Mrs J Salisbury
Situated in the picturesque hamlet of Abney, this traditional stone-built farmhouse is surrounded by a 70 acre sheep and beef cattle farm and can also offer livery for horses. Additionally, Jill Salisbury has produced a detailed nature trail around the farm and local area. The comfortable bedrooms are attractively decorated and furnished, whilst there is also a cosy lounge with an open log fire and a dining room offering fine views over the surrounding moorland.
3 rms (1 shr) No smoking in dining room No smoking in lounges Tea and coffee making facilities No dogs Cen ht CTV 10P Farm/nature trail Stabling for horses 74 acres beef sheep
ROOMS: s £25-£30; d £38-£50*

QQQ **Millstone** Sheffield Rd S32 1DA (on A625 from Sheffield, 0.5m before reaching Hathersage) ☎ 01433 650258 FAX 01433 651664
This stone built inn stands at the edge of the village and many of the rooms enjoy fine views along the Hope Valley. Bedrooms are nicely furnished and well equipped, while the cosy lounge bar offers a range of homemade meals. There is also a modern brasserie decorated with numerous musical instruments.

7 bth/shr (2 fmly) No smoking in 5 bedrooms CTV in all bedrooms Tea and coffee making facilities Direct dial from bedrooms Cen ht 80P No coaches Last d 9.30pm
ROOMS: s £35-£45; d £55-£65; wkly b&b £150-£200; wkly hlf-bd £240
MEALS: Lunch £9.95-£15 Dinner £9.95-£15&alc
CARDS:

QQQ **Moorgate** Castleton Rd S32 1EH
(on A625 100yds past George Hotel going towards Hope/Castleton, on right just before railway bridge which crosses road)
☎ 01433 650293
This large Victorian house is set well back from the road, just a few minutes from the centre of the village, and has the benefit of a colourful garden to the rear. Bedrooms are neatly decorated and comfortable, and there is a nicely furnished lounge. Breakfast is served at separate tables in the breakfast.
3 rms No smoking CTV in 2 bedrooms Tea and coffee making facilities No dogs (ex guide dogs) Cen ht 3P
ROOMS: s £17; d £30

QQQ **Moorview Cottage** Cannonfields, Jaggers Ln S32 1AG
☎ 01433 650110
Quietly situated, almost hidden away at the back of the village, this is a deceptively large cottage on one of the old tracks used by the 'jaggers', or travelling drapers. Comfortably furnished bedrooms, one of which is en suite, are located on two floors, whilst the combined lounge and dining room, on the ground floor, is where a varied and imaginative breakfast menu is offered.
3 rms (1 bth/shr) (2 fmly) No smoking CTV in all bedrooms Tea and coffee making facilities Cen ht No children 5yrs 3P
ROOMS: s fr £20; d fr £36.40; wkly b&b fr £120*

QQQ **The Mount** Castleton Rd S32 1EH
(on A625 200yds past George Hotel, towards Castleton, on right)
☎ 01433 650388 FAX 01433 650388
This carefully restored Victorian house lies on the edge of the village with Stanage Edge, frequented by climbers and hang gliding enthusiasts, to the rear. Spacious bedrooms have high ceilings and are attractively decorated, with comfortable easy seating, in addition to the lounge sited on the top floor to take advantage of the views. Breakfast is served around one table in the nicely furnished dining room.
2 rms 1 annexe rms (1 fmly) No smoking in bedrooms No smoking in dining room CTV in 2 bedrooms Tea and coffee making facilities Cen ht CTV 6P
ROOMS: s £20; d £36*

Selected

QQQQ **Old Barn** Sheffield Rd S32 1DA (on A6187 1m from the centre of Hathersage going towards Sheffield, 100yds below Millstone Inn, on same side of the road, with white B&B sign) ☎ 01433 650667 FAX 01433 650667
Mar-Oct
In a raised location, backed by Millstone Edge, this property enjoys fine views across the valley to the hills beyond. The original 16th-century barn was recently converted into comfortable modern guest accommodation, yet retained many features, particularly exposed timbers and stonework. Bedrooms are attractively furnished and comfortable. One of the main features is a large welcoming lounge leading off from the entrance hall with galleried landing.
3 bth/shr (1 fmly) No smoking CTV in all bedrooms Tea and coffee making facilities No dogs Cen ht No children 12yrs 5P No coaches
ROOMS: d £45-£65; wkly b&b £125-£187.50*
CARDS:

Selected

QQQQ ***The Old Vicarage*** Church Bank S32 1AJ
(Turn right off A625 into School Lane, proceed 100yds & turn left, opposite pub, up Church Bank into car park) ☎ 01433 651099
Closed Xmas
This 17th-century house is situated next to the parish church, with the grave of Little John in the churchyard. Another claim to fame is that Charlotte Bronte stayed in the house. Good sized bedrooms are neatly decorated and brightly furnished, with a number of thoughtful extras provided, including a decanter of sherry, sewing kits and a fridge for guest use. There is a spacious and comfortable sitting room and breakfast is served in the cottage-style dining room.
4 rms (2 shr) CTV in all bedrooms Tea and coffee making facilities 3P

QQQ **Scotsman's Pack** School Ln S32 1BZ (off A625 turning onto School Ln, inn 50 yds from the turning, follow signs to the church) ☎ 01433 650253 FAX 01433 650253
Closed 25 Dec

contd.

Situated on the edge of the village, this inn offers traditional hospitality, together with comfortable, en suite accommodation. All rooms are well equipped and attractively furnished. The open plan bar, with welcoming open fire, attracts locals as well as visitors to enjoy the home cooked meals. There is a separate breakfast room which can also be used as a games room.
5 bth/shr No smoking in dining room No smoking in 1 lounge CTV in all bedrooms Tea and coffee making facilities No dogs (ex guide dogs) Cen ht No children 14yrs 13P Last d 9.30pm
ROOMS: s £29-£36; d £55.50-£58; wkly b&b £203*
MEALS: Lunch £6.80-£11alc Dinner £6.80-£11alc*
CARDS:

HAVANT Hampshire

See Emsworth

HAVERIGG Cumbria Map **07** SD17

QQQ **Dunelm Cottage** Main St LA18 4EX
(in village next to Harbour Hotel) ☎ 01229 770097
Closed Jan
Converted from two cottages, Dunelm lies in the centre of the village next to the pub and can be recognised by its fresh white-painted facade and leaded windows. The little lounge has lots of reading material and breakfast is taken around one large pine table in the dining room. Bedrooms vary in size but all are tastefully decorated, thoughtfully equipped and although lacking en suites, they share two bathrooms.
3 rms No smoking in bedrooms Tea and coffee making facilities Cen ht CTV No children 10yrs No coaches Last d 6.30pm
ROOMS: s fr £26.50; d fr £46*

HAWES North Yorkshire Map **07** SD88

QQQ **Steppe Haugh** Town Head DL8 3RH (on A684)
☎ 01969 667645
Dating back over 350 years, this charming stone-built guest house lies in a quiet part of town. Bedrooms tend to be on the compact side but all are cosy, modern and prettily decorated. Thoughtful touches like hairdryers and TVs are provided. There is a comfortable sitting room, and a patio is available during the better weather.
6 rms (2 shr) No smoking in bedrooms No smoking in dining room CTV in all bedrooms Tea and coffee making facilities Licensed Cen ht CTV No children 7yrs 6P No coaches
ROOMS: s £18-£23; d £33-£50*

HAWKHURST Kent Map **05** TQ73

Selected

QQQQ **Southgate-Little Fowlers** Rye Rd TN18 5DA
(on A268, approx 0.25m from traffic lights in village eastwards on Rye Rd) ☎ 01580 752526 FAX 01580 752526
Mar-Oct
Set on the outskirts of the village of Hawkhurst, this pretty house dates from the late 17th century with later Victorian additions. Both en suite bedrooms have wonderful views over the surrounding countryside and have been individually furnished in keeping with the style of the house. Mrs Woodard provides an extensive breakfast in the flower filled conservatory during the summer. There is a comfortably appointed lounge for guest use and the delightful gardens provide a secluded place to relax.
2 bth/shr (1 fmly) No smoking CTV in all bedrooms Tea and coffee making facilities No dogs (ex guide dogs) Cen ht CTV 4P
No coaches
ROOMS: d £46-£50*

HAWKSHEAD Cumbria Map **07** SD39

See also Near Sawrey

QQQ **Ivy House Hotel** LA22 0NS (exit M6 junct 36 follow signs for Windermere and Ambleside. At Ambleside follow signs for Coniston, after 1m turn left onto B5286 to Hawkshead) ☎ 015394 36204
13 Mar-1 Nov
Ivy House Hotel is a fine Grade II listed Georgian building situated in the centre of an attractive conservation village. A comfortable family-run hotel, it offers a cosy lounge with log fire in season, and a spacious dining room where good-value meals are served. Bedrooms are attractively decorated and furnished in sensible, contemporary styles. Some rooms are also provided in a modern house just across the drive.
6 bth/shr 5 annexe bth/shr (2 fmly) No smoking in dining room CTV in all bedrooms Tea and coffee making facilities Licensed Cen ht 14P No coaches Fishing Last d 6pm
ROOMS: s £30-£32; d £60-£64; wkly hlf-bd £259-£273

QQ **Kings Arms Hotel** LA22 0NZ (on Main Sq) ☎ 015394 36372
FAX 015394 36372
Closed Xmas Day
This old traditional Lakeland inn lies right in the centre of the village and offers a good choice of food in both the lounge and the dining room. The cosy bedrooms are traditionally furnished but have a high level of equipment.
9 rms (6 shr) (2 fmly) No smoking in dining room CTV in all bedrooms Tea and coffee making facilities Direct dial from bedrooms Cen ht P Fishing Last d 9pm
ROOMS: s £27-£37; d £44-£64*
MEALS: Lunch £8.85-£19 Dinner £8.85-£19*
CARDS:

Selected

QQQQ **Rough Close Country House** LA22 0QF
(1.25m S on Newby Bridge road) ☎ 015394 36370
Apr-Oct rs Mar (wknds only)
This charming, small country hotel lies close to Esthwaite Water and is the home of Anthony and Marylin Gibson. The daily changing five-course evening meals are a delight, as are the substantial breakfasts. Reception rooms extend to a light and airy dining room next to the traditionally furnished lounge. Bedrooms are comfortably furnished, thoughtfully equipped and most have modern en suites. There is also a cosy bar.
5 bth/shr No smoking in bedrooms No smoking in dining room CTV in all bedrooms Tea and coffee making facilities No dogs (ex guide dogs) Licensed Cen ht No children 12yrs 10P No coaches Last d 7pm
ROOMS: s £37-£40.50; d £54-£61; wkly b&b £182-£206.50; wkly hlf-bd £255.50-£280
CARDS:

Selected

QQQQ **Sun** Main St LA22 0NT (from Windermere take A591 to Ambleside and then B5286 to Hawkshead. Establishment is situated in centre of village opposite 'Hawkshead Country Wear') ☎ 015394 36236 FAX 015394 36155

This 17th-century inn lies in the centre of the village and its cosy bedrooms combine the charm and character of beams, original wood panelling and natural Lakeland stone with tasteful fabrics, modern en suites and facilities that include hairdryer and trouser press. The bar has a flagstone floor and sets the scene for the accomplished cooking that is also provided in the spacious dining room.

8 bth/shr (1 fmly) No smoking in bedrooms No smoking in area of dining room CTV in all bedrooms Tea and coffee making facilities No dogs (ex guide dogs) Cen ht Last d 9.30pm

ROOMS: s £35-£50; d £50-£70; wkly b&b £190-£220

MEALS: Lunch £10-£25 Dinner £15-£30alc

CARDS:

HAWNBY North Yorkshire Map **08** SE58

Selected

QQQQ **Laskill** *(SE562007)* Hawnby YO6 5NB (6m N of Helmsley on the B1257) ☎ 01439 798268 Mrs S Smith

This 19th-century farmhouse is set in attractive gardens amidst wonderful scenery. The two comfortable bedrooms in the house share a charming Victorian bathroom, and there are spacious beamed rooms in adjacent converted farm buildings. The delightfully refurbished lounge is very inviting as is the smart dining room where dinner can be served by arrangement. Fishing is available on the River Seph that runs through the grounds.

2 bth/shr 4 annexe bth/shr No smoking CTV in all bedrooms Tea and coffee making facilities Licensed Cen ht CTV 20P Fishing Riding Last d 7pm

ROOMS: d £50-£60; wkly b&b £175.50-£210; wkly hlf-bd £259-£294*

CARDS:

HAWORTH West Yorkshire Map **07** SE03

QQQ ***Ferncliffe Hotel*** Hebden Rd BD22 8RS (on A6033 near junct with B6144) ☎ 01535 643405

This small hotel, enjoying fine views over the valley, offers comfortable modern bedrooms and a first-floor lounge for guests' use. Downstairs there is a small bar, and a wide range of meals is available in the spacious restaurant.

6 shr (1 fmly) No smoking in area of dining room No smoking in lounges CTV in all bedrooms Tea and coffee making facilities Licensed Cen ht CTV 12P No coaches Last d 8.30pm

CARDS:

HAYES Greater London Map **04** TQ08

Q **Shepiston Lodge** 31 Shepiston Ln UB3 1LJ (leave M4 junct follow signpost for Hayes from slip road lodge 50 yds from fire station almost opposite Great Western pub) ☎ 0181 573 0266 & 0181 569 2536 FAX 0181 569 2536

Close to Heathrow Airport, with some long-term parking available, this guest house offers simple, practical accommodation. Although none of the bedrooms are en suite, seven have in-room showers. The breakfast room boasts satellite TV and a dispense bar, plus some comfortable banquette seating. Dinners are by arrangement.

13 rms (3 fmly) CTV in all bedrooms Tea and coffee making facilities No dogs (ex guide dogs) Licensed Cen ht CTV 15P Last d 9pm

ROOMS: s £33.50-£36.50; d £46.50-£49.50*

CARDS:

HAYLE Cornwall & Isles of Scilly Map **02** SW53

Premier Selected

QQQQQ **Treglisson** *(SW576376)* Wheal Alfred Rd TR27 5JT (from rdbt om A30 follow Hayle signs, first turn left into Guildford Rd which then becomes Wheal Alfred Rd after bridge, 0.5m on left) ☎ 01736 753141 FAX 01736 753141 Mrs C Runnalls

Closed November

Surrounded by 40 acres of its own arable farmland, Treglisson was built in the 1780s, originally for a Mine Captain. Today it offers modern comforts in bedrooms that have been delightfully decorated and furnished with antiques. Fresh flowers add a homely touch, and guests are always offered a refreshing pot of tea on arrival. More antiques are to be found in day rooms which include an elegant lounge with plush blue Chesterfields, and a fine dining room with a huge old stone inglenook. In summer breakfast is taken in a charming conservatory. *contd.*

5 bth/shr (2 fmly) No smoking in bedrooms No smoking in dining room CTV in all bedrooms Tea and coffee making facilities No dogs Cen ht CTV No children 6yrs 6P Indoor swimming pool (heated)
ROOMS: s £26; d £42-£48*
CARDS:

HAYLING ISLAND Hampshire Map **04** SZ79

Premier Selected

QQQQQ ***Cockle Warren Cottage Hotel*** 36 Seafront PO11 9HL (take A3023 continue S to seafront then turn left & continue for 1m hotel on left) ☎ 01705 464961 FAX 01705 464838
Located on the sea front, this charming house has lots of character and a warm friendly atmosphere. The spacious bedrooms are individually furnished and many extras have been included. There are two cosy lounges, with a wood fire on chilly evenings, and a bright conservatory dining room that overlooks the swimming pool. An interesting menu is offered at dinner plus a well balanced wine list.
3 bth/shr 2 annexe bth/shr No smoking in bedrooms No smoking in dining room No smoking in 1 lounge CTV in all bedrooms Direct dial from bedrooms Licensed Cen ht No children 12yrs 7P No coaches Outdoor swimming pool (heated) Last d 6pm
CARDS:

HAYWARDS HEATH West Sussex Map **05** TQ32

Selected

QQQQ **Sliders Farm** *(TQ404257)* Furners Green TN22 3RT (1m S of Danehill village on A275, signposted at small crossroads) ☎ 01825 790258 FAX 01825 790258 Mr & Mrs D Salmon
Closed 21 Dec-1 Jan
Situated down a narrow country lane, and surrounded by fields and woodland, Sliders Farm is an idyllic retreat. Home to Jean and David Salmon, this 16th-century farmhouse offers charming antique-furnished bedrooms that are decorated in a bright sunny style. The rooms are furnished with thoughtful extras including a helpful and comprehensive guide to walks and other nearby attractions. The roomy and comfortable lounge boasts an inglenook fireplace and a snooker table. There is also an elegantly-appointed, beamed breakfast room. Self-catering accommodation is available in a converted barn and separate cottage.
3 bth/shr No smoking in bedrooms No smoking in dining room CTV in all bedrooms Tea and coffee making facilities No dogs Cen ht 12P Outdoor swimming pool (heated) Tennis (hard) Fishing Threequarter size snooker table 30 acres non working Last d 24hrs prior
ROOMS: s £34-£40; d £44-£60

HEATHFIELD East Sussex Map **05** TQ52

QQQ **Old Corner Cottage** Little London Rd TN21 0LT (A267 towards Heathfield take 1st right past Cross in Hand pub, signposted Horam & Eastbourne into Little London Rd) ☎ 01435 863787
This attractive cottage is well located for visitors to the many local National Trust properties, Glyndebourne and Tunbridge Wells. Accommodation is comfortable and well appointed with smart modern en suite facilities. There is a bright conservatory lounge overlooking the pretty garden.
3 bth/shr No smoking CTV in all bedrooms Tea and coffee making facilities No dogs (ex guide dogs) Cen ht CTV 8P No coaches
ROOMS: s £20-£25; d £38-£42*

HEATHROW AIRPORT Greater London Map **04** TQ07

See also Slough

QQ **Civic** 87/89 Lampton Rd TW3 4DP ☎ 0181 572 5107 FAX 0181 814 0203
Popular with holidaymakers using nearby Heathrow Airport, this guesthouse is close to the centre of Hounslow, and has the benefit of off-street parking. Rooms continue to be modernised and updated, many now having en suite showers, and all with satellite TV.
14 rms (8 shr) 14 annexe rms (6 bth/shr) (8 fmly) No smoking in 3 bedrooms CTV in all bedrooms Tea and coffee making facilities No dogs (ex guide dogs) Cen ht CTV 8P Last d 7.30pm
ROOMS: s £38-£43; d £50-£55*
CARDS:

QQQ **The Cottage** 150-152 High St, Cranford TW5 9PD (leave M4 junct3 onto A312 continue to traffic lights & turn left. Continue and turn left after first pub on left)
☎ 0181 897 1815 FAX 0181 897 3117
Behind the Jolly Gardener Pub on Cranford High street is a quiet cul de sac which could be miles away from Heathrow, yet is in fact only ten minutes away. The majority of bedrooms have good en suite showers and all have remote control TVs. Breakfast is served in the dining room facing the garden full of fruit trees.
11 rms (7 bth/shr) (2 fmly) No smoking CTV in all bedrooms No dogs Cen ht CTV 12P
ROOMS: s £46; d £55*
CARDS:

QQQ **Harmondsworth Hall** Summerhouse Ln, Harmondsworth Village UB7 0BG ☎ 0181 759 1824 & 0385 236597 FAX 0181 897 6385
Tucked away in the old part of Harmondsworth and close to two village pubs this guest house is ideal for those who are visiting the area or catching flights from Heathrow. Rooms are individual and vary in size. Hairdriers and remote control TVs are among the in-room facilities.
9 rms (4 bth/shr) (3 fmly) No smoking in 4 bedrooms No smoking in dining room No smoking in lounges CTV in all bedrooms Tea and coffee making facilities Direct dial from bedrooms Licensed Cen ht CTV 8P No coaches Last d by arrangement
ROOMS: s £30-£35; d £45-£55; wkly b&b £200-£245*

QQQ Longford 550 Bath Rd, Longford UB7 0EE
(approx 1.5m from junct 14 of M25)
☎ 01753 682969 FAX 01753 794189
Closed Xmas week
Situated on the edge of the village of Longford, this guest house is conveniently located for Heathrow Airport and the motorway network. The building, which dates from the 17th century, retains some of its original period features including timber-framed walls. Downstairs there is a comfortably furnished residents lounge and a breakfast room.
5 rms No smoking in bedrooms No smoking in dining room CTV in all bedrooms Tea and coffee making facilities No dogs Cen ht CTV No children 10yrs 5P No coaches
ROOMS: s fr £29; d fr £39*
CARDS:

QQQ Shalimar Hotel 215-221 Staines Rd TW3 3JJ
(exit M4 junc 3, road to Hounslow, at rdbt turn left, at next roundabout bear right, at third set of lights turn right, next lights turn left)
☎ 0181 577 7070 & 572 2816 & (free) 0500 238239 FAX 0181 569 6789
Ideally positioned for Heathrow Airport, this centrally located hotel is run by the Dar family and has established a loyal following. Bedrooms are simply decorated but well equipped, the majority having modern en suite facilities, and a number of new luxury rooms have recently been completed. There is an attractive open-plan restaurant, bar and lounge overlooking the garden.
39 rms (29 shr) (5 fmly) No smoking in 2 bedrooms No smoking in area of dining room CTV in all bedrooms Tea and coffee making facilities Direct dial from bedrooms No dogs (ex guide dogs) Licensed Cen ht CTV 10P Last d noon
ROOMS: s £40-£55; d £50-£65*
CARDS:

QQ Skylark 297 Bath Rd TW3 3DB ☎ 0181 577 8455
FAX 0181 577 8741
Located close to Heathrow Airport and Hounslow station, this guest house has been refurbished throughout. Some bedrooms are small but are adequately furnished in modern style and suitably equipped. English breakfast is included in the tariff.
11 rms (3 shr) (3 fmly) No smoking in 2 bedrooms No smoking in dining room No smoking in lounges CTV in all bedrooms Tea and coffee making facilities No dogs Cen ht 8P
ROOMS: s fr £40; d fr £55*
CARDS:

Remember to return your Prize Draw card for a chance to win an action-packed family weekend at one of the eleven Family Fun Hotels in the Hilton Hotels Directory. See inside the front cover for the card and competition details. Don't forget to fill in your name and address before posting!

HEBDEN BRIDGE West Yorkshire Map **07** SD92

Selected

Q Q Q Q **Redacre Mill** Redacre, Mytholmroyd HX7 5DQ (on A646 westbound at Mytholmroyd village turn right after fire station, cross hump back bridge and turn right)
☎ 01422 885563 FAX 01422 885563
This delightful private hotel lies alongside the Rochdale canal, and there are two acres of attractive landscaped gardens. A carefully converted cotton warehouse, it retains many original features including attractive wood panelling and the hoist used to lift the cotton bales. Bedrooms are comfortably furnished and attractively decorated. The sitting room leads into a spacious dining room where imaginative meals are served.
5 bth/shr (1 fmly) No smoking CTV in all bedrooms Tea and coffee making facilities No dogs (ex guide dogs) Licensed Cen ht No children 8P No coaches Fishing Last d 6.45pm
ROOMS: s £37.50-£39; d £55-£58; wkly b&b £192.50-£276.50; wkly hlf-bd £287-£367.50
CARDS:

HELMSLEY North Yorkshire Map **08** SE68

See also Hawnby

Q Q Q **Plumpton Court** High St, Nawton YO62 7TT (On entering Beadlam & Newton from Helmsley on A170, take 3rd turning on the left. Plumpton Court is 600yds on the left) ☎ 01439 771223
Peacefully situated in the village of Nawton, this attractive 17th century stone house offers modern and well equipped bedrooms. There is a cosy lounge bar with a real fire and good home cooking is served in the pleasant dining room. Friendly and attentive service is provided by the resident owners. There is a well tended garden to the rear.
7 rms (5 bth/shr) No smoking CTV in 5 bedrooms Tea and coffee making facilities No dogs Licensed Cen ht No children 5yrs 10P No coaches Last d noon
ROOMS: s £29.50-£33.50; d £42-£50; wkly b&b £147-£150; wkly hlf-bd £231-£234

HELSTON Cornwall & Isles of Scilly Map **02** SW62

Selected

Q Q Q Q ❦ ***Little Pengwedna** (SW638318)* Little Pengwedna Farm TR13 0AY (on B3302) ☎ 01736 850649 FAX 01736 850649 Mrs I White
Mrs White welcomes guests to this attractive stone-built farmhouse, situated midway between Helston and Hayle. The bedrooms are well equipped and attractively decorated with co-ordinated fabrics, and cleverly furnished to make the best use of available space. A spacious sitting room, with a log fire during the cooler months, is available for guests, enhanced by many pretty ornaments, pictures and fresh flowers from the well tended front garden. Breakfast is taken in the dining room.

3 rms (2 shr) No smoking in bedrooms Tea and coffee making facilities No dogs (ex guide dogs) Cen ht CTV No children 5yrs 6P 60 acres beef/sheep

Selected

Q Q Q Q ❦ **Nanplough Farm Country House** *(SW682214)* Cury Whitecross TR12 7BQ (Make way to Helston,take rd to Lisard,go straight across mini-rdbt,50-60yrds,then right to golf course,follow rd to Cury,farm on left up 1/4m drive)
☎ 01326 241088 FAX 01326 241088 Mrs J Makin
This large stone-built house dates back some 110 years. It is quietly located on a 26 acre holding, which is used mainly for the grazing of horses. It provides modern accommodation, which includes a bedroom on ground floor level. Separate tables are provided in the traditionally furnished dining room and there is a spacious and attractively decorated lounge.
3 shr No smoking in dining room CTV in all bedrooms Tea and coffee making facilities No dogs (ex guide dogs) Cen ht CTV 8P Outdoor swimming pool (heated) Games room, darts & table tennis 26 acres horses Last d 24hrs
ROOMS: wkly b&b £126-£196; wkly hlf-bd £220.50-£290.50
CARDS:

HENLEY-IN-ARDEN Warwickshire Map **07** SP16

Q Q Q **Ashleigh House** Whitley Hill B95 5DL (from Henley in Arden traffic lights turn off A3400 onto A4189 towards Warwick, house on left just after 'Old Victorian Nurseries')
☎ 01564 792315 FAX 01564 794126
This large Edwardian house stands in spacious grounds, one mile east of Henley. The traditionally furnished accommodation, which includes a family

room, is well equipped. Some bedrooms are located on the ground floor of a converted stable building. These have parking space immediately outside. Individual tables are provided in the breakfast room, and there is also an attractive and comfortable lounge.
6 bth/shr 4 annexe shr No smoking CTV in all bedrooms Tea and coffee making facilities Direct dial from bedrooms No dogs (ex guide dogs) Cen ht CTV No children 12yrs 18P No coaches Last d 7pm
ROOMS: s £35-£38; d £46-£49.50*
CARDS:

HENLEY-ON-THAMES Oxfordshire Map **04** SU78

Premier Selected

Q Q Q Q Q **Lenwade** 3 Western Rd RG9 1JL
(Leaving Henley on the Reading Rd turn right into Andrews over the crossroads, next left into Western Rd, premises on the left)
☎ 01491 573468 & 0374 941629 FAX 0149 573468
This turn of the century semi-detached property is situated in a quiet residential area. The smartly-furnished bedrooms are well equipped and there are many thoughtful extras. Breakfast is served around one large table in the attractive dining room and there is a comfortable lounge with satellite TV and an open fire in colder weather. Children are welcome and dogs accepted by prior arrangement.
3 bth/shr No smoking in dining room No smoking in lounges CTV in all bedrooms Tea and coffee making facilities Cen ht 2P
ROOMS: d £46-£50*

Q Q Q **Slater's Farm** Peppard Common RG9 5JL
(leave Henley up Gravel Hill at junct with B481 turn left. After 0.25miles after The Dog pub fork left farm on right after 200yds)
☎ 01491 628675 FAX 01491 628675
Located on the edge of the Chilterns this charming Georgian farmhouse is peacefully set in an attractive one acre garden, and has a warm friendly atmosphere. There are comfortable bedrooms, a cosy sitting room, and a small dining room where breakfast is served round a large, shared table.
3 rms No smoking in bedrooms CTV in 2 bedrooms No dogs (ex guide dogs) Cen ht CTV 5P No coaches Tennis (hard)
ROOMS: s £27.50; d £45*

HENSTRIDGE Somerset Map **03** ST71

Q Q Q ❦ ***Toomer** (ST708192)* Templecombe BA8 0PH (entrance to farm on A30 between Milborne Port and Henstridge traffic lights)
☎ 01963 250237 FAX 01963 250237 Mr P Doggrell & Mrs S White
Guests will enjoy the tranquil setting of this working dairy farm set in extensive grounds. The house retains much of its original character, and the three bedrooms have been furnished and decorated in keeping with the age of the building. Breakfast is served in the formal dining room, with guests being seated at one large table. There is also a spacious lounge in which to relax.
3 rms (2 shr) (2 fmly) CTV in all bedrooms Tea and coffee making facilities No dogs (ex guide dogs) Cen ht CTV 6P Fishing
600 acres arable dairy

Win a Family Fun Weekend with AA Lifestyle Guides in association with Hilton Hotels. 3 winners will be drawn every 2 months: December 1998; February 1999; April 1999; June 1999; August 1999; October 1999

HEREFORD Herefordshire Map **03** SO54

See also Little Dewchurch

Selected

Q Q Q Q **Dormington Court Country House Hotel**
Dormington, Bartestree HR1 4ES (5m E, off A438)
☎ 01432 850370 FAX 01432 850370
An impressive house with Georgian and Elizabethan origins surrounded by hop fields and apple orchards in addition to well maintained private gardens. Bedrooms are spacious, well equipped and comfortable, and all have modern en suite or private bathrooms. Public areas retain many original features including exposed beams and an inglenook fireplace.
6 bth/shr (1 fmly) No smoking in dining room CTV in all bedrooms Tea and coffee making facilities Cen ht No children 5yrs 20P No coaches
ROOMS: s £30-£35; d £45-£60; wkly b&b £140-£175*
CARDS:

Selected

Q Q Q Q **Felton House** Felton HR1 3PH
(turn off A417 at crossroads to Felton. After 300yds turn left. House on right after 400yds beside parish church)
☎ 01432 820366 FAX 01432 820366
Closed 24-28 Dec
This former rectory was built in 1851, and stands next to the church, on the edge of the village of Felton. The house has been carefully and tastefully furnished in a style befitting its age and character. The two rooms without en suite showers and toilets have their own private facilities nearby. There is a choice of lounges, where welcoming real fires burn in stoves during cold weather. Separate tables are provided in the pleasant breakfast room, which also has some fine period furniture.
4 bth/shr No smoking Tea and coffee making facilities Cen ht CTV 6P No coaches
ROOMS: s £22; d £44

Selected

Q Q Q Q ***Hermitage Manor*** Canon Pyon HR4 8NR
(3.5m NW off A4110 towards Canon Pyon) ☎ 01432 760317
Mar-mid Nov
Set right in the heart of rural Herefordshire and near the village of Canon Pyon, this large Manor House stands in eleven acres of gardens and woods and provides very spacious accommodation. The elegant public rooms are very grand, and the house also has its own spring-fed water supply.
3 bth/shr No smoking CTV in all bedrooms Tea and coffee making facilities No dogs Cen ht No children 10yrs 12P No coaches Bowling Croquet

Q Q Q **Hopbine Hotel** Roman Rd HR1 1LE (Take A49 from Hereford turn right onto A4103 establishment is 0.5 mile on left hand side)
☎ 01432 268722 FAX 01432 268722
This friendly, family-run hotel stands in its own extensive grounds, which include a helicopter landing pad. The accommodation has been considerably upgraded in recent times. The bedrooms, most of which are on ground floor level, have modern furnishings, equipment and facilities. Separate tables are provided in the cottage-style dining room, which has a small adjacent bar.
20 rms (16 bth) (4 fmly) No smoking in 5 bedrooms No smoking in dining room No smoking in lounges CTV in all bedrooms Tea and coffee making facilities Licensed Cen ht CTV 30P Last d 8.30pm

Selected

Q Q Q Q **Sink Green** *(SO542377)* Rotherwas HR2 6LE
(on B4399 2m from junct of A49) ☎ 01432 870223 Mr D E Jones
Closed Xmas
This charming 16th-century stone-built house is part of a 170-acre livestock farm that lies alongside the River Wye. It has a great deal of character, which is enhanced by original features such as low-beamed ceilings and stone-flagged floors. The attractively appointed bedrooms, which include one with a four-poster bed, have modern equipment and facilities. There is a large, comfortable lounge with several antique pieces and a welcoming fire in the stove. All guests share one table in the breakfast room.
3 bth/shr No smoking CTV in all bedrooms Tea and coffee making facilities No dogs (ex guide dogs) Cen ht CTV 10P
180 acres beef sheep
ROOMS: s £21-£25; d £38-£46*

HERNE BAY Kent Map **05** TR16

Selected

Q Q Q Q **Foxden** 5 Landon Rd, off Beltinge Rd CT6 6HP
(A299 turn into Herne Bay via A291, over small rdbt, at junct with lights turn right, 8th right turning, 2nd house on left)
☎ 01227 363514 369820
Built in 1928 this lovely house is very quietly located in a residential area. The accommodation has been tastefully furnished with antiques. Two spacious and comfortable bedrooms come well equipped with lots of thoughtful extras and very good quality furnishings. The breakfast room overlooks a well kept lawn garden and the atmosphere is very peaceful and relaxing.
3 rms (2 shr) No smoking CTV in all bedrooms Tea and coffee making facilities Cen ht No children 10yrs 4P No coaches Bowls croquet
ROOMS: s £18.50-£20; d £37-£40; wkly b&b £120-£130

HERSTMONCEUX East Sussex Map **05** TQ61

Selected

Q Q Q Q **Wartling Place** Wartling Place, Wartling BN27 1RY
(Take A271 signed Herstmonceux after Windmill Hill turn right continue following signs, at Wartling village, Wartling Pl is on right)
☎ 01323 832590 FAX 01323 832590
Set in two acres of gardens with impressive trees, this beautiful Georgian country house offers bedrooms that are furnished and decorated to a high standard. Two have four-posters and all have thoughtful extras. There is a comfortable guest drawing room and breakfast is served around one large polished table.
3 bth/shr (1 fmly) No smoking CTV in all bedrooms Tea and coffee making facilities Cen ht 10P No coaches
ROOMS: s £40-£50; d £50-£70; wkly b&b £157.50-£225
CARDS:

HEXHAM Northumberland Map **12** NY96

See also Barrasford

Selected

QQQQ **Dene House** Juniper NE46 1SJ (from town take B6306 and first right fork, then first left turn, both signposted Dye House. Follow road for 3.5m and Dene House past Juniper sign)
☎ 01434 673413 FAX 01434 673413
Set in the small village of Juniper, this former farmhouse is backed by attractive gardens and nine acres of meadow. Margaret and Brian Massey have converted it into a delightful family home. The lounge has a beamed ceiling and open fire, and there is a sun lounge for warmer weather. Aga-cooked breakfasts are taken in the farmhouse kitchen. The well proportioned bedrooms are furnished in pine and charmingly decorated.
3 rms (1 shr) No smoking Tea and coffee making facilities Cen ht CTV 4P No coaches
ROOMS: s £20; d £40*

QQQ **Dukeslea** 32 Shaws Park NE46 3BJ
(exit A69 onto B6305 towards Hexham West End, take 1st right past Hexham Golf club into Shaw's Park, keep right, premises at top of hill on right) ☎ 01434 602947
Closed Xmas
A modern detached private house set in a quiet residential estate on the western side of the town. Guests have use of the ground floor, where there are two compact but attractive bedrooms, as well as a cheery lounge with TV and lots of tourist literature. Breakfast is also taken here around the one table.
2 shr No smoking Tea and coffee making facilities No dogs Cen ht CTV 5P No coaches
ROOMS: d £36-£40*

QQQ **Rose & Crown** Main St, Slaley NE47 0AA
(exit A68 onto B6306, premises on the left)
☎ 01434 673263 FAX 01434 673305
This family-run inn lies in the sleepy village of Slaley, amidst open countryside. There are two bar areas, the main one featuring a collection of mugs hung from its low-beamed ceiling. Real ale is on tap and as well as bar meals. An a la carte menu is provided in the cosy dining room area. The pine-furnished bedrooms are cheerily decorated and well equipped.
3 bth/shr No smoking in bedrooms No smoking in area of dining room No smoking in 1 lounge CTV in all bedrooms Tea and coffee making facilities No dogs (ex guide dogs) Cen ht 35P No coaches
Last d 10pm
ROOMS: s £25-£32.50; d £40-£50*
MEALS: Lunch £7.50-£12.50 Dinner £10.95-£12.95&alc*
CARDS:

QQQ **Rye Hill** *(NY958580)* Slaley NE47 0AH (5m S of Hexham, off B6306) ☎ 01434 673259 FAX 01434 673608 Mrs E A Courage
The bedrooms at this hill farm offer lots of personal touches, are bright, and well equipped. There is a cosy lounge area with tourist information and also a games room, all contained in two converted barns within the main courtyard, close to working farm buildings. Meals are taken at two pine tables in the dining room which looks out onto the garden.
6 bth/shr (2 fmly) No smoking in bedrooms No smoking in dining room CTV in all bedrooms Tea and coffee making facilities Licensed Cen ht CTV 6P Games room 30 acres sheep Last d 6pm
ROOMS: s £24; d £40; wkly b&b £126-£151; wkly hlf-bd £196-£221
CARDS:

HIGHAM Suffolk Map **05** TM03

Selected

QQQQ **The Bauble** Higham CO7 6LA (on B1068, over the bridge at the foot of the hill approx 2 miles from A12) ☎ 01206 337254 FAX 01206 337263
This delightful 16th-century property has been carefully modernised, and lies in the heart of Dedham Vale, made famous by the paintings of John Constable. The house is set in two acres of gardens. The interior is decorated with period furniture, porcelain figurines and dried flower arrangements. One bedroom has an en suite shower while the remaining two have private bathrooms nearby. Breakfast is served around a single mahogany table in the dining room. Guests may enjoy use of the outdoor pool and tennis court.
3 bth/shr No smoking CTV in all bedrooms Tea and coffee making facilities No dogs Cen ht No children 12yrs 5P No coaches Outdoor swimming pool (heated) Tennis (hard)
ROOMS: s £25-£30; d £45-£50

HIGH CATTON East Riding of Yorkshire Map **08** SE75

QQQ **High Catton Grange** *(SE728541)* YO41 1EP
(leave A166 in Stamford Bridge opposite 'Corn Mill' left at church for approx 1.5m take first turning right to High & Low Catton,first farm on left)
☎ 01759 371374 FAX 01759 371374 Mrs S M Foster
Closed Xmas & New Year
A very pleasantly furnished 18th-century farmhouse standing in open countryside, where Mrs Foster proves to be a delightful and friendly host. There is a cosy lounge and breakfast is served in the pleasant dining room. Bedrooms are prettily decorated and pleasantly furnished.
3 rms (1 bth) (1 fmly) No smoking in 1 bedrooms No smoking in dining room No smoking in lounges CTV in 1 bedroom Tea and coffee making facilities Cen ht CTV 6P 300 acres mixed
ROOMS: s fr £20; d £34-£45*

HIGH WYCOMBE Buckinghamshire Map **04** SU89

Q Q **Amersham Hill** 52 Amersham Hill HP13 6PQ (300yds from High Wycombe Railway Station on the A404) ☎ 01494 520635
Closed 15 Dec-6 Jan
This pleasantly appointed, three-storey guest house offers comfortable accommodation, and is close to the town centre. Mrs Dowling is a charming host and offers a warm friendly welcome.
8 rms (1 shr) No smoking in dining room CTV in all bedrooms Tea and coffee making facilities No dogs (ex guide dogs) Cen ht No children 10yrs 9P No coaches
ROOMS: s £30-£32; d £48-£62*

Q Q Q ***Clifton Lodge Hotel*** 210 West Wycombe Rd HP12 3AR
☎ 01494 440095 & 529062 FAX 01494 536322
A privately owned and run commercial hotel located at the west of the town. The bedrooms, which vary in size are nicely decorated and well equipped. Public rooms are comfortably appointed, with bar, lounge and restaurant. A good carte menu is offered at dinner, and there is a choice of breakfast.
32 rms (12 bth 8 shr) (2 fmly) No smoking in dining room CTV in all bedrooms Tea and coffee making facilities Direct dial from bedrooms No dogs (ex guide dogs) Licensed Cen ht CTV 28P Sauna Jacuzzi
Last d 8.45pm
CARDS:

HILTON Cambridgeshire Map **04** TL26

Q Q Q **Prince of Wales** Potton Rd PE18 9NG
(follow B1040 to Biggleswade from A14 or B1040 to St Ives from A428)
☎ 01480 830257 FAX 01480 830257
Closed 25 Dec
With its picturesque village location, open log fire, real ales and hearty fare, the Prince of Wales has a traditional inn feel, but offers many modern comforts in its accommodation. The bedrooms may be slightly compact, but all are comfortable. The welcoming public areas include a lounge bar cum dining area, where guests can enjoy an appetising menu selection.
4 shr CTV in all bedrooms Tea and coffee making facilities Direct dial from bedrooms Cen ht CTV No children 5yrs 8P Pool table Darts
Last d 9.15pm
ROOMS: s £40-£45; d £60
MEALS: Bar Lunch £1.75-£7.50 Dinner £10-£18alc
CARDS:

HIMBLETON Worcestershire Map **03** SO95

Selected

Q Q Q Q **Phepson** *(SO941599)* WR9 7JZ
(from Droitwich take B4090 for 2m then turn right & proceed for 2m)
☎ 01905 391205 FAX 01905 391205 Mrs P Havard
Closed Xmas & New Year
This lovely old house dates back to the early 18th century and has a lot of character. The bedrooms, which include a family room, are traditionally furnished and well equipped. Two are situated in the main house, and two are on the ground floor of a separate building which was once a granary. Separate tables are provided in the breakfast room and there is also a comfortable lounge, with a welcoming solid fuel stove set in an inglenook fireplace.
2 shr 2 annexe bth (1 fmly) No smoking in bedrooms No smoking in dining room CTV in all bedrooms Tea and coffee making facilities Cen ht CTV 6P Fishing 170 acres beef sheep arable
ROOMS: s fr £25; d £40-£42*

HINCKLEY Leicestershire Map **04** SP49

Selected

Q Q Q Q **Ambion Court Hotel** The Green, Dadlington CV13 6JB (from Hinckley Police Station take Stoke Golding Rd pass Safeway Superstore. At Stoke Golding turn right into Dadlington)
☎ 01455 212292 FAX 01455 213141
Ambion Court, a restored collection of pleasant red brick farm cottages and outbuildings, sits overlooking Dadlington village green. The public rooms in the main house, characterised by old timbers and stonework, include a well stocked bar with easy chairs and an adjacent lounge with plump sofas and armchairs. A good variety of freshly prepared dishes is served at dinner in the attractive dining room. The bedrooms, all equally well equipped, are split between the modern-style courtyard bedrooms and a few character bedrooms in the main house.
2 shr 5 annexe bth/shr (1 fmly) No smoking in bedrooms No smoking in dining room CTV in all bedrooms Tea and coffee making facilities Direct dial from bedrooms Licensed Cen ht CTV 8P No coaches Last d 8.30pm
ROOMS: s £35-£45; d £50-£60
CARDS:

HINTON CHARTERHOUSE Somerset Map **03** ST75

Selected

Q Q Q Q **Green Lane House** Green Ln BA3 6BL (from Bath take A367 Exeter rd, at end of dual c'way turn left onto B3110 Frome rd, after 3m turn left at The Rose & Crown Inn, estab 1st on right)
☎ 01225 723631 FAX 01225 723773
Originally three 18th-century terraced cottages, Green Lane House has been lovingly restored and attractively furnished. Traditional features such as exposed beams and open fireplaces combine with modern comforts in the four distinctively decorated bedrooms and the homely resident lounge and breakfast room. Green Lane House is not far from two inns serving evening meals.

4 rms (2 shr) No smoking Tea and coffee making facilities No dogs (ex guide dogs) Cen ht CTV No children 8yrs No coaches
ROOMS: s £26-£42; d £40-£54
CARDS:

HITCHIN Hertfordshire Map **04** TL12

Q Q Q **Firs Hotel** 83 Bedford Rd SG5 2TY (premises on main A600 road to Bedford opposite Hitchins Football ground and swimming pool)
☎ 01462 422322 FAX 01462 432051
rs 25 Dec-2 Jan & Sun
Originally a manor house, this roadside hotel is located on the A600, a few minutes by car from the town centre. The public rooms include a comfortable lounge bar and a restaurant that specialises in Italian cooking. Bedroom styles and sizes vary quite considerably, most have en suite facilities, and they are all well equipped.
30 rms (24 bth/shr) (3 fmly) No smoking in dining room CTV in all bedrooms Tea and coffee making facilities Direct dial from bedrooms Licensed Cen ht CTV 30P Last d 9.30pm
ROOMS: s £31-£49; d £47-£59*
CARDS:

Q Q Q **The Greyhound** London Rd, St Ippollitts SG4 7NL (on B656 1m S of Hitchin) ☎ 01462 440989
The Greyhound is surrounded by farmland, and offers a cosy bar with open fires where informal bar meals are available, and a separate dining room in which breakfasts and an à la carte evening menu are served. Bedrooms are double glazed, soundly appointed and have modern en suite shower rooms; there are two ground floor bedrooms with direct access from the rear car park.
4 shr CTV in all bedrooms Tea and coffee making facilities Cen ht 25P Last d 10.30pm
ROOMS: s £42.50-£47.50; d £45-£55*
MEALS: Lunch £8.50-£12&alc Dinner £8.50-£12&alc*
CARDS:

HOARWITHY Herefordshire Map **03** SO52

Selected

Q Q Q Q **The Old Mill** HR2 6QH (From M50 travel W along A40 until A49 turn off, go along road take 2nd right and establishment is along this road) ☎ 01432 840602
A working mill until the 1930's, this 18th-century house, which is situated in the heart of the pretty village, provides comfortable accommodation within easy reach of the area's major attractions. Bedrooms are well equipped and homely and most have the benefit of modern en-suite facilities. Public areas include a spacious dining room, where imaginative dinners and tasty English breakfasts are served, and a comfortable sitting room. All areas are enriched by pretty soft furnishings and paintings, many of which are the work of hostess Carol Probert who extends a warm and caring welcome to her lovely home.
7 rms (1 bth 4 shr) No smoking in bedrooms No smoking in dining room Tea and coffee making facilities No dogs (ex guide dogs) Cen ht CTV 6P No coaches Last d 7pm
ROOMS: s £17-£19; d £34-£38; wkly b&b £108-£120; wkly hlf-bd £176-£189

The AA's professional Inspectors make regular and anonymous visits to all the establishments listed in the Guide. They accept no gifts or favours from proprietors

HOLBEACH Lincolnshire Map **08** TF32

Selected

Q Q Q Q **Pipwell Manor** Washway Rd, Saracens Head PE12 8AL (off A17) ☎ 01406 423119 FAX 01406 423119
Pipwell Manor is a period farmhouse sitting in its own beautiful grounds which feature a miniature railway that circles the gardens. Public rooms are tastefully furnished and consist of a dining room and lounge. The bedrooms are delightfully equipped and two of the rooms have modern en suite facilities. The house is fully no smoking.
4 bth/shr No smoking Tea and coffee making facilities No dogs Cen ht CTV No children 5yrs 4P No coaches Free use of cycles Large garden
ROOMS: s £30; d £40

HOLBECK Nottinghamshire Map **08** SK57

Selected

Q Q Q Q **Browns** The Old Orchard Cottage, Holbeck S80 3NF (6m from M1 junct 30, 0.5m off A616 Sheffield/Newark road)
☎ 01909 720659 FAX 01909 720659
Closed Xmas wk
This beautiful 18th-century cottage stands in lovely grounds with a dovecote, pond, and shallow ford on the drive. Both bedrooms are in converted farm buildings adjacent to the main house and have been well furnished. Joan Brown rightly prides herself on the breakfasts served in the elegant dining room. There is also a very welcoming lounge.

contd.

2 annexe shr (1 fmly) No smoking in 1 bedrooms No smoking in dining room No smoking in lounges CTV in all bedrooms Tea and coffee making facilities No dogs (ex guide dogs) Cen ht CTV No children 6yrs 3P No coaches
ROOMS: s £35; d £42*

HOLMFIRTH West Yorkshire Map 07 SE10

Selected

Q Q Q Q **Holme Castle Country Hotel** The Village, Holme HD7 1QG (2m SW of Holmfirth on A6024) (The Circle)
☎ 01484 680680 FAX 01484 686764

This delightful Victorian house stands at the head of the Holme Valley and enjoys superb views. The drawing room features oak panelling and parquet flooring, and an open fire burns on colder days. Bedrooms are generally spacious and are freshly decorated. Evening meals are available by arrangement and fresh local produce is used in the imaginative cooking. The house is fully no smoking.

8 rms (5 bth/shr) (3 fmly) No smoking CTV in all bedrooms No dogs (ex guide dogs) Licensed Cen ht CTV ch fac 12P No coaches Solarium Childrens playground Last d noon
ROOMS: s £30-£50; d £50-£70; wkly b&b £158-£315; wkly hlf-bd £233-£425*
CARDS:

Q Q Q **White Horse** Scholes Rd, Jackson Bridge HD7 7HF (off A616 towards Sheffield, 1m from New Mill)
☎ 01484 683940
Closed 24-25 Dec & 31 Jan

Good honest Yorkshire hospitality is provided by the Backhouse family at this pub which features in the TV series 'Last of the Summer Wine'. The walls are adorned with photographs of the stars of the programme, and Ron Backhouse, the landlord, is now a member of the cast. The bedrooms are cosy and well furnished, and a good range of food is served in the pleasant bar.

5 bth/shr (3 fmly) CTV in all bedrooms Tea and coffee making facilities No dogs (ex guide dogs) Cen ht 14P Last d 9.30pm
ROOMS: s £25; d £40*
MEALS: Lunch £1.90-£3.95 Dinner £1.90-£3.95*

HOLNE Devon Map 03 SX76

Selected

Q Q Q Q **Wellpritton** *(SX716704)* TQ13 7RX (from A38 follow signs for Ashburton, then take Princetown & Two Bridges road for approx 3m at AA telephone turn left then 1st right)
☎ 01364 631273 Mrs S Gifford

Tucked away in the fold of a hill on the edge of the Dartmoor National Park, Wellpritton is an ideal place for walkers and riders. The farm has a relaxed atmosphere and guests are assured of a friendly welcome. All the rooms are tastefully decorated and well equipped; two are suitable for families and all the rooms have many thoughtful extras. Evening dinners make good use of local produce. Visitors are welcome to bring well behaved dogs and good sized kennels are available.

4 rms (1 bth 2 shr) (2 fmly) No smoking in bedrooms No smoking in dining room CTV in 2 bedrooms Tea and coffee making facilities Cen ht CTV ch fac 6P Outdoor swimming pool Games room Snooker Table tennis Skittles 15 acres mixed Last d 12 noon
ROOMS: s £19-£22.50; d £38-£45*

HOLSWORTHY Devon Map 02 SS30

Selected

Q Q Q Q **Bickford Arms** Brandis Corner EX22 7XY (from A30 follow A3079 Hornsworthy road to Dunsland Cross and turn right. 400yds on left hand side is Brandis corner and hotel)
☎ 01409 221318 & 221693 FAX 01409 221781

Recently restored by the resident proprietors Keith and Laura Phipps, the inn now offers accommodation of a high standard. Five bedrooms have been tastefully furnished and equipped with modern comforts; one has a spacious wrought iron balcony. A blackboard menu offers a range of interesting meals and includes old fashioned homemade pies for which The Bickford Arms is well known. There is a beer garden and a games area where children can play while the adults relax.

5 bth/shr (5 fmly) No smoking in bedrooms No smoking in area of dining room No smoking in 1 lounge CTV in all bedrooms Tea and coffee making facilities Direct dial from bedrooms No dogs (ex guide dogs) Cen ht 46P Last d 9.30pm
ROOMS: s £35-£38; d £50-£59.50*
MEALS: Lunch £9-£15&alc Dinner £12-£26&alc*
CARDS:

Selected

Q Q Q Q ***Clawford Vineyard*** Clawton EX22 6PN (A388 Holsworth to Launceston road, turn left at Clawton cross roads, 1.5m to T-junct, turn left into village) ☎ 01409 254177

Situated in the peaceful Claw Valley, Clawford Vineyard, as its name suggests, is a working vineyard and cider orchard where guests can sample the produce. Extensive coarse fishing is available, with some monster carp awaiting anglers in several well-stocked lakes. The spacious bedrooms are a recent addition, all exceedingly well furnished and equipped. The lounge, spacious bar and games room look out over the lakes. Meals are served in the conservatory which offers views of the abundant wildlife.

2 rms (2 fmly) No smoking CTV in all bedrooms Tea and coffee making facilities No dogs Licensed Cen ht CTV No children 5yrs 46P Tennis (grass) Fishing Last d 8pm

Q Q Q **Leworthy** *(SS323012)* EX22 6SJ (leave Holsworthy via Bodmin St, past the Chapel in the direction of North Tamerton, Leworthy is signposted left after 3m)
☎ 01409 253488 FAX 01409 254671 Mr & Mrs J R Barrington
Closed 31 Mar-31 Oct

This friendly farmhouse is rurally located and benefits from a wealth of children's play equipment, a well-stocked fishing lake and a pitch and putt course. Bedrooms are comfortable and well equipped. A hearty breakfast is served in the spacious lounge/dining room which also has a table tennis table. There are a number of self-catering cottages also available.

3 shr (2 fmly) No smoking in bedrooms No smoking in dining room No smoking in lounges CTV in all bedrooms Tea and coffee making facilities No dogs (ex guide dogs) Cen ht 20P Outdoor swimming pool Tennis (hard) Fishing Darts Table tennis 1/2 size snooker table 200 acres mixed Last d 6pm

HOLT Norfolk Map **09** TG03

QQQ **Lawns Private Hotel** 26 Station Rd NR25 6BS (Hotel located opposite Greshams cricket ground, 20yds from town war memorial) ☎ 01263 713390 FAX 713390
This small family-run private hotel is close to the town centre and offers a good choice of accommodation. Rooms are individually decorated and equipped with radio alarms, colour television, beverage making facilities and hair dryers. All but one has en suite facilities. Public rooms offer a comfortable lounge, a separate bar and a bright dining room where guests can enjoy dinner by prior arrangement.
11 bth/shr No smoking CTV in all bedrooms Tea and coffee making facilities No dogs Licensed Cen ht No children 12yrs 12P No coaches Last d 6pm
ROOMS: s £35; d £70-£75
CARDS:

QQQ **The Old Telephone Exchange** The Old Telephone Exchange, 37 New St NR25 6JH (turn off A148 into Holt High St take New St which is beside Barclays Bank, establishment approx 200yds on left) ☎ 01263 712992
A non-smoking establishment with three well maintained bedrooms, offering a spacious open plan lounge/dining room with a widescreen television, books and games. Bedrooms are on the ground floor and are well appointed with co-ordinated decor and soft furnishings.
3 shr No smoking CTV in all bedrooms Tea and coffee making facilities Cen ht CTV No children 5yrs 2P
ROOMS: s £25-£30; d £30-£36

HONITON Devon Map **03** ST10

Selected

QQQQ **Colestocks House** Payhembury Rd, Feniton EX14 0JR (turn off A30 at Pattersons Cross, to Feniton/Payhembury. Hotel 2m on left) ☎ 01404 850633 FAX 01404 850901
Apr-Oct
This delightful 16th-century thatched property is only 500yds from Feniton main line railway station. The spacious bedrooms are individually decorated and the bar, with its collection of old clubs and prints, is a must for golf enthusiasts. The drawing room opens on to the sunny gardens. In the dining room guests can enjoy Mrs Broster's home-cooked meals which make use of local ingredients.
8 bth/shr No smoking in bedrooms No smoking in dining room No smoking in 1 lounge CTV in all bedrooms Tea and coffee making facilities No dogs (ex guide dogs) Licensed Cen ht CTV No children 10yrs 10P No coaches Last d 7pm
CARDS:

QQQ *The Crest* Moorcox Ln, Wilmington EX14 9JU (3m E of Honiton on A35 at eastern end of village, after the river bridge turn left, the Crest is 100 metres on right) ☎ 01404 831419
The Crest, with its two acres of lawns and gardens has superb views across the Umborne Valley. The guest wing, recently built, is self-contained and affords complete privacy; each room is equipped with modern comforts and has been tastefully decorated. Breakfast is served around one large table in the dining room and there is a bright conservatory overlooking the garden.
3 bth/shr (1 fmly) No smoking in bedrooms No smoking in dining room CTV in all bedrooms Tea and coffee making facilities Cen ht 6P No coaches

Selected

QQQQ *The Heathfield* Walnut Rd EX14 8UG (from A30 onto A375 Sidmouth road and in 0.5m at mini-rbt turn right the right again. Walnut Av 1st on right) (Old English Pub Co) ☎ 01404 45321 & 45322 FAX 01404 45321
This 16th-century traditional thatched Devon former farmhouse, is now a busy free house, with accommodation and bars retaining many original features. The bedrooms are furnished with modern pine furniture and one room has a unique hand crafted four-poster bed. The public areas include an attractive split level dining room and a function room suitable for small parties.
8 bth/shr (1 fmly) CTV in all bedrooms Tea and coffee making facilities Direct dial from bedrooms Cen ht ch fac 50P Skittle alley Last d 9.30pm
CARDS:

QQ *Roebuck (ST147001)* EX14 0PB (western end of Honiton-by-pass) ☎ 01404 42225 Mrs I Underdown
Conveniently situated just off the A30, outside Honiton, Roebuck Farm has been personally owned and run by Mrs Underdown for many years. There is a comfortable lounge and traditionally styled accommodation. Breakfast is served in the bright dining room.
3 rms (1 fmly) No smoking in bedrooms No smoking in dining room CTV in 2 bedrooms Tea and coffee making facilities Cen ht CTV 180 acres dairy mixed

HOOK Hampshire Map **04** SU75

QQ **Cedar Court Country** Reading Rd RG27 9DB (1m N of Hook on B3349) ☎ 01256 762178 FAX 01256 762178
This pretty guest house is tucked away at the end of a private drive. There is a lovely garden tended by owner Mrs Jennions. All bedrooms are well equipped and nicely furnished. There is a cosy lounge and smart dining room where breakfasts are served.
6 rms (5 shr) No smoking in dining room CTV in all bedrooms Tea and coffee making facilities No dogs (ex guide dogs) Cen ht CTV 6P No coaches
ROOMS: s £22-£29.50; d £39.50-£45*
CARDS:

QQ *Cherry Lodge* Reading Rd RG27 9DB (on B3349) ☎ 01256 762532 FAX 01256 762532
Closed Xmas
Cherry Lodge is an attractive brick built modern bungalow set back from the Reading Road. There is a pretty pond and fountain, and planters of flowers which greet guests at the entrance. Mr Phillips serves hearty dinners through the week and all bedrooms are well equipped.
6 bth/shr (1 fmly) No smoking in dining room CTV in all bedrooms Tea and coffee making facilities Direct dial from bedrooms Cen ht CTV 20P Last d midnight
CARDS:

Q Q ***Oaklea*** London Rd RG27 9LA (on A30, 200yds from centre of Hook)
☎ 01256 762673 FAX 01256 762150
Improvements continue at this friendly guest house which is not far from the M3 and Basingstoke. Mr and Mrs Volstaker Field are charming hosts who take great pride in The Oaklea. Most bedrooms are en suite, all have various home comforts. The comfortable lounge and licensed bar are further attractions.
10 rms (4 shr) (1 fmly) No smoking in 4 bedrooms No smoking in dining room CTV in all bedrooms Tea and coffee making facilities Licensed Cen ht CTV 11P No coaches Last d noon
CARDS:

HOPE Derbyshire Map **07** SK18

Selected

Q Q Q Q **Bowling Green** Smalldale, Bradwell S33 9JQ
☎ 01433 620450 FAX 01433 620890
Situated amidst glorious scenery, this welcoming 16th-century inn is popular with locals and visitors alike for the range of freshly prepared meals served. The adjacent barn has recently been converted to guest bedrooms, with attractive furnishings and a useful level of equipment provided. Many of the bedrooms, as with the restaurant, have fine views over the surrounding hills, whilst ground floor rooms also have direct access to the patio.
6 shr No smoking in bedrooms No smoking in area of dining room CTV in all bedrooms Tea and coffee making facilities No dogs Cen ht No children 12yrs 60P Last d 9pm
ROOMS: d £50-£65; wkly b&b £175-£227.50✻
MEALS: Lunch £11.45-£20.40alc Dinner £11.45-£20.40alc✻
CARDS:

Q Q Q **Round Meadow Barn** *(SK189836)* Parsons Ln S33 6RA (0.5m from Hope go N at staggered x-rds, 200yds over rail bridge. 200yds turn right into Hay barn yard, through gates across 3 fields house on left)
☎ 01433 621347 FAX 621347 Mr & Mrs J G Harris
A gated farm lane leads to this recently converted barn, set in open fields and enjoying fine views in all directions. Original features have been retained wherever possible, including stone walls and exposed timbers. The spacious bedrooms share an adjacent modern bathroom and breakfast is served around one table in the large farmhouse style kitchen.
2 rms (2 fmly) No smoking CTV in all bedrooms Tea and coffee making facilities 8P 4 acres non-working
ROOMS: s £25; d £38✻

Premier Selected

Q Q Q Q Q **Underleigh House** Edale Rd S33 6RF (from village church on A6187 (formerly A625) take Edale road for 1m then left into lane)
☎ 01433 621372 FAX 01433 621324
Set at the end of a private lane, this former barn has been tastefully converted into very comfortable accommodation by the owners, Barbara and Tony Singleton. Bedrooms have a cottagey feel, in keeping with the style of the house, and many thoughtful extras have been provided, even a resident teddy bear. Two of the rooms are on the ground floor and have patio doors leading to the award-winning garden. Tony takes charge in the kitchen, offering a choice of freshly prepared dishes, served around one large table in the stone-flagged dining room. The lounge is comfortable and spacious, with a small bar in the corner.
6 bth/shr No smoking CTV in all bedrooms Tea and coffee making facilities Direct dial from bedrooms No dogs (ex guide dogs) Licensed Cen ht No children 12yrs 6P No coaches Last d noon
ROOMS: s £44-£59; d £64-£94; wkly b&b £210-£315; wkly hlf-bd £325-£425
CARDS:

HORLEY Surrey

For accommodation details see under **Gatwick Airport, London**

HORNCASTLE Lincolnshire Map **08** TF26

Selected

Q Q Q Q ***Greenfield Farm*** *(TF175745)* Minting LN9 5RX (from Lincoln, A158 through Wragby and after 3m turn right at Midge Pub, farm 1m on right) ☎ 01507 578457 Mrs J Bankes Price
Closed Xmas & New Year
Standing in a rural setting, this spacious and modern farmhouse provides well furnished and comfortable bedrooms. There is a pleasant lounge and guests take breakfast around a large table in the cosy dining room. The gardens are well tended and include a large, well stocked pond.
3 rms (2 shr) No smoking Tea and coffee making facilities No dogs (ex guide dogs) Cen ht CTV No children 10yrs 12P 387 acres arable

HORN'S CROSS Devon Map **02** SS32

Premier Selected

Q Q Q Q Q **Lower Waytown** EX39 5DN (A39 from Bideford through Horns Cross, 0.5m past Hoops Inn, Roundhouse on left)
☎ 01237 451787 FAX 01237 451787
Closed Xmas & New Year
Lower Waytown is situated in 5 acres of beautifully kept gardens and grounds with stream-fed ponds, ornamental waterfowl and black swans. Many features of the old barn, and roundhouse from which it was converted, have been retained. The unique round sitting room with exposed beams and an inglenook fireplace is spacious and comfortable, and adjoins

the attractive dining room where guests can enjoy delicious home-cooked breakfasts at one large table. There are three tastefully furnished bedrooms, each with pretty co-ordinating fabrics and modern comforts.
3 bth/shr No smoking CTV in all bedrooms Tea and coffee making facilities No dogs Cen ht CTV No children 12yrs 8P No coaches
ROOMS: s £37-£40; d £47-£55*

HORSFORD Norfolk Map **09** TG11

Q Q Q **Church Farm** Church St NR10 3DB (A140, past airport take B1149, approx 1m turn right at Yeast & Feast Inn, premises 100 yards on left) ☎ 01603 898020 & 898582 FAX 01603 891649
Set peacefully in 2.5 acres of gardens, adjacent to the village church, this smart, well kept property is just four miles from the city centre. The bedrooms are bright and spacious with modern en suite shower rooms. There is a cosy guest TV lounge, and friendly proprietor Pat Hinchley serves a hearty breakfast in the attractive dining room.
6 shr (2 fmly) No smoking in dining room CTV in all bedrooms Tea and coffee making facilities No dogs (ex guide dogs) Cen ht CTV 20P No coaches
ROOMS: s £20-£25; d £36-£40*
CARDS:

HORSHAM ST FAITH Norfolk Map **09** TG21

Q Q Q **Elm Farm Country House** 55 Norwich Rd NR10 3HH (on A140 Cromer road from Norwich, pass airport, take right hand turning into village) ☎ 01603 898366 FAX 01603 897129
rs 25-26 Dec
Originally a collection of 17th-century farm buildings, this attractive property offers comfortable accommodation yet retains much of its historical charm. The chalet-style bedrooms have modern en suite facilities. In the enlarged farmhouse, guests can enjoy lunch and dinner and in the summer, afternoon tea is served.
16 annexe bth/shr (1 fmly) No smoking in 10 bedrooms No smoking in dining room No smoking in lounges CTV in all bedrooms Tea and coffee making facilities Direct dial from bedrooms No dogs (ex guide dogs) Licensed Cen ht CTV 20P No coaches
ROOMS: s £31-£36; d £50-£56; wkly b&b £173.25-£252; wkly hlf-bd £217-£252
CARDS:

HORTON Dorset Map **04** SU00

Q Q Q **Horton** Cranborne Rd BH21 5AD (on B3078 between Wimborne and Cranbourne) ☎ 01258 840252 FAX 01258 841400
Originally part of Lord Shaftesbury's estate, this 18th-century inn commands spectacular views of the surrounding downlands. The popular bar has a log fire in the winter months, and serves a range of hot and cold snacks. There is also a candlelit restaurant with a more extensive menu. Most rooms have en suite facilities, and are provided with such extra touches as bath robes.
9 rms (7 bth/shr) No smoking in dining room CTV in all bedrooms Tea and coffee making facilities Cen ht 100P Last d 9.30pm
ROOMS: s £19.50-£30; d £39-£55; wkly b&b £135-£200; wkly hlf-bd £240-£305
MEALS: Lunch £12.95-£20.95alc Dinner £12.95-£15.50&alc
CARDS:

HORTON IN RIBBLESDALE North Yorkshire Map **07** SD87

Q Q ***Crown Hotel*** BD24 0HF (take B6479 from Settle) ☎ 01729 860209 FAX 01729 860444
This popular village inn is located on the Pennine Way, with views over Pen-y-Ghent. Bedrooms are pleasantly furnished and a choice from the menu, or blackboard specials, is available in the character beamed bar or dining room, overlooking the garden.
9 rms (7 bth/shr) (4 fmly) Tea and coffee making facilities Cen ht CTV 15P Last d 8.30pm

HOUGH-ON-THE-HILL Lincolnshire Map **08** SK94

Selected

Q Q Q Q **Brownlow Arms** Grantham Rd NG32 2AZ
☎ 01400 250234 FAX 01400 250772
This quaint country inn stands on a hill surrounded by pretty stone cottages in an otherwise flat area of Lincolnshire. With stone mullioned windows, a real fire, a delightful restaurant and well equipped bedrooms, the inn offers the standards of a star-rated hotel. A blackboard menu has a good range of food to be eaten in the lounge-bar or the dining room.
7 bth/shr CTV in all bedrooms Tea and coffee making facilities Direct dial from bedrooms No dogs (ex guide dogs) Cen ht No children 5yrs 35P No coaches Last d 9.30pm
ROOMS: s £40; d £52-£60*
MEALS: Bar Lunch £6-£10alc Dinner £20-£30alc*
CARDS:

HOUNSLOW Greater London Map **04** TQ17

For accommodation details see under **Heathrow Airport**

HOVE East Sussex

See **Brighton & Hove**

HUBY North Yorkshire Map **08** SE56

Q Q **The New Inn Motel** Main St YO61 1HQ (between A19 & B1363)
☎ 01347 810219
The bedrooms here are well equipped and comfortable modern motel rooms. There is a cosy breakfast room and the resident owners provide a friendly and helpful style of service. There are plenty of good pubs in the village all serving quality food.
8 shr (3 fmly) No smoking in 2 bedrooms No smoking in dining room CTV in all bedrooms Tea and coffee making facilities Cen ht 8P No coaches
ROOMS: s fr £28; d fr £45; wkly b&b £115-£150

HUDDERSFIELD West Yorkshire Map **07** SE11

Selected

Q Q Q Q ***Weavers Shed Restaurant with Rooms*** Knowl Rd, Golcar HD7 4AN ☎ 01484 654284
Comfortable and well equipped bedrooms are offered at this recently converted mill owners house, situated in a quiet village just three miles from Huddersfield. There is an inviting bar lounge leading into the well-established restaurant where fresh produce, much of it from the Weavers Shed's own kitchen gardens, is used.
5 rms

HULL East Riding of Yorkshire Map **08** TA02

Q Q Q **Earlesmere Hotel** 76/78 Sunnybank, Spring Bank West HU3 1LQ (M62, under Humber Bridge, after 4m turn left, go over 2 rdbts to T-junct, turn left then left at next T-junct, 2nd left, hotel at bottom of street)
☎ 01482 341977 FAX 01482 473714
Closed Xmas
Situated in a quiet side road, this mainly commercial hotel offers modern bedrooms together with a cosy lounge and a separate breakfast room. Service is friendly and polite from the resident owners.
9 rms (7 shr) (4 fmly) No smoking in dining room No smoking in lounges CTV in all bedrooms Tea and coffee making facilities Licensed Cen ht CTV
ROOMS: s £18-£28; d £28-£38; wkly b&b £120-£200
CARDS:

HUNGERFORD Berkshire Map **04** SU36

Q Q Q **Marshgate Cottage Hotel** Marsh Ln RG17 0QX (from A338 turn right beside railway bridge into Church St, 0.5m pass used car garage & immediate right into Marsh Ln.At end on right)
☎ 01488 682307 FAX 01488 685475
Closed 24 Dec-15 Jan
This charming small hotel is situated by the Kennet and Avon Canal and only a short distance from the centre of Hungerford. The comfortable, well equipped bedrooms have many thoughtful extras including direct dial telephones. There is a small lounge for guests use, and the spacious dining room is where guests eat a hearty breakfast. Special diet are catered for by prior arrangement.
9 bth/shr (2 fmly) No smoking in 3 bedrooms CTV in all bedrooms Tea and coffee making facilities Direct dial from bedrooms Licensed Cen ht 9P
ROOMS: s fr £35.50; d £48.50-£55
CARDS:

HUNSTANTON Norfolk Map **09** TF64

Selected

Q Q Q Q **Claremont** 35 Greevegate PE36 6AF (off A149, turn left at Greevegate, opposite recreation ground. House is 300mtrs on right before St Edmunds church) ☎ 01485 533171
Guests can expect warm hospitality and friendly service at this attractively decorated and well maintained guest house. The bedrooms are nicely furnished and each has a good range of extras that include colour television, hair dryer and clock radio. There is also a ground floor room with disabled access and two feature rooms, one of which has a four poster, whilst the other has a canopied bed. The cosy public rooms include a comfortable lounge with books and magazines, and a dining room where guests can enjoy breakfast.
7 bth/shr (1 fmly) No smoking CTV in all bedrooms Tea and coffee making facilities Licensed Cen ht CTV No children 5yrs 4P No coaches
ROOMS: s £23-£25; d £38-£46; wkly b&b £120-£145

Q Q Q ***Gate Lodge*** 2 Westgate PE36 5AL (from A149 at Hunstanton rdbt turn left towards sea (Oasis Way), right at mini-rdbt at bottom of hill, Gate Lodge is approx 400yds on right) ☎ 01485 533549
Mar-Oct
Guests can expect a friendly welcome at this small family-run guest house, situated close to the beach. The bedrooms are bright and cheerful in appearance, most are of comfortable proportions and each has modern en suite facilities, mainly shower rooms. The public rooms feature a comfortable first floor lounge with a range of books and puzzles, and a ground floor dining room where guests can enjoy a hearty breakfast.
6 bth/shr No smoking in dining room No smoking in lounges CTV in all bedrooms Tea and coffee making facilities Licensed Cen ht CTV No children 5yrs 6P No coaches Last d 3pm

QQQ **Green Shutters** 44 Cliff Pde PE36 6EH (exit A147 into Cliff Parade at lighthouse, premises are 350 yards past lighthouse)
☎ 01485 533240 0468 384410 FAX 534874
Closed 20 Dec-5 Jan
Chris Wallace welcomes guests to his smartly appointed guest house, which sits in a prime location overlooking the sea, and is only a short distance from the town centre. Bedrooms have been individually decorated with cheerful soft furnishings and colour co-ordinated decor. There is a cheery breakfast room where good hearty breakfasts are served.
4 bth/shr No smoking in dining room No smoking in lounges
CTV in all bedrooms Tea and coffee making facilities No dogs Cen ht
No children 5yrs 4P No coaches
ROOMS: s £20-£35; d £30-£50; wkly b&b £105-£175*

QQQ **Narara House** 9 Lincoln Square PE36 6DW (from A149 take the coast road and turn off almost opposite bowling greens into Lincoln Square)
☎ 01485 534290
Closed Xmas-Jan
This delightful Edwardian house overlooks Lincoln Square green, gently sloping towards the seafront at the end of the road. The well maintained and attractively decorated bedrooms are spacious, and all have easy chairs or sofas and an excellent range of facilities, including hairdryer, clock/radio, and magazines. A hearty freshly prepared breakfast and a set three course evening meal are served in the elegant dining room at separate tables.
5 bth/shr No smoking CTV in all bedrooms Tea and coffee making facilities No dogs Cen ht No children 9yrs 3P No coaches Last d 9.30am
ROOMS: s £24-£25; d £42-£45

QQ ***Richmond House Hotel*** 6-8 Westgate PE36 5AL
☎ 01485 532601
Etr-Oct
This privately owned hotel is situated close to the seafront and offers well maintained accommodation throughout. Although the rooms vary in size they are equipped with a good range of extras which include TVs and beverage making equipment. Some of the rooms also have modern en suite facilities. The public areas feature a dining room and a well stocked bar where Dave Hallas entertains guests with live music on his Wurlitzer organ.
13 rms (1 bth 4 shr) No smoking in dining room CTV in all bedrooms
Tea and coffee making facilities Licensed Lift Cen ht No children 14yrs

---

QQQ **Sutton House Hotel** 24 Northgate PE36 6AP
(turn left off A149 into Greevegate, 2nd turning on right by Nat West bank, hotel is 300yds on right)
☎ 01485 532552 FAX 01485 532552
This friendly family-run guest house is close to the sea front and town centre. The public rooms feature a comfortable ground floor lounge, a small well stocked bar and a soundly appointed dining room. Guests can enjoy a freshly cooked breakfast or dinner by prior arrangement, choosing from the daily menu which features lovely home made desserts. The bedrooms are bright and cheerful and equipped with a useful range of extras including TVs and beverage making equipment.
8 bth/shr (2 fmly) No smoking in bedrooms No smoking in dining room
CTV in all bedrooms Tea and coffee making facilities Licensed Cen ht
CTV 5P No coaches Last d 2pm
ROOMS: s £25-£30; d £40-£55; wkly b&b £140-£175;
wkly hlf-bd £210-£245*

QQ **The White Cottage** 19 Wodehouse Rd PE36 6JW
☎ 01485 532380
In a tranquil setting close to the championship golf course and the beach, The White Cottage is surrounded by pretty lawns and gardens on all sides. The downstairs areas offer a cosy sitting room with a television and a spacious dining room with individual tables. The comfy bedrooms are spacious and attractively decorated, enjoying sea views on the horizon.
3 rms Cen ht No children 3yrs 11P No coaches Last d 6.30pm
ROOMS: s £17-£20*

225

HUNTON North Yorkshire Map 07 SE19

Selected

QQQQ **The Countryman's** DL8 1PY (just off A684 Bedale/Leyburn road between Patrick Brompton and Constable Burton)
☎ 01677 450554 FAX 01677 450570
The Countryman's is an attractive, traditional village inn offering a wide range of well cooked food as well as real ale. The bedrooms are well furnished and have been very thoughtfully equipped to include personal touches. The resident owners are very friendly and helpful.
7 bth/shr No smoking in bedrooms No smoking in dining room CTV in all bedrooms Tea and coffee making facilities No dogs (ex guide dogs) Cen ht No children 14yrs 20P No coaches Pool table Last d 9.30pm
ROOMS: s £35; d £45-£50*
MEALS: Bar Lunch £2.50-£6alc Dinner £5-£15alc*
CARDS:

HUTTON-LE-HOLE North Yorkshire Map 08 SE79

QQ **The Barn Hotel & Tearooms** YO62 6UA (turn off A170 towards Hutton Le Hole and contine for2.5m, premises are on the right in centre of village opposite stone cross on village green) ☎ 01751 417311
Closed Xmas
This converted and extended former barn is situated opposite the village green. Good value and modern accommodation is available and home cooked evening meals are a particular feature.
8 rms (3 bth/shr) (1 fmly) No smoking Tea and coffee making facilities No dogs (ex guide dogs) Licensed Cen ht CTV 15P Last d 7.30pm
ROOMS: s £22-£28; d £44-£56*
CARDS:

HYDE Greater Manchester Map 07 SJ99

Selected

Q Q Q Q **Needhams** *(SJ968925)* Uplands Rd, Werneth Low, Gee Cross SK14 3AQ (A560 at Gee Cross turn into Joel Lane, at top of hill turn left into Werneth Low Rd, 0.5 mile and Uplands Rd is on the right) ☎ 0161 368 4610 FAX 0161 367 9106 Mr & Mrs I Walsh

This is a delightful stone built farmhouse in an elevated position, which has been extensively restored and now provides modern accommodation. The bedrooms are well equipped and include many personal touches. The lounge and dining room are spacious and have open fires when needed. Good home cooking is served by arrangement and guests are welcome to use the courtesy bar.

7 rms (6 shr) (1 fmly) No smoking in bedrooms CTV in all bedrooms Tea and coffee making facilities Direct dial from bedrooms Licensed Cen ht CTV 14P Golf 12 Riding 30 acres beef Last d 9pm

ROOMS: s £20-£22; d £32-£34*

CARDS:

HYTHE Kent Map 05 TR13

Q Q Q **The White House** 27 Napier Gardens CT21 6DD (exit M20 junct 11 for Hythe, follow one-way system into Hythe town centre, turn right 100yds after Red Lion pub, then take 2nd left into Napier Gdns) ☎ 01303 266252

The White House is situated in quiet surroundings close to the seafront. The spacious bedrooms are individually decorated and thoughtfully furnished. The cosy dining room is located on the first floor and guests are seated at one polished wood table. Proprietor Mr Hutchison offers a generous freshly cooked breakfast.

2 shr No smoking CTV in all bedrooms Tea and coffee making facilities No dogs (ex guide dogs) Cen ht No children 10yrs 3P No coaches

ROOMS: d fr £40*

ILAM Staffordshire Map 07 SK15

Selected

Q Q Q Q **Stanshope Hall** Stanshope DE6 2AD (exit A515 towards Thorpe & Ilam, at Ilam turn right at memorial, premises are 3m further on towards Alstonefield) ☎ 01335 310278 FAX 01335 310470

Stanshope Hall is situated in the heart of the southern Peak District, on the brow of a hill between the rivers Dove and Manifold and features magnificent views across rolling countryside. It has been lovingly restored to maintain many of its original features, which include, an 18th century Hopton stone staircase, Georgian shutters and some of the old servant bell handles. The accommodation is neatly appointed and has been decorated by local artists to create interesting rooms. The public rooms feature a drawing room which has a moorland scene, complete with blue sky, clouds and birds, as well as a dining room, where guests can enjoy a freshly cooked breakfast or dinner which is available by prior arrangement.

3 bth No smoking in bedrooms No smoking in dining room CTV in all bedrooms Tea and coffee making facilities Direct dial from bedrooms No dogs (ex guide dogs) Licensed Cen ht 3P No coaches Trampoline Last d 8pm

ROOMS: s £25-£40; d £50-£80; wkly b&b £175-£280*

CARDS:

ILFORD Greater London Map 05 TQ48

Q Q Q ***Cranbrook Hotel*** 22-24 Coventry Rd IG1 4QR (exit A406 E onto A118, at top turn onto A123, second turning on right, at Ilford Station turn left, second right) ☎ 0181 554 6544 & 4765 FAX 0181 518 1463

This long-established, family-run hotel is conveniently situated close to the town centre, shopping mall and Gants Hill underground station. The smart modern bedrooms are well equipped. A well appointed bar-lounge is augmented by a beamed dining room where a daily three-course fixed-price dinner menu is offered Monday to Thursday.

30 rms (26 bth/shr) (5 fmly) No smoking in 10 bedrooms No smoking in dining room CTV in all bedrooms Tea and coffee making facilities Direct dial from bedrooms Licensed Cen ht CTV 30P Last d 7.30pm

CARDS:

See advertisement under LONDON

Q Q Q **Park Hotel** 327 Cranbrook Rd IG1 4UE (on A123 just south of junct with A12, Gantshill Rbt) ☎ 0181 554 9616 & 0181 554 7187 FAX 0181 518 2700

Situated directly opposite Valentines Park and convenient for the town centre, this attractive family-run hotel offers a good range of modern bedrooms designed to appeal to the corporate or leisure guest. A la carte dinner with daily specials is provided Monday to Thursday from 6.30 to 8pm and service of light refreshments is available throughout the day.

20 rms (7 bth 10 shr) (3 fmly) CTV in all bedrooms Tea and coffee making facilities Licensed Cen ht CTV 23P Last d 7.45pm

ROOMS: s £30.50-£46.50; d £42.50-£65*

CARDS: See advertisement under LONDON

Q Q Q **Woodville** 10-12 Argyle Rd IG1 3BQ (exit M25 onto M11, then A406, exit at Ilford junc, second turning on left off Cranbrook Rd, past station turn second left) ☎ 0181 478 3779 FAX 478282

Comfortable bedrooms and good shower facilities combine with double glazing and TV to provide good accommodation at this friendly guest house. Families with children are particularly welcome. Service of light refreshments is available throughout the day. There is a comfortable sitting area combined with a beamed dining room and a furnished rear garden and terrace.

16 rms (2 bth 4 shr) (5 fmly) No smoking in dining room CTV in all bedrooms No dogs (ex guide dogs) Cen ht 11P

ROOMS: s £25-£40; d £42-£50* See advertisement under LONDON

ILFRACOMBE Devon Map **02** SS54

See also West Down

Collingdale Hotel Larkstone Ter EX34 9NU
(on A339 travelling W from Combe Martin, 0.5m past Hele Bay on right. Travelling E through Ilfracombe, on left past B3230 turn off)
☎ 01271 863770 FAX 01271 863770
This small, family run hotel is within walking distance of the town centre and the town's beaches. Bedrooms are comfortably furnished and attractively decorated. A spacious lounge and bar are available for guests. An evening meal is served by prior arrangement.
9 rms (8 shr) (3 fmly) No smoking in bedrooms No smoking in dining room Tea and coffee making facilities Licensed CTV Last d 6pm
ROOMS: s £19.50; d £37-£39*
CARDS:

Cresta Hotel Torrs Park EX34 8AY ☎ 01271 863742
May-Oct
This well established private hotel has been owned and run by the Seddon Family for over 50 years. The present generation continue to make improvements and to maintain the friendly, relaxed atmosphere. Bedrooms are well furnished, bright and comfortable; several are on the ground floor and a lift serves all the upper floors. Some evening entertainment is organised in the bar.
29 shr (15 fmly) No smoking in area of dining room No smoking in 1 lounge CTV in all bedrooms Tea and coffee making facilities Licensed Lift Cen ht CTV 35P Putting green Last d 7pm
CARDS:

Dedes Hotel 1-3 The Promenade EX34 9BD
(on approach road into Ilfracombe follow signposts to seafront, hotel is on right) ☎ 01271 862545 FAX 01271 862234
Closed 23-26 Dec
Centrally situated on the seafront, this family-run, small hotel offers a relaxed atmosphere. The best use has been made of the available space in the well equipped bedrooms, with front-facing rooms benefiting from the views. Guests have a choice of eating options; the cafè, the more formal restaurant or lighter meals from the bar. The resident proprietors also own a championship clay-pigeon shooting ground.
17 rms (10 bth 2 shr) (6 fmly) No smoking in area of dining room CTV in all bedrooms Tea and coffee making facilities Licensed CTV 6P Clay pigeon shooting Last d 9.45pm
CARDS:

Southcliffe Hotel Torrs Park EX34 8AZ (on A361 from Barnstaple, left at 1st set of lights, left at 2nd set, then immediately left. Hotel 400mtrs on left) ☎ 01271 862958
Mar-Oct
This substantial, brick-built Victorian villa is run by young and enthusiastic owners, Adrian and Sarah Williams who are working through a programme of refurbishment and modernisation, retaining the original features of the property, such as stained glass windows. Each evening a short, well-balanced menu is offered for guests by prior arrangement. A comfortable lounge and cosy bar are also available.
12 bth/shr (2 fmly) No smoking in bedrooms No smoking in dining room No smoking in lounges CTV in all bedrooms Tea and coffee making facilities No dogs Licensed Cen ht CTV No children 5yrs 10P Games room/playroom Last d 6pm
ROOMS: s £19-£23; d £38-£45; wkly b&b £130-£150; wkly hlf-bd £175-£195*
CARDS:

Strathmore Hotel 57 St Brannocks Rd EX34 8EQ
(on A361 approach into Ilfracombe, 0.5 from Mullacot Cross roundabout)
☎ 01271 862248 FAX 01271 864044
Situated close to the town centre, Strathmore Hotel is personally supervised by the owner. Bedrooms are stylish, comfortable and very well equipped. In the smartly appointed dining room a choice of menu is offered each evening, accompanied by a good selection of wines. The cosy lounge and the well-stocked bar are ideal places to relax.
9 rms (8 bth/shr) (3 fmly) No smoking in dining room No smoking in 1 lounge CTV in all bedrooms Tea and coffee making facilities Licensed Cen ht CTV 8P No coaches Last d 7pm
ROOMS: s £16-£18; d £36-£44; wkly b&b £112-£126; wkly hlf-bd £177-£191*
CARDS:

Selected

Varley House 13 Chambercombe Park Ter, Chambercombe Park EX34 9QW (follow A399 Combe Martin road and at swimming pool turn right) ☎ 01271 863927 FAX 01271 863927
mid Mar-end Oct
Built at the turn of the century, Varley House offers a genuinely warm welcome. Hospitality is provided by Roy and Barbara Gable, who have

contd.

many guests who return on a regular basis. The spacious lounge is the ideal venue to relax after a busy day exploring the area; a cosy bar is also available. A choice of well presented, home-cooked meals is served each evening by arrangement. In addition to the traditional breakfast, an array of lighter fare is also offered.
9 rms (8 bth/shr) (3 fmly) No smoking in bedrooms No smoking in dining room CTV in all bedrooms Tea and coffee making facilities Licensed Cen ht CTV No children 5yrs 8P No coaches Last d 5.30pm
ROOMS: s £24-£25; d £50-£52; wkly b&b £152-£164; wkly hlf-bd £210-£230
CARDS:

Selected

QQQQ **Waterloo House Hotel** Waterloo Ter, Fore St EX34 9DJ ☎ 01271 863060
Situated in the heart of old Ilfracombe, this charming listed Georgian building was formerly three cottage properties built in 1820 to commemorate the Battle of Waterloo. Chrissie and Geoff Twigger welcome guests to their stylish property. Bedrooms are individually furnished and decorated, using colour to create an atmosphere. Interesting dishes are provided for dinner and breakfast, using the finest of ingredients. The Wellington lounge and bar, with its open fire and comfortable seating is the ideal place to enjoy a pre-dinner drink, whilst taking in the atmosphere of times gone by.
10 rms (5 bth/shr) (3 fmly) No smoking in bedrooms No smoking in dining room No smoking in 1 lounge CTV in all bedrooms Tea and coffee making facilities No dogs (ex guide dogs) Licensed Cen ht CTV No children 12yrs Last d 8pm
ROOMS: s £25; d £50-£70
CARDS:

QQQ **Westwell Hall Hotel** Torrs Park EX34 8AZ
(from Barnstaple on A361 on approaching Ilfracombe turn left into Church Hill, left into Langleigh Rd, right at T-junc then second left)
☎ 01271 862792 FAX 01271 862792
Adjacent to National Trust parkland, this impressive Victorian property is set in an acre of gardens and occupies an elevated position amid the famous Torrs, yet is convenient for the beaches and shops. The individually furnished and decorated bedrooms vary in size and are well equipped. Evening dinner is served in the restaurant which overlooks the sunken garden and patio. A cosy, well stocked bar and small lounge are also available.
10 bth/shr No smoking in dining room CTV in all bedrooms Tea and coffee making facilities Licensed Cen ht CTV 14P No coaches Croquet Table tennis Last d 6pm
ROOMS: s £20-£23; d £40-£46; wkly b&b £135-£149; wkly hlf-bd £198-£212✳
CARDS:

ILKESTON Derbyshire Map **08** SK44

Premier Selected

QQQQQ **Red House Hotel** Wharncliffe Rd DE7 5HL (from A6007 follow signs for 'Market Place')
☎ 0115 932 2965 FAX 0115 932 1253
Closed 2wks for Xmas
Conveniently located close to the town centre, this fine Victorian building is surrounded by gardens. Spacious bedrooms are nicely furnished and well equipped, and a bar-lounge leads off the oak-panelled entrance hall with its original green-tiled fireplace. A range of freshly prepared dishes is offered in the dining room.
8 rms (7 bth/shr) (2 fmly) No smoking in dining room CTV in all bedrooms Tea and coffee making facilities Direct dial from bedrooms
No dogs (ex guide dogs) Licensed Cen ht 10P No coaches Last d 7pm
ROOMS: s £37-£42; d £49.50-£59.50; wkly b&b £259-£294✳
CARDS:

ILKLEY West Yorkshire Map **07** SE14

Selected

QQQQ **Grove Hotel** 66 The Grove LS29 9EQ ☎ 01943 600298 FAX 01943 817426
This very well cared for, small hotel offers thoughtfully equipped bedrooms together with a cosy lounge and small bar. Breakfast is served in the bright dining room and the hotel is convenient for several local restaurants. Very friendly and attentive service is provided by the resident owners, Mr and Mrs Thompson.
6 bth/shr (2 fmly) No smoking in dining room No smoking in lounges CTV in all bedrooms Tea and coffee making facilities Direct dial from bedrooms Licensed Cen ht CTV 5P
ROOMS: s £39-£46; d £52-£62
CARDS:

ILMINSTER Somerset Map **03** ST31

Premier Selected

QQQQQ ***Keymer Cottage*** Buckland St Mary TA20 3JF (A303 from Ilminster 4 miles, turn right at Eagle Tavern- Keymer Cottage is 1 mile along road on left hand side)
☎ 01460 234460 FAX 01460 234226
Closed Xmas & New Year

Keymer Cottage is a Victorian farmhouse which Hilary and Ian Cumming have restored to its former glory. Hilary's motto is 3c's, 'comfort, cleanliness and care', and these she achieves to a high standard. Bedrooms vary in size but the lack of space is well compensated for by the excellent decor and appointments. The attractive sitting room features an inglenook fireplace and exposed beams. An evening meal is available by arrangement, and is served in the elegant dining room.
3 rms (1 bth/shr) No smoking Tea and coffee making facilities No dogs (ex guide dogs) Cen ht CTV No children 6P Golf 18 Riding Croquet Last d noon

Selected

Q Q Q Q **Old Rectory** Cricket Malherbie TA19 0PW (from rdbt junct A358/A303 take A358 S towards Chard. After village Donyatt left towards Ilminster, right to Cricket Malherbie, Old Rectory on left) ☎ 01460 54364 FAX 01460 57374
With golden hamstone walls and a thatched roof, this enchanting house fits in perfectly with its surroundings. Owners Michael and Patricia have devoted a considerable amount of time and effort to resurrecting this wonderful house. Bedrooms are furnished and equipped with comfort in mind and provide lovely views over the garden and countryside beyond. Relaxation is assured in the guest lounge, where drinks may be taken. Breakfast, and dinner by prior arrangement, are served in the striking dining room where the convivial atmosphere is akin to a house party.
5 bth/shr No smoking CTV in all bedrooms Tea and coffee making facilities No dogs (ex guide dogs) Licensed Cen ht No children 16yrs 5P No coaches
ROOMS: s £48; d £72*
CARDS:

INGLEBY GREENHOW North Yorkshire Map **08** NZ50

Selected

Q Q Q Q **Manor House Farm** *(NZ586056)* TS9 6RB (entrance to farm drive opposite church) ☎ 01642 722384 Mrs M Bloom
Closed 21-29 Dec
Set in woodland and parkland next to the ancient Ingleby Manor, this lovely house offers excellent accommodation and good home comforts. The bright and fresh bedrooms have been thoughtfully equipped and the comfortable lounge has a fine selection of reading matter. Good home cooking is provided in the pretty dining room, and warm and friendly service is assured from resident owners Dr and Mrs Bloom.
3 bth/shr No smoking Tea and coffee making facilities No dogs Licensed Cen ht CTV No children 12yrs 50P Fishing Riding Rough shooting 168 acres mixed Last d 3pm
ROOMS: (incl. dinner) d £85-£95
CARDS:

INGLETON North Yorkshire Map **07** SD67

Selected

Q Q Q Q **Ferncliffe** Main St LA6 3HJ (turn off A65 onto B6255, 75yds on right) ☎ 015242 42405
Closed Nov rs Dec-Jan
Louise and Allan Bruns offer a friendly welcome to their home, which is only a short walk from the village centre. The stone-built house dates back to 1897 and has been very nicefully furnished to create comfortable accommodation. The bright reception rooms extend to a cosy lounge with reading material and a tastefully decorated dining room, where guests can enjoy appetising evening meals and substantial breakfasts.
5 shr No smoking in dining room CTV in all bedrooms Tea and coffee making facilities Cen ht CTV 6P No coaches
ROOMS: s £22-£29; d £40-£46; wkly b&b £140-£180; wkly hlf-bd £220-£260*
CARDS:

Q Q Q **Inglenook** 20 Main St LA6 3HJ (turn off A65 towards village at Bridge Inn, house 300yds on left) ☎ 015242 41270
Phil and Carolyn Smith are certainly making their mark at this tastefully furnished Victorian house, standing on the edge of the village and surrounded by delightful scenery close to the River Greta. It provides modern bedrooms, - one with a small balcony - a cosy lounge and a pleasant dining room.
4 rms (3 shr) 1 annexe shr No smoking CTV in all bedrooms Tea and coffee making facilities Cen ht CTV No children 5yrs No coaches Last d previous evening
ROOMS: d £36-£46; wkly b&b £120-£155; wkly hlf-bd £170-£200
CARDS:

Q Q **Langber Country** Tatterthorne Rd LA6 3DT (off A65 between Mason's Arms and Pub car park, travelling in opposite direction to Ingleton, 1m on left) ☎ 015242 41587
Closed 23 Dec-3 Jan

contd.

Located in lovely open countryside about a mile from the village, this family-run guest house offers pleasant accommodation together with attentive, friendly service. There is a spacious lounge and a comfortable breakfast room.
7 rms (2 bth 1 shr) (3 fmly) No smoking in bedrooms No smoking in dining room Tea and coffee making facilities Cen ht CTV 7P Last d 5pm
ROOMS: s £16.75-£25; d £33.90-£42; wkly hlf-bd £115-£140*

Q Q Q **Riverside Lodge** 24 Main St LA6 3HJ (take A65 into Ingleton. Main Street is close to the "Ironbridge", River Side Lodge is 150yds from A65/Main St junc) ☎ 015242 41359
This delightful period house is on the main street of the village, and to the rear enjoys terraced gardens and lovely views over the River Greta. It offers comfortable bedrooms, two of which are contained in a coach house adjoining the main house. There is an inviting lounge with lots to read, and one can admire examples of Manuel Camacho's wood-turning skill. Breakfasts are taken in the conservatory which is also an ideal place to relax and take in the panoramic views.
6 bth/shr 2 annexe shr (2 fmly) No smoking in bedrooms No smoking in dining room CTV in all bedrooms Tea and coffee making facilities Licensed Cen ht CTV 8P Fishing Sauna Games room with pool table and dart board
ROOMS: s fr £26; d fr £44*
CARDS:

Q Q Q **Springfield Private Hotel** 26 Main St LA6 3HJ (from A65 towards Kendal take first left over iron bridge or from A65 towards Skipton turn right at Bridge Inn and hotel is 80yds on the left) ☎ 01524 241280 FAX 01524 241280
Situated close to the village with a delightful garden that leads down the river, the resident owners of this late Victorian house, Jack and Kathleen Thornton, provide a friendly service. There is a comfortable lounge and the bedrooms are well equipped, with radios, colour televisions and hairdryers. Private fishing is available on the River Greta.
5 shr (1 fmly) No smoking in dining room CTV in all bedrooms Tea and coffee making facilities Licensed Cen ht CTV 12P No coaches Fishing Last d 5pm
ROOMS: s £23; d £46; wkly b&b £126; wkly hlf-bd £196*
CARDS:

Q Q ***Stacksteads*** Tatterthorn Rd LA6 3HS (from A65 towards Settle, turn right at Masons Arms public house into Tatterthorn Rd , farm 300 yds on right) ☎ 015242 41386 FAX 015242 42407
Situated about a mile from the village in open countryside, this traditionally styled farmhouse is well furnished and offers good value for money with pleasant home comforts. A hearty breakfast is served in the cosy dining room and service is polite and friendly.
3 shr No smoking Tea and coffee making facilities No dogs (ex guide dogs) Cen ht CTV 3P No coaches

INSTOW Devon Map 02 SS43

Q Q Q **Anchorage Hotel** The Quay EX39 4HX
(exit A39 onto B3233, after 2.5m turn left into Instow village)
☎ 01271 860655 & 860475 FAX 01271 860767
Closed 16 Jan-Feb
Overlooking the Taw and Torridge estuary, the Anchorage Hotel is situated on the Quay and is only a few minutes walk from Instow's golden sands. This comfortable family-run house offers spacious and comfortable public areas and bedrooms which have been equipped with modern facilities. A varied choice of dishes is offered in the dining room, prepared where possible using fresh, local ingredients.
17 bth/shr (6 fmly) No smoking in dining room CTV in 15 bedrooms Tea and coffee making facilities Direct dial from bedrooms Licensed Cen ht CTV 18P Last d 9.30pm
CARDS:

IPSWICH Suffolk Map 05 TM14

Q Q Q **Bentley Tower Hotel** 172 Norwich Rd IP1 2PY (turn right off A12 at Chevalier roundabout) ☎ 01473 212142 FAX 01473 212142
Closed 24 Dec-4 Jan
This small, well-established family-run hotel has a welcoming atmosphere. The neat public rooms offer a comfortable lounge with satellite TV, an attractive dining room and a pleasant bar that opens out onto the garden. The individually decorated bedrooms are soundly appointed and all rooms have modern en suite facilities.
11 shr (2 fmly) No smoking in 2 bedrooms CTV in 13 bedrooms Tea and coffee making facilities No dogs (ex guide dogs) Licensed Cen ht 16P No coaches Last d 8.45pm
CARDS:

Selected

Q Q Q Q **Drumbeg** 4 Constitution Hill IP1 3RQ ☎ 01473 254479 FAX 01473 211103
Cilla Steed's charming Tudor house has a wealth of original features in the woodwork and architecture, and is matched by the tranquility and prettiness of the landscaped gardens. In a residential location to the north, there is easy access to the town centre. The homely yet elegant public rooms include a beamed lounge, a spacious dining room and a conservatory. Upstairs, the two attractive rooms have many personal touches and a well chosen interior design. An all-weather floodlit tennis court is a definite asset to the property.
2 bth/shr (1 fmly) No smoking in 1 bedrooms CTV in all bedrooms Tea and coffee making facilities No dogs Cen ht CTV 4P No coaches Tennis (hard)
ROOMS: s £20-£29; d fr £45; wkly b&b £140-£160*

Q Q Q **Highview House Hotel** 56 Belstead Rd IP2 8BE (pass railway station on right, first turning on right into Willoughby Rd, up hill to T-junct, turn right, house 300yds on right) ☎ 01473 601620 & 688659 FAX 688659
rs 24 Dec-1 Jan
This small family-run hotel is ideally situated for both the town centre and railway station. The accommodation is modern and well equipped. Most of the rooms have en suite facilities. The public areas feature an open-plan lounge-cum-dining room with lovely leather Chesterfield suites and a full size snooker table. A reasonably-priced dinner menu is available Monday to Thursday.
11 rms (9 bth/shr) (1 fmly) CTV in all bedrooms Tea and coffee making facilities Direct dial from bedrooms Licensed Cen ht CTV 15P No coaches Snooker Last d 7.30pm
ROOMS: s £33-£38.50; d £48.50*
CARDS:

IRONBRIDGE Shropshire Map 07 SJ60

Q Q Q **Broseley** The Square, Broseley TF12 5EW (from B4373 into Broseley and at petrol station turn right into Church St, the Square is on left) ☎ 01952 882043 FAX 01952 882043
This long-established guest house is just over the river from Ironbridge. It provides very well equipped and attractively decorated bedrooms, with those

on the first floor being more spacious. A cosy lounge is available for residents and good home cooking is offered in the traditionally furnished dining room.
6 bth/shr (2 fmly) No smoking in 3 bedrooms No smoking in dining room No smoking in lounges CTV in all bedrooms Tea and coffee making facilities Direct dial from bedrooms Licensed Cen ht No coaches Last d by arrangement
ROOMS: s £26-£30; d £45-£48*
CARDS:

Selected

QQQQ **The Library House** 11 Severn Bank TF8 7AN
(50yds from the Iron Bridge) ☎ 01952 432299 FAX 01952 433967
This delightful little 18th-century guest house, situated almost opposite the famous Iron Bridge, was once the village library. The house has been modernised to provide comfortable accommodation. One bedroom has its own private terrace with direct access to the garden. Other facilities include a comfortable lounge and an attractive breakfast room. Dinner is not served, but there are several restaurants and pubs close by which offer good variety and value.
4 bth/shr (1 fmly) No smoking CTV in all bedrooms Tea and coffee making facilities Licensed Cen ht CTV No children 4yrs P No coaches
ROOMS: s £40; d £50

ISLE OF

Placenames incorporating the words 'Isle of' or 'Isle' will be found under the actual name, eg Isle of Wight is under Wight, Isle of.

IVER HEATH Buckinghamshire Map **04** TQ08

QQQ **Bridgettine Convent** Fulmer Common Rd SL0 0NR
(from Iver Heath roundabout take Pinewood Road pass Film Studios to cross roads and turn left into Fulmer Common Road)
☎ 01753 662073 & 662645 FAX 01753 662172
This delightful house situated on the quiet Fulmer Common Road is run by the Order of St Bridget. The house offers clean, comfortable accommodation in a warm and friendly atmosphere. The bedrooms are brightly decorated, and simply furnished. Breakfast is served in the re-furbished dining room and guests have use of a large peaceful library. Dinner is available by prior arrangement.
13 rms (1 bth 7 shr) (2 fmly) No smoking No dogs Cen ht CTV No coaches Last d 2pm
ROOMS: s £18-£20; d £36-£40*

JACOBSTOWE Devon Map **02** SS50

Selected

QQQQ ❦ **Higher Cadham** *(SS585026)* EX20 3RB
(from Jacobstowe village take A3072 towards Hatherleigh/Bude, a few yards after church turn sharp right in front of Cottage Farm continue for 0.5m) ☎ 01837 851647 FAX 01837 851410 Mr & Mrs J King
Closed Dec
John and Jenny King have run this charming guest house for more than twenty years and know how to make guests comfortable. Bedrooms fall into two categories, rooms in the original farmhouse and those more recently converted from former farm buildings. Each is thoughtfully equipped, neatly decorated and furnished in modern pine. The restaurant is open to the public for morning coffees, lunches and cream teas, so booking for lunch is essential. Children enjoy the multitude of animals that are around, as well as the large children's play area. Forming part of the fascinating, Tarka Trail Scheme, guests have access to delightful riverside and country walks.
9 rms (3 fmly) No smoking in dining room No smoking in 1 lounge CTV in 3 bedrooms Tea and coffee making facilities Licensed Cen ht CTV 10P Play room Nature Trail 139 acres beef sheep Last d 6pm
ROOMS: s £18.50-£25; d £37-£50; wkly b&b £115-£160; wkly hlf-bd £190-£235
CARDS:
See advertisement under OKEHAMPTON

KEIGHLEY West Yorkshire Map **07** SE04

QQQ **Bankfield** 1 Station Rd, Cross Hills BD20 7EH
(turn off A650/A629 Aire Valley trunk road at Kildwick roundabout and take weight limit restriction road towards Cross Hills. 0.5m on right)
☎ 01535 632971
This stone-built house is situated midway between Keighley and Skipton, providing a good starting point for a tour of the Dales. Susan Dowgill is a welcoming hostess and also prepares a hearty breakfast, served family style. Neatly decorated bedrooms are spacious and there is a homely sitting room.
3 rms (2 shr) (1 fmly) No smoking in bedrooms No smoking in dining room CTV in 2 bedrooms Tea and coffee making facilities Cen ht CTV 5P No coaches
ROOMS: s £20-£22; d £40-£44*

KENDAL Cumbria Map **07** SD59

See also Brigsteer & Levens

Selected

QQQQ **Burrow Hall Country Guest House** Plantation Bridge LA8 9JR (on A591, 1.5m after Crook roundabout on right hand side)
☎ 01539 821711
Closed 23 Dec-9 Jan
Built in 1683, this delightful country house is home to Jack and Maureen Craig who offer a really friendly and warm welcome to all their guests. The stylish, spacious bedrooms are very comfortable and are thoughtfully equipped. Public areas include a quiet lounge and a neat dining room, where one can enjoy Maureen's freshly prepared, substantial breakfasts.
3 shr No smoking CTV in all bedrooms Tea and coffee making facilities No dogs Cen ht No children 12yrs 8P No coaches

ROOMS: d fr £45; wkly b&b fr £140*
CARDS:

Q Q Q ✓ **Garnett House** *(SD500959)* Burneside LA9 5SF (exit A591 at Ratherheath crossroads, farm is on left on Burneside Rd)
☎ 01539 724542 Mrs S Beaty
Closed Xmas & New Year
Set outside the village of Burneside within walking distance of the railway station and with a backdrop of rolling hills, this 15th-century farmhouse sits squarely in its farm yard and is fronted by a small cottage garden. It blends cosy and characterful bedrooms with modern facilities. Mrs Beaty will provide farmhouse dinners on request.
5 rms (4 shr) (2 fmly) No smoking in dining room CTV in all bedrooms Tea and coffee making facilities No dogs CTV 6P 750 acres Dairy Sheep Last d 5pm
ROOMS: d £33-£41; wkly b&b £115-£140

Q Q Q ✓ **Gateside** *(SD494955)* Windermere Rd LA9 5SE (2m from Kendal travelling towards Windermere on A591)
☎ 01539 722036 FAX 722036 Mrs J Ellis
Closed Xmas & New Year
Located just a few minutes drive from the busy town centre, this traditional Lakeland working farm enjoys an idyllic setting just off the Windermere road. It dates from the late 17th century and low ceilings and exposed timbers still feature. Bedrooms are tastefully decorated and well equipped with modern facilities.
5 rms (3 shr) (1 fmly) No smoking in bedrooms No smoking in dining room CTV in all bedrooms Tea and coffee making facilities Cen ht 6P Lovely walks from farm, maps provided 280 acres dairy sheep Last d 4.30pm
ROOMS: s £20-£27; d £35-£42*

Selected

Q Q Q Q **Higher House Farm** Oxenholme Ln, Natland LA9 7QH (exit M6 at junc 36, A65 to Kendal, at second sign for Natland turn left onto Oxenholme lane, premises at bottom of lane on right) ☎ 015395 61177 FAX 015395 61520

This 17th-century farmhouse retains much of its original character. There are a well-kept orchard and gardens where breathtaking views of the nearby fells can be enjoyed. On colder days a log fire warms the cosy lounge where you can find books on the local area. The snug dining room has a communal table where meals are served. Rooms are comfortable, individual in style, and include one with a four-poster bed.
3 bth/shr No smoking CTV in all bedrooms Tea and coffee making facilities Cen ht CTV 9P No coaches Golf 9 Last d 1pm
ROOMS: s £27.50-£30; d £45-£50*

Premier Selected

Q Q Q Q Q **Lane Head Country House Hotel** Helsington LA9 5RJ (exit M6 junct 36 and after 5m take sliproad for A6 and south Kendal. On reaching A6 take first left and continue up lane for 700yds to the top) ☎ 01539 731283 FAX 01539 721 023
Aptly named, Lane Head House affords spectacular views of the Kent Valley from its commanding location. The former 17th-century manor offers guests a tranquil haven in which to relax and enjoy the cuisine of the Miller family. Bedrooms are comfortable and well equipped with many personal touches. A spacious lounge allows guests to relax and the tastefully decorated dining room opens onto a sun terrace.
6 bth/shr No smoking in bedrooms No smoking in dining room CTV in all bedrooms Tea and coffee making facilities Direct dial from bedrooms No dogs (ex guide dogs) Licensed Cen ht 10P No coaches Last d 7pm
ROOMS: s £41; d £71-£82*
CARDS:

Premier Selected

Q Q Q Q Q **Low Jock Scar** Selside LA8 9LE (6m N of Kendal on A6 turn left down a small side road signposted to Selside)
☎ 01539 823259 FAX 01539 823259
Mar-Oct
Philip and Alison Midwinter are proud owners of this small country guest house, set in secluded gardens and woodland. Bedrooms are comfortable and the lounge is full of books and local maps. The conservatory dining room looks out onto the well tended gardens. Bedrooms are individual in style, some overlooking the beck.
5 rms (3 bth/shr) No smoking Tea and coffee making facilities Licensed Cen ht CTV No children 12yrs 7P No coaches Last d 10am
ROOMS: s £30.50-£35.50; d £45-£55

Q Q Q **Martindales** 9-11 Sandes Av LA9 4LL (N on A6, before Victoria Bridge) ☎ 01539 724028
This traditional guest house lies by the River Kent and within walking

distance of the town centre. Popular with commercial guests as well as tourists, it offers cheery modern bedrooms and a welcoming lounge bar complete with an open fire. Imaginative dinners prepared by Mrs Martindale are by prior arrangement.
8 shr No smoking in dining room CTV in all bedrooms Tea and coffee making facilities No dogs (ex guide dogs) Licensed Cen ht
No children 8yrs 7P No coaches Last d 12 noon
ROOMS: s £27-£30; d £42-£45*
CARDS:

Q Q Q Millers Beck Country Stainton LA8 0DU
(leave M6 at Junction 36 taking A65, take first left signed Crooklands/Endmoor, Millers Beck 3.5 miles on right) ☎ 015395 60877
Mar-Dec
Conveniently situated just outside Kendal, this 16th-century corn mill offers modern facilities in an idyllic setting. Original oak beams and traditional stonework are visible throughout, especially in the open plan lounges that extend to a delightful sun balcony. The dining room is an attractive and tasteful addition to the original building and sits besides the tumbling millrace. Bedrooms are well equipped and all benefit from modern en suite facilities.
3 shr No smoking in bedrooms No smoking in area of dining room
No smoking in 1 lounge CTV in all bedrooms Tea and coffee making facilities No dogs Cen ht 4P No coaches Last d 6pm
ROOMS: s £25; d £40*

Q Q Q ✔ Natland Mill Beck *(SD520907)* LA9 7LH
(1m from Kendal on A65, close to Westmoreland General Hospital, down short lane on the roundabout opposite store car park)
☎ 01539 721122 Mrs E M Gardner
Mar-Oct
This charming farmhouse lies peacefully secluded in its own attractive gardens, just 200 meters from the main road leading into the town. It has low-beamed ceilings and many original features that date back to the 1600s. The largest bedroom has an en suite shower room, while the smaller twin has a shower cubicle and shares a bathroom with the small double.
3 rms (1 shr) No smoking Tea and coffee making facilities No dogs
Cen ht CTV 3P 100 acres dairy
ROOMS: s £18.50-£20; d £37-£40*

KENILWORTH Warwickshire Map 04 SP27

Q Q Q Castle Laurels Hotel 22 Castle Rd CV8 1NG
(on A452, opposite castle) ☎ 01926 856179 FAX 01926 854954
Closed 21 Dec-4 Jan
New owners, Pam and Nick Moore, offer a warm welcome at this impressive and well maintained Victorian house, which sits close to the castle. Guests have the use of a comfortable and tastefully appointed lounge, and an attractive dining room in which home-made evening meals are served; a snack menu is also available. The bedrooms are currently being upgraded, each room is well equipped and comfortable.
11 shr (1 fmly) No smoking CTV in 12 bedrooms Tea and coffee making facilities Direct dial from bedrooms No dogs (ex guide dogs) Licensed
Cen ht No children 5yrs 12P No coaches Last d 6.45pm
CARDS:

Q Q Q Hollyhurst 47 Priory Rd CV8 1LL (on A452) ☎ 01926 53882
FAX 10926 53882
An inviting house which is proudly owned and run by Mary Millar who is a friendly and caring hostess. The house is well furnished throughout, and the public rooms include a spacious comfortable lounge and a smaller breakfast room. A dispense bar is also provided.
7 rms (3 shr) (1 fmly) No smoking CTV in all bedrooms Tea and coffee making facilities No dogs Licensed Cen ht CTV No children 5yrs 9P
No coaches Last d 10am
ROOMS: s £20-£24; d £40-£45*

Selected

Q Q Q Q Victoria Lodge Hotel 180 Warwick Rd CV8 1HU
(0.25m S on A452, opposite St Johns Church)
☎ 01926 512020 FAX 01926 858703
Victoria Lodge offers very smartly appointed, immaculately maintained accommodation. The individually styled bedrooms are well equipped and cheerfully decorated, and have co-ordinated, high-quality soft furnishings; ground-floor bedrooms are available, one with its own private access to a patio in the walled garden. Guests have the use of a small lounge and separate breakfast room; evening meals are available by prior arrangement.
9 bth/shr No smoking CTV in all bedrooms Tea and coffee making facilities Direct dial from bedrooms No dogs (ex guide dogs)
Licensed Cen ht No children 18mths 9P No coaches Last d 5.30pm
ROOMS: s £37.50-£45; d £52.50-£57.50*
CARDS:

See advertisement on p.235.

KESWICK Cumbria Map 11 NY22

See also Mungrisdale

Selected

QQQQ **Acorn House Hotel** Ambleside Rd CA12 4DL
(500yds from town centre opposite St John Church)
☎ 017687 72553 FAX 017687 75332
New Year, Feb-Nov
Set among its own colourful gardens, this fine Georgian house is within walking distance of the town centre. Most of the tastefully decorated bedrooms boast fine period furniture, plus some four-posters. The light and airy upper rooms have original features, fell views from velux windows and sturdy fitted units. The elegant lounge and dining room reflect the character of the house which is adorned with antiques.
10 rms (9 bth/shr) (3 fmly) No smoking CTV in all bedrooms Tea and coffee making facilities No dogs Licensed Cen ht No children 8yrs 10P No coaches
ROOMS: s £25-£40; d £50-£60; wkly b&b £165-£180*
CARDS:

QQQ ***Allerdale House*** 1 Eskin St CA12 4DH
☎ 017687 73891
A substantial end-terrace house, Allerdale has a delightful sitting room with a beautiful Japanese rosewood fire place. Bedrooms are very well equipped to include telephone/clock radios, hair dryers, tissues and towels. The home-cooked set dinners run to five courses and there is also a decent wine list.
6 bth/shr (2 fmly) No smoking CTV in all bedrooms Tea and coffee making facilities Direct dial from bedrooms Licensed Cen ht No children 5yrs 6P No coaches Last d 5pm

Selected

QQQQ **Avondale** 20 Southey St CA12 4EF
(take first left at Cenotaph into Southey St Avondale 100yds on right)
☎ 017687 72735
Mr and Mrs Williams offer a warm and friendly welcome to all their guests. Their house offers comfortable bedrooms which have recently been refurbished. They vary in size but all have hairdryers and clock-radios. Reception rooms extend to a cosy lounge with deep armchairs and collection of books. Breakfast can be enjoyed in the light and airy dining room.
6 shr No smoking CTV in all bedrooms Tea and coffee making facilities No dogs (ex guide dogs) Licensed Cen ht No children 12yrs No coaches
ROOMS: s £19.50-£21; d £39-£42; wkly b&b £130
CARDS:

QQQ **Beckside** 5 Wordsworth St CA12 4HU
(turn off A66 at Low Briery, turn right at junct onto Penrith Rd, Wordsworth St on left beyond pub & garage) ☎ 017687 73093
Closed 24-27 Dec
This slate-faced terraced house is situated in a quiet residential area of town and offers bright cheerful accommodation with bedrooms furnished mostly in pine. There is an attractive dining room.
4 bth/shr (1 fmly) No smoking CTV in all bedrooms Tea and coffee making facilities No dogs (ex guide dogs) Cen ht No coaches Last d 1pm
ROOMS: d £30-£39; wkly b&b £105-£129; wkly hlf-bd £175-£206*

See page 14-20 for a list of Premier Selected establishments

QQQ **Brierholme** 21 Bank St CA12 5JZ
(on A591, 100yds from post office) ☎ 017687 72938
Brierholme is situated right in the centre of the town and offers well kept accommodation with super views over the town to the surrounding mountains. Bedrooms are bright and modern and most are at the rear of the house, overlooking the pretty gardens. There is a comfortable lounge with an interesting collection of dolls from around the world, while home-cooked dinners are offered in the attractive dining room.
6 bth/shr (2 fmly) No smoking in bedrooms No smoking in dining room CTV in all bedrooms Tea and coffee making facilities No dogs (ex guide dogs) Licensed Cen ht 6P No coaches Last d 3pm
ROOMS: d £36-£45*

Selected

QQQQ **Brundholme Country House Hotel** Brundholme Rd CA12 4NL (from A66 take roundabout exit to Keswick. First left past garage, next left, first driveway on left)
☎ 017687 74495 FAX 017687 74495
Set in glorious gardens away from the hustle and bustle of the town, this splendid house is idyllically located high above the tumbling waters of the River Greta. Formerly an impressive Three Star Hotel, resident proprietors Ian and Sue have successfully converted the house to provide spacious, richly furnished bedrooms with stunning views. In the attractive dining room, Ian, an accomplished chef, provides a hearty breakfast to start the day.
3 bth/shr No smoking CTV in all bedrooms Tea and coffee making facilities No dogs (ex guide dogs) Cen ht No children 13yrs No coaches
ROOMS: s £35-£40; d £50-£60; wkly b&b £175-£210

QQQ **Charnwood** 6 Eskin St CA12 4DH
(0.5m S of A591 near town centre. Off A66 to Keswick,right at mini-rdbt into Penrith Rd, left into Greta St,this leads to Erskin St)
☎ 017687 74111
Closed 24-25 Dec
New proprietor Sue Banister is certainly ringing the changes at this attractive, welcoming guest house which has benefited from tasteful refurbishment. The well equipped bedrooms vary in size with a smart spacious suite topping the range. A comfortable lounge is provided and the traditional dining room sets the scene for imaginative cooking and good service.
5 bth/shr (2 fmly) No smoking CTV in all bedrooms Tea and coffee making facilities No dogs (ex guide dogs) Licensed Cen ht No children 5yrs No coaches Last d 10am
ROOMS: d £42-£54; wkly b&b £133-£182; wkly hlf-bd £322-£371*
CARDS:

QQQ ***Claremont House*** Chestnut Hill CA12 4LT (SE on A591)
☎ 017687 72089
Looking over the Lakeland town of Keswick, Claremont House is set in its own mature gardens. Rooms are comfortable and well equipped, and the lounge has a wealth of literature on local walks and places of interest. Meals are served in the neat, attractive dining room and a good wine list accompanies a home-made evening dinner.
5 bth/shr No smoking in bedrooms No smoking in dining room Tea and coffee making facilities No dogs Licensed Cen ht CTV 8P No coaches Last d 6pm

Premier Selected

QQQQQ Craglands Penrith Rd CA12 4LJ
(guesthouse at the foot of Chestnut Hill on right entering Keswick)
☎ 017687 74406

Now under new ownership this delightful house enjoys an elevated position 10 minutes walk east of the town centre. Plans are afoot to implement either a three or five course dinner – if the tasty breakfast is an early indicator of the cooking here, then dinner should be a treat! As the house is unlicensed guests are invited to bring their own wine. The bedrooms are richly furnished, in a modern style and equipped with all the expected facilities.

5 bth/shr No smoking CTV in all bedrooms Tea and coffee making facilities No dogs (ex guide dogs) Cen ht No children 8yrs 6P No coaches Last d 2pm

ROOMS: s £30; d £46-£50; wkly b&b £140-£150; wkly hlf-bd £275-£285

QQQ Cragside 39 Blencathra St CA12 4HX
(A66 1st turn left to Keswick, follow rd into town under rail bridge turn left at 'Millfield' house and follow rd to right, 1st house on right)
☎ 017687 73344

Proprietors Katie Norburn and David Low extend a warm welcome to all travellers. Situated just a short walk from the town centre, this Victorian house has splendid views of the surrounding fells. Accommodation is light, attractive and tastefully furnished. The two rooms at the top of the house enjoy en suite facilities, whilst the other three have the option of a shower or bathroom.

5 rms (2 shr) (2 fmly) No smoking CTV in all bedrooms Tea and coffee making facilities Cen ht No children 3yrs 2P No coaches Facilities are available nearby

ROOMS: s £20-£25; d £32-£38; wkly b&b £105-£120

Selected

QQQQ Dalegarth House Country Hotel Portinscale CA12 5RQ (approach Portinscale from A66 pass Farmers Arms approx 100yds on left to hotel) ☎ 017687 72817 FAX 017687 72817

This delightful house stands above landscaped gardens in a small lakeside village. Furnishings, décor and facilities are thoroughly modern and bright. The bedrooms on the ground floor are externally accessed, and all are generously proportioned. Dinners are home made and served in a relaxing and friendly atmosphere.

10 bth/shr (1 fmly) No smoking CTV in all bedrooms Tea and coffee making facilities No dogs (ex guide dogs) Licensed Cen ht CTV No children 5yrs 12P No coaches Last d 5.30pm

ROOMS: s £28-£30; d £56-£60; wkly b&b £180-£190; wkly hlf-bd £270-£280*

CARDS:

235

Premier Selected

QQQQQ Derwent Cottage Portinscale CA12 5RF
(A66 to Portinscale, pass the Farmers Arms , 200 mtrs turn right after left hand bend) ☎ 017687 74838
Mar-Oct

At the end of a private drive, Derwent Cottage sits in its own well cared for grounds and gardens. Enthusiastically run by Mr and Mrs Newman the house is comfortably furnished and offers cosy lounges and a small well-stocked bar. The dining room is the venue for freshly prepared, home cooked meals. Bedrooms are spacious, furnished to hotel standards and offer many additional facilities.

6 bth/shr No smoking CTV in all bedrooms Tea and coffee making facilities No dogs (ex guide dogs) Licensed Cen ht No children 12yrs 10P No coaches Last d noon

ROOMS: d £52-£78; wkly b&b £182-£224; wkly hlf-bd £280-£322*

CARDS:

QQ **Easedale Hotel** Southey St CA12 4HL (take A691 to Keswick fron A6 or Grasmere and then take a sharp left at the start of the shopping centre) ☎ 017687 72710 FAX 017687 71127
This sympathetically refurbished Victorian house is near the town centre and offers good value for money. The spacious bedrooms are particularly popular with families and cots are available upon request. Two television lounges are available, one especially reserved for non-smokers. The bright dining room connects to a small bar. Evening meals are provided upon request.
10 rms (3 bth/shr) (2 fmly) Tea and coffee making facilities No dogs (ex guide dogs) Licensed No coaches Last d 5pm
ROOMS: s £15-£18; d £30-£46; wkly b&b £90-£138; wkly hlf-bd £165-£213*
CARDS:

Selected

QQQQ **Goodwin House** 29 Southey St CA12 4EE (from A591 signed town centre, left before traffic lights and sharp left into Southey St. House 0.75 on left at crossroads with Church St) ☎ 017687 74634
Closed Xmas
Originally built in 1890 by the Lowther family to resemble a New England Villa with a mansard roof, this appealing house is now on the corner of an attractive terrace close to the town centre. The variously sized bedrooms are bright and cheery, well equipped and comfortable. New proprietors have plans to provide dinner during the winter months.
6 bth/shr No smoking CTV in all bedrooms Tea and coffee making facilities No dogs Licensed Cen ht No children 12yrs No coaches
ROOMS: s £20-£23; d £42-£48; wkly b&b £130-£180*

Premier Selected

QQQQQ **Grange Country House** Manor Brow, Ambleside Rd CA12 4BA (leave M6 at junct 40 and take A66 into Keswick, then head left on A591 towards Windermere for 0.5m. Take first right and estab is 200mtrs in right) ☎ 017687 72500
mid Feb-mid Nov
This elegant Lakeland Victorian residence is set in its own attractive gardens just a short stroll from the town centre. The spacious bedrooms are well equipped and traditionally furnished, with those at the top of the house featuring bare beams and delightful views across the town to the distant mountains. There is a stylish dining room, a comfortable lounge and a well equipped bar. Mr and Mrs Miller are accomplished hosts and with their team of friendly staff ensure a super standard of hospitality.
10 bth/shr No smoking CTV in all bedrooms Tea and coffee making facilities Direct dial from bedrooms No dogs (ex guide dogs) Licensed Cen ht No children 7yrs 11P No coaches
ROOMS: s £28-£38; d £50-£70; wkly b&b £175-£224
CARDS:

QQQ **Grasslees** Rickerby Ln, Portinscale CA12 5RH (off A66 Keswick-Cockermouth, signposted Portunscale. In village take second right marked 'Grasslees') ☎ 017687 71313
This comfortable house is located in Portinscale, a rural, residential suburb of Keswick. The attractive bedrooms vary in size and include a very spacious family room. Breakfast is served in the appealing dining room that also doubles as a television lounge.
3 rms (2 shr) (1 fmly) No smoking in dining room No smoking in lounges CTV in all bedrooms Cen ht 6P No coaches
ROOMS: d £45-£54*

Selected

QQQQ **Greystones** Ambleside Rd CA12 4DP (opposite St John's Church) ☎ 017687 73108
Closed Dec
This traditionally stonebuilt Lakeland house is the home of Janet and Robert Jones who offer a warm and friendly welcome to all their guests. Individually styled, the spacious bedrooms are comfortable and thoughtfully equipped. The lounge overlooks the garden, and the pleasantly decorated dining room is where one can enjoy breakfast. The house offers views of the local fells and is a short walk from the town centre.
8 rms (2 bth 5 shr) No smoking CTV in all bedrooms Tea and coffee making facilities No dogs Licensed Cen ht No children 10yrs 7P No coaches
ROOMS: s £23-£25; d £46-£50; wkly b&b £154
CARDS:

QQQ **Hall Garth** 37 Blencathra St CA12 4HX (off A591, turning by Millfield Nursing Home) ☎ 017687 72627
A Victorian house located in a quiet residential area but conveniently close to the town centre. Accommodation is modern, and every effort has been made to add personal extra touches. The inviting dining room is the venue for a hearty Cumbrian breakfast.
8 rms (2 shr) (1 fmly) No smoking CTV in 6 bedrooms Tea and coffee making facilities Cen ht No children 6yrs Last d night before
ROOMS: s £17; d £32-£40; wkly b&b £100-£126; wkly hlf-bd £170-£196*

QQQ **Heatherlea** 26 Blencathra St CA12 4HP (exit M6 onto A66 to Keswick, follow signs to Keswick, after second petrol station turn left) ☎ 017687 72430
Heatherlea is situated in a quiet residential area of this market town. At the end of a pretty terrace, Mr and Mrs Redfern offer friendly hospitality to all their guests. Bedrooms are thoughtfully equipped and tastefully decorated. A freshly prepared, substantial breakfast is served in the bright dining room, which looks onto the flower-filled garden.
4 shr (2 fmly) No smoking CTV in all bedrooms Tea and coffee making facilities No dogs (ex guide dogs) Cen ht No children 5yrs No coaches
ROOMS: d £37-£39; wkly b&b £126-£133*

Selected

QQQQ ***Howe Keld Lakeland Hotel*** 5/7 The Heads CA12 5ES (from town centre take road to Borrowdale. Turn right opposite main car park, first on left ☎ 017687 72417 FAX 017687 72417
Closed Xmas
This friendly, family run hotel is close to the town centre and lakeside. The bedrooms are thoughtfully designed and offer modern facilities throughout. Public rooms are spacious and extend to a first floor lounge, a cosy lounge bar and an appealing dining room, where the extensive menu using local and home-made produce. Vegetarians are well catered for.
15 rms (12 shr) (3 fmly) No smoking in bedrooms No smoking in dining room No smoking in 1 lounge CTV in all bedrooms Tea and coffee making facilities Licensed Cen ht 9P No coaches
Last d 7.30pm

Selected

QQQQ ***Littlebeck*** Chestnut Hill CA12 4LT (on A591 leaving town towards Windermere) ☎ 017687 72972 FAX 017687 72032
Closed Dec-Jan
Situated at the southern end of the town, this smart residential house is located on the Windermere road. Bedrooms are tastefully furnished and well equipped while the public areas include a breakfast room and a sun lounge. Ray and Christine Tuttles are the welcoming hosts.
3 bth/shr No smoking CTV in all bedrooms No dogs (ex guide dogs) Cen ht No children 15yrs 3P

QQQ **Lynwood Hotel** 12 Ambleside Rd CA12 4DL
(exit A591, take minor road signposted for Castlrigg Manor via Manor Brow, premises 0.5m on the right) ☎ 017687 72081 FAX 017687 75021
Closed 24-26 Dec rs November
This grand Victorian house is peacefully located just a few minutes walk from the town centre. The bedrooms have been decorated with attractive fabrics and furnishings, and there are interesting landscape photographs of the area throughout the house. There is a relaxing lounge and an attractive dining room, where dinner is served on request.
6 shr (1 fmly) No smoking CTV in all bedrooms Tea and coffee making facilities No dogs Licensed Cen ht No coaches Last d 4pm
ROOMS: s £24-£25.50; d £42-£49; wkly b&b fr £145; wkly hlf-bd fr £235
CARDS:

Selected

QQQQ **Ravensworth Hotel** 29 Station St CA12 5HH
(turn off A591 into Station Street at War Memorial, hotel is on right)
☎ 017687 72476
Closed Dec-Jan
Prominently sited close to the park and town centre, this substantial Victorian house offers attractively decorated bedrooms furnished with either pine or contemporary pieces. There is a delightful upstairs lounge, a bright and airy dining room and a cosy residents' bar.
8 rms (1 bth 6 shr) (1 fmly) No smoking CTV in all bedrooms Tea and coffee making facilities No dogs Licensed Cen ht CTV No children 6yrs 5P
ROOMS: s £17-£35; d £36-£52; wkly b&b £119-£154*
CARDS:

QQQ **Richmond House** 37-39 Eskin St CA12 4DG (follow signs to town centre, turn 4th left after passing under bridge into Greta St which continues into Eskin St) ☎ 017687 73965
Closed 25-26 Dec
This family-run guest house welcomes families and offers bright cheery bedrooms, a comfortable lounge and a cosy residents' bar off the dining room.
9 rms (8 shr) (1 fmly) No smoking CTV in all bedrooms Tea and coffee making facilities No dogs (ex guide dogs) Licensed Cen ht CTV No children 2yrs Last d 5pm
ROOMS: s £15-£23; d £30-£46; wkly b&b £110-£140; wkly hlf-bd £170-£190*
CARDS:

QQQ **Rickerby Grange Country House Hotel** Portinscale CA12 5RH (by-pass Keswick on A66 Cockermouth road turn left at Portinscale sign, pass Farmer Arms Inn on left & turn down second lane to the right)
☎ 017687 72344
20 Mar-mid Nov
Set in a quiet lane in the village of Portinscale, close to Lake Derwentwater, is this well proportioned and attractive house. As well as a comfortable lounge there is a residents' bar adjoining the dining room. The bright modern bedrooms are well equipped with first-class beds.
12 rms (11 bth/shr) (3 fmly) No smoking in dining room No smoking in 1 lounge CTV in all bedrooms Tea and coffee making facilities Licensed Cen ht No children 8yrs 20P No coaches Last d 5pm
ROOMS: s £27; d £54; wkly b&b £175; wkly hlf-bd £250

QQQ **Skiddaw Grove** Vicarage Hill CA12 5QB
(exit M6 junct 40 and follow A66 W, turn off at Keswick rbt, junc A591, into Keswick, immmediately turn right into Vicarage Hill hotel 20 yds on left) ☎ 017687 73324 FAX 017687 73324
Closed Xmas

contd.

Set in its own gardens in a quiet area of the town just off the by-pass, this private hotel enjoys fine panoramic views of Skiddaw with Bassenthwaite Lake in the distance. The spacious dining room offers this view and is a pleasant room to enjoy breakfast. Other reception rooms extend to a quiet lounge and a separate bar lounge. Bedrooms are individual in style and offer thoughtful extra facilities.
5 bth/shr (1 fmly) No smoking CTV in all bedrooms Tea and coffee making facilities No dogs Licensed Cen ht 8P No coaches
Outdoor swimming pool (heated) Table tennis
ROOMS: s £23-£25; d £46-£50; wkly b&b £160*

Q Q Q **Sunnyside** 25 Southey St CA12 4EF
(M6 take A66 West, turn off for Keswick, at T junct turn right towards town centre, under railway bridge, turn left at war memorial , 100yds on left)
☎ 017687 72446 FAX 017687 74447
Closed 19-28 Dec
This spacious guest house has recently been refurbished and the smart, stylish new bedrooms make good use of solid pine furniture and attractive decor. A comfortable lounge is provided on the first floor and breakfasts are taken in the inviting dining room.
7 rms (5 shr) (2 fmly) No smoking CTV in all bedrooms Tea and coffee making facilities Cen ht 8P No coaches
ROOMS: s £23; d £36-£46; wkly b&b £112-£147*

Selected

Q Q Q Q **Tarn Hows** 3-5 Eskin St CA12 4DH (from Penrith/Ambleside follow Keswick A591-Town centre onto A5271 to Conservative Club on left, turn right into Greta St and continue into Eskin St) ☎ 017687 73217 FAX 017687 73217
Formerly two grand Lakeland stone-clad houses this attractive house has recently benefited from a smart refurbishment. The bedrooms vary in size but all are stylishly furnished and well equipped. A cosy lounge has many books of local interest while the dining room provides the venue for both breakfast and optional dinners.
9 rms (7 shr) No smoking CTV in all bedrooms Tea and coffee making facilities Licensed Cen ht No children 6yrs 8P No coaches Last d 4pm
ROOMS: s £22; d £36-£44; wkly b&b £126-£154;
wkly hlf-bd £190-£225*

Q Q Q **Winchester House** 58 Blencathra St CA12 4HT (from Penrith take A591 for 0.5m then turn left opposite Texaco Garage into Wordsworth St and continue to first X-roads) ☎ 017687 73664
Situated in a quiet residential area just a short walk from the bustling town, this friendly house offers a warm welcome to all. Bedrooms offer comfort and modern facilities, and some have recently been refurbished. The attractive dining room provides the venue for a hearty Cumbrian breakfast.
6 rms (2 shr) (1 fmly) No smoking CTV in all bedrooms Tea and coffee making facilities No dogs (ex guide dogs) Cen ht No children 3yrs No coaches
ROOMS: s £16-£17.50; d £32-£38; wkly b&b £110-£125*

Q Q **Yew Tree House** 28 Eskin St CA12 4DG
(turn left off A591 opposite Fitz Park straight across two junctions into Eskin St, Yew Tree third GH on left) ☎ 017687 74323
This cosy Lakeland slate terraced house has an attractive dining room and neat, cheerily decorated bedrooms, some of which feature their original Victorian fireplaces.
5 rms (2 shr) (1 fmly) No smoking in dining room No smoking in lounges CTV in all bedrooms Tea and coffee making facilities Cen ht Last d 1pm
ROOMS: d £32-£38*

KETTERING Northamptonshire Map **04** SP87

Q Q Q **Headlands Hotel** 49-51 Headlands NN15 7ET (from market place) follow main rd to traffic lights, straight across into 'Headlands', hotel is 200yds on left) ☎ 01536 524624 FAX 01536 483367
This large Victorian house is located in a quiet residential road close to the centre of town. The accommodation is bright, attractive and well equipped. There is a comfortable guest lounge and a traditional breakfast is served in the dining room. Evening meals by prior arrangement.
14 rms (8 bth/shr) (2 fmly) No smoking in dining room CTV in all bedrooms Tea and coffee making facilities Direct dial from bedrooms No dogs (ex guide dogs) Cen ht CTV 10P Last d 5pm
ROOMS: s £25-£40; d £38-£50; wkly b&b £157-£280;
wkly hlf-bd £227.50-£385*
CARDS:

Q Q Q **Pennels** 175 Beatrice Rd NN16 9QR (A6003 from town centre, first right past football ground into Kingsley Avenue, second right and then first right into Beatrice Road)
☎ 01536 481940 & 0410 184715 FAX 01536 410798
Mrs Margaret Green is the landlady of this charming guest house and her attention to detail shines through. Rooms are well maintained and most benefit from en suite bathrooms. Pretty fabrics and quality bed linen feature throughout and Mrs Green will cook a tasty dinner by prior arrangement.
7 rms (5 bth/shr) (2 fmly) No smoking in 3 bedrooms No smoking in dining room No smoking in 1 lounge CTV in all bedrooms Tea and coffee making facilities No dogs (ex guide dogs) Cen ht CTV ch fac 10P No coaches Last d 6pm
ROOMS: s £19.50-£20; d £36-£39; wkly b&b £136.50-£140;
wkly hlf-bd £210-£213*
CARDS:

KETTLEWELL North Yorkshire Map **07** SD97

Selected

Q Q Q Q **Langcliffe Country** BD23 5RJ (off B6160, at 'Kings Head' take road marked 'Access Only') ☎ 01756 760243 & 760896
This detached stone house lies in the picturesque valley of Upper Wharfedale in the Yorkshire National Park. Richard and Jane Elliott are the hospitable and friendly hosts. Jane's 4-course home-cooked dinners are a strong feature, the daily-changing menu offering a choice of main course and starters, followed by a set dessert then cheese. Vegetarians

are welcomed. The pine-furnished bedrooms are thoughtfully equipped and include a two-bedroom family suite. Lots of interesting collectables and beautiful flower arrangements grace the house.
8 rms (6 bth/shr) No smoking in dining room No smoking in lounges CTV in 6 bedrooms Tea and coffee making facilities Direct dial from bedrooms Licensed Cen ht CTV 6P No coaches Last d 9am
CARDS:

KEXBY North Yorkshire Map **08** SE75

QQQ **Ivy House** *(SE691511)* YO41 5LQ
(On the A1079 approx 5 miles from York)
☎ 01904 489368 Mrs K R Daniel
Situated five miles from York city, this Victorian farmhouse is part arable, part dairy working farm. The house is very well furnished and has been in the same family for over a hundred years now. The bedrooms are pleasantly decorated and equipped. A good hearty Yorkshire breakfast is served in the cosy dining room, and a comfortable and inviting lounge is also provided for guests.
3 rms (1 shr) (1 fmly) No smoking in bedrooms No smoking in dining room CTV in all bedrooms Tea and coffee making facilities No dogs (ex guide dogs) Cen ht CTV 5P 132 acres mixed
ROOMS: s £20; d £38*

KIDDERMINSTER Worcestershire Map **07** SO87

QQ ***Gordonhouse Hotel*** 194 Comberton Rd DY10 1UE
(100yds from jct A449/A448) ☎ 01562 822900 FAX 01562 865626
This large Victorian house is close to Kidderminster Railway Station and the Severn Valley Steam Railway. The modern equipped bedrooms include family rooms; some rooms on the ground floor are in a separate wing with access from the large garden. There is a comfortable lounge and a small bar, and individual tables are provided in the dining room.
15 rms (1 shr) 3 annexe rms (2 fmly) No smoking in dining room CTV in all bedrooms Tea and coffee making facilities Licensed Cen ht CTV 25P No coaches Last d 7pm
CARDS:

QQQ ***Victoria Hotel*** 15 Comberton Rd DY10 1UA
(on A448, 0.5m from town centre) ☎ 01562 67240
This large semi-detached house is close to the railway station and the famous Severn Valley Steam Railway. The well maintained bedrooms vary in size and style, but all have similar modern equipment. Family bedded rooms are available. Separate tables are provided in the traditionally furnished breakfast room.
7 rms (4 shr) (2 fmly) No smoking in dining room No smoking in lounges CTV in all bedrooms Tea and coffee making facilities No dogs Cen ht No children 2yrs 5P No coaches Last d 9am
CARDS:

KIDLINGTON Oxfordshire Map **04** SP41

Selected

QQQQ ***Bowood House*** 238 Oxford Rd OX5 1EB
(on the A4260, 4m N of Oxford, opposite Thames Valley Police H.Q.)
☎ 01865 842288 FAX 01865 841858
Closed 24 Dec-4 Jan
This small hotel situated only four miles from the centre of Oxford on the old Banbury road, and popular with business guests. Bedrooms are well equipped with TV, telephone, radio alarm, trouser press and hairdryer. The majority of rooms are in the main house but a garden wing houses the remainder, one of which is equipped for disabled guests. There is a cosy lounge and well stocked bar. The attractive dining room is useful for guests wishing to choose from the well priced carte menu.

10 rms (8 bth/shr) 12 annexe bth/shr (4 fmly) No smoking in dining room No smoking in lounges CTV in all bedrooms Tea and coffee making facilities Direct dial from bedrooms No dogs (ex guide dogs) Licensed Cen ht CTV 26P Golf 18 Last d 8.30pm
CARDS:

See advertisement under OXFORD

KILBURN North Yorkshire Map **08** SE57

QQQ **Forresters Arms Hotel** YO61 4AH (from Thirsk take A170 for 2m then turn right for Kilburn. Follow the road for 3m into village)
☎ 01347 868386 & 868550 FAX 01347 868386
Standing in the shadow of the famous Kilburn white horse, this attractive old village inn offers a good range of food which is served either in the bar or the dining room. Bedrooms are well equipped and a refurbishment programme is ongoing.
10 bth/shr (2 fmly) CTV in all bedrooms Tea and coffee making facilities Direct dial from bedrooms Cen ht 40P Last d 9pm
ROOMS: s fr £38; d £49-£58; wkly b&b £171.50-£203; wkly hlf-bd £190-£226*
MEALS: Lunch £4-£10 Dinner £7-£10&alc*
CARDS:

Remember to return your Prize Draw card for a chance to win an action-packed family weekend at one of the eleven Family Fun Hotels in the Hilton Hotels Directory. See inside the front cover for the card and competition details. Don't forget to fill in your name and address before posting!

KILVE Somerset Map **03** ST14

Premier Selected

Hood Arms TA5 1EA (12m W of Bridgwater on the A39) ☎ 01278 741210 FAX 01278 741477
This former 17th-century coaching inn is in the centre of the village of Kilve which is just 10 miles from the town of Bridgwater. The Hood Arms is a favourite stopping place for travellers who wish to enjoy a lunchtime snack or a more substantial meal. The bars are very welcoming with wood burning stoves, oak beams and a warm atmosphere. There are five comfortable, well equipped bedrooms, and a newly created family area away from the central house.
5 bth (1 fmly) No smoking in 1 bedrooms No smoking in dining room CTV in all bedrooms Tea and coffee making facilities Direct dial from bedrooms Cen ht 12P Last d 9.45pm
ROOMS: s £30-£46; d £48-£60; wkly b&b £200-£280; wkly hlf-bd £285-£360
MEALS: Lunch £11-£13&alc Dinner £11-£13&alc
CARDS:

KINGSBRIDGE Devon

See **Aveton Gifford Bantham & Kingston**

KINGSLEY Cheshire Map **07** SJ57

Charnwood Hollow Ln WA6 8EF
(from Frodsham take B5152 for approx 3m, then turn onto B5153 for Kingsley Hollow Lane, hotel is just past church on right hand side)
☎ 01928 787097 FAX 01928 788566
Set on the edge of a peaceful village, close to Delamere Forest, this family home offers two nicely furnished bedrooms, sharing a spacious bathroom and comfortable lounge. Separate access is provided to the bedrooms, making it ideal for families as well as individuals. Breakfast is served around one table in the dining room, with sliding doors leading to the patio and colourful garden.
2 rms (1 bth/shr) (1 fmly) No smoking CTV in all bedrooms Tea and coffee making facilities Direct dial from bedrooms No dogs Cen ht CTV 5P
ROOMS: s £20-£30; d £36-£45; wkly b&b £140-£210

KING'S LYNN Norfolk Map **09** TF62

Selected

Andel Lodge 211 Station Rd, Watlington PE33 0JG
(2m from A10/A134 junction, adjacent to bank of river Ouse)
☎ 01553 811515 FAX 01553 811429
Set in quiet rural surroundings on the fringe of Watlington is this modern family-run guest house. The public areas are tastefully furnished, and feature a comfortable lounge and a smart dining room with a small dispense bar. Some of the accommodation is housed in the main building and there are more bedrooms in a separate annex. They are individually furnished and decorated, equipped with colourful soft furnishings. Each room has a good range of modern facilities. All rooms have en suite bathrooms. Dinner is available by prior arrangement.
3 bth 2 annexe bth No smoking in 3 bedrooms CTV in all bedrooms Tea and coffee making facilities No dogs (ex guide dogs) Licensed Cen ht CTV No children 8yrs 6P No coaches Last d 6.30pm

Buckingham Lodge 29 Tennyson Av PE30 2QG
(on the A47/A10/A149 lead into Kings Lynn follow town centre signs, at mini roundabout right onto Vancouver Av, leads into Tennyson Av)
☎ 01553 764469 FAX 01553 764469
Guests can expect a warm welcome from Hilda and George Braddick at this small family run guest house. The accommodation is soundly appointed and has a bright fresh appearance although, the rooms do vary in size and style; five of the rooms have shower cubicles . Breakfast is served in the small nicely furnished dining room and snacks are also available during the evening.
6 rms (1 fmly) No smoking CTV in all bedrooms Tea and coffee making facilities No dogs (ex guide dogs) Cen ht 6P Last d 4pm
ROOMS: s £20; d £36-£38*

Selected

Fairlight Lodge 79 Goodwins Rd PE30 5PE
(from A17/A10/A47 roundabout turn off onto Vancouver Av via the South Gates roundabout, premises on left before Exton Rd crossroads)
☎ 01553 762234 FAX 01553 770280
Closed 24-26 Dec
This Victorian house sits in attractive gardens. Attractively appointed accommodation is divided between the main house and 3 garden bedrooms. All are light and inviting with cheerful soft furnishings and complementing decor. The tastefully furnished public rooms include a comfortable lounge with open fire, books and music system, and a smaller dining room where breakfast is served.
7 rms (4 shr) (1 fmly) No smoking in 2 bedrooms No smoking in dining room No smoking in lounges CTV in all bedrooms Tea and coffee making facilities Cen ht 8P No coaches
ROOMS: s £18-£25; d £34-£40

Guanock Hotel South Gate PE30 5JG (follow signs to town centre, establishment immediately on right of South Gates)
☎ 01553 772959 FAX 01553 772959
The Guanock is located south of the centre just inside the town gate. Evening meals and breakfast are served in the cheerful dining room, or bar meals can be provided in the bar or lounge. Bedrooms have a fresh appearance and standard appointments; each room is equipped with a range of facilities.
17 rms (5 fmly) No smoking in 8 bedrooms No smoking in dining room CTV in all bedrooms Tea and coffee making facilities No dogs (ex guide dogs) Licensed Cen ht 12P Pool room Last d 5pm
ROOMS: s £21-£23; d £34-£36*
CARDS:

Havana 117 Gaywood Rd PE30 2PU
(opposite King Edward VII High School) ☎ 01553 772331
Closed 23 Dec-1 Jan
With the caring and friendly approach of its owners, Barry and Rosemary Breed, this turn-of-the-century, semi-detached building is continually being improved, and offers attractively appointed bedrooms. Most are en suite, and the ground floor bedrooms offer easy access and slightly larger accommodation. There is a shared lounge and breakfast room.
7 rms (4 shr) (1 fmly) No smoking in 1 bedrooms No smoking in dining room No smoking in lounges CTV in all bedrooms Tea and coffee making facilities No dogs Cen ht CTV 8P No coaches
ROOMS: s £18-£25; d £32-£40

Maranatha 115 Gaywood Rd PE30 2PU ☎ 01553 774596
Well suited to the needs of its varied clientele, this competitively-priced small guest house offers sound accommodation and public rooms, which tend to be of rather cosy dimensions. Consisting of the main-house rooms and newer, rear extension rooms, the accommodation is individually decorated and fresh in appearance. There is also a ground floor bedroom with en suite bath and shower. Light snacks are available for guests during the evening.

7 rms (2 shr) 1 annexe bth (2 fmly) No smoking in dining room CTV in all bedrooms Tea and coffee making facilities Cen ht CTV 12P Last d 6pm
ROOMS: s fr £17; d £28-£34*

KINGSTON Devon Map **03** SX64

Selected

Q Q Q Q ***Trebles Cottage Hotel*** TQ7 4PT ☎ 01548 810268 FAX 01548 810268
Trebles Cottage is a delightful 19th-century house easily located between Kingsbridge and Plymouth. The proprietors have succeeded in creating a tasteful, comfortable and friendly guest house to suit the discerning traveller. Dinner menus are creative and accompanied by an interesting wine list. All bedrooms are en suite and equipped with modern facilities.
5 bth/shr No smoking in 3 bedrooms No smoking in dining room CTV in all bedrooms Tea and coffee making facilities Licensed Cen ht No children 12yrs 10P No coaches Last d 4pm
CARDS:

KINVER Staffordshire Map **07** SO88

Q Q Q **Kinfayre Restaurant** 41 High St DY7 6HF (exit A449 into Kinver village, premises located in main High Street) ☎ 01384 872565 FAX 01384 877724
Henry and Ann Williams have run this 17th-century inn for well over twenty years. Bedrooms are situated in an adjacent purpose-built block. There is a heated outdoor swimming pool for the use of residents. Locals make use of the two skittle alleys and lounge bar, and there is a varied selection of freshly prepared meals served in the cottage-style restaurant.
11 shr (1 fmly) No smoking in 6 bedrooms No smoking in dining room No smoking in lounges CTV in all bedrooms Tea and coffee making facilities No dogs (ex guide dogs) Cen ht 22P Outdoor swimming pool (heated) Skittle alley Last d 10pm
ROOMS: s £35; d £50; wkly b&b fr £175*
MEALS: Lunch £5.95-£8.95&alc Dinner £4.95-£12.95alc*
CARDS:

KIRKBY-IN-FURNESS Cumbria Map **07** SD28

Selected

Q Q Q Q **Greyhound** Grizebeck LA17 7XJ (turn off A590 at Greenodd onto A5092 for Whitehaven, after 5.5m turn onto A595 Barrow-in-Furness road by petrol station. Premises immediately ahead) ☎ 01229 889224 FAX 01229 889900
Situated just off the A590 in the hamlet of Grizebeck this homely inn provides an ideal stepping stone from which to tour both the west coast of Cumbria and the National Park. A farmhouse of Jacobean origins this appealing inn now offers stylish, well equipped accommodation that has recently benefited from refurbishment. A traditional menu comprises many home cooked dishes and is served within the cosy bar. A comfortable lounge is also provided for residents.
3 rms (2 shr) (1 fmly) No smoking in 1 bedrooms No smoking in dining room CTV in all bedrooms Tea and coffee making facilities Cen ht 25P Pool table Last d 9pm
ROOMS: s £18-£22; d £30-£35; wkly b&b £108-£126; wkly hlf-bd £161-£179*
MEALS: Lunch £7.60-£14.15alc Dinner £7.60-£14.15alc*
CARDS:

KIRKBY LONSDALE Cumbria Map **07** SD67

Selected

Q Q Q Q ***Abbot Hall*** LA6 2AB ☎ 01524 271406 FAX 01524 271406
Closed Nov-1 Mar
This historic 16th-century farmhouse has been superbly restored, and features solid oak beams, sloping floors, ancient oak panelling and a plethora of antiques. The dining room features a huge stone-faced grate with a traditional log burner. The bedrooms, all with en suite facilities, are comfortable; one has a fine four poster bed. Proprietors Mike and Sue Paget-Tomlinson are accommodating hosts, and guests may relax in the orchard at the front of the house.
3 shr No smoking Tea and coffee making facilities No dogs (ex guide dogs) Cen ht No children 7P No coaches Last d 1pm

KIRKBYMOORSIDE North Yorkshire Map **08** SE68

Selected

Q Q Q Q **Appletree Court** 9 High Market Place YO62 6AT (left off A170 (Thirsk to Scarborough) into Kirbymoorside. Carry on up main street. House is on left immediately after the King's Head Public Head) ☎ 01751 431536
Closed 24-26 Dec
Appletree Court was once a working farm and has since been converted into a well-furnished and comfortable guest house. Breakfast is served in the bright and fresh country-style dining room, and there are ample good eating places within a short walk of the house. The house retains many original features, while the well-equipped and comfortable bedrooms are all named after apples.
5 rms (4 bth/shr) No smoking CTV in all bedrooms Tea and coffee making facilities No dogs (ex guide dogs) Cen ht No children 12yrs 2P No coaches
ROOMS: s £26-£28; d £44-£48; wkly b&b £182-£196
See advertisement on p.243.

KIRKBY THORE Cumbria Map **12** NY62

Premier Selected

Q Q Q Q Q **Bridge End** *(NY635252)* CA10 1UZ (On A66 at Kirkby Thore) ☎ 017683 61362 Mrs Y Dent
Closed Xmas
Yvonne Dent offers a friendly welcome to her comfortable farmhouse. Spacious bedrooms are very individual, with Yvonne's hand-made cushions and patchwork quilts adding a homely touch. Rooms are thoughtfully well equipped, stylishly furnished and have little extras

contd.

such as fruit, biscuits and reading material. Substantial home-made meals are served around one table in the dining room. The lounge is the ideal place in which to relax.

Bridge End

3 rms (2 bth/shr) No smoking CTV in all bedrooms Tea and coffee making facilities No dogs (ex guide dogs) Cen ht 3P Fishing 550 acres dairy & arable Last d noon
ROOMS: s £21-£22; d £41-£42; wkly b&b £140-£147; wkly hlf-bd £203-£210

KIRK IRETON Derbyshire Map **08** SK25

Q Q **Barley Mow** Main St, Kirk Ireton DE6 3JP ☎ 01335 370306
Closed Xmas wk
Barley Mow Inn is more than 300 years old, and in many respects nothing has changed. The bars are small rooms with quarry-tiled floors, walls worn by customers leaning on them over the centuries, old oak and pine settles to sit on, and beer still dispensed directly into jugs from barrels behind the counter. Across the courtyard though, are modern bedrooms, with fully tiled bathrooms, but here too there is a taste of the past, with attractive scrubbed pine furniture and Scandinavian sleigh beds in one room.
5 bth/shr (1 fmly) CTV in all bedrooms Tea and coffee making facilities Cen ht P No coaches Last d noon
ROOMS: s fr £25; d fr £42*
MEALS: Dinner fr £9*

KIRTLING Cambridgeshire Map **05** TL65

Q Q **Hill** *(TL685585)* CB8 9HQ ☎ 01638 730253 Mrs C A Bailey
This 400-year-old farmhouse nestles between Kirtling and Saxon Street, in a secluded position surrounded by arable farmland. A more modern exterior belies the historical charm inside where there are heavily beamed dining and sitting rooms, and the welcoming atmosphere of blazing log fires. Accommodation is full of character but rather compact. Breakfast is served communally and evening meals are offered by arrangement.
3 rms (2 shr) CTV in all bedrooms Tea and coffee making facilities Direct dial from bedrooms No dogs (ex guide dogs) Licensed Cen ht CTV 15P Games room 500 acres arable Last d 8.30pm
ROOMS: s £25; d £45; wkly b&b £175-£215; wkly hlf-bd fr £231*

See advertisement under NEWMARKET

KNARESBOROUGH North Yorkshire Map **08** SE35

Q Q Q **Newton House Hotel** 5-7 York Place HG5 0AD
(on A59, 2.5m from A1 turn off) ☎ 01423 863539 FAX 01423 869748
Closed Feb
Situated close to the town centre, this attractive Georgian house is approached through its own archway and courtyard. The rooms have good modern facilities to complement their mainly generous proportions. Guests have an inviting and comfortable lounge with a small dispense bar to relax in, while home-cooked meals are served from a set menu in the charming dining room.
9 bth/shr 3 annexe bth/shr (4 fmly) No smoking in dining room CTV in all

bedrooms Tea and coffee making facilities Direct dial from bedrooms Licensed Cen ht CTV 9P No coaches Last d 7pm
ROOMS: s £35-£45; d £53-£75
CARDS:

Q Q Q ***The Villa*** The Villa Hotel, 47 Kirkgate HG5 8BZ
☎ 01423 865370 FAX 01423 867740
Standing next to the railway station and within easy walking distance of the town, this charming house also enjoys lovely river views at the rear. One bedroom now has a beautiful hand-carved mahogany four-poster bed, while all rooms have been thoughtfully equipped.
6 rms (4 shr) (1 fmly) No smoking in dining room CTV in all bedrooms Tea and coffee making facilities Direct dial from bedrooms Licensed Cen ht CTV No coaches

KNOCKIN Shropshire Map **07** SJ32

Selected

Q Q Q Q **The Old Forge** Knockin SY10 8HQ (take B4396 from A5 N of Nesscliffe 3m establishment 1st white house on left next to Bradford Arms pub, 6m SE of Oswestry)
☎ 01691 682394 FAX 01691 682423
As the name suggests, this cottage originally housed the village blacksmith. It has undergone substantial renovation in recent years and now provides delightful accommodation. Just two bedrooms are available: one, a twin on the ground floor; the other, a family room on the first floor. Both are quite spacious, comfortably furnished and equipped with modern facilities. The sitting room is cosy and leads into the dining room where hearty breakfasts are served. The home-made venison sausages are not to be missed.
2 shr (1 fmly) No smoking CTV in all bedrooms Tea and coffee making facilities No dogs (ex guide dogs) Cen ht CTV ch fac 4P
ROOMS: s fr £25; d fr £40; wkly b&b fr £126*

Selected

Q Q Q Q ***Top Farm House*** *(SJ334214)* SY10 8HN
☎ 01691 682582 Mrs P A Morrissey
Dating back some 500 years, this impressive Grade I listed, black and white timbered farmhouse, has a wealth of exposed beams and wall timbers. The spacious and comfortably furnished drawing room is full of character, and an open log fire burns here during the colder months. Breakfast is served in the adjacent dining room. The three bedrooms are spacious and well equipped.
3 bth/shr (1 fmly) No smoking in dining room CTV in all bedrooms Tea and coffee making facilities Cen ht CTV 6P

KNUTSFORD Cheshire Map **07** SJ77

Selected

Q Q Q Q **The Dog Inn** Well Bank Ln, Over Peover WA16 8UP (from A50 turn left at Whipping Stocks continue straight on for approx 2m) ☎ 01625 861421 FAX 01625 861421

Nestling in the heart of the Cheshire countryside, hanging baskets and tubs adorn the front of this white-painted 18th-century inn. Bedrooms are attractively furnished and equipped with many extras. The lounge bar and dining room offer a wide range of freshly prepared meals and snacks throughout the day, as well as a choice of cask ales.

6 bth/shr (1 fmly) No smoking in dining room CTV in all bedrooms Tea and coffee making facilities No dogs (ex guide dogs) Cen ht 80P Pool table Last d 9.30pm

ROOMS: s £50; d £70*

MEALS: Lunch £9.50-£19.50 Dinner £9.50-£19.50*

CARDS:

Selected

Q Q Q Q **The Hinton** Town Ln, Mobberley WA16 7HH (On B5085 Hinton on right just past shops, if coming from Knutsford or just past car showroom if coming from Wilmslow) ☎ 01565 873484 FAX 01565 873484

This personally run guesthouse is within easy reach of Manchester Airport. The no smoking accommodation has modern furnishings and equipment and includes a two bedroom family suite. Other facilities include a small but comfortable lounge and a pleasant dining room, where separate tables are provided.

5 bth/shr (1 fmly) No smoking CTV in all bedrooms Tea and coffee making facilities No dogs (ex guide dogs) Licensed Cen ht 10P No coaches Last d 4.30pm

ROOMS: s £33-£38; d £45-£50*

CARDS:

Premier Selected

Q Q Q Q Q **Laburnum Cottage** Knutsford Rd, Mobberley WA16 7PU (premises situated on the B50851.5m from Knutsford town centre, 250 yards beyond "Welcome to Mobberley" sign on left) ☎ 01565 872464 FAX 01565 872464

Although close to the motorway network, and within easy reach of Manchester Airport, this delightful house offers peace and quiet, in its one-acre garden lovingly created by owners Shirley and Malcolm. The same care and attention to detail is evident inside the house, with prettily decorated bedrooms provided with many thoughtful extras. There is a homely feel to the sitting room, and the conservatory provides an ideal place to relax during the summer. Breakfast is served around the highly polished oak table and courtesy transport can be arranged into town for dinner.

5 rms (3 bth/shr) No smoking CTV in all bedrooms Tea and coffee making facilities No dogs (ex guide dogs) Cen ht CTV 12P No coaches Golf 6 Horseriding Last d 8pm

ROOMS: s £35-£39; d £50; wkly b&b £250*

The AA's professional Inspectors make regular and anonymous visits to all the establishments listed in the Guide. They accept no gifts or favours from proprietors

Selected

Q Q Q Q **Old Vicarage** Moss Ln, Over Tabley WA16 0PL (exit M6 at junct 19 on to A556 signposted Manchester Airport. Turn right after Little Chef into Moss Lane) ☎ 01565 652221 FAX 01565 755918

Closed 2 Jan-18 Jan

The Old Vicarage is a charming 19th-century house that lies in two acres of landscaped grounds and gardens. Bedrooms are attractively furnished, and trouser presses and hair dryers are some of the modern facilities provided. One room is located at ground floor level, and one is suitable for families. The pretty dining room is open throughout the day for teas and snacks. Light lunches and suppers are also served.

4 bth/shr (1 fmly) No smoking CTV in all bedrooms Tea and coffee making facilities No dogs (ex guide dogs) Licensed Cen ht CTV No children 10yrs 50P Arrangements with 2 golf courses Last d 9pm

ROOMS: s fr £45; d fr £55; wkly b&b £250-£385*

CARDS:

Q Q Q ***Pickmere House*** Park Ln, Pickmere WA16 0JX ☎ 01565 733433

Closed Xmas

This imposing Grade II listed building dates back to 1772 and was originally a farmhouse. Bedrooms are generally spacious and are well equipped with modern facilities. One room is located in a nearby building and is suitable for less mobile guests. Visitors have a choice of two comfortably furnished lounges and breakfast is served in an attractive dining room.

9 rms (5 shr) (3 fmly) CTV in all bedrooms Tea and coffee making facilities Cen ht CTV 9P No coaches

LACOCK Wiltshire Map 03 ST96

Premier Selected

Q Q Q Q Q **At the Sign of the Angel** 6 Church St SN15 2LB
☎ 01249 730230 FAX 01249 730527
Closed 23 Dec-30 Dec
Guests cannot fail to be impressed by the historic character of this former 15th-century wool merchant's house in the famous National Trust village of Lacock. Bedrooms are all different, some spacious, some cosy, and several are in an adjacent building, reached by a foot bridge across the charming enclosed garden. Even the beds themselves are unusual: one was owned by the Victorian engineer, Isambard Kingdom Brunel, another is 7ft long, and there is also a four-poster. Each room is well equipped and has been individually furnished in keeping with the age of the building. Good food is served in the beamed dining rooms and there is an inviting guests' lounge on the first floor.
6 bth 3 annexe bth (1 fmly) CTV in all bedrooms Tea and coffee making facilities Direct dial from bedrooms Licensed Cen ht No children 10yrs 1P No coaches Last d 9pm
ROOMS: s £65-£75; d £90-£125*
CARDS:

LAMBERHURST Kent Map 05 TQ63

Q Q ◀ ***George & Dragon*** School Hill TN3 8DQ ☎ 01892 890277 FAX 01892 890277
This popular inn is centrally located in the village, and offers spacious bedrooms that are well equipped with modern en suite facilities. The traditionally-furnished bar serves a wide range of bar meals, snacks and real ales. There is an attractive beamed restaurant offering an à la carte menu, and service is overseen by resident proprietors Sheila and John Eaton.
6 rms (4 bth/shr) CTV in all bedrooms Tea and coffee making facilities No dogs (ex guide dogs) Cen ht 30P Skittle alley Last d 9.30pm
CARDS:

LAMBOURN Berkshire Map 04 SU37

Selected

Q Q Q Q **Lodge Down** The Woodlands RG17 7BJ
(M4 at junc 14 N then 1st left turning to Baydon. Lodge Down entrance 1 mile from Baydown on RHS)
☎ 01672 540304 FAX 01672 540304
This farmhouse overlooking the gallops of Lambourn Downs will appeal to racing fans, but any guest will be enchanted by the warmth of welcome and the pretty bedrooms with their period furnishings. The spacious sitting room is a focal point in the evenings and although dinner is not available Mr and Mrs Cook are happy to recommend local hostelries. Breakfast is served round a large communal table.
3 bth/shr (1 fmly) No smoking in bedrooms No smoking in dining room Tea and coffee making facilities No dogs (ex guide dogs) Cen ht CTV No children 10yrs 10P No coaches
ROOMS: s fr £30; d fr £45*

See advertisement under HUNGERFORD

LANCASTER Lancashire Map 07 SD46

Q Q Q **The Malt House** 136 Main Rd, Slyne-With-Hest LA2 6BD
(M6 junct 34 follow Lancaster signs, A6 North, Carnforth signs, leave Lancaster, go 2m to signs Slyne-with-Hest, the hotel is on A6 in village on left ☎ 01524 822771 FAX 01524 822771
Set in a row of 17th-century stone cottages, this pleasantly furnished house offers well equipped and modern bedrooms. There is a cosy lounge for guests and breakfast is served around a large table. The resident owners, Mr & Mrs Lassey are very friendly and attentive hosts.
2 bth/shr No smoking in bedrooms No smoking in dining room CTV in all bedrooms Tea and coffee making facilities No dogs (ex guide dogs) Cen ht CTV 6P
ROOMS: s £22-£24; d £39-£40; wkly b&b £100*

LAND'S END Cornwall & Isles of Scilly

See Sennen

LANGPORT Somerset Map 03 ST42

Premier Selected

Q Q Q Q Q ***Hillards*** High St, Curry Rivel TA10 0EY
(exit M25 at junc5, A358, approx 3m turn left at traffic lights onto A378 towards Curry Rivel, premises on left)
☎ 01458 251737 FAX 01458 253233
A delightful Grade II listed former farmhouse dating from the 17th century, Hillards has wealth of oak and elm panelling, beamed ceilings and large open fireplaces. Each bedroom is furnished to a very high standard and the emphasis throughout is on guest comfort. A hearty breakfast is served in the impressive dining room around the beautiful oak table. The surrounding area offers a range of interesting places to visit and there is no better way to end a days' exploration than to enjoy a cup of tea in the warm atmosphere created by hosts Jeannie and Mike.
4 rms (1 bth/shr) 2 annexe bth/shr No smoking No dogs (ex guide dogs) Cen ht CTV No children 25P No coaches

Premier Selected

Q Q Q Q Q ♥ **Muchelney Ham Farm** *(ST438238)* Muchelney Ham TA10 0DJ (Podimore rdbt, 3rd exit onto A372, 5miles turn left to B3165 Long Load,right at church, 1 mile right at T junct 1st farm on the right) ☎ 01458 250737 Mrs A Woodborne
Situated in a unspoilt area of the Somerset Levels with glorious views, this delightful long-house is conveniently located near the towns of Langport, Yeovil and only 15 miles from the county town of Taunton. There are many interesting gardens and houses to visit in the locality, and the farm makes an excellent base for exploring. Jim and Ann

Woodborne welcome their guests personally to their family home. Oak beams and inglenook fireplaces lend character to the accommodation, and furnishings are all in keeping. Traditional English breakfast is served at separate tables in the attractive dining room. A set dinner is available by prior arrangement. Pretty gardens run down to a stream and the working farm provides an added interest.

3 bth/shr (1 fmly) No smoking CTV in all bedrooms Tea and coffee making facilities No dogs Cen ht CTV No children 7yrs 6P
107 acres beef arable
ROOMS: s £25-£30; d £42-£50*

Selected

Q Q Q Q Old Mill Knole, Long sutton TA10 9HY (turn off A372 (Podimore/Langport) opposite Lime Kiln Inn to Knole. Turn right after 0.5m at end of lane) ☎ 01458 241599 FAX 01458 241710
Closed Xmas & New Year rs £
Paula Barber's former Victorian water mill is ideally located for visiting the various historic houses and gardens in the area. The bedrooms are individually furnished and decorated, each having a 'cottagey' atmosphere. Guests take breakfast around one large table in the dining room; Cordon Bleu dinners are provided by prior arrangement. A spacious and comfortable sitting room is available, with a log burning fire for those cooler evenings.
3 bth/shr (1 fmly) No smoking in 3 bedrooms CTV in all bedrooms Tea and coffee making facilities No dogs Cen ht CTV No children 10yrs 6P No coaches
ROOMS: s £28-£45; d £48-£55; wkly b&b £161-£175*

Selected

Q Q Q Q ***Orchard Cottage*** Townsend, Curry Rivel TA10 0HT (from M5 take A358 to Henlade, then A378 to Curry Rivel) ☎ 01458 251511
This delightful property is set in its own pretty garden in the village of Curry Rivel. Brian and Sheila Adams are naturally welcoming, and invite guests to enjoy the friendly atmosphere of their family home. The bedrooms are tastefully decorated in styles which accentuate the character of the cottage and thoughtful touches like fresh flowers have not been forgotten. Dinner is available by prior arrangement and wherever possible fresh local produce is featured in Sheila's imaginative cooking.
3 rms (1 fmly) No smoking CTV in 2 bedrooms Tea and coffee making facilities No dogs (ex guide dogs) Cen ht CTV 20P
Last d 5pm

LAUNCESTON Cornwall & Isles of Scilly Map **02** SX38

Premier Selected

Q Q Q Q Q ❦ **Hurdon** *(SX333828)* PL15 9LS
(leave A30 at first Launceston exit (A388), at roundabout take exit for Hospital, second right signposted for Trebullett, premises first on right) ☎ 01566 772955 Mrs M Smith
Apr-Oct
An 18th-century, stone and granite farmhouse, Hurdon Farm is run by Margaret Smith and her daughter who have preserved many of the building's original features in their farmhouse, including the impressive granite fireplace in the kitchen with its original Dutch oven. Bedrooms are individually furnished and decorated and there is a family suite at ground floor level. Imaginative home cooking is served each evening in the dining room.
6 bth (1 fmly) No smoking CTV in all bedrooms Tea and coffee making facilities No dogs (ex guide dogs) Cen ht CTV 10P
400 acres mixed Last d 4.30pm
ROOMS: s £32-£34; d £62-£66; wkly b&b £133-£147; wkly hlf-bd £193-£214

Premier Selected

QQQQQ **Percy's at Coombeshead** EX21 5EA
(approx 3m N of Launceston, off A388)
☎ 01409 211236 FAX 01409 211275
Spacious accommodation with big beds, wonderful country views, superb food and set in 40 acres of open fields, this is an ideal stopping-off point when going to and from Cornwall. Come for one of Tina Bricknell-Webb's superb dinners and stay for breakfast. Simply decorated but with some style, bedrooms are exceptionally well equipped with good quality toiletries, fresh fruit and mineral water being amongst the thoughtful extra touches provided.
8 bth/shr (2 fmly) No smoking CTV in all bedrooms Tea and coffee making facilities Licensed Cen ht ch fac 50P No coaches Last d 10pm
ROOMS: s £49.50; d £79.50; wkly b&b £275; wkly hlf-bd £429*
CARDS:

LAVENHAM Suffolk Map **05** TL94

See also Boxford

Selected

QQQQ **The Great House** Market Place CO10 9QZ
(Turn off A1141 onto Market Ln, situated just behind the cross on the Market Place)
☎ 01787 247431 FAX 01787 248007
Closed last 3 wks Jan
This restaurant with rooms overlooks the market square, yet owners Mr and Mrs Crepy ensure their establishment is a little pocket of France. The menu offers rural French cuisine and features an incredible cheeseboard to finish. The delightfully furnished restaurant has a large log-burning inglenook fireplace. The charming bedrooms are furnished with some lovely pieces and all have modern en suite facilities.
4 bth/shr (2 fmly) No smoking in dining room CTV in all bedrooms Tea and coffee making facilities Direct dial from bedrooms Licensed Cen ht ch fac Tennis Riding Last d 9.30pm
ROOMS: s £55-£65; d £70-£82*
CARDS:

LAVERTON Gloucestershire Map **04** SP03

Selected

QQQQ **Leasow House** Laverton Meadows WR12 7NA
(take B4632 from town to Winchcombe for 2m & turn right to Wormington then 1st on right) ☎ 01386 584526 FAX 01386 584596
Parts of this house, in its peaceful rural setting, date from the 16th century. Bedrooms are comfortable, well equipped and homely, and some retain low beams. Two bedrooms are situated within the original barn and one has been adapted for the less able. Delicious breakfasts are taken in the attractive dining room which overlooks the gardens. The library lounge is comfortable and relaxing.
5 bth/shr 2 annexe bth/shr (2 fmly) No smoking in bedrooms CTV in all bedrooms Tea and coffee making facilities Direct dial from bedrooms Cen ht 10P No coaches
ROOMS: s £40-£50; d £55-£65*
CARDS:

See advertisement under BROADWAY

LEAMINGTON SPA (ROYAL) Warwickshire Map **04** SP36

QQ **Charnwood** 47 Avenue Rd CV31 3PF
(approaching from A452, under railway bridge, guesthouse on right in 0.5m)
☎ 01926 831074 FAX 01926 831074
This friendly little guest house just south of the town centre offers clean, bright, value-for-money accommodation. Bedrooms are soundly appointed and guests have the use of a comfortable small lounge, and breakfast is served in a separate dining room.
6 rms (1 bth 1 shr) (1 fmly) No smoking in dining room No smoking in lounges CTV in all bedrooms Tea and coffee making facilities Cen ht CTV 6P Last d noon
ROOMS: s £17-£25; d £34-£36*
CARDS:

Selected

QQQQ **Comber House** 2 Union Rd CV32 5LT (from main shopping centre, The Parade continues along Warwick St, after passing Fire Station on your left, take 4th turning on right into Union Rd)
☎ 01926 421332 FAX 01926 313930
Closed mid Dec-mid Jan
Comber House is a fine example of an early 19th-century quality residence, recently converted into a tastefully appointed guest house.

Brian and Roma Shorthouse are friendly and enthusiastic hosts. Public rooms include a comfortably furnished lounge, a billiards room and a cheerful breakfast room. Bedrooms are individually furnished and decorated, in keeping with the character of the house; most rooms have a smart modern en-suite shower or bathroom.

5 rms (1 bth 3 shr) (1 fmly) No smoking CTV in all bedrooms Tea and coffee making facilities No dogs (ex guide dogs) Cen ht No children 12yrs 5P No coaches Snooker
ROOMS: s £45-£55; d £75*
CARDS:

Q Q Q **Coverdale Private Hotel** 8 Portland St CV32 5HE (turn into Europa Way, continue into Princess Drive, under railway and right to mini roundabout, left over bridge to traffic lights, right then left)
☎ 01926 330400 FAX 01926 833388
Conveniently located for most of the town's amenities, this attractive Regency house is enhanced by colourful floral displays during the summer months. Sympathetically restored and modernised it offers bright, well decorated bedrooms with many facilities in addition to modern en suites. Two spacious bedrooms are located on the ground floor. Breakfast is served in the dining room, and there is also a small lounge.
7 bth/shr (2 fmly) No smoking in 2 bedrooms CTV in all bedrooms Tea and coffee making facilities Direct dial from bedrooms Cen ht 3P
CARDS:

Q Q Q **Hill** *(SP343637)* Lewis Rd, Radford Semele CV31 1UX (2m from Leamington Spa on the A425, in village turn right into Lewis Rd and continue to bottom) ☎ 01926 337571 Mrs R Gibbs
Closed Xmas & New Year
Rebecca Gibbs is an enthusiastic host who offers a warm welcome to this mid-Victorian farmhouse, which sits in 350 acres of mixed farmland east of Leamington Spa. The public rooms include a comfortable lounge and a conservatory breakfast room that looks out over the garden. Bedrooms sizes and styles may vary, but each room is pleasantly appointed and well maintained.
5 rms (3 shr) No smoking CTV in all bedrooms Tea and coffee making facilities No dogs Cen ht CTV 6P 350 acres arable beef mixed sheep
ROOMS: s £22-£25; d £36-£42*

LECHLADE Gloucestershire Map 04 SU29

Premier Selected

Q Q Q Q Q **Cottage-by-the-Church** Chapel Ln, Filkins GL7 3JG (off A361 between Burford and Lechlade, alongside Filkins church)
☎ 01367 860613 FAX 01367 860613
Situated opposite St Peter's church in the heart of the village, this 17th-century property of mellow Cotswold stone, a conversion of four separate cottages, has been sympathetically and tastefully restored to provide guest accommodation with charm and character. Bedrooms, reached via the original stone spiral stairways, are homely and comfortable, with modern en suite or private bathrooms and lots of thoughtful extras. The combined lounge and dining room is furnished with some good period pieces and the open inglenook fireplace is very welcoming during the colder months.
3 bth/shr No smoking in bedrooms Tea and coffee making facilities Cen ht CTV No children 6yrs 4P
ROOMS: s £30; d £45; wkly b&b £136.50

LEDBURY Herefordshire Map 03 SO73

Q Q Q **Barn House** New St HR8 2DX (Situated on the main Ross to Worcester Rd in town centre of Ledbury)
☎ 01531 632825
Closed Xmas-Boxing
This charming old house, situated close to the town centre, dates back in part to around 1612. Interesting period features include a staircase with Chinese Chippendale screens. The accommodation has modern equipment and consists of two double rooms and one twin. Separate tables are provided in the traditional breakfast room. Other facilities include a pleasant lounge, a small bar and a large, attractive garden.
3 rms (1 shr) No smoking CTV in all bedrooms Tea and coffee making facilities No dogs Licensed Cen ht CTV No children 14yrs 6P
ROOMS: d £48-£54*
CARDS:

Selected

Q Q Q Q **Moor Court Farm** *(SO639447)* Stretton, Grandison HR8 2TP (1.5m E of A417 at Upper Eggleton) ☎ 01531 670408 FAX 670408 Mrs E Godsall
This 15th-century timber-framed house, which is fronted by a pleasant garden, is quietly situated on a 200 acre mixed farm. The house has a wealth of charm and character, which is enhanced by original features such as beamed ceilings and exposed wall timbers. The traditionally furnished accommodation consists of three good size bedrooms, one a double and the others twins. Separate tables are available in the attractive dining room, which has antique furniture. There is also a cosy lounge.
3 bth/shr No smoking CTV in all bedrooms Tea and coffee making facilities No dogs (ex guide dogs) Licensed Cen ht No children 5P Fishing 200 acres Mixed livestock, hops Last d 6.30pm

LEEDS West Yorkshire Map 08 SE33

Q Q Q **Ash Mount Hotel** 22 Wetherby Rd, Oakham LS8 2QD (follow A58 signs through Leeds, look for signposts to Roundhay, proceed on Roundhay Rd, left at roundabout after dual carriageway, right at lights)
☎ 0113 265 8164 2654263 FAX 0113 265 8164

contd.

This pleasant Victorian house is fronted by an attractive garden and provides good accommodation for the modern traveller. The bedrooms have been thoughtfully equipped and a comfortable lounge is also provided for guests. The hotel stands in a leafy part of Leeds and is close to Roundhay Park.
12 rms (9 bth/shr) (2 fmly) No smoking in 6 bedrooms No smoking in dining room No smoking in lounges CTV in all bedrooms Tea and coffee making facilities Direct dial from bedrooms Licensed Cen ht CTV 10P Last d breakfast
CARDS:

Q Q Q **Merevale Hotel** 16 Wetherby Rd, Oakwood LS8 2QD (A58 from city centre, at first roundabout on a dual carriageway turn left onto Oakwood Lane, right at traffic lights onto Wetherby Rd)
☎ 0113 265 8933 & 273 7985 FAX 0113 265 8933
Set back behind a neat front garden and offering warm and friendly service, this comfortable house offers modern bedrooms which are well equipped. There is a good lounge while a car park is to the rear. The house is close to Roundhay Park.
14 rms (6 bth/shr) (1 fmly) No smoking in dining room No smoking in lounges CTV in all bedrooms Tea and coffee making facilities Direct dial from bedrooms No dogs (ex guide dogs) Licensed Cen ht CTV No children 3yrs 9P Last d 8pm
ROOMS: s £20-£40; d £38-£50*
CARDS:

Q Q Q **Pinewood Private Hotel** 78 Potter Newton Ln LS7 3LW (leave town centre on A61 Harrogate Road. Turn right at roundabout at top of hill, hotel 600yds on left) ☎ 0113 262 2561 FAX 0113 262 2561
Situated only two miles from the city centre, in a pleasant residential area, this family guest house offers well furnished bedrooms which have been delightfully decorated and thoughtfully equipped. There are two comfortable lounges available for guests and good home cooking is served in the traditional dining room.
10 bth/shr (2 fmly) No smoking in dining room No smoking in 1 lounge CTV in all bedrooms Tea and coffee making facilities Licensed Cen ht CTV P No coaches Last d 10am
ROOMS: s £36; d £44; wkly b&b £133-£219; wkly hlf-bd £209.65-£295.65*
CARDS:

Selected

Q Q Q Q **Temple Manor** 2 Field End Garth, Temple Newsam LS15 0QQ (A34 follow signs for Temple Newsam House pass Temple Motors and turn right into Field End Gardens to T junct turn right Temple Manor 200yds on right) ☎ 0113 264 1384
This modern detached house stands in a quiet suburban area convenient for the city. The house is very well furnished and is very much a home, with very friendly service being provided by the resident owners. The bedrooms have been very pleasantly furnished and thoughtfully equipped while the public rooms include a conservatory and a new lounge.
3 bth/shr (1 fmly) No smoking CTV in all bedrooms Tea and coffee making facilities No dogs Cen ht CTV No children 12yrs 5P No coaches
ROOMS: s £27.50-£29.50; d £37.50-£39.50; wkly b&b £192.50-£262.50; wkly hlf-bd £227-£292

Q Q Q **Trafford House & Budapest Hotel** 18 Cardigan Rd, Headingley LS6 3AG (off A660 Otley Rd)
☎ 0113 275 2034 & 275 6637 FAX 0113 274 2422
Closed 24 & 25 Dec
The hotel consists of three Victorian villas which retain much of their original charm and are well furnished to meet the expectations of today's traveller. Good lounge accommodation and attractively furnished bedrooms are provided, as is warm and friendly service. The house overlooks Headingley Cricket Ground to the rear.
18 rms (4 shr) (4 fmly) No smoking in dining room CTV in all bedrooms Tea and coffee making facilities Direct dial from bedrooms No dogs (ex guide dogs) Licensed Cen ht CTV 30P Last d noon
ROOMS: s £27-£41; d £38-£56*
CARDS:

LEEK Staffordshire Map 07 SJ95

Q Q Q **Abbey** Abbey Green Rd ST13 8SA (off A523, N of town take turning signposted Meerbrook and bear right at T-junction. Inn on left.)
☎ 01538 382865 FAX 01538 398604
Accommodation at this popular 17th-century inn is in the adjacent, converted sandstone barn. The rooms are neatly decorated, have attractive pine furniture and are well equipped. A range of freshly prepared meals and snacks is offered in the comfortable lounge bar and small dining room or, in the warmer months, on the patio. The inn is located just out of the town with easy access to the moorlands and Alton Towers.
7 annexe shr CTV in all bedrooms Tea and coffee making facilities Direct dial from bedrooms No dogs (ex guide dogs) Cen ht No children 14yrs 60P No coaches Last d 8pm
CARDS:

LEICESTER Leicestershire Map 04 SK50

Q Q Q **Burlington Hotel** Elmfield Av LE2 1RB (just off A6, 0.75m from railway station) ☎ 0116 270 5112 FAX 0116 270 4207
Closed 23 Dec-2 Jan
Popular with business guests and visitors to the nearby university, this family-run hotel lies in a quiet residential area. The enthusiastic owners are continually upgrading the bedrooms, which are now attractively furnished with co-ordinated soft furnishings; a recent addition is satellite television. The public rooms include a cosy bar area, a quiet oak panelled lounge and a separate dining room.
16 rms (11 bth/shr) (1 fmly) CTV in all bedrooms Tea and coffee making facilities No dogs (ex guide dogs) Licensed Cen ht CTV 23P Last d 8.15pm
ROOMS: s £32-£42; d £46-£50
CARDS:

Q Q ***Croft Hotel*** 3 Stanley Rd LE2 1RF (close to city, main line railway station and major attractions yet it is set in hearty Stoneygate)
☎ 0116 270 3220 FAX 0116 270 3220
Located in a residential part of the city, this family-run hotel dates from the turn of the century. The public rooms are cheerful, offering a quiet lounge and a dining room themed around film star Humphrey Bogart. Bedrooms are soundly appointed with modern facilities, several are suitable for families and some are at ground-floor level.
25 rms (7 bth/shr) (3 fmly) No smoking in dining room CTV in all bedrooms Tea and coffee making facilities Licensed Cen ht CTV 16P Last d 6.30pm
CARDS:

Q Q **Scotia Hotel** 10 Westcotes Dr LE3 0QR (take 3rd turning on the right after A46 leaves the A5460 west end of Leicester) ☎ 0116 254 9200 FAX 2549200
The Scotia was built at the turn of the century as a private residence. The period features are highlighted with cheerful decoration in the comfortably furnished public rooms. Bedrooms are homely, and each room is fitted with a small desk. 6 bedrooms are located in a separate house across the road. An evening meal is available by arrangement.
11 rms (4 bth/shr) (1 fmly) No smoking in dining room CTV in all bedrooms Tea and coffee making facilities Licensed Cen ht 5P No coaches Last d 8pm
ROOMS: s £22-£29*

The Stanfre House Hotel 265 London Rd LE2 3BE
(A6, turn left off ring road, premises 1m on left before Clarendon Park Church) ☎ 0116 270 4294
Closed 25 Dec-2 Jan
Stanfre House is located on the southern side of the city, about a mile from the city centre. Bedrooms are located to the rear of the house and are screened from traffic noise; room sizes and styles are mixed. The comfortable lounge is very welcoming, and the dining room has a cheerful air.
12 rms (1 fmly) No smoking in dining room CTV in all bedrooms Licensed Cen ht CTV 6P
ROOMS: s £20; d £32*

Stoneycroft Hotel 5-7 Elmfield Av LE2 1RB
(Near to city centre on main A6 to Market Harborough)
☎ 0116 270 7605 FAX 0116 270 6067
This large hotel is presently in the process of a major refurbishment, to provide all rooms with en suite facilities. The bedrooms have modern fittings which include desks and suitable chairs. The public areas include a foyer lounge area, breakfast room and conference facilities. There is also a large restaurant/bar area, which serves a good selection of freshly cooked dishes.
44 rms (25 bth/shr) (4 fmly) No smoking in dining room CTV in all bedrooms Tea and coffee making facilities Direct dial from bedrooms No dogs (ex guide dogs) Licensed Cen ht CTV 20P Pool table Last d 9.30pm
ROOMS: s £25-£38; d £45*
CARDS:

LEIGH Dorset Map 03 ST60

Selected

Huntsbridge Farm *(SD622075)* Batcombe Rd DT9 6JA (A352 towards Dorchester. after 1.5m turn right Lewiston/Leigh. Follow for 4m to Give Way sign, turn right to Leigh.Turn left before bridge, on right) ☎ 01935 872150 FAX 01935 872150
Mr & Mrs M Read
Closed Xmas & Jan
Set on the edge of the village of Leigh and close to the Batcombe Downs, this delightful farmhouse enjoys a peaceful setting. The three bedrooms are all furnished to a high standard, en suite, well equipped and feature many thoughtful touches such as fresh flowers. Guests can relax in the smartly appointed lounge and take breakfast in the adjacent conservatory.
3 bth/shr No smoking CTV in all bedrooms Tea and coffee making facilities No dogs Cen ht CTV 3P
ROOMS: s fr £28; d fr £40*
CARDS:

LELANT Cornwall & Isles of Scilly Map 02 SW53

Selected

Badger TR26 3JT (Take A3074 off Hayle bypass towards St Ives, The Badger Inn is situated in the heart of Lelant Village on the right hand side) ☎ 01736 752181 FAX 01736 752181
Conveniently situated for St Ives, this village inn has a spacious bar. In the conservatory, a hot carvery is available throughout the season and at weekends. A good choice is offered on both the bar menu and the blackboards and features delicious home made puddings. The first floor bedrooms are comfortable, attractive and well equipped, and guests can also enjoy the attractive award winning gardens and patio area.
6 bth/shr No smoking in dining room No smoking in lounges CTV in all bedrooms Tea and coffee making facilities Direct dial from bedrooms No dogs (ex guide dogs) Cen ht No children 12yrs 100P No coaches Last d 10.15pm
ROOMS: s £35-£45; d £50-£75*
MEALS: Lunch £6.50-£15alc Dinner £15.50-£25alc*
CARDS:

LEOMINSTER Herefordshire Map 03 SO45

See also Shobdon

Selected

Heath House Stoke Prior HR6 0NF
(take A44 from Leominster, after crosssing A49 take second turning right at Drum Farm. Heath House 1.3 miles on left)
☎ 01568 760385 FAX 01568 760385
Apr-Oct
Situated in a peaceful rural location, this former 17th-century farmhouse has a pretty garden and retains many original features including exposed beams and open fireplaces. Bedrooms are spacious and comfortable with fine period furniture, lots of thoughtful extras and modern en suite or private facilities. Public areas include a spacious lounge and a dining room where guests can enjoy imaginative dinners and delicious English breakfasts.
3 bth/shr No smoking in bedrooms No smoking in dining room Tea and coffee making facilities No dogs Cen ht CTV No children 9yrs 4P No coaches Last d 9am
ROOMS: s £25-£27; d £44-£48; wkly b&b £133-£147; wkly hlf-bd £238-£252*

Prices shown in the directory are meant as a guide only and are subject to change. Please check before you book

Premier Selected

Q Q Q Q Q **Hills Farm** *(SO564638)* Leysters HR6 0HP (exit A4112 Leominster to Tenbury Wells Rd on the edge of Leysters village) ☎ 01568 750205 FAX 01568 750205 Mrs J Conolly
Mar-Oct
This impressive 15th-century farmhouse lies on an arable farm. Jane looks after the kitchen and offers a daily set menu with a good choice of dishes. Several of the spacious bedrooms are located in converted outbuildings and these are equipped with modern facilities and high quality furnishings. A comfortable sitting room is available, and there is an abundance of information sheets on local beauty spots and leisure walks.
2 bth 3 annexe bth/shr No smoking CTV in all bedrooms Tea and coffee making facilities No dogs (ex guide dogs) Cen ht No children 12yrs 8P 120 acres arable Last d noon
ROOMS: s £34-£37; d £48-£54; wkly b&b £168-£259; wkly hlf-bd £287-£378
CARDS:

Selected

Q Q Q Q *Lower Bache* Kimbolton HR6 0ER (signposted from A4112 halfway between the villages of Kimbolton and Leysters) ☎ 01568 750304
This delightful, 350-year old, stone-built farmhouse is peacefully situated on a 14-acre holding. The bedrooms all have modern equipment and facilities, and one is located on the ground floor of a former stable. The dining room has sturdy antique furniture and original features, such as exposed beams and a stone-flagged floor. Rose Wiles prides herself on her cooking and set dinners.
3 bth/shr 1 annexe bth/shr No smoking CTV in all bedrooms Tea and coffee making facilities No dogs (ex guide dogs) Licensed Cen ht No children 8yrs 5P Last d noon

Q Q **Woonton Court Farm** *(SO548613)* Leysters HR6 0HL (take A49, 2.5m from town onto A4112 and pass through Kimbolton, turning right for Woonton before Leysters village. Farm 0.5m down lane) ☎ 01568 750232 FAX 01568 750232 Mrs E M Thomas
Closed 22-27 Dec
Parts of this old stone-built farmhouse date back to the 15th century. It has many original features, including low-beamed ceilings, and timber-framed walls. The house is located on a 300-acre cattle and sheep farm. The bedrooms have traditional furniture, including antique pieces. One is a cottage-style suite located in a converted outbuilding. Separate tables are provided in the breakfast room/lounge.
3 bth/shr No smoking in 1 bedrooms No smoking in area of dining room CTV in all bedrooms Tea and coffee making facilities Cen ht CTV ch fac 4P 250 acres mixed Last d previous day
ROOMS: d £36-£40; wkly b&b fr £125; wkly hlf-bd £180-£200.50*

LEVEN East Riding of Yorkshire Map 08 TA14

Q Q *The New Inn* 44 South St HU17 5NZ (off A1035, 6m NE of Beverley) ☎ 01964 542223
Providing a sound standard of accommodation, this red brick inn stands in the village centre and offers modern bedrooms together with a pleasant bar.
4 rms (3 shr) (1 fmly) No smoking in 1 bedrooms No smoking in area of dining room CTV in all bedrooms Tea and coffee making facilities Cen ht CTV 55P Golf 18 Last d 9pm
CARDS:

LEVENS Cumbria Map 07 SD48

Q Q Q *Birslack Grange* Hutton Ln LA8 8PA (exit M6 at junc 36, A591, A590, 1.5m turn right into village, past Hare & Hounds to village crossroads, turn left into Hutton Lane 300yds on left) ☎ 015395 60989
This attractive private residence - a modern conversion of an old barn - sits sedately in gardens on the fringe of the village, and enjoys fine views across meadowland to the south Lakeland hills. A stylish house with lots of personal touches, it offers bright cheerful pine-furnished bedrooms and well proportioned public rooms – a comfortable lounge and a Mediterranean style dining room.
4 rms (3 shr) No smoking Tea and coffee making facilities No dogs (ex guide dogs) Cen ht CTV 4P No coaches Cycle hire Fell walking Last d 8pm

Q Q Q **Gilpin Bridge** Bridge End LA8 8EP (on A5074, 100mtrs from junct with A590) (Frederic Robinson) ☎ 015395 52206 FAX 015395 52444
Just outside Levens, this traditional inn is ideally placed to attract both the business and leisure guest. A strong culinary theme provides an extensive bar and restaurant menu. Bedrooms are modern and well equipped and staff are friendly and keen to please.
10 bth/shr No smoking in 2 bedrooms No smoking in area of dining room No smoking in 1 lounge CTV in all bedrooms Tea and coffee making facilities Direct dial from bedrooms No dogs (ex guide dogs) Cen ht 100P Last d 9pm
ROOMS: s £29.50-£32; d £46-£60; wkly b&b £170-£180
MEALS: Lunch £5.75-£9.50&alc Dinner £5.95-£9.50&alc
CARDS:

LEWES East Sussex Map 05 TQ41

Selected

Q Q Q Q **Nightingales** The Avenue, Kingston BN7 3LL (2.5m SW of Lewes, turn off A27 signposted to Kingston, turn right after 30mph sign) ☎ 01273 475673 FAX 01273475673
Nightingales is situated at the foot of the South Downs along a quiet residential road, and is surrounded by beautifully kept gardens that are part of the National Garden Scheme. Exotic tender plants are housed in the conservatory where tea is happily provided. The rooms, one of which is en suite, are very comfortably furnished and come with a wide range of thoughtful extras from fresh fruit and sherry, to chocolate and fresh flowers. Dinner is not available but Geoff and Jean are happy to advise on local restaurants. Well behaved dogs are welcome and the Hudson's themselves have an black Labrador called Benny who provides a very warm welcome!
2 bth/shr (1 fmly) No smoking CTV in all bedrooms Tea and coffee making facilities Cen ht CTV No children 2P No coaches
ROOMS: s £35-£45; d £45-£55
CARDS:

LEYBURN North Yorkshire Map **07** SE19

Q Q Q **Clyde House** Railway St DL8 5AY (just off Market Square on A684) ☎ 01969 623941 FAX 01969 623941
Conveniently situated on the main road just off the market square, this interesting listed house is full of character and remarkably peaceful despite its location. Bedrooms are all individual and offer a variety of sizes, with those in the newly converted barn offering the added advantage of separate access. Breakfasts are taken in the cosy dining room which also doubles as a tea room in summer.
5 shr No smoking in dining room CTV in all bedrooms Tea and coffee making facilities Cen ht No children 12yrs
ROOMS: s £23-£26; d £36-£42; wkly b&b £126-£136.50*

Q Q Q ***Eastfield Lodge Private Hotel*** 1 St Matthews Ter DL8 5EL (on A684, near St Matthews Church) ☎ 01969 623196
This substantial house sits in its own gardens a short walk from the town centre. Well proportioned throughout, it has good sized bedrooms, an attractive dining room and a comfortable lounge which also has a small residents bar.
9 rms (4 shr) (2 fmly) CTV in all bedrooms Tea and coffee making facilities Licensed Cen ht 10P

Selected

Q Q Q Q **Foresters Arms** Carlton-in-Coverdale DL8 4BB (Off A1 at Catterick/Leeming Bar to Leyburn. M6 junct 37 to Gedbergh/Hawes. Carlton is situated off A684 5m from Leyburn and 18m from Hawes) ☎ 01969 40272 FAX 01969 40272
It's well worth making the journey to this delightful old inn. The traditional bar features low beams, stone flag floors and limestone walls, and in addition there is a more opulent restaurant offering an extensive range of imaginative and carefully produced dishes. The bedrooms are well furnished and offer restful, relaxing accommodation.
4 rms (1 bth 2 shr) (1 fmly) No smoking in area of dining room CTV in 3 bedrooms Tea and coffee making facilities Direct dial from bedrooms No dogs Cen ht 10P No coaches Last d 9pm
CARDS:

Selected

Q Q Q Q **Greenhills** 5 Middleham Rd DL8 5EY (on A6108 approx 100yds from the t-junction with the A684) ☎ 01969 623859
Closed Xmas/New Year
Mr and Mrs Pringle are the welcoming owners of this attractive detached house set in the lovely Yorkshire town of Leyburn. It consists of delightfully decorated bedrooms which have been thoughtfully equipped to include almost every possible extra. A delicious English breakfast is served around a large table in the elegant dining room.
3 bth/shr No smoking CTV in all bedrooms Tea and coffee making facilities No dogs Cen ht CTV No children 3P No coaches
ROOMS: s £25; d £40*

Selected

Q Q Q Q **Ivy Dene Country Guest House** Main St, West Witton DL8 4LP (A1 junct with A684 Bedale to Leyburn. 3.5 miles west of Leyburn on A684) ☎ 01969 622785
Closed 24-26 Dec
Standing in a peaceful village Ivy Dene is a 300-year-old Dales house which retains much of its original charm and character. The bedrooms have been thoughtfully equipped and delightfully furnished. Good home-cooking is served in the pleasant dining room and Bob and June Dickinson are very friendly hosts. The house is non-smoking throughout.
5 bth/shr (1 fmly) No smoking CTV in 3 bedrooms Tea and coffee making facilities Licensed Cen ht CTV No children 5yrs 6P No coaches Last d 4pm
ROOMS: s £30-£35; d £50-£52; wkly b&b £168-£182; wkly hlf-bd £245.80-£257.50

Premier Selected

Q Q Q Q Q **Park Gate House** Constable Burton DL8 5RG (on A684 opposite Constable Burton Hall) ☎ 01677 450466
Closed 25-26 Dec
Geoff and Sandra Thornber offer a friendly welcome at their delightful cottage set on the edge of Constable Burton. The house is adorned with plants and flowers grown in the beautiful garden. Both the lounge and dining room are furnished in a traditional style. Bedrooms come in a variety of sizes. Sandra's excellent breakfasts are a highlight, particularly her buffet selection of fruit compotes.
3 bth/shr 1 annexe shr No smoking CTV in all bedrooms Tea and coffee making facilities No dogs (ex guide dogs) Licensed Cen ht CTV No children 12yrs 6P No coaches
ROOMS: s £30-£35; d £46-£56*

LICHFIELD Staffordshire Map **07** SK10

Q Q **206 Beacon Street** WS13 7BH (locate Cathedral, drive past Cathedral Close out of the city, 0.25 mile down Beacon St, approach small island, house on right) ☎ 01543 262130
You are ensured of a warm welcome by the enthusiastic and friendly proprietors of 206 Beacon Street. There is a definite cottage-style feel to this house, located on the edge of the city but within easy reach of the cathedral. Bedrooms are comfortably appointed, bright and nicely decorated, while breakfast is served around one table in the dining room.
2 rms No smoking CTV in all bedrooms Tea and coffee making facilities Cen ht No coaches
ROOMS: s £18; d £30-£32*

Q Q Q **Coppers End** Walsall Rd, Muckley Corner WS14 0BG (on A461, 100yds from Muckley Corner rdbt off the A5) ☎ 01543 372910 FAX 01543 360423
Closed Xmas New Year
Converted from an old police station, this well maintained guest house is conveniently situated for both the city and major routes. Breakfast is served in the conservatory, overlooking the rear garden and patio. Guests also have use of a separate comfortably appointed lounge. Non-smoking bedrooms, two of which are on the ground floor, are well equipped and attractively furnished; new for this year are two smartly appointed and modern en suite shower rooms.
6 rms (3 bth/shr) No smoking in bedrooms No smoking in area of dining room CTV in all bedrooms Tea and coffee making facilities Licensed Cen ht CTV 12P No coaches Last d noon
ROOMS: s £25-£34; d £37-£46*
CARDS:

Q Q **Little Pipe Farm** *(SK078106)* Little Pipe Ln, Farewell, Chorley WS13 8BS (Litchfield A51, from Bowling Green Island left into Abnalls Lane right into Dark Lane follow Chorley signs left Little Pipe Lane) ☎ 01543 683066 Mrs E Clewley
This 19th-century farmhouse, which is still part of a working arable and beef farm, is the home of Mr and Mrs Clewley are friendly hosts who will provide a traditional evening meal by prior arrangement. Bedrooms are simply appointed and freshly decorated, and share a general bathroom.
contd.

Guests are encouraged to use the comfortable lounge, and both breakfast and dinner are served around one table in the character dining room.
3 rms (1 fmly) No smoking in bedrooms CTV in all bedrooms No dogs Cen ht CTV P Fishing 230 acres arable beef Last d by arrangement
ROOMS: s £17-£20; d £35-£40; wkly b&b £105-£126; wkly hlf-bd £161-£182*

Q Q **Main View** 18 Burton Rd DE13 7BB
(on A38 northbound 0.25 miles from A513, 200 yds past British Legion Club) ☎ 01283 790725
Closed 24 Dec-2 Jan
Situated on the slip road adjacent to the A38, this large detached house offers comfortable accommodation, including one en suite room on the ground floor. There is a lounge leading to the dining room which looks out on the garden to the rear of the property.
3 rms (1 shr) No smoking in dining room CTV in all bedrooms Tea and coffee making facilities No dogs (ex guide dogs) Cen ht CTV 6P No coaches
ROOMS: s £18-£20; d £34-£38; wkly b&b £112*

Q Q Q **Moat Cottage** 29 Gaia Ln WS13 7LW (A38 to A5026 Lichfield follow main road through city towards Cathedral, right into Gaia Lane, house is 200yds on left before bend) ☎ 01543 264591
Closed 20-31 Dec
This pretty white painted cottage, with mature gardens to the rear, is located close to the city and cathedral. The beamed ground floor twin bedroom has an en suite shower room, while the single has private use of an adjacent bathroom; both are attractively decorated and equipped with pine furniture. Breakfast is served around one table in the dining room.
2 rms (1 shr) No smoking CTV in all bedrooms Tea and coffee making facilities No dogs (ex guide dogs) Cen ht 2P
ROOMS: s £23-£25; d £40-£45; wkly b&b £100-£120

Q Q Q **Oakleigh House Hotel** 25 St Chads Rd WS13 7LZ
(A38 Northbound onto A5192, go straight on at 2 islands go into Eastern Ave, 3rd left by pub. Turn right at T-junct, first building on left)
☎ 01543 262688 255573 FAX 01543 418556
This is a busy commercial hotel with a very successful restaurant. It sits in its own grounds in a quiet residential area. Five rooms in the main building are more spacious than those in the annexe but all are well equipped with modern facilities. The conservatory restaurant is in several sections and there is a comfortable lounge and bar.
5 bth/shr 6 annexe bth/shr No smoking in dining room CTV in all bedrooms Tea and coffee making facilities Direct dial from bedrooms Licensed Cen ht 20P No coaches Last d 9pm
ROOMS: s £39-£49; d £55-£69.95*
CARDS:

Q Q Q **Park View** Shaw Ln WS13 7AG (follow directions to cathedral from city centre, follow road for approx 200 yds and take left turning into Shaw Lane, bungalow on right) ☎ 01543 256166
Closed 22-26 Dec
Park View is a family bungalow that lies in a quiet area near the Cathedral and Beacon Park. Two bedrooms are provided and these are attractively decorated and equipped with modern facilities. There is no breakfast room or lounge for guests but each room has comfortable armchairs and facilities for breakfasting in comfort.
2 bth/shr No smoking CTV in all bedrooms Tea and coffee making facilities No dogs Cen ht No children 6P No coaches
ROOMS: s £23; d £33-£35; wkly b&b £145; wkly hlf-bd £160*

Q Q Q **Stone House Farm** Farewell WS13 8DS
(Take A51 signed Rugeley/Stafford, take 2nd lane on left (Cross-in-Hand Lane). After 2m bear left establishment 2nd cottage on right) ☎ 01543 682575
Situated just outside the town this 17th-century house with livery stables is set in delightful gardens and enjoys views over open farmland. Bedrooms are bright and well furnished. The beamed lounge has a welcoming wood-burning stove in the inglenook fireplace, and breakfast is served in one of two separate dining areas.
3 rms No smoking CTV in all bedrooms No dogs Cen ht CTV No children 5yrs P Riding Golf and fishing nearby
ROOMS: s £15-£18; d £30-£36; wkly b&b £105*

Q Q Q ***Woodmuir*** Nether Beacon WS13 7AT ☎ 01543 251269
Woodmuir is a large detached house set in a residential cul-de-sac, just a short walk from the town centre and is very handily placed for access to the Cathedral. Bedrooms vary in sizes and styles, each room is individually furnished and soundly appointed, and guests have use of a comfortable lounge which overlooks the rear garden; breakfasts are taken communally around a large table in a tastefully appointed breakfast room.
3 rms (1 shr) No smoking CTV in 1 bedroom Tea and coffee making facilities No dogs (ex guide dogs) Cen ht CTV No children 7yrs 4P No coaches

LIGHTHORNE Warwickshire Map 04 SP35

Q Q Q **Redlands** *(SP334570)* Banbury Rd CV35 0AH
(off B4100, 5m S of Warwick) ☎ 01926 651241 Mrs J Stanton
Closed Xmas
Redlands Farm is surrounded by 100 acres of arable land which is ideal for short rambles. All the bedrooms are spacious, and one features a raised brass bedstead. Parts of the building date back to the 16th century but the overall impression is one of modern day comfort, now providing a comfortable guests' lounge and a cosy breakfast room.
3 rms (1 bth) (1 fmly) No smoking Tea and coffee making facilities No dogs (ex guide dogs) Cen ht CTV 7P Outdoor swimming pool 100 acres arable
ROOMS: s £17.50-£20; d £36-£42*

LINCOLN Lincolnshire Map 08 SK97

See also Horncastle, Marton, Sturton by Stow & Swinderby

Selected

Q Q Q Q **Carline** 1-3 Carline Rd LN1 1HL (left off the A1102, A15 N, premises 1m from A46 bypass and A57 into city) ☎ 01522 530422
Closed Xmas & New Year
John and Gill Pritchard are the friendly owners of this delightfully furnished guest house which is found in a quiet side road not far from the city. Bedrooms are attractive and have been very thoughtfully equipped, whilst the public rooms include a comfortable lounge and an attractive dining room. Service is very attentive and the house is fully no smoking.
9 bth/shr 3 annexe bth/shr (2 fmly) No smoking CTV in all bedrooms Tea and coffee making facilities No dogs (ex guide dogs) Cen ht No children 2yrs 13P No coaches
ROOMS: s £30-£40; d £40-£45*

Selected

Q Q Q Q **D'Isney Place Hotel** Eastgate LN2 4AA
(100yds away from Lincoln Cathedral, nearest main rd is A15 or A46)
☎ 01522 538881 FAX 01522 511321
This lovely 17th-century house stands in its own well tended walled garden and is within easy walking distance of the city centre. The bedrooms have been tastefully furnished with some delightful pieces and some have spa baths and four poster beds. As there are no public rooms, breakfast is served to each bedroom using the finest tableware.
17 bth/shr (2 fmly) No smoking in 10 bedrooms CTV in all bedrooms Tea and coffee making facilities Direct dial from bedrooms Cen ht 4P
ROOMS: s £48-£68; d £61-£92*
CARDS:

Selected

Q Q Q Q **Minster Lodge Hotel** 3 Church Ln LN2 1QJ (A15 five minutes from city centre) ☎ 01522 513220 FAX 01522 513220
A warm welcome can be expected from Mr and Mrs Baumber at this privately owned hotel, situated close to the city centre. This establishment recently changed hands, and the accommodation has been totally refurbished. Bedrooms are furnished with hand-made natural pine furniture, and have a good range of useful extras. All rooms also have modern en suite facilities with beautiful ceramic floor and wall tiles. There is a comfortable lounge as well as an attractive dining room where guests can enjoy a hearty breakfast.
6 bth/shr (2 fmly) No smoking CTV in all bedrooms Tea and coffee making facilities Direct dial from bedrooms No dogs (ex guide dogs) Licensed Cen ht CTV 6P No coaches
ROOMS: s £50-£65; d £65-£90*
CARDS:

Q Q Q **Tennyson Hotel** 7 South Park Av LN5 8EN (S of city centre on A15, nr South Park Common) ☎ 01522 521624 FAX 01522 521624
Closed 23 Dec-2 Jan
This comfortable house offers very well equipped bedrooms which include telephones and hairdryers. There is a cosy guest lounge and breakfast is served in the delightful cottage-style dining room. Friendly and attentive service is provided and the house is very convenient for the city centre.
8 bth/shr (1 fmly) No smoking in dining room CTV in all bedrooms Tea and coffee making facilities Direct dial from bedrooms No dogs Licensed Cen ht 8P No coaches
ROOMS: s £29; d £40-£42*
CARDS:

LISKEARD Cornwall & Isles of Scilly Map **02** SX26

Q Q Q **Elnor** 1 Russell St PL14 4BP (between town centre & railway station) ☎ 01579 342472 FAX 01579 345673
Closed Xmas
Located near the town centre, this personally run guest house caters for both the leisure and commercial markets. The well equipped bedrooms vary in size and a comfortable lounge is available at all times. Full English breakfast is served in the attractive dining room and a small bar is available for drinks in the evening.
9 rms (7 shr) (1 fmly) No smoking in dining room CTV in all bedrooms Tea and coffee making facilities Direct dial from bedrooms No dogs Licensed Cen ht CTV 6P No coaches Last d 5pm

Selected

Q Q Q Q **Tregondale** *(SX294643)* Menheniot PL14 3RG (E of Liskeard.Off A38 for Menheriot at Hayloft Rest. 1.5m to Menheriot,through village,1m left at junct.Signs on right.A390 follow signs to Menheriot) ☎ 01579 342407 FAX 01579 342407 Mrs S Rowe
rs 24-25 Dec

This 200 acre cattle and sheep farm is situated in a pleasant valley, about a mile from the village of Menheniot, east of Liskeard. The house is built on the site of an old manor dating back to the Domesday Book, and offers well equipped modern bedrooms, one suitable for family use. There is a comfortable lounge, where a wood-burning stove is lit in cold weather. All guests share one table in the pleasant dining room. Other facilities here include an all-weather tennis court.
3 bth/shr No smoking in bedrooms No smoking in dining room No smoking in 1 lounge CTV in all bedrooms Tea and coffee making facilities No dogs CTV No children 2yrs 3P Golf Tennis (hard) Fishing Cycling 200 acres arable beef mixed sheep Last d 6pm
ROOMS: s £22-£25; d £40-£45; wkly b&b £136.50-£140; wkly hlf-bd £199.50-£210*

LITTLEBOURNE Kent Map **05** TR25

Q Q Q ***King William IV*** 4 High St CT3 1ST
(turn off M2 at the Howletts Zoo junct, proceed to Littlebourne, when you join A257 establishment is directly opposite)
☎ 01227 721244 FAX 01227 721244
There is a lot of character in this popular village inn, and a friendly informal atmosphere. The four en suite bedrooms have been thoughtfully furnished and equipped to offer comfortable accommodation. The King William has a well deserved reputation for its food, offering an interesting menu which changes daily.
4 bth/shr (1 fmly) CTV in all bedrooms Tea and coffee making facilities No dogs (ex guide dogs) Cen ht No children 10yrs 20P No coaches Traditional pub games Last d 9.20pm
CARDS:

LITTLE DEWCHURCH Herefordshire Map **03** SO53

Selected

QQQQ ❦ **Cwm Craig** *(SO535322)* HR2 6PS
(take A49 from Ross rdbt, take 2nd turning on right from rdbt, continue to Little Dewchurch, turn right in village Cwm Craig is first farm on left) ☎ 01432 840250 FAX 01432 840250 Mrs G Lee
This large Georgian farmhouse is surrounded by farmland and its own large garden. The comfortable accommodation includes family rooms, and one of the two rooms without en suite facilities has a nearby private shower and toilet. There are two traditionally furnished dining rooms, where separate tables are provided, and a comfortable lounge. There is also a games room containing a three-quarter size snooker table and a dart board.
3 rms (2 bth/shr) (1 fmly) No smoking in dining room CTV in all bedrooms Tea and coffee making facilities No dogs (ex guide dogs) Cen ht CTV 5P Snooker/pool table Darts 190 acres arable beef
ROOMS: s £16-£18; d £32-£36; wkly b&b £105-£119*

LITTLE GRANSDEN Cambridgeshire Map **04** TL25

QQQ ❦ **Gransden Lodge** *(TL288537)* Longstowe Rd SG19 3EB
(2m off A1198 between Longstowe and Little Grandsden on B1046)
☎ 01767 677365 FAX 01767 677647 Mrs M Cox
Gransden Lodge Farm sits between the villages of Longstowe and Little Gransden. The comfortable bedrooms are attractively decorated and have modern en suite facilities. There is also a well appointed dining room and an inviting lounge with an open log fire. Please note that smoking is not permitted.
3 bth/shr No smoking CTV in all bedrooms Tea and coffee making facilities No dogs Cen ht CTV 6P 860 acres arable beef mixed
ROOMS: s £20; d £40*

LIVERPOOL Merseyside Map **07** SJ39

QQQ **Aachen Hotel** 91 Mount Pleasant L3 5TB (from M62 or M58 follow signs for city centre to Mount Pleasant car park)
☎ 0151 709 3477 709 3633 FAX 0151 709 1126
Closed 22 Dec-2 Jan
Situated in walking distance of both the Roman Catholic cathedral and the city centre, this small hotel provides comfortable accommodation. Smartly maintained bedrooms are particularly well equipped, and there is also a cosy bar and nicely furnished dining room offering a choice of evening meals.
17 rms (11 bth/shr) (6 fmly) No smoking in 10 bedrooms No smoking in dining room CTV in all bedrooms Tea and coffee making facilities Direct dial from bedrooms No dogs (ex guide dogs) Licensed Cen ht CTV 2P Snooker Bar games Last d 8.30pm
ROOMS: s £26-£35; d £40-£50; wkly b&b £140-£175; wkly hlf-bd £194.25-£229.25*
CARDS: MasterCard, American Express, Barclaycard Visa, Diners Club, Barclays Connect, Delta, Switch

QQQ **The Blenheim** 37 Aigburth Dr, Sefton Park L17 4JE
(turn off A561 into Sefton Park, 1st house on left in park)
☎ 0151 727 7380 FAX 0151 727 5833
This large Victorian house lies on the edge of Sefton Park and was once the family home of the late Stu Sutcliffe, a former bass player with The Beatles. Bedrooms are modern and well equipped and provide good-value accommodation for business travellers and visitors to the university. A cosy lounge bar is also provided for residents.
17 rms (8 shr) (4 fmly) No smoking in dining room CTV in all bedrooms Tea and coffee making facilities No dogs Licensed Cen ht CTV 22P Last d 8.30pm
ROOMS: s £19.50-£29; d £33-£39
CARDS: MasterCard, Barclaycard Visa, Delta

LIZARD Cornwall & Isles of Scilly Map **02** SW71

Premier Selected

QQQQQ ***Landewednack House*** Church Cove TR12 7PQ (left off A3083 at Lizard Village signed Church Cove then in 0.25m fork left) ☎ 01326 290909 FAX 01326 290192
This former 17th-century rectory located in a peaceful setting overlooking the sea, has been well-appointed throughout. The tastefully furnished and decorated bedrooms, which feature some fine period furniture and colourful co-ordinated soft furnishings include many thoughtful extras. An evening meal is available by arrangement, and guests can choose to eat at a communal table or at individual tables in a smaller dining room. There is also a sitting room.
3 bth/shr No smoking CTV in all bedrooms Tea and coffee making facilities Direct dial from bedrooms No dogs Licensed Cen ht No children 18yrs 4P No coaches Outdoor swimming pool (heated) Boules Croquet lawn Last d 8pm
CARDS: MasterCard, Barclaycard Visa

QQQ ***Penmenner House Hotel*** Penmenner Rd TR12 7NR
☎ 01326 290370
Guests will find a warm and friendly welcome at this Victorian house standing in its own grounds, and benefiting from a superb coastal location on the Lizard peninsula. In addition to a pretty dining room where home cooked dinners are served, there is a choice of comfortable lounges. Bedrooms are nicely furnished with a personal touch. Built in 1860, the property was once the haunt of the Bloomsbury set and has an interesting history.
6 rms (5 shr) No smoking CTV in all bedrooms Tea and coffee making facilities No dogs (ex guide dogs) Licensed Cen ht CTV 10P No coaches Table tennis Pool table Last d 5pm
CARDS: MasterCard, Barclaycard Visa, Delta

LONDON Greater London

Places within the London postal area are listed below in postal district order commencing East then North, South and West, with a brief indication of the area covered. Other places within the county of London are listed under their respective placenames.

E4 CHINGFORD

QQQ ***Ridgeway Hotel*** 115/117 The Ridgeway, North Chingford E4 6QU ☎ 0181 529 1964
A friendly and informal hotel, easily located in Chingford. It is family run and offers spacious and comfortable, well equipped bedrooms, all en suite. There is a combined restaurant, reception and bar and the menu has some Greek specialities.
20 rms

E11 LEYTONSTONE

Premier Selected

QQQQQ **Lakeside** 51 Snaresbrook Rd, Wanstead E11 1PQ
(half mile from end of M11 close to Snaresbrook Underground Station)
☎ 0181 989 6100
Mar-Nov
Located in an ideal setting overlooking the lake and within walking distance of the underground station, this house, which has many of its original features, has been thoughtfully furnished throughout. The spacious bedrooms are modern in style, comfortably appointed and well equipped with many modern facilities. A generous breakfast is served in the elegant lounge/dining room that overlooks the attractive garden, and afternoon tea can be served on the patio.
3 bth/shr No smoking CTV in all bedrooms Tea and coffee making facilities No dogs Cen ht CTV No children 12yrs 4P No coaches
ROOMS: s £43; d £47-£49*

E18 SOUTH WOODFORD

Q Q Q **Grove Hill Hotel** 38 Grove Hill, South Woodford E18 2JG (off A11 London Rd, close to South Woodford tube station. Grove Hotel is off A11 just beyond The George pub)
☎ 0181 989 3344 & 530 5286 FAX 0181 530 5286
A privately owned commercial hotel located in a quiet residential area. Bedrooms vary in size, and are comfortably furnished and thoughtfully appointed. Breakfast is served in the smart dining room and guests are offered a choice of English or continental.
21 rms (10 bth 2 shr) (2 fmly) No smoking in dining room CTV in all bedrooms Tea and coffee making facilities Direct dial from bedrooms Licensed Cen ht CTV 12P Last d 9pm
ROOMS: s £27.50-£39.50; d £46-£53*
CARDS:

N4 FINSBURY PARK

Premier Selected

Q Q Q Q Q **Mount View** 31 Mount View Rd N4 4SS (A406, A1 to Highgate tube station, left into Shepherds Hill, end of road turn right, drive through Crouch End, left fork by Midland Bank)
☎ 0181 340 9222 FAX 0181 342 8494
This elegant Victorian house in a quiet area of Crouch End with its village-like atmosphere is tastefully decorated and maintains a number of period features. Each bedroom has an original fireplace and a stripped wood floor with oriental rugs. Soft furnishings are stylish and beds are of a high quality. The open plan dining room and kitchen look on to a pretty garden. Friendly host Odette Hendrickx will pick up guests at Finsbury Park station. Breakfasts are hearty and feature vegetarian options if desired.
3 rms (2 bth/shr) No smoking CTV in all bedrooms Tea and coffee making facilities No dogs Cen ht No coaches
ROOMS: s £35-£45; d £45-£55*
CARDS:

Premier Selected

Q Q Q Q Q **Ossian House** 20 Ossian Rd N4 4EA (A406 A1 to Highgate tube station, left into Shepherds Hill, right at end, left fork at Nat West Bank)
☎ 0181 340 4331 FAX 0181 340 4331
Hosts Ann and John Ashman are from county Cork in Ireland and have created an atmosphere here that is informal, friendly and truly welcoming. The three rooms are delightfully furnished and reflect Ann's keen eye for detail and style. Guests can relax in deep comfy sofas in the lounge or retire to their rooms to watch TV. Though dinner is not available the Ashmans are delighted to recommend a local restaurant. Don't miss the hearty Irish breakfast which is a great start to a hectic day in London.
4 rms (2

bth/shr) (1 fmly) No smoking CTV in all bedrooms Tea and coffee making facilities Cen ht No coaches Last d 9am
ROOMS: s £35-£45; d £46-£55*

N8 HORNSEY

Q Q **Aber Hotel** 89 Crouch Hill N8 9EG (premises are 350yds S of junct of A1201/A103) ☎ 0181 340 2847 FAX 0181 340 2847
There is a friendly, homely atmosphere at this well-run guest house. Owners Mr and Mrs Jenkins provide comfortable well maintained accommodation and efficient attentive service. There is a small lounge for the guests use and a choice of breakfast is offered.
9 rms (4 fmly) No smoking No dogs Cen ht CTV No coaches
ROOMS: s £24-£26; d £36-£40; wkly b&b £126-£168*
CARDS:

Q Q **Oakley House** 7 Oakley Gardens, Crouch End N8 9PB
☎ 0181 340 1608
Conveniently located for Hornsey village and only 15 minutes by rail to the city, this attractively presented property is set in a quiet cul-de-sac. Rooms are neatly appointed and guests may enjoy an extensive continental breakfast in the small breakfast kitchen.
3 rms CTV in all bedrooms Tea and coffee making facilities No dogs (ex guide dogs) Cen ht
ROOMS: s £23-£29; d £40-£58*
CARDS:

Q Q Q **White Lodge Hotel** 1 Church Ln, Hornsey N8 7BU (A406 follow sign to Bounds Green, Hornsey High Rd and Church Lane)
☎ 0181 348 9765 FAX 0181 340 7851
There's a warm and friendly atmosphere at this family run guest house. The bedrooms are neatly furnished and well decorated. There is a small comfortable lounge and a continental breakfast is served in the cosy dining room.

16 rms (8 shr) (5 fmly) No smoking in 4 bedrooms No smoking in dining room No smoking in 1 lounge CTV in all bedrooms Tea and coffee making facilities No dogs (ex guide dogs) Cen ht CTV No coaches Last d at breakfast
ROOMS: s £26-£28; d £36-£44*
CARDS:

N10 MUSWELL HILL

Q Q Q **Grosvenor** 18 Grosvenor Rd, Muswell Hill N10 2DS
(take A406 and follow signs for Muswell Hill/Friern Barnet, turn right onto Colney Hatch Lane (B550). Take 5th turning on left to top and bear left)
☎ 0181 883 0487 FAX 0181 374 9518
Situated in a residential street in the heart of Muswell Hill, this property offers accommodation that is bright and well presented, with smart modern facilities. Families are welcome. Breakfast is served by a pretty bay window overlooking the garden. Tennis can be arranged nearby.
2 rms (1 shr) No smoking CTV in all bedrooms Tea and coffee making facilities No dogs Cen ht No children 10yrs No coaches
ROOMS: s £30-£35; d £50-£55
CARDS:

N19 UPPER HOLLOWAY

Q Q Q ***Parkland Walk*** 12 Hornsey Rise Gardens N19 3PR (premises situated at junc of the A103 and the B540, between Highgate and Crouch End) ☎ 0171 263 3228 & 0973 382982 FAX 0171 263 3965
This attractively presented house is well located and offers good access to the city and local amenities. Accommodation is comfortable and well equipped with lots of personal touches. Breakfast is served in the sunny dining room which overlooks the garden.
4 rms (2 bth/shr) 2 annexe bth/shr (1 fmly) No smoking CTV in 4 bedrooms Tea and coffee making facilities No dogs (ex guide dogs) Cen ht CTV
CARDS:

NW1 REGENT'S PARK

Q Q Q ***Four Seasons Hotel*** 173 Gloucester Place, Regents Park NW1 6DX (nearest tube station is Baker St, premises close to Regents Park) ☎ 0171 724 3461 & 0171 723 9471 FAX 0171 402 5594
A friendly welcome is assured at this family-run hotel, located in the heart of the West End. Bedrooms vary in size, are comfortably appointed in modern style and equipped with many useful facilities. Continental breakfast is included in the tariff, and English breakfast is available on request at a small additional charge. Room service is offered throughout the day and evening for light snacks and drinks.
16 rms (14 bth/shr) (2 fmly) No smoking in 4 bedrooms No smoking in dining room CTV in all bedrooms Direct dial from bedrooms No dogs Cen ht CTV
CARDS:

NW2 CRICKLEWOOD

Q Q Q **The Garth Hotel** 64-76 Hendon Way, Cricklewood NW2 2NL (on main A41 4.5m from Oxford Street. 1.5m from M1) ☎ 0181 455 4742 209 1511 FAX 0181 455 4742
Located to the north and within easy reach of the M1 and the West End, this family-run hotel continues to improve with the upgrading of the bar and lounge areas. The bright bedrooms are suitably furnished and equipped. An evening meal is available and served in the attractive Tivoli restaurant. Continental breakfast is included in the tariff, an additional charge is made for English.
53 bth/shr (9 fmly) No smoking in 25 bedrooms No smoking in dining room No smoking in 1 lounge CTV in all bedrooms Tea and coffee making facilities Direct dial from bedrooms No dogs (ex guide dogs) Licensed Cen ht CTV 58P Last d 11pm
ROOMS: s fr £65; d fr £80*
CARDS:

Q Q Q **Victorian London** 89 Somerton Rd NW2 1RU ☎ 0181 830 6589 FAX 0181 830 7589
Lovingly and painstakingly restored by Thalia Stobbe, this house is a step back in time to Victorian life. The decor and furnishings are all of that period or copies of original designs. The bedrooms, although compact, are comfortably appointed with flame fires and en suite showers. There is an attractive dining room and dinner can be provided by arrangement.
6 shr (2 fmly) No smoking CTV in all bedrooms Tea and coffee making facilities Direct dial from bedrooms No dogs Cen ht No children 4yrs Last d 10am
ROOMS: s fr £25; d fr £45*
CARDS:

NW3 HAMPSTEAD

Q Q **La Gaffe** 107-111 Heath St NW3 6SS (located at the top end of Heath St 200yds from Hampstead Underground) (Minotel) ☎ 0171 435 4941 & 435 8965 FAX 0171 794 7592
A warm Italian welcome is assured at this friendly family run guest house. Bedrooms are compact and modestly furnished but well equipped, and the colourful soft furnishings add to the comfort of the rooms. A popular Italian restaurant is available to guests.
18 annexe shr (1 fmly) No smoking in bedrooms CTV in all bedrooms Tea and coffee making facilities Direct dial from bedrooms No dogs (ex guide dogs) Licensed Cen ht CTV 2P Last d 11.30pm
ROOMS: s £55-£95; d £80-£115*
CARDS:

Selected

Q Q Q Q **The Langorf Hotel** 20 Frognal, Hampstead NW3 6AG (approx 3m N of Oxford St and 3m S of M1, just off A41 Finchley Rd) ☎ 0171 794 4483 FAX 0171 435 9055
This elegant Edwardian building has been thoughtfully and tastefully furnished and decorated throughout. The bedrooms are comfortably appointed with colourful decor and soft furnishings. There is a small cosy reception lounge and an attractive dining room, where light meals are available throughout the day. Guests also have a choice of breakfast.
31 bth/shr (4 fmly) No smoking in area of dining room CTV in all bedrooms Tea and coffee making facilities Direct dial from bedrooms No dogs Licensed Lift Cen ht CTV P No coaches Leisure centre 15min
ROOMS: s £73-£80; d £90-£99*
CARDS:

Premier Selected

Q Q Q Q Q **Sandringham Hotel** 3 Holford Rd, Hampstead NW3 1AD (from Hampstead Tube Station turn right into Heath St, right into fourth street on the right, first turning on left into Holford Rd) ☎ 0171 435 1569 FAX 0171 431 5932
This impressive Victorian House is located in a quiet residential street just a short walk from Hampstead village. There is a comfortable lounge with flame fire and honesty bar, and the breakfast room overlooks a pretty walled garden. Bedrooms vary in size but all have TV, telephone and thoughtful extras such as mineral water and a decanter of sherry. Breakfast is not to be missed, with choices such as

French toast, eggs Benedict and smoked salmon and scrambled eggs in addition to the traditional grill. Manageress Diana Sparks provides a warm welcome and creates a relaxed home-from-home atmosphere.
17 rms (15 bth/shr) (2 fmly) No smoking in bedrooms No smoking in dining room CTV in all bedrooms Direct dial from bedrooms No dogs (ex guide dogs) Licensed Cen ht No children 8yrs 5P No coaches
ROOMS: s £70-£85; d £115-£130*
CARDS:

NW4 HENDON

Q Q Q Peacehaven Hotel 94 Audley Rd, Hendon Central NW4 3HB (turn off A41 at Hendon Central, turn right into Vivian Avenue then 5th left into Audley Road)
☎ 0181 202 9758 & 0181 202 1225 FAX 0181 202 9758
Located in a quiet residential area, Peacehaven is within easy walking distance of Hendon Central tube station and has convenient parking in the street. Privately owned and run by Mr and Mrs Summers, it has a warm friendly atmosphere and offers modern accommodation with comfortable, well equipped bedrooms.
13 rms (7 bth/shr) CTV in all bedrooms Tea and coffee making facilities No dogs (ex guide dogs) Cen ht 2P
ROOMS: s £48-£60; d £65-£78*
CARDS:

NW6 KILBURN

Selected

Q Q Q Q ***Dawson House Hotel*** 72 Canfield Gardens NW6 3ED
☎ 0171 624 0079 & 624 6525 FAX 0171 372 3469
This small privately owned hotel is situated in a quiet residential area in South Hampstead. Dawson House offers easy access to the centre of London. The accommodation is comfortable and well equipped, with modern en suite facilities. There is a guest lounge and an attractive rear garden.
15 shr (2 fmly) No smoking in dining room CTV in all bedrooms Tea and coffee making facilities Direct dial from bedrooms No dogs Cen ht No children 5yrs No coaches
CARDS:

NW11 GOLDERS GREEN

Q Q Q **Anchor Hotel** 10 West Heath Dr, Golders Green NW11 7QH (North Circular A406 onto A598 Finchley Rd. At tube turn left then 1st right) ☎ 0181 458 8764 FAX 0181 455 3204
Privately owned and run, this popular guest house has brightly decorated and comfortably appointed bedrooms, all of which are equipped with modern facilities. A generous choice of breakfast is offered. New proprietor Dorrit Raab is especially friendly and takes every opportunity to welcome guests.
11 rms (8 shr) (3 fmly) No smoking in dining room No smoking in lounges CTV in all bedrooms Tea and coffee making facilities Direct dial from bedrooms No dogs (ex guide dogs) Cen ht CTV 6P No coaches
ROOMS: s £34-£44; d £48-£58*
CARDS:

Q Q **Central Hotel** 35 Hoop Ln, Golders Green NW11 8BS
(M11/M40 to A406 E, turn right at Finchley Rd onto the A598, premises near first traffic lights) ☎ 0181 458 5636 FAX 0181 455 4792
This privately owned and run commercial hotel is located off the Finchley Road with good access to the North Circular. Bedrooms are bright, fresh and well equipped with modern en suite facilities. Breakfast is served in the dining room located in the main building.
26 bth/shr CTV in all bedrooms Direct dial from bedrooms No dogs Cen ht 8P
ROOMS: s £40-£50; d £60-£70*
CARDS:

SE3 BLACKHEATH

Q Q Q ***Vanbrugh Hotel*** St Johns Park, Blackheath SE3 7TD
☎ 0181 853 4051 FAX 0181 858 7387
Just one mile from Greenwich, this small hotel is ideal for those seeking budget accommodation close to the Millennium celebrations. Bedrooms are all furnished and equipped to a high standard, with such extra amenities as trouser press, phone, TV and hair dryer. In addition to a comfy lounge area there is a small rear garden, and guests are served a simple continental breakfast in the dining room. More extensive meals and services may be enjoyed at the sister hotel, Bardon Lodge, across the road.
31 shr (3 fmly) CTV in all bedrooms Tea and coffee making facilities Direct dial from bedrooms Licensed Cen ht 30P
CARDS:

SE6 CATFORD

Selected

Q Q Q Q **Highfield** 12 Dowanhill Rd SE6 1HJ (on A205 Brownhill Road (South Circular), take Verdant Lane and Dowanhill Road is the second on the right) ☎ 0181 698 8038 FAX 0181 698 8039

This beautifully refurbished Victorian house enjoys a quiet residential location in Hither Green. The three bedrooms are decorated with bright colours, and have been thoughtfully equipped. Breakfast is served in the smartly appointed dining room. Warm hospitality is offered by Michel Tournier who is also happy to provide dinner by prior arrangement.
3 rms (1 bth/shr) (1 fmly) No smoking CTV in all bedrooms Tea and coffee making facilities No dogs (ex guide dogs) 1P
ROOMS: s £32-£48; d £40-£60
CARDS:

SE9 ELTHAM

Q Q ***Weston House Hotel*** 8 Eltham Green, Eltham SE9 5LB
(premises situated at junct of A205/A210, turn left at Kidbrooke BR Station, at first traffic lights turn left, premises opposite McDonalds)
☎ 0181 850 5191 FAX 0181 850 0030
An early Victorian villa located in the conservation area of Greenwich. It offers modestly furnished and adequately equipped bedrooms. A choice of breakfast is served in the brightly decorated dining room.
9 rms (7 shr) (1 fmly) No smoking in dining room CTV in all bedrooms Tea and coffee making facilities No dogs Cen ht 5P
CARDS:

Q Q Q **Yardley Court** 18 Court Rd, Eltham SE9 5PZ
(leave M25 junc3 onto A20 to London, turn right at traffic lights at Court Rd, Mottingham 0.5m on left)
☎ 0181 850 1850 FAX 0181 488 0421
Located in the centre of Eltham, this fine Victorian house is family run and offers modest accommodation for both business and tourist clientele. Bedrooms are adequately equipped and most have en suite facilities. Breakfast is served in the bright conservatory which overlooks the neat well kept garden.
9 bth/shr (1 fmly) No smoking in 3 bedrooms No smoking in dining room No smoking in lounges CTV in all bedrooms Tea and coffee making facilities Cen ht 9P No coaches
ROOMS: s £33-£37; d £49*
CARDS:

SE10 GREENWICH

Q Q **The Pilot Inn** 68 Riverway, Greenwich SE10 0BE
(follow signs for Greenwich Yacht Club)
☎ 0181 858 5910 FAX 0181 293 0371
There is a warm and friendly atmosphere at this popular inn situated close to the river and the new Millennium Dome. The bedrooms which are located in an adjacent annexe are furnished in a modern style, with bright decor and colourful soft furnishings. Sound British food is offered, plus a generous English breakfast.
7 rms (1 fmly) CTV in all bedrooms No dogs Cen ht P Last d 8.45pm
ROOMS: s £35; d £49.50*
MEALS: Lunch fr £5.45 Dinner £7.95-£15*
CARDS:

SE19 NORWOOD

Q Q Crystal Palace Tower Hotel 114 Church Rd, Crystal Palace SE19 2UB (premises situated on the A212 at Crystal Palace)
☎ 0181 653 0176
This privately owned and family run hotel enjoys a central location, convenient for the town centre. Bedrooms which vary in size, are modestly but comfortably furnished and are all en suite. A choice of breakfast is served in the small breakfast room located on the lower ground floor.
9 bth/shr (4 fmly) No smoking in dining room CTV in all bedrooms Tea and coffee making facilities Cen ht CTV 10P No coaches
ROOMS: s £39-£45; d £48*
CARDS: MasterCard, Barclaycard Visa, Barclays Connect, Delta, Switch

SE20 PENGE

Q Q Q Melrose House Hotel 89 Lennard Rd SE20 7LY (corner of Courtenay Road/Lennard Road between Penge High St and Sydenham High St) ☎ 0181 776 8884 FAX 0181 776 8480
Closed 25 Dec
Proprietor Frances Roberts offers a warm welcome at this attractive Victorian house close to the town. Bedrooms are individual in style, comfortably furnished and feature many thoughtful touches such as luxury toiletries, tissues and books. A hearty breakfast is served at a communal table, and guests are welcome to relax in the spacious conservatory which overlooks the pretty garden.
3 bth/shr (1 fmly) No smoking CTV in all bedrooms Tea and coffee making facilities No dogs (ex guide dogs) Cen ht 6P No coaches Pool table
ROOMS: s £25; d £35-£55*

SE22 EAST DULWICH

Q Q Q Bedknobs 58 Glengarry Rd, East Dulwich SE22 8QD (just N of Dulwich Village, opposite Dulwich Hospital in E Dulwich Grove)
☎ 0181 299 2004 FAX 0181 693 5611
There is a warm friendly atmosphere at this delightful guest house, where charming owner Mrs Jenkins provides comfortable accommodation which has benefited from recent refurbishment. Bedrooms are furnished to a high standard, equipped with quality beds, and offer many useful extras. Guest share a communal table at breakfast.

3 rms (1 fmly) No smoking CTV in all bedrooms Tea and coffee making facilities No dogs Cen ht No coaches
ROOMS: s £25-£45; d £50-£70; wkly b&b £150-£295
CARDS: MasterCard, Barclaycard Visa, Switch

SW1 WESTMINSTER

Q Q Annandale House Hotel 39 Sloane Gardens, Sloane Square SW1W 8EB (1min walk from Sloane Square and 1min walk from Sloane Sqaure Tube Station)
☎ 0171 7305051 & 7300360 & 7306291 & 7306292 FAX 0171 730 2727
This attractive red brick building is just a few minutes walk from Sloane Square. Annandale has recently undergone major refurbishment, the bedrooms now all have very smart en suite facilities although some are rather compact; all rooms have colour television and telephone, most also have a trouser press. Guests may enjoy the walled garden in the summer months.
15 bth/shr (2 fmly) No smoking in lounges CTV in all bedrooms Tea and coffee making facilities Direct dial from bedrooms No dogs Cen ht No coaches
ROOMS: s £60-£70; d £80-£110*
CARDS: MasterCard, American Express, Barclaycard Visa, Barclays Connect, Delta, Switch

Q Q Q The Executive Hotel 57 Pont St, Knightsbridge SW1X 0BD (turn left out of Knightsbridge Tube, walk past Harrods, turn left into Beecham Place, Pont Street is straight ahead, establishment on right hand side)
☎ 0171 581 2424 FAX 0171 589 9456
The upgrading of this attractive Victorian terrace house has been completed. It provides well appointed accommodation throughout. Bedrooms vary in size, are comfortably furnished and well equipped with many modern amenities. Continental breakfast is included in the tariff, extra is charged for English. It is served in the bright, newly decorated dining room. Guests also have use of a lounge and honesty bar.
27 bth/shr (3 fmly) No smoking in dining room CTV in all bedrooms Tea and coffee making facilities Direct dial from bedrooms Licensed Lift Cen ht 3P
CARDS: MasterCard, American Express, Barclaycard Visa, Diners, Barclays Connect, Delta, Switch

Melbourne House Hotel 79 Belgrave Rd, Victoria SW1V 2BG (From Pimlico tube stn, on Lypus St turn right into St Georges Sq, Belgrave Rd carries on) ☎ 0171 828 3516 FAX 0171 828 7120
A family run private hotel with a relaxed friendly atmosphere, within easy walking distance of Victoria Station. The bedrooms have all been re-furbished in a modern style and most have en suite bathrooms. Some family rooms are also available. A choice of breakfast is offered and this is included in the tariff.
14 rms (12 bth/shr) (2 fmly) No smoking in dining room No smoking in lounges CTV in all bedrooms Tea and coffee making facilities Direct dial from bedrooms No dogs Cen ht CTV P
ROOMS: s £40-£50; d £60-£70*
CARDS:

Victoria Inn 65-67 Belgrave Rd, Victoria SW1V 2BG
☎ 0171 834 6721 & 834 0182 FAX 0171 931 0201
Two fine Victorian houses located close to Victoria station. The accommodation continues to be upgraded and caters well for both business and tourist clientele. Bedrooms are comfortably appointed and provide many modern amenities. A choice of English, for which an extra charge is made, and continental breakfast is served in the newly decorated dining room. There is also a small lounge available to guests.
41 bth/shr (1 fmly) No smoking in dining room CTV in all bedrooms Tea and coffee making facilities Direct dial from bedrooms No dogs Lift Cen ht No coaches
ROOMS: s £64; d £82-£95*
CARDS:

Selected

Willett Hotel 32 Sloane Gardens, Sloane Square SW1W 8DJ ☎ 0171 824 8415 FAX 0171 730 4830
The Willett Hotel is a beautiful Victorian town house situated in a tree-lined street just off Sloane Square. The hotel has been furnished to a high standard with all rooms designed in keeping with the style of the building. Guests benefit from a good range of modern facilities and all rooms are en suite. Breakfast is served in the elegant dining room or room service is available.
19 bth/shr (4 fmly) CTV in all bedrooms Tea and coffee making facilities Direct dial from bedrooms No dogs (ex guide dogs) Cen ht No coaches
CARDS:

Winchester Hotel 17 Belgrave Rd SW1V 1RB (3min from Victoria Station) ☎ 0171 828 2972 Telex no 269674 FAX 0171 828 5191
The Winchester Hotel is a privately owned and family-run establishment, within walking distance of Victoria coach and railway stations. The accommodation offers comfortable rooms which all benefit from en suite facilities. Full English and continental breakfast is included in the tariff, and staff are happy to recommend places to dine in the evening.
18 bth/shr (2 fmly) No smoking in lounges CTV in all bedrooms No dogs Cen ht No children 10yrs No coaches

Selected

Windermere Hotel 142/144 Warwick Way, Victoria SW1V 4JE (head towards the coach stn on Buckingham Palace Rd. Opposite the stn turn left onto Elizabeth Bridge, then 1st right, hotel is at end of road)
☎ 0171 834 5163 & 834 5480 FAX 0171 630 8831
A fine example of early Victorian classical design, this family run hotel with a relaxed and informal atmosphere, is centrally located and within easy reach of Victoria station. Many bedrooms have been refurbished with modern furniture and attractive soft furnishings; all are well equipped. Delicious evening meals are available and served in the well appointed dining room, which has a small, but well stocked bar. A comfortable lounge area is available.
23 rms (20 bth/shr) (3 fmly) No smoking in area of dining room No smoking in lounges CTV in all bedrooms Tea and coffee making facilities Direct dial from bedrooms No dogs (ex guide dogs) Licensed Cen ht CTV Last d 10.30pm
ROOMS: s £62-£81; d £72-£104
CARDS:

SW3 CHELSEA

Selected

Claverley House 13-14 Beaufort Gardens, Knightsbridge SW3 1PS (take M4/A4 into London. Moving east down Brompton Road, Beaufort Gdns is 6th turning on the right after Victoria & Albert Museum) ☎ 0171 589 8541 FAX 0171 584 3410
Tucked away in a quiet tree-lined cul-de-sac, the Claverley Hotel is only a stroll from Harrods. Bedrooms have bath or shower en suite, and each has an individual style and character. Some have four-poster beds and all have TV and telephone. The reading room has comfortable leather Chesterfields, the day's newspapers and hot refreshment facilities. The tariff includes a substantial full English breakfast, served in the elegant dining room.
30 rms (27 bth/shr) (7 fmly) No smoking in 20 bedrooms No smoking in dining room CTV in all bedrooms Direct dial from bedrooms No dogs (ex guide dogs) Lift Cen ht No coaches
ROOMS: s £70-£120; d £120-£195*
CARDS:

262

SW5 EARLS COURT

Selected

QQQQ ***Henley House Hotel*** 30 Barkston Gardens, Earls Court SW5 0EN (turn off A4 Cromwell Rd at intersection with A3220, continue S on A3220 for 0.4km, Barkstons Gardens turning off to left past underground)
☎ 0171 370 4111 FAX 0171 370 0026
Close to Earls Court, and overlooking the well maintained garden square of Barkston Gardens, this attractive Victorian house is a haven from city life. The house has been thoughtfully furnished with rich decor and soft furnishings. Bedrooms vary in size, but are comfortably appointed and nicely equipped. Public areas include a cosy reception lounge and a breakfast room.
20 shr (2 fmly) No smoking in dining room CTV in all bedrooms Tea and coffee making facilities Direct dial from bedrooms No dogs (ex guide dogs) Cen ht No coaches
CARDS:

Q Q Q **Swiss House Hotel** 171 Old Brompton Rd, South Kensington SW5 0AN ☎ 0171 373 2769 & 373 9383 FAX 0171 373 4983
A warm friendly welcome is assured by Mr Vincenti and his staff at this popular guest house. All bedrooms have en suite facilities, and a number of extras such as hair dryers and telephones. A continental buffet breakfast is offered and served in the cosy dining room.
16 rms (15 bth/shr) (7 fmly) No smoking in 4 bedrooms No smoking in dining room No smoking in lounges CTV in all bedrooms Direct dial from bedrooms Cen ht CTV No coaches Last d 9.30pm
ROOMS: s £45-£62; d £77-£86*
CARDS:

SW7 SOUTH KENSINGTON

Selected

Q Q Q Q **Five Sumner Place Hotel** 5 Sumner Place, South Kensington SW7 3EE (300yds from South Kensington underground station) ☎ 0171 584 7586 FAX 0171 823 9962
Situated in the heart of South Kensington, this elegant Victorian terraced house has now been completely refurbished. All the bedrooms are individually designed and tastefully decorated. Guests are able to take breakfast amongst the shrubs and flowers in the bright Victorian style conservatory and complimentary newspapers and magazines are available.
13 bth/shr (4 fmly) No smoking in 6 bedrooms No smoking in dining room No smoking in lounges CTV in all bedrooms Tea and coffee making facilities Direct dial from bedrooms No dogs Lift Cen ht CTV No children 7yrs No coaches
ROOMS: s £85-£95; d £130-£150*
CARDS:

Selected

Q Q Q Q ***Gainsborough Hotel*** 7-11 Queensberry Place, South Kensington SW7 2DL (off Cromwell Rd, opposite Natural History Museum) ☎ 0171 957 0000 FAX 0171 957 0001
Located on a quiet street near the Natural History Museum and within easy reach of Knightsbridge and the West End. Bedrooms vary in size and are individually designed and decorated in fine fabrics, quality furnishings and carefully co-ordinated colours. Guests are offered a choice of breakfast, served in the very attractive dining room. There is a small lounge and 24-hour room service is available.
49 bth/shr (5 fmly) CTV in all bedrooms Tea and coffee making facilities Direct dial from bedrooms No dogs (ex guide dogs) Licensed Lift Cen ht
CARDS:

Premier Selected

Q Q Q Q Q ***Gallery Hotel*** 8-10 Queensberry Place, South Kensington SW7 2EA (turn off Cromwell Rd opposite Natural History Museum into Queensberry Place) ☎ 0171 915 0000 FAX 0171 915 4400
This quiet location so close to Kensington and Knightsbridge is popular with visitors from far and wide. Bedrooms are individually designed with fine fabrics and fittings. Some rooms have air conditioning. Public rooms include the mahogany panelled "4 Cats" lounge with bar, where daily newspapers are available. 24-hour room service is available and at breakfast guests have the option of buffet English or continental breakfast served in the elegant breakfast room.
36 bth/shr No smoking in area of dining room CTV in all bedrooms Direct dial from bedrooms No dogs (ex guide dogs) Licensed Lift Cen ht
CARDS:

Q Q Q ***Kensington Manor Hotel*** 8 Emperors Gate SW7 4HH (A4 towards central London from Heathrow, opposite Forum Hotel, turn left on Grenville Place, then left again. Hotel on right hand side)
☎ 0171 370 7516 FAX 0171 373 3163
This late Victorian terraced house is located just off the Cromwell Road and within easy walking distance of the museums and Knightsbridge shopping area. The bedrooms vary in size and offer modern, comfortable and well equipped accommodation. A choice of English and continental breakfast is available, and served in the cosy breakfast room.
14 rms (13 bth/shr) (4 fmly) Cen ht No coaches

SW19 WIMBLEDON

Q Q Q ***Kings Lodge Hotel*** 5 Kings Rd, Wimbledon SW19 8PL
☎ 0181 545 0191 FAX 0181 545 0381
Well appointed accommodation is available at this small privately-owned hotel within walking distance of Wimbledon station. Bedrooms vary in size and are furnished to meet the needs of both the commercial and tourist visitor. Evening meals (available by arrangement) and breakfast are served in the attractive dining room.
7 bth/shr (4 fmly) CTV in all bedrooms Tea and coffee making facilities Direct dial from bedrooms No dogs (ex guide dogs) Cen ht CTV 6P No coaches Last d 8pm
CARDS:

Q Q **Trochee Hotel** 21 Malcolm Rd, Wimbledon SW19 4AS (turn off ay A3 sign towards right, follow upto Worple Rd, proceed along Worple Rd and before end of road turn left into Malcolm Rd)
☎ 0181 946 1579 & 3924 FAX 0181 785 4058/9461579
This friendly hotel is located in a quiet residential area, within easy walking distance of the shops and Wimbledon station. Bedrooms are furnished in modern style and equipped with many amenities. Other public areas include a well appointed dining room/lounge, and a choice of breakfast is included in the tariff.
17 rms (2 fmly) CTV in all bedrooms Tea and coffee making facilities No dogs (ex guide dogs) Cen ht CTV 6P
ROOMS: s £40-£43; d £53-£56*
CARDS:

See advertisement on p.267.

Q Q **Wimbledon Hotel** 78 Worple Rd, Wimbledon SW19 4HZ (M25, A3, Merton exit) ☎ 0181 946 9265 & 946 1581 FAX 0181 946 9265
A small family-run hotel offering a warm comfortable atmosphere for both commercial and tourist guests, within walking distance of the town centre. Recently redecorated bedrooms are neat and adequately furnished. A small cosy lounge and a bright dining room are also available to guests.
14 rms (11 bth/shr) (6 fmly) No smoking in dining room CTV in all bedrooms Tea and coffee making facilities Direct dial from bedrooms No dogs Cen ht CTV 10P
ROOMS: s £45-£50; d £55-£65*
CARDS:

Elegant English Hotels
Classic Style
THE GALLERY
Cultured and traditional.
In the heart of South Kensington,
London's cultural centre.
8-10 Queensberry Place,
South Kensington, London SW7 2EA
Tel: +44 (0)171 915 0000
Fax: +44 (0)171 915 4400
THE GAINSBOROUGH
Vibrant and alive.
Minutes from London's
fashionable art world.
7-11 Queensberry Place,
South Kensington, London SW7 2DL
Tel: +44 (0)171 957 0000
Fax: +44 (0)171 957 0001
THE WILLETT
Superbly appointed.
Minutes from Harrods. Excellent
nightlife and shopping.
32 Sloane Gardens, Chelsea
London SW1W 8DJ
Tel: +44 (0)171 824 8415
Fax:+44 (0)171 730 4830
GDS: Access Code: WW
Freephone: (UK) 0-500 826 187 (USA) 1-800 270 9206 (JAPAN) 00-31 444 253
Internet Reservation Hotline: +44 (0)181 906 9650 Fax: +44 (0)181 906 3944
http://www.eeh.co.uk
reservations@eeh.co.uk

QQQ *Worcester House* 38 Alwyne Rd SW19 7AE (exit at A3 towards right, follow Worple Rd to the end, turn left and second right to Alwyne Rd)
☎ 0181 946 1300 FAX 0181 785 4058
Located in a quiet residential area, Worcester House offers modest accommodation in a warm and homely atmosphere. Bedrooms vary in size, and are suitably furnished and equipped. Public areas are limited to a small dining room, where guests are offered a choice of breakfast.
9 shr (1 fmly) CTV in all bedrooms Tea and coffee making facilities Direct dial from bedrooms No dogs (ex guide dogs) Cen ht CTV 1P
CARDS:

W1 WEST END

Selected

QQQQ **Bryanston Court** 60 Great Cumberland Place W1H 7FD (Best Western) ☎ 0171 262 3141 Telex no 262076 FAX 0171 262 7248
This peacefully located guest house is close to Oxford Street and a few minutes' walk from Marble Arch. Smart public areas include a club-like bar and a small breakfast room where a continental spread is provided each morning. A cooked breakfast is available on request. Bedroom sizes vary considerably but are all being steadily upgraded to provide bright, attractive accommodation.
54 bth/shr (3 fmly) CTV in all bedrooms Tea and coffee making facilities Direct dial from bedrooms No dogs Licensed Lift Cen ht No coaches Last d 10pm
ROOMS: s £90; d £110*
CARDS:

QQQ *Hotel Concorde* 50 Great Cumberland Place W1H 7FD (Minotel)
☎ 0171 402 6169 Telex no 262076 FAX 0181 724 1184
Closed 24 Dec-4 Jan
A family-run hotel conveniently situated for the West End. The bedrooms are compact and are shortly due to be upgraded to a more modern style. There is a cosy lounge and bar, and breakfast is served in the attractive basement restaurant.
28 bth/shr (1 fmly) CTV in all bedrooms Tea and coffee making facilities Direct dial from bedrooms No dogs (ex guide dogs) Licensed Lift Cen ht CTV 2P No coaches
CARDS:

QQQ **Georgian House Hotel** 87 Gloucester Place, Baker St W1H 3PG
☎ 0171 486 3151 FAX 0171 486 7535
This popular hotel provides good value for money and attracts both business and leisure guests. Bedrooms are modest but comfortable and all are spacious and well equipped. A limited choice of breakfast is served in the nicely appointed dining room.
19 bth/shr (4 fmly) No smoking in dining room CTV in all bedrooms Tea and coffee making facilities Direct dial from bedrooms No dogs Lift Cen ht No children 5yrs No coaches
ROOMS: s fr £70; d fr £85*
CARDS:

QQQ **Hart House Hotel** 51 Gloucester Place, Portman Sq W1H 3PE (just off Oxford St behind Selfridges, nearest underground is Baker St or Marble Arch) ☎ 0171 935 2288 FAX 0171 935 8516
Hart House Hotel is an elegant Georgian town house which is part of a terrace of mansions that were home to the French emigré nobility during the French Revolution. Now personally run by owner Andrew Bowden, the building has been restored to much of its original character, and offers modern bedrooms with a good range of facilities. Breakfast is served in the cosy dining room.
16 rms (11 bth/shr) (4 fmly) No smoking in dining room No smoking in lounges CTV in all bedrooms Tea and coffee making facilities Direct dial from bedrooms No dogs Cen ht CTV No coaches
ROOMS: s £49-£69; d £75-£95*
CARDS:

QQQ **London Continental Hotel** 88 Gloucester Place W1H 3HN (near Baker Street underground and off Oxford St, premises half way between Oxford St and Marylebone Rd)
☎ 0171 486 8670 FAX 0171 486 8671
Conveniently located close to Oxford Street and Marble Arch station, this small, privately-owned hotel offers modern, comfortable and well equipped accommodation. Breakfast is served in the bright conservatory breakfast room.
25 shr (4 fmly) No smoking in dining room No smoking in lounges CTV in all bedrooms Tea and coffee making facilities Direct dial from bedrooms No dogs (ex guide dogs) Lift Cen ht CTV 2P
ROOMS: s £50-£75; d £70-£90*
CARDS:

Selected

QQQQ **The Regency Hotel** 19 Nottingham Place W1M 3FF (A40 into Marylebone Rd, turn right at Baker St, left into Crawford St which leads into Nottingham Place)
☎ 0171 486 5347 FAX 0171 224 6057
Located close to the West End shops and theatres The Regency hotel offers a high standard of accommodation. The comfortable bedrooms are very well equipped with such extras as mini-fridges and ironing centres. There is as attractive breakfast room, where guests are offered a choice of breakfast.
20 bth/shr (2 fmly) No smoking in 2 bedrooms No smoking in area of dining room No smoking in 1 lounge CTV in all bedrooms Tea and coffee making facilities Direct dial from bedrooms No dogs (ex guide dogs) Licensed Lift Cen ht Last d 9pm
CARDS:

QQQ **22** W1H 1FD ☎ 0171 224 2990 FAX 0171 224 1990
This charming town house B&B close to Baker Street is ideally located for the West End shops and the Callis family extend a warm welcome. Bedrooms are comfortable and attractively decorated with charming antique pieces enhancing their appeal. Guest have access to hot and cold beverages in the lounge throughout the day; an extensive continental breakfast is served at the impressive family table.
6 bth/shr 6 annexe bth/shr (2 fmly) No smoking CTV in all bedrooms Direct dial from bedrooms No dogs Cen ht No children 5yrs No coaches
ROOMS: s £70-£82; d £94*
CARDS:

Q Q Q Wigmore Court Hotel 23 Gloucester Place W1H 3PB (turn off A40 onto Baker St, turn right at George St, turn right at Gloucester Place) (Minotel)

☎ 0171 935 0928 FAX 0171 487 4254

Custom-made for conferences this hotel has its own self-contained management centre. The public areas are inviting, with bedrooms equally appealing and equipped with a comprehensive range of modern facilities. There is a choice of dining options with two restaurants, and a good room-service menu.

18 rms (11 bth 5 shr) (4 fmly) CTV in all bedrooms Tea and coffee making facilities Direct dial from bedrooms No dogs (ex guide dogs) Cen ht CTV

ROOMS: s £55-£69; d £87-£97*

CARDS:

See advertisement on p.269.

W2 BAYSWATER, PADDINGTON, NOTTING HILL GATE

QQQ **Averard Hotel** 10 Lancaster Gate W2 3LH
(Opposite Hyde Park and Kensington Gdns, 2 mins walk from Lancaster Gate tube stn, 10 mins walk from Paddington main line stn)
☎ 0171 723 8877 FAX 0171 7060860
Closed 22-30 Dec
The Averard has 60 bedrooms all of which are en suite. There is a continuing programme of upgrading to provide modern, comfortably furnished and well equipped rooms. The public rooms include a comfortable lounge, a bar area and a superbly appointed restaurant where English or continental style breakfast can be enjoyed.
60 bth/shr (5 fmly) CTV in all bedrooms Direct dial from bedrooms Licensed Lift Cen ht No coaches
ROOMS: s £65-£70; d £85-£95*
CARDS:

QQQ **Blakemore Hotel** 30 Leinster Gardens W2 3AN
(just off Bayswater Rd turn onto Leinster Terrace, this road leads into Leinster Gardens, nearest tube stations are Bayswater and Queensway)
☎ 0171 262 4591 Telex no 291634 FAX 0171 724 1472
A large hotel that caters well for both the tourist and commercial guest. The bedrooms are in the process of being upgraded to provide more comfortable accommodation. The public areas are spacious and include a bar lounge and an attractive restaurant, where a choice of carte and set price menu is available at dinner.
163 bth/shr CTV in all bedrooms Tea and coffee making facilities Direct dial from bedrooms No dogs (ex guide dogs) Licensed Lift Cen ht CTV Last d 9pm
ROOMS: s £75-£85; d £120-£140*
CARDS:

Selected

QQQQ **Byron Hotel** 36-38 Queensborough Ter W2 3SH
(just off the Bayswater Rd close to Queensway)
☎ 0171 243 0987 FAX 0171 792 1957
This charming terraced house has been thoughtfully restored to provide comfortable accommodation, and maintains a number of its original features. Bedrooms are compact but have been tastefully decorated, comfortably furnished and equipped with modern facilities. Breakfast is served in the attractive dining room.
45 bth/shr (5 fmly) No smoking in bedrooms No smoking in dining room CTV in all bedrooms Tea and coffee making facilities Direct dial from bedrooms No dogs Licensed Lift Cen ht CTV
ROOMS: s £60-£75.50; d £70-£105
CARDS:

QQQ **Kingsway Hotel** 27 Norfolk Square, Hyde Park W2 1RX
(Follow the sign to Hyde Park/Marble Arch, then Paddington Station)
☎ 0171 723 7784 & 0171 723 5569 Telex no 885299 FAX 0171 723 7317
This family-run hotel with a warm friendly atmosphere continues to improve, with modern well appointed bedrooms that are equipped with many useful facilities. A choice of breakfasts is served in the bright breakfast room.
33 rms (30 bth/shr) (4 fmly) No smoking in dining room CTV in all bedrooms Tea and coffee making facilities Direct dial from bedrooms No dogs (ex guide dogs) Lift Cen ht CTV
ROOMS: s £38-£56; d £50-£76; wkly b&b £240-£360
CARDS:

We endeavour to be as accurate as possible but changes in personnel and data can occur in establishments after the Guide has gone to press

QQQ ***Mitre House Hotel*** 178-184 Sussex Gardens, Hyde Park W2 1TU
☎ 0171 723 8040 FAX 0171 402 0990
A family-run hotel conveniently located for easy access to the West End. Bedrooms vary in size but all are comfortably appointed and suitably equipped. Guests have use of a comfortable lounge and bar.
70 rms (64 bth/shr) (3 fmly) No smoking in 10 bedrooms No smoking in area of dining room CTV in all bedrooms Direct dial from bedrooms No dogs (ex guide dogs) Licensed Lift Cen ht CTV 25P
CARDS:

Selected

QQQQ **Mornington Hotel** 12 Lancaster Gate W2 3LG (located on the north of Hyde Park off A40-Bayswater Road) (Best Western)
☎ 0171 262 7361 FAX 0171 706 1028
A fine Victorian building located in a quiet road close to Lancaster Gate station for easy access to the West End. The bedrooms continue to be upgraded and provide comfortable, stylish accommodation. There are two comfortable lounges and an attractive dining room where a Scandinavian style continental breakfast is served.
66 bth/shr (6 fmly) No smoking in 20 bedrooms No smoking in dining room CTV in all bedrooms Tea and coffee making facilities Direct dial from bedrooms Licensed Lift Cen ht No coaches
ROOMS: s £99-£105; d £115-£145*
CARDS:

QQQ **Norfolk Plaza Hotel** 29/33 Norfolk Square, Paddington W2 1RX
(300 metres from Paddington station)
☎ 0171 723 0792 FAX 0171 224 8770
Located in a quiet residential square, within easy walking distance of the West End, this hotel has been thoughtfully furnished to provide comfortable and well equipped bedrooms, with a number of split level suites. The public areas include a well appointed bar and lounge, plus an attractive restaurant where breakfast is available.
87 bth/shr (28 fmly) No smoking in 5 bedrooms No smoking in dining room CTV in all bedrooms Tea and coffee making facilities Direct dial from bedrooms No dogs (ex guide dogs) Licensed Lift Cen ht
ROOMS: s £88-£98; d £108-£118*
CARDS:

Selected

QQQQ **Norfolk Towers Hotel** 34 Norfolk Place W2 1QW
(close to Paddington Station & St Mary's Hospital)
☎ 0171 262 3123 Telex no 268583 FAX 0171 224 8687
This elegant Victorian building is located close to the West End. It is one of the larger bed and breakfast hotels offering comfortable and well equipped accommodation. The public areas have recently been upgraded to provide modern and attractive lounge and bar facilities. A choice of breakfast is served in the spacious dining room and Cads café/bar is available for meals until 11pm.

85 bth/shr (3 fmly) CTV in all bedrooms Direct dial from bedrooms No dogs (ex guide dogs) Licensed Lift Cen ht Last d 10pm
ROOMS: s fr £80; d fr £120✱
CARDS:

Q Q Park Lodge Hotel 73 Queensborough Ter, Bayswater W2 3SU (Queensborough Terrace is just off the Bayswater Rd a short distance away from Kensington Gardens and Hyde Park)
☎ 0171 229 6424 FAX 0171 221 4772
Modest well equipped accommodation is offered at this friendly bed and breakfast hotel. It is located close to the Queensway station to give easy access to the West End.
29 bth/shr (2 fmly) No smoking in 5 bedrooms No smoking in dining room No smoking in lounges CTV in all bedrooms Tea and coffee making facilities Direct dial from bedrooms No dogs (ex guide dogs) Lift Cen ht Last d noon
ROOMS: s £70; d £85✱
CARDS:

Q Q ***Parkwood Hotel*** 4 Stanhope Place, Marble Arch W2 2HB (near Marble Arch tube station) ☎ 0171 402 2241 FAX 0171 402 1574
An attractive town house located in a quiet road within easy walking distance of Marble Arch. Bedrooms are not large, but have been comfortably furnished in modern style and benefit from many useful amenities. A choice of English and continental breakfast is offered and served in the small cosy dining room.
18 rms (12 bth/shr) (4 fmly) No smoking in 2 bedrooms No smoking in dining room CTV in all bedrooms Tea and coffee making facilities Direct dial from bedrooms No dogs Cen ht CTV No coaches
CARDS:

Rhodes Hotel 195 Sussex Gardens W2 2RJ (premises located between Lancaster Gate underground station and Edgware Rd)
☎ 0171 262 5617 & 0171 262 0537 FAX 0171 723 4054
A family-run terraced hotel within easy reach of the West End, the Rhodes offers a comfortable standard of accommodation in well equipped and adequately furnished bedrooms. Lounge facilities are restricted to a small reception lounge. Continental breakfast is included in the tariff and an additional charge is made for English; both are served in the bright dining room situated on the lower ground floor.
18 rms (15 bth/shr) (5 fmly) CTV in all bedrooms Tea and coffee making facilities Direct dial from bedrooms No dogs Cen ht CTV P
ROOMS: s £50-£60; d £65-£80*
CARDS:

Slavia Hotel 2 Pembridge Square W2 4EW (next to Public Library) ☎ 0171 727 1316 FAX 0171 229 0803
This attractive Victorian house, located in a quiet residential area, has been thoughtfully refurbished to retain many original features. Bedrooms are comfortably appointed and suitably equipped. Breakfast is served in the cellar-style dining room, guests also have use of a small cosy lounge.
31 shr (8 fmly) CTV in 12 bedrooms Direct dial from bedrooms Licensed Lift Cen ht CTV 1P
CARDS:

W4 CHISWICK

Selected

Chiswick Hotel 73 Chiswick High Rd W4 2LS (exit M4 junct 2 onto Chiswick High Rd-A315, Chiswick hotel approx 1m on right) ☎ 0181 994 1712 FAX 0181 742 2585
These fine Victorian houses have been thoughtfully converted to provide a high standard of comfort and facilities. Bedrooms are well furnished, have colourful decor and are nicely equipped. The hotel also features several apartments with separate kitchen and sitting facilities, a useful extra for long term residents. Guests have use of a well appointed lounge and an attractive dining room, where an evening meal with a short carte is available. There is a choice of breakfast, and a small additional charge is made for English.
33 bth/shr 20 annexe bth/shr (5 fmly) CTV in all bedrooms Tea and coffee making facilities Direct dial from bedrooms Licensed Cen ht 15P Last d 8.30pm
ROOMS: s £73.50-£80; d £99.75-£110*
CARDS:

W6 HAMMERSMITH

Premier West Hotel 28-34 Glenthorne Rd, Hammersmith W6 0LS (A4 for central London Hammersmith exit, take 2nd exit at Broadway rdbt into King St, take 2nd right to the end,turn into Glenthorne St-hotel on left) ☎ 0181 748 6181 FAX 0181 7482195
This popular hotel continues to upgrade, caters well for both commercial and tourist clientele, and is close to Hammersmith station for easy access to the West End. The comfortably furnished bedrooms vary in size and have many modern amenities. A short carte menu is offered at dinner plus a good choice of breakfast, served in the attractive restaurant.
26 bth/shr 15 annexe bth/shr (5 fmly) No smoking in dining room No smoking in lounges CTV in all bedrooms Tea and coffee making facilities No dogs (ex guide dogs) Licensed Cen ht CTV 5P Last d 9pm
ROOMS: s £70-£80; d £75-£90*
CARDS:

W7 HANWELL

Premier Selected

Wellmeadow Lodge 24 Wellmeadow Rd W7 2AL (from Boston Manor tube station turn left, take first road on the left, premises first house on the left) (The Circle)
☎ 0181 567 7294 FAX 0181 566 3468
A warm friendly atmosphere at this small well appointed hotel located close to Boston Manor station. Personally run by owners Francis Hornak and Kennie Davey offering delightfully appointed bedrooms, furnished in modern style and equipped with every modern amenity including cable TV and in some cases up to three telephones! Guests have use of a small cosy lounge, and service of light snacks is available throughout the day. Dinner is by arrangement and freshly cooked breakfast is served in the bright conservatory dining room.
8 bth/shr 2 annexe bth/shr (1 fmly) No smoking CTV in all bedrooms Tea and coffee making facilities Direct dial from bedrooms No dogs (ex guide dogs) Cen ht No coaches Last d 7pm
ROOMS: s £60-£70; d £65-£112
CARDS:

W8 KENSINGTON

Amber 101 Lexham Gardens, Kensington W8 6JN
☎ 0171 373 8666
Planters catch the eye outside this terraced hotel in a residential street just off Earls Court Road. There is a smart little lobby and a garden. Nicely appointed bedrooms do vary in size and outlook but all are thoughtfully equipped and comfortable.
40 bth/shr No smoking in 2 bedrooms No smoking in dining room CTV in all bedrooms Tea and coffee making facilities Direct dial from bedrooms Licensed Lift Cen ht Private garden
ROOMS: s £38-£90; d £50-£105
CARDS:

Q Q Atlas-Apollo Hotel 18-30 Lexham Gardens, Kensington W8 5JE (A4 into London, onto Cromwell Rd, first turning on left after Cromwell hospital, premises on right) (The Independents)
☎ 0171 835 1155 FAX 0171 370 4853
The Atlas and Apollo hotels have now been converted into one large hotel with most bedrooms having en suite facilities. Further improvements are being made throughout, with larger dining room, comfortable lounges and more modern bedrooms.
99 rms (47 bth 44 shr) (14 fmly) CTV in all bedrooms Direct dial from bedrooms No dogs (ex guide dogs) Licensed Lift Cen ht No coaches
ROOMS: s £70-£75; d £85-£90
CARDS:

W14 WEST KENSINGTON

Selected

Q Q Q Q *Aston Court Hotel* 25/27 Matheson Rd, West Kensington W14 8SN ☎ 0171 602 9954 FAX 0171 371 1338
Close to Olympia, and less than 15 minutes walk from the Earls Court Exhibition Centre, Aston Court is peacefully located in a quiet residential street. Bedrooms are particularly well equipped with such things as irons and ironing boards, mini-bars and remote control TVs in addition to the usual amenities. On the ground floor there is a comfortably furnished bar-lounge area and conservatory breakfast room.
29 bth/shr (3 fmly) No smoking in 14 bedrooms CTV in all bedrooms Tea and coffee making facilities Direct dial from bedrooms No dogs (ex guide dogs) Licensed Lift Cen ht CTV
CARDS:

See advertisement on p.273.

Q Q Q Avonmore Hotel 66 Avonmore Rd W14 8RS
(off Hammersmith Road opposite Olympia Exhibition Centre)
☎ 0171 603 4296 & 3121 FAX 0171 603 4035
The Avonmore Hotel is privately owned and located close to Olympia. The owners John and Margaret McKenzie pride themselves on the quality of their accommodation. The bedrooms have been refurbished and are attractively decorated and well equipped. A choice of breakfast is served in the welcoming dining room, which also has a small bar.
9 rms (7 bth/shr) (3 fmly) CTV in all bedrooms Tea and coffee making facilities Direct dial from bedrooms No dogs Licensed Cen ht CTV
ROOMS: s £55-£80; d £80-£90*
CARDS:

Q Q Q Centaur Hotel 21 Avonmore Rd W14 8RP (turn off A4 onto North End Rd, right hand fork into Mathesow Rd leads into Avonmore Rd)
☎ 0171 602 3857 & 603 5973 FAX 0171 603 9193
Located close to Olympia, this small family-run hotel has a warm and friendly atmosphere, with the owners always available to help. The bedrooms are not large but are furnished in modern style and with attractive soft furnishings. Breakfast is served in the cosy dining room situated on the ground floor.
10 shr (2 fmly) No smoking in dining room CTV in all bedrooms Tea and coffee making facilities Direct dial from bedrooms No dogs Cen ht CTV
ROOMS: s £65; d £85*
CARDS:

WC1 BLOOMSBURY, HOLBORN

Q Q *Euro Hotel* 51-53 Cartwright Gardens, Russell Square WC1H 9EL
☎ 0171 387 4321 FAX 0171 383 5044
This small bed and breakfast hotel in London's stylish Bloomsbury has improved greatly over the years and offers quality accommodation at a reasonable price. Bedrooms are well equipped and sparklingly clean. Breakfasts are served in a wood-floored room which overlooks the gardens outside.
33 rms (9 bth/shr) (9 fmly) No smoking in dining room CTV in all bedrooms Tea and coffee making facilities Direct dial from bedrooms No dogs (ex guide dogs) Cen ht
CARDS:

Q Q Mentone Hotel 54-56 Cartwright Gardens, Bloomsbury WC1H 9EL
(Between Euston Rd and Russell Square)
☎ 0171 387 3927 & 388 4671 FAX 0171 388 4671
The brightly decorated bedrooms at this recently refurbished guest house are adequately furnished and equipped. Breakfast is taken in the attractively decorated dining room at separate tables and there is a cosy lounge for guests.
42 rms (34 bth/shr) (14 fmly) No smoking in dining room CTV in all bedrooms Tea and coffee making facilities Direct dial from bedrooms No dogs Cen ht Tennis (hard)
ROOMS: s £39-£60; d £65-£78*
CARDS:

LONGLEAT Wiltshire Map 03 ST84

Q Q Q ❦ Stalls *(ST806439)* BA12 7NE
(turn off A362 at Corsley beside the White Hart, follow road for 2m towards Longleat House, farmhouse is on right hand side)
☎ 01985 844323 FAX 01985 844323 Mrs J Crossman
A delightful 18th-century farmhouse located in a tranquil setting and within walking distance of Longleat house. The 3 bedrooms are brightly decorated, furnished in modern style and suitably equipped. Breakfast is served at one end of the cosy lounge.
3 rms (1 fmly) No smoking in bedrooms No smoking in dining room CTV in all bedrooms Tea and coffee making facilities No dogs (ex guide dogs) Cen ht CTV 6P Childrens play area 400 acres dairy & arable
ROOMS: s fr £18; d fr £35*

Selected

Q Q Q Q ❦ Sturford Mead *(ST834456)* Corsley BA12 7QU
(on A362 half way between Warminster & Frome)
☎ 01373 832213 FAX 01373 832213 Mrs L N Corp
A delightful farmhouse with a warm and friendly atmosphere, located close to Longleat House. The attractive bedrooms have been thoughtfully furnished and have a few added features to give extra warmth to the rooms. Guests have use of a small cosy lounge and a traditional English breakfast is served in the brightly decorated dining room.
3 bth/shr No smoking CTV in all bedrooms Tea and coffee making facilities No dogs (ex guide dogs) Cen ht CTV 10P 5 acres pigs
ROOMS: s £28-£30; d £40

LONGNOR Shropshire Map 07 SJ40

Selected

Q Q Q Q Cobblers Cottage SY5 7PP
(in village centre 500yds E of A49, 8m S of Shrewsbury)
☎ 01743 718443
Feb-Nov
This delightful timber-framed, black and white cottage dates back to 1625. Set in its own pleasant gardens, it is located in Longnor village centre. The no smoking accommodation, which includes a ground floor bedroom, is attractively appointed and has modern equipment and facilities. All guests share one table in the dining room. Dinner is not served, but light suppers are available. There is also a spacious and comfortable lounge with an inglenook fireplace.
3 bth/shr (1 fmly) No smoking CTV in all bedrooms Tea and coffee making facilities No dogs (ex guide dogs) Cen ht 3P No coaches
ROOMS: d £40-£44

LONGRIDGE Lancashire Map 07 SD63

Selected

QQQQ **Jenkinsons** *(SD611348)* Alston Ln, Preston Rd PR3 3BD (off B6243 Preston to Longridge road - follow signs to Alston Hall College) ☎ 01772 782624 Mrs E J Ibison
rs Xmas
This substantial and traditional Lancashire farmhouse is immaculately furnished and provides excellent accommodation in a delightful rural setting. The lovely public rooms include a very comfortable lounge with a inglenook fireplace. Dinner is by arrangement and is served in the lovely dining room. The bedrooms, whilst not en suite, have been furnished with much care and include many antiques.
6 rms No smoking Tea and coffee making facilities No dogs (ex guide dogs) Cen ht CTV No children 12yrs 10P
100 acres dairy sheep
ROOMS: s £23.50; d £40*

LONGTOWN Cumbria Map 11 NY36

Premier Selected

QQQQQ **Bessiestown Farm** *(NY457768)* Catlowdy CA6 5QP (from Bush Hotel Longtown, 6.5m to Bridge Inn, turn right onto B6318, 1.5m to Catlowdy, farm first on left)
☎ 01228 577219 577019 FAX 01228 577219 Mr & Mrs J Sisson
Situated in the village of Catlowdy, set back from the road within secluded gardens, this charming farmhouse has been operating for over twenty years. The comfortable bedrooms are all individual, with either traditional or contemporary furnishings and many thoughtful touches, including radios, alarm clocks and hair dryers. There are two inviting lounges downstairs - one with an honesty bar - and a dining room. A recent addition includes a very smart conservatory lounge where guests can relax in the warmer months. The buildings across the courtyard have been converted to provide a modern heated swimming pool (summer months only) and a popular games room.
4 bth/shr (1 fmly) No smoking CTV in all bedrooms Tea and coffee making facilities No dogs Licensed Cen ht CTV 10P
Indoor swimming pool (heated) Games room 80 acres sheep
Last d 4pm
ROOMS: s £29-£31; d £45-£49; wkly b&b £155-£160
CARDS:

QQQ ***Craigburn*** *(NY474761)* Catlowdy CA6 5QP (leave A7 in Longtown, follow signs for Catlowdy and then Craigburn)
☎ 01228 577214 FAX 01228 577204 Mr & Mrs Lawson
This farmhouse lies at the end of winding mile-long road leading from the serene village of Catlowdy. Families will find the children's area of interest, and there is also a selection of rare breeds. Jane Lawson's traditional cooking proves popular with local trade as well as guests. Bedrooms are bright and modern, tastefully furnished with several having four-posters.
6 bth/shr (1 fmly) No smoking in bedrooms No smoking in dining room No smoking in lounges CTV in all bedrooms Tea and coffee making facilities No dogs (ex guide dogs) Licensed Cen ht CTV 20P
250 acres beef sheep Last d 6pm
CARDS:

LOOE Cornwall & Isles of Scilly Map 02 SX25

QQQ **Gulls Hotel** Hannafore Rd PL13 2DE
(take A38 from Plymouth then A387 to Looe, cross bridge from E. Looe to W. Looe, turn left by river to seafront, turn right by pub & right again)
☎ 01503 262531
Etr-Oct
Occupying a prime position, with uninterrupted views of both East and West Looe, Gulls Hotel is personally run by Jane and Robert Smalley. The cosy bedrooms are neatly furnished and decorated, with the fullest use being made of the available space. Guests can relax on the sun-terrace watching the boats. A wholesome dinner is served each evening in the dining room, after which guests can sit in comfort in the lounge.
10 rms (4 shr) (1 fmly) No smoking CTV in all bedrooms Tea and coffee making facilities Licensed Cen ht CTV 3P No coaches
Last d at breakfast
ROOMS: s £14-£16.50; d £28-£43; wkly b&b £84-£129; wkly hlf-bd £144-£189

Prices shown in the directory are meant as a guide only and are subject to change. Please check before you book

Selected

Q Q Q Q Harescombe Lodge Watergate PL13 2NE from Looe on road to Polperro, 1m after leaving Looe there is an isolated house on the right, 300yards past turn right, 1m on left) ☎ 01503 263158
Harescombe, a former hunting lodge built in the 18th century, is tucked away down a long winding lane, not far from Looe. There are delightful cottage-style bedrooms in the main house, with a further room in the adjoining Fig Tree Cottage. There are picturesque gardens and a new patio with a barbecue which sits alongside a gently cascading stream and tiny waterfalls.
2 bth 1 annexe shr No smoking in dining room Tea and coffee making facilities No dogs (ex guide dogs) Cen ht No children 12yrs 10P No coaches Last d 9am
ROOMS: d £40-£44; wkly b&b £126-£140

Q Q 'Kantara' 7 Trelawney Ter PL13 2AG (on main Looe/Polperro road, 120yds above Looe Bridge opposite Millpool car park) ☎ 01503 262093
A warm welcome awaits you at this well maintained guest house. There is satellite TV in all rooms and a selection of videos for guests to borrow as well as a marvellous array of fishing rods which owner, John Storer allows his guests to use. The centre of Looe is a short walk away.
6 rms (3 fmly) No smoking in dining room CTV in all bedrooms Tea and coffee making facilities Direct dial from bedrooms Licensed CTV 1P Fishing
ROOMS: s £13.50-£16; d £27-£32; wkly b&b £90-£107*
CARDS:

Selected

Q Q Q Q Panorama Hotel Hannafore Rd PL13 2DE (in West Looe overlooking pier & beach) ☎ 01503 262123 FAX 01503 265654
This delightful hotel certainly lives up to its name enjoying panoramic views over Looe. Bedrooms are tastefully furnished and decorated. Guests can enjoy the views from most of the bedrooms, some with balconies, or from the bar and attractive dining room where home-made cooking is produced by Jackie Russell.
10 bth/shr (4 fmly) No smoking in dining room CTV in all bedrooms Tea and coffee making facilities No dogs Licensed Cen ht CTV No children 5yrs 7P Last d 6.30pm
ROOMS: s £24.50-£34.50; d £49-£69*
CARDS:

Q Q Q *Polraen Country House Hotel* Sandplace PL13 1PJ (2m N, at junct of A387/B3254) ☎ 01503 263956
A fine stone-built house dating back to 1700, Polraen offers comfortable accommodation with a popular public bar and good cooking with a comprehensive wine list. Soundly decorated throughout, there is an attractive lounge looking on to the extensive gardens and a dining room where a full English breakfast is served.
5 bth/shr (2 fmly) No smoking in dining room CTV in all bedrooms Tea and coffee making facilities Licensed Cen ht 21P No coaches Last d 8pm
CARDS:

Selected

Q Q Q Q St Aubyns Marine Dr, Hannafore, West Looe PL13 2DH (from Looe Bridge take West Quay road signed Hannafore 0.75m, carry onto Marine Drive, guest house is on right facing sea)
☎ 01503 264351 FAX 01503 263670
Etr-end Oct
Personally run by Peter and Di Bishop since 1997, this impressive Victorian house is situated in its own attractive gardens, with uninterrupted sea views. Retaining its original character and charm, the house features some fine furniture, tapestries and paintings. Bedrooms are comfortable, well equipped and some rooms on the front of the building have access to balconies. Guests have use of the elegantly furnished lounge which is located adjacent to the breakfast room.
8 rms (6 bth/shr) (3 fmly) No smoking CTV in 7 bedrooms Tea and coffee making facilities No dogs (ex guide dogs) CTV No children 5yrs 4P No coaches
ROOMS: s £20-£22; d £40-£60; wkly b&b £126-£189*
CARDS:

Selected

Q Q Q Q Woodlands St Martins Rd PL13 1LP (on B3253, 1m from St Martins Church) ☎ 01503 264405
Situated on the outskirts of the fishing village of Looe, Woodlands is a small Victorian country house backing onto woodland, with views over the Looe River estuary. Ron and Kay Lundy recently took over the property and initiated a programme of redecoration. The bedrooms are cosy, neatly decorated and equipped with modern facilities. Breakfast is served each morning and dinner is available by prior arrangement.
5 rms (4 shr) No smoking in bedrooms No smoking in dining room CTV in all bedrooms Tea and coffee making facilities No dogs (ex guide dogs) Licensed Cen ht CTV 6P No coaches Last d breakfast
ROOMS: s £15; d £36-£40; wkly b&b £126-£140; wkly hlf-bd £224-£238*
CARDS:

LOPEN Somerset Map 03 ST41

Q Q Q Shores Farm Frogs St TA13 5JR (turn off A303 at South Petherton roundabout and take turning signed Lopen, continue to next roundabout and turn left into village, thatch on right) ☎ 01460 240587 FAX 01460 240587
Closed Xmas/New Year
This 17th-century listed former farmhouse, is built of the traditional hamstone of the area with a thatched roof, beautiful oak beams and inglenook fireplaces. Bedrooms are comfortable and well equipped with modern facilities. Dinner is available by arrangement and breakfast is served around one large table in the dining room. A lounge is available for guests.
4 rms (2 bth/shr) (1 fmly) No smoking CTV in all bedrooms Tea and coffee making facilities No dogs (ex guide dogs) Cen ht 4P No coaches Last d 10am
ROOMS: s £20-£22; d £36-£42*

LORTON Cumbria Map 11 NY12

Premier Selected

Q Q Q Q Q New House Farm CA13 9UU (6m S of Cockermouth, on B5289 between Lorton and Loweswater) ☎ 01900 85404 FAX 01900 85404
This carefully restored farm house, dating from 1650, is found in the picturesque Lorton Vale. Old beams and stone work along with the bold decorative colour schemes, all help to create a cosy, friendly, and traditional atmosphere. A wide ranging set menu changes daily and the freshly prepared dinner dishes are a delight. Breakfast depends heavily on local produce. Cosy lounges, with deep sofas, books and magazines are the main focal point as bedrooms have no TV. They do however, offer large beds, pine furniture and thoughtful extras such as fresh fruit, biscuits and flowers.

4 bth/shr No smoking Tea and coffee making facilities Licensed Cen ht No children 10yrs 30P No coaches Last d 7pm
ROOMS: s £40-£50; d £70-£76; wkly b&b £245-£266; wkly hlf-bd £371-£406

Selected

Old Vicarage Church Ln CA13 9UN
(turn off B5292 onto B5289 N of Lorton. Take first left signposted Church, house first on right) ☎ 01900 85656 FAX 01900 85656
Closed 2-31 Jan
This delightful Lakeland Victorian house is set in the Lorton Valley which is at the heart of the National Park. Roger and Helen Humphreys are at the helm and are refurbishing the bedrooms to an appealing standard. Two rooms located in the converted barn are self-contained and are ideal for families with youngsters. A fixed menu for dinner is served in the bright dining room and a lounge is available in which to relax.
6 bth/shr No smoking in bedrooms No smoking in dining room CTV in all bedrooms Tea and coffee making facilities No dogs (ex guide dogs) Licensed Cen ht 8P Last d 10am
ROOMS: s £23-£33; d £46-£54; wkly b&b £145-£208; wkly hlf-bd £243-£306
CARDS:

Premier Selected

Winder Hall CA13 9UP
(from Keswick take A66 West and B5292 Whinlatter pass at Braithwaite. Follow B5296 6m to B5289 junct, turn left, Winder Hall is 0.5m on right) ☎ 01900 85107 FAX 85107
Closed Jan & Xmas
Winder Hall is the original Manor House to the village and lies in extensive grounds leading down to the River Cocker. Its origins can be traced back to the 14th century, with stone mullions, leaded windows and matching Victorian bijouterie. Derek and Mary Denman have devoted years to restoring their property, yet Winder Hall is by no means stuffy or dated. The lounge has reading matter, games, coal fire, and luxurious furniture, and the commodious dining room is the setting for hearty breakfasts. Bedrooms are delightful, and range from a massive four poster to cosier rooms, all furnished with antiques or pine. Plans to extend the ambitious cooking to include dinner are to be implemented this year.

6 bth/shr (2 fmly) No smoking CTV in all bedrooms Tea and coffee making facilities No dogs Cen ht CTV No children 8yrs 6P No coaches Last d 10am
ROOMS: s £35; d £60-£70; wkly b&b £210-£245; wkly hlf-bd £285-£320*
CARDS:

See advertisement under KESWICK

LOSTWITHIEL Cornwall & Isles of Scilly Map **02** SX15

Ship Lerryn PL22 0PT (3m S off A390 at Lostwithiel)
☎ 01208 872374
Dating back to the 17th century, The Ship Inn is located in the village of Lerryn. Retaining much of its original character, such as flagstone floors and beams, the inn has a wide selection of traditional ales, malt whiskies and wine. In the restaurant a range of dishes is offered including vegetarian options and locally caught fish. Bedrooms are situated in an adjoining property, with one room on the ground floor.
4 bth/shr No smoking in 1 bedrooms No smoking in area of dining room CTV in all bedrooms Tea and coffee making facilities Cen ht No coaches Last d 9pm
CARDS:

All AA listed accommodation can also be found at the AA's Internet site, whose address is: http://www.theaa.co.uk/hotels

LOUGHBOROUGH Leicestershire Map 08 SK51

Q Q Q De Montfort Hotel 88 Leicester Rd LE11 2AQ
(on A6 Leicester road) ☎ 01509 216061 FAX 01509 233667
The De Montfort offers smart public rooms, which include a well appointed restaurant, a comfortable lounge furnished in a Victorian style, and a separate small bar with satellite television. Dinners are available from an à la carte menu which is supplemented by a daily special. Bedrooms, which vary in size, are continually being upgraded, offering co-ordinated colour schemes and a good range of facilities.
9 rms (7 bth/shr) (4 fmly) No smoking in dining room CTV in all bedrooms Tea and coffee making facilities No dogs (ex guide dogs) Licensed Cen ht CTV No coaches Last d 8pm
ROOMS: s £25-£35; d £35-£50
CARDS:

Q Q Q Garendon Park Hotel 92 Leicester Rd LE11 2AQ
(exit M1 at junc23, A512 to Loughborough, at second island turn right, at fourth island turn left, at traffic lights turn left, fourth lights right)
☎ 01509 236557 FAX 01509 265559
Friendly and enthusiastic proprietors are continually upgrading this small hotel which offers a comfortably appointed lounge, furnished with Chesterfield armchairs and sofas, and a cosy dining room; freshly cooked evening meals are available. Bedrooms are cheerfully decorated, individually furnished and each room has satellite TV, radio and tea-making facilities.
9 rms (7 bth/shr) (4 fmly) No smoking in 2 bedrooms No smoking in dining room CTV in all bedrooms Tea and coffee making facilities Licensed Cen ht CTV Last d 8pm
ROOMS: s £23-£32; d £38-£45*
CARDS:

LOUTH Lincolnshire Map 08 TF38

Selected

Q Q Q Q Masons Arms Cornmarket LN11 9PY
(from N M180/A18 past Humberside Airport to Laceby, A146 junc head to A18/A16 to Louth) ☎ 01507 609525 FAX 01507 602945
This delightful town centre inn is tucked away in a corner of the square and is a very popular meeting and dining place for locals and tourists alike. It provides modern and well equipped bedrooms and the inn has a very friendly, welcoming atmosphere. A good range of well produced home cooking is available, and a wide range of real ales are also on offer.
10 rms (5 bth/shr) No smoking in area of dining room CTV in all bedrooms Tea and coffee making facilities No dogs (ex guide dogs) Cen ht Cycling Nature Trail Last d 9.30pm
ROOMS: s £21; d £36-£50; wkly b&b £126-£136; wkly hlf-bd £162-£172*
MEALS: Lunch £7.50-£10&alc Dinner £7.50-£20&alc*
CARDS:

LOWER BRAILES Warwickshire Map 04 SP33

Q Q Q New House Farm *(SP300383)* Sutton Ln, Brailes OX15 5BD
(from Banbury B4035 to Brailes, turn left to Sutton Under Brailes, Farm 1m on right) ☎ 01608 686239 FAX 01608 686239 Mrs H Taylor
Closed Xmas
This well proportioned 400-year-old farmhouse is in a beautiful rural location and enjoys breathtaking views of the surrounding countryside. Bedrooms are cheerfully appointed with co-ordinated decor and soft furnishings, and each room has a good range of facilities. There is a comfortable lounge for guests, and breakfast is taken in the conservatory.
3 rms (2 shr) (1 fmly) No smoking in 2 bedrooms No smoking in dining room No smoking in 1 lounge CTV in all bedrooms Tea and coffee making facilities Cen ht CTV 10P Golf 18 Snooker 500 acres arable/sheep
ROOMS: s £18-£25; d £35-£40*

LOWESTOFT Suffolk Map 05 TM59

Selected

Q Q Q Q Abbe House Hotel 322 London Rd South NR33 0BG
(on main A12 London road on right travelling north 1.5 miles from town outskirts) ☎ 01502 581083 FAX 01502 581083
Guests can expect a warm friendly greeting from Nick and Diane Murphy at this family-run hotel. The Abbe features a lovely lounge/bar and a separate dining room, both of which are tastefully decorated and furnished with some nice pieces. The breakfast menu offers an imaginative choice of freshly cooked items, and dinner is available by prior arrangement. Although the bedrooms vary in size they are decorated and furnished to a high standard and an excellent range of extra little touches are supplied.
3 rms (2 shr) (1 fmly) No smoking in bedrooms No smoking in dining room CTV in all bedrooms Tea and coffee making facilities No dogs (ex guide dogs) Licensed Cen ht CTV 1P No coaches Last d 2.30pm
ROOMS: s £25-£34; d £40-£50; wkly b&b £125-£140; wkly hlf-bd £195-£210*

Q Q Fairways 398 London Rd South NR33 0BQ (S of town centre on A12, 1m from railway and bus station) ☎ 01502 572659
Gillian and Armando Montali are friendly proprietors, and they offer comfortable accommodation and a warm welcome in their well-run guest house at the southern end of town. The guest lounge has a TV and video and there is a dispense bar in the dining room.
7 rms (4 bth/shr) (2 fmly) No smoking in dining room CTV in all bedrooms Tea and coffee making facilities Licensed Cen ht CTV 2P Last d 6pm
ROOMS: s £17-£22; d £32-£36; wkly b&b £105-£140; wkly hlf-bd £157.50-£182.50*
CARDS:

Q Q Q *Kingsleigh* 44 Marine Pde NR33 0QN
(on the A12 overlooking the seafront) ☎ 01502 572513
Closed Xmas
Overlooking the Blue Flag beach and sea opposite, this Victorian house is centrally located and offers a friendly, relaxing atmosphere. The bedrooms are bright and well maintained. Traditional breakfasts are served in the dining room.
3 rms (2 shr) (1 fmly) No smoking CTV in 5 bedrooms Tea and coffee making facilities No dogs Cen ht No children 3yrs 4P No coaches

Q Q Q Longshore 7 Wellington Esplanade NR33 0QQ (on main A12 going south overlooking sea) ☎ 01502 565037 FAX 01502 582032
Closed 20 Dec-1 Jan
Sandra and Frank Nolan offer a warm welcome at their sea-facing guest house on the south side of town. This Grade II listed building has been well converted for the needs of guests, with all the attractively decorated and well equipped accommodation having en suite or private facilities. Four rooms enjoy panoramic sea views over the esplanade.
6 shr (1 fmly) No smoking in dining room No smoking in lounges CTV in all bedrooms Tea and coffee making facilities Cen ht 5P No coaches
ROOMS: s £20-£32; d £40-£42*
CARDS:

Q Q Q Rockville House 6 Pakefield Rd NR33 0HS
(enter town from south on A12, 1m past water tower take sharp turning right immediately after 'no entry' sign on right)
☎ 01502 581011 FAX 01502 574891
Situated in a residential area, Rockville is close to South Beach and Kensington Gardens. The enthusiastic proprietors offer welcoming hospitality in this well-maintained property which boasts antique furniture in the public rooms. A feature here is the selection of second-hand and collectable books for sale. A good breakfast choice is available in the dining room, where evening meals are served by prior arrangement. All bedrooms are comfortably furnished and immaculately presented.

4 bth/shr (1 fmly) No smoking in dining room CTV in all bedrooms Tea and coffee making facilities No dogs (ex guide dogs) Cen ht No children 12yrs No coaches Beach hut
ROOMS: s fr £25; d fr £45
CARDS:

Q Q Q **Somerton House** 7 Kirkley Cliff NR33 0BY
(On A12 southbound on seafront 100yds from Claremont pier)
☎ 01502 565665 FAX 01502 501176
This Grade II Sir Morton Peto-designed house has kept many of its original Victorian features, and is opposite the sandy beach. There is a comfortable lounge and evening meals include healthy options (special diets can be catered for). Bedrooms, which are attractively furnished, are continually being upgraded and retain much of their period character, with some lovely decoration and pieces of hardwood furniture; half have en suite facilities.
8 rms (4 shr) (2 fmly) No smoking in 2 bedrooms No smoking in dining room CTV in all bedrooms Tea and coffee making facilities Licensed Cen ht CTV Last d 7pm
ROOMS: s £18-£20; d £25-£36; wkly b&b £120-£192; wkly hlf-bd £169-£251*
CARDS:

LUDLOW Shropshire Map 07 SO57

See also Brimfield

Q Q Q **The Brakes** Downtown SY8 2LF
(take A49 N from Ludlow twds Shrewsbury. At Bromfield left onto A4113, after 2m left into Downton estates. Go on 3/4m. Est signed on right)
☎ 01584 856485 FAX 01584 856485
Parts of this charming house date back to the late 17th century and although it was extensively restructured in Victorian times, much of the original character remains. Surrounded by an attractive garden, it is located in picturesque countryside near the village of Downton. The accommodation, with twin and double bedded rooms, has modern facilities. Separate tables are provided in the dining room, where guests can enjoy 3-course Cordon Bleu dinners.
3 bth/shr (1 fmly) No smoking in dining room No smoking in lounges CTV in all bedrooms Tea and coffee making facilities Licensed Cen ht No children 12yrs 6P No coaches Croquet Badminton Last d 5pm
ROOMS: s £30-£35; d £50-£60; wkly b&b fr £150; wkly hlf-bd fr £300*

Q Q Q **Cecil** Sheet Rd SY8 1LR (From Shrewsbury right turn off A48 at 2nd roundabout. From Hereford left turn off A49 at 1st roundabout)
☎ 01584 872442 FAX 01584 872442
This much extended, detached house, with a pleasant rear garden provides soundly maintained, modern accommodation, which includes a family bedded room, and bedrooms on ground floor level. Facilities include a bright dining room, a small bar and a homely lounge.
9 rms (4 bth/shr) (1 fmly) No smoking CTV in all bedrooms Tea and coffee making facilities No dogs (ex guide dogs) Licensed Cen ht CTV 8P Last d 9am
ROOMS: s £19.50-£33; d £39-£54; wkly b&b £123-£170; wkly hlf-bd £195-£242*
CARDS:

Q Q Q **The Church** The Buttercross SY8 1AW (in Ludlow town centre) ☎ 01584 872174 FAX 01584 877146
This Grade II listed building lies between The Buttercross and the church in the centre of this bustling market town. An on-going refurbishment programme has resulted in comfortable and well maintained bedrooms, many having exposed beams, whilst downstairs there is a lounge bar offering a range of real ales. Meals and snacks are served either in the bar or the restaurant.
8 bth/shr (1 fmly) No smoking in dining room No smoking in lounges CTV in all bedrooms Tea and coffee making facilities No dogs (ex guide dogs) Cen ht P No coaches Last d 9pm
ROOMS: s £28-£45; d £45
MEALS: Lunch £4-£8.25alc Dinner £4.50-£8.25alc
CARDS:

Selected

Q Q Q Q **Five Ashes House** SY8 4BE ☎ 01568 750334 FAX 01568 750334

(For full entry see **Middleton-on-the-Hill**)

Premier Selected

Q Q Q Q Q **Line Farm** *(SO494668)* Tunnel Ln, Orleton SY8 4HY (signposted from A49 in Ashton. Follow the B&B signs in Tunnel Lane to Line Farm) ☎ 01568 780400 Mrs C Lewis
Mar-Oct
This large and very modern farmhouse stands in pretty lawns and gardens, and is surrounded by 54 acres of mixed farmland. It is owned and run by David and Carol Lewis, and guests are welcome to join them in farming activities. Pine furnished bedrooms are spacious and well equipped and attractive floral fabrics are used to good effect. A wood burning stove warms the comfortably furnished sitting room, and sliding doors lead on to the patio and garden. There are fine views over the surrounding area from all rooms.
3 bth No smoking CTV in all bedrooms Tea and coffee making facilities Direct dial from bedrooms No dogs (ex guide dogs) Cen ht CTV No children 6P 54 acres mixed
ROOMS: s £30-£35; d £45-£50*

Selected

QQQQ The Marcle Brimfield SY8 4NE
(turn left off A49 in centre of village, opposite post office)
☎ 01584 711459 FAX 01584 711459
Parts of this delightful and extensively renovated house date from the 16th century, and exposed beams, timbered walls in the spacious lounge, and traditionally furnished dining room, help to preserve the historic character. Bedrooms have modern facilities and meals are served at separate tables. The Marcle is set in a large garden in the centre of Brimfield, some 4 miles south of Ludlow.
3 bth/shr No smoking CTV in all bedrooms Tea and coffee making facilities No dogs Cen ht CTV 4P Last d by arrangement
ROOMS: s £35-£45; d £50-£60

Selected

QQQQ *Moor Hall* SY8 3EG ☎ 01584 823209 & 823333
FAX 01584 823387
This large Palladian-style Georgian country house, which is surrounded by extensive gardens and farmland, is about 5 miles north-east of Ludlow. The attractively appointed bedrooms consist of two doubles and one twin. One room is in fact a suite, with its own lounge. Other facilities include two comfortable lounges where log fires are lit during cold weather, a cosy bar and an elegant dining room with period furniture, where all guests share one table.
3 shr No smoking in bedrooms No smoking in dining room CTV in all bedrooms Tea and coffee making facilities Licensed Cen ht CTV 12P No coaches Fishing Archery Clay shooting Boules Croquet

Selected

QQQQ Mr Underhills Dinham Weir SY8 1EH
(located close to town centre below Ludlow Castle) ☎ 01584 874431
This delightful little hotel, or "restaurant with rooms" as the new owners prefer to describe it, enjoys a spectacular location on the bank of the River Teme, directly below Ludlow Castle. The town centre is but a few minutes walk away. Judy & Chris Bradley, who previously ran a well known restaurant of the same name in Stoneham, Norfolk, bought the place in November 1997. Since then they have made a lot of improvements to the bedrooms, which are well equipped and modern. The pleasant dining room has picture windows which overlook both the lovely garden and the river. There is also a lounge, where drinks can be served.
6 bth/shr No smoking in bedrooms No smoking in dining room CTV in all bedrooms Tea and coffee making facilities Direct dial from bedrooms No dogs (ex guide dogs) Licensed Cen ht 8P No coaches Fishing Last d 8.30pm
ROOMS: s £52.50-£67.50; d £70-£90
CARDS:

Premier Selected

QQQQQ Number Twenty Eight 28 Lower Broad St SY8 1PQ (A49, B4361, premises just off B4361) ☎ 01584 876996
FAX 01584 876860
Situated within the Georgian/Early Victorian area of this historic town, Number 28 is a combination of three separate houses, all retaining original features and enhanced by quality period furnishing and decor schemes. Each house has a comfortable sitting room in addition to well equipped bedrooms and pretty gardens. Breakfast is offered in the main house in the cosy dining room.
2 bth/shr 4 annexe bth/shr No smoking CTV in all bedrooms Tea and coffee making facilities Direct dial from bedrooms Licensed Cen ht No coaches
ROOMS: s £40-£65; d £60-£70; wkly b&b £215-£250*
CARDS:

Selected

QQQQ *Red Roofs* Little Hereford SY8 4AT
(on the A456 1.5m from A49) ☎ 01584 711439
This well maintained little guest house is some 5 miles south of Ludlow. It provides modern furnished and equipped accommodation which consists of a double-bedded room on ground floor level and a family room on the first floor. The latter does not have en suite facilities but a nearby private shower and toilet. There is a comfortable lounge and a pleasant dining room, where all guests share one table.
2 bth/shr (1 fmly) No smoking CTV in all bedrooms Tea and coffee making facilities Cen ht CTV 5P No coaches

LUSTLEIGH Devon Map 03 SX78

Selected

QQQQ Cleavelands TQ13 9SH (A382 Bovey Tracey/Moretonhampstead road, in 5m go left into Lustleigh, through village, turn left, cont to T-junc turn right, along on left)
☎ 01647 277349 FAX 01647 277349
Closed Xmas
Stunningly situated on the slopes overlooking Lustleigh and the Bovey Valley beyond, Cleavelands is a solid Victorian house set in two acres of well tended gardens. Bedrooms are individually furnished and decorated. One is located on the ground floor and is suitable for guests with a well behaved dog as it has its own access. Guests take breakfast around one large table in the dining room, where by arrangement evening meals are served. The sitting room is comfortable and benefits from a log fire and a grand piano, plus a selection of games and maps available in the library.
3 bth/shr (1 fmly) No smoking CTV in all bedrooms Tea and coffee making facilities Cen ht 7P No coaches Woodland walks/rides River & moor adjacent
ROOMS: s fr £25; d £40-£48; wkly b&b £140-£154

LUTON Bedfordshire Map 04 TL02

Q Q **Arlington Hotel** 137 New Bedford Rd LU3 1LF (on A6 opposite Wardown Park 0.75 mile from Luton Town Centre on the way to Bedford)
☎ 01582 419614 FAX 01582 459047
This predominantly commercial hotel offers guests the use of a small cosy bar with satellite TV and a traditionally appointed dining room. A variety of meals is available with daily specials and carte options in the dining room. Simpler snacks are served in the bar. Bedrooms have a good range of facilities, such as direct-dial telephone and TV.
22 rms (20 bth/shr) (3 fmly) No smoking in dining room CTV in all bedrooms Tea and coffee making facilities Direct dial from bedrooms No dogs (ex guide dogs) Licensed Cen ht 25P Last d 8pm
ROOMS: s £40-£45; d £45-£48*
CARDS:

Q Q **Leaside Hotel** 72 New Bedford Rd LU3 1BT (Access to car park via Old Bedford Road) ☎ 01582 417643 FAX 01582 734961
This large Victorian building is close to the town centre, and offers public rooms that include a popular restaurant serving international dishes and wines. There is also a bar which is open all day for light refreshments and drinks; residents have the use of a comfortable lounge area. The well equipped bedrooms vary in size and style, and some are located in a separate building.
13 bth/shr 1 annexe shr (1 fmly) CTV in 13 bedrooms Tea and coffee making facilities Direct dial from bedrooms No dogs (ex guide dogs) Licensed Cen ht CTV 30P No coaches Threequarter size snooker table Last d 9.30pm
ROOMS: s £40-£52.50; d £55-£65*
CARDS:

LYDFORD Devon Map 02 SX58

Selected

Q Q Q Q **Castle** EX20 4BH
(from A30 take A386 towards Tavistock and after 5m turn right signposted Lydford Gorge and Castle. Castle Inn is 1m down this road on right) ☎ 01822 820241 & 820242 FAX 01822 820454
Closed 25 Dec
Standing proudly beside the castle, just a short stroll from Lydford Gorge, this 16th-century country inn has charm in abundance. The wisteria clad exterior is a foretaste of the character within; aged darkened beams, crackling fires and bowed ceilings contribute to a wonderfully relaxed atmosphere. An imaginative range of freshly prepared bar food is supplemented by a dinner menu served in the intimate restaurant. The comfortably furnished lounge leads onto secluded gardens, and bedrooms are decorated and furnished in keeping with the period architecture.
9 bth/shr (1 fmly) No smoking in area of dining room CTV in all bedrooms Tea and coffee making facilities Direct dial from bedrooms Cen ht 8P No coaches Pets corner Last d 9.30pm
ROOMS: s £34.50-£67.50; d £62-£85; wkly b&b £241.50-£297.50; wkly hlf-bd £282.50-£328.08
MEALS: Dinner £15.95&alc
CARDS:

Premier Selected

Q Q Q Q Q **Moor View Hotel** Vale Down EX20 4BB
(turn off A30 at Sourton Cross onto A386 Tavistock road, hotel drive is approx 4m on right)
☎ 01822 820220 FAX 01822 820220

Built around 1870, Moor View has always welcomed guests, a tradition which current owners David and Wendy Sharples have carried on for the last 8 years. Beautifully furnished, this is a gracious and elegant abode with many fascinating pieces of family furniture and ephemera. Individually decorated bedrooms have an interesting collection of eclectic pieces and many thoughtful personal touches. Excellent food is carefully prepared by Wendy and enjoyed around the expansive oak dining table adorned with gleaming silverware.
4 bth/shr No smoking CTV in all bedrooms Tea and coffee making facilities Licensed Cen ht CTV No children 12yrs 15P No coaches Bowls Croquet Last d 3pm
ROOMS: s £45-£55; d £65-£80; wkly b&b £212-£248; wkly hlf-bd £280-£355*

See advertisement under OKEHAMPTON

LYME REGIS Dorset Map **03** SY39

See also Axminster

Q Q Q **Albany** Charmouth Rd DT7 3DP (situated on the eastern main road into Lyme Regis. 50yds past car park on left and before Anning Rd)
☎ 01297 443066
This attractive detached house, built in the 1920, is situated on the edge of town, and is just a few minutes walk from the seafront. The bedrooms are well equipped and comfortable; with one family room on the ground floor. Bedrooms at the rear of the property have delightful views over Lyme Bay.
4 rms (2 bth/shr) 1 annexe bth/shr (1 fmly) No smoking in 4 bedrooms No smoking in dining room No smoking in lounges CTV in all bedrooms Tea and coffee making facilities No dogs Cen ht CTV No children 5yrs 6P No coaches
ROOMS: d £36-£45*

Q Q Q **Coverdale** Woodmead Rd DT7 3AB (off A35 onto B3165 through Uplyme, over mini rbt the 2nd left before Mariners Hotel)
☎ 01297 442882
Closed Dec-Jan
Coverdale is just a few minutes from the town centre and seafront, situated in a quiet residential road. Bedrooms are comfortably furnished and equipped with TV, and all but one has modern en suite facilities. The dining room overlooks the pretty garden.
8 rms (6 shr) (1 fmly) No smoking CTV in all bedrooms Tea and coffee making facilities No dogs (ex guide dogs) Cen ht No children 10yrs 9P No coaches
ROOMS: s £16-£22; d £32-£44; wkly b&b £100-£133*

Q Q Q **St Michael's Hotel** Pound St DT7 3HZ ☎ 01297 442503
FAX 01297 442503
Located in the centre of town, this private hotel is only a short walk from the sea. Bedrooms are well maintained and equipped with modern comforts; those at the back have views over the sea. There is a spacious dining room and lounge, and a conservatory that leads into the pretty garden. There is an intimate cellar bar, as well as a sauna and solarium.
11 rms (4 bth 5 shr) (1 fmly) No smoking in 1 bedrooms No smoking in dining room No smoking in 1 lounge CTV in all bedrooms Tea and coffee making facilities Licensed Cen ht No children 3yrs 9P No coaches Sauna Solarium
ROOMS: s £21-£25; d £42-£50*
CARDS:

Q Q Q **The White House** 47 Silver St DT7 3HR
(on B3165 Axminster-Lyme Regis road approx 50mtrs from junct with A3052) ☎ 01297 443420
Apr-Sept
This charming personally-run guest house, built in 1770, offers bright attractively decorated rooms with modern en suite facilities. There is a comfortable lounge, a pretty breakfast room and Mr and Mrs Edmondson also provide detailed information on many local walks.
7 shr No smoking in dining room CTV in all bedrooms Tea and coffee making facilities Cen ht No children 10yrs 7P No coaches
ROOMS: d £38-£42; wkly b&b £119-£133*

LYMINGTON Hampshire Map **04** SZ39

Selected

Q Q Q Q **Albany House** Highfield SO41 9GB
(premises off the A337 100yards from the one way system in town)
☎ 01590 671900
Closed 2wks in winter
This attractive Regency property is situated on the western edge of the town and affords easy access to the Forest and the coast. Wendy Gallagher offers a warm welcome to her lovely house, which has a cosy lounge with large sofas, and a bright dining room. The spacious bedrooms have modern en suite facilities, and Wendy serves good home-cooked evening meals and hearty breakfasts.
3 bth/shr (1 fmly) No smoking in dining room CTV in all bedrooms Tea and coffee making facilities Cen ht CTV 4P No coaches
Last d noon
ROOMS: s £40-£46; d £52-£59; wkly b&b £166-£186; wkly hlf-bd £228-£268*

Selected

Q Q Q Q **Ash Barn** Walhampton Hill SO41 5RE (turn off A326 at Dibden rdbt, onto B3054. Walhampton Paddock 1m before Lymington opposite Walhampton School) ☎ 01590 673923 FAX 01590 673923
Set in an acre and a half of well tended gardens and a paddock, this ranch-style Colt Bungalow, is the home of Heather and Sid Cornish who welcome guests to their home. Situated on the edge of the New Forest, one mile from the centre of Lymington, this cosy single storey property, is the ideal centre for touring the area. The bedrooms are spacious and very comfortable, as is the sitting room with its adjoining dining area, where a traditional English breakfast is served each morning.
2 bth/shr (2 fmly) No smoking in 1 bedrooms No smoking in dining room No smoking in lounges CTV in all bedrooms Tea and coffee making facilities Cen ht CTV 5P No coaches
ROOMS: s £20-£25; d £40-£44; wkly b&b £140-£154*

Selected

Q Q Q Q **Auplands** 22 Southampton Rd SO41 9GG
(Situated on A337 just before town centre, almost opposite supermarket) ☎ 01590 675944 FAX 01590 675944
Closed Xmas & New Year
This friendly family-run guest house is located just 200 yards from Lymington High Street in the New Forest. The well furnished rooms are well equipped and have modern facilities. There is a comfortable lounge and the cosy breakfast room, where hearty English breakfasts are served, overlooks the garden. Guests are welcome to use the pool.
2 shr No smoking CTV in all bedrooms Tea and coffee making facilities Cen ht CTV 8P No coaches Outdoor swimming pool
ROOMS: s £20-£25; d £36-£45

Q Q Q ***Cherry Orchard Lodge*** 21 Waterford Ln SO41 3PT
☎ 01590 678406
Situated in a quiet residential area this well presented guest house is convenient for both the town centre and the harbour. Resident proprietor Julie Mansbridge provides a warm welcome and a relaxed informal atmosphere for all her guests. The bedrooms are neatly presented with comfortable furnishings throughout. Breakfast is taken communally around one of two tables in the cosy dining room.
4 rms

Selected

Q Q Q Q **Cottage Bed & Breakfast** Angel Cottage, Angel Ln, Downton BH25 5PT (A337 from Lymington, through Downton, 0.25 mile on left after Royal Oak pub) ☎ 01425 629506
This pretty house dates back to 1842 and has been skilfully restored by proprietors Mr and Mrs Jelley, who specialise in golfing holidays and will readily make all arrangements and drive guests to the nearby course. Bedrooms are spacious and attractively decorated in a cosy cottage-style and are equipped with lots of thoughtful home comforts.

There is also a family suite in a superb purpose built barn. Breakfast is served in the conservatory overlooking the attractive garden.

2 shr (1 fmly) No smoking CTV in all bedrooms Tea and coffee making facilities Cen ht 5P No coaches Golf 27 Last d 8pm
ROOMS: s £30-£50; d £40-£50✱

Premier Selected

QQQQQ Efford Cottage Milford Rd, Everton SO41 0JD
(on A337, 2m W of Lymington)
☎ 01590 642315 & 0374 703075
FAX 01590 641030/642315
Efford Cottage is well situated for both the New Forest and the coast. The spacious bedrooms are furnished with style and comfort, and the en suite shower rooms, although compact, are well equipped. There are many extras for the convenience of guests including trouser presses, hairdryers, fresh fruit and chocolates; also refrigerators with fresh milk, mineral water, fruit juice and chocolate biscuits. There is a large comfortable lounge to relax in. Patricia Ellis offers a good choice of freshly cooked food in the dining room at both at dinner and breakfast.
3 shr (1 fmly) No smoking in bedrooms No smoking in dining room CTV in all bedrooms Tea and coffee making facilities Direct dial from bedrooms Cen ht No children 14yrs 4P No coaches
Last d 90mins prior
ROOMS: d £44-£48; wkly b&b fr £154

Selected

QQQQ Harts Lodge 242 Everton Rd, Everton SO41 0HE
(At Everton turn off A337 into Everton Rd, 0.5m on left)
☎ 01590 645902
This attractive large bungalow enjoys a peaceful location in 3 acres of garden and paddock in the village of Everton. The three bedrooms are fully en suite, furnished to a high standard and feature many thoughtful touches such as alarm clocks. Guests can relax in the comfortable lounge and enjoy a hearty breakfast in the attractive dining room overlooking the surrounding, well tended gardens.
3 bth/shr (1 fmly) No smoking CTV in all bedrooms Tea and coffee making facilities Cen ht CTV 6P No coaches
ROOMS: s £20-£30; d £38-£45✱

QQQ Jevington 47 Waterford Ln SO41 3PT
(from High Street, turn right at St Thomas Church into Church Lane. Where road forks, take left fork into Waterford Lane) ☎ 01590 672148
Centrally situated in a quiet residential area, this attractive guest house provides an ideal base to explore the New Forest and surrounding areas. The

contd. on p.282.

Broadview Gardens,

East Crewkerne, Crewkerne,
Somerset/Dorset Border TA18 7AG
Tel/Fax: 01460-73424. Gillian & Robert Swann.

Unusual Colonial bungalow with en-suite rooms overlooking an acre of beautiful secluded gardens with lawns and hundreds of unusual plants. Furnished in keeping, in the Edwardian style. Extremely comfortable and relaxing in a friendly informal atmosphere. We offer the very best quality Traditional English home cooking. Stay a while and visit this wonderful area for garden visits, antique enthusiasts, Dorset coast and quaint old villages. A perfect touring base. Our list provides fifty varied places. A completely No Smoking house.
Open all year. En suite B&B £25-£28 pppn. Dinner £14.

AA QQQQQ | ETB ♛♛♛ DE-LUXE

Both Top Quality Awards. Also Recommended by 'Which'

Cottage Bed & Breakfast

Angel Cottage, Angel Lane, Downton, New Milton, Hampshire BH25 5PT
Tel: 01425 629506 Mobile: 0411 944280

Mariette and Trevor warmly welcome you to their Cottage, built in 1842. Situated down a country lane surrounded by fields and woods with a walk from the cottage to the beach. Mariette, one of the "Landlady of the Year" finalists for 1998, specialists in a home from home atmosphere – nothing is too much trouble. A scrumptious choice at breakfast, beautiful cottage style bedrooms and tranquil gardens all create the perfect ambience for relaxing and unwinding.

WHICH GUIDE | AA QQQQ

three bedrooms are pleasantly decorated, comfortably furnished and all offer smart en suite shower rooms. Guests enjoy a traditional cooked breakfast served around one large table in the downstairs dining room.
3 shr (1 fmly) No smoking CTV in all bedrooms Tea and coffee making facilities Cen ht No children 5 yrs 3P
ROOMS: s £25-£30; d £38-£40*

Premier Selected

QQQQQ **The Nurse's Cottage** Station Rd SO41 6BA
LYMINGTON ☎ 01590 683402 FAX 01590 683402

(For full entry see **Sway**)

Selected

QQQQ **Old Barn** Christchurch Rd, Downton SO41 0LA
(on A337 approx 3m from Lymington, approx 1m after Everton Nurseries on right hand side near Royal Oak Pub)
☎ 01590 644939 FAX 01590 644939
Julie and Simon Benford warmly welcome guests to their beautiful home, a carefully converted 17th-century barn. The well furnished and comfortable bedrooms have plain but attractive decor and the elegant bathrooms have power showers. There is a comfortable lounge where guests may relax. A traditional English breakfast is served around the farmhouse table in the dining room.
2 bth/shr (1 fmly) No smoking CTV in all bedrooms Tea and coffee making facilities No dogs (ex guide dogs) Cen ht CTV 6P
No coaches
ROOMS: s £35-£50; d £40-£50

Selected

QQQQ **Our Bench** Lodge Rd, Pennington SO41 8HH
(from A337 turn right signposted Pennington Village, pass the church, then 2nd right guesthouse on left)
☎ 01590 673141 FAX 01590 673141
Set in pretty gardens at Pennington village, this modernised bungalow is just a short walk from Lymington in the New Forest. Bedrooms have been designed to make good use of the available space and a further bedroom is available in a separate building in the garden. English breakfasts and enjoyable home-cooked evening meals are served in the attractive dining room, and guests can relax in the comfortable conservatory lounge. The small heated pool, sauna and jacuzzi are a popular feature, and available to guests at a small extra charge. Disabled facilities are available for guests with limited mobility (National Accessibility Scheme for the disabled Level 3).
2 shr 1 annexe shr No smoking CTV in all bedrooms Tea and coffee making facilities No dogs Cen ht CTV No children 14yrs 5P
No coaches Indoor swimming pool (heated) Sauna Jacuzzi
Mountain bikes
ROOMS: d £42-£50*
CARDS:

LYNDHURST Hampshire Map **04** SU30

See also Fritham

Selected

QQQQ ***Heather House Hotel*** Southampton Rd SO43 7BQ
☎ 01703 284409
This recently converted private residence has been transformed into a smart and stylish house by resident proprietors Mr and Mrs Swann. The hotel has a warm family atmosphere and, with a golfing background, Mr Swann is keen to meet fellow enthusiasts. The elegant restaurant serves freshly cooked dinners and the bar is a comfortable place for a chat and a drink.
7 rms

Selected

QQQQ **Ormonde House** Southampton Rd SO43 7BT
(turn off M27 onto A337, drive through Lyndhurst one way system and leave village, then 400 yds past fire station on left of A35)
☎ 01703 282806 FAX 01703 282004
Closed 8 days Xmas
Located just off the main Southampton-Lyndhurst road, this well presented property offers good value for money. Spacious bedrooms are comfortably appointed with co-ordinated furnishings and fabrics. Guests can relax in the bar or conservatory lounge which overlooks the gardens. Dinner is pre-ordered from a daily changing blackboard menu which offers a wide range of fresh, home-cooked dishes.

17 bth/shr (1 fmly) No smoking in 2 bedrooms No smoking in dining room No smoking in 1 lounge CTV in all bedrooms Tea and coffee making facilities Direct dial from bedrooms Licensed Cen ht 20P No coaches Last d 5pm
ROOMS: s £22-£32; d £44-£78; wkly b&b £191-£289; wkly hlf-bd £259-£357*
CARDS:

Selected

QQQQ Penny Farthing Hotel Romsey Rd SO43 7AA (from M27 junct 1 follow A337, hotel on left at entrance to village)
☎ 01703 284422 FAX 01703 284488
A warm welcome awaits guests at this small hotel on the edge of the village. Lyndhurst is close to the major routes and convenient for visiting the local attractions. The bedrooms vary in size but are well equipped, and attractively decorated; they have been named after types of bicycle. There is a spacious breakfast room, where breakfast is served, and a comfortable lounge bar.
11 rms (10 bth/shr) 4 annexe rms (2 fmly) No smoking in bedrooms No smoking in dining room No smoking in 1 lounge CTV in all bedrooms Tea and coffee making facilities Direct dial from bedrooms Licensed Cen ht CTV 15P No coaches Lock up bicycle store
ROOMS: s £25-£35; d £49-£70*
CARDS:

See advertisement on p.285.

The AA's professional Inspectors make regular and anonymous visits to all the establishments listed in the Guide. They accept no gifts or favours from proprietors

QQQ **Stable End** Emery Down SO43 7FJ
(follow A337 towards Lyndhurst and take 3rd turning on right. After 0.75m turn right at T-junction then immediatly left into gravel entrance)
☎ 01703 282504 FAX 01703 282504
Enjoying a peaceful rural setting on the edge of Lyndhurst, Mary and Warren Dibben provide a warm welcome to their family home. The two bedrooms are attractively decorated and furnished, and both offer en suite facilities. There is a bright conservatory style lounge and breakfast is served around one table in the adjacent dining room.
2 bth/shr No smoking CTV in all bedrooms Tea and coffee making facilities No dogs (ex guide dogs) Cen ht CTV 4P No coaches
ROOMS: s £21-£22; d £42-£44*

QQQ **Whitemoor House Hotel** Southampton Rd SO43 7BU
(entering town from west on A35, hotel first on right by golf course)
☎ 01703 282186 FAX 01703 282186
Closed 20 Dec-27 Dec
Located on the edge of the village of Lyndhurst this friendly hotel overlooking the golf course is in a good position for the attractions of the New Forest. En suite bedrooms are bright and spacious. The imaginative menu, served in the attractive dining room, is of top quality. The lounge is the place for drinks, and the terrace is a charming option in the summer months.
8 bth/shr (2 fmly) No smoking CTV in all bedrooms Tea and coffee making facilities Direct dial from bedrooms Licensed Cen ht 10P No coaches Golf 18 Last d 6pm
ROOMS: s £25-£50; d £40-£55*
CARDS:

LYNMOUTH Devon Map **03** SS74

Premier Selected

QQQQQ **Bonnicott House** Watersmeet Rd EX35 6EP
(opposite Anglican church and car park) ☎ 01598 753346
Mar-Nov
Built as a Rectory in 1820, Bonnicott stands in an elevated position overlooking the town and Lynmouth bay. The house is beautifully furnished with both modern and antique furniture and all bedrooms are of a high standard with modern facilities. The lounge is spacious and also has fine views.
7 bth/shr (1 fmly) No smoking CTV in all bedrooms Tea and coffee making facilities No dogs Licensed Cen ht No children 5yrs No coaches
ROOMS: s £25-£30; d £44-£60; wkly b&b £154-£189*

QQQ **Corner House** Riverside Rd EX35 6EH
(follow A39 to Lynton/Lynmouth, turn towards harbour at Lynmouth, Corner House is first building on left)
☎ 01598 753300 FAX 01598 753300
Mar-Oct
Situated close to the centre of the village, this popular restaurant and coffee shop has three spacious rooms, each smartly decorated and well equipped, and two have comfortable sofas. The restaurant is open throughout the day and serves an extensive range of meals and snacks.
3 shr No smoking in bedrooms CTV in all bedrooms Tea and coffee making facilities No dogs Licensed Cen ht No children 3P
ROOMS: d £44-£50
CARDS:

This symbol indicates a 'Child Friendly' establishment - see page 25 for details

Selected

QQQQ ***Countisbury Lodge Hotel*** Tors Park EX35 6NB
(enter town from A39 and down Countisbury Hill) ☎ 01598 752388
Mar-Dec
Close to the picturesque harbour, this former Victorian vicarage enjoys a secluded setting with fine views over the surrounding countryside. Bedrooms are well appointed, with modern facilities. In addition to the comfortable lounge, the exposed cliff wall is an unusual feature in the cosy bar. Breakfast is served in the attractive dining room and a small patio is also available. A self-catering cottage adjoins the house.
6 bth/shr (1 fmly) No smoking in bedrooms No smoking in dining room No smoking in lounges Tea and coffee making facilities Licensed Cen ht CTV 8P No coaches Last d 5pm
CARDS:

QQQ **Glenville House** 2 Torrs Rd EX35 6ET
(turn left off A39 at the bottom of Countisbury Hill) ☎ 01598 752202
mid Mar-mid Nov
Quietly located, overlooking the East Lyn River, this charming Victorian house is personally run by Tricia and Alan Francis, who welcome guests to their cosy home. The bedrooms are attractively co-ordinated and comfortable and there is a small lounge for guests on the first floor. A hearty breakfast is served each morning in the front facing dining room.
6 rms (3 shr) (1 fmly) No smoking Tea and coffee making facilities No dogs Licensed Cen ht CTV No children 8yrs
ROOMS: s £18.50; d £37-£42; wkly b&b £123-£140*

Selected

QQQQ **The Heatherville** Tors Park EX35 6NB
(1st left hand fork in Tors Rd) ☎ 01598 752327
Mar-Oct
A comfortable family-run guest house with commanding views over Lynmouth and the wooded areas surrounding. The bedrooms are well appointed with modern facilities and there is a bright lounge, dining room and bar with lovely views over the town.
9 rms (1 bth 4 shr) (2 fmly) No smoking in dining room CTV in 5 bedrooms Tea and coffee making facilities Licensed Cen ht CTV No children 7yrs 9P No coaches Last d 5.30pm

Selected

QQQQ **Rock House** Manor Grounds EX35 6EN (on A39)
☎ 01598 753508 FAX 01598 753508
This Grade II listed building, stands alone at the entrance to the harbour. The bedrooms are comfortable, with the majority having been totally refurbished to a very good standard. All the rooms are exceptionally well equipped and one room is located on the ground

floor. Guests have the option of either eating from the fixed price menu, or informally in the bar.
6 bth/shr No smoking CTV in all bedrooms Tea and coffee making facilities Licensed Cen ht No children 7yrs 6P No coaches Tennis (hard) Last d 8pm
ROOMS: s £26-£30; d £50-£70*
CARDS: MasterCard Barclaycard VISA Barclays CONNECT Delta Switch

Q Q Q **Tregonwell Riverside** 1 Tors Rd EX35 6ET ☎ 01598 753369
Closed 15 Dec-Jan
An elegant stone built Victorian house at the junction of the East and West Lyn Rivers, Tregonwell is a comfortable guest house with well appointed rooms and modern facilities. There is an abundance of interesting Far Eastern objets d'arts in the house. Morning coffees and afternoon teas are served in the garden.
7 rms (3 shr) (2 fmly) No smoking in 3 bedrooms No smoking in dining room No smoking in lounges CTV in 1 bedroom Tea and coffee making facilities Cen ht CTV 7P Last d noon

LYNTON Devon Map **03** SS74

Selected

Q Q Q Q **Alford House Hotel** Alford Ter EX35 6AT
(enter via Lynbridge and up hill past the Old Station then 2nd right into Normans Cleave) ☎ 01598 752359 FAX 01598 752359
Mid Feb-Mid Nov rs Xmas and New Year
This house, built in the 1840s, stands high over the town with commanding views. The proprietors extend a warm welcome and offer good home made fare, as Mr Pierce is a chef by trade. The bedrooms are bright and comfortable with modern facilities. The spacious lounge

contd. on p.286.

is enhanced by beautiful rosewood furniture bought in the Far East by the proprietors.
8 bth/shr No smoking CTV in all bedrooms Tea and coffee making facilities No dogs (ex guide dogs) Licensed Cen ht No children 12yrs No coaches Last d 3pm
ROOMS: s £30; d £44-£56; wkly b&b £139-£176; wkly hlf-bd £255-£270✻
CARDS:

Q Q Q **Castle Hill House** Castle Hill EX35 6JA (exit M5 junc 24, follow A39 to Lynton)
☎ 01598 752291 FAX 01598 752291
Situated in the heart of the village, this small Victorian hotel has recently been taken over by Chris and Sue Reeves-Jones. Each evening, an interesting range of imaginative dishes is available, and special dietary needs are always catered for, though prior notice is appreciated. Bedrooms are comfortable and especially well equipped; family suites are provided.
9 bth/shr (3 fmly) No smoking in 2 bedrooms No smoking in dining room No smoking in 1 lounge CTV in all bedrooms Tea and coffee making facilities Licensed Cen ht ch fac Last d 9.30pm
ROOMS: s £30; d £45-£55✻
CARDS:

Selected

Q Q Q Q **Fernleigh** Park St EX35 6BY (A39 to Lynmouth, up hill to Lynton. Through village, left after Post Office. From A39 Barbrook, downhill to Lynton, 2nd right by church off main st)
☎ 01598 753575 FAX 01598 753575
Feb-Nov
Fernleigh is a modern property situated in the centre of the village. Guests can expect a warm welcome from Hugh and Anne McDonnell who run Fernleigh in a very relaxed manner. The well appointed bedrooms vary in size, the most popular room being a family room, which enjoys splendid views. There is a ground floor room suitable for the less mobile guest. Evening meals are available by prior arrangement.
4 bth/shr (1 fmly) No smoking CTV in all bedrooms Tea and coffee making facilities No dogs (ex guide dogs) Cen ht CTV No children 10yrs 6P No coaches Last d noon
ROOMS: d £34-£40; wkly b&b £119-£129; wkly hlf-bd £189-£199✻

Selected

Q Q Q Q **Hazeldene** 27 Lee Rd EX35 6BP (100yds beyond town hall, opposite post office) ☎ 01598 752364 FAX 01598 752364
Closed 1 Nov-1 Feb
Conveniently situated near the centre of town, Hazeldene offers the guest every comfort. The bedrooms vary in style and size and offer modern amenities. There are comfortable lounges, a small bar and personal effects around the house adding to the homely atmosphere.
9 bth/shr (2 fmly) No smoking in 7 bedrooms No smoking in dining room No smoking in lounges CTV in all bedrooms Tea and coffee making facilities Licensed Cen ht CTV No children 5yrs 8P No coaches Last d 5pm
ROOMS: s £22-£27; d £40-£45; wkly b&b £138-£147; wkly hlf-bd £220-£234✻
CARDS:

Selected

Q Q Q Q **Ingleside Hotel** Lee Rd EX35 6HW (on private road between Town Hall & Methodist church on Lee Rd) ☎ 01598 752223
Apr-Oct
Standing in an elevated position above the town, with far reaching views, Ingleside offers the holidaymaker a stay in a homely and comfortable atmosphere provided by the resident proprietors. The bedrooms are bright, with modern amenities, and good home-made food is served in the dining room.
8 bth/shr (2 fmly) No smoking in dining room No smoking in lounges CTV in all bedrooms Tea and coffee making facilities No dogs Licensed Cen ht No children 12yrs 10P No coaches Last d 6pm
ROOMS: s £24-£26; d £48-£52; wkly b&b £154-£168; wkly hlf-bd £252-£266
CARDS:

Selected

Q Q Q Q **Longmead House** 9 Longmead EX35 6DQ (follow signs for 'Valley of Rocks') ☎ 01598 752523 FAX 01598 752523
mid Mar-Oct
Quietly situated towards the picturesque 'Valley of the Rocks', Longmead House is set in large gardens. The owners, John and Carol Pluck offer guests a warm welcome to their well presented small hotel. Bedrooms are well equipped, varying in size, but all attractively

decorated. A homely lounge with a well stocked bar is available for guests, while in the panelled dining room there is a magnificent oak fireplace. Evening meals are served by prior arrangement.
7 rms (5 bth/shr) (1 fmly) No smoking CTV in all bedrooms Tea and coffee making facilities No dogs Licensed Cen ht CTV 7P No coaches Last d 4pm
ROOMS: s £18-£20; d £40-£44✳
CARDS:

Selected

Q Q Q Q **Lynhurst Hotel** Lyn Way EX35 6AX
(drive to centre of Lynton, locate Lower Meadow car park opposite Royal Castle Pub, in far left corner is garden entrance to premises)
☎ 01598 752241 FAX 01598 752241
Mar-Oct rs Oct-Mar
Standing high above Lynton, The Lynhurst Hotel has commanding views over the town and the bay. Bedrooms are individual in style and size, and benefit from modern amenities. There is a dining room and spacious lounge with bar.
7 rms (2 bth 2 shr) (1 fmly) No smoking in bedrooms No smoking in dining room No smoking in 1 lounge CTV in all bedrooms Tea and coffee making facilities Licensed CTV No coaches Last d noon
ROOMS: s £26-£26; d £44-£54; wkly b&b £135-£175; wkly hlf-bd £233-£273✳

Selected

Q Q Q Q ***Mayfair Hotel*** Lynway EX35 6AY
(centre of Lynton, up Sinai Hill) ☎ 01598 753227 & 753327
From its elevated position, this former Victorian gentleman's residence has spectacular views over Lynton, across to Exmoor and the Welsh coastline. The public areas are comfortable and include a spacious lounge and cosy bar. In the smartly appointed dining room, separate tables are provided at breakfast, and special diets are catered for. Under the same ownership is a 14th-century pub about five minutes walk from the hotel, serving a range of meals at reasonable prices.
9 bth/shr No smoking in dining room CTV in all bedrooms Tea and coffee making facilities No dogs (ex guide dogs) Licensed Cen ht CTV No children 12yrs 10P No coaches Last d 11am
CARDS:

Selected

Q Q Q Q **Rockvale Hotel** Lee Rd EX35 6HW
(short private road to left of Lynton Town Hall and Tourist Information Office) ☎ 01598 752279 & 753343
Mar-Oct
A warm greeting awaits guests in this bright and cheerful small hotel. There are two lounges, one with a bar and with marvellous views out over the town and beyond. A five-course dinner is served each evening with many interesting dishes. Bedrooms are varied in style and size and offer modern facilities.
8 rms (5 bth 1 shr) (2 fmly) No smoking CTV in all bedrooms Tea and coffee making facilities Direct dial from bedrooms No dogs Licensed Cen ht No children 4yrs 8P No coaches Last d 5pm
CARDS:

Selected

Q Q Q Q **St Vincent** Castle Hill EX35 6JA (approx mid way between Barnstaple and Minehead, exit A39 to Lynton, premises located beside Exmoor Museum) ☎ 01598 752244 FAX 01598 752244
Closed Xmas
Situated in the heart of the village, this wisteria-clad Grade II listed property offers a warm welcome to guests. A comfortable lounge is provided, where drinks are served prior to dinner in the candle-lit dining room. The light and airy bedrooms vary in size, and all are well equipped.
7 rms (6 bth/shr) (1 fmly) No smoking CTV in all bedrooms Tea and coffee making facilities Licensed Cen ht CTV No children 8yrs 3P No coaches Last d 11.30am
ROOMS: s £19-£23✳

Premier Selected

Q Q Q Q Q **Victoria Lodge** Lee Rd EX35 6BS
(off A39 opposite Post Office) ☎ 01598 753203 FAX 01598 753203
Closed Dec-Jan rs Feb & March, & Nov
Ben and Jane Bennett have succeeded in transforming Victoria Lodge into a house of elegance and style. The fabrics, furniture and fittings are all of the highest quality and nothing has been overlooked to ensure guests are offered every comfort. Jane Bennett is also justifiably proud of the menus she offers to her guests at dinner, on certain days of the week.
9 bth/shr No smoking CTV in all bedrooms Tea and coffee making facilities No dogs Licensed Cen ht 7P No coaches Last d 12noon
ROOMS: d £46-£68; wkly b&b £147-£217
CARDS:

Selected

Q Q Q Q **Waterloo House Hotel** Lydiate Ln EX35 6AJ
☎ 01598 753391 FAX 01598 753391
Located in a residential area of Lynton, this Georgian property retains the character and charm of the period, while providing modern facilities. Bedrooms are individually furnished and well equipped, and two lounges are available at all times. Friendly owners Rosemary and Mel Edwards welcome guests and create a relaxed and informal atmosphere. An imaginative choice of home-cooked dishes is served in the elegant dining room.
9 rms (8 bth/shr) (2 fmly) No smoking in bedrooms No smoking in dining room No smoking in 1 lounge CTV in all bedrooms Tea and coffee making facilities No dogs (ex guide dogs) Licensed Cen ht CTV No children 5yrs 4P No coaches Last d 5pm
ROOMS: s £20-£24; d £40-£54; wkly b&b £119-£160; wkly hlf-bd £190-£232✳
CARDS:

LYTHAM ST ANNES Lancashire Map 07 SD32

Q Q **Cullerne Hotel** 55 Lightburne Av, St Annes on Sea FY8 1JE (on facing the pier turn left, premises seventh road along 100 yards from front) ☎ 01253 721753
This friendly family guest house is just off the Promenade and provides good value accommodation. There is a comfortable lounge for guests and breakfasts is served in the pleasant dining room.
5 rms (2 fmly) No smoking in dining room CTV in all bedrooms Tea and coffee making facilities No dogs Licensed Cen ht CTV 4P No coaches Last d noon
ROOMS: s £14.50; d £29; wkly b&b £101.50; wkly hlf-bd £116*

Q Q Q **Endsleigh Private Hotel** 315 Clifton Dr South FY8 1HN (premises located on A584 2.5m E of Blackpool, first hotel E of St Annes Sq shopping centre, opposite the main Post Office) ☎ 01253 725622
Peter and Elizabeth Robinson have run this small hotel for nearly two decades and the large number of repeat guests is testament to their success. Spacious bedrooms, two of which have separate access at the side of the building, are freshly decorated and comfortable. Family rooms are available. Home cooking is a feature of this hotel and there is a welcoming lounge.
15 bth/shr (3 fmly) No smoking in 6 bedrooms No smoking in dining room CTV in all bedrooms Tea and coffee making facilities No dogs Licensed Cen ht 8P No coaches Last d 4pm
ROOMS: s £19-£25; d £38-£50; wkly b&b £130-£140; wkly hlf-bd £182-£192*

Q Q Q **Strathmore Hotel** 305 Clifton Dr South FY8 1HN (premises situated on the main Preston to Blackpool Rd at the centre of St Annes opposite the Post Office) ☎ 01253 725478
Conveniently situated for both the town centre and the promenade, this small hotel offers light and airy bedrooms. First floor bedrooms are nicely spacious, while the standard rooms are slightly more compact. The spacious lounge is attractively decorated and leads into a cosy dining room, where freshly prepared evening meals are available.
10 rms (2 bth 3 shr) No smoking in dining room CTV in all bedrooms Tea and coffee making facilities No dogs Licensed Cen ht No children 9yrs 10P No coaches Last d 5pm
ROOMS: s £17-£23; d £34-£46; wkly b&b £119-£161; wkly hlf-bd £154-£182

MACCLESFIELD Cheshire Map 07 SJ97

Premier Selected

Q Q Q Q Q **Hardingland Farm Country House** *(SJ958725)* Macclesfield Forest SK11 0ND (A537, 2.5m out of Macclesfield at "Setter Dog" pub continue 100 yards past pub to millstone, turn right opposite stone up narrow lane, B&B signed) ☎ 01625 425759 FAX 615011 Mrs A Read
Mar-Nov
This delightful 18th-century farmhouse overlooks the Macclesfield Forest and the Teggs Nose Country Park. It is furnished throughout with many fine antique pieces, and exposed timbers and other original features remain. An elegantly furnished lounge is provided for residents and guests dine family-style in the charming dining room. Owner Anna Read is an accomplished cook and creates beautifully presented dinners. Fresh local produce is used whenever possible and breakfasts are also of excellent quality. The farm is surrounded by lovely countryside.
3 rms (2 bth/shr) No smoking Tea and coffee making facilities No dogs Cen ht CTV No children 16yrs 3P 17 acres smallholding beef sheep Last d 9am
ROOMS: s £35-£40; d £40-£46; wkly b&b £245-£322; wkly hlf-bd £320-£406*

Q Q Q **Moorhayes House Hotel** 27 Manchester Rd, Tytherington SK10 2JJ (on A538 0.5m N of town centre) ☎ 01625 433228 FAX 01625 433228
This large detached house is set well back from the main road and is surrounded by extensive and well tended gardens. Bedrooms vary in size and style and all are well maintained and attractively decorated. Some are located on the ground floor and are suitable for less mobile guests. There is no lounge but comfortable chairs are provided in each bedroom and breakfast is served in an attractive dining room.
9 rms (7 shr) (1 fmly) No smoking in 3 bedrooms No smoking in dining room No smoking in lounges CTV in all bedrooms Tea and coffee making facilities Cen ht 15P No coaches
ROOMS: s £28-£43; d £40-£54*
CARDS: BARCLAYCARD VISA

MAIDENHEAD Berkshire Map 04 SU88

Q Q **Antonio** 41 Switchback Rd North SL6 7UF (from Maidenhead take the B447 Cookham (about 1 mile) ☎ 01628 670537 & 0378 709207
Proprietor Mr Antinoro has converted three rooms of his family home into comfortable, quiet accommodation. All three rooms have cable TV, tea facilities and wash basin. There is a cosy breakfast room and although dinner is not available there are many local restaurants and pubs within easy reach.
3 rms No smoking in dining room CTV in all bedrooms Tea and coffee making facilities No dogs Cen ht 5P

Premier Selected

Q Q Q Q Q **Beehive Manor** Cox Green Ln SL6 3ET (exit M4 at junc 8/9, A404, exit at junc 9A, follow Cox Green signs and at second roundabout turn into Cox Green Rd, then left at Forresters Pub) ☎ 01628 620980 FAX 01628 621840
Closed Xmas
Barbara Barbour and Sue Lemin have upgraded this 16th-century house to give comfortable modern facilities, yet maintain the character of the building. Bedrooms are individually decorated and feature many useful amenities. There is a small lounge on the first floor where guests can enjoy tea and coffee and a spacious, elegantly appointed lounge

downstairs. A generous English breakfast is served around a large polished table in the adjoining dining room.
3 bth/shr No smoking No dogs Cen ht CTV No children 12yrs 6P No coaches
ROOMS: s £40; d £60*
CARDS:

Selected

Q Q Q Q **Woodpecker Cottage** Warren Row RG10 8QS
(turn N off A4 at Knowl Hill, after 1 mile turn left up dirt track, take left hand fork up into woods, house after 100yards 2nd on the left)
☎ 01628 822772 FAX 01628 822125
This charming cottage stands in an acre of well kept gardens and lawns. The location is peaceful yet still very convenient for Heathrow. Bedrooms are well equipped and comfortable, with many thoughtful extras. An excellent breakfast is served in the elegant dining room. There is a small cosy lounge with a wood burning stove in colder weather.
3 bth/shr (1 fmly) No smoking CTV in all bedrooms Tea and coffee making facilities No dogs Cen ht No children 8yrs 6P No coaches Croquet
ROOMS: s £25-£30; d £40-£50*

MAIDSTONE Kent Map **05** TQ75

Selected

Q Q Q Q **Conway House** 12 Conway Rd ME16 0HD
(exit M20 at junc 5, left onto A20, at crossroads with the BP petrol station and traffic lights turn right into Conway Rd)
☎ 01622 688287 FAX 01622 662589
Located in a quiet residential area with easy access to the M20. Bright, well appointed bedrooms are furnished in a modern style with attractive co-ordinating soft furnishings, and are equipped with many modern amenities. A choice of breakfast is offered and an evening meal is available by arrangement, both served to guests at a large table in the comfortable lounge/dining room.
3 rms (1 shr) (1 fmly) No smoking in 1 bedrooms No smoking in dining room No smoking in lounges CTV in all bedrooms Tea and coffee making facilities Cen ht CTV 5P No coaches Last d 24hrs
ROOMS: s £24-£28; d £34-£38; wkly b&b £105-£196; wkly hlf-bd £168-£259
CARDS:

See page 14-20 for a list of Premier Selected establishments

Selected

Q Q Q Q **Grove House** Grove Green Rd, Weavering St ME14 5JT
(M20 junct 7-follow signs to TV studios, at rdbt turn right, then left into Grovewood Dr, take 2nd left past Tesco & left again in to Grove Green Rd) ☎ 01622 738441
Situated in a quiet residential area, this is a well appointed house with a delightful garden, where guests are assured of a warm welcome from the owner Shirley Costella. Bedrooms are furnished in modern style, attractively decorated and are equipped with a wealth of quality extras including toiletries and bathrobes. Breakfast is served in the small cosy dining room where guests share one large table.
3 rms (1 bth) No smoking CTV in all bedrooms Tea and coffee making facilities No dogs Cen ht No children 10yrs 6P No coaches
ROOMS: s £25-£35; d £40-£45*
CARDS:

Selected

Q Q Q Q ***The Lime Tree*** 8-10 The Limes, Lenham Square ME17 2PQ ☎ 01622 859509 FAX 01622 850096
This family-run hotel and restaurant is located in the pretty village of Lenham, just five miles from Leeds Castle. The attractive bedrooms, one with a four-poster bed, have modern en suite facilities yet retain much of the character of the 14th-century building. The restaurant is among the best in the area and offers a good range of carefully prepared dishes in a delightful setting.
10 bth/shr (1 fmly) No smoking in bedrooms CTV in all bedrooms Tea and coffee making facilities Direct dial from bedrooms No dogs Licensed Cen ht P No coaches Last d 10pm
CARDS:

Q Q Q ***Rock House Hotel*** 102 Tonbridge Rd ME16 8SL (on A26, 0.5m from town centre) ☎ 01622 751616 FAX 01622 756119
This personally run guest house is conveniently located for the town centre and major routes. The bedrooms, some with en suite facilities, are bright, smart, well appointed and decorated in modern pastel colours. There is a comfortable guest lounge and an attractive breakfast room where guests are seated at individual tables.
12 rms (10 bth/shr) (4 fmly) No smoking in 3 bedrooms No smoking in dining room CTV in all bedrooms Tea and coffee making facilities No dogs (ex guide dogs) Cen ht CTV 7P
CARDS:

Selected

Q Q Q Q **Willington Court** Willington St ME15 8JW (1.5m E of Maidstone, at junct of A20 Asford Rd & Willington St)
☎ 01622 738885 FAX 01622 631790
Not far from the town centre, this Grade II listed building has been thoughtfully decorated and furnished to complement the character of the building. Bedrooms are of a good size and comfortably furnished and well equipped with many useful extras. A choice of breakfast is served in the oak-beamed dining room which has an inglenook fireplace. There are two small cosy lounges.
3 bth/shr No smoking in bedrooms No smoking in dining room No smoking in 1 lounge CTV in all bedrooms Tea and coffee making facilities Direct dial from bedrooms No dogs (ex guide dogs) Licensed Cen ht CTV No children 13yrs 8P No coaches Last d noon
ROOMS: s fr £27; d £42-£52; wkly b&b £170-£200; wkly hlf-bd £250-£350
CARDS:

MALDON Essex Map 05 TL80

Q Q ***Swan Hotel*** Maldon High St CM9 7EP ☎ 01621 853170 FAX 01621 854490
Popular with locals and residents alike, parts of The Swan date back to the 14th century. Bedrooms are light and fresh in appearance; each is equipped with TV and tea-making facilities and most have modern en suite shower rooms. Public areas are neatly divided into a bar and restaurant, with breakfasts served in a separate dining room.
6 bth/shr (2 fmly) No smoking in 2 bedrooms No smoking in dining room CTV in all bedrooms Tea and coffee making facilities No dogs Cen ht 31P Last d 9pm
CARDS:

MALHAM North Yorkshire Map 07 SD96

Q Q Q **Sparth House Hotel** BD23 4DA (from Skipton turn off A65 at Gargrave and follow main road up the dale to Malham. Hotel is located in the centre of the village) ☎ 01729 830315 FAX 830972
This large Victorian house, with a more modern extension to the rear, lies in the centre of this ever popular village. Bright and freshly decorated bedrooms, one of which is on the ground floor, are complemented by a comfortable lounge. There is also a cosy bar that leads into a spacious dining room where home cooked meals are available.
10 rms (7 bth/shr) No smoking in bedrooms No smoking in dining room No smoking in 1 lounge CTV in 7 bedrooms Tea and coffee making facilities No dogs (ex guide dogs) Licensed Cen ht CTV 4P Table-tennis Darts Riding stables next door Last d 5pm
ROOMS: s £22-£45; d £37-£54*
CARDS:

MALMESBURY Wiltshire Map 03 ST98

Premier Selected

Q Q Q Q Q **Horse & Groom** The Street, Charlton SN16 9DL (exit M4 junc 17, head towards Malmesbury, at second roundabout take B4040, premises through the village on the left)
☎ 01666 823904 FAX 01666 823390
This 16th-century coaching inn, situated in the village of Charlton, is built of Cotswold stone and conveniently located for visiting many interesting places. Resident proprietors Nicola King and Philip Gilder offer warm hospitality and spacious bedrooms that are attractively decorated and well equipped with modern comforts. Several little extras like mineral water, fresh fruit, flowers and bathrobes have been added. The restaurant has a deserving reputation for good food.
3 bth/shr CTV in all bedrooms Tea and coffee making facilities Direct dial from bedrooms No dogs (ex guide dogs) Cen ht 25P Last d 10pm
ROOMS: s £60; d £75*
MEALS: Lunch £1-£13.50alc Dinner £7-£13.50alc*
CARDS:

Selected

Q Q Q Q **Lovett Farm** *(ST974850)* Little Somerford SN15 5BP (3 miles from Malmesbury on B4042 (Wootton Bassett/Swindon road) on left hand side opposite signpost to the Somerfords)
☎ 01666 823268 FAX 01666 823268 Mrs S Barnes
Closed Christmas
Warm hospitality is provided by Mrs Sue Barnes at her lovely home, which is also a modern working farmhouse with lovely views over Dauntsey Vale. Bedrooms are comfortable and well equipped with many extras such as remote TV, hairdryer, clock radio, and fans. A

traditional home cooked breakfast is served at one large table in the guest lounge. Stabling for horses can be arranged.

3 bth/shr No smoking CTV in 2 bedrooms Tea and coffee making facilities No dogs Cen ht No children 3yrs 5P 70 acres beef
ROOMS: s £20-£25; d £40-£45

Q Q Q **Manby's Farm** Oaksey SN16 9SA
(M4 junct 15 take A419 towards Cirencester approx.13m, left onto B4696 signed Cotswold Water Park, in 6m at village of Oaksey left at mini rdbt)
☎ 01666 577399 FAX 01666 577241 Mrs A Shewry-Fitzgerald
A rural retreat close to the major Cotswold tourist destinations. At present there are two well appointed bedrooms with en suite facilities. Snooker and a private indoor pool are available for guests use. Dinner may be arranged at the time of booking.
3 rms (2 shr) No smoking CTV in all bedrooms Tea and coffee making facilities No dogs (ex guide dogs) Cen ht CTV 3P Indoor swimming pool (heated) Snooker 46 acres grassland Last d 6pm
ROOMS: s £22-£25; d £38-£42; wkly b&b £140; wkly hlf-bd £200
CARDS:

MALPAS Cheshire Map 07 SJ44

Premier Selected

Q Q Q Q Q **Tilston Lodge** Tilston SY14 7DR (3m N of Malpas)
☎ 01829 250223 FAX 01829 250223
Once a hunting lodge, this impressive Victorian house lies in 16 acres of pasture which is home to rare breeds of sheep and poultry. The pretty gardens have won awards. The three individually decorated bedrooms are furnished with fine period pieces, and public rooms are equally comfortable. Kathy Ritchie and her family offer a warm welcome to their guests.
3 bth/shr (1 fmly) No smoking CTV in all bedrooms Tea and coffee making facilities No dogs (ex guide dogs) Cen ht CTV 10P Croquet Table tennis Last d 6pm
ROOMS: s £40-£45; d £60-£68*

MALVERN Worcestershire Map 03 SO74

Selected

Q Q Q Q **The Chalet House** 24 Wyche Rd WR14 4EG
(take A449 from Great Malvern and fork right onto B4218 Colwall rd (this is Wynche Rd). Establishment is 0.75m further along this road on the right) ☎ 01684 572995
This beautifully preserved Edwardian house is situated high up on the Malvern Hills, overlooking the Cotswolds. There is direct access onto the hill footpaths from the terraced garden. The attractively appointed accommodation consists of a double-bedded room and a twin, both of which have modern facilities and equipment. A single-bedded room is also available for a child. Breakfast is served around one table. All parts of the house are no smoking.
2 bth/shr No smoking CTV in all bedrooms Tea and coffee making facilities No dogs (ex guide dogs) Cen ht
ROOMS: s £25-£28; d £38-£40*

Q Q **Chestnut Hill** Off Green Ln WR14 4HU
(take B4209 in either direction. On reaching telephone kiosk turn up Green Lane and then turn left past houses to end of the road and take 2nd right)
☎ 01684 564648
This large house is quietly situated in its own extensive grounds and gardens, on the eastern edge of Malvern Wells, with panoramic views of the Cotswolds. It provides no smoking accommodation, which takes the form of two doubles and one twin-bedded room. There is a bright and spacious lounge, which opens onto the garden, and a traditionally furnished breakfast room where separate tables are provided.
3 rms (1 bth/shr) No smoking Tea and coffee making facilities Cen ht No children 14yrs 4P No coaches Riding Outdoor riding arena Computers+tuition available
ROOMS: s fr £18; d £36-£40*

Q Q Q **Clevelands** 41 Alexandra Rd WR14 1HE
(From Malvern Link Station take the 3rd turning on the right after the railway station) ☎ 01684 572164 FAX 01684 576691
Closed Jan
Clevelands is a non-smoking guest house which is quietly located in a residential area to the north of Malvern. The well maintained house dates back to 1904. There are three comfortable bedrooms, comprising of a twin and two singles. A choice of lounges includes a conservatory. There is also a very attractive dining room, with good quality period furniture.
3 bth/shr No smoking CTV in all bedrooms Tea and coffee making facilities No dogs (ex guide dogs) Cen ht CTV 3P No coaches
ROOMS: s £17-£19; d £34-£38; wkly b&b £112-£113*

This symbol indicates a 'Child Friendly' establishment - see page 25 for details

Selected

Q Q Q Q The Dell House Green Ln, Malvern Wells WR14 4HU (located 2m south of Great Malvern on the A449. Turn left off A449 into Green Lane and premises are situated at the top of this road) ☎ 01684 564448 FAX 02684 893974

The Dell House dates back to 1820 and was once used as a rectory. Two of the tastefully appointed, comfortable bedrooms have en suite facilities, while the third room has a nearby private bathroom. Breakfast is served in a spacious room with period furniture, where all guests share one table. There is also a spacious and comfortable lounge. All parts of the house are non-smoking.

3 rms (2 bth/shr) No smoking CTV in 1 bedroom Tea and coffee making facilities No dogs Cen ht No children 10yrs 6P 2 acre grounds

ROOMS: s £25-£35; d £40-£50

Q Q Q ***Edgeworth*** 4 Carlton Rd WR14 1HH ☎ 01684 572565

Edgeworth is a well-maintained Edwardian, semi-detached house which is located in a quiet residential area to the north of Malvern. It is tastefully furnished in a style befitting its age and character. There are two letting bedrooms, one double and one single, both with period furnishings and modern equipment. Breakfast is served in a traditionally furnished room, which also contains a lounge area.

2 rms

Q Q Q Elm Bank 52 Worcester Rd WR14 4AB (located 0.5m S of junction of A449 & B4232/4219) ☎ 01684 566051

This large Regency house is close to the town centre. It provides modern equipped, traditionally furnished, no smoking accommodation, which includes family bedded rooms. The only room without an en suite facility has its own private bathroom. There is a comfortable lounge, and separate tables are provided in the breakfast room.

6 bth/shr (2 fmly) No smoking in bedrooms No smoking in dining room CTV in all bedrooms Tea and coffee making facilities Licensed Cen ht 9P

ROOMS: s £27-£38; d £40-£50*

CARDS:

Q Q Q Fairlight 234 West Malvern Rd, West Malvern WR14 4BD (from Gr Malvern take B4213 for Colwall, turn right onto B4232 (W. Malvern Rd)just after the Wyche cutting and after 1.25m estab is visible on left) ☎ 01684 892752

Closed 20 Dec-4 Jan

This large, semi-detached, Victorian house is situated on the western side of the Malvern Hills, and commands panoramic views towards the Welsh mountains. There are two soundly maintained, pretty bedrooms consisting of one twin and one double. Facilities here include a cosy lounge and a traditionally furnished breakfast room, where separate tables can be provided. The whole house is no smoking.

2 rms No smoking No dogs Cen ht 2P

ROOMS: s £18.50-£20; d £35*

Q Q Four Hedges The Rhydd, Hanley Castle WR8 0AD (located on the junction of B4211 and B4224, 4m from Malvern and 3m fron Upton on Severn) ☎ 01684 310405

Four Hedges is a large house set in three quarters of an acre of gardens, located north of the village of Hanley Castle. There is a private river mooring and fishing rights. The two bedrooms, can be let either as a family suite, or separately. In the case of the latter, one room has an en suite bathroom and the other a private facility. There is a spacious and comfortable lounge, which overlooks the garden and a traditionally furnished breakfast room, where all guests share one table.

4 rms (1 bth/shr) No smoking Tea and coffee making facilities 5P Fishing

ROOMS: s £15-£17; d fr £34

Selected

Q Q Q Q ***Grove House Farm (SO807459)*** WR14 3QZ ☎ 01684 574256 Mrs H Simpson

This large farmhouse is quietly located on a 365-acre mixed farm, some 2 miles east of Malvern. Personally run by young proprietors Helen and Mike Simpson, it provides two bedrooms, one a double and the other family-bedded, both of which are spacious and comfortably furnished with period pieces. All guests share one large table in the pleasant and homely breakfast room. There is also a comfortable lounge. Guests can also enjoy the attractively landscaped garden, as well as explore the farm.

2 rms

Selected

Q Q Q Q Guarlford Grange 11 Guarlford Rd WR14 3QW (turn off B4208 into Eston Ave left into Whitborn Close, Left to our entrance) ☎ 01684 575996

This large detached house, set in its own spacious pleasant garden, was built in 1990, but in a style which makes it look much older. The modern furnished and equipped accommodation is equally suitable for both business people and tourists. Facilities include a large and spacious lounge, where a welcoming wood-burning stove is lit during cold weather. Separate tables are provided in the traditionally furnished dining room, which has an adjacent conservatory. Dinner is available by prior arrangement. The whole house is no smoking.

4 rms (1 shr) No smoking CTV in all bedrooms Tea and coffee making facilities No dogs Licensed Cen ht CTV 4P No coaches Last d before noon

ROOMS: s £19-£25; d £40-£46; wkly b&b £127.50-£147.40; wkly hlf-bd £187-£206.90*

Selected

Q Q Q Q Hillside 113 Worcester Rd WR14 1ER (from A449 from Worcester, establishment on right at link top opposite common) ☎ 01684 565287 FAX 01684 565287

Situated on the outskirts of the town, this guest house offers homely and comfortable accommodation. Bedrooms are spacious and well equipped and both have the benefit of modern en suite bathrooms. Public areas include a bright dining room where English breakfasts are served and a small sitting room with TV, allocated for smokers. Free car parking is available nearby.

2 bth No smoking in bedrooms No smoking in dining room Tea and coffee making facilities No dogs (ex guide dogs) Cen ht No children 10yrs

ROOMS: d £40; wkly b&b fr £138*

Selected

Q Q Q Q **Link Lodge** 3 Pickersleigh Rd WR14 2RP (take A449 from Worcester passing straight through main traffic lights in Malvern Link. Take first left, establishment is first house on the left) ☎ 01684 572345
Link Lodge is an elegant Grade II listed Queen Anne house, where Elgar once taught music. Set in an acre of garden, it is located north of the town, with views across Malvern Link Common to the Malvern Hills. There are two tastefully appointed and comfortable bedrooms, plus a small single room which can be made available for a child accompanying its parents. Breakfast is served in the kitchen, where all guests share one large table in front of the Aga. The whole house is no smoking.
3 rms (1 shr) No smoking CTV in all bedrooms Tea and coffee making facilities Cen ht 5P No coaches Large landscaped gardens
ROOMS: s £20; d £40-£45✻

Q Q Q **The Mill House** 16 Clarence Rd WR14 3EH
(follow signs to car park/swimming pool, Clarence Rd adjacent to car park, house 200yds on right)
☎ 01684 562345 FAX 01684 562345
Parts of this charming old house date from the 13th century, when it was the water mill for the nearby Priory, but most of it is 17th century. Two of the bedrooms enjoy impressive views of the Malvern Hills. Facilities include a pleasant, comfortable lounge and a traditionally furnished breakfast room, with half-panelled walls, where separate tables are provided. There is also a croquet lawn in the garden.
3 rms (2 bth/shr) No smoking CTV in 1 bedroom Tea and coffee making facilities No dogs (ex guide dogs) Cen ht CTV No children 10yrs 6P No coaches
ROOMS: d £40-£50✻

Q Q Q **Rathlin** 1 Carlton Rd WR14 1HH
(take 3rd turning right past Malvern link station into Alexandra Rd and Carlton Rd is again the 3rd turning right. Rathlin is 1st house on left)
☎ 01684 572491
This nicely maintained house dates back to the turn of the century, and is located in a quiet residential area to the north of Malvern. The bedrooms have a mix of traditional and modern furniture. All guests share one large pine table in the pleasant breakfast room. There is also a comfortable lounge and a room containing a pool table. The whole house is non-smoking.
3 rms (1 bth/shr) No smoking CTV in all bedrooms Tea and coffee making facilities Cen ht 2P
ROOMS: s £16-£18; d £32-£36; wkly b&b £112-£126✻

Q Q Q **Robin's Orchard** New Rd, Castlemorton WR13 6BT
(B4208 Malvern-Gloucester rd to Castlemorton.Turn into New Rd opposite The Robin Hood pub.Robin's Orchard 100yrds on right)
☎ 01684 833251
Closed Dec-Feb
Robins Orchard was built in 1988. Set in a large garden, it is located in a quiet rural area on the outskirts of Castlemorton village. There are three modern furnished and equipped bedrooms, and a traditionally furnished breakfast room, where separate tables can be provided.
3 rms (1 bth/shr) (2 fmly) No smoking CTV in all bedrooms Tea and coffee making facilities Cen ht 10P No coaches
ROOMS: s £20-£30; d £35-£45; wkly b&b £122.50-£140✻

Q Q ***Rock House*** 144 West Malvern Rd, West Malvern WR14 4NJ
☎ 01684 574536
This former farm house, which dates back to 1804, is surrounded by an acre of garden, and commands panoramic views to the north. Bedrooms have recently been upgraded. Facilities here include a spacious lounge, a small bar and a traditionally furnished dining room, where separate tables are provided.
10 rms

Q Q Q ***Rosehurst*** 53 St Andrews Rd WR14 3PT ☎ 01684 569835
Rosehurst is a Victorian house, with views of the Malvern Hills. No smoking throughout, it provides well equipped accommodation, which takes the form of a double room with a king size bed. This has its own private bathroom and toilet facilities. Breakfast is served in a small elegant room, which has period furniture.
1 rm

Selected

Q Q Q Q **Rosendale** 66 Worcester Rd WR14 1NU
(on A449 0.5m N of town centre) ☎ 01684 566159
This detached, late Victorian house provides good quality accommodation, consisting of a double bedded room with an en suite shower and toilet, and a twin room with a nearby private bathroom. Both enjoy impressive views across the Severn Valley. All guests share one table in the homely combined breakfast room and lounge.
2 rms (1 shr) No smoking in bedrooms CTV in all bedrooms Tea and coffee making facilities No dogs Cen ht No coaches

Q Q Q ***Sidney House Hotel*** 40 Worcester Rd WR14 4AA
(alongside the A449 approx 200 yds from town centre)
☎ 01684 574994 FAX 01684 574994
Close to the town centre and offering superb views over the Cotswolds from the rear bedrooms, this Georgian detached house is enthusiastically run by resident hosts Len and Jan McLeod. Bedrooms are comfortable and furnished with antique pine pieces, and four rooms have the benefit of compact en suite showers. Tasty English breakfasts are eaten in the dining room and there is also a sitting room with honesty bar.
8 rms (5 shr) (1 fmly) No smoking in dining room CTV in all bedrooms Tea and coffee making facilities No dogs (ex guide dogs) Licensed Cen ht CTV 9P No coaches
CARDS: MasterCard, American Express, Barclaycard Visa, Barclays Connect

Selected

Q Q Q Q St Just 169 Worcester Rd WR14 1EU ☎ 01684 562023
Closed Xmas
This large house dates back to the 1850s and is close to Malvern Link Station. Non-smoking throughout, it provides traditionally furnished, spacious and well equipped accommodation. The room without en suite facilities has its own nearby private bathroom. The attractive breakfast room features walnut period furniture. There is also a pleasant and cosy sitting room.
3 bth/shr No smoking CTV in all bedrooms Tea and coffee making facilities No dogs (ex guide dogs) Cen ht No children 7yrs 7P
ROOMS: d £36-£56✻

Q Q Q Woodpeckers 66 Peachfield Rd, Malvern Wells WR14 4AL
☎ 01684 562827
This cosy, cottage-style bungalow is located midway between Malvern and the Three Counties Showground, and surrounded by woods, the Common and Golf Course. The accommodation takes the form of one traditionally furnished, well equipped twin-bedded room, with its own nearby private bathroom. Breakfast is served in a homely room, which overlooks the garden.
1 bth/shr No smoking CTV in all bedrooms Tea and coffee making facilities No dogs Cen ht 1P No coaches
ROOMS: s £25; d £40-£50✻

Selected

Q Q Q Q Wyche Keep 22 Wyche Rd WR14 4EG
(off B4218, Great Malvern to Colwall) ☎ 01684 567018
FAX 01684 892304
Situated in an elevated position with superb views of the Cotswolds, this late Victorian house offers comfortable accommodation. Bedrooms are well equipped and all have the benefit of modern en suite or private facilities. Public areas include a spacious lounge and dining hall where guests can enjoy meals served at the large family table. The Williams family are welcoming hosts with an excellent knowledge of the area and its many historical attractions.
3 bth/shr No smoking CTV in all bedrooms Tea and coffee making facilities No dogs Licensed Cen ht CTV No children 13yrs 6P No coaches Last d 7pm
ROOMS: s £35-£40; d £50-£60; wkly b&b £175-£210; wkly hlf-bd £301-£336

Selected

Q Q Q Q York House Walwyn Rd, Colwall WR13 6QG
(in centre of village on B4218) ☎ 01684 540449
This tastefully modernised and well maintained house dates back to 1906. It stands in the pleasant village of Colwall, on the western slopes of the Malvern Hills. Accommodation includes a bedroom on ground floor level. The one room without en suite facilities has its own nearby private bathroom. Facilities include a first floor lounge area and a breakfast room, where guests share one table.
3 bth/shr No smoking CTV in all bedrooms Tea and coffee making facilities No dogs Cen ht CTV 5P No coaches Arrangement with local riding stables
ROOMS: s £28-£35; d £38-£45; wkly b&b £120-£220✻

MANCHESTER Greater Manchester Map 07 SJ89

See also Altrincham

Q Q Cavendish Hotel 402 Wilbraham Rd, Chorlton M21 0UH
☎ 0161 881 1911 FAX 0161 881 1911
In the suburb of Chorlton-cum-Hardy, this large Victorian house is conveniently situated for the motorway network and the airport. The traditional-style public areas include a bar, a lounge and a dining room with individual tables. The bedrooms, which vary in size, have modern furnishings.
19 rms (9 bth/shr) (4 fmly) No smoking in 2 bedrooms No smoking in dining room CTV in all bedrooms Tea and coffee making facilities Cen ht CTV 30P darts Last d 8pm
ROOMS: s £20-£35; d £40-£50; wkly b&b £140-£200; wkly hlf-bd £175-£235✻
CARDS: MasterCard VISA

Q Q Kempton House Hotel 400 Wilbraham Rd, Chorlton-cum-Hardy M21 0UH (on A6010 W of A5103) ☎ 0161 881 8766 FAX 0161 881 8766
Closed 24 Dec-1 Jan
Value for money is the key at this well maintained and family-run small hotel, situated in the suburb of Chorlton-cum-Hardy. A cosy bar leads into the dining room, where dinner is available by prior arrangement, and there is also a separate lounge.
12 rms (5 shr) CTV in all bedrooms Tea and coffee making facilities No dogs (ex guide dogs) Licensed Cen ht CTV 9P No coaches Last d 5pm
ROOMS: s £24-£29; d £33-£39✻
CARDS: MasterCard VISA

Q Q New Central Hotel 144-146 Heywood St, Cheetham M8 0PD
(1.5m from city centre, off Cheetham Hill Rd Heywood Street is on the left opposite Esso Service Station) ☎ 0161 205 2169 FAX 0161 205 2169
Situated to the north of the city, just a mile from the centre, this family-run business offers good value accommodation. A choice of evening meals is available, with friendly service, and there is a comfortable lounge for guest use.
10 rms (5 shr) CTV in all bedrooms Tea and coffee making facilities Licensed Cen ht CTV 10P No coaches Last d 7.30pm
ROOMS: s £20.50-£21.50; d £33-£35
CARDS: MasterCard VISA

Q Q Q **Thistlewood Hotel** 203 Urmston Ln, Stretford M32 9EF
(leave M63 junct 7 towards Urmston, onto A56, take left onto Sandy Lane and left into Urston Lane. From M62 exit junct 3 in direction of Urmston)
☎ 0161 865 3611 FAX 866 8133
This large house stands in a pleasant residential area and is convenient for the M63. The bedrooms have been upgraded and all are well equipped. Public rooms include a spacious dining room and a comfortable lounge. Service is very friendly and helpful and evening meals are available.
9 shr (1 fmly) No smoking in dining room CTV in all bedrooms Tea and coffee making facilities No dogs (ex guide dogs) Licensed Cen ht CTV 8P No coaches Last d breakfast
ROOMS: s £30-£32; d £45-£47*
CARDS:

Q Q **Victoria Park Hotel** 4-6 Park Crescent, Victoria Park M14 5RE
(A6010 to B5117 Park Cres directly off Wilmslow Rd)
☎ 0161 224 1399 0161 224 2219 FAX 0161 225 4949
This large unlicensed guest house is situated in a residential area just a short drive from the city centre. Spacious bedrooms are simply furnished but comfortable. There is also a pleasant lounge and a continental breakfast is served in the lower ground floor dining room. No alcohol is allowed on the premises.
19 bth/shr (3 fmly) No smoking in dining room Tea and coffee making facilities Direct dial from bedrooms No dogs Cen ht 40P
ROOMS: s £31-£35; d £44-£48
CARDS:

MANCHESTER AIRPORT Greater Manchester Map **07** SJ88

Q Q Q **Rylands Farm** Altrincham Rd SK9 4LT
(leave M56 junct 6 take A538 towards Wilmslow guesthouse is 1m on left just past Wilmslow Moat House)
☎ 01625 535646 FAX 01625 535646
Closed 24-25 Dec
This well maintained guest house is conveniently located for the airport and lies in pleasant gardens. A modern conservatory houses a cosy sitting area and bar, as well as a dining room, where guests dine family style. Evening meals are available with prior notice. Bedrooms are located in nearby buildings and are attractively decorated with pretty wallpapers and fabrics.
6 annexe shr (2 fmly) No smoking in 4 bedrooms No smoking in dining room No smoking in lounges CTV in all bedrooms Tea and coffee making facilities Licensed Cen ht CTV 18P No coaches
ROOMS: s £33-£40; d £39.50-£45; wkly b&b £210-£280*
CARDS:

MANNINGTREE Essex Map **05** TM13

Q Q Q **Aldhams** Bromley Rd, Lawford CO11 2NE
(from south-A12 Colchester north exit, follow sign to Harwich joining A120 for 7.5m, turn left(Little Bromley), follow for 2.9m, house on right)
☎ 01206 393210 FAX 01255 393210
Closed 24-26 Dec
Aldhams is an elegant house which has been fashioned in the Lutyens style, and sits in three acres of gardens in rural surroundings. The bedrooms are all well maintained and furnished in period style. Guests have the use of a spacious lounge, with an open log fire and a selection of books and games. Breakfast is generally served at a large communal dining table in a separate breakfast room.

3 rms (2 bth) No smoking CTV in all bedrooms Tea and coffee making facilities No dogs (ex guide dogs) Cen ht CTV 6P No coaches
ROOMS: s £25-£30; d £40-£45

Selected

Q Q Q Q **Dairy House** *(TM148293)* Bradfield Rd CO11 2SR
☎ 01255 870322 FAX 01255 870186 Mrs B Whitworth

(For full entry see **Wix**)

MARAZION Cornwall & Isles of Scilly Map **02** SW53

Q Q Q **Glenleigh Hotel** Higher Fore St TR17 0BQ (off A394)
☎ 01736 710308
Dating back to 1898, this granite stone house has been owned by the Hales family for over 25 years. At the front of the property, there are glorious views over Mounts Bay to St Michael's Mount. A spacious and comfortable lounge is available for guests. Each evening in the dining room, a fixed price meal is offered, using local produce where possible. Bedrooms vary in size and shape, one room is located on the ground floor.
9 bth/shr (2 fmly) No smoking in dining room CTV in all bedrooms Tea and coffee making facilities Licensed Cen ht No children 10P No coaches Last d noon
ROOMS: s fr £23; d fr £46*

MARGARET RODING (NEAR GREAT DUNMOW)
Essex Map **05** TL51

Q Q **Greys** *(TL604112)* Ongar Rd CM6 1QR
(In Margaret Roding turn off A1060, Bishops Stortford to Chelmsford Rd, by telephone kiosk, 2nd house on left approx 0.5m, signed to Berners Roding) ☎ 01245 231509 Mr & Mrs J Matthews
Closed 24-26 Dec
Part of an arable and sheep farm, this guest house offers soundly appointed cottage-size bedrooms, which have the shared use of a newly refurbished bathroom. There is a delightful lounge with open fire, exposed brickwork and beams, and English breakfast is taken in an adjacent small dining room at individual pine tables.
3 rms No smoking No dogs Cen ht CTV No children 10yrs 3P
340 acres arable sheep
ROOMS: s fr £21; d fr £40*

See page 14-20 for a list of Premier Selected establishments

MARGATE Kent Map **05** TR37

Selected

Q Q Q Q **The Greswolde Hotel** 20 Surrey Rd, Cliftonville CT9 2LA ☎ 01843 223956
This comfortable house has a warm, friendly atmosphere and a high level of hospitality provided by charming proprietors Mr and Mrs Earle. There is a cosy guest lounge which has a fire in the winter months. The attractive bedrooms are spacious and offer lots of thoughtful extras.
6 bth/shr (2 fmly) No smoking in bedrooms No smoking in dining room CTV in all bedrooms Tea and coffee making facilities Licensed Cen ht No coaches
ROOMS: s £26; d £38
CARDS:

Q Q **Westbrook Bay House** 12 Royal Esplanade, Westbrook CT9 5DW ☎ 01843 292700
A homely guest house situated in a prime position overlooking a lovely sandy bay. Owners Maureen and Ken Richardson offer a friendly and relaxing stay with the emphasis on good home cooking. Bedrooms are pleasantly decorated and there is a comfortable lounge and bar.
11 rms (4 shr) (4 fmly) No smoking in dining room CTV in 10 bedrooms Tea and coffee making facilities No dogs (ex guide dogs) Licensed Cen ht CTV No coaches Last d 4.30pm
ROOMS: d £30-£34; wkly b&b £106-£114; wkly hlf-bd £132-£140*

MARKET DRAYTON Shropshire Map **07** SJ63

Selected

Q Q Q Q ❦ ***Mickley House*** *(SJ615325)* Faulsgreen, Tern Hill TF9 3QW (A41 to Tern Hill roundabout, then A53 towards Shrewsbury, first right for Faulsgreen, 4th house on right)
☎ 01630 638505 Mrs P Williamson
Closed Xmas
This impressive red-brick farmhouse is surrounded by rolling countryside and is very much a working farm. Two of the four bedrooms are at ground level. The first floor rooms look out over the attractive lawns and gardens. Two elegant lounges are available and the landscaped grounds contain several pools and a small wood where guests may roam.
3 bth/shr (1 fmly) No smoking CTV in all bedrooms Tea and coffee making facilities No dogs Cen ht CTV 10P 125 acres beef

MARKET RASEN Lincolnshire Map **08** TF18

Selected

Q Q Q Q **Blaven** Walesby Hill, Walesby LN8 3UW
(from Market Rasen take A46 towards Grimsby, turn right at junct with A1103 then left at T-junct) ☎ 01673 838352
Nestling at the foot of the Lincolnshire Wolds in the peaceful village of Walesby, this large modern house is surrounded by extensive and beautifully tended gardens. There are two delightfully furnished bedrooms and the public rooms include a cosy dining room and a comfortable conservatory.
2 rms No smoking CTV in all bedrooms Tea and coffee making facilities No dogs (ex guide dogs) Cen ht 4P No coaches
ROOMS: s £24; d £36*

MARLBOROUGH Wiltshire Map **04** SU16

Selected

Q Q Q Q ❦ **Clench Farmhouse** *(SU187629)* Clench SN8 4NT (from Marlborough take A346, in 3m right to Wootton Rivers, at Royal Oak PH turn right & drive 0.7m farmhouse after the single track to Clench Common)
☎ 01672 810264 FAX 01672 811458 Mrs C M Roe
All bedrooms at this friendly guest house are well equipped with thoughtful extras such as clock radio, hair dryer, and fresh flowers. Much of the food comes straight from the garden; fresh fruit and vegetables, plus free range eggs. Food is served at one large table in the elegant dining room. There is also a comfortable TV lounge. The house is set in landscaped gardens, with croquet lawn, tennis court and a heated outdoor swimming pool. Dogs are welcome by arrangement.
2 bth/shr 1 annexe bth/shr (1 fmly) No smoking in bedrooms No smoking in dining room CTV in 2 bedrooms Tea and coffee making facilities Cen ht CTV 8P Outdoor swimming pool (heated) Tennis (hard) 5 acres Last d afternoon

Selected

Q Q Q Q **Redlands** Elcot Ln SN8 2BA (turn off A4 eastbound at Roebuck Inn into Elcot Lane, Redlands on right opposite playing fields)
☎ 01672 515477 FAX 01672 516523 Etr-Nov
Redlands is located on the outskirts of Marlborough in a quiet residential area, overlooking playing fields. The spacious bedrooms have been thoughtfully furnished to a high standard. Mrs Camm is known for her home-cooking and meals are served in the smart dining room that doubles as a lounge.
3 rms (1 shr) No smoking CTV in all bedrooms Tea and coffee making facilities No dogs (ex guide dogs) Cen ht 3P No coaches
ROOMS: d £38-£45

Selected

Q Q Q Q **The Vines** High St SN8 1HJ (premises situated on left hand side of the main high street, approx 150 yards from St Peters Church) ☎ 01672 515333 FAX 01672 515338
Popular with holidaymakers and business travellers, The Vines is situated in the high street and offers well equipped bedrooms. Guests check in at The Ivy House Hotel across the road which is under the same ownership, where they are invited to use the range of attractive and very comfortable public areas. For those wishing to dine informally there is a bistro off the courtyard, while in the elegant restaurant table d'hôte and à la carte menus offer interesting dishes at reasonable prices.
6 bth/shr (2 fmly) No smoking in dining room No smoking in lounges CTV in all bedrooms Tea and coffee making facilities Licensed Cen ht 36P Last d 9.15pm
ROOMS: s £35-£40; d £55-£60
CARDS:

MARLOW Buckinghamshire Map **04** SU88

Selected

Q Q Q Q **Holly Tree House** Burford Close, Marlow Bottom SL7 3NF (from M40 junct4 take exit for Marlow Bottom, turn right into Marlow Bottom and follow road past shops. First left into Burford Close)
☎ 01628 891110 FAX 01628 481278

Situated in a peaceful valley on the edge of the village, this attractive house offers bright and well equipped bedrooms, all of which have en suite facilities, satellite TV and lots of thoughtful extras. There is a comfortable conservatory lounge, and guests are welcome to make use of the garden and the outdoor pool.
5 bth/shr (4 fmly) No smoking in bedrooms No smoking in dining room CTV in all bedrooms Tea and coffee making facilities Direct dial from bedrooms No dogs (ex guide dogs) Cen ht CTV 7P No coaches Outdoor swimming pool (heated)
ROOMS: s £64.50-£69.50; d £79.50-£84.50
CARDS:

MARTOCK Somerset Map 03 ST41

Selected

Q Q Q Q **Wychwood** 7 Bearley Rd TA12 6PG (exit A303 to centre of Martock, continue up East St from Post Office, Bearley Rd is on left opposite Nags Head) ☎ 01935 825601 FAX 01935 825601
Closed Xmas & New Year
A warm and friendly welcome awaits guests at the family home of Helen and Norman Turton, located only a short walk from the centre of this delightful Somerset village. Bedrooms are particularly well equipped and benefit from either en suite facilities or exclusive use of bath/shower rooms. A comfortable lounge and a conservatory, leading on to the pretty garden with its abundance of wild life, is available for guests. The Turtons are pleased to advise guests on places to dine in the village.
3 bth/shr No smoking CTV in all bedrooms Tea and coffee making facilities No dogs Cen ht CTV No children 4P No coaches
ROOMS: s £30-£34; d £40-£44*
CARDS:

MARTON (VILLAGE) Lincolnshire Map 08 SK88

Selected

Q Q Q Q **Black Swan Coaching Inn** 21 High St DN21 5AH (on A156, 12m from Lincoln, 6m from Gainsborough)
☎ 01427 718878 FAX 01427 718878
Myra and Brian Cunliffe have lovingly renovated this complex of farm buildings where Oliver Cromwell is believed to have stayed during the Battle of Gainsborough. Today it offers well equipped bedrooms together with two comfortable and inviting public lounges, and a small dispense bar. Breakfast is served in the dining room and very friendly service is provided.
6 shr 2 annexe shr (3 fmly) No smoking CTV in all bedrooms Tea and coffee making facilities No dogs (ex guide dogs) Licensed Cen ht CTV 8P No coaches Last d 8.30pm
ROOMS: s £27-£36; d £47-£57; wkly b&b £180-£190; wkly hlf-bd £250-£260
CARDS:

See advertisement under LINCOLN

MARY TAVY Devon Map 02 SX57

Q Q Q **Moorland Hall** Brentor Rd PL19 9PY (Turn off A30 onto A386, turn right at coach station onto Brentor Rd) ☎ 01822 810466
Sept-May
Moorland Hall is a family-run guest house of spacious dimensions, surrounded by five acres of gardens. Bedrooms are large and some include four posters. A comfortable lounge and bright conservatory are adjacent to the dining room where freshly prepared, home made meals are served.
6 bth/shr (3 fmly) No smoking in bedrooms CTV in all bedrooms Tea and coffee making facilities Licensed Cen ht 20P No coaches Outdoor swimming pool (heated) Bar billiards Assault course Licenced activity cnt Last d 8pm
ROOMS: s fr £40; d £64-£72

Q Q Q **Wringworthy** *(SX500773)* PL19 9LT (take A386 farm signed 2 miles after Mary Tavy) ☎ 01822 810434 FAX 01822 810434 Mrs B Anning
Mar-Oct rs Mar
Wringworthy Farm is mentioned in the Domesday Book, and is located in peaceful surroundings. Breakfast is served around an impressive, 16-foot antique table in a room with a polished flagstone floor. A comfortable lounge with log burning stove is provided, and bedrooms are spacious and comfortable.
3 rms (2 bth/shr) No smoking in bedrooms CTV in all bedrooms Tea and coffee making facilities No dogs (ex guide dogs) Cen ht CTV 3P 80 acres beef sheep
ROOMS: s £18-£20; d £36-£40*

MASHAM North Yorkshire Map 08 SE28

Selected

Q Q Q Q **Bank Villa** HG4 4DB (premises situated just after "30mph" sign on entering Masham on the A6108 from Ripon) ☎ 01765 689605
rs Xmas
This charming Georgian house features old beams and antique pine furniture in the bedrooms, and offers two comfortable and inviting lounges. Good home-cooking is served in the delightful dining room using fresh local produce where possible, and service is attentive and friendly.
6 rms (4 bth/shr) No smoking in bedrooms No smoking in dining room No smoking in 1 lounge No dogs (ex guide dogs) Licensed Cen ht CTV No children 5yrs 7P No coaches Last d noon
ROOMS: s fr £29.50; d fr £39; wkly b&b fr £125; wkly hlf-bd fr £225*

MATLOCK Derbyshire Map 08 SK36

Q Q **Bradvilla** 26 Chesterfield Rd DE4 3DQ (on A632 towards Chesterfield, below convent school) ☎ 01629 57147
Closed 22-28 Dec
Standing in an elevated position and set back from the main Chesterfield road on the edge of the town, Bradvilla has bright, fresh bedrooms. Smoking is discouraged in the bedrooms, but there is a conservatory overlooking the neatly tended garden where guests may smoke.
2 rms (1 bth) (2 fmly) No smoking CTV in all bedrooms Tea and coffee making facilities No dogs (ex guide dogs) Cen ht CTV 4P No coaches
ROOMS: s £17.50; d £32-£36; wkly b&b £100*

Q **5 Clarence Terrace** Holme Rd DE4 3NY (turn off A6 at County & Station Hotel, keep left for 200yds) ☎ 01629 55555
Mar-Nov
Located in a quiet residential area high above Matlock Bath, this house offers attractive, soundly appointed and well maintained accommodation. Breakfast is served in the lounge/dining room.
3 rms (2 fmly) No smoking No dogs Cen ht CTV No coaches large book selection for adults & children
ROOMS: s £18; d £26-£30; wkly b&b £130*

Q Q **Farley** *(SK294622)* Farley DE4 5LR
(A6 Buxton Bakewell first right after roundabout in Matlock turn right at top of hill then left up Farley Hill 2nd farm on left)
☎ 01629 582533 Mrs M Brailsford
Closed Xmas & New Year
Situated amongst open farmland parts of this traditional stone-built farmhouse date back to 1250. Mrs Brailsford offers a warm welcome to guests and provides a hearty breakfast that features home-produced milk, jam and eggs and is served communally around one large table; dinner is available by prior arrangement.
3 rms (1 shr) (2 fmly) No smoking in bedrooms No smoking in area of dining room CTV in 1 bedroom Tea and coffee making facilities Cen ht CTV 8P Riding 275 acres arable beef dairy Last d 5pm
ROOMS: s £18-£20; d £36-£40; wkly b&b £112-£126; wkly hlf-bd £161-£175*

Q Q Q **Glendon** Knowleston Place DE4 3BU
(M1 junct 28, take A615 Matlock road and premises are on left past Total Service Station. Turn into car-park just before 'Glendon B&B' sign)
☎ 01629 584732
Closed Dec
The Glendon is conveniently situated, set back from the A615, for easy access to the town and the adjacent Hall Leys park; guest can enjoy an attractive riverside walk into centre. The house offers spacious airy bedrooms that are pleasingly decorated and well equipped, with a comfortably appointed lounge on the third floor purely for residents - this room has some lovely views out over Bentley Brook and the local church. Breakfast is taken at separate tables in a breakfast room-cum-lounge on the ground floor. There is ample private car parking available.
3 rms (1 shr) (1 fmly) No smoking in 1 bedrooms No smoking in dining room No smoking in lounges CTV in all bedrooms Tea and coffee making facilities No dogs Cen ht CTV No children 3 yrs 4P No coaches
ROOMS: s £19-£20; d £35-£39; wkly b&b £115-£130*

Selected

Q Q Q Q **Hodgkinsons Hotel** 150 South Pde DE4 3NR
(on main A6 in centre of village)
☎ 01629 582170 FAX 01629 584891
Closed 24-27 Dec & 3-14 Jan
The limestone cliffs and steep wooded slopes of the Derwent Valley provide a dramatic backdrop to this distinctive small hotel. Lovingly restored by Malcolm and Nigel, the interior features period articles from Victorian times, sympathetically mixed with all the necessary modern comforts. Cooking features fresh local produce through traditional British menus in the restaurant.
7 shr No smoking in dining room CTV in all bedrooms Tea and coffee making facilities Direct dial from bedrooms Licensed Cen ht 6P No coaches Hairdressing salon within hotel Last d 8pm
ROOMS: s £35; d £60-£95; wkly b&b £210-£300; wkly hlf-bd £350-£500*
CARDS:

Q Q **Kensington Villa** 84 Dale Rd DE4 3LU
(exit M1 at junc 28, head towards Matlock, on entering Matlock follow signs for A6, premises 120 yards on right opposite Evans jewellers)
☎ 01629 57627
This terraced Victorian house offers brightly decorated bedrooms with colourful matching soft furnishings. Although there is no lounge, the bedrooms are comfortably appointed and all have colour TV. The dining room leads out onto a courtyard garden, and there are numerous guide books and maps to help you discover the delightful Peak District.
3 rms No smoking CTV in all bedrooms Tea and coffee making facilities No dogs (ex guide dogs) Cen ht 3P No coaches
ROOMS: s fr £20; d fr £40; wkly b&b £126

Selected

Q Q Q Q **Lane End House** Green Ln, Tansley DE4 5FJ (exit A615 into Church St, 500 yards to the Gate Inn, turn right into Green Lane) ☎ 01629 583981 FAX 01629 583981
Closed Xmas New Year
This Georgian farmhouse has been converted into a welcoming and comfortable guest house. Individually named bedrooms are equipped with all manner of extras, from fruit and fresh flowers to bath robes. The drawing room has a well stocked honesty bar. Freshly prepared evening meals are served around a large oval table in the dining hall, which leads out into the gardens.
4 bth/shr No smoking CTV in all bedrooms Tea and coffee making facilities Licensed Cen ht CTV 6P No coaches Croquet
ROOMS: s £30-£35; d £46-£57
CARDS:

Q Q **Manor House** Wensley DE4 2LL (from A6, turn onto B5057 signed Wensley, past Square & Compass pub and continue up the hill, house signposted on left 500 yds after Wensley sign)
☎ 01629 734360 FAX 01629 734360
Fine views are to be had over the valley and Riber Castle beyond, from this 18th-century farm cottage. Bedrooms are neatly decorated and furnished, with a shared modern bathroom. The comfortable lounge leads through into a sunny conservatory overlooking the extensive gardens.
2 rms No smoking Tea and coffee making facilities No dogs (ex guide dogs) Cen ht CTV No children 12yrs 6P No coaches Country Walks
ROOMS: s fr £25; d £39-£45*

Q Q Q **Red House Carriage Museum** Old Rd, Darley Dale DE4 2ER
(2 miles north of Matlock left off the A6 200yds on left)
☎ 01629 733583 FAX 01629 733583
The Red House Carriage Museum is a mix of working museum and soundly appointed accommodation. Bedrooms are either in the adjacent house or a clever stable conversion which provides a spacious en suite family bedroom. The one main house bedroom without en suite facilities has a private bathroom across the landing. Breakfast is taken in a small dining room around a large communal table.
2 bth/shr 1 annexe shr (1 fmly) No smoking CTV in all bedrooms Tea and coffee making facilities No dogs Cen ht 5P No coaches Carriage & horses trips/tuition Horse riding
ROOMS: d fr £45; wkly b&b £157.50-£175*

Selected

Q Q Q Q **Robertswood** Farley Hill DE4 3LL
(exit M1 at junc 28, A615 to Matlock, in Matlock take last exit of rdbt, up steep hill turn left into Smedley St, 1m turn right, first right)
☎ 01629 55642 FAX 01629 55642
This large stone-built Victorian house stands in an elevated position to the north of the town, from where it has panoramic views across the Derwent Valley. The accommodation is continually being upgraded to enhance guests comfort, and is equally well suited for business and leisure guests. Public rooms include a spacious comfortable lounge and a light attractively appointed dining room.
8 bth/shr (2 fmly) No smoking in bedrooms No smoking in dining room CTV in all bedrooms Tea and coffee making facilities Direct dial from bedrooms No dogs (ex guide dogs) Licensed Cen ht CTV 8P No coaches
ROOMS: s £35-£40; d £48-£54; wkly b&b £168-£189
CARDS:

QQ **Victoria House** 65 Wellington St DE4 3GS
(off A6 into Town Ctr, into Bank Road, bear right at T junct at the top into Wellington Street, 200yds on left hand side) ☎ 01629 55862
The Stevenson family invite guests to share their Victorian home. Spacious bedrooms, also suitable for families, are well presented and equipped, and there is also a comfortable lounge. Dinner is available by arrangement, featuring home-grown vegetables and bread baked on the premises.
2 rms (1 fmly) No smoking CTV in all bedrooms Tea and coffee making facilities No dogs Cen ht CTV 2P No coaches
ROOMS: d fr £36*

QQQ ♥ ***Wayside** (SK324630)* Matlock Moor DE4 5LF (from town centre take A632 to Chesterfield. Farm 2.5m on right) ☎ 01629 582967 Mrs J Hole
Closed Xmas & New Year
This working farm welcomes children, with a play area and access to the ducks, hens, pony and even pot-bellied pigs. Cottage style bedrooms have been refurbished recently and are attractively furnished, with built-in wooden furniture and modern en suite facilities. There is a comfortable lounge and dinner is available in the conservatory dining room.
4 rms (3 bth/shr) (2 fmly) No smoking CTV in all bedrooms Tea and coffee making facilities No dogs (ex guide dogs) Cen ht CTV 10P
35 acres mixed Last d 10am

QQQ **Woodside** Stanton Lees DE4 2LQ (A6 Bakewell 2 miles 1st left at Red House Hotel at crossroads left onto B5057 into Dartly Bridge, opposite pub right to Stanton Lees take right fork) ☎ 01629 734320
This stone-built cottage lies on the edge of a small village overlooking the valley and hills beyond. Bedrooms are attractively furnished, many of the items being made by the owner, Mrs Potter, and fine views are to be had. A hearty breakfast is served in the spacious combined lounge and dining room, heated by a wood burning stove in cooler weather.
3 bth/shr No smoking CTV in all bedrooms Tea and coffee making facilities No dogs Cen ht CTV No children 3yrs
ROOMS: d £36-£42

MATTERDALE END Cumbria Map 11 NY32

Selected

QQQQ **Bank House Farm** Matterdale End, Ullswater CA11 0LF ☎ 017684 82040 FAX 017684 82040
This fine period farmhouse sits in 12 acres high above Matterdale End, and enjoys delightful views across farmland and fells. The house has been restored by Rhona and David Longmire, to offer pretty bedrooms, most furnished in pine and all thoughtfully equipped. Public rooms are full of interest, adorned with memorabilia and period pieces. One can relax in the lounge, while Rhona's breakfasts complete with home-baked bread are taken in the cottage-style dining room.
4 shr No smoking No dogs (ex guide dogs) Cen ht No children 5P No coaches
ROOMS: d £50-£55; wkly b&b £175-£192.50

MAWGAN PORTH Cornwall & Isles of Scilly Map 02 SW86

QQQ **White Lodge Hotel** TR8 4BN
(on coast road between Newquay & Padstow opposite Mawgan Porth pitch & putt) ☎ 01637 860512 FAX 01637 860512
Closed Dec & Jan (ex Xmas)
Set in an elevated position and enjoying superb views of the sandy bay, this family-run hotel specialises in accommodating golfers and guests with dogs. Indeed, in the cosy residents' bar, one can buy a drink, a tin of dog food, or golf balls! The dining room spans the front of the hotel and along with the bar takes maximum advantage of the views.
16 rms (11 bth/shr) 3 annexe bth/shr (7 fmly) CTV in 18 bedrooms Tea and coffee making facilities Licensed CTV 21P Games room Last d 7.30pm
ROOMS: s £24-£26; d £48-£52; wkly b&b £140-£161; wkly hlf-bd £196-£217*
CARDS:

MAXEY Cambridgeshire Map 04 TF10

QQQ ***Abbey House*** West End Rd PE6 9EJ
(from roundabout on A15,1 mile south of Market Deeping, take Maxey direction, enter village by high street, take 1st right then in 50 yrds first left) ☎ 01778 344642 FAX 01778 344642
Parts of this delightful Georgian House actually date back to 1190, and its landscaped gardens include a yew tree, believed to be the oldest in the county. Consisting of the main building accommodation and annexe rooms in the converted coach house, all bedrooms are simply furnished and decorated in gentle pastel shades. There is a comfortable lounge and a breakfast room.

contd.

Abbey House

4 bth/shr 6 annexe bth/shr (1 fmly) No smoking in 6 bedrooms No smoking in dining room No smoking in lounges CTV in all bedrooms Tea and coffee making facilities Direct dial from bedrooms No dogs (ex guide dogs) Cen ht CTV 12P No coaches Fishing

See advertisement under STAMFORD

MELBOURNE Derbyshire Map **08** SK32

Selected

The Coach House 69 Derby Rd DE73 1FE (from Derby take A514 then the B587) ☎ 01332 862338 FAX 01332 862338

This comfortable Victorian House is in a conservation area, and has been carefully restored over recent years by the proprietors, Terry and June Lee. Bedrooms, two of which are in converted stables behind the main house, are attractively furnished. A cosy lounge leads through into the dining room where dinner is available by prior arrangement.

6 shr (1 fmly) No smoking in bedrooms No smoking in dining room CTV in all bedrooms Tea and coffee making facilities No dogs (ex guide dogs) Cen ht CTV 6P No coaches Last d 6pm

ROOMS: s fr £29.50; d fr £49

MELTON MOWBRAY Leicestershire Map **08** SK71

Cherry Trees Farmhouse 26 Middle Ln LE14 3HD (at Nether Broughton turn off the A606 Nottingham-Melton Mowbray Road at the Red Lion public house, Cherry Trees is 200 yards on the left hand side) ☎ 01664 822491 FAX 823406

This comfortable Victorian house is located in the centre of Nether Broughton, some six miles north of Melton Mowbray. The public rooms include a sitting room and a breakfast room; the original fireplaces in most rooms are worthy of note. Bedrooms are generally spacious and furnished with many period pieces.

3 bth No smoking CTV in all bedrooms Tea and coffee making facilities Cen ht CTV 4P No coaches

ROOMS: s £25; d £45; wkly b&b £150*

Home Farm Church Ln, Old Dalby LE14 3LB (6m NW of Melton Mowbray) ☎ 01664 822622 FAX 01664 823155

Closed Xmas

This delightful 18th-century farmhouse stands opposite the church in the village of Old Dalby. There is a cosy lounge for guests' use and breakfast is served family-style in a separate dining room. Bedrooms are individually styled and two rooms are situated in a converted outbuilding.

5 shr No smoking CTV in all bedrooms Tea and coffee making facilities No dogs Cen ht 5P No coaches

ROOMS: s £25-£26.50; d £40-£42.50*

CARDS:

MENDHAM Suffolk Map **05** TM28

Weston House *(TM292828)* IP20 0PB (from A143 or B1123 follow signs for Mendham then follow signs from centre of village) ☎ 01986 782206 FAX 01986 782414 Mrs J E Holden

Mar-Nov

Guests can expect a warm welcome at this 17th-century farmhouse, situated in 300 acres of farmland in the heart of the Waveny Valley. The accommodation is spacious, well appointed and en suite. There is also a soundly furnished lounge with TV and games as well as a dining room where guests can enjoy a hearty breakfast. Dinner is also available by prior arrangement.

3 shr (1 fmly) No smoking Tea and coffee making facilities Cen ht CTV 6P 300 acres Mixed Last d 2pm

ROOMS: s £23-£25; d £36-£40; wkly b&b £112-£140; wkly hlf-bd £189-£217

CARDS:

MERE Wiltshire Map **03** ST83

Selected

Chetcombe House Hotel Chetcombe Rd BA12 6AZ (off A303) ☎ 01747 860219 FAX 860111

This elegant country house is set in an acre of well tended gardens just a few minutes from the centre of Mere. Personally managed by the resident proprietors Colin and Susan Ross, Chetcombe House offers comfortable accommodation and a friendly atmosphere. Bedrooms are tastefully decorated and well equipped, and there is a delightful lounge for guests which has access to the garden. Traditional English Fare is served in the dining room making use of home-grown or local produce whenever possible.

5 bth/shr (1 fmly) No smoking CTV in all bedrooms Tea and coffee making facilities Direct dial from bedrooms Licensed Cen ht 10P No coaches Last d 5pm

ROOMS: s £29-£33; d fr £50; wkly b&b £150-£200; wkly hlf-bd £245-£295*

CARDS:

MEREWORTH Kent Map **05** TQ65

Queen's Head 133 Butchers Ln ME18 5QD (7m E of Maidstone) ☎ 01622 812534 FAX 01622 813630

A Grade II listed early Victorian country pub with three spacious and well equipped bedrooms. There are two bars open all day, featuring hand pulled cask ales, popular and good value home made bar food, lots of board games and a dart board. The separate dining room can be reserved for private parties, and families with children are very welcome. There is a large garden with a children's play area, barbecue, and wishing well with spring water.

3 shr No smoking in dining room CTV in all bedrooms Tea and coffee making facilities No dogs (ex guide dogs) Cen ht 50P Last d 8.45pm

CARDS:

MERIDEN West Midlands Map **04** SP28

Meriden Hotel Main Rd CV7 7NH (on B4104) ☎ 01676 522005 FAX 01676 523744

The Meriden is a licensed guest house within easy reach of the NEC. Bedrooms are comfortable and well equipped for the business user, and the owners, the Trippas family, are steadily improving overall quality throughout the house. There is a cheerful, cosy dining room, ideal for breakfasts and evening meals.

14 bth/shr (1 fmly) No smoking in dining room CTV in all bedrooms Tea and coffee making facilities Direct dial from bedrooms Licensed Cen ht 15P No coaches Last d 9pm

CARDS:

MEVAGISSEY Cornwall & Isles of Scilly Map **02** SX04

Q Q Q **Headlands Hotel** Polkirt Hill PL26 6UX (follow one way system through village & ascend towards Port Mellon, hotel on right 1m from village centre)
☎ 01726 843453 FAX 01726 844675
Set in an elevated position, with spectacular views over the bay, this hotel offers comfortable, well maintained accommodation. As well as the public areas and sun terrace, many of the bedrooms benefit from the glorious coastal views. At dinner an interesting selection of dishes is available.
14 rms (9 shr) (3 fmly) No smoking in dining room No smoking in lounges CTV in 13 bedrooms Tea and coffee making facilities Licensed Cen ht CTV ch fac 10P No coaches Last d 9.30pm
ROOMS: s £20; d £48-£54; wkly b&b £168-£189; wkly hlf-bd £231-£252
CARDS:

Selected

Q Q Q Q **Kerryanna** *(SX008453)* Treleaven Farm, Valley Rd PL26 6SA (off B3273 on entrance to village, turn right by tennis courts)
☎ 01726 843558 FAX 01726 843558 Mrs L Hennah
Mar-Oct
Linda and Percy Hennah run Kerryanna, situated in a quiet location on the edge of Mevagissey. There are fine views towards the sea from the comfortable lounge and an open air heated swimming pool in the attractive gardens. Bedrooms are furnished in pine. A freshly prepared evening meal is offered in the cosy dining room.
6 bth/shr (2 fmly) No smoking in bedrooms No smoking in dining room No smoking in 1 lounge CTV in all bedrooms Tea and coffee making facilities No dogs Licensed Cen ht CTV No children 5yrs 7P Outdoor swimming pool (heated) Games room Putting 200 acres arable beef Last d 5pm
ROOMS: d £44-£50; wkly b&b £160-£175*

Selected

Q Q Q Q **Mevagissey House** Vicarage Hill PL26 6SZ (exit A390 onto B3273 to Mevagissey, pass through Pentewan, at top of hill on crossroads turn left, at small roundabout turn right, premises on right)
☎ 01726 842427 FAX 01726 844327
Closed Nov-Feb
Recently refurbished by its enthusiastic owners, John & Gill Westmacott, Mevagissey House has smart newly decorated bedrooms and elegance is the key to the day rooms, where guests can enjoy the views over the four acre gardens to the sea beyond. After a leisurely breakfast, a short stroll down Vicarage Hill, to the village centre, makes a good beginning to the day.
5 rms (1 bth 3 shr) (2 fmly) No smoking in bedrooms No smoking in dining room No smoking in lounges CTV in all bedrooms Tea and coffee making facilities No dogs (ex guide dogs) Licensed Cen ht CTV No children 7yrs 12P No coaches
ROOMS: s £31-£39; d £44-£57; wkly b&b £126-£182
CARDS:

Q Q *The Ship* Fore St PL26 6UQ (St Austell Brewery)
☎ 01726 843324
A short stroll from the quay-side, the Ship Inn has a distinctly nautical feel, with the walls bedecked with maritime memorabilia. Popular with locals and holidaymakers alike, the bustling bar offers hearty informal fare with blackboard specials, and children are happily catered for. Though the rooms vary in size, all are attractively decorated and furnished in pine. The spacious public rooms include the cosy dining room on the first floor, where breakfast is served.
6 rms (2 fmly) CTV in all bedrooms Tea and coffee making facilities Cen ht Last d 8.30pm

Selected

Q Q Q Q **Spa Hotel** Polkirt Hill PL26 6UY (signed on Mevagissey-Portmellon road) ☎ 01726 842244
Mar-Oct
From its elevated position above this pretty, seaside village, many rooms enjoy distant coastal views. Since taking over Trevor and Valerie Hounslow have worked hard in upgrading this hotel. The bedrooms vary in size, but all are light, airy and well equipped, some having their own patio areas leading onto the well tended garden. A comfortable, cane-furnished lounge is provided for guests, together with a cosy bar.
11 bth/shr (4 fmly) No smoking in bedrooms No smoking in dining room No smoking in 1 lounge CTV in 12 bedrooms Tea and coffee making facilities Licensed Cen ht CTV 12P No coaches Pool table Putting green Last d noon
ROOMS: d £49-£60; wkly b&b £165-£200; wkly hlf-bd £249-£284*
CARDS:

Selected

Q Q Q Q ***Treleaven*** *(SX008454)* Valley Rd PL26 6SA (turn right at foot of hill when entering Mevagissey)
☎ 01726 842413 Mrs A Hennah
Closed 15 Dec-7 Jan
Treleaven enjoys a hilltop location with spectacular views over the fishing village of Mevagissey. Anne and Colin Hennah provide a welcoming atmosphere and also open their large dining room to non-residents where they offer a range of freshly prepared dishes. The bedrooms are well maintained and comfortable. The house is set in its own well tended gardens, and features an open air heated pool and an 18-hole putting green. *contd.*

Treleaven

6 shr (1 fmly) No smoking in dining room CTV in all bedrooms Tea and coffee making facilities No dogs Licensed Cen ht 6P Outdoor swimming pool (heated) Games room Putting 200 acres mixed Last d 8pm
CARDS:

MIDDLEHAM North Yorkshire Map **07** SE18

The Black Swan Hotel Market Place DL8 4NP
(exit A1 onto B6267 towards Masham, continue for 8m to Middleham)
☎ 01969 622221 FAX 01969 622221
rs 24-27 Dec
Located in the heart of this delightful village, famous for its racehorse connections, this 17th-century inn retains many period features. A good range of bar meals are provided within the cosy restaurants, plus an interesteing choice on the dinner menu. Bedrooms vary in size and despite being furnished in contemporary style, still retain the character of the inn.
7 bth/shr (1 fmly) CTV in all bedrooms Tea and coffee making facilities Direct dial from bedrooms Cen ht 3P Last d 9pm
ROOMS: s £27-£30; d £48-£65*
MEALS: Lunch £6-£10alc Dinner £10-£18alc*
CARDS:

MIDDLETON-IN-TEESDALE Co Durham Map **12** NY92

Brunswick House 55 Market Place DL12 0QH
(on B6277 opposite St Mary's Church) ☎ 01833 640393 FAX 640393
This charming house, with exposed beams and open fireplaces, is located in the heart of the village, and dates back to 1760. The bedrooms are bright and fresh and have been thoughtfully equipped, and the lounge provides a peaceful retreat and is the only area where smoking is permitted within the house. A good range of skilfully home-cooked food is available in the attractive dining room.
5 bth/shr No smoking in bedrooms No smoking in dining room CTV in all bedrooms Tea and coffee making facilities No dogs (ex guide dogs) Licensed Cen ht 5P No coaches Last d 7pm
ROOMS: s £30; d £45; wkly b&b £133; wkly hlf-bd £224
CARDS:

MIDDLETON-ON-THE-HILL Herefordshire Map **03** SO56

Selected

Five Ashes House SY8 4BE
(turn off A49 by Berrington Hall signed for Middleton on the Hill, 1m to crossroads, turn left, 1m and turn right, 100yds on right)
☎ 01568 750334 FAX 01568 750334
With the use of oak beams and natural stone, this modern house, situated on a ten acre holding and surrounded by delightful gardens, has been cleverly constructed to give the appearance of a much older property. There is an attractive and comfortable lounge, where a welcoming wood burning stove is lit in cold weather, and adjoining is the traditionally furnished dining area, where dinner is available on request.

2 shr No smoking CTV in all bedrooms Tea and coffee making facilities No dogs (ex guide dogs) Cen ht CTV No coaches Last d noon
ROOMS: d £42-£46; wkly b&b £147-£161*

MIDDLEWICH Cheshire Map **07** SJ76

Forge Mill *(SJ704624)* Forge Mill Ln, Warmingham CW10 0HQ
(M6 junc 18, in Middlewich turn left onto A533, after "40mph" sign turn right then first left, after 1.5m at T-junc turn right into Forge Mill Lane)
☎ 01270 526204 Mrs S Moss
This fine old farmhouse, built of Cheshire red brick, is surrounded by extensive gardens with views over open farmland. Bedrooms are spacious and furnished in traditional style, as is the comfortable lounge which is heated by a log fire during the cooler months. The large dining room, with its baby grand piano and separate tables, makes a pleasant setting for breakfast.
2 rms (1 fmly) No smoking in bedrooms No smoking in dining room No dogs (ex guide dogs) Cen ht CTV 10P 150 acres mixed
ROOMS: s fr £20; d fr £36*

MIDDLE WINTERSLOW Wiltshire Map **04** SU23

Premier Selected

Beadles Middleton SP5 1QS
(leave A30 at The Pheasant Hotel to Middle Winterslow. Enter village and turn first right into The Flood and right at end, first right after Trevano) ☎ 01980 862922 FAX 01980 862922
Quietly hidden away this charming house is just 8 miles from Salisbury. Hospitable hosts, Anne and David Yuille-Baddeley take great delight in welcoming guests and ensuring their stay is both relaxing and memorable. Anne, an accomplished cook, offers a variety of mouth-watering dishes which are served in the elegant dining room. Sightseeing trips are David's speciality and he will gladly plan an itinerary for you, to take in the many and varied sights in the area. The attractively decorated bedrooms all feature antique furniture and a host of thoughtful touches.
3 bth/shr No smoking CTV in all bedrooms Tea and coffee making facilities Direct dial from bedrooms No dogs (ex guide dogs) Cen ht No children 10yrs 5P No coaches Last d 3pm
ROOMS: d £50-£55; wkly b&b £157.50-£175*
CARDS:

This symbol indicates a 'Child Friendly' establishment - see page 25 for details

MIDHURST West Sussex Map 04 SU82

See also Rogate

Premier Selected

QQQQQ **Park House Hotel** Bepton GU29 0JB (from centre of Midhurst take B2226 to Bepton and the premises are 2m on the right hand side) ☎ 01730 812880 FAX 01730 815643

Michael and Liza O'Brien offer warm and friendly hospitality at Park House Hotel. The spacious drawing room overlooking the extensive landscaped gardens, the dining room where both lunch and dinner are served, and a well-stocked honesty bar, are furnished with antiques. Accommodation includes a two bedroom suite in Bay Tree Cottage, and another with private sitting room in an adjacent barn.

14 bth/shr (1 fmly) No smoking in 6 bedrooms No smoking in dining room CTV in all bedrooms Tea and coffee making facilities Direct dial from bedrooms Licensed Cen ht CTV 35P No coaches Outdoor swimming pool (heated) Golf 9 Tennis (grass) Croquet Pitch & putt, putting lawn Last d 7pm

ROOMS: s £49.50-£80; d £99-£140*

CARDS:

Selected

QQQQ **Redford Cottage** Redford GU29 0QF (from Petersfield-take A272 E, 1m outside Midhurst turn left towards Woolbeding/Redford after 2m enter Redford, house 500yds on left) ☎ 01428 741242 FAX 01428 741242

Ask for directions when booking, as David and Caroline Angela's delightful 16th-century former farmhouse is tucked away in the heart of the Sussex countryside. Of the antique-furnished bedrooms, the ground floor Garden Suite has its own small study and 'snug' with a real log fire in the winter, and sole use of a shower room. Two further rooms on the first floor have lovely views of the garden, and are usually let together sharing a bathroom. There is an attractive beamed lounge with a log fire, and French doors into the garden.

3 rms (1 shr) No smoking in bedrooms No smoking in dining room No smoking in 1 lounge CTV in 2 bedrooms Tea and coffee making facilities No dogs (ex guide dogs) Cen ht CTV 6P No coaches

ROOMS: s £34-£40; d £56-£65*

MIDSOMER NORTON Somerset Map 03 ST65

QQQ **Old Station** Wells Rd, Hallatrow BS18 5EN (A37 from Bristol to Wells turn left onto A39 directing you to Bath, 300yds on right) ☎ 01761 452228

This is an attractive roadside inn, located just off the A37, mid-way between the cities of Bath and Wells. Well situated for easy access to the many places of interest, and the beauty of North Somerset and the Mendip Hills to visit. Miles and Sue Davies, offer three comfortable, well equipped, bedrooms and a family suite in an adjacent converted stable block. A good menu for freshly cooked food is available from a blackboard in the beamed bar where a host of interesting memorabilia adorns the walls and ceilings. Dining in the State Car Restaurant, an old railway carriage overlooking the garden, offers a good menu in a delightful setting.

3 annexe bth/shr (1 fmly) No smoking in dining room CTV in all bedrooms Tea and coffee making facilities No dogs (ex guide dogs) Cen ht Last d 10pm

ROOMS: s fr £30; d fr £42*

MEALS: Lunch £5-£12alc*

CARDS:

MILFORD ON SEA Hampshire Map 04 SZ29

QQQ **Cherry Trees** Lymington Rd SO41 0QL (located at end of private lane between village centre and primary school just off B3058) ☎ 01590 643746

A comfortably appointed house set back from the road in attractive, peaceful surroundings, Cherry Trees is just a short distance from the village centre. The three bedrooms are well equipped and include many extra and thoughtful touches. Healthy eating is the order of the day on Sheri Gadd's dinner menu - vegetarian and fish dishes only are served. However, a traditional English breakfast can be provided. Aromatherapy, holistic massage and beauty treatments are available.

3 bth/shr (1 fmly) No smoking CTV in all bedrooms Tea and coffee making facilities No dogs (ex guide dogs) Cen ht ch fac 4P No coaches Holistic massage and beauty treatment room Last d 12 noon

ROOMS: s £22-£30; d £38-£46; wkly b&b £125-£175; wkly hlf-bd £175-£210*

MILLER'S DALE Derbyshire Map 07 SK17

QQ **Dale Cottage** SK17 8SN (turn off A6 between Buxton and Bakewell onto B6049 at signpost stating Millers Dale/ Tideswell. Opposite "Craft Supplies") ☎ 01298 872400

Closed Xmas holidays

contd.

Quietly situated in a wooded valley, this 19th-century cottage is close to the Monsal Trail and the proprietors keep maps of local walks for visitors to use. Bedrooms, both on the ground floor, are attractively furnished and share a modern bathroom. Upstairs, overlooking the river, breakfast is served around one table and dinner can be available by prior arrangement.
2 rms No smoking CTV in all bedrooms Tea and coffee making facilities No dogs (ex guide dogs) Cen ht 2P No coaches Last d 10am
ROOMS: s fr £25; d £36-£38*

MILTON KEYNES Buckinghamshire Map **04** SP83

See also Gayhurst

Selected

Q Q Q Q **Old Bakery** Main St MK19 7JL (off A508 towards Northampton. Take first right for Cosgrove, hotel on left after the bridge over Grand Union Canal) ☎ 01908 263103 & 262255 FAX 01908 263620
The pretty village of Cosgrove, just north of Milton Keynes, has many attractive features, not least of which is The Old Bakery. Ann Hepher the owner is a welcoming host and capable cook. All rooms are prettily furnished and particularly spacious. An excellent range of facilities is provided including satellite TV, and the en suite bathrooms really sparkle and quality toiletries are provided. A tasty range of both traditional and more imaginative cuisine is served in the restaurant.
8 bth/shr (1 fmly) No smoking in 3 bedrooms No smoking in lounges CTV in all bedrooms Tea and coffee making facilities Direct dial from bedrooms Licensed Cen ht 8P No coaches Last d 9pm
ROOMS: s £37.50-£55; d £47.50-£65; wkly b&b £166.50-£192.50; wkly hlf-bd £210-£236.50*
CARDS:

Q Q Q **Thurstons Private Hotel** 90 High St, Newport Pagnell MK16 8EH (exit M1 at junc 14, A509, pass Aston Martin Lagonda, over iron bridge, left onto A422, premises adjacent to Newport Pagnell Medical Centre) ☎ 01908 611377 FAX 01908 611394
Manager Sandra White has made a real impact on this substantial town house property. The accommodation sparkles and the bedrooms, most of which are newly refurbished, are spacious and bright. A small lounge adjoins the breakfast room.
8 bth/shr (1 fmly) No smoking in dining room CTV in all bedrooms Tea and coffee making facilities No dogs (ex guide dogs) Licensed Cen ht CTV 14P No coaches
CARDS:

MINEHEAD Somerset Map **03** SS94

See also Dunster

Q Q Q **Avill House** 12 Townsend Rd TA24 5RG (on entering Minehead from E, follow signs for town centre for 0.5m, premises on left before Esso Garage) ☎ 01643 704370
Conveniently situated within easy walking distance of the town centre and seafront, this Victorian mid-terraced property has a brightly painted facade, complemented by colourful flower beds in the summer. The comfortable bedrooms are neatly decorated and fitted with functional modern furniture. Breakfast is served in the front facing dining room and an evening meal can be provided by prior arrangement. A well-stocked bar is also available, the ideal place to sit, relax and socialise the night away!
9 rms (3 shr) (4 fmly) No smoking in bedrooms No smoking in dining room No smoking in 1 lounge CTV in all bedrooms Tea and coffee making facilities No dogs (ex guide dogs) Licensed CTV 9P Games room Last d 5.30pm
ROOMS: s fr £19.50; d £34-£40; wkly b&b £115-£133*

Q Q Q **Bactonleigh** 20 Tregonwell Rd TA24 5DU (premises located on A39 between Williton and Porlock, 3 min from seafront) ☎ 01643 702147
Mar-1 Nov
This small family-run hotel, situated within just a three minute and level walk of the beach and town centre, offers a relaxed and informal atmosphere. The fixed-price dinner features home cooking and, having a table license, guests can enjoy a glass of wine with their meal. Bedrooms are neatly decorated and furnished, and some are suitable for families.
8 rms (4 shr) (1 fmly) No smoking in bedrooms No smoking in dining room CTV in all bedrooms Tea and coffee making facilities Licensed Cen ht CTV 5P Last d 5pm
ROOMS: s fr £15.50; d fr £31; wkly b&b fr £105; wkly hlf-bd fr £157*

Selected

Q Q Q Q **Gascony Hotel** The Avenue TA24 5BB (premises situated on The Avenue at the corner of Tregonwell Rd) ☎ 01643 705939
Mar-Oct rs Nov-Feb
Over the last 12 years, John and Kay Luckett have transformed this Victorian property into an attractive and comfortable hotel. Close to the town centre and seafront, many regular guests view the Gascony Hotel as their second home. Bedrooms, varying in size, have bright and modern facilities and smart bathrooms. A spacious, open-plan lounge and bar is decorated with antiques and provides a welcoming atmosphere. A short table d'hôte menu features home cooked dishes complemented by a reasonably priced wine list.
13 bth/shr (2 fmly) No smoking in dining room CTV in all bedrooms Tea and coffee making facilities Licensed Cen ht 15P No coaches Last d 5.30pm
ROOMS: s £24-£27; d £46-£50; wkly b&b £148-£168; wkly hlf-bd £198-£206*
CARDS:

Selected

Q Q Q Q **Glendower Hotel** 32 Tregonwell Rd TA24 5DU ☎ 01643 707144 FAX 01643 708719
This small and friendly family run hotel, set in an attractive residential terrace, has plenty of parking at the rear and a pretty garden and patio. Ute and Herbert Lauben have recently restored the property which now provides modern creature comforts combined with the elegance and charm of the Victorian architecture. Bedrooms are spacious with gleaming en-suite shower rooms and there is a choice of cosy dining rooms where freshly prepared meals are available by arrangement. Glendower is licensed and a host of reading material is provided for guests enjoyment in the bar and lounge.
14 shr (2 fmly) No smoking in 3 bedrooms CTV in all bedrooms Tea and coffee making facilities Licensed Cen ht CTV 14P
ROOMS: s £18-£23; d £36-£46; wkly b&b £112-£133*
CARDS:

Kildare Lodge Townsend Rd TA24 5RQ
(Enter Minehead from east on A39, follow signs for town centre, establishment approx 0.5m on left) (The Independents)
☎ 01643 702009 FAX 01643 706516
Designed by a pupil of Sir Edwin Lutyens, this interesting inn has been sympathetically modernised. Situated within easy walking distance of the town centre and the seafront, motorists will also find the beautiful scenery of Exmoor easily accessible. Some of the well-equipped bedrooms are in a converted stable block adjacent to the main building, while the baronial-style restaurant offers a wide choice of dishes.
6 bth/shr 5 annexe bth/shr (1 fmly) No smoking in dining room No smoking in 1 lounge CTV in all bedrooms Tea and coffee making facilities Direct dial from bedrooms Cen ht CTV 25P Last d 9pm
ROOMS: s £25-£31; d £44-£74; wkly b&b £120-£210; wkly hlf-bd £180-£260*
MEALS: Lunch £12.50&alc Dinner £5-£18.95&alc*
CARDS:

Selected

Mayfair Hotel 25 The Avenue TA24 5AY
(main wide tree-line avenue between sea & main shopping area)
☎ 01643 702719
Mar-Nov
Situated a two minute, level walk from the beach and on the main high street, this delightful Victorian building offers comfortable accommodation and a relaxed and friendly atmosphere. The well equipped bedrooms are comfortably decorated. There is a charming, well furnished sitting room, part of which is used as a bar/lounge. A choice of dishes is offered from the menu and, as meals are freshly prepared, it is preferred that orders are taken in advance.
13 bth/shr (6 fmly) No smoking CTV in all bedrooms Tea and coffee making facilities No dogs (ex guide dogs) Licensed Cen ht 12P Last d 6pm
CARDS:

Selected

Red House Periton Rd TA24 8DT
(1m from Alacombe rdbt on A39 (Minehead to Porlock road))
☎ 01643 706519
Closed December
This smart, detached, Queen Anne-style property on the outskirts of Minehead, has easy access to the breathtaking scenery of Exmoor. Owners, Stan and Olive take a great pride in their home and offer high standards of hospitality and acccommodation. Bedrooms are neatly presented and furnished for comfort, some offering expansive views across the town to the sea. Breakfast is served around one large table in the delightful dining room, which overlooks the colourful garden.
3 bth/shr No smoking in dining room No smoking in lounges CTV in all bedrooms Tea and coffee making facilities No dogs (ex guide dogs) Cen ht CTV No children 10yrs 5P No coaches
ROOMS: s £20; d £40*

MINSTERLEY Shropshire Map 07 SJ30

Selected

Cricklewood Cottage Plox Green SY5 0HT
(on A488 towards Bishop Castle 1m past Minsterley on the left)
☎ 01743 791229
Closed 24 & 25 Dec
Dating from the 18th century, this delightful cottage has been restored to retain many original features, whilst providing modern comforts. The bedrooms have individual colour schemes and exposed beams. The sun room overlooks the surrounding hills and the welcoming sitting room has many books and local information. The lovely gardens include unusual plants and a trout stream. Debbie and Paul Costello are friendly and caring hosts.
3 bth/shr No smoking Tea and coffee making facilities No dogs Cen ht CTV No children 8yrs 4P No coaches
ROOMS: s £21-£35; d £42-£47; wkly b&b £147-£220*

Woodhouse Farm *(SJ388053)* Malehurst Bank SY5 0BS
(From A5 onto A488 for 6 miles, through Powtesbury village, farm 0.75m on left) ☎ 01743 791762 FAX 01743 791762
Mr & Mrs R Bromley
Closed 1 Nov-28 Feb
Set well back from the main road, at the end of a long drive, this 150-year old farmhouse is surrounded by open pasture. Both bedrooms are neatly decorated and feature traditional country furniture. At present, both share a bathroom, but plans are being made to create private facilities. A wood-burning stove heats the comfortable lounge, whilst meals are taken around the pine table in the welcoming dining room, next to the farmhouse kitchen.
2 rms (1 fmly) No smoking CTV in all bedrooms Tea and coffee making facilities No dogs Cen ht CTV 6P 40 acres sheep cattle
Last d by arrangement
ROOMS: s £20-£22; d £36*

MISTLEY Essex Map 05 TM13

Thorn Hotel High St CO11 1HE ☎ 01206 392821
FAX 01206 392133
Situated in the village centre, this popular inn is renowned for its connection with the infamous 17th-century Witchfinder General. The spacious bedrooms are attractively decorated and well equipped; there is a small reception sitting area and a dining room where a wide range of food is served at lunch and dinner.
4 shr CTV in all bedrooms Tea and coffee making facilities No dogs (ex guide dogs) Cen ht 4P Last d 9pm
ROOMS: s £30-£35; d £45-£50*
MEALS: Lunch £5-£10 Dinner £7.50-£12*
CARDS:

MOLESWORTH Cambridgeshire Map 04 TL07

Cross Keys PE18 0QF (turn off A14 follow signs to Molesworth) ☎ 01832 710283 FAX 01832 710098
In the quiet village of Molesworth, this whitewashed pub is very much the heart of the village. The pleasant and well-equipped accommodation is located within the main house and an adjacent building. Home-cooked fare is a speciality and a wide selection of hearty dishes is offered in the open-plan bar and dining area.
4 bth/shr 6 annexe bth/shr (1 fmly) CTV in all bedrooms Tea and coffee making facilities Direct dial from bedrooms Cen ht 30P Last d 10.15pm
CARDS:

MORCHARD BISHOP Devon Map **03** SS70

Premier Selected

QQQQQ **Wigham** *(SS757087)* EX17 6RJ
(1.5m NW of Morchard Bishop in the direction of Chulmleigh) ☎ 01363 877350 FAX 01363 877350
Mr & Mrs S Chilcott
Complete with thatch, beams and crackling log fires, this charming 16th-century longhouse is a haven of peace and tranquillity. Owners Dawn and Steve Chilcott provide a genuine welcome and serve imaginative dishes using organic meat and dairy produce straight from their adjoining farm. All the bedrooms, including one with a four-poster bed, have been tastefully decorated and feature hand-made furniture. There is a snooker lounge and a heated outdoor swimming pool.
5 bth/shr (1 fmly) No smoking CTV in all bedrooms Tea and coffee making facilities Direct dial from bedrooms No dogs Licensed Cen ht No children 9P Outdoor swimming pool (heated) Riding 7ft snooker table 31 acres pigs cattle sheep hay
ROOMS: (incl. dinner) d £110-£158*
CARDS:

MORECAMBE Lancashire Map **07** SD46

QQQ **Ashley Private Hotel** 371 Marine Rd, Promenade East LA4 5AH
☎ 01524 412034 FAX 01524 421390
Enjoying stunning views northwards over Morecambe Bay towards the Lake District, this comfortable hotel stands to the north of the town centre on the promenade. Bedrooms are bright and well equipped, some with spacious bathrooms and some large enough for family use. The comfortable first floor lounge makes the most of the views as does the combined dining room and cosy bar area. There is a neat patio at the front.
13 rms (11 bth/shr) (3 fmly) No smoking in dining room CTV in all bedrooms Tea and coffee making facilities Licensed Cen ht CTV 4P Last d 3pm
ROOMS: s £17-£19; d £34-£38; wkly b&b £108-£118; wkly hlf-bd £156-£174*
CARDS:

QQQ **Beach Mount** 395 Marine Rd East LA4 5AN ☎ 01524 420753
mid Mar-Oct
A modern, family owned hotel, with panoramic views of Morecambe Bay and the Lakeland fells beyond, offers a good range of facilities in bedrooms which have been furnished with an eye to comfort. The public rooms are designed to take advantage of the hotel's enviable location.
22 bth/shr (2 fmly) CTV in all bedrooms Tea and coffee making facilities Licensed Cen ht 6P No coaches Last d 7pm
ROOMS: s £22-£23.25; d £41-£43.50; wkly b&b £126.50-£139; wkly hlf-bd £152.50-£170*
CARDS:

QQQ **Hotel Prospect** 363 Marine Rd East Promenade LA4 5AQ
(exit M6 at junc 34/35, follow Morecambe Promenade, premises just before Gala Bingo) ☎ 01524 417819 FAX 01524 417819
Etr-Nov
This well established guest house has consistently maintained good standards. The bright and cheery en suite bedrooms meet modern standards of comfort, and half have good views over the bay. The dining room extends at the front into a small lounge area with its own well stocked bar and super sea views.
14 bth/shr (9 fmly) No smoking in 8 bedrooms No smoking in dining room CTV in all bedrooms Tea and coffee making facilities Licensed Cen ht CTV 18P Last d 3pm
ROOMS: s £17-£22; d £34-£40; wkly b&b £110-£120; wkly hlf-bd £150-£169*
CARDS:

QQQ **Wimslow Private Hotel** 374 Marine Rd East LA4 5AH
(400 yards from Broadway Hotel, 300 yards W of Town Hall)
☎ 01524 417804 FAX 01524 417804
Closed 1 week Nov & 1 week Jan
Mr and Mrs Beecroft have been welcoming hosts at their attractive hotel for more than five years. Although the en suite bedrooms vary in size, all are well equipped and freshly decorated, and some enjoy stuning views of the bay. On the first floor there is a neatly furnished dining room, and on the ground floor a sun lounge with a bar.
14 bth/shr (2 fmly) No smoking in dining room CTV in all bedrooms Tea and coffee making facilities No dogs (ex guide dogs) Licensed Cen ht 18P Last d 4.30pm
ROOMS: s £16-£19; d £32-£38; wkly b&b £115-£146; wkly hlf-bd fr £163
CARDS:

MORETONHAMPSTEAD Devon Map **03** SX78

Premier Selected

QQQQQ **Blackaller Hotel & Restaurant** North Bovey TQ13 8QY (A38, A382 to Moretonhampstead, on entering Moretonhampstead take first left by newsagents to North Bovey)
☎ 01647 440322 FAX 01647 440322
Closed Jan & Feb
This 17th-century woollen mill lies on the banks of the Bovey River, and is run by Peter Hunt and Hazel Phillips. Bedrooms are pleasing for their simplicity. The public areas include a charming sitting room, a well stocked bar and an attractive dining room with a lovely old inglenook fireplace and exposed granite walls. All produce on the daily changing menu comes from within the county and is carefully prepared with flair and imagination by Hazel Phillips.
5 bth/shr 1 annexe bth No smoking in bedrooms No smoking in dining room CTV in all bedrooms Tea and coffee making facilities Licensed Cen ht 6P No coaches Fishing Riding Bird watching Walking weekends Last d 8pm
ROOMS: s £30-£31; d £72-£74*

QQQ **Cookshayes** 33 Court St TQ13 8LG (Situated on B3213 Exeter/ Princetown road, approx 399yds from crossroads in Moretonhampstead with the A382 in direction of Princetown) ☎ 01647 440374
Mar-Oct
Set in nearly an acre of well tended gardens on the edge of the old moorland town of Moretonhampstead, this Victorian house has lovely views over Dartmoor. Most rooms have en suite facilities, one has a four-poster bed and two are on the ground floor. A set, home-cooked evening meal is served in the dining room and guests can enjoy relaxing in a comfortable lounge with bay windows overlooking the gardens.
8 rms (6 shr) (1 fmly) No smoking in dining room No smoking in lounges CTV in all bedrooms Tea and coffee making facilities Licensed Cen ht CTV No children 5yrs 8P No coaches Last d ordered when booking
ROOMS: s fr £19; d fr £41*
CARDS:

Selected

QQQQ **Great Sloncombe** *(SX737864)* TQ13 8QF
(from Moretonhampstead take A382 towards Chagford for 1.5m. At sharp double bend take left turning and farm is 0.5m up lane)
☎ 01647 440595 FAX 01647 440595 Mrs T Merchant
Built in the 13th century, this listed granite and cob-built longhouse provides guests with a peaceful environment in which to enjoy a relaxing stay. The Merchant family have retained all the characteristic features of the building, while ensuring that guests are comfortable. Inglenook fireplaces, low ceilings, exposed beams and flagstone floors are all features which will charm their visitors, and dinners are available by prior arrangement.
3 shr No smoking CTV in all bedrooms Tea and coffee making facilities Cen ht No children 8yrs 3P 170 acres dairy
Last d 10am
ROOMS: s £21-£22; d £42-£44*

Premier Selected

QQQQQ **Gate House** North Bovey TQ13 8RB
(Take A30, A382 to Moretonhampstead then take the B3212 to North Bovey) ☎ 01647 440479 FAX 01647 440479
A pot of tea and home-made cakes are part of the hospitality guests can expect at this 15th-century thatched cottage. The grounds feature an outdoor swimming pool, and bedrooms are stylishly furnished. Dinner is served in a candle-lit dining room and there is also beamed lounge with a large, granite fireplace.
3 bth/shr No smoking CTV in all bedrooms Tea and coffee making facilities Cen ht No children 15yrs 3P No coaches Outdoor swimming pool Riding Local riding Fishing Guided walks
Last d 3pm
ROOMS: s fr £34; d £52-£56*

Selected

Q Q Q Q **Moorcote** Chagford Cross TQ13 8LS
(A382 Chagford & Okehampton rd from Moretonhampstead for 350mtrs. Go past the hospital, Moorcote is on right)
☎ 01647 440966
Closed Nov-Feb
Overlooking the town, with some bedrooms benefiting from stunning views across Dartmoor, this Victorian house is set well back from the road in pretty country gardens. The location makes it an ideal base for those wishing to explore Dartmoor and it is also little more than a stroll to the town centre. Pat and Paul Lambert recently took over Moorcote and extend a warm welcome to guests. The comfortable bedrooms are well equipped and attractively co-ordinated.
6 rms (4 shr) (2 fmly) No smoking in dining room No smoking in lounges CTV in all bedrooms Tea and coffee making facilities No dogs Cen ht No children 5yrs 6P No coaches
ROOMS: d £38-£42; wkly b&b £126-£140

Selected

Q Q Q Q ♈ **Wooston** *(SX764890)* TQ13 8QA
(take Lime Street (opposite library) for 1.5 m over cattle grid. Fork left over second cattle grid and second house on right- S x 764890)
☎ 01647 440367 FAX 01647 440367 Mrs M Cuming
Standing high above the Teign Valley in the Dartmoor National Park, this delightful farm house is a peaceful haven surrounded by attractive gardens, with delightful views across the moors. All bedrooms are attractively decorated, and made homely with many personal touches. One room has a four poster bed. The two traditionally furnished lounges have wood burning stoves and a spacious dining room has a huge table, where guests are seated in house-party style.
3 rms (2 shr) No smoking CTV in all bedrooms Tea and coffee making facilities No dogs Cen ht CTV No children 8yrs 3P
280 acres mixed Last d by arrangement
ROOMS: d £38-£42; wkly b&b £130-£145*

MORETON-IN-MARSH Gloucestershire Map **04** SP13

Q Q **Acacia** 2 New Rd GL56 0AS
(premises just off A429, follow signposts to station opposite to Post Office)
☎ 01608 650130
Conveniently located close to the High Street in this popular little Cotswold town, the Acacia is an ideal touring base. Good use is made of the available space and the well-maintained rooms are bright and fresh. There is a small lounge with a log fire.
4 rms (1 shr) (1 fmly) No smoking in bedrooms No smoking in dining room CTV in all bedrooms Tea and coffee making facilities Cen ht CTV
ROOMS: s £20-£22; d £34-£36*

Q Q Q ♈ **Ditchford Farmhouse** *(SP223384)* Ditchford Farm, Stretton-on-Fosse GL56 9RD (on B4035 Shipston-on-Stour road within 50yds of junct with A429 (Fosse Way)) ☎ 01608 663307 Mr & Mrs B Hall
Mar-Oct
Some five miles from Moreton-in-Marsh, this period farmhouse is set on a large arable farm at the end of a long private drive. The bedrooms vary in size and style but most are quite spacious. The pleasant dining room features antique furniture, where dinner is available by prior arrangement. There is a comfortable lounge and a large garden.
6 rms (3 bth/shr) (2 fmly) No smoking in bedrooms No smoking in dining room CTV in all bedrooms Tea and coffee making facilities No dogs (ex guide dogs) Licensed Cen ht CTV 12P Fishing
1000 acres arable/sheep
ROOMS: s £27-£32; d £46-£52; wkly b&b £180-£210*

Q Q **Moreton House** High St GL56 0LQ (At junction of A44 & A429)
☎ 01608 650747 FAX 01608 652747
Moreton House has been in the Dempster family for nearly 100 years. The emphasis is on good home cooking in the traditionally furnished room, which serves as a tea room during the day and a restaurant at night. Homely comfort is offered in the bright and fresh-looking bedrooms.
11 rms (7 bth/shr) No smoking in area of dining room CTV in all bedrooms Tea and coffee making facilities Licensed Cen ht 7P
ROOMS: s £22-£24; d £42-£60*
CARDS:

Q Q Q **Rigside** Little Compton GL56 0RR ☎ 01608 674128
FAX 01608 674128
Conveniently located for Moreton-in-Marsh and the rest of the Cotswolds as well as Stratford, this very well kept guest house is situated in its own pretty gardens well off the main road. The bedrooms are simply decorated and carefully maintained with good levels of modern facilities. Breakfast can be taken in the attractive dining room which overlooks the garden and guests can also indulge in Mrs Cox's home-baking. The village of Little Compton, within walking distance, has a pub which serves evening meals.
3 rms (1 shr) No smoking in bedrooms No smoking in dining room CTV in 1 bedroom Tea and coffee making facilities No dogs (ex guide dogs) Cen ht CTV No children 6P No coaches
ROOMS: s £20; d £40

MORLAND Cumbria Map **12** NY62

Q Q Q ***Hill Top House*** Morland CA10 3AX (M6 junct 40 to A6 South. Turn left for Cliburn and right for Morland) ☎ 01931 714561
Set in a picturesque village, this traditional Georgian house is attractively maintained and offers an inviting lounge with a fire in cold weather. Meals are taken round one table in the adjoining dining room. Bedrooms are attractively furnished, the twin being the most spacious and the single having sole use of a bathroom just across the hall.
3 rms (1 bth 1 shr) No smoking in bedrooms No smoking in dining room CTV in all bedrooms Tea and coffee making facilities No dogs (ex guide dogs) Cen ht No children 7yrs 3P No coaches Last d 24hr notice

MORLEY West Yorkshire Map **08** SE22

Q Q Q **The Old Vicarage** Bruntcliffe Rd LS27 0JZ
(exit M62 at junc 27, follow signs for A650, A650, through traffic lights, past two garages, premises on left before St Andrews Church)
☎ 0113 2532174 FAX 0113 2533549
Standing on the A650, next to the church, this elegant stone building provides modern and well-equipped bedrooms. The interesting public rooms have a delightful Victorian theme and provide something that is very different. A good range of well-produced food is offered and service is attentive.
23 bth/shr No smoking in 17 bedrooms No smoking in dining room No smoking in 1 lounge CTV in all bedrooms Tea and coffee making facilities Direct dial from bedrooms No dogs (ex guide dogs) Licensed Cen ht CTV 23P No coaches Last d 7.45pm
ROOMS: s £25-£48; d £38-£62*
CARDS:

MORWENSTOW Cornwall & Isles of Scilly Map **02** SS21

Selected

Q Q Q Q **Darwood Country Guest House** Darwood, Shop EX23 9SL (at village shop, fork left passing Community Centre on left and follow grass bank to gate) ☎ 01288 331210
Peacefully located on the edge of the hamlet of Shop, Darwood is a charming home. The spacious bedrooms are comfortable and well appointed. Good home cooking, using the best of local produce, is

served, with evening meals available by prior arrangement. An ideal base for many local attractions, including the Coastal Footpath. The gardens are particularly pleasant.
2 bth (1 fmly) No smoking CTV in all bedrooms Tea and coffee making facilities No dogs Cen ht No children 11yrs 12P No coaches Last d 3pm
ROOMS: d £35-£40; wkly b&b £115.50-£126.50; wkly hlf-bd £203-£213.50*

MUCH BIRCH Herefordshire Map 03 SO53

Selected

Q Q Q Q **Oaklands House** Cross Collar, Llandinabo HR2 8JA (A49 from Hereford to Ross-on-Wye, 0.5m S of Axe & Cleaver Pub at Much Birch on right. A49 from Ross-on-Wye, 0.5 N of B4348 on left)
☎ 01981 540500
Feb-Oct
Situated exactly halfway between Ross-on-Wye and Hereford, this former Victorian staging post has been renovated to provide comfortable accommodation. The pretty bedrooms are modern in style and there is an attractive dining room and a choice of sitting rooms. Jenny Bishop ensures that a visit to Oaklands House is a happy and memorable one.
5 bth/shr No smoking in bedrooms No smoking in dining room No smoking in 1 lounge Tea and coffee making facilities Cen ht CTV 6P No coaches
ROOMS: d £40; wkly b&b £126*

MUCH WENLOCK Shropshire Map 07 SO69

Q Q Q ◀ ***The Plume of Feathers Inn*** Harley SY5 6LP (on A458, 1.5m on Shrewsbury side of Much Wenlock)
☎ 01952 727360 FAX 01952 727360
Dating back to the 17th century, this popular privately-owned hostelry stands on the A458 at Harley and is an ideal base for exploring Shrewsbury and the surrounding area. The bedrooms are well maintained and equipped. A wide choice of food is offered in the atmospheric bar or the spacious restaurant; there is a beer garden and a children's play area.
9 bth/shr (3 fmly) No smoking in bedrooms No smoking in dining room CTV in all bedrooms Tea and coffee making facilities No dogs (ex guide dogs) Cen ht 76P Last d 9.30pm
CARDS:

MUKER North Yorkshire Map 07 SD99

Q Q Q **Oxnop Hall** *(SD931973)* Low Oxnop, Gunnerside DL11 6JJ (off B6270 between the villages Muker and Gunnerside)
☎ 01748 886253 FAX 01748 886253 Mrs A Porter
Closed Xmas
Surrounded by breathtaking Swaledale scenery, this lovely 17th-century farmhouse has been furnished with thought and care. The prettily decorated bedrooms are well equipped and the attractive lounge is comfortable. Good home cooking, using local produce where possible, is served and the service is attentive and friendly.
5 bth/shr 1 annexe shr (1 fmly) No smoking CTV in 3 bedrooms Tea and coffee making facilities No dogs (ex guide dogs) Licensed Cen ht CTV No children 7yrs 10P 1000 acres beef sheep hill farming Last d 6.30pm
ROOMS: s £23-£24; d £46-£48; wkly b&b £154-£163; wkly hlf-bd £252-£261*

MUNGRISDALE Cumbria Map 11 NY33

Q Q Q ◀ **The Mill Inn** CA11 0XR (M6 junct 40 Penrith follow A66 Keswick, after 10 miles right to Mungrisdale. The Mill Inn is 2 miles down this road on left)
☎ 017687 79632 FAX 017687 79632
Closed 25 Dec
Located on the approach to the village, this charming 16th-century inn is set against a backdrop of woodland and is close to a tumbling steam. New proprietors are sympathetically refurbishing throughout to provide well-equipped, bright bedrooms. A wide range of dishes is provided in the popular restaurant and the atmospheric bar.
9 rms (7 bth/shr) (1 fmly) No smoking in bedrooms No smoking in dining room CTV in all bedrooms Tea and coffee making facilities Cen ht ch fac 30P Pool table Darts Last d 9pm
ROOMS: s £26-£28.50; d £59.90-£62.90; wkly b&b £149-£199*
MEALS: Lunch £11.90-£20.30alc Dinner £11.90-£20.30alc*
CARDS:

NANTWICH Cheshire Map 07 SJ65

See also Wybunbury

Premier Selected

Q Q Q Q Q **The Limes** 5 Park Rd CW5 7AQ (M6 junct 16 follow signs for Nantwich and Stapeley Water Gdns, cont into Nantwich, then follow signs for A530 Whitchurch.)
☎ 01270 624081 0402 332122 FAX 01270 624081
Lying in a quiet residential area not far from the town centre, this impressive Victorian house is impeccably maintained and has a warm and friendly atmosphere. The spacious bedrooms are well equipped; one has a four-poster bed. The lounge is elegantly furnished and breakfast is taken in a delightful dining room. The house is surrounded by pleasant gardens.
3 bth/shr No smoking CTV in all bedrooms Tea and coffee making facilities No dogs (ex guide dogs) Cen ht CTV No children 10yrs 3P No coaches
ROOMS: s £36-£40; d £40-£50; wkly b&b fr £200*

Premier Selected

Q Q Q Q Q **Oakland House** 252 Newcastle Rd, Blakelow, Shavington CW5 7ET (on A500 5m from M6 at junc 16 and 2m from Nantwich) ☎ 01270 567134 FAX 01270 651752
Conveniently situated near the M6 motorway, Oakland House has a friendly and relaxing atmosphere. The bedrooms are attractivley furnished and some are located in an adjacent building; one is suitable for families. There is a spacious and comfortably furnished sitting room and a modern conservatory overlooking the pretty rear garden. Hearty breakfasts are served.
3 shr 2 annexe bth/shr (1 fmly) No smoking in bedrooms No smoking in dining room No smoking in lounges CTV in all bedrooms Tea and coffee making facilities No dogs (ex guide dogs) Cen ht CTV No children 12yrs 10P No coaches
ROOMS: s £28-£32; d £35-£39*
CARDS:

NAYLAND Suffolk Map **05** TL93

Q Q Q **Hill House** Gravel Hill CO6 4JB (Enter village from A134 into Bear Street, continue past T junction into Birch Street, Gravel Hill is 100yds on left. Hill House is 50yds on right) ☎ 01206 262782
Closed 23 Dec-1 Jan
Situated in a peaceful village in the heart of Constable Country, this charming Grade II listed house is close to both the Stour Valley walk and the Essex Way. Two bedrooms have private facilities and overlook the pretty garden. A log fire burns in the elegant lounge in the winter months. A traditional breakfast is served and there are good local eating places serving evening meals nearby.
2 bth/shr (1 fmly) No smoking CTV in all bedrooms Tea and coffee making facilities No dogs Cen ht No children 9yrs 3P No coaches Croquet
ROOMS: s £22-£25; d £40-£44; wkly b&b £130-£150*

NEAR SAWREY Cumbria Map **07** SD39

Q Q Q **Beechmount Country House** LA22 0JZ (from Hawkshead take B5285 for 2m to sign for 'Near Sawrey'- house opposite) ☎ 015394 36356
Set in a village famous for its connections with the author, Beatrix Potter, this traditional Edwardian house features an interesting mix of period styles. There is an inviting lounge and dining room with board games and masses of books and magazines. Two bedrooms are spacious, and the smaller one has a private bathroom along the corridor.
3 bth/shr (1 fmly) No smoking in 1 bedrooms No smoking in dining room No smoking in lounges CTV in all bedrooms Tea and coffee making facilities Cen ht CTV 5P No coaches

Q Q Q **Buckle Yeat** LA22 0LF
(from M6 junct 36 proceed to Windermere and follow signs for Hawkshead via Ferry. Premises are located in the second village)
☎ 015394 36446 & 36538 FAX 015394 36446
Sitting next to Beatrix Potter's home Hill Top, this charming 200-year-old cottage is mentioned in her Tale of Tom Kitten. Still retaining much of its original character, despite the modern furniture in the bedrooms, the residents' lounge is most pleasant, while the beamed dining room, featuring a superb old cooking range, also doubles as a tea room. There is a small gift shop.
7 bth/shr (1 fmly) No smoking in bedrooms No smoking in dining room CTV in all bedrooms Tea and coffee making facilities Cen ht CTV 9P No coaches
ROOMS: s £25-£28; d £50-£56; wkly b&b £165-£175
CARDS:

Premier Selected

Q Q Q Q Q **Ees Wyke Country House** LA22 0JZ (1.5m outside Hawkshead on B5285. On the road to the ferry across Windermere)
☎ 015394 36393 FAX 015394 36393
Mar-Dec

Once a holiday home of Beatrix Potter, this fine Georgian country house has stunning views. Both John and Margaret Williams are super hosts and their care creates a friendly and relaxing atmosphere. Comfortable lounges and a spacious dining room set the scene for John's delightful five-course dinners. Breakfast offers a good selection of dishes which depend on local produce.
8 bth/shr No smoking in dining room CTV in all bedrooms Tea and coffee making facilities Licensed Cen ht No children 10yrs 12P No coaches Last d 7.15pm
ROOMS: s £56-£68; d £112-£116; wkly hlf-bd £385*

See advertisement under HAWKSHEAD

Selected

Q Q Q Q **Garth Country House** LA22 0JZ (from Hawshead village follow rd signposted Ferry. After 2 miles take first on the right the Garth is facing you) ☎ 015394 36373 FAX 015394 36373
Just a short walk from the village, this attractive Victorian residence is set in pleasant grounds. The new proprietors are ringing the changes with a complete and tasteful refurbishment of the house. The opulent lounge features deep modern sofas, whilst the attractive dining room is bright and cheery. The bedrooms are richly decorated and those at the rear of the house have delightful views over Esthwaite Water.
7 bth/shr (2 fmly) No smoking in bedrooms No smoking in dining room CTV in all bedrooms Tea and coffee making facilities Cen ht 12P No coaches
ROOMS: s £26-£35; d £50-£70; wkly b&b £150-£210
CARDS:

Q Q Q **High Green Gate** LA22 0LF (on B5285 between Bowness & Hawkshead via ferry) ☎ 015394 36296
Apr-Oct
Located just a stone's throw from Beatrix Potter's former home, this converted 18th-century farmhouse offers afternoon or evening tea in the pleasant garden or in one of the cosy lounges. Extra services are offered, such as morning tea in your room at a modest cost. Dinner and breakfast are served in the beamed dining room.
5 rms (1 bth 2 shr) (4 fmly) No smoking in dining room Tea and coffee making facilities Cen ht CTV 7P Last d 6pm
ROOMS: s £25-£28; d £44-£50; wkly b&b £154-£175; wkly hlf-bd £199-£220

Selected

Q Q Q Q **Sawrey House Country Hotel** LA22 0LF
(in village on B5285) ☎ 015394 36387 FAX 015394 36010
Closed Jan rs Nov-Feb (weekends only)
Shirley and Colin Whiteside offer a friendly welcome to their home, which is just a few minutes' walk from Beatrix Potter's former home.

Many of the comfortable bedrooms have views of Esthwaite Water and the charming lounges offer deep sofas to relax in. There are wonderful views from the restaurant, where a five-course dinner is served in spacious surroundings. Breakfast is a substantial affair.

11 bth/shr (2 fmly) No smoking in bedrooms No smoking in dining room No smoking in 1 lounge CTV in all bedrooms Tea and coffee making facilities Direct dial from bedrooms Licensed Cen ht 15P No coaches Fishing Last d 8pm
ROOMS: s £42; d £84-£106; wkly b&b £255-£330; wkly hlf-bd £350-£440*
CARDS:

NEATISHEAD Norfolk Map **09** TG32

QQQ **Regency** The Street NR12 8AD (Neatishead is 1m off the A1151 situated betwen Wroxham and Stalham)
☎ 01692 630233
Originally built in 1786, this attractive house is situated in the centre of a picturesque village set in the heart of the Norfolk Broads. The proprietors provide a warm welcome and pleasant accommodation. Pretty decor enhances the bedrooms and some have delightful views over the colourful rear garden. A quiet sitting room is available and light suppers can be served by prior arrangement.
5 rms (2 bth 1 shr) (1 fmly) No smoking in dining room No smoking in lounges CTV in all bedrooms Tea and coffee making facilities ch fac 6P No coaches
ROOMS: s £22-£29; d £40-£46*
CARDS:

NEEDHAM MARKET Suffolk Map **05** TM05

Selected

QQQQ **Pipps Ford** *(TM109537)* Norwich Rd rdbt IP6 8LJ (entrance off roundabout junct A14/A140)
☎ 01449 760208 FAX 01449 760561 Mrs Hackett-Jones
Closed mid Dec-mid Jan
Surrounded by meadows, this delightful 16th-century farmhouse sits beside the River Gipping. The lovely conservatory breakfast room features real grapevines growing across the ceiling, while the comfortable lounge has an inglenook fireplace and the dining room serves imaginative home-cooked dinners. There is a choice of traditionally styled bedrooms in the main house or contemporary rooms in the barn conversion.
3 bth/shr 4 annexe bth/shr No smoking in bedrooms No smoking in dining room No smoking in 1 lounge Tea and coffee making facilities No dogs (ex guide dogs) Licensed Cen ht CTV No children 5yrs 12P Tennis (hard) Fishing 8 acres Last d 5pm
ROOMS: s £20-£45; d £45-£70; wkly b&b £157.50-£245; wkly hlf-bd £287-£374.50

NETLEY Hampshire Map **04** SU40

QQQ **La Casa Blanca** 48 Victoria Rd SO31 5DQ (Exit M27 at junct 8, follow Hamble Lane past Tescos, turn right for Netley, at T-junct in village, turn right, premises 100 metres on the right)
☎ 01703 453718 FAX 01703 453718
Closed 26 Dec-2 Jan
Close to the village centre, this friendly, family-run hotel has views of Southampton Water. The comfortable bedrooms are attractively decorated; there is a welcoming bar and the pleasant dining room serves well-produced food. The pretty garden and conservatory are popular with guests in the summer months.
9 bth/shr (3 fmly) No smoking in dining room CTV in all bedrooms Tea and coffee making facilities Direct dial from bedrooms No dogs (ex guide dogs) Licensed Cen ht CTV 9P No coaches Last d 8.30pm
ROOMS: s £26; d £48*
CARDS:

NETTLECOMBE Dorset Map **03** SY59

Selected

QQQQ **Marquis of Lorne** DT6 3SY (from Bridport head N on A3066, after 1.5m after mini-rdbt turn right, pass through village of West Milton go straight over at junc, premises up hill) ☎ 01308 485236 FAX 01308 485666
Set in beautiful Dorset countryside, this welcoming 16th-century inn enjoys lovely views. The bedrooms are attractively decorated and the traditional public areas retain much of their original character, with stone walls and exposed beams. There is a choice of two bars and a small games room; the garden offers a pleasing option in summer with a play area for children.
6 shr No smoking in area of dining room CTV in all bedrooms Tea and coffee making facilities Direct dial from bedrooms No dogs (ex guide dogs) Cen ht No children 10yrs 50P Last d 9.30pm
ROOMS: s £38; d £58; wkly b&b £170*
MEALS: Lunch £10-£17alc Dinner £10-£17alc*
CARDS:

NETTLETON Wiltshire Map **03** ST87

Selected

QQQQ **Fosse Farmhouse Country Hotel** Nettleton Shrub SN14 7NJ (off B4039, 1.5m past Castle Combe race circuit take 1st left at Gib Village for farm 1m on right)
☎ 01249 782286 FAX 01249 783066
Decorated in an individual and interesting traditional style, this fascinating 18th-century farmhouse is owned by Caron Cooper, a television cook and writer, who provides excellent food and hospitality. Set in the quiet Wiltshire countryside close to Castle Combe, the hotel has well-equipped bedrooms and an attractive guests' lounge. Enjoy a hearty English breakfast, a cream tea in the tearoom situated in the old stables or an excellent dinner in the dining room of the farmhouse.
2 bth/shr 3 annexe shr No smoking in 1 bedrooms No smoking in dining room CTV in all bedrooms Tea and coffee making facilities Licensed Cen ht 10P Golf 18 Last d 8.30pm
ROOMS: s £55-£65; d £80-£125; wkly b&b £350-£400; wkly hlf-bd £500-£600*
CARDS:

NEWARK-ON-TRENT Nottinghamshire Map **08** SK75

Q Q Q **Willow Tree** Front St, Barnby in the Willows NG24 2SA (4m from Newark off the A17) ☎ 01636 626613 FAX 01636 626060
rs 25 December
Dating back to the 17th century, this attractive village inn is a Grade II listed building and features an abundance of exposed timbers. Two of the bedrooms are reached via the rear courtyard and further accommodation is being constructed. A wide range of freshly-prepared snacks and meals is offered in either the bar or the adjacent restaurant.
2 shr 5 annexe shr (1 fmly) No smoking in bedrooms No smoking in dining room CTV in all bedrooms Tea and coffee making facilities Direct dial from bedrooms Cen ht 50P Last d 9.30pm
ROOMS: s £35-£45; d £45; wkly b&b £245; wkly hlf-bd £350
MEALS: Lunch £11.95-£14.95&alc
CARDS:

NEWBIGGIN-ON-LUNE Cumbria Map **12** NY70

Q Q Q **Low Lane House** CA17 4NB (situated off A685, 0.5m W of Newbiggin-on-Lune village towards Kelleth) ☎ 015396 23269
Apr-Sept
Offering a peaceful haven, this 17th-century farmhouse has been sympathetically restored to retain many original features, such as wood panelling and parquet flooring. The bedrooms are traditional in style and although none have washhand basins, the bathroom is nearby. The dining room is a fine place to enjoy well-produced cooking, whilst admiring the country views; a feature is the solid oak spice cupboard in one corner.
3 rms No smoking Tea and coffee making facilities No dogs (ex guide dogs) Licensed Cen ht CTV No children 8yrs 3P No coaches Last d noon
ROOMS: s fr £18; d fr £36

NEWBURY Berkshire Map **04** SU46

See also Lambourn

Selected

Q Q Q Q **Rookwood Farm House** Stockcross RG20 8JX (from B4000 take 1st right (signed Woodspeen), bear immediately left Rookwood Farm is 1st house on right) ☎ 01488 608676 FAX 01488 608676
Charlotte Digby offers a warm welcome to her delightful former farmhouse set in attractive gardens. The individually-designed rooms are thoughtfully equipped and guests can relax in front of the open fire in the lounge and enjoy a hearty breakfast around the communal dining table. The large outdoor heated pool is a real plus.
3 bth/shr (1 fmly) No smoking CTV in all bedrooms Tea and coffee making facilities Direct dial from bedrooms No dogs Cen ht 3P Outdoor swimming pool (heated)
ROOMS: s fr £45; d fr £60*
CARDS:

NEWBY BRIDGE Cumbria Map **07** SD38

Q Q Q **The Coach House** Hollow Oak LA12 8AD (2.5m W of Newby Bridge turn off A590 onto B5278 (signposted Cark) then immediately left into car park) ☎ 015395 31622
Just a few miles from Newby Bridge, this delightful converted coach house features a charming dining room which was formerly the stables and where the original beams and woodwork have been retained. There is a welcoming lounge and bright, cheery bedrooms which are furnished in contemporary style.
2 bth/shr No smoking Tea and coffee making facilities No dogs Cen ht CTV 3P No coaches
ROOMS: d £38-£42; wkly b&b £125-£140*

Selected

Q Q Q Q **Cobblestones** Causeway End LA12 8JW (turn right off A590 at Haverthwaite x-rds follow signs to Grizedale Forest Visitor Ctr after 0.5m at t-junc turn right establishment on left) ☎ 015395 31391 FAX 015395 31391
Set in attractive grounds, this delightful 16th-century farmhouse is a peaceful haven with views of the distant fells. Many original features, such as little cupboards set into thick stone walls, have been preserved. The welcoming lounge is a focal point and the owners make their guests feel very much at home; breakfast is served round one large table. The bedrooms feature stripped pine furniture.
3 shr No smoking Tea and coffee making facilities Licensed Cen ht CTV 10P No coaches Cycle hire Last d 4.30pm
ROOMS: s £32-£36; d £44-£52; wkly b&b £140-£175; wkly hlf-bd £227.50-£269.50

Selected

Q Q Q Q **Hill Crest** Brow Edge LA12 8QP (1m after Newby Bridge on the A590 turn left into Brow Edge Rd, premises 0.75m on the right) ☎ 015395 31766 FAX 015395 31986
Mar-Nov & 27 Dec-5th Jan
Jane Jenkinson offers a warm welcome to her family home, which overlooks the southern fells of the scenic Lake District. The thoughtfully-equipped bedrooms feature pine furniture, whilst the pleasant lounge doubles as a breakfast room. The breakfast menu makes good use of local produce and shows off Jane's professional catering training.
2 shr (1 fmly) No smoking CTV in 3 bedrooms Tea and coffee making facilities No dogs Cen ht CTV 4P No coaches Free use of health & fitness club
ROOMS: s £25-£30; d £40-£50; wkly b&b £126-£154*

Q Q Q **Lakes End** LA12 8ND (on A590 in Newby Bridge, premises 100mtr from junc with A592) ☎ 015395 31260 FAX 015395 31260
With new proprietors at the helm, this friendly roadside guest house offers a good standard of accommodation and well-appointed bathrooms in a peaceful woodland setting. Each bedroom has been thoughtfully decorated and tastefully furnished. Hearty Lakeland breakfasts are served in the traditional-style dining room.
4 bth/shr (2 fmly) No smoking CTV in all bedrooms Tea and coffee making facilities Licensed Cen ht CTV 7P No coaches
ROOMS: d £40-£43; wkly b&b £130-£140*

NEWCASTLE-UNDER-LYME Staffordshire Map **07** SJ84

Q Q Q **Clayhanger** 42 King St ST5 1HX (on A53, exit M6 junct 15/16) ☎ 01782 714428 FAX 01782 714428
Within walking distance of the town centre, this pleasant little guest house is also close to the New Victoria Theatre. The accommodation includes a ground-floor bedroom and a family-bedded room; there is a cottage-style breakfast room and a welcoming lounge.
13 rms (7 shr) (1 fmly) No smoking in bedrooms No smoking in dining room No smoking in 1 lounge CTV in all bedrooms Tea and coffee making facilities Cen ht 13P No coaches
ROOMS: s £20-£28*

Q Q **Durlston** Kimberley Rd, Cross Heath ST5 9EG (on north side of town on A34 opposite the Hanging Gate pub) ☎ 01782 611708 FAX 01782 639770
Personally-run by David and Angela Stott for the past decade, this guest house offers comfortable and well-maintained accommodation. Although dinner is not served, there is a licence and drinks can be taken in the

welcoming lounge. There are a number of eating places nearby. Access from the M6 is straightforward and the property is only 10 minutes from Keele University.
7 rms (2 fmly) No smoking in bedrooms No smoking in dining room CTV in all bedrooms Tea and coffee making facilities Licensed Cen ht CTV No coaches
ROOMS: s £19-£20; d £34-£35*
CARDS:

NEWCASTLE UPON TYNE Tyne & Wear Map **12** NZ26

Q Q Q **Chirton House Hotel** 46 Clifton Rd, Grainger Park Rd NE4 6XH (exit A1 at Newcastle West junct, take A186 for 2m, turn right at the General Hospital into Grainger Park Rd, turn left into Clifton Rd)
☎ 0191 273 0407 FAX 0191 273 0407
New and enthusiastic owners Joan Cattenach and Pam Turnbull are working hard to improve all aspects of this well proportioned semi-detached mansion located in a quiet residential area to the west of the town centre. Guests can enjoy many hotel style facilities whilst the quiet relaxing atmosphere of a country house is retained, thus it attracts business persons as well as tourists. Tasty breakfasts can be enjoyed in the newly expanded dining room and the well stocked residents bar offers an alternative to relaxing in the comfortable lounge.
11 rms (2 bth 3 shr) (3 fmly) No smoking in 1 bedrooms No smoking in dining room No smoking in 1 lounge CTV in all bedrooms Tea and coffee making facilities Licensed Cen ht CTV 12P No coaches Last d 5.30pm
ROOMS: s £25-£35; d £35-£45; wkly b&b £125-£155; wkly hlf-bd £195-£245*
CARDS:

Q Q ***The George Hotel*** 88 Osborne Rd, Jesmond NE2 2AP (on B1600 off A1058) ☎ 0191 281 4442 FAX 0191 281 8300
This friendly hotel offers a diverse mix of facilities, with a stylish bistro and bar lounge for residents and diners offering a cosy and comfortable environment, whilst well equipped bedrooms blend practical furnishings with cheery fabrics.
14 rms (10 bth/shr) (4 fmly) CTV in all bedrooms Tea and coffee making facilities Direct dial from bedrooms Cen ht CTV 9P Last d 4pm
CARDS:

NEWMARKET Suffolk

See **Kirtling**

NEWPORT See **WIGHT, ISLE OF**

NEWPORT Shropshire Map **07** SJ71

Q Q Q **Fox & Duck** Pave Ln TF10 9LQ (1.5m S of Newport)
☎ 01952 825580 FAX 01952 825580
Located in the village of Pave Lane, this privately-owned hostelry is near the Lilleshall National Sports Centre. The inn provides modern accommodation and offers a choice of bars, which serve wholesome bar meals. There is an oak-panelled function room, a large garden and a children's play area.
9 rms (7 bth/shr) (2 fmly) No smoking CTV in all bedrooms Tea and coffee making facilities No dogs (ex guide dogs) Cen ht 75P Last d 10pm
ROOMS: s £25-£30; d £35-£45.50
MEALS: Lunch £3.95-£7.95&alc Dinner £3.95-£9.95&alc
CARDS:

NEWPORT PAGNELL Buckinghamshire Map **04** SP84

Premier Selected

Q Q Q Q Q **The Limes** North Square MK16 8EP (M1 junc15 Newport Pagnell pass Aston Martin factory and at T junct right into High St 1st left onto North Sq 3rd house on right) ☎ 01908 617041 FAX 01908 217292
Located on the edge of town, this lovely property is set in attractive gardens which back onto the river. The bedrooms are stylishly decorated with great attention to detail. Breakfast is served round one large table in the traditional dining room and an evening meal is available on request. A log fire burns in the winter months in the relaxing sitting room.
3 bth/shr (1 fmly) No smoking in bedrooms No smoking in dining room CTV in all bedrooms Tea and coffee making facilities No dogs (ex guide dogs) Cen ht No children 8yrs
ROOMS: s £35-£40; d £55-£60; wkly b&b £220-£250; wkly hlf-bd £340-£370
CARDS:

NEWQUAY Cornwall & Isles of Scilly Map 02 SW86

See also Watergate Bay

Q Q Q **Aloha Hotel** 124 Henver Rd TR7 3EQ (located on the A3058, on the northern side of Newquay adjacent to the junction with B3276 to Padstow) ☎ 01637 878366

Located about a mile from the town centre and close to Porth Beach, this small, family-run hotel offers a friendly service. The bedrooms vary in size, some of which are purpose built and located on the ground floor. There is a comfortable lounge, a bar and a games room. If required, the three-course set dinner should be ordered each day at breakfast.

13 rms (7 shr) (5 fmly) No smoking in dining room No smoking in lounges CTV in all bedrooms Tea and coffee making facilities No dogs Licensed Cen ht CTV 14P Games room Pool table Darts Last d 6pm

ROOMS: s £14-£22; d £28-£44; wkly b&b £90-£135

CARDS:

Q Q Q ***Arundell Hotel*** Mount Wise TR7 2BS (from Bodmin A392, at roundabout follow Mount Wise sign, premises half way up Mount Wise on the right) ☎ 01637 872481 & 874105 FAX 01637 850001

Situated close to the town centre and beaches, this family-run hotel offers a wide variety of leisure facilities. Spacious public areas include a lounge bar with a dance floor and entertainment is laid on throughout the season; the games room has a pool table. Soundly appointed bedrooms are easily reached via a lift.

35 bth/shr (8 fmly) No smoking in dining room CTV in all bedrooms Tea and coffee making facilities Direct dial from bedrooms No dogs Licensed Lift Cen ht CTV 34P Indoor swimming pool (heated) Sauna Solarium Min-gym Pool room Last d 7pm

CARDS:

Q Q Q **Bon-Ami Hotel** 3 Trenance Ln TR7 2HX (A392 after Quintrell Downs turn right at rdbt at junct with A3075 continue on A392. Straight ahead at next rdbt and first right into Trenance Lane) ☎ 01637 874009

May-Sep

Easily accessible to the town centre, yet away from the bustle, the Bon-Ami is pleasantly situated opposite Trenance Boating Lake and Gardens. All the rooms are bright and airy with modern facilities and decorated with co-ordinated fabrics. Home-made dinners are served in the pretty dining room adjacent to an intimate bar and lounge.

10 shr No smoking in dining room CTV in all bedrooms Tea and coffee making facilities No dogs Licensed Cen ht CTV No children 9P No coaches Last d 5pm

ROOMS: s £18-£29.50; d £34-£57; wkly b&b £115-£165.50; wkly hlf-bd £140-£195.50*

CARDS:

Selected

Q Q Q Q **Colan Barton** *(SW867612)* Colan TR8 4NB (take A392 to Newquay. At hamlet of Mountjoy turn second right signposted Colan Church and follow track for a mile, white-washed house on left) ☎ 01637 874395 FAX 01637 881388 Mrs A Machin-Weaver

Apr-Sep

Situated in a tranquil location, this 17th-century former farmhouse has been carefully restored to retain many original features. Guests can stroll across the fields to the river, or just relax by the duck pond and enjoy the wildlife. Breakfasts are memorable, with home-produced free-range eggs, local sausages and bacon, home-made marmalade and local honey.

3 rms (1 shr) No smoking CTV in all bedrooms Tea and coffee making facilities No dogs Cen ht 5P 11 acres horses chickens geese ducks

ROOMS: s £15-£20; d £30-£44*

Q Q Q ***Copper Beech Hotel*** 70 Edgcumbe Av TR7 2NN (follow main rd for bowling green, tennis courts at Trenance Leisure Park) ☎ 01637 873376

Etr-mid Oct & Xmas & New Year

Situated in a peaceful area of the town opposite Trenance Gardens, this family-run hotel is set amidst gardens. Bedrooms are light and airy, some of which are on the ground floor. The spacious bar lounge opens onto a sunny paved area and there is a relaxing lounge. Well-produced food is served in the dining room.

14 bth/shr (3 fmly) No smoking in dining room CTV in all bedrooms Tea and coffee making facilities No dogs (ex guide dogs) Licensed Cen ht CTV 14P Last d 6pm

Selected

Q Q Q Q ***Degembris*** *(SW852568)* Newlyn East TR8 5HY (from A30 turn left for Summercourt village, at crossroads turn right towards Newquay on A3058, take third left to St Newlyn East, turn second right) ☎ 01872 510555 FAX 01872 510230 Mrs K Woodley

Closed Xmas

This farmhouse, part of 165 acres of arable farmland, was built in the 18th century and retains much of its original character. The bedrooms are tastefully decorated, with co-ordinated soft furnishings and pine furniture. In the evening delightful four course meals are served, using fresh local ingredients. There is a comfortable lounge with a TV, and a selection of books and games. Guests can also enjoy the well tended garden, with its views of the local countryside.

5 rms (3 bth/shr) (2 fmly) No smoking CTV in all bedrooms Tea and coffee making facilities No dogs Cen ht CTV 8P Farm trail 165 acres arable Last d 10am

CARDS:

Q Q Q **Hotel Trevalsa** Whipsiderry Beach, Watergate Rd, Porth TR7 3LX (turn off A30 onto A392 follow signs for Porth Beach drive 500 metres up hill, premises is immediately on right) ☎ 01637 873336 FAX 01637 878843

Etr-31 Oct

Overlooking Porth Beach, and within a minute's walk of Whipsiderry Beach, this hotel offers spacious public areas - there is an informal bar where snacks are available, a separate lounge and an additional games room for children. Bedroom sizes vary; some have stunning sea views and some have four-poster beds. One even has its own private entrance and is conveniently located on the ground floor.

24 rms (20 bth/shr) (7 fmly) No smoking in 2 bedrooms No smoking in dining room No smoking in 1 lounge CTV in all bedrooms Tea and coffee making facilities Direct dial from bedrooms Licensed Cen ht CTV 20P Last d 7pm

ROOMS: (incl. dinner) s £22-£36*

CARDS:

Selected

Q Q Q Q ***Kellsboro Hotel*** 12 Henver Rd TR7 3BJ ☎ 01637 874620

Etr-Oct

This popular holiday hotel has been run successfully for the past twenty six years by the Matthews family. It is a spacious and airy hotel with well equipped bedrooms and bathrooms. There is an indoor swimming pool and pretty gardens. Good home-made food is served at dinner in the large and attractive dining room, adjoining the popular residents' bar.

14 bth/shr (8 fmly) No smoking in dining room CTV in all bedrooms Tea and coffee making facilities Licensed Cen ht CTV 20P Indoor swimming pool (heated) Pool table Last d 7pm

CARDS:

Q Q Q **Links Hotel** Headland Rd TR7 1HN ☎ 01637 873211
Jan-Oct rs Nov-Dec
The Links is situated midway between the famous Fistal Beach and the town centre and overlooks the golf course. Now run by Mr and Mrs Newton Jr, who offer guests a warm welcome. The dining room is large and sunny and the well equipped bar offers satellite TV. The bedrooms are tastefully decorated and well maintained, some rooms having fine views of the sea and golf course. Several of the rooms are suitable for families.
15 rms (10 bth 3 shr) (3 fmly) CTV in all bedrooms Tea and coffee making facilities No dogs (ex guide dogs) Licensed Cen ht CTV
ROOMS: s £22-£26; d £38-£46; wkly b&b £133-£161

Selected

Q Q Q Q **Manuels** *(SW839601)* Quintrell Downs TR8 4NY (Turn off A30 onto A392 continue to Quintrell Downs, farm signposted on A392 0.5m after Quintrell Downs rdbt approaching Newquay)
☎ 01637 873577 FAX 01637 873577 Mrs J C Wilson
Closed 23 Dec-1 Jan
Situated in a sheltered valley, just two miles from Newquay, this delightful 17th-century farmhouse has charming gardens. Subtle fabrics, dried flowers and quality furnishings feature in the stylish bedrooms. In the dining room, with its huge inglenook fireplace, guests gather around a large antique table for the traditional farmhouse breakfast; evening meals are available by prior arrangement. Children can help bottle feed the calves, collect the eggs and make friends with the ponies.
3 bth/shr (1 fmly) No smoking Tea and coffee making facilities No dogs (ex guide dogs) Cen ht CTV ch fac 6P Farm trail Pony rides Other Farm activities 100 acres mixed
ROOMS: s £18.50-£22; d £37-£44*

Selected

Q Q Q Q **Pendeen Hotel** Alexandra Rd, Porth TR7 3ND (turn off A3058 onto B3276 coastal road, premises located 0.25m on the right)
☎ 01637 873521 FAX 01637 873521
Closed Nov-Feb
Diana and Derek Woodfinden welcome you to their family run hotel, which enjoys fine views over Porth Beach. At dinner, a wide selection of freshly prepared dishes is available in the airy dining room. Light lunches and snacks are also available, served on the terrace. Bedrooms are tastefully decorated, many have excellent views, and three of the rooms are located on the ground floor.
15 bth/shr (3 fmly) No smoking in 10 bedrooms No smoking in dining room CTV in all bedrooms Tea and coffee making facilities No dogs (ex guide dogs) Licensed Cen ht 15P No coaches
Last d 6.30pm
ROOMS: s £21.50-£27; d £40-£50; wkly b&b £125-£165; wkly hlf-bd £149-£199*
CARDS: MasterCard American Express Visa

Selected

Q Q Q Q **Porth Enodoc** 4 Esplanade Rd, Pentire TR7 1PY
☎ 01637 872372 FAX 878219
Mar-Oct
Situated on the Esplanade, convenient for both shops and beaches. Many of the bedrooms, which are furnished to a high standard and offer a full range of modern comforts and facilities, enjoy stunning views across the bay. The spacious and comfortable lounge and elegant dining room also benefit from sea views.

12 shr (3 fmly) No smoking in bedrooms No smoking in dining room CTV in all bedrooms Tea and coffee making facilities No dogs Licensed Cen ht 12P No coaches Last d 6.45pm
ROOMS: s £18.50-£25.50; d £37-£51; wkly hlf-bd £153-£200*

Selected

Q Q Q Q **Priory Lodge Hotel** Mount Wise TR7 2BN (turn left at traffic lights in town centre on to the one way system & Berry Rd, right on to Mount Wise B3282 hotel is approx 0.5m on right) ☎ 01637 874111 FAX 01637 851803
Closed 11-22 Dec, 4 Jan-12 Feb rs Nov-Dec
Conveniently situated within walking distance of the town centre and enjoying splendid views of Towan Beach and Island. All the rooms are tastefully decorated and well maintained; some have balconies and some are suitable for families. Four of the rooms are located around the swimming pool at the rear of the hotel. There is a comfortable and well stocked bar where entertainment takes place on most evenings during the season. In the evening a good choice of freshly prepared dishes is offered in the wood-panelled dining room.
22 rms (7 bth 13 shr) 4 annexe shr (13 fmly) No smoking in dining room CTV in all bedrooms Tea and coffee making facilities Direct dial from bedrooms No dogs (ex guide dogs) Licensed Cen ht ch fac 30P Outdoor swimming pool (heated) Sauna Solarium Pool table Video machines Last d 7.30pm
ROOMS: s £20-£28; d £40-£56; wkly b&b £140-£196; wkly hlf-bd £175-£240
CARDS: MasterCard American Express Visa

QQQ *Rolling Waves* Alexandra Rd, Porth TR7 3NB (off A30 & join A3059 then onto B3276 into Porth) ☎ 01637 873236
22 May-23 Sep
The Rolling Waves is situated in a quiet area of Newquay within easy reach of the town centre. It enjoys a superb position overlooking Porth Beach. This establishment is personally run by Angela Pearson who offers her guests a warm and friendly welcome. The lounge and dining room are bright, airy, and have delightful views. The bedrooms are all tastefully decorated and equipped with all modern facilities, some situated on the ground floor.
9 rms (8 shr) (2 fmly) No smoking in bedrooms No smoking in dining room No smoking in lounges CTV in all bedrooms Tea and coffee making facilities Licensed Cen ht CTV 10P Last d 6.30pm
CARDS:

QQQ **Tir Chonaill Lodge** 106 Mount Wise TR7 1QP (Mount Wise is signposted from both boating lake rdbts on entering Newquay. The hotel is on the Mount Wise one-way system right above town centre)
☎ 01637 876492 FAX 01637 852676
Conveniently situated close to the town centre and beaches, this hotel offers true Celtic hospitality and service. Mr Watts is a chef, and prides himself on his cuisine. The bedrooms are decorated and furnished to a high standard.
22 rms (21 bth/shr) (10 fmly) No smoking in 2 bedrooms No smoking in dining room CTV in all bedrooms Tea and coffee making facilities Licensed Cen ht CTV 21P Darts Pool table Last d 5pm
ROOMS: s £18.50-£28.50; d £35-£54; wkly b&b £130-£160; wkly hlf-bd £154-£205✳
CARDS:

Selected

QQQQ **Towan Beach Hotel** 7 Trebarwith Crescent TR7 1DX (turn left off the one way system by the side of the main bus station, premises 200 yards on the right) ☎ 01637 872093 FAX 01637 872093
Etr-Nov
Situated in a quiet street, but close to the shops, beach and town centre, Anthony Baker and Andrew Medhurst have decorated and furnished this small hotel to a high standard. The bedrooms are comfortable and vary in size, some with their own en-suite facilities. There is a delightful lounge and small conservatory bar leading to a pretty garden.
6 rms (4 shr) (1 fmly) No smoking in dining room CTV in all bedrooms Tea and coffee making facilities No dogs Licensed Cen ht CTV No coaches Last d before lunchtime
ROOMS: s £17.50-£20; d £35-£40; wkly b&b £110-£120; wkly hlf-bd £155-£170✳
CARDS:

QQQ *Wheal Treasure Hotel* 72 Edgcumbe Av TR7 2NN
☎ 01637 874136
Apr-mid Oct
Situated in its own award-winning grounds in the delightful Trenance Valley, Wheal Treasure is owned and run by Mr and Mrs Franks. Each of the neatly furnished and decorated bedrooms is well equipped, and the majority of rooms are on the first floor. Each evening a home cooked, freshly prepared meal is served in the non-smoking dining room, with the adjoining conservatory and bar/lounge being the ideal location for a relaxing drink.
12 rms (3 bth 8 shr) (3 fmly) Tea and coffee making facilities No dogs Licensed Cen ht CTV No children 3yrs 10P No coaches Last d 5pm

Selected

QQQQ **Windward Hotel** Alexandra Rd, Porth TR7 3NB (Approaching Newquay on the A3508, turn right onto B3276 Padstow road, hotel is 1m on right) ☎ 01637 873185 FAX 01637 852436
Etr-end Oct rs mid Feb-Etr
The Windward Hotel enjoys panoramic views of Porth Beach and is personally run by Carole Sparrow who has created a relaxed and friendly atmosphere here. Bedrooms are light and airy, each is tastefully decorated and enhanced with pretty floral friezes. A good choice is offered on the menu at both breakfast and dinner and served in the attractive dining room, many of the dishes are home-made from fresh local ingredients.
14 bth/shr (3 fmly) No smoking in 2 bedrooms No smoking in dining room CTV in all bedrooms Tea and coffee making facilities No dogs (ex guide dogs) Licensed Cen ht CTV 14P Last d 6.30pm
ROOMS: s £29-£32; d £46-£52; wkly b&b £116-£170; wkly hlf-bd £165-£219✳
CARDS:

NEWTON ABBOT Devon Map 03 SX87

Selected

QQQQ *The Barn Owl* Aller Rd, Kingskerswell TQ12 5AN (turn off A380 at signpost for Aller Mills)
☎ 01803 872130 FAX 01803 875279
Closed 25-27 Dec
This 16th century former farmhouse is full of character and charm with beams, flagstone floors and exposed rustic stone walls. Each of three inter-connecting bars has either a log fire, a wood-burning stove or an inglenook fire place; the largest room has wood panelling and an ornate plaster ceiling. An extensive range of meals is offered from either the bar menu which includes salads, grills and sandwiches or on the speciality blackboards. In the restaurant an imaginative à la carte menu is offered and available six nights a week and for Sunday lunch. The bedrooms are all individually decorated and well equipped.
6 bth/shr CTV in all bedrooms Tea and coffee making facilities Direct dial from bedrooms No dogs Cen ht No children 14yrs 45P No coaches Last d 9.30pm
CARDS:

Q Q Q **Bulleigh Park** *(SX860660)* Ipplepen TQ12 5UA (turn off A381 for Compton at Jet garage follow for approx 1m. Signposted)
☎ 01803 872254 Mrs A Dallyn
Closed Christmas
This delightful family run farm, peacefully set down a quiet country lane, is only a short drive form Newton Abbot and is close to Compton Castle. The house is spacious and comfortable, and benefits from a lounge with an open fireplace, and a dining room which overlooks the countryside. Two en suite bedrooms are located in the main house and are well equipped with personal touches to ensure guests comfort. A family suite in an adjacent cottage is also let on a self-catering basis.
2 rms (1 shr) 1 annexe shr No smoking in bedrooms No smoking in dining room CTV in all bedrooms Tea and coffee making facilities No dogs (ex guide dogs) Cen ht CTV 6P Stabling available for own horse 60 acres beef ponies

NEWTON-LE-WILLOWS Merseyside Map 07 SJ59

Q Q Q **Pied Bull Hotel** 54 High St WA12 9SH (from M6 junct 23, follow A49 S and hotel is located in the centre of town)
☎ 01925 224549 FAX 291929
New owners are steadily upgrading this large inn, situated in the main street of the town. Bedrooms are neatly decorated, those in the adjacent cottage tending to be somewhat larger. There is a spacious lounge bar, popular with locals as well as visitors, and a range of snacks is offered in addition to the extensive menu served in the refurbished restaurant.
18 rms (10 bth 4 shr) No smoking in dining room CTV in all bedrooms Tea and coffee making facilities Direct dial from bedrooms No dogs (ex guide dogs) Cen ht 30P Last d 10pm
ROOMS: s £39.95-£44.25; d £50-£65
MEALS: Bar Lunch £1.95-£10.25alc Dinner £10.95-£14.95&alc
CARDS:

NITON See WIGHT, ISLE OF

NORTHALLERTON North Yorkshire Map 08 SE39

Q Q Q **Windsor** 56 South Pde DL7 8SL
(on A684 at southern end of High Street) ☎ 01609 774100
Closed 24 Dec-2 Jan
This attractively furnished Victorian house is conveniently located within easy walking distance of the town. It provides very pleasant and spotlessly clean bedrooms together with a cosy residents' lounge. Mrs Peacock, the resident owner, is very friendly and caring.
6 rms (3 shr) (1 fmly) No smoking in bedrooms No smoking in dining room CTV in all bedrooms Tea and coffee making facilities Cen ht CTV ch fac No coaches Last d 3pm
ROOMS: s £21-£27; d £35-£43; wkly b&b £122.50-£147; wkly hlf-bd £192.50-£217*
CARDS:

NORTHAMPTON Northamptonshire Map 04 SP76

Q **Hollington** 22 Abington Grove NN1 4QW
(1m from town centre on road to Kettering, take 1st right turn after White Elephant junct then 1st right again, premises opposite end of road)
☎ 01604 632584
Closed Xmas
This friendly guest house offers a warm welcome. The bedrooms though modestly furnished are attractive and well equipped featuring TVs and tea and coffee making facilities.
7 rms (2 fmly) No smoking in dining room CTV in all bedrooms Tea and coffee making facilities No dogs (ex guide dogs) Cen ht 7P No coaches
ROOMS: s £16-£20; d £35-£40*
CARDS:

Q Q Q **Poplars Hotel** Cross St, Moulton NN3 7RZ
(off A43 into Moulton Village and follow signs for Moulton College)
☎ 01604 643983 FAX 01604 790233
Closed Xmas wk
A long established hotel in the centre of Moulton village just north of Northampton. The Gillies family are great hosts and Peter is quick with a joke and a smile. All rooms are well furnished and comfortable, those in the new wing are particularly spacious. Home cooked meals are available most evenings and the cosy lounge features satellite TV.
18 rms (14 bth/shr) (7 fmly) No smoking in 14 bedrooms No smoking in area of dining room No smoking in 1 lounge CTV in all bedrooms Tea and coffee making facilities Direct dial from bedrooms Licensed Cen ht CTV 22P No coaches Last d 7.30pm
ROOMS: s £38-£45; d £50-£55*
CARDS:

Selected

Q Q Q Q **Quinton Green Farm** *(SP783532)* Quinton NN7 2EG (turn off A508 S of town, continue past Quinton village and farm is 1m on right) ☎ 01604 863685 FAX 01604 862230 Mrs M A Turney
Closed Christmas
This lovely stone built farmhouse dates back to the 17th century and is the hub of a farm of 1200 acres with a herd of 400 Friesian/Holstein cattle. Owner Mrs Turney is a charming host and her home is lovely. The three bedrooms are tastefully decorated and have smart modern en suite facilities. Breakfast is taken at a big dark wood refectory table, and there is a lounge featuring deep sofas and, in the winter months, a log fire.
3 bth/shr No smoking in dining room CTV in all bedrooms Tea and coffee making facilities Cen ht CTV 10P Snooker 1200 acres dairy arable
ROOMS: s £25-£27; d £45-£47*

NORTHLEACH Gloucestershire Map **04** SP11

Selected

Q Q Q Q **Cotteswold House** Market Place GL54 3EG (between Oxford and Cheltenham, off junction of A40/A429)
☎ 01451 860493 FAX 01451 860493
Closed 24 Dec-1 Jan
Situated on the edge of the market square, Cotteswold House, once the home of a prosperous merchant in Elizabethan times, retains much of its original character with oak beams, flagstone floors and panelling. Bedrooms are spacious, well equipped and offer modern en suite facilities. Elaine and Graham Whent are friendly and caring hosts, proud to welcome guests to their lovely home.
3 bth/shr No smoking CTV in all bedrooms Tea and coffee making facilities No dogs Cen ht No children 15yrs No coaches Last d 7pm
ROOMS: d £45-£75; wkly b&b £142-£220; wkly hlf-bd £246-£324*
CARDS:

Selected

Q Q Q Q **Northfield** Cirencester Rd GL54 3JL (just off A429 Northleach to Cirencester road, 1m from Northleach traffic lights. Well signed from main road) ☎ 01451 860427
Closed 23-27 Dec
Located just outside of the town this carefully maintained establishment has 12 acres of its own grounds with geese, chicken and sheep all kept by the owners. The bedrooms, two of which have external access, are comfortable and feature many thoughtful extra touches. In addition to a residents lounge, there is an attractive dining room which is the venue for some good home-cooking with an extensive menu on offer at dinner. There is plenty of private parking available.
2 shr 1 annexe shr (1 fmly) No smoking CTV in all bedrooms Tea and coffee making facilities No dogs Licensed Cen ht CTV 10P No coaches Last d 7pm
ROOMS: s £25; d £44-£50; wkly b&b £154-£175; wkly hlf-bd £224-£245*
CARDS:

NORTHLEW Devon Map **02** SX59

Selected

Q Q Q Q **East Worth Farmhouse** EX20 3PN (take Highhampton Road from Northlew Square, first right lane signposted 'Norley and Worth', follow for 1 mile, farmhouse is down lane to right)
☎ 01409 221757
This Grade II listed Devon longhouse, nestles in beautiful unspoilt countryside and is approached by narrow winding roads. Next to the farmhouse, which has preserved its oak beams and flagstone floors, stands a converted barn that houses two delightful bedrooms. Mary Hayes cooks with flair and imagination, and meals are served at a large table in the lounge, which has access to the lovely garden. A television can be provided but the focus of a stay here is on peace and relaxation.
2 annexe bth/shr No smoking in bedrooms No smoking in dining room No smoking in lounges Tea and coffee making facilities No dogs (ex guide dogs) Cen ht CTV No children 7yrs 3P No coaches
ROOMS: s fr £17; d fr £34; wkly b&b fr £119; wkly hlf-bd fr £196

NORTH WARNBOROUGH Hampshire Map **04** SU75

Q Q Q **The Jolly Miller** Hook Rd RG29 1ET
(from M3 junct 5 establishment is 2 minutes drive along the Alton Rd)
☎ 01256 702085 FAX 01256 704030
This friendly local pub has much to commend it, including a skittles alley and for the tasty home cooked meals served in an attractive room. In addition there is a good range of cask conditioned beers. Bedrooms are bright, airy and modern and some have en suite facilities.
9 rms (5 bth/shr) (1 fmly) No smoking in dining room CTV in all bedrooms Tea and coffee making facilities Direct dial from bedrooms No dogs (ex guide dogs) Cen ht CTV 60P Pool room Skittles
Last d 10.30pm
ROOMS: s £37-£47; d £47-£57*
CARDS:

NORTHWOOD Greater London Map **04** TQ09

Q Q **Frithwood House** 31 Frithwood Av HA6 3LY
(off Watford Rd past RAF & NATO Headquarters)
☎ 01923 827864 FAX 01923
A large detached Edwardian house very popular with guests from nearby NATO, yet situated in a quiet residential area. The modest but well maintained bedrooms continue to improve. Breakfast is served in the bright open plan kitchen/dining room around two large pine tables. Guests may also enjoy the peaceful and comfortably furnished lounge.
11 rms (1 bth 3 shr) (4 fmly) No smoking in bedrooms No smoking in dining room CTV in all bedrooms Direct dial from bedrooms No dogs (ex guide dogs) Cen ht CTV 10P
ROOMS: s £30-£36; d £50-£55; wkly b&b £210-£252*

NORTH WOOTTON Somerset Map **03** ST54

Q Q Q ***Barrow Farm** (ST553416)* BA4 4HL ☎ 01749 890245
Mrs M White
Closed Dec-Jan
Dating from the 15th century this stone built farmhouse is surrounded by beautiful open countryside. The bedrooms are neatly furnished and decorated, each equipped with beverage making trays and colour televisions. Two attractive sitting rooms are available and in the comfortable dining room guests can enjoy Mrs White's wholesome farmhouse food.
3 rms (1 fmly) No smoking in dining room No smoking in 1 lounge CTV in all bedrooms Tea and coffee making facilities No dogs CTV 4P 150 acres working dairy Last d 9am

Q Q Q **Greenacres** Barrow Ln BA4 4HL (A39 Wells-Glastonbury, turn at Browns gdn centre, follow campsite signs. A361 Shepton Mallet-Galstonbury, turn at Steanbow, follow campsite signs) ☎ 01749 890497
A modern chalet style bungalow, situated on a quiet country lane that offers uninterrupted views to Glastonbury Tor. Ros and David Harvie extend a warm welcome to their guests and invite them to enjoy the relaxed atmosphere of their family home. There are two brightly decorated bedrooms and the attractive sitting room and conservatory, where breakfast is served, overlook the garden.
2 bth/shr No smoking CTV in all bedrooms Tea and coffee making facilities No dogs (ex guide dogs) Cen ht CTV 4P No coaches
ROOMS: d £30-£40

The AA's professional Inspectors make regular and anonymous visits to all the establishments listed in the Guide. They accept no gifts or favours from proprietors

NORTON ST PHILIP Somerset Map **03** ST75

Premier Selected

Q Q Q Q Q **Bath Lodge Hotel** BA3 6NH (premises situated 7m S of Bath on the main A36 S of the junc with A366) ☎ 01225 723040 FAX 01225 723737

Built in 1806, this unique property stands in two acres of grounds. Careful restoration has resulted in tastefully decorated bedrooms of tremendous character. Original features have been cleverly incorporated; turrets double as circular shower rooms or breakfast rooms. Four-poster beds blend well with the battlements and heraldic shields to create a feeling of romance. Dinner is available on Friday and Saturday evenings.

6 bth/shr 2 annexe bth/shr (1 fmly) No smoking in bedrooms No smoking in area of dining room No smoking in lounges CTV in all bedrooms Tea and coffee making facilities Direct dial from bedrooms Licensed Cen ht No children 10yrs 25P No coaches Last d 4pm

ROOMS: s £40-£45; d £55-£95; wkly b&b £175-£260; wkly hlf-bd £280-£434

CARDS:

Premier Selected

Q Q Q Q Q **Monmouth Lodge** BA3 6LH (exit Bath on the A36, after 7m turn right onto the A366 to Norton St Philip)
☎ 01373 834367

Closed 20 Dec-2 Jan

Surrounded by lovely gardens with views to the Mendip Hills, this charming single-storey family home has been beautifully decorated and furnished to provide every modern comfort. The spacious lounge, with log fires on cooler evenings, is stylish and elegant. Some of the pleasant bedrooms have king-size beds, the largest of which opens onto the patio. Breakfast is served around the polished table. For dinner, there are several eating places nearby.

3 bth/shr (1 fmly) No smoking CTV in all bedrooms Tea and coffee making facilities No dogs Cen ht No children 5yrs 5P No coaches

ROOMS: s £50-£55; d £60-£65*

CARDS:

Selected

Q Q Q Q **The Plaine** BA3 6LE (from A36 Bath to Warminster Road turn right onto A366 signed Radstock, house at x-rds in village)
☎ 01373 834723 FAX 01373 834101

Closed Xmas/New Year

Dating from the 16th century, this charming family home is located in a peaceful village just 10 minutes' drive from Bath. The tastefully decorated bedrooms have four-poster beds and the welcoming lounge is most relaxing. Generous breakfasts are served around a large table in true family style.

3 bth/shr No smoking CTV in all bedrooms Tea and coffee making facilities No dogs (ex guide dogs) Cen ht No children 3yrs 6P No coaches

ROOMS: s £40-£45; d £48-£60

CARDS:

See advertisement under BATH

NORWICH Norfolk Map **05** TG20

See also Stoke Holy Cross

Q Q Q **Carr House** Low Rd, Strumpshaw NR13 4HT
(A47 Great Yarmouth to Brundall, through Brundall, follow signs for RSPB to Low Road. Take fourth turning on right into a by way system)
☎ 01603 713041

Backing onto the RSPB Strumpshaw Fen reserve, this charming property is popular with ornithologists. Margot Dunham is a delightful host and extends a warm welcome to her guests. A sympathetically designed extension has further enhanced the comfort of the guest rooms. Norwich is easily accessible by main road or by a regular bus service from the village.

3 bth/shr (1 fmly) No smoking in bedrooms No smoking in dining room CTV in all bedrooms Tea and coffee making facilities Direct dial from bedrooms Cen ht 6P No coaches Fishing Bird watching Fishing Walks Stables Boat hire

ROOMS: s £30; d £35-£45; wkly b&b £122.50

Q Q Q **Earlham** 147 Earlham Rd NR2 3RG
(from southern by-pass A47 take B1108 and follow signs City Centre. Over 2 rbts for guesthouse on left after Earlham House Shopping Centre)
☎ 01603 454169 FAX 01603 454169

Closed 23-26 Dec

Close to the city centre and the Roman Catholic cathedral, this Victorian house is owned and run by very committed owners, who offer a warm welcome to all their guests. The bedrooms vary in size but all are attractively decorated and lovingly cared for. There are plenty of local eating places for evening meals.

7 rms (2 shr) (1 fmly) No smoking CTV in all bedrooms Tea and coffee making facilities No dogs Cen ht CTV No children 5yrs No coaches

ROOMS: s £22-£36; d £38-£46; wkly b&b £147-£245

CARDS:

Selected

Q Q Q Q **Gables** 527 Earlham Rd NR4 7HN (Turn off Southern bypass onto B1108, follow signs to University of East Anglia, 300yds on left pass Fiveways roundabout, going towards city centre.)
☎ 01603 456666 FAX 01603 250320
Closed 20 Dec-1 Jan
Mr and Mrs Turner offer a warm welcome at this neatly appointed house, situated close to the city centre. The well equipped bedrooms are warm and comfortable with spacious, modern en suite facilities. The public rooms include a lounge, traditional dining room, conservatory where breakfast is served, and a snooker room with a full size table.
10 bth/shr (1 fmly) No smoking CTV in all bedrooms Tea and coffee making facilities Direct dial from bedrooms No dogs (ex guide dogs) Cen ht CTV 10P No coaches Snooker
ROOMS: s £35; d £50-£55✻
CARDS:

Q Q **Grange Hotel** 230 Thorpe Rd NR1 1TJ (from the by-pass A47 take A1042 for 2.5m through 2 sets traffic lights for hotel on right)
☎ 01603 434734 FAX 01603 434734
Closed 26-30 Dec
On the Yarmouth road, this large private hotel is especially popular with business guests. Evening meals can be taken in the bar or chosen from a daily changing menu in the dining room. The bedrooms tend to be functionally appointed, yet have a good range of facilities and the majority have en suite shower rooms.
35 bth/shr (1 fmly) No smoking in dining room CTV in all bedrooms Tea and coffee making facilities Direct dial from bedrooms Licensed Cen ht 40P Sauna Solarium Pool room Last d 9.30pm
ROOMS: s £37.50-£40; d £55-£60; wkly b&b £175-£210; wkly hlf-bd £245-£280
CARDS:

Q Q Q ***Hotel Belmonte*** 60-62 Prince of Wales Rd NR1 1LT
☎ 01603 622533 FAX 01603 760805
The Hotel Belmonte is conveniently situated close to the railway station and Norwich city centre and is therefore ideal for business people and commercial travellers. The bright, cheerful accommodation is thoughtfully furnished and well planned, all rooms have modern en suite facilities, some rooms have mini kitchens and are therefore generally more spacious. The bustling public areas include the 'Boss Hogg' American style restaurant and bar and a basement night club with live entertainment.
9 bth/shr CTV in all bedrooms Tea and coffee making facilities No dogs (ex guide dogs) Licensed Cen ht Last d 11pm
CARDS:

Q Q **Marlborough House Hotel** 22 Stracey Rd, Thorpe Rd NR1 1EZ (premises situated adjacent to Norwich railway station on A47 Thorpe to Yarmouth road) ☎ 01603 628005 FAX 01603 628005
This small private hotel is situated close to the railway station and football ground, just on the edge of Norwich city centre with its range of shops and amenities. It is popular with commercial travellers and business people and the bedrooms are soundly maintained although, they do vary in size. The public rooms feature an open plan lounge cum dining area with a corner bar. Dinner is available by prior arrangement.
12 rms (7 bth/shr) (2 fmly) No smoking in 3 bedrooms No smoking in area of dining room No smoking in 1 lounge CTV in all bedrooms Tea and coffee making facilities Licensed Cen ht CTV 10P Last d 4.30pm
ROOMS: s £22-£32; d £42-£50; wkly b&b £154-£224; wkly hlf-bd £210-£280

Q Q Q **Old Thorn Barn** Corporation Farm, Wymondham Rd, Hethel NR14 8EU (situated 6m S of Norwich and 3m E of Wymondham on B1135. Follow signs for Lotus cars from A11 or B1113)
☎ 01953 607785 FAX 01953 607785
Gina Pickwell offers a warm welcome to her delightful Grade II listed barn, which with her family she has recreated from cattle sheds and outbuildings in the grounds of the original farm. The spacious bedrooms are attractively decorated and well furnished. Breakfast is served in the long barn with its wood-burning stove and very comfortable dining and lounge area. Dinners are offered by arrangement, and in summer, the cobbled courtyard is a pleasant to relax in.
5 bth/shr No smoking CTV in all bedrooms Tea and coffee making facilities No dogs (ex guide dogs) Cen ht CTV 10P No coaches
ROOMS: s £29-£36; d £36-£42; wkly b&b £203-£252; wkly hlf-bd £259-£294✻

NOTTINGHAM Nottinghamshire Map 08 SK54

See also Ilkeston

Q Q **Fairhaven Private Hotel** 19 Meadow Rd, Beeston NG9 1JP (turn off B6005 for Beeston Railway Station, Hotel 200 yards after bridge)
☎ 0115 922 7509 FAX 9436217
Closed Xmas & NY
A well-established private hotel, situated in a quiet area of Beeston, where the new owners have started a programme of refurbishment. Public rooms include a spacious and comfortable lounge, with a small bar, and a traditionally furnished dining room to the rear. Bedrooms vary in style and sizes.
13 rms (1 bth 4 shr) (1 fmly) CTV in all bedrooms Tea and coffee making facilities Licensed Cen ht CTV 13P Last d 6pm
ROOMS: s £21-£27; d £32-£40✻

Q Q Q **Gallery Hotel** 8-10 Radcliffe Rd, West Bridgford NG2 5FW (on A52 20 min from junct 24 M1) ☎ 0115 981 3651 & 981 1346 FAX 0115 981 3732
Ideally situated for the cricket and football grounds, as well as the water sports centre, this popular guest house is run by Don Masson, a former international footballer, and his wife. Bedrooms are compact, but all offer attractive decor and are equipped to the same standard. Breakfast is served in the bright dining room and there is a bar as well as a homely visitors' lounge.
16 shr (3 fmly) No smoking in 10 bedrooms No smoking in dining room No smoking in lounges CTV in 15 bedrooms Tea and coffee making facilities No dogs (ex guide dogs) Licensed Cen ht CTV 35P Pool table
ROOMS: s £24-£32; d £40-£44✻
CARDS:

Q Q Q **Grantham Hotel** 24-26 Radcliffe Rd, West Bridgford NG2 5FW (follow signs for Nottingham South/Trent Bridge/National Water Sports Centre, hotel is 0.75km from E end of ring road A52)
☎ 0115 981 1373 FAX 0115 981 8567
Conveniently located just a mile from the city centre and within walking distance of Trent Bridge cricket ground, this guest house has been under the same ownership for over a quarter of a century. The comfortable lounge leads, via a cosy bar, to the bright dining room, where a selection of popular dishes and grills is available. Bedrooms, although not over large, are immaculate and carefully furnished.
22 rms (15 bth/shr) (2 fmly) No smoking in dining room CTV in all bedrooms Tea and coffee making facilities Licensed Cen ht CTV No children 3yrs 10P Last d 6.45pm
ROOMS: s £23-£30; d £40-£45; wkly b&b £140-£180; wkly hlf-bd £180-£220*
CARDS:

Selected

Q Q Q Q **Hall Farm House** *(SK679475)* Gonalston NG14 7JA (A612 towards Southwell then left into Gonalston. In 1.5m take 1st right in village)
☎ 0115 966 3112 FAX 0115 966 4844 Mrs A R Smith
Closed 20 Dec-2 Jan
In the small village of Gonalston this house can be found tucked away behind mature trees and shrubs. There is a heated outdoor swimming pool and tennis court to one side of a courtyard, plus a games room. Dinner is available by arrangement and can be served, around one large table in the beamed dining room or in the kitchen. Comfortable bedrooms, one of which is en suite, display a lot of character, as do the lounges.
4 rms (1 bth/shr) (1 fmly) No smoking CTV in 2 bedrooms Tea and coffee making facilities No dogs Cen ht CTV 5P Outdoor swimming pool (heated) Tennis (hard) Large playroom with piano and table tennis 22 acres sheep
ROOMS: s £20-£25; d £40-£45*

Q Q **P & J Hotel** 277-279 Derby Rd, Lenton NG7 2DP (on main Derby Rd A52, threequarters of a mile from the city centre)
☎ 0115 978 3998 FAX 0115 978 3998
rs 24-29 Dec
This popular guest house is located just a few minutes drive from the city centre. Bright furnishings are a feature of bedrooms that vary in shape and size. Snacks and simple evening meals are available and there is a comfortable bar/lounge with a pool table.
19 rms (9 shr) (8 fmly) No smoking in area of dining room No smoking in lounges CTV in all bedrooms Tea and coffee making facilities Licensed Cen ht CTV 15P No coaches Last d 7.30pm
CARDS:

Q Q Q ***Royston Hotel*** 326 Mansfield Rd, Sherwood NG5 2EF
☎ 0115 962 2947
One of a row of hotels just a mile from the city. The bedrooms are a good size, individually and comfortably furnished. The beds are inviting - made up with crisp starched co-ordinated fabrics and plump pillows. As well as a breakfast room there is a separate lounge.
8 rms (6 shr) 4 annexe shr (2 fmly) CTV in all bedrooms Tea and coffee making facilities No dogs (ex guide dogs) Cen ht CTV 16P
CARDS:

Q Q Q **St Andrews Private Hotel** 310 Queens Rd, Beeston NG9 1JA (Along A52 through 2 sets traffic lights then turn right to Beeston onto B6006, turn right at 4th set of lights onto Queens Rd, hotel 200m on right)
☎ 0115 925 4902 FAX 0115 925 4902
Bedroom sizes vary at this commercial hotel, but each is carefully maintained and attractively decorated using co-ordinated fabrics and wallcoverings. There is a comfortably furnished lounge and a home cooked set meal is offered.
10 rms (3 shr) (1 fmly) No smoking in 5 bedrooms No smoking in dining room CTV in all bedrooms Tea and coffee making facilities Cen ht CTV 6P No coaches Last d 1pm
ROOMS: s £21-£30; d £30-£40; wkly b&b £147-£210; wkly hlf-bd £206.50-£269.50

NUNEATON Warwickshire Map 04 SP39

Selected

Q Q Q Q **Leathermill Grange** Leathermill Ln, Caldecote CV10 0RX (from A5, take turning for Hartshill, at give way sign go under railway bridge follow road towards Nuneaton. Leathermill Ln 400yds on left) ☎ 01827 716094 & 716422 FAX 01827 716422
Closed 24-27 Dec & 2 wks annual holiday
Situated at the northernmost tip of the Neolithic Way in a peaceful rural setting, this impressive former farmhouse offers spacious and comfortable accommodation. Bedrooms are well equipped and all have the benefit of modern en suite shower rooms. Public areas include an elegant dining room, a sitting room with well-stocked bar and a conservatory extension overlooking the gardens. Jim Meacham is a friendly host.
4 bth/shr No smoking in dining room No smoking in 1 lounge CTV in all bedrooms Tea and coffee making facilities No dogs Licensed Cen ht CTV 30P No coaches Fishing Croquet Pool table Last d 6pm
ROOMS: s £30-£35; d £50-£55*
CARDS:

321

Q Q **La Tavola Calda** 68 & 70 Midland Rd CV11 5DY (through town centre take B4111 Atherstone/Coleshill rd for 0.5m)
☎ 01203 383195 & 381303 FAX 01203 381816
This friendly family owned and run Italian Trattoria provides well furnished bedrooms, with breakfast taken in a simple top floor dining room. The ground floor Italian restaurant offers guests a comprehensive choice of dishes at dinner.
8 bth/shr (2 fmly) CTV in all bedrooms Tea and coffee making facilities No dogs (ex guide dogs) Licensed Cen ht CTV 25P No coaches Last d 9.45pm
ROOMS: s £18-£20; d £32*
CARDS:

OAKAMOOR Staffordshire Map 07 SK04

Premier Selected

Q Q Q Q Q **Bank House** Farley Ln ST10 3BD (take B5417 from Cheadle, entering Oakamoor pass the church, then the pub, both on left, in 80yds turn right, Bank House is on right in ½ mile)
☎ 01538 702810 FAX 01538 702810
Closed Xmas week

contd.

Originally a farmhouse, this delightful property has been lovingly restored by John and Muriel Orme over many years. Bedrooms, one with four-poster, are spacious and well equipped and every conceivable luxury is provided. The comfort and well being of guests is the prime objective. An elegant drawing room is available and guests dine, family style with Muriel and John, in the dining room. Excellent meals are provided and the gardens are a joy to behold.
3 bth/shr (2 fmly) No smoking in bedrooms No smoking in dining room No smoking in 1 lounge CTV in all bedrooms Tea and coffee making facilities Direct dial from bedrooms Licensed Cen ht CTV 6P No coaches Last d 11am
ROOMS: s £43-£53; d £56-£76*
CARDS:

Selected

Q Q Q Q **Ribden Farm** *(SK075471)* Three Lows, Oakamoor ST10 3BW (on B5417 Cheadle/Ashbourne road, on right 0.5m before junction with A52)
☎ 01538 702830 & 702153 FAX 01538 702830 Mrs C Shaw
Mar-Nov
This Grade II listed, stone-built farmhouse dates back to 1748. Surrounded by the Staffordshire Moorlands it is located just two miles from Alton Towers theme park. The house has been extensively and tastefully modernised by friendly proprietors Chris and Peter Shaw, to provide well equipped, good quality accommodation, including family rooms and one room with a four-poster. There is a pine-furnished breakfast room and a cosy lounge. The gardens include a play area for children.
5 rms (4 shr) (1 fmly) No smoking in bedrooms No smoking in dining room CTV in all bedrooms Tea and coffee making facilities No dogs Cen ht CTV 6P 100 acres sheep
ROOMS: d £40-£46*
CARDS:

OAKFORD Devon Map **03** SS92

Selected

Q Q Q Q **Newhouse Farm** *(SS892228)* EX16 9JE (5m W of Bampton on B3227. Do not go into Oakford village) ☎ 01398 351347 Mrs A Boldry
Closed Xmas
Situated near Bampton, Newhouse Farm is a forty acre working sheep farm, set in undulating countryside. The friendly, informal atmosphere which is created by the owners, is complemented by the smart but rustic bedrooms equipped with all modern facilities and other little personal touches. Meals are taken around a large pine table.
2 bth (1 fmly) No smoking CTV in all bedrooms Tea and coffee making facilities No dogs Cen ht CTV No children 10yrs 3P Fishing 42 acres sheep Last d 4pm
ROOMS: s £20-£23; d £36-£42; wkly b&b fr £122; wkly hlf-bd fr £190

OAKHILL Somerset Map **03** ST64

Selected

Q Q Q Q **Oakhill House** Bath Rd BA3 5AQ (A367 from Bath, on entering village entrance to house is 75yds on right, drive through stone pillars to top of drive) ☎ 01749 840020 FAX 01749 840020
Closed 16-28 Dec

This substantial Grade II listed property, built in 1750, is surrounded by over three acres of parkland and is now home of the Spalding family. Three spacious bedrooms have been tastefully decorated and comfortably furnished and there is an attractive sitting room adjacent to the dining room where meals are served around one large table. Dinner is available by prior arrangement and the nearby village pub also serves food.
3 bth/shr No smoking CTV in all bedrooms No dogs (ex guide dogs) Cen ht CTV 20P No coaches
ROOMS: s £20-£25; d £40-£50*

OKEHAMPTON Devon Map **02** SX59

See also Holsworthy & Northlew

Q Q Q **Fairways Lodge** Thorndon Cross EX20 4NE (4m W, on A3079. On right hand side, before hump back bridge)
☎ 01837 52827 FAX 01837 52827
Etr-1 Jan
With stunning views over the local countryside, towards Dartmoor, guests are ensured of a warm welcome from Daphne and Andy Burgoine. On arrival the offer of a pot of tea and home made cakes should not be missed. One of the three bedrooms is on the ground floor and is suitable for the less able. Both breakfast and a delicious dinner, by prior arrangement, are taken around one large table in the dining room.
3 bth/shr (1 fmly) No smoking in 1 bedrooms No smoking in dining room CTV in 1 bedroom Tea and coffee making facilities Cen ht CTV 8P No coaches Tickets for Golf Cycle hire Horse riding Last d 6pm
ROOMS: s £19.50-£25; d £36; wkly b&b £136.50-£175; wkly hlf-bd £220.50-£259*

Selected

Q Q Q Q ***Heathfield House*** Klondyke Rd EX20 1EW (Okehampton Stn-under bridge 300yds up steep hill, through woods then straight ahead up drive into car park of hotel)
☎ 01837 54211 FAX 01837 54211
Closed 12 Dec-11 Jan
Once a Station Masters' house, Heathfield stands high above Okehampton with a vast expanse of Dartmoor National Park stretching out behind. Well kept bedrooms offer good standards of decoration and comfort. In addition to the residents' lounge there is a bright conservatory that overlooks the heated outdoor swimming pool. Scrumptious, home-cooked meals are served in the Victorian dining room, and dinner can fairly be described as the highlight of a stay here.
4 bth/shr (2 fmly) No smoking CTV in all bedrooms Tea and coffee making facilities Licensed Cen ht CTV ch fac 8P No coaches Outdoor swimming pool (heated) Table tennis Last d 7pm
CARDS:

Q Q Q *Luxridge (SX561932)* Hughslade Farm EX20 4LR (from town centre follow B3260 for 2m , past Petrol Station, bungalow on right)
☎ 01837 52883 Mrs K C Heard
Closed Xmas
With glorious views over the northern slopes of Dartmoor, Luxridge bungalow, part of Hughslade Farm is the home of the Heard family. Both bedrooms are light and airy, providing comfort and modern facilities. Mrs Heard has been welcoming guests for over 40 years and her naturally friendly approach encourages them to return year after year. Breakfast is served in the large conservatory.
2 bth/shr No smoking in dining room CTV in all bedrooms Tea and coffee making facilities Cen ht CTV 4P Snooker Games room Horse riding 600 acres mixed Last d 6pm

Selected

Pressland House Hatherleigh EX20 3LW
(A386 to Hatherleigh after 5.5 miles before reaching Hatherleigh Pressland House is on the right) ☎ 01837 810871
Mar-Nov
This impressive Victorian house, in over an acre of well tended grounds, is surrounded by open countryside. The bedrooms are spacious and have been tastefully decorated and equipped with modern facilities, two being on the ground floor and one with a four-poster. There is a choice of attractive lounges, one with a bar. Bett Cox's cooking uses the best local produce wherever possible.
4 bth 2 annexe shr No smoking CTV in all bedrooms Tea and coffee making facilities No dogs Licensed Cen ht No children 12yrs 10P No coaches Last d 6pm
ROOMS: s £27-£36; d £40-£58; wkly b&b £126-£182; wkly hlf-bd £220.50-£276.50✻

OLD SODBURY Gloucestershire Map 03 ST78

Premier Selected

The Sodbury House Hotel Badminton Rd BS37 6LU (M4 junct 18-A46 N for 2m, left at lights onto A432, hotel 1m on left. M5 junct 14-Wickwar, Chipping Sudbury, A432 towards A46, hotel 1.5m on right) (The Independents)
☎ 01454 312847 FAX 01454 273105
Closed 24 Dec-3 Jan rs Sundays
Hospitality abounds at this former farmhouse that dates back to the early 19th century. Now an hotel it stands in six acres of grounds and gardens, on the A432, on the western edge of the village. The comfortably furnished well equipped rooms in the house and adjacent buildings, and include bedrooms at ground floor level. There are many extras for guests comfort including hairdryers, trouser presses and in some room's mini bars. There is a pleasant lounge with comfortable seating, and where welcoming real fires burn during cold weather. The good choice of food at breakfast is served in the spacious, attractive breakfast room. Other facilities include a conference room for up to 25 delegates.
5 bth/shr 9 annexe rms (8 bth/shr) (2 fmly) No smoking in dining room CTV in all bedrooms Tea and coffee making facilities Direct dial from bedrooms Licensed Cen ht 20P No coaches Croquet Boules
ROOMS: s £45-£67.50; d £59-£88✻
CARDS:

OLNEY Buckinghamshire Map 04 SP85

Queen Hotel 40 Dartmouth Rd MK46 4BH
(on A509,situated in Olney town centre)
☎ 01234 711924 FAX 01234 711924
This attractive small hotel is smartly presented and shows a great deal of style. Owner Mr Neil Gregory is a charming host who enjoys making his guests feel at home. Bedrooms are a little compact but are tastefully furnished and well equipped.
4 rms (3 shr) 5 annexe shr No smoking in bedrooms CTV in all bedrooms Tea and coffee making facilities No dogs (ex guide dogs) Licensed Cen ht No children 9P No coaches
ROOMS: s £28-£33; d £40-£45✻
CARDS:

OSWESTRY Shropshire Map 07 SJ22

See also Llansilin (Powys)

Selected

Old Forge Knockin SY10 8HQ ☎ 01691 682394
FAX 01691 682423

(For full entry see **Knockin**)

Old Mill Inn The Candy SY10 9AZ
(from B5479 follow signs for Trefonen and Llansillin. After The Ashfield on right, take first right towards Llansillin, first right again down hill)
☎ 01691 657058 FAX 01691 657058
David Atkinson and his wife Sharon run this popular country inn near Offa's Dyke. David is an accomplished chef and his kitchen skills have earned him our prestigious one-rosette award. Bar food and blackboard specials supplement the carte menu. Bedrooms are on the small side but they are decorated with pretty wallpapers.
5 rms No smoking in bedrooms No smoking in area of dining room No smoking in lounges Tea and coffee making facilities No dogs (ex guide dogs) Cen ht CTV 200P Pool table Board games Dominoes Darts Last d 9.30pm
ROOMS: s £17; d £34; wkly b&b £119✻
MEALS: Lunch £9.15-£19.65alc Dinner £9.15-£19.65alc✻
CARDS:

Selected

The Pentre Trefonen SY10 9EE ☎ 01691 653952
This 400 year old, stone built former farmhouse is remotely and quietly located some three and a half miles from Oswestry and overlooks spectacular views of the surrounding hills and countryside. The house has a wealth of character, which is enhanced by features such as beamed ceilings and an inglenook fireplace, where a welcoming log burning stove burns when the weather is cold. The traditionally furnished, no smoking, modern equipped accommodation comprises of two family bedded rooms. The house is reached from the village of Trefonen by following the lane signposted for Pentre Issa. The Pentre is within a mile and a half and directional signs are provided.
2 bth/shr (2 fmly) No smoking CTV in all bedrooms Tea and coffee making facilities Cen ht CTV 10P No coaches Table tennis Child's snooker table Last d 9pm
ROOMS: s £20; d £39

Selected

Q Q Q Q *Top Farm House (SJ334214)* SY10 8HN
☎ 01691 682582 Mrs P A Morrissey

(For full entry see **Knockin**)

OTTERY ST MARY Devon Map **03** SY19

Q **Fluxton Farm** Fluxton EX11 1RJ ☎ 01404 812818
Apr-Oct & Xmas rs Nov-Apr
This delightful 16th-century Devon long house is situated just four miles from the coast. The home of Ann and Maurice Forth, and their famous cats, the property has a character all its own. Accommodation is simple, but well equipped and there is a choice of lounges for guests' use, Traditional English meals are served in the dining room. Railway enthusiasts will enjoy Mr Forth's narrow gauge railway.
12 rms (6 bth 4 shr) (2 fmly) No smoking in dining room No smoking in 1 lounge CTV in 11 bedrooms Tea and coffee making facilities Licensed Cen ht CTV 15P No coaches Fishing Putting Garden railway Last d 5.30pm
ROOMS: s £23-£25; d £46-£50; wkly b&b £150-£165; wkly hlf-bd £200-£215*

Selected

Q Q Q Q **Normandy House Hotel & Bistro** 5 Cornhill EX11 1DW (M5 junct29/A30 onto B3174. On approaching town centre bear left and follow directions for St Mary's church, house opposite)
☎ 01404 811088 FAX 01404 811023
An attractive Georgian town house, situated on a pretty square opposite the church, offers cosy accommodation and a friendly atmosphere. Emma and Michael Rice have carefully restored the property and Normandy House is becoming popular for its attractive bistro, where a range of interesting dishes are on offer.
5 bth/shr (1 fmly) No smoking in bedrooms No smoking in area of dining room CTV in all bedrooms Tea and coffee making facilities Direct dial from bedrooms No dogs (ex guide dogs) Licensed Cen ht No children 4yrs No coaches Last d 9.30pm
ROOMS: s £29.95-£37.50; d £52-£59.95; wkly b&b £140-£170*
CARDS:

Q Q Q **Venn Ottery Barton Hotel** Venn Ottery EX11 1RZ (take exit 30 from M5 going East on A3052, turn left to Venn Ottery (signposted) in the village of Newton Poppleford) ☎ 01404 812733 FAX 01404 814713
This fascinating 16th-century Devon longhouse has been lovingly restored by its proprietors to provide a comfortable and tastefully furnished small hotel. Refurbished bedrooms contain many modern facilities, including remote CTV. The conservatory style restaurant offers guests and non-residents a choice of home-made traditional and modern dishes.
14 rms (12 bth/shr) 1 annexe shr (3 fmly) No smoking in dining room No smoking in 1 lounge CTV in all bedrooms Tea and coffee making facilities Direct dial from bedrooms Licensed Cen ht CTV 20P No coaches 2 acres gdn Croquet Last d 9pm
ROOMS: s £34; d £68-£76; wkly b&b £224; wkly hlf-bd £322-£336*
CARDS:

OUNDLE Northamptonshire Map **04** TL08

Q Q Q *The Ship Inn* 18-20 West St PE8 4EF ☎ 01832 273918
A traditional inn on historic Oundle's main street has lots of atmosphere and a busy taproom which captures the essence of a rustic inn. The bedrooms are in three buildings to the rear of the pub. The older rooms are more traditionally furnished and the newer ones bright and attractive, featuring bold fabrics. All are well equipped and comfortable.
11 bth/shr (1 fmly) No smoking in area of dining room CTV in all bedrooms Tea and coffee making facilities Cen ht CTV 70P Last d 10pm
CARDS:

OXFORD Oxfordshire Map **04** SP50

See also Yarnton

Q **Acorn** 260/262 Iffley Rd OX4 1SE (From ring-road take A4158 north for 1m. On left opposite Volkswagan garage called Motor World)
☎ 01865 247998
Closed Xmas-New Year
There is a warm, homely atmosphere at this small guest house located south of the city centre. Bedrooms are well maintained and are suitably furnished and equipped.
12 rms (3 fmly) No smoking in 8 bedrooms No smoking in dining room No smoking in lounges CTV in all bedrooms Tea and coffee making facilities No dogs Lift Cen ht No children 9yrs 11P
ROOMS: s £24-£27; d £38-£42
CARDS:

Q Q Q **All Seasons** 63 Windmill Rd, Headington OX3 7BP (off North Eastern By-pass onto A420 then left at central traffic lights into Windmill Rd) ☎ 01865 742215 FAX 01865 432691
Personally run by Mr and Mrs Melbye this property is convenient for Oxford town centre; with the added advantage of rear parking and a small patio. Guests are offered a warm welcome and bedrooms have been thoughtfully equipped with extras such as TV, hair dryers and clock radios and several are en suite. Dinner is not served in this non-smoking establishment, but guests are welcome to use the cosy breakfast room.
6 rms (3 shr) No smoking CTV in all bedrooms Tea and coffee making facilities No dogs Cen ht No children 12yrs 6P
ROOMS: s £25-£30; d £35-£55*
CARDS:

Q Q Q *Ascot House* 283 Iffley Rd OX4 4AG (SE of city centre on A4158) ☎ 01865 240259 FAX 01865 727669
Business and tourist guests alike will enjoy being away from all the hustle and bustle at this quiet and comfortable guest house, situated just under a mile from the town centre. Bedrooms, one with a four-poster, are decorated with pretty matching fabrics, and well equipped with such thoughtful extras as mini fridges and phones. Proprietor Elizabeth Hall makes every effort to ensure that guests feel welcome and special diets are catered for at this no-smoking establishment.
6 bth/shr (2 fmly) No smoking CTV in 12 bedrooms Tea and coffee making facilities Direct dial from bedrooms No dogs (ex guide dogs) Cen ht CTV No children 5yrs 2P No coaches
CARDS:

See page 14-20 for a list of Premier Selected establishments

Q Q Q Balkan Lodge 315 Iffley Rd OX4 4AG ☎ 01865 244524 FAX 01865 251090
Situated to the east of the city Balkan Lodge offers easy access to the ring road and town centre. Now family owned, the property has recently undergone extensive refurbishment. The bright, attractive bedrooms, have modern en suite facilities and are equipped to a high level; one room has a four-poster bed and a jacuzzi. There is a comfortable guest lounge and a smartly furnished dining room.
13 bth/shr No smoking in bedrooms No smoking in dining room CTV in all bedrooms Tea and coffee making facilities Direct dial from bedrooms Licensed Cen ht CTV No children 13P
ROOMS: s £48.50-£55.50; d £58.50-£62.50*
CARDS:

Q Q Bravalla 242 Iffley Rd OX4 1SE
(On ring road take Iffley/Rosehill exit at Littlemore roundabout)
☎ 01865 241326 & 250511 FAX 01865 250 511
Situated on Iffley Road with good public transport links to the centre of the city, Bravalla is an semi-detached property with an informal atmosphere. Bedrooms all have remote TV and most have en suite facilities. Traditional and vegetarian breakfasts are available and served in the conservatory dining room.
6 rms (5 shr) (2 fmly) No smoking in dining room CTV in all bedrooms Tea and coffee making facilities Cen ht 6P No coaches
ROOMS: s £22-£35; d £38-£44*
CARDS:

Q Q Bronte 282 Iffley Rd OX4 4AA (Opposite VW garage on Iffley Rd)
☎ 01865 244594
A well presented, red brick Victorian semi-detached house situated within walking distance of the city centre. Bedrooms on two upper floors are neatly furnished and cheerfully decorated. There is a comfortable TV lounge, and the dining room opens out onto a pretty, well tended garden.
5 rms (2 shr) (1 fmly) No smoking CTV in all bedrooms Tea and coffee making facilities No dogs (ex guide dogs) Cen ht CTV No children 3yrs 5P
ROOMS: wkly b&b £126-£154
CARDS:

Q Q *Brown's* 281 Iffley Rd OX4 4AQ (from city centre take High St over Magdalen Bridge, Iffley Rd 3rd exit on roundabout)
☎ 01865 246822 FAX 01865 246822
This Victorian house has been suitably furnished and equipped to provide attractive, comfortable accommodation. A choice of breakfast is served in the small cosy breakfast room.
9 rms (2 shr) (3 fmly) No smoking in dining room CTV in all bedrooms Tea and coffee making facilities No dogs Cen ht 4P No coaches
CARDS:

Q Q Casa Villa 388 Banbury Rd OX2 7PW
(1.25m north of city centre 200yds from A40 link to M40, Banbury Rd is A4165 north side of Oxford City Centre)
☎ 01865 512642 FAX 01865 512642
Conveniently situated on the outskirts of the city, guests will be sure of a warm welcome by Mrs Duvnjak. Bedrooms, all with colour TV and radio and most with en suite shower, are simply decorated but comfortable. In addition to the breakfast room, where dinner can be served by prior arrangement, there is also a lounge for guests' use.
7 rms (5 shr) (1 fmly) No smoking CTV in all bedrooms No dogs Cen ht CTV 5P
ROOMS: s £29-£45; d £49-£64*
CARDS:

Premier Selected

Q Q Q Q Q Chestnuts 45 Davenant Rd, off Woodstock Rd OX2 8BU (off A40/A34 at Peartree rbt to Woodstock Rd rbt then on A4144 and second left)
☎ 01865 553375 FAX 01865 553375
Closed 23 Dec-5 Jan
This family-run guest house is just two miles north of the city. Bedrooms have been tastefully decorated with floral co-ordinating fabrics and furnished in pine; each room is en suite and equipped with a wealth of thoughtful extras. The cosy lounge features complimentary sherry and nibbles, and delicious freshly cooked breakfasts are served in the conservatory-style dining room which overlooks a colourful patio.
5 shr (1 fmly) No smoking CTV in all bedrooms Tea and coffee making facilities No dogs (ex guide dogs) Cen ht No children 12yrs 5P No coaches
ROOMS: s £38-£40; d £59-£69*

Q Q Combermere 11 Polstead Rd OX2 6TW (from jct with A40 proceed S down A4144 for 1.5m then turn right into Polstead road)
☎ 01865 556971 FAX 01865 556971
A three-storey red brick house, this establishment is located on a quiet residential street off the Woodstock road. Bedrooms vary in size and all have modern en suite showers. Limited off street parking is available.

9 shr (2 fmly) No smoking in dining room CTV in all bedrooms Tea and coffee making facilities Cen ht 3P No coaches
ROOMS: s £24-£40; d £34-£60
CARDS:

Q Q Q ***Conifer*** 116 The Slade, Headington OX3 7DX
(Turn off ring road at Green Rd/ Headington rdbt towards city centre, turn left at Windmill Rd straight down rd past hospital, hotel is on left)
☎ 01865 763055 FAX 01865 742232
Under the new ownership of Patsy and Helene Doran this family-run guest house, west of the city centre, sets a high standard in housekeeping. The en suite bedrooms are well equipped and comfortable. There is a separate guest lounge in addition to a breakfast room, and an outdoor swimming pool that guests can use in the summer months.
8 rms (1 bth 2 shr) (1 fmly) No smoking in dining room No smoking in lounges CTV in all bedrooms Tea and coffee making facilities No dogs Cen ht 8P No coaches Outdoor swimming pool (heated)
CARDS:

Premier Selected

Q Q Q Q Q **Cotswold House** 363 Banbury Rd OX2 7PL
(off A40,on a main road into Oxford city centre)
☎ 01865 310558 FAX 01865 310558
Conveniently located for the city, this modern house provides an ideal base away from the hustle and bustle. Jim and Anne O'Kane provide a friendly welcome and are very happy to offer advice on local places to visit. The bedrooms are equipped with modern facilities as well as thoughtful extras. A good variety of dishes are offered at breakfast that is served in a bright and spacious dining room.
7 shr (2 fmly) No smoking CTV in all bedrooms Tea and coffee making facilities No dogs Cen ht No children 6yrs 6P No coaches
ROOMS: s £41-£44; d £62-£66*

Q Q Q ***Courtfield Private Hotel*** 367 Iffley Rd OX4 4DP (on A4158, south east of city centre) ☎ 01865 242991 FAX 01865 242991
The Courtfield is a meticulously maintained house located just over a mile south of the centre, with plenty of off street parking. Bright bedrooms are spacious and the lounge, where tea and coffee are served, also acts as a breakfast room. There is a art deco marble bathroom, together with other touches from the same period.
6 rms (4 bth/shr) (1 fmly) No smoking in dining room No smoking in lounges No dogs Cen ht CTV No children 3yrs 8P No coaches
CARDS:

Selected

Q Q Q Q **Cumnor Hotel** 76 Abingdon Rd, Cumnor OX2 9QW (from Oxford take A420, take 2nd exit signposted Cumnor/ Abingdon.Follow signs for Cumnor (not Cumnor Hill) Hotel 1st on left after flyover) ☎ 01865 863098 FAX 01865 862217
Quietly situated this hotel is well located for Oxford and provides an ideal base for touring the Cotswolds. All rooms are tastefully furnished with co-ordinating fabrics and equipped with modern facilities, one with a four-poster. There is a comfortable lounge, a delightful dining room where guests can enjoy breakfast and home cooked evening meals, and a patio that provides the perfect place for relaxing in the summer.
7 bth/shr (1 fmly) No smoking CTV in all bedrooms Tea and coffee making facilities Direct dial from bedrooms Licensed Cen ht 7P No coaches Last d 4pm
ROOMS: s £46; d £62*
CARDS:

328

Selected

Q Q Q Q **Dial House** 25 London Rd, Headington OX3 7RE
☎ 01865 769944 FAX 01865 769944
This attractive half-timbered house is conveniently situated just 1.5 miles from the city centre and public transport is just a few steps away. The en suite bedrooms, several overlooking the attractive rear garden, are spacious and well equipped with TV, clock radios, hair dryers and hot water bottles. A cosy lounge is provided in addition to the front facing breakfast room.
8 bth/shr (2 fmly) No smoking CTV in all bedrooms Tea and coffee making facilities Cen ht No children 6yrs 8P
ROOMS: s £45-£50; d £55-£65; wkly b&b £190-£227.50*

Q Q Q **Earlmont** 322-324 Cowley Rd OX4 2AF ☎ 01865 240236
Closed 24 Dec-1 Jan
A double-fronted terraced property situated on the busy Cowley Road. There are eight bedrooms in the main building, with private bathrooms, and additional rooms are across the road in a small annexe. Public rooms are pleasantly furnished and decorated, although fairly small. Smoking is not permitted in the main building.
8 rms (1 bth 6 shr) (1 fmly) CTV in all bedrooms Tea and coffee making facilities No dogs Cen ht No children 5yrs 7P
ROOMS: s £28-£40; d £48-£50*
CARDS:

Q Q Q **Falcon Private Hotel** 88-90 Abingdon Rd OX1 4PX (from A34 South Hinksey jct-on to next rdbt on the Oxford ring road,take 1st exit into Oxford on the Abingdon Rd,Falcon hotel approx 1.5m on left) ☎ 01865 722995 FAX 01865 246642
Visitors can expect to receive a warm and friendly welcome from proprietor Mr Ellis at this small hotel situated just a ten minutes walk from the city centre. New ownership has brought about changes and refurbishment continues. Most rooms are spacious and all are well equipped with hair dryers, shoe cleaning kits and Sky TV. The newly redecorated smoking lounge benefits from an open fire in winter. A good English breakfast is served in the basement dining room, and dinner is available on request.
12 shr (3 fmly) No smoking in bedrooms No smoking in dining room CTV in all bedrooms Tea and coffee making facilities Direct dial from bedrooms No dogs (ex guide dogs) Cen ht CTV 10P Jacuzzi Last d 5pm
ROOMS: s £29-£29; d £52-£52; wkly b&b £147-£203*
CARDS:

Premier Selected

Q Q Q Q Q **Fallowfields Country House Hotel & Restaurant** Kingston Bagpuize, with Southmoor OX13 5BH (10 miles SW of Oxford turn off A420 signed Kingston Bagpuize and at mini-rbt turn right through the village to Southmoor) ☎ 01865 820416 FAX 01865 821275
Set in its own gardens and grounds, there is a warm and friendly welcome from hosts Peta and Anthony Lloyd. Each well equipped bedroom has a unique character with antique pieces of furniture. Richly co-ordinated fabrics and furnishings reflect the colourful history of this house, once home to the Begum Aga Khan. The kitchen garden provides many ingredients for the wide range of interesting dishes on the dinner menu. Fallowfields provides a popular venue for functions and weddings.
10 bth/shr No smoking in bedrooms No smoking in dining room No smoking in 1 lounge CTV in all bedrooms Tea and coffee making facilities Direct dial from bedrooms Licensed Cen ht No children 10rs 21P No coaches Outdoor swimming pool (heated) Tennis (hard) Croquet lawn Last d 8.30pm
ROOMS: s £85-£95; d £105-£145*
CARDS:

Selected

Q Q Q Q **Gables** 6 Cumnor Hill OX2 9HA (M40 junct 9 take A34 towards Newbury, at junct with A420 exit A34 to rdbt, take Oxford/Botley turn off, turn right at T-junct, then 500yds on right)
☎ 01865 862153 FAX 01865 864054
Closed 24 Dec-1 Jan

Gables is a charming, white Victorian house situated close to the railway station in a quiet suburb. Guests can relax in the large rear garden or if the weather is not so kind there is a bright and airy conservatory. All rooms are superbly equipped and prettily decorated. Linens are crisp and bedrooms impeccably maintained. Charming proprietor Sally Tompkins is the winner of the 1998 Landlady of the Year award so guests can be assured of a warm and friendly welcome.
7 rms (6 bth/shr) (1 fmly) No smoking CTV in all bedrooms Tea and coffee making facilities Direct dial from bedrooms No dogs Cen ht CTV 6P No coaches
ROOMS: s £25-£28; d £44-£48
CARDS:

Selected

Q Q Q Q ***Galaxie Private Hotel*** 180 Banbury Rd OX2 7BT
☎ 01865 515688 FAX 01865 556824
This popular, privately run hotel is in the Summertown area just north of the city centre, and is surrounded by shops and restaurants. The bedrooms are bright, modern and furnished with great taste and many accessories have been added for extra comfort. There is an attractive dining room and lounge area, housed in a modern conservatory, which has direct access to the carefully tended gardens and sun patio.
31 rms (27 bth/shr) (3 fmly) No smoking in bedrooms No smoking in dining room CTV in all bedrooms Tea and coffee making facilities Direct dial from bedrooms Lift Cen ht CTV 30P
CARDS:

Q Q Q **Green Gables** 326 Abingdon Rd OX1 4TE (off Oxford Ring Rd, south side, at the Kennington Rbt,toward city centre then. 5m on left)
☎ 01865 725870 FAX 01865 723115
Closed 23-31 Dec
This smartly maintained house has the added bonus of good parking. Friendly proprietors Mr and Mrs Ellis have compiled a personal guide to Oxford for guests and have introduced a book swap scheme where guests are welcome to take one of the many paperbacks on display and to perhaps leave one they have finished with. The breakfast room is smart and there is a cosy lounge.
9 rms (6 bth/shr) (3 fmly) No smoking in dining room No smoking in lounges CTV in all bedrooms Tea and coffee making facilities No dogs (ex guide dogs) Cen ht 8P No coaches
ROOMS: s £32-£44; d £37-£56*
CARDS:

Q Q Q ***Highfield*** 91 Rose Hill OX4 4HT (on A4158)
☎ 01865 774083 & 718524
This smartly presented and family run guest house provides a friendly welcome. Bedrooms, although varied in size, offer a good level of comfort and are stylishly decorated using bold fabrics. There is a comfortable lounge, and is also a bright attractive breakfast room.

contd. on p.330.

7 rms (5 shr) (2 fmly) No smoking in 3 bedrooms No smoking in dining room No smoking in lounges CTV in all bedrooms Tea and coffee making facilities No dogs Cen ht CTV 5P
CARDS:

QQQ ***Homelea*** 356 Abingdon Rd OX1 4TQ (on A4144, off ring road) ☎ 01865 245150
This well kept guest house is conveniently situated just one mile from the city centre, and on the main bus route. Bedrooms all have en suite facilities with showers and include a number of family rooms.
6 shr (3 fmly) No smoking in 2 bedrooms CTV in all bedrooms Tea and coffee making facilities No dogs (ex guide dogs) Cen ht CTV 6P

Selected

QQQQ **Marlborough House** 321 Woodstock Rd OX2 7NY (from A34/A44 junct north of city follow City Centre signs into Woodstock Rd for hotel on right adjacent to traffic lights) ☎ 01865 311321 FAX 01865 515329
Closed 23 Dec-2 Jan
Marlborough House is a three storey building of traditional style. The spacious bedrooms are decorated with colourful co-ordinating soft furnishings; they are well equipped, with kitchenette, fridge and microwave. A continental style breakfast is served in the room and placed on a tray the night before. There is a small cosy coffee lounge with free coffee and tea offered.
12 bth/shr 4 annexe bth/shr (2 fmly) No smoking in bedrooms CTV in all bedrooms Tea and coffee making facilities Direct dial from bedrooms No dogs Licensed Cen ht No children 5yrs 6P No coaches
ROOMS: s £62.50; d £73
CARDS:

QQQ **Pickwicks** 17 London Rd, Headington OX3 7SP (From A40 from London, at Shotover roundabout take exit to Headington. Guesthouse is 1.5 miles) ☎ 01865 750487 & 769413 FAX 01865 742208
Situated within easy walking distance of the town centre, and with the added benefit of car parking and access to public transport, Pickwicks is a good base for those wanting to explore the area. Bedrooms, many of which are en suite, are very well equipped with telephones, hair dryers and remote TV. A licensed bar is provided in the traditionally decorated lounge.
15 rms (3 bth 6 shr) (5 fmly) No smoking in 2 bedrooms No smoking in dining room CTV in all bedrooms Tea and coffee making facilities Direct dial from bedrooms Licensed Cen ht CTV 12P
ROOMS: s £28-£50; d £45-£60*
CARDS:

Selected

QQQQ **Pine Castle Hotel** 290/292 Iffley Rd OX4 4AE (off Ring Rd onto A4158,1.5 miles guesthouse is on left, after traffic lights) ☎ 01865 241497 & 728887 FAX 01865 727230
Closed Xmas

This detached Edwardian house, east of the city centre has much to commend it. Bedrooms are bright, fresh and attractive and all are very well equipped and furnished. In keeping with the name, pine furniture predominates. There is a comfortable lounge and bar. Breakfasts are a speciality, and guests should be sure to try the home-made yoghurt; vegetarians can be catered for.
8 bth/shr (1 fmly) No smoking in bedrooms No smoking in dining room CTV in all bedrooms Tea and coffee making facilities Direct dial from bedrooms No dogs (ex guide dogs) Licensed Cen ht CTV 4P No coaches
ROOMS: d £58-£67
CARDS:

Selected

QQQQ **Tilbury Lodge Private Hotel** 5 Tilbury Ln, Eynsham Rd, Botley OX2 9NB (A34-Oxford, stay on rd towards Swindon to Botley interchange go over rdbt, through lights, turn right go for ½ mile, right again, hotel on right) ☎ 01865 862138 FAX 01865 863700
Tilbury Lodge is a modern property run by resident proprietors Mr and Mrs Trafford. Bedrooms are bright and cheerfully decorated, and offer a range of modern comforts, including telephones, hair dryers, and remote control TV. One room has a four-poster, and there is also a spa bath available for guest use. There is a comfortable lounge and well tended garden with play equipment for children.
9 bth/shr (2 fmly) No smoking CTV in all bedrooms Tea and coffee making facilities Direct dial from bedrooms No dogs Cen ht CTV 10P No coaches Jacuzzi
ROOMS: s £42-£45; d £60-£68*
CARDS:

QQQ ***Westwood Country Hotel*** Hinksey Hill Top OX1 5BG (South off Ring Rd) (The Circle) ☎ 01865 735408
FAX 01865 736536
Closed 22 Dec-9 Jan
Located just three miles south of the city centre, this large, well established hotel is situated in it's own wooded nature conservation area. There is a

small function room, popular for conferences, a bar and dining area. The well-equipped bedrooms, of various sizes, are individually furnished in co-ordinated decor. Guests can also use a sauna spa bath and fitness machine.
21 bth/shr (2 fmly) No smoking in 7 bedrooms No smoking in dining room CTV in all bedrooms Tea and coffee making facilities Direct dial from bedrooms No dogs (ex guide dogs) Licensed Cen ht CTV ch fac 30P Sauna Jacuzzi Wildlife nature garden & trail Last d 8.15pm
CARDS:

OXHILL Warwickshire Map **04** SP34

Selected

Q Q Q Q Nolands Farm *(SP312470)* CV35 0RJ
(1m E of Pillarton Priors on A422)
☎ 01926 640309 FAX 01926 641662 Mrs S Hutsby
Closed 15 Dec-15 Jan
Peacefully situated in a small valley near the village, Nolands Farm has a well stocked trout lake, and clay pigeon shooting, bicycle hire and horse riding can be arranged. Breakfast is served in an attractive terracotta tiled dining room in the old granary and guests have use of a conservatory lounge that looks out over the colourful garden. Two of the bedooms have four-posters and all rooms are en suite and have a good range of facilities.
8 annexe bth/shr (2 fmly) No smoking in 2 bedrooms No smoking in dining room No smoking in 1 lounge CTV in all bedrooms Tea and coffee making facilities No dogs (ex guide dogs) Licensed Cen ht No children 7yrs 12P Fishing Clay pigeon shooting, bike hire, riding all nearby 200 acres arable Last d 24hrs notice
ROOMS: s £25-£40; d £36-£44*
CARDS:

PADSTOW Cornwall & Isles of Scilly Map **02** SW97

See also St Merryn

Selected

Q Q Q Q Cross House Hotel Church St PL28 8BG
(turn off A30 onto B3274. Follow signs to Padstow, on reaching town take 3rd right. Follow one way street past church for 50 yds and take sharp left) ☎ 01841 532391 FAX 01841 533633
Closed 19 Jan-12 Feb
Recently re-furbished to a very high standard throughout, Cross House Hotel is a charming Georgian property, situated in the centre of the town, and within walking distance of the harbour. Each of the bedrooms is individually designed and furnished, with every facility. Two comfortable lounges, one non-smoking, are provided for guests. A full English or continental breakfast with a variety of pastries is offered in the cosy dining room.

9 bth/shr (2 fmly) No smoking in bedrooms No smoking in dining room No smoking in 1 lounge CTV in all bedrooms Tea and coffee making facilities Direct dial from bedrooms No dogs (ex guide dogs) Licensed Cen ht 5P No coaches
ROOMS: s £60-£100; d £80-£120*
CARDS:

Q Q Q ***Newlands Hotel*** PL28 8QX (1.5m from Padstow on B3276)
☎ 01841 520469
A short walk from the sandy beach of Trevone Bay, this small friendly establishment is personally run by John and Beverley Philpott. There are two lounges and a cosy, well stocked bar, together with the recently re-decorated dining room where imaginative, home cooked meals are served. Bedrooms, some on the ground floor, are light and airy.
10 rms (3 bth 6 shr) (1 fmly) No smoking in dining room No smoking in 1 lounge CTV in all bedrooms Tea and coffee making facilities Licensed Cen ht CTV 12P No coaches Last d 4.30pm

Selected

Q Q Q Q The Old Cabbage Patch Trevone Rd, Trevone Bay PL28 8QL (from Padstow, take B3276 for approx 1.5m and turn right into Trevone Bay. Establishment is in the centre of the village) ☎ 01841 520956 FAX 01841 520956
Closed 2 Dec-30 Jan
Situated near the centre of the village, this single storey, modern property is the home of Tony and Sylvia Hending who offer a warm welcome to their guests. The comfortable bedrooms are attractively decorated, while the public rooms include a lounge and a sunny conservatory. Fresh flowers grace the tables in the well appointed dining room, where Tony is justly proud of the freshly cooked breakfasts.
3 bth/shr No smoking CTV in all bedrooms Tea and coffee making facilities No dogs Cen ht No children 15yrs 5P No coaches

Q Q Q Roselyn 20 Grenville Rd PL28 8EX
(on entering Padstow Grenville Road is 1st on left with new school on corner) ☎ 01841 532756 FAX 01841 532756
Etr-Oct
Within walking distance of the picturesque harbour, this detached property is located in a quiet residential area of the town. Friendly owners Les and Linda Green welcome guests to their home and are only too happy to supply any local information. The light and airy bedrooms are well equipped, and a good choice is offered at breakfast.
3 bth/shr (1 fmly) No smoking CTV in all bedrooms Tea and coffee making facilities No dogs Cen ht ch fac 5P No coaches
ROOMS: s £20-£25; d £40-£50*

Premier Selected

QQQQQ **St Petroc's House** 4 New St PL28 8EA
☎ 01841 532700 & 532485 FAX 01841 532942
Closed 19-26 Dec
St Petroc's, one of the oldest buildings in the town, is a small hotel just up the hill from the picturesque harbourside. It has a popular and lively bistro specialising in rustic French and Italian provincial cooking. There are lounges, a reading room and lovely gardens. The bedrooms are furnished with great style and quality throughout. Service is attentive and the welcome noteworthy.
13 bth/shr 16 annexe bth/shr (20 fmly) No smoking in dining room CTV in all bedrooms Tea and coffee making facilities Direct dial from bedrooms Licensed Cen ht 24P No coaches Last d 9.30pm
ROOMS: s £29-£35; d £60-£130*
CARDS:

PAIGNTON Devon Map **03** SX86

QQQ *Bay Cottage* 4 Beach Rd TQ4 6AY ☎ 01803 525729
Closed Nov
Bay Cottage guest house is situated just off the main esplanade and is therefore convenient for the beach, shops and theatre. All rooms are comfortably furnished, and some have en suite facilities. Home-cooked dinners are served in the pine-furnished dining room.
10 rms (5 shr) (1 fmly) CTV in all bedrooms Cen ht CTV Last d noon

QQQ **Beresford** 5 Adelphi Rd TQ4 6AW ☎ 01803 551560
Mar-Nov
This traditional, family-run establishment is situated in a quiet residential street, within easy reach of the seafront, pier, festival hall and main shopping area. Now under the new ownership of friendly proprietors, Janet and Martin Hunt, who like to provide such extra touches as fresh flowers. The bedrooms, including a large family room, are mostly spacious. Evening meals are served and there is a comfortable lounge for guests' use.
8 shr (1 fmly) No smoking in 2 bedrooms No smoking in dining room CTV in all bedrooms Tea and coffee making facilities No dogs Licensed Cen ht CTV 3P No coaches Last d 10am
ROOMS: s £17.50-£19.50; d £30-£35
CARDS:

Selected

QQQQ **Channel View Hotel** 8 Marine Pde TQ3 2NU
(from A380 Prestondown Rbt follow signs Preston down hill to traffic lights then forward under railway bridge and turn left)
☎ 01803 522432 FAX 01803 528376
Situated on the seafront, this friendly, family-run hotel is just yards from a safe sandy beach. The bedrooms are all well equipped, some suitable for families, and one on the ground floor. The bar and dining area are combined and guests can choose a full evening meal or a range of snacks. The large sun lounge enjoys panoramic views of Torbay.
12 bth/shr (3 fmly) No smoking in dining room No smoking in 1 lounge CTV in all bedrooms Tea and coffee making facilities No dogs (ex guide dogs) Licensed Cen ht CTV 10P Last d noon
ROOMS: s £18-£30; d £36-£60; wkly b&b £126-£210*
CARDS:

QQ *Cherra Hotel* 15 Roundham Rd TQ4 6DN
(Drive along seafront towards harbour, right at end along Sands Rd, 2nd left at church. Hotel is at top of St Andrews Rd on corner of Roundham Rd)
☎ 01803 550723
Mar-Nov
Found in a quiet residential area of Paignton, The Cherra Hotel distinguishes itself by the marvellous small gardens bursting with colour, and which have on past occasions been the winners of 'Torbay in Bloom'. The lounge is spacious and comfortable and includes a small residents bar. The bedrooms vary in style and size and have modern facilities. Food at dinner is traditional and home cooked.
14 rms (9 shr) (7 fmly) No smoking in dining room CTV in all bedrooms Tea and coffee making facilities Licensed Cen ht CTV 15P Putting green Last d 5.30pm

QQQ *Danethorpe Hotel* 23 St Andrews Rd TQ4 6HA
(past Festival Theatre towards Harbour but turn right ar rdbt & take 2nd left turn with church on corner)
☎ 01803 551251 FAX 01803 557075
Julie and John Chilcott take pride in their very friendly small hotel, where guests' comfort is paramount. It is situated in a quiet residential street and only a short walk from the shops, beaches and harbour. Danethorpe's bedrooms, most en suite, are well co-ordinated and offer a selection of modern facilities and personal touches. Both an a la carte and daily menu are offered at dinner, and are served in the attractive dining room.
10 rms (6 shr) (2 fmly) No smoking in bedrooms No smoking in dining room CTV in all bedrooms Tea and coffee making facilities No dogs Licensed Cen ht CTV 10P Last d 6pm
CARDS:

QQQ **Kingswinford Hotel** 30/32 Garfield Rd TQ4 6AX
☎ 01803 558358
Situated in a quiet residential street, just off the Esplanade and close to the beach. Many guests return each year enjoying the warm welcome, hospitality and home made dinners offered by experienced hoteliers, Mr & Mrs Self. This refurbished guest house offers comfortable bedrooms and lounges in addition to a cheerful bar where entertainment is often organised.
19 rms (12 shr) (5 fmly) No smoking in dining room No smoking in lounges CTV in all bedrooms Tea and coffee making facilities Licensed Cen ht CTV 13P Last d 5pm
ROOMS: s £13-£18.50; d £26-£39; wkly b&b £85-£125; wkly hlf-bd £115-£174*

QQQ **Redcliffe Lodge Hotel** 1 Marine Dr TQ3 2NL
(Situated at Northern end of Paignton seafront)
☎ 01803 551394 FAX 01803 551394
Apr-mid Nov
Situated opposite Paignton Green and close to the beach, Redcliffe Lodge is also conveniently placed for the theatre and all the other attractions Paignton has to offer. The bedrooms are well equipped and vary in style and size. There is an attractive sun lounge in addition to another lounge and a small residents bar. Views over the green to the sea are an added attraction for guests.
17 bth/shr (2 fmly) No smoking in dining room CTV in all bedrooms Tea and coffee making facilities No dogs Licensed Cen ht CTV 20P No coaches Last d 6.30pm
ROOMS: s £20-£30; d £40-£60; wkly hlf-bd £195-£260*
CARDS:

Q Q Q *St Weonard's Private Hotel* 12 Kernou Rd TQ4 6BA (Drive along esplanade, Kernou Rd is between the pier and Festival theatre) ☎ 01803 558842

Just a short walk from the seafront, shops and attractions, in a quiet street off the Esplanade, this friendly guest house has mostly en suite bedrooms with modern facilities. Traditional English cooking and bar snacks are served in the bright, spacious dining room, next to the popular residents' bar.

8 rms (5 shr) (2 fmly) No smoking in bedrooms No smoking in dining room CTV in 4 bedrooms Tea and coffee making facilities No dogs Licensed Cen ht CTV 2P No coaches Last d 4.30pm

CARDS:

Q Q Q **The Sealawn Hotel** Sea Front, 20 Esplanade Rd TQ4 6BE (on seafront between Festival Theatre & pier) ☎ 01803 559031

Closed 24 Dec-2 Jan

Ideally situated on the seafront, close to the town centre, with some of the rooms benefiting from views over the Bay and the pier. The rooms are spacious with both family rooms and a ground floor room available. Guests can enjoy traditional cooking as well as relaxing in the lounge and popular bar, both of which enjoy sea views.

12 bth/shr (3 fmly) No smoking in dining room CTV in all bedrooms Tea and coffee making facilities Direct dial from bedrooms No dogs Licensed Cen ht CTV 13P Solarium Last d 5.30pm

ROOMS: s £21-£30; d £42-£50; wkly b&b £140-£203; wkly hlf-bd £182-£245

CARDS:

Selected

Q Q Q Q **Sea Verge Hotel** Marine Dr, Preston TQ3 2NJ ☎ 01803 557795

Mar/Etr-Oct

Situated close to the seafront and Preston Green, this family run hotel continues to benefit from the dedicated approach of the Birchall family. Bedrooms are light and airy; several having balconies with views of the channel. Public areas are spacious and include a comfortable lounge with sun room off, a cosy bar and soundly appointed restaurant. Each evening a set home-cooked meal is served or guests have the option of choosing from the short a la carte menu.

11 rms (9 shr) (2 fmly) No smoking in dining room CTV in all bedrooms Tea and coffee making facilities No dogs Licensed Cen ht CTV No children 9yrs 14P Last d 6pm

ROOMS: d £32-£40*

Q Q Q **Torbay Sands Hotel** 16 Marine Pde, Preston Sea Front TQ3 2NU ☎ 01803 525568

This friendly family-owned hotel is located in a prime position overlooking Preston beach and within strolling distance of the Green. Many bedrooms, including one four poster, benefit from sea views, and all are comfortably furnished. There is a warm and cosy front facing lounge housing Mrs Hennequin's collection of china and ornaments, and a traditional dining room where three course dinners are served during the season.

13 rms (11 shr) (4 fmly) No smoking in dining room CTV in all bedrooms Tea and coffee making facilities Licensed Cen ht CTV 5P

ROOMS: wkly b&b £112-£126; wkly hlf-bd £154-£168

CARDS:

Q Q **Wentworth Hotel** 18 Youngs Park Rd, Goodrington TQ4 6BU (from Paignton on B3199-turn left at 1st rdbt, take 1st right(Roundham Rd) for 100m and turn right into Youngs Park Rd, hotel overlooks park on left) ☎ 01803 557843

This small Victorian house has been tastefully and carefully restored by Pam and Eddie Priest. Bedrooms are comfortable, and a fine choice of traditional English cuisine is served in the dining room.

8 bth/shr (3 fmly) No smoking in dining room CTV in all bedrooms Tea and coffee making facilities Licensed Cen ht 6P Last d 7pm

ROOMS: s £16-£20; d £28-£36*

PARKHAM Devon Map 02 SS32

Premier Selected

Q Q Q Q Q **The Old Rectory** EX39 5PL (take A39 from Bideford towards Bude, at Horns Cross turn left to Parkham, through village to Bell Pub turn left onto Rectory Ln, 3rd house on right) ☎ 01237 451443

1 Mar-31 Oct

The Old Rectory is the home of Jack and Jean Langton, charming hosts who take great delight in entertaining guests in the elegant surroundings of their country home. Close attention to detail is seen throughout; the bedrooms are tastefully decorated and include many thoughtful extras such as fresh fruit and flowers. Pre-dinner drinks are served in the lounge before moving through to the gracious dining room to enjoy imaginative meals of superb quality and presentation. *contd.*

The Old Rectory

3 bth/shr No smoking No dogs (ex guide dogs) Licensed Cen ht CTV No children 12yrs 12P No coaches Last d 6pm
ROOMS: s £50-£55; d £76-£80; wkly b&b £245-£252; wkly hlf-bd £406-£413*

PAWLETT Somerset Map **03** ST24

QQQ **Brickyard** *(ST298421)* River Rd TA6 4SE
(take A38 Highbridge to Pawlett road, after the large "Pawlett" sign turn sharp left into Vicarage Lane, turn left into River Rd)
☎ 01278 683381 FAX 01278 683381 Mrs Worgan
Overlooking open countryside to the rear and nature reserve to the front, this farmhouse, built about 450 years ago, is a peaceful place to stay. Located close to the main A38 and M5 motorway it is ideally situated for both the leisure and business guest. Furnished and decorated in an old world style the bedrooms are well equipped and comfortable. There is a cosy lounge with television and an attractive bar. Hearty English breakfasts are served in the dining room and dinner is available by prior arrangement.
3 rms (1 fmly) No smoking in bedrooms CTV in all bedrooms Tea and coffee making facilities No dogs Licensed Cen ht CTV 14P Fishing 2 acres non working Last d 6pm
ROOMS: s £18-£20; d £36-£40; wkly b&b £126-£140; wkly hlf-bd £168-£182*

PENRITH Cumbria Map **12** NY53

QQQ **Albany House** 5 Portland Place CA11 7QN
(from m-way, A592 into Penrith towards town centre. Left at bottom of hill, keep in right lane around block of buildings into left lane, GH on left)
☎ 01768 863072 FAX 01768 863072
This terraced house is the home of Cath Blundell who is a super host. In summer months, colourful flower-filled pots adorn the property. Whilst there is no lounge, bedrooms are tastefully decorated, have satellite TV and in-house movies. Good beverage facilities include hot chocolate, cappuccino coffee and biscuits. A substantial, freshly prepared breakfast is served in the cosy dining room.
5 rms (1 shr) (4 fmly) No smoking in dining room CTV in all bedrooms Tea and coffee making facilities No dogs (ex guide dogs) Cen ht 1P No coaches
ROOMS: s £20-£25; d £34-£38

QQQ ***Brandelhow*** 1 Portland Place CA11 7QN
(M6 junct 40 follow town centre signs, turn left into Portland Place at Town Hall) ☎ 01768 864470
Closed 24-25 Dec & 31 Dec
Spacious and attractively decorated bedrooms, which include a huge family room, compensate for lack of en suite bathrooms at this terraced guest house, within walking distance of the town centre. Public areas are comfortable, especially the lounge with the original fireplace its focal point.
6 rms (3 fmly) No smoking in 2 bedrooms No smoking in dining room CTV in all bedrooms Tea and coffee making facilities Cen ht CTV 1P No coaches

QQQ **Limes Country Hotel** Redhills, Stainton CA11 0DT
(0.5m W junct 40 M6 on A66 turn left immediately before Little Chef and follow road for 0.25 miles "The Limes" is on the right) ☎ 01768 863343
This Victorian country house is conveniently situated in quiet open countryside a short drive from the M6. Unassumingly decorated and traditionally furnished to reflect the character of the house, it offers comfortable, well proportioned bedrooms, a guests' lounge and spacious dining room.
6 bth/shr (2 fmly) No smoking in dining room CTV in all bedrooms Tea and coffee making facilities No dogs (ex guide dogs) Licensed Cen ht 7P No coaches Last d 3pm
ROOMS: s £27-£28; d £44-£46; wkly b&b £140-£155; wkly hlf-bd £215-£235
CARDS:

QQQ **Tymparon Hall** *(NY467300)* Newbiggin, Stainton CA11 0HS
(exit M6 at junct 40 and take A66 towards Keswick for approx 3m, then take right turn for village) ☎ 017684 83236 Mrs M Taylor
Closed 5 Nov-5 Mar
This 18th century working farm house lies on the fringe of Newbiggin village, within easy reach of Ullswater and the Lake District's northern fells. Bedrooms are lofty and well proportioned, with the reception rooms extending to a comfortable sitting room and the attractive dining room.
4 rms (2 bth/shr) (2 fmly) No smoking Tea and coffee making facilities No dogs Cen ht CTV P Last d 4pm
ROOMS: wkly b&b £140-£150; wkly hlf-bd £220-£230

QQ **Voreda View** 2 Portland Place CA11 7QN
(M6 junct 40-follow signs for town centre, at bottom of hill keep in right lane coming back on yourself and Portland Place is the first on the left)
☎ 01768 863395 & 0410 489301 FAX 01768 863395
An abundance of attractive floral arrangements grace this terraced row in summer, and on-going refurbishments continue despite its year round popularity. Pine furniture and stylish decor feature, and bedrooms are comfortable.
6 rms (4 fmly) No smoking in dining room CTV in all bedrooms Tea and coffee making facilities Cen ht CTV 1P No coaches
ROOMS: s £18-£19.50; d £30-£35

QQQ **Woodland House Hotel** Wordsworth St CA11 7QY
(at foot of Beacon Hill, close to Town Hall)
☎ 01768 864177 FAX 01768 890152
This Victorian terraced house with a quiet garden to the rear is in a residential area close to the town centre. The atmosphere is relaxed and Ivor Davies will happily advise guests on tours to places of interest. There are two lounges - the main one having a residents' bar - with lots of books, games and tourist information. The bedrooms are bright, cheery and sensibly furnished to suit both the tourist and business guest.
8 bth/shr (2 fmly) No smoking CTV in all bedrooms Tea and coffee making facilities No dogs Licensed Cen ht CTV 6P No coaches Last d 4.30pm
ROOMS: s £28-£38; d £45; wkly b&b £150-£186*
CARDS:

PENSHURST Kent Map **05** TQ54

Premier Selected

QQQQQ **Swale Cottage** Old Swaylands Ln, Off Poundsbridge Ln TN11 8AH (off A26 onto B2176 after 2.75m turn left onto Poundsbridge Lane) ☎ 01892 870738 FAX 01892 870738
This Grade II listed, beautifully converted Kentish barn was formerly part of a 13th-century yeoman farm. It is now home to Mrs Cynthia Dakin who offers three spacious and well appointed bedrooms, a sumptuous lounge and a beamed breakfast room all furnished in the English country cottage style. Many of the paintings that adorn the

public rooms are the work of the owner, an accomplished artist; and with views of the wooded Medway Valley over the lake and rose gardens, the setting is idyllic.

3 bth/shr No smoking CTV in all bedrooms Tea and coffee making facilities No dogs Cen ht No children 10yrs 5P No coaches
ROOMS: s £42-£52; d £60-£70*

PENZANCE Cornwall & Isles of Scilly Map **02** SW43

See also Porthcurno

Selected

Q Q Q Q **Blue Seas Hotel** 13 Regents Ter TR18 4DW
☎ 01736 364744 FAX 01736 330701
Situated in a quiet terrace location, yet within easy walking distance of the town centre, promenade and the Isles of Scilly ferry, this Victorian house offers comfortable accommodation. All bedrooms vary in style and size and offer modern facilities. There is a bright and airy lounge and a dining room where guests can enjoy a good English or Continental breakfast.
10 bth/shr (2 fmly) No smoking CTV in all bedrooms Tea and coffee making facilities No dogs Cen ht No children 5yrs 12P No coaches
ROOMS: s £18-£25; d £36-£50*
CARDS:

Selected

Q Q Q Q **Camilla House Hotel** 12 Regent Ter TR18 4DW (take seafront road to Promenade, Regent Terrace approx 30yds W of Jubilee Pool) ☎ 01736 363771 FAX 01736 363771
Rosemary and Bill Wooldridge offer a warm welcome to their guests at this attractive listed building where facilities have recently been upgraded. Set in a quiet terrace, parallel to the promenade, all the front-facing rooms benefit from delightful sea views. Bedrooms are tastefully furnished and well equipped with a number of thoughtful extras such as fresh flowers. There is a comfortable television lounge and Camilla House is fully licensed. Breakfast is served in the spacious dining room where a varied choice is offered and vegetarians are catered for.
8 rms (4 bth/shr) No smoking in bedrooms No smoking in dining room CTV in all bedrooms Tea and coffee making facilities Licensed Cen ht CTV No children 8yrs 8P
ROOMS: s £18-£21; d £36-£50
CARDS:

Q Q Q **Carlton Private Hotel** Promenade TR18 4NW (Take seafront rd past harbour, turn corner by Jubilee swimming, along prom, straight on for 30yds after mini-rdbt, pull in left, hotel is just opp) ☎ 01736 362081
Etr-mid Oct
With views over Mount's Bay and to St. Michael's Mount, this well established guest house has bedrooms which are furnished to make the best use of space. Furnishings are traditional, apart from the lounge where the owner's selection of Far Eastern furniture takes pride of place.
10 rms (8 shr) No smoking in bedrooms No smoking in dining room CTV in all bedrooms Tea and coffee making facilities No dogs (ex guide dogs) CTV No children 12yrs No coaches
ROOMS: s £18-£20; d £40-£50*

Premier Selected

Q Q Q Q Q **Chy-an-Mor** 15 Regent Ter TR18 4DW (A30-Penzance. Follow rd to rlwy stn in left hand lane to Newlyn. Pass harbour onto prom, pass Jubilee Pool on left, turn right at Stanley Hotel) ☎ 01736 363441 FAX 01736 363441
Closed Dec-Jan
Owners Mike and Jan Russell have done a splendid job of restoring this lovely Georgian property to its former glory. Bedrooms, several of which are on the ground floor, vary in size. They are all well equipped and beautifully decorated, individually-styled with quality co-ordinated fabrics and furnishings. In addition to the smart downstairs dining room with its art deco theme, there is an elegant ground floor lounge with fine views of Mounts Bay.
10 shr (1 fmly) No smoking CTV in all bedrooms Tea and coffee making facilities No dogs Licensed Cen ht No children 10yrs 10P No coaches
ROOMS: s £25-£27; d £42-£50*
CARDS:

Q Q **Coth'a Noweth** Catchall, Buryas Bridge TR19 6AQ (follow A30 beyond Penzance towards Lands End. Establishment, 0.25m past the left turn to St Buryan (B3283)) ☎ 01736 810572
Etr-Sep
Coth'a Noweth is Cornish for 'Old and New', and that is exactly what this detached granite house is. A real Cornish welcome is assured from Danny

contd.

and Margaret Craigue, both of whom are Cornish born and bred. Set in half an acre of gardens, bordered by a trout stream, this guest house is ideally located for visiting Land's End, The Minack Theatre, Penzance and all the other attractions in the surrounding area. Bedrooms are functional in their furnishings, with polished wood floors being a special feature.
4 rms (2 fmly) No smoking in dining room No dogs (ex guide dogs) Cen ht 8P No coaches
ROOMS: d £25-£29; wkly b&b £87.50-£101.50*

Q Q Q **Dunedin** Alexandra Rd TR18 4LZ (follow sea front along to mini roundabout, turn right into Alexandra road 500yds up on right)
☎ 01736 62652
Closed 10 Dec-10 Jan
Situated in a quiet street within walking distance from the promenade and town centre, Dunedin offers the traveller comfort and good home cooking. The bedrooms are equipped with modern facilities and are being continually upgraded.
9 bth/shr (4 fmly) No smoking in dining room CTV in all bedrooms Tea and coffee making facilities Licensed Cen ht CTV No children 3yrs
ROOMS: s £16-£20; d £32-£40; wkly b&b £110-£135

Premier Selected

Q Q Q Q Q **Ennys Farm** *(SW559328)* St Hilary TR20 9BZ
☎ 01736 740262 FAX 01736 740055 Miss G Charlton

(For full entry see **St Hilary**)

Selected

Q Q Q Q **Georgian House** 20 Chapel St TR18 4AW
(follow A30 into Penzance and then signs for town centre, with Lloyds Bank on the right turn left, premises 400 yards on the right)
☎ 01736 365664 FAX 01736 365664
Closed Xmas
Midway between the town centre and the beach, and within walking distance of the Isles of Scilly ferry, the Georgian House offers comfortable bedrooms, which are well equipped with all modern facilities. The public areas include a lounge and bar. Breakfast is taken in the Matisse and Picasso inspired dining room.
11 rms (9 bth/shr) (3 fmly) No smoking in 2 bedrooms No smoking in dining room CTV in all bedrooms Tea and coffee making facilities No dogs (ex guide dogs) Licensed Cen ht CTV 11P Last d 8pm
ROOMS: s £18-£25; d £36-£42; wkly b&b £130-£162.50*
CARDS:

Q Q **Kimberley House** 10 Morrab Rd TR18 4EZ
(take Promenade road, pass Harbour and turn right into Morrab Road)
☎ 01736 362727
Closed Dec-Jan
The proprietors, Mr & Mrs Mudway, are experienced hoteliers who run this friendly guest house. Kimberley House is near to the town centre and all the attractions of Penzance. The bedrooms, some of which are en-suite are comfortable and vary in style and size. There is a small bar and lounge, and a dining room where good home cooked breakfasts are served.
8 rms (2 shr) (3 fmly) No smoking in dining room CTV in all bedrooms Tea and coffee making facilities No dogs (ex guide dogs) Licensed Cen ht CTV No children 5yrs 4P Last d 5pm
ROOMS: s £15-£18; d £30-£38; wkly b&b £105-£126; wkly hlf-bd £175-£189*

Q Q Q ***Hotel Minalto*** Alexandra Rd TR18 4LZ ☎ 01736 362923
FAX 01736 62923
This spacious Victorian house is located in a quiet residential street, within easy walking distance of the centre of town. There are two lounges, one of which has a small bar. The dining room, like the rest of the house, is bright and airy and the bedrooms are well equipped and have modern facilities.
10 rms (8 shr) (3 fmly) No smoking in dining room CTV in 12 bedrooms Tea and coffee making facilities Licensed Cen ht CTV 8P No coaches Last d 7.30pm
CARDS:

Q Q Q **Mount Royal Hotel** Chyandour Cliff TR18 3LQ
(on the old A30 entering Penzance) ☎ 01736 362233
Mar-Oct
Three generations of the Cox family have run and owned Mount Royal. An imposing, part-Georgian, part-Victorian house, with beautifully appointed and spacious rooms. Many original features, like the fireplace and sideboard, can still be seen in the dining room. The bedrooms are very large, and some have marvellous views over Mounts Bay.
9 rms (5 bth) (3 fmly) No smoking in dining room No smoking in lounges CTV in 8 bedrooms Tea and coffee making facilities Cen ht 10P No coaches
ROOMS: s £25-£30; d £30-£55; wkly b&b £105-£175*

Q Q Q **Penalva** Alexandra Rd TR18 4LZ
(Follow seafront from railway station and along harbour to promenade, Alexandra Rd is at end of the promenade on right)
☎ 01736 369060 FAX 01736 369060
Situated in a quiet part of town and yet within easy walking distance of the centre and harbour, Penalva has been owned and run by the Buswell family for the past eleven years. The rooms vary in size and style and offer modern amenities.
5 rms (4 shr) (3 fmly) No smoking CTV in all bedrooms Tea and coffee making facilities No dogs Cen ht CTV No children 3yrs No coaches Last d 6.30pm

Q Q Q ***Pendennis*** Alexandra Rd TR18 4LZ
(enter Penzance on A30 and at railway station take sea front road to small roundabout and turn right into Alexandra Rd) ☎ 01736 363823
Situated in a quiet residential area, Pendennis benefits from being within walking distance of the shops and harbour. This well appointed guest house offers comfortable, modern en suite bedrooms. Good home made cooking is available both at breakfast and dinner.
8 rms (6 bth/shr) (5 fmly) No smoking in dining room CTV in all bedrooms Tea and coffee making facilities Licensed Cen ht CTV Last d 4.30pm
CARDS:

Q Q Q **Penmorvah Hotel** Alexandra Rd TR18 4LZ
(250 yards up from promenade) ☎ 01736 363711
Closed Xmas
Situated in a quiet tree-lined avenue off the promenade, this hotel is also conveniently located for the town centre. Friendly owners Colin and Mary

Williams welcome guests, many of whom return on a regular basis. Bedrooms are simply furnished and decorated and include one room on the ground floor. A choice of menus is offered at both breakfast and the evening meal. In addition to a comfy ground floor lounge there is a licensed bar in the downstairs dining room.
8 bth/shr (4 fmly) No smoking in dining room CTV in all bedrooms Tea and coffee making facilities Licensed Cen ht Last d 6pm
ROOMS: s £16-£22.50; d £32-£45; wkly b&b £105-£148; wkly hlf-bd £178-£225*
CARDS:

Selected

Q Q Q Q **Rose Farm** *(SW446290)* Chyanhal, Buryas Bridge TR19 6AN (take A30 to Land's End, at Drift turn left (behind phone box), 0.75m down lane on left) ☎ 01736 731808 FAX 01736 731808
Mrs P Lally
Closed 24-27 Dec
Situated three miles from Penzance and dating back some 200 years, this is a small working farm occupying 25 acres. Penny and John Lally offer a warm welcome to guests and create a relaxed atmosphere. The Barn Room is the largest bedroom with a romantic 17th-century four-poster bed. The other two rooms are located in the farmhouse, and one is situated on the ground floor and has its own entrance. In addition to the many animals kept on the farm, there is a beautifully maintained Pets Memorial Garden which guests can visit. The famous open-air theatre at Minack is nearby.
2 shr 1 annexe shr (1 fmly) No smoking in bedrooms No smoking in dining room CTV in all bedrooms Tea and coffee making facilities No dogs (ex guide dogs) Cen ht 8P 23 acres beef
ROOMS: d £40-£43*

Q Q Q **Tremont** Alexandra Rd TR18 4LZ (follow promenade towards Newlyn and at rdbt turn right into Alexandra Rd) ☎ 01736 362614
Closed 24 Dec- 1 Jan
Situated in a quiet residential street, but near the sea front this attractive guest house has recently been comprehensively upgraded and re-furbished. All bedrooms are comfortable and include many modern facilities. Home made dinner and a hearty English breakfast are served in the bright and cheerful dining room.
10 shr (1 fmly) No smoking in dining room CTV in all bedrooms Tea and coffee making facilities No dogs (ex guide dogs) Licensed Cen ht CTV No children 5yrs 5P Last d 5.50pm
ROOMS: s £16-£19; d £32-£38; wkly b&b £100-£120

Q Q Q *Trenant Private Hotel* Alexandra Rd TR18 4LX (from A30 at Penzance Station follow road by harbour for about 1m, turn right into Alexandra Road) ☎ 01736 362005
Situated in a quiet residential area, Trenant is within easy walking distance of the town. All rooms are individual in style and decor and most have en suite facilities. Mrs Hood specialises in catering for guests with special diets and has awards from the Celiac Society.
9 rms (5 shr) (3 fmly) No smoking in dining room No smoking in lounges CTV in all bedrooms Tea and coffee making facilities Licensed Cen ht CTV No coaches Last d 7pm

Q Q **Trevelyan Hotel** 16 Chapel St TR18 4AW (Turn left at the top of the town centre into Chapel St hotel halfway along on right) ☎ 01736 62494
Located centrally, near to antique shops and restaurants, the Trevelyan offers its guests comfortable accommodation. There is also a small cottage at the rear which provides a self-contained unit, suitable for a family.
6 rms (5 shr) 2 annexe bth/shr (4 fmly) No smoking in 4 bedrooms No smoking in dining room CTV in all bedrooms Tea and coffee making facilities No dogs (ex guide dogs) Cen ht CTV 8P No coaches Last d am
ROOMS: s £15-£20; d £32-£35; wkly b&b £100-£112

Q Q Q **Treventon** Alexandra Rd TR18 4NE (Enter Penzance via A30, bear left at stn, take coastal rd to Newlyn, after rdbt turn right into Alexandra Rd, 3rd turning on right approx 200yds) ☎ 01736 361873
Treventon has been owned and run successfully by Gloria and John Glover for the past ten years. Their immaculate house is comfortably furnished and offers accommodation with modern facilities. There is a separate lounge and a dining room where traditional English breakfast is served.
7 rms (4 shr) (2 fmly) No smoking in dining room CTV in all bedrooms Tea and coffee making facilities No dogs Cen ht CTV No children 5yrs No coaches
ROOMS: s fr £15; d £30-£36; wkly b&b £112-£118

Q Q Q **Trewella** 18 Mennaye Rd TR18 4NG ☎ 01736 363818
Mar-Oct
Mr and Mrs Glenn have owned and run Trewella for 14 years and have made many improvements to the guest house in that time. Bedrooms, mostly en suite, provide comfortable, well equipped accommodation. Traditional cooking is offered and special diets are catered for.

contd.

8 rms (6 shr) (2 fmly) No smoking CTV in all bedrooms Tea and coffee making facilities No dogs Licensed Cen ht CTV No children 5yrs No coaches Last d 24hrs before
ROOMS: s £14.50-£15.50; d £33-£35; wkly b&b £91-£112

Q Q Q **Woodstock** 29 Morrab Rd TR18 4EZ (From the rlwy stn along seafront 1km turn right at approach to Queens Hotel. Woodstock is 200 metres on right)
☎ 01736 369049 FAX 01736 369049
This Victorian terraced property is the home of John and Cherry Hopkins, and is located in a quiet residential road between the Promenade and the town centre. Bedrooms vary in style but are all well equipped; one en suite room is situated on the ground floor. A hearty breakfast is served in the strikingly decorated blue dining room, and there is also a large lounge for guest use.
8 rms (4 shr) (1 fmly) No smoking in bedrooms No smoking in dining room CTV in all bedrooms Tea and coffee making facilities No dogs (ex guide dogs) Cen ht CTV No children 14yrs
ROOMS: s £14-£22.50; d £28-£50; wkly b&b £98-£157.50*
CARDS:

PERRANUTHNOE Cornwall & Isles of Scilly Map 02 SW52

Selected

Q Q Q Q **Ednovean Farm** *(SW912299)* TR20 9LZ (from the A394 Penzance/Helston turn off towards Perranuthnoe at Dynasty Cantonese restaurant, farm drive is on the left on bend by the post box)
☎ 01736 711883 FAX 01736 710480 Mr & Mrs C Taylor
This granite 17th-century barn has been lovingly restored by Charles and Christine Taylor who welcome guests to their informal home. The small farm of 22 acres and is situated above the village with glorious views over Mount's Bay and St Michael's Mount. The ground floor bedrooms are decorated and furnished in a country style, with pretty chintz fabrics and thoughtful extras such as fresh fruit, flowers and magazines. Guests take breakfast around a communal table in the open plan, first floor living area. There are many restaurants in the area for dinner, two within walking distance.
3 bth No smoking CTV in all bedrooms Tea and coffee making facilities No dogs Cen ht CTV No children 9yrs 6P 22 acres arable grassland horticultural
ROOMS: s £20-£40; d £40-£55*

Q Q Q **Ednovean House** TR20 9LZ (turn off A394 at Perran x-rds, then take first lane on the left and continue to very end of the lane)
☎ 01736 711071
Closed Xmas
A spacious Victorian house with fine views over farmland and across to Mounts Bay and St Michael's Mount, Ednovean House has comfortable accommodation, set in one acre of gardens with a small putting and croquet course. Most rooms are en suite and public rooms include an intimate lounge and bar.
9 rms (6 shr) (1 fmly) No smoking in dining room Tea and coffee making facilities Licensed Cen ht CTV No children 7yrs 12P No coaches 9 hole putting green Last d 6pm
ROOMS: s £23; d £38-£50; wkly b&b £119.70-£157.50; wkly hlf-bd £224.70-£262.50*
CARDS:

PERSHORE Worcestershire Map 03 SO94

Q Q **Brook Cottages** Upton Rd, Defford WR8 9BA (located 2.5m SW of Pershore on A4104 in village of Defford)
☎ 01386 750229
The original part of this property dates back to the 1870s, but it was considerably extended 100 years later. It stands two and a half miles south-west of Pershore. To the rear is a delightful garden and private fishing is available in the adjacent brook. The accommodation comprises a double and a twin room, plus a third single bedded room, which is suitable for a child accompanying parents. Guests share one table in the pleasant combined lounge/breakfast room, which overlooks the garden.
2 rms No smoking CTV in 1 bedroom Tea and coffee making facilities No dogs (ex guide dogs) Cen ht CTV ch fac 9P No coaches Fishing
ROOMS: s £18.50-£22.50; d £37*

PETERBOROUGH Cambridgeshire Map 04 TL19

See also **Maxey**

Q Q Q **Hawthorn House Hotel** 89 Thorpe Rd PE3 6JQ (from the South take the A1, A1139, A1260, A1179, straight over next roundabout, hotel 0.25m on the right)
☎ 01733 340608 & 313470 FAX 01733 440032
Caring proprietors Mr and Mrs Warren warmly welcome guests to their lovely Victorian house, within walking distance of the Cathedral and city centre. Evening meals are available in the pleasant dining room, which has a corner bar and is adjacent to a small conservatory lounge area. The well equipped bedrooms are decorative and of good proportions. Most have direct-dial telephones and remote control television; bedrooms on the front of the house also have secondary glazing.
8 bth/shr (2 fmly) No smoking in 5 bedrooms No smoking in dining room CTV in all bedrooms Tea and coffee making facilities Direct dial from bedrooms No dogs (ex guide dogs) Licensed Cen ht CTV 5P No coaches Last d 8pm
ROOMS: s £30-£40; d £49.50-£52
CARDS:

Q Q Q **Lodge Hotel** 130 Lincoln Rd PE1 2NR (N of city at junct with Lincoln Road and Limetree Avenue)
☎ 01733 341489 FAX 01733 753437
With its relaxing atmosphere and parking to the rear, this small welcoming hotel offers easy access to the ciy centre and is just ten minutes' walk from the Cathedral. The enthusiastic and friendly owners maintain good standards of housekeeping, and each of the pleasant cosy bedrooms has a modern en-suite shower room. Guests have the use of a small comfortable bar and an attractive, non-smoking restaurant where a range of home cooked dishes is available from a set price three course menu.
9 shr No smoking in dining room CTV in all bedrooms Tea and coffee making facilities Licensed Cen ht No children 10yrs 6P No coaches Last d 8.30pm
ROOMS: s £37-£40; d £45-£50
CARDS:

PETERSFIELD Hampshire Map 04 SU72

See **Rogate**

PEVENSEY East Sussex Map **05** TQ60

Q Q **Napier** The Promenade BN24 6HD
(exit A27 onto the A259 through Pevensey Bay village, premises situated on the corner of Collier Rd and seafront) ☎ 01323 768875
Apr-Oct
With a splendid location by the sea shore, the Napier Guest House is neatly kept by the friendly proprietors Pat and Alan Silver. Day rooms include a small sun lounge and cosy bar and a short all-day snack menu can be enjoyed either here or at tables set out on a lawned garden beside the pebble beach. Dinners are not offered. Two of the bedrooms, ideal for a family group, share a large balcony overlooking the sea.
10 rms (5 shr) (3 fmly) No smoking in dining room CTV in all bedrooms Tea and coffee making facilities No dogs Licensed Cen ht CTV 7P No coaches Fishing Swimming in sea Last d 4pm
ROOMS: s £18-£21; d £36-£42*

PEWSEY Wiltshire Map **04** SU16

Q Q Q **Woodbridge** North Newnton SN9 6JZ (2.5m SW on A345)
☎ 01980 630266 FAX 01980 630266
Closed 25 Dec
This 16th century inn is situated beside the River Avon in four and a half acres. Lou and Terry Vertessy offer a warm welcome and the atmosphere is cheerful and relaxed. Bedrooms are brightly decorated and equipped with thoughtful extras such as mineral water and reading material. There is an extensive range of meals available from the blackboard menu, in both the bar and restaurant, and a good choice of breakfast dishes, also available to non-residents
4 rms (3 shr) No smoking in dining room CTV in all bedrooms Tea and coffee making facilities No dogs (ex guide dogs) Cen ht CTV 60P No coaches Fishing Petanque Table games Last d 10.30pm
ROOMS: s £30-£35; d £35-£40; wkly b&b £210-£245; wkly hlf-bd £297-£364*
MEALS: Lunch £8.50-£15.50&alc Dinner £8.50-£15.50&alc*
CARDS:

PICKERING North Yorkshire Map **08** SE88

Q Q Q ***Bramwood*** 19 Hallgarth YO18 7AW (off A169) ☎ 01751 474066
Closed 20-31 Dec
Steve and Georgina Hackett have carefully and tastefully restored this Grade II listed building, dating from around 1740. Further improvements are continuing, with all rooms now en suite, and additional bedrooms are planned. Bedrooms are very comfortably furnished, as is the cosy lounge, whilst freshly prepared evening meals are offered in the charming dining room.
5 shr (1 fmly) No smoking Tea and coffee making facilities No dogs (ex guide dogs) Cen ht CTV No children 5yrs 6P No coaches Last d 10.30am

Premier Selected

Q Q Q Q Q ***Burr Bank*** Cropton YO18 8HL
(from A170 take road to Wrelton/Cropton. Turn right after the New Inn. Go through village and house on left 500yds past post office)
☎ 01751 417777 FAX 01751 417789
Set in attractive natural gardens, amidst 70 acres of farmland, this recently built stone house, designed to fit sympathetically into surrounding countryside, enjoys fine views over Rosedale and the fells. Comfortable bedrooms are delightfully furnished and equipped to a high standard. The spacious lounge leads into a welcoming dining room where freshly prepared evening meals are available by arrangement.
3 bth/shr No smoking CTV in all bedrooms Tea and coffee making facilities No dogs Cen ht 10P No coaches Last d 7pm

Selected

Q Q Q Q **Rawcliffe House Farm** *(SE797917)* Stape YO18 8JA
(off A170 at traffic lights in Pickering,through Newton-upon-Rawcliffe(4m) after 1.5m take right fork signed Stape,farm first left bottom of hill) ☎ 01751 473292 FAX 01751 473766 Mrs S Ducat
Etr-Oct
Set amidst glorious countryside, about six miles from Pickering, the bedrooms are situated in converted farm outbuildings around a pleasant courtyard. The beamed rooms are spacious and attractively furnished with a number of thoughtful extras provided. A short walk past the duck pond leads to the stone built farmhouse where there is a welcoming lounge and dining room, meals being served around one table.
3 annexe bth/shr No smoking CTV in all bedrooms Tea and coffee making facilities No dogs (ex guide dogs) Cen ht No children 8yrs 20P 40 acres non-working Last d 24hrs prior
ROOMS: d £42-£48; wkly b&b fr £147; wkly hlf-bd fr £210

PIDDLETRENTHIDE Dorset Map **03** SY79

Q Q Q **The Poachers** DT2 7QX (8m along on B3143 from Dorchester) ☎ 01300 348358 FAX 01300 348153
Closed 24-26 Dec
Located on the edge of this sleepy Dorset village, and within easy reach of Dorchester, guests will find a warm welcome at this friendly family run inn. Built in the 16th century, the majority of rooms are situated in a modern extension building to the rear of the inn, beside the outdoor swimming pool. Offering good value, and popular with families, bedrooms are spacious and well appointed. All are very well equipped with a host of extras such as clock radio, hot water bottle, hair dryer and shoe cleaning kit. Fresh home-cooking is a feature of the house, with an interesting choice of dishes, plus daily specials.
3 bth/shr 15 annexe bth/shr (1 fmly) CTV in all bedrooms Tea and coffee making facilities Direct dial from bedrooms Cen ht 40P Outdoor swimming pool (heated) Last d 9pm
ROOMS: d £52; wkly b&b £164; wkly hlf-bd £239*
MEALS: Lunch £8-£10alc Dinner £10-£15alc*
CARDS:

See advertisement under DORCHESTER

PINNER Greater London Map **04** TQ18

Q Q Q **Tudor Lodge Hotel** 50 Field End Rd, Eastcote HA5 2QN
(Turn off A40 at Swakeleys rdbt to Ickenham, A466 to Eastcote. Or Turn off A40 at A312 towards Harrow, then left at Northot Stn to Eastcote)
☎ 0181 429 0585 & 0181 866 6027 FAX 0181 429 0117
Guests will find a warm welcome at this friendly little hotel with a real family atmosphere provided by long serving staff. Located with 11 golf courses within five miles, just 20 minutes from Heathrow, and a short walk to Eastcote station, it provides the perfect base for out of town visitors. Bedrooms, which vary in size and style, are well equipped, those in the adjacent building proving very popular with families. A good choice for those seeking budget accommodation. *contd.*

Tudor Lodge Hotel

26 rms (22 bth/shr) 8 annexe bth/shr (18 fmly) No smoking in 10 bedrooms No smoking in dining room CTV in all bedrooms Tea and coffee making facilities Direct dial from bedrooms No dogs (ex guide dogs) Licensed Cen ht CTV 49P All above faclities are available nearby
ROOMS: s £35-£75; d £55-£85; wkly b&b £293-£503*
CARDS:

PLUCKLEY Kent Map **05** TQ94

Selected

Q Q Q Q ♥ ***Elvey Farm Country Hotel** (TQ916457)* TN27 0SU
(exit M20 at junc 8, take A20 to Charing, at Charing take turning to Pluckley, at village down steep hill, right at Tea Room, next right, then right) ☎ 01233 840442 FAX 01233 840726 Mr & Mrs V Harris
This charming farmhouse enjoys a beautiful setting on the edge of the village. The comfortably furnished rooms are located in the barn, stables and oast house which have been sympathetically restored to preserve many of the original features. Some of the rooms can accommodate families. An evening meal is available on request, and a good choice of breakfast is served in the beamed dining room. There is also a well appointed bar lounge and guests can relax and enjoy the gardens in the summer months.
10 bth/shr (6 fmly) CTV in all bedrooms Tea and coffee making facilities Licensed Cen ht 20P 75 acres mixed Last d 7pm
CARDS:

PLYMOUTH Devon Map **02** SX45

Selected

Q Q Q Q **Bowling Green Hotel** 9-10 Osborne Place, Lockyer St, The Hoe PL1 2PU
(exit A38, follow signs for Plymouth city centre, follow signs to "The Hoe", left at traffic lights, at T-junc turn right into Citadel Rd)
☎ 01752 209090 FAX 01752 209092
Closed 23-27 Dec

Overlooking Sir Francis Drake's Bowling Green on The Hoe, this Victorian property boasts distant views to Dartmoor on the horizon. Friendly owners, Mr and Mrs Dawkins, continue to upgrade and improve bedrooms, most of which are spacious. All are well decorated and furnished, and equipped with such extras as phone, satellite TV, hair dryer and clock radio. Breakfast is served in the bright open-plan dining room with a lounge area at one end. The ferry port, city centre and The Barbican are within easy walking distance.
12 bth/shr (2 fmly) No smoking in lounges CTV in all bedrooms Tea and coffee making facilities Direct dial from bedrooms Cen ht CTV 4P
ROOMS: s £36-£40; d £48-£50*
CARDS:

Q Q Q **Caraneal** 12/14 Pier St, West Hoe PL1 3BS
(from A38 follow signs for city centre, then follow signs for The Hoe and seafront, on the seafront pass Plymouth Dome, turn right after Dome)
☎ 01752 663589 & 261931
Just a short walk from the sea front and The Hoe this neat mid-terrace house is located in a quiet residential area. Pleasant sensibly furnished accommodation and attractive public areas include a smart lounge and residents bar. A range of bar meals is available during the evening and local restaurants are close by.
9 bth/shr (1 fmly) No smoking in 3 bedrooms No smoking in dining room CTV in all bedrooms Tea and coffee making facilities No dogs (ex guide dogs) Licensed Cen ht CTV 2P Last d 7.30pm
ROOMS: s £25-£30; d £35-£40; wkly b&b fr £120*
CARDS:

Q Q **Citadel House** 55 Citadel Rd, The Hoe PL1 3AU
☎ 01752 661712 FAX 01752 202192
Closed 23 Dec-1 Jan
Conveniently located for easy access to the city centre, The Hoe and Barbican, this Victorian property offers soundly decorated, well equipped bedrooms. In addition to the front facing dining room, where a hearty breakfast is served, a cosy sitting room is available for guests use.
13 rms (7 shr) (3 fmly) No smoking in dining room CTV in all bedrooms Tea and coffee making facilities No dogs (ex guide dogs) Cen ht CTV
CARDS:

Q Q Q **Cranbourne Hotel** 282 Citadel Rd, The Hoe PL1 2PZ
☎ 01752 263858 & 661400 FAX 01752 263858
An attractive end of terrace, Georgian property, conveniently located with easy access to the city centre, The Barbican and The Hoe. Bedrooms are neatly furnished and decorated, with several rooms being especially suited to families. Breakfast is served in the light and airy dining room.
13 rms (8 shr) (1 fmly) No smoking in dining room CTV in all bedrooms Tea and coffee making facilities Licensed Cen ht 3P
ROOMS: s £17-£25; d £30-£45*
CARDS:

Q Q Q **Devonshire** 22 Lockyer Rd, Mannamead PL3 4RL (at Hyde Park public house on traffic island turn left into Wilderness Road. After 60mtrs turn left into Lockyer Rd) ☎ 01752 220726 FAX 01752 220766
Conveniently close to the shopping area of Mutley Plain, with its regular bus service to the city centre, this friendly well maintained property is located in a mainly residential street. The well proportioned bedrooms are furnished in a bright, contemporary style. A comfortable lounge is available, the dining room being located on the lower ground floor at the rear of the property. Evening meals are provided by prior arrangement.
10 rms (3 shr) (4 fmly) No smoking in 1 bedrooms No smoking in dining room CTV in all bedrooms Tea and coffee making facilities No dogs Licensed Cen ht CTV 6P Last d 2pm
ROOMS: s £19-£28; d £34-£40; wkly b&b £126-£140; wkly hlf-bd £182-£196
CARDS:

Q Q Q **Dudley Hotel** 42 Sutherland Rd, Mutley PL4 6BN
(A38-signs to city centre, before centre follow signs to rlwy stn, when reached Nth Rd East by stn stay on rd for 200yds, left at lights, left again) ☎ 01752 668322 FAX 01752 673763
A warm welcome awaits you at this family-run guest house. Bedrooms are very well equipped, spacious and cheerfully decorated. A family room is available, complete with cot and single bed. There is a separate sitting room and a pretty front facing dining room. Dinner is available on request and an information board provides guidance for those wishing to sample the local cuisine.
6 rms (5 shr) (2 fmly) No smoking in dining room CTV in all bedrooms Tea and coffee making facilities Cen ht CTV 2P Last d 9am
ROOMS: s £17-£25; d £36; wkly b&b £102-£150*
CARDS:

Q Q Q **Four Seasons** 207 Citadel Rd East, The Hoe PL1 2JF
(From A38 follow Hoe/Seafront signs to Notte St, turn left into Hoegate St, turn right off road) ☎ 01752 223591
Closed 23 Dec-1 Jan
This well presented property is located close to the seafront, The Hoe and the city centre. Ralph and Lynn Whitworth ensure a friendly and relaxed atmosphere. Bedrooms are light, airy and equipped with modern facilities. A full English Breakfast is served in the front facing dining room.
8 rms (7 shr) (3 fmly) No smoking in dining room CTV in all bedrooms Tea and coffee making facilities No dogs (ex guide dogs) Cen ht No coaches
CARDS:

Q Q Q **Georgian House Hotel** 51 Citadel Rd, The Hoe PL1 3AU
(Citadel Rd opposite Plymouth Pavillion conference centre. House 500yds on left) ☎ 01752 663237 FAX 01752 253953
Closed 25 Dec-1 Jan
Ideally located within walking distance of the city centre and The Hoe, this family run establishment is also conveniently situated for the ferry terminal. The comfortable bedrooms are well equipped, light and airy. An attractive bar is provided, and in the cosy restaurant both fixed price and an a la carte menus are available.
10 bth/shr (1 fmly) No smoking in 2 bedrooms No smoking in dining room CTV in all bedrooms Tea and coffee making facilities Direct dial from bedrooms Licensed Cen ht 2P No coaches Last d 8.30pm
ROOMS: s £26-£31; d £37-£42*
CARDS:

See advertisement on p.343.

This symbol indicates a 'Child Friendly' establishment - see page 25 for details

Q Q Q **Jewell's** 220 Citadel Rd, The Hoe PL1 3BB
☎ 01752 254760
Ideally situated within walking distance of the city centre and The Hoe, and completely renovated during 1998, a warm welcome is assured at Jewell's. Bedrooms are smartly presented, and breakfasts are served in the front facing dining room.
10 rms (7 shr) (5 fmly) No smoking in 3 bedrooms No smoking in dining room CTV in all bedrooms Tea and coffee making facilities Cen ht P
ROOMS: s £15-£20; d £30-£35; wkly b&b £105-£140*

Q Q Q **The Lamplighter Hotel** 103 Citadel Rd, The Hoe PL1 2RN
(exit A38, follow signs to city centre, first exit at roundabout, left at third set of traffic lights, right at fifth set of lights, second right)
☎ 01752 663855
Closed 24-26 Dec
This relaxed guest house is conveniently located for easy access to The Hoe, Barbican and the city centre. The light and airy bedrooms vary in size and shape. Public areas include a soundly appointed breakfast room with adjoining lounge area.
9 shr (2 fmly) CTV in all bedrooms Tea and coffee making facilities Cen ht CTV 4P
ROOMS: s £22-£25; d £32-£35; wkly b&b £84-£112.50*
CARDS:

Q Q Q **Rosaland Hotel** 32 Houndiscombe Rd, Mutley PL4 6HQ
(from A38 follow signs for city centre, keep left for Mitley, straight across at Freebooker/Firkin pub, right at lights, right again at next lights)
☎ 01752 664749 FAX 01752 256984
Convenient for the station and University this is a small family run hotel. Home cooked set meals are served in the cheerful, dining room, by prior arrangement. Bedrooms are well equipped with extras such as hair dryers, colour TV and beverage making facilities.
8 rms (4 shr) (2 fmly) No smoking in dining room No smoking in lounges CTV in all bedrooms Tea and coffee making facilities Direct dial from bedrooms No dogs (ex guide dogs) Licensed Cen ht CTV 3P Last d noon
ROOMS: s £18-£26; d £30-£37*
CARDS:

Q Q Q *Roscoff* 32 Grand Pde, West Hoe PL1 3DJ ☎ 01752 257900 FAX 01752 675192
Ideally situated for easy access to The Hoe and the ferry terminal, this smartly presented, and recently refurbished, small guest house is managed by friendly Winifred Rowlings. Bedrooms vary in size and some rooms are suitable for families. Breakfast is served in the rear facing dining room, with evening meals available by prior arrangement.
9 rms (2 shr) (2 fmly) No smoking CTV in all bedrooms Tea and coffee making facilities No dogs (ex guide dogs) Licensed Cen ht CTV
Last d 7pm

POLPERRO Cornwall & Isles of Scilly Map 02 SX25

Selected

Q Q Q Q **Landaviddy Manor** Landaviddy Ln PL13 2RT
(Turn right at mini rdbt at Polperro main car park, follow ln for 1m until T-junct, Landaviddy is signposted to the left) ☎ 01503 272210
mid Mar-end Sep
This former magistrates' house, built in 1785, stands in two acres of well tended gardens, just outside Polperro. Most of the bedrooms are en suite; two with their own private bathrooms. The bedrooms, some with sea views, are prettily decorated. There is a cosy bar, spacious dining room and a comfortable lounge. The hospitality extended by the proprietors, Mr & Mrs Rowe, leads to a many guests making a return visit.
7 shr No smoking CTV in all bedrooms Tea and coffee making facilities No dogs Licensed Cen ht CTV No children 14yrs 9P No coaches
ROOMS: d £48-£68*
CARDS:

Q Q Q **Penryn House Hotel** The Coombes PL13 2RQ
(follow A387 to village, hotel on main road 200 metres after main car park)
☎ 01503 272157 FAX 01503 273055
This privately owned and personally run small hotel is situated opposite the East Cornwall Artists building, near the entrance to the village. The well equipped bedrooms vary in their style of furnishings and a family suite is available. The hotel has a cosy lounge, a traditional style bar and in the dining room, both fixed price and a la carte menu are offered at separate tables. The hotel's own car park is certainly an added bonus in this much visited village.
10 bth/shr No smoking in bedrooms No smoking in dining room No smoking in lounges CTV in all bedrooms Tea and coffee making facilities Direct dial from bedrooms Licensed Cen ht CTV 13P No coaches Last d 9pm
ROOMS: s £30-£37; d £44-£58; wkly b&b £154-£203; wkly hlf-bd £231-£280
CARDS:

Premier Selected

Q Q Q Q Q **Trenderway** *(SX214533)* Pelynt PL13 2LY
(from Looe take A387 to Polperro, farm is signposted on main road)
☎ 01503 272214 FAX 01503 272991 Mrs L Tuckett
Closed Xmas
A 16th-century farmhouse set in 400 acres of beautiful countryside. The en suite bedrooms, in the main house and adjacent barn, are luxurious. Free-range eggs, from the farm's own chickens are used in the substantial breakfasts served in the sunny conservatory. Guests can also relax by the log fire in the large sitting room. The Meadow Barn is available as self-catering accommodation.
2 bth/shr 2 annexe bth/shr No smoking CTV in all bedrooms Tea and coffee making facilities No dogs Cen ht No children 4P 400 acres arable mixed sheep cattle
ROOMS: s £30-£45; d £60-£70; wkly b&b £392-£450*

POOLE Dorset Map **04** SZ09

Selected

Q Q Q Q **Acorns** 264 Wimborne Rd, Oakdale BH15 3EF
(On A35 1m from town centre)
☎ 01202 672901 FAX 01202 672901
Closed 23 Dec-1 Jan
A family-run hotel with a unique and homely style of hospitality, where the relaxed atmosphere ensures guests are made to feel at ease. Although the bedrooms are not large, this is compensated for by the excellent quality of the decor and soft furnishings. An evening meal, served in the bright dining room, is available by arrangement.
6 shr No smoking in bedrooms No smoking in dining room CTV in all bedrooms Tea and coffee making facilities No dogs Licensed Cen ht CTV No children 14yrs 7P No coaches Last d noon
ROOMS: s fr £27.50; d fr £45*
CARDS:

Q Q Q **Blue Shutters Hotel** 109 North Rd, Parkstone BH14 0LU (located 2 mins from Poole Park and Civic Centre buildings) ☎ 01202 748129
A well-kept guest house that is especially popular with the many business people who return here regularly. Good home-cooked food and a pleasant, bright and comfortable lounge and bar all add to the atmosphere. Bedrooms are all en suite and equipped with modern facilities.
8 shr No smoking in bedrooms No smoking in dining room CTV in all bedrooms Tea and coffee making facilities No dogs Licensed Cen ht CTV No children 5yrs 8P No coaches Last d 7pm(can be flexible)
ROOMS: s £27.50-£35; d £45-£48*
CARDS:

Q Q ***Burleigh Private Hotel*** 76 Wimborne Rd BH15 2BZ (off A35 onto A349) ☎ 01202 673889 FAX 01202 685283
Conveniently located close to the town centre, this friendly guest house offers clean, comfortable accommodation and homely hospitality. A choice of breakfast is available and served in the well appointed dining room. There is also a small lounge.
8 rms (4 shr) (1 fmly) No smoking in 3 bedrooms No smoking in dining room CTV in all bedrooms Tea and coffee making facilities Licensed Cen ht CTV 5P
CARDS:

Q Q Q **Centraltown** 101 Wimborne Rd BH15 2BP (A350 to town centre and take A349. Barclays International building on left and guest house 500mtrs on same side) ☎ 01202 674080 FAX 01202 674080
Closed mid Dec-mid Jan
The atmosphere is warm and friendly at this small, well-maintained guest house. The bedrooms are attractively decorated, furnished in modern style and suitably equipped. Full English breakfast is served in the bright cosy dining room.
6 rms (3 bth/shr) (2 fmly) No smoking in dining room No smoking in lounges CTV in all bedrooms Tea and coffee making facilities Cen ht 6P No coaches
ROOMS: s £22.50-£30; d £36-£45*

Q Q **Harbour View** 157 Longfleet Rd BH15 2HS ☎ 01202 672421
This small well run guest house continues to improve. The bright bedrooms are adequately furnished and equipped. Guests are offered a choice of breakfast which is served in the cosy dining room.
3 bth/shr No smoking in 2 bedrooms No smoking in dining room No smoking in lounges CTV in all bedrooms Tea and coffee making facilities Cen ht 4P No coaches
ROOMS: s £25; d £40-£50

Q **Holly House** 97 Longfleet Rd BH15 2HP (Just off A35) ☎ 01202 677839 FAX 01202 461722
This small guest house offers comfortable accommodation for those on a budget or working in the area. Conveniently located for easy access to the town centre and just a few minutes drive from the ferry port.
7 rms (4 bth/shr) (1 fmly) CTV in all bedrooms Tea and coffee making facilities Cen ht CTV 7P Harley Davidson hire
ROOMS: s £16-£30; d £34-£42; wkly b&b £112-£210*
CARDS:

Q Q **Lewina Lodge** 225 Bournemouth Rd, Parkstone BH14 9HU (leave A31 in either direction and proceed along A338. At Frizzell's roundabout join A35 and continue past next roundabout into Bournemouth Rd) ☎ 01202 742295
A warm welcome is particularly extended to guests with children although commercial visitors also find the location convenient. Breakfast, which includes a wide variety of cooked dishes, is provided in an atmospheric dining room. A garden to the rear is available to guests who wish to relax during the summer months.
6 rms (3 shr) (2 fmly) No smoking in dining room CTV in all bedrooms Tea and coffee making facilities No dogs (ex guide dogs) Cen ht 6P No coaches
ROOMS: s £20-£25; d £38-£42; wkly b&b £140-£182*

Q Q Q **Marric Hotel** 145 Bournemouth Rd, Parkstone BH14 9HT (on A35, midway between Poole and Bournemouth)
☎ 01202 732207 FAX 01202 747255
On the main road to Bournemouth, this pleasant hotel is well suited to the needs of both business visitors and tourists. With several family rooms and extra touches like hairdryers and ironing centres, the well-equipped rooms are comfortable and spacious. There is a new dining room, a large timbered bar and lounge.
6 shr 6 annexe bth/shr No smoking in 2 bedrooms No smoking in dining room CTV in all bedrooms Tea and coffee making facilities No dogs (ex guide dogs) Licensed Cen ht CTV 30P Last d 9pm
ROOMS: s £25-£27; d £40-£45*
CARDS:

Q Q Q **Marrick** 151 Bournemouth Rd, Parkstone BH14 9HT (midway between Poole and Bournemouth town centre on the A35, premises near the "Grasshopper" pub)
☎ 01202 721576 FAX 01202 747255
Mrs Graham extends a warm welcome at this family run hotel. Situated between Bournemouth and Poole, it is popular with commercial and holiday guests. The rooms are bright and well equipped, and most have en suite facilities. There is also a comfortable lounge and bar.
9 rms (7 shr) (1 fmly) No smoking in dining room No smoking in lounges CTV in all bedrooms Tea and coffee making facilities No dogs (ex guide dogs) Licensed Cen ht CTV 11P No coaches Last d 5pm
ROOMS: s £25-£30; d £39-£45; wkly b&b £175-£210; wkly hlf-bd £227-£262*
CARDS:

Q Q Q **Seacourt** 249 Blandford Rd, Hamworthy BH15 4AZ (Turn off A3049/A35 signposted to Hamworthy)
☎ 01202 674995
Run by the Hewitt family, this establishment is just a short drive from the ferry port. The comfortable bedrooms, some on the ground floor, are en suite and well decorated. In addition to the attractive breakfast room, a small lounge with TV and video is also available.
5 bth/shr (1 fmly) No smoking in 1 bedrooms CTV in all bedrooms Tea and coffee making facilities Cen ht CTV 5P No coaches
ROOMS: s £25-£30; d £36-£40; wkly b&b £126

Q Q ***Sheldon Lodge*** 22 Forest Rd, Branksome Park BH13 6DH (turn off A35 at Frizzel rdbt & take second exit signed Canford Cliffs. Then take first right into Western Road and first left into Forest Road)
☎ 01202 761186 FAX 01202 769891
Situated in Branksome Park, a quiet residential area, this hotel is close to the beaches and all amenities. It provides comfortable and adequately equipped bedrooms. An evening meal is available and is served in the pleasant refurbished dining room. Other public rooms include a bar lounge and a snooker room.
14 bth/shr (4 fmly) No smoking in dining room CTV in all bedrooms Tea and coffee making facilities Licensed Cen ht CTV 7P No coaches Snooker Last d 7pm
CARDS:

Q Q Q ***Southern Comfort*** 192 Bournemouth Rd, Parkstone BH14 9HZ
☎ 01202 722250
There is a warm and friendly welcome from Pam Richmond at this guest house conveniently located for both Poole and Bournemouth. There is a spacious lounge/dining room and the bedrooms are comfortable and tastefully decorated. Evening meals are available by prior arrangement.
6 rms (2 shr) (2 fmly) No smoking CTV in all bedrooms Tea and coffee making facilities No dogs Cen ht CTV 6P No coaches Last d 4pm
CARDS:

Q Q Q Towngate 58 Wimborne Rd BH15 2BY (take A349 towards centre of Poole, guest house on left before the town centre) ☎ 01202 668552
Closed mid Dec-early Jan
Conveniently located within walking distance of the town centre and a few minutes drive of ferry port, this small guest house offers a warm welcome. John and Ann Young have worked hard at upgrading this semi-detached property and the well equipped bedrooms, one on the ground floor, are now furnished and decorated in a modern style. Guests may choose a full breakfast or a one of the lighter alternatives.
3 shr (1 fmly) No smoking in dining room CTV in all bedrooms Tea and coffee making facilities No dogs (ex guide dogs) Cen ht 5P
ROOMS: s £30; d £40-£45✱

PORLOCK Somerset Map **03** SS84

Premier Selected

Q Q Q Q Q The Cottage Hotel Porlock Weir TA24 8PB (A39 from Minehead to Porlock, through village and take first right signposted Harbour (Porlock Weir) for 1.5m) ☎ 01643 863300 FAX 01643 863311
Feb-Nov
The subject of extensive renovations, The Cottage Hotel enjoys a delightful location overlooking Porlock Bay. Furnished and decorated in a style akin to a country house hotel, bedrooms are spacious and exceedingly comfortable, one boasting a magnificent four-poster bed. The sitting room is sumptiously elegant and a log fire burns on cooler evenings. Interesting and freshly prepared dinners are available by prior arrangement.
6 bth No smoking in dining room CTV in all bedrooms Tea and coffee making facilities No dogs Licensed Cen ht No children 10yrs 6P No coaches Last d 8pm
ROOMS: d £60-£110; wkly b&b £210-£332; wkly hlf-bd £364-£486
CARDS:

PORTESHAM Dorset Map **03** SY68

Selected

Q Q Q Q Millmead Hotel Goose Hill DT3 4HE (turn off A35 at Winterborne Abbas onto B3157 Portesham road. On reaching Portesham turn right at Kings Arms pub and hotel 100yds on right) (Minotel)
☎ 01305 871432 FAX 01305 871884
Situated in the peaceful village of Portesham, this comfortable hotel is being given a new lease of life thanks to owners Amanda and Mark Bowley. The attractive bedrooms are well equipped and benefit from views over the extensive gardens. Substantial breakfasts are served in the sunny conservatory with an interesting range of teas and coffees on offer. This is an ideal base from which to explore the beautiful countryside and spectacular coast. At the end of a hard day visiting the sleepy villages and historic towns, why not relax in the lounge and plan the itinerary for the following day! Although dinner is not available, there are a number of pubs and restaurants are nearby.
6 bth/shr No smoking in 3 bedrooms No smoking in area of dining room No smoking in 1 lounge CTV in all bedrooms Tea and coffee making facilities Cen ht 35P No coaches
ROOMS: s £35-£45; d £50-£60; wkly b&b £245-£315✱
CARDS:

PORTHCURNO Cornwall & Isles of Scilly Map **02** SW32

Q Q Q Corniche Trebehor TR19 6LX (at Sennen turn left off the A30 at the Wreckers Inn on to B3315, establishment 1m on left)
☎ 01736 871685 FAX 01736 871685
Feb-Oct
This detached, modern property, run by John and Wyn Ring, is within easy walking distance of both the Minack Theatre and Land's End and has stunning views over the surrounding countryside. Bedrooms are neatly decorated and soundly appointed. In the spacious lounge/dining room, cream teas are available during the day and each evening a selection of dishes is offered.
6 rms (1 fmly) No smoking CTV in 3 bedrooms Tea and coffee making facilities No dogs Licensed Cen ht CTV No children 5yrs 7P No coaches Last d 7pm
ROOMS: s £16; d £32; wkly b&b £112; wkly hlf-bd £157.15✱

Q Q Q ***Porthcurno Hotel*** The Valley TR19 6JX (Turn off A30 from Penzance onto B3283 at Catchall. On entering village, hotel is approx 200yds past post office)
☎ 01736 810119 FAX 01736 810711
Built in 1935, this building was formerly owned by Cable and Wireless and run as a hostel. The present owners, Richard Sweet and Alan Singer are in the process of restoring the house and grounds. The bedrooms are comfortable and neatly decorated, and other areas are attractively furnished with flair. Nearby are coastal paths to explore and the world famous Minack Theatre.
13 rms (2 shr) No smoking in dining room Tea and coffee making facilities Licensed Cen ht CTV No children 5yrs 14P No coaches Tennis courts available for hire opposite hotel

PORT ISAAC Cornwall & Isles of Scilly Map **02** SW98

Selected

Q Q Q Q **Archer Farm Hotel** Trewetha PL29 3RU
(on B3267 0.5 mile from Port Isaac) ☎ 01208 880522
Etr-Oct
Quietly located this Cornish stone farmhouse has been modernised and extended to provide comfortable accommodation. Vicki Welton is the charming hostess who welcomes guests, many returning on a regular basis, to her attractive home. Bedrooms are well equipped and look out onto open countryside; a family suite with two interconnecting rooms is popular. One of the two lounges has a bar and a hearty breakfast is served in the spacious dining room.
5 bth/shr (1 fmly) No smoking in dining room No smoking in 1 lounge CTV in all bedrooms Tea and coffee making facilities Licensed Cen ht CTV 8P No coaches
ROOMS: s £22.50-£28.50; d £45-£57; wkly b&b £150-£200*

Q Q **Bay Hotel** 1 The Terrace PL29 3SG
(turn off A39 onto B3314 then onto B3267) ☎ 01208 880380
Etr-Oct
In a prominent position overlooking the sea and cliffs of Port Isaac Bay, this hotel is only a three minute walk from the village and Port Gaverne beach. Front-facing bedrooms are, for obvious reasons, the most popular but all offer acceptable modern standards. In addition to the residents' lounge there is a cosy bar and spacious dining room where a fixed-price menu is served each evening.
10 rms (4 bth/shr) (4 fmly) No smoking in dining room CTV in all bedrooms Tea and coffee making facilities Licensed Cen ht 10P Last d 7pm
ROOMS: s £20-£23; d £40-£57; wkly b&b £120-£178;
wkly hlf-bd £186.50-£243

PORTLAND Dorset Map **03** SY67

Q Q Q **Alessandria Hotel & Italian Restaurant** 71 Wakeham Easton DT5 1HW (off A354) ☎ 01305 822270 & 820108 FAX 01305 820561
Rosa and Giovanni Bisogno have been running this friendly little hotel for almost ten years and offer their guests a warm welcome. Bedrooms are compact but neatly furnished, most have en suite facilities and some have wonderful sea views. The Alessandria has gained a good local reputation for its restaurant food and has a loyal following. Many of the dishes include home-grown fruit and vegetables.
15 rms (1 bth 10 shr) 1 annexe bth/shr (3 fmly) No smoking in dining room CTV in all bedrooms Tea and coffee making facilities No dogs (ex guide dogs) Licensed Cen ht CTV 16P No coaches Last d 9pm
ROOMS: s £29-£45; d £48-£55; wkly b&b £150-£180;
wkly hlf-bd £245-£280*
CARDS:

Selected

Q Q Q Q ***Queen Anne House*** 2/4 Fortuneswell DT5 1LP
(A354 to Portland and then Fortuneswell. House on left 200m past Royal Portland Arms) ☎ 01305 820028 FAX 01305 824389
This beautiful Grade II listed building, in an elevated position, offers bedrooms that are individually furnished to a high standard. The sitting and dining rooms are elegantly furnished and decorated in a style in keeping with this old house. Guests take breakfast around one large table, with a wide choice of options available.
3 bth/shr No smoking CTV in all bedrooms Tea and coffee making facilities No dogs (ex guide dogs) Cen ht CTV

PORTREATH Cornwall & Isles of Scilly Map **02** SW64

Selected

Q Q Q Q **Benson's** 1 The Hillside TR16 4LL
(exit A30 for Portreath onto B3300 and turn left by Portreath school. Fork left by Glenfeadon Castle) ☎ 01209 842534
Closed 22-30 Dec
Recently built overlooking the village, harbour and coast this guest house offers ground floor bedrooms which are attractively decorated, comfortably furnished and well equipped with many thoughtful extras. Christine and Peter Smythe offer a friendly welcome to their guests. Breakfast is taken in the conservatory, which enjoys splendid views.
4 shr No smoking CTV in all bedrooms Tea and coffee making facilities No dogs Cen ht No children 12yrs 6P No coaches
ROOMS: s £25; d £35; wkly b&b £100-£122.50*

Q Q **Cliff House** The Square TR16 4LB
(turn off A30 onto the Redruth to Portreath Rd) ☎ 01209 842008
Situated in the centre of this coastal village, Cliff House is an attractive stone cottage dating back about 200 years. The cosy, well equipped bedrooms are neatly decorated and furnished. A hearty breakfast is served in the rear dining room opening onto the kitchen.
4 shr CTV in all bedrooms Tea and coffee making facilities No dogs Cen ht No children 7yrs 6P No coaches
ROOMS: s £20-£25; d £33-£35*

PORTSMOUTH & SOUTHSEA Hampshire Map **04** SZ69

Abbey Lodge 30 Waverley Rd, Southsea PO5 2PW
(follow sea front signs towards pier turn left into Granada, Clarendon or Burgoyne Road to roundabout for Waverley Road)
☎ 01705 828285 FAX 01705 872943
Closed Xmas
Mr and Mrs Forbes offer a warm welcome at this conveniently located guest house. Situated a short distance from the shops and seafront, Abbey Lodge is brightly decorated and has well equipped bedrooms, some with en suite facilities. There is a comfortable lounge and a traditionally furnished dining room.
9 rms (1 bth 2 shr) (2 fmly) No smoking in dining room CTV in all bedrooms Tea and coffee making facilities No dogs Cen ht CTV
ROOMS: s £16-£18; d £30-£34*
CARDS:

Bembell Court Hotel 69 Festing Rd, Southsea PO4 0NQ
(road opposite Natural History Museum)
☎ 01705 735915 & 750497 FAX 01705 756497
Located close to the sea front, this friendly family run guest house has neatly decorated and well equipped bedrooms. There is a comfortable lounge and bar and an evening meal is available.
13 rms (9 bth/shr) (3 fmly) No smoking in 4 bedrooms No smoking in dining room No smoking in 1 lounge CTV in all bedrooms Tea and coffee making facilities Direct dial from bedrooms No dogs (ex guide dogs) Licensed Cen ht CTV 10P Last d 4pm
CARDS:

Collingham 89 St Ronans Rd, Southsea PO4 0PR
(follow signs for Southsea, at seafront east to canoe lake, take left fork & travel to Festing Road at top turn left then left into St Ronans Road)
☎ 01705 821549
Closed 25 Dec
This small and friendly guest house is situated a short distance from the shops and the seafront. The bedrooms are neatly decorated and simply furnished. A traditional cooked breakfast is served in the comfortable dining room.
6 rms (3 fmly) No smoking in 4 bedrooms No smoking in dining room No smoking in lounges CTV in all bedrooms Tea and coffee making facilities Cen ht CTV
ROOMS: s £16-£17; d £30-£32; wkly b&b £90-£95*

The Elms 48 Victoria Rd South, Southsea PO5 2BT
(left at roundabout at end of M275, straight ahead at next 3 roundabouts & traffic lights guesthouse 300yds on right)
☎ 01705 823924 FAX 01705 823924
This Victorian property is conveniently located close to the shops and seafront. The rooms, which are being steadily upgraded, are comfortably furnished. Several are suitable for families. There is a lounge, and a traditional breakfast can be served early for those catching ferries.
5 bth/shr (1 fmly) No smoking in dining room CTV in all bedrooms Tea and coffee making facilities No dogs (ex guide dogs) Cen ht CTV No children 4yrs 2P No coaches
ROOMS: d £38-£42; wkly b&b £125-£140
CARDS:

Fairlea 19 Beach Rd, Southsea PO5 2JH
(Follow signs for seafront and head for the Pyramids, facing east take the 1st left and 2nd right onto Beach Rd
☎ 01705 733090
Convenient for both seafront and town centre this neat and well maintained guesthouse is owned and personally run by Miss Johnson Walker. The bedrooms are bright and well appointed with modest furnishings. Breakfast is served in the pretty dining room.
4 rms (2 fmly) No smoking in dining room No smoking in lounges CTV in all bedrooms Tea and coffee making facilities Cen ht
ROOMS: s £12-£13; d £25-£26; wkly b&b £75-£80

The Festing Grove 8 Festing Grove, Southsea PO4 9QA
(follow signs to seafront, east along seafront to South Parade Pier, after pier immediate left, around lake 3rd left & 2nd right) ☎ 01705 735239
In a quiet residential street minutes from the seafront, this well presented guest house is personally run by Keith Newton. The bedrooms are brightly decorated and sensibly furnished and there's also a comfortable lounge and pleasant dining room where breakfast is served.
6 rms (2 bth/shr) (3 fmly) No smoking CTV in all bedrooms Tea and coffee making facilities Cen ht CTV No coaches
ROOMS: s £15-£17; d £28-£34

Gainsborough House 9 Malvern Rd, Southsea PO5 2LZ
(take M275 into Portsmouth, follow signs for seafront and Pyramids, opposite Pyramids turn into Florence Rd, take second left) ☎ 01705 822604
Closed Xmas
This personally run guest house is conveniently located for both town centre and seafront. The bedrooms are bright and comfortably appointed. The public areas are divided into a guest lounge and a separate dining room where a traditional breakfast is served.
7 rms (1 fmly) No smoking in dining room No smoking in lounges CTV in all bedrooms Tea and coffee making facilities No dogs Cen ht CTV No children 3yrs No coaches
ROOMS: s £16; d £30-£32; wkly b&b £98-£105*

Glencoe 64 Whitewell Rd, Southsea PO4 0QS ☎ 01705 737413 FAX 01705 737413
Located in a quiet residential area this well presented guest house is convenient for both seafront and town. Proprietor Mrs June Gwilliam offers a warm welcome and creates a friendly atmosphere. The bedrooms are bright and comfortably furnished, and breakfast is taken in the attractive dining room overlooking a small patio garden.
7 rms (5 shr) (1 fmly) No smoking CTV in all bedrooms Tea and coffee making facilities No dogs Cen ht CTV No children 3yrs
CARDS:

Selected

Q Q Q Q Hamilton House 95 Victoria Rd North, Southsea PO5 1PS (take M275 into Portsmouth, at roundabout take first exit and follow road to right and then to the left, cross three roundabouts into Victoria Rd N) ☎ 01705 823502 FAX 01705 823502

This spacious Victorian property has been carefully renovated by Graham and Sandra Tubb to provide bright, comfortable accommodation. The bedrooms all have colour television and four of them offer en suite facilities. There is a comfortable lounge where guests can relax, and easy parking is available in the adjoining street. This is an ideal stopover point for the ferry which is five minutes away and full English breakfast is available from 6.15am for those catching the boat.

8 rms (4 shr) (3 fmly) No smoking in 3 bedrooms No smoking in dining room No smoking in lounges CTV in all bedrooms Tea and coffee making facilities No dogs Cen ht CTV Last d noon

ROOMS: s £18-£23; d £36-£46; wkly b&b £123-£162; wkly hlf-bd £165-£203*

Q Q Q *Mallow* 82 Whitwell Rd, Southsea PO4 0QS (M275 to Portsmouth, head for Southsea seafront, after South Parade Pier bear left, turn second left, premises on the left)

☎ 01705 293829 & 293892 FAX 01705 293829

A warm welcome is assured from friendly hosts Jayne and George Gentle at their well run guest house. Bedrooms are attractively decorated with many thoughtful touches throughout. Guests can enjoy the comfortable lounge which has a licensed bar and the smart dining room where breakfast and home cooked evening meals are served.

7 rms (3 shr) (1 fmly) No smoking in 1 bedrooms No smoking in dining room CTV in all bedrooms Tea and coffee making facilities Licensed Cen ht CTV No coaches Last d 1pm

CARDS: MasterCard, Barclaycard Visa, Barclays Connect, Delta, Switch

Q Q Marmion Lodge 71 Marmion Rd, Southsea PO5 2AX (leave M27 for M275, over fly-over then bear left (bus lane), on rdbt bear left round S-bend, over next 3 rdbts,through lights, take 6th right turn)

☎ 01705 822150 FAX 01705 822150

This friendly guest house enjoys a central location convenient for both town centre and the sea front. Bedrooms are well equipped and offer comfortable accommodation. There is a lounge for guests' use and breakfasts are served in the downstairs dining room.

9 rms (6 shr) (3 fmly) No smoking in 3 bedrooms No smoking in dining room No smoking in lounges CTV in all bedrooms Tea and coffee making facilities Cen ht 3P No coaches Last d 5pm

ROOMS: s £20-£25; d £38-£45; wkly b&b £126-£145; wkly hlf-bd £170-£185*

CARDS: MasterCard, Barclaycard Visa, Barclays Connect, Delta, Switch

Q Q Sherwood 21 Beach Rd, Southsea PO5 2JH (Leave M27 take seafront road to Pyramids, turn left into Florence Rd then 2nd right) ☎ 01705 734108

Closed 23 Dec- 2 Jan

This friendly little guest house is within easy walking distance of the sea front with its many attractions. The bedrooms are fresh and bright and a hearty breakfast is served in the cosy breakfast room.

6 rms (1 fmly) No smoking in dining room CTV in all bedrooms Tea and coffee making facilities No dogs (ex guide dogs) Cen ht Last d 8am

ROOMS: s £13; d £26; wkly hlf-bd £115*

Q Q Uplands Hotel 34 Granada Rd, Southsea PO4 0RH (off seafront by South Parade pier) ☎ 01705 821508 FAX 01705 870126

This well established hotel is owned and personally run by the Zanellotti family, who provide a warm welcome and friendly atmosphere. Located close by the seafront the property is convenient for both city centre and ferries. Guests can enjoy home cooking in the downstairs dining room and relax in the cosy lounge.

9 rms (6 bth/shr) (4 fmly) No smoking in 2 bedrooms No smoking in dining room CTV in all bedrooms Tea and coffee making facilities No dogs Cen ht CTV No children 5yrs Last d day before

ROOMS: s £18-£25; d £36-£44; wkly b&b £126-£175; wkly hlf-bd £182-£231*

CARDS: MasterCard, American Express, Barclaycard Visa, Barclays Connect, Delta, Switch

Selected

Q Q Q Q Upper Mount House Hotel The Vale, Clarendon Rd, Southsea PO5 2EQ (exit M275 and head for D-Day Museum, turn down road opposite museum, turn right at T-junc, then turn right)

☎ 01705 820456

Located in a quiet residential area only a short distance from the seafront and shops you will find this colonial-style house that is over 150 year old. The bedrooms are attractively decorated and well equipped with modern en suite facilities. The elegant dining room is where good home cook food is served. There is a comfortable lounge and a cosy, well stocked bar.

12 bth/shr (3 fmly) No smoking in dining room CTV in all bedrooms Tea and coffee making facilities No dogs (ex guide dogs) Licensed Cen ht CTV 12P Last d 6pm

ROOMS: s £25-£28; d £40-£50

CARDS: MasterCard, Barclaycard Visa, Delta, Switch

Q Q Q *Victoria Court* 29 Victoria Rd North, Southsea PO5 1PL

☎ 01705 820305 & 0800 174911(booking)

A fine terraced Victorian house, retaining many of its original features. Personally run by owners Mr & Mrs Johnson, they offer smart, comfortable and well equipped bedrooms. The dinner menu is predominantly organic vegetarian and the vegetables are all home grown, the meals are served in the small cosy dining room located on the lower ground floor.

7 shr (3 fmly) No smoking in dining room CTV in all bedrooms Tea,and coffee making facilities Direct dial from bedrooms No dogs (ex guide dogs) Licensed Cen ht No coaches Last d am
CARDS:

POUNDSGATE Devon Map **03** SX77

Selected

Q Q Q Q **New Cott Farm** *(SX703727)* TQ13 7PD (take Two Bridges/Princetown turning off A38 at 2nd Ashburton junct (Pear Tree). Through Poundsgate village then 1st left and follow farm signs) ☎ 01364 631421 FAX 01364 631421 Mrs M Phipps
Closed 25 Dec
Set amongst thatched cottages in well tended gardens, New Cott Farm is a modern bungalow which enjoys breathtaking moorland views. Margaret Phipps offers wholesome farmhouse cooking in the comfortable dining room. A pine furnished conservatory is ideal for relaxing, and the bedrooms are bright and airy with co-ordinated fabrics.
4 bth/shr (1 fmly) No smoking Tea and coffee making facilities No dogs (ex guide dogs) Cen ht CTV No children 5yrs 4P 130 acres sheep Last d 4.30pm
ROOMS: d £37-£38; wkly hlf-bd £190-£195✳

PRESTON Lancashire Map **07** SD52

See also Longridge

Q Q Q **Birley Arms Motel** Bryning Ln, Warton PR4 1TN (leave M55 at junct 3 then A585 to Kirkham, follow signs to Wrea Green & Warton, Birley Arms between the two) ☎ 01772 679988 FAX 01772 679435
Modern bedrooms are offered at this popular country inn, situated in the village of Warton, midway between Preston and Lytham St Annes. The rooms are nicely spacious, as is the well kept bar which attracts locals as well as visitors. An extensive menu is available in the separate dining area, whilst service is friendly and willing.
16 bth/shr No smoking in area of dining room CTV in all bedrooms Tea and coffee making facilities Direct dial from bedrooms No dogs (ex guide dogs) Cen ht 80P Last d 9.15pm
ROOMS: s £27-£39; d £40-£45✳
MEALS: Lunch £8-£14alc Dinner £12.50&alc✳
CARDS:

Q Q Q **Tulketh Hotel** 209 Tulketh Rd, Ashton-on-Ribble PR2 1ES (from M6 junct 31, turn left onto A59 Preston then right onto A5085 towards Blackpool. Turn left at St Andrews Church after 3m onto Tulketh Rd) ☎ 01772 726250 & 728096 FAX 01772 723743
Closed 20 Dec-4 Jan
Many original features have been retained in this fine Edwardian house, home of Margaret and Derrick Butterworth. The hotel is situated in the residential area of Ashton, north-west of the town centre just off the Blackpool Road. Reception rooms extend to a bar lounge and dining room off an impressive

period hallway. Dinner is freshly prepared to order and breakfast is a substantial affair with a choice of Continental or English menus.
12 rms (11 bth/shr) (1 fmly) No smoking in 3 bedrooms No smoking in dining room CTV in all bedrooms Tea and coffee making facilities Direct dial from bedrooms No dogs Licensed Cen ht CTV 12P No coaches Last d 7.30pm
ROOMS: s £36.50-£38.50; d fr £48.50✳
CARDS:

Q Q Q **Withy Trees** 175 Garstang Rd, Fulwood PR2 8JQ (M6 junct 32, left at roundabout, establishment just before third set of traffic lights on right) ☎ 01772 717693 FAX 01772 718010
Well positioned for easy access to the motorway network, Withy Trees offers comfortable accommodation and a relaxed and friendly atmosphere. Bedrooms are well equipped and have modern facilities and two rooms are located on the ground floor. A comfortably furnished lounge is provided and breakfast is served in the bright and spacious dining room. An evening meal is served by prior arrangement.
10 bth/shr (4 fmly) No smoking in 7 bedrooms No smoking in dining room CTV in all bedrooms Tea and coffee making facilities Cen ht CTV 20P
ROOMS: s £30; d £40✳

RAMSGATE Kent Map **05** TR36

Q Q ***Eastwood*** 28 Augusta Rd CT11 8JS (east side of harbour near Granville Theatre) ☎ 01843 591505 FAX 01843 591505
This family run guest house is located close to the beach, the ferry port and the town centre. The accommodation is in two houses, each having its own breakfast room. The bedrooms are bright and well presented with modern furnishings and facilities. Set evening meals are served in the main house, and lock-up garages are available.
7 rms (2 bth/shr) (4 fmly) No smoking in 4 bedrooms No smoking in dining room No smoking in 1 lounge CTV in 13 bedrooms Tea and coffee making facilities Cen ht CTV 18P Last d 6pm

RAVENSCAR North Yorkshire Map 08 NZ90

Q Q Q **The Smugglers Rock Country** YO13 0ER
(leave A171 towards Ravenscar guesthouse half mile before Ravenscar opposite an old stone windmill) ☎ 01723 870044
Mar-Nov
Standing in open countryside, this friendly house offers well furnished and equipped bedrooms together with comfortable and cosy public rooms. A games room is also provided. The house's history links it with smuggling activities along the coast when a light from a window in the east wall would signal that it was safe to bring contraband through the tunnels from the beach.
8 bth/shr (1 fmly) No smoking in dining room No smoking in lounges CTV in all bedrooms Tea and coffee making facilities Licensed Cen ht CTV No children 3yrs 12P Last d 9am
ROOMS: s £24-£26; d £44-£46; wkly b&b £139-£145; wkly hlf-bd £195-£199*

READING Berkshire Map 04 SU77

Selected

Q Q Q Q **Abbey House Hotel** 118 Connaught Rd RG30 2UF
(take A329 towards Pangbourne after Reading West Railway bridge take 3rd left) ☎ 0118 9590549 FAX 0118 9569299
Closed Xmas-New Year
Abbey House is located in a quiet residential area off the main Oxford road, and is convenient for both Reading West station and the town centre. Bedrooms are well equipped, stylish and comfortable. Mr & Mrs Peck take pride in ensuring their guests have a relaxing stay. Dinners are available in the bright airy dining room which incorporates a cosy bar area and a quiet lounge.
19 bth/shr (1 fmly) No smoking in dining room CTV in all bedrooms Tea and coffee making facilities Direct dial from bedrooms No dogs (ex guide dogs) Licensed Cen ht CTV 14P Last d 8.00pm
ROOMS: s £54.50; d £72*
CARDS:

REDCAR North Yorkshire Map 08 NZ62

Q Q Q **Claxton Hotel** 196 High St TS10 3AW (leave A174 at double rdbt signed Redcar continue across railway crossing turn right at traffic lights by St Peter's Church hotel on left) ☎ 01642 486745 FAX 01642 486522
This friendly family owned commercial hotel overlooking the sea is also a popular venue for local functions. Bedrooms are bright and fresh with practical modern furnishings while public areas include a small lounge and an attractive dining room. It is hoped to extend the lounges in the near future and add more bedrooms.
28 rms (24 shr) (2 fmly) No smoking in dining room CTV in all bedrooms Tea and coffee making facilities Licensed Cen ht CTV 10P Last d 9pm
ROOMS: s £20-£23; d £38-£40*
CARDS:

REDDITCH Worcestershire

See **Studley**

REDHILL Surrey Map 04 TQ25

Selected

Q Q Q Q **Ashleigh House Hotel** 39 Redstone Hill RH1 4BG
(on the A25 Redhill to Sevenoaks 500yds from Redhill railway station)
☎ 01737 764763 FAX 01737 780308
Closed Xmas
Built at the turn of the century, this hotel is conveniently located a short walk from both Redhill Station and the shopping centre. The tastefully co-ordinated bedrooms are equipped with all modern facilities. Breakfast is served in a delightful dining room overlooking the gardens and swimming pool.
8 rms (6 bth/shr) (2 fmly) No smoking in dining room CTV in all bedrooms Tea and coffee making facilities No dogs (ex guide dogs) Cen ht 9P No coaches Outdoor swimming pool (heated)

Q Q Q **Lynwood House** 50 London Rd RH1 1LN
(on A23 going from Redhill to Croydon 500yds from the railway station)
☎ 01737 766894 & 778253
Closed 18 Dec-3 Jan
Lynwood House enjoys a central location on the London road close to both the town centre and railway station. Bedrooms are comfortably furnished and feature either en suite facilities or in-room showers. There is a cosy lounge and also a smart breakfast room.
9 rms (3 shr) (4 fmly) No smoking in dining room CTV in all bedrooms Tea and coffee making facilities No dogs (ex guide dogs) Cen ht 8P
ROOMS: s £28-£32; d £42-£50*
CARDS:

REDMILE Leicestershire Map 08 SK73

Q Q Q **Peacock Farm & The Feathers Restaurant** NG13 0GQ
(follow signs for Belvoir Castle Peacock Farm half a mile from village) ☎ 01949 842475 FAX 01949 843127
Located just north of the village, this house dates back to 1780 and retains many original features. Most bedrooms are situated in converted outbuildings and these are brightly decorated and well equipped with modern amenities. Two of the main house floors have been converted to family units comprising two rooms each and shared bathroom facilities. The restaurant is now managed by Chef Paul Reisenbuchler whose interesting carte and set priced menus are fully deserving of AA Rosette recognition. There are plans to open an Arts and Craft centre within one of the farm buildings; local artists' works decorate many of the public rooms.
8 rms (3 shr) (5 fmly) No smoking in dining room No smoking in 1 lounge CTV in all bedrooms Tea and coffee making facilities No dogs (ex guide dogs) Licensed Cen ht CTV ch fac 30P Indoor swimming pool Solarium Half-size snooker table Croquet Last d 8.30pm
ROOMS: s £35; d £49; wkly b&b £157.50-£245; wkly hlf-bd £259-£346.50*
CARDS:

REEDHAM Norfolk Map 05 TG40

Q Q Q **Briars** 10 Riverside NR13 3TF
(approach on B1140 Acle to Beccles road, turn into Reedham village at railway station, 0.5m to war memorial and fork right, Briars 200yds on left)
☎ 01493 700054 FAX 01493 700054
On the banks of the River Yare, this village is the end of the road before you approach the ferry crossing, so tranquility is virtually assured, as are the wonderful views, the waters lap the moorings opposite. The public rooms include a hairdressing salon and a teashop, where breakfast is offered, and dinner by arrangement. On the first floor, the intimate lounge and adjoining conservatory are an impressive vantage point over the surrounding Broads. The three comfortable bedrooms are furnished in a traditional cottage style and each has its own smartly appointed bathroom.
3 bth/shr No smoking in dining room No smoking in 1 lounge CTV in all bedrooms Tea and coffee making facilities Cen ht CTV 6P No coaches Fishing Last d 8pm
ROOMS: s £35; d £50
CARDS:

REETH North Yorkshire Map **07** SE09

Premier Selected

QQQQQ **Arkleside Hotel** DL11 6SG (follow B6160 then B6270 from Richmond to Reeth. Hotel on top right corner of village green) ☎ 01748 884200 FAX 01748 884200
Closed Jan-9 Feb
This charming private hotel is situated just off the village green and offers relaxing accommodation in each of its distinctive bedrooms. Spectacular views of the Swaledale can be enjoyed from the lounge and conservatory bar and guests have use of the patio and gardens. The dining room offers delicious candlelit dinners. Dorothy Kendall and Richard Beal are attentive hosts as well as being keen walkers and are pleased to arrange walking tours in the area.
8 shr 1 annexe bth (1 fmly) No smoking in bedrooms No smoking in dining room No smoking in lounges CTV in all bedrooms Tea and coffee making facilities Licensed Cen ht CTV No children 10yrs 6P No coaches Walking & painting trips arranged Last d 6.30pm
ROOMS: s £32-£42; d £64; wkly b&b £210-£224; wkly hlf-bd £310
CARDS:

REIGATE Surrey Map **04** TQ25

Selected

QQQQ **Cranleigh Hotel** 41 West St RH2 9BL
(on A25 at end of High St heading towards Dorking)
☎ 01737 223417 FAX 01737 223734
Closed 24 Dec-1 Jan
Mr and Mrs Bussandri have been welcoming guests here for over twenty years and the hospitality they provide ensures that many return. The hotel is within walking distance of the centre of Reigate and is also well placed for visitors flying into Gatwick. The rooms are all furnished in modern fabrics and feature many extra facilities. The bar and restaurant, which are open to the public, are a great asset to this hotel. Dinner can be taken Monday to Thursday and the menu reflects the proprietor's enthusiasm for good food and drink with an Italian influence. The hotel offers extensive gardens and a pool and tennis court is available for guests use.
9 rms (8 bth) No smoking in area of dining room CTV in all bedrooms Tea and coffee making facilities Direct dial from bedrooms No dogs (ex guide dogs) Licensed Cen ht CTV 6P No coaches
Outdoor swimming pool (heated) Last d 9pm
ROOMS: s £65-£75; d £85-£95*
CARDS:

RETFORD Nottinghamshire

See **North Wheatley**

RICHMOND North Yorkshire Map **07** NZ10

See also East Layton, Reeth and Thwaite

Q Q Q **Oak House** High St, Gilling West DL10 5JB (take A66 Penrith Rd, turn left after 1m for Gilling West/Richmond and travel 1m into village, house on right)
☎ 01748 826916 & 0410 584238
This delightfully inviting stone house stands in the lovely village of Gilling West and offers two bright and fresh bedrooms together with a cosy lounge and an attractive dining room. Guests may also use the well tended rear garden while very friendly service is provided by the resident owner.
2 bth/shr (1 fmly) No smoking CTV in all bedrooms Tea and coffee making facilities Cen ht CTV ch fac 3P No coaches Aromatherapy/reflexology Last d 6pm
ROOMS: s £25-£28; d £40-£45; wkly b&b £126-£139; wkly hlf-bd £210-£223✳

Selected

Q Q Q Q **Old Brewery** 29 The Green DL10 4RG (A6108 to Richmond, turn at second roundabout along Victoria Rd and then second turning left into Cravengate leading to the Green)
☎ 01748 822460 FAX 01748 825561
Feb-Nov
Set in the older part of this historic town overlooking the green, guests can enjoy the feeling of being in a quaint village whilst being able to take advantage of the town's many amenities. With views of the castle, this guest house was once an inn adjoining the brewery. In summer it is recognised by its hanging baskets and has an attractive mews garden to the rear. There is a cosy lounge with lots to read and the dining room overlooks the garden. Bedrooms are all individual and lean towards a period style. Yvonne Mears' home-cooked meals are a feature, breakfasts are delicious and her dinners offer an impressive choice.
5 bth/shr No smoking in dining room No smoking in lounges CTV in all bedrooms Tea and coffee making facilities No dogs Cen ht CTV No children 10yrs No coaches Puzzles Needlepoint Books Last d 5pm
ROOMS: s fr £30; d £42-£44; wkly b&b £147-£154; wkly hlf-bd £238-£245✳
CARDS:

Selected

Q Q Q Q **West End** 45 Reeth Rd DL10 4EX (on A6108 West End of Richmond going out to the Dales) ☎ 01748 824783
Closed Xmas/New Year
This beautiful mid 19th-century house lies well back from the road, secluded in its own garden dominated by a large monkey puzzle tree. Guests are assured of a warm welcome at Kath and Trevor Teeley's home which offers an attractive lounge and an inviting dining room where Kath's home cooked meals are proving to be a hit with guests. Bedrooms come in a variety of sizes and styles, all are comfortably furnished and prettily co-ordinated.
5 shr (1 fmly) No smoking in bedrooms No smoking in dining room CTV in all bedrooms Tea and coffee making facilities Licensed Cen ht 14P No coaches Last d 5pm
ROOMS: s £21; d £42; wkly b&b £147; wkly hlf-bd £231✳

Premier Selected

Q Q Q Q Q ♥ ***Whashton Springs*** *(NZ149046)* DL11 7JS (in Richmond turn right at traffic lights towards Ravensworth, 3m down steep hill farm at bottom on left)
☎ 01748 822884 FAX 01748 826285 Mrs M F Turnbull
Closed late Dec-Jan
Warm and friendly hospitality coupled with excellent service is assured at this delightful Georgian farmhouse set in the lovely countryside to the north of Richmond. The house is beautifully furnished and offers an attractive lounge complete with an open fire. All bedrooms have been

thoughtfully equipped, with those in the main house being more traditional than the more modern garden rooms. Delicious Yorkshire breakfasts make use of quality produce.
3 bth/shr 5 annexe bth/shr (2 fmly) No smoking in 3 bedrooms No smoking in dining room CTV in all bedrooms Tea and coffee making facilities Direct dial from bedrooms No dogs (ex guide dogs) Licensed Cen ht No children 5yrs 10P 600 acres arable beef mixed sheep

RICHMOND UPON THAMES Surrey Map **04** TQ17

Q Q Q **Hobart Hall Hotel** 43-47 Petersham Rd TW10 6UL (on A307, 200yds from Richmond Bridge) ☎ 0181 940 0435 FAX 0181 332 2996
Built around 1690, this pleasant historic hotel is located on the fringe of the town by the bridge. Many of the spacious bedrooms have views of the river and all offer a good range of modern facilities. The hotel benefits from a comfortably furnished lounge and attractive breakfast room - its walls painted with murals - where a good choice of breakfasts is served. There is also a fine meeting room, overlooking the river, which can accommodate up to 60 persons.
19 bth/shr (4 fmly) No smoking in bedrooms No smoking in dining room CTV in all bedrooms Tea and coffee making facilities Direct dial from bedrooms No dogs Cen ht CTV 19P
ROOMS: s £55-£60; d £75-£120*
CARDS:

RINGWOOD Hampshire Map **04** SU10

Premier Selected

Q Q Q Q Q **Little Forest Lodge** Poulner Hill BH24 3HS (1.5m E on A31) ☎ 01425 478848 FAX 01425 473564
This charming small hotel is well positioned for exploring the New Forest, and Judith Harrison offers a warm and friendly welcome to her guests. The well equipped bedrooms are attractively decorated and have many little extras. There is a comfortable bar lounge leading onto a terrace where guests can relax in the summer. Judith offers honest home-cooked food in the beautiful panelled dining room. Children are welcome here as are well behaved dogs, but only by prior arrangement.
6 bth/shr (1 fmly) No smoking in bedrooms No smoking in dining room CTV in 5 bedrooms Tea and coffee making facilities Licensed Cen ht 12P No coaches Last d 9pm
ROOMS: s £25-£35; d £45-£80; wkly b&b £150-£245; wkly hlf-bd £210-£300
CARDS:

Selected

Q Q Q Q **The Nest** 10 Middle Ln, off School Ln BH24 1LE (off A31 into B3347 at 2nd pedestrian lights turn sharp left into School Lane then left again) ☎ 01425 476724 & 0589 854505 FAX 01425 476724
This smartly maintained house, home of the Nixon family, is set in a quiet residential area. The bedrooms are comfortable and attractively decorated with co-ordinated Laura Ashley style fabrics and modern facilities. Breakfast is served in the conservatory dining room which overlooks the pond and garden.
3 rms No smoking CTV in all bedrooms Tea and coffee making facilities No dogs (ex guide dogs) 6P No coaches
ROOMS: s £18-£25; d £35-£39; wkly b&b £126-£140*

Selected

Q Q Q Q **Old Stacks** 154 Hightown Rd BH24 1NP (A31 West 1m before Ringwood, take slip road signed 'Hightown' & 'Owl Sanctuary'. Left into Eastfield Ln, after 0.5m turn right, Old Stacks on left)
☎ 01425 473840 FAX 01425 473840
Closed Xmas
Joan and Brian Peck ensure a warm welcome at this charming family home, where two spacious bedrooms are full of thoughtful extras such as fresh flowers, pot plants, chocolates and mineral water. There is a comfortable lounge with a piano and the charming dining room where breakfast is taken round a communal table. Although dinner is not available Joan is happy to recommend local pubs and restaurants.
2 bth/shr No smoking CTV in all bedrooms Tea and coffee making facilities Cen ht CTV No children 12yrs 4P No coaches
ROOMS: s £25-£30; d £39-£45

Selected

Q Q Q Q **Picket Hill House** Picket Hill BH24 3HH (from Ringwood take A31 Southampton, in approx 2m slip off left Burley/Services, under A31 turn right A31 Ringwood 250yds turn left Hightown & Crow) ☎ 01425 476173 FAX 01425 470022
Closed 23 Dec-2 Jan
Audrey and Norman Pocock's lovely home is located in the tranquillity of the New Forest, ideal for exploring the area or for quiet relaxation.

contd.

On arrival complimentary tea and home made cakes are served in the sun room which overlooks the pretty garden. The well furnished bedrooms are a haven of peace without TV - but if you can't live without it, there is a comfortable first floor TV lounge where books and games are also provided. Excellent breakfasts are enjoyed at one large table in the dining room. Stabling for horses can be arranged.
3 shr No smoking in bedrooms No smoking in dining room Tea and coffee making facilities No dogs (ex guide dogs) Cen ht CTV No children 12yrs 6P No coaches
ROOMS: s £25-£30; d £40-£48*
CARDS:

RIPON North Yorkshire Map **08** SE37

Selected

QQQQ **Bay Tree** *(SE263685)* Aldfield HG4 3BE
(approx 4m W, take unclass road S off B6265)
☎ 01765 620394 FAX 01765 620394 Mrs V Leeming
Situated in the quiet village of Aldfield, this delightful farmhouse lies close to Fountains Abbey. Accommodation is provided in a converted barn and offers both family and ground-floor rooms. Val Leeming and husband Andrew are the welcoming owners and nothing is too much trouble for them. Wholesome, home-cooked food is served and a comfortable lounge is provided for guests, where a wood-burning stove glows during colder weather.
6 bth/shr (1 fmly) No smoking CTV in all bedrooms Tea and coffee making facilities Licensed Cen ht ch fac 10P 400 acres beef, pigs, arable Last d 10am
ROOMS: s £25-£27.50; d £45-£50*
CARDS:

QQQ **St George Court** *(SE237697)* Old Home Farm, Grantley HG4 3EU (from Ripon, take B6265 and pass Fountains Abbey and right hand sign to Grantley & Wintersley, up hill for 1m past 'Risplith' sign and next right) ☎ 01765 620618 Mrs S Gordon
This delightful farm lies in secluded and attractive countryside close to Fountains Abbey and provides a peaceful haven. Bedrooms are around a courtyard and each has its own front door; all are well proportioned and thoughtfully equipped. One comprises two bedrooms to make an ideal family unit.
5 bth/shr (1 fmly) No smoking in 3 bedrooms No smoking in dining room No smoking in lounges CTV in all bedrooms Tea and coffee making facilities Cen ht 12P 20 acres beef sheep
ROOMS: s £30-£35; d £42-£45; wkly b&b £145-£150*
CARDS:

ROADWATER Somerset Map **03** ST03

Selected

QQQQ ***Wood Advent*** TA23 0RR ☎ 01984 640920
FAX 01984 640920
Dating back to the 19th century this working farm is surrounded by the beautiful rolling hills of Exmoor National Park and offers guests peace and quiet. Owners Diana and John Brewer have been welcoming guests for several years, with many returning on a regular basis. The spacious bedrooms are well equipped and comfortable and there is drawing room with a log fire on chilly evenings. Home cooked dinners are available by prior arrangement and the wine list offers some tempting choices.
4 bth/shr (1 fmly) No smoking in bedrooms No smoking in dining room No smoking in lounges CTV in all bedrooms Tea and coffee making facilities No dogs Cen ht CTV No children 9yrs 10P Outdoor swimming pool (heated) Tennis (grass) Clay pigeon shooting Last d 8.30am
CARDS:

ROCHDALE Greater Manchester Map **07** SD81

QQ **Leaches** *(SD837139)* Ashworth Valley OL11 5UN
(M62 J19 Heywood, Bamford Rd, left into B6222, right Ashworth Rd farm on left. M66 J1a Edenfield, A680, right into Ashworth Rd farm on right)
☎ 01706 641116 , 641117 & 224307 Mrs J Neave
Closed 22 Dec-2 Jan
Standing high on the moors above the town, this 300 year old stone built farmhouse enjoys fine views over the surrounding area. Nicely furnished bedrooms are complemented by a homely lounge. Breakfast is served in the adjacent sitting room.
3 rms (2 fmly) No smoking in bedrooms No smoking in dining room CTV in all bedrooms Tea and coffee making facilities Cen ht CTV No children 8yrs 6P Fishing Moorland Walks 140 acres beef sheep
ROOMS: s £20; d £36*

ROCK Cornwall & Isles of Scilly Map **02** SW97

QQ **Roskarnon House Hotel** PL27 6LD ☎ 01208 862329
FAX 01208 862785
Mar-Nov
Under the same family ownership for many years, this detached Edwardian property has stunning views over the Camel Estuary. Public rooms and some of the bedrooms benefit from the glorious view; several ground floor rooms are available. A fixed price menu is served using local produce wherever possible. Water sports can be arranged locally.
12 rms (10 bth/shr) (5 fmly) No smoking in dining room CTV in all bedrooms Tea and coffee making facilities No dogs (ex guide dogs) Licensed CTV 16P No coaches Last d 8pm
ROOMS: s £25-£35; d £50-£60; wkly b&b fr £175; wkly hlf-bd £210-£260*
CARDS:

RODE Somerset Map 03 ST85

Premier Selected

Q Q Q Q Q **Irondale** 67 High St BA3 6PB
(from Bath take A36 towards Warminster at Wolverton, turn left for a mile and cross small bridge. Take 3rd turning on right, 4th house on right) ☎ 01373 830730 FAX 01373 830730
Closed 24-27 Dec
Dating from the late 18th century, Irondale is located in the centre of the quiet village of Rode. Public areas include an elegant drawing room and a balcony overlooking the beautiful walled garden. Bedrooms are well equipped, tastefully decorated and offer high standards of comfort. Being just 10 miles south of Bath, this is an ideal location from which to tour the many and varied attractions of the area.
2 bth/shr (1 fmly) No smoking in bedrooms No smoking in dining room CTV in all bedrooms Tea and coffee making facilities No dogs (ex guide dogs) Cen ht CTV 3P No coaches
ROOMS: s £50; d £60-£65*
CARDS:

ROGATE West Sussex Map 04 SU82

Premier Selected

Q Q Q Q Q **Mizzards** *(SU803228)* GU31 5HS
(from x-rds in Rogate go S for 0.50miles cross river continue for 300yds then turn right, signed Mizzards Farm)
☎ 01730 821656 FAX 01730 821655 Mrs J C Francis
Closed Xmas
The 16th-century, stone-built Mizzards Farm enjoys an idyllically tranquil setting in a designated Area of Outstanding Natural Beauty. Surrounded by delightful landscaped gardens which include a carp-filled lake, swimming pool and croquet lawn, and extensive grounds that support a flock of pedigree Chorales sheep. Roses climb around the front door that leads into a fine galleried inner hall where breakfast is served. There is a split-level drawing room with grand piano (kept at concert pitch) and a real log fire in winter; there is also a charming first floor, wicker-furnished conservatory. The largest of the three individually decorated and antique-furnished bedrooms boasts a splendid canopied bed set on a dais and a mirrored marble bathroom. This is a no smoking house.
3 bth/shr No smoking CTV in all bedrooms Tea and coffee making facilities No dogs Cen ht No children 9yrs 12P Outdoor swimming pool (heated) Croquet 13 acres sheep non-working
ROOMS: s £34-£40; d £54-£62

ROMFORD Greater London Map 05 TQ58

Q Q **The Orchard Guest House** 81 Eastern Rd RM1 3PB
(Turn off main road into Junction Rd opposite Romford Police Station, Eastern Rd is 3rd turning on the right) ☎ 01708 744099 FAX 01708 768881
This attractive Edwardian house is located in a quiet residential cul-de-sac just minutes from the town centre. The bedrooms are bright and attractively pine furnished with en suite facilities. There is a comfortable lounge/dining room where guests may enjoy a traditional breakfast.
5 rms (1 shr) (2 fmly) CTV in all bedrooms Tea and coffee making facilities No dogs (ex guide dogs) Cen ht CTV 6P No coaches Last d am
ROOMS: s £25-£35; d £35-£45; wkly b&b £175-£245*

ROMSEY Hampshire Map 04 SU32

See also East Tytherley

Selected

Q Q Q Q **Country Accommodation** The Old Post Office, New Rd, Michelmersh SO51 0NL (leave A3057 at Timsbury New Rd, Michelmersh, guesthouse at top of hill) ☎ 01794 368739
This attractive bed and breakfast started life as a forge back in the 1920s. It then became the post office and later a bakery and village shops were added. These became the attractive bedrooms, which have many interesting pieces of memorabilia from those bygone days adorning the walls. All have modern en suite facilities, TV, books, and unlimited supplies of tea and coffee. Freshly cooked English breakfasts are served in the breakfast room, using home produced eggs and homemade preserves.
3 annexe shr (1 fmly) No smoking in dining room CTV in all bedrooms Tea and coffee making facilities No dogs Cen ht 5P No coaches
ROOMS: s £28; d £45*
CARDS:

Selected

Q Q Q Q **Cranford Farm** *(SU360252)* Braishfield SO51 0PU
(from A3057 follow Stockbridge signs pass the Dukes Head pub on reaching sign for Hilliers turn right then immediately left signed Michelmarsh)
☎ 01794 368216 FAX 01794 368216 Mr B J C Brooks
A warm welcome from Tina and Brian Brooks awaits guests visiting Cranford Farm. Set in the Test Valley between the picturesque villages of Braishfield and Michelmarsh, the idyllic surroundings and the charming scene of sheep grazing viewed from bedroom windows make this a peaceful place to stay. The rooms are spacious and well furnished with such thoughtful extras as fresh milk for tea and coffee.
3 bth/shr CTV in all bedrooms Tea and coffee making facilities No dogs Cen ht No children 7yrs 12P 3 acres sheep
ROOMS: s £28; d £45*

Premier Selected

QQQQQ **Highfield House** Newtown Rd, Awbridge SO51 0GG (take A27 signed Salisbury/Whiteparish for 3 miles then 1st right into Danes Rd for 1 mile the 1st left signed Newtown, Highfield 1st house on right) ☎ 01794 340727 FAX 01794 341450
Set in one and a half acres of beautiful gardens in a peaceful setting outside the village of Awbridge, this welcoming house has a friendly and relaxing atmosphere. Bedrooms have lovely old furnishings and are thoughtfully equipped to include items such as radio alarm clocks, hair dryers and bathrobes; you'll even find flowers from the gardens. Downstairs there is a cosy lounge where a log fire burns on chilly days. Home-cooked breakfasts and dinner are served around the one large table in the dining room.
3 bth/shr No smoking CTV in all bedrooms Tea and coffee making facilities No dogs (ex guide dogs) Cen ht CTV No children 14yrs 10P No coaches Golf horse riding & fishing can be arranged Last d 4pm
ROOMS: d fr £55*

ROSEDALE ABBEY North Yorkshire Map **08** SE79

Selected

QQQQ **Sevenford House** Thorgill YO18 8SE (turn off A170 at sign for Rosedale Abbey, in village turn sharp left at Coach House Restaurant & right at White Horse) ☎ 01751 417283 FAX 01751 417505
Located in the heart of a National Park, this delightful Victorian house stands in peaceful grounds and was built from the stones of Rosedale Abbey. It has been delightfully furnished by the resident owners and provides three comfortable bedrooms, a traditional lounge and a spacious breakfast room. Two self-catering cottages are also available within the grounds.
3 shr (1 fmly) No smoking CTV in all bedrooms Tea and coffee making facilities No dogs (ex guide dogs) Cen ht 6P No coaches
ROOMS: d £42-£45; wkly hlf-bd £294-£315

ROSS-ON-WYE Herefordshire Map **03** SO52

See also Much Birch

Selected

QQQQ **The Arches Hotel** Walford Rd HR9 5PT (take B4234 from town centre continue for approx half a mile The Arches is on the left just below Chasedale Hotel) ☎ 01989 563348
Situated within walking distance of the town, The Arches Hotel has been under the same ownership for over thirty years. Well equipped bedrooms are furnished in modern style and most have en suite facilities. Public areas include a dining room where breakfast and dinner are served. The conservatory/lounge overlooks the pretty gardens and is filled with ornaments and memorabilia.
8 rms (2 bth 3 shr) (1 fmly) No smoking CTV in all bedrooms Tea and coffee making facilities No dogs (ex guide dogs) Licensed Cen ht CTV 9P No coaches Last d 5pm
ROOMS: d £40-£44; wkly b&b £130-£150*
CARDS: Mastercard Visa

Q **Brookfield House** Ledbury Rd HR9 7AT (approaching town from M50 via Ledbury road Brookfield House is on the left at the bottom of the hill before town centre)
☎ 01989 562188
Closed 3 days Xmas rs Dec-Jan
This large detached property stands just north of the town centre, and in easy reach of the A40. It is an 18th-century building, part of which dates from the Queen Anne period, and part from the Georgian era. The accommodation is well equipped and represents good value for money. Separate tables are provided in the traditionally furnished breakfast room and there is also a bright and comfortable lounge.
8 rms (1 bth 2 shr) No smoking in dining room CTV in all bedrooms Tea and coffee making facilities Licensed Cen ht No children 5yrs 10P No coaches
ROOMS: s £16-£20; d £28-£35; (room only)
CARDS: Mastercard American Express Visa

Selected

QQQQ **Brynheulog** Howle Hill HR9 5SP (from Ross take B4234 and turn left signed 'Howle Hill'. After 250yds take 1st right for Howle Hill, proceed to x-roads. Turn left, house past church) ☎ 01989 562051 FAX 01989 562051
This recently built detached house stands near the tiny, peaceful village of Howle Hill, 100 yards past the church, in picturesque countryside. One of its bedrooms has an antique four-poster bed, and on the ground floor there is a private suite of two bedrooms, lounge, kitchen and bathroom which can be let on a self-catering basis. The lounge and dining room are pleasant and comfortable.
4 bth/shr (1 fmly) No smoking in 2 bedrooms No smoking in dining room No smoking in 1 lounge CTV in 2 bedrooms Tea and coffee making facilities Cen ht CTV 5P No coaches
ROOMS: s fr £15; d fr £30*

Selected

QQQQ **Lumleys** Kern Bridge, Bishopswood HR9 5QT (A40 turn off at Goodrich onto B4229 over Kern Bridge. Right at Inn On The Wye aprox 400yds past inn opposite picnic ground)
☎ 01600 890040
Lumleys is a former Victorian roadside hostelry which has been transformed into a guest house while retaining much original character.

Bedrooms are comfortable, tastefully decorated and filled with lots of extra personal touches to make guests feel at home. Public areas are spacious and have some fine period pieces and ornaments very much in keeping with a bygone era.

3 bth/shr No smoking CTV in all bedrooms Tea and coffee making facilities Direct dial from bedrooms Cen ht No children 10yrs 15P No coaches Last d 7pm
ROOMS: s £30-£40; d £44-£50*

QQQ **Sunnymount Hotel** Ryefield Rd HR9 5LU
(M50 junct 4-at 1st rdbt follow signs for A449 Ross, at 2nd take A40 Gloucester turnoff, at 3rd turn right to Ross town centre, then take 2nd right)
☎ 01989 563880
rs 21-31 Dec (B & B only)
Situated in a quiet residential area east of the town centre, this large house is in easy reach of the M50 and A40. The accommodation is well maintained, and meals are served at separate tables in the bright, pleasant dining room.
6 bth/shr No smoking in dining room No smoking in 1 lounge Tea and coffee making facilities No dogs (ex guide dogs) Licensed Cen ht CTV 7P No coaches Last d 4pm
ROOMS: s £20-£27; d £50; wkly hlf-bd £235*
CARDS:

QQQ *White Lion* Wilton Ln, Wilton HR9 6AQ
☎ 01989 562785
This stone-built inn dates from 1770 and is situated on the bank of the River Wye at Wilton Bridge. The bar has kept its traditional character, and its dining room once served as the local jail! The wide range of dishes on the menu can be served in either the dining room or the bar. The bedrooms all have modern equipment and facilities.
5 rms

ROTHBURY Northumberland Map 12 NU00

QQQ **Orchard** High St NE65 7TL
(turn off A697 onto B6334 to Orchard Guesthouse on right side of village)
☎ 01669 620684
Closed Dec-Feb
The hospitality extended by owners Jean and Martin Pickard is the lynch pin of this comfortable guest house in the main street of this popular tourist village. Guests will be greeted on arrival with tea in the lounge, whilst breakfasts are taken in the attractive dining room.
6 rms (4 shr) (1 fmly) No smoking CTV in all bedrooms Tea and coffee making facilities No dogs Cen ht No coaches
ROOMS: s £21-£30; d £40-£46

Prices shown in the directory are meant as a guide only and are subject to change. Please check before you book

ROTHERHAM South Yorkshire Map 08 SK49

Selected

QQQQ **Black Lion Country Inn** 9 New Rd, Firbeck S81 8JY (M18 junct 1 to Maltby, take A64 (East Retford) 3m signpost Firbeck) ☎ 01709 812575 FAX 01709 819892
This lovely 400-year-old inn stands in the delightful village of Firbeck, providing good-value meals in both the restaurant and photograph-lined bar. The bedrooms here are of high quality, large, well furnished and equipped with all the comforts guests could need. Continental breakfast is provided in the bedrooms although guests can also opt for a full breakfast in the restaurant.
2 bth/shr (1 fmly) CTV in all bedrooms Tea and coffee making facilities Direct dial from bedrooms No dogs (ex guide dogs) Cen ht 50P Last d 9.30pm
ROOMS: s £50-£65; d £55-£75*
MEALS: Lunch £7.95-£12.95 Dinner £12.95-£15.95&alc*
CARDS:

Selected

Q Q Q Q **Stonecroft** Main St, Bramley S66 2SF
(M18 junct1, towards Rotherham on A631, after 300yds turn right at Sportsman Inn, continue through village to Stonecroft on right after 400yds) ☎ 01709 540922 FAX 01709 540922
This small creeper-clad cottage, liberally festooned with colourful hanging baskets, offers attractively furnished bedrooms, with many useful amenities, including video players and an extensive video library. A delightful courtyard with lawns and a fountain separates the main house from the mews, and there is a warm, inviting lounge. All in all Stonecroft is very much a home from home.
3 bth/shr 5 annexe shr (1 fmly) No smoking in bedrooms No smoking in dining room No smoking in 1 lounge CTV in all bedrooms Tea and coffee making facilities Licensed Cen ht CTV 10P No coaches
ROOMS: s £31-£34; d £41-£44; wkly b&b £210-£240*
CARDS:

ROTTINGDEAN East Sussex Map **05** TQ30

Q Q ***Braemar House*** Steyning Rd BN2 7GA ☎ 01273 304263
A colourful display of flowers in hanging baskets makes a welcoming first impression at Chris and Susan Gregory's guest house, situated near the centre of the village. Inside all is spick-and-span with neat, well kept bedrooms, a comfortable TV lounge and welcoming breakfast room.
15 rms (2 fmly) No smoking in dining room Cen ht CTV No coaches

ROWSLEY Derbyshire Map **08** SK26

Q Q Q **Grouse and Claret** Station Rd DE4 2EL
(on A6 between Matlock and Bakewell) ☎ 01629 733233
A popular and attractive roadside inn, the Grouse and Claret has comfortable, spacious bedrooms decorated in an attractive modern style. Although they are not en suite, they are close to the well equipped bathrooms. The themes of grouse and claret have inspired the downstairs decor, and the bar serves a range of popular dishes.
5 rms No smoking in area of dining room No smoking in 1 lounge CTV in all bedrooms Tea and coffee making facilities No dogs (ex guide dogs) Cen ht 77P Boules pitch Last d 9.30pm
ROOMS: s £20; d £35*
MEALS: Lunch fr £10 Dinner £10-£15*
CARDS:

RUFFORTH North Yorkshire Map **08** SE55

Q Q Q **Wellgarth House** Wetherby Rd YO23 3QB
(from A1237, at 2nd rdbt turn left onto B1224 signposted Wetherby, after 1m 1st house on left entering village)
☎ 01904 738592 FAX 01904 738595
Standing on the edge of the village in open countryside, Wellgarth is a large, detached house, offering comfortable modern bedrooms. There is a small guests' lounge and a substantial breakfast is served in the bright dining room.
7 shr (1 fmly) No smoking in bedrooms No smoking in dining room CTV in all bedrooms Tea and coffee making facilities Cen ht CTV No children 16yrs 8P No coaches
ROOMS: s £18.50-£20; d £37-£45
CARDS:

Take the guesswork out of choosing somewhere to eat with AA Best Restaurants, featuring more than 1800 inspected places to eat throughout the country

RUSHLAKE GREEN East Sussex Map **05** TQ61

Premier Selected

Q Q Q Q Q **Great Crouchs** TN21 9QD
(off B2096, 200yds past village green on right) ☎ 01435 830145
Closed 20-26 Dec
This delightful, listed house, dating from the early 18th century, is in a tranquil rural setting on the fringe of the small village. Pride of place, of the two letting rooms, goes to the converted barn - more a small suite - with its high, beamed ceiling, and wood-burning fire. The other room in the main building, has its own private bathroom adjacent. A generous English breakfast is served in the cosy dining room in the main house. The hospitality of owners Ruth and Richard Thomas is of the highest standard and adds to the relaxing and informal atmosphere.
2 bth/shr No smoking CTV in all bedrooms Tea and coffee making facilities No dogs (ex guide dogs) Cen ht No children 6P No coaches Indoor swimming pool (heated)
ROOMS: d £60-£65*

RUSTINGTON West Sussex Map **04** TQ00

Selected

Q Q Q Q **Kenmore** Claigmar Rd BN16 2NL
(from A259 follow signs for Rustington turn off for Claigmar Rd between War Memorial & Alldays Shop. Kenmore on right as Claigmar Rd bends) ☎ 01903 784634 FAX 01903 784634
Located in a quiet residential road just of the main shopping street, the Kenmore is personally run by Ray and Sylvia Dobbs' who provide a warm and friendly welcome. This well kept house provides comfortable accommodation and extras in the rooms include fridges and hairdryers along with nice touches like pot-pourri, tissues and face cloths. The lounge offers books, magazines and comfortable seating and there is a bright and airy dining room where a good choice of breakfast is provided. Dinners are no longer available but there are plenty of options within walking distance. The Kenmore offers off street parking.
7 rms (1 bth 5 shr) (2 fmly) No smoking in dining room No smoking in lounges CTV in all bedrooms Tea and coffee making facilities Cen ht CTV 7P No coaches Last d noon
ROOMS: s £22.50-£25; d £45-£50; wkly b&b £145-£160*
CARDS:

RUYTON-XI-TOWNS Shropshire Map **07** SJ32

Q Q Q **Brownhill House** SY4 1LR (Off A5 onto B4397 2 miles to Ruyton-XI-Towns through village Brownhill House is situated on the left on a right hand bend) ☎ 01939 261121 FAX 01939 260626
rs Xmas

Situated in the unusually named Ruyton-XI-Towns, some eight miles from Shrewsbury, this cottage has a most attractive, steeply sloping garden leading down to the River Perry. Inside, the bedrooms are thoughtfully equipped, including desk space for business visitors. The beamed lounge has a large open fireplace and a hearty breakfast is served around one large table in the kitchen. There is a secure lock-up for bicycles.
3 bth/shr No smoking in bedrooms No smoking in dining room Tea and coffee making facilities No dogs (ex guide dogs) Cen ht CTV 5P No coaches Fishing Canoeing Garden Last d midday
ROOMS: s £22-£29; d £37-£41; wkly b&b £108.50-£133; wkly hlf-bd £192.50-£217*
CARDS:

RYDAL Cumbria

See **Ambleside**

RYDE See **WIGHT, ISLE OF**

RYE East Sussex Map **05** TQ92

See also **Winchelsea**

Premier Selected

QQQQQ **Benson Hotel** 15 East St TN31 7JY
(in direction of town centre and high street, pass under stone landgate arch and continue 200 metres to High St. East St is first on the left)
(The Circle) ☎ 01797 225131 FAX 01797 225512
Closed Jan
Situated in the heart of the conservation area of Rye, this listed building has been sympathetically converted into an elegant small hotel. The rooms have been individually decorated in period style and are comfortably appointed with a range of thoughtful extras, some enjoying views of the marsh and surrounding countryside. At dinner guests can choose from a good selection of home cooked food, and a good choice of breakfast is served in the bistro-style dining room. The attractive lounge, conservatory and terrace overlook the River Rother and Romney Marsh, and the hotel offers both bar and room service.
4 bth (1 fmly) No smoking in bedrooms No smoking in area of dining room CTV in all bedrooms Tea and coffee making facilities Direct dial from bedrooms No dogs (ex guide dogs) Licensed Cen ht No coaches Last d 9pm
ROOMS: s £47-£60; d £64-£100
CARDS:

Premier Selected

QQQQQ **Cadborough Farm** *(TQ908197)* Udimore Rd TN31 6AA (on B2089) ☎ 01797 225426 FAX 01797 224097
Mrs J Apperly
Closed 24-26,31 Dec 1 Jan
Cadborough Farm was rebuilt in 1952 on the original foundations of the 17th-century farmhouse. In an excellent position on the outskirts of Rye, the farm benefits from magnificent views across the Brede Valley towards the sea overlooking Rye and Winchelsea. Individually decorated bedrooms, one a full suite, are spacious and comfortable and come with little extras like fresh flowers, sweets, home-made biscuits, books and magazines. Three rooms are in the main house and another two, soon to be converted to self-catering apartments, are in the newly converted stables close by. Day rooms, warmed by real fires in winter, include a fine, beamed sitting room, and a separate breakfast room where the day starts with a delicious spread including free range eggs from the farm's own hens.

3 bth/shr No smoking CTV in all bedrooms Tea and coffee making facilities Cen ht No children 8yrs 5P 24 acres non-working
ROOMS: d £45-£55
CARDS:

QQ **Cliff Farm** *(TQ933237)* Iden Lock TN31 7QE
(2m along the Military Road to Appledore turn left at hanging milk churn)
☎ 01797 280331 FAX 01797 280331 Mrs P Sullivin
Mar-Oct
A couple of miles out of town, Cliff Farm is set well back from the road and enjoys fine views across Romney Marsh. Run in friendly fashion by Pat and Jeff Sullivin, the three well kept bedrooms are traditionally furnished and prettily decorated. Downstairs there is a comfortable residents' lounge, warmed by a log-burning stove when needed, with TV and plenty of board games and magazines.
3 rms (1 fmly) No smoking in bedrooms Tea and coffee making facilities Cen ht CTV 6P 6 acres smallholding
ROOMS: d £31-£32*

359

Premier Selected

QQQQQ **Jeake's House** Mermaid St TN31 7ET
(within the cobbled medieval town centre, approached either from High St or from The Strand Quay)
☎ 01797 222828 FAX 01797 222623
Set in one of the prettiest cobbled streets of this ancient town, the creeper-covered Jeake's House has a long and interesting history. With its origins in the 16th century it has by turns been a wool store, Friends Meeting House (one of the bedrooms is named after Elizabeth Fry, a frequent visitor) and a Baptist Chapel. Today, under the friendly administration of Jenny Hadfield, it provides charming antique-furnished bedrooms. All are individually decorated and well appointed with modern amenities and comforting extras. Day rooms comprise a

contd.

comfortable bar/lounge with chintz sofas and easy chairs and shelves full of books, a beamed parlour with piano and a delightful galleried breakfast room where a good vegetarian breakfast is among the options.
12 rms (8 bth 2 shr) (2 fmly) No smoking in dining room No smoking in 1 lounge CTV in all bedrooms Tea and coffee making facilities Direct dial from bedrooms Licensed Cen ht No children 12yrs 20P No coaches
ROOMS: s £25.50-£59; d £49-£65; wkly b&b £171.50-£227.50*
CARDS:

Premier Selected

Q Q Q Q Q **King Charles II Guest House** 4 High St TN31 7JE (centrally in Rye High St) ☎ 01797 224954
Known locally as the Black Boy (due to its association with King Charles II, a frequent visitor) this listed medieval building dates back to 1420. In the 1930s it was home to the novelist Radclyffe Hall; today it has been lovingly and sensitively restored by Margrit Berger and Nicola Fischbach. The day rooms boast old black beams and ancient brick fireplaces made homely by fresh flowers and plants while the two bedrooms combine character and charm with modern convenience and various comforting extras like mineral water and magazines. There is also a tiny flower-filled walled garden/patio. Dinner is not available but Nicola and Margrit are happy to recommend local restaurants, as well as advise on local history and places of interest. There is restricted on-road parking opposite the house.
2 shr No smoking CTV in all bedrooms Tea and coffee making facilities No dogs Licensed Cen ht
ROOMS: d £70-£82; wkly b&b £210-£240*

Q Q **Little Saltcote** 22 Military Rd TN31 7NY (turn off A268 onto Military Rd, signposted to Appledore. House a quarter mile on left) ☎ 01797 223210 FAX 01797 223210
Little Saltcote is peacefully located on the edge of town; the tile-hung, turn-of-the-century house overlooks the River Rother and Romney Marsh beyond. The rooms are comfortably furnished, and some are suitable for families, all have either river or garden views. Proprietors Barbara and Denys Martin offer a warm welcome and serve a hearty breakfast in the dining room.
5 rms (2 shr) (3 fmly) No smoking in dining room CTV in all bedrooms Tea and coffee making facilities Cen ht 3P No coaches
ROOMS: s £22.50-£25; d £37-£42*

Selected

Q Q Q Q ***Manor Farm Oast*** Windmill Orchard, Main Rd TN36 4AJ (A259 Rye to Hastings road, from Rye in Icklesham pass church on left, turn left at crosslands into Workhouse Lane. After sharp left bend turn left) ☎ 01424 813787 FAX 01424 813787
Closed 28 Dec-31 Jan
Surrounded by orchards, this mid-19th century oast house is set in a peaceful rural location. The three bedrooms have been attractively decorated and tastefully converted to preserve the original features of the building. There are lots of thoughtful extras provided, such as bathrobes, home-made biscuits, bottled water and fresh flowers. Owner Kate Mylrea offers a very warm welcome and guests can enjoy tea and home-made cake in one of the two lounges. Kate provides very good home-cooking, offering four courses, all prepared using healthy recipes and local ingredients where possible.
3 rms (2 bth/shr) (1 fmly) No smoking CTV in all bedrooms Tea and coffee making facilities No dogs (ex guide dogs) Cen ht No children 12yrs 8P No coaches Last d 7.30pm
CARDS:

Selected

Q Q Q Q **Mint Lodge** 38 The Mint TN31 7EN (High Street Rye) ☎ 01797 223268 FAX 01797 223268
With its central location, The Mint is an extension of the High Street. This neat little establishment, offering a friendly welcome from proprietor Yvonne Cronshaw, has prettily decorated en suite bedrooms featuring pine furniture, patchwork bedcovers and extras like mineral water and sweets. There is a bright, appealing breakfast room on the ground floor. No evening meals, but there is a wide range of eating options available in the town.
3 bth/shr CTV in all bedrooms Tea and coffee making facilities No dogs Cen ht No children 3yrs
ROOMS: d £38-£44*
CARDS:

Selected

Q Q Q Q **Old Borough Arms** The Strand TN31 7DB (off A259) ☎ 01797 222128 FAX 01797 222128
This former sailor's inn dates back to 1720, and part of the much older town wall forms part of one of the bedroom corridors. The beamed public areas are particularly charming with a pine-floored, split-level bar/lounge and open-plan dining room sporting a collection of antique carpenter's tools among other interesting artefacts. Well-appointed bedrooms feature comfortably cushioned rattan easy chairs.
9 shr (2 fmly) CTV in all bedrooms Tea and coffee making facilities Licensed Cen ht CTV 2P Last d 8pm
ROOMS: s £25-£30; d £45-£60; wkly b&b £157.50-£175*
CARDS:

Premier Selected

Q Q Q Q Q **The Old Vicarage Guesthouse** 66 Church Square TN31 7HF (follow Town Centre signs from A259, enter town via Landgate Arch, 3rd left in High St into West St, by St Mary's Church footpath leads to Vicarage) ☎ 01797 222119 FAX 01797 227466
Closed 24-26 Dec
Ask any local where the "Pink House on the Square" is and they will know that you are seeking the Old Vicarage Guest House. Personally run by Julia and Paul Masters guests can be assured of a warm and friendly stay. Each bedroom is individually designed and decorated with Laura Ashley fabrics and prints. Breakfast offers a great start to a day with home-made preserves, bread, local produce and Paul's renowned scones.

5 bth/shr (1 fmly) No smoking in bedrooms No smoking in dining room CTV in all bedrooms Tea and coffee making facilities No dogs (ex guide dogs) Cen ht No children 8yrs 5P No coaches
ROOMS: s £35-£55; d £44-£64; wkly b&b £131-£190

Premier Selected

Q Q Q Q Q **Playden Cottage** Military Rd TN31 7NY
(leave Rye in direction of Appledore, Playden Cottage is last house on left, at the de-limit sign) ☎ 01797 222234
Run in friendly fashion by Sheelah Fox, Playden Cottage has enormous appeal. Inside, individually furnished and decorated bedrooms combine comfort with charm in equal measure. Antique-furnished day rooms include a split-level lounge with a plentiful supply of books, and a piano for musically inclined guests. The elegant dining room offers first rate breakfasts, including 'mix-your-own' muesli, soft fruits from the garden, home-made yoghurt and a special gooseberry and elderflower puree. Dinner is available by arrangement. From November to Easter every third nights' stay is free.
3 shr (1 fmly) No smoking in dining room Tea and coffee making facilities No dogs (ex guide dogs) Cen ht CTV No children 12yrs 5P No coaches Close to tennis & squash courts Golf
Last d by arrangement
ROOMS: d £50-£62; wkly b&b £157.50-£217;
wkly hlf-bd £241.50-£301
CARDS:

SAFFRON WALDEN Essex Map **05** TL53

Q Q Q ***Cricketer's Arms*** Rickling Green and Quendon CB11 3YG
(exit B1383 at Quendon, premises 300yds on the left opposite the cricket green) (Minotel) ☎ 01799 543210 FAX 01799 543512
Very much a traditional inn, full of historical charm and character, the Cricketers Arms is popular with local diners and residents alike. A mellow red brick building, it sits beside the village green, and Mr & Mrs Proctor and their friendly team create a welcoming and informal atmosphere. Most of the attractively decorated accommodation is housed in a modern extension.
10 shr (2 fmly) CTV in all bedrooms Tea and coffee making facilities Direct dial from bedrooms Cen ht 48P Last d 10pm
CARDS:

Q Q Q **Rowley Hill Lodge** Little Walden CB10 1UZ
(1.25m N of town centre on B1052. On left of road with three tall chimneys) ☎ 01799 525975 FAX 01799 516622
Originally built in 1830 as the lodge to the nearby farmhouse, the house, of delightful character, has been modernised and enlarged by the caring proprietors, Edward and Kate Haslam. The views from the two well proportioned bedrooms stretch across open countryside around the property. Breakfasts are served around the large wooden table in the dining room, and there are many recommendations for good local restaurants.
2 bth/shr No smoking in bedrooms No smoking in dining room CTV in all bedrooms Tea and coffee making facilities No dogs (ex guide dogs) Cen ht 4P No coaches
ROOMS: s £25; d £44; wkly b&b £138-£160

ST AGNES Cornwall & Isles of Scilly Map **02** SW75

Q Q **Penkerris** Penwinnick Rd TR5 0PA (A30 to B3277 to St Agnes for 3 miles. Penkerris is the 1st house on the right after the village sign) ☎ 01872 552262 FAX 01872 552262
This creeper-clad Edwardian house on the edge of the village has been home to Dorothy Gill-Carey for many years. The lounge is comfortable and homely, with a piano, magazines and videos plus a real log fire for guests to enjoy in the winter. The breakfast room boasts collections of blue glass and brassware and it is here that dinners, by prior arrangement, can be enjoyed. There are double, twin and family rooms and one has its own kitchenette. There is a children's play area.

contd.

6 rms (3 shr) (3 fmly) CTV in all bedrooms Tea and coffee making facilities Licensed CTV ch fac 9P No coaches Badminton Volleyball Last d 10am
ROOMS: s £15-£30; d £30-£50; wkly b&b £95-£130; wkly hlf-bd £135-£195*
CARDS:

Selected

Q Q Q Q ***Porthvean Hotel*** Churchtown TR5 0QP
(off A30 at Chiverton rdbt onto B3277, hotel opposite parish church)
☎ 01872 552581 FAX 01872 553773
Closed 18 Dec-22 Jan
The Porthvean Hotel is situated in the centre of Churchtown and guests are assured of a warm and friendly welcome by the Robinsons, who have personally run this hotel for many years. The public areas are very comfortable and there is a well equipped bar, with a log fire on cold evenings. The bedrooms are individually furnished and equipped with all modern facilities. Frin's Restaurant is very popular with guests and locals alike, offering a wide choice to suit all tastes, including vegetarian dishes, and using only fresh local ingredients.
7 shr (2 fmly) No smoking in dining room CTV in all bedrooms Tea and coffee making facilities Direct dial from bedrooms No dogs (ex guide dogs) Licensed Cen ht 8P No coaches Last d 9pm
CARDS:

ST ALBANS Hertfordshire Map 04 TL10

Selected

Q Q Q Q **Ardmore House** 54 Lemsford Rd AL1 3PR
☎ 01727 859313 & 853642 FAX 01727 859313
rs 25-26 Dec & 1 Jan
This fine Edwardian property is situated in a residential road close to the town centre. Personally run by Mr and Mrs Guddemi, it goes from strength to strength. Friendly service matches the welcoming atmosphere in the elegant lounge bar; in the adjoining dining room evening meals or bar snacks are readily available. The breakfast room overlooks a beautifully landscaped rear garden. The bedrooms are attractively decorated and have smart modern bathrooms and stylish decor.
40 bth/shr (5 fmly) No smoking in 1 bedrooms No smoking in dining room No smoking in 1 lounge CTV in all bedrooms Tea and coffee making facilities Direct dial from bedrooms No dogs (ex guide dogs) Licensed Cen ht CTV 40P Last d 8.30pm
ROOMS: s £45-£65; d £65-£85*
CARDS:

ST AUSTELL Cornwall & Isles of Scilly Map 02 SX05

Q Q **Alexandra Hotel** 52-54 Alexandra Rd PL25 4QN (take A391 into St Austell and at 3rd set of lights turn right, continue to close-coupled mini rdbts and proceed up hill to hotel on left) ☎ 01726 66111 FAX 01726 66111
Closed 2 wks Xmas
A detached, stone built property, within walking distance of the town centre, the Alexandra Hotel is personally run by Rita and John Staples. The bedrooms vary in size and style; two rooms are located on the ground floor. There is a comfortable lounge with television, together with a cosy bar. A fixed price menu is available on request, with bar meals served during the evening.
12 rms (4 shr) (1 fmly) No smoking in dining room CTV in all bedrooms Tea and coffee making facilities Licensed Cen ht CTV No children 20P Last d 5.30pm
ROOMS: s £28-£33; d £49-£60; wkly b&b £162-£196; wkly hlf-bd £225-£281*
CARDS:

Premier Selected

Q Q Q Q Q **Anchorage House** Nettles Corner, Tregrehan PL25 3RH (2m E of St Austell on A390, follow road signed Tregrehan (opposite Garden Centre) and in 50 metres, turn left into drive leading to courtyard) ☎ 01726 814071
A recently constructed Georgian style property, set in neatly tended gardens and convenient for golf and visiting attractions like Carlyon Bay Beach, Heligan Gardens and National Trust properties. The house is furnished and decorated in attractive and comfortable style, and bedrooms are well equipped. Mrs Epperson loves to cook, and it shows in her popular four-course gourmet dinners, which are served in house-party style and usually hosted by both Steve and Jane Epperson.
3 bth/shr No smoking CTV in all bedrooms Tea and coffee making facilities No dogs Cen ht CTV No children 15yrs 5P No coaches Outdoor swimming pool (heated) Last d 10am
ROOMS: s £28-£42; d £56-£64
CARDS:

Selected

Q Q Q Q **Poltarrow** *(SW998518)* St Mewan PL26 7DR (off A390 turn right at St Mewan School entrance to farmhouse within 0.25m on left) ☎ 01726 67111 FAX 01726 67111 Mrs J Nancarrow
Closed 16 Dec-5 Jan
Set in 45 acres of rolling pasture, Poltarrow Farm is full of charm and character. Bedrooms are individually furnished and decorated, and equipped with thoughtful extra touches, such as mineral water and toiletries. The sitting room has a log fire. A traditional breakfast is served at separate tables in the dining room. Three large self-catering cottages are also available.
3 bth/shr 2 annexe bth/shr (1 fmly) No smoking in bedrooms No smoking in dining room CTV in all bedrooms Tea and coffee making facilities No dogs (ex guide dogs) Licensed Cen ht CTV 10P Pool table 45 acres mixed
ROOMS: s £25; d £46*
CARDS:

Q Q Q **Rashleigh Arms** Quay Rd, Charlestown PL25 3NJ (A390, signposted on St Austell roundabout) ☎ 01726 73635 FAX 01726 73635
Popular with locals and tourists alike, this busy inn is located on the hill towards the delightful port of Charlestown. The two bars offer a range of real ales and an extensive range of bar meals in addition to the carvery operation, salad bar and daily special dishes. The bedrooms are furnished with pine and well equipped.
5 shr CTV in all bedrooms Tea and coffee making facilities No dogs (ex guide dogs) Cen ht 120P Last d 10pm
ROOMS: s £26; d £48*
MEALS: Lunch £5.25-£8.95 Dinner £5.95-£13.95alc*
CARDS:

Selected

QQQQ *T'Gallants* 6 Charlestown Rd, Charlestown PL25 3NJ (exit A390 at roundabout signposted for Charlestown, premises at the bottom of hill) ☎ 01726 70203

With marvellous views down the hill to the quayside, where yachts are often moored, this attractive Georgian house is situated in the small picturesque fishing village of Charlestown, just one mile from St Austell. Bedrooms are smart and well maintained, providing comfortable and generally spacious accommodation. Breakfasts are freshly prepared and often feature smoked haddock from the excellent local smokery.

8 rms (6 shr) No smoking in area of dining room No smoking in 1 lounge CTV in all bedrooms Tea and coffee making facilities No dogs Licensed Cen ht CTV 20P No coaches

CARDS:

Selected

QQQQ **Wheal Lodge** 91 Sea Rd, Carlyon Bay PL25 3SH ☎ 01726 815543 FAX 01726 815543

Closed 23 Dec-2 Jan

On a secluded private road and set in its own attractive grounds, Wheal Lodge stands high above the pictursque Carlyon Bay, opposite the golf club. With a regular stream of loyal guests returning every year, one of the main attractions of this delightful guest house is the warmth and charm of owners Jeanne and Don Martin. Most of the accommodation is on the ground floor, overlooking the grounds, and all the bedrooms are attractively decorated, comfortable and spacious . Guests in one first-floor room enjoy a balcony. The downstairs public areas include a guests' lounge, and a cosy licensed bar. Mrs Martin is an excellent home baker, who serves generous portions of freshly prepared food in the bright, airy dining room.

6 bth/shr (1 fmly) No smoking in bedrooms No smoking in dining room CTV in all bedrooms Tea and coffee making facilities No dogs (ex guide dogs) Licensed Cen ht CTV No children 10yrs 20P No coaches Carlyon Bay golf club is opposite

ROOMS: s £39-£50; d £65-£75*

CARDS:

ST BLAZEY Cornwall & Isles of Scilly Map 02 SX05

Premier Selected

QQQQQ **Nanscawen House** Prideaux Rd PL24 2SR (A38 from Plymouth, turn left at Dobwalls to A390-St Austell, in St Blazey turn right after railway, opposite garage, Nanscawen is 0.75m on right) ☎ 01726 814488 FAX 01726 814488

Closed 25-26 Dec

This delightful stone built house dates from the 15th century, and has been considerably extended and tastefully modernised in more recent times. One of the three double bedrooms is exceptionally large, and one has a four-poster bed. All have luxurious en suite bathrooms with air spa baths. There is a spacious and comfortable drawing room with an honesty bar, and breakfast is served in the conservatory.

3 bth/shr No smoking CTV in all bedrooms Tea and coffee making facilities Direct dial from bedrooms No dogs Licensed Cen ht No children 6P No coaches Outdoor swimming pool (heated) Jacuzzi Whirlpool

ROOMS: s £55.50-£58.50; d £74-£78*

CARDS:

ST HILARY Cornwall & Isles of Scilly Map 02 SW53

Premier Selected

QQQQQ **Ennys** *(SW559328)* St Hilary TR20 9BZ (1m N of B3280, Redruth to Goldsithney road) ☎ 01736 740262 FAX 01736 740055 Miss G Charlton

Closed 20 Nov-15 Feb

Ennys is a beautiful 17th-century Cornish manor house situated amidst sheltered gardens. A small working farm, it is an ideal spot for a peaceful holiday, and guests return year after year to enjoy its tranquility and comfort. Bedrooms are tastefully furnished in country-house style, two with four-poster beds. Adjoining the house, there is a family suite in a converted barn. A grass tennis court and outdoor heated swimming pool are also available to guests.

contd.

Ennys

3 bth/shr 2 annexe bth/shr (1 fmly) No smoking in bedrooms No smoking in dining room CTV in all bedrooms Tea and coffee making facilities No dogs Cen ht CTV No children 2yrs 10P Outdoor swimming pool (heated) Tennis (grass) 20 acres non-working
ROOMS: s £40; d £55-£65*
CARDS:

ST IVES Cornwall & Isles of Scilly Map **02** SW54

Q Q Q ***Bay View*** Headland Rd, Carbis Bay TR26 2NX
☎ 01736 796469
Mar-Oct
Situated close to the beach and within easy access of St Ives, this friendly guest house has a relaxed atmosphere. Rooms are light, well decorated and all are now en suite. A large homely and comfortable lounge is available where guests can relax. There is a combined bar and dining room where hearty English breakfasts and traditional evening meals are served.
9 rms (8 shr) (3 fmly) No smoking in bedrooms CTV in all bedrooms Tea and coffee making facilities No dogs (ex guide dogs) Licensed Cen ht CTV No children 5yrs 11P Last d 6pm

Q Q Q **Channings Hotel** 3 Talland Rd TR26 2DF
(on entering St Ives on the A3074 fork left at Porthminster Hotel then turn 1st left & 1st left again into Talland Rd. Hotel 2nd on right)
☎ 01736 795681 FAX 01736 797863
A spacious house with neat, well equipped rooms, many available for family use, is provided by the friendly Juggins family. There is an attractive dining room serving traditional dishes at dinner as well as a comfortable bar and lounge.
10 bth/shr (6 fmly) No smoking in 10 bedrooms No smoking in dining room CTV in all bedrooms Tea and coffee making facilities Licensed Cen ht CTV 10P Last d 4pm
ROOMS: s £20-£27; d £40-£54; wkly b&b £140-£189; wkly hlf-bd £185-£250*
CARDS:

Q Q Q **Chy-an-Creet Private Hotel** Higher Stennack TR26 2HA
(on B3311 to harbour, opposite Leach Pottery)
☎ 01736 796559 FAX 01736 796559
Closed 1-28 Dec
Situated on the outskirts of the town, Chy-an-Creet offers comfortable, modern accommodation, with some rooms on ground level for the less mobile. The friendly owners have plans to upgrade their small hotel, increasing the facilities.
9 bth/shr (2 fmly) No smoking in bedrooms No smoking in dining room No smoking in 1 lounge CTV in all bedrooms Tea and coffee making facilities Licensed CTV 16P No coaches Last d 9pm
ROOMS: s £19-£25; d £38-£50; wkly b&b £120-£169*
CARDS:

Q Q **Chy-Roma** 2 Seaview Ter TR26 2DH
(on entering St Ives on A3074 fork left at Porthminster Hotel, then 1st left, 1st right, down slope 2nd guest house on left)
☎ 01736 797539
This small family-run guest house has superb views over the town to the harbour and sea beyond. The bedrooms are neatly furnished and decorated, with two now having en suite facilities. The cosy lounge has splendid views and leads into the dining room, where traditional home cooking is served and home baking is a speciality.
7 rms (2 shr) (2 fmly) No smoking in dining room CTV in all bedrooms Tea and coffee making facilities Cen ht CTV No children 5yrs 5P No coaches Last d 4pm
ROOMS: s £15-£20; d £50-£80; wkly b&b £120-£195*

Selected

Q Q Q Q **Dean Court Hotel** Trelyon Av TR26 2AD
(take A3074 through Lelant and Carbis Bay. The hotel is located on right hand side on entering St Ives.)
☎ 01736 796023 FAX 01736 796233
Mar-Oct
Dean Court is situated just out of town in a superb position, with commanding views over St Ives and the coastline around. The house has spacious private and public rooms and all are equipped to a high standard with modern facilities. The proprietors pride themselves on their personal service which explains why many guests return on a regular basis.
12 bth/shr (2 fmly) No smoking in dining room No smoking in 1 lounge CTV in all bedrooms Tea and coffee making facilities No dogs Licensed Cen ht No children 14yrs 12P No coaches Last d 6.30pm
ROOMS: s £32-£39; d £60-£76; wkly b&b £190-£240; wkly hlf-bd £240-£290*
CARDS:

Q Q Q **The Hollies Hotel** 4 Talland Rd TR26 2DF
(A30 to St Ives, entering town go down Trelyon Ave to Porthminster Hotel, fork left, cont for approx 500yds, fork left again, hotel 3rd on right)
☎ 01736 796605
Situated in an elevated position and only a few minutes' walk from the town centre, harbour, and beaches this very friendly guest house offers well maintained and thoughtfully equipped bedrooms, several of which are suitable for families. Many also have sea views. The cheerful Dowland family are always on hand and provide breakfast in the pine-panelled dining room. Guests can relax in either the large comfortable lounge or separate bar.
10 bth/shr (4 fmly) No smoking in dining room CTV in all bedrooms Tea and coffee making facilities No dogs Licensed Cen ht CTV 12P
ROOMS: s £14-£24; d £28-£48; wkly b&b £112-£150

Q Q Q ***Island View*** 2 Park Av TR26 2DN ☎ 01736 795111
Mar-Oct
Standing high above the town centre with the bus and rail stations nearby, Island View is a small family-run establishment where comfort and service are a high priority. The bedrooms vary in size and some benefit from excellent views across the harbour and bay. There is a cosy lounge and adjoining dining room where traditional home-cooked meals are provided.
10 rms (2 shr) (4 fmly) CTV in all bedrooms Tea and coffee making facilities Cen ht No coaches Last d 6.30pm

Q Q Q **Kandahar** 11 The Warren TR26 2EA
(follow Railway Station and car park signs. Park in station car park and follow Kandahar sign on foot to obtain parking permit) ☎ 01736 796183
Mar-1 Nov rs part Nov & part Feb
This unique house is as close to the water's edge as anyone could wish to get. The Kandahar is in the quaint Warren area of this delightful fishing

community, close to the harbour and almost on the beach! The rooms vary in size and style and one has a balcony over the beach. Others are well suited for families, and almost all have superb views. There is a comfortable lounge and separate dining room where a choice of breakfast dishes is served. The house is fully no smoking.

5 rms (3 bth/shr) (1 fmly) No smoking CTV in all bedrooms Tea and coffee making facilities No dogs Cen ht CTV No children 6yrs 6P No coaches
ROOMS: s £20-£40; d £38-£52*
CARDS:

Selected

Q Q Q Q Kynance The Warren TR26 2EA
(take A3074 into town centre taking sharp right hand turn before bus/coach terminus, into railway station approach road. Kynance 20yds on left) ☎ 01736 796636
Mar-mid Nov
Situated within easy, level walking distance of the picturesque harbour and sandy Porthminster Beach, The Kynance is a charming old property in the heart of the village. The bedrooms are attractively decorated and well equipped and have either private or en suite facilities. Several are suitable for families and some benefit from stunning views. Guests can enjoy a varied choice at breakfast including a vegetarian option. Dawn and Simon Norris are welcoming hosts, always on hand to advise guests on attractions, and restaurants for evening dining. The house operates a no smoking policy.
6 bth/shr (1 fmly) No smoking CTV in all bedrooms Tea and coffee making facilities No dogs Cen ht CTV No children 7yrs 4P No coaches
ROOMS: d £38-£48; wkly b&b £133-£168
CARDS:

Selected

Q Q Q Q Longships Hotel Talland Rd TR26 2DF
(turn off A30 through main route into St Ives, take left fork at Porthminster Hotel, follow road around to the left)
☎ 01736 798180 FAX 01736 798180
Mar-Dec
Located high above the town, Longships offers good views over the harbour and sea. All bedrooms are furnished with care and quality. There is an attractive bar with fine sea views and regular entertainment is provided.
25 bth/shr (7 fmly) No smoking in dining room No smoking in 1 lounge CTV in all bedrooms Tea and coffee making facilities No dogs (ex guide dogs) Licensed Cen ht CTV 18P
Last d 7pm
CARDS:

Selected

Q Q Q Q Lyonesse Hotel 5 Talland Rd TR26 2DF
(A3074 to St Ives fork left at Porthminster, left again at Albert Rd. Lyonesse 50yds on right) ☎ 01736 796315 FAX 01736 796315
Apr-Sep
Situated above the town, with fine sea and harbour views, the Herbert Family run a comfortable small hotel with excellent standards of hospitality and housekeeping. All bedrooms are of good quality and have their own en suite facilities.
10 shr (3 fmly) No smoking CTV in all bedrooms Tea and coffee making facilities No dogs Licensed Cen ht CTV No children 5years 10P No coaches
ROOMS: d £40-£50
CARDS:

Selected

Q Q Q Q ***Monowai*** Headland Rd, Carbis Bay TR26 2NR
(on entering Carbis Bay turn right off A3074 into Porthrepta Rd, Headland Rd is on the right after 300yds) ☎ 01736 795733
Mar-Sep
This delightful property set above Carbis Bay enjoys stunning views out over the garden and swimming pool and across the bay. Each of the bedrooms are tastefully decorated with co-ordinated fabrics, well equipped, and comfortably furnished. The service is quiet, friendly and unobtrusive and all the food is local and freshly produced. The dining room is to be refurbished this winter whilst the peaceful sitting room is ideal for relaxation. The new conservatory provides outstanding views over the sea.
8 shr (3 fmly) No smoking Tea and coffee making facilities Licensed Cen ht CTV No children 5yrs 7P No coaches Outdoor swimming pool (heated)

Q Q Q The Old Vicarage Hotel Parc-en-Creet TR26 2ET
(as the first hill of shops in St Ives levels out, turn left at Nat West bank on B3306 to Lands End. Parc-en-Creet is right turn 0.5m from town)
☎ 01736 796124 FAX 01736 796124
Etr-Oct
This former Victorian rectory is situated in a quiet area of St Ives, yet close to the town centre. It is personally run by Jack and Irene Sykes who offer guests a warm and friendly welcome. The bedrooms are tastefully decorated and well equipped, all with modern facilities, some of the rooms are suitable for families. There is a comfortable lounge, a separate residents bar and in the extensive grounds, guests can enjoy badminton, putting and other games.
8 rms (4 bth/shr) (3 fmly) No smoking in bedrooms No smoking in dining room CTV in all bedrooms Tea and coffee making facilities Licensed Cen ht CTV 12P No coaches Putting green
ROOMS: s £23-£27; d £38-£52; wkly b&b £119-£161
CARDS:

Selected

Q Q Q Q Pondarosa Hotel 10 Porthminster Ter TR26 2DQ
(approach town by A3074, fork left at Porthminster Hotel and follow road to left hand bend then take 1st left and we are situated 50yds on right) ☎ 01736 795875 FAX 01736 797811
This charming terraced guest house is set above the town, close to the train and bus stations and within easy walking distance of the harbour and beaches. Pat and Alan Tyldesley continue to improve the facilities they offer to their guests, and cheerful service is the order of the day. All of the bedrooms now have en suite or private facilities and each is

contd.

neatly co-ordinated and equipped with many thoughtful extras. There is a cosy lounge and cheerful dining room and conservatory where guests can take coffee.
9 rms (8 bth/shr) (4 fmly) No smoking CTV in all bedrooms Tea and coffee making facilities Licensed Cen ht CTV 12P Last d 4pm
ROOMS: s £17-£21; d £34-£42; wkly b&b £119-£147; wkly hlf-bd £178-£210✻
CARDS:

QQQ **Queens Tavern** High St TR26 1RR (in centre of town opposite Boots chemist on High Street) (St Austell Brewery)
☎ 01736 796468 FAX 01736 796468
This popular inn is situated in the centre of this seaside Cornish town, and within easy walking distance of the harbour and sandy beaches. The bedrooms are all equipped with modern facilities. There is a dining room on the first floor, with traditional bar food available in the main bar area.
5 shr (3 fmly) CTV in all bedrooms Tea and coffee making facilities No dogs (ex guide dogs) Cen ht Last d 8.30pm
ROOMS: s £21.50; d £43; wkly b&b £129✻
MEALS: Bar Lunch £3.50-£6.50alc✻
CARDS:

Selected

QQQQ **Regent Hotel** Fernlea Ter TR26 2BH (in centre of town, close to bus & railway station)
☎ 01736 796195 FAX 01736 794641
The Regent Hotel is located near the bus and railway stations, with the harbour and sandy beaches just a few minutes walk away. Bedrooms are fresh, bright and well equipped with some non-smoking and family rooms available. The restaurant is open to the public during the day but is reserved for residents in the evening. Friendly owners, Keith and Sandi Varnals, have been welcoming guests for more than twenty years.
9 rms (7 shr) No smoking in 4 bedrooms No smoking in area of dining room CTV in all bedrooms Tea and coffee making facilities No dogs Licensed Cen ht CTV No children 7yrs 12P No coaches Last d 7pm
ROOMS: s £25-£29; d £55-£70; wkly b&b £190-£230✻
CARDS:

Selected

QQQQ **Sloop** The Wharf TR26 1LP (St Ives harbour by middle slipway) ☎ 01736 796584 FAX 01736 793322
Dating from at least 1312, this historic inn is situated right on the harbour with many rooms enjoying panoramic views. Although rooms differ in size, all exude a distinctly historic atmosphere and contain the modern facilities expected by today's guest. Breakfast is served in the bedrooms whilst dinner is offered in the Lounge or Cellar bar, where fresh seafood and fine ales are specialities. Enjoy the collection of original paintings and drawings by artists such as Hyman Segal, which hang next to other famous St Ives artists.
15 rms (2 bth 10 shr) (3 fmly) No smoking in 2 bedrooms CTV in all bedrooms Tea and coffee making facilities Direct dial from bedrooms No dogs (ex guide dogs) Cen ht No coaches Last d 8.45pm
ROOMS: s £35-£45; d £50-£65✻
MEALS: Lunch £5.95-£9.95&alc Dinner £5.95-£9.95&alc✻
CARDS:

QQQ **Sunrise** 22 The Warren TR26 2EA
(take A30 onto B3074, continue to St Ives railway station, premises on the left 50 mtrs left of the station approach) ☎ 01736 795407
Closed 6 Apr-1 May & Oct
Situated in the ancient Warren area of this delightful fishing village, and only yards from the harbour and beaches. Bedrooms are cleverly designed, prettily decorated, and well equipped - some have stunning views over the harbour. There is a comfortable lounge and charming dining room, where Mrs Adams has built up a good reputation for her adventurous and varied breakfast menu.
7 rms (5 bth/shr) No smoking in dining room CTV in all bedrooms Tea and coffee making facilities No dogs (ex guide dogs) Cen ht CTV No children 6yrs 5P
ROOMS: d £38-£60✻
CARDS:

QQQ **Thurlestone Private Hotel** St Ives Rd, Carbis Bay TR26 2RT (off A30 follow A3074 St Ives signs. Go through Lelant onto Carbis Bay, pass Cost-Cutters and Londis stores on left. Hotel is 0.75m on left)
☎ 01736 796369
Closed Jan
Opposite the hotel, an attractive house built of granite in 1843, is a footpath leading down to a sandy beach which is only a five minute walk away. The ground floor public areas are beamed and retain lots of original character and charm, they include a comfortable lounge and a cosy, well presented bar. The bedrooms, some with sea views, are tastefully decorated and well equipped. The house has a no smoking policy except for the bar.
7 rms (6 bth/shr) (3 fmly) No smoking in bedrooms No smoking in dining room No smoking in lounges CTV in 6 bedrooms Tea and coffee making facilities No dogs Licensed Cen ht CTV 5P No coaches
ROOMS: s £20-£24; d £34-£42; wkly b&b £112-£140✻
CARDS:

Selected

QQQQ **Tregorran Hotel** Headland Rd, Carbis Bay TR26 2NU (at Carbis Bay turn right down to beach along Porthrepta Rd. Take last turning on the right into Headland Rd, Tregorran Hotel halfway along)
☎ 01736 795889
Etr-1 Oct
Situated in a prominent position, overlooking Carbis Bay with its sandy beach, the Tregorran offers comfortable accommodation with modern facilities. The hotel has a choice of comfortable lounges, one with a bar.

There are many facilities available for families, including a multi-gym, outdoor heated pool and a games room. The bedrooms are well furnished and, in some, children have their own separate room.
18 shr (8 fmly) No smoking in dining room CTV in all bedrooms Tea and coffee making facilities Licensed Cen ht CTV 20P Outdoor swimming pool (heated) Gymnasium Pool table Games room Last d 3pm
ROOMS: s £20.50-£38.50; d £41-£77; wkly b&b £143.50-£269.50; wkly hlf-bd £210-£336
CARDS:

Selected

Q Q Q Q **Trewinnard** 4 Parc Av TR26 2DN
(A3074 to St Ives, on entering town turn left at Nat West bank and then turn left at mini roundabout. Go past car park and house 150yds on right) ☎ 01736 794168 FAX 01736 798161
Apr-Oct
Trewinnard, which offers comfortable accommodation for holidaymakers, enjoys an enviable position with views over the town and beach. Rooms have clock radio, colour TV and hairdryers. There is a comfortable residents lounge and an attractive small bar. Natural hospitality is provided by the owners, Mr & Mrs Sears.
7 shr (1 fmly) No smoking CTV in all bedrooms Tea and coffee making facilities No dogs Licensed Cen ht No children 6yrs 4P No coaches Last d 8.30pm
ROOMS: s £22-£29; d £40-£56; wkly b&b £133-£175
CARDS:

ST JUST (NEAR LAND'S END) Cornwall & Isles of Scilly Map 02 SW33

Q Q Q **_Wellington Hotel_** Market Square TR19 7HD (take the A3071 from A30. St Just is 6m W of Penzance. Hotel overlooks Main Square)
☎ 01736 787319 FAX 01736 787906
This historic 14th-century inn is situated in the market square and is popular with local residents and holidaymakers alike. The modern bedrooms are well equipped and some are housed in the former stable block at the rear of the inn. This year saw the addition of four newly refurbished rooms in the main building. A good range of beers and home-cooked food is available.
7 rms (2 bth 2 shr) 6 annexe bth/shr (4 fmly) No smoking in 1 bedrooms CTV in all bedrooms Tea and coffee making facilities Direct dial from bedrooms Cen ht CTV Last d 9pm
CARDS:

ST MARY'S See SCILLY, ISLES OF

ST MAWES Cornwall & Isles of Scilly Map 02 SW83

Selected

Q Q Q Q **Polsue Manor** Ruan High Lanes TR2 5LU
(A390 Truro to St Austell Rd take B3078 St Mawes Rd. On reaching the village of Ruan High Lanes 2nd right signposted Philleigh, hotel 1 mile on left) ☎ 01872 501270 FAX 01872 501177
Having only recently purchased Polsue Manor, the proprietors, Mr & Mrs Sylvester intend to refurbish all bedrooms to a stunning standard. Rooms are spacious and look out over five acres of grounds and the surrounding countryside. Guests can relax in the newly re-decorated sitting room before enjoying dinner which features interesting and innovative dishes, cooked by Mrs Sylvester.

8 bth/shr (1 fmly) No smoking in 1 lounge CTV in all bedrooms Tea and coffee making facilities Direct dial from bedrooms Licensed Cen ht 20P Board games Last d 7.30pm
ROOMS: s £27-£37; d £54-£74; wkly b&b £189-£259; wkly hlf-bd £315-£385✳

ST MAWGAN Cornwall & Isles of Scilly Map 02 SW86

Q Q Q **The Falcon** TR8 4EP (from A30 follow signs RAF St Mawgan, then St Mawgan village. Pub at bottom of hill in village centre)
☎ 01637 860225 FAX 01637 860884
Situated in a charming old village, opposite the church, this 16th-century stone-built inn has plenty of atmosphere. The bedrooms are individual in style and size and two have en suite bathrooms. The bar and dining room are beamed and have an open log fire.
3 rms (2 shr) No smoking in dining room CTV in all bedrooms Tea and coffee making facilities Direct dial from bedrooms Cen ht 20P Last d 10pm
ROOMS: s £18; d £47-£57✳
MEALS: Lunch £6-£12alc Dinner £8-£17alc✳
CARDS:

ST MERRYN Cornwall & Isles of Scilly Map 02 SW87

Q Q Q ■ ***Farmers Arms*** PL28 8NP (St Austell Brewery)
☎ 01841 520303
Located in a small village a few miles south of Padstow, the Farmer's Arms is a friendly, informal inn - extremely popular for bar meals, especially during the season. Bedrooms are attractively decorated and have modern furnishings. A choice is offered at breakfast.
4 shr (2 fmly) CTV in all bedrooms Tea and coffee making facilities Cen ht 100P Last d 9.30pm
CARDS:

ST NEOT Cornwall & Isles of Scilly Map 02 SX16

Selected

Q Q Q Q ■ **London** St Neot PL14 6NG (turn off A30 at junct after Jamaica Inn signposted St Neot. Follow this road to St Neot, drive through village and establishment is next to church)
☎ 01579 320263 FAX 01579 320263
This delightful 17th-century inn is located adjacent to the church and claims to be the first over-night stop on the coach route from Penzance to London. The recently refurbished bedrooms are comfortable, well equipped and attractively co-ordinated. The beamed bar and dining area are a popular haunt for locals and visitors alike. An extensive range of meals is offered with a choice of five real ales. A skittle alley is available and salmon and brown trout fishing nearby.
3 shr No smoking in bedrooms No smoking in dining room CTV in all bedrooms Tea and coffee making facilities No dogs (ex guide dogs) 14P Last d 9pm
ROOMS: s £30-£36; d £40-£48; wkly b&b £238-£294*
MEALS: Lunch £5-£20 Dinner £5-£20&alc*
CARDS:

SALCOMBE Devon Map 03 SX73

Selected

Q Q Q Q ***Devon Tor Hotel*** Devon Rd TQ8 8HJ ☎ 01548 843106
Closed Dec
Enjoying an enviable position, with stunning views of the Salcombe Estuary, this family-run establishment offers comfortable accommodation. Resident proprietor, Malcolm Barlow, extends a warm and friendly welcome to his guests. Bedrooms are all tastefully decorated, well maintained and equipped with modern amenities. There is also a comfortable lounge, and home cooked meals, using fresh local ingredients, are served in the sunny front-facing conservatory dining room.
6 bth/shr (2 fmly) No smoking CTV in all bedrooms Tea and coffee making facilities No dogs Licensed Cen ht CTV 5P No coaches Last d 4.30pm

Selected

Q Q Q Q ***The Lodge*** Malborough, Kingsbridge TQ7 3RN (A381 from Kingsbridge to Salcombe. On reachimg Marlborough village turn sharp right into Higher Town. The Lodge is 100yds on left)
☎ 01548 561405
Guests will find a warm welcome awaits them at this charming little family-run hotel with a popular local restaurant business. Ideally placed for exploring the local area, yet away from all the tourist hustle and bustle, first impressions are favourable from the pretty rear garden, where parking is also provided. Bedrooms are stylishly decorated with stencilled walls, pretty fabrics and pine furniture. In addition to the lounge bar there is a separate cosy guest lounge in this non-smoking establishment.
6 bth/shr (2 fmly) No smoking CTV in all bedrooms Tea and coffee making facilities No dogs Licensed Cen ht 8P No coaches Last d 8pm
CARDS:

SALE Greater Manchester Map 07 SJ79

Selected

Q Q Q Q **Brooklands Luxury Lodge** 208 Marsland Rd M33 3NE (premises situated on the A6144 1.5m from M60 junc 6 near Brooklands tram station) ☎ 0161 973 3283 FAX 0161 282 0524
This well maintained private hotel lies in a residential area convenient for the airport. Well furnished bedrooms are provided and these are equipped with mini fridges, hair dryers and other useful facilities. Breakfasts and cooked dinners are normally served in the bedrooms and all are furnished appropriately. A complimentary light breakfast is included in room charges but guests may pay extra for cooked or continental varieties. Resident owners Les and Ann Bowker are friendly and welcoming and offer warm hospitality to their guests.
9 rms (5 shr) (2 fmly) No smoking in 7 bedrooms No smoking in dining room No smoking in lounges CTV in all bedrooms Tea and coffee making facilities No dogs (ex guide dogs) Cen ht CTV 6P No coaches Jacuzzi Last d noon
ROOMS: s £27-£36; d £46-£48
CARDS:

SALFORD Greater Manchester Map 07 SJ89

Q Q Q **Hazeldean Hotel** 467 Bury New Rd, Kersal M7 3NE (on A56 2.25m from Manchester centre)
☎ 0161 792 6667 FAX 0161 792 6668
Closed 24 Dec-2 Jan
An imposing Victorian house which has recently been refurbished throughout to provide comfortable and attractive accommodation. There is a cosy lounge and a good range of food is served from Monday to Thursday in the pleasant dining room. A feature here is the very friendly and caring attention provided by all the staff.
21 rms (17 bth/shr) (3 fmly) No smoking in dining room CTV in all bedrooms Tea and coffee making facilities Direct dial from bedrooms No dogs (ex guide dogs) Licensed Cen ht CTV 27P No coaches Last d 9pm
ROOMS: s £30-£40; d £44-£50; wkly b&b £194-£252*
CARDS:

SALISBURY Wiltshire Map **04** SU12

See also **Cholderton, Downton, Whiteparish, Wilton & Winterbourne Stoke**

Q Q Q **Barford Inn** Barford St Martin SP3 4AB (on B3089)
☎ 01722 742242 FAX 01722 743606
A fine 17th century former coaching inn just 5 miles west of Salisbury. The bright well appointed bedrooms are located in the annexe building a short distance from the main house. The cosy bars with wooden beams and inglenook fireplace is the ideal setting in which to relax and enjoy a meal chosen from chef Mark Routledge's carte or bar menu.
4 annexe bth/shr No smoking in dining room No smoking in 1 lounge CTV in all bedrooms Tea and coffee making facilities Direct dial from bedrooms No dogs (ex guide dogs) Cen ht 30P private 0.5 acre lake Last d 9.30pm
ROOMS: s £35-£40; d £45-£50
MEALS: Lunch £13-£20&alc Dinner £13-£20&alc
CARDS:

Premier Selected

Q Q Q Q Q **Beadles** Middleton SP5 1QS ☎ 01980 862922 FAX 01980 862922

(For full entry see **Middle Winterslow**)

Q Q Q ***Briden House*** West St, Barford St Martin SP3 4AH (close to junct of A30/B3089 in the village of Barford St Martin)
☎ 01722 743471 FAX 01722 743471
This Grade II listed family home in the village of Barford St Martin is a short drive from Salisbury, and the surrounding countryside and pretty villages have much to offer holidaymakers. Resident proprietors Patsy and Tim Barter have restored the house to its former glory. The spacious bedrooms are tastefully co-ordinated, and breakfast is served at separate tables in the beamed dining room.
4 rms (1 bth 2 shr) No smoking in dining room No smoking in lounges CTV in all bedrooms Tea and coffee making facilities No dogs Cen ht 6P No coaches

Q Q Q **Byways House** 31 Fowlers Rd SP1 2QP
(at junc of A36 with A30 at major roundabout turn first left signposted "Youth Hostel", right at junc, left at traffic lights, first right)
☎ 01722 328364 FAX 01722 322146
Closed Xmas & New Year
Situated in a quiet residential area of Salisbury, just a short downhill stroll to the city centre, this Victorian property is well run by its friendly proprietor, Mrs Arthey. Bedrooms, including a number of family rooms, are nicely decorated in pale co-ordinating fabrics. Many are on the ground floor, and one has been specially adapted for disabled access. Breakfast is served in the dining room overlooking the rear garden. Off street parking is available.
23 rms (19 bth/shr) (5 fmly) No smoking in dining room No smoking in lounges CTV in all bedrooms Tea and coffee making facilities Licensed Cen ht 15P
ROOMS: s £25-£33; d £39-£55
CARDS:

Q Q Q ***Clovelly*** 17-19 Mill Rd SP2 7RT
(approx 5 minutes from the Market Square and the Cathedral)
☎ 01722 322055 FAX 01722 327677
In an enviable position in the historic city of Salisbury, set in its own grounds close to the railway station and within easy walking distance of the city centre. Hadyn and Rowena Ingram continue to upgrade, with additional en suite facilities and modern attractive bedrooms. A good choice of breakfast is offered and is served in the colourful dining room. Rowena is a Blue Badge Guide specialising in Salisbury and Stonehenge – tours can be arranged.
12 bth/shr (1 fmly) No smoking CTV in all bedrooms Tea and coffee making facilities Licensed Cen ht 15P Golf 18
CARDS:

Q Q Q **The Coach & Horses** Winchester St SP1 1HG
☎ 01722 336254 FAX 01722 414319
Guests can be sure of a warm and friendly welcome from Martin and Angie Cooper at this 500 year old Grade II listed inn, which has stacks of character, and is located in the centre of the city. Two cosy bedrooms, one with a corner bath, have been sympathetically restored in keeping with the age of the property and provide comfortable accommodation. A wide range of AA Rosette worthy meals may be enjoyed in the main bar and dining areas.
2 bth/shr No smoking in bedrooms No smoking in area of dining room CTV in all bedrooms Tea and coffee making facilities No dogs Cen ht ch fac Last d 10pm
ROOMS: s £39.50; d £49.50*
MEALS: Lunch £10-£25alc Dinner £10-£25alc*
CARDS:

Selected

Q Q Q Q **Cricket Field Cottage** Skew Bridge, Wilton Rd SP2 7NS (off A36 Warminster road between Salisbury and Wilton) ☎ 01722 322595 FAX 01722 322595
Closed 24-25 Dec
This is a charming property conveniently situated just one mile from the town centre. Adjacent to the South Wiltshire Cricket Ground, fans will enjoy the subtle, whimsical cricket theme of the decor and can watch a match from inside the bright conservatory where breakfast is served. The majority of the bedrooms, including one designed specifically for the disabled, are situated in an annexe behind the main house which overlooks a pleasant courtyard. All are smart and spacious, with quality furnishings and fabrics. Mrs James ensures a friendly welcome, and a very good choice of evening meals is available by prior arrangement.
4 shr 10 annexe shr No smoking CTV in all bedrooms Tea and coffee making facilities No dogs (ex guide dogs) Cen ht No children 14yrs 14P Last d 3pm
ROOMS: s £32.50-£42; d £45-£55
CARDS:

Selected

Q Q Q Q **The Edwardian Lodge** 59 Castle Rd SP1 3RH (0.5m North of city centre on A345)
☎ 01722 413329 FAX 01722 503105
This spacious property has been recently redecorated and provides comfortable accommodation. A considerable selection of freshly prepared meals is available at dinner. A riverside walk of approximately fifteen minutes will lead you into the City of Salisbury and the Cathedral.
7 shr (2 fmly) No smoking CTV in all bedrooms Tea and coffee making facilities No dogs (ex guide dogs) Cen ht CTV No children 6years 8P Last d 7pm
ROOMS: s £25-£30; d £38-£44*

All AA listed accommodation can also be found at the AA's Internet site, whose address is: http://www.theaa.co.uk/hotels

Selected

Glen Lyn 6 Bellamy Ln, Milford Hill SP1 2SP
(from A36 turn into Tollgate Road and at traffic lights turn right up Milford Hill. Bellamy Lane at top on left)
☎ 01722 327880 FAX 01722 327880
Closed Xmas New Year
Close to the town centre, this elegant Victorian house, in well tended gardens on a tree-lined lane, has been considerably improved and upgraded since Patrick Fairbrother took over. Breakfast, and evening meals with the family, if required, are served in the cosy dining room, and there is also a lounge. The house is entirely no-smoking.
7 rms (4 bth/shr) (1 fmly) No smoking CTV in all bedrooms Tea and coffee making facilities Licensed Cen ht CTV No children 12yrs 5P No coaches Last d by request
ROOMS: s fr £28.50; d £39.50-£49.50; wkly b&b £199.50-£227.50; wkly hlf-bd £269.50-£297.50
CARDS:

Hayburn Wyke 72 Castle Rd SP1 3RL
(0.5m N on A345 from Salisbury town centre) ☎ 01722 412627
FAX 01722 412627
This small, friendly guest house is personally run by Dawn and Alan Curnow. It is situated on the northern side of the city, adjacent to Victoria Park and within walking distance of the city centre. The bedrooms are comfortable and well maintained, all equipped with modern facilities. One ground floor bedroom is available.
7 rms (3 shr) (3 fmly) No smoking in dining room No smoking in lounges CTV in all bedrooms Tea and coffee making facilities No dogs (ex guide dogs) Cen ht CTV 7P
ROOMS: s £26-£48; d £37-£48
CARDS:

Holmhurst Downton Rd SP2 8AR
(follow ring road around city taking A338-South coast route)
☎ 01722 410407 FAX 01722 323164
Conveniently located on the Ringwood Road, within walking distance of the city centre and the Cathedral, Holmhurst is the family home of Karen and Trevor Hayward. The bedrooms are comfortable and well equipped with modern facilities. In the neatly presented breakfast room, guests eat at separate tables.
6 rms (4 shr) (2 fmly) No smoking in dining room No smoking in lounges CTV in all bedrooms Tea and coffee making facilities No dogs (ex guide dogs) Cen ht 9P
ROOMS: s £20-£26; d £38-£42
CARDS:

Kelebrae 101 Castle Rd SP1 3RP
(on A345 from Amesbury, house on left opposite Victoria Park)
☎ 01722 333628
Owners Mr & Mrs De Soto provide well maintained and comfortable accommodation, with attractively and traditionally furnished bedrooms, all having their own bathrooms. A generous traditional English breakfast is served in the smart dining room, with guests sharing one large table.
3 bth/shr No smoking CTV in all bedrooms Tea and coffee making facilities No dogs Cen ht CTV No children 10yrs 4P No coaches
ROOMS: d £38-£40*

Leena's 50 Castle Rd SP1 3RL
(off A303 onto A345 to Castle Road and establishment is on the right)
☎ 01722 335419 FAX 01722 335419
Guests are welcomed at this attractive, family-run guesthouse by Leena herself, a native of Finland - the comfortable, well equipped bedrooms have a Scandanavian feel. Guests take breakfast at lace clothed tables in the rear facing dining room, and there is a spacious lounge with big leather chairs, ideal for relaxing after a busy day exploring the many attractions of the area. The city centre is a ten minute level walk away.
6 rms (5 shr) (1 fmly) No smoking in bedrooms No smoking in dining room CTV in all bedrooms Tea and coffee making facilities No dogs (ex guide dogs) Cen ht CTV 6P No coaches
ROOMS: s fr £22; d £39-£44

Selected

Malvern 31 Hulse Rd SP1 3LU (from A30 take Amesbury sign at second roundabout, then first left into Butts Rd, then first left) ☎ 01722 327995
Situated in a peaceful cul-de-sac and within easy, level walking distance of the city centre. Guests are ensured a warm welcome from Freda and Jack Elkins. The attractively furnished lounge has a friendly atmosphere and is adorned with lots of personal ornaments. The conservatory dining room opens onto colourful gardens which lead down to the River Avon. Bedrooms are individually furnished and decorated to a high standard, each equipped with thoughtful extras.
3 bth/shr No smoking CTV in all bedrooms Tea and coffee making facilities No dogs (ex guide dogs) Cen ht CTV No children 10yrs 3P No coaches
ROOMS: d £40-£42*

Selected

The Old House 161 Wilton Rd SP2 7JQ
(on the A30 between Wilton and Salisbury, close to the police station)
☎ 01722 333433 FAX 01722 416144
Conveniently located and within walking distance of the city centre, this delightful property dates back to the 17th century. Hilary and Patrick Maidment welcome guests to their charming home, where the ground floor areas have been gracefully furnished to enhance the character of the building. The cosy cellar bar is the ideal location for a quiet drink and the only place in the house where smokers are allowed! Dinner is served by prior arrangement, in the dining room which overlooks the garden at the rear. Bedrooms have been tastefully decorated and are equipped with modern facilities; two ground floor rooms are available.

7 bth/shr (2 fmly) No smoking in bedrooms No smoking in dining room No smoking in 1 lounge CTV in all bedrooms Tea and coffee making facilities No dogs (ex guide dogs) Licensed Cen ht CTV 10P No coaches Games room Table tennis Last d 3.30pm
ROOMS: s £25-£30; d £40-£45; wkly b&b fr £157.50*

Q Q **Richburn** 23/25 Estcourt Rd SP1 3AP
(from A30 take 5th exit off Weeping Cross rdbt) ☎ 01722 325189
A detached Victorian house, situated within a few minutes walk of the city centre, and offering attractively decorated and co-ordinated bedrooms. A comfortable and spacious lounge is available for guests' use, with breakfast being served in the light and airy dining room.
10 rms (2 bth/shr) (2 fmly) No smoking in bedrooms No smoking in dining room Tea and coffee making facilities No dogs (ex guide dogs) Cen ht CTV 10P
ROOMS: s £20-£21; d £34-£44*

Q Q Q **Rokeby** 3 Wain-a-Long Rd SP1 1LJ
(premises situated just off St Marks Church roundabout, on A30 take Laverstock exit into Wain-a-Long Rd)
☎ 01722 329800 FAX 01722 329800
Set in half an acre of landscaped gardens and within ten minutes walk of the city centre, this elegant Edwardian family home offers comfortable accommodation and a friendly atmosphere. Bedrooms are equipped with modern facilities and maintained to a high standard. The two-storey conservatory houses the galleried restaurant which leads downstairs to the residents' lounge overlooking the garden. Guests are requested to book for dinner. Off street parking available.
7 bth/shr (3 fmly) No smoking in dining room No smoking in lounges CTV in all bedrooms Tea and coffee making facilities No dogs Licensed Cen ht No children 10yrs 7P No coaches Gymnasium Last d 5pm
ROOMS: s £30-£32; d £40-£45*

Q Q Q **Springfields** Lyndhurst Rd, Landford SP5 2AS
(M27 junct 1,B3078 to Brook then B3079 passing through Bramshaw into Landford, establishment on left 0.5m after Landford perimeter sign)
☎ 01794 390093
Springfields is the family home of Jim and Glenda Hickman, who welcome guests to their large, detached property on the edge of the New Forest, situated midway between Salisbury and Southampton. The two well equipped bedrooms have exclusive use of an adjacent bathroom, both rooms are at the rear of the house and enjoy peace and quiet. A hearty breakfast is served each morning and guests have a varied choice of local pubs and restaurants for other meals.
2 rms No smoking CTV in all bedrooms Tea and coffee making facilities No dogs (ex guide dogs) Cen ht CTV 4P No coaches
ROOMS: s £24; d £34; wkly b&b £119-£168*

Selected

Q Q Q Q **Stratford Lodge** 4 Park Ln, off Castle Rd SP1 3NP
(take A345 Castle Rd past St Francis Church on on right and Victoria Park on left. Park Lane is an unadopted road between park and Alldays store) (The Circle) ☎ 01722 325177 FAX 01722 412699
Closed 23 Dec-1 Jan
Under the new ownership of Mr and Mrs Lawrence, but with Gemma still on hand to welcome returning guests, this charming property, tucked away down an unadopted lane, is within easy walking distance of the town centre, and has all the charm of the Victorian era. Bedrooms are equipped and furnished to a high standard, and benefit from numerous personal touches to provide a warm and welcoming environment. In addition to a bright and sunny conservatory, where guests might want to sample such delights as smoked haddock kedgeree for breakfast, there is an elegant dining room where lovely home cooked dinners are the highlight of the day, and an attractive lounge in which to sleep off your over-indulgence.

8 bth/shr (2 fmly) No smoking CTV in all bedrooms Tea and coffee making facilities Direct dial from bedrooms No dogs (ex guide dogs) Licensed Cen ht CTV No children 5yrs 8P Last d 8.30pm
ROOMS: s £36-£38.50; d £56-£58.50*
CARDS:

Q Q **Swaynes Firs Farm** *(SU068221)* Grimsdyke, Coombe Bissett SP5 5RF (7m SW Salisbury & 3m SW of Coombe Bissett on left side of A354 Blandford road) ☎ 01725 519240 Mr A Shering
Arthur Shering is the landlord at this friendly farmhouse with a sense of history. The Grimsditch, constructed in the bronze age, runs through the property. Just seven miles from the city of Salisbury, guests can enjoy farm life, shared with horses, steers and poultry. The dining room, where breakfast is served, overlooks an ornamental duck pond. Accommodation is comfortable, with all rooms en suite and equipped with TV.
3 shr (1 fmly) No smoking in bedrooms No smoking in dining room CTV in all bedrooms Tea and coffee making facilities Cen ht CTV 6P 11 acres beef horses poultry
ROOMS: d £40-£44*

Victoria Lodge 61 Castle Rd SP1 3RH
(take A345 off Salisbury ring road. Castle Road 400yds on right. Turn into Victoria Rd for access to car park)
☎ 01722 320586 FAX 01722 414507
Closed 25-26 Dec
A fine Victorian house, ideally located within easy walking distance to the city centre. Brightly decorated bedrooms are comfortably appointed in modern style, and there is now a small cosy lounge.
15 bth/shr (3 fmly) No smoking in bedrooms No smoking in dining room No smoking in 1 lounge CTV in all bedrooms Tea and coffee making facilities Licensed Cen ht CTV 15P Last d 8.30pm
ROOMS: s £25-£32.30; d £35-£44*
CARDS:

Selected

Websters 11 Hartington Rd SP2 7LG
(from city centre take A360 Devizes road and Hartington Road is 500yds from St Pauls roundabout on left hand side)
☎ 01722 339779 FAX 01722 339779
Amiable hosts, Mary and Peter Webb take great pleasure in welcoming guests into their delightful home. Conveniently situated in a quiet cul-de-sac, the fascinating sights of Salisbury are just a short stroll away. Bedrooms are well equipped and immaculately presented with attractive co-ordinating soft furnishings and some lovely pieces of furniture. A ground floor room is available which has been specifically designed for use by those with disabilities. Generous breakfasts are served on bright and cheerful crockery in the attractive dining room, a perfect start to the day!
5 bth/shr No smoking in bedrooms No smoking in dining room CTV in all bedrooms Tea and coffee making facilities No dogs (ex guide dogs) Cen ht No children 12yrs 5P No coaches
ROOMS: s £22-£25; d £34-£38*

SALTASH Cornwall & Isles of Scilly Map 02 SX45

Selected

The Crooked Inn Stoketon PL12 4RZ ☎ 01752 848177 FAX 01752 843203
The Arnold family create a friendly atmosphere for their guests at this well run inn. The courtyard is home to pigs, ducks, dogs and cats that wander about happily and freely. The bedrooms are located across the courtyard from the main buildings and are furnished to a high standard with many modern facilities, including satellite TV, radio and hairdryers. The public house restaurant offers an extensive menu.
12 annexe rms (9 bth/shr) (2 fmly) CTV in 8 bedrooms Tea and coffee making facilities Cen ht CTV 45P Outdoor swimming pool (heated) Childrens play area Last d 9.30pm
CARDS:

Selected

Weary Friar Pillaton PL12 6QS (2m W of A388, between Saltash/Callington) ☎ 01579 350238 FAX 01579 350238
This 12th-century inn prides itself on its food with an extensive carte and bar menu. The Weary Friar has an intimate 'olde worlde' atmosphere with suits of armour and a baronial style private dining room. Tucked away in the country, yet convenient for Plymouth, its 12 bedrooms offer traditional comfort with modern facilities.
12 bth (1 fmly) No smoking in area of dining room CTV in all bedrooms Tea and coffee making facilities No dogs (ex guide dogs) Cen ht CTV 30P Last d 9.30pm
ROOMS: s £35; d £50*
MEALS: Lunch £6.50-£10.50 Dinner £6.50-£10.50&alc*
CARDS:

SANDBACH Cheshire Map 07 SJ76

Poplar Mount 2 Station Rd, Elworth CW11 3JG
(off A533 into Station Rd) ☎ 01270 761268 FAX 01270 761268
Close to the railway station and only 3 miles from junction 17 of the M6, this friendly guest house is well situated for visitors to the area. There is a cosy lounge and dinner is available, choosing from a selection of popular dishes, whilst neatly decorated bedrooms are bright and well equipped.
7 rms (2 bth 2 shr) (1 fmly) No smoking in dining room CTV in all bedrooms Tea and coffee making facilities No dogs (ex guide dogs) Cen ht CTV 7P No coaches Last d 7.30pm
ROOMS: s £20-£28; d £40*
CARDS:

SANDHURST Kent Map 05 TQ82

Hoads Farm *(TQ805282)* Crouch Ln TN18 5PA
(on A268 0.5m from Sandhurst village turn right into Crouch lane)
☎ 01580 850296 FAX 01580 850296 Mrs A Nicholas
Dating from the 16th century and set in tranquil countryside on the edge of the village of Sandhurst, Hoads Farm has been beautifully restored and is personally run by Mrs Anne Nicholas. There is a spacious beamed lounge with log burning fire, and a separate candlelit dining room overlooking the garden; dinner can be arranged with 24 hours notice. Families are especially welcome and the Nicholas family also own the adjoining Sandhurst Vineyard (and a wine shop) which has produced some award-winning English table wines. There are plenty of signposted local walks.
3 rms Tea and coffee making facilities No dogs Licensed Cen ht CTV 350 acres apple hops vines sheep
ROOMS: s fr £19; d fr £38*
CARDS:

See page 14-20 for a list of Premier Selected establishments

SANDOWN See **WIGHT, ISLE OF**

SANDY Bedfordshire Map **04** TL14

Selected

Q Q Q Q **Highfield** *(TL166515)* Great North Rd SG19 2AQ
(1.5m N of Sandy roundabout on the A1 or 2.5m S of Black Cat roundabout on the A1)
☎ 01767 682332 FAX 01767 692503
Mrs M Codd
Mrs Codd is an enthusiastic and friendly hostess who takes great pride in this immaculately maintained farmhouse which is surrounded by farmland. Tastefully furnished bedrooms are divided between the main house and a nicely converted stable block with many thoughtful extras adding to guest comfort. Breakfast is taken communally at a large table in a pleasantly appointed dining room and guests also have the use of an inviting and comfortable lounge, decorated with pictures and dried flower arrangements and providing a range of books and games for guests' use.
3 rms (1 bth 1 shr) 3 annexe shr (2 fmly) No smoking CTV in 3 bedrooms Tea and coffee making facilities Cen ht CTV 14P
300 acres arable
ROOMS: s £25-£45; d £40-£50*
CARDS:

SCARBOROUGH North Yorkshire Map **08** TA08

Q Q Q **Anatolia Hotel** 21 West St YO11 2QR ☎ 01723 503205 & 360864
Closed Nov-Etr
This friendly family-run hotel is found in a quiet side road close to the south beach and has been pleasantly furnished by the resident owners, Pat and Tony Simpson. The bedrooms are bright and fresh and a comfortable lounge is provided for guests. Good home cooking is served in the cosy dining room.
9 shr (3 fmly) No smoking in dining room No smoking in lounges CTV in all bedrooms Tea and coffee making facilities No dogs (ex guide dogs) Licensed Cen ht CTV No coaches Last d 3.30pm

Q Q **Argo Hotel** 134 North Marine Rd YO12 7HZ
(close to Scarborough Cricket Ground main entrance)
☎ 01723 375745
The Argo has particularly appealing public areas, with a cosy lounge and a dining room which also has a residents bar. Bedrooms are all bright and cheerful, with rear-facing ones having splendid views overlooking the town's cricket ground.
8 rms (3 shr) (5 fmly) No smoking in dining room CTV in all bedrooms Tea and coffee making facilities No dogs Licensed Cen ht CTV No coaches Last d 3pm
ROOMS: s £14-£16; d £28-£38; wkly b&b £93-£107; wkly hlf-bd £125-£135

Q Q **Avoncroft Hotel** 5-7 Crown Ter YO11 2BL
(from Station take Filey road A165 over Valley Bridge and left opposite St Andrews Church then left again for Crown Crescent, then turn right)
☎ 01723 372737 FAX 01723 372737
This family owned and run hotel is in the centre of an attractive Georgian terrace and is convenient for both the seafront and the town centre. Bedrooms are pleasantly furnished and decorated and there is a comfortable lounge for residents together with a spacious dining room and an adjoining lounge bar.
34 rms (1 bth 20 shr) (13 fmly) No smoking in area of dining room CTV in all bedrooms Tea and coffee making facilities Licensed Cen ht CTV Games room Pool table Last d 6.15pm
ROOMS: s £20.50-£26.50; d £41-£53; wkly b&b £143.50-£185.50; wkly hlf-bd £176-£216

Lyness 145 Columbus Ravine YO12 7QZ
(M62 junct 37, then A165 to North Bay and North Marine Drive. Turn left at Peasholme Park to Columbus Ravine, house on left)
☎ 01723 375952 & 0966 404219
Attractive public areas are a feature of the Lyness, with a comfortable and inviting lounge and a cosy dining room which also has a well stocked residents bar. Bedrooms are brightly decorated and good hospitality is assured from the resident owner, Mrs Laycock.
8 rms (6 bth/shr) (2 fmly) No smoking in 4 bedrooms No smoking in area of dining room No smoking in 1 lounge CTV in all bedrooms Tea and coffee making facilities No dogs (ex guide dogs) Licensed Cen ht CTV P Last d 6pm
ROOMS: s £16-£18; d £32-£36; wkly b&b £112-£126; wkly hlf-bd £161-£175*

Lysander Hotel 22 Weydale Av YO12 6AX
(located between Peasholm Park and Northstead Manor Gardens within 100yards of indoor swimming pool) ☎ 01723 373369
Apr-Oct
A pleasant hotel standing in a quiet side road and convenient for all the many attractions of the North Shore. There is a cosy lounge bar, and a good range of home cooked food is available in the bright dining room. Bedrooms are delightfully furnished with matching fabrics and have been thoughtfully equipped. Friendly service is provided by the resident owners Joan and Mike Atack.
18 rms (15 bth/shr) (2 fmly) No smoking in 12 bedrooms No smoking in dining room CTV in all bedrooms Tea and coffee making facilities No dogs (ex guide dogs) Licensed Cen ht CTV No children 2yrs 10P Golf 18 Last d 7pm
ROOMS: s £21-£26.50; d £42-£53; wkly b&b £140-£175; wkly hlf-bd £180-£224*
CARDS:

Manor Heath Hotel 67 Northstead Manor Dr YO12 6AF
(follow signs for North Bay and Peasholme Park)
☎ 01723 365720 FAX 01723 365720
Closed Dec-1 Jan
Situated on the North Bay beside Peasholm Park, this pleasantly furnished and family-owned and run small hotel offers a newly furnished and comfortable lounge together with a very attractive dining room. The bedrooms are modern and bright and there is also the benefit of a car park to the rear.
14 bth/shr (6 fmly) No smoking in dining room CTV in all bedrooms Tea and coffee making facilities No dogs Licensed Cen ht CTV 16P No coaches Last d 4.30pm
ROOMS: s £20-£23; d £40-£46; wkly b&b £126-£146; wkly hlf-bd £175-£195*
CARDS:

North End Farm Country Main St, Seamer YO12 4RF
(A64/B1261, farmhouse adjacent to only roundabout in village)
☎ 01723 862965
Apr-Oct
Situated in the village of Seamer, this charming cottage offers well equipped bedrooms together with a cosy residents lounge. Generous hospitality is provided by the resident owner.
4 rms (3 bth/shr) No smoking CTV in all bedrooms Tea and coffee making facilities No dogs Cen ht CTV No children 8yrs 6P No coaches
CARDS:

Selected

Paragon Hotel 123 Queens Pde YO12 7HU
(on A64, follow signs for the North Bay, premises situated on the cliff top) ☎ 01723 372676 FAX 01723 372676
25 Jan-Oct
The Paragon occupies a prime position overlooking the sea and is a delightful small hotel which has been carefully furnished throughout. The pretty bedrooms, although not over spacious, are delightfully decorated with matching fabrics and have been thoughtfully equipped. There is a very comfortable and inviting lounge which enjoys superb sea views, whilst the owners are very caring and friendly hosts. There is also a car park to the front of the hotel.
15 bth/shr (2 fmly) No smoking in 6 bedrooms No smoking in dining room CTV in all bedrooms Tea and coffee making facilities Direct dial from bedrooms Licensed Cen ht No children 2yrs 6P No coaches Last d 7pm
ROOMS: s £23-£25*
CARDS:

Parmelia Hotel 17 West St YO11 2QN ☎ 01723 361914
Apr-Oct
This comfortable private hotel is situated on the South Cliff only a short distance from the Esplanade and Cliff tramway. Bedrooms are modern and pleasantly furnished with attractive co-ordinated fabrics. There is a relaxing guests lounge and also a spacious lounge bar. Five-course evening meals are served in the attractive dining room and the standards of both hospitality and maintenance are very high.
15 rms (1 bth 12 shr) (3 fmly) No smoking in dining room CTV in all bedrooms Tea and coffee making facilities No dogs (ex guide dogs) Licensed Cen ht CTV Last d 5.45pm

Pickwick Huntriss Row YO11 2ED
(A64 to town centre, come to a T-junct with Scarborough stn on right, turn right and take 1st left, through lights over rdbt, hotel is 50 yds on left)
☎ 01723 375787 FAX 01723 374284
Closed 25 Dec
A listed building, Pickwick Inn stands in the centre of town and is close to all amenities. Modern, well equipped and pleasantly appointed bedrooms are provided, with some having four-poster beds. Public rooms include a first floor breakfast room and popular bars on the ground floor.
10 bth/shr CTV in all bedrooms Tea and coffee making facilities Direct dial from bedrooms No dogs (ex guide dogs) Lift Cen ht No children 10yrs No coaches
ROOMS: s £25-£32; d £39-£55; wkly b&b £150-£162*
MEALS: Lunch £1.95-£3.50*
CARDS:

Plane Tree Cottage Farm *(SE999984)* Staintondale YO13 0EY
(7m N) ☎ 01723 870796 Mrs M A Edmondson
May-Oct
Plane Tree Farm is certainly off the beaten track, about 8 miles north of Scarborough and near to the coast. There are two cosy and comfortable bedrooms together with a peaceful lounge and a charming dining room. Guests are usually welcomed by the friendly sheep dog, the cat, and of course, Mrs Edmondson! Good home cooking is provided and the eggs at breakfast could not be fresher, coming straight from the hens.
2 rms No smoking Tea and coffee making facilities No dogs Cen ht CTV No children 2P 60 acres rare breed sheep pigs hens Last d am
ROOMS: d £36; wkly b&b £120; wkly hlf-bd £190*

Premier Hotel 66 Esplande, South Cliffe YO11 2UZ
(A165 from Bridington-turn right opp Bowling Club onto Holbrick Road, at end turn left onto Esplanade, hotel approx 100yds on left with Union Jack)
☎ 01723 501062 FAX 01723 501112
Standing in a delightful position overlooking the south bay this well furnished and comfortable hotel offers a delightful lounge together with well equipped bedrooms and a separate bar. Many of the original Victorian features have been retained and the atmosphere is enhanced by friendly and attentive service.
19 bth/shr (3 fmly) No smoking in dining room CTV in all bedrooms Tea and coffee making facilities Licensed Lift Cen ht 6P Last d 5pm
ROOMS: s £27-£34; d £54-£80; wkly b&b £189-£245; wkly hlf-bd £259-£315
CARDS:

The Ramleh 135 Queens Pde YO12 7HY
(from A64 left at Station, then right at traffic lights, left at roundabout, second right, first left) ☎ 01723 365745 FAX 01723 365745
Mar-Oct
Standing in a prime position and enjoying fine sea views, this friendly family-owned and run hotel offers fresh and bright bedrooms together with a comfortable lounge and a recently refurbished cosy dining room which overlooks the sea. The hotel has a small car park and provides very good value-for-money together with very friendly and attentive service.
9 bth/shr (3 fmly) No smoking in dining room CTV in all bedrooms Tea and coffee making facilities No dogs (ex guide dogs) Licensed Cen ht CTV 5P Last d 2pm
ROOMS: s £22; d £38; wkly b&b £126; wkly hlf-bd £168
CARDS:

Rose Dene 106 Columbus Ravine YO12 7QZ ☎ 01723 374252 FAX 01723 507356
Mar-Oct
This semi-detached guest house is cheerfully decorated throughout and provides a comfortable guests lounge and pleasant dining room. Bedrooms come in a variety of sizes, with contemporary furnishings making the best use of space in the smaller ones.
9 bth/shr (3 fmly) No smoking in 5 bedrooms No smoking in dining room No smoking in lounges CTV in all bedrooms Tea and coffee making facilities No dogs (ex guide dogs) Cen ht CTV No children 3yrs 7P No coaches Last d 3pm

Sefton Hotel 18 Prince of Wales Ter YO11 2AL ☎ 01723 372310
Mar-Oct
The Sefton is a traditional and long-established hotel on the South Cliff which offers comfortable and spacious public rooms together with bright and fresh bedrooms. It overlooks a small park and there is the benefit of a lift between floors. Service is provided by Mrs Kelly and her family.
14 rms (10 bth) No smoking in 8 bedrooms No smoking in dining room No smoking in lounges No dogs (ex guide dogs) Licensed Lift Cen ht CTV No children 12yrs No coaches Last d 6pm

West Lodge Private Hotel 38 West St, South Cliff YO11 2QP (A165 towards centre turn left into Seacliff Rd along Holbeck Hill onto West Street) ☎ 01723 500754
Situated in a side road and close to the South Cliff, this Victorian house offers very good value accommodation. There is a comfortable lounge available and home-cooked dinners are served in the dining room which incorporates a small bar.
7 rms (3 shr) (4 fmly) No smoking in dining room CTV in all bedrooms Tea and coffee making facilities Licensed Cen ht CTV Garden swing Last d 10am
ROOMS: s £16-£18; d £32-£36
CARDS:

The Whiteley Hotel 99/101 Queens Pde YO12 7HY
(follow signs to North Bay. By Alexander Bowls Centre turn into Queens Parade. Hotel is then situated on cliff top)
☎ 01723 373514 FAX 01723 373007
Closed 30 Nov-Jan
This family-run hotel offers superb views over the bay and provides bright, fresh and well equipped bedrooms which have been delightfully co-ordinated. There is a comfortable and inviting lounge as well as a smaller no-smoking lounge to the rear. Good home-cooking is served in the cosy and traditional-style dining room and very friendly service is provided by the resident owners, Mr & Mrs Smith.
10 shr (3 fmly) No smoking in 4 bedrooms No smoking in dining room No smoking in 1 lounge CTV in all bedrooms Tea and coffee making facilities Licensed Cen ht CTV 10P No coaches Last d 2pm
ROOMS: d £40-£44; wkly b&b £133-£147; wkly hlf-bd £185.50-£199.50*
CARDS:

SCILLY, ISLES OF Map 02

ST MARY'S Map 02

Selected

Carnwethers Country House Carnwethers, Pelistry Bay TR21 0NX (2.5m from Hugh Town, St Marys) ☎ 01720 422415 FAX 422415
30 Apr-2 Oct
Located on the far side of the island, this house is a ten-minute drive from the town and Roy and Joyce Graham ensure a warm welcome. Bedrooms are bright and comfortably equipped with modern en suite facilities, and decorated with attractive local watercolours and prints. Guests can enjoy the garden with its lovely views, heated pool and croquet lawn; indoors there is a cosy lounge and well stocked bar. Home-cooked evening meals are served in the smart dining room.
8 bth/shr 1 annexe bth/shr (2 fmly) No smoking in bedrooms No smoking in dining room No smoking in 1 lounge CTV in all bedrooms Tea and coffee making facilities Licensed Cen ht CTV No children 7yrs 4P No coaches Outdoor swimming pool (heated) Golf 9 Sauna Pool table,Table tennis,Croquet,Golf is 1m away
ROOMS: wkly hlf-bd £280-£385

Selected

Crebinick House Church St TR21 0JT
(one third of a mile from the quay through Hugh Town)
☎ 01720 422968 FAX 01720 422968
30 Mar-Sep rs 1-26 Oct
This house is located in the centre of the town just two minutes from the sea, and although dating back to 1760, offers bright, well equipped rooms with modern en suite showers. There is a comfortable sitting room with TV, and good home-cooked evening meals are served in the smart dining room. There are two ground-floor bedrooms.
6 shr No smoking Tea and coffee making facilities No dogs Licensed Cen ht CTV No children 7yrs No coaches Last d 9.30am
ROOMS: wkly b&b £161-£245; wkly hlf-bd £252-£315

SCOTCH CORNER North Yorkshire Map 08 NZ20

Vintage Hotel DL10 6NP (leave A1 at Scotch Corner and take A66 towards Penrith, hotel is 200yds on left)
☎ 01748 824424 & 822961 FAX 01748 826272
Closed 25 Dec & 1 Jan rs Nov-Mar (closed Sun pm)
You'll be assured of a warm welcome and excellent service at this hotel and restaurant situated just off the main road. Comfortable and well equipped bedrooms are available in a variety of sizes, many of which include trouser presses. For relaxation, guests can enjoy a drink in the fully licensed bar, or choose from a mouth watering selection of evening meals served in the cheery restaurant. Breakfast is not included in the prices.
8 rms (5 bth/shr) No smoking in dining room CTV in all bedrooms Tea and coffee making facilities Direct dial from bedrooms No dogs (ex guide dogs) Licensed Cen ht CTV 50P Last d 9.15pm
ROOMS: s £23.50-£35.50; d £29.50-£39.50; (room only) *
CARDS:

SEAFORD East Sussex Map 05 TV49

Selected

Q Q Q Q Avondale Hotel Avondale Rd BN25 1RJ (on A259 edge of town opposite town memorial) ☎ 01323 890008 FAX 01323 490598
This family run hotel is close to both town centre and seafront. A winner of the 'Seaford in Bloom' award, the hotel is a picture in the summer with hanging baskets and window boxes. Most of the rooms are en suite and comfortably furnished in a modern style. Lunch and evening meals are served by prior arrangement and guests have use of a comfortable lounge.
16 rms (10 shr) (6 fmly) No smoking CTV in all bedrooms Tea and coffee making facilities Direct dial from bedrooms No dogs (ex guide dogs) Lift Cen ht CTV No coaches Seaford leisure centre is nearby Last d 12.30pm
ROOMS: s £20-£25; d £40-£50*
CARDS:

Selected

Q Q Q Q Maycroft Eastbourne Rd BN25 4BB (on main A259 caost road, at Eastbourne end of Seaford, close to Seven Sisters Country Park) ☎ 01323 491755
This charming family home has three super bedrooms two of which have four poster beds. Guests are assured of a warm welcome by genial host Jackie Duncan and her husband. There is a spacious comfortable lounge with deep leather sofas and breakfast is eaten in a very smart dining room.
3 shr (1 fmly) No smoking CTV in all bedrooms Tea and coffee making facilities Licensed Cen ht CTV 4P No coaches
ROOMS: s £25-£35; d £40-£45

Q Q Q Silverdale 21 Sutton Park Rd BN25 1RH (on A259 in the centre of Seaford, close to War Memorial) ☎ 01323 491849 FAX 01323 891131
Expect a friendly welcome from Ted and Gilly Cowdrey at this appealing establishment close to the town centre. Well-equipped bedrooms are decorated in pretty pastel shades and come with extras like books, pot-pourri and face cloths. Public rooms include a comfortable no smoking lounge and a well-stocked conservatory bar that is open plan to a dining room that, although small, offers and extensive range of home-cooked dishes for both lunch and dinner; breakfasts include home-made jams. Some bedrooms are reserved for non smokers.
8 rms (4 bth/shr) (3 fmly) No smoking in 2 bedrooms No smoking in area of dining room No smoking in lounges CTV in all bedrooms Tea and coffee making facilities Direct dial from bedrooms Licensed Cen ht CTV 6P No coaches Last d 8pm
ROOMS: s £20-£40; d £30-£60; wkly b&b £105-£175; wkly hlf-bd £160-£230
CARDS:

SEAHOUSES Northumberland Map 12 NU23

Selected

Q Q Q Q *Railston House* 133 Main St, North Sunderland NE68 7TS (exit A1 N of Alnwick signposted Seahouses & Beadnell. Turn left at first roundabout after Beadnell, house 400yds on left)
☎ 01665 720912 FAX 01665 720912
Closed Xmas & New Year
This interesting Georgian house lies within walking distance of the centre of this popular seaside village. Chippy and Jill McConnell-Wood have refurbished it with style and imagination. Bedrooms are furnished with pine and traditional pieces and enhanced with thoughtful personal touches. The room without en suite has sole use of a super bathroom with twin basins, a bath, and separate shower cubicle. Downstairs the flagstone hall leads to a small conservatory and secluded garden. Breakfast is taken round one large table in the period dining room.
3 rms (2 shr) No smoking CTV in all bedrooms Tea and coffee making facilities Cen ht 2P No coaches

SEATON Devon Map 03 SY29

Selected

Q Q Q Q Beach End at Seaton 8 Trevelyan Rd EX12 2NL (at eastern end of seafront near yacht club and harbour)
☎ 01297 23388 FAX 01297 625604
Mar-Oct
This attractive Edwardian guest house enjoys a quiet position on Seaton seafront. The bedrooms all have delightful sea views, are individually decorated and furnished and have been equipped with all modern comforts. Proprietors, Philip and Joan Millard, afford a warm welcome and offer guests fine, freshly prepared food.
4 bth/shr No smoking in dining room CTV in all bedrooms No dogs Licensed Cen ht CTV 5P No coaches Last d 3pm
ROOMS: d £47*

Selected

CLOSED

Q Q Q Q *Harepath Farm* Harepath Hill EX12 2SZ (on main coastal road A3052 between Lyme Regis and Sidmouth)
☎ 01297 20606
This beautiful stone-built Devon longhouse, situated beside the A3052, is ideally placed for exploring the coastal areas around Seaton, Beer, Lyme Regis and Sidmouth. June and David Palmer have recently restored the former farmhouse, which dates from the 15th century and now, with original flagstone floors, inglenook fireplaces and oak beams, it offers a wealth of character and charm. Bedrooms, which are spacious and equipped with modern comforts, have been tastefully decorated and furnished. There is a cosy sitting room for guests, and breakfast is served at separate tables in the elegant dining room. Dinner is also available by prior arrangement.
4 shr No smoking in 4 bedrooms No smoking in area of dining room CTV in all bedrooms Tea and coffee making facilities CTV No children 14yrs 12P No coaches Last d 11am

The AA's professional Inspectors make regular and anonymous visits to all the establishments listed in the Guide. They accept no gifts or favours from proprietors

Selected

QQQQ **Mariners Hotel** Esplanade EX12 2NP
(situated on middle of seafront) ☎ 01297 20560
This small privately run hotel, situated on Seaton seafront, overlooks Lyme Bay. All bedrooms are en suite, tastefully decorated and well furnished. There is a spacious and comfortable lounge, with an additional sea facing sun lounge and an adjacent bar. In the relaxed atmosphere of the dining room a choice of home cooked meals is offered.
10 bth/shr (1 fmly) No smoking in dining room CTV in all bedrooms Tea and coffee making facilities Licensed Cen ht CTV 10P No coaches Last d 6pm
ROOMS: s £23-£28; d £40-£44*
CARDS:

SEAVIEW See **WIGHT, ISLE OF**

SEDBERGH Cumbria Map **07** SD69

QQQ **Cross Keys Temperance Inn** Cautley LA10 5NE (M6 junct 37 to A683 through Sedbergh. Hotel 4 miles north of Sedbergh on the left)
☎ 015396 20284 FAX 015396 21966
Idyllically situated within the Yorkshire Dales National Park, this traditional and historic Inn is ideally placed for the tourist seeking restful peace and quiet. Uniquely, this is a 'Temperance Inn', so no alcohol is sold although guests are invited to bring their own selection to complement the ambitious menu of home cooked dishes. Stunning views over the surrounding fells and wildlife are enjoyed from the conservatory.
2 bth/shr (1 fmly) No smoking Tea and coffee making facilities No dogs (ex guide dogs) Cen ht 9P Riding Last d 9pm
ROOMS: s £27.50-£37.50; d £55-£65; wkly b&b £165-£200; wkly hlf-bd £240-£290
CARDS:

QQQ **St Mark's** Cautley LA10 5LZ (3m N of Sedbergh on the A683)
☎ 015396 20287 FAX 015396 21585
Closed 22-27 Dec rs 28 Dec-2 Jan (b & b only)
Lying in a valley three miles north of Sedbergh and with striking views of the hills, this fine old Victorian vicarage formerly served Cautley Church. It is now a family home and guest house which promotes leisure activity breaks. The pine-furnished bedrooms retain their original character and have modern en suite bathrooms. There is a small lounge, and meals are taken house-party style at one long antique table in the dining room.
5 bth/shr (1 fmly) No smoking in bedrooms No smoking in dining room No smoking in 1 lounge CTV in all bedrooms Tea and coffee making facilities Cen ht CTV 7P No coaches Leisure courses Golf Fishing Stables Tennis Last d 7.45pm
ROOMS: s £21.50-£25; d £43-£50; wkly b&b £143.80-£166.25; wkly hlf-bd £212.80-£249.38

SEDGEFIELD Co Durham Map **08** NZ32

QQQ ◖ ***Dun Cow*** High St TS21 3AT
(Sedgefield is at junct of A177 and A689, premises in the centre of the village by village green and Parish church) (Ramside)
☎ 01740 620894
The archetypal English inn, the Dun Cow is full of character and offers an excellent range of food both in its restaurant and various bar areas, all of which are interesting and adorned with bric-a-brac. Bedrooms are in the process of being completely refurbished to include en suite facilities.
6 rms CTV in all bedrooms Tea and coffee making facilities Direct dial from bedrooms Cen ht 25P Last d 10pm
CARDS:

SELBY North Yorkshire Map **08** SE63

QQ **Hazeldene** 32-34 Brook St, Doncaster Rd YO8 4AR
(off A19 south of town centre)
☎ 01757 704809 FAX 01757 709300
A friendly family owned and run guest house offering generally spacious, comfortable bedrooms and modern bathroom facilities. The house is close to the town centre and has parking facilities to the rear.
8 rms (3 shr) No smoking CTV in all bedrooms Tea and coffee making facilities No dogs No children 12yrs 5P No coaches
ROOMS: s £20-£30; d £36-£46*

SELSEY West Sussex Map **04** SZ89

Selected

QQQQ **St Andrews Lodge** Chichester Rd PO20 0LX
(on right past Police Station just before the church)
☎ 01243 606899 FAX 01243 607826
Closed Xmas
Close to the sea on the peninsula south of Chichester, and on the main street of this peaceful village, this well kept establishment offers neat, bright bedrooms. Valma Kennedy runs a friendly, informal house, putting her guests at ease on arrival. Newly created rooms in a single storey building in the garden include one that has been well adapted for disabled guests. Day rooms include a convivial bar, the only place where smoking is allowed, and an appealing lounge with picture windows and a wood-burning stove to keep things cosy in winter. Dinner is served by arrangement.
5 bth/shr 1 annexe shr (2 fmly) No smoking in bedrooms No smoking in dining room No smoking in lounges CTV in all bedrooms Tea and coffee making facilities Licensed Cen ht CTV 15P Golf Golf and riding nearby Last d 1pm
ROOMS: s £25-£50; d £45-£65*
CARDS:

SEMLEY Wiltshire Map 03 ST82

Q Q **Benett Arms** SP7 9AS
(2m N of Shaftesbury on A350, turn right for 1m. On village green, opposite church) ☎ 01747 830221 FAX 01747 830152
Closed 25 & 26 Dec
Resident proprietor, Joe Duthie, offers guests cheerful hospitality at this country inn set in a pretty village just off the A303. Bedrooms, although simply furnished, are well equipped. Three rooms are located on the ground floor in an adjacent annexe. The popular split-level bar is informal and friendly and has an open fire in winter. Guests may dine in the more formal restaurant or sample one of the many bar meals available.
2 bth/shr 3 annexe shr CTV in all bedrooms Tea and coffee making facilities Direct dial from bedrooms Cen ht ch fac 30P Last d 9.45pm
ROOMS: s £31-£34; d £48-£54
MEALS: Lunch £8.95-£11.95&alc Dinner £11.95-£19.50alc
CARDS:

SENNEN Cornwall & Isles of Scilly Map 02 SW32

Q Q **The Old Manor Hotel** TR19 7AD (on A30, opposite St Sennens Church) (The Circle) ☎ 01736 871280 FAX 01736 871280
Situated close to Lands End, this charming 18th-century house is under new ownership. Shirley & David Evans, with their partner Janet Aldridge, offer guests a very friendly welcome. Rooms are simply furnished, some en suite, but have lots of facilities. Dinner is served in the cottage-style dining room, overlooking the pretty gardens.
8 rms (4 shr) (2 fmly) No smoking in 1 bedrooms No smoking in dining room CTV in all bedrooms Tea and coffee making facilities Direct dial from bedrooms No dogs Licensed Cen ht CTV 10P No coaches Last d 8.30pm
ROOMS: s £17; d £44-£54; wkly b&b £107-£170.50; wkly hlf-bd £176-£233
CARDS:

Q Q ***Sunny Bank Hotel*** Sea View Hill TR19 7AR
(on A30, 8m W of Penzance just after sign for Sennen) ☎ 01736 871278
Closed Dec
A relaxed and friendly atmosphere is created by Ralph and Valerie Comber at their family-run hotel. There is a spacious lounge with colour television, plus a separate reading room and there is a dispense bar in the dining room. Evening meals are popular, bringing guests back to Sunny Bank year after year. Sennen Cove, Land's End and the Minack Theatre are all a short distance away. With prior notice Mrs Comber will provide special picnics to take to the unique Minack Theatre.
11 rms (2 fmly) Tea and coffee making facilities No dogs (ex guide dogs) Licensed Cen ht CTV 12P No coaches Last d 7pm

SETTLE North Yorkshire Map 07 SD86

Q Q **Golden Lion** 5 Duke St BD24 9DU (in town centre opposite Barclays Bank) ☎ 01729 822203 FAX 01729 824103
Situated in the centre of the town, this popular inn offers an extensive range of food, served in the character bar or restaurant. Bedrooms, a number of them recently refurbished, are comfortable and there is an inviting lounge, exclusively for residents, on the first floor.
14 rms (1 bth 4 shr) (2 fmly) CTV in all bedrooms Tea and coffee making facilities No dogs (ex guide dogs) Cen ht 11P Last d 10pm
ROOMS: s £22.50-£29.50; d £45-£56*
MEALS: Bar Lunch £3-£5 Dinner £5-£12*
CARDS:

Q Q **Liverpool House** Chapel Square BD24 9HR
(turn off B6480 by side of police station (Chapel Street) and take 2nd turning on right) ☎ 01729 822247
Within walking distance of the town centre, this Grade II listed building, dating from the mid-19th century, has great character, particularly in the top floor beamed bedrooms. There are no TVs in bedrooms, but there is a comfortable TV lounge and breakfast is served in the nicely furnished dining room. This is a non smoking guest house.
7 rms (1 shr) No smoking Tea and coffee making facilities No dogs (ex guide dogs) Licensed CTV 8P No coaches
ROOMS: s £17-£18.50; d £34-£44; wkly b&b £115-£125*
CARDS:

Q Q Q **The Oast Guest House** 5 Pen-y-Ghent View, Church St BD24 9JJ (entering through Settle town heading N shambles and the market place on the right, Royal Oak Pub and car park on left, premises on left 100yds on) ☎ 01729 822989
Set in an attractive row of Edwardian cottages close to the town centre, many of the bedrooms enjoy views of the surrounding hills. Pleasantly furnished bedrooms either have en suite facilities or shower cubicles, sharing an adjacent toilet. Dinner is available by arrangement and there is a comfortable sitting room for guest use.
5 rms (3 bth/shr) No smoking CTV in all bedrooms Tea and coffee making facilities No dogs (ex guide dogs) Licensed Cen ht CTV No children 4P No coaches Golf Fishing Riding Last d noon
ROOMS: s £18-£19.50; d £36-£39*

Q Q Q **Whitefriars Country Guesthouse** Church St BD24 9JD
(from A65 follow signs into Settle Market Place, exit market place on Kendal Rd, premises signposted) ☎ 01729 823753
Closed Xmas Day
Standing in its own delightful grounds and close to the town centre, this family owned hotel offers traditional and pleasantly furnished accommodation. There are two lounges provided together with a beamed dining room where good home cooking is served. The house is fully no smoking.
9 rms (6 shr) (2 fmly) No smoking CTV in all bedrooms Tea and coffee making facilities No dogs (ex guide dogs) Licensed Cen ht CTV 9P No coaches Last d 5pm
ROOMS: s fr £18; d £36-£45; wkly b&b £135.40-£141.75; wkly hlf-bd £179.40-£207.75*

Q Q **Yorkshire Rose** Duke St BD24 9AJ
(turn off A65 at rdbt towards Settle. Establishment is located on the left just before town centre) ☎ 01729 822032
This Grade II listed building, dating back to 1839, is situated on the edge of the town, with fine views over the surrounding fells from many bedrooms. Enthusiastic new owners are steadily improving the guest house and currently offer good value accommodation. There is a comfortable lounge and dinner can be available by arrangement in the traditionally furnished dining room.
5 rms (2 shr) (2 fmly) No smoking in bedrooms No smoking in dining room CTV in all bedrooms Tea and coffee making facilities No dogs Licensed Cen ht CTV 7P Last d by prior arrangement
ROOMS: s £15-£20; d £30-£40; wkly b&b £105-£140; wkly hlf-bd £140-£210*

SEVENOAKS Kent Map 05 TQ55

See also **Wrotham**

Q Q **Barn Cottage** Seven Mile Ln, Borough Green TN15 8QY
(turn onto A20 and take B2016 (Seven Mile Lane) for 1m over cross roads, Barn cottage on left, entrance opposite sign for Viking Oak Kennels)
☎ 01732 883384
This white boarded cottage is set back off the B2016 in a pretty courtyard. The bedrooms are neat and comfortably furnished. Guests are welcome to use the lounge and enjoy the attractive garden; a traditional breakfast is served in the flower filled conservatory.
2 rms No smoking CTV in 1 bedroom No dogs Cen ht 5P No coaches Walking Cycling Garden Woods & Bridleways nearby
ROOMS: s £22.50-£25; d £45-£50*

SHACKLEFORD Surrey Map 04 SU94

Q Q Q **Seven Pines** Shackleford Rd GU8 6AE
(take A3 south from Guildford, 3m after A3/A31 junction exit A3 following Shackleford signs and then first right into Grenville Rd premises on left)
☎ 01483 425286 FAX 01483 425286
Closed 15 Dec-10 Jan
This comfortable country house situated in 1.5 acres of garden offers warm hospitality and good service. One bedroom is en suite and the other shares the owners' bathroom. There are also many extra touches such as ornaments and books. Good home cooked dinners and breakfasts are served in the dining room, and Wendy and Douglas Hamilton invite guests to share in the comfort of their own sitting room.
2 rms (1 bth/shr) (1 fmly) No smoking CTV in all bedrooms Tea and coffee making facilities No dogs (ex guide dogs) Cen ht CTV 6P No coaches Croquet Livery stable Golf course Fishing Walking
Last d by arrangement
ROOMS: s £20-£25; d £36-£44; wkly b&b £126-£157.50; wkly hlf-bd £182-£213.50

SHAFTESBURY Dorset Map 03 ST82

See also **Tollard Royal**

Selected

Q Q Q Q **The Knoll** Bleke St SP7 8AH (A350/A30 turn at Esso rdbt to town centre, after 200yds house is last on right before sharp right) ☎ 01747 855243 FAX 01747 850559
Closed Xmas week
This delightful family home offers easy level access to the famous Gold Hill (featured in the Hovis advertisements) and also commands glorious country views as far as Glastonbury Tor on clear days. Attractively decorated, and individually furnished, bedrooms have been equipped with lots of thoughtful extras. Bryan is a professional artist and his paintings decorate the walls and many are for sale. Breakfast is served around one large table in the dining room which overlooks the delightful garden.
3 bth/shr No smoking CTV in all bedrooms Tea and coffee making facilities No dogs Cen ht No children 4P No coaches
ROOMS: s £30-£40; d £46-£50*

Selected

Q Q Q Q ***Old Forge*** Chapel Hill, Compton Abbas SP7 0NQ
(A350 from Shaftsbury signed to Blandford, go through Cann village, Compton Abbas is the next village. The Old Forge is the 1st building on the left) ☎ 01747 811881 FAX 01747 811881
Closed Xmas
The Old Forge dates back to 1700 and is located in the village of Compton Abbas, next to a National Trust area of outstanding beauty. The blacksmith's forge has been restored as a museum, and sells country antiques. Owners Tom and Lucy Kerridge and family offer a warm welcome. The bedrooms retain much of their original character with antique furnishings, sloping ceilings and pretty decor. There is a lounge with a log-burning stove and a selection of games and books. A farmhouse breakfast is served using local organic produce and free-range eggs.
3 rms (1 bth 1 shr) No smoking CTV in 2 bedrooms Tea and coffee making facilities No dogs (ex guide dogs) Cen ht CTV 4P

SHALDON Devon

See **Teignmouth**

SHANKLIN See WIGHT, ISLE OF

SHAP Cumbria Map 12 NY51

Q Q Q **Brookfield** CA10 3PZ (two minutes off junct 39 of M6)
☎ 01931 716397 FAX 716397
Closed 21 Dec-Jan
At this friendly guest house, attractive bedrooms provide comfort and most rooms offer tastefully appointed en suite showers. Good home cooking is offered in the evening and served in the light and airy dining room, where substantial breakfasts can be enjoyed too.
5 rms (4 shr) (3 fmly) No smoking in bedrooms No smoking in dining room CTV in all bedrooms Tea and coffee making facilities No dogs Licensed Cen ht CTV 36P No coaches Last d 8.15pm
ROOMS: s £19-£25; d £37-£46

Q **Green Farm** *(NY565143)* CA10 3PW (on A6 in Shap village)
☎ 01931 716619 Mr & Mrs E Hodgson
Etr-Sep
Proprietor Mrs Hodgson has been welcoming guests to her traditional farmhouse for thirty years. The bedrooms offer comfort as well as dramatic views across the rolling fells. Downstairs there is a cosy lounge and a dining room were individual tables are set up for a hearty Cumbrian breakfast.
3 rms (2 fmly) No smoking in bedrooms No smoking in dining room Tea and coffee making facilities No dogs CTV 4P 200 acres mixed
ROOMS: d £32-£34*

SHEFFIELD South Yorkshire Map 08 SK38

Q Q Q **The Briary** 12 Moncrieffe Rd S7 1HR (turn right off A621 from Abbeydale Rd at Yorkshire Bank traffic lights, up Shedson Rd to next traffic lights, turn right onto Moncrieffe Rd) ☎ 0114 255 1951
This large Victorian house, originally a doctor's surgery, is situated in a leafy suburb with easy access to the city centre. It provides attractively decorated and furnished bedrooms. Room sizes vary, and the larger ones are suitable for families. Good home cooking is offered, meals being served in a combined dining room and lounge. *contd.*

6 bth/shr (1 fmly) No smoking CTV in all bedrooms Tea and coffee making facilities No dogs Cen ht No children 10yrs 4P No coaches Last d evening before
ROOMS: s £28; d £46-£50; wkly b&b fr £176*
CARDS:

Q Q Q Endcliffe Villa 50 Endcliffe Rise Rd, Endcliffe S11 8RU
☎ 0114 266 1232 FAX 267 6115
Closed Xmas
Situated in a quiet residential area close to the Botanical Gardens, this friendly guest house has recently been totally refurbished. Attractively furnished bedrooms are full of character and the owner Sue Hoey prides herself on the freshly prepared evening meals; a wide choice of dishes is offered and the breakfast menu is equally extensive.
3 shr (1 fmly) No smoking CTV in all bedrooms Tea and coffee making facilities No dogs (ex guide dogs) Cen ht No children 5yrs P Last d lunchtime same day
ROOMS: s £30-£36; d £44-£50
CARDS:

Q Q Q Hunter House Hotel 685 Ecclesall Rd, Hunters Bar S11 8TG (on A625 overlooking Endcliffe Park, 1m from City Centre)
☎ 0114 266 2709 FAX 0114 268 6370
A popular and mainly commercial hotel part of which is a 250 year old toll house. The spacious bedrooms are geared towards the business guest and the public rooms include a cosy bar and an attractive breakfast room. A good range of bar meals is provided and service is very friendly.
24 rms (11 bth/shr) (9 fmly) No smoking in 1 bedrooms No smoking in dining room CTV in 23 bedrooms Tea and coffee making facilities Direct dial from bedrooms No dogs (ex guide dogs) Licensed Cen ht CTV 8P Last d 8.30pm
ROOMS: s £25-£42; d £40-£52*
CARDS:

Q Q Q Lindrick Hotel 226 Chippinghouse Rd S7 1DR
(Turn off A621 Abbydale Rd into Chippinghouse Rd hotel is 200yds on right) ☎ 0114 258 5041 FAX 0114 255 4758
Closed 24 Dec-first Sat in Jan
This well kept, family run hotel is found in a leafy residential area of the city. It provides well equipped and modern bedrooms together with a spacious bar and a cosy breakfast room on the ground floor. The resident owners are very friendly and provide attentive service.
23 rms (15 shr) (2 fmly) No smoking in dining room No smoking in 1 lounge CTV in all bedrooms Tea and coffee making facilities Direct dial from bedrooms Licensed Cen ht CTV 20P Last d 8.45pm
ROOMS: s £22-£38; d £44-£50
CARDS:

Q Q Q Millingtons 70 Broomgrove Rd S10 2NA
(off A625, signposted Castleton, Eccleshall Rd) ☎ 0114 266 9549
This delightful guest house is in a quiet side road not far from the university and the city. It provides bright and fresh bedrooms and good breakfasts, taken around a large table. A cosy lounge is also provided.
6 rms (3 bth/shr) No smoking in dining room CTV in all bedrooms Tea and coffee making facilities No dogs (ex guide dogs) Cen ht CTV No children 12yrs 4P No coaches
ROOMS: s £25-£28; d £39-£42*

Selected

Q Q Q Q Westbourne House Hotel 25 Westbourne Rd, Broomhill S10 2QQ ☎ 0114 266 0109 FAX 0114 266 7778
Conveniently situated for the city and the university, this former gentleman's residence, dating from 1860, has recently changed hands. New owner Christine Ratcliffe is upgrading bedrooms, each individually designed, and equipped with a range of extras. The comfortable lounge, overlooking the patio and garden, has already been refubished. Substantial breakfasts are served in the dining room and the atmosphere throughout is most welcoming.
11 rms (10 bth/shr) (2 fmly) No smoking in dining room CTV in all bedrooms Tea and coffee making facilities Direct dial from bedrooms Cen ht 7P
ROOMS: s £38-£52; d £70-£78; wkly b&b £230-£250*
CARDS:

SHEPTON MALLET Somerset Map 03 ST64

Selected

Q Q Q Q ***Brottens Lodge*** Doulting BA4 4RB
(A361 towards Frome, turn right just before Abby Barn pub, over railway, at fork in road take either way, as both roads lead to Brottens Lodge) ☎ 01749 880352 FAX 01749 880601
rs Sun/Mon
Nestling in the heart of the countryside, this former Gamekeeper's Lodge dates from 1810 and now offers a warm welcome from hosts Roger and Santa. Three delightful bedrooms are available which are well equipped and tastefully furnished and decorated. Pre-dinner drinks can be taken in a choice of lounges before enjoying Santa's excellent cuisine in the dining room.
3 bth/shr No smoking in bedrooms No smoking in dining room No smoking in 1 lounge CTV in all bedrooms Tea and coffee making facilities Licensed Cen ht CTV 12P No coaches Outdoor swimming pool (heated) Last d 9pm
CARDS:

Q Q ◖ Stumbles Inn 27-29 Town St BA4 5BE
(Town Street located at the bottom end of Shepton Mallet main high street)
☎ 01749 344995 FAX 01749
This popular inn is situated off the pedestrianised high street in the quaint old Somerset town of Shepton Mallet. Accommodation comprises two comfortable en suite bedrooms. Whilst staying, why not take advantage of the range of interesting dishes available in either the bar or the adjoining restaurant.
2 bth/shr (2 fmly) No smoking in bedrooms No smoking in area of dining room CTV in all bedrooms Tea and coffee making facilities No dogs (ex guide dogs) Cen ht P Last d 9pm
ROOMS: s £26-£30; d £45-£60*
CARDS:

SHERBORNE Dorset Map **03** ST61

See also Henstridge & Leigh

Selected

Q Q Q Q **The Alders** Sandford Orcas DT9 4SB (from town take B3148 towards Marston Magna, after 2.5m take turning signed 'Sandford Orcas', at T-junc in village turn left towards Manor House)
☎ 01963 220666 FAX 220106
In the peaceful village of Sandford Orcas, The Alders is set in a lovely walled garden. The bedrooms are attractively decorated and well equipped. There are charming watercolours on the walls, painted by the owner. A comfortable sitting room is provided for guests, featuring a huge inglenook fireplace with a log burning stove. Good breakfasts are served round a large farmhouse table in the open plan dining room. A short walk away, the village pub serves good food at reasonable prices.
2 bth/shr No smoking CTV in all bedrooms Tea and coffee making facilities No dogs (ex guide dogs) Cen ht CTV 5P No coaches Arrangement with Sherborne Golf Club
ROOMS: d £45-£48*

Selected

Q Q Q Q ❦ **Almshouse Farm** *(ST651082)* Hermitage, Holnest DT9 6HA (from Sherborne take A352 Dorchester rd for 5m, at Holnest crossrds turn right signed Hermitage for farm 1.2m on left)
☎ 01963 210296 FAX 01963 210296 Mrs J Mayo
Feb-Dec
This farmhouse is part of a working dairy farm. The oldest part of the building is a former monastery, dating from the 16th century. Two of the spacious bedrooms overlook the lovely garden, and all offer modern en suite facilities. They are well equipped, with many thoughtful extras. A hearty breakfast is served in the dining room, which is in the oldest part of the house and has a magnificent inglenook fireplace. There is also a comfortable lounge for the use of guests.
3 bth/shr No smoking in dining room No smoking in lounges CTV in all bedrooms Tea and coffee making facilities No dogs (ex guide dogs) Cen ht CTV 6P Horse-riding, fishing and golf nearby
300 acres dairy
ROOMS: d £40-£46; wkly b&b £133-£150

Premier Selected

Q Q Q Q Q **Old Vicarage** Sherborne Rd, Milborne Port DT9 5AT (off A30) ☎ 01963 251117 FAX 01963 251515
Feb-Dec
Situated in the delightful Dorset village of Milborne Port, The Old Vicarage is a charming, listed Victorian abode. Originally built in 1870, this is a house where quality and history have been stylishly interwoven. Three spacious bedrooms are provided in the main house, all individually styled with flair and considerable taste. The remaining bedrooms, located within the adjacent coach house, are smaller but still offer high levels of comfort. Enjoy a drink in the gracious surroundings of the lounge, whilst contemplating accomplished dishes from the menu, available on both Friday and Saturday evenings. The southern facing terrace provides a sheltered haven in which to soak up the sunshine and admire the glorious copper beech tree, standing guard over the extensive lawns.
7 bth/shr (1 fmly) No smoking in bedrooms No smoking in dining room CTV in all bedrooms Tea and coffee making facilities Direct dial from bedrooms Licensed Cen ht No children 5yrs 10P No coaches Last d 6pm
ROOMS: s £25-£55; d £50-£90*
CARDS:

Selected

Q Q Q Q **Pheasants Restaurant with Rooms** 24 Greenhill DT9 4EW (centre of town on A30) ☎ 01935 815252 FAX 01935 815252
Closed 2 wks mid-Jan rs Sun & Mon
This popular establishment in the high street of Sherborne serves modern English cuisine. The bedrooms, furnished and decorated to a high standard, offer comfort and well equipped modern bathrooms. The restaurant offers top quality food, making skillful use of local produce; an ideal place to celebrate a special occasion or from which to explore Hardy Country.
6 bth/shr (2 fmly) No smoking in 3 bedrooms CTV in all bedrooms Direct dial from bedrooms No dogs (ex guide dogs) Licensed Cen ht 8P No coaches Last d 10pm
ROOMS: s £40; d £55
CARDS:

Q Q ❦ ***Venn*** *(ST684183)* Milborne Port DT9 5RA
(on the A30 3m E of Sherborne, on edge of village of Milborne Port)
☎ 01963 250598 Mrs P T Tizzard
Guests will find simply decorated, bright and cheerful accommodation at this working dairy farm, located on the outskirts of Sherborne. There is a pleasant lounge for guests' use, and Mrs Tizzard provides a hearty breakfast and a warm welcome.
3 rms (1 fmly) No smoking CTV in all bedrooms Tea and coffee making facilities No dogs (ex guide dogs) Cen ht CTV P 375 acres dairy/beef

SHERIFF HUTTON North Yorkshire Map **08** SE66

QQQ **Rangers House** Sheriff Hutton Park YO60 6RH
(off A64 between York and Malton signed Sheriff Flaxton/Sheriff Hutton and through Flaxton and West Lilling to T-junct take sharp right turn)
☎ 01347 878397 FAX 01347 878397
Next to the hall in Sheriff Hutton Park, with peacocks wandering round the peaceful garden, the Ranger's House is full of character. Built in 1639 as a brew house and stable for the Royal Hunting Lodge, the spacious lounges are overflowing with interesting and unusual items. The comfortable bedrooms overlook the extensive grounds.
6 rms (2 bth 2 shr) (1 fmly) No smoking in area of dining room Tea and coffee making facilities No dogs Licensed Cen ht CTV 30P No coaches Multigym Last d 9.30pm
ROOMS: s £34; d £64-£68; wkly b&b £224-£240; wkly hlf-bd £300-£399✳

SHERINGHAM Norfolk Map **09** TG14

Selected

QQQQ **Fairlawns** 26 Hooks Hill Rd NR26 8NL
(from A149 turn into Holt Road opposite Police Station then 2nd left and at T-junct turn right) ☎ 01263 824717 FAX 01263 824717
Feb-Nov & Dec-Jan
This charming Victorian guest house, which sits in its own attractive grounds in a secluded cul-de-sac, is just a few minutes from the town centre and the sandy beaches of Sheringham. The accommodation is bright and cheerful, and rooms are well equipped with a good range of useful extras as well as modern en suite bathrooms. Public areas include a comfortable lounge with a small corner bar. There is also a lovely garden with a croquet pitch. As Fairlawns has a heartbeat award, guests are assured of a healthy home cooked breakfast, dinner is also available by prior arrangement.
5 bth/shr No smoking in bedrooms No smoking in dining room CTV in all bedrooms Tea and coffee making facilities No dogs (ex guide dogs) Licensed Cen ht CTV 6P No coaches Croquet Last d noon
ROOMS: d £44-£48; wkly b&b £145; wkly hlf-bd £230

QQQ **Knollside Lodge** 43 Cliff Rd NR26 8BJ (from A148 turn off onto A1082 towards the sea. Turn right before Lobster PH and Cliff Rd is at the bottom. Estab on left before putting green) ☎ 01263 823320
Avril Millar's very pleasant Victorian house sits high above the beach. Guests are offered a warm welcome and a glass of sherry on arrival. Mrs Millar enjoys making her small but pretty gardens flourish with flowers. Inside, she has made every effort to add personal touches and little luxuries everywhere, from trouser presses and comfy seating in the rooms, to excellent breakfasts, making good use of home-made sausages and local Binham smoked bacon. The spacious en suite accommodation and relaxing public areas make for an enjoyable stay.
3 bth/shr (1 fmly) No smoking CTV in all bedrooms Tea and coffee making facilities No dogs Cen ht 3P No coaches
ROOMS: s fr £30; d £43-£48✳

382

QQQ **The Birches** 27 Holway Rd NR26 8HW
(situated on A1082 main road into Sheringham next to the Baptist church 3mins walk from railway station) ☎ 01263 823550
Etr-Oct
Pat Pearce is a charming host, and gets to know her valued guests over a cup of tea and home made biscuits. Delightful home cooked dinners and breakfasts are offered in the cosy dining/sitting room. The two attractive rooms feature many personal touches.
2 bth/shr No smoking CTV in all bedrooms Tea and coffee making facilities No dogs (ex guide dogs) Cen ht No children 12yrs 2P
ROOMS: d £44; wkly b&b £133; wkly hlf-bd £259✳

SHIPBOURNE Kent Map **05** TQ55

Selected

QQQQ **The Chaser** Stumble Hill TN11 9PE (next to church on the A227 between Wrotham and Tonbridge) (The Circle)
☎ 01732 810360 FAX 01732 810941
This colonial-style building has all the ingredients of a country inn and remains as popular as ever. It offers comfortable, well appointed accommodation, some rooms are in the main building and others are in the converted stable block. In the old village hall, there is a formal restaurant where an extensive menu is offered at lunch and dinner, plus a varied selection of bar meals.
15 bth/shr (1 fmly) CTV in all bedrooms Tea and coffee making facilities Direct dial from bedrooms Cen ht 30P Last d 9.30pm
ROOMS: s fr £45; d fr £65✳
MEALS: Lunch £13.50-£14.50 Dinner £16.50-£22.50✳
CARDS:

See advertisement under TONBRIDGE

We endeavour to be as accurate as possible but changes in personnel and data can occur in establishments after the Guide has gone to press

SHIPSTON ON STOUR Warwickshire Map 04 SP24

See also Lower Brailes

Selected

Q Q Q Q **Folly Farm Cottage** Ilmington CV36 4LJ (7 miles South of Stratford-upon-Avon off A3400. 4 miles North of Chipping Campden) ☎ 01608 682425 FAX 01608 682425
Enjoying some fine rural views, this mellow stone house has been carefully renovated to provide accommodation of character and quality. Bedrooms have lots of homely extras as well as quality fabrics, fine period furniture and ornaments. Two bedrooms have four-poster beds, and all have the benefit of modern en suite facilities. English breakfast is taken at one family table in the cosy dining room.
3 bth/shr No smoking CTV in all bedrooms Tea and coffee making facilities No dogs Cen ht No children 8P No coaches
ROOMS: d £50-£72

Q Q Q **The Manor** Main St, Long Compton CV36 5JJ (centre of Long Compton village on A3400 50yds S of St Peter & St Pauls church)
☎ 01608 684218 FAX 01608 684218
Closed 23 Dec-8 Jan
This spacious 16th-century house, built of Cotswold stone, offers guests a separate dining room in which good home cooked evening meals are served (by prior notice), and a choice of three comfortable lounges; one of which houses a small bar with an open log fire. Bedrooms are traditionally appointed and spacious, each has its own en suite bathroom.
5 bth/shr (1 fmly) No smoking in dining room Tea and coffee making facilities No dogs (ex guide dogs) Licensed Cen ht CTV
No children 12yrs 8P Last d 6.45pm
ROOMS: s £40; d £60; wkly b&b £210; wkly hlf-bd £254-£324
CARDS:

SHOBDON Herefordshire Map 03 SO46

Selected

Q Q Q Q **The Paddock** HR6 9NQ
(off A49 onto B4362 at Wooferton, follow road through Shobdon village. The Paddock is located on outskirts of village near Pearl Lake caravan park) ☎ 01568 708176
Situated on the outskirts of the village, this modern chalet style house offers comfortable accommodation close to major attractions and is an ideal base for walking holidays. Bedrooms are very well equipped and extras include controllable under floor heating, ceiling fans and modern en-suite facilities. Tasty home cooked dinners and English breakfasts are taken in the pretty dining room, there is also a homely and comfortable sitting room. Sheila Womersley is a friendly and caring hostess.

5 bth/shr (1 fmly) No smoking CTV in all bedrooms Tea and coffee making facilities No dogs Cen ht CTV 5P Last d 4pm
ROOMS: s £25-£28; d £40-£44*

SHREWSBURY Shropshire Map 07 SJ41

See also Cressage Longnor Ruyton-XI-Towns & Wem

Selected

Q Q Q Q ♥ ***The Day House** (SJ465104)* Nobold SY5 8NL
(turn for Shrewsbury off A5 at rdbt with Esso service stn, follow signs for Nuffield hospital, continue for 0.5m past hospital, turn right into drive) ☎ 01743 860212 FAX 01734 860212 Mrs P A Roberts
Closed Xmas & New Year
Dating from the 18th century and extended in early Victorian times, this impressive mellow brick house is situated in beautiful gardens, teeming with wildlife. The public areas retain many of the building's original features and are enhanced by fine period furniture and ornaments. Bedrooms are spacious and comfortable and all have the benefit of en suite or private bathrooms.
3 bth/shr (3 fmly) No smoking in 2 bedrooms CTV in all bedrooms Tea and coffee making facilities No dogs (ex guide dogs) Cen ht CTV 11P Rough & game shooting 400 acres arable dairy

Selected

Q Q Q Q **Fieldside** 38 London Rd SY2 6NX (from A5 take A5064, premises 1m on the left) ☎ 01743 353143 FAX 01743 358645
Closed 18 Dec-18 Jan
This well maintained house lies in a quiet residential area of the town, but within easy reach of the centre. Well equipped bedrooms are very nicely presented, with thoughtful attention to guest comfort.
Downstairs, a cosy lounge area leads into the spacious dining room where a hearty breakfast is served.
4 shr No smoking CTV in all bedrooms Tea and coffee making facilities No dogs Cen ht No children 9yrs 12P No coaches
ROOMS: s £30-£35; d £45-£50; wkly b&b fr £147*
CARDS:

Q Q Q ♥ **Grove** *(SJ537249)* Preston Brockhurst SY4 5QA (6m N on A49) ☎ 01939 220223 FAX 01939 220223 Mrs J M Jones
Closed 16 Dec-14 Jan
Set in the small village of Preston Brockhurst, this 17th-century farmhouse is flanked by pretty lawns, and overlooks the surrounding countryside. The traditionally furnished bedrooms are well-equipped, and a family room is available. There is a spacious and comfortable lounge and a traditionally furnished breakfast room, where separate tables can be provided.

contd.

4 rms (1 fmly) No smoking CTV in 2 bedrooms Tea and coffee making facilities No dogs (ex guide dogs) Cen ht CTV 6P
322 acres arable pigs
ROOMS: s £18.50-£20; d £40-£42*

Premier Selected

Q Q Q Q Q **Mytton Hall** Montford Bridge SY4 1EU (from A5 turn right to Montford Bridge, turn left in Montford Bridge to Forton Fitz & Leaton, after 1m turn right to Mytton & Fitz, driveway on left)
☎ 01743 850264
In a delightful rural setting by the River Perry, this fine Georgian house retains its original features, complemented by the period furnishings and paintings. Bedrooms are spacious and well equipped, and all have modern en suite facilities. Breakfast is taken in the magnificent dining room at a large family table and served buffet style from the sideboard.
3 bth No dogs Cen ht CTV No children 14yrs 6P No coaches Tennis (hard) Fishing
ROOMS: s £30; d £50*

Q Q Q **Restawhile** 36 Coton Crescent SY1 2NZ (on the junction of A528 to Ellesmere and B5067 to Baschurch) ☎ 01743 240969
This well maintained, small and friendly guest house is located just north of the town centre. It provides modern accommodation, has a homely lounge and a pleasant dining room, where individual tables are provided. Dinner is by prior arrangement.
4 bth/shr No smoking in dining room CTV in all bedrooms Tea and coffee making facilities Direct dial from bedrooms No dogs Cen ht CTV No children 14yrs 5P No coaches Last d 6pm
ROOMS: s £25-£32; d £35-£42; wkly b&b £112-£133; wkly hlf-bd £203-£238
CARDS:

Selected

Q Q Q Q ***Roseville*** 12 Berwick Rd SY1 2LN (0.75m N of town centre and 80yds from junct of B5067/A528) ☎ 01743 236470
Closed 17 Dec-Jan
This beautifully preserved, late Victorian town house is tastefully decorated, and furnished in a style befitting its age and character. The no-smoking accommodation comprises one twin and one double bedded room, both with en suite WC, plus a single which has its own private bathroom just along the corridor. Separate tables can be provided in the traditionally furnished breakfast room and there is a cosy lounge.
3 rms (2 shr) No smoking No dogs Cen ht CTV No children 12yrs 3P No coaches

Selected

Q Q Q Q **Sandford House Hotel** St Julians Friars SY1 1XL (cross River Severn over 'English Bridge' and take first sharp left)
☎ 01743 343829 FAX 01743 343829
This fine Grade II listed Georgian townhouse is situated near the River Severn, within easy walking distance of the town centre. The brightly decorated bedrooms are mostly spacious. There is a large and comfortable lounge for visitors and a pretty breakfast room.
11 rms (10 bth/shr) (3 fmly) No smoking in 6 bedrooms No smoking in dining room No smoking in lounges CTV in all bedrooms Tea and coffee making facilities Licensed Cen ht CTV 3P
ROOMS: s £27.50-£37.50; d £54*
CARDS:

Q Q Q **Stiperstones** 18 Coton Crescent, Coton Hill SY1 2NZ (from town centre head for Ellesmere road A528. Left at sign for Baschurch B5067. Next right , at x-rds, house opposite on right)
☎ 01743 246720 & 350303 FAX 01743 350303
This guest house is situated in a quiet residential area of the town, within easy walking distance of the river and shopping area. Bedrooms are split between the main house and an adjoining property, both having a guest lounge, the second one with a patio. Breakfast is served in the traditional dining room.
3 rms 3 annexe rms (1 fmly) No smoking in 1 bedrooms No smoking in dining room No smoking in lounges CTV in all bedrooms Tea and coffee making facilities No dogs (ex guide dogs) Cen ht CTV 6P No coaches
ROOMS: s £18-£20; d £34-£36; wkly b&b £112-£126

Q Q Q **Sydney House Hotel** Coton Crescent, Coton Hill SY1 2LJ (junct of A528/B5067) ☎ 01743 354681 0800 2981243 FAX 01743 354681
Closed 25 Dec-2 Jan
This friendly, family run private hotel lies within a few minutes walk of the town centre. Bedrooms are smart and modern and many extra facilities are provided. An attractively panelled lounge bar is available for residents and there is a pretty restaurant.
7 rms (4 shr) (1 fmly) No smoking in dining room CTV in all bedrooms Tea and coffee making facilities No dogs (ex guide dogs) Licensed Cen ht 7P No coaches Piano Board games Books Last d 8.30pm
ROOMS: s £30-£50; d £44-£66; wkly b&b £154-£315*
CARDS:

Selected

Q Q Q Q **Tudor House** 2 Fish St SY1 1UR (enter town by crossing English Bridge, ascend Wyle Cop after 50yds first right) ☎ 01743 351735
Closed 23-26 Dec
Dating back to 1460 this historic house stands in the centre of the medieval town; an ideal location for exploring Shrewsbury. There is a wealth of exposed wall timbers and beams adding to the charm of the cosy bedrooms. Downstairs, the lounge is attractively furnished and a hearty breakfast is served in the traditional dining room. Mr and Mrs Harris are very friendly proprietors who ensure guest comfort at every turn.
3 rms (2 shr) No smoking in 2 bedrooms No smoking in dining room CTV in all bedrooms No dogs Licensed Cen ht CTV No children 12yrs No coaches
ROOMS: s £26-£34; d £40-£48*

SIDMOUTH Devon Map 03 SY18

See also Harpford & Ottery St Mary

Q Q Q ***Cotfordbridge Hotel & Orchardside Restaurant*** Cotford Rd, Sidbury EX10 0SQ (N end of Sidbury on A375) ☎ 01395 597351
Set well back from the road overlooking the village of Sidbury, this attractive hotel is only three miles from the seafront at Sidmouth. Bedrooms are comfortable and attractively decorated, and have modern facilities. There is a smart restaurant with a choice of imaginative and traditional dishes and an adjoining bar with a small pool table, both look out onto the well tended gardens.
4 rms (3 shr) (1 fmly) No smoking in bedrooms No smoking in dining room CTV in all bedrooms Tea and coffee making facilities No dogs (ex guide dogs) Licensed Cen ht CTV 30P Last d 9pm
CARDS:

This symbol indicates a 'Child Friendly' establishment - see page 25 for details

Selected

QQQQ ♈ **Higher Weston Farm** *(SY166880)* Weston EX10 0PH (M5 junct 30 to A3052 Lyme Regis Rd, after 9 miles pass through Sidford at top of hill right and follow signs for Weston, house is 1 mile on right) ☎ 01395 513741 Mr S MacFadyen
Feb-Nov Closed Jan
This attractive farmhouse is surrounded by over one hundred acres of pasture and arable land which sweeps down to the sea. The three bedrooms have been tastefully decorated and comfortably furnished, each has its own spacious bathroom. In the lounge a wood burning stove gives warmth on cooler evenings and a host of books have been provided. Breakfast is quite a feature of a stay here; fresh fruit, free range eggs, local bread and honey, and homemade preserves all make for a special start to the day.
3 bth/shr No smoking in bedrooms No smoking in dining room CTV in all bedrooms Tea and coffee making facilities No dogs Cen ht CTV 12P Badminton Croquet 170 acres cattle corn
ROOMS: d £38-£44*

QQQ **Jubilee Cottage** 75 Chapel St, Sidbury EX10 0RQ (on A375 between Honiton and Sidmouth just pass the church in Sidbury) ☎ 01395 597295
Closed Xmas/New Year
This 16th-century thatched cottage is situated in the peaceful village of Sidbury. Bedrooms, many with exposed beams, are nicely furnished and there is also a cosy lounge for guests' use. Home cooked evening meals are a feature, whilst breakfast can be served at individual tables in the dining room, or on the patio.
3 rms No smoking CTV in all bedrooms Tea and coffee making facilities No dogs Licensed Cen ht CTV P No coaches Last d when booking
ROOMS: s fr £19; d fr £34; wkly b&b fr £112; wkly hlf-bd fr £182*
See advertisement on p.387.

Selected

QQQQ **Mariners** 69 Sidford High St EX10 9SH (exit M5 at junct 30 and take A3052) ☎ 01395 515876
Mariners is a delightful Victorian residence, set in an acre of terraced gardens. Bedrooms are tastefully decorated, and equipped with modern comforts. There is an attractive guest lounge, and a bright dining room where breakfast is served. Home cooked dinners feature local produce whenever possible.
7 shr (1 fmly) No smoking in bedrooms No smoking in dining room CTV in all bedrooms Tea and coffee making facilities No dogs Cen ht No children 7yrs 10P No coaches
ROOMS: s £18-£20; d £36-£40; wkly b&b £122.22-£135.80; wkly hlf-bd £196.91-£210.49*

385

Selected

Q Q Q Q **Number Four** 4 Fortfield Place, Station Rd EX10 8NX (leave A3052 towards Sidmouth for approx 2 m house on right just before Fortfield Hotel) ☎ 01395 578733
Closed 24 Dec-1 Jan
This semi-detached Victorian property, situated within easy walking distance of both the town centre and Sidmouth's attractive promenade, is a convenient place from which to explore the delights of East Devon. The three en suite rooms have been tastefully decorated and equipped with all modern comforts.
3 bth/shr No smoking CTV in all bedrooms Tea and coffee making facilities Cen ht 3P No coaches
ROOMS: s £25-£40; d £36-£44; wkly b&b £120-£195

Selected

Q Q Q Q **The Old Farmhouse** Hillside Rd EX10 8JG (from Exeter A3052 to Sidmouth, Bowd crossrds turn right, 2miles, left at rdbt, left at minirdbt, next right over humpbacked bridge, left on corner) ☎ 01395 512284
Closed Dec & Jan
This is a picturesque thatched 16th-century farmhouse in a residential area. It is full of character, with exposed beams and original fireplaces. Bedrooms, some in a cottage across the patio, are decorated with pretty floral papers and co-ordinated soft furnishings. There are two lounges and an attractive dining room, where evening meals are served.
3 bth/shr 4 annexe rms (1 bth 2 shr) (1 fmly) No smoking CTV in 3 bedrooms Tea and coffee making facilities Licensed Cen ht CTV 4P No coaches Last d am
ROOMS: s £21-£25; d £42-£50; wkly b&b £125-£160; wkly hlf-bd £185-£235
CARDS:

Q Q Q 🛏 **Ryton House** 52-54 Winslade Rd EX10 9EX (A3052-Exeter to Sidmouth-approx 10m, turn right B3176, 2m towards Sidmouth, left into Alexandria Rd, right into Winslade Rd, GH down hill on left) ☎ 01395 513981
Mar-11 Nov
This well maintained guest house is just a short stroll from the seafront. Most of the bright bedrooms enjoy private facilities, and are decorated with co-ordinated fabrics. There is a comfortable lounge where drinks are served, and a cheerful dining room in which to sample Mrs Williams' home cooked evening meals.
9 rms (2 bth 4 shr) (4 fmly) No smoking in dining room No smoking in lounges CTV in all bedrooms Tea and coffee making facilities Licensed Cen ht CTV 9P Last d 4.30pm
ROOMS: s £18-£25; d £35-£45; wkly b&b £130-£150; wkly hlf-bd £185-£195

Q Q Q **Southcombe** Vicarage Rd EX10 8UQ (100mtrs from police station) ☎ 01395 513861 FAX 01396 512912
Mar-Oct Closed Dec rs Nov/Jan/Feb
This attractive detached family home, situated just a short level walk from the centre of the town and the sea, offers comfortable accommodation and a relaxed and friendly atmosphere. The prize-winning gardens stretch down to the River Sid. Home made food at dinner is prepared from fresh produce and Mrs Dann prides herself on her delicious desserts.
6 rms (5 shr) No smoking in dining room No smoking in lounges CTV in all bedrooms Tea and coffee making facilities No dogs Cen ht CTV No children 14yrs 7P No coaches Last d 4pm
ROOMS: s £18.50-£20; d £37-£40; wkly b&b £128-£135; wkly hlf-bd £183-£190✱

Selected

Q Q Q Q ***Willow Bridge Private Hotel*** Millford Rd EX10 8DR (A3052 from Exeter, right at Sidmouth sign, follow rd past Knole park, left-All Saints Rd-at bottom turn left, then right over bridge, then turn left) ☎ 01395 513599 FAX 013195 513599
Dec, Mar to end Oct
Willow Bridge, set in its own attractive gardens, overlooks the River Sid. Bedrooms are pleasantly decorated, and equipped with modern facilities. There is a comfortable lounge with plenty of reading material and games. The dining room serves five course dinners based on fresh local produce, complemented by an excellent wine list.
6 rms (5 shr) No smoking CTV in all bedrooms Tea and coffee making facilities Licensed Cen ht CTV 6P No coaches

SILECROFT Cumbria Map 06 SD18

Q Q **Miner's Arms** Main St LA18 5LP (from M6 follow A590 signposted Barrow as far as Greenwood at which point turn right and follow signs for A595 Whitehaven/Broughton.)
☎ 01229 772325 & 773397 FAX 01229 772325
This popular family run inn boasts a growing reputation for its imaginative food, served in one of the several lounges or the cosy dining area. Bedrooms come in a variety of sizes and are bright, cheerfully decorated and have modern bathrooms. There is also a cosy residents' lounge upstairs.
4 bth/shr No smoking in bedrooms No smoking in dining room CTV in all bedrooms Tea and coffee making facilities No dogs (ex guide dogs) Cen ht CTV 50P Last d 9.30pm
ROOMS: s £20-£32; d £32✱
MEALS: Lunch £7-£15&alc Dinner £7-£15&alc✱

SILLOTH Cumbria Map 11 NY15

Q Q Q 🛏 **Nith View** 1 Pine Ter CA5 4DT (B5302 into Silloth. At 'T' junct turn right for 200 metres, overlooking tennis court and sea)
☎ 016973 31542 FAX 016973 31037
Closed Xmas
Popular with golfers, this attractive Victorian terraced guest house enjoys panoramic views across the Solway Firth. Tastefully decorated throughout, the bedrooms are large and two have fridges. A good choice is offered at breakfast.
6 rms (4 shr) (4 fmly) No smoking in 3 bedrooms No smoking in dining room CTV in all bedrooms Tea and coffee making facilities Cen ht 7P No coaches
ROOMS: s £16-£21; d £37; wkly b&b £105.60-£138.60

SILSOE Bedfordshire Map 04 TL03

Q Q **The Old George Hotel** High St MK45 4EP (Slip Rd off A6 halfway between Bedford and Luton) ☎ 01525 860218
Formerly a coaching inn, The Old George Hotel is popular with locals. Public areas include the large, busy bar (which serves informal snacks and a

range of real ales), and the cheerful restaurant offering a good choice from an a la carte menu. Bedrooms vary in size and style, each is well equipped and soundly appointed.
7 rms (3 fmly) No smoking in 2 bedrooms No smoking in dining room No smoking in 1 lounge CTV in all bedrooms Tea and coffee making facilities Cen ht 50P Last d 9pm
ROOMS: s fr £32; d fr £48*
MEALS: Lunch £10-£30&alc Dinner £10-£30&alc*
CARDS:

SILVERSTONE Northamptonshire Map **04** SP64

Q Q Q **Silverthorpe** *(SP661456)* Silverthorpe, Abthorpe Rd NN12 8TW (off A43 for Silverstone Village Abthorpe Rd north out of village house 0.5 mile on left) ☎ 01327 858020 Mr & Mrs Branch
Closed 23 Dec-2 Jan
This spacious modern bungalow is set in five acres of pastureland and features a lovely garden. All three bedrooms are smart and well furnished. The house is particularly convenient for the Silverstone circuit.
3 rms (1 fmly) No smoking CTV in all bedrooms Tea and coffee making facilities Cen ht 4P
ROOMS: s £20-£25; d £38-£45*

SIMONSBATH Somerset Map **03** SS73

Selected

Q Q Q Q **Barkham** Sandyway EX36 3LU (exit A361 to North Molton, through North Molton onto the moor signposted Sandyway, left at crossroads signposted to Simonsbath, 400 mtrs turn right)
☎ 01643 831370 FAX 01643 831370
In the heart of Exmoor National Park lies this Georgian farmhouse, with twelve acres of pastureland and streams. The grounds also include a delightful wooded valley with a 'tree-house' for the young at heart! The individually furnished and tastefully decorated bedrooms are comfortable and there is a fabulous drawing room. Interesting and imaginative dinners are available by prior arrangement, along with a traditional breakfast served in the oak-panelled dining room. Self catering cottages are also available.
3 rms (1 bth) No smoking No dogs Licensed Cen ht CTV 6P No coaches Croquet, tree house Last d 10am
ROOMS: d £40-£50*

Situated 3 miles from Sidmouth our garden and 2 Double bedrooms boast open views over the Sid Valley up to Buckley Hill. A further Twin or Single bedroom at the front of the building has Secondary double glazing. All have CTV, Radio, Tea and Coffee making facilities. 2 Bathrooms – one with shower – plus separate Shower room. Cosy Guest Lounge with CTV and games. No Dogs. No smoking. £16-£18. Major (retired) and German born Marianne Coles offer delicious old fashioned and international dishes. It is our ambition not to serve you the same meal twice. Apfelstrudel, Tiramisu, home made Ice creams and sorbets are favourite sweets. £15 (4 course). ***German & Spanish spoken.***

The Old Farmhouse

Sidmouth

Quietly situated in residential area on the edge of the Byes and only a few minutes walk from both sea and shops. A delightful 16th century farmhouse with an adjoining cottage which once housed the local cider mill. Whilst all modern amenities have been provided the originality has been preserved with no two rooms the same but all sharing the pretty decor and homely feel. Relax in the cosy, low beamed lounge or the intimate Inglenook bar with a pre dinner drink. Delicious old fashioned recipes form the basis of the menus with the same meal never served twice in a fortnight. Car parking space available.

Hillside Road, Sidmouth, Devon EX10 8JG
Telephone: 01395 512284

SITTINGBOURNE Kent Map 05 TQ96

Premier Selected

QQQQQ **Hempstead House** London Rd, Bapchild ME9 9PP (on A2, 1.5m E of Sittingbourne opposite turning to Tonge) ☎ 01795 428020 FAX 01795 428020

This very attractive Victorian country house hotel is set in three acres of mature grounds and gardens, the accommodation is designer furnished to provide the best in quality and comfort. Guests will enjoy the conservatory, the spacious drawing room furnished with antiques, and the elegant dining room which features a polished dining table, cut glass, fresh flowers and fine table appointments. Dinner, which can be taken in the kitchen or conservatory, is available for resident guests; service and all meals are provided personally by Mrs Holdstock. A friendly, relaxed and informal atmosphere prevails. The facilities can also be used for private parties and small functions, and a marquee is available to cater for wedding receptions.

13 bth/shr (3 fmly) No smoking in bedrooms No smoking in dining room No smoking in 1 lounge CTV in all bedrooms Tea and coffee making facilities Direct dial from bedrooms Licensed Cen ht CTV ch fac 100P Outdoor swimming pool (heated) Play area Croquet Last d 10pm

ROOMS: s £62; d £72*

CARDS:

SIXPENNY HANDLEY Dorset Map 03 ST91

QQ **Town Farm Bungalow** SP5 5NT (from Salisbury take A354 S towards Blandford Forum at Handley rdbt turn right to Sixpenny Handley B3081, 200yds on right) ☎ 01725 552319 FAX 01725 552319

Guests receive a warm welcome from Ann Inglis at this pretty property. Bedrooms are comfortable, and in addition to the smart sitting room, opening onto the garden, there is a dining room where tea and coffee are available and hearty breakfasts are served at one table.

3 rms (1 bth 1 shr) No smoking in 2 bedrooms No smoking in dining room CTV in 1 bedroom Cen ht CTV 6P No coaches Golf

ROOMS: s £22.50-£25; d £35-£39; wkly b&b £110.25-£122.85*

SKEGNESS Lincolnshire Map 09 TF56

QQQ **Crawford Hotel** South Pde PE25 3HR ☎ 01754 764215

Standing in a prime position on the promenade, this family run hotel offers bright and fresh bedrooms with good facilities. A lovely warm atmosphere is assured and there is the added attraction of an indoor pool together with very pleasant public rooms.

23 rms (9 bth 11 shr) (8 fmly) No smoking in dining room CTV in all bedrooms Tea and coffee making facilities No dogs Licensed Lift Cen ht CTV Indoor swimming pool (heated) Sauna jacuzzi games room Last d 5pm

ROOMS: s fr £28.79; d fr £47; wkly b&b fr £135; wkly hlf-bd fr £170*

CARDS:

QQQ **Northdale** 12 Firbeck Av PE25 3JY ☎ 01754 610554

Enthusiastic proprietors Janet and Christopher Smith run this pleasant guest house, located in a quiet residential road just a short walk from the town, seafront and attractions. The bedrooms are bright and airy, and most have en suite facilities. There is a lounge and a separate bar; a choice of menu is offered in the dining room.

12 rms (2 bth 7 shr) (3 fmly) No smoking in dining room No smoking in lounges CTV in 10 bedrooms Tea and coffee making facilities Licensed Cen ht CTV 8P Last d 5.30pm

SKIPTON North Yorkshire Map 07 SD95

QQ **Alton House** 5 Salisbury St BD23 1NQ ☎ 01756 794780 FAX 01756 793999

Closed 24 Dec-1 Jan

Situated in a quiet residential area, just ten minutes walk from the town centre, this friendly guest house offers attractively furnished bedrooms, being ideal for families. A substantial breakfast is served at separate tables in the homely dining room.

3 bth/shr (2 fmly) No smoking CTV in all bedrooms Tea and coffee making facilities No dogs Cen ht No children 10yrs No coaches

ROOMS: s fr £20; d fr £40*

QQ **Craven House** 56 Keighley Rd BD23 2NB (situated on A629 coming in from Keighley) ☎ 01756 794657 FAX 01756 794657

Closed 25 Dec-3 Jan

Situated just a short walk from the town centre, this Victorian house offers well maintained bedrooms. Breakfast is served at individual tables in the traditionally furnished dining room.

7 rms (2 bth 1 shr) No smoking in dining room CTV in all bedrooms Tea and coffee making facilities Cen ht 3P

ROOMS: s £18-£26; d £36-£44*

CARDS:

QQQ **Highfield Hotel** 58 Keighley Rd BD23 2NB (on A629 heading towards Keighley, 0.25m from town centre) ☎ 01756 793182 FAX 01756 793182

Closed 23-27 Dec rs New Years Eve

Further improvements have been made at this stone-built corner house. Freshly decorated bedrooms, including two on the ground floor, have comfortable seating and have been carefully equipped with the needs of visitors in mind. The comfortable lounge bar leads into a cosy dining room where a selection of dishes is offered.

10 rms (3 bth 6 shr) No smoking in dining room CTV in all bedrooms Tea and coffee making facilities Licensed Cen ht CTV No coaches Last d 6pm

ROOMS: s £18.50-£30; d £35-£37; wkly b&b £122.50*

CARDS:

QQQ **Low Skibeden Farmhouse** *(SD013526)* Skibeden Rd BD23 6AB (at E end of Skipton bypass off A65/59) ☎ 01756 793849 07050 207787 FAX 01756 793804 Mrs H Simpson

Situated just a mile from the town centre, this large farmhouse is surrounded by neatly tended gardens and enjoys delightful views over the nearby hills.

Bedrooms are comfortably furnished, as is the homely lounge. A hearty breakfast is served.
5 rms (4 bth/shr) (3 fmly) No smoking Tea and coffee making facilities No dogs Cen ht CTV No children 10yrs 6P 40 acres Beef & sheep
ROOMS: s £25-£38; d £34-£44; wkly b&b £119-£154
CARDS:

Q Q ◄ ***Red Lion Hotel*** High St BD23 1DT (Whitbread) ☎ 01756 790718
Dating back to the early 13th century, and believed to be one of the oldest buildings in the town, this popular inn stands proudly in the centre of the High Street. Comfortably furnished bedrooms are all en suite and the lively bars serve a good range of meals and snacks which can be accompanied by a range of beers.
3 bth/shr (2 fmly) CTV in all bedrooms Tea and coffee making facilities No dogs Cen ht 4P Last d 7.30pm
CARDS:

SLAIDBURN Lancashire Map **07** SD75

Premier Selected

Q Q Q Q Q ***Parrock Head Farm House Hotel*** Woodhouse Ln BB7 3AH (from village of Slaidburn turn left at the Hark to Bounty Inn, pass health centre on right, hotel under a mile on left)
☎ 01200 446614 FAX 01200 446313
For those seeking peace and tranquillity, Parrock Head is ideal. A delightfully converted 17th-century 'long' farmhouse, it occupies a beautiful hidden corner of Lancashire in the heart of the Forest of Bowland. Well equipped and very comfortable bedrooms are on offer, some in the garden rooms, others in the main house. Public rooms are very special and include a spacious beamed lounge with an open log fire and a cosy bar where guests can relax with a pre-dinner drink. Meals are carefully prepared and use the best of local produce.
3 bth/shr 6 annexe bth/shr (1 fmly) No smoking in dining room CTV in all bedrooms Tea and coffee making facilities Direct dial from bedrooms Licensed Cen ht 25P Last d 9pm
CARDS:

SLEAFORD Lincolnshire

See **Aswarby**

SLEDMERE East Riding of Yorkshire Map **08** SE96

Premier Selected

Q Q Q Q Q **Old Rectory** Cowlam YO25 0AD
(off B1253 York to Bridlington Road) ☎ 01377 267617 & 267403
FAX 01377 267403
The Old Rectory is home to Annabel and Jeremy Mooney who provide a friendly and a relaxed atmosphere in which to stay. The house boasts uninterrupted panoramic views of the Yorkshire Wolds and offers thoughtfully appointed bedrooms. Antique furniture together with collectables can be seen throughout this 19th-century house. Both public rooms are warmed by open fires in the colder months, and the drawing room has an honesty bar. The most memorable features, however, must be the superb dinners and the impressive breakfast menu; both meals are freshly prepared by Annabel and are deserving of praise.
3 bth/shr No smoking CTV in all bedrooms Tea and coffee making facilities No dogs Licensed Cen ht No children 15yrs 10P No coaches Tennis (grass) Country walks Last d 11am
ROOMS: d £55-£59*
CARDS:

Q Q ◄ **Triton** YO25 3XQ (leave A166 at Garton on the Wolds on B1252 signed Sledmere House. Inn is situated on left opposite rd junct to Luttons, adjacent to Sledmere House) ☎ 01377 236644
Situated in the centre of the village and next to the popular tourist attraction of Sledmere House, this 18th-century inn offers neat bedrooms and a good selection of home made food, available mainly in the oak-panelled bar. There is also a cosy dining room and a separate pool room.
5 rms (2 bth/shr) (1 fmly) No smoking in bedrooms No smoking in dining room CTV in all bedrooms Tea and coffee making facilities No dogs (ex guide dogs) Cen ht 20P Last d 9pm
ROOMS: s £22-£24; d £44-£50; wkly b&b £132-£144*
MEALS: Lunch £5.90-£9.45alc Dinner £8.40-£14.45alc*
CARDS:

SLOUGH Berkshire Map **04** SU97

Q Q **Colnbrook Lodge** Bath Rd, Colnbrook SL3 0NZ (Airport side of Colnbrook Village between Punchbowl Pub & level crossing) ☎ 01753 685958 FAX 01753 685164
Closed 23 Dec-2 Jan
This interesting Edwardian house is within easy reach of Heathrow Airport. Bedrooms, which vary in size, are furnished in modern style and decorated in pastel colours. A choice of breakfast is served in the small cosy breakfast room.
8 rms (6 bth/shr) (2 fmly) No smoking in dining room CTV in all bedrooms Tea and coffee making facilities No dogs (ex guide dogs) Licensed Cen ht CTV ch fac 26P
ROOMS: s fr £39; d fr £49*
CARDS:

SOLIHULL West Midlands Map **07** SP17

Q Q Q **The Gate House** Barston Ln, Barston B92 0JN
(A4141 Warwick 1.2 miles to Hampton Rd, left at Wilson Arms, 2 miles to Wyevale Gdn Cntr. Turn right into Barston Ln, The Gate House is on right)
☎ 01675 443274 FAX 01675 443274
This large, well maintained Victorian house is set in three acres of lovely gardens on the edge of Barston village. The traditionally furnished accommodation is well equipped and equally suitable for business people and tourists. Separate tables can be provided in the cosy and attractive breakfast room.
4 rms (2 bth/shr) No smoking CTV in all bedrooms Tea and coffee making facilities No dogs (ex guide dogs) Cen ht CTV 20P No coaches
ROOMS: s £22-£30; d £40-£50*

Q Q Q ***Ivy House*** Warwick Rd, Heronfield, Knowle B93 0EB
(3m from junct 5 of M42, on A4141) ☎ 01564 770247 FAX 01564 778063
This charming old house stands in six acres of grounds, south of Solihull. It provides well equipped, modern, no-smoking accommodation which is equally suitable for business people and tourists. Separate tables are provided in the traditionally furnished breakfast room, which adjoins a comfortable lounge area.
8 shr (1 fmly) No smoking CTV in all bedrooms Tea and coffee making facilities Cen ht CTV 20P Fishing

Q Q Richmond House Hotel 47 Richmond Rd, Olton B92 7RP (M6 junct4, to M42 South junct6 and take A45 towards Birmingham. At third set small traffic lights turn left into Lyndon Rd and follow road for 1.5m) ☎ 0121 707 9746 FAX 0121 707 9746

Richmond House offers homely accommodation, and soundly appointed bedrooms which vary quite considerably in both sizes and styles. The public areas are dominated by a large restaurant in which a traditional carte and a Portuguese set menu are offered. The remainder of the public rooms consist of a small quiet lounge area and a cosy bar.

10 bth/shr No smoking in 1 lounge CTV in all bedrooms Tea and coffee making facilities Direct dial from bedrooms Licensed Cen ht CTV ch fac 20P Pool table

ROOMS: s fr £63; d fr £63*

CARDS:

SOMERTON Somerset Map **03** ST42

Q Q Q Church Farm Compton Dundon TA11 6PE ☎ 01458 272927

Closed 20 Dec-7 Jan

This part thatched cottage is located in a tranquil village setting, close to the interesting towns of Street and Somerton. The majority of the comfortably appointed bedrooms are located in a converted stable block although there is one room in the main house. Dinner is available on request.

1 bth/shr 5 annexe bth/shr (2 fmly) No smoking CTV in all bedrooms Tea and coffee making facilities Licensed Cen ht No children 5yrs 6P No coaches Fishing

ROOMS: s £25; d £39; wkly b&b £150-£234; wkly hlf-bd £186*

Q Q Q ✦ Lower Farm *(ST527309)* Kingweston TA11 6BA (A303 take A37 north Shepton Mallet to traffic lights at Lydford-on-Fosse, left onto B3153 through Keinton Mandeville & onto Kinweston Farm on right) ☎ 01458 223237 FAX 01458 223276 Mrs J Sedgman

Closed Xmas/New Year

This Grade II listed stone-built farmhouse is the focus of a 500 acre working farm within a site of special scientific interest. Bedrooms combine old world charm with modern comforts. A hearty breakfast is served in the attractive farmhouse dining room.

3 shr (1 fmly) CTV in all bedrooms Tea and coffee making facilities No dogs (ex guide dogs) Cen ht 6P Badminton net Large Garden 1005 acres Arable

ROOMS: s fr £20; d fr £40; wkly b&b fr £133*

CARDS:

Premier Selected

Q Q Q Q Q Lydford House Lydford-on-Fosse TA11 7BU (A303 to Podimore rdbt take A37 Bath/Bristol after 3 miles crossroads B3153 Lydford House is on the left after traffic lights) ☎ 01963 240217 FAX 01963 240413

The cities of Bath and Wells are within easy driving distance of Lydford House, and the Bath and West showground is only a few miles away. Spacious bedrooms have been imaginatively decorated, and equipped with modern facilities and thoughtful touches. The large sitting room is furnished with style, and delicious breakfasts are served around one table in the open plan dining room. Part of the house is run as an antique shop, and guests are welcome to browse.

4 bth/shr No smoking in 1 bedrooms CTV in all bedrooms Tea and coffee making facilities No dogs (ex guide dogs) Cen ht CTV 35P No coaches

ROOMS: s £40; d £60*

See page 14-20 for a list of Premier Selected establishments

Premier Selected

Q Q Q Q Q The Lynch Country House 4 Behind Berry TA11 7PD (leave A303 at Podimore rdbt and follow signs to Somerton) ☎ 01458 272316 FAX 01458 272590

Closed Xmas New Year

This is a quiet, personally run establishment that has a variety of rooms to offer. The beautifully proportioned house is set on the edge of this picturesque town, with its own extensive gardens and a lake. The Lynch Country House is an ideal place to relax and enjoy gracious surroundings, and it retains the feel of a friendly family home. Spacious rooms offer wonderful views over the fields and provide excellent facilities.

5 bth/shr (1 fmly) No smoking CTV in all bedrooms Tea and coffee making facilities Direct dial from bedrooms No dogs (ex guide dogs) Licensed Cen ht 15P No coaches

ROOMS: s £45-£53; d £49-£75*

CARDS:

Q Q Q ✦ Rookery *(ST534288)* Charlton Mackrell TA11 7AL (A303 to Podimore rdbt, A37 N, 1m turn left signed Charlton Mackrell to mini rdbt, turn right past school & church, farm on left hand side) ☎ 01458 224030 FAX 01458 224090 Mr D Grindley

Peace and tranquility are in abundance at this friendly farmhouse. Philomena and David Grindley have renovated this property, that partly dates back to the 15th century. The farm is just a short drive from the A37 in the beautiful Somerset countryside. Breakfast is served around a large pine table in the kitchen where there is an impressive inglenook fireplace. A comfortable sitting room is available where guests can relax.

3 rms (1 fmly) No smoking CTV in all bedrooms Tea and coffee making facilities No dogs Cen ht CTV No children 5yrs 10P Sauna Gymnasium 9 acres sheep

ROOMS: s £20-£28; d £38-£42; wkly b&b £130-£145*

Selected

Q Q Q Q Somerton Court Country House TA11 7AH (turn off A303 at Podimore rdbt onto A372 in 2m turn right A3165 to Somerton road in 3m at bad right hand bend turn left & follow B&B signs) ☎ 01458 274694

Closed Xmas & New Year

A dwelling has been on this site since 1200 and parts of the current building are believed to date from the 17th century. Surrounded by 55 acres of parkland and gardens, this is a tranquil haven for those wishing to escape the clutter of urban life. Owners Pauline and Owen Stephens have tastefully refurbished the house and the results are a fitting testament to their efforts. The spacious bedrooms are attractively styled, equipped for comfort, and offer lovely views across the grounds. Breakfast is served in the delightful dining room which overlooks the garden, a popular haunt for wildlife.

3 bth/shr (1 fmly) No smoking CTV in all bedrooms Tea and coffee making facilities No dogs (ex guide dogs) Cen ht 30P
ROOMS: d £50-£60*
CARDS:

SOUTHAMPTON Hampshire Map **04** SU41

Q Q **Ashelee Lodge** 36 Atherley Rd, Shirley SO1 5DQ (from M27 to Shirley High Rd, turn into Hill Lane, into Languard 4th left, 1st right into Atherley Rd) ☎ 01703 222095 FAX 01703 222095
Closed 24 & 25 Dec
Mrs Ward offers a warm welcome at this small guest house in a quiet residential location close to the city centre. The four bedrooms are brightly decorated and comfortably furnished. Guests can enjoy the smart television lounge and a hearty breakfast, served in the dining room.
4 rms No smoking in dining room No dogs Cen ht CTV 3P Outdoor swimming pool
ROOMS: s £17-£19; d £32-£36*
CARDS:

Q Q **Banister House Hotel** Banister Rd SO15 2JJ (0.5m NE of city centre off A33) ☎ 01703 221279 & 225753 FAX 01703 221279
Closed 25-31 Dec
Banister House stands in a residential area close to the city centre, and convenient for the university. The bedrooms are attractively decorated and well equipped, several rooms have en suite showers. There is a well appointed restaurant with a bar, and evening meals are available Monday to Thursday.
23 rms (13 bth/shr) (3 fmly) CTV in all bedrooms Tea and coffee making facilities Direct dial from bedrooms Licensed Cen ht CTV 14P No coaches Last d 7.45pm
ROOMS: s £22.50-£26.50; d £32-£36
CARDS:

Q Q Q ***Capri*** 52 Archers Rd SO1 2LU (in city centre near Railway Station) ☎ 01703 632800 FAX 01703 630100
With easy access to the city centre and The Dell, this guest house continues to attract a regular clientele. The majority of bedrooms feature en suite showers and are individually furnished. The Ambassador Suite offers a water bed and spa bathroom. Guests can enjoy home cooked meals in the dining room and relax in the lounge.
15 rms (11 bth/shr) (2 fmly) No smoking in 1 bedrooms No smoking in 1 lounge CTV in all bedrooms Tea and coffee making facilities Direct dial from bedrooms No dogs (ex guide dogs) Licensed Cen ht 15P Last d 5pm
CARDS:

Selected

Q Q Q Q ***Hunters Lodge Hotel*** 25 Landguard Rd, Shirley SO1 55DL ☎ 01703 227919 FAX 01703 230913
Closed 17 Dec-7 Jan
This Victorian property is situated in a residential area, close to the main routes to the ferry and docks. Original stained glass panels and other features have been retained in the public areas and bright, co-ordinated decor and soft furnishings make the bedrooms attractive. Guests can relax in the bar/TV lounge and the dining room is a pleasant area in which to enjoy breakfast. Dinner is available on request.
18 shr (2 fmly) No smoking in 4 bedrooms No smoking in area of dining room No smoking in 1 lounge CTV in all bedrooms Tea and coffee making facilities Direct dial from bedrooms Licensed Cen ht CTV 20P Last d 6pm
CARDS:

Selected

Q Q Q Q **Landguard Lodge** 21 Landguard Rd SO15 5DL (north of railway station between Shirley Rd and Hill Lane) ☎ 01703 636904 FAX 01703 632258
Located in the a quiet residential area, this well maintained property is ideal for the city centre, ferry terminals and docks. Owner Mr McCowan is a warm and friendly host and will provide an evening meal on request. All the bedrooms have en suite shower rooms, are comfortable and attractively decorated. Guests can also use the lounge and dining room.
10 shr No smoking in bedrooms No smoking in dining room CTV in all bedrooms Tea and coffee making facilities No dogs (ex guide dogs) Cen ht CTV No children 5yrs 4P No coaches Last d 9am
CARDS:

Q Q Q **Linden** 51-53 The Polygon SO15 2BP (Central situation 5 mins walk from Southampton central station) ☎ 01703 225653 FAX 10703 630808
Closed 2wks Xmas
This family run guest house is located close to the city centre and offers well maintained accommodation. The bedrooms are brightly decorated and suitably furnished. There is a comfortable lounge and a well appointed dining room.
12 rms (4 fmly) No smoking in dining room No smoking in lounges CTV in all bedrooms Tea and coffee making facilities No dogs Cen ht CTV 7P No coaches
ROOMS: s £15-£17; d £30-£34; wkly b&b £94.50-£101.50*

Q Q Q **Lodge** 1 Winn Rd, The Avenue SO17 1EH (take A33 into city and at end of Common, and at Cowherds pub turn left) (The Independents) ☎ 01703 557537 FAX 553586
Closed 23-27 Dec
Located close to the city centre, this family run commercial hotel has a relaxed and informal atmosphere. The bedrooms are modern in style, and adequately furnished and equipped. Public areas include a comfortably appointed lounge, small bar and a cosy dining room. An evening meal is available.
14 rms (1 bth 7 shr) (2 fmly) No smoking in dining room CTV in all bedrooms Tea and coffee making facilities Direct dial from bedrooms Licensed Cen ht CTV 10P No coaches Last d 9pm
ROOMS: s £25-£34.50; d £42.50-£46.50
CARDS:

Q Q Q **Madison House** 137 Hill Ln SO15 5AF (A33 then A35, at next roundabout turn left, straight over mini-roundabout into Hill Ln, 0.75m on left) ☎ 01703 333374 FAX 01703 909923
Closed 24 Dec-1 Jan
Mrs Foley offers a warm and friendly welcome at this well maintained guest house. The comfortably appointed rooms are gradually being refurbished to offer en suite showers. Breakfast is served in the front dining room and guests can take advantage of the small lounge.
9 rms (3 bth/shr) (1 fmly) No smoking in dining room No smoking in lounges CTV in all bedrooms Tea and coffee making facilities No dogs (ex guide dogs) Cen ht CTV 6P
ROOMS: s fr £16; d fr £32*
CARDS:

Q **Wayside Lodge** 2 Midanbury Ln, Bitterne SO18 4HP (On main road from junct 7 or 8 to city centre. hotel is approx 1.5 miles from city centre) ☎ 01703 228780 & 322780
Located just off the Bitterne Road, Wayside Lodge is personally run by Bob and Ingrid Tyley. All the bedrooms are comfortably furnished and some have their own showers. Guests have access to the proprietor's lounge where home cooked dinners are available by prior arrangement.
8 rms (2 fmly) CTV in all bedrooms Tea and coffee making facilities Cen ht CTV 6P No coaches Last d 8.30pm
ROOMS: s £17; d £32; wkly b&b £112*

SOUTH BRENT Devon Map 03 SX66

See also Totnes

Selected

Q Q Q Q **Coombe House** North Huish TQ10 9NJ (A38 from Exeter, exit at Ermington/Modbury/Yealmpton, take A3210, at cross roads straight along B3196 towards Loddiswell. 2nd left and 2nd lane left) ☎ 01548 821277 FAX 01548 821277

Coombe House is set in four acres of gardens and grounds, with a large pond and two streams, attracting much wildlife. The spacious public areas are comfortable and enjoy delightful views over the surrounding countryside. The individually furnished and decorated bedrooms are well equipped and have modern facilities. Adjacent barns have been skilfully converted to provide self catering accommodation. Dinner is served by prior arrangement, and is made with as much local produce as possible.

4 bth/shr (1 fmly) No smoking CTV in all bedrooms Tea and coffee making facilities No dogs (ex guide dogs) Cen ht ch fac 10P No coaches Special arrangement with local golf club Last d 10am

ROOMS: s £25; d £40-£50; wkly b&b fr £140; wkly hlf-bd £210-£245*

SOUTH CAVE East Riding of Yorkshire Map 08 SE93

Selected

Q Q Q Q **Rudstone Walk** South Cave HU15 2AH (from junct 38 of M62 take A1034 to South Cave turn right onto B1234 Rudstone Walk is on left 200yds) ☎ 01430 422230 FAX 01430 424552

Rudstone Walk Farm is mentioned in the Domesday Book and has a long and interesting history. Today it provides good accommodation for the discerning traveller, with well furnished bedrooms and delightful public areas. Both dinner and breakfast are served around a large table in the elegant dining room, where the service is attentive yet relaxed. The farm enjoys lovely views over the Vale of York and the Humber estuary, and is very convenient for the Wolds.

14 bth/shr (1 fmly) No smoking in 7 bedrooms No smoking in dining room CTV in all bedrooms Tea and coffee making facilities Direct dial from bedrooms Licensed Cen ht 50P Last d 7pm

ROOMS: s £43-£45; d £58-£61; wkly b&b £301-£315; wkly hlf-bd fr £402.50*

CARDS:

SOUTHEND-ON-SEA Essex Map 05 TQ88

Q Q **Marine View** 4 Trinity Av, Westcliff on Sea SS0 7PU (turn right off A13 into Milton Road and continue a short distance and over a railway bridge. Turn left and then immediately right into Trinity Ave) ☎ 01702 344104

Closed 23 Dec-1 Jan

Marine View is personally run by Mrs Miller, a hard working and friendly landlady who ensures sound standards of accommodation. Bedrooms are quite traditional in their appointment and each is well equipped. Guests have the use of a small lounge which adjoins the neat breakfast room.

6 rms (1 fmly) No smoking in dining room CTV in all bedrooms Tea and coffee making facilities No dogs (ex guide dogs) Cen ht CTV No children 3yrs No coaches

ROOMS: s £16-£17.50; d £30-£35; wkly b&b £105-£115*

Q Q Q **Mayflower Hotel** 5-6 Royal Ter SS1 1DY (premises overlooking the pier and estuary. Approach from seafront) ☎ 01702 340489

Closed 10 days Xmas & New Year

The ironwork balcony of this prominent Georgian building is ablaze with geraniums in the summer months. The neatly furnished accommodation is spread over 4 floors. A lounge on the first floor has communal tea and coffee-making facilities and a pool table.

23 rms (4 shr) (3 fmly) No smoking in dining room CTV in all bedrooms Tea and coffee making facilities Cen ht CTV 2P Pool table

ROOMS: s £19-£23.50; d £35.25-£42.30

Q Q ***Terrace Hotel*** 8 Royal Ter SS1 1DY (Royal Terrace can only be approached from Southend seafront, via Pier Hill, opposite the pier) ☎ 01702 348143 FAX 01702 348143

This small hotel is part of a smart Georgian terrace in a conservation area. Guests have the use of a comfortable lounge, small dining room and a cosy bar. The accommodation is generally of comfortable proportions, light, fresh and modestly appointed.

9 rms (3 shr) (3 fmly) No smoking in lounges CTV in all bedrooms Tea and coffee making facilities Licensed Cen ht CTV No coaches

Q Q Q **Tower Hotel** 146 Alexandra Rd SS1 1HE (off A13 at Cricketers Inn into Milton Rd then left into Cambridge Rd and take 3rd turn on right into Wilson Rd) (The Independents) ☎ 01702 348635 FAX 01702 433044

Accommodation at this former gentleman's residence is split between the main hotel and a nearby annexe. Room sizes vary, and the annexe bedrooms are generally more spacious but more modestly appointed. Basil's restaurant on the lower ground floor restaurant offers table d'hôte and à la carte dining in the evening; alternatively bar snacks are available in the large Victorian bar on the ground floor.

15 rms (14 bth/shr) 17 annexe bth/shr (4 fmly) No smoking in area of dining room CTV in all bedrooms Tea and coffee making facilities Direct dial from bedrooms Licensed Cen ht CTV 4P Residents membership of nearby sports club Last d 9pm

ROOMS: s £39-£49; d £45-£65*

CARDS:

SOUTH MOLTON Devon Map 03 SS72

Premier Selected

QQQQQ **Kerscott** *(SS793255)* Ash Mill EX36 4QG (6m east of South Molton on B3227. Sign 1.5m from A361 at bottom of lane) ☎ 01769 550262 Mrs T Sampson

Closed Nov-Jan

Theresa and John Sampson welcome guests to their farm which has lovely views over the Devon countryside. Kerscott is mentioned in the Domesday Book and the farmhouse retains many interesting features such as exposed beams, flagstone floors and impressive inglenook fireplaces. Mrs Sampson's delicious farmhouse cooking includes home-baked breads, and meals are served at a single large table in the traditionally furnished dining room.

3 bth/shr No smoking CTV in all bedrooms Tea and coffee making facilities No dogs Cen ht No children 4P 120 acres beef sheep Last d 10am

ROOMS: s fr £22; d £38-£40

SOUTHPORT Merseyside Map 07 SD31

QQQ **Ambassador Private Hotel** 13 Bath St PR9 0DP ☎ 01704 543998 & 530459 FAX 01704 536269

Closed Xmas & New Year

Harry and Margaret Bennett have run this private hotel, found between the promenade and Lord Street shopping area, for well over 30 years. The lounge is on the first floor, and the dining room and bar are on the ground floor. The bar serves snacks at lunch-time and in the evening, and Harry Bennett entertains on the electric organ. Bedrooms are neat and well equipped.

8 shr (2 fmly) No smoking in 4 bedrooms No smoking in dining room No smoking in 1 lounge CTV in all bedrooms Tea and coffee making facilities Licensed Cen ht No children 5yrs 6P No coaches Leisure club nearby Last d 6pm

ROOMS: s £36; d £50; wkly b&b £150; wkly hlf-bd £210-£210*

CARDS: [MasterCard] [American Express] [Barclaycard Visa]

Q **Lyndhurst** 101 King St PR8 1LQ (off A570 at MacDonalds on corner of King St) ☎ 01704 537520

This well maintained and friendly guest house, just a short walk from the main shopping area, offers value-for-money accommodation. The cosy lounge is brightly decorated and leads into a nicely furnished breakfast room.

7 rms CTV in all bedrooms Tea and coffee making facilities No dogs (ex guide dogs) Licensed Cen ht CTV No children 5yrs 2P No coaches Last d noon

ROOMS: s £14; d £28; wkly b&b fr £91; wkly hlf-bd fr £130*

QQQ **Rosedale Hotel** 11 Talbot St PR8 1HP (enter by A570 and left into Talbot St) ☎ 01704 530604 FAX 01704 530604

Closed 21 Dec-3 Jan

This friendly guest house is situated in a quiet part of the town, yet within easy walking distance of Lord Street and the main attractions. Public areas include a bar overlooking the garden, a separate comfortable lounge, and traditionally furnished dining room where a set dinner is available. Bedrooms are bright and cheerful, most of them being quite spacious.

10 rms (7 shr) (1 fmly) No smoking in bedrooms No smoking in dining room CTV in all bedrooms Tea and coffee making facilities No dogs (ex guide dogs) Licensed Cen ht CTV 8P Last d 4pm

ROOMS: s £22-£25; d £45-£50; wkly b&b £135-£165; wkly hlf-bd £195-£235*

CARDS: [MasterCard] [Barclaycard Visa] [Delta]

Selected

QQQQ **Sidbrook Hotel** 14 Talbot St PR8 1HP ☎ 01704 530608 FAX 01704 531198

This private hotel is conveniently situated for access to the centre of town and surrounding leisure attractions. Comfortable bedrooms are individually decorated, and have good facilities. Reception rooms include a dining room a separate bar and a peaceful lounge. There is a good choice of home-cooked meals, and a range of snacks. A sauna and solarium are available to guests, and there is also a garden.

8 bth/shr (2 fmly) No smoking in dining room No smoking in 1 lounge CTV in all bedrooms Tea and coffee making facilities Direct dial from bedrooms Licensed Cen ht CTV 9P No coaches Sauna Solarium Pool table Games room Last d 7.30pm

ROOMS: s £24.99-£28.50; d £35-£50*

CARDS: [MasterCard] [American Express] [Barclaycard Visa] [Diners]

QQQ **The White Lodge Private Hotel** 12 Talbot St PR8 1HP (in town centre, off Eastbank St) ☎ 01704 536320 FAX 01704 536320

Just a short stroll from the centre of the town, this guest house offers a warm welcome. Bedrooms are thoughtfully equipped and one is on the ground floor. The lounge is comfortably furnished, whilst the bar has a good atmosphere. A home-cooked evening meal is served in the bright dining room.

8 rms (1 bth 4 shr) (2 fmly) No smoking in dining room CTV in all bedrooms Tea and coffee making facilities No dogs (ex guide dogs) Licensed Cen ht CTV 6P Last d 6pm

ROOMS: s £22-£28; d £40-£55; wkly b&b £120-£160; wkly hlf-bd £149-£199

QQ ***Whitworth Falls Hotel*** 16 Lathom Rd PR9 0JH (towards N end of promenade, adjacent to municipal golf course) ☎ 01704 530074 FAX 01704 530074

Colourful gardens surround this large building which lies in a quiet residential area. Its well maintained bedrooms include some on the ground floor, and an inter-connecting family suite. There is a comfortable lounge and the bar stocks an interesting range of malt whiskies, whilst good home cooking is provided in the bright dining room.

13 rms (8 shr) (2 fmly) No smoking in dining room CTV in all bedrooms Tea and coffee making facilities No dogs (ex guide dogs) Licensed Cen ht CTV 8P Last d 3pm

SOUTHSEA Hampshire

See **Portsmouth & Southsea**

SOUTHWELL Nottinghamshire Map 08 SK65

QQ **Crown Hotel** 11 Market Place NG25 0HE (Take A617 from Newark towards Southwell. Crown Hotel is next to Southwell Minster) ☎ 01636 812120

Set between the Minster and main thoroughfare of a popular market town, this attractive Georgian inn offers spacious, well furnished bedrooms. The public bar, where breakfast is served, is open-plan, comfortably furnished and decorated, and the atmosphere is warm and convivial.

7 rms (5 shr) CTV in all bedrooms Tea and coffee making facilities No dogs (ex guide dogs) Cen ht 10P Last d 5.45pm

ROOMS: s £30-£38; d £45*

CARDS: [MasterCard] [Barclaycard Visa] [Delta] [Switch]

SOUTHWOLD Suffolk Map 05 TM57

QQQ ***The Cricketers*** Wangford Rd, Reydon IP18 6PZ (2m past Blythburgh turn right off A12 towards Reydon/Southwold onto A1095, at Reydon sharp left into Wangford Rd, Cricketers on left) ☎ 01502 723603 FAX 01502 722194

contd.

The Cricketers is a charming pub restaurant with rooms and is equally popular with locals and tourists. The twice daily changing blackboard menu and the carte selection are complemented by the famed Adnams ales. The accommodation offers much comfort and all rooms are attractively decorated and equipped with a good range of extra facilities.
10 rms (8 bth/shr) (3 fmly) No smoking in dining room CTV in all bedrooms Tea and coffee making facilities Direct dial from bedrooms No dogs (ex guide dogs) Licensed Cen ht CTV 40P No coaches Last d 9pm
CARDS:

Q Q Q ***Oldhurst*** 24 High St IP18 6AD
(opposite Kings Head at start of High Street) ☎ 01502 723829
This small well maintained Victorian guest house offers a good standard of accommodation throughout. The bedrooms are quite spacious and furnished with some well chosen antique pieces, all rooms have en suite facilities. There is a breakfast room on the ground floor which also has armchairs to relax in.
3 bth/shr No smoking in dining room CTV in all bedrooms Tea and coffee making facilities Cen ht No coaches

SOUTH ZEAL Devon Map 03 SX69

Q Q Q **Poltimore** EX20 2PD
(leave A30 at Whiddon Down towards South Zeal and turn left at Rising Sun public house) ☎ 01837 840209
This charming thatched cottage has two comfortable, beamed lounges for guests. Each evening in the oak-panelled dining room, home made specialities are served, cooked with as much local produce as possible. The cosy bedrooms are well equipped and comfortable. Self catering apartments are available in an adjacent converted barn.
7 rms (4 bth/shr) No smoking in dining room CTV in all bedrooms Tea and coffee making facilities Licensed Cen ht CTV 25P No coaches Last d 9pm
ROOMS: s £19-£25; d £38-£50; wkly b&b £129-£139.50; wkly hlf-bd £206-£220*
CARDS:

STADHAMPTON Oxfordshire Map 04 SU69

Selected

Q Q Q Q **Crazy Bear** Bear Ln OX44 7UR
(M40 junct 7 signposted Thame & Wallingford-turn left onto A329, continue for 5m and turn left immediately after petrol station and left again) ☎ 01865 890714 FAX 01865 400481
For travellers who seek something just a little different, this out of the way 17th-century inn is just the ticket. Recently refurbished, the bedrooms are vibrantly designed with a 60s and 70s renaissance in mind. This is blended with superb art deco and cartoon style features including copper plated doors with slanting frames, wrought iron banisters that resemble trees and leopard skin effect carpets. The outlandish decor continues in the jazz/blues bar where a seven-foot stuffed bear looks on. In the stylish restaurant there is even a ceiling of wine bottles! A separate cellar dining room has seats resembling six-foot petals which surround the tables and add an air of privacy. The cooking is superb, and represents terrific value for money, an eclectic range is provided with enthusiasm and imagination.
5 bth/shr 4 annexe rms (2 fmly) No smoking in area of dining room No smoking in 1 lounge CTV in 8 bedrooms No dogs Cen ht 50P No coaches Last d 10pm
ROOMS: s £50-£80; d £60-£100
MEALS: Lunch fr £12.95 Dinner fr £19.95
CARDS:

STAFFORD Staffordshire Map 07 SJ92

See also Adbaston

Q Q **Bailey Hotel** 63 Lichfield Rd ST17 4LL
(on A34 1m south of town centre) ☎ 01785 214133 FAX 01785 227920
Closed 20 Dec-2 Jan
This large well maintained house provides modern accommodation, which includes a room on ground floor level. There is a comfortable lounge and a cosy dining room, where separate tables can be provided. Evening meals are available Monday to Thursday.
11 rms (3 shr) (1 fmly) No smoking in dining room CTV in all bedrooms Tea and coffee making facilities Direct dial from bedrooms Licensed Cen ht CTV 11P No coaches Last d 6.45pm
ROOMS: s £17-£27; d £34-£41; wkly b&b £97-£167*
CARDS:

Q Q Q **Leonards Croft Hotel** 80 Lichfield Rd ST17 4LP
(from junct 13 on M6 follow A449 for 2m, turn right at Esso Garage then left onto A34, on right after railway bridge) ☎ 01785 223676
Closed Xmas
This large and very impressive detached house stands in pleasant and spacious gardens opposite the GEC Alsthom factory. Much of the accommodation has recently been upgraded. The guest house has a spacious and comfortable lounge and separate tables are provided in the dining room, which also contains a bar.
10 rms (3 shr) (3 fmly) No smoking in dining room CTV in all bedrooms Tea and coffee making facilities Licensed Cen ht CTV 11P No coaches Last d 8.30pm
ROOMS: s £20-£28; d £38-£48

Q Q Q ***Old School*** Newport Rd, Haughton ST18 9JH
(from centre of Stafford take A518 for 3m in direction of Telford. House next to church in centre of Haughton village)
☎ 01785 780358 FAX 01785 780358
Apr-Oct
As the name would suggest, this Grade II listed property once served as Haughton village school. It now provides well maintained accommodation comprising of one double, one twin and one single bedded room. All guests share one large table in the traditionally furnished breakfast room and there is a spacious and comfortable lounge.
3 rms No smoking CTV in all bedrooms Tea and coffee making facilities No dogs Cen ht CTV 3P No coaches

Q Q Q **Stone Cliff** Brook Ln, Brocton ST17 0TZ
(M6 junct 13-signs to Stafford, A34-Cannock turn left into Brocton 2m past Police HQ, through village and Brook Lane is 2nd right past village gdns)
☎ 01785 662217
On the edge of Cannock Chase country park, this house comes complete with a duck pond! The comfortable first floor lounge is an ideal spot for admiring the peaceful surroundings. All guests share one table in the adjacent breakfast room. Two of the modern equipped bedrooms have their own private balconies.
3 rms (1 bth/shr) (1 fmly) No smoking CTV in all bedrooms Tea and coffee making facilities No dogs Cen ht CTV 3P No coaches
ROOMS: s £25; d £40-£44*

Selected

QQQQ **Whitgreave Manor** Whitgreave ST18 9SP (off M6 junct 14 onto A34 towards Stone and in 0.5m left into Whitgreave Lane)
☎ 01785 251767 FAX 01785 257078
This is a large house set in spacious grounds that is believed to be early Victorian, although a dwelling existed on the site much earlier. It provides modern furnished accommodation, which is equally suitable for business people and tourists. All share one table in the breakfast room, which has attractive antique furniture. Period furniture is also on display in the spacious and comfortable lounge, where welcoming log fires are lit in cold weather. A newly constructed conservatory provides alternative lounge space and there is a small library.
5 bth/shr (1 fmly) No smoking in bedrooms No smoking in dining room No smoking in 1 lounge CTV in all bedrooms Tea and coffee making facilities Direct dial from bedrooms No dogs (ex guide dogs) Cen ht CTV 20P Tennis (grass) Fishing Table tennis
ROOMS: s £20-£35; d £40-£60*

See advertisement under Stone

QQ **Windsor Hotel** 69 Lichfield Rd ST17 4LW ☎ 01785 258531
Closed 21 Dec-7 Jan
This commercial guest house is under the same ownership as the two star Abbey hotel next door, where bookings for the Windsor are taken and guests may use the hotel bar and dining room. It stands close to the GEC Alsthom factory, within easy reach of the motorway.
14 rms (2 bth/shr) No smoking in dining room No smoking in 1 lounge CTV in all bedrooms Tea and coffee making facilities Cen ht CTV 10P No coaches Last d 8.30pm
CARDS:

STAMFORD Lincolnshire Map **04** TF00

Selected

QQQQ **The Mill** Mill Ln, Tallington PE9 4RR
(Tallington is on A16, 4m fron Stamford. Mill Lane is 2nd turning on the right by the old school. Signposted on A16)
☎ 01780 740815 FAX 01780 740280 Sue & John Olver
This delightful mill, built in 1682, sits in a picturesque and quiet setting, surrounded by open farmland and mature water meadows within the village of Tallington, just a short drive from Stamford. Every room in this renovated mill has a tremendous character and charm, with an abundance of exposed beams throughout the bedrooms, and original mill equipment in the public rooms; in the breakfast room sits a huge mill wheel. Bedrooms are tastefully furnished in a country style, are well equipped and generally quite spacious, all have superb modern bathrooms; the views from many of the rooms are a real treat, overlooking the River Welland, water meadows and the mill pond.

6 bth (2 fmly) No smoking CTV in all bedrooms Tea and coffee making facilities Cen ht 8P Tennis (hard) Fishing 100 acres Sheep Last d by arrangement
ROOMS: s £30-£45; d £45-£55*

Premier Selected

QQQQQ ***The Priory*** Church Rd, Ketton PE9 3RD (off A6121 Morcot rd 3m from A1, opposite village church)
☎ 01780 720215 FAX 01780 721881
Closed 23-30 Dec
The Priory, located in the centre of Ketton village has been tastefully restored and decorated with contemporary fabrics. All rooms have modern facilities, and a warm and friendly welcome can be expected on arrival. A balanced range of home cooked dinners, requiring short notice, can be served in the splendid dining room or in the conservatory, which overlooks the beautiful garden.
3 bth/shr No smoking in bedrooms No smoking in dining room CTV in all bedrooms Tea and coffee making facilities Direct dial from bedrooms No dogs (ex guide dogs) Licensed Cen ht ch fac 9P No coaches Fishing Croquet Last d 7pm
CARDS:

STAMFORD BRIDGE East Riding of Yorkshire

See **Low Catton & High Catton**

STANLEY Co Durham Map **12** NZ15

Q Q ♥ **Bush Blades Farm** *(NZ168533)* Harperley DH9 9UA (Leave A1(m) at Chester-le-St for Stanley on A693 then sign for Consett - 0.5m after Stanley follow sign for Harperley.Farm on right 0.5m from crsrds)
☎ 01207 232722 Mrs P Gibson
Closed 20 Dec-2 Jan
This substantial farmhouse sits peacefully in its own garden enjoying fine views towards Tyneside. The traditionally furnished bedrooms are spacious and comfortable, whilst the breakfast room doubles as a lounge.
3 rms (1 bth) No smoking in 3 bedrooms No smoking in dining room No smoking in lounges CTV in all bedrooms Tea and coffee making facilities No dogs Cen ht CTV No children 12yrs 4P 50 acres sheep
ROOMS: s £20-£25; d £34-£39; wkly b&b £259*

STANTON Staffordshire Map **07** SK14

Q Q Q **Homesclose House** DE6 2DA
(A52 to Stok-on-Trent, left to Stanton 1.5 miles through narrow lane to middle of village) ☎ 01335 324475
Feb-Nov
This little guest house lies in a lovely rural setting. It is excellently maintained and provides two pretty and well equipped bedrooms, each has use of a nearby bathroom, and one has an adjoining single room. The breakfast room looks out over the lawns and gardens and there are fine views over the local countryside.
3 rms (1 fmly) No smoking CTV in all bedrooms Tea and coffee making facilities Cen ht 4P
ROOMS: s £16-£20; d £32-£36*

STANTON PRIOR Somerset Map **03** ST66

Q Q Q ♥ **Poplar Farm** *(ST679630)* Stanton Prior BA2 9HX
(from Bath take A4 (Bath/Bristol). At 1st rdbt take A39 and after 2m turn left opposite Wheatsheaf Pub. Farm first on left in village)
☎ 01761 470382 FAX 01761 470382 Mrs V Hardwick
Guests here can share in the life of a working family farm. The spacious bedrooms are comfortably furnished in keeping with the style of the 17th-century house. A large inglenook fireplace is the centrepiece of the cosy sitting and dining room where guests share a large table at breakfast.
2 rms (1 bth/shr) 1 annexe shr (1 fmly) No smoking CTV in 1 bedroom Tea and coffee making facilities No dogs Cen ht CTV 10P
400 acres arable/beef
ROOMS: s £20-£30; d £36-£48

STEEPLE ASTON Oxfordshire Map **04** SP42

Q Q Q **Westfield Farm Motel** The Fenway OX6 3SS (off A4260, 0.5m into village) (The Circle) ☎ 01869 340591 FAX 01869 347594
Accommodation at Westfield Farm is in the old milking parlour and stables. Rooms are comfortable and attractively decorated. Julie Wayne is a keen cook and her hearty breakfasts are sure to please. The cosy breakfast room, with its dark wood furniture, adjoins a small bar where drinks are served prior to dinner. Several self catering units are also available.
7 shr (2 fmly) No smoking in 2 bedrooms CTV in all bedrooms Tea and coffee making facilities Direct dial from bedrooms Licensed Cen ht CTV 12P No coaches Riding Last d 8.30pm
ROOMS: s £45-£50; d £55-£65
CARDS:

STEYNING West Sussex Map **04** TQ11

Selected

Q Q Q Q ***Springwells Hotel*** 9 High St BN44 3GG (from A283,by-pass, take main road through village for house on right opposite Methodist Church) ☎ 01903 812446 & 812043 FAX 01903 879823
Closed 24 Dec-1 Jan
Public areas at this former Georgian merchant's house include a period lounge and separate breakfast room as well as an appealing conservatory bar where complimentary cheese and biscuits are served in the evenings. Individually decorated bedrooms come with many extras such as biscuits and magazines. Snacks are available by prior arrangement.
10 rms (8 bth/shr) (1 fmly) No smoking in 1 lounge CTV in all bedrooms Tea and coffee making facilities Direct dial from bedrooms Licensed Cen ht CTV 6P No coaches Outdoor swimming pool (heated) Sauna Last d 8.45pm
CARDS:

STOCKBRIDGE Hampshire Map **04** SU33

Q Q Q **Carbery** Salisbury Hill SO20 6EZ (on A30) ☎ 01264 810771 FAX 01264 811022
Closed 2 wks Xmas
This attractive Georgian property is located at the northern end of Stockbridge. Hosts Mrs and Mrs Hooper create a friendly atmosphere. The bedrooms are nicely furnished and most have en suite facilities. A home-cooked evening meal is served in the smart dining room, and there is a bright conservatory lounge, a terrace and an acre of garden.
11 rms (2 bth 6 shr) (2 fmly) No smoking in dining room CTV in all bedrooms Tea and coffee making facilities No dogs Licensed Cen ht 14P Outdoor swimming pool (heated) Pool table Last d 6pm
ROOMS: s £26-£33; d £49-£52; wkly b&b £179-£227; wkly hlf-bd £265-£312*

STOKE-BY-NAYLAND Suffolk Map **05** TL93

Selected

Q Q Q Q **The Angel Inn** Polstead St CO6 4SA
(off A12 onto B1068 midway between Colchester and Ipswich)
☎ 01206 263245 FAX 01206 263373
Closed 25-26 Dec
The Angel Inn has offered hospitality to travellers since the 16th century and is situated in one of Suffolk's most interesting villages. Its

popular bars and restaurant are much frequented by local customers. The inn has been tastefully refurbished and retains its original features, such as rough brickwork, high rafted ceilings, exposed beams, open fireplaces and a deep well. The bedrooms are individually decorated and furnished to a high standard with some well chosen pieces, and all rooms have modern en suite facilities. Guests can have a hearty breakfast in the Well Room restaurant, as well as an extensive choice of items available from the blackboard menu for dinner.
5 bth/shr 1 annexe bth/shr No smoking in area of dining room CTV in all bedrooms Tea and coffee making facilities Direct dial from bedrooms No dogs (ex guide dogs) Cen ht No children 8yrs 25P No coaches Last d 9pm
ROOMS: s £46; d £59.50*
MEALS: Lunch £12.75-£20alc Dinner £15.50-£20alc*
CARDS:

STOKE HOLY CROSS Norfolk Map 05 TG20

QQ **Salamanca** *(TG235022)* NR14 8QJ (at A47/A140 intersection take minor road to Caistor St Edmunds, then first right, farm approx 1m on left) ☎ 01508 492322 Mrs Harrold
Closed 15 Dec-15 Jan & Etr
Salamanca Farm offers peace and quiet, and spacious bedrooms with en suite or private facilities. Parts of this large red brick farmhouse date back to the 16th century and the farm is still working today. There is a guest lounge with TV and a comprehensive list of restaurants and pubs is provided.
3 rms (1 bth 1 shr) 1 annexe bth No smoking CTV in 1 bedroom Tea and coffee making facilities No dogs Cen ht CTV No children 6yrs 7P 165 acres beef mixed
ROOMS: s £20-£22; d £36-£44*

STOKE-ON-TRENT Staffordshire Map 07 SJ84

See also Audley & Cheddleton

QQQ **Corrie** 13 Newton St, Basford ST4 6JN (in cul de sac off A53, 250 yds from junction of the A500/A53 in the direction of Newcastle under Lyme)
☎ 01782 614838 FAX 01782 614838
This large Victorian house is quietly situated in a cul-de-sac. It provides well maintained accommodation, which includes family bedded rooms. Separate tables are available in the bright and pleasant breakfast room and there is a lounge.
8 rms (3 shr) (4 fmly) No smoking in bedrooms No smoking in dining room CTV in all bedrooms Tea and coffee making facilities No dogs (ex guide dogs) Cen ht 11P No coaches
ROOMS: s £19-£26; d £34-£40*

All AA listed accommodation can also be found at the AA's Internet site, whose address is: http://www.theaa.co.uk/hotels

Premier Selected

QQQQQ ***Hanchurch Manor*** Hanchurch ST4 8SD (off A519 Eccleshall) ☎ 01782 643030 FAX 01782 643035
Closed 25-31 Dec
This impressive 17th-century Grade II listed building lies in nine acres of landscaped gardens which include a fishing lake. Spacious bedrooms are provided and one has a four-poster bed. All are individually styled, and equipped with many thoughtful extras. There is a choice of elegantly furnished sitting rooms and dinner is available by arrangement. Breakfasts are wholesome and a good choice is provided.
7 bth/shr No smoking in dining room No smoking in 1 lounge CTV in all bedrooms Tea and coffee making facilities Direct dial from bedrooms No dogs Licensed Cen ht No children 12yrs 52P No coaches Fishing Last d 9pm
CARDS:

QQQ **The Hollies** Clay Lake, Endon ST9 9DD (turn off A53 at Endon onto B5051 and continue uphill for 300yds) ☎ 01782 503252
This traditionally furnished Victorian house enjoys a peaceful location close to the Staffordshire moorlands. Spacious bedrooms, including some family rooms, are individually furnished and decorated, many having views over the extensive gardens. There is a comfortable lounge, and breakfast is served in the adjacent dining room.
5 bth/shr (2 fmly) No smoking CTV in all bedrooms Tea and coffee making facilities Cen ht CTV 7P No coaches
ROOMS: s £22-£30; d £36-£40; wkly b&b £119-£140*

QQQ **Rhodes Hotel** 42 Leek Rd ST4 2AR (turn off M6 onto A500 and then onto A52 (Ashbourne road), 0.25m on right) ☎ 01782 416320
This personally run guest house is located on the Leek road, conveniently close to Stoke-on-Trent station. It provides modern furnished and equipped accommodation which includes family bedded rooms and a bedroom on ground floor level. Separate tables are provided in the cosy breakfast room and there is also a guests' lounge, with a horse racing theme. The house is popular with both commercial guests and tourists.
7 rms (4 shr) (3 fmly) No smoking in dining room CTV in all bedrooms Tea and coffee making facilities Cen ht CTV
ROOMS: d £32-£39*

QQQ **Trentside Hotel** 260 Stone Rd, Hanford ST4 8NJ (off M6 junct 15 onto A500, at 2nd rdbt turn right onto A34, establishment on right 0.25m (dual carriageway, turn at lights).) ☎ 01782 642443 FAX 01782 641910
New owners are upgrading facilities at this friendly guest house, conveniently situated for Trentham Gardens and the pottery factories and museums. Additional en suite facilities are being added and a programme of redecoration continues. There is a cosy lounge and breakfast is served in the bright dining room.
8 rms (1 bth 1 shr) (1 fmly) No smoking in bedrooms No smoking in dining room CTV in all bedrooms Tea and coffee making facilities Cen ht CTV 10P No coaches Golf 18
ROOMS: s £20; d £32-£38; wkly b&b £80-£100
CARDS:

QQQ **The White House Hotel** 94 Stone Rd, Trent Vale ST4 6SP (1.5m from junct 15 of M6 at crossroads of A500 and A34) ☎ 01782 642460 FAX 01782 657189
Conveniently situated for visitors to The Potteries, this family run house offers comfortable and neatly furnished bedrooms. Some rooms are on the ground floor and two are in an adjacent building. There is a cosy lounge area and breakfast is served in the bright dining room.
10 rms (3 shr) 2 annexe shr (2 fmly) No smoking in bedrooms No smoking in dining room CTV in all bedrooms Tea and coffee making facilities Direct dial from bedrooms Licensed Cen ht CTV 12P No coaches
ROOMS: s £25-£38; d £38-£48*
CARDS:

STONE Staffordshire Map **07** SJ93

QQQ **Norton Farm** *(SJ898322)* Eccleshall Rd ST15 0NF
(turn off A34 onto Eccleshall Rd (B5026), over motorway bridge, farm off left layby 0.75m into farmyard) ☎ 01785 760224 Mrs M Brown
rs 20 Dec-5 Jan
This Georgian farmhouse is set within a 400-acre dairy farm and is close to the golf course. Bedrooms are spacious and furnished with sturdy wooden furniture. In the dining room, a hearty farmhouse breakfast is served, plus dinner by prior arrangement. There is a comfortable lounge and guests can use the well stocked ponds for coarse fishing.
3 rms (1 fmly) No smoking in bedrooms No smoking in 1 lounge Tea and coffee making facilities Cen ht CTV Golf 18 300 acres dairy/beef

STONEHOUSE Gloucestershire Map **03** SO80

QQQ **Rose & Crown Inn** Nympsfield GL10 3TU
(turn off B4066 at Coaley Peak, 0.75m to village where Inn is situated in the centre) (The Circle)
☎ 01453 860240 FAX 01453 860900
Located in the peaceful village of Nympsfield, this attractive Cotswold inn attracts a bustling trade to its two large bars. The character of the building has been carefully retained and log fires burn in the inglenook fireplace during colder weather. The bedrooms are all spacious with comfortable furnishings and modern equipment.
4 rms (3 bth/shr) (3 fmly) CTV in all bedrooms Tea and coffee making facilities No dogs (ex guide dogs) Cen ht CTV 20P Last d 9.30pm
ROOMS: s £33-£35; d £55-£60
MEALS: Lunch £13.50-£21alc Dinner £13.50-£21alc
CARDS:

STOW-ON-THE-WOLD Gloucestershire Map **04** SP12

Premier Selected

QQQQQ **College House** Chapel St, Broadwell GL56 0TW
(North of Stow-on-the-Wold turn off. A429 follow signs to Broadwell, then Evencode, premises on Chapel St)
☎ 01451 832351
Closed 24-26 Dec
Situated in a pretty village, this 17th-century house retains many of its original features including exposed beams and flagstone floors. Decor and soft furnishings enhance the building's character, while fine period pieces and pictures create a warm and homely atmosphere. Bedrooms are spacious, comfortable and well equipped. Home cooked breakfasts are taken in the dining hall at one family table and there is a cosy sitting room for guests' use.
3 bth No smoking in bedrooms No smoking in dining room CTV in all bedrooms Tea and coffee making facilities No dogs Cen ht No children 16yrs 5P No coaches Last d noon
ROOMS: d £55-£68

QQQ **Corsham Field** *(SP217249)* Bledington Rd GL54 1JH
(take A436 out of Stow-on-the-Wold towards Chipping Norton. After 1m fork right onto B4450 Bleddington road. First farm on right)
☎ 01451 831750 Mr R Smith
A farmhouse of Cotswold stone with some exceptional views, just a short drive from Stow-on-the-Wold. Bedrooms are appointed in a simple farmhouse style with modern equipment and good maintenance throughout. Breakfast is served in an attractive dining room.
7 rms (5 bth/shr) (3 fmly) No smoking in dining room No smoking in lounges CTV in all bedrooms Tea and coffee making facilities Cen ht 10P 100 acres arable beef sheep
ROOMS: s £15-£30; d £33-£45; wkly b&b £105-£157.50*

Premier Selected

QQQQQ **Crestow House** GL54 1JY (at junct of A429 and B4068) ☎ 01451 830969 FAX 01451 832129
Closed Jan
Situated close to the centre of town, Crestow House is an early Victorian manor which has retained many if its original features. Bedrooms are spacious, comfortable and very individual in style with many homely extras. Public areas include a lovely dining room and a large comfortable sitting room with conservatory extension overlooking the immaculate gardens and swimming pool.
4 bth/shr No smoking CTV in all bedrooms Tea and coffee making facilities No dogs Cen ht CTV No children 15yrs 4P No coaches Outdoor swimming pool (heated) Sauna Solarium Gymnasium Last d noon
ROOMS: s £44*
CARDS:

Selected

QQQQ **Kings Head Inn & Restaurant** The Green, Bledington OX7 6XQ (4m SE off B4450) ☎ 01608 658365
FAX 01608 658902
Closed 24-25 Dec

This most delightful Cotswold Inn offers warm and inviting bars with a superb selection of meals. The bedrooms are well equipped with fresh flowers, magazines and boiled sweets. Bledington is a lovely village, situated four miles from the market town of Stow-on-the-Wold; it also boasts the best kept village award.
6 bth 6 annexe bth/shr (2 fmly) No smoking in bedrooms
No smoking in area of dining room No smoking in 1 lounge CTV in all bedrooms Tea and coffee making facilities Direct dial from bedrooms No dogs (ex guide dogs) Cen ht CTV 70P Last d 9.45pm
ROOMS: s £45; d £65-£75*
MEALS: Lunch £10.95 Dinner £10.95&alc*
CARDS:

Q Q Q **Limes** Evesham Rd GL54 1EJ
(turn off A429 towards Evesham on A424. The Limes 800yds on left)
☎ 01451 830034
Closed 24 Dec-2 Jan
Located just on the outskirts of historic Stow, The Limes is well situated for visitors to the Cotswolds. Recently upgraded, the bedrooms are comfortable, prettily decorated and have modern facilities. Breakfast is taken in the sunny dining room which looks out onto the garden.
4 rms (2 shr) 1 annexe shr (1 fmly) No smoking in dining room CTV in all bedrooms Tea and coffee making facilities Cen ht CTV 4P No coaches
ROOMS: d £35-£40*

Selected

Q Q Q Q **Woodlands** Woodlands, Upper Swell GL54 1EW (one mile from Stow-on-the-Wold, situated in village of Upper Swell on B4077) ☎ 01451 832346
Situated in a hamlet on the outskirts of the town, this mellow stone house has pretty gardens and superb views of the countryside. Bedrooms are well equipped and comfortable. The dining room is used as a small sitting area during the evening. The Sykes family are very friendly and attentive hosts.
5 bth/shr CTV in all bedrooms Tea and coffee making facilities Cen ht 8P No coaches
ROOMS: s fr £29; d fr £52; wkly b&b fr £182*
CARDS:

STRATFORD-UPON-AVON Warwickshire Map 04 SP25

Q Q Q **Aberfoyle** 3 Evesham Place CV37 6HT ☎ 01789 295703
FAX 01789 295703
This small personally run guest house is conveniently located for the town centre and the major road access. The rooms are well maintained, bright, cheerfully decorated and comfortably appointed with smart en suite facilities. There is a cosy breakfast room.
2 shr (1 fmly) No smoking CTV in all bedrooms Tea and coffee making facilities Cen ht No children 5yrs 2P No coaches
ROOMS: s £22-£25; d £38-£42; wkly b&b £112-£125*

Q Q Q **Ambleside** 41 Grove Rd CV37 6PB
(turn off A3400 onto B439, through traffic lights, guesthouse on right)
☎ 01789 297239 & 295670 FAX 01789 295670
Closed Xmas
Mr Mullis offers all his guests a warm welcome at this centrally located guest house which offers smartly appointed bedrooms and an airy breakfast room; guests can also use the comfortable lounge.
7 rms (3 shr) (3 fmly) No smoking CTV in all bedrooms Tea and coffee making facilities Cen ht 8P
ROOMS: s £20-£25; d £38-£50
CARDS:

Q Q Q **Brook Lodge** 192 Alcester Rd CV37 9DR
(W on A422 opposite turning to Anne Hathaway's Cottage)
☎ 01789 295988 FAX 01789 295988
Closed 22 Dec-1 Jan
Located within walking distance of Anne Hathaway's Cottage, this well maintained modern house with its large private car park offers compact but well equipped bedrooms. Giovanni and Barbara Renna are very friendly and attentive hosts.

contd.

Brook Lodge

7 shr (3 fmly) No smoking CTV in all bedrooms Tea and coffee making facilities No dogs (ex guide dogs) Cen ht CTV No children 5yrs 10P No coaches
ROOMS: s £34-£40; d £42-£52; wkly b&b £140-£175
CARDS:

QQQ **Craig Cleeve House** 67-69 Shipston Rd CV37 7LW
(follow A3400 out of Stratford towards Oxford. Hotel 150yrds on right)
☎ 01789 296573 FAX 01789 299452
New owners have begun a programme of refurbishment at this small hotel. Bedrooms are comfortably furnished and well equipped, several are located on the ground floor. There is a cosy lounge/bar and a cheerful restaurant that overlooks an attractive rear garden; a good choice of popular dishes is readily available.
15 rms (9 shr) (5 fmly) No smoking in bedrooms No smoking in dining room CTV in all bedrooms Tea and coffee making facilities Licensed Cen ht 15P Last d 8pm
ROOMS: s £19.50-£45; d £42-£54; wkly b&b £126-£300; wkly hlf-bd £196-£370*
CARDS:

QQQ **The Croft** 49 Shipston Rd CV37 7LN
(on A3400, 400 yds from Clopton Bridge) ☎ 01789 293419
FAX 01789 293419
Situated close to Clopton Bridge and with private rear garden access to the sports fields, this extended Victorian house offers simply appointed but well equipped bedroom accommodation close to major attractions.
9 rms (4 shr) (5 fmly) No smoking in 2 bedrooms No smoking in dining room CTV in all bedrooms Tea and coffee making facilities Licensed Cen ht CTV 4P Outdoor swimming pool (heated) Last d noon
ROOMS: s £20-£39; d £40-£52*
CARDS:

QQ **Curtain Call** 142 Alcester Rd CV37 9DR
(follow A46 then left onto A422 towards Stratford. Curtain Call on the brow of the hill, just past turn off for Shottery & Anne Hathaways Cottage)
☎ 01789 267734 FAX 01789 267734
The new owners of this small guest house are both experienced hoteliers. Whilst bedroom sizes may vary, they are all soundly appointed; each room has a good range of facilities and several have four-posters. Breakfasts are taken in the ground floor dining room, and dinners are readily available by prior request.
5 rms (3 shr) (1 fmly) No smoking CTV in all bedrooms Tea and coffee making facilities Cen ht CTV 6P Last d 9pm
ROOMS: s £18-£21; d £36-£50; wkly b&b £126-£147; wkly hlf-bd £178.50-£199
CARDS:

The AA's professional Inspectors make regular and anonymous visits to all the establishments listed in the Guide. They accept no gifts or favours from proprietors

QQQ **The Dylan** 10 Evesham Place CV37 6HT
(from A439 Evesham road, pass Shell Garage and continue over traffic island. Guesthouse 200yds towards Stratford on the right)
☎ 01789 204819
This friendly family guest house is centrally located and features in its breakfast room a Wurlitzer juke box that plays many of Bob Dylan's hits. Bedrooms are bright and comfortable, many of them have stylish Victorian fireplaces.
5 shr (1 fmly) No smoking CTV in all bedrooms Tea and coffee making facilities Cen ht 5P No coaches
ROOMS: s £20-£24; d £38-£44*

Selected

QQQQ **Eastnor House Hotel** Shipston Rd CV37 7LN
(follow A3400 Shipston Rd hotel 1st on right close to Clopton Bridge)
☎ 01789 268115 FAX 01789 266516
Closed Xmas
Situated close to Clopton Bridge and conveniently located for all the major tourist attractions, this spacious double fronted Victorian house offers comfortable accommodation with efficient services. Bedrooms are well equipped and extras include modern en suite bathrooms with additional showers. Public areas include the original tiled hallway and staircase, a small cosy sitting room and a pretty dining room where delicious English breakfasts are served. Friendly and attentive service is offered by the Everitt Family.
9 bth/shr (3 fmly) No smoking CTV in all bedrooms Tea and coffee making facilities No dogs Licensed Cen ht 9P No coaches
ROOMS: s £20-£60; d £50-£64*
CARDS:

QQQ **Emsley** no 4 Arden St CV37 6PA ☎ 01789 299557
This Victorian town house sits close to the town centre and several Shakespearean properties. The public rooms offer a comfortable airy lounge and a separate dining room for breakfast. Bedrooms are soundly appointed and generally of good comfortable proportions.
5 bth/shr (2 fmly) No smoking in dining room CTV in all bedrooms Tea and coffee making facilities No dogs (ex guide dogs) Cen ht CTV 1P
ROOMS: d £40-£50*
CARDS:

QQQ **Eversley Bears** 37 Grove Rd CV37 6PB ☎ 01789 292334
FAX 01789 292334
Situated close to town centre and attractions, this semi-detached private hotel offers good value accommodation. Bedrooms are comfortable and well equipped and the house is well known for its large collection of Teddy Bears which has grown to over 700.
6 rms (2 shr) (2 fmly) No smoking CTV in all bedrooms Tea and coffee making facilities No dogs (ex guide dogs) Cen ht No children 14yrs 3P
ROOMS: s £20-£24; d £40-£48*
CARDS:

Premier Selected

Q Q Q Q Q **Glebe Farm House** *(SP248533)* Loxley CV35 9JW (S from Stratford crossing River Avon, turn immediately left onto Tiddington road, then immediately right onto Loxley road, farm 2.5 miles on left) ☎ 01789 842501 FAX 01789 841194
Mrs K M McGovern
Situated in landscaped grounds, this house dates from the 18th century and has been modernised and extended in recent years. Bedrooms are spacious and comfortable, fitted with antique pine furniture. Facilities include lots of homely extras and modern en suite shower rooms. Public areas feature a spacious and very comfortable lounge with an open fire for the cooler months, plus the conservatory dining room which is reached via the charming farmhouse kitchen. Kate McGovern is a friendly and caring hostess as well as being a fine artist and cook.
2 bth/shr No smoking CTV in all bedrooms Tea and coffee making facilities No dogs Cen ht No children 40P
30 acres rare breed animals
ROOMS: s £69.50-£80; d £80-£110*
CARDS:

Selected

Q Q Q Q **Gravelside Barn** Binton CV37 9TU
☎ 01789 750502 & 297000 FAX 01789 298056
Gravelside Barn is a clever conversion of a stone-built barn. Each of the smartly appointed bedrooms has a delightful view of the open Warwickshire countryside, a modern en suite shower room and a range of useful facilities. Guests also have the use of a comfortable open plan lounge and breakfast room.
3 shr No smoking CTV in all bedrooms Tea and coffee making facilities No dogs (ex guide dogs) Cen ht No children 12yrs 6P
No coaches Golf 18 Tennis (hard)
ROOMS: s £35-£40; d £50-£60*
CARDS:

Q Q Q **Hardwick House** 1 Avenue Rd CV37 6UY
(Turn right off A439 at St Gregory's Church into St Gregory's Rd, Hardwick House 200yds on right) ☎ 01789 204307 FAX 01789 296760
Situated in a residential area a few minutes from both the river and Birthplace, this late Victorian house offers comfortable bed and breakfast accommodation with friendly and attentive service. Bedrooms are comfortable and equipped with modern en suite or private facilities.
14 rms (13 bth/shr) (3 fmly) No smoking in bedrooms No smoking in dining room CTV in all bedrooms Tea and coffee making facilities No dogs (ex guide dogs) Cen ht 12P
ROOMS: s £28-£35; d £42-£62
CARDS:

Highcroft Banbury Rd CV37 7NF
(on A422 out of town towards Banbury, 2m from river bridge on left)
☎ 01789 296293 FAX 01789 415236
This attractive property is set in an attractive rural setting two miles outside Stratford. There are two pretty bedrooms which combine period furnishings with modern facilities. Breakfast is taken in a comfortable open plan lounge and dining room.
1 bth/shr 1 annexe bth/shr (1 fmly) No smoking CTV in all bedrooms Tea and coffee making facilities Cen ht CTV 5P No coaches Tennis (hard)
ROOMS: s £25; d £38; wkly b&b £120

Hollies 'The Hollies', 16 Evesham Place CV37 6HQ
☎ 01789 266857
This cosy, personally run guest house is well positioned just a few minutes walk from the town centre. Bedrooms have a range of modern furnishings and equipment. Breakfasts are served in an attractively appointed dining room.
6 rms (3 bth/shr) (3 fmly) No smoking CTV in all bedrooms Tea and coffee making facilities Cen ht CTV 6P

Hunters Moon 150 Alcester Rd CV37 9DR
(on A422 5m from M40 junct 15) ☎ 01789 292888 FAX 01789 204101
Situated on the northern outskirts of the town close to Anne Hathaway's Cottage, this modern house offers compact well equipped accommodation convenient for the area's major attractions. Rosemary and David Austin are very friendly and attentive hosts with a wide knowledge of the area and its amenities.
6 shr 1 annexe shr (4 fmly) CTV in all bedrooms Tea and coffee making facilities No dogs (ex guide dogs) Cen ht CTV 6P
ROOMS: s £23-£28; d £40-£50
CARDS:

Marlyn 3 Chestnut Walk CV37 6HG
(from Evesham Road A439 towards town centre, second right after roundabout) ☎ 01789 293752 FAX 01789 293752
A well furnished and comfortable house which is personally run by the enthusiastic and friendly owners, Andrew & Rosie Evans. The bedrooms are soundly appointed and there is a cosy lounge and a pleasant dining room; guests also have use of the rear gardens in summer months. The town centre and the theatre are only a short walk away.
8 rms (4 shr) (1 fmly) No smoking in 2 bedrooms No smoking in dining room CTV in all bedrooms Tea and coffee making facilities Licensed Cen ht No coaches Aromatherapy & reflexology treatment
Last d breakfast/midday
ROOMS: s £20; d £40-£50*
CARDS:

Selected

Melita Private Hotel 37 Shipston Rd CV37 7LN
(south on A3400 towards Shipston, 200 yds on right from Clopton Bridge) ☎ 01789 292432 FAX 01789 204867
Closed 20-27 Dec
A spacious Victorian house offering good value accommodation with friendly service. Bedrooms are varied in style and all are well equipped for the needs of the modern traveller. The public areas include a cosy dining room where breakfast is served and a sitting room with feature fireplace and an honesty bar.
12 bth/shr (3 fmly) No smoking in bedrooms No smoking in dining room CTV in all bedrooms Tea and coffee making facilities Direct dial from bedrooms Licensed Cen ht CTV 12P
ROOMS: s £35-£45; d £49-£79*
CARDS:

Monk's Barn *(SP206516)* Shipston Rd CV37 8NA
(on A3400 approx 1.25m S)
☎ 01789 293714 FAX 01789 205886 Mrs R M Meadows
Closed 25-26 Dec
Monk's Barn Farm, two miles south of Stratford, has its origins in the 16th century, although the pretty house is more recent. Friendly proprietors help to create a welcoming atmosphere. The public areas include a split level lounge and dining room with traditional furnishings and an open fire. The cosy bedrooms, some with delightful countryside views, are situated in both the main house and the cleverly converted milking parlour.
4 rms (3 shr) 2 annexe shr (1 fmly) No smoking in 2 bedrooms No smoking in dining room No smoking in lounges CTV in all bedrooms Tea and coffee making facilities No dogs (ex guide dogs) Cen ht CTV 5P Fishing 75 acres mixed
ROOMS: s £17.50-£19.50; d £32-£36; wkly b&b £98-£122.50*

Moonraker House 40 Alcester Rd CV37 9DB
(on A422, 900yds NW of town centre) (Minotel)
☎ 01789 299346 & 267115 FAX 01789 295504
Moonraker House is actually four different properties in the same street and with this diversity come a number of individually styled bedrooms, including two luxurious four-poster rooms with garden terraces. All are spacious and furnished to a high standard. There are several ground floor bedrooms and an attractive sun lounge.
10 bth/shr 12 annexe bth/shr (4 fmly) No smoking in 14 bedrooms No smoking in dining room No smoking in lounges CTV in all bedrooms Tea and coffee making facilities Cen ht 22P
ROOMS: s £35-£38; d £45-£70*
CARDS:

The Myrtles 6 Rother St CV37 6LU
(In town centre opposite market place in Rother Street)
☎ 01789 295511
Standing opposite the market square, this welcoming guest house, dating from 1900, offers cheerful, ground-floor bedrooms with smart modern bathrooms. Breakfast is served either in the open-plan kitchen/breakfast room, or sometimes on the attractive patio.
3 shr No smoking CTV in all bedrooms Tea and coffee making facilities Cen ht 2P No coaches
ROOMS: s £30-£40; d £45-£50*
CARDS:

Nando's 18-19 Evesham Place CV37 6HT
(on B439, 5min walk from railway station)
☎ 01789 204907 FAX 01789 204907
Standing close to the town and theatre, this busy guest house provides modern accommodation and there is also a lounge and large dining room.
20 rms (1 bth 16 shr) (11 fmly) No smoking in bedrooms No smoking in dining room CTV in all bedrooms Tea and coffee making facilities Cen ht CTV 8P
ROOMS: s £23-£35; d £46-£54
CARDS:

QQQ *Parkfield* 3 Broad Walk CV37 6HS
(just off B439 to left on way out of Stratford, immediately before first rdbt)
☎ 01789 293313 FAX 01789 293313
Within easy walking distance of the town centre, this charming Victorian house is an ideal base for visitors to the Royal Shakespeare Theatre. Owners Mr and Mrs Pettitt are also keen theatre goers. Bedrooms are well equipped with helpful extras such as sewing kits, tissues and clock radios, and are furnished in an individual mix of styles. A vegetarian breakfast is on offer as an alternative to the full British, and there are other 'healthy eating' choices. The owners are glad to recommend local restaurants for evening meals.
7 rms (5 shr) (1 fmly) No smoking CTV in all bedrooms Tea and coffee making facilities No dogs (ex guide dogs) Cen ht No children 5yrs 8P No coaches
CARDS:

QQQ **Penryn House** 126 Alcester Rd CV37 9DP
(0.5m past railway station, right hand side of A422, going out of Stratford)
☎ 01789 293718 FAX 01789 266077
Situated on the outskirts of the town, close to Anne Hathaway's Cottage, this modern dormer bungalow offers comfortable accommodation within easy reach of the major attractions. Bedrooms are well equipped and most have en-suite facilities. Breakfast is served in an attractive dining room overlooking the back garden. Service is friendly.
6 rms (4 shr) 1 annexe shr (1 fmly) No smoking CTV in all bedrooms Tea and coffee making facilities No dogs (ex guide dogs) Cen ht No children 5yrs 7P
ROOMS: s £22-£30; d £36-£48*
CARDS:

Take the guesswork out of choosing somewhere to eat with AA Best Restaurants, featuring more than 1800 inspected places to eat throughout the country

Q Q ***Salamander*** 40 Grove Rd CV37 6PB
(on A439 towards Evesham, just behind the police station and Firs Park)
☎ 01789 205728 FAX 01789 205728
Conveniently located close to the town centre, this Edwardian house, overlooking Firs Park, continues to improve. The bedrooms are comfortably furnished and have colour TV, and most have modern en suite showers.
7 rms (5 shr) (2 fmly) No smoking in dining room No smoking in lounges CTV in all bedrooms Tea and coffee making facilities No dogs (ex guide dogs) Cen ht No children 12yrs 6P No coaches

Selected

Q Q Q Q **Sequoia House Private Hotel** 51-53 Shipston Rd CV37 7LN (on A3400 close to Clopton Bridge)
☎ 01789 268852 FAX 01789 414559
Closed 21-27 Dec
Close to town centre and with direct access through the beautifully tended rear garden, this large Victorian house retains many original features. Bedrooms are well equipped and comfortable, and some in the main house are furnished with fine period pieces and decorated with complementary colour schemes. Breakfast is taken in the air conditioned dining room. There are two sitting rooms and a well stocked bar. Proprietors Jean and Philip Evans are constantly making improvements to enhance their guests' comfort.
19 rms (15 bth/shr) 5 annexe shr (2 fmly) No smoking in bedrooms No smoking in dining room CTV in all bedrooms Tea and coffee making facilities Direct dial from bedrooms No dogs Licensed Cen ht CTV No children 5yrs 26P
ROOMS: s £35-£55; d £45-£79*
CARDS:

Q Q Q **Stretton House Hotel** 38 Grove Rd CV37 6PB
(A39 central Stratford-upon-Avon road behind police station)
☎ 01789 268647 FAX 01789 268647
This attractive semi-detached property, which is close to the town centre, offers bright, attractively appointed bedrooms with fresh bold fabrics and decor; some family rooms are available. The house is very well maintained throughout and offers a combined lounge and breakfast room for guests' use.
7 rms (4 shr) (2 fmly) No smoking CTV in all bedrooms Tea and coffee making facilities No dogs (ex guide dogs) Cen ht No children 8yrs 4P
ROOMS: s £20-£30; d £30-£50

Selected

Q Q Q Q **Twelfth Night** Evesham Place CV37 6HT
(on B439. Town centre approx 200metres from police station)
☎ 01789 414595
Situated on the edge of the town close to Anne Hathaway's Cottage, this Victorian Villa (once owned by the Royal Shakespeare Company), was an actors' pied à terre for 25 years. Recently restored and refurbished, it provides comfortable and well equipped accommodation. Bedrooms are homely with pretty decor and soft furnishing schemes and lots of little extras. Breakfast is served in the elegant dining room and there is a comfortable sitting room for guests' use.

6 shr No smoking CTV in all bedrooms Tea and coffee making facilities No dogs Cen ht No children 12yrs 8P No coaches
ROOMS: d £45-£58
CARDS:

Selected

Q Q Q Q **Victoria Spa Lodge** Bishopton Ln CV37 9QY
(1.5m N on A3400 intersected by A46. 1st exit left Bishopton Lane, 1st house on right) ☎ 01789 267985 FAX 01789 204728
Mr and Mrs Tozer's attractive early Victorian house is peacefully located on the outskirts of the town. The dramatic lounge with its stripped hardwood floor is a lovely room that has many period features. Bedrooms are well equipped and spacious with tasteful use of fabrics, quality furnishings and welcome extra touches; all rooms have efficient showers. Vegetarians are well catered for at breakfast. The house is no-smoking throughout.
7 shr (3 fmly) No smoking CTV in all bedrooms Tea and coffee making facilities No dogs Cen ht 12P No coaches
ROOMS: d £55-£60*
CARDS:

Q Q Q **Virginia Lodge** 12 Evesham Place CV37 6HT
(In town centre off A34 turn right 2nd set of lights into Rother Street past small car park on right) ☎ 01789 292157
Closed Xmas
A friendly welcome and soundly maintained accommodation are provided here. The modern furnished and well equipped rooms are attractively decorated. Three bedrooms have four-poster beds and there is a ground floor annexe bedroom which opens onto a patio and garden. Breakfast is taken in a separate dining room and there is a guests' lounge.
7 rms (6 shr) (1 fmly) No smoking CTV in all bedrooms Tea and coffee making facilities No dogs (ex guide dogs) Licensed Cen ht CTV 9P
ROOMS: s £18-£22; d £36-£46*

STROUD Gloucestershire Map **03** SO80

Selected

QQQQ **Crown** Frampton Mansell GL6 8JG (turn off A419 Cirencester-Stroud following signs to Frampton Mansell. Premises are 6m into village just past St Lukes Church on right) ☎ 01285 760601 FAX 01285 760681

LIONHEART Arms

Dating back to the 16th century, this charming inn is located in a Cotswold village, six miles south of Stroud, overlooking the Golden Valley. The beamed bar is full of character, with three areas for drinking and taking advantage of the extensive menu which is also served in the cosy restaurant. The well equipped bedrooms are located in a separate building across the car park.

12 bth/shr (1 fmly) No smoking in dining room CTV in all bedrooms Tea and coffee making facilities Direct dial from bedrooms Cen ht 50P No coaches Last d 10pm

ROOMS: s £39; d £59; wkly b&b £273; wkly hlf-bd £378*

MEALS: Lunch £4.95-£15&alc Dinner £4.95-£15&alc*

CARDS: MasterCard, American Express, Visa, Switch

SEQUOIA HOUSE HOTEL

51 Shipston Road
Stratford-upon-Avon
CV37 7LN
Tel: (01789) 268852
Fax (01789) 414559

Superbly situated across the River Avon opposite the Theatre. Beautifully appointed private hotel accommodation with friendly personal; attention of resident proprietors. Residential lounge with licensed bar and open Victorian fireplace. All 24 bedrooms have colour television, tea/coffee facilities, shaver point, central heating and direct dial telephone. Most bedrooms have private bathroom/shower/wc.

- **Fully Air Conditioned Dining Room**

Large private car park and beautifully mature gardens in which stands the "Sequoia" tree that gives the house its name – a delightful garden walk leads to the theatre. Riverside gardens, Shakespeare Properties, Shops and Leisure complex.

http://www.stratford-upon-avon.co.uk/sequoia.htm

Victoria Spa Lodge

Paul and Dreen Tozer.

BISHOPTON LANE, STRATFORD-UPON-AVON, WARWICKSHIRE CV37 9QY

Tel: 01789 267985 & 204728 Fax: 01789 204728

http://www.scoot.co.uk/victoria_spa/

E-mail: ptozer@victoriaspalodge.demon.co.uk

Victoria Spa Lodge was opened in 1837. A Grade II listed building in a peaceful setting overlooking the Stratford-upon-Avon canal. Named after the then Princess Victoria, her coat of Arms can still be seen built into the gables of the building.

The lodge has seven well appointed ensuite bedrooms. Facilities include colour TV, hairdryers, radio alarm and hostess trays.

Breakfast is served in a large elegant dining room.

Completely non-smoking, no pets.

Ample car parking.

AA QQQQ Selected

English Tourist Board HIGHLY COMMENDED

VISA MASTERCARD EUROCARD accepted

Q Q Q ***Downfield Hotel*** 134 Caincross Rd GL5 4HN
(2m W on A419 from Stroud town. or 5 miles East from M5 junct 13)
☎ 01453 764496 FAX 01453 753150
Closed 2 wks Xmas & New Year
This comfortable, medium sized hotel is ideal for the tourist and business visitor alike. The bedrooms are well appointed and offer modern facilities. There is a lounge bar and a dining room where freshly cooked food is served.
21 rms (11 bth/shr) (4 fmly) CTV in 17 bedrooms Tea and coffee making facilities Direct dial from bedrooms Licensed Cen ht CTV 25P No coaches Last d 8pm
CARDS:

Selected

Q Q Q Q **Hunters Lodge** Dr Browns Rd, Minchinhampton GL6 9BT ☎ 01453 883588 FAX 01453 731449
Closed Xmas
Situated on the edge of Minchinhampton Common, this impressive Victorian Cotswold-stone house is conveniently situated for the towns of Stroud and Cirencester. Margaret and Peter Helm are friendly and caring hosts, justly proud of their home which offers spacious comfortable public rooms with some nice period pieces and spacious bedrooms with lots of homely extras including personal dressing gowns.
3 bth/shr (1 fmly) No smoking CTV in all bedrooms Tea and coffee making facilities No dogs Cen ht CTV No children 10yrs 8P No coaches Golf 18
ROOMS: s £26-£30; d £40-£46

STUDLEY Warwickshire Map **04** SP06

Q Q Q ***Ardendane Manor*** Henley Rd, Outhill B80 7DT
(on A4189 halfway between Redditch and Henley-in-Arden)
☎ 01527 852808
Closed 24 Dec-1 Jan
Dating from the 1930s, this lovely house stands in 25 acres of grounds. It has been extensively renovated by the present owners, and provides well equipped accommodation, currently comprising a room in the main house and another in the grounds. All guests share one table in the charming breakfast room, which overlooks the garden.
1 bth/shr 1 annexe shr No smoking CTV in all bedrooms Tea and coffee making facilities No dogs Cen ht No children 10P No coaches Last d 1pm

STURMINSTER NEWTON Dorset Map **03** ST71

Q Q Q **Holebrook** *(ST743117)* Lydlinch DT10 2JB
☎ 01258 817348 FAX 817747 Mr C Wingate-Saul
2 Jan-24 Dec
Holebrook Farm has a wealth of facilities available to guests. Bedrooms are located in converted farm buildings adjacent to the main house. They have been sympathetically renovated and individually furnished. Several are equipped for families and disabled guests. All benefit from mini kitchens and their own sitting rooms.
2 rms (1 bth/shr) 4 annexe rms (3 bth/shr) No smoking in dining room No smoking in 1 lounge CTV in 4 bedrooms Tea and coffee making facilities No dogs (ex guide dogs) Licensed Cen ht CTV 12P Outdoor swimming pool Games room Mini-gym 126 acres mixed Last d 4pm
ROOMS: s fr £34; d fr £46*

Selected

Q Q Q Q **Stourcastle Lodge** Goughs Close DT10 1BU
(small lane off Town Square opposite Cross)
☎ 01258 472320 FAX 01258 473381
This lovely house is quietly tucked away just opposite the market square. Owners Jill and Ken Hookham-Bassett provide a warm welcome. The property has been skilfully renovated to provide five delightful bedrooms that are individually and traditionally decorated with beautiful brass bedsteads and antique pine furnishings; they have modern bathrooms, some with whirlpool tubs. Jill is a talented cook and provides a hearty breakfast with home made bread and preserves. Guests can enjoy the peace of the pretty walled garden (complete with dovecot) which provides the herbs and vegetables that Jill uses to prepare dinner.
5 bth/shr No smoking in bedrooms No smoking in dining room CTV in all bedrooms Tea and coffee making facilities Direct dial from bedrooms No dogs (ex guide dogs) Cen ht 8P No coaches Last d 7pm
ROOMS: s £35-£44; d £55-£70; wkly b&b £173.25-£220.50; wkly hlf-bd £280.35-£327.60*
CARDS:

STURTON BY STOW Lincolnshire Map **08** SK88

Selected

Q Q Q Q **Gallows Dale Farm** *(SK874809)* Stow Park Rd LN1 2AH (From Lincoln A57 to Saxilby turn right onto B1241 to Sturton By Stow, turn left to A1500, 1 mile on right hand side)
☎ 01427 788387 FAX 01427 788387 Mrs B Williams
This attractive 18th-century farmhouse has been sympathetically restored and extended to emphasise its original features. The bedrooms are decorated and furnished to a high standard and offer comfort and countryside views; two rooms have four-poster beds. There is a cosy guest lounge and a hearty farmhouse breakfast is served in the dining room. The house is no-smoking.
3 rms (2 shr) (1 fmly) No smoking CTV in 1 bedroom Tea and coffee making facilities No dogs Cen ht CTV 5P 33 acres cattle & horses
ROOMS: s £20-£25; d £36-£40*

SUDBURY Suffolk Map 05 TL84

Q Q Q ***Hill Lodge Private Hotel*** 8 Newton Rd CO10 6RL
(on A134 Colchester/Ipswich road - as approaching Sudbury town, left hand side. 2 mins walk from town, bus & rail station)
☎ 01787 377568 or 373636 FAX 373636
Closed Christmas week
Jim and Anita French run this hotel which offers attractive, well equipped rooms. There is a spacious bar and lounge area, with evening meals served in the bright dining room. Popular with local businesses, the smart conference facilities have been recently refurbished, and weddings ceremonies can be performed and catered for.
17 rms (7 shr) No smoking in dining room CTV in all bedrooms Direct dial from bedrooms No dogs (ex guide dogs) Licensed Cen ht CTV 27P No coaches
CARDS:

Q Q Q **Old Bull Hotel & Restaurant** Church St CO10 6BL
(On main A131 Halstead Rd. 0.25 mile from town centre)
☎ 01787 374120 FAX 01787 379044
Located on the Chelmsford road near the town centre, this 16th-century coaching inn offers a friendly relaxed atmosphere, combined with useful amenities. Public areas include a cosy residents' lounge, and a small bar linked to the elegant and popular restaurant.
7 rms (5 bth/shr) 2 annexe bth/shr (4 fmly) No smoking in area of dining room CTV in all bedrooms Tea and coffee making facilities Direct dial from bedrooms Licensed Cen ht 15P No coaches Last d 7.30pm
ROOMS: s £27.50-£38; d £40-£54
CARDS:

SULHAMSTEAD Berkshire Map 04 SU66

Premier Selected

Q Q Q Q Q **The Old Manor** Whitehouse Green, Sulhamstead RG7 4EA (M4 junct 2, A4 west left for Theale Station, over railway turn right 0.75 miles to crossroads turn left and Old Manor entrance on left)
☎ 01189 832423
This fine period manor house is situated near the village of Sulhamstead. The house is set in over 4 acres with well cared for gardens. Both bedrooms are elegantly furnished, one has a four-poster bed and a spa bath. Afternoon tea can be taken in the drawing room; good food and a complimentary glass of wine are on offer at dinner in the dining room. Breakfast is served in the cosy second dining room.
2 bth/shr No smoking No dogs Cen ht CTV No children 8yrs 8P Bowls Volley ball Last d previous day
ROOMS: s £50; d £70; wkly b&b £350*

See advertisement under READING

407

SURBITON Greater London Map 04 TQ16

Q Q **Warwick** 321 Ewell Rd KT6 7BX
(Turn off A3 onto A240 towards Kingston. Warwick Guesthouse is half a mile on the right)
☎ 0181 296 0516 FAX 0181 296 0517
This guest house has mostly single rooms which are attentively decorated and well equipped. Several rooms have integral showers, one room is en suite. The Warwick is well located for access to Kingston and the A3.
9 rms (1 bth/shr) (1 fmly) CTV in all bedrooms Tea and coffee making facilities Direct dial from bedrooms Cen ht CTV 8P
ROOMS: s £32-£38; d £42-£48; wkly b&b £175-£200
CARDS:

See advertisement on p.409.

SUTTON Greater London Map 04 TQ26

Selected

Q Q Q Q ***Ashling Tara Hotel*** 50 Rosehill SM1 3EU
(opposite Rose Hill Park, on A297) ☎ 0181 641 6142
FAX 0181 644 7872
A well established family run property which has gained a loyal following over the years. The bedrooms are split between the main building and a separate house, all are smartly decorated and well equipped. The spacious public areas include a cosy lounge, a well stocked bar and a dining room serving good home cooked food.
14 bth/shr (2 fmly) No smoking in 2 bedrooms CTV in 16 bedrooms Tea and coffee making facilities Direct dial from bedrooms No dogs Licensed Cen ht CTV 25P Hard tennis courts available in park opposite Last d 8.45pm
CARDS:

SUTTON West Sussex Map **04** SU91

Premier Selected

QQQQQ **The White Horse** RH20 1PS
(turn off A29 at foot of Bury Hill. After 2m pass Roman Villa on right. Follow road 1m to Sutton) ☎ 01798 869221 FAX 01798 869291
The White Horse is a charming Georgian country inn hidden away in the peaceful South Downs Village of Sutton. The six bedrooms, each with their own bathroom, are traditionally furnished and combine a cottagey feel with modern comforts and extras such as fresh flowers, magazines and mineral water. Five of the rooms are in the main building, and the garden cottage is hidden away at the end of a pathway. A wide choice of home cooked food is offered in the restaurant and guests can choose from a frequently changing blackboard menu. A good selection of wines is also available.
5 bth No smoking in bedrooms CTV in all bedrooms Tea and coffee making facilities Direct dial from bedrooms No dogs Cen ht 10P No coaches Last d 9.30pm
ROOMS: s £48; d £58-£68; wkly b&b £134-£218*
MEALS: Lunch £11.20-£24alc Dinner £11.20-£24alc*
CARDS:

SUTTON COLDFIELD West Midlands Map **07** SP19

QQ **Standbridge Hotel** 138 Birmingham Rd B72 1LY (1m S on A5127) ☎ 0121 354 3007
This large Edwardian house, with its pleasant rear garden stands just one mile south of Sutton Coldfield town centre. It provides modern accommodation, including a bedroom on ground floor level. Separate tables are provided in the traditionally furnished dining room and there is a comfortable, homely lounge.
8 rms (5 shr) No smoking in 6 bedrooms No smoking in dining room No smoking in lounges CTV in all bedrooms Tea and coffee making facilities Licensed Cen ht CTV No children 5yrs 8P No coaches Jacuzzi Spa bath Last d 6pm
ROOMS: s £23-£28.50; d £42*
CARDS:

QQQ **Windrush** 337 Birmingham Rd, Wylde Freen B72 1DL
(On main A5127 to Sutton Coldfield from Birmingham. House immediately before Doctors' Surgery, "The Hawthorns" on right hand side) ☎ 0121 384 7534
Closed 20 Dec-2 Jan
Located between Sutton Coldfield and the city centre, this house offers accommodation for both the business and leisure traveller. Bedrooms are comfortable, well equipped and tastefully decorated. Lynne Bridgwater is a very friendly and caring hostess as well as an excellent cook.
3 rms No smoking CTV in all bedrooms Tea and coffee making facilities No dogs Cen ht No children 5P No coaches Last d 6pm
ROOMS: s £23; d £46; wkly b&b £161; wkly hlf-bd £213.50*

SUTTON MANDEVILLE Wiltshire Map **03** ST92

QQQ **The Lancers** SP3 5NL (on A30 midway between Salisbury and Shaftesbury, directly opposite the Sutton Mandeville Hillside Chalk Badges) ☎ 01722 714220
Situated midway between Salisbury and Shaftesbury, this family run freehouse is the ideal place to break a journey to the West Country or as a base to explore the Dorset and Wiltshire countryside. Bedrooms are neatly presented and well equipped. In addition to the convivial bar, there is a spacious restaurant and comfortable lounge.
4 shr (2 fmly) No smoking in 2 bedrooms No smoking in area of dining room No smoking in 1 lounge CTV in all bedrooms Tea and coffee making facilities Direct dial from bedrooms Cen ht 40P Snooker table Darts Video machines. Last d 9pm
ROOMS: s £25-£30; d £40-£45*
MEALS: Lunch £8-£18.50&alc Dinner £8-£18.50&alc*
CARDS:

CLOSED

SUTTON UPON DERWENT East Riding of Yorkshire Map **08** SE74

QQQ **Manor Farmhouse** Main St YO41 4BN (7.5m S of York off B1228. Follow B1228 through Elvington over stone bridge to Sutton upon Derwent, on right next to church) ☎ 01904 608009
Next to the church in the delightful village of Sutton upon Derwent, this well furnished house provides pleasant bedrooms and a cosy lounge. Very friendly service is provided by the resident owner, Diana Arnold and a well produced and hearty breakfast is served in the cosy dining room around a large table.
3 shr No smoking CTV in all bedrooms Tea and coffee making facilities No dogs (ex guide dogs) Cen ht CTV 6P No coaches Riding & golf arranged locally Fishing
ROOMS: s £25; d £40-£45*
See advertisement under YORK

SWAFFHAM Norfolk Map **05** TF80

Selected

QQQQ **Corfield House** Sporle PE32 2EA (3m E, of Swaffham on S edge of village, 0.5m from A47) ☎ 01760 723636
end Mar-mid Dec
A warm, friendly welcome is on offer from Mr and Mrs Hickey at this charming guest house, which is situated in the peaceful village of Sporle close to the market town of Swaffham. The bedrooms are individually decorated, maintained to a high standard and equipped with a range of useful extras. The public rooms comprise a comfortable, tastefully furnished lounge with an array of books maps and games and a neat dining room, where guests can enjoy a freshly prepared four course dinner, by prior arrangement. Mr Hickey is chairman of the local tourist board and is always pleased to pass on his knowledge of the area.
4 bth/shr No smoking CTV in all bedrooms Tea and coffee making facilities No dogs (ex guide dogs) Licensed Cen ht 5P No coaches Last d 5.30pm
ROOMS: d £37-£43; wkly b&b £129.50-£150.50; wkly hlf-bd £205-£220
CARDS:

QQQ ***Red Lion Hotel*** 87 Market Place PE37 7AQ
(Off A47 at Swaffham sign, all roads to market place. Red Lion on market place- next to Woolworths) ☎ 01760 721022
This is a popular, centrally located public house with a cheerful team of staff. Motel-style accommodation is located to the rear of the pub. Bedrooms are bright and colourfully furnished, each with a shower room; a few bedrooms are designed to take family groups.
9 annexe shr CTV in all bedrooms Tea and coffee making facilities No dogs (ex guide dogs) Cen ht 8P Last d 9.30pm
CARDS:

SWANAGE Dorset Map **04** SZ07

Q Q Q **Bella Vista Hotel** 14 Burlington Rd BH19 1LS (from A351 travel towards Studland, take 2nd right opposite Crows Nest PH. Bella Vista is next to Grand Hotel) ☎ 01929 422873
Apr-Oct Closed Nov-Jan rs Feb-Mar
Situated off a tree-lined road in a quiet part of Swanage, this smart and friendly guest house is just five minutes from the beach. As the name suggests, there are wonderful views across the bay from some of the attractively decorated bedrooms, and the dining room where freshly prepared meals are served.
7 bth/shr (4 fmly) No smoking CTV in all bedrooms Tea and coffee making facilities No dogs Licensed Cen ht 7P No coaches Last d 10am
ROOMS: s £20.50-£24.50; d £41-£49; wkly b&b £129-£154; wkly hlf-bd £198-£217*

Q Q Q **Burlington House Hotel** 7 Highcliffe Rd BH19 1LW ☎ 01929 422422
This friendly hotel overlooks Swanage Bay and is a short distance from the beach and town centre. The bedrooms are brightly decorated, and suitably furnished and equipped. A set dinner menu and a good choice at breakfast is offered, and served in the attractive dining room. There is a nicely appointed lounge and a small cosy bar.
8 rms (7 bth/shr) (6 fmly) No smoking in dining room CTV in all bedrooms Tea and coffee making facilities No dogs (ex guide dogs) Licensed Cen ht CTV No children 6yrs 8P Last d 5pm
ROOMS: s £20-£22; d £44-£48; wkly b&b £118-£168; wkly hlf-bd £188-£238
CARDS:

Q Q Q **Chines Hotel** 9 Burlington Rd BH19 1LR ☎ 01929 422457
2 Mar-2 Oct
This family run hotel has a cheerful atmosphere and offers bright rooms, most with en suite facilities. There is a cosy lounge and a well stocked bar, and good home cooked meals are served in the smart dining room.
12 rms (9 shr) (4 fmly) No smoking in bedrooms No smoking in dining room No smoking in 1 lounge CTV in all bedrooms Tea and coffee making facilities No dogs Licensed Cen ht CTV 10P Last d 4pm
ROOMS: s fr £18; d fr £41; wkly b&b fr £126*

Q Q **Cluny Croft** 19 Cluny Crescent BH19 2BP (Follow one-way system to pier, turn right after zebra crossing into Taunton Rd. Est at top of hill) ☎ 01929 424322
Closed Dec
Set high above the town, with wonderful views, and only a short stroll from the beach, Cluny Croft is a comfortable hotel that attracts many returning visitors. The hospitable owners are particularly children friendly and welcome families wholeheartedly. Good home cooked food is served in the dining room and guests have use of a small bar.
3 bth/shr No smoking in dining room CTV in all bedrooms Tea and coffee making facilities No dogs (ex guide dogs) Cen ht CTV No children 3P
ROOMS: d £40-£48*

Q Q Q **Eversden Private Hotel** 5 Victoria Rd BH19 1LY (follow Swanage to Studland road past Ferry Boat Inn. Third road on the right past the Ferry Boat Inn) ☎ 01929 423276 FAX 01929 427755
Pleasantly located in a quiet residential area, this hotel offers a high standard of accommodation. Bedrooms are brightly decorated and thoughtfully furnished. There is a comfortable lounge and bar, and an attractive dining room with separate tables. Evening meals are served and packed lunches are available.
13 rms (2 bth 5 shr) (3 fmly) No smoking in bedrooms No smoking in dining room No smoking in 1 lounge CTV in 10 bedrooms Tea and coffee making facilities No dogs (ex guide dogs) Licensed Cen ht CTV 12P No coaches Last d 2pm
ROOMS: s £18-£25; d £36-£50; wkly b&b £120-£165; wkly hlf-bd £200-£250*
CARDS:

Q Q Q **Firswood Hotel** 29 Kings Rd BH19 1HF (take the Swanage road from Wareham. 2 minutes from town centre, opposite Health Centre) ☎ 01929 422306
Closed Dec
Mr and Mrs Baker take delight in welcoming guests to their hotel which is just a short walk from the town centre and seafront. The Firswood is both bright and well maintained and offers comfortable and cheery bedrooms. Breakfast is served in the pretty dining room and a guest lounge is available.
6 rms (2 bth 3 shr) (2 fmly) No smoking in dining room CTV in all bedrooms Tea and coffee making facilities No dogs Cen ht CTV No children 5yrs 7P No coaches
ROOMS: s £16-£17; d £32-£36; wkly b&b £112-£126

Q Q Q **St Michael Hotel** 31 Kings Rd BH19 1HF (Swanage Town Centre opposite bus station) ☎ 01929 422064
Closed Xmas
This friendly, family run guest house is conveniently close to the town centre and seafront. The attractively decorated bedrooms are comfortably appointed. There is a cosy lounge in which guests can relax, and an evening meal is available with a choice of menus.
5 shr (3 fmly) No smoking in dining room CTV in all bedrooms Tea and coffee making facilities Licensed Cen ht CTV No children 5yrs 5P No coaches Last d 2pm

Q Q Q **Sandringham Hotel** 20 Durlston Rd BH19 2HX (follow signs for Durlston Country Park) ☎ 01929 423076 FAX 01929 423076
Peacefully located high above the town, this family run private hotel offers brightly decorated and well equipped bedrooms. An evening meal is available, served in the well appointed dining room, there is also a comfortable lounge and small conservatory bar.
11 rms (9 shr) (5 fmly) No smoking in dining room CTV in 6 bedrooms Tea and coffee making facilities No dogs (ex guide dogs) Licensed Cen ht CTV 8P No coaches Last d 6pm
ROOMS: s £23-£27; d £46-£54; wkly b&b £155-£180; wkly hlf-bd £199-£228
CARDS:

Q Q Q **White Lodge Hotel** Grosvenor Rd BH19 2DD (Along seafront turn right before pier into Seymer Rd heading into Durlston Rd, hotel on corner of Durlston Rd & Grosvenor Rd) ☎ 01929 422696 FAX 01929 425510
rs Dec-Feb
Many of the rooms at this impressively refurbished hotel have superb views across the bay. All offer a combination of space and comfort. In addition to a choice of lounges, guests have use of the conservatory. Dinner is available, if required, with dishes displaying imagination and skill.
13 bth/shr (3 fmly) No smoking in bedrooms No smoking in dining room No smoking in 1 lounge CTV in all bedrooms Tea and coffee making facilities Licensed Cen ht CTV No children 4yrs 12P Last d 6.30pm
ROOMS: s £23-£27; d £46-£54; wkly b&b £140-£165;
wkly hlf-bd £205-£265
CARDS:

SWAY Hampshire Map **04** SZ29

Premier Selected

Q Q Q Q Q **The Nurse's Cottage** Station Rd
SO41 6BA (off B3055 in village next to post office)
☎ 01590 683402 FAX 01590 683402
Closed 15 Nov-15 Dec
Tony Barnfield continues to improve this delightful guest house that was once the District Nurse's cottage. The bedrooms are comfortable and come with many welcome extras such as biscuits, chocolates, fruit and fresh flowers. A fridge with mineral water, fruit juices and fresh milk is provided in each room. The quality en suite bathrooms feature lovely toiletries and good fluffy towels. Guests can enjoy Tony's excellent home cooking (now available to non-residents) in The Garden Room which also serves as the lounge. Meals are backed up by a very respectable wine list. In summer guests can enjoy a drink in the pretty garden.
3 bth/shr No smoking CTV in all bedrooms Tea and coffee making facilities Direct dial from bedrooms Licensed Cen ht No children 10yrs 4P No coaches Last d 8pm
ROOMS: s £50-£60; d £85; wkly b&b £297.50-£420;
wkly hlf-bd £315-£437.50
CARDS:

See advertisement under LYMINGTON

SWINDERBY Lincolnshire Map **08** SK86

Q Q Q ***Halfway Farm Motel & Guest House*** A46 LN6 9HN
(8m N of Newark on A46, 8m SW Lincoln)
☎ 01522 868749 FAX 01522 868082
This 300-year-old farmhouse combines the old with the new. There are some traditional bedrooms in the main house and contemporary rooms in a modern motel block to the rear. The accommodation is well furnished and thoughtfully equipped, and good breakfasts are served in one of the two cosy dining rooms; a comfortable lounge is also provided for guests.
7 rms (5 shr) 10 annexe shr (3 fmly) No smoking in dining room CTV in all bedrooms Tea and coffee making facilities Direct dial from bedrooms Cen ht CTV 20P No coaches
CARDS:

SWINDON Wiltshire Map **04** SU18

Q Q Q **Fir Tree Lodge** 17 Highworth Rd, Stratton St Margaret SN3 4QL (opposite 'The Rat Trap' public house. Follow A419 until Highworth/Burford turn right at rdbt Fir Tree Lodge 100yds on right) ☎ 01793 822372
Comfortable and well appointed accommodation is offered by owners Mr & Mrs Duggan at their well maintained and friendly guest house. The colourful bedrooms are furnished in modern style and are suitably equipped. A choice of breakfast is offered, served in the attractive dining room.
11 shr No smoking in 6 bedrooms CTV in all bedrooms Tea and coffee making facilities No dogs (ex guide dogs) Cen ht 14P No coaches
ROOMS: s £25-£30; d £40-£47*

Q Q ***Grove Lodge*** 108 Swindon Rd, Stratton St Margaret SN3 4PT (turn off A417 to Stratton St Margaret, follow to Swindon town centre, house on right after a mile) ☎ 01793 825343 FAX 01793 825343
Comfortable accommodation is offered at this family run guest house in Stratton St Margaret. Bedrooms are all en suite and are equipped with satellite TV and tea trays.
10 bth/shr (2 fmly) No smoking in dining room No smoking in lounges CTV in all bedrooms Tea and coffee making facilities Cen ht 12P

Selected

Q Q Q Q **Portquin** Highworth Rd, Blunsdon SN2 4DH
(turn off A419 at Blunsdon onto B4019 signposted Highworth, half a mile from A419) ☎ 01793 721261 FAX 01793 721261
Portquin is a comfortable family run guest house only a short drive from Swindon. It has views to the Berkshire Downs and the surrounding countryside. The rooms here are all well equipped, warm and comfortable, and some are very spacious. There is an attractive open plan dining room which also has a pleasant and relaxing lounge area.
7 shr 3 annexe shr (2 fmly) No smoking in 6 bedrooms No smoking in dining room No smoking in lounges CTV in 9 bedrooms Tea and coffee making facilities Direct dial from bedrooms Cen ht 12P No coaches
ROOMS: s £28-£30; d £38-£45*

SYDLING ST NICHOLAS Dorset Map **03** SY69

Q Q Q **Lamperts Cottage** DT2 9NU
(from Dorchester A37 turn off right just beyond Grimstone, follow valley road to Sydling St Nicholas, Lamperts Cottage 1st thatched cottage on right)
☎ 01300 341659 FAX 01300 341699
This pretty 17th-century cottage is situated close to the historic town of Dorchester. Bedrooms are simply decorated and comfortably furnished.

Guests might enjoy the tranquility provided by the absence of TV. A choice of breakfasts, including home made jams and vegetarian options, is served in the cosy dining room.
3 rms No smoking in 3 bedrooms No smoking in dining room No smoking in lounges Tea and coffee making facilities Cen ht No children 8yrs 3P
ROOMS: s fr £25; d fr £40*

SYMONDS YAT (EAST) Herefordshire Map **03** SO51

Selected

QQQQ **Garth Cottage** HR9 6JL (turn off A40 at Little Chef, Whitchurch & follow signs for Symonds Yat East) ☎ 01600 890364
Apr-Oct
Situated in the heart of this renowned beauty spot overlooking the River Wye, Garth Cottage dates back to the 18th century and was once the post office in this tranquil community. Bedrooms are comfortable, well equipped and extras include modern en suite facilities and little touches to enhance guests' comfort. Public areas include a small well stocked bar, a sun lounge and a comfortable sitting room. Home cooked breakfasts, and dinner by arrangement, are served in the attractive dining room overlooking the river towards Symonds Yat West.
4 shr No smoking in dining room Tea and coffee making facilities No dogs (ex guide dogs) Licensed Cen ht CTV No children 12yrs 9P No coaches Fishing Last d 3pm
ROOMS: d £46; wkly b&b £120; wkly hlf-bd £228.50*

TAMWORTH Staffordshire Map **04** SK20

QQ **Broadfields Farm** *(SK211125)* Pessal Ln, Edingale B79 9JW (Off A513 towards Croxall, take first right towards Edingale. Entering the village turn left into Pessall Lane and continue to first farm on right) ☎ 01827 383225 0385 917824 Mrs K Cliffe
Parts of this farmhouse date back to the 17th century. The accommodation consists of one twin and one double bedded room. All share one table in the cosy combined lounge and breakfast room.
3 rms (1 bth 1 shr) (1 fmly) No smoking Tea and coffee making facilities No dogs (ex guide dogs) Cen ht CTV ch fac P 650 acres arable sheep horses
ROOMS: s £20-£22.50; d £35-£40; wkly b&b £130-£140*

QQQ **Harlaston Post Office** Main Rd, Harlaston B79 9JU (turn off M42/A42 at junct 11 onto B5453 to No Man's Heath, turn right for Clifton Campuille and then straight on for Haunton and Harlaston) ☎ 01827 383324
This pleasant little guest house shares the same premises as the post office in the village of Harlaston. The soundly maintained accommodation consists of a twin room plus a two bedroom family suite. All guests share one table in the breakfast room, which has an adjacent conservatory lounge.
4 bth/shr (1 fmly) No smoking in dining room No smoking in lounges CTV in all bedrooms Tea and coffee making facilities Direct dial from bedrooms No dogs Cen ht CTV 3P No coaches
ROOMS: s £20-£22.50; d £34-£40; wkly b&b £105-£140*

Premier Selected

QQQQQ ***Oak Tree Farm*** *(SK180047)* Hints Rd, Hopwas B78 3AA (take A51 Lichfield to Tamworth road and turn in to Hints Road at the Tame Otter public house. Last house on left where road divides) ☎ 01827 56807 FAX 01827 56807 Mrs S Purkis
This renovated farmhouse is set in spacious gardens overlooking the River Tame. Bedrooms are comfortably furnished and contain many thoughtful extras. Two rooms are located in the main house while others are in a converted grain store and shed. There is a spacious lounge, as well as a breakfast room where separate tables are provided.

2 bth/shr 5 annexe bth/shr (3 fmly) No smoking in bedrooms CTV in all bedrooms Tea and coffee making facilities Cen ht CTV No children 6yrs 10P Indoor swimming pool (heated) Fishing 4 acres ducks hens

QQQ **The Old Rectory** Churchside, Harlaston B79 9HE (situated in the centre of Harlaston village 4.5m N of Tamworth) ☎ 01827 383583 FAX 01827 383583
This large early Victorian rectory, surrounded by over an acre of mature gardens, is in the centre of the village of Harlaston, four and a half miles north of Tamworth. The house, which is no smoking throughout, provides modern accommodation, including two rooms which can be let as a family suite with its own private bathroom. The breakfast room overlooks a pleasant patio, which guests are welcome to use.
4 rms (1 shr) No smoking CTV in all bedrooms Tea and coffee making facilities Cen ht 7P No coaches
ROOMS: s £18-£20; d £36-£40; wkly b&b £119-£133
CARDS:

QQQ The Sleepy Owl 20 Church Ln, Edingale B79 9JD (from Tamworth take Wigginton Rd to Harlaston and turn left at White Lion pub for Edingale, right over bridge and left at Black Horse pub) ☎ 01827 383436 & 383853

This modern detached house is quietly located in a cul-de-sac in the village of Edingale, about 5 miles north of Tamworth. It provides modern furnished and equipped accommodation, which is soundly maintained. There is a spacious and comfortable lounge, plus a pleasant breakfast room where separate tables are provided.

2 rms No smoking in bedrooms No smoking in dining room CTV in all bedrooms Tea and coffee making facilities Direct dial from bedrooms No dogs (ex guide dogs) Cen ht CTV No children 16yrs 3P No coaches Last d 8pm

ROOMS: s £20; d £33-£35*

TAUNTON Somerset Map 03 ST22

See also Burrowbridge & Churchinford

Premier Selected

QQQQQ ❦ **Allerford Farm** *(ST183249)* Norton Fitzwarren TA4 1AL (from Taunton on B3227, go through village, over railway bridge, take first turning left signposted Allerford. Follow this road for 1m to T junction) ☎ 01823 461210 FAX 01823 461210

Mr & Mrs M James

Surrounded by rolling countryside, the farm dates back 300 years. Every room has received the same care and attention to detail, resulting in a house which combines comfort with style. The oak staircase leads to two enchanting bedrooms adorned with carefully chosen fabrics and fine furniture. Very much a working farm, Mr James has devoted equal care and attention to his prize winning Heritage Herd, currently the third highest milk yielders in the country. Breakfast is served in the elegant dining room, where the pervading sense of quality is again evident. Dinner is available by arrangement.

2 bth/shr No smoking CTV in all bedrooms Tea and coffee making facilities No dogs Cen ht No children 10yrs 4P 200 acres Dairy Last d 4pm

ROOMS: s £30-£35; d £50-£60; wkly b&b £155-£180*

Selected

QQQQ Beaufort Lodge 18 Wellington Rd TA1 4EQ (M5 junct 25, follow A38 through town. It becomes Wellington Rd and house on right) ☎ 01823 326420 FAX 01823 326420

This Victorian house, within five minutes level walk of the town centre, has recently been upgraded to a high standard. The bedrooms have been tastefully decorated and equipped with modern facilities and thoughtful touches like sweets, biscuits and fresh flowers. There is a charming dining room overlooking the garden, where home cooked breakfasts are served. Pauline and Brian Adams invite guests to enjoy the relaxed atmosphere of Beaufort Lodge.

3 shr No smoking CTV in all bedrooms Tea and coffee making facilities No dogs (ex guide dogs) Cen ht No children 16yrs 6P No coaches

ROOMS: s £30; d £50*

QQQ Blorenge House 57 Staple Grove TA1 1DG (M5 junct 25 head to cricket ground which is on left through traffic lights, at 2nd set turn left, then right at next lights, hotel is 300yds on left) ☎ 01823 283005 FAX 01823 283005

This substantial Victorian gothic-style property is within walking distance of the town centre. Bedrooms are individually furnished and decorated, some have four-poster beds. A comfortable bar-lounge is available for guests. During the summer months, wedding receptions are held in the gardens.

22 rms (17 shr) (4 fmly) No smoking in 2 bedrooms No smoking in dining room CTV in all bedrooms Tea and coffee making facilities Licensed Cen ht CTV 22P Outdoor swimming pool (heated) Last d 10am

CARDS:

QQQ Brookfield 16 Wellington Rd TA1 4EQ (just out of town on A38) ☎ 01823 272786 FAX 01823 326420

This neat property, within a five minute level walk of the town centre, offers well equipped bedrooms and a relaxed and friendly atmosphere. Breakfast is served in the spacious dining room, where there is also some comfortable seating for guests.

8 rms (6 bth/shr) (2 fmly) No smoking in 2 bedrooms No smoking in dining room CTV in all bedrooms Tea and coffee making facilities Cen ht 8P No coaches

ROOMS: s £20-£25; d £40*

QQQ The Coach House Pitminster TA3 7AZ (M5 junct25 to Taunton, left following racecourse signs at crossroads/lights, right at White Hart, continue to Queens Arms, 1st house on right) ☎ 01823 421571

The Coach House is peacefully located in the small village of Pitminster. Bedrooms are spacious, decorated and furnished in a country style. Guests breakfast around a large table in the dining room, adjacent to the charming sitting room with French windows opening onto the neatly tended gardens.

4 rms (2 bth/shr) (1 fmly) CTV in all bedrooms Cen ht CTV 4P No coaches

ROOMS: s £17.50-£20; d £35-£40*

Selected

QQQQ Creechbarn Vicarage Ln, Creech-St-Michael TA3 5PP (exit M5 junct25 onto A358. Turn to Creech St Michael via Ruishton. Follow canal boat signs to end of Vicarage Lane) ☎ 01823 443955 FAX 01823 443955

Closed 15 Dec-15 Jan

A warm welcome is extended to visitors by Hope and Mick Humphreys, who run this lovingly converted stone-built Longbarn, surrounded by nearly an acre of well tended gardens. It has access to the Taunton/Bridgwater canal. The two bedrooms have been comfortably furnished and there is a studio sitting room where books, table tennis and a television are provided for guests. Dinner and breakfast are taken around one large table.

2 bth/shr No smoking in bedrooms No smoking in dining room Tea and coffee making facilities Cen ht CTV ch fac 4P No coaches Last d breakfast

ROOMS: s £20-£27; d £36-£40*

Premier Selected

QQQQQ **Cutsey House** Cutsey, Trull TA3 7NY (M5 junct 26, take West Buckland turning and after 0.5 mile turn right at T-junction. Take 2nd turning left adjacent motorway bridge. House on right) ☎ 01823 421705 FAX 01823 421294 Etr-Xmas
Set in the midst of over twenty acres of gardens and grounds, Cutsey House is just a short drive from Taunton. Many of the original 15th and 16th century features have been retained. Glorious views can be had from the spacious bedrooms. Dinner is available by arrangement, and drinks can be enjoyed in the library.
3 bth/shr (1 fmly) No smoking in 1 bedrooms No smoking in dining room CTV in all bedrooms No dogs Cen ht CTV 11P No coaches Riding Snooker Last d 5pm
ROOMS: s £30-£35; d £45-£55; wkly b&b £115-£210; wkly hlf-bd £175-£270

Selected

QQQQ ***Forde House*** 9 Upper High St TA1 3PX (on A38 in town centre) ☎ 01823 279042 FAX 01823 279042 Closed Xmas & New Year
This elegant Georgian property with a secluded garden at the rear, has been carefully renovated and provides spacious bedrooms now tastefully decorated and comfortably furnished. Downstairs, the drawing room has access to the garden, and the breakfast room boasts an inglenook fireplace. Breakfasts are substantial; a wide range of freshly prepared hot and cold items is always on offer. 5 bth/shr No smoking in dining room CTV in all bedrooms Tea and coffee making facilities No dogs (ex guide dogs) Cen ht No children 10yrs 5P No coaches

Premier Selected

QQQQQ ***Heathfield Lodge*** Heathfield, Hillcommon TA4 1DN (from Taunton travel W, take B3227 towards Wiveliscombe, pass through Norton Fitzwarren and proceed for approx 2.5m, Heathfield is on the right) ☎ 01823 432286 Closed 20 Dec-2 Jan
Surrounded by five acres of beautiful landscaped gardens, this delightful Regency house is the family home of Sue and Phil Thornton. The coast and Exmoor National Park are within easy driving distance. Bedrooms are well equipped and there is a spacious guests' sitting room. Home cooked suppers are available and special diets can be catered for with adequate notice.
3 shr (5 fmly) No smoking CTV in all bedrooms Tea and coffee making facilities No dogs (ex guide dogs) Cen ht No children 16yrs 6P No coaches Snooker Croquet Last d 6.30pm

Selected

QQQQ ❦ **Higher Dipford** *(ST216205)* Trull TA3 7NU (from County Hall Taunton signed Trull, pass Queens College on Honiton Trull Rd, right to Dipford Rd, before the fork Higher Dipford Farm on right) ☎ 01823 275770 & 257916 Mrs M Fewings
This Grade II listed, 600-year-old long house is part of a working dairy farm. Only three miles from Taunton, it is well situated for both leisure and business guests. The comfortable en suite bedrooms are well equipped with large televisions, hairdryers and electric blankets. There is a large comfortable lounge with an inglenook fireplace and a cosy honesty bar for guests. In the attractive dining room where guests sit at one large table, Maureen Fewings serves excellent food.
3 bth/shr No smoking in bedrooms No smoking in dining room No smoking in 1 lounge CTV in all bedrooms Tea and coffee making facilities No dogs (ex guide dogs) Licensed Cen ht CTV 6P 120 acres beef dairy Last d 8pm
ROOMS: s £27-£30; d £50-£54
CARDS:

Q Q Q **Lower Farm** *(ST281241)* Thornfalcon TA3 5NR (2m SE from junct 25 M5 on A358 Ilminster/Yeovil Rd, turn left opposite Nags Head PH, Lower Farm in 1m on left hand side, signed on driveway) ☎ 01823 443549 FAX 01823 443549 Mrs D J Titman

A charming thatched farmhouse, with pretty garden, situated about three miles from the centre of Taunton. Owners, Doreen and John Titman, welcome guests to their peaceful retreat, with genuine friendliness. Bedrooms are attractively furnished and decorated. A hearty breakfast is served in the kitchen/dining room, with home produced eggs being especially popular. By prior arrangement, dinner is available. A comfortable sitting room, with a log fire on those cooler evenings is provided.

3 rms (2 bth) (1 fmly) No smoking No dogs CTV No children 4yrs 8P 10 acres beef cows poultry Last d 7.30pm

ROOMS: s £23; d £45; wkly b&b fr £140*

Selected

Q Q Q Q **Lower Marsh Farm** *(ST224279)* Kingston St Mary TA2 8AB (2m N of Taunton, between Taunton/Kingston-St-Mary) ☎ 01823 451331 Mr & Mrs J Gothard

At the foot of the Quantock Hills, Lower Marsh Farm has recently been lovingly refurbished. It is the family home of Richard and Jill Gothard, who thoroughly enjoy welcoming guests to their charming home. Bedrooms are attractively co-ordinated and equipped with modern facilities. Breakfast is served around a large table in the dining room, and by arrangement, a traditionally cooked evening meal is available. A comfortable drawing room is provided, with a log fire on cooler evenings.

3 bth/shr (1 fmly) No smoking CTV in all bedrooms Tea and coffee making facilities No dogs Cen ht CTV ch fac P 3/4 snooker table Croquet 300 acres arable beef sheep working Last d noon

CARDS:

The AA's professional Inspectors make regular and anonymous visits to all the establishments listed in the Guide. They accept no gifts or favours from proprietors

Selected

Q Q Q Q **Meryan House Hotel** Bishop's Hull TA1 5EG (take A38 from town towards Wellington. After crematorium on left take first right and house approx 600yds) ☎ 01823 337445 FAX 01823 322355

rs Sundays

Meryan House is over 350 years old and each bedroom has its own unique blend of period furniture and modern comforts. A selection of interesting dishes, carefully prepared by Mrs Clark, are available from a nicely balanced a la carte menu, which is extended by a choice of daily specials. The public areas include an attractive bar-lounge and a spacious and comfortable sitting room. All of this combined with friendly, yet efficient, service make this a special place to stay!

12 bth/shr (2 fmly) No smoking in 4 bedrooms No smoking in dining room No smoking in 1 lounge CTV in all bedrooms Tea and coffee making facilities Direct dial from bedrooms Licensed Cen ht CTV 17P No coaches Last d 7.30pm

ROOMS: s £40-£55; d £55-£65

CARDS:

Q Q Q **Old Wheelwrights** Stoneyhead, Wrantage TA3 6BZ (M5 junct 25 take A358 to Chard, approx 2m take A378 to Langport, 0.25m to Wrantage sign, house 1st on left) ☎ 01823 481047

Mar-Nov

An interesting history surrounds the charming home of Barry and Sharon Williams. Originally built some 200 years ago, this was, as the name suggests, the wheelwrights abode and workshop. More recently it was a pub, before last orders were called and the final pint was pulled! However the doors are once again open to customers of a different variety - those looking for a comfortable place to relax, enjoy genuine hospitality and explore the many and varied delights of the area. Two attractive and tastefully decorated bedrooms are available, together with a guest lounge. Breakfast is served in the intimate dining room, with eggs supplied by the resident chickens!

2 rms (1 fmly) No smoking in bedrooms No smoking in dining room No dogs Cen ht CTV No children 10yrs 3P No coaches

ROOMS: s fr £20; d fr £35; wkly b&b fr £140

Q Q Q **Pare Mill** Hagley Bridge, Hagley, Waterrow TA4 2AS (M5 junct 25-follow signs for Minehead A358 around outskirts of Taunton. At junct with A358 W, continue along B3227 to Wiveliscombe for 13m) ☎ 01984 623865

Closed 24-26 Dec

This is a 19th-century Mill House set in an area of outstanding natural beauty. The best possible use has been made of space in the bedrooms, which are neatly furnished and decorated. Evening meals are available on request, served around one large table and using excellent local produce. Home made marmalade, honey and home reared lamb are especially noteworthy here.

3 rms No smoking in bedrooms No smoking in dining room Tea and coffee making facilities Cen ht CTV ch fac 7P No coaches Fishing Walking in open country, Bird-watching Last d previous day

ROOMS: s fr £17; d fr £32; wkly b&b fr £105; wkly hlf-bd fr £164*

Selected

Q Q Q Q **The Spinney** Curland TA3 5SE (off A358, Taunton to Ilminster road) ☎ 01460 234362 FAX 01460 234362

The delightful family home of Ann and John Bartlett lies on the slopes of the Blackdowns, six miles from Taunton. The surroundings are rural and part of the charm of The Spinney is its peaceful location. The bedrooms are attractively decorated, comfortable and equipped with modern amenities. Two rooms are located on the ground floor, one being designed for the less able. An evening meal is available by prior arrangement, with a choice of either two or three courses.

Ann cooks using fresh local and home-grown produce whenever possible. Guests are welcome to bring their own wine to enjoy with the meal. During summer months, breakfast can be taken in the well tended gardens.
3 bth/shr (2 fmly) No smoking CTV in all bedrooms Tea and coffee making facilities No dogs (ex guide dogs) Cen ht CTV 5P
No coaches Riding stables at end of lane Last d 4pm
ROOMS: s £25; d £39-£44; wkly b&b fr £136;
wkly hlf-bd £209.50-£223.50*

TAVISTOCK Devon Map **02** SX47

See also Bere Alston & Mary Tavy

Premier Selected

Q Q Q Q Q **Tor Cottage** Chillaton PL16 0JE ☎ 01822 860248
FAX 01822 860126

(For full entry see **Chillaton**)

TEBAY Cumbria Map **07** NY60

Q Q **Cross Keys** CA10 3UY (from M6 junct 38 turn right at rdbt onto A685 to Kendal and the establishment is located after 0.25m)
☎ 015396 24240 FAX 015396 24240
This popular family-run inn lies in the centre of the village and conveniently just a stone's throw from the motorway. The bright cheery bedrooms are furnished in contemporary style and offer good value, as does the selection of food which can be taken in the cosy low beamed bar or adjoining dining room.
6 rms (2 fmly) No smoking in dining room CTV in all bedrooms Tea and coffee making facilities No dogs (ex guide dogs) Cen ht CTV 30P
Tennis (hard) Fishing Pool darts Last d 9pm
ROOMS: s £20-£25; d £27-£35*
MEALS: Lunch £4.50-£4.95alc Dinner £4.50-£11.50alc*
CARDS:

TEDBURN ST MARY Devon Map **03** SX89

Q Q Q **Kings Arms** Tedburn St Mary EX6 6EG ☎ 01647 61224
FAX 01647 61931
Situated in the centre of the village, the Kings Arms is conveniently located for exploring nearby Dartmoor. The bedrooms are simply decorated, furnished in keeping with the age and charm of the building. Downstairs the bars are full of character with log fires and exposed beams. A wide selection of meals is offered.
8 rms (1 shr) (3 fmly) No smoking in dining room CTV in all bedrooms Tea and coffee making facilities No dogs (ex guide dogs) Cen ht 40P
Last d 9.30pm
ROOMS: s £21; d £42-£48*
MEALS: Lunch £8-£28alc*
CARDS:

TEIGNMOUTH Devon Map **03** SX97

Q Q Q **Glenside Hotel** Ringmor Rd, Shaldon TQ14 0EP
(cross bridge from Teignmouth, turn right and then bear right again signed Ringmore, hotel on left) ☎ 01626 872448
Built in 1820, this cottage style hotel has views across the Teign Estuary. Owners Keith and Tricia Underwood welcome guests to their cosy hotel, many of whom return on a regular basis. The bedrooms are comfortable and well equipped, the most popular being the rooms with views across the river.

contd. on p.416.

A relaxing lounge and separate bar are available for guests, while in the summer months what could be more pleasant than sitting in the garden with a pot of tea? Home cooked, traditional evening meals are served, using local produce as available; special diets and vegetarians are catered for with prior arrangement.
9 rms (8 bth/shr) (1 fmly) CTV in all bedrooms Tea and coffee making facilities Licensed No children 3yrs 10P
ROOMS: s £19-£24; d £38-£50*

Q Q Q *Hill Rise Hotel* Winterbourne Rd TQ14 8JT
(A381, Teignmouth railway station turn left into Shute Hill, over crossroads hotel on left) ☎ 01626 773108
This charming red-brick Edwardian house is set in a quiet residential area with some lovely views. The Potters continue to upgrade and improve the hotel, which offers comfortable bedroom accommodation. There is a cosy bar, separate lounge and cheerful dining room, overlooking the well-tended garden.
8 rms (3 shr) (2 fmly) No smoking in bedrooms No smoking in dining room No smoking in 1 lounge CTV in all bedrooms Tea and coffee making facilities No dogs (ex guide dogs) Licensed Cen ht CTV 5P No coaches

Premier Selected

Q Q Q Q Q **Thomas Luny House** Teign St TQ14 8EG (A381 to Teignmouth, at 3rd lights turn right to quay, 50yds turn left into Teign St, after 60yds turn right through white archway) ☎ 01626 772976
Closed Jan
This beautifully proportioned house was built in the late 18th century by the marine artist Thomas Luny. An elegant drawing room with French windows leads into a walled garden with a sunny, terraced sitting area. Breakfast is served in the charming dining room around one large table. Bedrooms are individually decorated and comfortably furnished with many fine antique pieces. The en suite bathrooms are spacious and well equipped.
4 bth/shr No smoking in dining room No smoking in lounges CTV in all bedrooms Direct dial from bedrooms No dogs (ex guide dogs) Licensed Cen ht No children 12yrs 8P No coaches
ROOMS: s £30-£35; d £50-£70*

TELFORD Shropshire Map **07** SJ60

Selected

Q Q Q Q *Church Farm* Wrockwardine, Wellington TF6 5DG
(in centre of village, opposite church) ☎ 01952 244917
This Grade II listed farmhouse enjoys a village location just opposite the church in Wrockwardine. Beams and exposed timbers remain and the comfortable lounge features an inglenook fireplace where logs burn during the colder weather. Bedrooms include one on the ground floor and another in an adjacent building. All are well equipped and are furnished in keeping with the style of the house. Dinner is available by arrangement, guests dine family style, and hospitality from Mrs Jo Savage is warm and friendly.
5 rms (2 bth/shr) 1 annexe shr (1 fmly) No smoking in dining room CTV in all bedrooms Tea and coffee making facilities Cen ht CTV 10P No coaches Last d 9am
CARDS:

Q Q Q **Swan Hotel** Watling St, Wellington TF1 2NH
(leave M54 junct 6, right at rbt then over next rbt, left at next rbt, 0.5m on right by traffic lights) ☎ 01952 223781 FAX 01952 223782
This popular inn is situated on the old Holyhead road at Wellington and provides modern bedrooms and smart public areas. The bar is attractively cane-furnished and leads into several dining areas. Excellent value-for-money food is offered from an extensive choice, including a popular carvery.
12 rms (8 bth/shr) (2 fmly) No smoking in area of dining room CTV in all bedrooms Tea and coffee making facilities Cen ht 120P Last d 9.30pm
ROOMS: s £20-£35*
MEALS: Lunch £2.95-£8&alc Dinner £5-£8&alc*
CARDS:

TENBURY WELLS Worcestershire Map **07** SO56

Selected

Q Q Q Q **Peacock** Worcester Rd, Boraston WR15 8LL
(on A456 from Worcester follow A443 to Tenbury Wells and the inn is situated 1.25m E of Tenbury Wells)
☎ 01584 810506 FAX 811236
This roadside hotelry dates back to the 14th Century. It stands on the A456, just to the east of Tenbury Wells. Now a small privately owned hotel, it provides spacious, comfortable and luxuriously appointed accommodation, which includes two room four-poster beds. All three bedrooms are located in a separate building to the main part of the inn. Public areas are also nicely appointed and have a lot of character. A wide range of dishes is available.
3 shr No smoking in bedrooms No smoking in area of dining room CTV in all bedrooms Tea and coffee making facilities No dogs (ex guide dogs) Cen ht CTV 30P No coaches Fishing Last d 9.30pm
ROOMS: s £55; d £65*
MEALS: Lunch £10-£25alc Dinner £16-£25alc*
CARDS:

TENTERDEN Kent Map **05** TQ83

Selected

Q Q Q Q **White Lion** The High St TN30 6BD
(situated in the centre of Tenterden High Street on the A28 Ashford/Hastings road)
☎ 01580 765077 FAX 01580 764157

LIONHEART Inns

Situated in the centre of this charming town, the 16th-century White Lion provides a convivial bar atmosphere, together with a separate restaurant serving an extensive range of popular dishes. The recently refurbished bedrooms vary in size and are especially well equipped to meet the demands of the travelling public.
15 bth/shr (2 fmly) No smoking in 2 bedrooms No smoking in area of dining room CTV in all bedrooms Tea and coffee making facilities Direct dial from bedrooms Cen ht 35P Last d 10pm
ROOMS: s £49; d £79*
MEALS: Lunch £9-£18alc Dinner £9-£18alc*
CARDS:

TETBURY Gloucestershire Map **03** ST89

Premier Selected

QQQQQ **Tavern House** Willesley GL8 8QU
(From m-way follow A46, at Petty France take right fork to Tetbury/ Didmarton, onto the A433, 4m to Willesley, tavern is on right away from road) ☎ 01666 880444 FAX 01666 880254
This 17th-century inn has been lovingly restored to provide comfortable accommodation. Bedrooms are homely, well equipped, furnished with antique country pieces and have the benefit of modern en suite bathrooms. Home cooked English breakfasts are taken in the cosy dining room or the garden during the warmer months. The sitting room retains all of the original features including a fine open fireplace.
4 bth/shr No smoking in bedrooms No smoking in dining room CTV in all bedrooms Tea and coffee making facilities Direct dial from bedrooms No dogs Cen ht No children 10yrs 8P No coaches Golf and riding both available locally
ROOMS: s £45-£55; d £59-£65; wkly b&b £199-£210
CARDS:

TEWKESBURY Gloucestershire Map **03** SO83

QQ **The Abbey Hotel** 67 Church St GL20 5RX
(from M5 junct 9 take A38 to Gloucester. Church St is on A38)
☎ 01684 294247 FAX 01684 297208
Closed 24 Dec-New Year
A small family run commercial hotel situated close to the Abbey. Bedrooms vary in size and are modestly furnished. An evening meal is provided by arrangement from Monday to Thursday.
16 rms (7 bth 7 shr) (3 fmly) No smoking in 8 bedrooms CTV in all bedrooms Tea and coffee making facilities Licensed Cen ht 11P No coaches Last d 9.30pm
ROOMS: s £30-£42; d £40-£50*
CARDS:

THAME Oxfordshire Map **04** SP70

Premier Selected

QQQQQ **The Dairy** Moreton OX9 2HX
(M40 junct 8 left to Thame, right at rdbt, 400yds left to Moreton, left at War Memorial, left again after 150yds) ☎ 01844 214075
This former milking parlour provides a beautifully peaceful and comfortable environment. All the bedrooms in this stylish conversion are en suite and have king size beds. The proprietor, Peter Cole, provides a warm welcome and adds thoughtful extras such as hair dryers, writing desks, fresh flowers, biscuits and comfortable sofas and chairs to the rooms. Bedrooms are beautifully decorated as are the en suite facilities which offer excellent showers as well as baths. The open plan lounge area is available for guests' use, and breakfast is served at one long table off the kitchen. Guests are requested not to smoke.

3 bth/shr No smoking CTV in all bedrooms Tea and coffee making facilities No dogs Cen ht CTV No children 12yrs 8P No coaches
ROOMS: s £52; d £75
CARDS:

QQQ **Julia's Kitchen** Pymroyd House, Thame Rd OX33 1JW
☎ 01844 339631
Situated just off the M40 and close to Thame, this pretty guest house is popular with travellers wanting good hearty breakfasts. All bedrooms are prettily furnished with pine furniture and pastel colours, and include all the expected facilities. There is also a comfortable lounge.
3 shr CTV in all bedrooms Tea and coffee making facilities Cen ht No children
ROOMS: s £30-£40; d £45-£55*
CARDS:

Premier Selected

QQQQQ **Upper Green** *(SP736053)* Manor Rd, Towersey OX9 3QR (take Towersly Road off Thame ring road. Farm is the first on the left after Towersly Manor)
☎ 01844 212496 FAX 01844 260399 Mr & Mrs E Aitken
Closed Xmas and New Year
Guests will thoroughly enjoy a visit to this delightful property. In a peaceful rural setting with views of the Chiltern Hills, Upper Green Farm is conveniently situated for exploring the Cotswolds. Guests can even use one of the bikes provided by the Aitkens family, who offer a very warm welcome. The en suite bedrooms are tastefully furnished, each with its own theme, and are all well equipped with a number of thoughtful extras, including the use of a video. Two rooms are in the main house, the remainder, including several ground floor rooms, are in an attractive separate barn, which also offers a lounge. Guests can

contd.

wander around the beautiful grounds and in the summer months can relax under a shady tree beside the lake. Mind the geese as you drive in, they may be providing the eggs for your breakfast!
2 bth/shr 8 annexe bth/shr No smoking CTV in all bedrooms Tea and coffee making facilities No dogs Cen ht No children 13yrs 11P
6 hole pitch & putt cycle loan croquet lawn 7 acres poultry
ROOMS: s £38-£40; d £48-£60*

THEALE Berkshire

See **Sulhamstead**

THIRLMERE Cumbria Map **11** NY31

Q Q Q **Stybeck** *(NY319188)* CA12 4TN (on A591 near junct B5322)
☎ 017687 73232 Mr & Mrs J Hodgson
Closed 25 Dec
Set well back from the main road, this traditional farmhouse has a striking flower garden to the front and a backdrop of the dramatic fells. Cosy public rooms comprise two lounges, one doubling as the dining room where breakfast is taken around one table. Bedrooms are prettily decorated and, in keeping with the rest of the house, are graced by teddies, dolls and other homely touches.
3 rms (1 shr) (1 fmly) No smoking Tea and coffee making facilities No dogs Cen ht CTV No children 5yrs 4P 200 acres dairy mixed sheep working

THIRSK North Yorkshire Map **08** SE48

Selected

Q Q Q Q **Spital Hill** York Rd YO7 3AE (From A1(M) take A168,then take A170, at rdbt take A19 to York for 1m, house set back 200yds from road on right, drive marked by two white posts)
☎ 01845 522273 FAX 01845 524970
Robin and Ann Clough will welcome you warmly to their home, a fine Victorian country house set in over two acres of gardens and parkland and surrounded by open countryside. The atmosphere is very much that of a country house, with a lovely lounge and meals taken at the one table in the dining room, house party style. Ann produces a set dinner each evening using fine fresh produce, much of which comes from the garden. Bedrooms are very inviting and thoughtfully equipped to include items such as bathrobes, fresh fruit and shortbread, mineral water, books, alarm clocks and hairdryers, but no tea-making equipment, Ann preferring to offer tea as a service. The largest room has its own piano and a superb bathroom.
3 bth/shr 2 annexe bth/shr No smoking Direct dial from bedrooms No dogs (ex guide dogs) Licensed Cen ht CTV No children 12yrs 6P No coaches Croquet Last d 2pm
ROOMS: d £69.50-£79.50*
CARDS:

THORPE BAY Essex

See **Southend-on-Sea**

THRESHFIELD North Yorkshire Map **07** SD96

Selected

Q Q Q Q **Long Ashes** Long Ashes Park BD23 5PN
(turn off B6160 1m from centre of Threshfield and continue for 0.5m along the driveway) ☎ 01756 752434 FAX 01756 752927
This Dales inn is situated outside the village, adjacent to a holiday park. Visitors are welcome to use the leisure centre on the park. A wide choice of dishes is offered either in the popular bar or in the spacious restaurant. Bedrooms are comfortably furnished and have good quality bathrooms.
5 bth/shr (1 fmly) No smoking in bedrooms No smoking in dining room CTV in all bedrooms Tea and coffee making facilities Direct dial from bedrooms Cen ht 10P Indoor swimming pool (heated) Squash Sauna Solarium Gymnasium Last d 9.30pm
ROOMS: s £47.50; d £75; wkly b&b £225; wkly hlf-bd £300*
MEALS: Lunch £12.95-£20alc Dinner £12.95-£20alc*
CARDS:

THRUXTON Hampshire Map **04** SU24

Selected

Q Q Q Q **May Cottage** SP11 8LZ
(from A303 take sign Thruxton (village only), situated between George Inn and post office on opposite side)
☎ 01264 771241 & 0468 242166 FAX 01264 771770
Closed Xmas
Guests will find that a warm and friendly welcome awaits them at this attractive creeper clad property. Built in 1740, and partly thatched, May Cottage is situated in a tranquil village, yet very convenient for the

A303 and such nearby attractions as Stonehenge and Salisbury. Tom and Fiona Biddolph make every effort to ensure guests will feel at home, whether taking tea, with home made cake, in the pretty enclosed garden, or relaxing in the private guest lounge. Bedrooms are comfortable and thoughtfully furnished in a traditional style, with quality furnishings. Off street parking is available, and home cooked dinners are served by arrangement.

4 bth/shr (1 fmly) No smoking CTV in all bedrooms Tea and coffee making facilities No dogs Cen ht CTV No children 6yrs 5P No coaches Last d by arrangement
ROOMS: s £25-£30; d £45-£50*

THURNING Norfolk Map **09** TG02

Q Q **Rookery** *(TG078307)* NR24 2JP (Leave A148 Thursford to B1354, through Bristol village, pass Green Man pub, bear right then left, then left. Farm is 1st on left after 1 m)
☎ 01263 860357 Mrs A M Fisher
Closed Dec-Jan
Guests can expect a friendly welcome from Mrs Fisher at this delightful 300-year-old red brick farmhouse. The accommodation features an extremely large bedroom and a further single room and is therefore ideally suited to families. The public rooms comprise a large sitting and dining room where guests can enjoy a hearty home cooked breakfast, and dinner by prior arrangement.
2 rms (1 shr) (1 fmly) No smoking Tea and coffee making facilities No dogs CTV ch fac P 400 acres arable Last d By arrangement
ROOMS: s £17-£18; d £34-£36

THWAITE North Yorkshire Map **07** SD89

Q Q **Kearton** DL11 6DR ☎ 01748 886277 FAX 01748 886590
Mar-Dec
Standing in the centre of the village, this attractive little guest house boasts a tea room and restaurant serving an extensive range of food. There is a comfortable lounge and the bedrooms are modern and generally spacious with showers provided in most. The house is surrounded by inspiring Dales scenery.
13 rms (2 fmly) No smoking in dining room Tea and coffee making facilities No dogs (ex guide dogs) Licensed Cen ht 50P Last d 6.30pm
ROOMS: s fr £27; d fr £54; wkly hlf-bd fr £185.50
CARDS:

TIDESWELL Derbyshire Map **07** SK17

Q Q Q **Courtyard Barn** Buxton Rd SK17 8PG
(turn off A623 onto B6049, house 50yds past Horse & Jockey public house)
☎ 01298 871180
Located in the centre of a pretty Peak District village, this small family run guest house has been cleverly created from a farm barn. Just two bedrooms are provided and these are spacious and well equipped with modern facilities. The pretty breakfast room with an attractive flagstone floor is where good breakfasts are served. The guest house is owned and run by the friendly Roberts family.
2 shr (2 fmly) No smoking CTV in all bedrooms Tea and coffee making facilities Cen ht 2P No coaches
ROOMS: d £42-£46*

Q Q **Jaret House** Queen St SK17 8JZ (Situated on main road B6049 which runs through village linking A6/A623. Opposite Hills and Dales Tearooms) ☎ 01298 872195 FAX 01298 872982
Closed 13 Dec-13 Jan
This stone built cottage is situated in the centre of the village. Straightforward bedrooms include one with a private adjacent bathroom. There is also a comfortable sitting room, warmed by a log fire during cooler months. Breakfast is served around one table.
3 bth/shr (1 fmly) No smoking CTV in all bedrooms Tea and coffee making facilities Cen ht
ROOMS: s £18-£22; d £40-£42; wkly b&b £120-£125*

TINTAGEL Cornwall & Isles of Scilly Map **02** SX08

Q Q Q **Castle Villa** Molesworth St PL34 0BZ
(on entering Tintagel on B3263 turn left onto Camelford/Trebar Rd, Castle Villa is 150 yards on the left) ☎ 01840 770373 & 770203
Situated in the picturesque and much visited village of Tintagel, this charming stone cottage is the family home of Karen and Andrew Hill, who offer a relaxed and friendly welcome to guests, many of whom return on a regular basis. Bedrooms are cosy and well equipped, and mealtimes are a homely affair.
4 rms (1 shr) No smoking in bedrooms No smoking in area of dining room CTV in all bedrooms Tea and coffee making facilities Licensed Cen ht CTV 4P No coaches Last d 8.30pm
ROOMS: d £31-£40; wkly b&b £195.30-£252
CARDS:

Q Q Q **Cornishman** Fore St PL34 0DB ☎ 01840 770238
FAX 01840 770078
Situated in the centre of the village, within walking distance of the breathtaking scenery along the cliffs and mythical home of King Arthur at Tintagel Castle, The Cornishman is a traditional inn. The three bars feature a display of rural bygones, one boasts a roaring log fire during the winter, and offering an extensive range of meals throughout the year. Bedrooms are approached from the flower-filled terrace at the rear of the property, each is light and airy, with several specifically designed for families.
10 shr (2 fmly) No smoking in bedrooms CTV in all bedrooms Tea and coffee making facilities No dogs Cen ht 40P Last d 9.30pm
ROOMS: s £25-£30; d £40-£50*
CARDS:

The AA's professional Inspectors make regular and anonymous visits to all the establishments listed in the Guide. They accept no gifts or favours from proprietors

Selected

Q Q Q Q ***Polkerr*** PL34 0BY (Leave A30 just S of Launceston onto A395 towards Camelford, A3314 follow signs to Tintagel. Hotel on right just after the Tintagel village sign) ☎ 01840 770382
Closed 25 Dec
Polkerr benefits from the care lavished upon it by owners Robert and June Fry. The rooms are attractively decorated and thoughtfully furnished. Similarly, the ground floor public areas, which include an elegant dining room and a sunny conservatory, are well presented and comfortable. An evening meal is readily available.
7 rms (6 shr) (2 fmly) No smoking CTV in all bedrooms Tea and coffee making facilities No dogs Cen ht 9P Last d noon

Selected

Q Q Q Q **Port William** Trebarwith Strand PL34 0HB (Off B3263 from Camelford to Tintagel) ☎ 01840 770230 FAX 01840 770936
The Port William has a spectacular location, perched on the cliffside looking down onto the bay. The charming and busy public areas are furnished with old church pews and large wooden tables. A wide range of dishes is on offer with an emphasis on locally caught fish. The bedrooms are decorated and furnished to a high standard with good modern facilities.
5 bth/shr (1 fmly) No smoking in bedrooms No smoking in area of dining room No smoking in 1 lounge CTV in all bedrooms Tea and coffee making facilities Direct dial from bedrooms Cen ht 50P Last d 9.30pm
ROOMS: s £40-£55; d £57-£80*
MEALS: Lunch £10-£20&alc Dinner £10-£20&alc*
CARDS:

Q Q Q **Tintagel Arms Hotel** Fore St PL34 0DB
(from M5 take A30, turn right for North Cornwall on the B395, follow signs for Camelford, premises situated in Tintagel centre opposite Lloyds Bank)
☎ 01840 770780
This Cornish stone property is popular with locals and tourists alike. Margaret and George Hunter offer attractively appointed accommodation with a high level of comfort and several extras. A wide choice of dishes is available in the spacious bar/bistro, from usual favourites to Greek specialities and vegetarian options. In addition to the bar area, there is a small lounge.
7 bth/shr No smoking in bedrooms No smoking in area of dining room CTV in all bedrooms Tea and coffee making facilities No dogs (ex guide dogs) Cen ht 8P Golf available close by Last d 9.30pm
ROOMS: d £36-£45*
MEALS: Lunch £3-£10.50alc Dinner £5.50-£10.50alc*
CARDS:

TISSINGTON Derbyshire Map 07 SK15

Q Q Q **Bent** *(SK187523)* DE6 1RD (A515 Ashbourne to Buxton Rd turn off at Tissington, follow down the avenue of trees to the village, past the pond Bent farm is on the left) ☎ 01335 390214 Mrs H Herridge
Etr-Oct
Rolling hills and open pasture land surround this stone-built farmhouse, parts of which date back to the 16th century. Two spacious rooms are available, both of them en suite and furnished to match the character of the house. Breakfast is served in the traditional dining room and there is a large, comfortable lounge.
2 bth (1 fmly) No smoking Tea and coffee making facilities No dogs (ex guide dogs) Cen ht CTV No children 5yrs 6P 280 acres beef dairy mixed sheep
ROOMS: d £38-£40*

TIVERTON Devon Map 03 SS91

Q Q Q **Bridge** 23 Angel Hill EX16 6PE (in centre of Tiverton, beside River Exe) ☎ 01884 252804 FAX 01884 253949
This family run guest house enjoys a riverside location close to the town centre and benefits from its own small garden overlooking the river. Bedrooms are comfortable and well decorated and most are equipped with modern en suite facilities. There is a choice of lounges for guests' use, one with bar games. Good home cooked dinners are served in the lower ground floor dining room.
9 rms (5 shr) (2 fmly) No smoking in dining room CTV in all bedrooms Tea and coffee making facilities Licensed Cen ht CTV 7P No coaches Fishing Last d 7pm
ROOMS: s £19.50-£24.50; d £38-£49; wkly b&b £135-£165; wkly hlf-bd £210-£240*

Premier Selected

Q Q Q Q Q **Hornhill** *(SS965117)* Exeter Hill EX16 4PL (follow signs to Grand Western Canal, take right fork up Exeter Hill farmhouse on left at top of hill) ☎ 01884 253352 FAX 01884 253352
Mrs B Pugsley
From its peaceful hilltop setting, Hornhill enjoys panoramic views over the town and beautiful Exe Valley. Parts of this delightful farmhouse, the home of the Pugsley family for more than 100 years, date back to the 18th century. The bedrooms are tastefully decorated, comfortably furnished, and equipped with modern facilities; many thoughtful extras like bottled water, herbal tea and locally produced toiletries are also provided. There is a lovely sitting room with log fires on chilly evenings, and meals are served around one large table in the elegant dining room, where the emphasis is on home cooking using local produce whenever possible. Barbara Pugsley is a friendly host, and affords a warm welcome to all of her guests.
3 bth/shr No smoking CTV in all bedrooms Tea and coffee making facilities No dogs No children 12yrs 5P 75 acres beef sheep Last d 24hr in advance
ROOMS: s fr £25; d fr £40*

Q Q *Lodge Hill (SS945112)* EX16 5PA (1m S of town centre, off A396)
☎ 01884 252907 FAX 01884 242090 Mr & Mrs B Reader
A warm welcome awaits guests at this large detached farmhouse situated in an attractive location with a well tended garden. Rooms vary in size, with family suites available in beamed lofts. Guests can relax in the charming bar or comfortable lounge, and home cooked evening meals are available.
8 rms (7 shr) (2 fmly) No smoking in dining room CTV in all bedrooms Tea and coffee making facilities Licensed Cen ht CTV 12P 10 acres non-working Last d noon
CARDS:

Selected

Q Q Q Q Lower Collipriest *(SS953117)* EX16 4PT (off Great Western Way, approx 1m)
☎ 01884 252321 FAX 01884 252321 Mrs R Olive
Etr-Oct
This delightful farmhouse has a peaceful rural location in the beautiful Exe Valley but is only one mile from the market town of Tiverton and has easy access to the North Devon Link and the M5. Bedrooms are spacious, tastefully decorated and have many thoughtful extras. There is a character lounge with an inglenook fireplace and access to the attractive courtyard garden where drinks are served in the summer evenings. The dining room has a large communal table where guests can enjoy Mrs Olive's home cooking and friendly atmosphere.
3 bth/shr No smoking Tea and coffee making facilities No dogs (ex guide dogs) Cen ht CTV No children 16yrs 6P Fishing 220 acres dairy Last d noon
ROOMS: s £30-£32; d £60-£64; wkly b&b £150; wkly hlf-bd fr £210
CARDS:

TIVETSHALL ST MARY Norfolk Map 05 TM18

Selected

Q Q Q Q Old Ram Coaching Inn Ipswich Rd NR15 2DE (on A140 15 min S of Norwich) ☎ 01379 676794 FAX 01379 608399
Closed 25-26 Dec
This delightful 17th-century coaching inn is well known for its quality food and offers a wide variety of freshly cooked dishes, daily fish specials and home made desserts. The accommodation is superb, decorated and furnished to provide extremely comfortable bedrooms which are thoughtfully equipped with lots of useful extras as well as beautiful en suite bathrooms. The public rooms are full of character and have a wealth of exposed beams, open log fires and rustic furniture, there is also a lovely terraced garden where guests can enjoy a meal al fresco. Breakfast is not included in the price.
11 bth/shr (1 fmly) No smoking in area of dining room CTV in all bedrooms Tea and coffee making facilities Direct dial from bedrooms No dogs (ex guide dogs) Cen ht 120P Last d 10pm
ROOMS: s £42.50-£45; d £55-£57.50 (room only); wkly b&b £343-£360; wkly hlf-bd £465-£478;
MEALS: Lunch £11.65-£22.40alc Dinner £11.65-£22.40alc
CARDS:

TOLLARD ROYAL Wiltshire Map 03 ST91

Q Q Q King John SP5 5PS (on B3081 about 7 m E of Shaftsbury, 2nd property on the left after entering the village of Tollard Royal)
☎ 01725 516207 FAX 01725 516459
Closed 25 Dec
This privately owned free house enjoys a hideaway village location, and offers a good selection of wines by the glass, and locally brewed real ales, in addition to good home cooked food. Bedrooms are all en suite and equipped with modern facilities.
3 bth/shr No smoking in bedrooms CTV in all bedrooms Tea and coffee making facilities Cen ht 17P No coaches Last d 9.30pm
ROOMS: s £33.50; d £40-£55*
MEALS: Lunch £1.95-£15alc Dinner £7.50-£20alc*
CARDS:

TONBRIDGE Kent

See **Penshurst and Shipbourne**

See also advertisement on p.423.

TORBAY Devon

See **Brixham, Paignton and Torquay**

TORQUAY Devon Map 03 SX96

Q Q Arran Lodge 97 Avenue Rd TQ2 5LH
(on main approach from Newton Abbot, the road splits right for beach & left for town, take right, Arran approx 75yds on left)
☎ 01803 292273 FAX 01803 292273
New owners, Mary and John Palmer offer their guests a warm welcome to this friendly and informal guest house where the bedrooms are smartly decorated, with many modern and convenient facilities and personal touches. Dinner is served in the cosy dining room where guests can also relax after dinner.
4 shr (1 fmly) No smoking in bedrooms No smoking in dining room CTV in all bedrooms Tea and coffee making facilities Cen ht CTV 4P No coaches Last d 2pm
ROOMS: s £12-£20; d £24-£40; wkly b&b £80-£115; wkly hlf-bd £129-£164*
CARDS:

QQQ **Atlantis Hotel** 68 Belgrave Rd TQ2 5HY (from M5 proceed to A380 and follow signs to Torquay, then follow signs to central area)
☎ 01803 292917 FAX 292917
The proprietors, Gill & Tom Saunders extend a warm welcome to their guests in this attractive and comfortably furnished guest house. Rooms have extra personal touches including bottled mineral water, toiletries and shoe shine packs. A comfortable lounge/bar is situated on the ground floor adjacent to the dining room.
10 bth/shr (7 fmly) No smoking in bedrooms No smoking in dining room CTV in all bedrooms Tea and coffee making facilities Licensed Cen ht CTV 3P Last d 5pm
ROOMS: s £18-£21; d £36-£42; wkly b&b £126-£147; wkly hlf-bd £168-£199*
CARDS:

QQQ **Bahamas Hotel** 17 Avenue Rd TQ2 5LB
(Take A380 for 18m through Kings Kerswell. At rdbt straight on Riviera Way, at 6th lights fork right onto Avenue Rd) ☎ 01803 296005
The Bahamas Hotel is only a few minutes walk from the centre of Torquay and a stone's throw from Torre Abbey. All bedrooms are en suite and offer modern facilities. There is a spacious lounge, and a dining room where home made food is served in the form of a five course dinner. There is now the added attraction of a pretty patio where dinner can be taken 'al fresco' in the summer.
11 bth/shr (3 fmly) No smoking in bedrooms No smoking in dining room CTV in all bedrooms Tea and coffee making facilities Licensed Cen ht CTV 12P Last d 6.30pm
ROOMS: s £19-£23; d £38-£46; wkly b&b £135-£155; wkly hlf-bd £190-£215*
CARDS:

QQQ **Beauly** 503 Babbacombe Rd TQ1 1HL
(600yds from Torquay Harbour on the B3199 Babbacombe Rd)
☎ 01803 296993 FAX 01803 296993
This small and comfortable terraced guest house is 600 yards from Torquay harbour and within easy walking distance of the town centre. The bedrooms are equipped with all modern facilities including hairdryers.
5 bth/shr (3 fmly) No smoking in dining room No smoking in lounges CTV in all bedrooms Tea and coffee making facilities Cen ht CTV No coaches
ROOMS: s £21-£28; d £36-£50; wkly b&b £121-£170*

Selected

QQQQ **Belmont Hotel** 66 Belgrave Rd TQ2 5HY
☎ 01803 295028
Located in the centre of town and close to all the attractions of the Bay, this charming, well run small hotel is impeccably decorated and maintained, providing comfortable accommodation with many modern facilities and extra thoughtful personal touches. Breakfast is served in the attractive dining room, surrounded by many mementoes donated by thoughtful guests over the past fourteen years.
13 rms (10 shr) (4 fmly) No smoking in dining room CTV in all bedrooms Tea and coffee making facilities Licensed Cen ht CTV No children 6yrs 3P Last d 4pm
ROOMS: s £16-£22; d £36-£50*
CARDS:

Selected

QQQQ **The Berburry Hotel** 64 Bampfylde Rd TQ2 5AY
(at Torre Railway Station bear right into Avenue Rd signposted Seafront hotel 50yds before2nd set of lights, 300yrds from seafront)
☎ 01803 297494 FAX 01803 215902
Closed Dec ex Xmas
Bernard and Rosemary Sellick pride themselves on their delightful detached hotel, close to the town centre and a level stroll from the seafront. Being former restaurateurs they are keen to maintain their reputation for fine food, and enjoy a high level of repeat business from satisfied guests. The bedrooms, three of which are situated on the ground floor, are all tastefully decorated and comprehensively equipped. Also available a drawing room and a cocktail bar.
10 bth/shr 5 annexe bth/shr (2 fmly) No smoking CTV in all bedrooms Tea and coffee making facilities No dogs Licensed Cen ht CTV No children 8yrs 14P Last d 5pm
CARDS:

Selected

QQQQ **Blue Haze Hotel** Seaway Ln TQ2 6PS
(follow signs to seafront, right at lights by Grand Hotel, turn right then left, turn right at crossroads with Seaway Lane Blue Haze 200yds on right) ☎ 01803 607186 & 606205 FAX 01803 607186
Apr-Oct rs Wed
This delightful Victorian property, set in a quiet elevated position only 500 yards from the sea, is within easy walking distance of both the town and the harbour. The large, secluded and well tended garden is an ideal place to relax and enjoy the sunny position. The bedrooms are spacious, comfortable, tastefully decorated and are well equipped with many extras; two are situated on the ground floor. There is a stylish lounge with a coal fire, and a separate bar and spacious dining room where guests can enjoy delightful four-course home cooked meals, including a complimentary glass of wine. Dinner is not available on Wednesday evenings.
9 bth/shr (3 fmly) No smoking in bedrooms No smoking in dining room CTV in all bedrooms Tea and coffee making facilities No dogs Licensed Cen ht CTV 20P No coaches Last d 4pm
ROOMS: d £58-£62; wkly b&b £189-£203; wkly hlf-bd £259-£273
CARDS:

QQQ **Braddon Hall Hotel** Braddons Hill Rd East TQ1 1HF
(from Torquay seafront follow signs for harbour, turn left at clock tower onto the Babbacombe road, 1st left after museum and estab is on right)
☎ 01803 293908 FAX 01803 293908

This imposing south facing hotel, with easy access to the town centre and harbour, offers a friendly relaxed atmosphere in attractive surroundings. All bedrooms are individually decorated and furnished and offer en suite facilities. There is a separate lounge in addition to the bar. The home cooked dishes are a treat.
12 bth/shr (2 fmly) No smoking in 2 bedrooms No smoking in dining room CTV in all bedrooms Tea and coffee making facilities No dogs Licensed Cen ht No children 5yrs 8P No coaches
ROOMS: s £16-£20; d £32-£40
CARDS:

Q Q Q ***Burleigh House*** 25 Newton Rd TQ2 5DB ☎ 01803 291557
Closed Xmas & New Year
Within walking distance of all the attractions of Torquay, this large detached house offers comfortably furnished and well equipped bedrooms with modern facilities. In addition is a splendid self-contained flat to suit all the needs of a family on holiday.
9 rms (7 bth/shr) CTV in all bedrooms Tea and coffee making facilities No dogs (ex guide dogs) Cen ht CTV 12P No coaches Last d 5pm

Selected

Q Q Q Q **Chesterfield Hotel** 62 Belgrave Rd TQ2 5HY (follow signs to seafront and harbour leads to Belgrave Rd, premises located 500 yards from seafront) ☎ 01803 292318 FAX 01803 293676
Closed 20-31 Dec
John and Donna Daglish have made a great impression in the short time they have owned and run Chesterfield. Rooms are all en suite and have been successfully upgraded, blending quality with modern facilities. Children are welcome, and play facilities are thoughtfully provided for them. A spacious lounge is available on the ground floor, and breakfast and dinner are served in the welcoming dining room.
10 shr (3 fmly) No smoking in 2 bedrooms No smoking in dining room No smoking in lounges CTV in all bedrooms Tea and coffee making facilities No dogs (ex guide dogs) Licensed Cen ht CTV 3P Last d 4pm
ROOMS: d £34-£50; wkly b&b £110-£160; wkly hlf-bd £160-£220✻
CARDS:

Q Q Q **Clevedon Hotel** Meadfoot Sea Rd TQ1 2LQ
(from Torquay harbour take Babbacombe rd for 100yds, right at lights for Meadfoot beach. Follow rd for 0.5m, hotel is on right 300yds before beach) ☎ 01803 294260 FAX 01803 299396
This detached Victorian villa is close to Torquay town centre. All bedrooms are en suite and have radio alarm clocks. The public areas, including a spacious lounge, separate bar, and dining room, are nicely furnished. There is also a sunny conservatory where guests may relax. Home-cooked evening meals are served.
10 bth/shr (4 fmly) No smoking in dining room No smoking in 1 lounge CTV in all bedrooms Tea and coffee making facilities Licensed CTV 9P No coaches Last d 6.30pm
ROOMS: s £22-£28; d £44-£76; wkly b&b £154-£196; wkly hlf-bd £268-£325✻
CARDS:

Q Q **Clovelly** 91 Avenue Rd TQ2 5LH (at Torre Station take right hand lane into Avenue Rd guesthouse 100yds on left)
☎ 01803 292286
This is a cheerful family run guest house. Rooms vary in size, one boasting a four-poster bed, whilst another is suitable for families, but all are nicely decorated, and have thoughtful touches. There is a comfortable, plant-filled lounge, and a separate sunny dining room where generous breakfasts and traditional home cooked evening meals are served.
7 rms (2 shr) (3 fmly) No smoking in 2 bedrooms No smoking in dining room No smoking in lounges CTV in all bedrooms Tea and coffee making facilities Cen ht CTV ch fac 4P Last d 7.30pm
ROOMS: s £12-£14; d £24-£28; wkly b&b £84-£98; wkly hlf-bd £126-£140✻
CARDS:

Selected

Q Q Q Q **Court Prior** St Lukes Rd South TQ2 5NZ
(M5 to A380 Torquay, pass Halfords on right, right at lights into Avenue Rd, proceed to sea front, left at next lights up Sheddon Hill St Lukes Rd) ☎ 01803 292766 FAX 01803 292766
Located in a quiet residential part of the town yet within easy walking distance of the centre, the harbour front and beach, this spacious Victorian villa has large rooms and a high standard of decor and furnishing throughout. All the well equipped rooms are comfortable, en suite and offer modern facilities. Dinner menus provide traditional home made dishes, including a separate children's menu.
10 bth/shr (3 fmly) No smoking in dining room CTV in all bedrooms Tea and coffee making facilities CTV No children 4yrs 10P Last d 4pm
ROOMS: s £16-£19; d £32-£38; wkly b&b £105-£126; wkly hlf-bd £141-£167✻
CARDS:

Q Q Q ***Craig Court Hotel*** 10 Ash Hill Rd, Castle Circus TQ1 3HZ (from Castle Circus (town hall) take St Mary Church Road (left by Baptist Church) first on right is Ash Hill Road) ☎ 01803 294400

A large Victorian villa, once the summer home of Lord Haldon, which Ann and Bob Box have dedicated themselves to transforming into a home-from-home for guests. Craig Court is in a quiet residential area, close to the centre and beaches.

10 rms (5 shr) (3 fmly) No smoking in dining room No smoking in lounges CTV in all bedrooms Tea and coffee making facilities Licensed Cen ht CTV 12P Last d 10am

Selected

Q Q Q Q **Cranborne Hotel** 58 Belgrave Rd TQ2 5HY (M5, A380, follow signs to Torquay, at Torre Station follow signs for seafront which leads to Belgrave Rd, premises on right by traffic lights) ☎ 01803 298046 FAX 01803 298046

Closed Xmas & New Year

This Victorian property is owned by Peter Tinto who has transformed it into a bright and welcoming establishment that is within easy walking distance of the town centre. All the rooms have recently been decorated and are equipped with modern facilities. Well prepared meals can be taken in the bright and airy dining room.

12 rms (11 bth/shr) (6 fmly) No smoking in dining room No smoking in lounges CTV in all bedrooms Tea and coffee making facilities No dogs Licensed Cen ht CTV 3P Last d 3pm

ROOMS: s £20-£30; d £40-£50*

CARDS:

Q Q Q **Cranmore** 89 Avenue Rd TQ2 5LH (A380 onto A3022, from Newton Abbot at the Torre station turn right at traffic lights, premises 200yds on the left) ☎ 01803 298488

Closed Xmas

Guests are assured of a warm and friendly welcome from new hosts, Joy and Dave Smale. This small hotel offers attractively decorated bedrooms, some of which are suitable for families. There is also a comfortable lounge and adjoining dining room where home cooked evening meals are served.

8 bth/shr (2 fmly) No smoking in dining room No smoking in lounges CTV in all bedrooms Tea and coffee making facilities No dogs (ex guide dogs) Cen ht CTV 4P No coaches Last d 3.30pm

ROOMS: s £15-£18; d £30-£36; wkly b&b £105-£126; wkly hlf-bd £158-£177.50*

CARDS:

Q Q Q **Crown Lodge** 83 Avenue Rd TQ2 5LH (A30 onto A3022, from Newton Abbot at the Torre station fork right at traffic lights, premises 200yards on left) ☎ 01803 298772

Winners of the Torbay Heart Beat award, for high standards of hygiene and healthy eating, Crown Lodge is situated within walking distance of the harbour and seafront. The well equipped bedrooms are delightfully furnished and decorated. For guests' comfort there is spacious and homely lounge.

5 shr No smoking in 4 bedrooms No smoking in dining room CTV in all bedrooms Tea and coffee making facilities No dogs (ex guide dogs) Cen ht CTV No children 6P No coaches Card table

ROOMS: s £25; d £32-£44*

Q Q Q **Elmdene Hotel** Rathmore Rd TQ2 6NZ (enter Torquay on the A3022, follow seafront signs, turn right for Chelston and Cockington) ☎ 01803 294940 FAX 01803 294940

The Elmdene is in a good position, near to the seafront and railway station. A large number of decorative improvements have been carried out in the bedrooms. There is an attractive sun lounge and a cosy bar. Hearty breakfasts, and a choice of traditional dinners, are served in the recently refurbished dining room.

11 rms (2 bth 5 shr) (4 fmly) No smoking in dining room No smoking in 1 lounge CTV in all bedrooms Tea and coffee making facilities Licensed Cen ht CTV 11P Last d 4pm

ROOMS: s £19-£20.50; d £38-£41; wkly b&b £125-£131; wkly hlf-bd £177-£187.50*

CARDS:

Q Q Q ***Everglades Hotel*** 32 St Marychurch Rd TQ1 3HY (A380 from Newton Abbot, turn left at Reeds Ford Garage traffic lights into Hele Rd. 1.5m to next traffic lights, turn right into St Marychurch Rd) ☎ 01803 295389 FAX 01803 214357

The spacious en suite bedrooms here are currently being upgraded by new owner Mr Margiotta. Everglades is just a short walk from the shops and main attractions of the town. The bright, comfortable dining room benefits from fine views over Torquay.

11 bth/shr (2 fmly) No smoking in dining room No smoking in 1 lounge CTV in all bedrooms Tea and coffee making facilities No dogs Licensed Cen ht CTV No children 5yrs 8P Last d 5pm

CARDS:

Q Q Q **Exmouth View Hotel** St Albans Rd, Babbacombe Down TQ1 3LG (from St Marychurch town centre follow Babbacombe Rd towards Torquay after 500yds turn left into St Albans Rd) ☎ 01803 327307 FAX 01803 329967

Close to the Babbacombe Downs and beaches, this friendly hotel offers comfortable accommodation. Traditional fare features on its dinner menu. There is regular evening entertainment in the spacious lounge and bar areas.

29 rms (27 bth/shr) (9 fmly) No smoking in dining room No smoking in 1 lounge CTV in all bedrooms Tea and coffee making facilities No dogs (ex guide dogs) Licensed Cen ht CTV 25P Last d 6.30pm

ROOMS: s £18-£29.50; d £36-£59; wkly b&b £121.25-£195.75; wkly hlf-bd £164-£245*

CARDS:

Q Q **Gainsboro Hotel** 22 Rathmore Rd TQ2 6NY (from seafront turn at traffic lights by Grand Hotel. Past cricket/rugby ground, fork left. Hotel is 50mtrs from junct) ☎ 01803 292032 FAX 01803 292032

Mar-Sep

Gainsboro is but a short walk from the seafront and Torre Abbey and its gardens. Bedrooms are mostly en suite and are mainly spacious, with atttractive decor. Breakfast is served in the sunny dining room with a comfortably furnished lounge adjacent.

6 rms (4 shr) No smoking CTV in all bedrooms Tea and coffee making facilities No dogs Cen ht CTV No children 5P No coaches

ROOMS: s £13-£18; d £26-£36; wkly b&b £87-£119*

CARDS:

Selected

Q Q Q Q **Glenorleigh Hotel** 26 Cleveland Rd TQ2 5BE (follow A3022 Newton Abbot/Torquay road until traffic lights at Torre Station, bear right into Avenue Road A379 and Cleveland Road is first left) ☎ 01803 292135 FAX 01803 292135

Closed Dec-11 Feb rs 12 Feb-Etr & 30 Sep-Nov

New owners Toni and Rob Maddison plan to upgrade their hotel to offer an even greater degree of comfort. Situated in a quiet residential area, yet within easy reach of the town centre, Glenorleigh offers pleasant accommodation with many facilities, including an outdoor heated swimming pool and secluded garden area, a solarium and a games room. The comfortably appointed bar is adjacent to the dining room where both breakfast and dinner are served.
16 rms (9 shr) (5 fmly) No smoking in bedrooms No smoking in dining room CTV in all bedrooms Tea and coffee making facilities Licensed Cen ht CTV 10P Outdoor swimming pool (heated) Solarium Pool table Darts Last d 6pm
ROOMS: s £16-£30; d £32-£60; wkly b&b £112-£210; wkly hlf-bd £172-£269*
CARDS:

Q Q Q **Grosvenor House Hotel** Falkland Rd TQ2 5JP
(From Newton Abbot continue to Torquay. At Torre station turn right by Halfords. At 2nd set of traffic lights turn sharp left into Falkland Road)
☎ 01803 294110
Situated in a quiet part of Torquay, yet within easy walking distance of the centre and beach, Mr & Mrs Pearce, committed Christians, offer guests comfortable accommodation with spacious bedrooms and modern facilities. There is a lounge-bar and a separate comfortable lounge nearby.
10 shr (4 fmly) No smoking in bedrooms No smoking in dining room No smoking in 1 lounge CTV in all bedrooms Tea and coffee making facilities No dogs (ex guide dogs) Licensed Cen ht CTV 7P Last d 4.30pm
ROOMS: s £18-£23; d £36-£46; wkly b&b £112-£147; wkly hlf-bd £168-£199.50
CARDS:

Selected

Q Q Q Q **Headland View** 37 Babbacombe Downs Rd, Babbacombe TQ1 3LN (follow A379 coast road to Babbacombe and turn left onto seafront) ☎ 01803 312612 FAX 01803 312612
Apr-Oct
This delightful seafront property has unbeatable views. Rita and Brian Gallimore extend a warm welcome to their guests and assure them of attentive and friendly service. The bedrooms are all well equipped and attractively decorated with good co-ordinated fabrics and furnishings. There is a choice of sea-facing rooms each with a balcony or quieter rooms at the rear with four poster beds. Breakfasts are of particular note and will set you up for a good day's sightseeing.
6 shr (2 fmly) No smoking in 2 bedrooms No smoking in dining room No smoking in lounges CTV in all bedrooms Tea and coffee making facilities No dogs (ex guide dogs) Cen ht CTV No children 3yrs 6P No coaches
ROOMS: d £32-£40; wkly b&b £112-£133*

Selected

Q Q Q Q **Hotel Blue Conifer** Higher Downs Rd, The Seafront, Babbacombe TQ1 3LD (follow signs for Babbacombe & seafront, hotel 500yds from model village) ☎ 01803 327637
Etr-Oct
Situated on the level, only 50 yards from the lovely Babbacombe Downs, overlooking Lyme Bay, Hotel Blue Conifer is set in attractive gardens. Tom and Ann Ingram welcome guests to their well maintained small hotel. Bedrooms are attractively co-ordinated and comfortable, several benefiting from coastal views; one ground floor room is available. Each morning, a hearty breakfast is served in the comfortable and well appointed dining room. An ideal centre for touring and exploring the many local attractions, or just relaxing in charming surroundings.
7 bth/shr (3 fmly) No smoking in 3 bedrooms No smoking in dining room No smoking in 1 lounge CTV in all bedrooms Tea and coffee making facilities Cen ht CTV 9P
ROOMS: s £26-£33; d £42-£56*
CARDS:

Selected

Q Q Q Q **Hotel Fleurie** 50 Bampfylde Rd TQ2 5AY
(M5 junct 31-follow signs for Torquay. Hotel located just off A3022 (main seafront approach road) between Torre station and Torre Abbey)
☎ 01803 294869
This is a comfortable, well equipped and tastefully decorated guest house with many personal touches in the bedrooms including hairdryers, books and sweets in all rooms. Located in a quiet tree lined avenue, and yet within easy walking distance of the beach and town centre.
8 shr (2 fmly) No smoking in dining room No smoking in lounges CTV in all bedrooms Tea and coffee making facilities No dogs (ex guide dogs) Cen ht No children 2yrs 6P
ROOMS: s £18-£22; d £36-£44; wkly b&b £120-£150*

Q Q Q **Hotel Trelawney** 48 Belgrave Rd TQ2 5HS
(Belgrave Rd is main road into Torquay, hotel is approx 250yds up from beach) ☎ 01803 296049 FAX 01803 296049
Conveniently situated within close walking distance of the centre and the beaches, Hotel Trelawney offers comfortable accommodation with many extra bedroom facilities. There is a spacious lounge and a pretty front patio decorated with hanging baskets and tubs of colourful flowers.
14 rms (13 bth/shr) (2 fmly) CTV in all bedrooms Tea and coffee making facilities Direct dial from bedrooms No dogs (ex guide dogs) Licensed Cen ht CTV 3P Use of facilities at nearby hotel Last d 2pm
ROOMS: wkly b&b £112-£147; wkly hlf-bd £168-£203
CARDS:

Q Q Q **Ingoldsby Hotel** 1 Chelston Rd TQ2 6PT
☎ 01803 607497
In a quiet part of Torquay, within walking distance of the centre and harbour, this imposing Victorian villa offers spacious rooms and a comfortable lounge that has an adjoining residents' bar. A five course dinner can be taken in the dining room. There are attractive gardens for guests to enjoy.
15 rms (3 bth 9 shr) (3 fmly) No smoking in bedrooms No smoking in dining room CTV in all bedrooms Tea and coffee making facilities No dogs (ex guide dogs) Licensed Cen ht CTV 12P No coaches Last d 7pm
ROOMS: s £16-£21; d £32-£42; wkly b&b £128-£144; wkly hlf-bd £177-£216*
CARDS:

Q Q Q **Kelvin House Hotel** 46 Bampfylde Rd TQ2 5AY
(from A3002 turn into Avenue Rd after next traffic lights turn left into Bampfylde Rd, Kelvin House Hotel 100yds on right)
☎ 01803 297313 FAX 01803 297313
Closed Dec-Jan
Kelvin House is situated close to the seafront, within easy walking distance of the town centre. Though the rooms vary in size, all are en suite and smartly decorated and furnished, including a number of extra facilities. In addition to a cosy and comfortable lounge there is a pleasant dining room where home cooked dinners are served.
8 shr (1 fmly) No smoking CTV in all bedrooms Tea and coffee making facilities Licensed Cen ht CTV No children 5yrs 6P Last d 7pm
ROOMS: d £32-£40; wkly b&b £108-£135; wkly hlf-bd £170-£198*
CARDS:

Selected

QQQQ **Kings Hotel** 44 Bampfylde Rd TQ2 5AY
(from A3022 to Torquay, turn right at Torre Railway station into Avenue Rd, after 0.5m turn left into Bampfylde Rd)
☎ 01803 293108 FAX 01803 292482
Closed 15 Dec-20 Jan
Situated close to Torre Abbey and only a short walk to the seafront, this comfortable, friendly guest house is now under the ownership of Marie Burke, who is gradually re-furbishing the house. The bedrooms are comfortable and well equipped, with modern facilities. There is a small bar and a bright and cheerful dining room where a daily menu offers guests good home cooked fare.
8 bth/shr (3 fmly) No smoking in dining room No smoking in 1 lounge CTV in all bedrooms Tea and coffee making facilities Direct dial from bedrooms No dogs (ex guide dogs) Licensed Cen ht CTV 5P Last d 3pm
ROOMS: s fr £21; d fr £42; wkly b&b fr £140; wkly hlf-bd fr £203*
CARDS:

Selected

QQQQ **Kingston House** 75 Avenue Rd TQ2 5LL
(from A3022 to Torquay turn right at Torre Station down Avenue Road, Kingston House approx a quarter of a mile on left)
☎ 01803 212760
In the capable hands of owners Anita and Brian Sexon, a relaxed atmosphere prevails at this charming guest house. Careful planning has gone into the furnishing and decorating of the bedrooms, with tasteful co-ordinated colour schemes and a good range of facilities. Although evening meals are no longer served, guests may relax in the attractive lounge and enjoy a good home-cooked breakfast in the separate dining room.
6 bth/shr (2 fmly) No smoking in dining room CTV in all bedrooms Tea and coffee making facilities No dogs Cen ht No children 8yrs 6P No coaches
ROOMS: s £20-£22.50; d £32-£40; wkly b&b £109-£129*
CARDS:

QQQ **Kingsway Lodge** 95 Avenue Rd TQ2 5LH
(at Torre station with Halfords on right, take right hand filter at traffic lights signed 'to sea front'. House 20yds on left)
☎ 01803 295288
Closed 22 Dec-5 Jan
Situated near to the town centre and seafront, within walking distance of Torre Abbey, this small guesthouse offers the visitor a comfortable stay. All rooms are very well equipped with modern facilities and Mr & Mrs Barrett ensure their guests are well cared for.

5 bth/shr (3 fmly) No smoking CTV in all bedrooms Tea and coffee making facilities Direct dial from bedrooms No dogs (ex guide dogs) Cen ht CTV 4P
ROOMS: s £15-£20; d £30-£40; wkly b&b £100-£140*
CARDS:

Selected

QQQQ ***Millbrook House*** Old Mill Rd, Chelston TQ2 6AP
(Turn off A380 onto A3022 follow signs to seafront-Millbrook on junct of Avenue Rd and Old Mill Rd) ☎ 01803 297394 FAX 01803 297394
Under the enthusiastic ownership of the Branch family, guests can be sure of a warm and friendly welcome at this small hotel. Rooms, including one with its own sitting room, are exceedingly well equipped, with all the expected comforts, and some have extras like mini-bars. There is a downstairs bar where guests can enjoy a quiet drink before a good home-cooked dinner. There is also an attractively decorated lounge. Millbrook House is close to the seafront and just a pleasant stroll to the town centre.
10 bth/shr (1 fmly) No smoking CTV in all bedrooms Tea and coffee making facilities No dogs Licensed Cen ht CTV 10P No coaches Last d 4pm
CARDS:

Premier Selected

QQQQQ **Mulberry House** 1 Scarborough Rd TQ2 5UJ
(from Torquay seafront turn up Belgrave Rd, then turn first right up Scarborough Rd, premises on the left) ☎ 01803 213639
This delightful Victorian property, set in a quiet residential area within walking distance of the seafront, is most accurately described as a restaurant with rooms. There are three attractive bedrooms which all have their own individual character and charm. In the restaurant log fires burn on cooler evenings and a choice of freshly prepared dishes is offered from blackboard menus. Look out for local fish and meat and hearty portions of mouth-watering puddings.
3 bth/shr No smoking CTV in all bedrooms No dogs Licensed Cen ht Leisure centre near Last d 9.30pm
ROOMS: s £25-£35; d £44-£50; wkly b&b £150; wkly hlf-bd £255*

Selected

QQQQ **Newlyn Hotel** 62 Braddons Rd East TQ1 1HF
(follow B3199 round sea front to harbour turn left to Babbacombe Rd, 4th turning on left) ☎ 01803 295100
Conveniently located close to both the town centre and the beaches at Babbacombe, The Newlyn Hotel is under the new ownership of Barbara and John Eggleston, who have re-furbished and decorated their

bedrooms to a high standard. Barbara offers her guests splendid four-course dinners, served in the attractive and brightly decorated dining room.

9 rms (6 shr) (3 fmly) No smoking CTV in all bedrooms Tea and coffee making facilities No dogs (ex guide dogs) Cen ht CTV 10P No coaches Last d breakfast
ROOMS: s £16-£18; d £36-£44; wkly b&b £120-£148; wkly hlf-bd £200-£228*

Q Q Q ***Newton House*** 31 Newton Rd, Torre TQ2 5DB ☎ 01803 297520
Closed 21 Dec-1 Jan
Newton House is in an accessible position close to the town centre and all the main attractions. Guests benefit from many little luxuries in each of the pleasantly decorated bedrooms. There is a sunny breakfast room and comfortable lounge.
8 rms (6 shr) (2 fmly) CTV in all bedrooms Tea and coffee making facilities No dogs Cen ht No children 5yrs 12P No coaches

Q Q Q **Redlands** 317 Babbacombe Rd TQ1 3TB (from Torquay harbour take B3199 signposted Babbacombe, 1.5m is Palace Hotel is on right, premises on left just past Palace Hotel) ☎ 01803 298702
Apr-Oct rs Oct-Apr
Redlands is situated on the Babbacombe Road and is within easy reach of the town centre. Beautiful beaches and the Babbacombe Downs, with their fine views, are within easy walking distance. The bedrooms are spacious and comfortable, offer all modern facilities and have either en suite or private bathrooms.
3 bth/shr No smoking CTV in all bedrooms Tea and coffee making facilities Cen ht No children 6P No coaches
ROOMS: d £34-£40*

Selected

Q Q Q Q **Robin Hill Hotel** 74 Braddons Hill Rd East TQ1 1HF (from Torquay Harbour head towards Babbacombe, on the B3199 Babbacombe Rd take fourth turning on left, premises are first hotel on right) ☎ 01803 214518 FAX 01803 291410
Etr-Oct
Built in 1896 as a colonial style gentleman's residence, Robin Hill, standing in its own terraced gardens, was designed for gracious living, and the stairs and galleried landing are an impressive feature of the hotel. Jo and David Kitson are the friendly, outgoing owners, who continue to upgrade and improve the property. All the attractively furnished bedrooms offer the expected modern comforts, and many interesting period features have been preserved. Public rooms are spacious and inviting, and in the dining room, a short fixed-price dinner menu is offered (guests are asked to make their choice at breakfast).
18 shr (3 fmly) No smoking in bedrooms No smoking in dining room CTV in all bedrooms Tea and coffee making facilities Direct dial from bedrooms Licensed Cen ht CTV 12P No coaches Last d 6pm
ROOMS: s £22-£30; d £44-£60; wkly b&b £140-£195; wkly hlf-bd £210-£265
CARDS:

Q Q Q **Sceptre Lodge Hotel** 533 Babbacombe Rd TQ1 1HQ (on B3199. 400mtrs from harbour, via Torwood St on left hand side before museum ,overlooking gardens) ☎ 01803 292668 FAX 01803 292668
Pamela and Arthur Mee epitomise the ideal hosts and have run Sceptre Lodge for some years, warmly welcoming their guests. Comfortable accommodation with modern facilities is on offer. An attractive lounge and dining room has views towards Torwood Park. The harbour and shops are but a short stroll away.
10 rms (8 shr) (2 fmly) No smoking in dining room CTV in all bedrooms Tea and coffee making facilities Licensed Cen ht CTV 6P No coaches
ROOMS: s £16-£22; d £32-£44; wkly b&b £100-£150; wkly hlf-bd £199*
CARDS:

Q Q Q **Seaway Hotel** Chelston Rd TQ2 6PU (turn off Torquay seafront at the Grand Hotel, left into Hennapyn Rd, at crossroads turn right, then first right into Chelston Rd) ☎ 01803 605320 FAX 01803 605320
This well kept Victorian property is situated in a quiet area of Torquay in easy reach of the harbour and town centre. There is a sunny terrace where guests are welcome to relax. Guests can also enjoy the large sun lounge overlooking the garden, and a separate dining room with an adjacent bar. Meals and snacks are available each evening.
13 bth/shr (3 fmly) No smoking in dining room CTV in all bedrooms Tea and coffee making facilities Licensed Cen ht CTV 18P Last d 6.30pm
ROOMS: s £18.50-£23.50; d £37-£47; wkly b&b £123-£152; wkly hlf-bd £170-£213
CARDS:

Q Q Q **Shirley Hotel** Braddons Hill Rd East TQ1 1HF (follow signs for seafront, turn left to harbour, at harbour turn left along Babbacombe Rd. 1st left past museum) ☎ 01803 293016
Closed Xmas & New Year
Located in a quiet residential road, yet within easy walking distance of the harbour and centre of the town, The Shirley Hotel is a friendly well run guest house which the Stephens family have owned and personally run for

contd.

the last nine years. The spotless bedrooms are comfortable and attractively decorated with modern facilities. Breakfast is taken in the spacious dining room, adjacent to the comfortable lounge/bar, where guests can relax and enjoy a drink, after taking a swim in the outdoor pool or enjoying the views from the hotel's patio and garden.
13 rms (12 bth/shr) (2 fmly) No smoking in dining room CTV in all bedrooms Tea and coffee making facilities No dogs Licensed Cen ht CTV No children 12yrs 8P Outdoor swimming pool (heated) Sauna Jacuzzi
ROOMS: s £18-£25; d £36-£50; wkly b&b £100-£160
CARDS:

QQQ ***Silverlands Hotel*** 27 Newton Rd TQ2 5DB
(on A3022 after Torre Station traffic lights)
☎ 01803 292013
Silverlands Hotel is an attractive Tudor-style house located close to the town centre. The smart bedrooms are all thoughtfully decorated with attractive fabrics and furnishings. There is a large sunny dining room, where breakfast is served, and a cosy lounge area that is combined with the entrance hall.
12 rms (8 shr) (2 fmly) No smoking in dining room CTV in 11 bedrooms Tea and coffee making facilities Cen ht 13P

Selected

QQQQ **Suite Dreams** Steep Hill, Maidencombe TQ1 4TS
(2m from St Marychurch on A379, turn right at Maidencombe garage. Approx halfway between Torquay and Teignmouth) (The Independents)
☎ 01803 313900 FAX 01803 313841
Suite Dreams provides guests with a peaceful and relaxing environment. There is a pretty cove just a short walk away, and the property is within easy driving distance of a variety of local tourist attractions. Purpose built, the hotel offers a high standard of accommodation in comfortable well equipped bedrooms, many having the benefit of sea views and several being on the ground floor. An interesting selection of dishes is available at breakfast, and owners Ken and Lorraine James make every effort to ensure guests are made to feel welcome.
12 bth/shr (3 fmly) No smoking in 4 bedrooms No smoking in dining room CTV in all bedrooms Tea and coffee making facilities Direct dial from bedrooms Cen ht 12P No coaches
ROOMS: s £29.50-£43; d £39-£66; wkly b&b £136-£231
CARDS:

QQ **Torbay Rise** Old Mill Rd, Chelston TQ2 6HL
(into Torquay,right at Halfords trffc lights Next set of lights right into Old Mill Rd,under railway bridge,through shops to top of hill.Est on right)
☎ 01803 605541
Apr-Oct
Set a little way above the town centre, and benefiting from lovely views, Torbay Rise Hotel is surrounded by well tended gardens. One bedroom boasts a four-poster bed whilst another is on the ground floor, ideal for the less able. There is a sunny dining room where traditional English fare is served, and a separate cosy bar lounge.
15 bth/shr (3 fmly) No smoking in dining room CTV in all bedrooms Tea and coffee making facilities Licensed Cen ht 8P No coaches Outdoor swimming pool (heated) Last d noon
ROOMS: s £16-£27; d £32-£54; wkly b&b £112-£189; wkly hlf-bd £147-£224*
CARDS:

QQ ***Tor Dean Hotel*** 27 Bampfylde Rd TQ2 5AY ☎ 01803 294669
Apr-Oct
Popular with guests attending conferences at the nearby English Riviera Centre, this Victorian villa is situated within walking distance of the many attractions of Torquay. Dinner is available in the bright dining room and there is a cosy bar as well as a comfortable sitting room for guests. Courtesy pickup from the stations is provided on request.
12 rms (7 shr) (3 fmly) No smoking in bedrooms No smoking in dining room No smoking in 1 lounge CTV in all bedrooms Tea and coffee making facilities No dogs Licensed Cen ht CTV 10P Last d 4.30pm
CARDS:

QQ **Wayland Hotel** 31 Belgrave Rd TQ2 5HX ☎ 01803 293417
FAX 01803 293417
Within easy walking distance of the seafront and the town centre, The Wayland Hotel offers comfortable en suite accommodation. Breakfast is served in the front-facing dining room.
10 shr (3 fmly) No smoking in lounges CTV in all bedrooms Tea and coffee making facilities No dogs Cen ht
ROOMS: d £20-£50; wkly b&b £70-£140*
CARDS:

Selected

QQQQ **Westgate Hotel** Falkland Rd TQ2 5JP
(A380 turn right at Torre stn down Avenue Rd, at 2nd lights-left into Falkland Rd.)
☎ 01803 295350 FAX 01803 295350
The Westgate is conveniently situated for the beach and Torquay's many attractions. Friendly owners Sid and Ann Fuller are constantly looking for ways to improve their charming hotel, spending the quieter months redecorating and refurbishing. The bedrooms are well equipped, and one is on the ground floor. Many guests return regularly to enjoy the relaxing atmosphere and the traditional home cooking. The huge games room with darts, table tennis and a pool table opens onto a pretty outdoor terrace.
13 bth/shr (2 fmly) No smoking in 3 bedrooms No smoking in dining room No smoking in lounges CTV in all bedrooms Tea and coffee making facilities No dogs Licensed CTV No children 5yrs 13P Games room Pool table Table tennis Last d 8pm
ROOMS: s £25-£27; d £50-£54; wkly b&b £147-£157.50; wkly hlf-bd £227.50-£237.50*
CARDS:

TOTLAND BAY See **WIGHT, ISLE OF**

TOTNES Devon Map **03** SX86

See also South Brent

Selected

QQQQ **Durant Arms** Ashprington TQ9 7UP
☎ 01803 732240
Situated in the centre of picturesque Ashprington, The Durant Arms certainly adds charm and character to a quiet village. Inside this 18th-century inn, guests can enjoy fine ales, and excellent food prepared by William Steer, the chef. There are three bedrooms with their own

private entrance and each is furnished to a high standard. All the rooms are en suite, comfortable, and offer modern facilities.

3 bth/shr (1 fmly) No smoking in bedrooms No smoking in area of dining room No dogs Cen ht 3P Last d 9.15pm
ROOMS: s £25-£30; d fr £47*
MEALS: Lunch £11-£14 Dinner £15-£19alc*
CARDS:

Selected

QQQQ **The Old Forge at Totnes** Seymour Place TQ9 5AY (turn off A38 towards Totnes, from town centre cross river bridge and take second right) ☎ 01803 862174 FAX 01803 865385
rs Xmas wk
Quietly situated just a short walk from the town centre, this attractive 600 year old property is personally supervised by Jeannie Allnutt. The bedrooms are cosy, being individually decorated and furnished in a cottage style, with many extras. Guests can relax in the lounge or the new conservatory which overlooks the gardens. There is a wide selection at breakfast, served in a Tudor style dining room and in the summer months, afternoon teas are a speciality. An added attraction is the working smithy and pottery.
10 bth/shr (4 fmly) No smoking CTV in all bedrooms Tea and coffee making facilities Direct dial from bedrooms No dogs (ex guide dogs) Licensed Cen ht CTV ch fac 10P No coaches Whirlpool Spa
ROOMS: s £40-£50; d £52-£72; wkly b&b £182-£252*
CARDS:

QQQ *Penny Rowden (SX805545)* Washbourne TQ9 7DN (Off A3122 at Forces Tavern towards Washbourne, Penny Rowden Drive is on right after approx 0.25 mile.) ☎ 01803 712485 FAX 01803 712485 Mrs A Parsons
Peacefully set at the end of a lane, this smallholding is surrounded by open countryside, yet close to the many areas of beauty in the South Hams. Ann Parsons assures her guests of a warm welcome and provides comfortable accommodation and honest home cooking.
3 shr (1 fmly) No smoking in bedrooms No smoking in dining room Tea and coffee making facilities Cen ht CTV P 11 acres variable

Selected

Q Q Q Q **Red Slipper** Stoke Gabriel TQ9 6RU (from A385, take either of the two southbound turnings to Stoke Gabriel. Hotel is opposite Church House Inn) ☎ 01803 782315 FAX 01803 782315
Mar-Dec
Situated in the heart of the picturesque and unspoilt village of Stoke Gabriel, this restaurant with rooms is within easy reach of Paignton and Torquay and their many attractions. Morning coffee and afternoon teas are popular, as are the imaginative dinners served to guests and residents of the area. Bedrooms, many of which are on the ground floor, are equipped with clock radio and a number of extra touches, such as sweets and fresh flowers.
6 rms (4 bth/shr) (1 fmly) No smoking in bedrooms No smoking in dining room CTV in 5 bedrooms Tea and coffee making facilities Licensed Cen ht 7P No coaches Last d 8.30pm
ROOMS: d £53-£55; wkly b&b £180
CARDS:

Premier Selected

Q Q Q Q Q **The Watermans Arms** Bow Bridge, Ashprington TQ9 7EG (A38, A381, folow signs for Kingsbridge out of Totnes, at top of hill turn left for Ashprington and Bow Bridge)
☎ 01803 732214 FAX 01803 732314
Situated on the banks of the River Harbourne at the head of Bow Creek, this historic property has one of the most delightful locations of any country inn. Only two miles from the Elizabethan town of Totnes, guests have all the advantages of a rural location, yet are within easy reach of many nearby attractions. The popular bars are full of character, with exposed beams and log fires and offer an extensive range of meals, all cooked to order using local produce whenever possible. In addition to the printed menu, daily special dishes are available, the list displayed on blackboards. Bedrooms, one with a four-poster, are attractively decorated, those in the new annexe being particulary spacious. All are furnished with modern pine, and well equipped.
15 bth/shr (2 fmly) CTV in all bedrooms Tea and coffee making facilities Direct dial from bedrooms Cen ht 60P Fishing
Last d 9.30pm
ROOMS: s £40-£44; d £40-£64*
MEALS: Lunch £10.95-£19.95&alc*
CARDS:

TROUTBECK (NEAR KESWICK) Cumbria Map 11 NY32

Q Q Q **Lane Head Farm** CA11 0SY
(midway between Penrith and Keswick on A66) ☎ 017687 79220
Closed 6 Jan-15 Mar rs Nov-Dec
Dating from the mid 1700s, this country guest house is full of character and has a friendly, welcoming atmosphere. Bedrooms offer a variety of styles and include two attractive four-poster rooms. There is a cosy lounge and small sun lounge, while breakfast and a skilfully prepared dinner are served in the well proportioned dining room.
9 rms (5 bth/shr) No smoking in bedrooms No smoking in dining room No smoking in 1 lounge CTV in all bedrooms Tea and coffee making facilities No dogs (ex guide dogs) Licensed Cen ht CTV 9P No coaches
ROOMS: s £25-£30; d £36-£44; wkly b&b £126-£154;
wkly hlf-bd £192.50-£220.50*

Q Q Q **Netherdene** CA11 0SJ (off A66, on A5091) ☎ 017684 83475
FAX 017684 83475
Closed 25 Dec
Sitting at the foot of Blencathra, Netherdene is an ideal spot for ramblers and countryside lovers. Rooms are cosy and guarantee a comfortable stay. Breakfast is served in the nicely appointed dining room. In the cooler months an open log fire burns in the lounge, while in summer guests can relax on the patio.
5 shr (1 fmly) No smoking CTV in all bedrooms Tea and coffee making facilities No dogs Cen ht CTV No children 7yrs 6P No coaches
ROOMS: s £21-£25; d £36-£44; wkly b&b £125-£130*

TROUTBECK (NEAR WINDERMERE) Cumbria Map 07 NY40

Q Q Q **Queens Head Hotel** Town Head LA23 1PW
(M6 junct 36, take A590/591 Westbound towards Windermere, turn right at mini-rdbt oto A592 signed Penrith/Ullswater, Queens Head 2m on right)
☎ 015394 32174 FAX 015394 31938
Closed 25 Dec
Steeped in history, this 17th-century coaching inn enjoys stunning views of the Troutbeck Valley. In the spacious bar a selection of real ales complement the nationally acclaimed standard of cooking whilst upstairs there is a restaurant featuring varied and imaginative dishes. Bedrooms - some contained in an adjacent converted barn - provide modern facilities but are furnished to retain the character of the inn.
5 bth/shr 3 annexe bth/shr No smoking in bedrooms CTV in all bedrooms Tea and coffee making facilities Cen ht 110P No coaches Last d 9pm
ROOMS: s £45; d £60-£70*
MEALS: Lunch £10-£22.50alc Dinner £10-£22.50alc*
CARDS:

TRURO Cornwall & Isles of Scilly Map **02** SW84

See also St Mawes

Premier Selected

QQQQQ **Arrallas** *(SW886526)* Ladock TR2 4NP (do not go to Ladock - find Summercourt at junct of A30/A3058 (Newquay to St Austell road) signposted from forecourt of Clock Garage W end of village)
☎ 01872 510379 FAX 01872 510200 Mrs B Holt
Feb-Oct

This is very much a working arable farm that is part of the Duchy of Cornwall estate. Barbara and Ian Holt are the very welcoming hosts and nothing is too much trouble for them. Hearty meals are served using only fresh produce. Bedrooms enjoy the lovely views of the Cornish countryside and all are comfortably furnished. Televisions and other modern facilities are provided and thoughtful touches like hot water bottles are also available.

3 bth/shr No smoking CTV in all bedrooms Tea and coffee making facilities No dogs Cen ht CTV No children 10yrs 10P 317 acres arable
ROOMS: d £42-£46; wkly b&b £136-£149✱

Selected

QQQQ **Bissick Old Mill** Ladock TR2 4PG (7m NE on B3275) ☎ 01726 882557 FAX 01726 884057
Closed 14 Dec-4 Jan

Dating back over 300 years, Bissick Old Mill has been lovingly restored by Liz and Keith Henderson. The beamed dining room with its Delabole slate floor provides an ideal setting for Liz Henderson's cooking, and meals are always imaginative, puddings being a speciality. During the summer months the Hendersons run a tea shop, offering some delicious home made cakes. The individually decorated bedrooms are furnished in pine and are well equipped.

4 bth/shr No smoking in bedrooms No smoking in dining room CTV in all bedrooms Tea and coffee making facilities Licensed Cen ht No children 10yrs 9P No coaches Last d 5pm
ROOMS: s £39.95; d £54-£65; wkly b&b £190-£279.65; wkly hlf-bd £295.40-£384.65✱
CARDS:

QQQ **Conifers** 36 Tregolls Rd TR1 1LA (on A39 opposite Alverton Manor Hotel) ☎ 01872 79925

This attractive Victorian house, which stands in an elevated position above the town is conveniently situated for both the business and leisure traveller. Just a short walk from the centre, Conifers has attractive rooms with modern facilities.

4 rms No smoking in bedrooms No smoking in dining room CTV in all bedrooms Tea and coffee making facilities No dogs (ex guide dogs) Cen ht CTV No children 8yrs 3P No coaches
ROOMS: s £21-£22; d £37-£38; wkly b&b £147-£154✱

Selected

QQQQ **Lands Vue Country House** Lands Vue, Three Burrows TR4 8JA (at Chiverton rdbt where A30 crosses A390 due W of Truro, take the A30 to Bodmin, after 0.5m turn right, premises 400yds on the right) ☎ 01872 560242
Closed Xmas & New Year

contd. on p.432.

Lands Vue is surrounded by 2 acres of peaceful gardens, with its own croquet lawn. The bedrooms are well equipped and most have delightful views of the Cornish countryside. Molly Hutchings is a very hospitable hostess. In the attractive dining room, guests are served a hearty breakfast complete with Mrs Hutching's home made marmalade. There is a cosy lounge with an open fire on winter evenings.
3 bth/shr 1 annexe shr No smoking in bedrooms No smoking in dining room CTV in 3 bedrooms Tea and coffee making facilities No dogs (ex guide dogs) Cen ht CTV No children 12yrs 6P No coaches Croquet
ROOMS: d £40-£44

QQQ **Manor Cottage** Tresillian TR2 4BN
(2.5m from Truro on the A39 St Austell road) ☎ 01872 520212
Closed 24-26 Dec
Situated between Truro and St Austell, Manor Cottage is comfortably furnished with many interesting and individual pieces. Some rooms are being made into en suite accommodation. The popular restaurant is open Thursday to Saturday evenings and provides an interesting modern English menu.
5 rms (3 bth/shr) (1 fmly) No smoking in dining room CTV in all bedrooms Tea and coffee making facilities No dogs (ex guide dogs) Licensed Cen ht 9P No coaches Last d 9pm
ROOMS: s £19-£25; d £36-£50; wkly b&b £115.50-£154
CARDS:

Selected

QQQQ **Rock Cottage** Blackwater TR4 8EU (takethe A30 to Chiverton rdbt, follow sign to Blackwater, premises next to Red Lion Inn just past crossroads)
☎ 01872 560252 FAX 01872 560252
Closed Xmas & New Year
This 18th-century miner's home, with its oak beams, and cob and stone walls has been carefully restored by Brian and Shirley Wakeling. The bedrooms, one of which is on the ground floor, are extremely well equipped and comfortable, with good use being made of the space available. Guests can enjoy the choice of two comfortable and spacious lounges. Meals are served in the original cottage kitchen with its antique Cornish range; although Rock Cottage is not licensed, guests are welcome to bring their own drinks. This is a good place from which to sight-see, the Cathedral City of Truro and the sea are both nearby, not forgetting Cornwall's other attractions.
3 shr No smoking CTV in all bedrooms Tea and coffee making facilities No dogs Cen ht CTV No children 18yrs 3P No coaches
ROOMS: s fr £28; d fr £48
CARDS:

Selected

QQQQ *Trevispian Vean (SW850502)* St Erme TR4 9BL
(from A30 take A35 for Truro, in 2.5m in Trispen village take 2nd left in 0.5m bear sharp left, farm entrance 500yds on left)
☎ 01872 79514 FAX 01872 263730 Mr & Mrs E Dymond
Mar-Oct
Trevispian Vean Guest House has been successfully run by Mr & Mrs Dymond for many years, alongside their farm. The comfortable bedrooms are well equipped and furnished and all have en suite bathrooms. The lounges and dining room are spacious and visitors enjoy the good home cooking provided by Mrs Dymond.
12 rms (2 bth 8 shr) (7 fmly) No smoking Tea and coffee making facilities No dogs (ex guide dogs) Licensed Cen ht CTV 20P Fishing Pool table Table tennis 300 acres arable pigs Last d 4.30pm

TUNBRIDGE WELLS (ROYAL) Kent Map 05 TQ53

Premier Selected

QQQQQ **Danehurst House** 41 Lower Green Rd, Rusthall TN4 8TW (from Tunbridge Wells take the A264 out of town, 1.5m turn right past Spa Hotel, right at crossroads, Lower Green Rd 200yds on left) (The Circle) ☎ 01892 527739 FAX 01892 514804
This delightful Victorian house is home to Angela and Michael Godbold, and combines traditional levels of comfort with warm hospitality. The bedrooms are individually furnished in the style of the house and are particularly well equipped with lots of thoughtful extras. There is an elegant drawing room with a grand piano and library, and a new conservatory breakfast room which can also be used for private meetings. Full English breakfast offers a good choice of dishes and is served in the attractive conservatory. Service is especially helpful and light refreshments are available throughout the day.
5 bth/shr No smoking CTV in all bedrooms Tea and coffee making facilities No dogs Licensed Cen ht CTV No children 8yrs 6P No coaches Last d 6pm
ROOMS: s £35-£49.50; d £55-£69.50; wkly b&b £245-£346
CARDS:

QQQ **Dewspel** Bird-In-Hand St, Old Groombridge TN3 9QJ
(take A264 from Tunbridge Wells, then B2188 at Langton Green, turn right in front of Crown PH and right again up hill to Dewspel 0.25m on right)
☎ 01892 864369 FAX 01892 864369
Closed Dec 23-2 Jan
Dewspel is set on a hillside and offers tranquility and lovely countryside views. Bedrooms are very comfortable, and decorated in a modern style; they are equipped with a range of thoughtful extras. Guests may use the sunny lounge with views across the rolling hills; breakfast is served around a large communal table in the adjoining breakfast room.
3 rms (1 bth/shr) (1 fmly) No smoking CTV in all bedrooms Tea and coffee making facilities No dogs Cen ht CTV 8P No coaches
ROOMS: s £30; d £40

Premier Selected

QQQQQ **The Old Parsonage** Church Ln, Frant TN3 9DX
(2m S of Tunbridge Wells, off A267 in Frant, East Sussex)
☎ 01892 750773 FAX 01892 750773
This elegant Georgian house is set in three acres of grounds in the tranquil village of Frant. The beautifully renovated and spacious interior has striking furnishings and decor (which features photographs taken by the owner Mr Dakin). Bedrooms are generous both in size and facilities, and the bathrooms are luxurious. Summertime guests are encouraged to take advantage of the attractive gardens and terrace or relax with afternoon tea in the conservatory.

3 bth/shr No smoking CTV in all bedrooms Tea and coffee making facilities Cen ht CTV 12P Croquet lawn Sun terrace
ROOMS: s £45-£55; d £62-£72*
CARDS:

TWO BRIDGES Devon Map **02** SX67

Selected

Q Q Q Q Cherrybrook Hotel PL20 6SP (on B3212)
☎ 01822 880260 FAX 01822 880260
Closed 24 Dec-2 Jan
Cherrybrook Hotel is situated in the rugged expanse of Dartmoor National Park, and owners Margaret and Andy Duncan make every effort to ensure their guests' stay is both enjoyable and memorable. Over the years, this farmhouse has been upgraded, resulting in a selection of comfortable, well equipped bedrooms and a cosy lounge with a bar. A four-course meal is available each evening with the emphasis on fresh local produce.
7 rms (6 shr) (2 fmly) No smoking in dining room CTV in all bedrooms Tea and coffee making facilities Licensed Cen ht 12P No coaches Last d 7.15pm
ROOMS: s £26-£43.90; d £52-£82.80; wkly b&b £175-£185; wkly hlf-bd £255-£270*

TYWARDREATH Cornwall & Isles of Scilly Map **02** SX05

Selected

Q Q Q Q Elmswood Tehidy Rd PL24 2QD
(turn off A390 at junct for Fowey, follow road for 3m B3269. Turn left at junct for Tywardreath & Par Hotel opposite St Andrews Church)
☎ 01726 814221 FAX 01726 814221
Peacefully located in a quiet village, this impeccably maintained gabled house is conveniently located for St Austell and Fowey. Richard and Pam Warren offer a warm welcome and take pride in their establishment. The bedrooms are individually decorated with co-ordinated fabrics and good quality furnishings. There is a ground floor family room, and all rooms have modern facilities. Downstairs there is a small bar and attractive dining room which overlooks the beautifully kept garden and offers the opportunity to sample the home cooked dishes which make up the set menu.
7 rms (1 bth 5 shr) (1 fmly) No smoking in dining room CTV in all bedrooms Tea and coffee making facilities No dogs (ex guide dogs) Licensed Cen ht CTV 8P No coaches Last d noon
ROOMS: s £20-£26; d £43-£46; wkly b&b £140-£182; wkly hlf-bd £150-£245*

UCKFIELD East Sussex Map **05** TQ42

Selected

Q Q Q Q Highlands Framfield TN22 5SA
(turn off A22 to Uckfield, follow signs to B2102. Just before Framfield turn left at Hammonds Green into lane signposted Buxted,house 500yds on right) ☎ 01825 890788 FAX 01825 890803
Closed 20 Dec-7 Jan
Highlands is situated in its own gardens near the village of Framfield. Now fully restored by David and Maria Andrews, parts of the house are over 400 years old. The two spacious bedrooms are in the original house and offer comfort with good extra facilities. Meals are substantial and can be enjoyed in the dining room, which features antique furniture. There is also a guest lounge with plenty of reading matter.
2 bth No smoking CTV in all bedrooms Tea and coffee making facilities No dogs (ex guide dogs) Cen ht CTV 5P No coaches Fishing Last d 6pm
ROOMS: s £33; d £56; wkly b&b £180-£196; wkly hlf-bd £305-£336

Premier Selected

[Q] [Q] [Q] [Q] [Q] **Hooke Hall** 250 High St TN22 1EN (N end of Uckfield High St) ☎ 01825 761578 FAX 01825 768025
Closed 25-31 Dec
Lovingly restored by the owners, this classic Queen Anne townhouse features pleasant day-rooms full of antique furniture, fine paintings and ornaments, creating a wonderful country house feel. The bedrooms have been individually decorated in great style. Breakfast (charged as an extra) is taken in the elegant setting of the restaurant, which serves Italian dishes at other times.
9 bth/shr No smoking in dining room CTV in all bedrooms Tea and coffee making facilities Direct dial from bedrooms No dogs Licensed Cen ht No children 10yrs 8P No coaches Last d 9pm
ROOMS: s £47.50-£80; d £65-£120
CARDS:

Selected

[Q] [Q] [Q] [Q] **South Paddock** Maresfield Park TN22 2HA (in centre of Maresfield village, enter the park under the lodge opp the church & The Chequers Hotel, cross 5 speed bumps, South Paddock is on left)
☎ 01825 762335
An extended 1920s house furnished with antiques and set in three and a half acres of glorious grounds, Graham and Jennifer Allt's home is one of enormous charm. The three bedrooms, all south-facing, are spacious, individually decorated and provided with extras such as magazines, plants and bathrobes. The breakfast room, Major Allt's particular responsibility, features over 50 small flags, representing the countries of origin of all their guests. His home-made preserves round off breakfasts that are well worth getting up for. There are two delightful lounges warmed by log fires in winter. Comprehensive information, including maps, on all the local places of interest is freely offered.
3 rms (1 bth) No smoking in bedrooms No smoking in 1 lounge CTV in all bedrooms Tea and coffee making facilities No dogs (ex guide dogs) Cen ht CTV No children 10yrs 7P No coaches Croquet
ROOMS: s £35-£39; d £53-£57

UFFCULME Devon Map 03 ST01

[Q] [Q] **Houndaller** *(ST058138)* EX15 3ET (0.25m from junct 27 of M5)
☎ 01884 840246 Mrs S R Farley
This 16th-century Devonshire longhouse is part of a 600-acre mixed farm. The bedrooms are spacious and comfortable, the atmosphere relaxed and friendly. There is a cosy lounge/dining room with a wood-burning stove where breakfast is served around one large family table.
2 rms (2 fmly) CTV in all bedrooms Tea and coffee making facilities Cen ht CTV 3P 210 acres arable beef sheep

ULEY Gloucestershire Map 03 ST79

Selected

[Q] [Q] [Q] [Q] **Hodgecombe Farm** *(ST783993)* GL11 5AN (Uley is on B4066. In Uley take road to Coaley up Fop Street, follow signs to Coaley until you come to farm track on sharp left bend)
☎ 01453 860365 Mrs C Bevan
Mar-Oct
Reached by a farm track and set in three acres of its own grounds, Hodgecombe Farm is convenient for the Severn Vale and the many attractions of this delightful area. Mrs Bevan is a very welcoming hostess and bedrooms are comfortable and prettily decorated.
3 rms (1 bth/shr) No smoking Tea and coffee making facilities No dogs (ex guide dogs) Cen ht No children 5yrs 3P 3 acres non-working Last d previous day
ROOMS: d £17-£21; wkly b&b £102-£126

ULVERSTON Cumbria Map 07 SD27

[Q] [Q] [Q] **Church Walk House** Church Walk LA12 7EW (follow 'Town Centre' at main rdbt, turn sharp right at junct opposite the Kings Arms, establishment is opposite Stables furniture shop). ☎ 01229 582211
Discreetly set in the town centre, this elegant residence dates back to the 17th century and features a tasteful mix of period styles. It has a peaceful and relaxing atmosphere. There is a charming little lounge and breakfast is taken around one large table.
3 bth/shr (2 fmly) No smoking Tea and coffee making facilities Cen ht CTV No coaches
ROOMS: s £18-£25; d £35-£42; wkly b&b £75-£110*

UPPINGHAM Rutland Map 04 SP89

Selected

[Q] [Q] [Q] [Q] **Rutland House** 61 High St East LE15 9PY (off A47 onto A6003 turn left into High St East past Market Square Rutland house on left near end of High St) ☎ 01572 822497 FAX 01572 822497
Rutland House sits at the quieter end of High Street East. Bedrooms are spacious and comfortably appointed, each room is thoughtfully equipped and has a modern en suite bathroom; there is a ground floor bedroom available. Breakfasts are taken in the cheerfully decorated breakfast room.
5 bth/shr (1 fmly) No smoking in 1 bedrooms No smoking in dining room CTV in all bedrooms Tea and coffee making facilities Cen ht No children 5yrs 3P No coaches
ROOMS: s £30; d £40
CARDS:

UTTOXETER Staffordshire Map **07** SK03

Selected

Q Q Q Q **Hillcrest** 3 Leighton Rd ST14 8BL
(follow Race Course signs along A518 to B5017, right at mini-rdbt 400m, right Wood Leighton right again Leighton Road, end on right)
☎ 01889 564627 FAX 01889 564627
Closed Xmas Day
This privately owned and personally run guesthouse is located in a residential area, within easy reach of the town centre and close to the JCB factory. It provides modern equipped accommodation, which includes family bedded rooms. Separate tables are provided in the traditionally furnished dining room and there is a spacious, comfortable lounge.
7 bth/shr (5 fmly) No smoking in bedrooms No smoking in dining room CTV in all bedrooms Tea and coffee making facilities No dogs (ex guide dogs) Licensed Cen ht CTV 12P No coaches Last d 4pm
ROOMS: s £30-£32; d £40-£42*
CARDS:

VENTNOR See **WIGHT, ISLE OF**

VOWCHURCH Herefordshire Map **03** SO33

Selected

Q Q Q Q **Upper Gilvach Farm** *(SO336340)* St Margarets HR2 0QY (off B4348, towards Michaelchurch Escley, after approx 3m follow signs for Gilvach)
☎ 01981 510618 FAX 01981 510618 Mrs R Watkins
Closed Xmas
In an unspoilt area between the Black Mountains and the Golden Valley, this farmhouse offers comfortable accommodation especially suited to walkers and nature lovers. Bedrooms are well equipped and homely and all have the benefit of modern en suite or private facilities. Public areas include a dining room where four course dinners and tasty English breakfasts are served and a comfortable sitting room and separate conservatory. Alan and Ruth Watkins are friendly and caring hosts with a good knowledge of the area and its attractions.
3 bth/shr (1 fmly) No smoking CTV in all bedrooms Tea and coffee making facilities No dogs (ex guide dogs) Licensed Cen ht CTV P 90 acres mixed working
ROOMS: s £20-£30; d £40-£60*

WADEBRIDGE Cornwall & Isles of Scilly Map **02** SW97

Q Q Q **Swan Hotel** Molesworth St PL27 7DD (St Austell Brewery)
☎ 01208 812526 FAX 812526
The Swan Hotel is a popular haunt for locals and residents alike. The well equipped bedrooms are neatly decorated and furnished with country-style pine. An extensive range of bar meals is served at midday and during the evening. Residents can dine in the Victorian-themed restaurant, where breakfast is served.
6 bth (1 fmly) CTV in all bedrooms Tea and coffee making facilities Cen ht 6P Last d 9pm
ROOMS: s fr £27.50; d fr £49.50; wkly b&b fr £165*
MEALS: Lunch £1.95-£10.95alc Dinner £5-£15alc*
CARDS:

See page 14-20 for a list of Premier Selected establishments

WADHURST East Sussex Map **05** TQ63

Q Q Q **Four Keys** Station Rd TN5 6RZ ☎ 01892 782252 FAX 01892 784113
A small country inn situated just north of the town. The spacious bedrooms, comfortably appointed and with modern furnishings, are located in a building adjacent to the main house. Home cooked meals are offered throughout the day and can be taken in the restaurant or bar.
7 annexe bth/shr (1 fmly) CTV in all bedrooms Tea and coffee making facilities Direct dial from bedrooms Cen ht 24P Last d 10pm
CARDS:

WAKEFIELD West Yorkshire Map **08** SE32

Q Q Q **Kirklands Hotel** 605 Leeds Rd, Owtwood WF1 2LU
(turn off junct 41, take A650 signed Wakefield at 2nd rdbt take A61. Hotel approx 1.5m on left next to Parish church)
☎ 01924 826666 FAX 01924 826682
Situated a short way from the city on the Leeds road, this friendly inn is well furnished and offers modern and well equipped bedrooms. A good range of food is available as is a selection of real ales.
6 bth/shr (1 fmly) CTV in all bedrooms Tea and coffee making facilities Direct dial from bedrooms No dogs (ex guide dogs) Cen ht 30P Last d 8.30pm
ROOMS: s £42.50-£46; d £54.50-£59.50*
MEALS: Bar Lunch £2-£8 Dinner £10-£15alc*
CARDS:

Selected

Q Q Q Q **Stanley View** 226 / 228 Stanley Rd WF1 4AE
(2m off M62 junct 30 on A642 to York, close to city centre)
☎ 01924 376803 FAX 01924 369123
This attractive terraced property has been pleasantly furnished by the resident owners Mr & Mrs Heppinstall. The spacious bedrooms are furnished in contemporary style. A cosy lounge and a small conservatory bar are provided, alongside an airy dining room where home cooking is provided.
10 rms (8 shr) (6 fmly) No smoking in bedrooms CTV in all bedrooms Tea and coffee making facilities Direct dial from bedrooms Licensed Cen ht CTV ch fac 8P Last d 8.30pm
CARDS:

WANTAGE Oxfordshire Map **04** SU38

Selected

Q Q Q Q **Star** Watery Ln, Sparsholt OX12 9PL
(Sparsholt is 4m West of Wantage, take the B4507 Wantage to Ashbury road and turn off right to the village, The Star Inn is signposted)
☎ 01235 751539 & 751001 FAX 01235 751539 *contd.*

400 years old, and with log fires and oak beams, guests cannot fail to be charmed by The Star Inn. Accommodation is in a separate building to the rear of the property. Rooms are tastefully decorated with good quality furnishings, one on the ground floor is suitable for the disabled guest. Meals may be had either in the cosy bar, along with the racing fraternity, or at big old pine tables in the dining room. The inn is shut from 2.30 to 6pm on weekdays and it is advisable for guests planning to arrive early to give advance notice.

7 annexe bth/shr (1 fmly) No smoking in bedrooms CTV in 8 bedrooms Tea and coffee making facilities Direct dial from bedrooms No dogs (ex guide dogs) Cen ht 18P Stabling for guests horses Last d 9.30pm

ROOMS: d £55*

MEALS: Lunch £10.70-£18.50*

CARDS:

WAREHAM Dorset Map **03** SY98

See also Bere Regis

Q Q **Luckford Wood** *(SY873865)* East Stoke BH20 6AW
(turn left off A352 at East Stoke Church, over manned level crossing follow lane for approx 0.5m large house on right)
☎ 01929 463098 FAX 01929 405715 Mr & Mrs Barnes

Set in a peaceful country setting, this homely farmhouse has modestly furnished and suitably equipped bedrooms. A typical English breakfast is served in the very attractive dining room. Guests have use of the owners' private lounge.

4 rms (1 bth 2 shr) (3 fmly) No smoking CTV in all bedrooms Tea and coffee making facilities Cen ht 5P 167 acres dairy

ROOMS: s £20-£26; d £37-£50; wkly b&b £112-£175

Selected

Q Q Q Q **Redcliffe** *(SY932866)* BH20 5BE ☎ 01929 552225
Mrs J Barnes
Closed Xmas

This modern farmhouse enjoys a superb location on the River Frome just a short riverbank walk from Wareham. Mr and Mrs Barnes offer a warm welcome and create a relaxed and friendly atmosphere. The bedrooms are bright and attractively decorated, two of them have balconies to take full advantage of the views. A hearty farmhouse breakfast is served at a communal table, and the Barnes' provide a wealth of local information.

4 rms (1 bth 1 shr) No smoking CTV in 1 bedroom No dogs (ex guide dogs) Cen ht CTV 4P 250 acres dairy mixed

WARMINSTER Wiltshire Map **03** ST84

Selected

Q Q Q Q **Granary** Manor Farm, Upton Scudamore BA12 0AG
(From Granada Services rdbt take the A350, 1st left after railway bridge then 1st right. The Granary is the 2nd house on the left)
☎ 01985 214835 FAX 01985 214835
Closed Dec-11 Jan

Situated close to many places of interest, this is a luxurious base from which to explore the picturesque area. William and Marcia Candy are justifiably proud of their recently created ground floor accommodation. Three bedrooms are provided, individually styled with different themes. Breakfast is served in the privacy of rooms, two of which offer south facing patios. Each tastefully decorated bedroom has a fridge for keeping both the milk and white wine chilled!

3 annexe shr No smoking CTV in all bedrooms Tea and coffee making facilities No dogs Cen ht No children 12yrs 4P

ROOMS: d £44-£48*

WARREN STREET (NEAR LENHAM) Kent Map **05** TQ95

Q Q Q **Harrow** Hubbards Hill ME17 2ED
(turn off A20 marked Warren St, opposite Lenham, follow the road 0.5 mile The Harrow Inn is on the right hand side)
☎ 01622 858727 FAX 01622 850026
Closed 25 & 26 Dec

The comfortable, good sized rooms all have modern en suite facilities. The bar and restaurant offer a wide variety of good food, and are popular with tourists and locals alike. A full English breakfast is served in the sunny conservatory, or if preferred a continental breakfast can be served in your room. The inn also caters for small functions and conferences.

15 bth/shr (6 fmly) No smoking in area of dining room CTV in all bedrooms Tea and coffee making facilities Direct dial from bedrooms No dogs (ex guide dogs) Cen ht 80P No coaches Last d 9.30pm

ROOMS: s fr £39.50; d fr £49.50*

CARDS:

WARRINGTON Cheshire Map **07** SJ68

Selected

Q Q Q Q ***Kenilworth Hotel*** 2 Victoria Rd, Grappenhall WA4 2EN
(on A50) ☎ 01925 262323 FAX 01925 268320

This family run small hotel is situated just south of the town centre, close to the swing bridge over the Manchester Ship Canal. Well maintained bedrooms are attractively furnished, and there is a comfortable lounge for guests' use. A hearty breakfast is served and evening meals are offered.

14 shr (2 fmly) CTV in all bedrooms Tea and coffee making facilities Direct dial from bedrooms Licensed Cen ht CTV 14P No coaches

CARDS:

WARSASH Hampshire Map 04 SU40

Selected

Q Q Q Q Dormy House Hotel 21 Barnes Ln, Sarisbury SO31 7DA (take A27 towards Fareham, turn right at Warsash)
☎ 01489 572626 FAX 01489 573370
This family run hotel is strong on hospitality making it a very pleasant place to stay. Well located for access to major motor routes it is suited to leisure and business guests alike. The bedrooms are bright and well equipped, with modern en suite facilities. There is a comfortable lounge and a good home cooked evening meal is served in the attractive dining room.
12 bth/shr (1 fmly) No smoking in 3 bedrooms No smoking in dining room CTV in all bedrooms Tea and coffee making facilities Direct dial from bedrooms Licensed Cen ht CTV 18P No coaches Last d 5pm
ROOMS: s £30-£37.60; d £40-£46*
CARDS:

Selected

Q Q Q Q Solent View Private Hotel 33-35 Newtown Rd SO31 9FY (leave M7 junct 9 left onto A27, at next large rdbt take 2nd left towards Warsash for 2.5m, 1st left at rdbt in village, left again for Newton Rd) ☎ 01489 572300 FAX 01489 572300
Located in the quiet village of Warsash this attractive, well maintained house is in a good position for reaching Portsmouth, Fareham and Southampton and their many attractions. The bedrooms are well equipped, comfortably furnished and have modern en suite facilities. The bright dining room overlooks the garden and patio, and after a good home cooked dinner guests may relax in the lounge and enjoy a drink in the bar.
8 bth/shr (1 fmly) No smoking in 2 bedrooms No smoking in dining room CTV in all bedrooms Tea and coffee making facilities Direct dial from bedrooms Licensed Cen ht CTV 12P No coaches Last d noon
ROOMS: s fr £36; d fr £46*
CARDS:

WARWICK Warwickshire Map 04 SP26

See also Lighthorne

Q Q Agincourt Lodge Hotel 36 Coten End CV34 4NP (2m from junct 15 of M40 on the A445)
☎ 01926 499399 FAX 01926 499399
Mr & Mrs Blackband offer guests a warm welcome to the Agincourt Lodge and provide comfortable, double glazed and well equipped bedrooms; guests also have the use of a spacious lounge bar and pleasant breakfast room.
7 bth/shr (2 fmly) No smoking in bedrooms No smoking in dining room CTV in all bedrooms Tea and coffee making facilities Licensed Cen ht CTV 9P No coaches
ROOMS: s £26.50-£29.50; d £45-£52*
CARDS:

Q Q Austin House 96 Emscote Rd CV34 5QJ (on A445 Warwick to Leamington Spa) ☎ 01926 493583
FAX 01926 493583
Mr & Mrs Winter are the pleasant and enthusiastic owners of this small and friendly guest house which is within walking distance of the city. The bedrooms are modern and bright, and good hearty breakfasts are served in the cosy dining room. There is also a comfortable sitting room.
6 rms (4 shr) (4 fmly) No smoking in 2 bedrooms No smoking in dining room No smoking in lounges CTV in all bedrooms Tea and coffee making facilities No dogs Cen ht 6P No coaches
ROOMS: d £34-£40*
CARDS:

Selected

Q Q Q Q Croft Haseley Knob CV35 7NL (from Warwick By-Pass take A4177 towards Solihull and in 4.5m turn right signed M6 Stonebridge then 0.5m turn right to Haseley Knob follow B&B signs)
☎ 01926 484447 FAX 01926 484447
Closed Xmas wk
Situated close to the area's major attractions, this constantly improving guest house, which is part of a smallholding, has been popular for many years. Bedrooms are comfortable and modern in style and most are equipped with small en suite shower rooms. Pat and David Clapp are very friendly and their conservatory dining room is a lovely place to enjoy one of Pat's excellent breakfasts which include free range eggs and home made preserves.
5 bth/shr (2 fmly) No smoking CTV in all bedrooms Tea and coffee making facilities Cen ht CTV 8P No coaches
ROOMS: s £30-£36; d £44-£50
CARDS:

Q Q Q Dockers Barn Farm Oxhill Bridle Rd, Pillerton Hersey CV35 0QB (A422 Stratford-upon-Avon to Banbury, turn left in Pillerton Priors to Pillerton Hersey, 1st right in village onto Oxhill Bridle Rd for0.75m)
☎ 01926 640475 FAX 01926 641747
Closed Xmas rs Daily
This delightful 18th-century threshing barn is set in 27 acres. The pretty bedrooms have modern en suite facilities and overlook the countryside. Proprietors Mr and Mrs Howard provide a warm welcome and offer good local knowledge for walks, pubs, restaurants and sightseeing. Mr Howard speaks fluent French and Spanish.
3 bth/shr (1 fmly) No smoking CTV in all bedrooms Tea and coffee making facilities Cen ht No children 8yrs 9P No coaches Stabling and grazing available for horses
ROOMS: d £38-£44*

Selected

High House Old Warwick Rd, Rowington CV35 7AA (N from Warwick on A4177 turning left after Waterman Inn onto B4439. After 3rd set of crossroads half mile on left down long farm drive) ☎ 01926 843270 FAX 01203 257943
Closed Xmas
John and Beryl Penn are enthusiastic and friendly hosts who welcome guests to their home, a charming Queen Anne, listed farmhouse which sits at the end of a long winding drive in a secluded and tranquil setting. Bedrooms and public rooms are tastefully appointed with period and antique furniture and have an abundance of exposed beams. Breakfast is served at a large communal table in a delightful dining room which has a superb inglenook fireplace. Fresh breads are baked for breakfast most mornings; there is also a separate comfortable sitting room for guests use, with French windows that open onto a colourful garden. Bedrooms are full of character too, each equipped with a thoughtful range of useful extras; both rooms have en suite showers and one of the bedrooms has an antique four-poster.
4 rms (3 bth/shr) No smoking in bedrooms CTV in all bedrooms Tea and coffee making facilities No dogs (ex guide dogs) Cen ht CTV No children 12yrs 20P No coaches
ROOMS: s £28-£35; d £60*

Selected

The Old Rectory Vicarage Ln, Sherbourne CV35 8AB (from M40 juct 15 take A46 Stratford road, 0.25m on left sign 'Old Rectory') ☎ 01926 624562 FAX 01926 624995
Convenient for both Stratford-upon-Avon and Warwick, this 17th-century rectory has been renovated to provide comfortable accommodation. Bedrooms, some of which are located in the former stable block, are well equipped and comfortable, with period furniture and decor. The public rooms include a comfortable sitting room with open inglenook fireplace and honesty bar, and a dining room where imaginative dinners and tasty English breakfasts are served.
7 shr 7 annexe bth/shr (2 fmly) No smoking in dining room CTV in all bedrooms Tea and coffee making facilities Direct dial from bedrooms Licensed Cen ht 14P No coaches Last d 8.30pm
ROOMS: s £30-£35; d £40-£65*
CARDS:

Premier Selected

Shrewley House Shrewley CV35 7AT (take A4177 from Warwick, 1.5m take left fork B4439 to Shrewley. Shrewley House 1.5m on left before village)
☎ 01926 842549 FAX 01926 842216
Close to the village of Shrewley, amidst beautifully maintained grounds, Shrewley House is a Grade II listed Georgian farmhouse. Bedrooms are very individual, tastefully decorated and comfortable. Lots of homely extras are provided and all rooms have the benefit of modern en suite facilities. The elegant drawing room opens on to the lawned gardens and the attractive dining room serves excellent home cooked breakfasts.
4 bth/shr (1 fmly) No smoking CTV in all bedrooms Tea and coffee making facilities Direct dial from bedrooms Cen ht CTV 17P
ROOMS: s fr £45; d fr £62*
CARDS:

Tudor House 90-92 West St CV34 6AW (off A46 onto A429, opposite entrance to castle) (Old English Pub Co)
☎ 01926 495447 FAX 01926 492948
Built in 1472, this is one of the few buildings to survive the Great Fire of Warwick in 1694. It has a wealth of character with exposed timbers and an abundance of bric-a-brac in the public rooms. Each room has a good range of modern facilities. A wide choice of home made meals is available.
11 rms (8 bth/shr) (1 fmly) No smoking in area of dining room No smoking in 1 lounge CTV in all bedrooms Tea and coffee making facilities Direct dial from bedrooms No dogs (ex guide dogs) Cen ht Last d 8.45pm
ROOMS: s £30-£50; d £65-£70
MEALS: Lunch £16.50&alc Dinner £16.50&alc
CARDS:

Woodside Country House Langley Rd CV35 8PJ (6m W of Warwick and 0.75m S of A4189. Turn towards Langley off A4189 in Claverdon village, after a mile, house on right)
☎ 01926 842446 FAX 01926 842410
Closed 24 Dec-1 Jan
Woodside is a pretty cottage which sits in a very peaceful setting amongst 22 acres of attractive gardens and woodland on the edge of the small village of Claverdon. Mrs Bromilow is a charming host who offers traditionally furnished accommodation and with a cosy shared lounge; breakfast is served in a separate room with large picture windows.
4 rms (1 shr) (1 fmly) No smoking CTV in all bedrooms Tea and coffee making facilities Cen ht CTV 12P No coaches Croquet Walks in nature reserve Last d 2pm
ROOMS: s £22-£30; d £44-£50*

WASHFORD Somerset Map 03 ST04

Washford TA23 0PP (on A39 Taunton-Minehead road)
☎ 01984 640256 FAX 01984 641288
This country inn offers easy access to the north coast of Somerset and the beautiful scenery of Exmoor. For train enthusiasts, the West Somerset Steam Railway runs behind the inn and the station is only a stone's throw away. Bedrooms are equipped with modern comforts and a wide range of dishes is available from the menu served in the open plan bar.
8 shr No smoking in area of dining room CTV in all bedrooms Tea and coffee making facilities Direct dial from bedrooms No dogs (ex guide dogs) Cen ht CTV 40P Last d 9.30pm
ROOMS: s £24; d £48; wkly b&b fr £150*
MEALS: Lunch £7.85-£17.45alc Dinner £7.85-£17.45alc*
CARDS:

WASHINGTON Tyne & Wear Map 12 NZ35

Ye Olde Coppe Shop 6 The Green, Washington Village NE38 7AB (follow signs Washington village/Washington Old Hall proceed over cross roads and in 20yds turn left next to the library)
☎ 0191 4165333 FAX 0191 4165333
Mr and Mrs Henderson's delightful home has been converted to include cosy, prettily decorated bedrooms which have been very well equipped with

many thoughtful touches. The rooms are situated above a lovely little tea room where delicious evening meals are served on request.
4 rms (2 shr) No smoking CTV in all bedrooms Tea and coffee making facilities No dogs (ex guide dogs) Cen ht CTV 8P No coaches
Last d 12pm
ROOMS: s £24-£28; d £38-£44✱
CARDS:

WATERHOUSES Staffordshire Map **07** SK05

Q Q **Ye Olde Crown** ST10 3HL (in centre of village, on A523)
☎ 01538 308204
This traditional village inn features bars and sound modern bedrooms. The bars offer a wide range of food options and are popular with locals. Several of the bedrooms are located in a nearby cottage and some of these are suitable for families.
7 rms (6 bth/shr) (2 fmly) CTV in all bedrooms Tea and coffee making facilities No dogs (ex guide dogs) Cen ht 50P Last d 9.30pm
ROOMS: s £15-£25; d £40✱
MEALS: Lunch £8-£14alc Dinner £8-£14alc✱
CARDS:

WATERROW Somerset Map **03** ST02

Q Q Q **The Rock** TA4 2AX (on B3227 14m W of Taunton)
☎ 01984 623293 FAX 01984 623293
rs 24-26 Dec
Built against the rock face in the 16th century this inn is located in the beautiful Tone Valley. The bar with its rock wall and brass topped bar retains much of its original character and charm. A wide range of freshly prepared meals is available in either the bar or the restaurant areas. The comfortable bedrooms are well equipped, and there is a spacious first floor lounge.
7 bth/shr (1 fmly) No smoking in 2 bedrooms CTV in all bedrooms
Direct dial from bedrooms Cen ht CTV 25P Last d 10pm
ROOMS: s £22; d £44✱
MEALS: Lunch £6-£12alc Dinner £7-£14alc✱
CARDS: See advertisement under TAUNTON

WATFORD Hertfordshire Map **04** TQ19

Q Q Q **Upton Lodge** 26-28 Upton Rd WD1 2EL
☎ 01923 237316 FAX 01923 233109
rs Xmas
Upton Lodge sits in the town centre opposite the White House Hotel, which is the point of contact for reservations and arrival; breakfasts are also taken here. The accommodation is housed in two buildings, and each room has a good range of amenities, such as direct dial telephones and en suite facilities.
26 annexe bth/shr (1 fmly) No smoking in 5 bedrooms No smoking in dining room No smoking in 1 lounge CTV in all bedrooms Tea and coffee making facilities Direct dial from bedrooms Licensed Cen ht CTV 35P
Last d 9.45pm
ROOMS: s £64-£79; d £79-£89✱
CARDS:

WEETON Lancashire Map **07** SD33

Q **High Moor** *(SD388365)* Singleton Rd PR4 3JJ
(M55 junct 3 Fleetwood Rd 3m N, left to Singleton. T-junct turn left, 1m on left opposite Weeton Barracks)
☎ 01253 836273 FAX 01253 836273 Mr & Mrs J Colligan
Closed mid Jan-mid Feb, Xmas & New Year
Hearty breakfasts are a feature of this well established farmhouse, situated opposite Weeton Barracks. Two comfortable bedrooms, one suitable for families, are available and service is willingly provided in a friendly environment.
2 rms (1 fmly) CTV in all bedrooms Tea and coffee making facilities
No dogs Cen ht CTV 10P 7 acres non-working
ROOMS: d fr £30✱

WELLINGBOROUGH Northamptonshire Map **04** SP86

Q Q Q **Oak House Private Hotel** 8-11 Broad Green NN8 4LE
(turn off A45 & head towards Kettering on A509, hotel on edge of town near cenotaph) (The Independents) ☎ 01933 271133 FAX 01933 271133
Closed Xmas
A comfortable guest house which is fully en suite and serves dinner. Bedrooms are thoughtfully appointed and well equipped. Guests can enjoy a drink in the pleasant bar.
16 rms (15 shr) (1 fmly) CTV in all bedrooms Tea and coffee making facilities Licensed Cen ht CTV 12P No coaches Last d noon
ROOMS: s £30-£32.50; d £40-£42✱
CARDS:

WELLS Somerset Map **03** ST54

Premier Selected

QQQQQ **Beaconsfield Farm** *(ST515475)* Easton BA5 1DU (2.5m from Wells on A371, on right just before village of Easton)
☎ 01749 870308 Mrs C Lloyd
2 Apr-16 Nov
This delightful farmhouse, surrounded by some lovely countryside in the lee of the Mendip Hills, is home to the Lloyd family. Bedrooms have been equipped with modern facilities which include fridges and telephones. There is an attractive lounge, and gardens to enjoy in the warmer months. Although dinner is not available, the Lloyds are always happy to recommend one of the many good pubs and restaurants in the area.
3 bth/shr No smoking in bedrooms No smoking in dining room CTV in all bedrooms Tea and coffee making facilities Direct dial from bedrooms No dogs (ex guide dogs) Cen ht CTV No children 7yrs 10P 4 acres non-working
ROOMS: s £28-£30; d £40-£45; wkly b&b £140-£155*

Selected

QQQQ **Bekynton House** 7 St Thomas St BA5 2UU (St Thomas Street is the B3139 from Wells to Radstock signed The Honningtons)
☎ 01749 672222 FAX 01749 672222
Closed 24-26 Dec
Desmond and Rosaleen Gripper extend a warm welcome to their delightful period home. Bedrooms are well furnished and have spacious bathrooms. The lounge is an ideal place to relax. The breakfast menu offers a choice of traditional items, and vegetarians and other special diets are always willingly catered for.
6 bth/shr (1 fmly) No smoking CTV in all bedrooms Tea and coffee making facilities No dogs (ex guide dogs) Cen ht CTV No children 5yrs 6P No coaches
ROOMS: s £28-£38; d £44-£51*
CARDS:

Selected

QQQQ **Box Tree House** Westbury-sub-Mendip BA5 1HA (on A371 between Wells & Cheddar next to Westbury Inn)
☎ 01749 870777
Located between Wells and Cheddar, this 17th-century farmhouse serves scrumptious breakfasts, including fresh fruit and home-made muffins served around the communal dining table. A small lounge, packed with games and reading material is also available. A short stroll will take you to the village inn which is fast developing a reputation for excellence. Mrs White has a stained-glass workshop at the rear, adjacent to the lovely gardens and patio, and she is happy to show guests her designs.
3 bth/shr No smoking in bedrooms No smoking in dining room Tea and coffee making facilities No dogs (ex guide dogs) Cen ht CTV 4P No coaches
ROOMS: s £28-£30; d £40-£42*

QQQ **Double-Gate Farm** *(ST484424)* Godney BA5 1RX (from Wells A39 towards Glastonbury, at Polsham turn right signed "Godney/Fenny Castle", continue approx 2m to x-roads, farmhouse on left after inn)
☎ 01458 832217 & 0585 443336 FAX 01458 835612 Mrs H Millard
Feb-Nov
Tom and Hilary Millard warmly welcome you to their listed Georgian farmhouse, in a pleasant position on the Somerset levels, where it is quiet and peaceful with wonderful views to the Mendip Hills. The accommodation is attractive and well equipped, and families are welcomed. There is a large games room complete with full-size snooker and table tennis tables. Self catering is also offered for more independent longer stays, and another five rooms have recently been added.
3 bth/shr 5 annexe shr (1 fmly) No smoking CTV in all bedrooms Tea and coffee making facilities No dogs (ex guide dogs) Cen ht CTV 9P Snooker Table tennis Darts 200 acres beef
ROOMS: d fr £40; wkly b&b fr £135*
CARDS:

Selected

Q Q Q Q Furlong House Lorne Place, St Thomas St BA5 2XF (Lorne Pl is a mews turning on the southside of St Thomas Street, 0.25m E of the Cathedral) ☎ 01749 674064

Peace and tranquillity are assured in the secluded grounds of this Grade II listed Georgian house. Just a five minute stroll from the magnificent Cathedral, this is an ideal base from which to explore the many and varied attractions of the area. Bedrooms are attractively decorated and feature a number of personal touches to enhance comfort. The south facing terrace overlooks the walled garden, with views of the Cathedral and National Trust woodland. Lovely views over the Somerset countryside can be enjoyed from many of the rooms, with glimpses of Glastonbury Tor to the west.

4 rms (2 shr) No smoking CTV in 1 bedroom Tea and coffee making facilities No dogs (ex guide dogs) Cen ht CTV 4P No coaches

ROOMS: s £20-£22; d £40-£44; wkly b&b £140-£154*

Selected

Q Q Q Q Hillview Cottage Paradise Ln, Croscombe BA5 3RL (from Wells take A371 to Croscombe, right at red telephone box then immediately right into lane, house is up hill on the left after 0.25m) ☎ 01749 343526 FAX 01749 676134

Once a quarryman's dwelling, Hillview Cottage, built in 1863, has been sympathetically extended over the years. From an elevated setting in eight acres of pasture with its own rose garden, the property enjoys views over the village of Croscombe and the Mendip Hills. Bedrooms are comfortable, and an open fire blazes in the sitting room. The breakfast room leads onto the garden, and Catherine and Michael Hay are very welcoming hosts.

2 bth/shr No smoking CTV in all bedrooms Tea and coffee making facilities Cen ht 4P No coaches Tennis (grass) Table tennis Drum kit

ROOMS: s fr £25; d fr £40*

Selected

Q Q Q Q ❧ Hollow Tree Farm Launcherley BA5 1QJ (take A39 Glastonbury road out of Wells, take 1st left at Brownes Garden Centre and farm is approx 0.75m on the right) ☎ 01749 673715 Mrs J Coombes

Hosts Jean and Harold are justifiably proud of their home and take great delight in sharing its abundant charms with guests. Bright and cheery colour schemes combined with polished wooden floors create an uplifting and happy house. The panoramic views are quite superb, with the magnificent Wells Cathedral to the north, and to the south, the striking silhouette of Glastonbury Tor. Many hours of dedication are reflected in the wonderful, flower filled garden, a lovely place to relax. Home baked bread is a speciality of the house, and a highlight of the delicious breakfasts served in the dining room.

3 bth/shr (1 fmly) No smoking CTV in all bedrooms Tea and coffee making facilities No dogs (ex guide dogs) Cen ht 4P

27 acres Grazing

ROOMS: d £32; wkly b&b fr £100*

Selected

Q Q Q Q Infield House 36 Portway BA5 2BN (from city centre, on right hand side of A371, driveway immediately after traffic lights at junction with Strawberry Way) ☎ 01749 670989 FAX 01749 679093

This handsome stone built house is situated conveniently close to the centre of the historic City of Wells. The proprietors have managed to retain the Victorian atmosphere in the decor, furnishings, pictures and personal effects. The spacious and comfortable bedrooms are traditionally furnished, some with antiques. The en suite bathrooms are extremely modern and well equipped.

3 bth/shr No smoking CTV in all bedrooms Tea and coffee making facilities No dogs (ex guide dogs) Cen ht CTV No children 16yrs 3P No coaches Last d 10.30am

ROOMS: d £42-£49; wkly b&b £147

CARDS:

Premier Selected

Q Q Q Q Q Littlewell Farm Coxley BA5 1QP (1m from centre on A39 towards Glastonbury) ☎ 01749 677914

Situated in the hamlet of Coxley, this 200 year-old farmhouse is the ideal base from which to explore the many delights of the area. Bedrooms are well equipped, comfortably furnished and tastefully decorated to a high standard. Dinner is skillfully prepared and beautifully presented, utilising only the best of local produce.

contd.

Littlewell Farm

5 bth/shr No smoking CTV in all bedrooms Tea and coffee making facilities No dogs (ex guide dogs) Licensed Cen ht No children 10yrs 10P No coaches Riding Last d 3pm
ROOMS: s £21-£25; d £39-£48*

QQQ **Milton Manor** *(ST546474)* Old Bristol Rd, Upper Milton BA5 3AH (1m W A39 towards Bristol, turn left into Old Bristol Rd. Farm 0.75miles up on left) ☎ 01749 673394 Mrs J Gould
Closed 24-2 Jan
Located in a hamlet of outstanding natural beauty, this gracious Grade II Elizabethan farmhouse is set on a 130-acre farm with glorious views across rolling Somerset countryside to Brent Knoll. Guests can sit out in the delightful gardens or visit the nearby City of Wells. Each of the bedrooms is pleasantly furnished and decorated. Breakfast is taken in the cosy panelled dining room which also serves as a lounge.
3 rms (1 fmly) No smoking Tea and coffee making facilities No dogs (ex guide dogs) Cen ht CTV 6P 130 acres beef
ROOMS: s £18-£19; d £32-£34*

Selected

QQQQ **Old Farmhouse** 62 Chamberlain St BA5 2PT
☎ 01749 675058
Closed 24-26 Dec
Dating from the 17th century, this former farmhouse has been sensitively and sympathetically restored to provide accommodation of quality, character and considerable style. Just a five minute stroll from the Cathedral, why not leave the car behind and launch a pedestrian exploration of this historic city. As a retired diplomat, Chris is well versed in the art of hospitality, a factor which contributes to the warm and convivial atmosphere which pervades. Dinner is available by prior arrangement and provides an opportunity for Felicity to demonstrate her Cordon Bleu skills. Afterwards, relax beside the fire before climbing the stairs for a sound nights sleep in the tastefully decorated bedrooms.
2 shr No smoking CTV in all bedrooms Tea and coffee making facilities No dogs Cen ht No children 12yrs 3P No coaches
ROOMS: d £39-£43

Selected

QQQQ **Riverside Grange** Tanyard Ln, North Wootton BA4 4AE (take A39 towards Glastonbury. On leaving Wells take first left signed North Wootton, proceed through village to T-junct turning left and 2nd left) ☎ 01749 890761
This delightful property, built in 1853 as a tannery to supply leather to Clarks shoe factory, has been sympathetically converted yet retains many of its original features. The setting next to the River Redlake is charming, and the surroundings are peaceful and very rural. Two bedrooms have been tastefully decorated and furnished to offer a high standard of accommodation. Breakfast is served around one large table in the dining room, and there is a village pub serving good food just a two minute walk away.
2 bth/shr No smoking CTV in all bedrooms Tea and coffee making facilities Cen ht 4P
ROOMS: s £25; d £37-£39*

Selected

QQQQ **Southway** *(ST516423)* Polsham BA5 1RW (between Wells/Glastonbury, off A39)
☎ 01749 673396 FAX 01749 670373 Mr & Mrs Frost
Feb-Nov
Southway Farm is a working farm between Glastonbury and Wells. Bedrooms are presented in true country style with some lovely antiques and thoughtful touches. There is a comfortable sitting room where guests are welcome to relax after a day exploring the delights of this Somerset region and a cosy dining room with separate tables.
3 bth/shr No smoking CTV in all bedrooms Tea and coffee making facilities No dogs (ex guide dogs) Cen ht CTV 3P 170 acres dairy
ROOMS: s £22-£26; d £37-£42

Selected

QQQQ **Tor House** 20 Tor St BA5 2US (situated in Wells on the A3139 off A371 main Wells-Shepton Mallet road) ☎ 01749 672322 & 0589 530253 (mobile) FAX 01749 672322
Situated just behind the magnificent Cathedral at Wells, Tor House is over 400 years old and has been lovingly restored to its former beauty by its present owner, and now provides modern comforts. The house is furnished to the highest standards and all bedrooms and bathrooms have been decorated and equipped with great care.
8 rms (5 bth/shr) (2 fmly) No smoking CTV in all bedrooms Tea and coffee making facilities No dogs Cen ht CTV No children 3yrs 12P Golf 18
ROOMS: s £22-£40; d £40-£55*
CARDS:

WEM Shropshire Map 07 SJ52

Selected

QQQQ **Foxleigh House** Foxleigh Dr SY4 5BP (11m N of Shrewsbury, take B5476 Wem/Whitchurch road and second turning right after Hawkstone public house, then immediately left onto Foxleigh Drive) ☎ 01939 233528 FAX 01939 233528
Closed Xmas
This large 19th-century mansion lies in pleasant gardens on the outskirts of the town. The traditionally furnished bedrooms are well equipped; one has a private bathroom and the others can be let as a family suite. There is a large and comfortably furnished sitting room and a very pleasant dining room, both fitted with fine period furniture.
2 bth (1 fmly) No smoking CTV in 3 bedrooms Tea and coffee making facilities No dogs Cen ht No children 8yrs 4P No coaches Croquet lawn Last d previous day
ROOMS: d £39-£44*

Selected

QQQQ ❦ ***Soulton Hall*** *(SJ543303)* Soulton SY4 5RS (turn off A49 onto B5065 towards Wem, 2m on left after small bridge) ☎ 01939 232786 FAX 01939 234097 Mrs A P Ashton

This impressive hall run by the Ashton family, who can trace their tenure back to the 16th century, has many reminders of the antiquity of the building, most notably the sloping floors! The comfortable entrance lounge leads to the bar on one side and a restaurant on the other. Bedrooms have mullioned windows with many exposed timbers and one room is wood-panelled. There are also rooms in the converted coach house across the garden. Open farmland surrounds the house and guests are welcome to explore the grounds.

3 bth/shr 2 annexe bth/shr (4 fmly) No smoking in bedrooms No smoking in dining room CTV in all bedrooms Tea and coffee making facilities Direct dial from bedrooms Licensed Cen ht ch fac 12P Fishing Riding Birdwatching in 50 acre woodland 560 acres arable Last d 9pm

CARDS:

WEMBLEY Greater London Map **04** TQ18

QQQ ***Adelphi Hotel*** 4 Forty Ln HA9 9EB ☎ 0181 904 5629 FAX 0181 908 5314

This popular, modern hotel is conveniently situated near the Wembley complex. The en suite bedrooms offer modern comfortable accommodation.

11 rms (7 shr) (2 fmly) No smoking in dining room CTV in all bedrooms Tea and coffee making facilities No dogs Cen ht CTV 12P No coaches Last d 8pm

CARDS:

See advertisement on p.445.

QQQ **Arena Hotel** 6 Forty Ln HA9 9EB (M1 North Circular close to stadium) ☎ 0181 908 0670 & 0181 904 0019 FAX 0181 908 2007

This friendly guest house is situated near the Wembley complex and offers modern accommodation with en suite facilities. There is a comfortable guest lounge and a traditional breakfast is served in the bright dining room.

13 bth/shr (3 fmly) No smoking in dining room CTV in all bedrooms Tea and coffee making facilities Direct dial from bedrooms No dogs (ex guide dogs) Cen ht CTV 15P Last d 10.30pm

ROOMS: s £41-£45; d £51-£55*

CARDS:

WEST BAGBOROUGH Somerset Map 03 ST13

Premier Selected

QQQQQ ❦ **Bashfords Farmhouse** *(ST172333)* TA4 3EF (follow main road through village for approx 1.5m. Bashfords is third on left after pub) ☎ 01823 432015 FAX 01823 432520 Mr & Mrs C Ritchie

Bashfords Farmhouse is in the centre of the village, on the southern slopes of the Quantocks. Over the last few years owners Charles and Jane Ritchie have renovated the property. Bedrooms are attractively decorated and furnished in country style. Meals, dinner by prior arrangement, are taken around an impressive pine table in the dining room with its huge inglenook fireplace. All dishes are prepared with flair and imagination from the best of fresh, and if possible, local ingredients.

3 bth/shr No smoking CTV in all bedrooms Tea and coffee making facilities No dogs Cen ht No children 10yrs 4P Last d 48hrs in advance

ROOMS: s £22.50-£25; d £40-£45*

Selected

QQQQ ***Higher House*** TA4 3EF (turn off A358 (Taunton-Minehead) signposted to West Bagborough. Higher House approx 1.5m from main road, last house on right before leaving village) ☎ 01823 432996 FAX 01823 433568

Closed 24-26 Dec

Higher House stands at the far edge of the village, 650 feet up on the southern slopes of the Quantock Hills. The views from the house, gardens and tennis court are spectacular, across the Vale of Taunton to the Brendon Hills and Exmoor beyond. The principal part of the house is 17th-century and is built around two courtyards, one of which contains a heated outdoor swimming pool. The bedrooms are attractively decorated and exceedingly well equipped. Imaginative three-course dinners are available by prior arrangement, and on other occasions a simple, two-course supper can be provided.

3 bth (1 fmly) No smoking CTV in all bedrooms Tea and coffee making facilities Direct dial from bedrooms No dogs Licensed Cen ht 8P No coaches Outdoor swimming pool (heated) Tennis (hard) Tennis coaching available

Premier Selected

QQQQQ ❦ **Tilbury Farm** *(ST177334)* Cothelstone TA4 3DY (take A358 towards Minehead and 0.75m after second railway bridge take sharp right towards West Bagborough. Through village, on left up steep hill) ☎ 01823 432391 Mrs P Smith

This delightful, recently restored, farmhouse is said to be the highest dwelling on the Quantocks. From this elevated, and very peaceful position, Tilbury Farm affords spectacular country views over the vale of Taunton. Pamela and Mike Smith have taken enormous care in the renovation of their wonderful home, which still retains impressive original features such as flagstone floors, oak beams, and inglenook fireplaces. Bedrooms, each with their own individual style, have been tastefully furnished and equipped with modern facilities. Dinner is available by arrangement and served around a splendid 17th-century table. Pam is an innovative cook and prepares dishes from the best of fresh ingredients.

3 bth/shr No smoking CTV in all bedrooms Tea and coffee making facilities No dogs Cen ht CTV No children 8yrs 20P Riding Stabling 20 acres none working Last d 11am

ROOMS: s £25-£30; d £46-£50*

WESTCLIFF-ON-SEA Essex

See **Southend-on-Sea**

WEST DOWN Devon Map 02 SS54

QQQ **Sunnymeade Country House Hotel** Dean Cross EX34 8NT (1m W on A361 between Braunton and Ilfracombe set back off A361) ☎ 01271 863668

Located about three miles south of Ilfracombe, this family-run hotel has excellent views of the rolling Devon countryside and offers a warm welcome to guests. Devonshire cream teas are served in the afternoons. In the evenings there is a fixed-price menu with a varied choice of dishes. Guests have the use of a lounge and bar. The well equipped bedrooms are neatly furnished and include two on the ground floor, one of which is suitable for guests with disabilities. British sign language can be provided – please enquire when booking.

9 rms (8 shr) (1 fmly) No smoking in dining room No smoking in 1 lounge CTV in all bedrooms Tea and coffee making facilities Direct dial from bedrooms Licensed Cen ht CTV 14P Last d 6pm

ROOMS: s £20-£31; d £40-£50; wkly b&b £125-£155; wkly hlf-bd £214-£228*

CARDS:

WEST DRAYTON Greater London

For accommodation details see **Heathrow Airport**

WEST MALLING Kent Map 05 TQ65

Selected

QQQQ **Scott House** High St ME19 6QH (on A228) ☎ 01732 841380 FAX 01732 870025

Closed Xmas

Scott House is a fine Georgian House in the centre of delightful West Malling, offering a very high standard of well furnished

accommodation. The entrance to the house is via the main entrance of the proprietor's very stylish interior design business downstairs. This expertise shows in the beauty of the building as a whole, especially the antique-laden drawing room, with its high ceiling and huge bay window. Breakfast is taken at separate tables downstairs, and amenable service is provided by the attentive and genial proprietor.
3 shr No smoking CTV in all bedrooms Tea and coffee making facilities No dogs (ex guide dogs) Cen ht No children 12yrs No coaches
ROOMS: s £49; d £69✳
CARDS:

Selected

QQQQ **Woodgate** Birling Rd, Leybourne ME19 5HT
(exit M20 at junc 4, take the A228 to West Malling, first right, first left)
☎ 01732 843201
This pretty rural cottage offers comfortable accommodation in a peaceful location. The bedrooms are attractively decorated with many beautiful paintings and objets d'art from around the world, and all have colour televisions and radio alarms. Breakfast is served at a huge wooden table in the conservatory which overlooks the well tended gardens.
4 rms (2 bth/shr) No smoking CTV in 3 bedrooms Tea and coffee making facilities Cen ht CTV 5P No coaches Last d 9.30pm
ROOMS: s £22-£25; d £44-£50; wkly b&b £145-£154✳

WESTON-SUPER-MARE Somerset Map **03** ST36

Selected

QQQQ **Ashcombe Court** 17 Milton Rd BS23 2SH
(M5 junct 21 follow signs for Seafront, over 4 rdbts at 5th take 3rd exit over old railway bridge, at 2nd lights left and right into Elmhurst Rd)
☎ 01934 625104 FAX 01934 625104
This family run hotel is strong on hospitality making it a very pleasant place to stay. It is an attractive Victorian house only a short walk from the seafront. The bedrooms are attractively decorated and well equipped with modern en suite facilities. There are many extras including hairdryers, shoe cleaning kits and many other thoughtful touches. There is a comfortable lounge and good home cooked food is served in the dining room.
6 bth/shr (1 fmly) No smoking CTV in all bedrooms Tea and coffee making facilities No dogs Cen ht CTV No children 11years 6P No coaches Last d 6pm
ROOMS: s £25-£35; d fr £39; wkly b&b £131-£139; wkly hlf-bd £158-£171

QQQ ***Baymead Hotel*** Longton Grove Rd BS23 1LS ☎ 01934 622951 FAX 01934 628110
Closed Jan & Feb
This friendly family run hotel, located close to the town and only a short walk to the seafront, is ideal for both holiday makers and business travellers. The cosy bedrooms are well equipped and are attractively decorated. The traditional bar has a dance floor and entertainment three nights a week. There is an attractive dining room where hearty home cooked meals are served.
33 rms (30 bth/shr) (3 fmly) No smoking in dining room CTV in all bedrooms Tea and coffee making facilities Licensed Lift Cen ht CTV 10P Half size snooker table Darts Last d 7pm

Beverley 11 Whitecross Rd BS23 1EP (follow town cntr/rlwy stn signs. When rlwy stn on left, turn left, drive past stn taking 2nd left into Ellenborough Park Rd leading to Whitecross Rd) ☎ 01934 622956
This comfortable family home, located in a peaceful residential area of the town, is only a short walk from the beaches, the shopping centre and Weston-Super-Mare's many other places of interest. The bedrooms are comfortably furnished and good home-cooked food is served in the attractive dining room.
5 shr (3 fmly) No smoking in dining room CTV in all bedrooms Tea and coffee making facilities No dogs (ex guide dogs) Cen ht No coaches Last d 2pm
ROOMS: s £19-£21; d £32-£40; wkly b&b £107-£120; wkly hlf-bd £147-£154*

Selected

Braeside 2 Victoria Park BS23 2HZ
(with sea on left, take 1st right after Winter Gardens then 1st left into Lower Church Rd. Victoria Park is on right after left-hand bend)
☎ 01934 626642 FAX 01934 626642
A warm and friendly welcome from Hugh and Bronwyn Wallington awaits guests to this small hotel, only a short walk from the seafront. Some of the comfortably furnished and well equipped bedrooms overlook Weston Bay. There is a cosy lounge and an attractive and well laid-out dining room where meals are served. The hotel is licensed and guests can also enjoy a drink on the patio in the good weather. Hugh Wallington plays the organ on some evenings for the enjoyment of guests.
9 bth/shr (3 fmly) No smoking in dining room CTV in all bedrooms Tea and coffee making facilities Licensed Cen ht No coaches Last d 2pm
ROOMS: s £24; d £48; wkly b&b £144; wkly hlf-bd £228

Selected

Clifton Lodge 48 Clifton Rd BS23 1BN
(follow main road to sea front, Clifton Rd is 1st turning on left past the Tropicana) ☎ 01934 629357
Located within walking distance of the seafront, town centre and other amenities, this charming house is ideal for tourists. Well equipped and comfortable bedrooms have many thoughtful extras. Home-cooked food, including English roasts and delicious desserts are served in the attractive dining room, and there is also a comfortable lounge.
6 rms (3 shr) (3 fmly) No smoking CTV in all bedrooms Tea and coffee making facilities No dogs (ex guide dogs) Cen ht CTV 2P No coaches Last d 10.30am
ROOMS: s £16-£17; d £32-£38; wkly b&b £105-£126; wkly hlf-bd £150-£178*

Conifers 63 Milton Rd BS23 2SP (turn off M5 at junct 21 and follow A370 towards Weston turn right into Bay Tree Rd left turn at lights into Milton Rd) ☎ 01934 624404 FAX 01934 624404
Closed 22 Dec-3 Jan
A comfortable, family-run guest house within walking distance of the town centre, beaches, and other amenities. The bedrooms are modern, attractively decorated and well equipped. There is a cosy breakfast room overlooking the pretty garden.
3 rms (1 bth/shr) No smoking in dining room CTV in all bedrooms Tea and coffee making facilities No dogs Cen ht No children 14yrs 4P
ROOMS: s £16-£20; d £30-£40

Goodrington 23 Charlton Rd BS23 4HB ☎ 01934 623229
Apr-Sep
Quietly tucked away in a smart residential area of the town , Goodrington is a charming Victorian house which exudes a warm and welcoming atmosphere. Hosts Reg and Vera make every effort to ensure guests leave with happy memories and thoughts of a return visit! Bedrooms are spacious and comfortably furnished and in addition, an attractive lounge is available. Being just a short distance form the shops, beach and amenities, this is an ideal base from which to explore the local area.
3 rms (2 shr) (1 fmly) No smoking CTV in all bedrooms Tea and coffee making facilities No dogs (ex guide dogs) Cen ht CTV No coaches Last d 24hr notice
ROOMS: s £14-£17; d £28-£34; wkly b&b £90-£110; wkly hlf-bd £125-£140

Ivy Lodge 18 Clifton Rd BS23 1BL ☎ 01934 626884
Cosy and personally-run guest house with bright, individually styled bedrooms, all equipped with a good range of modern facilities. Very conveniently positioned for the beach, and within walking distance of the town centre. Ivy Lodge represents very good value for money and is suitable for business guest and tourist alike.
3 rms (1 shr) (2 fmly) No smoking in 1 bedrooms No smoking in dining room No smoking in lounges CTV in all bedrooms Tea and coffee making facilities No dogs (ex guide dogs) Cen ht No coaches Last d noon

Selected

Milton Lodge 15 Milton Rd BS23 2SH
(M4 junct 21 to town centre take the B3440, right at mini rdbt for Milton and Sea Front North, at lights left into Milton Rd)
☎ 01934 623161 FAX 01934 623210
Now under the new ownership of Val and Les Bullock, returning guests will not be disappointed. Guests are greeted by the welcome offer of tea before being whisked up to one of the six attractive en suite bedrooms. All are well equipped and maintained to a high standard, and there is a spacious guest lounge to relax in. A short stroll will take you to the town centre or the sea front. Traditional home-cooked meals are a strong feature.
6 bth/shr (1 fmly) No smoking in dining room CTV in all bedrooms Tea and coffee making facilities No dogs (ex guide dogs) Cen ht CTV No children 16yrs 6P No coaches Last d 7pm
ROOMS: s £24-£40; d £36-£44; wkly b&b £110-£140; wkly hlf-bd £155-£186*

Oakover 25 Clevedon Rd BS23 1DA (follow signs for seafront/ Tropicana, Clevedon Rd is opposite the Tropicana Pleasure beach on seafront, Oakover is on left just before traffic lights) ☎ 01934 620125
Oakover is a substantial Victorian property, situated a short level walk from the town centre and the seafront. The bedrooms are comfortable and well equipped. Hearty breakfasts are served in the bright and airy dining room. Diane Hill is the friendly proprietor.
8 bth/shr (1 fmly) No smoking in dining room CTV in all bedrooms Tea and coffee making facilities No dogs (ex guide dogs) Cen ht 8P
ROOMS: s £15-£19; d £30-£38; wkly b&b £100-£125*
CARDS:

Purn House *(ST331571)* Bleadon BS24 0QE
(just off A370 Weston-super-Mare/Bridgwater rd, 3m from Weston seafront, turn opposite Anchor Inn signposted Bleadon, third house on the left)
01934 812324 FAX 01934 811029 Mrs T G Moore
Feb-Nov
Situated three miles from town, this attractive creeper-clad 17th-century farmhouse, part of a working farm, provides warm hospitality, and comfortable accommodation. The bedrooms have retained much of the building's original character, and there is also a lounge and games room for the use of guests. The attractive dining room is where Mrs Moore serves breakfast, and there is a pub only a short stroll from the house that can provide good meals in the evening.
6 rms (4 bth/shr) (3 fmly) No smoking in bedrooms No smoking in dining room CTV in 4 bedrooms Tea and coffee making facilities No dogs (ex guide dogs) Cen ht CTV 10P Fishing Childrens playroom Snooker Table tennis 700 acres arable dairy

Sarnia Hotel 28 Upper Church Rd BS23 2DX 01934 629696
The Sarnia Hotel is located close to the seafront, and a colourful mass of tubs and hanging baskets greet you on arrival. The rooms are bright and well maintained and facilities include a television.
8 rms (5 shr) (3 fmly) No smoking in dining room CTV in all bedrooms Tea and coffee making facilities No dogs (ex guide dogs) Licensed CTV Last d breakfast
CARDS:

Scots Hotel 36 Beach Rd BS23 1BG 01934 629529
This attractive Victorian seaside property, situated a level ten minute walk from the pier, is run by friendly proprietor Mrs Carter. Bedrooms, most en suite, are equipped with such facilities as TV and phone, and many benefit from bay windows and sea views. There is a smart lounge for guest use and a cosy licensed bar, where guests may also order sandwiches and snacks, while a full cooked breakfast is served in the dining room.
11 rms

The Weston Bay Hotel 2/4 Clevedon Rd BS23 1DG
(exit M5 at junc 21, 15 min to Weston Bay Hotel by Locking Rd, premises on sea front) 01934 628903 FAX 01934 417661
Mar-Nov
Located on the seafront, this family hotel provides spacious well equipped bedrooms, all of which have modern en suite facilities. There is a comfortable lounge for the use of guests, and an attractive dining room where Mr and Mrs Hui serve evening meals and breakfast.
9 bth/shr (4 fmly) No smoking in 2 bedrooms No smoking in dining room CTV in all bedrooms Tea and coffee making facilities No dogs (ex guide dogs) Cen ht CTV 12P No coaches Last d 6pm
ROOMS: s £25-£30; d £40-£47; wkly b&b £140-£155; wkly hlf-bd £170-£185

Selected

Wychwood Hotel 148 Milton Rd BS23 2UZ
01934 627793
Closed 24 Dec-3 Jan
This small family hotel is under the personal supervision of Sue and Tony Pearce and is located within easy reach of the seafront. Bedrooms are well decorated and have been equipped with modern facilities. There is a comfortable bar-lounge and an attractive dining room where meals are served. The heated swimming pool in the garden is popular in the warmer weather.
8 bth/shr (3 fmly) No smoking in dining room CTV in all bedrooms Tea and coffee making facilities No dogs (ex guide dogs) Licensed Cen ht CTV 12P No coaches Outdoor swimming pool (heated) Last d 4.30pm
ROOMS: s £27; d £44; wkly b&b £140-£175; wkly hlf-bd £196-£231
CARDS:

WESTON UNDERWOOD Derbyshire Map 08 SK24

Premier Selected

Park View Farm *(SK293425)* DE6 4PA
(6m NW of Derby off A38 1.5m Kedleston Hall National Trust property) 01335 360352 FAX 01335 360352 Mrs L Adams
Closed 24 & 25 Dec
Set in a small village and surrounded by 370 acres of arable land, this delightful early Victorian farmhouse has been furnished with great care by Linda and Michael Adams. Each bedroom has an antique four-poster bed and period furniture. The comfortable sitting room provides an ideal place in which to relax and breakfast is served around one table in the dining room.
3 bth/shr No smoking CTV in 1 bedroom Tea and coffee making facilities No dogs Cen ht CTV No children 6yrs 10P 375 acres mixed
ROOMS: s £28-£35; d £45-£50*

WESTOW North Yorkshire Map 08 SE76

Blacksmith Arms Main St, Westow YO60 7NE (turn right off A64 between York and Malton onto unclassified road signposted Kirkham Priory and Westow for 1.5m) 01653 618365 & 618343 FAX 01653 618365
Closed Xmas
Situated in the village of Westow in a quiet backwater between York and Malton, the Blacksmith is a traditional old inn. It is well furnished and throughfully equipped bedrooms are located in newly converted stables to the rear. A wide range of home cooking is available and a good local pub atmosphere prevails in the bars.
6 annexe shr No smoking in bedrooms No smoking in dining room CTV in all bedrooms Tea and coffee making facilities Direct dial from bedrooms No dogs (ex guide dogs) Cen ht CTV 18P Last d 9.30pm
ROOMS: s £21.50; d £43-£48*
MEALS: Lunch £9.25-£19 Dinner £9.25-£19*
CARDS:

WEST PENNARD Somerset Map 03 ST53

Ashcombe Farm *(ST573395)* Stean Bow BA6 8ND
(between Glastonbury and Shepton Mallet on A361, 4m from Glastonbury opposite Apple Inn) 01749 890153 Mrs D Frayne
Closed 21 Dec-2nd Jan
Di and Peter take great delight in welcoming guests to their home just a few miles outside Glastonbury. In their three years of ownership, many improvements have been made and the accommodation now offered is bright, spacious and comfortable. In addition to a lounge, a large garden lies at the rear.
3 bth/shr No smoking in dining room No smoking in lounges CTV in all bedrooms Tea and coffee making facilities No dogs (ex guide dogs) Cen ht CTV No children 5yrs 6P 6 acres non-working
ROOMS: s £20-£25; d £36-£38; wkly b&b £119-£126

WESTWARD HO! Devon Map **02** SS42

QQQ **The Buckleigh Lodge** 135 Bayview Rd EX39 1BJ
(0.75m W of rdbt near Torridge Bridge, Bideford turn off A39 onto B3236 signed Westward Ho!, Buckleigh Lodge approx 0.75m on right) ☎ 01237 475988
This Victorian house is situated just five minutes away from the beach at Westward Ho! It offers comfortable bedrooms and a spacious lounge with its own bar for residents.
6 bth/shr (1 fmly) No smoking in bedrooms No smoking in dining room CTV in all bedrooms Tea and coffee making facilities No dogs (ex guide dogs) Licensed Cen ht CTV ch fac 8P No coaches Last d 4pm
ROOMS: s £20-£22; d £40-£44; wkly b&b £133-£146; wkly hlf-bd £214-£227

WETHERBY West Yorkshire Map **08** SE44

QQ **Prospect House** 8 Caxton St LS22 6RU
(A1 to Wetherby rdbt, turn left to Wetherby, cont through 1st set lights, at 2nd set turn left, continue until Kwiksave on left, house on corner)
☎ 01937 582428
Situated close to the town centre, this family-owned and run guest house offers bright bedrooms, some of which are en suite. There is a combined lounge and dining room available to guests and service from the owners is very friendly.
6 rms (4 shr) CTV in 1 bedroom Tea and coffee making facilities Cen ht CTV 6P No coaches
ROOMS: s £20-£22.50; d £45-£50; wkly b&b £140-£157.50*

WEYMOUTH Dorset Map **03** SY67

See also Portland

QQQ **Bayview Hotel** 35 The Esplanade DT4 8DH
(from Dorchester take A354 to Weymouth and follow signs for Ferry. Hotel is situated on the seafront 100yds before Ferry terminal)
☎ 01305 782083 FAX 78083
1 Mar-30 Nov
A newly refurbished family run hotel overlooking Weymouth Bay conveniently situated for town centre, old harbour and ferry. The tastefully decorated bedrooms all have very comfortable beds. Cooked breakfasts are served in the smart dining room. There is also a lounge and cosy bar.
8 bth/shr (3 fmly) No smoking in 1 bedrooms No smoking in dining room No smoking in lounges CTV in all bedrooms Tea and coffee making facilities No dogs Licensed Cen ht 8P No coaches
ROOMS: s £20-£25; d £40-£50; wkly b&b £130-£170*
CARDS:

QQQ **Birchfields** 22 Abbotsbury Rd DT4 0AE
(from Jubilee Clock on Esplanade turn into King St 2nd exit continue over bridge, 2nd exit from rdbt into Abbotsbury Rd, hotel 100yds on right)
☎ 01305 773255 FAX 01305 773255
Mar-Oct
A small guest house personally run by Dave and Pam Dutton who give guests a warm and friendly welcome. Situated on the main Weymouth to Bridport road and near the town centre and beach it is ideal for the leisure and business visitor. Some of the bright and comfortable rooms have en suite facilities and two have WC. There is a cosy lounge with an honesty bar. In addition to hearty breakfasts a varied menu is on offer in the evening.
9 rms (3 shr) (3 fmly) No smoking in dining room CTV in all bedrooms Tea and coffee making facilities Licensed Cen ht CTV 3P Last d 3pm
ROOMS: s £15-£20; d £30-£40; wkly b&b £88-£116; wkly hlf-bd £128-£156*

This symbol indicates a 'Child Friendly' establishment - see page 25 for details

Selected

QQQQ **Channel View** 10 Brunswick Ter, The Esplanade DT4 7RX (at Manor rdbt by Safeway go straight on,at St John's Church go to sea front,pass church,double back left at pedestrian crossing into Brunswick Ter) ☎ 01305 782527 FAX 01305 782527
Closed 5 Dec-15 Jan
A pretty guest house overlooking beautiful Weymouth Bay where guests will receive warm hospitality from Ian and Ruth Cowley. The well equipped bedrooms are located on three floors, with the front facing rooms having the benefit of glorious views. Hearty breakfasts are served in the light and airy dining room that has sea views. There is also a cosy lounge.
7 rms (4 shr) (1 fmly) No smoking CTV in all bedrooms Tea and coffee making facilities No dogs (ex guide dogs) Licensed Cen ht CTV No children 12yrs No coaches
ROOMS: s £19-£22.50; d £38-£45; wkly b&b £133-£157
CARDS:

Selected

QQQQ **Cumberland Hotel** 95 Esplanade DT4 7BA
☎ 01305 785644
Closed Xmas
Located on the Esplanade, this small friendly hotel, under the personal supervision of Will and Valerie Hampshire for over 20 years, has superb views of the Bay. The comfortable bedrooms, all with en suite facilities, are well equipped and attractively decorated. On the lower ground floor the well laid out dining room offers good home cooked food, and there is also a cosy bar and small lounge for guests' use.
12 bth/shr (4 fmly) No smoking in 6 bedrooms No smoking in dining room No smoking in lounges CTV in all bedrooms Tea and coffee making facilities No dogs Licensed Cen ht No children 10yrs 2P Last d 5pm
ROOMS: d £48-£60; wkly b&b £160-£185; wkly hlf-bd £235-£260*

Premier Selected

QQQQQ **Esplanade Hotel** 141 The Esplanade DT4 7NJ
(E end of Esplanade, opposite pier bandstand) ☎ 01305 783129
Apr-Oct
Owners Kathy and Len Paul provide caring hospitality at their attractive Georgian property located on the seafront. Most of the bedrooms enjoy sea views, and although the rooms vary is size they are particularly well furnished and attractively decorated, and include many extras. There is a first floor lounge overlooking the Bay and Kathy's good home-cooked meals, including a 'light bite' menu, are served in the elegant dining room.

11 bth/shr (2 fmly) No smoking CTV in all bedrooms Tea and coffee making facilities No dogs Licensed Cen ht CTV 9P
Last d by arrangement
ROOMS: s £28-£35; d £42-£65; wkly b&b £154-£210

Q Q Q **Ferndown** 47 Walpole St DT4 7HQ
(in town, go past church on 2-way traffic system, right into William St, over x-roads past Waterloo pub & Scuba Cntr. Ferndown opposite & painted pink) ☎ 01305 775228
Closed 25 Dec-9 Jan
This neat little flower-fronted guest house is situated in a quiet residential area, close to the seafront and town centre. The bedrooms are pretty and individually decorated with welcoming extra touches, and public areas are compact but comfortable. The whole Waddell Family are involved in the running of this establishment where the atmosphere is friendly and relaxed.
8 rms No smoking in dining room CTV in all bedrooms Tea and coffee making facilities CTV 2P Last d noon
ROOMS: s £14-£16; d £24-£32; wkly b&b £90-£100; wkly hlf-bd £120-£130*

Q Q Q **Kenora** 5 Stavordale Rd DT4 0AB
(from Esplanade left at Jubilee Clock into King St, 2nd exit off rdbt over bridge to next rdbt 2nd exit into Abbotsbury Rd left & then right)
☎ 01305 771215
Etr & 1 May-25 Sep
Located in a quiet, tree lined cul-de-sac, close to the Marina, sandy beaches and town centre, Jean and Chris Lamb have been welcoming guests to their hotel for over twenty years. Each evening, in the smartly decorated dining room, a choice of menu is offered including a vegetarian option. The delightful rear gardens have received various awards. A comfortable bar/lounge is available for guests.
15 rms (4 bth 9 shr) (3 fmly) No smoking in dining room CTV in all bedrooms Tea and coffee making facilities No dogs (ex guide dogs) Licensed Cen ht CTV 20P Last d 4.30pm
ROOMS: s £29-£35; d £50-£60; wkly b&b £160-£185; wkly hlf-bd £195-£220*
CARDS:

Q Q Q **Sou'west Lodge Hotel** Rodwell Rd DT4 8QT
☎ 01305 783749
Closed 22 Dec-1 Jan
Now under the ownership of William and Margaret Bradley, who give a warm welcome to their guests, the hotel is set away from the hustle and bustle of the town centre. It is however within easy walking distance of all the main attractions, and has the added advantage of parking facilities. Bedrooms, some on the ground floor, are simply decorated but offer a good level of comfort and many extras. There is a spacious lounge/bar, and a separate dining room where evening meals are served.
8 bth/shr (2 fmly) No smoking in dining room CTV in all bedrooms Tea and coffee making facilities Licensed Cen ht CTV 12P No coaches Last d 3pm
ROOMS: d £39-£50*
CARDS:

Q Q Q **Sunningdale Private Hotel** 52 Preston Rd, Overcombe DT3 6QD (on A353 near Overcombe Corner beach, 2m E of town centre)
☎ 01305 832179 FAX 01305 832179
Mar-Oct rs Nov-Feb
A friendly, family run hotel, that has been in the ownership of the same family for over 35 years. Located a short walk from the seafront and only 2 miles from the town centre is ideal for both holiday makers and business travellers. The comfortable, well equipped bedrooms are attractively decorated. There is a traditional style bar, a large television lounge, a games room and comfortable dining room where hearty dinners and English breakfasts are served.

18 rms (11 bth 2 shr) (8 fmly) No smoking in dining room CTV in all bedrooms Tea and coffee making facilities Licensed CTV 20P Outdoor swimming pool (heated) Table tennis Games room Extensive garden Last d 6.45pm
ROOMS: s £24-£29; d £48-£58; wkly b&b £140-£187; wkly hlf-bd £182-£229*
CARDS:

Q Q Q **Tamarisk Hotel** 12 Stavordale Rd, Westham DT4 0AB
(follow A354 to Westham rdbt, take 3rd exit left to Bridport & then immediately left into Stavordale Rd) ☎ 01305 786514 FAX 01305 786514
Mar-Oct
A small comfortably appointed guest house, located in a quiet residential area and within easy reach of the beach and town centre. The new owners plan to upgrade the suitably equipped bedrooms. There is a small lounge and bar and a bright dining room.
14 rms (4 bth 8 shr) (5 fmly) No smoking in dining room CTV in all bedrooms Tea and coffee making facilities No dogs (ex guide dogs) Licensed Cen ht CTV 19P Last d 4pm
ROOMS: s £20-£25; d £40-£50; wkly b&b £125-£160; wkly hlf-bd £170-£210*
CARDS:

Trelawney Hotel 1 Old Castle Rd DT4 8QB
(follow signs Portland on leaving Harbourside for hotel in 700yds on left)
☎ 01305 783188 FAX 01305 783181
Nov-Mar
Located in a quiet area, this charming Victorian house is set in its own well maintained garden. The accommodation continues to be upgraded, with spacious and nicely appointed bedrooms. A generous English breakfast and a home-cooked dinner is offered in the light and airy dining room. There is also a comfortable lounge.
10 bth/shr No smoking in 2 bedrooms CTV in all bedrooms Tea and coffee making facilities No dogs (ex guide dogs) Licensed Cen ht CTV 13P No coaches Putting green Last d 7pm
ROOMS: s £30-£35; d £54-£58*
CARDS:

Warwick Court Hotel 20 Abbotsbury Rd DT4 0AE
(right at Manor rdbt on Dorchester Rd, onto Weymouth Way, left at Chafrey's rdbt right at next rdbt onto Abbotsbury Rd, hotel 150yds on right)
☎ 01305 783261 FAX 01305 783261
Closed Xmas
Warm hospitality awaits guests at this small, family run hotel, located only a short walk from the town centre and sea front, the picturesque Radipole Lake and swimming pool complex. A choice of hearty home cooked food is provided at breakfast and in the evening. The bedrooms vary in size and style, but all are comfortably equipped. There is a comfortable lounge for guests.
9 shr (3 fmly) No smoking in bedrooms No smoking in dining room CTV in all bedrooms Tea and coffee making facilities No dogs Licensed Cen ht CTV 6P No coaches Last d 4pm
ROOMS: s £16-£24; d £32-£48; wkly b&b £105-£152; wkly hlf-bd £149-£196
CARDS:

The Westwey 62 Abbotsbury Rd DT4 0BJ ☎ 01305 784564
A warm welcome from Pam and Dave, the resident proprietors, sets the scene for a relaxing stay at this small hotel, located just half a mile from the town centre and the Esplanade. The bedrooms are all en suite and well equipped, including television, tea making facilities and hair dryers. Generous portions of fresh home cooked meals are offered with a choice at each course; special diets can be catered for by prior arrangement.
11 rms (1 bth 8 shr) (2 fmly) No smoking in dining room No smoking in lounges CTV in all bedrooms Tea and coffee making facilities No dogs Licensed Cen ht CTV No children 6yrs 10P Last d 6.30pm
ROOMS: s £17-£21; d £34-£42; wkly b&b £107-£137; wkly hlf-bd £142-£176*

WHEATLEY Oxfordshire Map 04 SP50

Bat & Ball 28 High St, Cuddesdon OX44 9HJ
☎ 01865 874379 FAX 01865 873363
Just 15 minutes drive from Oxford, this lovely rural inn, seems to be removed from the rat-race of modern life. There is a cricketing theme throughout, including the smart bedrooms and the stylish tap room with its wooden tables and floors. Breakfast is a hearty affair, and both full meals and lighter meals are available at lunch and dinner from an interesting menu.
7 shr CTV in all bedrooms Tea and coffee making facilities No dogs (ex guide dogs) Cen ht 20P Last d 9.45pm
ROOMS: s fr £39.95; d fr £49.95*
MEALS: Lunch £4.75-£15alc Dinner £4.75-£15alc*
CARDS:

WHEDDON CROSS Somerset Map 03 SS93

Premier Selected

Little Brendon Hill Farm *(SS933377)* TA24 7BG (from Wheddon Cross take B3224 towards Taunton, farm on left after 1m) ☎ 01643 841556 FAX 01643 841556 Mr L Maxwell
Closed Xmas
Situated within the Exmoor National Park, this charming family run farmhouse offers a high standard of accommodation. The bedrooms are comfortably appointed and equipped with many amenities. Guest can enjoy a well prepared dinner by candlelight, beside a crackling log fire in colder weather. The hospitality of Shelagh and Larry Maxwell, carried out in a quiet relaxing manner, is a real delight.
3 bth/shr No smoking CTV in all bedrooms Tea and coffee making facilities No dogs Cen ht CTV No children 7yrs 10P 5 acres horses sheep Last d noon
ROOMS: s £28; d £42; wkly b&b £132; wkly hlf-bd £221

Selected

Rest and be Thankful Inn Wheddon Cross TA24 7DR (set on the cross roads of the A396 and B3224, 5m S of Dunster)
☎ 01643 841222 FAX 01643 841222
rs 24-26 Dec
Surrounded by unspoilt countryside, the "Rest and Be Thankful" - once a coaching inn - is situated in this moorland village and looks over Dunkery Beacon, the highest point of Exmoor. The comfortable bedrooms are well equipped with modern facilities and there is a cosy lounge for residents. The restaurant, popular with non-residents, offers a wide selection of dishes which range from bar snacks to more substantial house specialities. Warm hospitality is assured from the resident proprietors who know just what it takes to make guests feel welcome.
5 shr No smoking in bedrooms No smoking in dining room CTV in all bedrooms Tea and coffee making facilities Direct dial from bedrooms No dogs (ex guide dogs) Cen ht No children 11yrs 35P Pool Darts Skittle alley Last d 10pm
ROOMS: s £27; d £54; wkly b&b £165; wkly hlf-bd £240*
MEALS: Lunch £8-£16alc Dinner £2.95-£11.95alc*
CARDS:

WHIMPLE Devon Map 03 SY09

Selected

Down House EX5 2QR (from Exeter or Honiton, leave A30 signed Whimple, turn right at 30mph sign by Woodhayes Hotel. Proceed for 0.75m and house is up hill on left) ☎ 01404 822860
This delightful country house, where Michael and Joanne Sanders offer old style hospitality in Edwardian elegance with 20th-century comfort. It stands in six acres of peaceful gardens, paddocks and orchard. Many improvements have taken place especially to the bedrooms, many with lovely views and equipped with such thoughtful extras as fresh flowers, trouser press, hairdryers and clock radios. On fine days guests may enjoy a variety of lawn games, such as croquet and badminton. There is a spacious, elegant sitting room and light and airy dining room.
6 rms (4 bth/shr) (1 fmly) No smoking CTV in all bedrooms Tea and coffee making facilities Cen ht CTV 13P No coaches 18 hole putting Badminton Boules Croquet Skittles
ROOMS: s £20-£30; d £40-£48*

Premier Selected

QQQQQ *Woodhayes* EX5 2TD ☎ 01404 822237
Set peacefully in four acres of carefully kept gardens and grounds and yet only one mile away from the A30, Mr & Mrs Rendle offer their guests a warm welcome and fine hospitality. This beautifully appointed Georgian country house offers the choice of two delightfully decorated lounges and six individual and tastefully furnished en suite bedrooms, with many personal touches provided.
6 bth/shr

WHITBY North Yorkshire Map **08** NZ81

QQQ **Corra Lynn Hotel** 28 Crescent Av YO21 3EW
(corner of A174 & Crescent Avenue) ☎ 01947 602214 FAX 01947 602214
Mar-Oct rs Nov-Apr
This well presented guest house occupies a corner site on the West Cliff, within walking distance of the town and harbour. Light and airy bedrooms, those on the first floor being especially spacious, are attractively decorated and furnished. Breakfast is a particular highlight of a stay at Corra Lynn, and there is a comfortable visitors' lounge.
5 bth/shr (1 fmly) No smoking in dining room CTV in all bedrooms Tea and coffee making facilities Licensed Cen ht CTV No children 5yrs 4P No coaches
ROOMS: d £42-£52; wkly b&b £147-£161*

QQQ **Glendale** 16 Crescent Av YO21 3ED (off Upgang Lane Rd)
☎ 01947 604242
Apr-Oct
Situated on the West Cliff, with views over to the Abbey from some rooms, this is a well maintained and friendly guest house offering good value for money. Bedrooms, many of which are suitable for families, are attractively decorated and well equipped. The newly refurbished lounge is very comfortable and a set dinner is available in the traditional dining room.
6 rms (5 shr) (3 fmly) No smoking in dining room CTV in all bedrooms Tea and coffee making facilities Licensed CTV 6P No coaches
Last d 4.15pm
ROOMS: s £17-£18; d £40-£42; wkly b&b £130-£135;
wkly hlf-bd £190-£195*

QQQ **Haven** 4 East Crescent YO21 3HD
(West Cliff at top of Khyber Pass) ☎ 01947 603842
rs Nov-Mar
After 16 years running this family guest house, Joan and Brian Smith often welcome many guests back year after year. Comfortable bedrooms, some of them having sea and harbour views, are neatly decorated, whilst downstairs, there is a cosy lounge and breakfast is served at individual tables in the airy dining room.
8 rms (5 bth/shr) (1 fmly) No smoking in dining room CTV in all bedrooms Tea and coffee making facilities No dogs (ex guide dogs) Licensed Cen ht CTV No children 5yrs No coaches
ROOMS: s £20-£22; d £40-£44; wkly b&b £115-£147

QQQ ***Lavinia House*** 3 East Crescent YO21 3HD
☎ 01947 602945 & 820656
Enjoying fine views over the harbour and sea, this guest house has been fully refurbished by owners Jill and Tony Campbell. Attractively decorated bedrooms are comfortable, whilst there is also a welcoming lounge, with breakfast being served in the bright and airy dining room.
5 rms (3 bth/shr) (2 fmly) No smoking in 1 bedrooms No smoking in dining room No smoking in lounges CTV in all bedrooms Tea and coffee making facilities No dogs Cen ht 2P No coaches

Q Q Q **Sandbeck Hotel** 2 Crescent Ter, West Cliff YO21 3EL (on West Cliff, opposite the theatre and Pavilion booking office)
☎ 01947 604012
Closed Xmas period
There are fine sea views from front facing bedrooms at this family run guest house. Bedrooms, those on the lower floors tending to be larger, are equipped with modern appointments. There is a comfortable sitting room and breakfast is served at separate tables in the traditional dining room.
15 bth/shr (6 fmly) No smoking in dining room No smoking in lounges CTV in all bedrooms Tea and coffee making facilities Licensed Cen ht CTV No coaches
ROOMS: s £20-£27.50; d £40-£55*
CARDS:

Selected

Q Q Q Q **Seacliffe Hotel** North Promenade, West Cliff YO21 3JX (follow signs for West Cliff & West Cliff car park, hotel on sea front)
☎ 01947 603139 FAX 01947 603139
Situated on the West Cliff, this holiday hotel offers fine sea views. The bedrooms may be compact in size, but are comfortably furnished and one even features a water bed. Top floor rooms can also be used as a family suite. The visitors' lounge leads into a bar with a patio that proves to be a real sun trap in summer months. An extensive menu is offered and served in the bright, beamed restaurant.
19 bth/shr (4 fmly) No smoking in 1 bedrooms No smoking in dining room CTV in all bedrooms Tea and coffee making facilities Direct dial from bedrooms Licensed Cen ht CTV 8P Golf available nearby Last d 8.45pm
ROOMS: s £32.50-£37.50; d £59-£65*
CARDS:

WHITCHURCH Shropshire Map **07** SJ54

Premier Selected

Q Q Q Q Q **Dearnford Hall** *(SJ543389)* Tilstock Rd SY13 3JJ (at Tilstock rdbt on southerly Whitchurch by-pass take B5476 to Tilstock. Establishment is 0.25m on the left)
☎ 01948 662319 FAX 01948 666670 Mrs J Bebbington
Closed Xmas
This impressive country house combines 20th-century comfort and 18th-century elegance and charm. Surrounded by its own farmland, that includes a spring-fed trout pool and many interesting walks, Dearnford Hall is only a mile from Whitchurch. Inside, the beauty of the architecture has been further enhanced by Jane Bebbington's stylish selection of antique furniture, rich fabrics and family treasures which adorn the sitting and dining rooms. The genuine hospitality of the Bebbingtons makes a stay here truly memorable.

2 bth/shr No smoking CTV in all bedrooms Tea and coffee making facilities Cen ht CTV No children 15yrs 10P Fishing Grand piano, unspoilt walking areas 500 acres Arable
ROOMS: s £35-£45; d £60-£80; wkly b&b £210-£245*

WHITEHAVEN Cumbria Map **11** NX91

Q Q Q ***Queens Hotel*** Main St CA27 0DE ☎ 01946 822287
This traditional inn is decorated with a mass of colourful window boxes and shrubs and is just a short walk from the railway station. Despite its pub origins this friendly hostelry boasts rich town house decor, subdued lighting and a cosy atmosphere. There is a stylish, spacious conservatory which serves a wide ranging menu. The bedrooms are generously proportioned and furnished in stripped pine.
15 bth/shr Last d 9.30pm

WHITEPARISH Wiltshire Map **04** SU22

Selected

Q Q Q Q ***Brickworth*** *(SU217240)* Brickworth Ln SP5 2QE (on A36 travelling S from Salisbury, Brickworth Ln is on left by bus stop, just before traffic lights at junc with A27 to Romsey and Whiteparish) ☎ 01794 884663 FAX 01794 884581 Mrs S Barry
Closed 23 Dec-2 Jan
This delightful farmhouse, partly dating back to the 18th century, is set in a peaceful rural setting and within easy reach of the city of Salisbury. The spacious bedrooms have been thoughtfully furnished to reflect the character of the house and are equipped with many modern amenities. A generous English breakfast is served in the attractive dining room and guests also have use of a small but cosy lounge.
4 bth/shr (1 fmly) No smoking CTV in all bedrooms Tea and coffee making facilities No dogs Cen ht CTV 20P 5 acres non-working

Selected

QQQQ **Newton Farmhouse** Southampton Rd SP5 2QL (on the A36 1m S of the junc with the A27) ☎ 01794 884416
A 16th-century farmhouse on the borders of the New Forest, formerly part of the Trafalgar Estate, is situated just eight miles south of Salisbury. All bedrooms, three with four-poster beds, are delightfully decorated with co-ordinated fabrics, and are equipped with a number of thoughtful extras. The beamed dining room houses a collection of Nelson memorabilia, flagstone floors, and an inglenook fireplace. Home-made breads and preserves are a feature of the breakfasts, and dinners, using home grown produce from the extensive garden, are popular. There is an outdoor swimming pool in the well stocked gardens.
8 bth/shr No smoking CTV in all bedrooms Tea and coffee making facilities No dogs (ex guide dogs) Cen ht CTV 10P Outdoor swimming pool Last d 24hrs notice
ROOMS: d £38-£50* See advertisement under SALISBURY

WHITEWELL Lancashire Map **07** SD64

Selected

QQQQ ◀ ***The Inn at Whitewell*** BB7 3AT ☎ 01200 448222 FAX 01200 448298
A delightful old inn, owned and run by Richard Bowman and family, is situated in the Forest of Bowland. The stone flagged entrance leads to a delightful bar with an open fire and also to the reception which doubles as an art gallery and small wine shop. An excellent range of food is served in the bar and in the elegant restaurant. The well equipped bedrooms, now with CD players, are full of antiques. Warm and very friendly service is provided by the dedicated staff.
11 bth/shr (4 fmly) CTV in all bedrooms Direct dial from bedrooms Cen ht 60P Fishing Clay pigeon shooting by arrangement
Last d 9.30pm
CARDS:

WHITLEY BAY Tyne & Wear Map **12** NZ37

QQQ **Cherrytree House** 35 Brook St NE26 1AF (on seafront facing St Mary's church, first on the left past Marlborough Hotel) ☎ 0191 251 4306 FAX 0191 2514306
One will find a warm and inviting atmosphere at this homely house situated in a quiet street between the town centre and the sea front. The traditionally furnished bedrooms are cosy, appealing and spotlessly clean, and Mr and Mrs Coleman are happy to offer their comfortable lounge to guests.
4 rms (3 shr) No smoking in dining room CTV in all bedrooms Tea and coffee making facilities Cen ht CTV 1P No coaches
ROOMS: s £30-£40; d £38-£50*

QQQ **Marlborough Hotel** 20-21 East Pde, Central Promenade NE26 1AP (A19 follow signs for Tynemouth/Whitley Bay. From S use A1058 to seafront turn N into Whitley Bay. From N use A186 to seafront, turn S into Bay) ☎ 0191 251 3628 FAX 0191 251 3628
Closed Xmas and New Year
With its sandstone terraced façade, this attractive and well maintained hotel enjoys a beach front and promenade location. The smart, modern bedooms, two on the ground floor, offer as good standard of accommodation. Several rooms have comfortable seating areas from which to enjoy the sea views. There is a bright, cheery dining room and a comfortable lounge. Small groups and parties can be accommodated.
17 rms (13 bth/shr) (4 fmly) No smoking in bedrooms No smoking in dining room CTV in all bedrooms Tea and coffee making facilities Direct dial from bedrooms No dogs (ex guide dogs) Licensed CTV No children 3yrs 7P No coaches Last d 5.30pm
ROOMS: s £22-£38; d £52-£58*
CARDS:

York House Hotel 30 Park Pde NE26 1DX (A19 onto A193 and turn left at Baptist church) ☎ 0191 252 8313 FAX 0191 251 3953
Michael and Marissa Ruddy offer personal attention at their friendly hotel. The lovely bedrooms are well equipped with a host of accessories and thoughtful touches, ensuring maximum comfort. The dinner menu offers excellent value for money and can be enjoyed in the spacious dining room, or alternatively one can order a cold supper tray to take in one's bedroom. Business travellers can take advantage of the fax and e-mail facilities.
8 rms (7 bth/shr) 7 annexe rms (5 bth/shr) (6 fmly) No smoking in dining room CTV in all bedrooms Tea and coffee making facilities Direct dial from bedrooms Licensed Cen ht CTV 3P Last d 7.30pm
ROOMS: s £25-£50; d £40-£60; wkly b&b £170-£300; wkly hlf-bd £260-£400*
CARDS:

WHITNEY-ON-WYE Herefordshire Map 03 SO24

Premier Selected

Rhydspence HR3 6EU (N side of A438 1m W) ☎ 01497 831262 FAX 01497 831751
Dating back to the 14th century this large privately owned and personally run hostelry stands three miles north of Hay-on-Wye. Surrounded by attractive gardens and with a stream that forms part of the boundary between England and Wales, the inn provides modern accommodation and the public rooms include a very attractive restaurant and two quaint bars with low beamed ceilings and log fires.
7 bth/shr No smoking in area of dining room CTV in all bedrooms Tea and coffee making facilities No dogs (ex guide dogs) Cen ht 60P No coaches Last d 9.30pm
ROOMS: s £32.50-£37.50; d £65-£75*
MEALS: Lunch £18-£35alc Dinner £18-£35alc*
CARDS:

WHITSTABLE Kent Map 05 TR16

Selected

Barnfield at Windy Ridge Wraik Hill CT5 3BY (from M2/A299, rdbt 3rd exit, 2nd rdbt 2nd exit, and continue for 0.5m) ☎ 01227 263506 FAX 01227 771191
A warm welcome is extended to all guests by owners Elizabeth and Colin Dyke. The accommodation is comfortable and tastefully furnished with many thoughtful extras, and most bedrooms have panoramic views of the sea or countryside. A room on the ground floor is designed specifically for disabled guests. Windy Ridge makes an ideal setting for wedding receptions, and ceremonies are conducted in the attractive garden. There is a spacious lounge and an attractive dining room where an evening meal is available to parties of four and over by prior arrangement.

8 shr (2 fmly) No smoking in area of dining room CTV in all bedrooms Tea and coffee making facilities Direct dial from bedrooms Licensed Cen ht CTV 16P No coaches Last d 8pm
CARDS:

WIDECOMBE-IN-THE-MOOR Devon Map 03 SX77

Selected

Torcroft TQ13 7TE (Bovey Tracy exit on A38 head for town and left at 2nd rdbt follow signs for Widecombe. Torcroft is on left on steep hill to village) ☎ 01364 621229 FAX 01364 621370
rs 24 Dec-2 Jan
A charming country house, set in three acres of secluded woodland and well tended gardens, boasts an unrivalled position and stunning views. Torcroft is a haven for those looking to relax. Owners Sally and Dave make their guests feel instantly at home and provide many thoughtful extra touches such as fresh fruit, flowers and even foot balm for weary walkers. One of the bedrooms features a delightful four-poster bed, hand crafted by Dave himself. The accommodation is to a high standard. Breakfast is served around a large communal table in the attractive dining room which leads to a sunny conservatory. The delightful home-cooked meals are a highlight of a stay at Torcroft.
3 bth/shr No smoking CTV in all bedrooms Tea and coffee making facilities Cen ht No children 14yrs 6P No coaches Last d 4pm
ROOMS: s £26-£32.50; d £37-£50*
CARDS:

WIGHT, ISLE OF Map 04

COWES Map 04 SZ49

Busigny 16 Castle Rd PO31 7QZ
(A3020 from Newport, left onto B3325 at Northwood Garage, right at mini-rdbt onto Park Rd, left into Union Rd after a 1m, left into Church Rd)
☎ 01983 291919 FAX 01983 294004
This well presented small guest house enjoys a central location convenient for both town centre and the ferry. The bedrooms are neatly furnished and decorated with the bathrooms currently being upgraded. There is a spacious combined lounge and dining room where guests can relax and enjoy freshly prepared breakfasts. Rear parking is a real plus.
4 rms (2 shr) (2 fmly) No smoking in dining room No smoking in lounges CTV in 3 bedrooms Tea and coffee making facilities CTV 3P
ROOMS: s £25-£35; d £30-£40 (room only); wkly b&b £140-£175

Salty Seadog 31 Marsh Rd, Gurnard PO31 8JQ
(from ferry, cross floating bridge up Medina Rd, right down Victoria Rd, left down Park Rd, over rdbt, left into Solvent View Rd, to bottom of hill)
☎ 01983 200330 FAX 01983 200330
Both adults and children will find a warm and friendly welcome from owners Jon and Sally Peach, whose policy is 'nothing is too much trouble'.

In an enviable location on the waterfront, just 2 miles from Cowes, the area is famous for its sunsets. The en suite bedrooms, although not spacious, are smart and clean, and equipped with remote TV and tea facilities. Guests take all meals in the restaurant, a popular summer venue with outdoor BBQs a feature. Guest parking and two private slipways provided. Off shore sporting activities arranged.
3 bth/shr (1 fmly) CTV in all bedrooms Tea and coffee making facilities No dogs (ex guide dogs) Licensed Cen ht 40P No coaches
Watersports available in summer Last d 9.30pm
ROOMS: s £20-£30; d £40-£60
CARDS:

Q Q Q Windward House 69 Mill Hill Rd PO31 7EQ
(A320 Cowes-Newport, halfway up Mill Hill Rd on right hand side from 'floating bridge' from E Cowes (Red Funnel Ferries)) ☎ 01983 280940
Popular with yachtsmen in summer and business travellers in winter, Sue Ogston-Brown's friendly, late Victorian establishment is just five minutes from the centre of town and chain ferry to East Cowes. Bedrooms are bright and cheerful and day rooms comprise a homely lounge with TV, videos and music centre, and a separate dining room where guests share a table for breakfast. Guests also have use of a laundry and drying room. There is a patio and neatly kept garden to the rear.
6 rms (4 shr) (2 fmly) No smoking in dining room CTV in all bedrooms Tea and coffee making facilities Cen ht CTV 4P No coaches
ROOMS: s £20-£22.50; d £40-£45*

NEWPORT Map 04 SZ48

Q Q Elizabeth House 21 Carrisbrooke Rd PO30 1BU ☎ 01983 521389 FAX 01983 521389
A small, homely guest house, conveniently located close to the town centre. The bedrooms are attractively decorated, comfortably furnished and well maintained. A hearty cooked breakfast can be enjoyed in the breakfast room or alternatively served in the bed room.
4 rms (2 shr) (1 fmly) No smoking in 2 bedrooms No smoking in dining room CTV in all bedrooms Tea and coffee making facilities No dogs (ex guide dogs) Cen ht CTV 4P No coaches
ROOMS: s £18-£20; d fr £36; wkly b&b £116-£130*

NITON Map 04 SZ57

Q Q Q Pine Ridge Country House Niton Undercliff PO38 2LY
(on A3055 main Niton to Ventor road, just after BP garage on the right)
☎ 01983 730802 FAX 01983 731001
Closed 25 Dec
Set in several acres of grounds with panoramic sea views to the front and The Undercliff as a backdrop, Pine Ridge is situated in a peaceful village near St Catherine's Lighthouse. Bedrooms are bright and comfortably furnished offering good facilities. The public areas include separate lounge and bar, and guests can enjoy Mrs Lake's home cooking in the well appointed dining room.
7 bth/shr (3 fmly) No smoking in 2 bedrooms No smoking in dining room CTV in all bedrooms Tea and coffee making facilities Direct dial from bedrooms Licensed Cen ht CTV 10P No coaches Last d 9pm
ROOMS: d £55-£80*
CARDS:

RYDE Map 04 SZ59

Q Q Q Teneriffe Hotel 36 The Strand PO33 1JF ☎ 01983 563841 FAX 01983 615692
Closed Dec-Feb
Just one street back from the sea front, near the swimming pool and boating lake, this well-kept hotel has been personally run by the Brown Family for over 30 years. Spacious public rooms include a comfortable lounge and a large red plush bar, with dance floor, where live entertainment is provided most nights of the week. Attractively decorated bedrooms are en suite and a lift serves most floors.
50 bth/shr (7 fmly) No smoking in dining room CTV in all bedrooms Tea and coffee making facilities No dogs (ex guide dogs) Licensed Lift Cen ht CTV 9P Last d 7pm
ROOMS: s £18.95-£19.95; d £37.90-£39.90; wkly b&b £132.65-£139.65; wkly hlf-bd £152-£180*
CARDS:

SANDOWN Map 04 SZ58

Q Q Q Bertram Lodge 3 Leed St PO36 9DA
(Turn off A3055 prior to leisure centre turn right into Leed St)
☎ 01983 402551
Jan-Sep
With neat gardens to front and rear, this well-kept establishment is personally run by Cheryl and Dennis Flowers. Day rooms include a small cosy bar off the well-appointed dining room and a comfortable, non-smoking residents' lounge. Bar snacks are available as an alternative to the full dinners offered. Bedrooms, some reserved for non-smokers and some on the ground floor, are en suite and prettily decorated.
8 shr No smoking in 4 bedrooms No smoking in dining room No smoking in lounges CTV in all bedrooms Tea and coffee making facilities No dogs (ex guide dogs) Licensed Cen ht CTV 7P No coaches New gams room American pool Darts Last d 4.30pm
ROOMS: s £17-£21; d £34-£42; wkly b&b £115-£125; wkly hlf-bd £150-£164
CARDS:

Q Q Q Carisbrooke House Hotel 11 Beachfield Rd PO36 8NA
(200yds along the High Street on right hand side) ☎ 01983 402257
Mar-Oct
Well placed for both town centre and seafront, this friendly hotel has been run by Anne and Bernard McHugh for over ten years. Bedrooms are bright and fresh with five particularly suitable for families. Public areas include a cosy lounge with books and games and an open-plan bar/dining room. Evening meals are available by prior arrangement.
12 rms (1 bth 6 shr) (5 fmly) CTV in all bedrooms Tea and coffee making facilities No dogs (ex guide dogs) Licensed Cen ht CTV
ROOMS: s £18-£20; d £36-£44; wkly b&b £120-£145*
CARDS:

Q Q Chester Lodge Hotel Beachfield Rd PO36 8NA
☎ 01983 402773
Etr-end Sept
In the same family ownership for over 30 years, Chester Lodge is just a few steps from the sea front and the shops. Public rooms include a roomy bar lounge and bright dining room where evening meals are available. Bedrooms, several on the ground floor, include a television.
18 rms (2 bth 12 shr) (5 fmly) No smoking in bedrooms No smoking in dining room CTV in all bedrooms Tea and coffee making facilities Licensed Cen ht No children 2yrs 15P
ROOMS: s £16-£23; d £32-£46; wkly b&b £130-£155; wkly hlf-bd £150-£185
CARDS:

Q Q Q Culver Lodge Hotel Albert Rd PO36 8AW
(turn off The Broadway Sandown into Station Rd and left into Albert Rd)
☎ 01983 403819 & 402902 & 0500 121252 FAX 01983 403819
Mar-Nov
A splendid new swimming pool and patio with stone balustrade are the latest improvements at this friendly, well-kept hotel located just a short walk from the sea front and town centre. Spacious public areas include an inviting lounge furnished with cushioned rattan easy chairs and a smart, comfortable bar. Bedrooms are well-presented and comfortable.
21 bth/shr (5 fmly) No smoking in dining room CTV in all bedrooms Tea and coffee making facilities No dogs (ex guide dogs) Licensed Cen ht CTV 20P Outdoor swimming pool (heated) Pool room Darts
Video games Last d 9pm
ROOMS: s £20-£26; d £40-£52
CARDS:

See advertisement on p.457.

QQQ *Cygnet Hotel* 58 Carter St PO36 8DQ ☎ 01983 402930
FAX 01983 405112
This family run hotel benefits from the friendly and dedicated approach of the Teasdale family. The bedrooms are comfortably furnished and well equipped. Public areas are extensive with two lounge areas and a large bar where there is live entertainment at least three nights a week in season. Guests can also enjoy both indoor and outdoor swimming pools, solarium and spa bath.
50 rms (36 bth/shr) (8 fmly) No smoking in dining room CTV in 30 bedrooms Tea and coffee making facilities No dogs (ex guide dogs) Licensed Lift Cen ht CTV 30P Indoor swimming pool (heated) Outdoor swimming pool (heated) Sauna Solarium Gymnasium Spa pool Last d 6.30pm
CARDS:

QQ **Hazelwood Private Hotel** 19 Carter St PO36 8BL
☎ 01983 402536
Close to the town centre, and just a short stroll from the sea front, guests here can be sure of a friendly welcome from proprietor Pauline Wright and her daughter Gemma. Public areas include a cosy bar/lounge and an L-shaped dining room where dinner usually includes one of Pauline's home-made fruit pies among the desserts. Several of the neatly-kept bedrooms are suitable for families and in one dogs are allowed by prior arrangement.
7 rms (3 fmly) No smoking in 5 bedrooms No smoking in dining room Tea and coffee making facilities Licensed CTV ch fac 10P

Selected

QQQQ **St Catherine's Hotel** 1 Winchester Park Rd PO36 8HJ
(from Ryde pass under a rail bridge on edge of Sandown, come to an island with a garage on either side. Turn right up hill, hotel 0.25m on left) ☎ 01983 402392 FAX 01983 402392
Kept in immaculately good order by Stuart and Marlene Barker, this hotel was originally built as a retirement home by the Dean of Winchester in 1860. A comfortable lounge and a small bar, retain a period feel, but the prettily decorated bedrooms come with every modern convenience including satellite TV. There is a substantial room service menu and a good choice of meals served in the well-appointed dining room.
19 bth/shr (4 fmly) No smoking in dining room CTV in all bedrooms Tea and coffee making facilities Direct dial from bedrooms Licensed Cen ht CTV 8P No coaches Last d 8pm
ROOMS: s £23-£25; d £46-£50; wkly b&b £136.50-£149.50; wkly hlf-bd £195-£221
CARDS:

The AA's professional Inspectors make regular and anonymous visits to all the establishments listed in the Guide. They accept no gifts or favours from proprietors

SEAVIEW Map 04 SZ69

QQ **Northbank Hotel** Circular Rd PO34 5ET ☎ 01983 612227
Etr-Sep
Families return year after year to enjoy traditional family holidays at Mary and Michael Shaw-Yates' charmingly old fashioned hotel where the garden runs down to the sea. Antiques, objets d'art and bygones are to be found in public areas which include a large, well-furnished lounge, intimate bar and TV room where 16mm cartoon films are shown to keep younger guests amused on wet days. Traditionally furnished bedrooms are kept in good decorative order and make up for limited facilities. Only a few have TV but the others have splendid old wireless sets.
18 rms (6 fmly) No smoking in dining room CTV in 2 bedrooms Licensed CTV ch fac 12P Fishing Snooker Last d 8pm
ROOMS: s £25-£30; d £50-£60; wkly b&b £175; wkly hlf-bd £250-£285*

SHANKLIN Map 04 SZ58

Selected

QQQQ **Aqua Hotel** The Esplande PO37 6BN
(turn off Arthurs Hill/North Rd at fiveways junct into Hope Rd and follow through to esplanade) ☎ 01983 863024 FAX 01983 864841
Etr-5 November
Personally run in friendly fashion by James and Annette Blanchett, this well-kept hotel is fronted by a spacious patio that takes full advantage of the hotel's fine sea front location. Public areas include a comfortably appointed bar/lounge with parquet dance floor and all-day snack menu, and the attractive Boaters restaurant. Immaculate bedrooms, six with sea-facing balconies, are comfortable and well-equipped.
22 bth/shr (4 fmly) No smoking in dining room CTV in all bedrooms Tea and coffee making facilities No dogs Licensed Cen ht 2P Darts board Pool table Last d 4.30pm
ROOMS: s £25-£30; d £50-£60; wkly b&b £175-£210; wkly hlf-bd £210-£245
CARDS:

QQQ **Bay House Hotel** 8 Chine Av PO37 6AG
(A3055 from Sandown, at traffic lights located at end of Arthurs Hill take Queens Rd to end then turn left)
☎ 01983 863180 FAX 01983 866604
Adjacent to Keats Green, and with glorious views over Shanklin Bay, this hotel has been run by the Hughes family for 20 years. Bedrooms are bright and very well kept and the public areas are extensive and comfortable and include a well-stocked bar. In high summer a snack menu is served on the extensive patio. The restaurant offers home cooking from the proprietors' son, David, whose Sunday lunches prove popular throughout the year. Other amenities include an indoor swimming pool, sauna and solarium.
23 bth/shr (3 fmly) No smoking in bedrooms No smoking in dining room CTV in 22 bedrooms Tea and coffee making facilities Licensed CTV 15P Indoor swimming pool (heated) Sauna Last d 7.30pm
CARDS:

QQQ **Culham Lodge** 31 Landguard Manor Rd PO37 7HZ
(take A3055 from Ryde through the traffic lights, at Lake turn right into Green Lane, then right into Landguard Manor Rd)
☎ 01983 862880 FAX 01983 862880
Feb-Nov
Mr and Mrs Metcalf offer a warm welcome to all their guests at this well established small hotel. Bedrooms are attractively furnished and decorated, and all feature modern en suite facilities. In addition to the comfortable lounge and dining room, guests may enjoy the heated outdoor swimming pool.

10 shr No smoking in dining room No smoking in lounges CTV in all bedrooms Tea and coffee making facilities No dogs (ex guide dogs) Cen ht CTV No children 12yrs 8P Outdoor swimming pool (heated) Last d 4pm
ROOMS: s £22-£23; d £44-£46; wkly b&b £143-£150;
wkly hlf-bd £178-£185✻
CARDS:

Q Q Q Curraghmore Hotel 22 Hope Rd PO37 6EA ☎ 01983 862605
FAX 01983 867431
Mar-Oct
The Curraghmore has sea views from its elevated position and it is only a short stroll down to the beach and the Esplanade. Margaret and Colin Andrews are the friendly hosts while sons Garry and Derek are the chefs. Day rooms include a cosy bar with its own terrace. There is live entertainment three nights a week through the season and on a fourth night a film show extolling the Island's attractions. Bedrooms are fresh and bright and central heating has now been installed.
24 bth/shr (9 fmly) CTV in all bedrooms Tea and coffee making facilities Licensed Cen ht 20P Putting Last d 6.30pm
ROOMS: s £20-£23; d £40-£46; wkly b&b £140-£161;
wkly hlf-bd £175-£209

Selected

Q Q Q Q Hambledon Hotel Queens Rd, Queens Rd PO37 6AW (off A3055) ☎ 01983 862403 & 863651 FAX 01983 867894
A warm, friendly, family run hotel that caters for all ages, and where owners Beryl and Norman Birch provide a high standard of comfortable accommodation. The bedrooms are attractively decorated, furnished in modern style, and have many modern amenities. A choice of menu is offered at dinner and is served in the elegant dining room. Other public rooms include two lounges, one non-smoking, and a well stocked bar.
11 shr (4 fmly) No smoking in dining room No smoking in 1 lounge CTV in all bedrooms Tea and coffee making facilities Direct dial from bedrooms Licensed Cen ht CTV ch fac 8P Free use of nearby indoor leisure facilities Last d 6pm
ROOMS: s £19-£25; d £38-£50; wkly b&b £130-£175;
wkly hlf-bd £160-£210✻
CARDS:

Q Q Q Keats Cottage Hotel 76 High St, Old Village PO37 6NJ (located at the top end of Shanklin High St, looking down into the old village, public car park 50 yds down road on same side)
☎ 01983 866351 FAX 01983 866351
Originally the home of the poet John Keats back in 1819, this small hotel has undergone major refurbishment to offer comfortable accommodation. Bedrooms have been smartly appointed and feature thoughtful touches such as a complimentary half bottle of wine. Public areas include a first floor lounge, bar and popular bistro which specialises in seafood. Resident proprietors Gabriella and Keith Hazelwood provide warm hospitality in a relaxed informal atmosphere.
5 rms (2 shr) No smoking in 2 bedrooms No smoking in area of dining room No smoking in 1 lounge CTV in 2 bedrooms Tea and coffee making facilities No dogs (ex guide dogs) Licensed Cen ht CTV No children 14yrs No coaches Last d 10pm
ROOMS: d £50-£80✻
CARDS:

Q Q Q Mount House Hotel 20 Arthurs Hill PO37 6EE
(on A3055 on outskirts of town on corner of Clarence Road)
☎ 01983 862556 FAX 01983 867551
Closed 31 Dec-1 Jan
This Edwardian house is ideally located for both town centre and seafront, and is run by the friendly Scott family. Bright bedrooms are well kept and comfortably appointed. Hearty home-cooked food is served in the dining room and guests may also enjoy the small bar lounge.

9 shr (2 fmly) No smoking in dining room CTV in all bedrooms Tea and coffee making facilities Licensed Cen ht CTV 5P No coaches Last d 7pm
ROOMS: s £19-£27.50; d £38-£55; wkly b&b £121-£140;
wkly hlf-bd £154-£179✻
CARDS:

Selected

Q Q Q Q Osborne House Esplanade PO37 6BN
(on Seafront opposite Clock Tower)
☎ 01983 862501 FAX 01983 862501
Jan-18 Oct
Fronted by a flower bedecked terrace and lawn, Osborne House is located on the Esplanade, and run in friendly fashion by Mike and Liz Hogarth. Well kept bedrooms are simply furnished but are en suite and provided with all sorts of extras including fresh fruit and a vacuum flask of iced water. Dinners are no longer served but Mike's breakfasts, served on the terrace when the weather allows, are well worth getting up for.
12 bth/shr No smoking in dining room CTV in all bedrooms Tea and coffee making facilities No dogs Licensed Cen ht No children 13yrs No coaches
ROOMS: s fr £30; d fr £50✻
CARDS:

Q Q Q Rowborough Hotel 32 Arthurs Hill PO37 6EX (1m S of Lake at junct of A3055/A3056) ☎ 01983 866072 FAX 01983 867703
Mar-28 Oct
Hospitable new owners, Jim and Mary Pearce, offer a warm welcome to this small, well-kept hotel just a short walk from the centre of town. Fresh flowers grace the tables in the dining room which is open plan to a well-stocked bar.
contd.

Other day rooms include a comfortable sitting room and a conservatory lounge looking out onto the front garden. Bowls of fresh fruit are a nice touch in the neat, comfortable bedrooms. Mary is responsible for the home-cooked dinners while Jim is particularly proud of his substantial breakfasts.
9 bth/shr (5 fmly) No smoking in dining room No smoking in 1 lounge CTV in all bedrooms Tea and coffee making facilities No dogs (ex guide dogs) Licensed Cen ht CTV 5P No coaches Last d 8pm
ROOMS: s £26-£30.50; d £52-£61; wkly b&b £120-£140; wkly hlf-bd £160-£185*
CARDS:

Q Q Q White House Hotel Eastcliff Promenade PO37 6AY
(A3055 from Sandown, at first set of traffic lights, take B3328, second turning on the left, at top of hill turn right into Park Rd)
☎ 01983 862776 & 867904 FAX 01983 865980
Closed Nov
Well positioned on the cliff top, this small and friendly hotel commands great views over Shanklin Bay. Car access and parking are via Park Road but the public lift down to the Esplanade is close by. The bedrooms are gradually being refurbished and are comfortably appointed with some enjoying a seaview. Public areas are spacious and include a sun lounge, homely bar and TV lounge. The dining room offers home-cooked food and overlooks the well tended garden.
11 bth/shr (1 fmly) No smoking in dining room CTV in all bedrooms Tea and coffee making facilities Direct dial from bedrooms No dogs (ex guide dogs) Licensed Cen ht CTV 12P No coaches Last d 5pm
ROOMS: s £24-£28; d £48-£56; wkly b&b £160-£190; wkly hlf-bd £205-£245*
CARDS:

TOTLAND BAY Map 04 SZ38

Q Q Frenchman's Cove Country Hotel Alum Bay Old Rd PO39 0HZ
(off B3322, signposted to Freshwater Bay. Hotel 500yds on right)
☎ 01983 752227 FAX 01983 755125
Personally run by friendly owners Sue and Chris Boatfield, the hotel enjoys a peaceful rural location with views across the Solent. The property is well suited to families, with pine bunk beds in many rooms, the majority of which feature en suite facilities. There is also a self-catering apartment in a separate coach house. Guests can enjoy the large garden and the cosy bar which has a real fire.
12 bth/shr (9 fmly) No smoking in bedrooms No smoking in dining room No smoking in 1 lounge CTV in all bedrooms Tea and coffee making facilities No dogs (ex guide dogs) Licensed Cen ht CTV ch fac 17P Badminton Table tennis Last d 6pm
ROOMS: s £25-£30; d £46-£52; wkly b&b £145-£170; wkly hlf-bd £205-£240
CARDS:

Q Q Q Littledene Lodge Granville Rd PO39 0AX (on approaching Totland from Yarmouth ferry terminal turn right at Totland Bay post office)
☎ 01983 752411
rs Nov-Mar (excl. Xmas)
A colourful display of flowers fronts this small establishment just a short walk from sea front. Personally run by Jennifer Barnes, the bedrooms are prettily decorated and neatly kept, and on the ground floor there is comfortable residents' lounge and, at one end of the dining room, a copper-topped dispense bar.
7 rms (6 bth/shr) (3 fmly) No smoking in dining room Tea and coffee making facilities Licensed Cen ht CTV 5P No coaches Free entry to local swimming complex Last d 4.30pm
ROOMS: d £39-£44; wkly b&b £132-£145; wkly hlf-bd £198-£210*
CARDS:

Q Q Q The Nodes Country Hotel Alum Bay Old Rd PO39 0HZ
(from Yarmouth head for Totland, then for Alum Bay. 0.25m from Alum Bay turn left into Alum Bay Old Road. Hotel 500 yds on right)
☎ 01983 752859 FAX 01705 201621
Mr and Mrs Sanchis offer a warm welcome at this well established guest house. Enjoying a peaceful countryside location close to Alum Bay the rooms offer en suite facilities and are divided between the main building and a purpose built extension. The public areas include a cosy lounge and bar, and guests can enjoy freshly prepared meals in the dining room.
5 rms (3 bth) 6 annexe shr (5 fmly) No smoking in bedrooms No smoking in dining room CTV in all bedrooms Tea and coffee making facilities Licensed Cen ht CTV 15P Badminton Table tennis Last d 3pm
ROOMS: s £24.50-£29.50; d £49-£59; wkly b&b £166.50-£210; wkly hlf-bd £228-£255*
CARDS:

VENTNOR Map 04 SZ57

Selected

Q Q Q Q Hillside Private Hotel Mitchell Av PO38 1DR
(exit A3055 onto B3327, premises 600 yards on right behind tennis courts) ☎ 01983 852271 FAX 01983 852271
Run in friendly fashion by Brenda and Peter Hart, this substantial thatched house dates back to 1807 and enjoys an elevated position above the town. Day rooms include a homely lounge, separate bar (the only place where smoking is allowed) and charming plant-filled conservatory verandah. Brenda's home-cooked dinners, always with good vegetarian options (the Harts are themselves vegetarian), encourage many guests to return year after year. Of the variously furnished bedrooms, the three that are not en suite each have their own private facilities nearby.
11 bth/shr (1 fmly) No smoking in dining room No smoking in lounges CTV in all bedrooms Tea and coffee making facilities Licensed Cen ht No children 5yrs 12P Last d 8.30pm
ROOMS: s £20-£23; d £40-£46; wkly b&b £140.50-£161.50; wkly hlf-bd £200-£224
CARDS:

Selected

Q Q Q Q Lake Hotel Shore Rd, Bonchurch PO38 1RF
(opposite Bonchurch Pond in Bonchurch village)
☎ 01983 852613 FAX 01983 852613
Mar-Oct
Set in one of the most beautiful parts of the Island, this lovely Georgian house still has an air of informal charm and atmosphere. It continues to be upgraded, now with re-furbished lounge and newly tiled bathrooms. The spacious bedrooms are brightly decorated and comfortably furnished. In addition to the lounge there is a large bar and an attractive conservatory overlooking the well maintained garden.
11 bth/shr 9 annexe bth/shr (7 fmly) No smoking in 11 bedrooms No smoking in dining room No smoking in 1 lounge CTV in 21 bedrooms Tea and coffee making facilities Licensed Cen ht CTV No children 3yrs 20P No coaches Last d 6.30pm
ROOMS: s £23-£35; d £46-£70; wkly b&b £159-£189; wkly hlf-bd £199.50-£220

Q Q Q Llynfi Hotel 23 Spring Hill PO38 1PF
(A3055 from Shanklin, before sharp S bend go right into St Boniface Rd. Next left into Spring hill. Est 200yrds on right)
☎ 01983 852202 FAX 01983 852202
Closed Jan
This well-kept hotel located just a short way up a hill from the High Street. Bedrooms are bright and there are several sitting areas including a sunny conservatory, well-appointed lounge, and separate bar.
10 rms (7 shr) (4 fmly) No smoking in dining room CTV in all bedrooms Tea and coffee making facilities No dogs (ex guide dogs) Licensed 7P Last d 3.30pm
ROOMS: s £18-£23; d £36-£46
CARDS:

Q Q Medina House Hotel Alma Rd PO38 1JU (just off Ventnor seafront)
☎ 01983 852424
Dulcie and Alan are the friendly hosts at this mid-Victorian house set at the top of a short (but steep) hill off the Esplanade. The majority of the bright well-kept bedrooms, three with their own balconies, enjoy fine views of the bay. Downstairs there is a bar/lounge that is open-plan to the breakfast room and there is also a small sun-trap patio.
10 rms (7 bth/shr) (1 fmly) No smoking in bedrooms No smoking in dining room No smoking in 1 lounge CTV in 9 bedrooms Tea and coffee making facilities No dogs (ex guide dogs) Licensed Cen ht CTV No children 10yrs 4P Pool table Last d 12am
ROOMS: s £17-£20; d £37-£40*
CARDS:

Q Q Q Hotel Picardie Esplanade PO38 1JX (on Ventnor seafront)
☎ 01983 852647
Mar-Sep
This friendly, no-smoking hotel with its enviable location on the Esplanade just yards from the beach, is run by Brian and Pauline Sparks. Fresh flowers adorn tables in the dining room beyond which is a small, sea-facing, rattan-furnished conservatory bar. There is also a well-appointed lounge and a little terrace. Of the neat bedrooms, half are en suite but the others have their own private facilities nearby. A stair-lift serves the first floor bedrooms.
10 bth/shr (3 fmly) No smoking CTV in all bedrooms Tea and coffee making facilities Licensed CTV Last d 4.30pm
ROOMS: s £18.50-£20; d £37-£40; wkly b&b £129.50-£140; wkly hlf-bd £195-£210*
CARDS:

Q Q Q St Maur Hotel Castle Rd PO38 1LG
(exit A3055 at the end of Park Ave onto Castle Rd, premises 150 yards on the left) ☎ 01983 852570 FAX 01983 852306
Closed Dec-Jan
From its elevated position above the town, this immaculately kept Victorian villa enjoys fine views across Ventnor Park towards the sea. In the same family ownership since 1966, guests can be sure of a warm welcome from David and Jan Groocock. Day rooms include a spacious, comfortable lounge, a separate bar, and a well-appointed dining room in which to enjoy David's home cooking. Good-sized, comfortable bedrooms are bright and fresh.
14 rms (13 bth/shr) (4 fmly) No smoking in bedrooms No smoking in dining room Tea and coffee making facilities No dogs Licensed Cen ht No children 5yrs 12P No coaches Last d 7pm
ROOMS: d £70-£74*
CARDS:

Q Q Q St Andrews Hotel Belgrave Rd PO38 1JH (from town centre left from Poer St to Church St signposted Niton/Blackgang, past St Catherine's church, hotel is on the left on Belgrave Rd)
☎ 01983 852680 FAX 01983 856828
New owners Mick and Nava Young provide a warm welcome at this small charming hotel. Just a few minutes walk from the town the property enjoys a cliff top location with superb sea views and direct access down to the beach. The bedrooms are tastefully decorated and comfortably furnished, all

offering en suite facilities. Public areas include a sun lounge, cosy bar and smart dining room where guests can enjoy Nava's Oriental cuisine.
10 bth/shr (2 fmly) No smoking CTV in all bedrooms Tea and coffee making facilities No dogs Licensed Cen ht ch fac 8P Last d 5.30pm
ROOMS: s £17-£23; d £34-£40; wkly b&b £110-£130; wkly hlf-bd £160-£185*
CARDS:

459

WIGMORE Herefordshire Map 07 SO46

Q *Compasses Hotel* HR6 9UN
☎ 01568 770203 FAX 01568 770705
This traditional village inn dates back to the 16th century. Privately owned and personally run, it provides value for money accommodation in two twin and one double-bedded room. Other facilities include a choice of bars, a quaint dining room and a function room for up to 80 people.
4 rms (1 fmly) No smoking in 1 bedrooms No smoking in dining room CTV in 3 bedrooms Tea and coffee making facilities Cen ht 36P Last d 9.30pm
CARDS:

WIGTON Cumbria Map 11 NY24

Q Q Q Fiddleback Farm Tea Rooms *(NY487493)* West Woodside, Thursby CA7 8BA (on A595, 7m W of Carlisle, in direction of Cockermouth and lakes) ☎ 016973 42653 Mr D Knight
Adorned with antiques, bric-a-brac and pine furniture - which can be bought in the shop in the barn beneath - this 17th-century round house is an interesting property. A spiral staircase leads to three comfortable bedrooms, furnished in the style of the house and thoughtfully equipped to include radios, alarm clocks and magazines.
2 rms (1 shr) (1 fmly) No smoking CTV in all bedrooms Tea and coffee making facilities No dogs Cen ht 6P 9 acres non-working
ROOMS: d £36-£40*

WILBERFOSS East Riding of Yorkshire Map 08 SE75

Q Q ♥ **Cuckoo Nest** *(SE717510)* YO4 5NL (on Hull Rd A1079 between Kexby and Wilbefoss on the right) ☎ 01759 380365 Mrs J M Liversidge
Closed 24-26 Dec
Dating back over 200 years, this traditional red brick farmhouse is surrounded by attractive and well tended gardens. There is a spacious split-level lounge with a selection of board games and a TV, and breakfast is served at a large table in the dining room close to the kitchen. The neat and tidy bedrooms, one en suite, are all non-smoking and are pleasantly furnished. Friendly Yorkshire hospitality is provided by Mrs Liversidge, the resident owner.
3 rms (1 shr) No smoking in bedrooms Tea and coffee making facilities No dogs Cen ht CTV 150 acres arable beef dairy mixed sheep
ROOMS: s £22-£25; d £36-£44*

WILMINGTON East Sussex Map 05 TQ50

Selected

Q Q Q Q **Crossways Hotel** Lewes Rd BN26 5SG (on A27 between Lewes and Polegate, 2m E of Alfriston rdbt) ☎ 01323 482455 FAX 01323 487811
Closed 24 Dec-23 Jan
Set back from the road, this green shuttered Georgian house is in the heart of the Cuckmere Valley under the gaze of the famous Neolithic 'Long Man of Wilmington' carved into the South Downs. A small country hotel, surrounded by well tended informal gardens that include a pretty pond with attendant ducks that form a greeting party on arrival ! Very much a 'restaurant with rooms', the latter are attractively decorated and equipped with a host of thoughtful extras including mini-bars, direct-dial phones and even a TV programme guide. Downstairs the elegant dining room provides cooking to a high standard (AA 2 rosettes). There is also a separate breakfast room. The resident proprietors, David Stott and Clive James, provide a warm welcome and excellent hospitality.
7 bth/shr No smoking in dining room CTV in all bedrooms Tea and coffee making facilities Direct dial from bedrooms No dogs (ex guide dogs) Licensed Cen ht No children 12yrs 30P No coaches Last d 8.45pm
ROOMS: s £48; d £72-£76
CARDS:

WILMSLOW Cheshire Map 07 SJ88

See also Manchester Airport

Q Q Q ***Fernbank*** 188 Wilmslow Rd, Handforth SK9 3JX (2m N on A34) ☎ 01625 523729 FAX 01625 539515
Closed 24 Dec-2 Jan rs Limited reception times
This large detached corner house is well situated for both the motorway network and the airport. Bedrooms are well equipped and attractively decorated, whilst public areas include a comfortable lounge and, during the summer months, the conservatory is used for breakfast.
3 bth/shr (1 fmly) No smoking CTV in all bedrooms Tea and coffee making facilities Cen ht CTV 4P No coaches

Q Q Q ***Grove*** 16 Grove Av SK9 5EG (from A34 turn onto A538 turn right into Grove Way 50yds from junct, Grove Way leads to Grove Av) ☎ 01625 548484 FAX 01625 548640
This small family-run guest house lies near the town centre with all local amenities just a short walk away. There are just three bedrooms – modern and comfortably furnished with trouser presses and telephones. Hearty breakfasts are served and Alison Jackson and her family are friendly and welcoming.
3 bth/shr (1 fmly) No smoking in dining room CTV in all bedrooms Tea and coffee making facilities Direct dial from bedrooms Cen ht P No coaches

WILTON (NEAR SALISBURY) Wiltshire Map 04 SU03

Q Q Q **Swan** Stoford SP2 0PR (6m N from Salisbury on A36 and S of A303) ☎ 01722 790236 FAX 01722 790115
This popular family run inn is located in the village of Stoford just west of Wilton. The comfortably appointed bedrooms are attractively decorated and equipped with many useful additions. Guests can enjoy sound home cooking, bar snacks in the relaxing atmosphere of the bars and also sample one of fine ales offered.
6 bth/shr (1 fmly) No smoking in bedrooms No smoking in dining room CTV in all bedrooms Tea and coffee making facilities No dogs Cen ht 50P Fishing Skittle alley Pool table Last d 9.30pm
ROOMS: s fr £30; d fr £45
CARDS:

WIMBORNE MINSTER Dorset Map 04 SZ09

Q Q Q **Aston Lodge** 10 Oakley Hill BH21 1QH (off A31 Dorchester/Pool Road) ☎ 01202 883423 FAX 01202 886180
Hanging baskets provide a riot of colour at the front of this smart, modern house, and guests may relax in the pretty enclosed rear garden. Bedrooms are bright and comfortable, and nicely decorated in co-ordinated fabrics. All are equipped with such extras as remote TV, mineral water, radio, hair dryer, biscuits, fresh flowers, and reading material. There is also a lounge/diner where a 'proper' cooked breakfast is served at one large table.
4 bth/shr CTV in all bedrooms Tea and coffee making facilities No dogs 4P
ROOMS: s fr £20; d £40-£45

Q Q Q **Twynham** 67 Poole Rd BH21 1QB (A31 or A35 to Wimborne, take A349 the Poole to Bournemouth road) ☎ 01202 887310
Located within walking distance of the town centre and Wimborne Abbey. Attractively presented bedrooms are comfortably furnished and with many amenities. There is a conservatory in which to relax, and guests are served breakfast in communal style at one large table in the cosy dining room.
3 rms No smoking in bedrooms No smoking in lounges CTV in all bedrooms Tea and coffee making facilities No dogs (ex guide dogs) Cen ht 3P No coaches
ROOMS: s £15-£18; d £25-£30*

WINCHCOMBE Gloucestershire Map 04 SP02

Selected

Q Q Q Q ♥ **Postlip Hall Farm** *(SP020280)* GL54 5AQ (leave Winchcombe on B4632 heading for Cheltenham, 1m up hill on left sign for "Farmhouse B & B". Turn left and keep bearing left 0.75m up drive) ☎ 01242 603351 Mr & Mrs J Albutt
Closed Xmas
Situated south of the town amidst magnificent countryside, this impressive mellow stone house offers comfortable accommodation close to all the major attractions. Bedrooms are spacious, well equipped and all have the benefit of en suite or private facilities in addition to

homely extras to enhance guest comfort. Public areas include a cosy dining room where delicious English breakfasts are taken and a spacious and comfortable lounge. The Albutt family are friendly and caring hosts, proud to welcome guests to their lovely home.
3 bth/shr No smoking CTV in all bedrooms Tea and coffee making facilities No dogs (ex guide dogs) Cen ht CTV 8P Riding Golf available nearby 300 acres beef sheep
ROOMS: s £20-£30; d £40-£44; wkly b&b £135-£140*

Selected

Q Q Q Q **Sudeley Hill Farm** *(SP038276)* GL54 5JB
(turn off B4632 in Winchcombe into Castle St, White Hart Inn on corner. Farm 0.75m on right)
☎ 01242 602344 FAX 01242 602344 Mrs B Scudamore
Closed Xmas
This delightful old house is situated on a large mixed arable and sheep farm and is built of mellow stone. Dating back to the 15th century, it has a wealth of charm and character, with a large inglenook fireplace in the lovely lounge and period furniture in the breakfast room, where all guests share one table. The well equipped, no smoking accommodation includes a family room. Bedrooms have views over the surrounding countryside.
3 bth/shr (1 fmly) No smoking in bedrooms No smoking in dining room CTV in all bedrooms Tea and coffee making facilities No dogs (ex guide dogs) Cen ht CTV 10P 800 acres sheep arable
ROOMS: s fr £28; d fr £44; wkly b&b fr £138*

Selected

Q Q Q Q **Wesley House** High St GL54 5LJ ☎ 01242 602366 FAX 01242 602405
Closed 14 Jan-10 Feb rs Sun evenings except BH Sun
There is a lot of character in this charming early 15th-century half-timbered building, and a warm friendly atmosphere. The log fire and comfortable seating add to the old-world charm, and guests can enjoy the culinary skills of chef Jonathan Lewis in the attractive dining room. Bedrooms vary in size and have been individually decorated and suitably equipped.
5 shr No smoking in bedrooms No smoking in dining room CTV in all bedrooms Tea and coffee making facilities Direct dial from bedrooms No dogs (ex guide dogs) Licensed Cen ht Last d 9.30pm
ROOMS: s £48-£55; d £70-£80
CARDS:

This symbol indicates a 'Child Friendly' establishment - see page 25 for details

WINCHELSEA East Sussex Map **05** TQ91

Selected

Q Q Q Q **The Strand House** The Strand TN36 4JT
(2m W of Rye on A259, 1st buliding on left after passing town sign)
☎ 01797 226276 FAX 01797 224806
Once on the harbourside - the sea is now over a mile away - Strand House dates back to the 15th century, with part of the building being even older. Lovingly renovated, the interior is full of charm and character with a wealth of old beams, inglenook fireplaces and not a straight wall or level floor to be found anywhere. The lounge is well supplied with books and warmed by a real fire in winter.
10 bth/shr (1 fmly) No smoking CTV in all bedrooms Tea and coffee making facilities No dogs Licensed Cen ht No children 1yrs 12P No coaches
ROOMS: s £34; d £50-£64
CARDS:

WINCHESTER Hampshire Map **04** SU52

Selected

Q Q Q Q **Acacia** 44 Kilham Ln SO22 5PT
(M3 junct 11 follow signs for Oliver's Battery, at rdbt take A3090 for Winchester, turn left at lights into Kilham Lane and estab is 200yds on left) ☎ 01962 852259 FAX 01962 852259
mid Mar-mid Nov
Situated in a quiet residential area, this charming, non-smoking property is run by Shirley Buchanan who ensures that all her guests are made welcome. The three bedrooms are all individual in style, comfortably appointed and equipped with en suite shower rooms. There is a pleasant lounge where guests can relax with breakfast served in the conservatory.
3 shr No smoking Tea and coffee making facilities No dogs Cen ht CTV No children 10yrs 4P No coaches
ROOMS: d £42-£46*

Selected

Q Q Q Q ***Shawlands*** 46 Kilham Ln SO22 5QD
(take A3090 from Winchester, straight over rdbt and turn right at second set of traffic lights)
☎ 01962 861166 FAX 01962 861166
Situated in a peaceful location on the outskirts of Winchester. This attractive well-maintained house offers comfortable well appointed accommodation. Clever design makes best use of available space in the bedrooms. All are furnished in modern style and adequately equipped. Kathy and Bill Pollock are enthusiastic and welcoming hosts and they offer a generous breakfast which features home-made bread and preserves.
5 rms (1 bth/shr) (2 fmly) No smoking CTV in 4 bedrooms Tea and coffee making facilities Cen ht CTV 5P No coaches
CARDS:

Premier Selected

Q Q Q Q Q **The Wykeham Arms** 75 Kingsgate St SO23 9PE
(immediately south of the Cathedral, by Kingsgate and opposite Winchester College) ☎ 01962 853834 FAX 01962 854411
This charming 250-year-old inn is located in the old part of the city. Bedrooms in the main house are well appointed and furnished to reflect the character of the building. The annexe is a recent addition and the bedrooms are spacious and comfortable. The restaurant is unique, having several eating areas and a fine collection of military memorabilia, tankards and pictures. A daily changing menu offers an interesting choice of traditional pub food.
7 bth/shr 6 annexe bth/shr No smoking in 7 bedrooms No smoking in area of dining room CTV in all bedrooms Tea and coffee making facilities Cen ht No children 14yrs 12P No coaches Sauna Last d 8.45pm
ROOMS: s £45-£99; d £79.50-£117.50*
MEALS: Lunch £11-£15alc Dinner £15-£21alc*
CARDS:

WINDERMERE Cumbria Map **07** SD49

Selected

Q Q Q Q **Archway** College Rd LA23 1BU
(turn off A591 into Windermere village. At Elltray corner turn into College Road. Establishment is on the left half way down)
☎ 015394 45613
This delightful guest house is delightfully furnished - beautiful antique and Welsh quilts decorate the beds and original pictures and tapestries adorn the walls. Bedrooms vary in size and offer a plethora of books, magazines, curios and bric-a-brac. Mrs Greenhalgh bakes various fresh breads daily, and muesli, preserves and yoghurts are all home-made. Sausages and bacon come from the finest suppliers and all the eggs are free range.

4 shr No smoking CTV in all bedrooms Tea and coffee making facilities Direct dial from bedrooms No dogs Licensed Cen ht No children 10yrs 2P No coaches Last d 3pm
ROOMS: d £44-£58*
CARDS:

10 bth/shr (1 fmly) No smoking CTV in all bedrooms Tea and coffee making facilities No dogs Licensed Cen ht CTV No children 10yrs 10P No coaches
ROOMS: s £32-£38; d £50-£90
CARDS:

Selected

Q Q Q Q **The Beaumont** Holly Rd LA23 2AF (follow town centre signs through one-way system then 2nd left into Ellerthwaite Rd then 1st left into Holly Rd)
☎ 015394 47075 FAX 01539 447075
Closed mid Dec-mid Jan
This Lakeland Victorian house is home to the Casey family. Located just a short walk from the town, the house provides well appointed bedrooms, which offer the choice of four poster beds and a whole host of thoughtful extras. The reception rooms are tastefully co-ordinated with the elegant lounge offering deep comfortable sofas and the dining room is bright and inviting.

Q Q Q ***Belgrave*** 2 Ellerthwaite Rd LA23 2AH ☎ 015394 43335
This semi-detached house lies just off the Bowness road and offers bright modern bedrooms, two smart comfortable lounges and an attractive dining room.
3 rms (2 shr) No smoking CTV in all bedrooms Tea and coffee making facilities No children 5P No coaches
CARDS:

Q Q Q **Belsfield House** 4 Kendal Rd, Bowness-on-Windermere LA23 3EQ (from A592 in Bowness, take first left after mini-rdbt, then at St Martins church turn left onto Kendal road, house on right) ☎ 015394 45823
Victoria and Marie Harrison are now at the helm here and changes are afoot. Close to the centre of the village and within yards of the lake, this extremely

contd. on p.464.

well kept guest house offers a warm welcome. The dining room and adjacent lounge feature magnificent original marble fire surrounds. Parking is situated to the rear.
9 shr (4 fmly) No smoking in dining room CTV in all bedrooms No dogs (ex guide dogs) Cen ht 9P No coaches
ROOMS: s £24-£26; d £36-£52*

Selected

QQQQ **Blenheim Lodge** Brantfell Rd, Bowness-on-Windermere LA23 3AE (A591 Bowness village, across mini-rdbt, turn first left and left again, house is at the top) ☎ 015394 43440 FAX 015394 43440
Backed by woodland, Blenheim Lodge lies in a quiet cul-de-sac above Bowness with panoramic views of Windermere. Jackie and Frank Sanderson have established a country guest house of charm and character. Public rooms are adorned with paintings and prints, whilst the bar displays old photographs and prints of naval vessels. The thoughtfully equipped bedrooms are individually styled, some having four-poster or half-tester beds. Jackie's home-cooked dinners and breakfasts continue to draw praise and a recipe booklet is for sale. Frank is a trained artist and runs residential courses in oil painting for beginners.
11 bth/shr (1 fmly) No smoking CTV in all bedrooms Tea and coffee making facilities No dogs Licensed Cen ht CTV No children 6yrs 12P No coaches Membership of country club Last d 4pm (7pm if needed)
ROOMS: s £32-£40; d £56-£80*
CARDS:

QQQ ***Braemount House*** Sunny Bank Rd LA23 2EN
(from A591 turn into Windermere, drive along one way system towards lake, left after clock tower into Queens Drive, take 1st right into Sunny Bank Rd) ☎ 015394 45967 FAX 015394 45967
Closed Xmas
This comfortably furnished house is conveniently situated between Windermere and Bowness within a peaceful residential area. Bedrooms throughout are thoughtfully furnished, especially the loft rooms. 5 bth/shr (2 fmly) No smoking CTV in all bedrooms Tea and coffee making facilities No dogs Licensed Cen ht No children 10yrs 6P No coaches
CARDS:

QQQ ***Brendan Chase*** 1 & 3 College Rd LA23 1BU ☎ 015394 45638 FAX 015394 45638
Brendan Chase is a well established and friendly guest house to which Mrs Graham, a native of the area, draws visitors from far afield. Bedrooms are cosy, traditional and boast attractive co-ordinated furnishings.
8 rms (4 shr) (4 fmly) No smoking in bedrooms No smoking in dining room No smoking in 1 lounge CTV in all bedrooms Tea and coffee making facilities Cen ht CTV 8P No coaches

QQQ **Broadlands** 19 Broad St LA23 2AB (from A591 to town centre follow one way system for 300 metres to pelican crossing, Broad Street is next on the left) ☎ 015394 46532 FAX 015394 46532
Mr and Mrs Pearson run this friendly guest house with great enthusiasm. It stands opposite the park and library with the town's shops just around the corner. Bedrooms boast attractive colour schemes and furnishings, whilst in the cosy lounge there are many books to read and a selection of board games.
4 shr (2 fmly) No smoking in 2 bedrooms No smoking in dining room No smoking in lounges CTV in all bedrooms Tea and coffee making facilities No dogs (ex guide dogs) Cen ht CTV No coaches Mountain bike hire
ROOMS: d £34-£46; wkly b&b £119-£154*
CARDS:

QQQ ***Brooklands*** Ferry View, Bowness LA23 3JB
(in Bowness, follow Kendal/Lancaster road A5074 in 0.75m establishment on left) ☎ 015394 42344
This family run guest house is pleasantly situated in a rural setting just south of Bowness at the junction of the A5074 and B5284. Its elevated position gives glimpses of the lake and the fells from the comfortable ground floor combined lounge/dining room and the front bedrooms.
6 rms (5 shr) (3 fmly) No smoking CTV in all bedrooms Tea and coffee making facilities Cen ht CTV 6P

Selected

QQQQ **The Chestnuts** Princes Rd LA23 2EF ☎ 015394 46999
Set back from the main road between Bowness and Windermere, this fine Victorian house nestles within its own well tendered gardens. Peter and Chris Reed have sympathetically refurbished the entire house and blend contemporary style tastefully with the traditional architecture of the building. Bedrooms are attractively furnished with pretty fabrics and papers and several offer four poster beds. The inviting dining room provides the venue for a hearty Cumbrian breakfast to start the day and doubles as a lounge during the evening.
6 bth/shr No smoking CTV in all bedrooms Tea and coffee making facilities Cen ht 6P No coaches Free use of nearby leisure facilities
ROOMS: d £45-£84; wkly b&b £152-£210*

Selected

QQQQ **Coach House** Lake Rd LA23 2EQ
(M6 junct36, take A591, in Windermere turn left towards Bowness, 0.5m on right opposite St Herbert's church)
☎ 015394 44494 FAX 015394 43476
Closed 24-30 Dec
This stylish house offers something a little different. Decorated throughout with soothing colours the house provides a minimalist, chic ambience enhanced with stunning lighting and brand new cosmopolitan furnishings. The bedrooms - all boasting power showers - reflect cutting-edge interior design. A hearty Cumbrian breakfast is served in the more traditional dining room.
5 shr (1 fmly) No smoking CTV in all bedrooms Tea and coffee making facilities No dogs (ex guide dogs) Cen ht 5P No coaches
ROOMS: d £48-£56; wkly b&b £125-£165
CARDS:

QQQ **Corner Cottage** Old Hall Rd, Troutbeck Bridge LA23 1HF
(from A591, over mini rdbt, at the two road signs on left, turn left and house is big white one over brow of hill)
☎ 015394 48226
Distinguished by its white façade, this detached house lies in an acre of secluded wooded gardens. Bedrooms are bright and cheery and offer a variety of sizes, some suitable for family occupancy. Downstairs there is a homely lounge and an attractive dining room. Babies and infants are very welcome.
4 shr (2 fmly) No smoking in 1 bedrooms CTV in all bedrooms Tea and coffee making facilities No dogs (ex guide dogs) Cen ht CTV ch fac 10P No coaches Last d breakfast
ROOMS: d £39-£45*

QQQ **Eastbourne Hotel** Biskey Howe Rd LA23 2JR
(from A591 turn left into town and proceed towards Bowness and lake. Take 2nd left after police station) ☎ 015394 43525
Closed Jan
This family-run guest house is situated in a quiet side road and is within easy walking distance of the centre of Bowness. The house is well maintained throughout and provides bright and fresh bedrooms which are furnished in pine and are also well equipped. There is an honesty bar together with a comfortable and cosy lounge.
8 shr (2 fmly) No smoking CTV in all bedrooms Tea and coffee making facilities No dogs Licensed Cen ht 6P No coaches
ROOMS: d £36-£56; wkly b&b £120-£160
CARDS:

We endeavour to be as accurate as possible but changes in personnel and data can occur in establishments after the Guide has gone to press

Selected

Q Q Q Q **Fairfield** Brantfell Rd, Bowness LA23 3AE
(follow Bowness signs and at mini rdbt take rd to lake, turn left opp church & left again in front of Spinnery Restaurant, house up hill on right) ☎ 015394 46565 FAX 015394 46565
Feb-Nov & New Year
Ray and Barbara Hood's comfortable and relaxing country house lies in a quiet lane high above the town but within walking distance of the centre. There is a cosy residents' bar, a lounge with a log fire for chilly evenings, and an attractive dining room where Barbara's breakfasts and home-cooked dinners are served. Bedrooms vary in size but all are bright, cheery and thoughtfully equipped.
9 rms (8 bth/shr) (2 fmly) No smoking CTV in all bedrooms Tea and coffee making facilities No dogs Licensed Cen ht CTV 12P No coaches Corporate membership of leisure club Last d breakfast
ROOMS: s £24-£31; d £48-£62; wkly b&b £165-£195
CARDS:

Q Q Q **Firgarth** Ambleside Rd LA23 1EU
(situated on the A591, Windermere to Ambleside road, opposite Wynlass Beck Riding Stables) ☎ 015394 46974
This is a friendly roadside guest house benefiting from panoramic views to the rear. Bedrooms are furnished with a mix of styles but, like the lounge and dining room, are bright and cheery.
8 shr (1 fmly) No smoking in 5 bedrooms No smoking in dining room CTV in all bedrooms Tea and coffee making facilities Licensed Cen ht 10P No coaches
ROOMS: s £17.50-£22.50; d £35-£42; wkly b&b £122.50-£136.50✳
CARDS:

Selected

Q Q Q Q **Fir Trees** Lake Rd LA23 2EQ
(0.5m below town centre on left going toward lake)
☎ 015394 42272 FAX 015394 42272
This large detached Victorian dwelling is the home of enthusiastic Californian owners, Allene and Ira Fishman, who provide a wealth of local information for their guests. Over the years they have furnished each of the well proportioned rooms with excellent quality beds and powerful shower fittings. Breakfasts are traditionally English but supplemented by freshly baked muffins, hash browns and fruit compôtes.
8 bth/shr (2 fmly) No smoking CTV in all bedrooms Tea and coffee making facilities No dogs Cen ht 9P No coaches
ROOMS: s £25-£40; d £44-£56; wkly b&b £145-£180
CARDS:

Selected

Q Q Q Q **Glencree Private Hotel** Lake Rd LA23 2EQ
(0.5m from town centre after leaving one way system keeping stone clock tower on left at junct of New Rd & Lake Rd, Glencree is on right)
☎ 015394 45822 FAX 015394 45822
This substantial Lakeland-stone house is found midway between Bowness and Windermere and is backed by a tumbling stream in a woodland valley. Bedrooms are very well furnished and have been thoughtfully equipped. Guests have the use of a comfortable lounge, and there are individual tables in the dining room.
5 bth/shr (1 fmly) No smoking in 3 bedrooms No smoking in dining room No smoking in lounges CTV in all bedrooms Tea and coffee making facilities Licensed Cen ht CTV 6P No coaches
Last d 2pm
ROOMS: s £20-£35; d £40-£60; wkly b&b £140-£175; wkly hlf-bd £210-£259✳
CARDS:

Q Q Q *Glenville Hotel* Lake Rd LA23 2EQ
(turn left off A591 into Windermere Village, follow main road for 0.5m, Glenville is on the right next to St Johns Church)
☎ 015394 43371
This traditional Lakeland-stone house sits in its own gardens a short walk from both the town centre and Lake Windermere. The atmosphere is relaxed and evening meals are provided by arrangement. A comfortable lounge offers a wide screen television with satellite channels, and breakfast is served in the cosy dining room. The well kept garden to the rear is delightful in summer.
8 bth/shr (3 fmly) No smoking in area of dining room No smoking in 1 lounge CTV in all bedrooms Tea and coffee making facilities No dogs (ex guide dogs) Licensed Cen ht CTV 10P No coaches Last d 2pm
CARDS:

Q Q Q Green Gables 37 Broad St LA23 2AB
(off A591 at Windermere town centre sign, follow one-way system through village and turn left at last shop into Broad Street)
☎ 015394 43886
The Green Gables is found in a side street within easy walking distance of the town and ample restaurants and pubs. The house is pleasantly furnished and offers bright and fresh bedrooms and is available for guests.
8 rms (3 shr) (3 fmly) No smoking in bedrooms No smoking in dining room No smoking in 1 lounge CTV in all bedrooms Tea and coffee making facilities No dogs (ex guide dogs) Licensed Cen ht CTV 2P No coaches
Golf & riding can be arranged. Tours booked
ROOMS: s £15-£22; d £32-£42*

Prices shown in the directory are meant as a guide only and are subject to change. Please check before you book

Selected

Q Q Q Q Haisthorpe House Holly Rd LA23 2AF
(turn off A591, onto A5074 and after 0.25m turn left into Ellerthwaite Road and then 1st left)
☎ 015394 43445 FAX 015394 43445
Mick and Angela Brown offer a warm welcome to their home, which is just a short stroll from the town centre. Tastefully decorated bedrooms are comfortable and are well equipped. A substantial breakfast is served in the light and airy dining room, and the homely lounge looks out onto the neat garden.
6 bth/shr (1 fmly) No smoking in bedrooms No smoking in dining room CTV in all bedrooms Tea and coffee making facilities No dogs (ex guide dogs) Cen ht CTV 3P No coaches
Free use of nearby pravate leisure complex
ROOMS: s £18-£22; d £36-£44; wkly b&b £112-£140*
CARDS: MasterCard VISA DELTA

Q Q The Haven 10 Birch St LA23 1EG
(on A5074, take 3rd left after entering one way system into Birch Street, post office on corner) ☎ 015394 44017
Patricia and Edward Wood warmly welcome guests to their Victorian house that sits in a quiet road just yards from the town centre. Some of the bedrooms are spacious including one with an original brass bed, and whilst furnishings have been kept simple, attractive fabrics make for a bright cheerful appearance. The lounge also doubles as the breakfast room where vegetarian breakfasts are an option.
4 rms (1 bth/shr) (2 fmly) No smoking CTV in all bedrooms Tea and coffee making facilities No dogs (ex guide dogs) Cen ht No children 3yrs 4P No coaches
ROOMS: d £36-£39; wkly b&b fr £94*

Selected

Q Q Q Q ***Hawksmoor*** Lake Rd LA23 2EQ
(follow Windermere town centre one-way system for approx 0.5m to establishment opposite church) ☎ 015394 42110
11 Feb-24 Nov & 27 Dec-7 Jan
Although set on the main road between Windermere and Bowness, this extended house lies in well tended gardens set away from the road and backed by a wooded valley. Smartly decorated throughout it offers bright modern bedrooms in a variety of sizes, some with four-poster beds and most with contemporary fitted furniture. A feature of the house is its attractive dining room, and there is also a comfortable lounge. The set dinner menu is accompanied by an extensive and reasonably priced wine list.
10 bth/shr (3 fmly) No smoking in 5 bedrooms No smoking in dining room CTV in all bedrooms Tea and coffee making facilities No dogs (ex guide dogs) Licensed Cen ht No children 6yrs 12P No coaches Last d 5pm
CARDS:

Selected

Q Q Q Q **Hazel Bank** Hazel St LA23 1EL
(off A591 opposite Windermere Hotel, turn left into Oak St at Walter Willsons supermarket, 2nd on left into Hazel St)
☎ 015394 45486 FAX 0153494 45486
Closed 23-30 Dec
Resident proprietors Mr and Mrs Gray extend a warm welcome to guests at their late Victorian home. Bedrooms are light and airy with thoughtful extra touches. Brightly decorated reception rooms extend to a lounge with deep sofas and a cosy dining room where breakfast is served.
3 bth/shr No smoking in bedrooms No smoking in dining room CTV in all bedrooms Tea and coffee making facilities No dogs Cen ht No children 7yrs 4P No coaches
ROOMS: d £38-£56*

Q Q Q **Hilton House** New Rd LA23 2EE (turn off A591 onto road signposted Windermere and Bowness town centres. Premises are located 0.5m on the left) ☎ 015394 43934
Standing on the main road between Windermere and Bowness, this substantial Edwardian house offers modern bedrooms together with a spacious lounge and dining room. The house is fully no smoking.
7 shr (1 fmly) No smoking CTV in all bedrooms Tea and coffee making facilities No dogs Licensed Cen ht CTV No children 6yrs 10P No coaches
ROOMS: s £20-£28; d £40-£56; wkly b&b £130-£170*

Q Q Q **Holly Lodge** 6 College Rd LA23 1BX
(from the A591 opposite Windermere Hotel follow the road downhill towards Bowness through the village turn right into College Rd)
☎ 015394 43873 FAX 015394 43873
Set in side street close to the town centre, this Victorian house offers a variety of bedroom styles and comfortable public rooms, which include an inviting lounge and a cosy dining room which has a dispense bar. The en suite bedrooms are attractively decorated, and the others may be let as multi-room units with their own bathroom, depending upon availability.
11 rms (6 shr) (3 fmly) No smoking in bedrooms No smoking in dining room CTV in all bedrooms Tea and coffee making facilities No dogs (ex guide dogs) Licensed Cen ht 7P No coaches
ROOMS: s £18-£21; d £36-£42*

Selected

Q Q Q Q **Holly Park House** 1 Park Rd LA23 2AW
(from A591 through town centre one way system beyond shops, turn left along Broad St and turn right at the end, estab on the next left hand corner) ☎ 015394 42107 FAX 015394 48997
Roger Wallis and James Peters have continued their quest to ensure that Holly Park is at the forefront of value-for-money guest accommodation in picturesque Windermere. Interesting features include tasteful period furnishings, paintings and lots of personal touches. The attractive dining room and inviting lounge, along with comfortable, well laid out bedrooms and warm hospitality all combine to create a relaxing and peaceful atmosphere.

6 bth/shr (3 fmly) No smoking in 4 bedrooms No smoking in dining room CTV in all bedrooms Tea and coffee making facilities Licensed Cen ht CTV 4P No coaches Last d 5pm
ROOMS: s £28-£32; d £40-£48; wkly b&b £130-£135
CARDS:

Selected

QQQQ **Howbeck** New Rd LA23 2LA (left off A591 through Windermere town centre 300yrds on left. Maw Rd to Bowness)
☎ 015394 44739 FAX 015394 44739
Howbeck sits just outside Windermere on the way to Bowness, with the lake just minutes walk away. Bedrooms are spacious, offering good facilities and comfort. The reception rooms extend to a dining room with a small bar and a cosy lounge at the front of the house. Meals are freshly prepared and Roger displays his culinary skills at dinner and breakfast, using fresh, local produce whenever possible.

10 bth/shr (1 fmly) No smoking CTV in all bedrooms Tea and coffee making facilities No dogs Licensed Cen ht CTV No children 5yrs 12P No coaches Last d 7pm
ROOMS: d £45-£70*
CARDS:

QQQ **Ivy Bank** Holly Rd LA23 2AF
(turn off A591 by Nat West Bank, take first left after pedestrian crossing, into Broad Street turn right at end and right again into Holly Road)
☎ 015394 42601
Closed 23-28 Dec
New owners have put a lot of work into this semi-detached Lakeland stone house and improvements continue to display the high standards already achieved. Bedrooms, which come in a variety of sizes, are furnished with a mix of traditional and period pieces. There is a lounge, and breakfast is taken at two large pine tables in the bright, attractive dining room.
5 bth/shr (1 fmly) No smoking CTV in all bedrooms Tea and coffee making facilities Cen ht 7P No coaches Free membership to local leisure club
ROOMS: s £18-£25; d £34-£42; wkly b&b £105-£147
CARDS:

Remember to return your Prize Draw card for a chance to win an action-packed family weekend at one of the eleven Family Fun Hotels in the Hilton Hotels Directory. See inside the front cover for the card and competition details. Don't forget to fill in your name and address before posting!

QQQ Kenilworth Holly Rd LA23 2AF (drive through one way system, take 2nd left, Ellerthwaite Rd then 1st left into Holly Rd) ☎ 015394 44004 FAX 015394 46554
This semi-detached Victorian property lies in a quiet residential street close to the town centre. Well maintained and comfortably furnished, it offers a spacious and comfortable lounge with a TV and video player and an attractively decorated rear dining room.
6 rms (3 shr) (1 fmly) No smoking CTV in 1 bedroom Tea and coffee making facilities No dogs (ex guide dogs) Cen ht CTV ch fac 3P No coaches
ROOMS: s £15-£20; d £32-£40; wkly b&b £99.75-£133

Selected

QQQQ **Kirkwood** Prince's Rd LA23 2DD ☎ 015394 43907 FAX 015394 43907
This Lakeland-stone house with its colourful garden occupies a corner position in a residential area between Windermere and Bowness. Nicely maintained throughout, it has stylishly decorated bedrooms, some furnished with contemporary pieces and some with pine, and all are well equipped. There is a comfortable lounge and an attractive little dining room where a good choice is offered at breakfast.
7 bth/shr (4 fmly) No smoking in bedrooms No smoking in dining room CTV in all bedrooms Tea and coffee making facilities Cen ht 1P No coaches
ROOMS: d £44-£52*
CARDS:

Selected

QQQQ **Langthwaite** Crook Rd, Ferry View LA23 3JB (M6 junct36, follow A591 signposted Windermere, at first roundabout take left B5284 signposted Hawkshead via ferry, house 6m on left before T-junct) ☎ 015394 43329
mid Feb-mid Nov
Nestling in attractive woodland away from the hustle and bustle of the town lies this smart and well maintained cottage. Two of stylishly decorated bedrooms are situated in the main house and a pine furnished room with its own entrance is located separately. Breakfast is served in the delightful conservatory, enjoying a pleasant outlook onto the colourful moorland garden.
2 bth/shr No smoking CTV in all bedrooms Tea and coffee making facilities No dogs Cen ht No children 5P No coaches
ROOMS: d £40-£52*

QQQ **Laurel Cottage** Saint Martins Square, Kendal Rd LA23 3EF (from A592 turn right at St Martins church onto A5074 then first cottage on left) ☎ 015394 45594 FAX 015394 45594
Conveniently located in the heart of Bowness this charming 17th-century guest house provides an ideal base for the Lakeland tourist. A choice of accommodation is offered including bedrooms in the original cottage, with stools or window seats and fitted furniture, or more spacious rooms with pine furniture and wicker chairs in the Victorian part of the house. There is a cosy lounge and cottagey dining room with a low beamed ceiling.
14 rms (12 shr) (2 fmly) No smoking in 5 bedrooms No smoking in dining room No smoking in lounges CTV in all bedrooms Tea and coffee making facilities No dogs (ex guide dogs) Cen ht CTV 14P No coaches Membership of local leisure club
ROOMS: s £19-£25; d £40-£60; wkly b&b £130-£175*

QQQ **Lynwood** Broad St LA23 2AB ☎ 015394 42550 FAX 015394 42550
This friendly guest house is situated at the end of a Victorian terrace within easy walking distance of the village centre. There are two attractively appointed dining rooms and a cosy and comfortable lounge, where some of the proprietor's doll collection may form part of a window display. Individually decorated bedrooms are fresh and inviting, and fully en suite - a few are suitable for families.
9 shr (4 fmly) No smoking CTV in all bedrooms Tea and coffee making facilities No dogs (ex guide dogs) Cen ht No children 5yrs 4P No coaches
ROOMS: s £15-£22; d £30-£44*

QQQ **Montfort** Princes Rd LA23 2DD (from A590 take A591 through Windermere village, take 4th turn on left after pelican crossing by clock tower, then 1st right and estab on the right) ☎ 015394 45671
Situated in a quiet corner of Windermere, this friendly and pleasantly furnished house offers modern and well equipped bedrooms together with personal attention from the resident owners. Two of the bedrooms have four-poster beds.
5 bth/shr No smoking CTV in all bedrooms Tea and coffee making facilities Cen ht No children Complimentary use of local country club
ROOMS: s £25-£30; d £36-£48*
CARDS:

QQQ **Mylne Bridge House** Brookside, Lake Rd LA23 2BX (At the top of Lake Road behind New Road adjacent to the Carver Church) ☎ 015394 43314 FAX 015394 48052
This substantial Victorian house lies in a residential area just south of the town centre and offers comfortable accommodation of varying styles as well as an attractive dining room which doubles successfully as a lounge.

8 rms (7 shr) (2 fmly) No smoking CTV in all bedrooms Tea and coffee making facilities No dogs (ex guide dogs) Cen ht No children 1yr 10P No coaches
ROOMS: s £20-£25; d £40-£50; wkly b&b £140-£150*
CARDS:

Premier Selected

QQQQQ Newstead New Rd LA23 2EE (0.5m from A591 between Windermere/Bowness) ☎ 015394 44485
Sue and Bill Jackson offer a warm welcome to their substantial home, minutes walk away from the town centre. Bedrooms are tastefully furnished in pine, with the comfort of guests a major consideration of each individual room. Thoughtful extra facilities and homely touches ensure a memorable stay. The light and airy reception rooms include a most comfortable lounge which looks onto the neat garden. Sue's freshly prepared breakfasts are served in the attractive dining room.
7 bth/shr (1 fmly) No smoking CTV in all bedrooms Tea and coffee making facilities No dogs Cen ht No children 7yrs 10P No coaches
ROOMS: d £44-£52; wkly b&b £151-£173*

Q ***Oakthorpe Hotel*** High St LA23 1HF
(turn off A591 at Rockside guest house, inn entrance is 100yds on left opposite Gray Walls hotel) ☎ 015394 43547
Closed 25 Dec-24 Jan rs All day mon in winter. Lunch other times
Located centrally in the town this family run business continues to attract the Lakeland tourist. The Lamplighter bar serves good fresh food from an interesting blackboard menu and residents have the choice of eating either in the bar or homely dining room. Bedrooms are traditionally furnished and offer a variety of standards, most rooms being of a good size.
16 rms (4 bth 3 shr) (3 fmly) No smoking in dining room CTV in all bedrooms Tea and coffee making facilities Cen ht 18P Fishing
Last d 8.30pm
CARDS:

QQQ The Old Court House Lake Rd LA23 3AP
(on Windermere/Bowness road on right at junct with Longlands Road)
☎ 015394 45096
Formerly a Victorian police station and courthouse, this stylish house enjoys a central location in the town. Thanks to a sympathetic conversion it has plenty of character and there are many features left from the past. The bedrooms are comfortable with attractive decor and several four poster beds. The breakfast room is bright and appealing.
6 shr No smoking CTV in all bedrooms Tea and coffee making facilities No dogs Cen ht No children 7yrs 6P No coaches
ROOMS: d £40-£50*

See page 14-20 for a list of Premier Selected establishments

Oldfield House Oldfield Rd LA23 2BY
(from A591 continue through Windermere village beyond village turn left into Ellerthwaite Road then 2nd right & 1st left)
☎ 015394 88445 FAX 015394 43250
Closed Jan
This charming Victorian house lies in a quiet residential area south of the town centre and has a local pub right across the road. Both the lounge and dining room are attractive and comfortable, and each bedroom has pretty co-ordinated decor and good facilities. Bob and Maureen Theobold are able to recommend a host of activities within the area as well as places to eat. Breakfast provides a good range of hearty Cumbrian produce.
8 bth/shr (2 fmly) No smoking CTV in all bedrooms Tea and coffee making facilities Direct dial from bedrooms No dogs (ex guide dogs) Cen ht 7P No coaches Free membership to leisure club
ROOMS: s £20-£34.50; d £40-£69; wkly b&b £126-£217*
CARDS:

Orrest Close 3 The Terrace LA23 1AJ
(turn off A591, 300yds beyond the Windermere town sign entering from the south) ☎ 015394 43325 FAX 015394 43325
Built in 1840 this is a delightful period Pugin villa of stone and slate with mullioned trefoil windows. There is a lovely dining room with a willow pattern china display, a comfortable, relaxing lounge and thoughtfully designed bedrooms each of which has its own private bathroom either en suite or adjacent.
6 rms (4 shr) (2 fmly) No smoking CTV in all bedrooms Tea and coffee making facilities No dogs (ex guide dogs) Cen ht CTV 7P No coaches Last d 3.30pm
ROOMS: d £40-£48
CARDS:

Selected

Parson Wyke Country House Glebe Rd, Bowness on Windermere LA23 3GZ (500yds beyond steamer piers & Bowness Bay Tourist Information Centre on the one way system)
☎ 015394 42837
Wyke means 'a bay or inlet', and the house lies amid one and a half acres of meadowland overlooking the lake, a short stroll from the bustling piers and town. A very warm welcome is offered by the resident proprietors Jean and David Cockburn and their family. The house is fascinating, retaining features ranging from mediaeval cottage to spacious early Victorian. The bedrooms are amply proportioned, very comfortable and provided with extras such as hot water bottles, books and fresh flowers.
3 bth/shr (1 fmly) No smoking in bedrooms No smoking in dining room CTV in all bedrooms Tea and coffee making facilities No dogs (ex guide dogs) Cen ht CTV No children 4yrs 9P No coaches
ROOMS: s £35-£45; d £55-£75*

Rocklea Brookside, Lake Rd LA23 2BX
(proceed through village towards Bowness and after approx 0.5m turn sharp left at monument into Lake Road)
☎ 015394 45326
This Lakeland stone house lies in a quiet residential area south of the town adjacent to Mylne Beck, a bubbling brook which flows from Orrest Head into Lake Windermere. New proprietors have set about upgrading the accommodation which offers bright modern bedrooms that come in a variety of sizes. A hearty breakfast is taken in a combined open plan dining room and lounge. Off street car parking is a bonus.
7 rms (5 shr) (1 fmly) No smoking in dining room No smoking in lounges CTV in all bedrooms Tea and coffee making facilities Cen ht No children 3yrs 5P No coaches
ROOMS: s £16-£23; d £33-£46; wkly b&b £105-£145*
CARDS:

Rosemount Lake Rd LA23 2EQ
(turn off A591 continue through village Rosemount is on left side of road just beyond modern Catholic church)
☎ 015394 43739 FAX 015394 48978
Closed 24 Dec-31 Jan
A traditional semi-detached house conveniently situated on the main road between Windermere and Bowness. An inviting dining room provides the venue for breakfast and bedrooms are freshly decorated and thoughtfully furnished.
8 bth/shr (1 fmly) No smoking CTV in all bedrooms Tea and coffee making facilities No dogs Licensed Cen ht 3P Golf can be arranged
ROOMS: s £19.50-£27; d £39-£54; wkly b&b £130-£170*
CARDS:

The Royal Queens Square LA23 3DB
(M6 junct 36, follow signs for Windermere/Ambleside, head into Windermere taking one way road into Bowness. Hotel at bottom of hill on right) ☎ 015394 43045 FAX 015394 44990
Dating back to the 16th century, The Royal is reputed to be the oldest hotel in the Lake District and once inspired Wordsworth - some of his work is displayed in the first floor breakfast room. Downstairs are two very contrasting bars, one an ultra-modern sports bar with giant TV screens, the other a traditional Irish Pub. Bedrooms are variable in size and offer mixed modern appointments. Two unusually themed rooms are available and these have particular appeal for the children.
29 bth/shr (5 fmly) No smoking in dining room CTV in all bedrooms Tea and coffee making facilities Direct dial from bedrooms Licensed Cen ht 20P Use of leisure facilities at nearby hotel
CARDS:

St Johns Lodge Lake Rd LA23 2EQ
(on A5704 between Windermere village and Lake Windermere)
☎ 015394 43078
rs Xmas
New proprietors Mr and Mrs Watts offer an enthusiastic welcome to all guests. Refurbishment plans are under way and completed work is of a high standard. The house is situated on the main road half way between Windermere and Bowness and limited parking is provided at the front of the house. The bedrooms vary in size but all are nicely decorated. A cosy breakfast room is located in the smartly converted cellar. An optional 4-course dinner is available which always includes a fish and vegetarian choice.
14 rms (12 shr) (3 fmly) No smoking CTV in all bedrooms Tea and coffee making facilities No dogs (ex guide dogs) Licensed Cen ht No children 4yrs 11P No coaches Facilities at private leisure club Last d 6pm
ROOMS: s £18-£26; d £36-£52*
CARDS:

QQQ ***Villa Lodge*** Cross St LA23 1AE
(exit M6 at junc 36 onto A590/A591 into Windermere, fork left into village past tourist information, left at Elleray Hotel along Cross Street)
☎ 015394 43318 FAX 015394 43318
Located in a quiet cul-de-sac close to the town centre, this inviting guest house is well maintained throughout. Public areas are particularly attractive and include a relaxing sun lounge and bright dining room. Bedrooms come in a variety of sizes, and those without en suites each have their own private shower room. Those rooms facing the front enjoy stunning views over and across the town to the distant mountains.
7 rms (5 shr) No smoking in 2 bedrooms No smoking in dining room No smoking in 1 lounge CTV in all bedrooms Tea and coffee making facilities No dogs (ex guide dogs) Cen ht No children 6yrs 8P No coaches
CARDS:

QQQ **Westwood** 4 Ellerthwaite Rd LA23 2AH
(from A591 follow signs for Windermere drive through village and take 2nd road on right, house is second on right opposite library entrance)
☎ 015394 43514
Closed 24-26 Dec
Nicely decorated throughout, this immaculately maintained and friendly little guest house has bright contemporary bedrooms, and an attractive open plan dining room and small cosy sun lounge.
5 bth/shr No smoking CTV in all bedrooms Tea and coffee making facilities No dogs Cen ht No children 12yrs 5P No coaches
ROOMS: s £20-£30; d £30-£40*

Prices shown in the directory are meant as a guide only and are subject to change. Please check before you book

Selected

Q Q Q Q **White Lodge Hotel** Lake Rd LA23 2JJ (on main lake road, on right) ☎ 015394 43624 FAX 015394 44749
Mar-Nov
This stately Victorian house lies in its own gardens just north of Bowness. The lounge and main dining room are attractively furnished with antiques whilst the modern bedrooms offer a high level of comfort and make good use of pine furniture. There is a bright, attractive residents' bar that during the morning is used as a breakfast room.
12 bth/shr (3 fmly) No smoking in dining room CTV in all bedrooms Tea and coffee making facilities No dogs (ex guide dogs) Licensed Cen ht CTV 14P No coaches Free membership of leisure club Last d 6.30pm
ROOMS: s £25-£33; d £48-£66; wkly b&b £175-£200; wkly hlf-bd £240-£275
CARDS:

Selected

Q Q Q Q **Woodlands** New Road LA23 2EE (from railway station turn left through village) ☎ 015394 43915 Fax 015394 48558
A semi-detached property that features a comfortable lounge, cosy residents' bar and an attractive dining room with views of the garden and small stream. The bedrooms are bright and modern. The new owners have exciting plans to enhance Woodlands.
rs Dec-Jan (Thu-Sun only)
14 bth/shr 1 fmly) No smoking in dining room CTV in all bedrooms. Tea and coffee making facilities. No dogs. Licensed Cen ht. No children 5yrs. 14P. No coaches Last d5pm
ROOMS: s£22-45; d£44-90*
CARDS:

WINDSOR Berkshire Map **04** SU97

Q Q **Clarence Hotel** 9 Clarence Rd SL4 5AE (from M4 junct 6 follow dual carrriageway to Windsor, turn left at 1st rdbt into Clarence Rd) ☎ 01753 864436 FAX 01753 857060
This Victorian villa is situated in the heart of Windsor within walking distance of the castle. Bedrooms vary in size and are attractively decorated and nicely furnished, some look out over the newly built garden. Guests have use of a well stocked and comfortable bar with giant TV screen. Breakfast is served in the bright dining room.
20 bth/shr (6 fmly) No smoking in dining room CTV in all bedrooms Tea and coffee making facilities Licensed Cen ht CTV 4P Sauna Steam room
ROOMS: s £33-£43; d £44-£55
CARDS:

AA
QQQQ

English Tourist Board
HIGHLY COMMENDED

The Woodlands Hotel

New Road, Windermere,
Cumbria LA23 2EE
Tel: (015394) 43915
Fax: (015394) 48558

The Secret to a truly wonderful holiday is the right hotel, experience our delightful surroundings, renowned breakfasts and a warm welcome from resident proprietors Juliet and Andrew Wood who take great pride in maintaining high Standards throughout the hotel.

All 14 rooms are tastefully furnished, en-suite with colour television, tea/coffee making facilities, hairdryers, radio/alarm clocks and independently controlled central heating. Large private car park.

In the evenings you may wish to sample our excellent four course Table d'Hote dinner or simply relax in our residents bar or lounge. Flowers and/or champagne can be requested and will be in your room on arrival for that special occasion.

Experience the Woodlands and we are sure you will become one of our regular guests

Selected

Q Q Q Q **Melrose House** 53 Frances Rd SL4 3AQ
(M4 Junct 6 signposted Windsor, follow signs for Staines, left into Frances Rd, 3rd rdbt from M4) ☎ 01753 865328 FAX 01753 865328
Recent improvements have been made to this elegant Victorian house, located in a peaceful residential area within walking distance of the town centre and castle. Bedrooms vary in size but are brightly decorated and well equipped. Guests are offered a choice of breakfast which is served in the spacious breakfast room. The house benefits from off street parking.
9 bth/shr (2 fmly) No smoking in 3 bedrooms No smoking in dining room CTV in all bedrooms Tea and coffee making facilities Direct dial from bedrooms Cen ht CTV 10P No coaches
ROOMS: s £45-£55; d £50-£65*
CARDS:

Q Q Q ***Netherton Hotel*** 96 St Leonards Rd SL4 3DA ☎ 01753 855508
An attractive Edwardian villa, this hotel has bright fresh bedrooms all featuring co-ordinating fabrics and modern facilities. There is a small lounge available for guest use and a light and airy breakfast room. Dedicated facilities for disabled guests are also available. Off street parking is provided at the rear of the property.
11 bth/shr (5 fmly) CTV in all bedrooms Tea and coffee making facilities No dogs Cen ht CTV 9P
CARDS:

WINFORTON Herefordshire Map **03** SO24

Selected

Q Q Q Q **Winforton Court** HR3 6EA (on A438 in village centre)
☎ 01544 328498 FAX 01544 328498
This large, delightful 16th century timber framed house has an abundance of charm and character. Surrounded by three-quarters of an acre of lovely gardens, it stands on the A438 in the village centre. It has a fascinating history and what is now the breakfast room was a court room in Civil War times, and the infamous Judge Jeffrey presided here when he was the circuit judge. The spacious no smoking bedrooms are tastefully appointed and have period style furnishings. Two have four-poster beds and all have modern facilities plus extra thoughtful touches. An adjacent two bedroom cottage is also available either as bed & breakfast or self catering accommodation. Welcoming real fires burn during cold weather, in both the spacious elegant lounge and the breakfast room. There is also a small library containing a good selection of tourist information and other reading material.
3 bth/shr No smoking in bedrooms No smoking in dining room Tea and coffee making facilities CTV No children 10yrs 10P No coaches
ROOMS: s £28.50-£36; d £47-£62

WINSFORD Somerset Map **03** SS93

Premier Selected

Q Q Q Q Q **Savery's at Karslake House** Halse Ln TA24 7JE
(leave A396 signposted Winsford into village turn left beyond village stores signed Karslake House continue around corner just beyond Royal Oak)
☎ 01643 851242 FAX 01643 851242
Closed February rs Dec-mid Mar
This country hotel is situated in a peaceful Exmoor village and is continuously improving, offering a high standard of comfort and facilities. The bedrooms have been thoughtfully furnished, and a number of useful extras have been added. Pat Carpenter is most hospitable, and John Savery's cooking is skilful.
7 rms (5 bth/shr) No smoking in bedrooms No smoking in dining room CTV in all bedrooms Tea and coffee making facilities Licensed Cen ht No children 15yrs 12P No coaches Shooting or fishing Clay pigeon shooting Last d 9pm
ROOMS: d £50-£80
CARDS:

WINTERBOURNE ABBAS Dorset Map **03** SY69

Q Q Q **Churchview** DT2 9LS (approach Winterbourne Abbas on A35, Church View is in centre of village opposite the church) ☎ 01305 889296
rs Nov-Feb
This delightful 17th-century house is situated five miles west of Dorchester making it an ideal base from which to explore the beautiful countryside and the Hardy Trail. Michael and Jane Deller offer a warm welcome and are always upgrading the facilities. The bedrooms have pretty co-ordinated decor and retain much of their original character, although most have modern en suite facilities. Jane prepares an interesting range of good home-cooked evening meals which are served in the attractive dining room. There are two comfortable lounges, both non-smoking.
9 rms (7 bth/shr) (1 fmly) No smoking CTV in all bedrooms Tea and coffee making facilities Licensed Cen ht No children 3yrs 10P No coaches Last d 7pm
ROOMS: s £21-£30; d £41-£54
CARDS:

WINTERBOURNE STOKE Wiltshire Map **04** SU04

Selected

Q Q Q Q **Scotland Lodge** SP3 4TF
(from Salisbury take A360 to the A303 junct and turn left 0.25m W of village beyond turning to Berwick St James on right)
☎ 01980 620943 FAX 01980 620943
Set in its own grounds, this large family home is situated alongside the A303 and offers comfortable accommodation. Owners Jane and John Singleton offer guests a warm welcome and a host of thoughtful extras are provided in the bedrooms. Breakfast is taken in the dining room around one large table, with a sitting room available for guests.
3 bth/shr (1 fmly) No smoking CTV in all bedrooms Tea and coffee making facilities No dogs (ex guide dogs) Cen ht 5P No coaches Stabling available
ROOMS: s £25-£30; d £35-£50; wkly b&b £125-£150*

WISBECH Cambridgeshire Map **05** TF40

Selected

Q Q Q Q ❦ **Stratton Farm** *(TF495144)* West Drove North, Walton Highway PE14 7DP (leave A47 at Little Chef onto B198, right into West Walton Highway. After 1m turn left into West Drove North, 0.5m farm on left)
☎ 01945 880162 Mrs S M King
Set in 22 acres of peaceful countryside, Stratton Farm is home to Mrs King, an enthusiastic and caring hostess who maintains high standards. Bedrooms (all non-smoking) are well appointed and comfortable, with a thoughtful range of extras. Tasty breakfasts, which are taken around a communal dining table, include home produced bacon, sausage, eggs and marmalades. There is a quiet and comfortable Library, and guests are also welcome to use the heated outdoor swimming pool in season and to fish in the small lake which is stocked with carp.

3 bth/shr No smoking CTV in all bedrooms Tea and coffee making facilities No dogs Cen ht No children 7yrs 6P Outdoor swimming pool (heated) Fishing 22 acres beef
ROOMS: s £20.50-£25; d £45-£50; wkly b&b £157.50*

WITHERIDGE Devon Map 03 SS81

Selected

Q Q Q Q **Marchweeke** *(SS797115)* Thelbridge EX16 8NY (on B3042 towards Thelbridge) ☎ 01884 860418 Mrs A Webber
Easter-November
This Devon long house, set at the end of a private drive in sheltered gardens amid beautiful rolling countryside, is the family home of Ann and Ken Webber. Each room is tastefully decorated using co-ordinating soft furnishings, and has either en suite or private facilities. There is a comfortable lounge where guests can relax, and a spacious dining room where dinner and breakfast are served.
2 rms (1 bth) No smoking Tea and coffee making facilities No dogs (ex guide dogs) Cen ht CTV No children 5yrs 2P Small snooker table 80 acres beef sheep cereal
ROOMS: s £15-£18; d £30-£36; wkly b&b fr £100

Selected

Q Q Q Q **Thelbridge Cross** Thelbridge EX17 4SQ
(2m W of Witheridge on the B3042)
☎ 01884 860316 FAX 01884 861318
rs 26 Dec
This charming inn is locally renowned for both its well prepared, fresh food, and the excellent hospitality extended to guests by the Ball family. The prettily co-ordinated bedrooms are well equipped and of the three on the ground floor, one is available as a family suite. One bar has open log fire and comfortable sofas, the other larger bar has a log burner and tables where bar snacks and light lunches are served. Restaurant meals are also available, the dining room being used in the mornings for breakfast.
8 bth/shr (1 fmly) No smoking in bedrooms No smoking in area of dining room CTV in all bedrooms Tea and coffee making facilities Direct dial from bedrooms No dogs (ex guide dogs) Cen ht 40P No coaches Forest and cycling trails Last d 9pm
ROOMS: s fr £35; d fr £50; wkly b&b fr £350*
MEALS: Lunch £5-£15&alc Dinner £11.50-£20alc*
CARDS:

WITNEY Oxfordshire Map 04 SP30

Q Q Q *Greystones Lodge Hotel* 34 Tower Hill OX8 5ES
(off A40 at junct of A415,follow signs to town centre at 1st traffic lights straight on to rdbt take 2nd exit into Tower Hill,hotel 300yds on left)
☎ 01993 771898 FAX 01993 771898
Closed 24 Dec-1 Jan
This attractive house is conveniently located on the edge of the town; new proprietors Anthony and Christine Pugh offer a warm welcome. Bedrooms, which are bright and attractively decorated, continually improve. There is a comfortable lounge and the breakfast room overlooks the garden and outdoor pool.
11 shr (1 fmly) No smoking in 4 bedrooms No smoking in dining room CTV in all bedrooms Tea and coffee making facilities Licensed Cen ht CTV 15P No coaches Outdoor swimming pool (heated) Last d 8.30pm
CARDS:

WIVELISCOMBE Somerset Map 03 ST02

Selected

Q Q Q Q **Alpine House** 10 West Rd TA4 2TF
(on B3227, opposite cricket ground, at western edge of village)
☎ 01984 623526
This elegant Victorian House, on the edge of Wiveliscombe, overlooks the playing fields, tennis courts and open air swimming pool. The unusual terraced garden is stocked with a wide range of shrubs and plants, and enjoys superb views. Bedrooms are individually furnished and decorated, one being located on the ground floor. Dinners are provided by prior arrangement and the speciality of the house is a Sri Lankan meal, for which several days notice is required and generally for parties of 6 or more.
4 bth/shr No smoking CTV in all bedrooms Tea and coffee making facilities No dogs Cen ht No children 15yrs No coaches
ROOMS: s £35; d £50
CARDS:

WIX Essex Map 05 TM12

Selected

Q Q Q Q **Dairy House** *(TM148293)* Bradfield Rd CO11 2SR
(between Colchester and Harwich, turn off A120 into Wix village. At crossroads take road signposted Bradfield and farm is 1m on left)
☎ 01255 870322 FAX 01255 870186 Mrs B Whitworth
At the end of a long drive alongside arable farmland, this Victorian farmhouse retains a great deal of character, and has been sympathetically converted to offer high quality accommodation. Both day rooms and bedrooms are furnished in keeping with the house, with some delightful period pieces. Guests are welcomed with a cup of tea and home-made cakes, and breakfasts are served at a large mahogany dining table. There are no evening meals, but the village of Bradfield is only about a 20-minute walk away and has some good pubs.
2 shr No smoking in bedrooms No smoking in dining room CTV in all bedrooms Tea and coffee making facilities No dogs (ex guide dogs) Cen ht CTV No children 12yrs 6P Games room Pool table Croquet Table tennis 700 acres arable fruit
ROOMS: s £26-£28; d £37-£40

Q Q Q **New Farm House** *(TM165289)* Spinnel's Ln CO11 2UJ
(turn off A120 into Wix, at village crossroads take Bradfield road, under A120 to top of hill turn right New Farm House 200yds on left)
☎ 01255 870365 FAX 01255 870837 Mr & Mrs B R Winch
Surrounded by arable farmland, New Farm benefits from attractive gardens and a children's play area. Bedrooms are divided between the main house and the adjacent ground floor annexe (two of the annexe rooms are especially suited to the less able). Rooms are especially well equipped. Two lounges are available for guests, one a no smoking room and the other with television. Drinks and light refreshments are available, and a small kitchenette provided. Traditional home cooking is served in the dining room.
5 rms (3 bth/shr) 6 annexe shr (5 fmly) No smoking in 9 bedrooms No smoking in dining room No smoking in 1 lounge CTV in all bedrooms Tea and coffee making facilities Licensed Cen ht CTV ch fac 20P Last d 6.30pm
ROOMS: s £23-£28; d £40-£48; wkly b&b £120-£144
CARDS:

WOLD NEWTON East Riding of Yorkshire Map 08 TA07

Selected

Q Q Q Q ***The Wold Cottage** (TA042723)* YO25 0HL (from B1249 head for Wold Newton, turn right by pond, round double bend, first on right, past bungalow, 200yds to farmhouse) ☎ 01262 470696 FAX 01262 470696 Mrs K Gray
Set in open Wold countryside, within its own grounds and overlooking new and mature woodland, this lovely house dates back to about 1750. The house is delightfully furnished and offers two very comfortable and spacious bedrooms together with a cosy lounge and pleasant dining room where good home cooking is served using much home grown produce. There is a monument to mark where a meteorite landed in 1795. Very friendly and attentive service is provided by the resident owners.
2 bth No smoking Tea and coffee making facilities No dogs Cen ht CTV ch fac P 450 acres arable sheep

WOODBRIDGE Suffolk Map 05 TM24

Q Q **Grove House** 39 Grove Rd IP12 4LG (on A12, 400yds beyond junct with B1079) ☎ 01394 382202 FAX 01394 380652
Conveniently located on the A12 to the north-west of Woodbridge, this pleasant private hotel offers a warm welcome from Mrs Kelly, the friendly owner, and is being dramatically upgraded. Bedrooms are bright, tastefully decorated and well maintained. There is a small lounge with an honesty bar, and a dining room, where breakfast includes healthy options. Reasonably priced, home-cooked evening meals are also offered.
13 rms (11 shr) (2 fmly) No smoking in 3 bedrooms No smoking in dining room CTV in all bedrooms Tea and coffee making facilities Licensed Cen ht CTV 14P No coaches Last d 7.30pm
ROOMS: s £34-£39; d £48-£55; wkly b&b £215-£245; wkly hlf-bd £265-£295*
CARDS:

WOODFALLS Wiltshire Map 04 SU12

Premier Selected

Q Q Q Q Q ***Woodfalls*** The Ridge SP5 2LN (on B3080) ☎ 01725 513222 FAX 01725 513220
In a village location between Salisbury and Southampton, this attractive inn offers a good base for exploring the Forest. Bedrooms are attractively decorated and well equipped, two have four poster beds and there is one suite. The public rooms have a relaxed atmosphere, there is a comfortably furnished lounge with a log fire and an intimate restaurant; the popular public bar also offers a good range of snacks, and breakfast is served in a brightly decorated conservatory.
10 bth/shr (2 fmly) No smoking in 5 bedrooms No smoking in dining room No smoking in 1 lounge CTV in all bedrooms Tea and coffee making facilities Direct dial from bedrooms Cen ht CTV ch fac 30P Fishing Bike hire Last d 9.30pm
CARDS:

WOODHALL SPA Lincolnshire Map 08 TF16

See also Horncastle

Q Q **Claremont** 9/11 Witham Rd LN10 6RW (on B1191 Horncastle/Kirkstead Bridge road, at the centre of Woodhall Spa close to mini rdbt) ☎ 01526 352000
This attractive property enjoys a good central location and is personally run by Mrs Brennan. The bedrooms are generally quite spacious and traditionally furnished; there is a comfortable guest lounge, and a home-cooked breakfast is served in the sunny dining room.
9 rms (2 shr) (5 fmly) No smoking in dining room CTV in 10 bedrooms Tea and coffee making facilities 5P No coaches
ROOMS: s £12.50-£20; d £30-£35*

Q Q **Pitchaway** The Broadway LN10 6SQ (follow B1192 toward Woodhall Spa then turn right onto B1191 Pitchaway is on right) ☎ 01526 352969
New proprietors, Mr & Mrs Tomkinson, offer a warm welcome to this attractive Victorian house, which is conveniently located for the famous local golf course. The bedrooms are bright, fresh and comfortably furnished, and breakfast is taken in pleasant light and airy dining room; guests also have use of a comfortable foyer lounge area and off street parking.
7 rms (2 bth/shr) (2 fmly) No smoking in 3 bedrooms No smoking in dining room CTV in all bedrooms Tea and coffee making facilities No dogs (ex guide dogs) Cen ht CTV 8P Last d 8pm

Q Q Q **Village Limits Motel** Stixwould Rd LN10 6UJ (in village of Woodhall Spa, large sign for the Pettwood hotel, Village Limits is approx 500yds further on same road) ☎ 01526 353312 FAX 353312
Guests are assured a warm welcome from their enthusiastic hosts, Mr and Mrs Sloan, at this well established motel style establishment, which sits

peacefully on the edge of the town. Bedrooms are comfortable and attractively decorated with modern en suite facilities.
8 annexe bth/shr (1 fmly) No smoking in 4 bedrooms No smoking in dining room CTV in all bedrooms Tea and coffee making facilities Cen ht 30P 1m from EGU HQ. Hotchkin/Bracken course Last d 9pm
ROOMS: s £30-£35; d £40-£50✳
MEALS: Lunch £5-£8&alc Dinner £7.50&alc✳
CARDS:

WOODSTOCK Oxfordshire Map **04** SP41

Selected

Q Q Q Q **Kings Head Inn & Restaurant** Chapel Hill, Wootton OX20 1DX (1m N of Woodstock on A44, turn right (signposted Wootton), the inn is located in the centre of the village close to the church) ☎ 01993 811340 FAX 01993 811340
A lovely little inn with a reputation for tasty, home-cooked meals, served in the restaurant. The three well equipped bedrooms are nicely furnished with pine furniture; one room is located in the pretty courtyard, and has a separate sitting room and four-poster bed. The tap room serves a range of well kept real ales and excellent wines by the glass. The atmosphere is most convivial.
2 bth/shr 1 annexe bth/shr (1 fmly) No smoking in bedrooms No smoking in dining room CTV in all bedrooms Tea and coffee making facilities No dogs (ex guide dogs) Cen ht 8P No coaches Last d 9.30pm
ROOMS: s £49.95-£54; d £65-£92; wkly b&b £227.50-£378; wkly hlf-bd £290-£356✳
MEALS: Lunch £15-£25alc Dinner £15-£25alc✳
CARDS:

Selected

Q Q Q Q **The Laurels** Hensington Rd OX20 1JL
(from A44 turn into Hensington Rd by the Punchbowl PH, The Laurels is approx 500yds on right opposite a small Catholic church)
☎ 01993 812583 FAX 01993 812583
Closed Xmas
Built in 1890, this fine Victorian house is full of character and charmingly furnished with the Lloyd's collection of antique furniture. The pretty bedrooms are well equipped and have been sympathetically decorated in keeping with the age of the building. Home cooked breakfasts are served at one large polished wooden table in the front facing dining room. The property is situated just a short walk from Blenheim Palace, and provides a convenient base for exploring The Cotswolds.
3 bth/shr No smoking CTV in all bedrooms Tea and coffee making facilities No dogs Cen ht No children 7yrs 3P No coaches
ROOMS: s £32-£40; d £42-£50✳
CARDS:

WOOLACOMBE Devon Map **02** SS44

Q Q Q **The Castle** The Esplanade EX34 7DJ
(A361 from Barnstaple to Ilfracombe, turn right at Woolacombe sign)
☎ 01271 870788 FAX 01271 870788
Apr-Oct
Built in 1898 as a summer residence for a Colonel Pickering and his young bride this Victorian folly has the architectural features of a castle. Many guests return on a regular basis to this friendly, small hotel with stunning views over Woolacombe Bay. Most of the bedrooms benefit from these views, all are light, airy and well equipped. The comfortable, spacious lounge features an unusual, wood-carved ceiling, and breakfast is served in the dining room. Evening meals are available by prior arrangement.
8 shr (2 fmly) No smoking in dining room CTV in all bedrooms Tea and coffee making facilities No dogs (ex guide dogs) Licensed Cen ht CTV No children 5yrs 8P No coaches Last d 6pm
ROOMS: s £21.50-£23.50; d £43-£49; wkly b&b £147-£167; wkly hlf-bd £199-£220.50✳

Selected

Q Q Q Q **Cleeve House Hotel** Mortehoe EX34 7ED
(from A361 onto B3343 at Mullacutt Cross. Turn right towards Mortehoe, then right at post office, hotel 300yds on left)
☎ 01271 870719 FAX 01271 870719
Apr-Oct
Quietly located in Mortehoe, Cleeve House is personally owned and run by David and Anne Strobel who welcome guests to their small hotel. The bedrooms are tastefully co-ordinated and well equipped; one room is specifically designed for the less able. They benefit either from a distant sea view or a view of the village or the surrounding countryside. Dinner is served each evening in the elegantly furnished

contd.

dining room, an imaginative and interesting choice is always offered. Guests can relax in either of the cosy sitting rooms, in addition there is a tea room and garden where morning coffees, light lunches and cream teas are served during the summer months.
7 bth/shr (1 fmly) No smoking CTV in all bedrooms Tea and coffee making facilities No dogs (ex guide dogs) Licensed Cen ht No children 12yrs 9P No coaches Last d 5.30pm
ROOMS: s £23.50-£38.50; d £47-£57; wkly b&b £164.50-£178.50; wkly hlf-bd £259-£280
CARDS:

Q Q Q ***Holmesdale Hotel*** Bay View Rd EX34 7DQ ☎ 01271 870335 FAX 01271 870088
Closed Feb
From its slightly elevated position, this friendly, personally run hotel has spectacular views over the bay. The comfortably furnished bedrooms are soundly decorated and well equipped. In the cosy restaurant, an extensive carte and a set menu is offered to guests, cooked by the chef/proprietor.
15 shr (10 fmly) No smoking in bedrooms No smoking in dining room No smoking in 1 lounge CTV in all bedrooms Tea and coffee making facilities Licensed Cen ht CTV 14P Last d 8.30pm
CARDS:

Selected

Q Q Q Q **Sunnycliffe Hotel** EX34 7EB (turn off A361 at Mullacott Cross onto B3343, Sunnycliffe on right just after end of Woolacombe esplanade) ☎ 01271 870597 FAX 01271 870597
Closed Dec & Jan
A quiet hotel, enjoying a unique hillside position overlooking the rocky inlets and pools, as well as the rugged North Devon coastline. Bedrooms all benefit from the views. A choice of meals are offered each evening in the dining room, and a comfortable lounge is available..
8 bth/shr No smoking in bedrooms No smoking in dining room No smoking in 1 lounge CTV in all bedrooms Tea and coffee making facilities No dogs Licensed Cen ht No children 10P No coaches Last d 6pm
ROOMS: d £50-£64; wkly b&b £179-£195; wkly hlf-bd £245-£275
CARDS:

WOOLSTONE Oxfordshire Map **04** SU28

Selected

Q Q Q Q **The White Horse** SN7 7QL ☎ 01367 820726 FAX 01367 820566
This quaint 16th-century inn, reputed to be one of the oldest inns in the country, offers a warm and friendly welcome. Bedrooms are well equipped with modern facilities including colour television, direct dial telephone and hairdryers. There is also a luxury suite with lounge, two bedrooms and bathrooms. The intimate a la carte restaurant offers good fresh food, while the oak beamed bar has olde worlde ambience and a fine selection of malt whiskies.
6 annexe bth/shr No smoking in 2 bedrooms No smoking in area of dining room CTV in all bedrooms Tea and coffee making facilities Direct dial from bedrooms No dogs (ex guide dogs) Cen ht 60P Last d 10pm
ROOMS: s £50; d £65*
MEALS: Lunch £15.95-£16.95&alc Dinner £15.95-£16.95&alc*
CARDS:

WORCESTER Worcestershire Map **03** SO85

Selected

Q Q Q Q ***Burgage House*** 4 College Precincts WR1 2LG (M5 junct 7 towards city centre, 4th set of traffic lights see Edgar Ston left, College Precincts is next left where there is parking) ☎ 01905 25396 FAX 01905 25396
Closed 23-30 Dec
Situated adjacent to the Cathedral in an ideal location for the city centre, this fine Georgian building retains many original features including an impressive stone staircase and carvings. Bedrooms are comfortable and well equipped, and public areas include a spacious dining room where breakfast is served, and a homely, small sitting room.
4 rms (2 shr) (1 fmly) No smoking in bedrooms No smoking in dining room CTV in all bedrooms Tea and coffee making facilities Cen ht

Q Q **Wyatt** 40 Barbourne Rd WR1 1HU (M5 junct 6 follow signs for city centre (A449). At junction with A38 turn right, house is on left after approx 0.25m) ☎ 01905 26311 FAX 01905 26311
This privately owned guest house stands on the A38, just north of the city centre. The modern furnished and equipped bedrooms include a room on ground floor level and family bedded rooms. There is a homely lounge, and separate tables are provided in the breakfast room.
8 rms (4 shr) (4 fmly) No smoking in dining room CTV in all bedrooms Tea and coffee making facilities Cen ht CTV
ROOMS: s £20-£22; d £34-£40*
CARDS:

WORKSOP Nottinghamshire Map **08** SK57

Q Q Q ***Leaf Lodge Hotel*** 20 Park St S80 1HB ☎ 01909 486194 FAX 01909 486194
Modern bedrooms have been given character with antique furniture, and one has a four poster bed. Breakfast, and dinner if required, is served in the adjacent Friar Tuck's restaurant; although it is not licensed, diners are welcome to bring their own wine.
4 annexe shr No smoking CTV in all bedrooms Tea and coffee making facilities No dogs (ex guide dogs) Cen ht 8P Last d 10pm
CARDS:

Q Q Q ***Old Blue Bell Hotel & Restaurant*** 30 Park St S80 1HF (in town centre 100yds from Market Square) ☎ 01909 500304
Very friendly hospitality is provided by Linden and Janice Pearson at their small and well furnished inn and restaurant. The bedrooms have been thoughtfully equipped, and an extensive range of home cooked English food is available in the spacious restaurant. Very good value accommodation.
3 bth/shr No smoking in dining room CTV in all bedrooms Tea and coffee making facilities No dogs (ex guide dogs) Cen ht 15P Last d 9.45pm
CARDS:

WORTHING West Sussex Map 04 TQ10

Selected

Q Q Q Q **Moorings** 4 Seldon Rd BN11 2LL
(on A259 towards Brighton, pass indoor swimming pool on right and hotel opposite garage) ☎ 01903 208882
Closed 19 Dec-4 Jan
Set in a quiet residential street to the east of the town centre only a short walk from the sea front, this elegant late Victorian villa offers a warm welcome to guests. Bedrooms are spacious and smart and offer a good range of extras. There is a cosy lounge and breakfasts are served in an airy dining room.
6 shr (2 fmly) No smoking CTV in all bedrooms Tea and coffee making facilities Direct dial from bedrooms Cen ht No coaches
ROOMS: s £22-£28; d £42-£49*
CARDS:

Q Q **Wolsey Hotel** 179-181 Brighton Rd BN11 2EX (on A259, facing sea, 0.75m E of town centre) ☎ 01903 236149 & 234255 FAX 01903 235875
Closed Xmas/New Year
Look out for colourful hanging baskets and window boxes in order to find this guest house, which is on the sea front to the east of the town. Well-kept bedrooms all boast satellite TV, but the many regular guests tend to get together in the small bar, which opens into the lounge where glass cases display dolls from around the world. Dinner is by arrangement.
13 rms (5 bth/shr) (2 fmly) CTV in all bedrooms Tea and coffee making facilities Licensed Cen ht CTV Last d 10am
CARDS:

Q Q Q **Woodlands** 20-22 Warwick Gardens BN11 1PF
(from A27/A24 follow town centre signs after railway bridge at 3rd rdbt take 1st exit,next rdbt 2nd exit-High St 1st left after Safeways,then right)
☎ 01903 233557 FAX 01903 233557
Although set in a quiet, tree-lined street, this double-fronted Edwardian house is close to both the town centre and the sea front. Bedrooms are bright and cheerful - six are now reserved for non-smokers - and there is a comfortably furnished lounge. The set dinners are all home-made and special diets can be catered for with advance notice.
11 rms (6 bth/shr) (3 fmly) No smoking in 6 bedrooms No smoking in dining room CTV in all bedrooms Tea and coffee making facilities Licensed Cen ht CTV 8P No coaches Last d 6pm
ROOMS: s £19-£26; d £36-£50; wkly b&b £130-£172; wkly hlf-bd £170-£225
CARDS:

WROTHAM Kent Map 05 TQ65

Q Q Q **The Bull Hotel** Bull Ln TN15 7RF (off A20)
(The Independents) ☎ 01732 885522 FAX 01732 886288
The owners, Mike and Elaine Dunnell, offer friendly hospitality, good food and comfortable accommodation. Bedrooms are brightly decorated, nicely furnished and well equipped. The oak beam restaurant with inglenook fireplace, which is open every day, serves French/English à la carte as well as a set price menu.
10 rms (6 bth/shr) (1 fmly) CTV in all bedrooms Tea and coffee making facilities Direct dial from bedrooms Cen ht 50P Last d 10pm
CARDS:

WYBUNBURY Cheshire Map 07 SJ64

Q Q **Lea** *(SJ717489)* Wrinehill Rd CW5 7NS
(A500 towards Nantwich over 2 rdbts over split railway bridge take 1st road on left to T-junct, turn left 2nd farm on right)
☎ 01270 841429 FAX 01270 841429 Mrs J E Callwood
Closed Xmas
Surrounded by open countryside, this large house and working dairy farm offers spacious farmhouse bedrooms, furnished in a mixture of styles. The well tended and mature gardens are home to a number of peacocks. The large lounge includes a small snooker table, and breakfast, as well as an evening meal by arrangement, is taken in the dining room.
3 rms (2 shr) (1 fmly) No smoking in bedrooms No smoking in area of dining room CTV in all bedrooms Tea and coffee making facilities CTV 24P Fishing Pool table 150 acres dairy Last d 5pm
ROOMS: s £18-£25; d £32-£36; wkly b&b fr £150; wkly hlf-bd fr £210*

YARNTON Oxfordshire Map 04 SP41

Q Q Q **Eltham Villa** 148 Woodstock Rd OX5 1PW (on A44)
☎ 01865 376037 FAX 01865 376037
This small guest house just off the A44 between Oxford and Woodstock offers attractive, well maintained accommodation with en suite facilities. There is a charming pine furnished breakfast room and cosy guest lounge.
7 bth/shr (2 fmly) No smoking in bedrooms No smoking in dining room CTV in all bedrooms Tea and coffee making facilities Direct dial from bedrooms No dogs Cen ht CTV 7P No coaches Last d 10am
ROOMS: s £25-£35; d £40-£50; wkly b&b £140-£200; wkly hlf-bd £180-£250*
CARDS:

See advertisement under WOODSTOCK

YEALAND CONYERS Lancashire Map **07** SD57

Premier Selected

QQQQQ **The Bower** LA5 9SF (leave M6 at junct 35, follow A6 towards Milnthorpe for 0.75m, after passing under narrow bridge, take next left and bear left at end)
☎ 01524 734585
Michael & Sally Rothwell are the proud and very friendly hosts at this delightfully elegant house which stands in its own grounds close to the village centre. The two bedrooms are attractively and thoughtfully furnished whilst guests have the use of a lovely lounge with an open fire. Excellent dinners are served around a large table and breakfast is served in the delightful kitchen area. The house is very convenient for the M6.
2 bth/shr (1 fmly) No smoking CTV in all bedrooms Tea and coffee making facilities No dogs (ex guide dogs) Cen ht CTV No children 12yrs 6P No coaches Croquet lawn Last d noon
ROOMS: s £36-£41; d £52-£62; wkly b&b £165-£260; wkly hlf-bd £305-£400
CARDS:

YELVERTON Devon Map **02** SX56

Selected

QQQQ **Greenwell** *(SX536659)* Meavy PL20 6PY (from Yelverton rbt take A386 signed Plymouth, then immediately left, signed Cadover Bridge and in 2m over cattle grid, farm lane in 100yds)
☎ 01822 853563 FAX 01822 853563 Mrs B Cole
Closed Xmas
With parts of the property dating back to the 15th Century, Greenwell Farm is situated south of Yelverton, near Cadover Bridge on the edge of Dartmoor. Owners Bridget and Arnold Cole welcome guests to their traditional farmhouse, with panoramic views onto the garden, fields and moors beyond. The individually bedrooms are well equipped with guest comfort in mind. Three course suppers are a speciality using home produced, naturally reared meat and fresh local produce whenever possible. These are served at one large table in the traditionally furnished dining room.
3 bth/shr No smoking in bedrooms CTV in all bedrooms Tea and coffee making facilities No dogs Licensed Cen ht CTV 10P Stabling for guests horses Clay shooting 300 acres beef sheep Last d 4pm
ROOMS: s £26-£40; d £42-£48; wkly b&b £147-£154; wkly hlf-bd £215-£225*

Selected

QQQQ **Harrabeer Country House Hotel** Harrowbeer Ln PL20 6EA (at Yelverton rdbt take Princetown road for 20yds turn left at signpost for Harrowbeer Ln. Hotel 300yds on right)
☎ 01822 853302 FAX 01822 853302
Closed 24 Dec-2 Jan
Ask for directions to this 400 year old property, tucked behind the village of Yelverton, with glorious views towards Dartmoor at the rear of the house. A warm welcome is assured from owners Sonia and Graham Williams who obviously thoroughly enjoy running this small hotel. Bedrooms vary in size, but all are equipped with thoughtful extras. In cooler months a log fire roars in the cosy bar, and in addition there is a spacious lounge. Honest, home cooking is featured and special diets are provided with prior arrangement.
7 rms (5 bth/shr) (1 fmly) No smoking in 3 bedrooms No smoking in dining room No smoking in lounges CTV in all bedrooms Tea and coffee making facilities Direct dial from bedrooms Licensed Cen ht CTV 10P No coaches Last d by arrangement
ROOMS: s £20; d £40-£53; wkly b&b £119-£182; wkly hlf-bd £185.50-£238*
CARDS:

See advertisement under PLYMOUTH

YEOVIL Somerset Map **03** ST51

See also Cary Fitzpaine, Crewkerne & Langport

QQQ **The Half Moon** Main St, Mudford BA21 5TF (leave A303 at Sparkford, onto A359 continues for approx 4m)
☎ 01935 850289 FAX 01935 850842
Closed Xmas
Situated three miles north of Yeovil in the small village of Mudford, the property dates back to the 17th Century. The inn comprises a bar, village bar and two restaurants, one of which is no-smoking. The bedrooms are set on ground floor level to the rear of the building, in a delightful paved courtyard.
11 annexe bth/shr No smoking in 6 bedrooms No smoking in dining room CTV in all bedrooms Tea and coffee making facilities Direct dial from bedrooms Cen ht 40P Last d 9.30pm
CARDS:

Win a Family Fun Weekend with AA Lifestyle Guides in association with Hilton Hotels. 3 winners will be drawn every 2 months: December 1998; February 1999; April 1999; June 1999; August 1999; October 1999

Premier Selected

Q Q Q Q Q **Holywell House** Holywell, East Coker BA22 9NQ (leave Yeovil on A30 Crewkerne road, turn left in 2m past Yeovil Court Hotel signed East Coker, continue down lane Holywell House is on right).
☎ 01935 862612 FAX 01935 863035
Closed Xmas & New Year
A beautiful house, built in the 18th century from mellow Hamstone, and set in three acres. Quality is high throughout, with three superb bedrooms each offering individual touches of charm and character. The Masters Suite has fine antique furniture and a Victorian-style panelled bathroom. The award-winning gardens are exceptional and extend to include water and herb gardens, croquet lawns and a tennis court.
3 bth/shr No smoking in dining room No smoking in lounges CTV in all bedrooms Tea and coffee making facilities No dogs (ex guide dogs) Cen ht ch fac 12P No coaches Tennis (hard) Croquet Garden games
ROOMS: s £40-£45; d £60-£65*

YORK North Yorkshire Map **08** SE65

See also Acaster Malbis, Rufforth & Sutton upon Derwent

Q Q Q **Acorn** 1 Southlands Rd, Bishopthorpe Rd YO23 1NP (turn off A64 onto A1036 into city centre and in 0.6m turn right into Scarcroft Rd then right again into Scott St)
☎ 01904 620081 FAX 01904 613331
This stone-fronted house is situated a short walk from the historic centre of York. Bedrooms have been thoughtfully equipped and are pleasingly co-ordinated. Both lounge and dining room are comfortably furnished and the latter is a bright, airy room in which one can take breakfast.
5 shr (2 fmly) No smoking CTV in all bedrooms Tea and coffee making facilities Direct dial from bedrooms No dogs Cen ht CTV Last d 10am
ROOMS: d £30-£41
CARDS:

Q Q Q **Adams House Hotel** 5 Main St, Fulford YO10 4HJ (turn left off A64 onto A19, hotel is 1m on right just beyond St Oswalds Church & traffic lights) ☎ 01904 655413 FAX 01904 643203
This Tudor-style house sits back from the main road in the suburban village of Fulford. It has many fine period features and enjoys well proportioned bedrooms and an attractive dining room.
8 rms (7 bth/shr) (3 fmly) No smoking in dining room CTV in all bedrooms Tea and coffee making facilities No dogs (ex guide dogs) Licensed Cen ht 8P Last d 6.30pm
ROOMS: s £18-£30; d £36-£60; wkly b&b £125-£200; wkly hlf-bd £200-£275*
CARDS:

Q Q Q **Alfreda** 61 Heslington Ln, Fulford YO10 4HN (approach city centre from A19 and at 1st traffic lights turn right for house 200yds on left)
☎ 01904 631698 FAX 01904 411215
Closed Christmas and New Year
Set in its own grounds, this large and attractive Edwardian house is very well furnished throughout. It is found to the south of the city and is close to Fulford golf course. Meals are taken around a large table in the very pleasant dining room and the bedrooms are thoughtfully equipped and a small lounge is also provided for guests.
10 rms (8 bth/shr) (4 fmly) No smoking in dining room CTV in all bedrooms Tea and coffee making facilities Direct dial from bedrooms Cen ht CTV 22P No coaches Play area for children Gardens
ROOMS: s £20-£45; d £38-£50; wkly b&b £150-£175*
CARDS:

See advertisement on p.485.

Q Q Q **Ambleside** 62 Bootham Crescent YO30 7AH ☎ 01904 637165 FAX 01904 637165
Closed Jan
Spotlessly clean and well maintained throughout, this guest house offers bright contemporary bedrooms which are well equipped and include ceiling fans, an added bonus in warmer weather. There is also a comfortable lounge.
8 rms (6 shr) (1 fmly) No smoking CTV in all bedrooms Tea and coffee making facilities No dogs Cen ht CTV No children 9yrs No coaches
ROOMS: d £36-£56*
CARDS:

Premier Selected

QQQQQ **Arndale Hotel** 290 Tadcaster Rd YO24 1ET
(turn off A64 on to A1036 towards city centre for 2m, on left overlooking racecourse) ☎ 01904 702424
Closed Xmas & New Year
Gillian and David Reynard's home offers both views of the racecourse and their immaculately kept gardens. The reception rooms extend to a cosy dining room and a first floor lounge offering comfort and space in which to relax. An extensive breakfast menu is available and the dishes are freshly prepared using much local produce. A small bar is an additional feature in the lounge.
10 bth/shr (1 fmly) No smoking in bedrooms No smoking in dining room CTV in all bedrooms Tea and coffee making facilities No dogs (ex guide dogs) Licensed Cen ht No children 7yrs 20P No coaches
ROOMS: d £47-£75*
CARDS:

QQQ **Arnot House** 17 Grosvenor Ter, Bootham YO30 7AG
(from Bootham Bar drive along Bootham on the A19 towards Thirsk, Grosvenor Terrace is second on right)
☎ 01904 641966 FAX 01904 641966
Situated in a quiet side road, this well furnished and delightful house stands within easy walking distance of the city and the Minster. Reflecting a Vitorian theme throughout the bedrooms have been thoughtfully equipped and are a delight to occupy. There is a good choice at breakfast and the service provided is both attentive and friendly. The house is fully no smoking.
4 bth/shr No smoking CTV in all bedrooms Tea and coffee making facilities No dogs Cen ht No children 12yrs 4P No coaches
ROOMS: d £48-£55
CARDS:

This symbol indicates a 'Child Friendly' establishment - see page 25 for details

QQQ **Ascot House** 80 East Pde YO31 7YH
(A1079 into city after 2m take centre lane at Shell petrol station and right into Melrosegate, at lights left and Ascot House 200yds on left)
☎ 01904 426826 FAX 01904 431077
Dating back to 1869 this well furnished house stands in its own grounds. Family owned and run, friendly service is provided together with well equipped bedrooms, some having antique beds. The wide staircase features a rare and impressive oriel stained glass window. There is a comfortable lounge and spacious breakfast room and security car parking at the rear.
15 rms (5 bth 7 shr) (3 fmly) No smoking in dining room CTV in all bedrooms Tea and coffee making facilities Licensed Cen ht CTV 14P Sauna
ROOMS: s £19-£23; d £38-£48; wkly b&b £130-£155*
CARDS:

Selected

QQQQ **Ashbourne House** 139 Fulford Rd YO10 4HG (on A19)
☎ 01904 639912 FAX 01904 631332
David and Aileen Minns offer a friendly welcome at their family home, just a short distance from York's centre. Bedrooms are well equipped, offering comfort and modern facilities. The lounge provides plenty of literature on the local sights and countryside. Wedgwood Flower Fairy plates adorn the walls of the dining room where Aileen serves freshly prepared meals and breakfast.
6 bth/shr (1 fmly) No smoking CTV in all bedrooms Tea and coffee making facilities Direct dial from bedrooms Licensed Cen ht CTV 6P No coaches Last d 6pm
ROOMS: s £34-£40; d £40-£60; wkly b&b £140-£210; wkly hlf-bd £262-£332.50*
CARDS:

QQQ ***Barbican Hotel*** 20 Barbican Rd YO10 5AA
(from A1 N take A64, A19 and from A1 S take A59 to city centre, follow signs for Barbican Leisure Centre, premises 100yds on)
☎ 01904 627617 FAX 01904 647140
A pleasant Victorian residence, with its own rear car park, that is well furnished throughout and provides attractive and well equipped bedrooms that include direct dial telephones. There is a cosy lounge and the house has a strict no smoking policy. A Yorkshire breakfast is served in the cosy dining room.
6 bth/shr (1 fmly) No smoking CTV in all bedrooms Tea and coffee making facilities Direct dial from bedrooms No dogs (ex guide dogs) Cen ht CTV 6P No coaches
CARDS:

Ascot House

80 East Parade · York · YO3 7YH
Tel: (01904) 426826
Fax: (01904) 431077

- ★ En-suite rooms of character
- ★ 4-Poster & Canopy Beds
- ★ 15 mins. walk to city centre
- ★ Private car park ★ Sauna
- ★ Residential Licence

English Tourist Board COMMENDED · Yorkshire Tourist Board MEMBER · AA QQQ Recommended · Les Routiers · RAC ACCLAIMED

Contact Mrs J. Wood for colour brochure

ALFREDA GUEST HOUSE

BED & BREAKFAST

61 HESLINGTON LANE • FULFORD
YORK YO1 4HN TEL: 01904 631698

A family run Edwardian residence standing in 1.5 acres of ground and situated off the main Fulford Road. Enjoy the comforts of en-suite rooms, colour TV, radio, direct dial telephone, tea and coffee facilities in all rooms. Excellent English and Continental breakfasts. Fully double glazed, gas central heating and a large car park with security lighting. Only 5 minutes walk from Fulford Golf Course and close to the University.

Please call Elizabeth or Bert for reservations.

Access · VISA

ARNDALE HOTEL

AA QQQQQ Premier Selected

Highly Commended

290 Tadcaster Road, York YO2 2ET
Telephone: (01904) 702424

David and Gillian Reynard warmly welcome you to their delightful award winning Victorian Hotel directly overlooking York's famous racecours beautiful enclosed walled gardens giving a country house atmosphere within the City.

Spacious elegant lounge complete with an abundance of antiques, fresh flowers and paintings. Beautiful antique half-tester/four-poster beds. Modern whirlpool baths. Quality English Breakfast.

Large enclosed walled car park.

Q Q Q **The Beckett** 58 Bootham Crescent YO30 7AH
(take A64 for York turn onto A1237 York ring road, turn onto A19 past traffic lights at Clifton take 3rd turn on right into Bootham Cres)
☎ 01904 644728
The Beckett is situated in a side road only a short walk from the city and offers well equipped bedrooms together with a comfortable guests' lounge. A Yorkshire breakfast is served in the cosy dining room and the friendly resident owners are always helpful.
7 rms (5 shr) (2 fmly) No smoking in 2 bedrooms No smoking in dining room CTV in all bedrooms Tea and coffee making facilities No dogs (ex guide dogs) Cen ht CTV 3P
ROOMS: s £18-£20; d £38-£46; wkly b&b £140-£154*
CARDS:

Q Q Q **Bedford** 108/110 Bootham YO30 7DG
(a few hundred yards N of the Minster)
☎ 01904 624412 FAX 01904 632851
Recognised by its Tudor façade, the Bedford is well maintained throughout and offers spacious bedrooms with modern amenities. Also provided is a residents' bar, a separate lounge and an attractive dining room, where freshly prepared meals are served.
17 bth/shr (5 fmly) No smoking in dining room CTV in all bedrooms Tea and coffee making facilities No dogs (ex guide dogs) Licensed Cen ht CTV 17P No coaches Last d 6.30pm
ROOMS: s £30-£40; d £46-£60*
CARDS:

Q Q Q **Beech House** 6-7 Longfield Ter, Bootham YO03 7DJ
(from A64, A1237, A19, follow city centre signs for 1.5m, under pedestrian flyover, second right into Bootham Terr which leads into Longfield Terr)
☎ 01904 634581 & 630951
Closed Dec-Jan
The combination of two adjoining terraced houses, this guest house has cheerfully decorated public rooms, which include a cosy lounge and attractive dining room, whilst bedrooms are bright and well equipped.
10 bth/shr No smoking in dining room No smoking in lounges CTV in all bedrooms Tea and coffee making facilities Direct dial from bedrooms No dogs Cen ht No children 10yrs 5P No coaches
ROOMS: s £27-£30; d £46-£52*

Q Q Q ***Bloomsbury Hotel*** 127 Clifton YO30 6BL
(from by-pass take A19 to city centre and Clifton, hotel in 1m on right opposite Parish Church)
☎ 01904 634031
This very well furnished hotel is close to Clifton Green and only a short walk from the city. It is family owned and run and offers delightfully furnished bedrooms and both the lounge and dining room are equally inviting and comfortable. There is a car park to the rear.
8 shr (3 fmly) No smoking CTV in all bedrooms Tea and coffee making facilities No dogs (ex guide dogs) Cen ht 10P Last d noon
CARDS:

Q Q Q **Bootham** 56 Bootham Crescent YO30 7AH
(off A19, N of city centre) ☎ 01904 672123
Situated in a side road and within walking distance of the city, this friendly guest house has been well furnished and provides good comforts. There is a cosy lounge which is combined with the attractive dining room.
7 rms (5 shr) (1 fmly) No smoking in bedrooms No smoking in dining room CTV in all bedrooms Tea and coffee making facilities No dogs Cen ht CTV 5P No coaches
ROOMS: s £18-£25; d £40-£45*

Q Q Q **Bootham Bar Hotel** 4 High Petergate YO1 7EH
(100yds from Minster) ☎ 01904 658516
Situated in a narrow lane just within the city walls, and having the advantage of its own coffee shop and restaurant attached, this friendly house offers bedrooms which are attractively furnished and well equipped. Secure parking can be arranged by prior notice.

14 rms (11 bth/shr) (3 fmly) No smoking in 3 bedrooms No smoking in area of dining room CTV in all bedrooms Tea and coffee making facilities No dogs (ex guide dogs) Licensed Cen ht 6P No coaches Gardens
ROOMS: s £20-£23; d £40-£70
CARDS:

See advertisement on p.489.

Q Q **Brontë House** 22 Grosvenor Ter, Bootham YO30 7AG
(from A19 north follow signs for city centre, take left turn immediately after Churchill Hotel into Grosvenor terrace, house is along the road)
☎ 01904 621066 FAX 01904 653434
Closed 23-29 Dec
This small hotel is set in the centre of an imposing Victorian terrace of town houses and is within reasonable walking distance of the town centre. A delightful lounge is available together with a very attractive dining room where breakfast and pre-arranged dinners are served. The bedrooms, all en suite, are pleasantly furnished with good facilities. Service is very friendly from the resident owners Peter and Margot Chalkley.
6 rms (4 shr) (2 fmly) No smoking in dining room No smoking in lounges CTV in all bedrooms Tea and coffee making facilities No dogs (ex guide dogs) Cen ht 2P No coaches
ROOMS: s £17-£22; d £34-£50; wkly b&b £112-£644*
CARDS:

Q Q Q **Burton Villa** 22 Haxby Rd YO31 8JX (take ring road A1237, leave on B1363, pass hospital then sharp left)
☎ 01904 626364 FAX 01904 626364
Situated on a corner this house is within easy walking distance of the city and has the benefit of a rear car park. The bedrooms are attractively decorated and well furnished and hearty breakfasts are served in two dining rooms. Service is friendly and helpful.
11 rms (1 bth 7 shr) (3 fmly) No smoking in dining room CTV in all bedrooms Tea and coffee making facilities Cen ht 7P
ROOMS: s £17.50-£25; d £34-£52*
CARDS:

See page 14-20 for a list of Premier Selected establishments

Q Q **Carousel** 83 Eldon St, Stanley St, Haxby Rd YO31 7NH
☎ 01904 646709
Standing in a quiet side road and only a short walk from the city this one time dairy is a now a cosy guest house that has recently undergone extensive refurbishment and now provides modern style accommodation. Breakfast is served in a pleasant and lofty dining room.
7 shr (2 fmly) No smoking in dining room No smoking in lounges CTV in all bedrooms Tea and coffee making facilities No dogs Licensed Cen ht CTV No children 4yrs 4P
ROOMS: s £20-£25; d £40-£50

Q Q Q ***Cavalier Private Hotel*** 39 Monkgate YO31 7PB
(situated on the A1036 (A64) York to Malton Road, 250mtrs from York Inner Ring road and City Wall (Monkgate))
☎ 01904 636615 FAX 01904 636615
Conveniently located within easy walking distance of the city, this well cared for hotel provides modern and well equipped bedrooms. There is a cosy lounge and attentive and knowledgeable service is provided by the resident owner.
10 rms (2 bth 5 shr) (4 fmly) No smoking in dining room CTV in all bedrooms Tea and coffee making facilities No dogs (ex guide dogs) Licensed Cen ht CTV 6P No coaches Sauna
CARDS:

Q Q Q **City** 68 Monkgate YO31 7PF (from A1 take A64 to York, at rdbt take A1036 to York in 2.5m blue sign on left) ☎ 01904 622483
Situated within easy walking distance of the city, this well cared for guest house offers a cosy lounge together with fresh, bright and well equipped bedrooms. Friendly service is provided by the resident owner.
7 rms (1 bth 5 shr) (2 fmly) No smoking CTV in all bedrooms Tea and coffee making facilities No dogs Cen ht No children 3years 5P No coaches
ROOMS: s £16-£24; d £28-£48
CARDS:
See advertisement on p.491.

Cornmill Lodge 120 Haxby Rd YO31 8JP (York Dist Hops is on B1363. We are 500 yds to the East on Haxby Rd) ☎ 01904 620566
Closed Nov-Feb
Situated just a ten minute walk away from the city, this attractive guest house provides comfortable, well furnished andf thoughtfully equipped bedrooms. Hearty breakfasts are served in the cosy dining room and there is car parking to the rear of the house.
5 rms (3 shr) (1 fmly) No smoking CTV in all bedrooms Tea and coffee making facilities No dogs (ex guide dogs) Cen ht CTV No children 6yrs 4P No coaches
ROOMS: s £18-£22; d £34-£45

Crescent 77 Bootham YO30 7DQ (approach city on A19 city centre road, hotel 5mins for centre) ☎ 01904 623216 FAX 01904 623216
Positioned a short walk from the walls of the city, this guest house offers bedrooms with thoughtfully provided extra facilities. Breakfast is taken in the small first floor dining room and the lounge offers comfy seating on the quieter, lower ground floor.
10 rms (8 bth/shr) (5 fmly) No smoking in dining room CTV in all bedrooms Tea and coffee making facilities Direct dial from bedrooms No dogs Licensed Cen ht CTV 4P
ROOMS: s £18.50-£28; d £37-£56; wkly b&b £126-£182*
CARDS:

Cumbria House 2 Vyner St, Haxby Rd YO31 8HS (take ring road A1247, leave on B1363, past hospital, sharp left at traffic lights) ☎ 01904 636817
Cumbria House, conveniently situated within a ten minute walk of the city, is extremely well furnished and provides pretty bedrooms with a good range of equipment. A Yorkshire breakfast is served in the bright and attractive dining room and service is warm and friendly.
5 rms (2 shr) (2 fmly) No smoking in dining room No smoking in lounges CTV in all bedrooms Tea and coffee making facilities No dogs (ex guide dogs) Licensed Cen ht No children 4years 5P No coaches
ROOMS: s £18-£25; d £34-£45; wkly b&b £119-£140*
CARDS:

Selected

Curzon Lodge and Stable Cottages 23 Tadcaster Rd, Dringhouses YO24 1QG (from A64 take the A1036 towards the city centre, 2m on the right twixt Post House and Swallow Hotel) ☎ 01904 703157
Closed 24-26 Dec
This detached 17th-century house, with well tended gardens, is situated close to the racecourse. The comfortable bedrooms are in either the main house or the converted stable block, and are all well furnished with antique stripped pine pieces. Breakfast is served in the cosy dining room and there is also an inviting lounge. The service is very friendly and attentive.
5 bth/shr 5 annexe bth/shr (1 fmly) No smoking CTV in all bedrooms Tea and coffee making facilities No dogs Cen ht No children 7yrs 16P No coaches
ROOMS: s £39-£49; d £55-£75*
CARDS: See advertisement on p.491.

Selected

Four Seasons Hotel 7 St Peters Grove, Bootham YO30 6AQ (leave Ring Rd (A1237) at A19 signed York Centre. After 2m St Peter's Grove on left by pedestrian bridge)
☎ 01904 622621 FAX 01904 620976
Closed 24-26 Dec-Jan
This spacious and attractive house has been comfortably furnished and stands in a leafy side road that is within easy walking distance of the city centre. A spacious and comfortable lounge is provided and the bedrooms are all well equipped. Guests can expect attentive and friendly service.
5 bth/shr (2 fmly) No smoking CTV in all bedrooms Tea and coffee making facilities Licensed Cen ht CTV 8P No coaches
ROOMS: d £56-£62*
CARDS:

Galtres Lodge Hotel 54 Low Petergate YO1 7HZ (from ring road take A1036 into city via Heworth Green and Monkgate)
☎ 01904 622478 FAX 01904 627804
Galtres Lodge is a fine Georgian building standing in the heart of the city, that is not only a small hotel but a restaurant open to non residents. The bedrooms, one with four-poster and two having half-tester beds, are attractive and freshly decorated. A good range of well prepared food is available in the attractive restaurant.
12 rms (5 shr) No smoking CTV in all bedrooms Tea and coffee making facilities No dogs (ex guide dogs) Licensed Cen ht No children 14yrs 9P Last d 9.30pm
ROOMS: s £25-£30; d £50-£75*
CARDS:

Georgian 35 Bootham YO30 7BT
(A19 into York centre, then into Bootham, premises on left just before Bootham Bar) ☎ 01904 622874 FAX 01904 635379
Parts of this family owned and run guest house date back to 1668, and it is an easy two minute walk to the city and the Minster. The accommodation is pleasant and the present owners are carrying out continual improvements.
14 rms (9 bth/shr) (1 fmly) No smoking CTV in all bedrooms Tea and coffee making facilities No dogs (ex guide dogs) Cen ht 8P
ROOMS: s £20-£35; d £32-£50*
CARDS:

Selected

Grasmead House Hotel 1 Scarcroft Hill, The Mount YO24 1DF (follow York West signs into city and after Racecourse cross at traffic lights and immediately turn right)
☎ 01904 629996 FAX 01904 629996
Just a short walk from the city centre, this 19th-century house offers individually styled bedrooms, each with an antique four-poster bed. All
contd. on p.490.

are well equipped and it is clear that the comfort of guests is a priority. The house is tastefully decorated with many period features retained. A comfortable bar lounge offers a place to relax with deep sofas and a substantial freshly-cooked breakfast is served in the comfortable dining room.
5 bth/shr (1 fmly) No smoking in bedrooms No smoking in dining room CTV in all bedrooms Tea and coffee making facilities No dogs (ex guide dogs) Licensed Cen ht CTV 1P No coaches
ROOMS: d £60-£70*
CARDS:

Q Q **Greenside** 124 Clifton YO30 6BQ (approach city centre on A19 N and at traffic lights straight on for Greenside on the left opposite Clifton Green) ☎ 01904 623631
Standing overlooking Clifton Green, this attractive detached house is within easy walking distance of the city. It provides pleasantly furnished bedrooms together with a cosy lounge and a nicely furnished dining room where a hearty breakfast is served.
6 rms (3 shr) (2 fmly) No smoking in dining room No smoking in lounges CTV in all bedrooms Tea and coffee making facilities Licensed Cen ht CTV ch fac 6P Garden & Children's play area Last d 6pm
ROOMS: s fr £18; d fr £30*

Selected

Q Q Q Q **Hazelwood** 24-25 Portland St, Gillygate YO31 7EH (approaching York from north on A19 turn left before City Gate and take 1st turning left) ☎ 01904 626548 FAX 01904 628032
Set in a quiet side road in the centre of York and only 400 yards from the Minster, Ian and Carolyn McNabb's Victorian house is being carefully refurbished. The breakfast room is graced with stylish fabrics and smart linen, and lounge offer lots of reading material and features a small kitchen area which guests are free to use. Bedrooms, all well equipped, come in a variety of sizes and include a choice of superior rooms.
14 bth/shr (2 fmly) No smoking CTV in all bedrooms Tea and coffee making facilities No dogs Licensed Cen ht No children 8yrs 11P No coaches
ROOMS: s £30-£55; d £48-£72
CARDS:

Selected

Q Q Q Q **The Heathers** 54 Shipton Rd, Clifton - Without YO30 6RQ (North of York on the A19 York/Thirsk road, mid-way between the A1237 ring road and York city centre)
☎ 01904 640989 FAX 01904 640989
Closed Xmas & Jan
The Heathers is a comfortable and welcoming establishment where the proprietors have designed each bedroom individually using quality fabrics to provide a feeling of luxury. Two of the rooms are conveniently situated on the ground floor. There is pleasant breakfast room that looks out onto well tended gardens. Heather and Graham Fisher operate this guest house with great pride and care.
8 rms (5 shr) (3 fmly) No smoking CTV in all bedrooms

Tea and coffee making facilities No dogs Cen ht No children 10yrs 9P
No coaches
ROOMS: s £30-£70; d £34-£90
CARDS:

Q Q Q ***Heworth*** 126 East Pde, Heworth YO31 7YG
(from Outer Ring Rd take East turning towards city centre and at traffic lights turn right into Melrose Gate then at next lights turn left)
☎ 01904 426384 FAX 01904 426384
This guest house is convenient for the city centre yet is located in a quiet residential area. Bedrooms are pleasantly decorated and offer thoughtful extra facilities. A freshly prepared breakfast is served at individual tables in the light and airy dining room. Friendly, hospitable service is provided by the resident owners.
6 rms (3 shr) No smoking in dining room No smoking in lounges CTV in all bedrooms Tea and coffee making facilities No dogs Cen ht 4P No coaches

Q Q Q **Hillcrest** 110 Bishopthorpe Rd YO23 1JX
(follow signs A1036 for city centre and take 1st right after Swallow Hotel and at T-junct turn left) ☎ 01904 653160 FAX 01904 656168
The house is conveniently situated for the city and racecourse and there is a park just a few minutes' walk away. The bedrooms are thoughtfully furnished and the guests' lounge offers a comfortable place to relax in. Breakfast is served in the tastefully decorated dining room.
13 rms (7 shr) (4 fmly) No smoking in 11 bedrooms No smoking in dining room No smoking in lounges CTV in all bedrooms Tea and coffee making facilities No dogs Cen ht CTV 8P Last d noon
ROOMS: s £16-£22; d £30-£46
CARDS:

Greenside

124 Clifton, York. Tel: York (01904) 623631
Martyn & Lynne Tattersall

Greenside is a charming detached conservation house fronting on to Clifton Green.
Situated in a most convenient location just outside the city walls, close to the many attractions that York has to offer.
Spacious fully equipped large bedrooms are all situated on ground or first floor, all have tea/coffee facilities, colour TV and central heating. En suite rooms available but there are also ample bath, shower and WC facilities. Enclosed car park. First class English breakfast and evening meals. Licensed. Fire certificate.
Winter Break Specials.
Registered with English Tourist Board.

Church Cottage

Family run, licensed private hotel on the A19 at Escrick, convenient for York & Selby. Standing in two acres of lawn and woodland, with large private car park. Local bus service available directly into York.
At Church Cottage we have first class en suite accommodation with tea & coffee making facilities and remote control TV in all rooms.

Contact: The Robinson Family, Church Cottage, Escrick, York YO19 6EX

Telephone: 01904 728462
Fax: 01904 728896

Yorkshire and Humberside Tourist Board

AA QQQ

Access · MasterCard · VISA · AMERICAN EXPRESS

Curzon Lodge & Stable Cottages

23 Tadcaster Road, Dringhouses, York, North Yorkshire YO24 1QG
Tel: 01904 703157

AA Selected QQQQ · **Highly Commended** · MEMBER Yorkshire and Humberside Tourist Board

A charming 17th century listed house and former stables, in a conservation area overlooking York Racecourse, once a home of the Terry 'chocolate' family. Stay in a unique atmosphere with antiques, beams, cottage style bedrooms, pretty lounge and hearty breakfasts in 'Farmhouse Kitchen' dining room. All rooms en-suite with colour TV and tea/coffee facilities. AA awards. Large car park within grounds. Please ask for our colour brochure.

City Guest House

5 minutes walk to York Minster

★ Central location ★ Private car park
★ En-suite rooms ★ B&B from £15

We are a small family-run B&B offering friendly helpful service at the heart of York

AA QQQ

68 Monkgate
York YO31 7PF
Tel: 01904 622483

VISA · MasterCard

COMMENDED

QQQ **The Hollies** 141 Falford Rd YO10 4HG
(situated on A19 approx 0.75m S of city centre) ☎ 01904 634279
This pleasantly furnished house provides well equipped bedrooms, one of which has a four poster bed. There is combined lounge and breakfast room and friendly service is offered by the resident owners.
4 rms (3 shr) (1 fmly) No smoking CTV in all bedrooms Tea and coffee making facilities No dogs (ex guide dogs) Cen ht 4P No coaches
ROOMS: d £32-£48*
CARDS:

QQQ **Holly Lodge** 204-206 Fulford Rd YO10 4DD
(located on the A19 Southside, 1.5 miles on the left from A64/A19 junct or follow A19 Selby signs from city centre to Fulford Rd)
☎ 01904 646005
Closed 24-27 Dec
This family owned and run Georgian house hotel is within easy walking distance of the city and is well furnished throughout. The bedrooms are well equipped and there is also a comfortable lounge complete with a grand piano and large television. Hearty breakfasts are served in the delightful dining room. There is a walled garden and parking is provided.
5 bth/shr (1 fmly) No smoking in dining room CTV in all bedrooms Tea and coffee making facilities No dogs (ex guide dogs) Cen ht CTV 6P No coaches
ROOMS: s £40-£60; d £48-£60*
CARDS:

Selected

QQQQ **Holmwood House Hotel** 114 Holgate Rd YO24 4BB
(on A59 Harrogate road on right 300yds past traffic lights at The Fox pub) ☎ 01904 626183 FAX 01904 670899
Holmwood House is set in an attractive row of substantial Victorian houses and is within easy walking distance of the city centre. Well equipped, richly decorated and pleasantly furnished bedrooms with many antiques are offered and there is also a cosy lounge provided for guests together with an 'honesty' bar. Lots of fresh flowers create a welcoming effect in the hall, and friendly and attentive service is provided by the resident owners. Breakfast is served in the pleasant lower ground floor dining room.

12 bth/shr (2 fmly) No smoking CTV in all bedrooms Tea and coffee making facilities Direct dial from bedrooms No dogs Licensed Cen ht No children 8yrs 8P No coaches
ROOMS: d £55-£75; wkly b&b £150-£250*
CARDS:

QQQ ***Linden Lodge Hotel*** Nunthorpe Av, Scarcroft Rd YO23 1PF
☎ 01904 620107 FAX 01904 620985
Closed 24-28 Dec
Warm and friendly service is provided by Mr & Mrs Wharton at this well furnished and comfortable house. It is situated in a quiet side road that is only a short walk from the city. The bedrooms are well equipped and there is a cosy and comfortable lounge provided for guests.
12 rms (9 shr) (2 fmly) No smoking in bedrooms No smoking in dining room CTV in all bedrooms Tea and coffee making facilities No dogs Licensed Cen ht CTV
CARDS:

Selected

QQQQ **Midway House Hotel** 145 Fulford Rd YO10 4HG
(Midway House is 1m S of city centre on A19 just beyond Broadway Junction and the 'Gimcrack' public house)
☎ 01904 659272 FAX 01904 659272
Well presented throughout, this Victorian house offers comfortable accommodation in well equipped bedrooms, two of which are situated on the ground floor. There is a cosy lounge and breakfast is served in the attractive dining room. Dinner is also available by prior arrangement.
12 rms (11 shr) (2 fmly) No smoking CTV in all bedrooms Tea and coffee making facilities No dogs (ex guide dogs) Licensed Cen ht 14P Last d 7pm
ROOMS: s £20-£40; d £32-£58; wkly b&b £135-£260; wkly hlf-bd £205-£330*
CARDS:

QQQ **Minster View** 2 Grosvenor Ter YO30 7AG (turn off A64 onto Clifton Moor, head towards York on the Bootham Rd, turn left at Churchills Hotel, premises on left) ☎ 01904 655034
This well proportioned, Victorian guest house lies in a terraced row close to the city centre. Bedrooms are of good size with several suitable for families. Breakfast is taken in the attractive dining room on tables laid with lace tablecloths.
7 rms (5 bth/shr) (4 fmly) No smoking in dining room No smoking in lounges CTV in all bedrooms Tea and coffee making facilities Direct dial from bedrooms Licensed Cen ht CTV 6P Last d 10am
ROOMS: s £15-£19; d £30-£44; wkly b&b £105-£133; wkly hlf-bd £210-£238

QQQ ***Moat Hotel*** Nunnery Ln YO23 1AA ☎ 01904 652926 FAX 01904 652926
This family owned and run hotel is well situated beside the city walls and has the advantage of its own car parking. The well equipped bedrooms, some with half-tester beds, are bright and fresh. This is a non-smoking establishment.
8 bth/shr (1 fmly) No smoking CTV in all bedrooms Tea and coffee making facilities No dogs (ex guide dogs) Licensed Cen ht CTV 10P No coaches Fishing
CARDS:

Selected

QQQQ **Nunmill House** 85 Bishopthorpe Rd YO23 1NX (400yds outside City Wall at SE corner) ☎ 01904 634047 FAX 01904 655879
Closed Dec-Jan
An elegant Victorian house standing in an elevated position with a pleasant well tended front garden. The house has been carefully furnished by the present owners and includes a comfortable and inviting lounge and a cosy dining room where good hearty breakfasts are served. Bedrooms have been individually furnished, are no-smoking and have been thoughtfully equipped. Parking permits are available for guests.
8 bth/shr (1 fmly) No smoking CTV in all bedrooms Tea and coffee making facilities No dogs Cen ht CTV 4P No coaches
ROOMS: d £44-£52* See advertisement on p.495.

QQQ **Orchard Court Hotel** 4 St Peters Grove YO30 6AQ ☎ 01904 653964 FAX 01904 653964
An attractive and well cared for Victorian house standing in a quiet side road and is within walking distance of the city. There is a pleasant residents' lounge plus a separate bar. Bedrooms are modern in style and are well equipped to include all of today's needs. The service from Mr & Mrs Noble is both friendly and attentive.
14 rms (11 bth/shr) (4 fmly) No smoking in 8 bedrooms No smoking in dining room CTV in all bedrooms Tea and coffee making facilities No dogs (ex guide dogs) Licensed Cen ht CTV 14P No coaches Last d 6pm
ROOMS: s £25-£35; d £50-£65
CARDS: See advertisement on p.495.

Selected

Priory Hotel 126 Fulford Rd YO10 4BE
(On A19, on S side of city) ☎ 01904 625280 FAX 01904 625280
Closed Xmas
Ancient stone archways lead through the quiet gardens of this town hotel toward the reception rooms, which extend to a dining room, lounge and cosy bar. These rooms are decorated to complement the period of the house whilst bedrooms are more modern with colour TV. Dinner is served in the restaurant.
20 bth/shr (5 fmly) CTV in all bedrooms Tea and coffee making facilities No dogs (ex guide dogs) Licensed Cen ht CTV 25P Last d 9.15pm
ROOMS: s £35-£45; d £48-£50*
CARDS:

Riverside Walk 8 & 9 Earlsborough Ter, Marygate YO30 7BQ
(A19 Bootham, turn right after stone tower onto Marygate. Right before 'Bay Horse' and 1st left) ☎ 01904 620769 FAX 01904 646249
Delightfully situated just a short walk from the city this small and very friendly hotel benefits from a riverside location. The charming patio area to the front features many colourful flowers tubs in season. Bedrooms are thoughtfully equipped, some with ceiling fans. There is a small comfortable sitting area. There are several good restaurants nearby.
10 rms (8 bth/shr) (1 fmly) No smoking CTV in all bedrooms Tea and coffee making facilities No dogs (ex guide dogs) Licensed Cen ht 10P No coaches Last d noon
ROOMS: s £24-£30; d £40-£52; wkly b&b £105-£128.34*
CARDS:

Selected

St Denys Hotel St Denys Rd YO1 9QD
(turn off A1079 York/Hull straight on for approx 2.5m, through Walmgate Bar, then left after 200yds, left again to house opposite St Denys Church) ☎ 01904 622207 FAX 01904 624800
Closed 2 wks Xmas
This former vicarage is very close to the city centre and the en suite bedrooms have recently been updated with new pine furniture. There is a cosy lounge with a bar and pool table and the hotel has its own car park. There are plans to extend the lounges in the near future.
10 bth/shr (4 fmly) No smoking in 2 bedrooms No smoking in dining room CTV in all bedrooms Tea and coffee making facilities Direct dial from bedrooms Licensed Cen ht CTV 9P Last d noon
CARDS:

St Georges House Hotel 6 St Georges Place, Tadcaster Rd YO24 1DR (from A64 take A1036, as the racecourse finishes, St Georges Place is on the left)
☎ 01904 625056 FAX 01904 625009
This well furnished, family-owned and run hotel is within walking distance of the city and is also very convenient for the racecourse. Bedrooms are well equipped and have been pleasantly furnished and decorated and there is a cosy lounge and a delightful dining room where a good standard of home cooking is available.
10 bth/shr (5 fmly) No smoking in dining room CTV in all bedrooms Tea and coffee making facilities Licensed Cen ht 7P No coaches Last d 7pm
ROOMS: s £30-£55; d £45-£55*
CARDS:

St Raphael 44 Queen Anne's Rd, Bootham YO30 7AF
(A19 north road to City Centre)
☎ 01904 645028 FAX 01904 658788
Standing in a quiet side road and close to the city and the Minster this family owned and run guest house offers good comforts. The house is pleasantly furnished and offers well equipped bedrooms together with friendly and personal service from the resident owners.
8 rms (5 shr) (1 fmly) No smoking in dining room CTV in all bedrooms Tea and coffee making facilities Cen ht 2P No coaches
ROOMS: s £17-£25; d £34-£44*
CARDS:

Sycamore 19 Sycamore Place, Bootham YO30 7DW
(approach from A19 and at Churchill Hotel turn right into Bootham Terrace then in 200yds turn right)
☎ 01904 624712 FAX 01904 624712
Closed 19-27 Dec
This very pleasantly furnished house with an attractive front garden is within easy walking distance of the city and is family owned and run. The homely bedrooms are attractively decorated and well equipped and the dining room is also pleasingly furnished. There is no lounge but guests have access to the bedrooms at all times.
7 rms (3 shr) (1 fmly) No smoking CTV in all bedrooms Tea and coffee making facilities No dogs Cen ht No children 8yrs 2P No coaches n
ROOMS: s £18-£25; d £32-£42

Tower 2 Feversham Crescent, Wigginton Rd YO31 7HQ
(on B1363 adjacent to district hospital)
☎ 01904 655571 & 635924
This corner situated house is well furnished and provides attractive and comfortable bedrooms. Service is both friendly and attentive from the resident owners and a good hearty breakfast is served in the cosy dining room. The house has its own car park and is within walking distance of the city centre.
6 bth/shr (2 fmly) No smoking CTV in all bedrooms Tea and coffee making facilities No dogs (ex guide dogs) Cen ht 7P No coaches Last d noon
ROOMS: s £32-£36; d £40-£44; wkly hlf-bd £210-£230*
CARDS:

THE INN ON THE RIVER

A 17th century coaching inn on the banks of the River Ouse, about a mile from York Racecourse and 3½ miles from York city centre. The Ship offers 8 bedrooms with private facilities, including one four poster bedded room. Guests can dine by candlelight in the cottage style restaurant or enjoy a drink by a roaring log fire in the original old bar. The Inn's garden, with its array of floral tubs and window boxes, affords attractive river views. Car parking is no problem or you may arrive by boat and make use of the Inn's private moorings.
The Inn now boasts a seventy seat conservatory.

Ship Inn, Acaster Malbis, York.
Tel: York (01904) 705609/703888

NUNMILL HOUSE

85 Bishopthorpe Road, York, YO23 1NX

AA QQQQ

Tel: 01904 634047
Fax: 01904 655879

English Tourist Board HIGHLY COMMENDED

Nunmill House is an elegant Victorian residence lovingly restored to enhance the original architectural features now offers Bed and Breakfast and the benefit of an easy walk to all of York's historic attractions. Each bedroom, individually furnished and smoke-free is for those are looking for a comfortable yet affordable accommodation and also includes complimentary tea/coffee facilities, colour television, etc. Nunmill is a non smoking hotel.

The Priory Hotel, York

The Priory offers comfortable accommodation with full English breakfast, and is situated 600 yards south of York's medieval city walls, within easy direct reach of the nearby inner and outer ring roads. The city centre can be reached by a pleasant riverside walk.
The 20 bedrooms, all equipped with colour TV and tea/coffee making facilities, include single, double and family accommodation, all with en suite shower and toilet facilities.
The hotel is AA listed, and has full central heating, a licensed bar and restaurant. The pleasant garden leads to the large private car-park.
Reductions are available for children sharing accommodation with their parents. Please send for brochure and tariff.
Proprietors: George and Barbara Jackson
The Priory Hotel, Fulford Road, York YO1 4BE
Telephone York (01904) 625280

ORCHARD COURT HOTEL

A delightful small Victorian Hotel with **private car park.** Pleasantly situated in a **quiet location**, within easy walking distance of the city centre.

Comfortable, centrally heated en-suite bedrooms all with colour TVs, radios & complimentary tea/coffee trays. A friendly, family run hotel with a relaxed atmosphere, offering full English breakfast & traditional home-cooked evening meals.

St Peter's Grove · Bootham · York · YO3 6AQ
Tel/Fax (01904) 653964

Q Q **Tree Tops** 21 St Marys, Bootham YO30 7DD (from A1237 follow signs towards York, straight on at Clifton Green lights & under pedestrian footbridge. St Marys is 3rd road on right) ☎ 01904 658053
Situated in a quiet side road and with parking to the rear, this friendly guest house is pleasantly furnished. The bedrooms are well equipped and a hearty breakfast is served in the pleasant dining room. The house is within easy walking distance of the city.
9 rms (5 shr) No smoking CTV in 17 bedrooms Tea and coffee making facilities No dogs Cen ht No children 7P No coaches
ROOMS: s £18-£25; d £36-£48*

Q Q Q **Turnberry House** 143 Fulford Rd YO10 4HG (Fulford Road is on the A19 York to Selby road, linked to the A1 by the A64 Leeds to Scarborough road) ☎ 01904 658435
Closed 25 Dec
Well maintained throughout and offering friendly and attentive service, this Edwardian house provides good sized bedrooms suitable for family use. There is an attractive dining room featuring the fireplace that housed the original range.
4 shr (2 fmly) No smoking CTV in all bedrooms Tea and coffee making facilities No dogs (ex guide dogs) Cen ht No children 5yrs 6P

CHANNEL ISLANDS Map 16

ALDERNEY Map 16

Selected

Q Q Q Q ***The Georgian House*** Victoria St, St Anne GY ☎ 01481 822471 FAX 01481 822471
A bustling bar and popular restaurant occupy the ground floor of this Georgian house, and in summer there is an outdoor bar at the rear and a barbeque at weekends. Bedrooms consist of one neat, well-equipped single room and a suite that extends the full depth of the building with a little balcony overlooking the garden. There is a small residents' lounge and a first floor breakfast room.
3 bth/shr (1 fmly) CTV in all bedrooms Tea and coffee making facilities Direct dial from bedrooms No dogs (ex guide dogs) Cen ht CTV No children 8yrs Last d 9.30pm
CARDS:

GUERNSEY Map 16

ST PETER PORT

Selected

Q Q Q Q **Farnborough Hotel** Les Damouettes Ln GY1 1ZN (left at Fermain Tavern) ☎ 01481 37756 FAX 01481 34082
Apr-Sep
This delightful small hotel, peacefully situated away from the main road and within walking distance of Fermain Bay, is personally run by the friendly proprietor. The double-glazed bedrooms are furnished in a modern style; some are larger than others and many overlook the rear garden. The two attractive lounges, one reserved for non-smokers, are comfortably furnished and there is also a cosy bar and a tastefully appointed breakfast room.
11 shr No smoking in dining room CTV in all bedrooms Tea and coffee making facilities Direct dial from bedrooms No dogs Licensed Cen ht CTV No children 12yrs 11P No coaches
ROOMS: s £28-£35; d £46-£60; wkly b&b £161-£210*
CARDS:

Q Q Q **Marine Hotel** Well Rd GY1 1WS (situated just off Glatengy Esplanade, opposite Queen Elizabeth II Marina) ☎ 01481 724978 FAX 01481 711729
This family-run hotel, situated 30 metres from the sea-front and the Queen Elizabeth II Marina, and a few minutes' walk from the centre of St Peter Port, offers well equipped bedrooms and a comfortable lounge. There is an attractive sun terrace which boasts the island's only functioning red telephone box, and breakfast is served in a smart dining room. Evening meals can be taken at one of the many eating places close by.
11 bth/shr (3 fmly) No smoking in dining room No smoking in lounges Tea and coffee making facilities No dogs (ex guide dogs) Cen ht CTV No coaches
ROOMS: s £16.50-£26.50; d £32-£49; wkly b&b £112-£168
CARDS:

Premier Selected

Q Q Q Q Q **Midhurst House** Candie Rd GY1 1OP (adjacent to Candie Gardens) ☎ 01481 724391 FAX 01481 729451
Etr-mid Oct
This well established, elegant Regency house enjoys a central location just five minutes' walk from the harbour and the town centre. Personally run by friendly owners Brian and Jan Goodenough who provide a warm welcome to all their guests. The bedrooms are all individual in style, well equipped and feature many thoughtful touches such as fresh flowers and mineral water. Day rooms include a comfortable lounge, lit by an unusual octagonal skylight, that looks out on to a very pretty walled garden. Guests can sample Brian's cooking, based on market-fresh ingredients, in the elegant dining room.
5 bth/shr 1 annexe shr (1 fmly) No smoking in dining room CTV in all bedrooms Tea and coffee making facilities Direct dial from bedrooms No dogs Licensed Cen ht No children 8yrs 1P No coaches Last d 6.45pm
ROOMS: d £52-£78; wkly b&b £182-£273; wkly hlf-bd £259-£350*
CARDS:

JERSEY Map 16

GREVE DE LECQ BAY

Selected

Q Q Q Q **Hotel Des Pierres** JE3 2DT (on B65 near beach) ☎ 01534 481858 FAX 01534 485273
Closed 15 Dec-15 Jan
From its elevated position overlooking the beautiful north coast bay of Greve de Lecq, this small, family-run hotel is just a few minutes walk from the sandy beaches. Bedrooms which offer either sea or country views, are neatly presented with comfortable furnishings and modern facilities throughout. In addition to a small, colourfully-furnished lounge there is a split level bar and dining room where the daily-changing dinner menu offers a good choice, especially for vegetarians.

16 bth/shr (4 fmly) No smoking in bedrooms No smoking in dining room No smoking in lounges CTV in all bedrooms Tea and coffee making facilities No dogs Licensed Cen ht CTV 13P Gymnasium cycling, walking Last d 8pm
CARDS:

GROUVILLE

Selected

Q Q Q Q Lavender Villa Hotel Rue A Don JE3 9DX (approx 3m from St Helier on East Coast Road just off A3)
☎ 01534 854937 FAX 01534 856147
mid Mar-early Nov
Personally run by friendly owners Janine and Tony Davies, Lavender Villa enjoys a splendid location overlooking the famous Royal Jersey Golf Course. All bedrooms are en suite and tastefully decorated in a variety of soft colour schemes. Public areas include a beamed dining room, comfortable lounge and cosy bar. Guests can also enjoy the hotel's outdoor swimming pool.
21 bth/shr (3 fmly) No smoking in dining room No smoking in lounges CTV in all bedrooms Tea and coffee making facilities No dogs Licensed Cen ht CTV No children 3yrs 20P No coaches Outdoor swimming pool Last d 7.45pm
CARDS:

ST AUBIN

Q Q Q Bryn-y-Mor Private Hotel Route de la Haule, St Aubins Bay JE3 8BA (on A1, overlooking St Aubin's Bay)
☎ 01534 20295 FAX 01534 24262
A substantial Victorian house overlooking St Aubin's Bay, this small hotel offers traditionally furnished, particularly well-equipped bedrooms. There is a bar area attached to the wood-panelled dining room where a good choice of evening meals is accompanied by a substantial wine list. Lunches are served on request and light refreshments are available throughout the day. Fronted by pleasant gardens, the hotel also provides off-road parking.
13 rms (11 bth/shr) (4 fmly) No smoking in dining room CTV in all bedrooms Tea and coffee making facilities Direct dial from bedrooms Licensed CTV ch fac 6P No coaches Last d 8.00pm
ROOMS: s £20-£32; d fr £40; wkly b&b £140-£224; wkly hlf-bd £175-£259*
CARDS:

Selected

Q Q Q Q The Panorama La Rue du Crocquet JE3 8BZ
☎ 01534 742429 FAX 01534 745940
Mid Mar-Mid Dec
An attractive property standing in a peaceful elevated position with beautiful views over St Aubin Bay. Owners John and Jill Squires provide a warm welcome to all their guests. Stylishly decorated bedrooms, many with sea views, boast a host of facilities including mini-fridge, microwave (dinners are not available), 20-channel TV and bathrobes. Tea is a big thing here, with a fascinating collection of over 400 tea pots, and several times a week Jill's home-baked cream teas are available either in the tea-room or on the grassed terrace.
17 bth/shr No smoking in 4 bedrooms No smoking in dining room No smoking in lounges CTV in all bedrooms Tea and coffee making facilities No dogs Cen ht No children 12yrs No coaches Tea garden
ROOMS: s £23-£45; d £46-£78; wkly b&b £163-£210*
CARDS:

Selected

Q Q Q Q Peterborough House La Rue Du Croquet JE3 8BZ (from St Helier turn right (sign Red Houses) 400mtrs before St Aubin, take 1st left and follow road until cobbles, located on left)
☎ 01534 41568 FAX 01534 46787
Mar-Oct Closed Nov-Feb
Dating back to 1690 this well presented guest house still retains some of the original features such as the oak beams. Friendly new owner Fernando Cabral offers a warm welcome to all guests. Bedrooms are tastefully decorated and comfortably furnished with solid pine furniture throughout. There is a cosy, downstairs dining room, two comfortable lounges, one for non-smokers, and a small terrace overlooking the bay.
14 rms (12 shr) No smoking in bedrooms No smoking in dining room No smoking in 1 lounge CTV in all bedrooms Tea and coffee making facilities No dogs Licensed Cen ht CTV No children 12yrs No coaches
ROOMS: s £23.50-£31; d £37-£52; wkly b&b £129.50-£217*
CARDS:

ST CLEMENT

Selected

Q Q Q Q Bon Air Hotel Coast Rd, Pontac JE2 6SE
☎ 01534 855324 FAX 01534 857801
Mar-Oct
Resident proprietors John and Frances Hutton provide a warm welcome to all their guests, at this attractive small hotel. There is a well-furnished and comfortable lounge that includes a no smoking area, a convivial bar with plush banquette seating and a beamed dining room. Other facilities include a games room and a covered, heated swimming pool that opens onto a sun patio. Bedrooms, four with balconies, are well-equipped and, although varying in size and shape, identically furnished and decorated.
18 bth/shr (3 fmly) No smoking in dining room No smoking in lounges CTV in all bedrooms Tea and coffee making facilities No dogs (ex guide dogs) Licensed Cen ht CTV 20P No coaches Indoor swimming pool (heated) Games room Last d 7.20pm
ROOMS: d £44-£70*

Q Q Q ***Les Grandes Vagues*** Pontac JE2 6SE (on A4)
☎ 01534 51198 FAX 01534 856120
15 Jan-15 Dec
Based on a traditional Jersey farmhouse dating back to 1825, Les Grandes Vagues has been well modernised and extended by Brian and Ruth Styles to create a comfortable and appealing small hotel. Bedrooms are light and airy and well equipped. Day rooms include a well-stocked bar and separate lounge near the reception area. The menu for the home-cooked set dinner is displayed at breakfast time in case an alternative to that night's main dish is required. The hotel is close to the beach and has ample parking.
12 rms (10 bth/shr) (2 fmly) No smoking in dining room CTV in all bedrooms Tea and coffee making facilities Licensed Cen ht CTV No children 4yrs 18P No coaches Garden with table tennis & snooker Last d 11am
CARDS:

ST HELIER

Q Q Q *Cliff Court Hotel* St Andrews Rd, First Tower JE2 3JG
☎ 01534 34919 FAX 01534 66715
Mar-Oct
From its elevated position in the First Tower area to the west of town, this family-run hotel offers generally good-sized bedrooms that are all en suite. Spacious public rooms include a bar with pool table, comfortable red plush lounge area plus a separate TV lounge. The hotel also offers a small outdoor pool and a sun-trap patio.
17 bth/shr (3 fmly) No smoking in area of dining room Tea and coffee making facilities No dogs (ex guide dogs) Licensed Cen ht CTV 14P No coaches Outdoor swimming pool (heated) Last d 7.30pm
CARDS:

Selected

Q Q Q Q **Domino Central** Rue Du Val Vauxhall JE2 4TJ (from harbour take ring rd,right at traffic lights into New St, pass St Thomases Church turn left into Rue du Val Vauxhall,hotel first on left) ☎ 01534 30360 FAX 01534 31546
Closed 11 Dec-19 Feb
Roger and Mary Lishman's well-kept, licensed establishment is in a quiet street near the centre of town. A comfortable and appealing lounge, generously provided with fresh flowers, is at the heart of the day rooms while bedrooms are bright and neatly furnished. Breakfast includes such treats as brioche and toasted tea cakes in addition to a traditional cooked meal. Dinners are not provided but the menus of local restaurants are available to help guests make an informed choice.
13 rms (11 bth/shr) No smoking in dining room CTV in all bedrooms Tea and coffee making facilities No dogs (ex guide dogs) Licensed Cen ht CTV No children 12yrs
ROOMS: s £25-£40; d £40-£60; wkly b&b £140-£210*
CARDS:

Selected

Q Q Q Q **Gloster House** Gloster Ter, Rouge Bou Illon JE2 3ZA
☎ 01534 20365 FAX 01534 69144
Apr-Oct
With classic columns supporting the entrance portico, Gloster House is an impressive building dating back to the early 1800s. Set back from the road in a tree-lined terrace, it is in easy walking distance of the town centre and ample parking is provided. Most popular of the well-equipped bedrooms are the half dozen Garden Rooms that overlook the rear garden and swimming pool. Day rooms include a high-ceilinged lounge and separate, beamed dining room, and also a quiet room with a supply of books.
24 bth/shr (2 fmly) No smoking in dining room CTV in all bedrooms Tea and coffee making facilities Direct dial from bedrooms Licensed Cen ht No children 24P Indoor swimming pool (heated)
CARDS:

Selected

Q Q Q Q **The Haven** 7 Kensington Place JE2 3PA
(Go to St Helier on Victoria Ave A2 to Esplanade.Kensington Plc is from townside of Grand Hotel up to Cheapside/The Parade A9 rd junct)
☎ 01534 21619 FAX 01534 888842
Right in the heart of town, yet just a very short walk from the sea front, this well-kept establishment has been personally run by Connie and Carlo Mausolle for over ten years. Bedrooms are bright and fresh and all but two have en suite shower rooms. There is a cosy bar and separate sitting room in addition to a neat breakfast room. Dinners are not served but there is a wide choice of restaurants in the neighbourhood.
10 rms (8 shr) (2 fmly) No smoking in dining room CTV in all bedrooms Tea and coffee making facilities No dogs Licensed Cen ht CTV No coaches
ROOMS: s £16-£24; d £36-£52*
CARDS:

Selected

Q Q Q Q **Millbrook House** Rue de Trachy, Millbrook JE2 3JN (1.5m W of town on A1) ☎ 01534 33036 FAX 01534 24317
18 Apr-5 Oct
This greatly extended Georgian mansion enjoys a peaceful location set in ten acres of its own grounds. Bright, well appointed bedrooms are comfortably furnished, and are equipped with many modern amenities. Extensive public areas include two cosy lounges, one for non-smokers and a separate bar. Guests can enjoy good home-cooking in the dining room where an extensive range of wines are also available.
27 bth/shr (2 fmly) No smoking in dining room No smoking in 1 lounge CTV in all bedrooms Tea and coffee making facilities Direct dial from bedrooms No dogs Licensed Lift CTV 20P No coaches Golf 5 Last d 7pm
ROOMS: s £26.80-£34.80; d £53.60-£69.60*
CARDS:

ST MARY

Selected

Q Q Q Q **Roc Annick** La Rue es Boeufs JE3 3EQ (turn off A10 onto B39 300m (C112 St Peters Valley). Right at T junct. Right (C112 Carrefour Selous), follow (C112). Roc Annick 250m on right) ☎ 01534 862272 FAX 01534 865709
Closed Nov-Mar
Run by Fred and Anne Coote in friendly fashion for over 20 years, Roc Annick is peacefully located in the centre of the island (ask for directions when booking). A modern building, surrounded by neat gardens and with ample parking, it offers bedrooms of good size, conveniently appointed and decorated with matching bedcovers and curtains. The lounge has been comfortably refurbished and there is a bright breakfast room.
11 rms (9 bth/shr) (2 fmly) No smoking in dining room CTV in all bedrooms Tea and coffee making facilities No dogs (ex guide dogs) Cen ht CTV No children 7yrs 10P No coaches
ROOMS: s £16.50-£24.50; d £28-£49; wkly b&b £98-£171.50
CARDS:

ST SAVIOUR

Selected

Q Q Q Q *Champ Colin* Rue du Champ Colin JE2 7UN
☎ 01534 851877 FAX 01534 854902
Closed Xmas
Enjoying a delightfully peaceful location in the Island's interior, close to La Hougue Bie Museum, Champ Colin is a fine old stone house dating back to 1815. It offers charming accommodation in three antique-furnished bedrooms, two with fine half-tester beds. More antiques are to be found in the day rooms which include a recently refurbished drawing room and well-appointed breakfast room with an impressive granite fireplace.
3 bth/shr (1 fmly) No smoking CTV in all bedrooms Tea and coffee making facilities Cen ht CTV No children 2yrs 10P
CARDS:

SARK

Selected

QQQQ **Hotel Petit Champ** GY9 0SF
(from the Methodist Chapel take lane, signposted, towards sea & turn left) ☎ 01481 832046 FAX 01481 832469
Etr-Oct
Hotel Petit Champ enjoys a secluded position on Sark's beautiful west coast. Guests can not only enjoy the peace and tranquillity but also the magnificent views of the sea and neighbouring islands of Herm, Jethou and Guernsey. All the comfortably furnished bedrooms offer en suite facilities, and three have a private balcony. Day rooms include several sun lounges, a small TV room, no-smoking library lounge and cosy, well-stocked bar plus dining rooms candlelit at night.
16 bth/shr (2 fmly) No smoking in dining room No smoking in 1 lounge No dogs (ex guide dogs) Licensed Cen ht CTV No children 7yrs Outdoor swimming pool (heated) Putting green Last d 8.30pm
ROOMS: (incl. dinner) s £46-£53; d £88-£112;
wkly b&b £220.50-£304.50; wkly hlf-bd £308-£392
CARDS:

MAN, ISLE OF Map 06

DOUGLAS Map 06 SC37

QQQ **Ainsdale Guest House** 2 Empire Ter, Central Promenade IM2 4LE (from sea terminal, 4th turn left after Villa Marina building, situated on left hand side) ☎ 01624 676695 FAX 01624 676695
A small, privately owned and personally run hotel is located just up from the Central Promenade and is convenient for the sea front and most of the other amenities in Douglas. The well maintained accommodation has modern equipment and facilities. Family rooms are available and indeed children are especially welcome here. There is an attractively appointed dining room and a comfortable lounge. The house is fronted by a small, attractive garden and terrace area.
13 rms (10 bth/shr) (3 fmly) No smoking in dining room CTV in 10 bedrooms Tea and coffee making facilities No dogs (ex guide dogs) Cen ht CTV P Last d 1pm
ROOMS: s £22-£24; d £44-£48

QQQ **All Seasons** 11 Clifton Ter, Broadway IM2 3HX
(turn off Central Prom Villa Marina in 1st row of hotels on left)
☎ 01624 676323 FAX 01624 676323
A personally run, friendly and pleasant guest house that is conveniently situated for access to most of the town's amenities. The promenade and sea front of just a few minutes walk away. It has well equipped, soundly maintained accommodation. Separate tables are provided in the dining room, which has an adjacent lounge bar. A second lounge is available upstairs.
6 rms (5 shr) No smoking in dining room No smoking in lounges CTV in all bedrooms Tea and coffee making facilities No dogs (ex guide dogs) Licensed Cen ht No coaches Last d 6pm
ROOMS: s £18.25-£23.75; d £39.50-£40.50
CARDS:

QQ **Ashley House** 6 Clifton Ter, Broadway IM2 3HU (from the ferry port, go towards the Villa Marina and turn left. House 300mtrs on left) ☎ 01624 675408
This privately owned and personally run small hotel is located a few minutes' walk from the promenade and sea front. It is convenient for many of the town's amenities and attractions. It provides modern furnished accommodation and at the time of our last inspection the new owner was planning to upgrade. The open plan breakfast room and bar is ultra modern and bright. There is also a lounge.
8 rms (4 bth/shr) (3 fmly) No smoking in bedrooms No smoking in dining room No smoking in 1 lounge CTV in 4 bedrooms Tea and coffee making facilities Licensed Cen ht CTV
ROOMS: s £16; d £37; wkly b&b £112✳

QQQ **Blossoms Hotel** 4 The Esplanade IM2 4LR
(situated in centre of promenade. Straight ahead through traffic lights at Villa Marina, second turning on left. Hotel set back on private road)
☎ 01624 673360 FAX 01624 673360
This well maintained, small personally run guest house is centrally situated on the promenade, overlooking Douglas Bay. It provides attractively appointed, modern accommodation which includes a bedroom on ground floor level. There is a comfortable, attractive lounge and separate tables are provided in the pleasant breakfast room.
6 bth/shr No smoking in dining room No smoking in lounges CTV in all bedrooms Tea and coffee making facilities No dogs (ex guide dogs) Cen ht CTV No coaches
ROOMS: s £17.50-£20; d £33-£40; wkly b&b £140✳

QQQ ***The Laurels*** 2 Mona Dr, Central Promenade IM2 4LG
(25yds from sea front off Central Prominade)
☎ 01624 674884 FAX 01624 618287
This small, privately owned and personally run guest house is situated just off the Central Promenade, a few yards from the sea front. It provides fairly modern accommodation, that includes a comfortable lounge and a bar. Separate tables are provided in the attractively appointed dining room. The new owners Celia and Michael Gardner are planning a scheme of improvements.
14 rms (8 bth/shr) (2 fmly) No smoking in dining room CTV in all bedrooms Tea and coffee making facilities Licensed CTV No children 2yrs No coaches Last d 9.00pm
CARDS:

QQQ **Rosslyn Guest House** 3 Empire Ter, Central Promenade IM2 4LE ☎ 01624 676056 FAX 01624 674122
Closed Dec-1 Jan
This personally run, friendly guest house is situated just a few yards from the promenade and sea front and top floor rooms have fine views out to sea. The neatly decorated bedrooms are complemented by a welcoming lounge, traditionally furnished dining room and a cosy bar.
12 rms (6 bth/shr) No smoking in 4 bedrooms No smoking in dining room No smoking in lounges CTV in 6 bedrooms Tea and coffee making facilities No dogs (ex guide dogs) Licensed Cen ht CTV No children 5yrs
ROOMS: s £18-£28; d £36-£46; wkly b&b £126-£161;
wkly hlf-bd £175-£210

ONCHAN Map 06 SC37

Premier Selected

QQQQQ **Engelwood Lodge** 105 King Edward Rd IM3 2AS
(1m N from Douglas promenade on King Edward road on left after Churchill of India restaurant. Private road parallel to main road over railway line)
☎ 01624 616050 FAX 01624 616051
Mar-Oct
Built just a few years ago this is a modern detached house situated at Onchan from where it commands superb panoramic views of Douglas Bay and the harbour. The luxuriously and tastefully appointed, well equipped accommodation comprises of two double and one twin bedded room. There is a choice of spacious and comfortable lounges, one overlooking the rear patio and pleasant garden. There is also a very attractive breakfast room with high quality furnishings.
3 bth/shr No smoking CTV in all bedrooms Tea and coffee making facilities No dogs Cen ht CTV No children 14yrs 3P No coaches Pool table
ROOMS: s £30-£37.50; d £57-£60

SCOTLAND

Inspectors selected bed & breakfast of the year:
Farmhouse Kitchen, Arbroath, Angus

ABERDEEN Aberdeen City Map **15** NJ90

Q Q Q **Arkaig** 43 Powis Ter AB25 3PP (on main A96/A956 Inverness-Aberdeen road, 0.5m N of city centre, close to university and hospital)
☎ 01224 638872 FAX 01224 622189
Good value for money is offered at this personally run granite-built guest house located north of the city centre and convenient to the university. The bedrooms have been designed to make best use of available space and offer attractive colour schemes together with a good range of amenities. The small sun lounge leads out onto the patio at the rear of the house.
9 rms (7 shr) (1 fmly) No smoking in dining room No smoking in lounges CTV in all bedrooms Tea and coffee making facilities Direct dial from bedrooms Cen ht CTV 10P Last d 6pm
ROOMS: s £30-£32; d £42-£44
CARDS:

Q Q **Bimini** 69 Constitution St AB24 5ET
(5mins walk from town centre, 15-20mins walk from Rail/Bus station,near University) ☎ 01224 646912 FAX 01224 646755
Ongoing improvements are taking place at this personally run guest house which is situated in the east end convenient to both the seafront and central amenities. Three rooms have recently benefited from the upgrade and now offer en suite facilities. Remaining rooms are more practical in style but represent good value for money. Hearty breakfasts are served at shared tables in the dining room which adjoins the cosy lounge. This is a non-smoking establishment.
8 rms (3 shr) (1 fmly) No smoking CTV in all bedrooms Tea and coffee making facilities No dogs (ex guide dogs) Cen ht CTV 7P No coaches
ROOMS: s £20-£30; d £40-£50*
CARDS:

Q Q Q **Corner House Hotel** 385 Great Western Rd AB10 6NY (on A93)
☎ 01224 313063 FAX 01224 313063
A welcoming atmosphere prevails at this family run establishment, a detached granite-built house conveniently situated at the city's west end. Modern bedrooms offer a good range of modern amenities, which are especially suited to the business guest. There is a comfortable lounge and an attractive restaurant where the menu offers a good range of dishes.
17 bth/shr (3 fmly) No smoking in dining room CTV in all bedrooms Tea and coffee making facilities Direct dial from bedrooms Licensed Cen ht CTV 12P No coaches Last d 8pm
ROOMS: s £38-£50; d £50-£60; wkly b&b £180-£270; wkly hlf-bd £250-£340
CARDS:

Premier Selected

Q Q Q Q Q **Ewood House** 12 Kings Gate AB15 4EJ (Turn off A90 ring rd W of Aberdeen City onto King's Gate - Elwood Hse is 1/2m on left past Atholl Hotel) ☎ 01224 648408 FAX 01224 648408
Sheila and Fred Hawkey have adapted their delightful, detached, granite-built Victorian home, situated in a desirable west-end residential area, to provide top-class accommodation for visitors to the city. Set in its own award winning gardens, Ewood has a relaxed, informal atmosphere and Sheila, a genial host, welcomes her guests with freshly brewed tea and delicious home baking. Most of the attractive bedrooms are well proportioned and comfortably furnished in either period or modern styles, and the thoughtful touches include fresh fruit and flowers. One room is suitable for travellers with disabilities, and one has a four-poster bed. The spacious lounge, with ample reading material, invites relaxation, and to start the day, excellent breakfasts are served in the bright dining room.
6 shr No smoking CTV in all bedrooms Tea and coffee making facilities No dogs (ex guide dogs) Cen ht CTV No children 8P No coaches
ROOMS: s £45-£45; d £65-£65; wkly b&b fr £270*
CARDS:

Q Q Q **Fourways** 435 Great Western Rd AB10 6NJ ☎ 01224 310218 FAX 01224 310218
Good parking facilities are available at this family run guest house which stands beside the ring road at its junction with the Deeside road. Attractive fabrics have been used to good effect in the tastefully decorated bedrooms and there is a smart dining room which also contains a lounge area.
7 rms (6 bth/shr) (2 fmly) CTV in all bedrooms Tea and coffee making facilities No dogs (ex guide dogs) Cen ht CTV 7P
ROOMS: s £20-£25; d £40-£50*
CARDS:

Selected

Q Q Q Q **The Jays** 422 King St AB24 3BR (A90 from the South to Main St - Union St, continue on A92 to King St (North))
☎ 01224 638295 FAX 01224 638295
Closed Aug & Jan
Alice and George Jennings have extended their attractive, detached, granite-built home in the north of the city to provide quality accommodation. A warm personal welcome is assured and this, together with meticulous attention to detail, ensures that many guests return time and again. The comfortable bedrooms are furnished to a high standard and feature pretty decor and co-ordinated fabrics. Freshly prepared breakfasts are served in the smart dining room.
10 shr No smoking CTV in all bedrooms Tea and coffee making facilities No dogs Cen ht No children 12yrs 9P No coaches
ROOMS: s £30-£40; d £50-£60*
CARDS:

Kildonan 410 Great Western Rd AB10 6NR
(100mtrs from the junct of the A90, A93 and A96) ☎ 01224 316115
Closed Xmas & New Year
Enthusiastic new owners Anne and Alan Dey are making good progress with their refurbishment programme at this comfortable end terrace house in the west end. More en suites have been added and most bedrooms have benefited from enhanced decoration and new furnishings. There is no lounge but hearty breakfasts are served in the upgraded ground floor dining room. This is a non smoking house.
6 rms (3 shr) No smoking CTV in all bedrooms Tea and coffee making facilities No dogs Cen ht 3P No coaches
ROOMS: s £22-£27; d £40-£60
CARDS:

Selected

Mannofield Hotel 447 Great Western Rd AB10 6NL
(from the south-cross the Bridge of Dee and follow signs for Inverness, A96 South Anderson Drive) ☎ 01224 315888 FAX 01224 208971
Under the enthusiastic ownership of Dorothy and Bruce Cryle, a major transformation has taken place at this delightful hotel in the west end. All the refurbished bedrooms are decorated to a high standard and are comfortably furnished in the modern style. Public areas include an inviting lounge and a tastefully appointed dining room were freshly prepared breakfasts and, by prior arrangement, enjoyable home cooked evening meals are served at individual tables. A warm welcome is assured.
9 rms (6 shr) (3 fmly) No smoking in 7 bedrooms No smoking in dining room CTV in all bedrooms Tea and coffee making facilities Direct dial from bedrooms Licensed Cen ht CTV 12P Last d 7pm
CARDS:

Selected

Manorville 252 Gt Western Rd AB10 6PJ
☎ 01224 594190 FAX 01224 594190
Mr & Mrs Marshall enjoy meeting new guests and welcoming them to their comfortable granite-built home, situated in the west end and offering easy access to the city centre. The well appointed rooms are comfortable and offer all the expected amenities. There is a delightful lounge which is a haven for relaxation. Hearty breakfasts are served in a pleasant dining room.
3 bth/shr (2 fmly) No smoking in 3 bedrooms No smoking in dining room CTV in all bedrooms Tea and coffee making facilities No dogs (ex guide dogs) Cen ht 4P
ROOMS: s £25-£28; d £40-£42*
CARDS:

Open Hearth 349 Holburn St AB10 7FQ ☎ 01224 596888
A welcoming atmosphere prevails at this comfortable and well maintained guest house which is situated in the west end. Bedrooms, though variable in size, are comfortable modern in style and offer high standards of cleanliness. Hearty breakfasts are served at shared tables in the attractive dining room. Parking is available.
12 rms (2 fmly) No smoking in dining room CTV in all bedrooms Tea and coffee making facilities Cen ht CTV 5P No coaches
ROOMS: s £22; d £36*

We endeavour to be as accurate as possible but changes in personnel and data can occur in establishments after the Guide has gone to press

Selected

Strathisla 408 Gt Western Rd AB10 6NR (off A93)
☎ 01224 321026
High levels of comfort and hospitality are the hallmarks of this welcoming terraced guest house which is situated in a desirable west end residential area close to the bypass. Most of the attractive bedrooms are spacious and offer a bright airy feel together with quality appointments. Both continental and traditional style breakfasts are served at separate tables in the smart dining room.
5 bth/shr (1 fmly) No smoking CTV in all bedrooms Tea and coffee making facilities No dogs Cen ht No children 8yrs 1P
No coaches

262 Great Western Road AB10 6PJ ☎ 01224 574486
FAX 01224 574486
Closed 22 Dec-8 Jan
Sheila Young's comfortable semi-detached home is situated in a desirable west end residential area and offers good value accommodation. At present there are two bedrooms comfortably furnished in period style, and although they lack wash basins they are situated beside a shared bathroom. Hearty breakfasts are served at the communal table in the dining room to the rear of the house. A collection service from the railway station/airport can be arranged.
4 rms (2 fmly) No smoking CTV in all bedrooms Tea and coffee making facilities No dogs (ex guide dogs) Cen ht CTV
ROOMS: s £18-£25; d £36-£50; wkly b&b £126-£175*

ABERDOUR Fife Map 11 NT18

The Aberdour Hotel 38 High St KY3 0SW (on A921)
☎ 01383 860325 FAX 01383 860808
Situated beside the main street, this welcoming inn appeals to the visiting businessman and tourist alike. Although the original house dates back to the 17th century, the comfortable bedrooms offer a good range of modern amenities. The most spacious rooms are to be found in the stable block annexe to the rear. Traditional home cooking and real ales are the house specialities.
16 bth/shr (4 fmly) No smoking in 5 bedrooms CTV in all bedrooms Tea and coffee making facilities Direct dial from bedrooms Cen ht 7P No coaches Last d 9pm
ROOMS: s £41.50-£45; d £50-£58; wkly b&b £170-£310; wkly hlf-bd £240-£410
MEALS: Lunch £8-£10&alc Dinner £8-£10
CARDS:

Premier Selected

Hawkcraig House Hawkcraig Point KY3 0TZ
(turn off A921 in Easter Aberdour and follow Hawkcraig Rd to large car park, then continue down very steep access. Guest parking in front of premises) ☎ 01383 860335
mid Mar-late Oct
Hawkscraig House is a converted ferryman's house set beside the shore, commanding fantastic views across the Firth of Forth. The steep narrow access can be a little daunting but with care, there should be no problem. Both the comfortable en suite bedrooms are on the ground floor next to a lounge and conservatory where breakfast is served. There is also an elegant dining room, and a comfortable lounge.
2 bth/shr No smoking CTV in all bedrooms No dogs (ex guide dogs) Cen ht CTV No children 10yrs 3P No coaches
Last d 24hr notice
ROOMS: s £36; d £52*

ABERFELDY Perth & Kinross Map 14 NN84

Premier Selected

Q Q Q Q Q **Fernbank House** Kenmore St PH15 2BL
(on way out of town on A827 to Kenmore and Killin)
☎ 01887 820345
This large Victorian house, set in lovely, well kept gardens, provides attractive accommodation and a warm welcome. The well equipped, simply decorated bedrooms vary in size, and the delightful lounge offers plenty of information on the surrounding area. Substantial breakfasts are served in the bright dining room.
7 bth/shr (2 fmly) No smoking CTV in all bedrooms Tea and coffee making facilities No dogs Cen ht CTV 8P No coaches
ROOMS: s £28-£37; d £48-£60

Q Q Q **West Park Farm** *(NN887506)* PH15 2EQ
(A9 onto A827, 7m on left just beyond Grantully Castle. From W, 2m from Aberfeldy on A827 in direction of Ballinluig)
☎ 01887 840415 Mrs C Thomson
Catriona Thomson looks forward to welcoming guests old and new to her delightful home, a late 17th-century farmhouse. The immaculately maintained bedrooms are decorated and furnished in a style appropriate to the character of the house. Public areas include a cosy lounge with CTV, and the adjacent porch which overlooks the garden, has another lounge area as well as individual tables for the hearty farmhouse breakfasts.
2 rms No smoking No dogs (ex guide dogs) Cen ht CTV 3P Fishing permits can be arranged
ROOMS: s £18-£20; d £36-£40; wkly b&b £100-£120

ABERLOUR Moray Map 15 NJ24

Q Q **Roys Croft** *(NJ246411)* AB38 9NR (1.75m S of village)
☎ 01340 871408 FAX 01340 871408 Mrs S Mitchell
A warm welcome is assured at this small croft house which is situated just south of the village. The smartly decorated bedrooms are well maintained and comfortably modern in style. The conservatory doubles as the lounge and dining room where hearty breakfasts are served at the communal table.
2 rms (1 shr) No smoking CTV in all bedrooms Tea and coffee making facilities No dogs (ex guide dogs) Cen ht No children 4P 8 acres croft Last d noon (Oct-Apr)
ROOMS: wkly b&b £94.50-£125.50

Prices shown in the directory are meant as a guide only and are subject to change. Please check before you book

ABOYNE Aberdeenshire Map 15 NO59

Premier Selected

Q Q Q Q Q **Arbor Lodge** Ballater Rd AB34 5HY (on A93 0.5m W of village centre) ☎ 01339 886951 FAX 01339 886951
Mar-Oct Closed Dec-Feb rs Nov
Set in extensive and well-manicured gardens beside the Ballater Road, Arbor Lodge offers a welcoming atmosphere together with high standards of comfort and quality. The carefully appointed bedrooms are well proportioned, furnished in the modern style and feature walk-in dressing rooms and luxurious bathrooms. Attractive public areas include a choice of sitting rooms, and there is direct access to the patio in the rear garden. Substantial freshly prepared breakfasts are served around the communal table in the dining room.
3 bth/shr No smoking in bedrooms No smoking in dining room No smoking in 1 lounge CTV in all bedrooms Tea and coffee making facilities Cen ht CTV No children 12yrs 6P No coaches
ROOMS: s £25-£32; d £50-£64
CARDS:

AIRDRIE North Lanarkshire Map 11 NS76

Q Q **Rosslee** 107 Forrest St ML6 7AR (1m E on A89) ☎ 01236 765865 FAX 01236 748535
Situated at the east end of town, this family-run licensed guest house offers good value accommodation with its modern styled bedrooms. The public areas include a pleasant lounge with a dispense bar and a separate dining room with individual tables where evening meals can be ordered.
6 rms (4 shr) (2 fmly) No smoking in dining room CTV in all bedrooms Tea and coffee making facilities Licensed Cen ht CTV 8P No coaches Last d 11am
ROOMS: s £20-£25; d £40-£50; wkly b&b £140-£165; wkly hlf-bd £210-£235

ALYTH Perth & Kinross Map 15 NO25

Q Q *Losset* Losset Rd PH11 8BT
(take A926 turn into Alyth, A952 Losset Inn 1m into town on road to the "Glens") ☎ 01828 632393
Dating back to 1690, this family run village inn combines a welcoming atmosphere with good value accommodation and has particular appeal for visiting golfers. Bedrooms, although compact, are all en suite and offer all the expected amenities. Natural stone and exposed beams add to the character of the well stocked lounge bar, which has a small inviting dining area adjacent.
3 shr No smoking in area of dining room CTV in all bedrooms Tea and coffee making facilities Cen ht 10P No coaches Last d 9pm

ANSTRUTHER Fife Map **12** NO50

Selected

QQQQ **Beaumont Lodge** 43 Pittenweem Rd KY10 3DT
(take the B9131 from St Andrews to Anstruther. Turn right at the crossroads, Beaumont Lodge is on left side past the Hotel)
☎ 01333 310315 FAX 01333 310315
This large house is located on the western edge of Anstruther, at the heart of the Kingdom of Fife. Bedrooms are bright and offer modern appointments and a great range of accessories. One is situated on the ground floor and has a four-poster bed. Home cooked dinners and breakfasts are served at individual tables in the attractive dining room. This is a non smoking establishment.
5 rms (4 shr) (1 fmly) No smoking CTV in all bedrooms Tea and coffee making facilities No dogs (ex guide dogs) Cen ht 10P
Last d 4pm
ROOMS: s £22-£30; d £44-£52
CARDS:

Premier Selected

QQQQQ **Hermitage** Ladywalk KY10 3EX
(from Shore St (Harbour Area) turn left at the Ship Inn, turn left along lane, establishment is on the left)
☎ 01333 310909 FAX 01333 311505
Sea views can be enjoyed from this charming Georgian house which is peacefully set in its own carefully tended walled garden. Lovingly restored by the enthusiastic owners, the house offers the elegance of a former era combined with modern day comforts. Bedrooms have individual colour schemes and can be let individually or, as the owners prefer, as two suites each with two bedrooms, a bathroom and comfortable sitting room. When let individually, the bathroom and lounge are shared. The carefully prepared breakfasts served in the attractive dining room provide the guest with a really good start to their day. For the comfort of all, smoking is not permitted.
4 rms (2 fmly) No smoking Tea and coffee making facilities
Direct dial from bedrooms No dogs (ex guide dogs) Licensed Cen ht CTV 6P No coaches
ROOMS: d £40-£50; wkly b&b £126-£157.50
CARDS:

Selected

QQQQ **The Spindrift** Pittenweem Rd KY10 3DT (from W first building on left when entering town and from E last building on right when leaving) ☎ 01333 310573 FAX 01333 310573
Closed 17 Nov-10 Dec & Xmas
Maintained to a very high standard, this comfortable Victorian house is located at the western edge of a picturesque fishing village and offers a welcoming atmosphere and good value holiday accommodation. The comfortable bedrooms have a wide range of amenities and the timber-clad Captains Cabin has particular appeal. The elegant lounge features an open fire and honesty bar and good home cooking is the order of the day at both breakfast and dinner. A non-smoking establishment.
8 bth/shr (2 fmly) No smoking CTV in all bedrooms Tea and coffee making facilities Direct dial from bedrooms No dogs Licensed
Cen ht CTV 12P No coaches Last d 7pm
ROOMS: d £55-£65; wkly b&b £192.50-£231; wkly hlf-bd £280-£315
CARDS:

ARBROATH Angus Map 12 NO64

Premier Selected

QQQQQ ❦ ***Farmhouse Kitchen** (NO582447)* Grange of Conon DD11 3SD (6m N, signposted from A933 just beyond Colliston) ☎ 01241 860202 FAX 01241 860424 Mrs S A Caldwell
Sandra Caldwell's delightful family farmhouse is situated in the heart of the peaceful Angus countryside. Bedrooms are comfortable and feature a host of thoughtful extras. The ground floor bedroom boasts a canopied sleigh bed. Guests are encouraged to make the most of the facilities available - including the lovely sun lounge overlooking the garden and a games room offering a full size snooker table, exercise bike, table tennis and sun bed. Breakfast is served around a communal table in the kitchen.
3 rms (2 bth/shr) No smoking in bedrooms No smoking in dining room CTV in all bedrooms Tea and coffee making facilities No dogs (ex guide dogs) Cen ht CTV No children 3yrs 4P Fishing Snooker Solarium Games room 560 acres arable

QQ **Kingsley** 29 Market Gate DD11 1AU (from A92 follow sign for harbour then 1st road on the left (100 metres from harbour))
☎ 01241 873933 FAX 01241 873933
Situated just a short walk from the harbour and central amenities, this family run guest house offers good value accommodation. Though they vary in size, bedrooms are brightly decorated and offer mixed modern furnishings. Public areas include a residents' bar, lounge and smart dining room.
16 rms (8 bth/shr) (3 fmly) No smoking in dining room CTV in all bedrooms Licensed Cen ht CTV 4P Childrens play ground
ROOMS: s £17-£22; d £30-£36*
CARDS:

ARDBRECKNISH Argyll & Bute Map 10 NN02

QQQ ❦ ***Rockhill** (NN072219)* PA33 1BH (from Inverary take A819 turning on to B840 at Cladich for 3 miles to Rockhill)
☎ 01866 833218 Mr & Mrs Whalley
May-Sep
Beautifully situated in a quiet position on the eastern shore of Loch Awe and providing lovely views towards Ben Cruachan and its dam, this family-owned and run farmhouse offers traditionally styled bedrooms. There is a cosy lounge which is well stocked with reading material and good home-cooking is provided in the neat dining room. Hanoverian horses are bred on the farm and can be seen in the fields.
5 rms (1 bth/shr) (3 fmly) No smoking in dining room No smoking in lounges CTV in all bedrooms Tea and coffee making facilities Licensed No children 8yrs 8P Fishing 200 acres horses sheep Last d 7pm
See advertisement under INVERARAY

ARRAN, ISLE OF North Ayrshire Map 10

BRODICK Map 10 NS03

QQQ **Allandale** KA27 8BJ (2 mins from Brodick Pier, turn left at junc follow sign to Lanlash, up the hill take 2nd left at the Corriegills sign Allandale on corner of main rd) ☎ 01770 302278
Closed Nov-Dec
This detached house lies in its own gardens just outside the village and features attractive, comfortable public areas and bright cheery bedrooms that includes two spacious rooms contained in a small bungalow in the gardens.
4 bth/shr 2 annexe bth/shr (4 fmly) No smoking in dining room No smoking in 1 lounge CTV in all bedrooms Tea and coffee making facilities Licensed Cen ht 6P Last d 7pm
ROOMS: s £22-£24; d £44-£48*

Selected

QQQQ **Dunvegan House** Dunvegan Shore Rd KA27 8AJ (Turn right from ferry terminal, 500yds along Shore Road)
☎ 01770 302811 FAX 302811
David and Naomi Spencer extend a warm welcome to guests at their lovely detached home, which is centrally situated overlooking the bay towards the castle and mountains beyond. The tastefully decorated no-smoking bedrooms feature pretty co-ordinated fabrics and are comfortably furnished in pine. Guests can relax and enjoy coffee or after dinner drinks in the lounge, and a choice of carefully prepared Taste of Scotland dishes and hearty breakfasts in the dining room.
9 bth/shr (1 fmly) No smoking in bedrooms CTV in all bedrooms Tea and coffee making facilities No dogs (ex guide dogs) Licensed Cen ht CTV No children 10yrs 10P No coaches Last d 4pm
ROOMS: s £28.50-£30; d £57-£60*

LAMLASH Map 10 NS03

Selected

QQQQ **Lilybank** Shore Rd KA27 8LS (4m S of Brodick Ferry Terminal) ☎ 01770 600230 FAX 01770 600230
Closed Nov-Feb
An 18th-century house has been carefully restored and extended to create a welcoming small hotel, located in the centre of the village overlooking the bay towards the Holy Isle. The no-smoking bedrooms are smartly decorated and feature attractive co-ordinated fabrics together with comfortable modern furnishings. Public areas include a choice of relaxing lounges, one of which has a dispense bar. Throughout there is an interesting pig theme to the ornaments and wall decorations. The attractively decorated dining room offers a range of Taste of Scotland dishes carefully prepared from quality raw ingredients.
8 rms (7 shr) (1 fmly) No smoking in bedrooms No smoking in dining room CTV in all bedrooms Tea and coffee making facilities Licensed Cen ht No children 13yrs 8P No coaches Last d 7pm
ROOMS: s £25-£42.50; d £45-£55; wkly b&b £175-£192.50; wkly hlf-bd £245-£280*

LOCHRANZA Map 10 NR95

Q Q ***Kincardine Lodge*** KA27 8HL ☎ 01770 830267
Apr-Oct
Convenient for the Kintyre ferry terminal and enjoying a picture postcard outlook over the bay and castle, this spacious Victorian lodge offers good value tourist accommodation. It has two lounges, one no-smoking, and the well proportioned bedrooms that vary in style from modern to traditional. Wild deer often visit the hillside immediately behind the house.
6 rms (3 shr) (2 fmly) No smoking in bedrooms No smoking in dining room No smoking in 1 lounge CTV in all bedrooms Tea and coffee making facilities CTV 6P No coaches Last d 12pm

WHITING BAY Map 10 NS02

Selected

Q Q Q Q **Grange House Hotel** KA27 8QH (from the Ferry Terminal turn left signposted Whiting Bay. After approx 8m enter village, house 0.25m on right hand side) ☎ 01770 700263 FAX 01770 700263
Etr-Oct
Clive and Janet Hughes' fine Victorian house lies in attractive gardens and looks out across the bay towards the mainland. The lounge, with its open fire in cooler evenings, boasts lots of books and takes advantage of the sea views. Spotless table appointments, including sparkling silverware, are a feature of the dining room that is the perfect setting for Janet's excellent breakfasts which include smoked fish, croissants and home-made marmalade. Bedrooms are furnished with period pieces and guests have use of a sauna during the day.
7 bth/shr (1 fmly) No smoking CTV in all bedrooms Tea and coffee making facilities No dogs Licensed Cen ht CTV 7P No coaches Sauna 8 hole putting lawn
ROOMS: s £30-£35; d £60-£70; wkly b&b £210*
CARDS:

Q Q Q **Invermay Hotel** Shore Rd KA27 8PZ ☎ 01770 700431
Apr-Oct
Spotlessly clean and well maintained, this detached red sandstone house looks out over the sea shore to the Ayrshire coast. Public areas include a comfortable lounge and a cosy very well stocked residents' bar where guests can enjoy the relaxed and friendly atmosphere.
7 rms (5 shr) No smoking in bedrooms No smoking in dining room Tea and coffee making facilities No dogs (ex guide dogs) Licensed Cen ht CTV 8P No coaches Last d 2pm
ROOMS: s fr £25; d fr £50; wkly b&b fr £175; wkly hlf-bd fr £259 *

All AA listed accommodation can also be found at the AA's Internet site, whose address is: http://www.theaa.co.uk/hotels

ARROCHAR Argyll & Bute Map 10 NN20

Q Q Q ***Bemersyde*** Tarbet, Loch Lomond G83 7DE (on A82) ☎ 01301 702230
Mar-Oct
Good value accommodation is offered at Bridget and Robert Munro's extended detached bungalow, situated just off the A82. There are two first floor bedrooms, one of which has an adjoining room suitable for family use and is en suite. A further en suite room is available at ground level. There is a cosy sitting room with CTV, and hearty breakfasts are served in the separate dining room.
3 bth/shr (1 fmly) No smoking CTV in 1 bedroom Tea and coffee making facilities Cen ht CTV 3P No coaches

AUCHTERARDER Perth & Kinross Map 11 NN91

Selected

Q Q Q Q **Allandale House** 17 High St PH3 1DB (turn off A9 onto A824, house at North End of Auchterarder beside police station) ☎ 01764 663329 FAX 01764 663329
Enthusiastic owner Maureen Langlands welcomes you to her comfortable home just off the High Street. The house dates back to the early 18th century and has recently been extensively renovated and refurbished to provide guests with a high standard of accommodation. The brightly decorated bedrooms, enhanced by attractive co-ordinated fabrics, are comfortably modern in style. Breakfast is served at individual tables in the tastefully appointed dining room.
5 rms (3 shr) (1 fmly) No smoking in dining room No smoking in lounges CTV in all bedrooms Tea and coffee making facilities No dogs (ex guide dogs) Cen ht CTV 6P No coaches
ROOMS: s £18-£25; d £36-£46; wkly b&b £112-£161
CARDS:

Q Q Q ***Morven Hotel*** 196 High St PH3 1AF ☎ 01764 662578 FAX 01764 664710
A relaxed informal atmosphere prevails at this small hotel in the centre of town that enjoys a good level of local support, especially for the popular weekend disco. The bedrooms are comfortably modern in style and offer a good range of amenities. Public areas include a choice of well stocked bars and a small dining area.
9 bth/shr (3 fmly) CTV in all bedrooms Tea and coffee making facilities Direct dial from bedrooms 7P Pool table Last d 8.30pm
CARDS:

AUCHTERMUCHTY Fife Map 11 NO21

Premier Selected

Q Q Q Q Q **Ardchoille** *(NO248096)* Dunshalt KY14 7EY (A91 to Auchtermuchty, B936 southwards to Dunshalt through main street over bridge 1st right) ☎ 01337 828414 FAX 01337 828414 Mrs I Steven
Guests receive warm and friendly hospitality at this lovely modern farmhouse run by Isobel and Donald Steven. The standard of service is excellent and the well-kept bedrooms have been thoughtfully equipped to include all sorts of welcome extras. Expertly home cooked food is the order of the day, and guests will enjoy enormous afternoon teas, shortbread, delicious evening meals and sumptuous breakfasts.
2 shr No smoking CTV in all bedrooms Tea and coffee making facilities No dogs (ex guide dogs) Cen ht CTV 6P 2 acres Last d 6pm
ROOMS: d fr £70*
CARDS:

Q Q Q *Forest Hills Hotel* 23 High St, The Cross KY15 7AP
☎ 01337 828318 FAX 01337 828318
A relaxed informal atmosphere prevails at this popular inn in the centre of the village. The bedrooms vary in size and in style, but all offer a wide range of modern amenities. Charming public rooms include an attractive restaurant featuring Flemish murals and candlelit tables, and a less formal atmosphere can be found in the small Bistro. The bar is cosy and well stocked.
10 rms (8 bth/shr) No smoking in 2 bedrooms CTV in all bedrooms Tea and coffee making facilities Direct dial from bedrooms Cen ht No coaches Last d 9.45pm
CARDS:

Q Q Q **Wester Cash Farmhouse** *(NO217089)* Wester Cash Farm, Strathmiglo KY14 7RG (turn off M90 junct 8 onto A91, pass through Gateside, take 2nd signpost for Strathmiglo & Falkland) the A912, 2nd right, farm up on hill)
☎ 01337 860215 FAX 01337 860215 Mrs S Black
A warm welcome is assured at Sandra Black's 200-year old farmhouse set on the edge of the village overlooking the Lomond Hills. The smartly decorated bedrooms are furnished in both modern and traditional styles and offer a good range of amenities. In the cooler evenings, a coal fire burns in the sitting room. Breakfast and, by prior arrangement, enjoyable home cooked evening meals, are served at the communal table in the dining room.
3 rms (1 fmly) No smoking in bedrooms No smoking in dining room CTV in all bedrooms Tea and coffee making facilities No dogs Cen ht CTV 6P 400 acres arable Last d 8pm
ROOMS: s £19-£23; d £38-£38; wkly b&b £133-£161; wkly hlf-bd £210-£238
CARDS:

AVIEMORE Highland Map 14 NH81

Q Q Q **Ravenscraig** Grampian Rd PH22 1RP
(At north end of Main St on left. 250m north of Police Station)
☎ 01479 810278 FAX 01479 811800
Robert and Christine Thompson look forward to welcoming you to their comfortable guest house which stands beside the main road at the north end of the village. Bedrooms, including those in the adjacent annexe, are comfortably modern and offer a good range of amenities. Public areas include a inviting lounge with lots of books and an attractive dining room where breakfast is served at individual tables.
8 bth/shr 6 annexe shr (2 fmly) No smoking in dining room CTV in all bedrooms Tea and coffee making facilities Cen ht CTV 15P
ROOMS: s £20-£24; d £40-£48*
CARDS:

AYR South Ayrshire Map 10 NS32

See also Dalrymple & Dunure

Selected

Q Q Q Q **Brenalder Lodge** 39 Dunure, Doonfoot KA7 4HR (2m S on A719) ☎ 01292 443939
With a style reminiscent of a Spanish villa, this modern house stands on the southern edge of town. The bedrooms vary in size and are en suite. Irrespective of size, all are attractively decorated, smartly furnished and thoughtfully equipped. The spacious and comfortable lounge boasts an impressive stone fireplace, whilst the dining room is particularly appealing, with bright, colourful decor.
3 bth/shr (1 fmly) No smoking CTV in all bedrooms Tea and coffee making facilities Cen ht CTV No children 7yrs 10P
ROOMS: s £30-£35; d £50-£60; wkly b&b £175-£210

Q Q Q **Craggallan** 8 Queens Ter KA7 1DU ☎ 01292 264998
Nancy and Bill Hamilton offer a true Scottish welcome at their immaculately maintained guest house which is located in a residential street just off the seafront, and only a short walk from the town centre. Bedrooms are brightly decorated with good modern amenities; family rooms are also available and all are en suite. A comfortable lounge is provided for residents.
4 shr (1 fmly) No smoking in bedrooms No smoking in dining room CTV in all bedrooms Tea and coffee making facilities Cen ht CTV 4P No coaches
ROOMS: s £18-£25; d £36-£44*

Q Q Q **Dargill** 7 Queens Ter KA7 1DU (situated on the seafront, just off Wellington Square) ☎ 01292 261955
Now owned by Tina MacNeill and her family this guest house forms part of a terrace of attractively painted Victorian properties close to the town centre. It backs on to the promenade and has fine views over the garden towards the Firth of Clyde and Island of Arran. There is a spacious and comfortable lounge and pine furnished dining room. Bedrooms, some suitable for families, are brightly decorated and well equipped.
5 rms (3 shr) (2 fmly) No smoking in dining room CTV in all bedrooms Tea and coffee making facilities Cen ht CTV 5P No coaches Last d 2pm
ROOMS: s £17-£22; d £30-£40; wkly b&b £95-£125; wkly hlf-bd £130-£160
CARDS:

Selected

Q Q Q Q *Glenmore* 35 Bellevue Crescent KA7 2DP (into Ayr on A77 from South or A71 from North. Take town centre turn, left at Tourist info, left at lights, first right then left into Bellevue Cres)
☎ 01292 269830 FAX 01292 269830
Marie and Tom Mitchell's fine Victorian house lies in a quiet tree-lined terrace to the south of the town centre. Bedrooms are stylishly

decorated, and the large ones are graced with magnificent period furniture. There is also a comfortable lounge together with a neat dining room where Tom's breakfasts attract much praise.
5 bth/shr (2 fmly) No smoking in dining room No smoking in lounges CTV in all bedrooms Tea and coffee making facilities No dogs (ex guide dogs) Cen ht CTV No coaches

Q Q **Windsor Hotel** 6 Alloway Place KA7 2AA
(from the centre of Ayr, take the A19 through Wellington Square and establishment is first on the right) ☎ 01292 264689
Closed Xmas & New Year
A friendly private hotel, situated within easy walking distance of the seafront and town centre. Bedrooms are bright and modern, several are on the ground floor and some are suitable for families. Ann Hamilton produces good fresh home cooking that is served in the attractive dining room, furnished with chairs and tables once used aboard the SS France.
10 rms (7 bth/shr) (4 fmly) No smoking in dining room CTV in all bedrooms Tea and coffee making facilities Cen ht CTV No coaches
ROOMS: s fr £22; d fr £44; wkly b&b fr £140; wkly hlf-bd fr £210
CARDS:

BALLACHULISH Highland Map **14** NN05

Selected

Q Q Q Q **Fern Villa** East Laroch PA39 4JE
(leave A82 & take left turn on entering village from Glencoe, house 150yds on left) ☎ 01855 811393 FAX 01855 811727
June and Kenneth Chandler extend a warm welcome to guests at their comfortable granite-built Victorian villa. There are no TVs in the rooms, but the cosy and comfortable lounge is the focal point for guests. June's cooking makes dining at Fern Villa quite special. Bedrooms are mixed in size and style and upgrading continues.
5 bth/shr No smoking CTV in all bedrooms Tea and coffee making facilities No dogs (ex guide dogs) Licensed Cen ht CTV No children 10yrs 5P No coaches Last d 5pm
ROOMS: d £40-£44; wkly b&b £126-£140; wkly hlf-bd £196-£210 *

Remember to return your Prize Draw card for a chance to win an action-packed family weekend at one of the eleven Family Fun Hotels in the Hilton Hotels Directory. See inside the front cover for the card and competition details. Don't forget to fill in your name and address before posting!

Selected

Q Q Q Q **Lyn-Leven** West Laroch PA39 4JP (off A82)
☎ 01855 811392 FAX 01855 811600
Closed Xmas
Genuine Highland hospitality together with high standards are part of the appeal of this comfortable modern guest house, that enjoys lovely views over Loch Leven. The smart bedrooms, varying in size, are all on the ground floor. The spacious lounge and attactive dining room look out over the Loch. Traditional home cooking is featured on daily-changing menus.
8 shr 1 annexe bth/shr (1 fmly) No smoking in 1 bedrooms CTV in 8 bedrooms Tea and coffee making facilities Licensed Cen ht CTV 12P Last d 7pm
ROOMS: s £25-£26; d £36-£44; wkly b&b £140-£154; wkly hlf-bd £197-£205
CARDS:

BALLANTRAE South Ayrshire Map **10** NX08

Q Q **Cafe Ballantrae** 49 Main St KA26 0NA
(midway between Girvan and Stranraer on A77, adjacent to Royal Bank of Scotland) ☎ 01465 831293
Set on the main street, and convenient for the Irish ferries, this cheerful café serves meals into the evening, whilst upstairs are attractive bedrooms, two having modern shower rooms.
3 shr (1 fmly) CTV in all bedrooms Tea and coffee making facilities Cen ht No children 5yrs No coaches Last d by arrangement
ROOMS: s £15-£18; d £30-£36; wkly b&b £105; wkly hlf-bd £140

All AA listed accommodation can also be found at the AA's Internet site, whose address is: http://www.theaa.co.uk/hotels

Premier Selected

Q Q Q Q Q **Cosses Country House** Cosses KA26 0LR (from A77 follow caravan sign) ☎ 01465 831363 FAX 01465 831598
Closed 24 Dec-5 Jan
Set in 12 acres of woodland and gardens in a secluded valley this delightful country house has been lovingly converted into very comfortable accommodation, all on ground floor level. Two of the bedrooms, with their own sitting rooms, are located across a courtyard and provide spacious family accommodation. A beautiful lounge with a welcoming log fire is available. Susan and Robin Crosthwaite offer warm hospitality to their guests and dogs are welcome too. Susan's Cordon Bleu cooking is the order of the day, with freshly prepared dishes offered house-party style in the elegant dining room.
3 bth/shr (2 fmly) No smoking in bedrooms No smoking in dining room CTV in all bedrooms Tea and coffee making facilities Licensed Cen ht 8P No coaches Games room Table tennis Snooker Darts Last d 7pm
ROOMS: s £42-£48; d £64-£76; wkly b&b £191-£228; wkly hlf-bd £331-£450*
CARDS:

Q Q Q **The Haven** 75 Main St KA26 0NA (on A77) ☎ 01465 831306 FAX 831306
rs Xmas & 1 Jan
This well maintained bungalow lies its own neat garden and is a handy stop-off to and from Ireland. There are two pleasant bedrooms offering good standards and each with its own adjacent bath or shower room. The larger ground floor room has its own TV, whilst the upper room has the use of a 'viewing gallery' with sofa and small TV. From here there are fine views over the estuary of the River Stinchar towards the Irish Sea.
2 bth/shr (1 fmly) No smoking CTV in 1 bedroom Tea and coffee making facilities No dogs Cen ht CTV 2P No coaches
ROOMS: s fr £21; d fr £36

BALLATER Aberdeenshire Map **15** NO39

Selected

Q Q Q Q ***Bank House*** Station Square AB35 5QB (centre of town, opposite the old station adjacent to Albert & Victoria Halls) ☎ 013397 55996
Situated opposite the old railway station, Bank House is full of interesting artefacts which have been collected by the owners over many years. Bedrooms vary in size, but offer many extra touches such as heated rollers and fully tiled bathrooms. Breakfast is served round one table, with a good selection of cold and hot dishes being offered.
4 bth/shr (2 fmly) No smoking CTV in all bedrooms Tea and coffee making facilities Cen ht 4P No coaches

Selected

Q Q Q Q **Glen Lui Hotel** Invercauld Rd AB35 5RP (Invercauld Road is a turning off A93 in Ballater) ☎ 013397 55402 FAX 013397 55545
Glen Lui Hotel commands some astounding views of both the golf course and the mountains beyond. The hospitality and service is of a professional standard and is matched by the cuisine. The bedrooms are varied and spacious and immaculately maintained.
10 bth/shr 9 annexe bth/shr (2 fmly) No smoking in bedrooms No smoking in dining room No smoking in 1 lounge CTV in all bedrooms Tea and coffee making facilities Direct dial from bedrooms Licensed Cen ht CTV 30P Last d 9pm
ROOMS: s £29-£54; d £58-£108*
CARDS:

Selected

Q Q Q Q **Green Inn Restaurant with Rooms**
9 Victoria Rd AB35 5QQ (on A93 in the centre of Ballater on the green) ☎ 013397 55701 FAX 013397 55701
Closed Sun Oct-Mar & 2 wks in Oct
A "restaurant with rooms" is the appropriate description for this charming small inn set beside the village green. Over the years Jeff and Carol Purves have earned much praise for the their innovative style of cooking and welcoming hospitality. The three en suite bedrooms have recently been completely refurbished and are now smartly decorated and furnished in pine. There is also an inviting lounge where house guests can mingle with the restaurant customers after enjoying Jeff's delicious food at dinner.
3 bth/shr No smoking in bedrooms No smoking in dining room CTV in all bedrooms Tea and coffee making facilities Licensed Cen ht CTV Last d 9pm
ROOMS: (incl. dinner) s £69.50; d £98-£110; wkly hlf-bd £285*
CARDS:

Selected

Q Q Q Q **Inverdeen House** 11 Bridge Square AB35 5QJ (on A93, near bridge over River Dee, adjacent to Alexandra Hotel) ☎ 01339 755759
Sandy and Heli Munroe look forward to welcoming guests, old and new, to their delightful home close to the River Dee. There are three charming bedrooms, each individually furnished with antique or period furnishings, and equipped with all the expected amenities. Breakfast remains one of the highlights of any visit to Inverdeen, and is served around the communal farmhouse style table. The menu includes a substantial Scottish breakfast with venison sausages, home-made pancakes - Canadian style, as well as muffins and various vegetarian options. This is a strictly non-smoking house.

3 rms (1 bth) (1 fmly) No smoking CTV in all bedrooms Tea and coffee making facilities No dogs (ex guide dogs) Cen ht No coaches
ROOMS: s £25-£35; d £40-£45; wkly b&b £135-£152

Selected

Q Q Q Q **Moorside** Braemar Rd AB35 5RL (on left hand side of main road when entering Ballater on A93 from SW) ☎ 013397 55492 FAX 013397 55492
Closed Nov-Feb
Enthusiastic owners Mr & Mrs Walker have made good progress with bedroom refurbishment at their welcoming guest house. Accommodation is mostly spacious with attractive decor and smart modern furnishings. There is a comfortable lounge and freshly prepared breakfasts are served at individual tables in the attractive dining room. Guests are welcome to use the rear garden.
9 bth/shr (3 fmly) No smoking in bedrooms No smoking in dining room CTV in all bedrooms Tea and coffee making facilities No dogs (ex guide dogs) Cen ht 10P No coaches
ROOMS: d £38-£40; wkly b&b £130-£135*
CARDS:

Q Q Q **Netherley** 2 Netherley Place AB35 5QE ☎ 013397 55792 FAX 55792
This friendly family run guest house is located beside the village square and is easily recognised by its smartly painted blue and white facade. Bedrooms are variable in size and in style while public areas include a choice of lounges on the first floor, one of which is non smoking. Hearty breakfasts and, by prior arrangement, home cooked evening meals are served in the traditional dining room.
9 rms (4 bth/shr) (3 fmly) No smoking in dining room No smoking in 1 lounge CTV in all bedrooms Tea and coffee making facilities Cen ht CTV
ROOMS: s £18-£25; d £32-£50*

BALMAHA Stirling Map 10 NS49

Selected

Q Q Q Q ***Moniack*** Moniack G63 0TQ ☎ 01360 870388 & 870357 FAX 01360 870350
Moniack stands in its own grounds on the east side of Loch Lomond in Balmaha village, a well known beauty spot. The attractive bedrooms, all en suite, are well appointed with co-ordinating decor. Hearty breakfast are served in the open plan kitchen/diner overlooking the garden and terrace. Guests are also welcome to eat in the new restaurant situated directly opposite the house.
3 bth/shr (1 fmly) No smoking in bedrooms No smoking in dining room CTV in all bedrooms Tea and coffee making facilities No dogs Cen ht CTV 10P No coaches Fishing

BANCHORY Aberdeenshire Map 15 NO69

Q Q **The Stag Hotel** 40 High St AB31 5SR (in the centre of village) ☎ 01330 824671 FAX 01330 824020
Easy to spot by its black and white mock Tudor frontage, this popular hostelry offers a relaxed and informal atmosphere. One of the two buildings houses rustic bars, and comfortable, compact, en suite accommodation is found in the other situated across a small courtyard. Here too you will find the atmospheric panelled bar/lounge, and the dining room which offers a good choice of competitively priced Scottish fare.
9 bth/shr CTV in all bedrooms Tea and coffee making facilities Direct dial from bedrooms Cen ht 5P Last d 9.30pm
ROOMS: s £27.50-£35; d £40-£55*
CARDS:

BANFF Aberdeenshire Map 15 NJ66

Selected

Q Q Q Q ***Bryvard*** Seafield St AB45 1EB (on A98 100mtrs from junct with Castle Street near the War Memorial) ☎ 01261 818090
Enthusiastic owner Kathleen Moffat is making good progress with her ambitious programme of renovation of her lovely detached Edwardian house. Pretty fabrics have been used in the attractively decorated bedrooms, furnished in period style. Thoughtful touches include fresh flowers and sweets. At present there is one comfortable lounge but a further non-smoking lounge is planned. Breakfasts are served at the communal table in the dining room, soon to have a conservatory extension.
5 rms (2 shr) No smoking in bedrooms No smoking in dining room No smoking in 1 lounge CTV in all bedrooms Tea and coffee making facilities No dogs (ex guide dogs) Cen ht

Q Q Q ***Morayhill*** Bellevue Rd AB45 1BJ (turn off A947 onto A97, direction Aberchirder, second on right and third house on left) ☎ 01261 815956 FAX 01261 818717
An elegant detached Victorian house, situated within a few minutes of the central amenities. The comfortable, non-smoking bedrooms offer a wide range of amenities and are enhanced by fresh floral displays. The inviting lounge has an original marble fire place and freshly prepared breakfasts are served at individual tables in the dining room. Golf and fishing can be arranged on request by the friendly owners.
3 rms (2 shr) (2 fmly) CTV in all bedrooms Tea and coffee making facilities Cen ht CTV 5P

BEAULY Highland Map 14 NH54

Selected

Q Q Q Q **Chrialdon Hotel** Station Rd IV4 7EH (situated on the main street of the village of Beauly) ☎ 01463 782336 FAX 01463
Apr-Oct
Nicoll and Val Reid continue to improve standards at their comfortable and well appointed detached Victorian home beside the main road. First floor bedrooms have been refurbished to a high standard although those on the top floor do not have private facilities. Refreshments are served in the lounge and Nicoll, a chef of some experience, offers a tempting range of traditional Scottish fare in the attractive dining room. Smoking is only permitted in the lounge.
9 rms (2 bth 4 shr) (2 fmly) No smoking in bedrooms No smoking in dining room CTV in all bedrooms Tea and coffee making facilities Licensed Cen ht CTV 14P No coaches Last d 7.30pm
ROOMS: s £26-£40; d £36-£60
CARDS:

QQQ **Heathmount** Station Rd IV4 7EQ (20mtrs from Post Office)
☎ 01463 782411
Closed Xmas & New Year
Good value accommodation is offered at this detached Victorian house situated beside the main road. The brightly decorated bedrooms are spacious and well maintained with modern furnishings. The lounge is ideal for relaxation and freshly prepared breakfasts are served at individual tables in the dining room.
5 rms (2 fmly) No smoking in bedrooms No smoking in dining room CTV in all bedrooms Tea and coffee making facilities Cen ht CTV 5P No coaches
ROOMS: s £18; d £36*

BEITH North Ayrshire Map 10 NS35

Selected

QQQQ **Garnock Lodge** Boydstone Rd, Lochwinnoch PA12 4JT (1m N of Beith, just off A737) ☎ 01505 503680 FAX 01505 503680
Vivienne and Jim McMeechan's comfortable bungalow is situated one mile north of Beith and has recently been substantially refurbished. The bedrooms have been decorated to a high standard and offer modern appointments with many personal touches. There is an additional single room available in conjunction with one first floor room, for family use. There is a small and attractive sitting area with French windows that leads onto the patio - this is the only area where smoking is permitted. Vivienne's enjoyable home cooking and substantial breakfasts are served at separate tables in the dining room.
4 rms (1 bth 2 shr) No smoking CTV in all bedrooms Tea and coffee making facilities Cen ht 7P No coaches Last d 6.30pm
ROOMS: s £11-£16; d £36-£42; wkly b&b £120-£140; wkly hlf-bd £200-£225*
CARDS:

QQQ **Shotts Farm** *(NS363500)* KA15 1LB (from A736 or A737 take B706 to Barnhill or Greenhills and follow Bed & Breakfast signs)
☎ 01505 502273 Mrs J Gillan
A relaxed friendly atmosphere prevails at this modernised farmhouse situated in quiet rolling countryside four miles east of Beith. Bedrooms vary in size and offer comfortable modern appointments. There is a pleasant and spacious dining room overlooking the garden where breakfasts and home cooked dinners are served at the communal table.
3 rms (1 shr) (1 fmly) CTV in all bedrooms Tea and coffee making facilities No dogs Cen ht CTV 3P 200 acres dairy Last d 10am
ROOMS: s fr £14; d fr £26; wkly b&b fr £84; wkly hlf-bd fr £140*

BIGGAR South Lanarkshire Map 11 NT03

Selected

QQQQ **Toftcombs Country House & Restaurant** Peebles Rd ML12 6QX (A702 from Biggar towards Edinburgh, take A72 Peebles turning on right, house 50yds from junction)
☎ 01899 220142 FAX 01899 221771
Charles and Vivian Little completed a magnificent restoration job on this fine red sandstone building in June 1998. Toftcombs now combines the comfort and elegance of a country house with the convivial atmosphere a country restaurant. The same menu can also be enjoyed in the bar lounge, and there are other lounges in which to relax with a magazine or over coffee. Upstairs, the tastefully appointed bedrooms retain the character of the house.
4 bth/shr (1 fmly) No smoking in bedrooms No smoking in dining room No smoking in 1 lounge CTV in all bedrooms Tea and coffee making facilities Direct dial from bedrooms No dogs Licensed Cen ht ch fac 50P Last d 9.30pm
ROOMS: s £45; d £60*
CARDS:

BLAIR ATHOLL Perth & Kinross Map 14 NN86

Selected

QQQQ **Dalgreine** Bridge of Tilt PH18 5SX (turn off A9 at Blair Atholl sign. Dalgreine is situated between garage and butchers shop one row back from main road) ☎ 01796 481276
The new owners look forward to welcoming old and new guests to their comfortable home which stands in its own colourful garden in a residential area close to Blair Castle. Though variable in size, the bedrooms are smartly decorated and offer comfortable pine furnishings. There is a lounge and separate dining room where home cooked evening meals are served by prior arrangement. This is a non-smoking house.
6 rms (3 shr) (1 fmly) No smoking Tea and coffee making facilities No dogs (ex guide dogs) Cen ht CTV 6P No coaches Small snooker table Last d 3pm
ROOMS: s £15.50-£17.50; d £31-£37; wkly b&b £103.95-£116.55; wkly hlf-bd £173.95-£186.55

BLAIRGOWRIE Perth & Kinross Map 15 NO14

QQQ **Dalmore House Hotel** Rosemount PH10 6QB (on A93)
☎ 01250 872150
Feb-Nov
A relaxed and friendly atmosphere prevails at this comfortable small hotel in its own well tended garden close to the golf course. Attractive colour schemes have been used to good effect in the comfortably furnished bedrooms. There is a well stocked bar and a smartly appointed dining room. The putting green in the garden is a popular practice facility for the golfers.
5 shr (1 fmly) No smoking in bedrooms No smoking in dining room CTV in all bedrooms Tea and coffee making facilities No dogs Cen ht CTV 60P Pool table Mini golf course Last d 10pm

QQQ **Duncraggan** Perth Rd PH10 6EJ (on A93 from Perth pass Shell service station on left, 2 bungalows, Duncraggon on corner of Essendy and Perth road) ☎ 01250 872082 FAX 01250 872098
Christine McClement looks forward to welcoming guests old and new to her lovely detached home standing in its own secluded garden. Two of the attractively decorated en suite bedrooms are comfortably furnished in pine while the other room has a four-poster bed and private bathroom. The comfortable lounge, with ample reading material and board games, invites peaceful relaxation. There is a separate dining room where hearty breakfasts, light suppers and dinners are served. A non-smoking establishment.
4 rms (2 shr) No smoking CTV in all bedrooms Tea and coffee making facilities No dogs Cen ht CTV 6P No coaches 9 hole putting and table tennis Last d 5pm
ROOMS: s £18.50-£20*

QQQ **Gilmore House** Perth Rd PH10 6EJ (situated on the main A93 from Perth at the beginning of Blairgowrie) ☎ 01250 872791
Improvements are ongoing at this comfortable, detached house. Throughout the house, the atmosphere is relaxed and welcoming and public areas include

a choice of inviting lounges as well as an attractive dining room. Hearty breakfasts and, by prior arrangement, evening meals are willingly served at individual tables. Bedrooms are gradually being enhanced. This is a non-smoking house.
3 bth/shr (1 fmly) No smoking CTV in all bedrooms Tea and coffee making facilities Cen ht CTV 3P No coaches Last d 8pm
ROOMS: s fr £17.50; d £32-£37

Q Q Q ***Heathpark Lodge*** Coupar Angus Rd PH10 6JT (on A923 at Rosemount) ☎ 01250 874929 FAX 01250 874929
A warm welcome is assured at Ruth Mitchell's inviting lodge-style home, located on the south side of town. There are two bedrooms, one traditional and one modern, and although they do not have wash basins they are both located near the bathroom. The attractive sun lounge invites peaceful relaxation and leads onto the garden. Freshly prepared breakfasts, including fish dishes, are served at the communal table in the combined TV lounge/dining room.
2 rms No smoking in bedrooms No smoking in dining room CTV in all bedrooms No dogs (ex guide dogs) CTV No children 3yrs 5P No coaches

BOAT OF GARTEN Highland Map 14 NH91

Premier Selected

Q Q Q Q Q **Glenavon House** Kinchurdy Rd PH24 3BP (turn off A9, follow signs for Grantown-on-Spey until sign for Boat of Garten. At Boat of Garten Post Office turn right into Kinchurdy Rd, on right) ☎ 01479 831213 FAX 01479 831213
New Year, Apr-Oct
Ian and Rosemary Strain look forward to welcoming guests to their charming home, a detached Victorian house in landscaped gardens. Bedrooms, all en suite, are decorated and furnished to a high standard and offer a wide range of amenities. In the evening, relax with a pre-dinner drink in front of the cosy log fire in the delightful sitting room and peruse Ian's tempting menu. Dinner is served 'house party' style around the communal table in the elegant dining room. Dinner is a gourmet experience and there is a carefully chosen wine list.
5 bth/shr No smoking in bedrooms No smoking in dining room CTV in all bedrooms Tea and coffee making facilities Licensed Cen ht 8P No coaches Last d 5.30pm
ROOMS: s fr £25; d fr £50; wkly b&b fr £161; wkly hlf-bd fr £287*
CARDS:

BONAR BRIDGE Highland Map 14 NH69

Q Q **Kyle House** Dornoch Rd IV24 3EB (on A949, 4th house on left after newsagents going N out of village) ☎ 01863 766360
Feb-Nov
This spacious roadside house has splendid views over the Kyle of Sutherland towards the Ross-shire hills and offers guests good value accommodation. Bedrooms are furnished in traditional style with central heating, electric blankets and double glazing as well as TVs. There is a comfortable lounge with a colour TV, and a coal fire for the colder months. The spacious dining room is to the front of the house and has separate tables.
6 rms (3 bth/shr) (2 fmly) No smoking in bedrooms No smoking in dining room CTV in all bedrooms Tea and coffee making facilities No dogs (ex guide dogs) Licensed Cen ht CTV No children 5yrs 6P No coaches
ROOMS: s £17.50-£20; d £35-£40; wkly b&b £120-£135*

BO'NESS Falkirk Map 11 NS98

Q Q Q **Kinglass** *(NT006803)* Borrowstoun Rd EH51 9RW (from M9 junct 3, turn right, first left for 1.5m, farm on right hand side) ☎ 01506 822861 & 824185 FAX 01506 824433 Mrs B Kirk

Many visitors to the area, businessman and holidaymakers alike, return regularly to this welcoming farmhouse which stands in its own garden beside the main farm complex. The bedrooms are variable in size and offer mixed modern furnishings together with a good range of amenities. Hearty breakfasts and, by prior arrangement, enjoyable home cooked evening meals are served at individual tables in the attractive dining room.
6 rms (2 shr) (1 fmly) CTV in all bedrooms Tea and coffee making facilities Direct dial from bedrooms Licensed Cen ht CTV 20P 750 acres arable Last d 5.30pm

BRAEMAR Aberdeenshire Map 15 NO19

Selected

Q Q Q Q **Callater Lodge Hotel** 9 Glenshee Rd AB35 5YQ (adjacent to A93, 300yds S of Braemar village centre) ☎ 013397 41275 FAX 013397 41275
rs Nov-Dec
Standing in over an acre of grounds beside the Glenshee road, this detached Victorian house offers mostly spacious bedrooms with comfortable modern furnishings. A welcoming fire burns in the lounge on cooler evenings and in the separate dining room a good choice of dishes are offered at breakfast. Enjoyable home cooked dinners are available by arrangement.
7 rms (6 bth/shr) No smoking in 2 bedrooms No smoking in dining room No smoking in lounges CTV in all bedrooms Tea and coffee making facilities Licensed Cen ht CTV No children 4yrs 6P No coaches Last d noon
ROOMS: s £24-£31; d £46-£62; wkly b&b £168-£217; wkly hlf-bd £259-£308
CARDS:

BRIDGE OF WEIR Renfrewshire Map **10** NS36

QQQ **Garth House** Bank End Rd PA11 3EU
(M8 junct 27A. A789 Houston/Bridge of Weir. A761 BOW. At sign for BOW left into Locher Rd to T junct, turn right then right again. Bankend Rd)
☎ 01505 614414 FAX 01505 614414
This substantial late Victorian house, in attractive gardens, is in a quiet residential crescent, yet only 15 minutes from the airport. The bedrooms are spacious and some have fine views. Guests have use of a cosy wood panelled lounge which opens on to a small sun porch and the back garden. Dinner can be served by arrangement in the attractive dining room.
3 rms (2 bth/shr) (2 fmly) No smoking in bedrooms No smoking in dining room No smoking in 1 lounge CTV in all bedrooms Tea and coffee making facilities No dogs (ex guide dogs) Cen ht 4P No coaches
Last d noon
ROOMS: s £25-£50; d £50-£60; wkly b&b £140-£160*
CARDS:

BRODICK See **ARRAN, ISLE OF**

BRORA Highland Map **14** NC90

Selected

QQQQ **Lynwood** Golf Rd KW9 6QS
(turn off A9 by river bridge onto Golf Rd, 500 yards on left)
☎ 01408 621226 FAX 01408 621226
Closed Jan & Feb
This welcoming family home stands within its own pretty walled garden close to the golf course. Bedrooms are tastefully decorated and offer comfortable modern furnishings. One room with external access is suitable for disabled guests. There is a homely lounge and attractive dining room with a conservatory extension where Mary Cooper's enjoyable home cooking and hearty breakfasts earn much praise.
3 rms (1 bth 1 shr) 1 annexe shr (1 fmly) No smoking in bedrooms No smoking in 1 lounge CTV in all bedrooms Tea and coffee making facilities Cen ht CTV 4P No coaches
ROOMS: s £25-£28; d £40-£46; wkly b&b £130-£150; wkly hlf-bd £210-£230*
CARDS:

BURNMOUTH Scottish Borders Map **12** NT96

QQQ **Greystonelees** *(NT958604)* Greystonelees TD14 5SZ
(6m N of Berwick on Tweed, 1/4m before village of Burnmouth on A1)
☎ 01890 781709 FAX 781709 Mrs P Goff
Although it's no longer a working farm, this farmhouse is an animal lover's paradise. The Goffs have assembled a varied collection of livestock which includes geese, ducks, sheep and family pets, with more exotic species such as owls and squirrels coming and going as they wait for new homes following injury or abandonment. The house itself is attractive and inviting. There are lots of books in the guests' lounge and the dining room houses a variety of stuffed birds and animals, most of which have perished on the main road nearby. Bedrooms are thoughtfully equipped to include a radio and hair dryer, as well as a montage of the occupants of Greystonelees!
3 bth/shr No smoking CTV in all bedrooms Tea and coffee making facilities Cen ht CTV No children 5yrs 10P 140 acres mixed
Last d 4pm
ROOMS: s £20-£25; d £38-£42; wkly b&b £135-£150; wkly hlf-bd £198-£250
CARDS:

See page 14-20 for a list of Premier Selected establishments

BUTE, ISLE OF Argyll & Bute

MOUNT STUART Map **10** NS15

Selected

QQQQ **New Farm** *(NS098584)* PA20 9NA (Left after coming off Wemyss Bay Rothesay Ferry. New Farm is app. 6m on right - 1m past Mount Stuart House) ☎ 01700 831646 Mrs C Howard
Unique, personal, different and *homely* are some of the words best used to describe this highly individual farmhouse, set in over 1000 acres of land where sheep, pigs and dairy cattle are reared. Carole Howard has developed a dining experience that is reminiscent of farmhouse family gatherings, when all guests are seated at a communal table and help themselves to the dishes created from the farm's own produce; guests are welcome to bring their own drinks. Bedrooms reflect the farmhouse style, being simply furnished, yet having many nice touches.
3 rms (1 bth/shr) (1 fmly) CTV in all bedrooms Tea and coffee making facilities No dogs (ex guide dogs) Cen ht 25P 1080 acres dairy/sheep/arable/hens/pigs
ROOMS: s £20-£27.50; d £40-£60

CALLANDER Stirling Map **11** NN60

QQQ *Abbotsford Lodge* Stirling Rd FK17 8DA
(off A84 eastern approach to town) ☎ 01877 330066
This welcoming family run hotel, a detached Victorian house standing to the east of town, offers good value accommodation. The well maintained bedrooms are variable in size and in style while public areas include a comfortable lounge, small dispense bar, and a restaurant with conservatory extension.
18 rms (5 bth 5 shr) (7 fmly) No smoking in dining room Tea and coffee making facilities Licensed Cen ht CTV 20P Last d 7pm

QQQ **Almardon** Leny Rd FK17 8AJ (W of town adjacent to Meadows Park) ☎ 01877 331597
Situated beside the main road at the west end of town, Margaret Cameron's attractive detached bungalow offers good value accommodation. The house is maintained to a high standard and the comfortable modern bedrooms have fitted pine units, and all offer a wide range of amenities. There is also a combined lounge/dining room where hearty breakfasts are served at individual tables. A warm welcome is assured.
3 shr No smoking in dining room CTV in all bedrooms Tea and coffee making facilities No dogs Cen ht CTV No children 12yrs 6P
ROOMS: d £40-£42; wkly b&b £125-£130

QQQ **Annfield** 18 North Church St FK17 8EG ☎ 01877 330204
Closed 20 Dec-5 Jan
Good value accommodation is offered at this comfortable detached Victorian house is situated close to central amenities. Bedrooms are spacious and comfortably furnished in both modern and traditional styles, and there is an inviting first floor lounge which features a collection of dolls from around

the world. Hearty breakfasts are served at individual tables in the attractive dining room. No smoking in bedrooms.
7 rms (4 shr) (1 fmly) No smoking in bedrooms No smoking in dining room Tea and coffee making facilities Cen ht CTV No children 10yrs 9P No coaches
ROOMS: s £25; d £40

Selected

QQQQ **Arden House** Bracklinn Rd FK17 8EQ
(from A84 in Callander turn right into Bracklinn Rd, signposted to golf course and Bracklinn Falls. House 200yds on left)
☎ 01877 330235 FAX 01877 330235
31 Mar-1 Nov
This substantial Victorian family home stands in a quiet location just a short walk up the hill from the main street. Now under enthusiastic new ownership, the association of the house as the home of television's Dr Finlay is a theme. Bedrooms are comfortable and have many thoughtful and personal touches. There is a homely lounge and the breakfast room has been redecorated with individual tables.
6 bth/shr No smoking CTV in all bedrooms Tea and coffee making facilities No dogs Cen ht No children 14yrs 10P No coaches
ROOMS: s fr £25; d £50-£60; wkly b&b £150-£175*
CARDS:

Premier Selected

QQQQQ **Arran Lodge** Leny Rd FK17 8AJ
(on W outskirts on the A84) ☎ 01877 330976
mid Mar-Oct
Robert and Pasqua Moore's immaculately kept bungalow is over 150 years old and has lovely gardens with lawns leading down to the River Leny. It is immaculately maintained and adorned with mementoes from around the world as well as photographs of Robert's days in television. Three of the bedrooms have four-poster beds and all have purpose-fitted furniture to make good use of space. Two rooms are accessed from outside, each having its own door leading onto the garden. Public rooms are delightful, a beautiful lounge looking onto the garden and an elegant dining room.
4 bth/shr (1 fmly) No smoking CTV in all bedrooms Tea and coffee making facilities No dogs Cen ht CTV No children 12yrs 5P No coaches Fishing
ROOMS: d £30-£40; wkly b&b £210-£260.50*

We endeavour to be as accurate as possible but changes in personnel and data can occur in establishments after the Guide has gone to press

Selected

QQQQ **Brook Linn Country House** Leny Feus FK17 8AU
(take A84 through Callander from Stirling, turn right at Pinewood Nursing Home into Leny Feus. Right again and uphill at "Brook Linn" sign) ☎ 01877 330103 FAX 01877 330103
Etr-Oct
Fiona and Derek Home have sympathetically restored their elegant Victorian home to provide their guests with consistently high standards. The bedrooms are bright and airy with attractive decor and pretty fabrics. Some are furnished in period style while others have more modern appointments. Public areas include an inviting sitting room and enjoyable home cooked fare is served at individual tables in the tastefully appointed dining room. The house stands peacefully in 2 acres of mature grounds above the town. This is a non smoking establishment.
6 shr (1 fmly) No smoking CTV in all bedrooms Tea and coffee making facilities Licensed Cen ht 10P No coaches Last d £
ROOMS: s £22-£26; d £44-£52
CARDS:

CARDROSS Argyll & Bute Map **10** NS37

Premier Selected

QQQQQ **Kirkton House** Darleith Rd G82 5EZ (0.5m N of village - turn N off A814 into Darleith Road at W end of village. Kirkton House is half mile on right) (The Circle)
☎ 01389 841951 FAX 01389 841868
Closed Dec-Jan
Stewart and Gillian McDonald are the owners of this spacious and traditional farmhouse. Inside the atmosphere is rustic and this, together with Gillian's splendid home cooking ensures that many guests return regularly. The well equipped bedrooms enjoy panoramic views over the River Clyde. Linda Mcdonald, the daughter, is an accomplished jewellery designer who specialises in creating tailor made, fine quality pieces to commemorate your visit.
6 bth/shr (4 fmly) No smoking in dining room CTV in all bedrooms Tea and coffee making facilities Direct dial from bedrooms Licensed Cen ht ch fac 12P No coaches Riding Last d 7.30pm
ROOMS: s £40; d £59.50-£65; wkly b&b £208.25; wkly hlf-bd £301*
CARDS:
See advertisement under HELENSBURGH

This symbol indicates a 'Child Friendly' establishment - see page 25 for details

CARNOUSTIE Angus Map 12 NO53

Selected

QQQQ **Park House** 12 Park Av DD7 7JA (turn off A92 on to the Muirdrum A930 road) ☎ 01241 852101 FAX 01241 852101
A substantial detached Victorian house with a welcoming atmosphere, centrally situated and within a short walk of the famous Championship golf course. The tastefully decorated bedrooms are comfortably furnished and one room offers a superb bathroom which includes a Jacuzzi. Substantial breakfasts are served in the dining room overlooking the garden. This is a non smoking establishment.
3 bth/shr No smoking CTV in all bedrooms Tea and coffee making facilities No dogs (ex guide dogs) Cen ht CTV 5P No coaches large lawn, BBQ area,
ROOMS: s fr £22; d fr £44*
CARDS:

CARRADALE Argyll & Bute Map 10 NR83

QQQ **Dunvalanree** Port Righ PA28 6SE (in middle of Carradale village turn left at sign for Portrigh Bay and follow road to end)
☎ 01583 431226 FAX 01583 431339
This comfortable detached home is peacefully situated beside a small bay with glorious views over the water to the hills of Arran beyond. Bedrooms are bright and fresh, mostly furnished in traditional style. The comfortable lounge and attractive dining room have a relaxed and friendly atmosphere. Home baking is a speciality.
7 rms (3 shr) (1 fmly) No smoking Tea and coffee making facilities Licensed CTV ch fac 19P No coaches Golf 9 Fishing Squash Last d 8.30pm
ROOMS: s £20-£23; d £40-£46; wkly b&b £120; wkly hlf-bd £190*

CARRBRIDGE Highland Map 14 NH92

Selected

QQQQ **Carrmoor** Carr Rd PH23 3AD (first right after bistro)
☎ 01479 841244 FAX 01479 841244
Enthusiastic owners Michael and Christine Stitt have tastefully modernised and refurbished their charming village home. The brightly decorated bedrooms have been carefully designed to make best use of available space and offer modern furnishings. There is a comfortable TV lounge and a small dining room where Michael's enjoyable food, carefully prepared from fresh local produce, is presented. The daily-changing fixed-price menu, which is supported by an extensive carte, also caters for vegetarians and children. When space is available, non-residents can also make use of the restaurant.
6 shr (1 fmly) No smoking in bedrooms No smoking in dining room Tea and coffee making facilities Licensed Cen ht CTV 6P No coaches Last d 8pm
ROOMS: s £21.50-£26; d £38-£42; wkly b&b £126-£175; wkly hlf-bd £210-£259
CARDS:

QQQ **Feith Mhor Country House** Station Rd PH23 3AP (off A9 to Carrbridge. Station Road is opposite grocers shop. Continue for 1.25m and house is on right) ☎ 01479 841621
Closed 30 Nov-26 Dec
Feith Mhor is a substantial Victorian house which is peacefully set in its own well tended gardens amid beautiful countryside. Bedrooms are furnished in both traditional and modern styles and offer all the expected amenities. Public areas include an inviting lounge with well filled book shelves and a dining room where breakfast is served at individual tables that overlook the garden.
6 bth/shr (1 fmly) No smoking in dining room No smoking in lounges CTV in all bedrooms Tea and coffee making facilities Licensed Cen ht No children 12yrs 8P No coaches
ROOMS: s £25-£26; d £50-£52; wkly b&b £168-£175*

CASTLE DOUGLAS Dumfries & Galloway Map 11 NX76

QQQ **Barrington House** 39 St Andrew St DG7 1EN (turn off A75 (Gretna to Stranraer road) to first rdbt at edge of town and take second left exit, down Queen St and 3rd left into St Andrew St)
☎ 01556 502601
This delightful period house lies just off the town centre and offers spacious and comfortable accommodation in a traditional environment. Impressive woodwork and a fine staircase, plus plenty of ornaments and personal items feature in what is a friendly and welcoming family home. All guest rooms are on the ground floor, and there is a relaxing lounge, and all meals come freshly cooked.
2 bth/shr No smoking CTV in all bedrooms Tea and coffee making facilities Cen ht No children 12yrs No coaches Last d 5pm
ROOMS: d £40-£44; wkly b&b £120-£132; wkly hlf-bd £183-£209*

QQQ **Rose Cottage** Gelston DG7 1SH (beside B727, 2m S)
☎ 01556 502513
Feb-Oct
This cosy little cottage sits in its own gardens bordered by a small stream with fields at the bottom, in the small village of Gelston, about two miles from Castle Douglas. Bedrooms are all on the ground floor, with two chalet-style rooms behind the house that are ideal for families. There is a comfortable lounge and a bright cheery dining room.
3 rms (1 bth/shr) 2 annexe rms (1 fmly) No smoking in dining room CTV in 3 bedrooms Tea and coffee making facilities Cen ht CTV 15P No coaches Last d 5pm
ROOMS: s £18; d £36-£41; wkly b&b £126-£143.50; wkly hlf-bd £195-£212.50

COATBRIDGE North Lanarkshire Map 11 NS76

QQQ **Auchenlea** 153 Langmuir Rd, Bargeddie G69 7RS (turn off A8 onto A752, 0.5m on right before A89) ☎ 0141 771 6870
There's a welcoming atmosphere at this comfortable semi-detached cottage-style house which is backed by farmland. The two modern styled bedrooms provide all expected amenities. Satisfying breakfasts are served at the communal table in the comfortable combined lounge/dining room.
2 bth/shr (1 fmly) No smoking CTV in all bedrooms Tea and coffee making facilities No dogs (ex guide dogs) Cen ht CTV 8P
ROOMS: s £18-£20; d £36-£40*

COMRIE Perth & Kinross Map 11 NN72

QQQ **Mossgiel** Burrell St PH6 2JP (on A85 opposite Parish Church)
☎ 01764 670567 FAX 01764 670567
The Griffiths family look forward to welcoming guests old and new to their comfortable home which stands at the west end of the village. Popular golfing packages are arranged, and tourists are equally welcome. The

bedrooms are bright and cheerful with attractive fabrics and smart pine furnishings. Guests have their own cosy lounge, and hearty breakfasts and enjoyable home cooked evening meals are offered in the timber clad dining room.
3 shr No smoking in bedrooms No smoking in dining room Tea and coffee making facilities No dogs Cen ht CTV No children 5yrs 6P No coaches Golf packages Physical therapy clinic Last d 6pm
ROOMS: s £25-£30; d £44-£50; wkly b&b £140-£160
CARDS:

CONNEL Argyll & Bute Map **10** NM93

Premier Selected

Q Q Q Q Q **Ards House** PA37 1PT (on A85, 4m N of Oban) ☎ 01631 710255
Closed Dec-Jan rs 1-23 Dec
Jean and John Bowman welcome guests to their detached house on the western side of the village. The view from front facing rooms towards the Morven Hills beyond the Firth of Lorn is spectacular especially at sunset. All bedrooms are individually decorated and comfortably furnished in mixed styles with many thoughtful touches. The house is licensed and guests can relax in the spacious lounge before moving to the dining room for dinner.
7 bth/shr No smoking CTV in 1 bedroom Tea and coffee making facilities No dogs Licensed Cen ht CTV No children 14yrs 12P No coaches Last d 6.30pm
ROOMS: s £40-£50; d £80-£102; wkly hlf-bd £270-£320
CARDS:

See advertisement under OBAN

Q Q Q ***Kilchurn*** PA37 1PG (on A85) ☎ 01631 710581
Etr-Oct
This Victorian villa is on the east side of the village and offers fine views across the turbulent Loch Etive towards Ben Lora on the opposite shore. Attractive standards of decoration are provided in the comfortable bedrooms, which have some nice personal touches. The homely lounge has a television and breakfast is served at three tables in the elegant dining room which overlooks the loch.
3 bth/shr No smoking in bedrooms No smoking in dining room CTV in all bedrooms Tea and coffee making facilities No dogs No children 12yrs 3P No coaches

Selected

Q Q Q Q **Loch Etive House Hotel** Main St PA37 1PH (Turn off A85 in village of Connel, 5 miles from Oban)
☎ 01631 710400 FAX 01631 710680
Etr-28 Oct
The genuine warm welcome together with good food are all part of the appeal of this personally-run private hotel in the centre of the village, just off the A85. The comfortable bedrooms vary in size with both modern and traditional furnishings; one top floor room has a natural stone wall and beamed ceiling while another is fully pine clad. There is also a comfortable combined lounge/dining room.
6 rms (4 bth/shr) (2 fmly) No smoking in 3 bedrooms No smoking in dining room No smoking in lounges CTV in all bedrooms Tea and coffee making facilities Licensed Cen ht 7P No coaches
ROOMS: s £25-£50; d £40-£60 ✳
CARDS:

Selected

Q Q Q Q **Ronebhal** PA37 1PJ (on A85 Oban road. 4th house past turn off for Fort William overlooking the bay)
☎ 01631 710310 FAX 710310
Apr-Oct
This attractive detached Victorian house stands in its own well-tended garden beside the A85 with a lovely outlook over Loch Etive. It has a welcoming atmosphere and offers high standards of comfort. Bedrooms, with pretty dècor and attractive fabrics, are comfortably furnished in the modern style. Most are en suite, though one room has a private bathroom opposite, and the single room has private use of a shower room downstairs. There is a relaxing and homely lounge and substantial breakfasts are served at individual tables in the dining room.
5 rms (4 shr) (1 fmly) No smoking CTV in all bedrooms Tea and coffee making facilities No dogs Cen ht No children 7yrs 6P No coaches
ROOMS: s £18-£35; d £36-£60; wkly b&b £119-£196
CARDS:

COWDENBEATH Fife Map **11** NT19

Q Q Q ***Struan Bank Hotel*** 74 Perth Rd KY4 9BG
(turn E at junct 3 M90 to Cowdenbeath, drive through town centre & up hill)
☎ 01383 511057 FAX 01383 511057
Situated on the north side of town, this welcoming and personally run small hotel offers good value for money. Though variable in size, the well equipped bedrooms are comfortable, most with smart pine furnishings. Public areas include a well stocked and comfortable lounge bar and a dining room which is open to non residents.
9 rms (6 shr) (2 fmly) No smoking in dining room CTV in all bedrooms Tea and coffee making facilities Licensed Cen ht CTV 8P No coaches Last d 6pm
CARDS:

CRAIL Fife Map **12** NO60

Q Q **Caiplie** 53 High St KY10 3RA
(from the South on left hand side of the High St) ☎ 01333 450564
FAX 01333 450564
Mar-Nov
The welcoming atmosphere together with enjoyable home cooking are all part of the appeal of this family run guest house in the centre of the village. Public areas include an inviting first floor lounge and separate dining room on the ground floor. The house is licensed.
7 rms (3 shr) (1 fmly) No smoking in dining room Tea and coffee making facilities Licensed Cen ht CTV 3P No coaches Last d 4pm
ROOMS: s £18-£22; d £32-£48; wkly b&b £112-£140;
wkly hlf-bd £168-£196✳

Q Q Q **Golf Hotel** 4 High St KY10 3TD
(Follow A917 along coast, hotel on corner of High St, opposite Royal Bank)
☎ 01333 450206 & 450500 FAX 01333 450795
rs 26 Dec & 1 Jan
Personally run by Graham Guthrie, this historic inn in the centre of the village has a welcoming atmosphere and is especially popular with visiting golfers. Bedrooms have been designed to make best use of available space and are comfortably furnished in pine. Public areas include a homely first floor lounge, a choice of old world bars with exposed beams and natural stone walls. A wide range of meals are served in both bars and the recently refurbished dining room.
5 shr (1 fmly) CTV in all bedrooms Tea and coffee making facilities Cen ht CTV 15P Last d 9pm
ROOMS: s £26-£29; d £46-£50✳
MEALS: Lunch £8.45-£10.50 Dinner £12-£17✳
CARDS:

Q Q Q **Selcraig House** 47 Nethergate KY10 3TX (opposite the Marine Hotel) ☎ 01333 450697 FAX 01333 451113
Margaret Carstairs has lovingly restored her charming home, a stone built semi-detached house which dates back to the 1700s. Many of the original features have been carefully retained. The dining room, with its lovely conservatory extension, has been furnished in the style of an Edwardian parlour and provides a perfect setting for breakfast. Upstairs is an inviting and relaxing lounge. Bedrooms are individual in style with the best rooms being on the first floor. Those at the top of the house are limited in size, but best use has been made of available space. This is a non smoking house.
6 rms (1 fmly) No smoking CTV in all bedrooms Tea and coffee making facilities CTV 2P No coaches Last d noon
ROOMS: s £18-£20; d £36-£40; wkly b&b £120-£135

CRIANLARICH Stirling Map 10 NN32

Q Q Q **The Lodge House** FK20 8RU (on A82, 1m NW of Crianlarich) ☎ 01838 300276
Mar-Oct
A true Scottish welcome awaits at this superbly located guest house. The well proportioned bedrooms offer all expected amenities and the adjacent Scandinavian-style chalet is ideal for family use. A cosy residents' bar adjoins the comfortable lounge. Dinners and breakfasts are served in an attractive dining room with stunning views of the mountains.
5 bth/shr 1 annexe shr No smoking in bedrooms No smoking in dining room CTV in all bedrooms Tea and coffee making facilities Licensed Cen ht CTV 10P No coaches Last d noon
ROOMS: s £25-£45; d £45-£55*
CARDS:

CRIEFF Perth & Kinross Map 11 NN82

Selected

Q Q Q Q **Comeley Bank** 32 Burrell St PH7 4DT (on A822) ☎ 01764 653409
A welcoming atmosphere prevails at this family-run guest house which forms part of a terraced row close to the town centre. The ground floor bedroom has been made en suite and completely refurbished to provide suitable accommodation for either disabled guests or families. Other rooms are tastefully decorated and feature attractive fabrics and pine furnishings. There is also an inviting lounge (the only part of the house where smoking is permitted.) Enjoyable home cooked fare is served at individual tables in the dining room.
5 rms (3 bth/shr) (2 fmly) No smoking in bedrooms No smoking in dining room CTV in all bedrooms Tea and coffee making facilities Licensed Cen ht CTV No coaches Last d 4pm
ROOMS: s fr £17; d fr £38; wkly b&b fr £119; wkly hlf-bd fr £190*

Q Q Q **Gwydyr House Hotel** Comrie Rd PH7 4BP (on A85, Comrie Road, 0.25m from town centre, on right opposite Macrosty Park entrance) ☎ 01764 653277 FAX 01764 653277
Now under the care and direction of the Blackie family, various improvement projects are planned for this lovely Victorian house. Set in its own informal gardens, the house stands beside the A85 at the west side of town and enjoys wonderful views over the Vale of Strathearn. The bright airy bedrooms are generally spacious and offer mixed modern and traditional furnishings. Public areas include an inviting lounge which has a dispense bar and hearty breakfasts are served at individual tables in the bright dining room.
8 rms (7 bth/shr) (2 fmly) No smoking in 4 bedrooms No smoking in dining room CTV in all bedrooms Tea and coffee making facilities Licensed Cen ht CTV 12P No coaches nearby leisure centre
ROOMS: s £25-£28; d £50-£64; wkly b&b £175-£210; wkly hlf-bd £225-£275*
CARDS:

CRINAN Argyll & Bute Map 10 NR79

Selected

Q Q Q Q **Tigh-na-Glaic** *(NR787943)* Crinan PA31 8SW (signposted on B841) ☎ 01546 830245 FAX 01546 830243
Mr M C Anderson
Situated in a picturesque position just above Lock 15 of the Crinan Canal with views across the bay towards Duntrune Castle, this is a cottage-style farmhouse. Wensleydale sheep are reared on the 50 acres of land that lead down to the sea. The accommodation is charming, with one room having its own lounge with good views, whilst the other twin room is accessed from the spacious main lounge. Breakfast is served in the conservatory at a communal table.
2 bth/shr No smoking CTV in all bedrooms Tea and coffee making facilities No dogs (ex guide dogs) Cen ht CTV 4P 55 acres sheep

CULLEN Moray Map **15** NJ56

Q Q **Torrach** 147 Seatown AB56 4SL (A98 fron Elgin, on entering Cullen turn first left after viaduct at Royal Oak Hotel, then first right afer 150yds. Cream house next to post box) ☎ 01542 840724
Etr-Sep
The genuine home from home atmosphere is all part of the appeal of Ann Mair's delightful home, a former fisherman's cottage which has been completely renovated and modernised. The house, situated close to the harbour and golf course, has two comfortable and well equipped bedrooms on the first floor.
2 rms (1 fmly) CTV in all bedrooms Tea and coffee making facilities Cen ht CTV 2P
ROOMS: s £18; d £32✳

CULLODEN MOOR Highland Map **14** NH74

Q Q **Culdoich** *(NH755435)* Culloden Moor IV1 2EP
☎ 01463 790268 Mrs E M C Alexander
May-Oct
Situated south east of Inverness amid pleasant rural countryside overlooking the famous battlefield, this traditional farmhouse has a relaxed, homely atmosphere. Bedrooms are spacious and there is a comfortable lounge. Mrs Alexander provides hearty breakfasts and enjoyable home-cooked evening meals at the communal table, and the complimentary tea and shortbread provided in the evening is a nice touch.
2 rms (1 fmly) No smoking in dining room Tea and coffee making facilities No dogs CTV P 200 acres mixed Last d 5pm
ROOMS: d £34✳

CUPAR Fife Map **11** NO31

Q Q Q **Rathcluan** Carslogie Rd KY15 4HY
(on A91, adjacent to main Cupar police station, house sits behind trees)
☎ 01334 657856/7 FAX 01334 657856/7
This substantial building lies in its own gardens on the main road off the town centre, close to Elmwood College. Formerly government offices it is now a well proportioned B&B offering practical yet spacious accommodation, including a large comfortable lounge and a dining room which features a magnificent old cooking range. A ground floor bedroom has been adapted for use by disabled guests.
10 rms (2 shr) (2 fmly) No smoking in bedrooms No smoking in dining room CTV in all bedrooms Tea and coffee making facilities Licensed Cen ht CTV 30P Tennis (grass) Last d 5pm
ROOMS: s £20-£30✳
CARDS:

Premier Selected

Q Q Q Q Q **Todhall House** Dairsie KY15 4RQ (2m E of Cupar, on A91 - sign for Todhall on left. House half mile from road end)
☎ 01334 656344 FAX 01334 656344
Closed Nov-mid Mar
This beautiful house lies in countryside to the east of Cupar. The tastefully decorated bedrooms are comfortably furnished and have thoughtful extras such as books and fruit. The master bedroom has a four poster bed. During the summer months guests can enjoy the fabulous views whilst taking tea in the two acre garden or swim in the outdoor pool. Dinner and breakfast can be enjoyed in front of a roaring log fire in the dining room.
3 bth/shr No smoking CTV in all bedrooms Tea and coffee making facilities No dogs Cen ht No children 10yrs 5P No coaches Outdoor swimming pool Golf net Last d noon
ROOMS: s £30-£36; d £50-£60; wkly b&b £157.50-£189
CARDS:

DALBEATTIE Dumfries & Galloway Map **11** NX86

Q Q Q **Anchor Hotel** Kippford DG5 4LN (off A710)
☎ 01556 620205 FAX 01556 620205
Set in a picturesque village overlooking the marina and estuary, this inn is foremost a food pub popular for its wide range of dishes served in a variety of different bar areas. Bright modern bedrooms are provided upstairs.
7 rms (6 bth/shr) (2 fmly) No smoking in 2 bedrooms No smoking in area of dining room No smoking in lounges CTV in all bedrooms Tea and coffee making facilities No dogs 6P Golf 12 Children's games room Last d 9pm
ROOMS: s £22.50-£40; d £48-£50✳
MEALS: Lunch £4-£14✳
CARDS:

Premier Selected

Q Q Q Q Q **Auchenskeoch Lodge** DG5 4PG (5m SE off B793)
☎ 01387 780277 FAX 01387 780277
Closed Nov-Mar
This fine Victorian shooting lodge is peacefully situated in 20 acres of grounds that include a vegetable garden, croquet lawn, small fishing loch and a maze. Christopher and Mary Broom-Smith have carefully retained the original character of the house, full of charm and graced with antiques and period furniture. Two of the well proportioned bedrooms have a lounge area and one of these can be also be used as an additional single bedroom. The spacious ground-floor room is ideally suited for disabled or elderly guests. A set four course dinner is served house party style at 8pm and features Mary's home-cooked dishes

contd.

which include vegetables picked from the garden. There is a good wine list and guests are invited to help themselves to drinks in the billiard room.

Auchenskeoch Lodge

3 bth/shr No smoking in dining room CTV in all bedrooms Tea and coffee making facilities Licensed Cen ht No children 12yrs 22P No coaches Fishing Snooker Croquet lawn Last d 8pm
ROOMS: s £37-£40; d £58-£64
CARDS:

Q Q **Pheasant Hotel** 1 Maxwell St DG5 4AH
(A74 onto A75 (Dumfries) onto A711, hotel at junct of A711/High St)
☎ 01556 610345 FAX 01556 612362
Located in the centre of the town the Pheasant has built up a reputation for its good value meals and friendly service. The popular public bar serves real ale and has a giant video screen, ideal for sporting events, whilst the upstairs dining room also has a bar. Bedrooms are bright, modern and well equipped.
8 bth/shr (3 fmly) CTV in all bedrooms Tea and coffee making facilities Direct dial from bedrooms Cen ht CTV discounts on Golf courses Last d 9pm
ROOMS: s £22.50-£25; d £38-£45
MEALS: Lunch £6&alc Dinner £6&alc
CARDS:

DALCROSS Highland Map 14 NH75

Q Q Q **Easter Dalziel Farmhouse** *(NH755509)* Easter Dalziel Farm, Dalcross IV1 2JL (between A96 and B9039, 6m E of Inverness)
☎ 01667 462213 FAX 01667 462213 Mrs M Pottie
Closed 20 Dec-6 Jan rs 1-20 Dec & 6 Jan-28 Feb
A welcoming atmosphere prevails at Margaret Pottie's comfortable early Victorian farmhouse, which stands amid pleasant wooded countryside near Inverness Airport. Bedrooms are comfortably furnished in both period and traditional styles. There is a relaxing lounge with a piano, stereo and TV, and breakfasts are served at the communal table in the adjacent dining room.
3 rms Tea and coffee making facilities CTV 10P
210 acres arable/beef/sheep Last d 10am
ROOMS: d £34-£40; wkly b&b £119-£133
CARDS:

DALGETY BAY Fife Map 11 NT18

Q Q Q **The Coach House** 1 Hopeward Mews KY11 5TB
(M90 junct1, take A921 for Kirkcaldy, right at NCR factory rdbt in Dalgety Bay, over next 2 rdbts, estab at end of road, driveway marked 'Keep clear')
☎ 01383 823584 FAX 01383 823584
Tom and Patricia Mead look forward to welcoming you to their delightful home, a smart modern bungalow with splendid views over the Firth of Forth to Edinburgh. Although variable in size, bedrooms are comfortably furnished in mixed modern styles. There is a cosy guest lounge where French windows give access to the patio. This is a no-smoking house.
4 rms (1 fmly) No smoking Tea and coffee making facilities No dogs Cen ht CTV No children 10yrs 5P No coaches
ROOMS: s £19-£22; d £38-£44; wkly b&b £130-£140

DALRYMPLE East Ayrshire Map 10 NS31

Q Q Q **Kirkton Inn** 1 Main St KA6 6DF (between A77 and A713 approx 5m from Ayr, signed from both roads. In village large black and white building) ☎ 01292 560241 FAX 01292 560835
A friendly village inn popular for the wide range of good value meals served in its lounge bar. There is also a cosy second bar open in the evening; ask for their list of malt whiskies.
3 bth/shr No smoking in area of dining room CTV in all bedrooms Tea and coffee making facilities Cen ht 40P Last d 8.45pm
ROOMS: s £22.50-£35; d £45-£70; wkly b&b £150-£210; wkly hlf-bd £185-£350; (room only) ✱
MEALS: Lunch £2.50-£15.50&alc Dinner £7.75-£15.50&alc✱
CARDS:

DARVEL East Ayrshire Map 11 NS53

Premier Selected

Q Q Q Q Q **Scoretulloch House** KA17 0LR
(turn off the A71 just east of Darvel and follow signs for 1m)
☎ 01560 323331 FAX 01560 323441
Closed Boxing Day & New Years Day

Donald and Annie Smith have restored a former ruin and created a dream house. Set high on a hillside, sheltered by landscaped gardens, it enjoys fine views across the valley of the River Irvine. The original walls date back 500 years, otherwise everything is new, but the style is that of a Scottish shooting lodge and country home. The very personal service and relaxed atmosphere is in keeping with this style, with Donald and Annie fully involved in looking after their guests. Scoretulloch is however first and foremost a restaurant with rooms. The elegant dining room is the perfect setting for first class cooking which has earned our award of Two Rosettes. There is a cosy library with masses of wildlife books, (Donald is a naturalist, author and photographer) as well as a conservatory bar. Bedrooms are quietly gracious and match perfectly the style of the house.
4 bth/shr No smoking in bedrooms No smoking in dining room No smoking in lounges CTV in all bedrooms Tea and coffee making facilities Direct dial from bedrooms Licensed Cen ht No children 12yrs 50P No coaches Pheasant & clay pigeon shooting Last d 9pm
ROOMS: s fr £65; d fr £95*
CARDS:

DENNY Falkirk Map **11** NS88

The Topps *(NS757843)* Fintry Rd FK6 5JF
(just off B818, 4m W) ☎ 01324 822471 FAX 01324 823099 Mr & Mrs Steel
The Topps really does feel like the top of the world, its elevated position ensuring that most of the bedrooms have panoramic views of the Ochil Hills, as does the popular restaurant. Although part of a working farm, specialising in sheep and cashmere goats, the house is more of a small hotel, popular with business guests and tourists and renowned for the quality of its dinners and hearty breakfasts. Bedrooms vary in size, all are well-equipped and most are furnished in pine. Two family rooms with bunk beds are available.
8 bth/shr (2 fmly) No smoking CTV in all bedrooms Tea and coffee making facilities Direct dial from bedrooms Licensed Cen ht CTV 12P Fishing 3 pitch & put greens Bowls M.Bikes 300 acres cashmere goats sheep Last d 6pm
ROOMS: s £28-£34; d £40-£44
CARDS:

DERVAIG See **MULL, ISLE OF**

DINGWALL Highland Map **14** NH55

Millcraig 18 Millcraig Rd IV15 9PS (turn off the A834, no 18 is approx 100yds on Left) ☎ 01349 862194
Closed Dec-Jan
Situated in a quiet residential street close to the town centre and sports centre, is this well maintained semi-detached home with an attractive garden. The first floor bedrooms are light and bright, and have clock radios and tea - making facilities. Guests can watch TV or listen to the stereo in the small but comfortable combined lounge/breakfast room.
3 rms No smoking Tea and coffee making facilities No dogs (ex guide dogs) Cen ht CTV No children 2P No coaches
ROOMS: s £14-£17; d £28-£34

DIRLETON East Lothian Map **12** NT58

Castle EH39 5EP (off A198) ☎ 01620 850221
This 19th-century coaching inn is situated beside the village green and overlooks Dirleton Castle. A popular base for visiting golfers, it offers tastefully decorated bedrooms in the main house and more modest rooms in the adjacent annexe. There is a choice of 'olde worlde' bars and a spacious dining room.
4 bth/shr 4 annexe rms Tea and coffee making facilities Cen ht CTV 10P Pool table Darts Last d 8.30pm
ROOMS: s £20-£42; d £40-£54; wkly b&b fr £180*
MEALS: Bar Lunch £7.50-£14.90*
CARDS:

DORNOCH Highland Map **14** NH78

Premier Selected

Fourpenny Cottage Skelbo IV25 3QF
(Take A949, until square in Dornoch. At tourist board left on Embo Rd, but carry on straight past turning)
☎ 01862 810727 FAX 01862 810727
Closed 20 Dec-20 Jan
Glorious views over the Dornoch Firth towards Golspie are enjoyed from this welcoming and comfortable guest house, two miles north of Dornoch. Ted and Sheila Board and family have considerably extended the former croft and byre as well as building modern houses within their grounds, one of which is currently used as an annexe. The comfortable lounge and pine tabled dining room are on the first floor and capitalise on the views, whilst the spacious well appointed bedrooms are on the ground floor. An enjoyable dinner, cooked by Ted, can be served at 7pm.
2 bth/shr 2 annexe shr No smoking in bedrooms No smoking in dining room No smoking in 1 lounge CTV in all bedrooms Tea and coffee making facilities Cen ht CTV ch fac 10P No coaches bird watching
ROOMS: d £54-£60; wkly b&b £175-£190*

Premier Selected

Highfield Evelix Rd IV25 3HR (take A9 N over Dornoch Bridge. After 2m turn right onto A949. After 1.5m, pass schools on left, Highfield 500yds on left)
☎ 01862 810909 FAX 01862 810909
Located close to the town centre and overlooking the Dornoch Firth, this modern house is set in its own pleasant gardens, which are still being developed by Stephen and Jane Dooley. Bedrooms are individually decorated with a good range of facilities, the most spacious

contd.

room offering a jacuzzi bath. Guests can relax and enjoy the views either in the pretty sun lounge or the upper landing, where a collection of books and magazines is always to hand. There is a wide range of breakfasts, with a combination of continental and Scottish specialities being available.
3 bth/shr No smoking CTV in all bedrooms Tea and coffee making facilities Cen ht No children none 6P No coaches
ROOMS: d £48-£50

DRUMNADROCHIT Highland Map **14** NH52

Selected

Q Q Q Q **Borlum Farmhouse** *(NH518291)* IV3 6XN
(0.5m S of Lewiston village on A82 Inverness - Fort William road)
☎ 01456 450358 FAX 01456 450358 Mr A D MacDonald-Haig
From its elevated position south of the village, this charming Georgian farmhouse enjoys panoramic views over Loch Ness. The spacious bedrooms, with pretty decor, have traditional furnishings, although amenities such as television and a tea tray are provided only in the cottage family unit. There is an inviting sun lounge with glorious views of the loch and an attractive breakfast room with a log-burning stove and individual tables. Riding is available, including facilities for disabled riders.
6 rms (2 bth) No smoking No dogs Cen ht CTV 10P Fishing Riding BHS app. riding centre on the farm 300 acres Sheep/horses
ROOMS: d £41-£48
CARDS:

Q Q Q **Enrick Cottage** IV3 6TZ (Turn off A82 onto A831 establishment 0.5m on left)
☎ 01456 450423 FAX 01456 450423
Mar-Oct
Excellent value accommodation combined with a tremendously welcoming atmosphere are all part of the appeal of Avis and Alan Raper's pleasant cottage, which stands outside the village on the Cannich road. The two en suite bedrooms are comfortable, with most of the wooden furnishings having been made by Alan in his workshop. Freshly prepared breakfasts are served at individual pine tables in the lounge/dining room.
2 shr No smoking CTV in all bedrooms Tea and coffee making facilities Cen ht CTV No children 15yrs 3P No coaches Chair making course Wood turning
ROOMS: d £32-£36*
CARDS:

Selected

Q Q Q Q **Glen Rowan** West Lewiston IV3 6UW
(A82 to Fort William untill Drumnadrochit, keep on A82 to village of Lewiston right after Esso Garage Glen Rowan 600yds up on the left)
☎ 01456 450235 FAX 01456 450817
2 Feb-27 Nov Closed 28 Nov-1 Feb
A welcoming atmosphere prevails at this comfortable detached house which stands in its own well tended garden beside the River Coiltie. Well equipped bedrooms offer individual and pleasant colour schemes, and two overlook the rear garden towards the river. Hearty breakfasts are served at individual tables in the upper area of the split level lounge.
3 shr No smoking CTV in all bedrooms Tea and coffee making facilities No dogs (ex guide dogs) Cen ht 3P No coaches
Last d 6.30pm
ROOMS: s £28-£40; d £32-£44
CARDS:

Selected

Q Q Q Q **Kilmore Farm House** IV3 6UH
(coming from Inverness and following A82 take first road on left after leaving Drumnadrochit village - signposted)
☎ 01456 450524
This attractive modern detached house is surrounded by pleasant countryside in a quiet location at the east end of the village, close to Loch Ness. The atmosphere is warm and welcoming and the comfortable modern ground floor bedrooms offer all the expected amenities. A sauna is also available. The comfortable lounge invites relaxation and enjoyable home cooking is served at individual tables in the small dining room.
3 shr (1 fmly) No smoking CTV in all bedrooms Tea and coffee making facilities Cen ht CTV 6P No coaches Sauna Last d 6pm
ROOMS: d £30-£36
CARDS:

Selected

Q Q Q Q **Woodlands** East Lewiston IV3 6UL ☎ 01456 450356
Closed 25-26 Dec
Jim and Janette Drysdale welcome guests to their comfortable modern villa which is quietly situated at the south end of the village. The attractive bedrooms are spacious and offer comfortable, modern, pine furnishings together with a range of thoughtful amenities. There is a cosy lounge on the first floor, and Janette's enjoyable home cooking is offered in the dining room which overlooks the neat garden.
3 bth/shr No smoking in bedrooms No smoking in dining room CTV in all bedrooms Tea and coffee making facilities No dogs (ex guide dogs) Cen ht CTV 3P No coaches
ROOMS: d £34-£40*
CARDS:

DRYMEN Stirling Map **11** NS48

Q Q Q **Croftburn Cottage** Croftamie G63 0HA (2m S of Drymen on A809 adjacent to Dalmair House) ☎ 01360 660796 FAX 01360 660796
Dorothy Reid looks forward to welcoming guests to this former keeper's cottage, set in spacious gardens with views of the Campsie Fells. Attractive public areas include a spacious and comfortable lounge with French windows giving access to the patio, and enjoyable home cooked fare is served around the communal table in the dining room. Bedrooms are cheerfully decorated, comfortably furnished, and thoughtfully equipped.
3 bth/shr No smoking in bedrooms No smoking in dining room CTV in all bedrooms Tea and coffee making facilities Cen ht CTV No children 12yrs 20P No coaches Croquet Putting Last d 10am
ROOMS: d £36-£44; wkly b&b £120-£150; wkly hlf-bd £190-£220*
CARDS:

Q Q Q **Easter Drumquhassle Farm** *(NS486871)* Gartness Rd G63 0DN (From Drymen By-pass (A811) take minor rd Gartnes. Farm 1m on right) ☎ 01360 660893 FAX 01360 660282 Mrs J Cross
Actually situated on the route of the West Highland Way, this delightful farm property with 40 acres of grazing land for sheep and horses is the ideal stop for the first or last night of the trek. Bedrooms are very individual in decorative style and have many thoughtful touches in addition to the usual facilities. Breakfast, and dinner if pre-booked, is served in the bright sun lounge around a communal table, giving fine views of the Endrick Valley.
2 bth/shr 1 annexe shr (1 fmly) No smoking CTV in all bedrooms Tea and coffee making facilities Cen ht 6P 40 acres sheep/horses Last d 9.00am
ROOMS: s fr £22; d fr £35*

Q Q Q **Strathvern** *(NS493910)* Strathvern, Balfron Station G63 0NQ ☎ 01360 660619 Mr & Mrs W Harrower
23 May-Nov
This newly built bungalow sits amidst rolling farmland with sheep and hill cattle up a mile long track, with lovely views across Strathendrick towards Killearn and the Campsie Fells. The two bedrooms are spacious and bright and guests can use the large and comfortable lounge. Breakfast is served in the open plan kitchen/dining room.
2 shr No smoking CTV in all bedrooms Tea and coffee making facilities Cen ht CTV No children 3yrs 4P 760 acres beef sheep
ROOMS: s fr £20; d fr £40; wkly b&b fr £120*

DUFFTOWN Moray Map **15** NJ34

Q Q **Fife Arms Hotel** 2 The Square AB55 4AD (turn off A96 onto A920 at Huntly to Dufftown hotel in village square)
☎ 01340 820220 FAX 01340 821137
Situated in the centre of the village, this family run inn offers good value accommodation, with all the bedrooms housed in an annexe to the rear. All are comfortably furnished in pine and one room is suitable for disabled use. Public areas include a homely public bar as well as a combined bar and dining room where a good range of tempting dishes are offered from the varied menus.
6 annexe shr (2 fmly) CTV in all bedrooms Tea and coffee making facilities Cen ht ch fac 8P Children's play area Last d 8pm
ROOMS: s £25-£27; d £40-£44*
MEALS: Lunch £5-£15alc Dinner £5-£25alc*
CARDS:

DULNAIN BRIDGE Highland Map **14** NH92

Q Q **Bydand** PH26 3LU (10m N of Aviemore, take A938 house is 200 metres on right) ☎ 01479 851278
Betty and Stewart Crabb extend a personal welcome to guests both old and new. Their detached home stands in pine-studded grounds south of the village. The two upstairs bedrooms offer homely comforts and share a bathroom. Guests are more than welcome to share the owners' comfortable lounge, and breakfasts, together with honest home-cooked fare are served at individual tables in the dining room. Good access for the less able is offered.
2 rms No smoking in bedrooms No smoking in dining room Cen ht CTV 6P No coaches Last d 8.30pm
ROOMS: d £30-£32
CARDS:

DUMBARTON West Dunbartonshire

See **Cardross**

DUMFRIES Dumfries & Galloway Map **11** NX97

Q Q Q **Orchard House** 298 Annan Rd DG1 3JE
☎ 01387 255099
This smart guest house is conveniently situated on the approach to the town centre from the south east, and is surrounded by attractive gardens. Accommodation is contained in what was originally a stable block and now offers ground floor bedrooms that are bright, cheery and well equipped. There is a lounge in the house and breakfasts are also taken there. Hostess Carole Murphy looks after her guests with great care and enthusiasm.
3 annexe bth/shr (1 fmly) No smoking CTV in all bedrooms Tea and coffee making facilities No dogs Cen ht CTV 10P No coaches

DUNBAR East Lothian Map 12 NT67

QQQ ***Overcliffe*** 11 Bayswell Park EH42 1AE
(off A1, opposite Lauderdale Park) ☎ 01368 864004
This attractive semi-detached red sandstone villa is situated in a residential area within easy reach of the town centre and seafront. Bedrooms vary in size and offer mixed modern furnishings together with the expected amenities and there is also a tastefully decorated combined lounge/dining room.
6 rms (3 shr) (3 fmly) No smoking in dining room CTV in all bedrooms Tea and coffee making facilities Licensed Cen ht CTV 2P No coaches Last d 5pm

QQQ **Springfield** Edinburgh Rd EH42 1NH
(Turn off A1 onto Dunbar Loop, establishment is on main road west side of Dunbar near Belhaven Church) ☎ 01368 862502
Jan-Nov
Situated on the west side beside the main road, this substantial detached Victorian house has a welcoming atmosphere which has special appeal for family visitors and golfers. The spacious bedrooms are bright and airy and offer modern furnishings together with the expected amenities. The first floor lounge is especially inviting and enjoyable home cooked meals are served downstairs in the dining room.
5 rms (1 bth/shr) (2 fmly) No smoking in dining room CTV in all bedrooms Tea and coffee making facilities Licensed Cen ht CTV 7P Last d 5pm
ROOMS: s £16-£20; d £30-£40; wkly b&b £105-£119; wkly hlf-bd £147-£170
CARDS:

DUNBLANE Stirling Map 11 NN70

Selected

QQQQ **Rokeby House** Doune Rd FK15 9AT
(M9 North, Dunblane exit and then take next turn-off to Doune along Doune Road. Premises are located 0.5m on left)
☎ 01786 824447 FAX 01786 821399
Mar-Dec rs Feb
This substantial late Victorian dwelling house is being sympathetically and fully restored to a high standard by enthusiastic proprietor Richard Beatts. Bedrooms are comfortable and appointed to a very high standard, one being a suite. Guests have a comfortable first floor lounge in which to relax and breakfast is served in a bright conservatory with marble-topped tables and wicker chairs, with an outlook over the splendid gardens which are also being lovingly restored.
3 bth/shr (1 fmly) No smoking CTV in all bedrooms No dogs Cen ht No children 14yrs 6P No coaches
ROOMS: s £45; d £60; wkly b&b £210-£315*
CARDS:

Selected

QQQQ **Westwood** Doune Rd FK15 9ND
(leave A9 on A820, turn towards Doune 0.5m on left)
☎ 01786 822579 FAX 01786 822579
Closed Nov-Feb
Situated to the west of town just off the Doune Road, this comfortable detached modern house has a welcoming atmosphere and is maintained to a high standard. Bedrooms are tastefully decorated and modern in style; one room is available on the ground floor. There is a spacious and inviting lounge with CTV and lots of tourist information, while freshly prepared meals are served at individual tables in the adjacent dining room.
3 bth/shr No smoking CTV in 1 bedroom Tea and coffee making facilities No dogs (ex guide dogs) Cen ht CTV No children 6P No coaches
ROOMS: s £30-£30; d £40-£48; wkly hlf-bd £135-£150

DUNDEE Dundee City Map 11 NO43

QQQ **Anlast Three Chimneys** 379 Arbroath Rd DD4 7SQ
(turn off A90 onto A92, house 200yds on right, next to tennis court)
☎ 01382 456710
The Stewart family look forward to welcoming you to their comfortable detached home which stands on the eastern edge of the city. High standards are maintained in the attractive bedrooms where pretty fabrics complement the modern fitted furnishings. Breakfast is served at the communal table in the dining room which forms part of the owners private lounge. This is a non smoking house.
3 bth/shr No smoking CTV in all bedrooms Tea and coffee making facilities No dogs Cen ht 6P No coaches
ROOMS: s £25-£30; d £40-£45; wkly b&b £140-£210*

Selected

QQQQ **Beach House Hotel** 22 Esplanade, Broughty Ferry DD5 2EN ☎ 01382 775537 & 776614 FAX 01382 480241
A warm welcome and wonderful service await you at this lovely beach front property, situated in a pretty village just east of the city. Bedrooms are very well equipped and are popular with business guests and tourists alike. A spacious and inviting lounge offers an excellent environment in which to relax and take advantage of the plentiful reading material, videos, or to enjoy a drink from the bar. Good value evening meals and tasty breakfasts are served in the dining room.
5 bth/shr (1 fmly) No smoking in 2 bedrooms No smoking in dining room CTV in all bedrooms Tea and coffee making facilities Direct dial from bedrooms No dogs Licensed Cen ht CTV 1P No coaches Last d 8pm
ROOMS: s £35-£38; d £45-£48
CARDS:

QQQ **Homebank** 9 Ellieslea Rd, Broughty Ferry DD5 1JH
☎ 01382 477481
Good value bed & breakfast accommodation is offered at this family run guest house, a substantial late Victorian house set in well cared for gardens in a Broughty Ferry residential area. Two attractively decorated en suite bedrooms are available, each with modern furnishings. There is an inviting lounge on the first floor with an additional seating area in the combined lounge/dining room.
4 rms (2 shr) No smoking in bedrooms No smoking in dining room CTV in all bedrooms Tea and coffee making facilities No dogs (ex guide dogs) Cen ht CTV No children 6P No coaches
ROOMS: s £22.50-£30; d £45*

QQQ **Invermark House** 23 Monifeith Rd, Broughty Ferry DD5 2RN (3m E A930) ☎ 01382 739430 FAX 01382 739430
Sharon Cummings looks forward to welcoming you to her comfortable detached Victorian home which stands beside the main road through Broughty Ferry. All bedrooms are now en suite and good progress is being made with the refurbishment programme. Public areas include a lounge with well filled book shelves and board games, and hearty breakfasts are served at individual tables in the dining room. This is a strictly non smoking establishment.
4 bth/shr (1 fmly) No smoking CTV in all bedrooms Tea and coffee making facilities No dogs (ex guide dogs) Licensed Cen ht CTV 16P
ROOMS: s £30; d £45*
CARDS:

DUNFERMLINE Fife Map **11** NT08

Selected

QQQQ **Clarke Cottage** 139 Halbeath Rd KY11 4LA
(exit M90 at junct 3, follow signs for Dunfermline, pass Halbeath Retail Park, Clarke Cottage situated on left after second set of lights)
☎ 01383 735935
Aileen Neill's detached Victorian home has recently been extended to provide additional stylish accommodation. Bedrooms are comfortably furnished in matching pine and offer a wide range of amenities including mini bars. Public areas include a conservatory dining room where freshly prepared breakfasts are served at individual tables.
9 shr No smoking CTV in all bedrooms Tea and coffee making facilities No dogs (ex guide dogs) Licensed Cen ht 11P No coaches
ROOMS: s £29-£31; d £42-£46

QQQ **Hillview House** 9 Aberdour Rd KY11 4PB
(from Edinburgh exit M90 junct 2 and follow A823 for Dunfermline, right at T-junction by Cottage Inn pub into Aberdour Rd, estab 100yds on right)
☎ 01383 726278 FAX 01383 726278
A welcoming atmosphere prevails at this family run guest house. The three comfortable bedrooms have recently been upgraded to provide en suite facilities. All are tastefully decorated and offer modern furnishings and fittings. Freshly prepared breakfasts are served at individual tables in the combined lounge/dining room.
3 rms No smoking CTV in all bedrooms Tea and coffee making facilities No dogs (ex guide dogs) Cen ht CTV 3P No coaches Video library
ROOMS: s £18-£23; d £32-£40*

Selected

QQQQ **Hopetoun Lodge** 141 Halbeath Rd KY11 4LA
(exit M90 at junct 3 and travel 1.5m through Halbeath, past Retail Park on right, over the rdbt and two sets of lights. On left after Kwik-Fit)
☎ 01383 620906 & 624252
Closed 25-26 Dec, 1-2 Jan
This small and friendly house is conveniently located on the western side of Dunfermline. The spacious bedrooms are attractively decorated with bright floral wall coverings and co-ordinated furnishings. There are also many thoughtful extras provided. A delicious breakfast is served at individual tables.
3 rms (1 shr) (1 fmly) No smoking CTV in all bedrooms Tea and coffee making facilities No dogs (ex guide dogs) Cen ht CTV 4P No coaches
ROOMS: s £23-£30; d £46-£54*

QQQ **Pitreavie** 3 Aberdour Rd KY11 4PB (At west end of Aberdour road at junct with A823. Half mile south of Dunfermline town centre.)
☎ 01383 724244 FAX 01383 724244
Anne Walker looks forward to welcoming guests old and new to her comfortable home, a semi-detached house within easy reach of central facilities. Bedrooms, with attractive fabrics and comfortable pine furnishings, offer a good range of amenities including bathrobes. Hearty breakfasts and, by arrangement, evening meals are served in the combined lounge/dining room.
6 rms (1 fmly) No smoking CTV in all bedrooms Tea and coffee making facilities Cen ht CTV 6P No coaches Last d 6.45pm
ROOMS: s £20-£27; d £37-£39*
CARDS:

DUNKELD Perth & Kinross Map **11** NO04

QQQ **Waterbury** Murthly Ter PH8 0BG (Turn off A9 to Birnam, Dunkeld, on main street next to church and post office)
☎ 01350 727324 FAX 01350 727023
The Neil family look forward to welcoming you to their comfortable home, an end terraced house in the centre of Birnam. The bright airy bedrooms are comfortably furnished in both modern and traditional styles. Refreshments are served in the inviting lounge from the small dispense bar while hearty breakfasts and, by prior arrangement, home cooked evening meals are served in the attractive dining room. Smoking is permitted in the lounge only.
7 rms (3 bth/shr) (32 fmly) No smoking in bedrooms No smoking in dining room CTV in all bedrooms Tea and coffee making facilities Licensed Cen ht 3P No coaches Last d noon
ROOMS: s £18-£22; d £36-£40; wkly b&b £120-£133; wkly hlf-bd £180-£194*
CARDS:

DUNLOP East Ayrshire Map **10** NS44

QQQ **Struther Farmhouse** Newmill Rd KA3 4BA
(within village approx 200yds from railway station) ☎ 01560 484946
Closed 2wks spring & autumn rs Sun & Mon
This beautiful old period house, standing in its own garden and grounds, is situated in a small village mid-way between Glasow and Ayr. Spacious bedrooms offer old fashioned charm without the addition of modern facilities. The public areas reflect a similar style and log fires and the friendly family dogs create a welcoming atmosphere. Fresh ingredients are used to produce tasty meals and a good choice is available from the set priced menu.
4 rms (2 fmly) Tea and coffee making facilities Cen ht CTV 16P Last d 8.30pm
ROOMS: s £18; d £36; wkly b&b fr £100; wkly hlf-bd fr £180*

DUNOON Argyll & Bute Map **10** NS17

Premier Selected

QQQQQ **The Anchorage** Lazaretto Point, Shore Rd, Ardnadam, Holy Loch PA23 8QG (3m N on A815)
☎ 01369 705108 FAX 01369 705108
Closed Nov
Overlooking the Holy Loch towards Benmore Forest this pleasantly renovated and extended house is handy for the ferry terminals. Friendly owners Dee and Tony Hancock have considerably improved the property over the years and have created pretty, well equipped bedrooms and an attractive lounge which overlooks the loch. A small bar lounge and the Conservatory Restaurant are proving popular locally. A truly Scottish breakfast is served.
5 bth/shr (1 fmly) No smoking CTV in all bedrooms Tea and coffee making facilities No dogs (ex guide dogs) Licensed Cen ht 14P No coaches Discount on membership of country club Last d 9.30pm
ROOMS: s £45-£70; d £60-£70*
CARDS:

Q Q Q The Cedars 51 Alexandra Pde, East Bay PA23 8AF (situated on the seafront close to the town centre) ☎ 01369 702425 FAX 01369 706964
Good value accommodation is offered at this friendly guest house which stands on the esplanade overlooking the Firth of Clyde. Bedrooms are smartly decorated and offer comfortable modern furnishings together with a good range of amenities. Hearty breakfasts are provided at individual tables in the dining room, which overlooks the sea.
11 bth/shr (1 fmly) No smoking in 8 bedrooms No smoking in dining room No smoking in lounges CTV in all bedrooms Tea and coffee making facilities Direct dial from bedrooms No dogs Licensed Cen ht
ROOMS: s £19.50-£29.50; d £39-£55*
CARDS:

DUNURE South Ayrshire Map **10** NS21

Selected

Q Q Q Q Dunduff *(NS265160)* Dunure KA7 4LH
(on A719, 400yds past village school on left) ☎ 01292 500225
FAX 01292 500222 Mrs A Gemmell
Closed Nov - Feb
Parts of this substantial farmhouse date back to the 15th and 17th centuries and it occupies a wonderful elevated position above the Firth of Clyde, with lovely views towards Arran, and on clearer days, beyond to Northern Ireland. Bedrooms are comfortable, well equipped and modern with two being especially spacious. A very comfortable lounge is provided for residents and Agnes Gemmell and her family offer genuine Scottish hospitality. Animals, including Highland Cows, graze peacefully in the fields to the front of the house.
3 rms (2 shr) (2 fmly) No smoking CTV in all bedrooms Tea and coffee making facilities No dogs (ex guide dogs) Cen ht CTV 10P Fishing 600 acres beef sheep - working
ROOMS: s £30-£35; d £45-£47; wkly b&b £157-£175*
CARDS:

DUNVEGAN See **SKYE, ISLE OF**

EAGLESHAM East Renfrewshire Map **11** NS55

Q Q Q New Borland Glasgow Rd G76 0DN (9 miles S of Glasgow city centre at junction of B764 and B767)
☎ 01355 302051 FAX 01355 302051
Quietly situated in its own gardens outside the village and within easy distance of East Kilbride, New Borland started life as a barn and was cleverly converted and extended in the seventies to create a comfortable family home. Fiona Allison has upgraded all her bedrooms to a smart contemporary style which appeals to business persons as well as tourists. Relaxing public areas retain the feel of a family home and include a cosy lounge, a games room and a comfortable dining room where breakfasts are served at one large table.
4 rms (2 shr) No smoking CTV in all bedrooms Tea and coffee making facilities No dogs (ex guide dogs) Cen ht CTV No children 12yrs 10P No coaches
ROOMS: s £20-£25; d £45-£50*

EAST CALDER West Lothian Map **11** NT06

Selected

Q Q Q Q Ashcroft Farmhouse *(NT095682)* EH53 0ET
(on B7015, off A71) ☎ 01506 881810 FAX 01506 884327
Mr & Mrs D Scott
Derek and Elizabeth Scott will ensure your stay at their lovely farmhouse is so memorable you'll want to return time and again. Set in beautiful landscaped gardens, this modern home comprises of ground floor bedrooms where pretty fabrics complement the smart pine furnishings. One room has a four poster bed. The residents' lounge includes a library and the newly extended dining room is bright, comfortable and adorned with fascinating golf bric-a-brac. After early morning tea in your room, you can enjoy Derek's home-made sausages - one of the many highlights of the delicious breakfast.

6 shr (2 fmly) No smoking CTV in all bedrooms Tea and coffee making facilities No dogs (ex guide dogs) Cen ht CTV No children 3yrs 8P 5 acres cattle sheep
ROOMS: s fr £38; d fr £54; wkly b&b fr £182*
CARDS:
See advertisement under EDINBURGH

Q Q Q Overshiel Farm *(NT099689)* EH53 0HT (head west out of Edinburgh along the A71, turn off A71 onto B7015, then turn second right, 0.5m on right) ☎ 01506 880469 FAX 01506 883006 Mrs J Dick
Good value bed and breakfast accommodation is offered at this welcoming Victorian farmhouse which stands in sheltered gardens adjacent to the farm complex just east of the village. There is a spacious twin room with a private bathroom on the first floor, while two further rooms with en suite facilities are located at ground level. These rooms have external access. The spacious lounge is ideal for relaxation while farmhouse breakfasts are served around the communal table in the attractive dining room. This is a non smoking house.
1 rms 2 annexe shr No smoking CTV in all bedrooms Tea and coffee making facilities No dogs (ex guide dogs) Cen ht 6P Children's playground 340 acres mixed
ROOMS: s £25-£30; d £32-£40*

EAST LINTON East Lothian Map **12** NT57

Selected

Q Q Q Q Kippielaw Farmhouse EH41 4PY (Leave A1 at E Linton, follow Traprain sign 3/4m, take single track road on right after farm. Estab ½m on left opposite CP) ☎ 01620 860368 FAX 01620 860368
Set in an elevated position but sheltered by gardens, Kippielaw Farmhouse enjoys magnificent views of the Tyne Valley. Liz and Bill

Campbell are very welcoming proprietors. A cosy lounge with open staircase and log fire is the focal point, and meals are also served here around a cherry wood dining table. The country-style bedrooms are thoughtfully equipped to include hair dryers and radios, but no TVs.
3 bth/shr No smoking Tea and coffee making facilities No dogs Cen ht 3P No coaches Boules Last d 24hr prior
ROOMS: s £22-£26; d £44-£52; wkly b&b £154-£182; wkly hlf-bd £252-£2800

EDINBURGH City of Edinburgh Map **11** NT27

See also South Queensferry

Q Q Q **Abcorn** 4 Mayfield Gardens EH9 2BU (1.5m S from city centre) ☎ 0131 667 6548 FAX 0131 667 9969
A friendly atmosphere prevails at this well maintained and attractively decorated Victorian house. Bedrooms are generally of good size and with modern en suite bathrooms; a particularly large bay windowed room being very popular with families.
7 shr (1 fmly) No smoking in dining room No smoking in lounges CTV in all bedrooms Tea and coffee making facilities No dogs (ex guide dogs) Cen ht CTV 7P
ROOMS: s £26-£34; d £52-£68*

Q Q Q **Abercorn** 33 Abercorn Ter, Joppa, Portobello EH15 2DF (directly off the A1 main road) ☎ 0131 669 6139
Angela McDonald's hospitality is second to none at this friendly family home on the east side of the city, close to Portobello Beach. Tastefully decorated throughout, it offers bedrooms which have a host of extra touches - radios, hair dryers, magazines, biscuits and even a bottle opener and wine glasses. Bedrooms share a smart general bathroom and huge bath sheets are an added luxury.
4 rms (2 shr) (2 fmly) No smoking in 1 bedrooms No smoking in dining room No smoking in lounges CTV in all bedrooms Tea and coffee making facilities Cen ht ch fac
ROOMS: s £15-£30; d £30-£60; wkly b&b £75-£140*

Selected

Q Q Q Q **Acorn Lodge** 26 Pilrig St EH6 5AJ ☎ 0131 555 1557 FAX 0131 555 4475
This tastefully appointed Georgian terraced home is situated just off Leith Walk and is only a ten minute walk from central amenities. Warm hospitality and excellent service encourages guests to return time and again. Attractive decor and fabrics have been used to good effect in the bright airy bedrooms, all of which are comfortably furnished in antique pine and offer a wide range of facilities. Guests can choose from an extensive range breakfast choices, served at individual tables in the pretty dining room. Arrangements can be made for those who require organised trips, theatre tickets or restaurant bookings.
7 bth/shr (2 fmly) No smoking CTV in all bedrooms Tea and coffee making facilities Direct dial from bedrooms No dogs (ex guide dogs) Cen ht
ROOMS: s £30-£45; d £55-£90*
CARDS:

Selected

Q Q Q Q **Adam Hotel** 19 Lansdowne Crescent EH12 5EH (from Airport follow signs City Centre, on reaching Haymarket Terrace turn left opp Station car park, follow road which bears right) ☎ 0131 337 1148 FAX 0131 337 1729
Part of a Georgian terrace facing a park, this beautiful house is only a short distance from Princes Street. The bedrooms are varied in size and type but all are attractively decorated and comfortably furnished. Many period features have been retained in the smart public areas including an interesting cupola surrounded by cherubs and varnished paper panels in the grand entrance hallway.
13 bth/shr (3 fmly) No smoking CTV in all bedrooms Tea and coffee making facilities Direct dial from bedrooms No dogs (ex guide dogs) Licensed Cen ht CTV ch fac No coaches Last d 7.30pm
ROOMS: s £40-£60; d £75-£120; wkly b&b £245-£315; wkly hlf-bd £385-£455*
CARDS:

Q Q **The Adria Hotel** 11-12 Royal Ter EH7 5AB
(East end of city centre, round corner from Playhouse theatre. Nearest main roads-Leith Walk & London Rd)
☎ 0131 556 7875 FAX 0131 558 7782
Closed Nov-Dec
Good value bed and breakfast accommodation is offered at this personally run hotel which forms part of an elegant Georgian terrace beside Calton Hill. Most of the bedrooms are spacious with traditional furnishings and those with en suite facilities are also provided with CTV. The lounge is comfortable, while breakfast is served in the smart dining room.
24 rms (6 bth/shr) (8 fmly) No smoking in dining room CTV in 8 bedrooms Tea and coffee making facilities No dogs (ex guide dogs) Cen ht CTV
ROOMS: s £20-£40; d £40-£70*
CARDS:

Q Q Q **Allan Lodge** 37 Queens Crescent EH9 2BA ☎ 0131 668 2947 FAX 0131 668 2947
Situated in a quiet residential area on the south side, this period home has been tastefully refurbished to enhance its many fine features. Bedrooms are well proportioned and the attractive dining room also doubles as a comfortable lounge.
6 rms (4 shr) (2 fmly) No smoking CTV in all bedrooms Tea and coffee making facilities Cen ht
ROOMS: d £45-£56

Q Q Q **Amaryllis** 21 Upper Gilmore Place EH3 9NL (directly opposite The King's Theatre) ☎ 0131 229 3293 FAX 0131 229 3293
This friendly guest house is situated in a quiet residential side street just south of the city centre. Most of the bedrooms are spacious and furnished in pine, while breakfast is served at individual tables in the breakfast room which has the cheerful style of a continental farmhouse kitchen.
5 rms (4 shr) (3 fmly) No smoking in dining room CTV in all bedrooms Tea and coffee making facilities No dogs (ex guide dogs) Cen ht 2P
ROOMS: s £25-£40; d £36-£60
CARDS:

[symbols] Q Q Q **An Fuaran** 35 Seaview Ter, Joppa EH15 2HE
☎ 0131 669 8119 FAX 0131 669 8119
Closed 24-26 Dec
This terraced house has a small garden with patio. The seafront is just across the road and front-facing rooms enjoy fine panoramic views of the Firth of Forth. One of the family bedrooms comprises a unit of two separate rooms.
5 shr (3 fmly) No smoking CTV in all bedrooms Tea and coffee making facilities No dogs Cen ht No coaches
ROOMS: s £18-£25; d £35-£50
CARDS: [card logos]

Q Q **Anvilla** 1a Granville Ter EH10 4PG
(west end of Princes St, up Lothian Road to Kings Theatre, located in road opposite which is Gilmore Place, Granville Terrace is a continuation)
☎ 0131 228 3381 FAX 0131 228 3381
Situated in a residential area to the south west of the city centre, Anvilla is a comfortable detached Victorian house where the atmosphere is warm and relaxed. The attractive bedrooms are furnished in both period and modern styles, and there is an inviting lounge with a beautiful ornate ceiling on the first floor.
6 rms (2 fmly) No smoking in dining room No smoking in lounges CTV in all bedrooms Tea and coffee making facilities Cen ht CTV 5P No coaches
CARDS: [card logos]

Q Q Q **Arden** 126 Old Dalkeith Rd EH16 4SD (on A7) ☎ 0131 664 3985 FAX 0131 621 0866
This extended detached house provides good value accommodation for the visiting businessman and tourist alike. The attractive bedrooms, all on the ground floor, have been designed to make best use of available space and offer a wide range of amenities. There is no lounge, but hearty breakfasts are served around the communal table in the neat dining room.
8 shr No smoking in 2 bedrooms No smoking in dining room No smoking in lounges CTV in all bedrooms Tea and coffee making facilities Cen ht CTV 8P No coaches
ROOMS: s £25-£45; d £45-£55*
CARDS: [card logos]

Selected

Q Q Q Q **Arden House** 26 Linkfield Rd, Musselburgh EH21 7LL
(follow signs to Musselburgh/Racecourse opposite racecourse on A199)
☎ 0131 665 0663 FAX 0131 665 0663
Drew Threlfell runs his substantial end terraced guest house with commitment and enthusiasm. It lies opposite the racecourse and golf course and is popular with both business guests and tourists. Spotlessly clean and with modern bathrooms, bedrooms come in a variety of sizes - some very spacious. There is a lounge for guests use and an attractive breakfast room.
4 bth/shr (2 fmly) No smoking CTV in all bedrooms Tea and coffee making facilities Cen ht CTV
ROOMS: s £25-£40; d £42-£54*
CARDS: [card logos]

Selected

Q Q Q Q **Ashgrove House** 12 Osborne Ter EH12 5HG
(on the main A8 road between Murrayfield & Haymarket opposite Donaldson's College for Deaf, under 1 mile to Princes Street)
☎ 0131 337 5014 FAX 0131 313 5043
A friendly welcome awaits you at this charmingly elegant Victorian guest house. Bedrooms are comfortably furnished in the modern style and are

thoughtfully equipped with many extras. Freshly prepared breakfasts and, by prior arrangement, evening meals are served at individual tables in the attractive dining room. An inviting sun lounge overlooks the rear garden and this is the only area where smoking is permitted.
7 shr (2 fmly) No smoking CTV in all bedrooms Tea and coffee making facilities Direct dial from bedrooms No dogs (ex guide dogs) Cen ht CTV 10P No coaches Last d 11am
ROOMS: s £25-£35; d £50-£70
CARDS:

QQQ **Auld Reekie** 16 Mayfield Gardens EH9 2BZ
(follow A701 joining city bypass turn off at Straiton Junction follow signs for city centre, drive approx 2.5km city centre approx 1.5km)
☎ 0131 667 6177 FAX 0131 662 0033
A recently refurbished Victorian terraced house offering bedrooms which are mostly spacious with comfortable modern furnishings. Both Scottish and vegetarian breakfasts are available in the attractive combined lounge/dining room.
7 bth/shr (2 fmly) No smoking in 4 bedrooms No smoking in dining room No smoking in lounges CTV in all bedrooms Tea and coffee making facilities Cen ht CTV 2P No coaches
ROOMS: s £25-£40; d £40-£70*

Q **Averon** 44 Gilmore Place EH3 9NQ (turn left at the west end of Princes Street and follow A702 and turn right at Kings Theatre)
☎ 0131 229 9932 FAX 0131 228 9265
This terraced guest house is situated south west of the city centre close to the Kings Theatre and offers good value bed and breakfast accommodation. Bedrooms vary in size with both traditional and modern furnishings. The dining room features a large stone fireplace and breakfast is served at shared tables.
10 rms (3 fmly) No smoking in dining room CTV in all bedrooms Tea and coffee making facilities No dogs Cen ht 14P
ROOMS: s £21-£28; d £36-£48*
CARDS:

See advertisement on p.531.

Q Q **Ben Doran** 11 Mayfield Gardens EH9 2AX
(from east side of Princes Street, take A701, Ben Doran is on left side, about 1.5 miles) ☎ 0131 667 8488 FAX 0131 667 0076
Improvements continue at this welcoming south side guest house. Bedrooms come in a variety of sizes and include a number of family rooms, whilst more en suites are being installed. Breakfasts are served at individual tables in the spacious dining room.
10 rms (4 bth/shr) (5 fmly) No smoking CTV in all bedrooms Tea and coffee making facilities No dogs (ex guide dogs) Cen ht 6P
ROOMS: s fr £20; d fr £40
CARDS:

Q Q Q **Beverley Hotel** 40 Murrayfield Av EH12 6AY (the hotel is situated near Murrayfield Rugby Ground on main A8 road on north east of city) ☎ 0131 337 1128 FAX 0131 445 1994
Closed 20-27 Dec
A welcoming atmosphere prevails at this comfortably family run hotel which is situated in a tree lined avenue in the west end. The well maintained bedrooms are comfortably modern in style and there is a relaxing lounge with beverage making facilities and well filled book shelves on the first floor. Breakfast is served at shared tables in the attractive dining room. Street parking available.
7 bth/shr (3 fmly) No smoking in bedrooms No smoking in dining room CTV in all bedrooms Tea and coffee making facilities Licensed Cen ht CTV
ROOMS: s £25-£40; d £50-£70*
CARDS:

Q Q ***Boisdale Hotel*** 9 Coates Gardens EH12 5LG ☎ 0131 337 1134 FAX 0131 313 0048
A welcoming, personally run licensed guest house, part of a terraced row near the Haymarket station. Bedrooms are vary in size and offer mixed modern appointments together with all the expected amenities. Freshly prepared breakfasts and, by prior arrangement, home cooked evening meals, are offered in the smart basement dining room. Refreshments can be served in either the lounge or bedroom.
11 bth/shr (6 fmly) CTV in all bedrooms Tea and coffee making facilities Licensed Cen ht CTV Last d 7pm

Selected

Q Q Q Q ***Bonnington*** 202 Ferry Rd EH6 4NW
☎ 0131 554 7610
David and Eileen Watt are the enthusiastic owners of this Georgian house located to the north of the city. Bedrooms are comfortable and offer both modern and traditional furnishings. The lounge, with its grand piano and ample provision of books and board games is very relaxing, while Eileen's carefully prepared breakfasts continue to earn much praise.
6 rms (2 bth 2 shr) (3 fmly) No smoking in bedrooms No smoking in dining room CTV in all bedrooms Tea and coffee making facilities Cen ht CTV 9P No coaches Last d 10am

Q Q Q **Borthwick** 23 Mayfield Gardens EH9 2BX
(from the city centre go to E end of Princes St, turn right into North Bridge (A7) after 1.4m establishment on left hand side)
☎ 0131 667 8475 FAX 0131 667 6763
Huge comfortable bedrooms, several ideal for family use, are hallmarks of this well proportioned detached period house which also features impressive stained glass windows. There is a small lounge area in the dining room.
7 shr (5 fmly) CTV in all bedrooms Tea and coffee making facilities No dogs (ex guide dogs) Cen ht CTV 20P No coaches
ROOMS: s £25-£45; d £50-£90*
CARDS:

Selected

Q Q Q Q **Brunswick Hotel** 7 Brunswick St EH7 5JB
(London rd, Hillsdie Crescent then Brunswick Street)
☎ 0131 556 1238 FAX 0131 557 1404
Closed Xmas
Designed by William Playfair, this elegant Georgian terraced house in now a comfortable guest house, within easy walking distance of the city centre. The spacious lounge has plush, deep seating and a black marble fireplace, while the dining room is situated on the lower ground floor. Well equipped bedrooms include two on the ground floor and two with four-poster beds.
11 shr (1 fmly) No smoking CTV in all bedrooms Tea and coffee making facilities Direct dial from bedrooms No dogs Cen ht No children 2yrs No coaches
ROOMS: s £25-£45; d £50-£90
CARDS:

Q Q ***Buchanan*** 97 Joppa Rd EH15 2HB
(turn off A1 onto A199. At lights turn left to B6415. Establishment 1m on left) ☎ 0131 657 4117
Guests are made to feel at home in this friendly guest house set in the east of the city, with the sea front just across the road. Bedrooms are bright and cheerful and breakfasts are well presented at smartly set up tables in the owners lounge.
4 rms (1 shr) (1 fmly) CTV in all bedrooms Tea and coffee making facilities No dogs Cen ht CTV No coaches
CARDS:

Q Q ***Chalumna*** 5 Granville Ter EH10 4PQ ☎ 0131 229 2086 FAX 0131 221 0880
Ongoing improvements continue at this friendly family run guest house on the south side. Top floor bedrooms have been smartly upgraded while those of the first floor remain practical in style. Hearty breakfasts are served at shared tables in the refurbished dining room.
9 rms (5 bth/shr) (2 fmly) No smoking in dining room CTV in all bedrooms Tea and coffee making facilities Cen ht CTV 4P
CARDS:

Q Q Q Classic House 50 Mayfield Rd EH9 2NH
(turn off the by pass road on to A701, establishment 0.5 mile on left just after the Kings Building)
☎ 0131 667 5847 FAX 0131 662 1016
The atmosphere is welcoming at this comfortable personally-run guest house on the south side. The tastefully decorated and well-equipped bedrooms have been cleverly designed to make best use of available space. Hearty breakfasts are served at individual tables in the conservatory dining room.
7 rms (6 bth/shr) No smoking CTV in all bedrooms Tea and coffee making facilities No dogs Cen ht CTV
ROOMS: s £20-£30; d £40-£60*
CARDS:

Q Q Clifton Private Hotel 1 Clifton Ter, Haymarket EH12 5DR
(just opposite Haymarket Railway Station on main Glasgow Road near city centre) ☎ 0131 337 1002 FAX 0131 337 1002
Good value bed and breakfast accommodation is offered at this family run private hotel which is situated in the west end opposite Haymarket station. Bedrooms, though compact, are brightly decorated and offer mixed styles and standards of furnishings.
11 rms (4 shr) No smoking in dining room CTV in all bedrooms Tea and coffee making facilities Direct dial from bedrooms Cen ht CTV No coaches
ROOMS: s £25-£40; d £40-£70; wkly b&b fr £175*
CARDS:

Q Q Q Corstorphine 188 St Johns Rd, Corstorphine EH12 8SG
(along M8 take city bypass north and head for city centre for 1 mile along A8, guest house on the left)
☎ 0131 539 4237 & 0131 539 7092 FAX 0131 539 4945
The Fowdar family look forward to welcoming you to this detached Victorian house in the west end convenient for both the airport and central amenities. Bedrooms vary in size and are tastefully decorated, with a good range of amenities. There is also a combined lounge/dining room where guests can choose from either the traditional, continental, or vegetarian menus at breakfast. This is a non smoking establishment.
4 bth/shr (2 fmly) No smoking CTV in all bedrooms Tea and coffee making facilities No dogs (ex guide dogs) Cen ht CTV ch fac 5P
ROOMS: s £20-£40; d £40-£80; wkly b&b £126-£196*
CARDS:

Selected

Q Q Q Q Dorstan Private Hotel 7 Priestfield Rd EH16 5HJ
(turn off A68 at Priestfield Road, just before Commonwealth Swimming Pool)
☎ 0131 667 6721 & 667 5138 FAX 0131 668 4644
A warm welcome from enthusiastic owner Mairae Campbell and her efficient staff is assured at this beautiful Victorian house, set in a residential area on the south side of the city. Bedrooms vary in size and are comfortably furnished and decorated to a high standard. The small aquarium is an interesting feature in the inviting lounge, and by prior arrangement, good value meals are served in the attractive dining room.
14 rms (12 bth/shr) (2 fmly) No smoking CTV in all bedrooms Tea and coffee making facilities Direct dial from bedrooms No dogs (ex guide dogs) Cen ht 8P No coaches Last d 3pm
ROOMS: s £34-£39; d £70-£80*
CARDS:
See advertisement on p.533.

The AA's professional Inspectors make regular and anonymous visits to all the establishments listed in the Guide. They accept no gifts or favours from proprietors

Premier Selected

QQQQQ ***Drummond House*** 17 Drummond Place EH3 6PL (premises on NW corner of Drummond Place at E end of Great King St) ☎ 0131 557 9189 FAX 0131 557 9189
Closed Xmas
Lovingly restored by the present owners, this distinctive Georgian house provides an ideal base for exploring the city's attractions and shops. Set in a quiet residential town square, around well kept gardens, Drummond House offers bedrooms and public areas furnished with artefacts collected by Josephine and Alan Dougall during their travels around the world, whilst modern conveniences have been added to ensure a comfortable and relaxing stay. The freshly prepared breakfast is served around one table in the dining room.
4 bth/shr No smoking No dogs Cen ht CTV No children 12yrs No coaches
CARDS:

QQQ **Dunstane House** 4 West Coates, Haymarket EH12 5JQ (on A8 between Murrayfield and Haymarket. 5 mins from city centre) ☎ 0131 337 6169 & 337 5320 FAX 0131 337 6169
The new owners of this detached Victorian house have embarked on a major upgrade. Bedrooms, some of which are generously proportioned, offer mixed modern furnishings along with the expected amenities. Public areas include a relaxing lounge with dispense bar, and an elegant dining room where breakfast is served.
15 rms (14 shr) (5 fmly) No smoking in 8 bedrooms No smoking in dining room CTV in all bedrooms Tea and coffee making facilities No dogs (ex guide dogs) Licensed Cen ht CTV 10P
ROOMS: s £30-£49; d £55-£88
CARDS:

QQQ **Ecosse International** 15 McDonald Rd EH7 4LX (E end Princes St exit to Leith St. Down past roundabout, Playhouse Theatre on right. Turn left at service station, McDonald Rd on right) ☎ 0131 556 4967
Situated just off Leith Walk to the north of the city centre, this well maintained guest house offers bright cheerful accommodation. The lower ground floor offers a comfortable lounge area adjacent to the attractive dining room.
5 bth/shr (3 fmly) No smoking CTV in all bedrooms Tea and coffee making facilities No dogs (ex guide dogs) Cen ht CTV No coaches
ROOMS: s £30-£35; d £50-£70*
CARDS:

QQQ **Eglinton Hotel** 29 Eglinton Crescent EH12 5BY ☎ 0131 337 2641 FAX 0131 337 4495
Recent renovation and refurbishment of this elegant terraced Victorian town house has created tastefully decorated bedrooms of generous proportions with modern furnishings and a wide range of amenities. The Pictures and Prints Restaurant offers a good-value fixed-price menu, whilst more serious food is to be found on the innovative carte. There is a pleasant small bar adjacent.
12 bth/shr (1 fmly) CTV in all bedrooms Tea and coffee making facilities Direct dial from bedrooms Licensed Cen ht Last d 9pm
ROOMS: s £50-£65; d £80-£110*

QQQ **Elder York** 38 Elder St EH1 3DX ☎ 0131 556 1926 FAX 0131 624 7140
Occupying the fourth and fifth floors of a Victorian building close to the bus station and city centre, this friendly guest house offers good value bed and breakfast accommodation. Bedrooms are smartly decorated and offer both modern and traditional furnishings, while freshly prepared breakfasts are served in the large dining room.
13 rms (4 shr) (2 fmly) No smoking in 4 bedrooms No smoking in dining room No smoking in lounges CTV in all bedrooms Tea and coffee making facilities No dogs (ex guide dogs) Cen ht
ROOMS: s £25-£30; d £44-£60*
CARDS:

Selected

QQQQ **Ellesmere House** 11 Glengyle Ter EH3 9LN (central Edinburgh off the A702) ☎ 0131 229 4823 FAX 0131 229 5285
You will receive a warm greeting and personal attention at Celia and Tommy Leishman's delightful, centrally located, terraced home overlooking Bruntsfield Links. The attractive bedrooms are individually decorated, comfortably furnished in a modern style and offer an extensive range of thoughtful accessories and facilities. A delicious breakfast can be enjoyed in the lovely dining/living room.
6 bth/shr (1 fmly) No smoking in dining room CTV in all bedrooms Tea and coffee making facilities No dogs (ex guide dogs) Cen ht CTV No children 10yrs No coaches
ROOMS: s £25-£35; d £50-£70; wkly b&b £175-£245*

CENTRAL EDINBURGH

Ellesmere House

11 Glengyle Terrace, Edinburgh EH3 9LN
Telephone: 0131-229 4823 Fax: 0131-229 5285

A warm welcome is extended to all visitors to this attractive and comfortable Victorian house overlooking the meadows. 6 bedrooms, decorated and furnished to a very high standard, all bedrooms en-suite, and equipped with every comfort in mind. Delicious breakfasts and special diets are provided. Comfortable lounge available throughout the day. Convenient for the Castle, Princes Street, the Royal Mile and International Conference Centre.

Scottish Tourist Board HIGHLY COMMENDED

AA Selected QQQQ

Dunstane House Hotel

Shirley and Derek Mowat welcome you to Dunstane House, a beautifully preserved B Listed Victorian Mansion house occupying a prime corner site in Edinburghs exclusive West End, close to City centre, Murrayfield and Edinburgh International Conference Centre with airport 15 minutes drive away. Residents Lounge Bar. Dinners provided. Four poster bedroom available. Private secluded car park and excellent bus service to all amenities.

4 West Coates, Haymarket, Edinburgh,
Scotland, EH12 5JQ
Tel/Fax: 0131 337 6169
Web:http://members.edinburgh.org/mowat/
E-Mail:smowat@compuserve.com

EDINBURGH

DORSTAN

PRIVATE HOTEL

7 Priestfield Road,
Edinburgh, EH16 5HJ

Tel: 0131 667 6721 / 5138
Fax: 0131 668 4644

A tastefully furnished Victorian house, The Dorstan offers a warm welcome and comfortable accommodation. Situated in a quiet southside residential area conveniently located for bypass and city centre. Come and enjoy the friendly personal service of this family run hotel.

Proprietor:
Mairae Campbell.
Send for colour brochure.

AA Selected QQQQ

Scottish Tourist Board HIGHLY COMMENDED

533

Premier Selected

Q Q Q Q Q **Elmview** 15 Glengyle Ter EH3 9LN
(take A702 S up Lothian Road, turn first left past Kings Theatre into Valley Field Street one way system leading to Glengyle Terrace)
☎ 0131 228 1973 FAX 0131 622 3271
Elmview is a luxurious guest house offering a high standard of accommodation, service and hospitality to either the business person or holidaymaker. All bedrooms are equipped with many useful facilities, including ironing boards, mini bar fridges and towelling bath robes. There is an elegant dining room which faces on to a pretty paved garden with pot plants and flowers.
3 bth/shr No smoking CTV in all bedrooms Tea and coffee making facilities Direct dial from bedrooms No dogs Cen ht No children 15yrs No coaches
ROOMS: s £70-£85; d £75-£90*
CARDS:

Q Q Q ***Finlay*** 4 Hartington Place, Bruntsfield EH10 4LE
☎ 0131 229 1620 FAX 0131 229 1548
Terance and Annette Hazzard look forward to welcoming you to their comfortable home, a terraced Victorian house set in a cul-de-sac in the fashionable Bruntsfield area. The delightful bedrooms with attractive lemon and green colour schemes are furnished in antique pine. Hearty breakfasts are served at individual tables in the pine furnished dining room.
6 rms (1 fmly) No smoking in 2 bedrooms No smoking in area of dining room CTV in all bedrooms Tea and coffee making facilities No dogs (ex guide dogs) Cen ht No coaches
CARDS:

Q Q Q **Galloway** 22 Dean Park Crescent EH4 1PH
(½m from Princes St West end on £A9)
☎ 0131 332 3672 FAX 332 3672
Robert and Sheila Clark look forward to welcoming you to their lovely terraced home which is situated in a residential area close to shops and bistros in the Stockbridge area. The tastefully decorated bedrooms are comfortably furnished in a modern style and feature en suite bathrooms. Carefully prepared breakfasts are served in the attractive dining room.
10 rms (6 bth/shr) (6 fmly) CTV in all bedrooms Tea and coffee making facilities Cen ht
ROOMS: s £30-£45; d £36-£54; wkly b&b £108-£270

Q Q Q **Glenalmond** 25 Mayfield Gardens EH9 2BX (on A701)
☎ 0131 668 2392 FAX 0131 668 2392
On-going improvements are taking place at this welcoming, family-run guest house, situated on the south side within ten minutes of the city centre. The mostly spacious bedrooms are smartly decorated and new pine furnishings are gradually being introduced. A new Fraser tartan carpet has been laid in the attractive dining room where breakfasts are served at individual tables.

10 shr (4 fmly) No smoking in 3 bedrooms No smoking in dining room No smoking in 1 lounge CTV in all bedrooms Tea and coffee making facilities No dogs (ex guide dogs) Cen ht CTV 10P

Q Q ***Glenisla Hotel*** 12 Lygon Rd EH16 5QB
(off A7 at first exit on right after rdbt at Lady Road Junction, heading into Town) ☎ 0131 667 4877 FAX 0131 667 4098
A warm welcome is assured at this family run guest house on the south side of the city. Bedrooms are variable in size and in style but offer a good range of amenities including telephones. There is a spacious and comfortable lounge on the first floor and enjoyable home cooking is served in the bright dining room.
8 rms (5 shr) (1 fmly) No smoking in dining room Tea and coffee making facilities Direct dial from bedrooms Licensed Cen ht CTV 6P No coaches Last d 8pm
CARDS:

Q Q Q **Greenside Hotel** 9 Royal Ter EH7 5AB
(follow A1 into London Road, Royal Terrace is at the end of London Road turning left at the rdbt)
☎ 0131 557 0022 & 557 0121 FAX 0131 557 0022
A comfortable private hotel, which forms part of an elegant Georgian terrace close to the east end of Princes Street. Much of the hotel is being gradually upgraded, and the smart newly refurbished rooms are finished to a high standard. All the accommodation is soundly furnished, attractively decorated with pretty fabrics and suitably equipped, though the bedrooms may vary in

size. The recently redecorated dining room includes a small residents bar and offers hearty breakfasts, and evening meals are available by arrangement.
14 bth/shr (5 fmly) No smoking in dining room CTV in all bedrooms Tea and coffee making facilities Direct dial from bedrooms No dogs (ex guide dogs) Licensed Cen ht CTV Arrangement with 4 star hotel to use facilities Last d 4pm
ROOMS: s £30-£50; d £45-£85; wkly b&b £210-£280; wkly hlf-bd £280-£315*
CARDS:

Selected

Q Q Q Q Grosvenor Gardens Hotel 1 Grosvenor Gardens EH12 5JU ☎ 0131 313 3415 FAX 0131 346 8732
Situated in a quiet cul-de-sac, this elegant guest house is a converted Victorian town house. Bedrooms are nicely furnished and decorated and offer a wide range of thoughtful extras. The elegant drawing room has deep cushioned sofas, and guests are welcome to use the baby grand piano.
8 bth/shr (3 fmly) No smoking in 5 bedrooms No smoking in dining room No smoking in lounges CTV in all bedrooms Tea and coffee making facilities Direct dial from bedrooms No dogs (ex guide dogs) Cen ht CTV No children 5yrs No coaches
ROOMS: s £35-£50; d £60-£100*
CARDS:

Q *Halcyon Hotel* 8 Royal Ter EH7 5AB ☎ 0131 556 1033 & 0131 556 1032
Situated in the east end and forming part of an elegant Georgian terrace, this friendly family run guest house offers good value accommodation. The variable sized bedrooms offer mixed simple appointments with those on the upper floors enjoying views of the Firth of Forth. There is a spacious traditional first floor lounge and hearty breakfasts are served in the ground floor dining room.
16 rms (2 shr) (6 fmly) Tea and coffee making facilities Cen ht CTV Tennis (hard)

Q Q Harvest 33 Straiton Place, Portobello EH15 2BA (From city centre by pass (A720) take A1 to Edinburgh follow sign Portobello, from Portobello High St take Bath St to Straiton Pl) ☎ 0131 657 3160 FAX 0131 468 7028
This family run terraced guest house is situated to the east of the city overlooking Portobello Beach, and offers good value bed and breakfast accommodation. Bedrooms are mostly compact and offer both modern and traditional furnishings while hearty breakfasts are served at shared tables in the cosy dining room.
7 rms (2 shr) (2 fmly) No smoking CTV in all bedrooms Tea and coffee making facilities No dogs Cen ht CTV 4P
ROOMS: s £15-£25; d £30-£50; wkly b&b £105-£150*
CARDS:

Selected

Q Q Q Q A Haven 180 Ferry Rd EH6 4NS (The Circle)
☎ 0131 554 6559 FAX 0131 554 5252
You'll be assured of a warm welcome from Moira and Ronnie Murdoch at their elegant house, situated to the north of the city centre. The tastefully decorated bedrooms, though varied in size, are comfortably furnished and offer a wide range of amenities to suit the needs of both the business and leisure guest. Oil paintings by the owners' daughter feature in the welcoming open plan lounge/dining room where Moira's delicious home cooked Scottish fare continues to earn praise.
12 shr (2 fmly) No smoking in bedrooms No smoking in dining room CTV in all bedrooms Tea and coffee making facilities Direct dial from bedrooms No dogs (ex guide dogs) Licensed Cen ht CTV 6P Last d 8pm
ROOMS: s £40-£60; d £60-£90*
CARDS:

Q Q Heriott Park 256 Ferry Rd, Goldenacre EH5 3AN
☎ 0131 552 6628 FAX 0131 552 6628
This welcoming, friendly family-run guest house lies on the north side of city and enjoys lovely panoramic views of the city skyline with the Castle and Arthur's Seat prominent. Bedrooms come in a variety of sizes and those without en suites are served by two good modern bathrooms. The breakfast menu offers a decent choice.
6 rms (3 shr) (3 fmly) No smoking CTV in all bedrooms Tea and coffee making facilities No dogs Cen ht CTV
CARDS:

Q Q Hermitage 16 East Hermitage Place, Leith Links EH6 8AB
☎ 0131 555 4868 FAX 07070 600705
Set in a terraced row overlooking Leith Links on the northern side of the city, this guest house has bright, cheerfully decorated bedrooms and an attractive dining room which also doubles as a lounge. Business facilities are provided.
5 rms (2 fmly) No smoking in dining room No smoking in lounges CTV in all bedrooms Tea and coffee making facilities No dogs (ex guide dogs) Cen ht
ROOMS: s £21-£26; d £32-£44*
CARDS:

Q Q Hopetoun 15 Mayfield Rd EH9 2NG
(south side of city near Edinburgh University Kings Buildings Campus. North end of Mayfield Road, near Mayfield church)
☎ 0131 667 7691 FAX 0131 466 1691
Closed xmas
Located on the south side of the city, close to the University buildings, this small family run guest house has a strict no smoking policy, which ensures that rooms are kept fresh and bright. Bedrooms, including two family rooms, are a good size and have working wooden shutters. A wide choice is available at breakfast.
3 rms (2 shr) (2 fmly) No smoking CTV in all bedrooms Tea and coffee making facilities No dogs Cen ht CTV No children 4yrs 2P No coaches
ROOMS: s £25-£45; d £40-£56
CARDS:

Q Q Q House O'Hill 7 House O'Hill Ter, Queensferry Rd EH4 2AA
(On A90 Queensferry Rd between Kwik-Fit & The Holiday Inn, going towards city centre)
☎ 0131 332 3674 FAX 0131 343 3446
Chrissy White provides a warm welcome and friendly service which gives a genuine home-from-home atmosphere. The house is stylishly decorated throughout, with bedrooms in a variety of sizes, all of smart appearance and with modern en suite bathrooms. They are very well equipped and include radios, hair dryers and fridges. Breakfasts are served on glass topped tables in the cosy dining room.
4 shr (2 fmly) No smoking CTV in all bedrooms Tea and coffee making facilities No dogs Cen ht 6P No coaches
ROOMS: s £25-£40; d £44-£60*
CARDS:

Selected

Q Q Q Q International 37 Mayfield Gardens EH9 2BX
(1.5m S of Princes Street on the main A701 and only 4m from the Straiton Junction on the Edinburgh City by-pass)
☎ 0131 667 2511 FAX 0131 667 1112
You'll receive a delightfully warm welcome and enthusiastic service from Mr and Mrs Niven at their attractive Victorian terraced house on the south side of the city. Recent improvements have provided consistently high standards and earned much praise from their guests. Bedrooms are attractively decorated and comfortably furnished, and breakfast is served in the lounge/dining room which boasts a beautiful ornate ceiling.

contd.

International

9 bth/shr (3 fmly) No smoking in 4 bedrooms No smoking in dining room No smoking in lounges CTV in all bedrooms Tea and coffee making facilities Direct dial from bedrooms No dogs (ex guide dogs) Cen ht CTV 3P
ROOMS: s £22-£45; d £40-£80*
CARDS:

Q Q Q ***Inveresk House*** 3 Inveresk Village, Musselburgh EH21 7UA
☎ 0131 6655855 FAX 0131 6650578
Situated in three and a half acres of grounds on the outskirts of Musselburgh, this historic mansion house, used as a base by Cromwell at the battle of Dunbar, is today run by Alice Chute. Public areas include an expansive sitting room on the first floor which has been furnished in sympathy with the character of the house. Downstairs, enjoyable home cooking is offered in the dining room which boasts an ornate ceiling and a fine carved fire place. The upstairs bedroom is well proportioned and very comfortable while those on the ground floor are of more standard size and traditional style. These rooms have private bathrooms adjacent.
3 bth/shr (1 fmly) No smoking CTV in all bedrooms Tea and coffee making facilities No dogs (ex guide dogs) Cen ht 10P No coaches Last d 4pm
CARDS:

Q Q Q **Ivy House** 7 Mayfield Gardens EH9 2AX (on A701 1.5m S of Princes Street) ☎ 0131 667 3411 FAX 0131 620 1422
This Victorian terraced guest house offers large bedrooms (which compensates for the lack of a lounge) all with modern en suite or private bathrooms. The ivy motif is reflected throughout the house's decor.
8 shr (4 fmly) No smoking in dining room CTV in all bedrooms Tea and coffee making facilities Cen ht 9P
ROOMS: s £18-£50; d £36-£62

Q Q **Kariba** 10 Granville Ter EH10 4PQ ☎ 0131 229 3773
A welcoming atmosphere prevails at this family run guest house which stands in a residential area a short distance from the Kings Theatre. Attractive fabrics have been used to good effect in the variable sized modern bedrooms. Public areas include a comfortable lounge and dining room.
9 rms (8 bth/shr) (3 fmly) No smoking in dining room No smoking in lounges CTV in all bedrooms Tea and coffee making facilities Cen ht CTV 6P No coaches
ROOMS: s £25-£40; d £36-£60*

Selected

Q Q Q Q **Kew** 1 Kew Ter, Murrayfield EH12 5JE (situated on the main A8 Glasgow Road, 1m west of city centre and close to Murrayfield Rugby Stadium) ☎ 0131 313 0700 FAX 0131 313 0747
This immaculately maintained house is beautifully decorated and furnished to a very high standard throughout. Bedrooms have been thoughtfully equipped with an emphasis on guest comfort and include many personal touches which will ensure a memorable stay. Public areas include a stylish lounge and dining room where an extensive breakfast menu and delicious selection of light evening meals and snacks can be enjoyed.
6 shr (2 fmly) No smoking CTV in all bedrooms Tea and coffee making facilities Direct dial from bedrooms Licensed Cen ht 6P No coaches Last d 9pm
ROOMS: s £40-£45; d £68-£82*
CARDS:

Selected

Q Q Q Q ***Kilmaurs*** 9 Kilmaurs Rd EH16 5DA (Kilmaurs Road lies parallel to A7 Dalkeith Road close to Commonwealth Swimming Pool) ☎ 0131 667 8315 FAX 0131 662 6949
Situated in the residential area south of the city, this pleasant guest house offers a welcoming atmosphere. The attractive bedrooms boast a quality selection of pine furnishings and many thoughtful extra touches to ensure maximum comfort. Public areas include a pleasing dining room where guests can enjoy a choice of freshly cooked breakfast dishes.
4 shr (2 fmly) No smoking CTV in all bedrooms Tea and coffee making facilities No dogs (ex guide dogs) Cen ht
CARDS:

Q Q **Kingsley** 30 Craigmillar Park, Newington EH16 5PS (S on A701) ☎ 0131 667 8439 FAX 0131 667 8439
This family run guest house offers good value accommodation, including some family rooms. There is a spacious lounge and a bright dining room where full Scottish breakfast is served.
6 rms (5 shr) (3 fmly) No smoking in bedrooms No smoking in dining room CTV in all bedrooms Tea and coffee making facilities No dogs Cen ht CTV No children 6yrs 6P
ROOMS: d £36-£50*
CARDS:

Q Q **Kirklea** 11 Harrison Rd EH11 1EG (leave city bypass at Calder Junction A71, follow signs for city centre turn right after passing Hearts FC, Kirklea on left after next traffic lights) ☎ 0131 337 1129 FAX 0131 337 1129
The atmosphere is relaxed at Moira and Vic Kielnar's guest house, which can be found in a residential area just a five minute drive from central

amenities. Bedrooms are well maintained and offer mixed modern appointments. Breakfast is served at individual tables in the attractive dining room and as well as a full Scottish selection, continental, vegetarian, and light alternatives are available. Dutch, French, German, and Italian are spoken here.
6 rms (1 shr) (1 fmly) No smoking CTV in all bedrooms Tea and coffee making facilities Cen ht
ROOMS: s £22-£30; d £36-£60
CARDS:

Q Q Q **Leamington** 57 Leamington Ter EH10 4JS (off Bruntsfield Place - 1m from W end of Princes Street) ☎ 0131 228 3879 FAX 0131 221 1022
Charles and Louise Hodkinson are the welcoming hosts at this comfortable guesthouse. Bedrooms at the lower levels of the house have been tastefully refurbished and offer attractive pine furnishings. Those on the top floor are gradually being upgraded to the same standard. Breakfast is served in the delightful dining room overlooking the rear garden. This is a non smoking establishment.
8 rms (4 shr) (3 fmly) No smoking CTV in all bedrooms Tea and coffee making facilities Cen ht No coaches
ROOMS: s £22-£28; d £44-£56*
CARDS:

Q Q **Lindsay** 108 Polwarth Ter EH11 1NN (turn off A720 bypass at Colinton/Redford link to 2nd rdbt, go to end turn left past Napier University. Bottom of hill left at mini rdbt) ☎ 0131 337 1580 FAX 0131 337 9174
Set in a residential area in the city's western suburbs, this semi-detached Victorian house has bedrooms which come in a variety of sizes, some being particularly spacious, which compensates for the lack of a lounge. Breakfasts are served in the attractive dining room.
7 rms (3 shr) (4 fmly) No smoking CTV in all bedrooms Tea and coffee making facilities No dogs (ex guide dogs) Cen ht 6P No coaches
ROOMS: s £18-£35; d £36-£70*
CARDS:

Selected

Q Q Q Q **The Lodge Hotel** 6 Hampton Ter, West Coates EH12 5JD (on A8, 1m W of city centre) ☎ 0131 337 3682 FAX 0131 313 1700
Closed 10-26 Dec
A warm welcome awaits you at Linda and George Jarron's attractive Georgian home. Ideally located in Edinburgh's West End, guests can relax after a long days sightseeing in the comfortable living room, cosy bar or beautifully presented bedrooms. For new arrivals, fresh fruit and a welcoming glass of sherry is thoughtfully provided. Freshly prepared breakfasts and evening meals are served in the elegant dining room.
10 shr No smoking in bedrooms No smoking in dining room CTV in all bedrooms Tea and coffee making facilities Direct dial from bedrooms No dogs Licensed Cen ht CTV 10P Last d 8.00pm
ROOMS: s £38-£48; d fr £58*
CARDS:

Selected

Q Q Q Q **Maitland Hotel** 25-33 Shandwick Place EH2 4RG (west end of Princes Street) (The Circle) ☎ 0131 229 1467
FAX 0131 229 7549
This comfortable Town House hotel enjoys the superb location of being situated right in the heart of Edinburgh's West End, just off Princes Street. The attractively decorated and comfortably furnished bedrooms offer a wide range of amenities to suit the business traveller and tourist alike. Ten executive rooms have been created, all with CD players and complimentary wine. There is an attractive and well stocked bar, and a wide range of dishes are available from the breakfast buffet in the extended dining room. *contd. on p.538.*

65 bth/shr (1 fmly) No smoking in 10 bedrooms No smoking in dining room CTV in all bedrooms Tea and coffee making facilities Direct dial from bedrooms No dogs (ex guide dogs) Licensed Lift Cen ht
ROOMS: s £69.50-£75; d £80-£105*
CARDS:

Q Q **Marchhall Hotel** 14-16 Marchhall Crescent EH16 5HL
(off A720 city bypass onto A7, over Cameron toll rdbt staying on A7, after 0.5m at traffic lights turn into Priestfield Road, 1st right)
☎ 0131 667 2743 FAX 0131 662 0777
Major improvements are taking place at this personally run small hotel in the south side of the city. Bedrooms are being refurbished to provide improved standards of accommodation. The lounge bar is an ideal place to relax and enjoy a drink or bar meal. More formal meals are available from the small carte in the dining room.
14 rms (11 bth/shr) (4 fmly) No smoking in 4 bedrooms No smoking in dining room No smoking in lounges CTV in all bedrooms Tea and coffee making facilities Direct dial from bedrooms No dogs (ex guide dogs) Licensed Cen ht CTV Last d 8.30pm
ROOMS: s £23-£40; d £46-£62; wkly b&b £160-£270; wkly hlf-bd £221-£350*
CARDS:

Q Q Q **Mardale** 11 Hartington Place EH10 4LF (city centre)
☎ 0131 229 2693 FAX 0131 229 2693
Situated in a residential cul-de-sac on the south side, this cosy well maintained B&B offers attractive thoughtfully equipped bedrooms and a bright cheerful breakfast room.
6 shr (2 fmly) No smoking in dining room No smoking in lounges CTV in all bedrooms Tea and coffee making facilities Direct dial from bedrooms Cen ht No coaches
CARDS:

Q **Menzies** 33 Leamington Ter EH10 4JS
(from Princes Street, left up Lothian Road, right into Home Street (Toll Cross) straight ahead to Brunstfield Hotel, on right and turn right)
☎ 0131 229 4629 FAX 0131 229 4629
Situated in the south side and forming part of a terraced row, this personally run guest house offers good value accommodation. Bedrooms are well equipped and offer mixed practical appointments. Breakfast is served at shared tables in the combined lounge/dining room.
6 rms (2 shr) (3 fmly) No smoking in dining room No smoking in lounges CTV in all bedrooms Tea and coffee making facilities No dogs Cen ht CTV 5P
ROOMS: d £30-£60*
CARDS:

Q Q Q **The Newington** 18 Newington Rd EH9 1QS
(between A7 and A68 routes into Edinburgh)
☎ 0131 667 3356 FAX 0131 667 8307
Traditional values and comforts are all part of the appeal of this welcoming guest house on the south side of the city. Bedrooms, some of which have lovely antique furnishings, are quite individual and offer a wide range of amenities. Far Eastern bric-a-brac features in the comfortable first floor lounge while the attractive dining room provides an appropriate setting for the carefully prepared breakfasts. A no smoking establishment.
8 rms (5 bth/shr) (1 fmly) No smoking CTV in all bedrooms Tea and coffee making facilities Licensed Cen ht CTV 3P
ROOMS: s £30-£40; d £49-£70*
CARDS:

Q Q Q **Parklands** 20 Mayfield Gardens EH9 2BZ (1.5m S of Princes Street on the main A7/A701) ☎ 0131 667 7184 FAX 0131 667 2011
For almost thirty years Mrs Drummond has been welcoming guests to her comfortable terraced home on the south side of the city. Bedrooms are tastefully decorated and comfortably furnished and freshly prepared breakfasts are served in the attractive dining room.
6 rms (5 shr) (1 fmly) No smoking in 1 bedrooms No smoking in dining room No smoking in lounges CTV in all bedrooms Tea and coffee making facilities No dogs (ex guide dogs) Cen ht 1P No coaches
ROOMS: d £40-£60*

Selected

Q Q Q Q **Priory Lodge** The Loan EH30 9NS ☎ 0131 331 4345 FAX 0131 331 4345

(For full entry see **South Queensferry**)

Q Q Q **Quaich** 87 St John's Rd EH12 6NN
(M74 to M8 & A8 to Edinburgh,pass airport, through underpass at Gogar rdbt, through Maybury traffic lights into Glasgow Rd, & into St John's Rd)
☎ 0131 334 4440 FAX 476 9002
Good value accommodation is offered at this friendly, family run guesthouse which stands beside the Glasgow Road in the west end. The well maintained bedrooms are bright and cheery with modern furnishings, and some are generously proportioned. Breakfast is served in the attractive front facing dining room. This is a non smoking house.
6 rms (4 bth/shr) (4 fmly) No smoking CTV in all bedrooms Tea and coffee making facilities No dogs (ex guide dogs) Cen ht 8P
ROOMS: s £20-£26; d £40-£52; wkly b&b £126-£154*

Q Q Q **Ravensdown** 248 Ferry Rd EH5 3AN
(A1-A199 Leith & Granton, round the corner from the Royal Botanic Gardens, north side of Princess Street) ☎ 0131 552 5438 FAX 0131 552 7559
Len and Sue Welch look forward to welcoming you to their comfortable home which enjoys wonderful views over Edinburgh, especially from the upper levels. The tastefully decorated bedrooms, some now en suite, are bright and airy and offer both modern and traditional furnishings. Guests are welcome to use the music centre and piano in the inviting lounge and freshly prepared breakfasts are served at individual tables in the dining room. This is a non smoking establishment.
7 shr (4 fmly) No smoking CTV in all bedrooms Tea and coffee making facilities No dogs Licensed Cen ht CTV 4P
ROOMS: s £25-£35; d £40-£60*

Selected

Q Q Q Q Roselea 11 Mayfield Rd EH9 2NG
(on A701, 1m N of the Royal Observatory) ☎ 0131 667 6115
FAX 0131 667 3556
Closed 1 week Xmas
This family run Victorian terraced house is conveniently located to the south of the city centre. The individually decorated bedrooms vary in size but guests can be assured of the highest standards of comfort and a host of thoughtful extras. Public areas include a smart lounge and attractive dining room where a delicious breakfast choice is served at individual tables.
7 rms (5 shr) (1 fmly) No smoking in dining room No smoking in lounges CTV in all bedrooms Tea and coffee making facilities No dogs (ex guide dogs) Cen ht 4P
ROOMS: s £35-£50; d £60-£90*
CARDS:

Q Q Q Rowan 13 Glenorchy Ter EH9 2DQ
(just off A70, left at Bright's Crescent, 1.5 miles South of Princes St)
☎ 0131 667 2463 FAX 0131 667 2463
Sparklingly clean and meticulously maintained, this welcoming guest house lies in a quiet residential terrace on the south side of the city. The atmosphere is friendly and relaxing and the breakfast room becomes an inviting lounge during the day and evening. Breakfasts themselves offer a good choice, with loose leaf tea and Mrs Vidler's delicious home-made scones a bonus. Bedrooms come in a variety of sizes and are solidly furnished with either pine or traditional pieces.
9 rms (3 shr) (2 fmly) No smoking in dining room No smoking in lounges CTV in all bedrooms Tea and coffee making facilities Cen ht CTV P
ROOMS: s £22-£27; d £42-£60*
CARDS:

Q Q Q *Rutland Hotel* 1 Rutland St EH1 2AE (Scottish & Newcastle)
☎ 0131 229 3402
Situated at the west end of Princes Street in the heart of the city, The Rutland Hotel offers fifteen smartly appointed and thoughtfully equipped bedrooms, as well as two lively bars and a gallery restaurant. The views of Princes Street and Edinburgh Castle, especially from the restaurant, are outstanding. When making a reservation, the friendly staff will be more than happy to provide information with regard to parking.
15 rms

Q Q Q **St Margaret's** 18 Craigmillar Park EH16 5PS (St Margarets is situated N from junct A701. From the city bypass A720, turn off at Straiton junction on A701 3m on) ☎ 0131 667 2202 FAX 0131 667 2202
Enthusiastic owners Harold and Alison Levey look forward to welcoming guests old and new to their comfortable terraced home on the south side of the city. The immaculately kept bedrooms vary in size and offer mixed modern furnishings. Public areas include a spacious and inviting lounge while freshly prepared breakfasts are served in the dining room.
8 rms (5 bth/shr) (3 fmly) No smoking in bedrooms No smoking in dining room CTV in all bedrooms Tea and coffee making facilities No dogs Cen ht CTV 7P No coaches
ROOMS: s £30-£50; d £44-£60*
CARDS:

Q Q Q **Salisbury** 45 Salisbury Rd EH16 5AA (left off A7 - opposite Royal Commonwealth Pool) ☎ 0131 667 1264 FAX 0131 667 1264
Closed Xmas-New Year
There is a welcoming atmosphere at this personally run guest house, a conversion of two Georgian houses situated just off the main thoroughfare on the south side. The comfortable bedrooms are mostly spacious, as are public areas which include a lounge where refreshments are available, and an attractive dining room.
12 bth/shr (3 fmly) No smoking CTV in all bedrooms Tea and coffee making facilities No dogs (ex guide dogs) Licensed Cen ht CTV No children 5yrs 12P No coaches
ROOMS: s £25-£32; d £48-£60*
CARDS:

Q Q Q **Salisbury View Hotel** 64 Dalkeith Rd EH16 5AE
(on A7/A68, 5 mins from city centre, adjacent to Holyrood Park)
☎ 0131 667 1133 FAX 0131 667 1133
A large detached sandstone house with a welcoming atmosphere, this hotel provides comfortable accommodation in well equipped bedrooms. The comfortable lounge contains a small dispense bar and the restaurant provides a good range of carefully prepared dishes for guests and non residents alike.
8 shr (1 fmly) No smoking in dining room CTV in all bedrooms Tea and coffee making facilities Direct dial from bedrooms Licensed Cen ht 8P No coaches
ROOMS: s £28-£47; d £54-£74; wkly b&b £196-£259*
CARDS:

Q Q Q **Sandaig** 5 East Hermitage Place, Leith Links EH6 8AA
(once in Edinburgh follow signs for Leith. Establishment is located facing Leith Links Park)
☎ 0131 554 7357 FAX 0131 554 7313
Occupying a terraced row overlooking Leith Links, Sandaig offers bedrooms in various sizes, all being very well equipped to include extras such as telephone, hairdryer and radio, and most having been refurbished. The attractive breakfast room and inviting lounge mirror the period character of the house.
10 rms (4 shr) (3 fmly) No smoking in 2 bedrooms No smoking in dining room CTV in all bedrooms Tea and coffee making facilities Direct dial from bedrooms CTV
ROOMS: s £20-£30; d £35-£65*
CARDS:

Q Q Q **Sherwood** 42 Minto St EH9 2BR
(one mile up North Bridge from Princes St) ☎ 0131 667 1200
Closed 20-29 Dec
Enthusiastic owner Mrs Greig is constantly striving to improve standards at her comfortable and welcoming guest house on the south side. All bedrooms now have smart pine furnishings and all but one are en suite with newly tiled shower units. Hearty breakfasts are served at pretty lace clothed tables in the cosy combined lounge/dining room.
6 shr (2 fmly) No smoking CTV in all bedrooms Tea and coffee making facilities No dogs Cen ht CTV 3P
ROOMS: d £46-£70*
CARDS:

Q Q Q **Six Mary's Place** 6 Mary's Place, Raeburn Place, Stockbridge EH4 1JD ☎ 0131 332 8965 FAX 0131 624 7060
Situated in the village suburb of Stockbridge, this terraced Georgian house offers friendly service in a comfortable and relaxed environment. A vegetarian guest house, it provides good home-cooked two or three course dinners and tasty breakfasts, served refectory style at the one large table in an attractive conservatory. There is also a comfortable guests lounge with TV.
8 rms (2 shr) No smoking Tea and coffee making facilities No dogs (ex guide dogs) Cen ht CTV Last d 10am
CARDS:

Q Q Q ***Sonas*** 3 East Mayfield EH9 1SD (from A720 bypass turn off Edinburgh/Peebles sign follow for city centre through 4 lights, 1 rdbt, turn right at the next lights) ☎ 0131 667 2781 FAX 0131 667 0454
Closed 21-26 Dec
Bright and cheerful in both atmosphere and appearance, Sonas offers bedrooms with thoughtful touches such as hair dryers, tissues and note pads with mapped directions to the local bus services into the city centre.
7 bth/shr (3 fmly) No smoking in dining room CTV in all bedrooms Tea and coffee making facilities No dogs (ex guide dogs) Cen ht CTV 6P

Q Q Q **Stra'ven** 3 Brunstane Rd North, Joppa EH15 2DL
(A1 over rdbt approaching Edinburgh, at 2nd right to Joppa turn left into Brunstane Rd, house behind St Philips church)
☎ 0131 669 5580 FAX 0131 657 2517
Friendly, attentive service is a feature of this enthusiastically run guest house which lies in a quiet cul-de-sac just a couple of minutes walk from Portobello Beach. Attractive and well maintained public areas include an inviting upstairs lounge and cheery dining room, where breakfast offers a good choice of both hot and cold dishes. Bedrooms come in a variety of sizes and there is an excellent family room.
7 shr (3 fmly) No smoking CTV in all bedrooms Tea and coffee making facilities No dogs (ex guide dogs) Cen ht CTV
ROOMS: s £20-£32; d £40-£60*

See page 14-20 for a list of Premier Selected establishments

Selected

QQQQ **Stuart House** 12 East Claremont St EH7 4JP
(east along Princes Street, turn onto Leith Street, left down Broughton Street, located bottom of Broughton Street 2nd road on right)
☎ 0131 557 9030 FAX 0131 557 0563
Closed 18-27 Dec
June Watson's delightful Georgian-style town house is situated in a quiet residential area near to Leith Walk and is within easy reach of central amenities. The lovingly tended bedrooms are decorated to a high standard and attractive fabrics have been used to stunning effect. All are comfortably furnished and offer a wide range of amenities together with useful extras. Carefully prepared breakfasts are served at two long tables in the dining room. For the comfort of all, smoking is not permitted in the house.
6 rms (5 bth/shr) No smoking CTV in all bedrooms Tea and coffee making facilities Direct dial from bedrooms No dogs Cen ht No coaches
ROOMS: s £35-£50; d £60-£90
CARDS:

QQQ **The Stuarts** 17 Glengyle Ter EH3 9LN
(E of A702, between the Kings Theatre and Bruntsfield Links)
☎ 0131 229 9559 FAX 0131 229 2226
Closed 18-28 Dec
Overlooking Bruntsfield Links, this guest house offers comfortable accommodation within its generously proportioned rooms. Breakfast is served in the bright dining room at two communal tables.
3 bth/shr No smoking CTV in all bedrooms Tea and coffee making facilities Direct dial from bedrooms Cen ht No coaches
ROOMS: d £40-£45*
CARDS:

QQ ***Sylvern*** 22 West Mayfield EH9 1TQ ☎ 0131 667 1241
Closed 22-29 Dec
Spacious bedrooms, most with modern en suites and comfortable chairs, are a feature of this well maintained detached villa situated in a south side residential area, which has good public transport links with the city centre.
6 rms (4 shr) (4 fmly) No smoking in dining room No smoking in lounges TV available Tea and coffee making facilities No dogs Cen ht 8P

QQQ ***Terrace Hotel*** 37 Royal Ter EH7 5AH
(from Waverley Station/Princes St travel East along Regent Road turn left Regent Terrace - leads into Royal Terrace)
☎ 0131 556 3423 FAX 0131 556 2520
This well proportioned property is part of an impressive Georgian terrace offering fine views across the city to the Firth of Forth from its upper floors. Bedrooms come in a variety of sizes, most being spacious and furnished with quality pieces.
14 rms (11 bth/shr) (7 fmly) No smoking in dining room CTV in all bedrooms Tea and coffee making facilities No dogs Cen ht
CARDS:

Q Q *Tire* 26 Craigmillar Park EH16 5PS
(on the A701 close to the Cameron Toll shopping centre)
☎ 0131 667 7477 FAX 0131 662 1608
This family-run guest house forms part of a terraced row on the south side of the city, close to the Cameron Toll shopping centre. Bedrooms vary in size and appointment, while the dining room is situated on the ground floor.
7 rms (5 shr) (2 fmly) No smoking in dining room No smoking in lounges CTV in all bedrooms Tea and coffee making facilities Cen ht 7P

Selected

Q Q Q Q The Town House 65 Gilmore Place EH3 9NU
(city centre location, access from A1, A8 and A702, entrance to Gilmore Place opposite the Kings Theatre) ☎ 0131 229 1985
This former manse is located in central Edinburgh, a short distance from the King's Theatre. Over the years, Susan Virtue has completely restored the house, carefully preserving many of the original features. The stylish bedrooms are attractively decorated and offer comfortable furnishings. Public areas include an elegant lounge and separate, small dining room where breakfast is served at individual tables.
5 bth/shr (1 fmly) No smoking CTV in all bedrooms Tea and coffee making facilities No dogs (ex guide dogs) Cen ht CTV
No children 10yrs 5P No coaches
ROOMS: s £25-£35; d £50-£70

See advertisement on p.541.

Q Q Truva 2 East Hermitage Place, Leith Links EH6 8AA
(At bottom of Leith Walk turn right at traffic lights, then left at roundabout. House is on right opposite park)
☎ 0131 554 3763 FAX 0131 554 0853
This nicely decorated guest house lies in a terraced row looking out onto Leith Links. Bedrooms come in a variety of sizes and are served by attractive bathrooms, and breakfast is served in the cosy dining room. A short selection of hot snacks is available from 4pm to 7pm.
5 rms (2 shr) (3 fmly) No smoking CTV in all bedrooms Tea and coffee making facilities Cen ht
ROOMS: s £17-£25; d £30-£52 ✱
CARDS:

Q Q Q Yellow Rose (Buidhe Rôs) 9 Hawkshead Crescent EH16 6LR
(turn off A720 city by-pass onto A701 city centre, Hawkeshead Cres is on left 1.75m) ☎ 0131 621 7111 FAX 0131 621 7111
Jun-Sep 26 Dec-5 Jan
Maureen Brett and Peter Livingstone look forward to welcoming you to their comfortable semi-detached home which has good public transport links to the city centre. The house offers excellent value bed and breakfast accommodation in bedrooms which have been decorated to a very high standard. Hearty breakfasts are served at the communal table in the combined lounge/dining room. Street parking is readily available.
2 shr (2 fmly) No smoking CTV in all bedrooms Tea and coffee making facilities No dogs Cen ht CTV 1P
ROOMS: d £40-£50✱

ELGIN Moray Map 15 NJ26

Q Q Q Auchmillan 12 Reidhaven St IV30 1QG
(take A96 to Elgin then A941 Perth road to Elgin Station, Reidhaven St is opposite this and estab is on left at top end next to the bowling green)
☎ 01343 549077
This substantial Victorian house is beside the bowling green, and used to be a doctor's house and surgery. Currently being developed, the bedrooms are bright and modern with all expected facilities. The combined lounge and dining room has individual tables and a lounge suite.

3 rms (1 bth/shr) No smoking in 2 bedrooms No smoking in dining room No smoking in lounges CTV in all bedrooms Tea and coffee making facilities No dogs (ex guide dogs) Cen ht 6P No coaches
Last d breakfast same day
ROOMS: s £17-£25; d £32-£48; wkly b&b £105-£140✱
CARDS:

Q Q Q Belleville 14 South College St IV30 1EP
(on entering town follow signs to Elgin museum, turn right at end of Glover St. 200 yds on right opposite Safeway car park)
☎ 01343 541515 FAX 01343 540033 - quote 'Belleville'
The Belleville lies in the shadow of Elgin's oldest monument, The Cathedral. Hugh & Frances McMillan are superb hosts and offer two comfortable, well equipped bedrooms. Breakfast is taken at one table in the dining room where a bright coal fire glows in winter.
2 shr No smoking CTV in all bedrooms Tea and coffee making facilities No dogs (ex guide dogs) Cen ht No children 12yrs 2P No coaches
ROOMS: s £18-£24; d £34-£36

Premier Selected

Q Q Q Q Q The Croft 10 Institution Rd IV30 1QX
(turn off A96 at Safeway and down Queen St turn right at bottom)
☎ 01343 546004 FAX 546004
Guests find it easy to relax in Ann Cartmell's welcoming home, a lovely period mansion set in its own mature grounds. Bedrooms are well proportioned and offer high standards of decoration together with comfortable modern furnishings. A beautiful marble fire place is the focal point in the inviting lounge and Ann's wonderful freshly prepared breakfasts, served around the communal table in the dining room, continue to earn much praise. This is a non smoking establishment.
3 rms (2 shr) (1 fmly) No smoking CTV in all bedrooms Tea and coffee making facilities No dogs Cen ht 6P No coaches
ROOMS: s £21-£30; d £44-£48✱

Q Q Q *Lodge* 20 Duff Av IV30 1QS (turn off A9 N of Aviemore onto A95 (signposted Elgin) until Craigellachie where road becomes A941)
☎ 01343 549981 FAX 01343 549981
This large detached Victorian house is set in its own grounds, not far from the station. Bedrooms are attractively furnished in pine and have neat en suite bathrooms. There is a spacious lounge with a beautiful turret window overlooking the well tended garden and breakfast is served at separate tables in the dining room.
8 bth/shr (1 fmly) No smoking in bedrooms No smoking in dining room CTV in all bedrooms Tea and coffee making facilities No dogs (ex guide dogs) Cen ht CTV 9P No coaches
CARDS:

Q Q **Non Smokers Haven** 37 Duff Av IV30 1QS (follow signs for Railway St or Perth, Duff Avenue is approx 150mtrs east of Railway St) ☎ 01343 541993 & 07050 371891
This neat guest house which stands on the corner of the street not far from the station, is true to its name and is freshly maintained throughout. The two bedrooms, each with a spacious wash basin unit, are nicely appointed and comfortable, with posies of flowers, pretty ornaments and many other thoughtful extras which add a homely touch. The breakfast room is quite compact and has a single table.
2 rms No smoking CTV in all bedrooms Tea and coffee making facilities No dogs (ex guide dogs) Cen ht No children 14yrs 3P No coaches
ROOMS: d £30-£34

Premier Selected

Q Q Q Q Q **Pines** East Rd IV30 1XG (on the eastern approach of the A96 Aberdeen/Inverness road) ☎ 01343 542766 FAX 542766
Dedicated owners Dave and Kath Findlay look forward to personally welcoming you to their charming detached home which stands in its own well tended garden close to the historic cathedral. The attractive bedrooms are decorated and furnished to a high standard and one room offers a four poster bed. Guests are welcome to make use of the large range of books and videos which are provided in the inviting lounge. This is a non smoking house.
4 rms (3 shr) (1 fmly) No smoking CTV in all bedrooms Tea and coffee making facilities Cen ht CTV 10P No coaches Last d 9am
ROOMS: s £18-£42; d £36-£52*

FALKIRK Falkirk Map 11 NS88

Q Q Q **Denecroft** 8 Lochgreen Rd, Off Slamannan Rd FK1 1NJ
☎ 01324 629258
This pre-war family home is quietly located in an elevated area south of the town and has glimpses of the Firth of Forth. The double room on the ground floor has a spacious shower room adjacent whilst the two first floor rooms share a spacious spa bathroom. There is a cosy lounge overlooking the well tended garden and guests share the breakfast table in the elegant dining room.
3 rms (1 fmly) No smoking in bedrooms CTV in all bedrooms Tea and coffee making facilities No dogs (ex guide dogs) Cen ht CTV No children 1yr 5P No coaches
ROOMS: s £23-£26; d £44-£48*

FORGANDENNY Perth & Kinross Map 11 NO01

Q Q Q *Craighall (NO081176)* PH2 9DF (0.5m W off B935 Bridge of Earn-Forteviot Rd) ☎ 01738 812415 FAX 01738 812415 Mrs M Fotheringham
A warm welcome is assured at Mrs Fotheringham's comfortable modern home set amid gentle countryside adjacent to the main farm complex. Bedrooms are all located at ground level. The comfortable lounge invites peaceful relaxation and hearty breakfasts are served at the communal table in the owner's private sitting room.
3 rms (2 shr) (1 fmly) Tea and coffee making facilities No dogs Cen ht CTV 4P Fishing 1000 acres beef mixed sheep Last d 9pm

FORRES Moray Map 14 NJ05

Q Q Q **Knockomie Lodge** IV36 0SG (A940, Forres to Grantown-on-Spey road, a mile outside Forres on right) ☎ 01309 676785
Just south of the town Knockomie Lodge is the former gate house to the grander house up the drive, which is now a hotel. Bedrooms are well equipped and pretty, and one is on the ground floor. Guests share the breakfast table in the small combined lounge/breakfast room and Olga Foran will provide lots of useful local information.
3 bth/shr (2 fmly) No smoking CTV in all bedrooms Tea and coffee making facilities No dogs (ex guide dogs) Cen ht 6P No coaches
ROOMS: s £20-£35; d £34-£42
CARDS:

Selected

Q Q Q Q **Mayfield** Victoria Rd IV36 0BN (opposite Grant Park car park on main road through town) ☎ 01309 676931
An attractive Victorian house, quietly situated in its own well tended garden. Bedrooms are bright and airy and offer comfortable modern facilities. Lots of useful tourist information is provided for the benefit of guests, and breakfast is served at the communal table in the attractive dining room.
3 rms (2 shr) (1 fmly) No smoking in bedrooms No smoking in dining room CTV in all bedrooms Tea and coffee making facilities No dogs Cen ht CTV 4P No coaches
ROOMS: s £20-£30; d £32-£50; wkly b&b £112-£175*
CARDS:

Selected

Q Q Q Q **The Milton of Grange Farmhouse** *(NJ049599)* Milton of Grange IV36 0TR (leave A96 at East End rdbt take the B9011 to Kinloss, turn off at first left where you will see the sign for B&B)
☎ 01309 676360 FAX 01309 676360 Mrs Massie
Closed 1 Dec-31 Jan
A warm welcome is assured at Hilda Massie's comfortable renovated farmhouse. There are three attractive first floor bedrooms, where the pretty colour schemes are complemented by comfortable antique pine furnishings. There is no lounge, but excellent farmhouse breakfasts are served around the communal table in the tastefully appointed dining room. Hilda's menu includes cheese, fresh fruit, and smoked fish as well as more traditional dishes. This is a no smoking establishment.
3 shr (2 fmly) No smoking CTV in all bedrooms Tea and coffee making facilities No dogs (ex guide dogs) Cen ht CTV 4P 400 acres Arable
ROOMS: s £20-£25; d £36-£44*

FORT AUGUSTUS Highland Map **14** NH30

Selected

QQQQ ***Brae Hotel*** PH32 4DG ☎ 01320 366289
FAX 01320 366702
Standing in well tended grounds and in an elevated position, close to a multitude of wonderful forest walks, the hotel has a cosy bar with natural fire, interesting canal memorabilia, books and games and there is also a comfortable and spacious lounge. Bedrooms are all fresh, attractively furnished and well equipped. Dinner is no longer available.
7 rms

FORT WILLIAM Highland Map **14** NN17

Premier Selected

QQQQQ **Ashburn House** 8 Achintore Rd PH33 6RQ
(junc A82 and Ashburn Ln 500yds from large rbt at south end of Fort William High St or 400yrds on right after entering 30mph zone from S)
☎ 01397 706000 FAX 01397 706000
Feb-Nov
Dedicated owners Allan and Sandra Henderson have lovingly restored and renovated their charming detached Victorian home overlooking Loch Linnhe to provide their guests with commendable standards of quality and comfort. The spacious bedrooms are decorated and furnished to a high standard and offer a wide range of amenities as well as thoughtful extras. The conservatory lounge invites peaceful relaxation while noteworthy breakfasts are served at individual tables in the dining room. This is a non smoking establishment.
7 bth/shr No smoking CTV in all bedrooms Tea and coffee making facilities No dogs (ex guide dogs) Cen ht 8P
ROOMS: s £30-£35; d £60-£70; wkly b&b £200-£240
CARDS:

QQQ ***Benview*** Belford Rd PH33 6ER
(A82 Glasgow-Inverness Road, near town centre) ☎ 01397 702966
Apr-Oct
Good value bed and breakfast accommodation is offered at this friendly personally-run guest house which stands beside the A82 at the north end of town. The non-smoking bedrooms combine tasteful dècor with comfortable modern appointments. Public areas include a choice of relaxing lounges and a separate, spacious dining room which has a fine outlook.
12 rms (9 bth/shr) No smoking in bedrooms No smoking in dining room CTV in all bedrooms Tea and coffee making facilities No dogs (ex guide dogs) Cen ht CTV 20P

Selected

QQQQ **Clintwood** 23 Hillview Dr, Corpach PH33 7LS
(500 mtrs past village sign on left "Clintwood" sign board at entrance to Hillview Dr, house 400 mtrs on left)
☎ 01397 772680
Etr-Oct
Located in the village of Corpach is the well presented villa home of Ian and Cristina MacLeod. The comfortable lounge, with its solid Chesterfield seating, adjoins the pretty dining room that overlooks the rear garden. The three spacious bedrooms are on the first floor and have all expected facilities as well as many personal touches.
3 bth/shr No smoking CTV in all bedrooms Tea and coffee making facilities No dogs Cen ht No children 12yrs 3P No coaches
ROOMS: d £50-£53*

Selected

QQQQ **Distillery House** Nevis Bridge, North Rd PH33 6LR
(from S A82 3rd rdbt on left hand side, from N A82 just before the Glen Nevis rdbt, right hand side)
☎ 01397 700103 FAX 01397 702980
Situated at the north end of town in the grounds of the former Glenlochy Distillery, this friendly guest house was once the distillery manager's home. The tastefully decorated bedrooms are comfortably furnished in a modern style and offer a wide range of amenities. The spacious reading lounge is furnished with Chesterfield sofas and hearty breakfasts are served at individual tables in the attractive dining room.
7 bth/shr (1 fmly) No smoking CTV in all bedrooms Tea and coffee making facilities Direct dial from bedrooms Cen ht 7P Fishing
Last d 5.30pm
ROOMS: s £25-£38; d £44-£70*
CARDS:

QQQ **Glenlochy** Nevis Bridge PH33 6PF (0.5m N on A82)
☎ 01397 702909
In the garden of this friendly family run guest house is the bridge which marks the official end of the West Highland Way walk. The bedrooms are nicely decorated and come with comfortable traditional furnishings. There is a lounge on the first floor and breakfast is served at individual tables in the bright dining room.
10 rms (8 shr) (2 fmly) No smoking in bedrooms No smoking in dining room CTV in all bedrooms Tea and coffee making facilities No dogs (ex guide dogs) Cen ht CTV 12P No coaches
ROOMS: s £20-£24; d £32-£52*
CARDS:

Premier Selected

Q Q Q Q Q **The Grange** Grange Rd PH33 6JF
(leave Fort William on A82 S-300yds from rdbt take left onto Ashburn Ln. The Grange is at top on left)
☎ 01397 705516 FAX 701595
Closed Nov-Mar
Over the years, a lot of careful planning and hard work has gone into the restoration of this house to ensure that only the highest standards are offered to guests. Throughout the house, a meticulous attention to detail is self evident. Attractive decor and pretty fabrics have been used to stunning effect in the charming bedrooms, two of which enjoy beautiful views over Loch Linnhe. Ample provision of books and fresh flowers enhance the comfortable lounge, while the dining room is a lovely setting for the extensive breakfast which provides guests with a good start to their day.
4 bth/shr No smoking CTV in all bedrooms Tea and coffee making facilities No dogs (ex guide dogs) Cen ht CTV No children 13yrs 4P
ROOMS: d £72-£90*
CARDS:

Q Q Q **Guisachan House** Alma Rd PH33 6HA (off A82, 100yds past St Marys Church) ☎ 01397 703797 FAX 01397 703797
High standards of maintenance are the hallmarks of this friendly guest house which stands in an elevated position at the north end of town. The bedrooms are variable in size and offer mixed modern appointments. Public areas include a relaxing lounge with dispense bar, and enjoyable home cooking is served at individual tables in the attractive split-level dining room.
13 bth/shr (2 fmly) No smoking in bedrooms No smoking in dining room CTV in all bedrooms Tea and coffee making facilities No dogs (ex guide dogs) Licensed Cen ht CTV 16P
ROOMS: s £18-£28; d £36-£56*
CARDS:

Q Q Q **Lochview** Heathercroft, Argyll Rd PH33 6RE
(up hill at rdbt at West End Hotel on A82. Left into Argyll Terrace and first right up private road and follow to end)
☎ 01397 703149 FAX 01397 703149
May-Sept
From its position on the hillside above the town this modern house in its own gardens enjoys fine views over Loch Linnhe. The bright, cheery bedrooms are tastefully decorated and offer mixed modern furnishings. Public areas, where the atmosphere is relaxed and friendly, include a comfortable lounge and small dining room, where hearty breakfasts are served at individual tables.
8 bth/shr No smoking CTV in all bedrooms Tea and coffee making facilities No dogs Cen ht 8P No coaches
ROOMS: s £25-£30; d £40-£52
CARDS:

Q Q Q **Mansefield House** Corpach PH33 7LT
(turn off A82 onto A830 , establishment is 2m from junct on left hand side on corner of Hill View Drive)
☎ 01397 772262 FAX 01397 772262
Closed 24-28 Dec
Enthusiastic owners Doug and Sue Pearse are raising standards at this former Victorian manse. The inviting lounge has been carefully refurbished to reflect its Victorian character. Sue's enjoyable home cooking is served at individual tables in the bright dining room.
6 rms (5 bth/shr) (2 fmly) No smoking in bedrooms No smoking in dining room CTV in all bedrooms Tea and coffee making facilities No dogs (ex guide dogs) Cen ht 6P No coaches Last d 5pm
ROOMS: d £36-£48*

Q **Rhu Mhor** Alma Rd PH33 6BP
(N on A82, after hospital turn first right then first left)
☎ 01397 702213
Closed Nov-Easter
Genuine hospitality from the kilted proprietor together with thoroughly enjoyable home cooking are all part of the appeal of this sturdy Edwardian house which stands in its own interesting grounds on the hill above the town overlooking Loch Linnhe. Bedrooms are compact with mixed practical appointments. Public areas include a choice of lounges, one non-smoking, and an attractive dining room where, at peak times, you can expect to share your table with other guests.
7 rms (1 fmly) No smoking in dining room No smoking in 1 lounge Tea and coffee making facilities Cen ht CTV 7P No coaches 1 acre of wild gardens Last d 2pm
ROOMS: d £36-£37
CARDS:

FOYERS Highland Map **14** NH42

Selected

Q Q Q Q **Foyers Bay House** Lochness IV1 2YB (From Inverness B862 to Dores,right (B852) 10m to Foyers.From Ft Augustus take A82 to B862 10m then left onto B852 to Foyers.)
☎ 01456 486624 FAX 01456 486337
Many guests return time and time again to this lovely restored Victorian house which, from its elevated position, enjoys glorious views of Loch Ness and is an ideal touring base. Bedrooms are maintained to a high standard and offer comfortable modern appointments together with a wide range of amenities. In addition to the comfortable lounge there is an attractive conservatory café/restaurant offering snacks and meals.
5 bth/shr No smoking in bedrooms CTV in all bedrooms Tea and coffee making facilities Direct dial from bedrooms No dogs (ex guide dogs) Cen ht CTV 6P No coaches Last d 8.00pm
ROOMS: s £32-£37; d £44-£54*
CARDS:

GAIRLOCH Highland Map **14** NG87

Q Q ***Bains*** Strath IV21 2BZ
(A332 to Gairloch turn onto B8021 Strath is 0.25m past car park on right)
☎ 01445 712472
Bryan Thornton continues to improve this pleasant roadside house in the western part of the village. At the moment there are no en suite facilities but bedrooms do have radios, TV's and tea making facilities. Breakfast is served in a cosy room overlooking the road and overall good value for money is given.
6 rms (3 fmly) No smoking in dining room No smoking in lounges CTV in all bedrooms Tea and coffee making facilities Cen ht 6P No coaches

Premier Selected

Q Q Q Q Q **Birchwood** IV21 2AH (A832 to Gairloch. Cross cattle grid on entering village and Birchwood signed on right) ☎ 01445 712011
Mar-Nov rs Dec-Feb
Set in two acres of well tended gardens, its elevated position providing lovely views over the old harbour, this attractive, traditional and extended Highland house has been sympathetically refurbished by the enthusiastic owners Ruth and Bill Swann. The bedrooms offer attractive decor and fabrics together with appropriate furniture. The guest lounge has traditional, comfortable seating and a range of reading material, and at dinner, although no choice is offered, the emphasis is very much on quality local produce, often fish, cooked with flair and imagination.
5 shr No smoking Tea and coffee making facilities No dogs Cen ht CTV No children 14yrs 5P No coaches Last d noon
ROOMS: s £42-£48; d £64-£70; wkly b&b £214-£245; wkly hlf-bd £354-£385

GALASHIELS Scottish Borders Map **12** NT43

Q Q Q ***Ashlyn*** 7 Abbotsford Rd TD1 3DP ☎ 01896 752416 FAX 01896 752416
A warm welcome awaits you at this substantial period house which has been completely upgraded, and now offers attractive bedrooms with modern shower rooms. Two rooms are particularly spacious and comfortable and there is a well proportioned lounge where breakfasts are served.
3 bth/shr No smoking CTV in all bedrooms Tea and coffee making facilities Cen ht 3P

Selected

Q Q Q Q **Binniemyre** Abbotsford Rd TD1 3HP (S side of Galashiels just off A7) ☎ 01896 757137 FAX 01896 757137
This beautiful period house is on the south side of town, and has been sympathetically restored by Carol Murray and Bill Elliot. Teddy bears and ducks adorn the house along with many home-made flower baskets. The entrance hall is a welcoming lounge with a wood-burning stove for cooler weather. There is a second lounge as well as an attractive dining room. Bedrooms vary in size but are all thoughtfully equipped. The two rooms without their own facilities have the use of two bathrooms.
5 rms (3 shr) (3 fmly) No smoking in bedrooms No smoking in dining room No smoking in 1 lounge CTV in all bedrooms Tea and coffee making facilities Cen ht CTV 5P Snooker Last d 8pm
ROOMS: s £25-£35; d £36-£58*
CARDS:

Q Q Q **Island House** 65 Island St TD1 1PA (opposite B & Q store) ☎ 01896 752649
Guests can expect a warm and friendly welcome here. The modern bedrooms are comfortable and attractively decorated and one is located on the ground floor. Breakfast is served in the snug, pine finished dining room.
3 rms (2 shr) No smoking in bedrooms No smoking in dining room CTV in all bedrooms Tea and coffee making facilities Cen ht CTV 2P
ROOMS: d £30-£40*

Premier Selected

Q Q Q Q Q **Maplehurst** 42 Abbotsford Rd TD1 3HP (on A7) ☎ 01896 754700 FAX 01896 754700
Closed Xmas & New Year
This magnificent detached house was originally built for a mill owner and his wife in 1907. Many of the original features of the house have been retained, including art deco stained glass, wood panelling, a tapestry wall covering and recessed dresser. The guest bedrooms are located on the first floor and are individual in character; the turret suite, with views of the surrounding Border hills, has a cast iron bath in the turret. Janice Richardson's home cooking is well worth sampling, dinner has to be requested in advance. There is also a first floor lounge and a beautiful sunken garden surrounds the house.
3 bth/shr (1 fmly) No smoking CTV in all bedrooms Tea and coffee making facilities No dogs (ex guide dogs) Cen ht 12P No coaches Last d 6pm
ROOMS: s £30-£35; d £50-£55*
CARDS:

GARTOCHARN West Dunbartonshire Map **10** NS48

Selected

Q Q Q Q **Ardoch Cottage** Main St G83 8NE (on A811 midway between Balloch & Drymen, past Balloch on A811, first cottage on left in Gartocharn village) ☎ 01389 830452 FAX 01389 830452
Enthusiastic owners Mabel and Paul Lindsay have lovingly restored their roadside cottage which overlooks rolling countryside towards Ben Lomond to provide a welcoming base for visiting holidaymakers. Attractive fabrics enhance the prettily decorated and comfortably furnished bedrooms. The sun lounge is where guests like to relax and unwind before sampling Mabel's enjoyable home cooking, which is served at the communal table in the combined lounge/dining room.
3 shr No smoking CTV in all bedrooms Tea and coffee making facilities Cen ht CTV 5P Last d 5pm
ROOMS: d £48-£52*
CARDS:

Selected

Q Q Q Q **Mardella** *(NS442866)* Old School Rd G83 8SD (off A811 into Old School Road, 200m 2nd house on right) ☎ 01389 830428
FAX 01389 830428 Mrs S MacDonell
Expect a warm welcome from the enthusiastic owners, Sally and Angus MacDonnell, whose delightful modern farmhouse is situated at the northern end of the village. Enjoy the spectacular views across the River Endrick towards Loch Lomond. Welcoming bedrooms are complemented by an elegant sitting room, which overlooks a paddock with its collection of wild fowl and sheep. Sally's love of ducks permeates throughout the house with ornamental ducks nesting in every corner. Breakfast is a treat - expect goose eggs and home-baked bread.
3 rms (1 bth/shr) (2 fmly) No smoking Tea and coffee making facilities Cen ht CTV ch fac 4P 9 acres sheep poultry Last d 9am
ROOMS: s £31-£38; d £37-£44*

GARVE Highland Map 14 NH36

Q Q Q **Old Manse** IV23 2PX
(turn off A835 by AA telephone 0.5m W of village) ☎ 01997 414201
Closed 24 Dec-1 Jan
This former manse, situated west of the village, is enthusiastically run by Jean and Pete Hollingdale to provide comfortable bed and breakfast accommodation for touring holidaymakers. Guests can be served tea in bed in the morning, whilst breakfast is served at the communal table in the attractive dining room, and there is also a comfortable lounge with natural stone walls. Both rooms offer super views towards Ben Wyvis.
3 rms (1 shr) No smoking No dogs (ex guide dogs) Cen ht
No children 10yrs 6P No coaches Good Walks
ROOMS: s £15.50-£16.50; d £31-£33; wkly b&b £108.50-£115.50

GLASGOW City of Glasgow Map 11 NS56

See also Eaglesham

Q Q Q **Angus Hotel** 970 Sauchiehall St G3 7TH (W on M8 exit fast lane jnct 18, at 2nd set traffic lights turn right, Berkeley St, Right at end, 1st left to Sauchiehall St. hotel in 400m) ☎ 0141 357 5155 FAX 0141 339 9469
Occupying a corner position adjacent to Kelvingrove Park and convenient for the University, Kelvin Hall and Art Gallery, this attractive and friendly guest house has good modern standards of accommodation, with all the expected facilities. The bright breakfast room is quite compact but does have a pleasant outlook across to the park.
18 bth/shr (7 fmly) No smoking in bedrooms No smoking in dining room CTV in all bedrooms Tea and coffee making facilities Direct dial from bedrooms No dogs (ex guide dogs) Cen ht
ROOMS: s £34-£42; d £46-£52*
CARDS:

Q Q **Belgrave** 2 Belgrave Ter, Hillhead G12 8JD
(diagonally opposite the Kelvinbridge Post Office, off Great Western Rd)
☎ 0141 337 1850 & 337 1741 FAX 0141 429 8608
Enthusiastic young owner Amir Khokhar is making good progress with refurbishment of this welcoming guesthouse which forms part of a Victorian terrace beside Great Western Road in the west end. The upgraded bedrooms, though mostly compact, are smartly decorated and offer modern furnishings; this contrasts with the more simple appointments of the older rooms. Hearty breakfasts are served in the pleasant dining room, though at peak periods it may be necessary to share a table.
11 rms (2 shr) (2 fmly) No smoking in 5 bedrooms No smoking in dining room CTV in all bedrooms Tea and coffee making facilities No dogs (ex guide dogs) Cen ht 15P
ROOMS: s £20-£25; d £36-£46; wkly b&b £130-£175
CARDS:

Q Q Q ***Botanic Hotel*** 1 Alfred Ter, Great Western Rd G12 8RF (off M8 at junct 17, turn right for hotel in 1m on left, directly above A625 Great Western Road) ☎ 0141 339 6955 FAX 0141 339 6955
This Victorian property occupies a corner position in a raised terrace off Great Western Road and is convenient for the attractions of the west end of the city. Rooms, on three floors, are generally well appointed and spacious. Breakfasts is served in the pleasant breakfast room on the ground floor.
17 rms (11 bth/shr) (4 fmly) No smoking in dining room CTV in 11 bedrooms Tea and coffee making facilities Cen ht CTV Last d 7.30pm
CARDS:

See advertisement on p.547.

Q Q **Charing Cross** 310 Renfrew St, Charing Cross G3 6UW (off M8 into Sauchiehall St up Scott St to Buccleugh St, turn left & proceed into Renfrew St) ☎ 0141 332 2503 FAX 0141 353 3047
Convenient for city centre attractions this Victorian property offers mostly compact bedrooms, some fully en suite. There is a small comfortable lounge and the breakfast room is attractively furnished and can cater for both larger parties or individuals.
24 rms (7 bth/shr) (8 fmly) CTV in all bedrooms Tea and coffee making facilities Direct dial from bedrooms No dogs (ex guide dogs) Cen ht CTV
ROOMS: s £21-£27; d £38-£46*
CARDS:

Q Q Q ***Greek Thomson Hotel*** 140 Elderslie St G3 7AW
☎ 0141 332 6556
This conveniently located city centre hotel is just off Suchiehall Street and west of Charing Cross. The bedrooms are all well equipped and have an attractive decorative theme and the breakfast room has an airy feel where a traditional Scottish breakfast is served. If a space can be found, the street parking is free.
17 rms

Q Q Q **Hotel Enterprise** 144 Renfrew St G3 6RF (Leave M8 at Charing Cross. Straight along Sauchiehall St, left into Scott St then right into Renfrew St. Look out for 2 trees & 2 lamp posts)
☎ 0141 332 8095 FAX 0141 332 8095
This city centre hotel is set in a Victorian terrace, close to the Art School and Suchiehall Street and has been well furnished to provide comfortable modern accommodation. The mostly spacious and comfortable bedrooms include telephones and TVs. Hearty breakfasts are served in the cosy dining room where an evening meal can also be served if arranged in advance. Service is friendly and attentive from the proprietors Alexander and David Ross.
6 bth/shr (2 fmly) No smoking in 1 bedrooms No smoking in dining room CTV in all bedrooms Tea and coffee making facilities Direct dial from bedrooms Licensed Cen ht CTV No coaches Last d 1pm
CARDS:

Q Q **Kelvin Private Hotel** 15 Buckingham Ter, Great Western Rd, Hillhead G12 8EB (leave M8 at junct 17 follow A82 Kelvinside/Dumbarton 1m from motorway on right before Botanic Gardens)
☎ 0141 339 7143 FAX 0141 339 5215
Two Grade I Victorian terraced houses have been linked to create this friendly private hotel off Great Western Road close to the Botanic Gardens and the BBC. Upper floor bedrooms tend to be well proportioned while the single rooms on the lower floor are somewhat more limited in size. Public areas include a quiet lounge and a breakfast room, both on the first floor.
21 rms (9 bth/shr) (5 fmly) CTV in all bedrooms Tea and coffee making facilities Cen ht 5P
ROOMS: s £23-£39; d £42-£56*
CARDS:

Q Q **Lomond Hotel** 6 Buckingham Ter, Great Western Rd, Hillhead G12 8EB (Leave M8 at junct 17. Follow A82 Dumbarton 1m from motorway, on right before Botanic Gardens)
☎ 0141 339 2339 FAX 0141 339 5215
Good value bed and breakfast accommodation is offered at this friendly hotel, which stands in a tree-lined Victorian terrace in the west end off Great Western Road. Bedrooms offer mixed modern appointments along with the expected amenities. There is also a combined lounge/dining room where, at busy periods, it may sometimes be necessary to share your breakfast table with other guests.
17 rms (6 bth/shr) (6 fmly) CTV in all bedrooms Tea and coffee making facilities Cen ht
ROOMS: s £23-£39; d £42-£56*
CARDS:

Q Q **McLays** 264/276 Renfrew St, Charing Cross G3 6TT (from M8 head for Charing Cross) ☎ 0141 332 4796 FAX 0141 353 0422
Situated close to the Art School in the city centre, in a street running parallel to the famous Suchiehall Street is this large budget hotel which has been created from three buildings. Standards of accommodation vary from spacious family rooms to more compact doubles and there are many single rooms; all are reasoanably equipped and have mixed standards of decor. There are three breakfast rooms and two simple lounges available.
62 rms (39 bth/shr) (14 fmly) No smoking in dining room No smoking in 1 lounge CTV in all bedrooms Tea and coffee making facilities Direct dial from bedrooms No dogs (ex guide dogs) Lift Cen ht CTV
ROOMS: s £21-£27; d £38-£46*
CARDS:

Premier Selected

Q Q Q Q Q ***62 St Andrews*** 62 St Andrews Dr, Pollockshields G41 5EX ☎ 0141 427 1106 FAX 0141 427 1106
This imposing large Victorian villa is well situated in the leafy suburb of Pollockshields, and is handy for the city centre and museums. All the rooms are spacious and tastefully furnished, and bedrooms are well equipped with extra touches such as tissues, toiletries, sparkling water and shortbread. There is a spacious conservatory where breakfast is taken. Dinner is available by arrangement
6 rms (4 bth/shr) (1 fmly) CTV in all bedrooms Tea and coffee making facilities Direct dial from bedrooms Licensed 40P
CARDS:

GLASGOW AIRPORT Renfrewshire Map **11** NS46

Premier Selected

Q Q Q Q Q **Myfarrclan** 146 Corsebar Rd PA2 9NA (passing Royal Alexandra Hospital on left, house half mile up hill on right with tall evergreen hedge) ☎ 0141 884 8285 FAX 0141 884 8285

The warmth of the welcome combined with high standards of comfort and quality appointments have brought success to Brenda and Keith Farr who have lovingly converted their charming home in a leafy suburb on the south side of town. Bedrooms offer quality furnishings and fittings together with a wide range of useful extras. Keith, a genial host, dispenses his own brand of hospitality in the comfort of the relaxing sitting room and there is also a conservatory lounge overlooking the back garden. In the attractive dining room Brenda provides hearty breakfasts and, by prior arrangement, a substantial 3-course dinner. Tours of Scotland and transport for the airport and city bus/rail terminal can be arranged.

3 bth/shr No smoking CTV in all bedrooms Tea and coffee making facilities No dogs Cen ht CTV 2P No coaches Conservatory/sun lounge Last d 3.00pm

ROOMS: s £50-£65; d £70; wkly b&b £210-£245; wkly hlf-bd £336-£371

CARDS:

GLENCOE Highland Map **14** NN15

Q Q Q **Scorrybreac** PA39 4HT (off A82 just outside village, 500 metres from Bridge of Coe) ☎ 01855 811354 FAX 01855 811354

Closed Nov

A relaxed friendly atmosphere prevails at this comfortable non-smoking guest house which stands on a wooded hillside above the village with views towards the loch. Bedrooms vary in size with mixed modern appointments and offer the expected amenities. There is a small lounge with a range of books and board games, and a pleasant dining room where hearty breakfasts and (by prior arrangement) home-cooked evening meals are served at individual tables.

6 rms (5 bth/shr) No smoking CTV in all bedrooms Tea and coffee making facilities Cen ht 8P No coaches Permits available for fishing 500m

ROOMS: s £17-£40; d £32-£44*

GLENLIVET Moray Map **15** NJ12

Q Q Q ***Roadside Cottage*** Tomnavoulin AB37 9JL (on B9008 Tomintoul to Dufftown road, 0.75m S of Tomnavoulin) ☎ 01807 590486

A genuine country welcome is assured at this renovated roadside cottage which is located in the heart of the Speyside distillery country. Though compact, the attractive bedrooms are furnished in comfortable modern styles and share a bathroom. Public areas include a homely lounge where a log fire burns on the cooler evenings and enjoyable home-cooked evening meals and breakfasts are served at the communal table in the open-plan kitchen.

3 rms (1 fmly) CTV in all bedrooms Tea and coffee making facilities Cen ht 9P No coaches Last d on request

GLENMAVIS North Lanarkshire Map **11** NS76

Q **Braidenhill** *(NS742673)* ML6 0PJ (on B803 on outskirts of Airdrie/Coatbridge) ☎ 01236 872319 Mrs M Dunbar

Braidenhill is a working farm, offering good value accommodation in pleasantly appointed bedrooms, and there is a comfortable lounge that gives fine unrestricted views over open countryside towards the Campsie Fells. Good hearty breakfasts are served and service is friendly and honest.

3 rms (1 shr) (1 fmly) No smoking in bedrooms No smoking in dining room CTV in 2 bedrooms Tea and coffee making facilities No dogs Cen ht CTV 4P 50 acres arable mixed

ROOMS: s £16; d £32-£40*

GRANTOWN-ON-SPEY Highland Map **14** NJ02

Premier Selected

Q Q Q Q Q **Ardconnel House** Woodlands Ter PH26 3JU (from SW approach to town off A95, on the left hand side near the Craislynne Hotel) ☎ 01479 872104 FAX 01479 872104

Closed Nov-Etr

Now under the ownership of Barbara and Michel Bouchard, this fine Victorian house, within its own attractive grounds, continues to provide high standards of comfort and appointment. Michel prepares dinner with care making use of local produce, whilst Barbara is responsible for the front of house duties. The elegant dining room has individual tables and there is also a comfortable lounge which invites complete relaxation. Bedrooms are comfortably furnished in antiques or pine and offer all the expected amenities.

6 shr (2 fmly) No smoking CTV in all bedrooms Tea and coffee making facilities No dogs Licensed Cen ht No children 10yrs 6P No coaches Last d by arrangement

ROOMS: s £25-£36; d £50-£70*

CARDS:

Selected

Q Q Q Q **Ardlarig** Woodlands Ter PH26 3JU (just off A95 on entrance to Grantown-on-Spey) ☎ 01479 873245 FAX 01479 873245

Closed 22 Dec-2 Jan

Under the enthusiastic ownership of Neil Cairns, this attractive Victorian house on the south side of the town provides a warm welcome. Neil produces Cordon Bleu style cooking using fresh Scottish produce; vegetarian and special diets can be catered for. The lounge is most comfortable and offers a range of interesting books and magazines and the dinner is served in the attractive dining room. Bedrooms are mostly spacious, well furnished and offer mixed modern appointments.

contd.

7 rms (4 bth/shr) No smoking CTV in all bedrooms Tea and coffee making facilities No dogs Licensed Cen ht CTV 10P No coaches Golf shooting & fishing can be arranged Last d 4.30pm
ROOMS: s £19.50-£35; d £39-£57; wkly b&b £130-£190; wkly hlf-bd £255-£319*
CARDS:

Selected

QQQQ Garden Park Woodside Av PH26 3JN
(turn off High Street at Forest Road, Garden Park is at junc of Forest Road & Woodside Avenue) ☎ 01479 873235
Mar-Oct
A home from home is how regular visitors view this comfortable Victorian house close to the golf course. The bedrooms vary in size and all but one has a TV. The lounge, with its welcoming fire, invites peaceful relaxation, while carefully prepared meals are served in the small dining room.
5 bth/shr No smoking in dining room CTV in 4 bedrooms Tea and coffee making facilities No dogs (ex guide dogs) Licensed Cen ht CTV No children 12yrs 8P No coaches Last d 5pm
ROOMS: s £20.50-£23; d £41-£46; wkly b&b £135-£145; wkly hlf-bd £197-£222

QQQ The Pines Woodside Av PH26 3JR (at traffic lights follow Elgin signs then take first right) ☎ 01479 872092 FAX 01479 872092
Jan-Oct
Big changes are taking place at this charming detached Victorian house under the caring ownership of the Stewart family. Recent refurbishment has completely transformed the delightful public areas, which include a choice of inviting lounges and an elegant restaurant which has two adjoining dining areas. This is a most appropriate setting for the enjoyable Highland fare which is carefully prepared from quality local produce.
9 rms (5 shr) (1 fmly) No smoking in bedrooms No smoking in dining room No smoking in 1 lounge CTV in all bedrooms Tea and coffee making facilities Licensed Cen ht CTV No children 6yrs 9P No coaches Last d noon
ROOMS: s £20-£32; d £38-£60; wkly b&b £126-£203; wkly hlf-bd £210-£301
CARDS:

QQQ Rossmor Woodlands Ter PH26 3JU (take A95 from Aviemore to Grantown-on-Spey. Left fork at r'about on approach to town through pine woods, on left hand side opposite park)

☎ 01479 872201 FAX 01479 872201
Dedicated owners Sue and Davis Say extend a warm welcome at their charming home, a detached Victorian house situated at the south side of town with views over the garden to the Cromdale Hills. The bedrooms are spacious and offer both modern and traditional furnishings. Public areas include an inviting lounge and dining room where freshly prepared breakfasts are served at individual tables.
6 bth/shr No smoking Tea and coffee making facilities No dogs Cen ht CTV No children 6P No coaches
ROOMS: s £21-£23; d £40-£46; wkly b&b £140-£144*
CARDS:

GRETNA (WITH GRETNA GREEN)
Dumfries & Galloway Map **11** NY36

QQQ The Beeches Loanwath Rd, off Sarkfoot Rd DG16 5EP
(turn left off B7076 at Crossways Garage down Sarkfoot Road for a quarter of a mile) ☎ 01461 337448
Closed Dec-Jan
This former farmhouse is situated on the edge of the town, looking across open countryside towards the Solway Firth and distant Lakeland Hills. Both of the bedrooms enjoy these stunning views, and are comfortably furnished. The charming breakfast room also doubles as a TV lounge in the evenings.
2 shr (1 fmly) No smoking CTV in all bedrooms Tea and coffee making facilities No dogs Cen ht CTV No children 10yrs 3P No coaches
ROOMS: d £38-£42

QQ Greenlaw DG16 5DU (off A74) ☎ 01461 338361
Conveniently located opposite the railway station, this large, red brick house is popular with wedding parties as well as tourists to the Old Smithy, which is within walking distance. Bedrooms vary in size, with some being quite compact and the largest having a four-poster bed and en suite facilities. There is a comfortable lounge and a bright breakfast room.
9 rms (5 shr) (1 fmly) No smoking in dining room CTV in all bedrooms Tea and coffee making facilities Cen ht CTV 13P
ROOMS: s £18-£25; d £38-£42*
CARDS:

QQ The Mill Grahams Hill, Kirkpatrick Fleming DG11 3BQ
(A74 Nthbd: Exit 1/2m after services N of Gretna, right at end of slip. A74 Sthbd: Exit juct for Canonbie/Kirkpatrick Flemming, follow hotel signs)
☎ 01461 800344 FAX 01461 800255
Situated just north of Gretna Green, The Mill has evolved from former farm buildings. It offers lodge style accommodation in two single storey stone chalet buildings set around two courtyards. Some of the bedrooms offer spacious family accommodation and there is also a room fully equipped for disabled guests. The restaurant and function suite form part of the complex.
24 annexe bth/shr (7 fmly) No smoking in area of dining room CTV in all bedrooms Tea and coffee making facilities Licensed Cen ht 50P Last d 8.45pm
ROOMS: s £38; d £58*
CARDS:

QQQ Surrone House Annan Rd DG16 5DL
(exit M74 onto B721, turn onto B7076, town centre 500yds on right)
☎ 01461 338341 FAX 01461 338341
A former farmhouse, Surrone sits in its own grounds well back from the main street. It offers bright sensibly furnished bedrooms including a honeymoon suite, a comfortable lounge and cheery dining room. A choice of menus is available at dinner, as well as a full wine list.
7 rms (6 bth/shr) (4 fmly) CTV in all bedrooms Tea and coffee making facilities No dogs (ex guide dogs) Licensed Cen ht CTV 10P No coaches Last d 8pm
ROOMS: s £30; d £45*
CARDS:

GULLANE East Lothian Map **12** NT48

Selected

QQQQ Faussetthill House 20 Main St EH31 2DR
(on A198, from A1 follow A198 to Gullane) ☎ 01620 842396
FAX 01620 842396
Mar-Dec

George and Dorothy Nisbet welcome you to their elegant detached Edwardian home, which stands in its own well-tended garden in the picturesque village of Gullane. Bedrooms are tastefully decorated and very comfortably furnished. There is a bright and inviting first floor lounge with well filled bookshelves. Breakfast is served in the elegant dining room on the ground floor. Smoking is not permitted in the house.
4 rms (2 shr) No smoking Tea and coffee making facilities No dogs Cen ht CTV No children 12yrs 4P No coaches
ROOMS: s £30-£40; d £44-£52*
CARDS:

HELENSBURGH Argyll & Bute Map **10** NS28

See **Cardross**

Selected

Q Q Q Q **Lethamhill** West Dhuhill Dr G84 9AW
(turn off A82 onto B831 and left onto B832, follow sign for Hillhouse. Take second right after 30mph sign)
☎ 01436 676016 FAX 01436 676016
From the red telephone box in the garden, to old typewriters and slot machines inside, Douglas and Jane Johnston's fine house is an Aladdin's cave of collectables and memorabilia accrued over the years by Douglas and could mean hours of enjoyable browsing in every corridor and corner. Beyond this unique insight into British heritage is a house offering spacious comfortable bedrooms of individual style and thoughtfully equipped. Whilst downstairs Jane's home-cooked meals and delicious baking draw praise.
3 bth/shr (1 fmly) No smoking CTV in all bedrooms Tea and coffee making facilities No dogs (ex guide dogs) Cen ht CTV 6P No coaches Last d 10am
ROOMS: s £40-£48; d £50-£70*

HOPEMAN Moray Map **15** NJ16

Selected

Q Q Q Q **Ardent House** 43 Forsyth St IV30 2SY
(A9 to Inverness, on to A96 to Elgin, B9012 to Hopeman, Ardent House on main road opposite Bowling Green)
☎ 01343 830694 FAX 01343 830694
Closed 13 Dec-3 Jan
A warm welcome is assured at Norma McPherson's delightful detached home which stands in its own walled garden, with well manicured lawns and colourful rose beds. The pretty bedrooms are modern in style and equipped with thoughtful extras. The conservatory lounge overlooks the garden, while Norma's speciality breakfasts, which include home smoked fish, garden produce and delicious home baking, provide an excellent start to the day. This is a non smoking establishment.
3 rms (1 shr) No smoking CTV in all bedrooms Tea and coffee making facilities No dogs Cen ht CTV 4P No coaches
ROOMS: s £17-£25; d £33-£44; wkly b&b £100-£160*

Remember to return your Prize Draw card for a chance to win an action-packed family weekend at one of the eleven Family Fun Hotels in the Hilton Hotels Directory. See inside the front cover for the card and competition details. Don't forget to fill in your name and address before posting!

HOUNDWOOD Scottish Borders Map **12** NT86

Selected

Q Q Q Q **Westwood House** TD14 5TP (just off A1 at Houndwood 3m N of Reston turn off 2m S of Grantshouse. Can be seen from A1)
☎ 01361 850232 FAX 01361 850333
Set in landscaped gardens, this former 18th century coaching inn has been tastefully renovated by owners Tricia and Dennis Davison and is now a friendly family home. Guests can relax in the comfortable living room and enjoy traditional home cooking and garden produce. Dennis' speciality is praise-winning seafood and local shellfish dishes during the summer months. Children can hunt in the garden for freshly laid eggs for breakfast.
6 bth/shr (2 fmly) No smoking CTV in all bedrooms Tea and coffee making facilities No dogs Licensed Cen ht CTV 6P No coaches Last d noon
ROOMS: s £22.50-£30; d £40-£45; wkly b&b £126-£157.50; wkly hlf-bd £213.50-£297.50*

HUNTLY Aberdeenshire Map **15** NJ53

QQQ **Drumdelgie House** Cairnie AB54 4TH
(4m NW of Huntly, off A96 (signed)) ☎ 01466 760368
end Mar-Oct
A Victorian home, peacefully set amid gentle rolling countryside overlooking the River Deveron and Strathbogie. The main house offers a family suite, and additional accommodation is available in the adjacent cottages, converted steadings which have been have been designed for self catering use or annexe accommodation for the main house - one cottage is suitable for disabled use. The cottages have either two or three bedrooms, bathroom, and a sitting room with open plan kitchen. Enjoyable home cooked fare is offered in the delightful oak beamed dining room.
1 bth/shr 3 annexe bth/shr (4 fmly) No smoking in bedrooms CTV in all bedrooms Tea and coffee making facilities No dogs (ex guide dogs) Licensed Cen ht 16P No coaches Last d 5pm
ROOMS: s £23; d £46; wkly b&b £144.90; wkly hlf-bd £242.90*
CARDS:

INNERLEITHEN Scottish Borders Map **11** NT33

QQQ **Traquair Arms Hotel** Traquair Rd EH44 6PD (from A72 Peebles to Galashiels road take B709 for St Mary's Loch & Traquair) ☎ 01896 830229 FAX 01896 830260

This small hotel enjoys a reputation for its good-value meals, served throughout the day and evening, in either the dining room or the cosy bar, where open fires burn in season and where real ales are on tap, including one brewed at historic Traquair House nearby. Bedrooms come in a variety of sizes, are well equipped and include a two-bedroom family suite on the top floor.
10 bth/shr (2 fmly) No smoking in dining room CTV in all bedrooms Tea and coffee making facilities Direct dial from bedrooms Cen ht ch fac 18P No coaches Fishing Last d 9pm
ROOMS: s £45; d £58-£80*
MEALS: Bar Lunch £10-£18alc Dinner £16-£20*
CARDS:

INVERARAY Argyll & Bute

See **Ardbrecknish**

INVERGARRY Highland Map **14** NH30

QQQ **Craigard** PH35 4HG (off A82 onto A87 for house 1m on right)
☎ 01809 501258
Closed 24-31 Dec
A welcoming atmosphere prevails at this attractive family-run guesthouse which stands in its own gardens and is backed by a wooded hillside. Bedrooms are spacious and comfortable with pretty fabrics, while several retain their original fireplaces. A collection of wall plates and the dispense bar are features of the warmly decorated dining room where evening meals are served by arrangement.
7 rms (2 bth 1 shr) No smoking CTV in all bedrooms Tea and coffee making facilities No dogs (ex guide dogs) Licensed CTV No children 10P No coaches Last d 11am
ROOMS: s £18-£22; d £36-£44*

QQQ **Forest Lodge** South Laggan PH34 4EA
(3m SW off Invergarry on north side of A82)
☎ 01809 501219 FAX 01809 501476
A purpose-built, modern guest-house standing in its own well tended gardens. The bright and individual bedrooms have a mix of traditional and modern styles, with the best use being made of the available space. There is a choice of two lounges: the sun lounge where smoking is permitted, and a spacious lounge with plenty of local information, games and jigsaws. Home-cooked dinners are served in the attractive dining room, which has many points of interest including details of the owners' family trees.
7 shr (2 fmly) No smoking Tea and coffee making facilities Cen ht CTV 10P No coaches Last d 6.30pm
ROOMS: d £34-£40; wkly hlf-bd £200-£214

INVERKEILOR Angus Map **15** NO64

QQQ **Gordon's Restaurant** Main St DD11 5RN
(take A92 Arbroath to Montrose and turn off at sign for Inverkeilor. On reaching main street continue to end, premises located on left)
☎ 01241 830364
Closed last 2 wks Jan
Situated beside the main street at the north end of the village, there are two tastefully decorated en suite bedrooms on the first floor. However, the restaurant is really what this business is all about. Guests are guaranteed fine dining in the recently refurbished restaurant which is also open to non residents. Gordon and Garry Watson have deservedly earned two AA Rosettes.
2 shr No smoking in bedrooms No smoking in dining room CTV in all bedrooms Tea and coffee making facilities Licensed Cen ht 7P Last d 9pm
ROOMS: s £25-£28; d £47*
CARDS:

INVERKEITHING Fife Map **11** NT18

QQQ **Forth Craig Private Hotel** 90 Hope St KY11 1LL
(off A90 at 1st exit after Forth Bridge, signed Inverkeithing, for hotel in 0.5m on right next to church)
☎ 01383 418440
Views over the Firth of Forth are enjoyed from this welcoming family run private hotel which stands beside the main road at the south side of the village. The well maintained bedrooms are furnished in the modern style and offer a good range of amenities. Enjoyable home cooking is served at individual tables in the attractive dining room and refreshments can be served in the cosy lounge.
5 shr No smoking in bedrooms No smoking in dining room CTV in all bedrooms Tea and coffee making facilities Licensed Cen ht 8P No coaches Last d 6pm
ROOMS: s £26-£30; d £42-£48
CARDS:

Selected

QQQQ **The Roods** 16 Bannerman Av KY11 1NG
(off A90/M90 onto B981) ☎ 01383 415049 FAX 01383 415049
Set in a secluded garden, Isabel Marley's charming home has delightful bedrooms appointed to a high standard, offering a wide range of amenities and lots of thoughtful personal touches. There is also an inviting lounge. Breakfast is served at individual tables in the conservatory. This is a non-smoking establishment.
2 shr No smoking CTV in all bedrooms Tea and coffee making facilities Direct dial from bedrooms No dogs (ex guide dogs) Cen ht CTV 4P No coaches Last d 9am
ROOMS: s £22-£27; d £40-£48

INVERNESS Highland Map **14** NH64

See also Culloden Moor, Dalcross & Tomatin

Q Q Q **Aberfeldy Lodge** 11 Southside Rd IV2 3BG
(Head for Inverness town centre from A9 at Marks & Spencer, proceed S on Crown Rd to Southside Rd)
☎ 01463 231120 FAX 01463 234741
This family run guest house located within easy reach of central amenities now has keen new owners. The bedrooms, which vary in size, are comfortable and offer the expected facilities, with two on the ground floor having access for the disabled to the car park. In addition to the attractive dining room there also is a small lounge area.
9 shr (2 fmly) No smoking in 3 bedrooms No smoking in dining room No smoking in lounges CTV in all bedrooms Tea and coffee making facilities Cen ht No children 4yrs 9P No coaches Last d 3pm
ROOMS: s fr £30; d £38-£58*
CARDS:

Q Q Q **Acorn House** 2A Bruce Gardens IV3 5EN ☎ 01463 717021 FAX 01463 714236
In spite of the attractive traditional appearance, this detached house, just a ten minute walk from the town centre, was built in 1995. Inside there is a strong Scottish theme, with bold use of tartan in the decor and fabrics. Bedrooms are well equipped and guests also have a comfortable lounge to relax in. A good choice of dishes are offered at dinner and served in the pretty dining room which has stained glass windows.
6 bth/shr (3 fmly) No smoking in bedrooms No smoking in dining room CTV in all bedrooms Tea and coffee making facilities Cen ht CTV 7P Last d 8pm
ROOMS: s £27.50-£35; d £55-£60; wkly b&b £175-£192.50; wkly hlf-bd £245-£262.50*
CARDS:

Selected

Q Q Q Q **Ardmuir House** 16 Ness Bank IV2 4SF
(on E bank of river, opposite the cathedral)
☎ 01463 231151 FAX 231151
Genuine hospitality is a feature of this small private hotel, which stands on the east bank of the River Ness opposite the cathedral. The smartly decorated bedrooms are enhanced by attractive fabrics and offer modern fitted furnishings together with a good range of facilities. The house is licensed and refreshments are readily available in the comfortable lounge which overlooks the river. Enjoyable home cooking is served at individual tables in the tastefully appointed dining room.
11 shr (2 fmly) No smoking in 8 bedrooms No smoking in dining room CTV in all bedrooms Tea and coffee making facilities Direct dial from bedrooms No dogs (ex guide dogs) Licensed Cen ht 4P No coaches Last d 7pm
ROOMS: s £31.50-£36; d £51-£66; wkly b&b £178.50-£234.50
CARDS:

Selected

Q Q Q Q *Ardross House* 18 Ardross St IV3 5NS
(first turning on right at St Andrews Cathedral) ☎ 01463 241740
Good value bed and breakfast accommodation is offered at this detached Victorian house which is situated in a residential area close to Eden Court Theatre. Bedrooms are bright and airy with pleasant modern furnishings, are well equipped and have many personal touches. Substantial breakfasts are served at separate tables in the bright and attractive dining room.
8 rms (6 bth/shr) (2 fmly) No smoking in 1 bedrooms No smoking in dining room No smoking in lounges CTV in all bedrooms Tea and coffee making facilities Cen ht 2P

Premier Selected

Q Q Q Q Q **Ballifeary House Hotel** 10 Ballifeary Rd IV3 5PJ
(off A82, 0.5m from town centre,turn left into Bishops Road and sharp right into Ballifeary Road)
☎ 01463 235572 FAX 01463 717583
Closed mid Oct-Etr
Many guests have become regular visitors to Margaret and Danny Luscombe's large detached house, situated in an attractive residential area of Inverness, close to the Eden Court Theatre. There is a warm welcoming atmosphere throughout and comfortable, spotlessly clean bedrooms ensure a peaceful night's sleep.
5 bth/shr No smoking CTV in all bedrooms Tea and coffee making facilities No dogs (ex guide dogs) Licensed Cen ht No children 15yrs 8P No coaches
ROOMS: s £46-£56; d £68-£72; wkly b&b £231-£245
CARDS:

Selected

Q Q Q Q **Borve** 9 Old Edinburgh Rd IV2 3HF
(past Inverness Castle, up Castle Street, about 200yds on left Old Edinburgh Road. First house on left hand side - parking opposite)
☎ 01463 234728 FAX 711017
Good value bed and breakfast accommodation is offered at this friendly personally-run guest house close to the town centre. Well maintained bedrooms are brightly decorated and comfortably furnished in pine, and substantial breakfasts are served at individual tables in the combined lounge/dining room.
4 shr (2 fmly) No smoking CTV in all bedrooms Tea and coffee making facilities Cen ht CTV 8P No coaches Last d 12pm
ROOMS: s fr £25; d £50-£60∗

Selected

Q Q Q Q *Braemore* 1 Victoria Dr IV2 3QB
(Millburn Rd into town centre. Victoria Drive second turning on left and house 100 metres on left, clearly signed)
☎ 01463 243318
A lovely detached Victorian house with its own well tended garden, set in a quiet residential area on the southern side of town, where Susan Moodie treats visitors very much as house guests. Public areas include a spacious and comfortable lounge and an elegant breakfast room. Bedrooms are very individual and reflect the Victorian theme present throughout the house, though all the expected facilities are provided.
3 bth/shr (1 fmly) No smoking CTV in all bedrooms Tea and coffee making facilities No dogs (ex guide dogs) Cen ht 5P No coaches

Selected

Q Q Q Q **Brae Ness Hotel** 17 Ness Bank IV2 4SF
(0.25m along river bank below Inverness Castle in direction of Dores (B862) from town centre) ☎ 01463 712266 FAX 01463 231732
Closed Nov-Apr
Pleasantly situated by the riverside, close to the town centre and the Eden Court Theatre, Brae Ness is a friendly personally-run establishment. Bedrooms, though variable in size, are smartly decorated and comfortably furnished. There is a lounge on the first floor, and enjoyable home-cooked meals are served in the front facing dining room.
10 bth/shr (2 fmly) No smoking in 7 bedrooms No smoking in dining room CTV in all bedrooms Tea and coffee making facilities No dogs (ex guide dogs) Licensed Cen ht 7P No coaches
Last d 6.30pm
ROOMS: s £28-£38; d £50-£66∗
CARDS:

Q Q Q **Craigside** 4 Gordon Ter IV2 3HD (from town centre take Castle Street, then first turning on left (Old Edinburgh Road) then three first left turns) ☎ 01463 231576 FAX 01463 713409
Janette and Wilf Skinner's welcoming Georgian lodge is situated in a residential area close to the town centre and has super views over the castle towards the Firth and Ben Wyvis beyond. The bright bedrooms are cleverly designed to make best use of available space and offer a wide range of amenities. The lounge is comfortable and relaxing with well filled book shelves, and hearty breakfasts are served at individual tables in the dining room.
6 bth/shr No smoking in bedrooms No smoking in dining room CTV in all bedrooms Tea and coffee making facilities No dogs (ex guide dogs) Cen ht 4P No coaches
ROOMS: s £18-£22; d £36-£40*
CARDS:

Premier Selected

Q Q Q Q Q **Culduthel Lodge** 14 Culduthel Rd IV2 4AG (follow B861 Castle St from town centre) ☎ 01463 240089 FAX 01463 240089
This charming Grade II Georgian residence has been lovingly restored by dedicated owners David and Marion Bonsor to provide a superior standard of accommodation. The house stands in an elevated position close to the town centre in its own landscaped garden with views of the River Ness and the countryside beyond. Bedrooms are individually decorated and furnished to a high standard and are thoughtfully provided with many personal touches. Elegant public areas include a comfortable sitting room with an ornate ceiling and a welcoming open fire, while the attractive dining room is the appropriate setting for Marion's enjoyable freshly prepared dishes offered on the daily-changing menu.
12 bth/shr (1 fmly) No smoking in bedrooms No smoking in dining room CTV in all bedrooms Tea and coffee making facilities Direct dial from bedrooms Licensed Cen ht 13P No coaches Last d 7.30pm
ROOMS: s £45; d £80-£95; wkly b&b £275-£325; wkly hlf-bd £400-£450
CARDS:

Selected

Q Q Q Q ***Dionard*** 39 Old Edinburgh Rd IV2 3HJ ☎ 01463 233557 FAX 01463 710526
This immaculately maintained detached Victorian house stands in its own attractive garden in a residential area close to central amenities. There is a welcoming atmosphere and the comfortable bedrooms are bright and airy, appropriately modern in style and well equipped. Breakfast is served at the communal table in the attractive combined lounge/dining room.
3 shr No smoking in 1 bedrooms No smoking in dining room No smoking in lounges CTV in all bedrooms Tea and coffee making facilities Cen ht CTV No children 6yrs 6P

[Q] [Q] ***Hawthorn Lodge*** 15 Fairfield Rd IV3 5QA (from town centre, turn up Waterside to bridge and cross bridge onto Kenneth St and second left into Fairfield Rd)
☎ 01463 715516 FAX 01463 221578
A recently restored, detached family home with its own garden, just a short walk from the town. The house is currently undergoing renovations and the bedrooms, some of which are suitable for families, are all attractively decorated. The breakfast room is cosy and modern in style.
5 rms (1 bth/shr) (3 fmly) No smoking in dining room No smoking in lounges CTV in all bedrooms Tea and coffee making facilities No dogs Cen ht CTV ch fac 6P
CARDS:

[Q] [Q] [Q] ***Heathfield*** 2 Kenneth St IV3 5NR ☎ 01463 230547 FAX 01463 230547
Located in a terraced row with a neat front garden, close to the centre of the city, this homely guest house retains many of its original Victorian features, including well proportioned bedrooms. Individual dècor with a floral theme has been used in the bedrooms, which are comfortable and well equipped. There is an attractive lounge/breakfast room which has a collection of pretty figurines and oil paintings.
3 rms (1 bth/shr) No smoking CTV in all bedrooms Tea and coffee making facilities No dogs (ex guide dogs) Cen ht

[Q] [Q] [Q] ***Heathmount*** Kingsmills Rd IV2 3JU ☎ 01463 235877 FAX 01463 715749
Closed 31 Dec-2 Jan rs 25 Dec
The well proportioned and comfortable modern bedrooms are a feature of this friendly family-run hotel which dates back to 1868. Public areas are strikingly decorated in an attractive black and gold colour scheme which reflects the Victorian character of the house. The bars, with real ale, are popular with locals and guests alike and the restaurant, with a separate non-smoking area, offers a wide range of carefully prepared dishes at very reasonable prices.
7 bth/shr (2 fmly) No smoking in area of dining room CTV in all bedrooms Tea and coffee making facilities Direct dial from bedrooms Cen ht 20P No coaches Last d 9.30pm
CARDS:

[Q] [Q] [Q] **Inchberry House** Lentran IV3 6RJ (A862 from Inverness to Beauly. Housis signposted on left 5m past B & Q.
☎ 01463 831342 FAX 01463 831342
Etr-Oct rs Xmas week
A substantial farm house with fine views across the Beauly Firth to the mountains beyond. Pedigree Limousin cattle are raised on the property. The house has been completely renovated by the new owners, and bedrooms all have individual decor and good facilities. There is a spacious and comfortable lounge in addition to the traditional dining room which provides good sized individual tables.
6 bth/shr (1 fmly) No smoking in bedrooms No smoking in dining room CTV in all bedrooms Tea and coffee making facilities No dogs Licensed Cen ht No children 12yrs 6P No coaches Last d day before
ROOMS: wkly b&b £130-£165
CARDS:

[Q] [Q] [Q] **Inverglen** 7 Abertarff Rd IV2 3NW
(head for town centre, follow directions for Crown, establishment only 4 mins walk from town centre, quiet residential area) ☎ 01463 237610
Closed Xmas rs 24-26 Dec
Margaret Bews offers exemplary standards at her comfortable detached home, located in a residential area within easy reach of the town centre. The bright airy bedrooms have been carefully designed to make best use of available space and offer comfortable modern appointments. Hot drink facilities are provided in the small inviting lounge and breakfast is served at individual tables in the refurbished dining room.
5 shr (2 fmly) No smoking CTV in all bedrooms Tea and coffee making facilities No dogs (ex guide dogs) Cen ht 6P
ROOMS: s £18-£25; d £36-£48; wkly b&b £120-£150*

[Q] [Q] [Q] **Macrae House** 24 Ness Bank IV2 4SF
(5 mins from Castle/town centre on the town side of river, opposite Eden Court Theatre) ☎ 01463 243658
Located close to the town centre and looking across the river to the Eden Court Theatre, this attractive home, with a neat front garden, provides comfortable accommodation and good facilities. There are many items of interest around the house with the cosy breakfast room to the rear being the only public room. One bedroom is conveniently located on the ground floor with its own shower room adjacent, whilst the rest of the rooms are on the first floor.
4 rms (2 shr) (1 fmly) No smoking CTV in all bedrooms Tea and coffee making facilities No dogs (ex guide dogs) Cen ht 8P No coaches
ROOMS: s fr £18; d £40-£48*

Premier Selected

[Q] [Q] [Q] [Q] [Q] ***Millwood House*** 36 Old Mill Rd IV2 3HR
(from A9 towards town centre through rdbt & traffic lights to mini-rdbt left fork pass golf course through traffic lights house 2nd turning on right) ☎ 01463 237254 FAX 01463 719400
Apr-Oct
Millwood House is situated in a residential area, and stands in beautifully secluded gardens. Bill and Gillian Lee have transformed their family home into a top class establishment, with every possible luxury being offered. The bedrooms have many thoughtful extras and best use has been made of the available space. The sitting room has an open fire and fresh flowers are always a feature, while the extensive breakfast is offered at a communal oak table which enjoys views over the garden. Afternoon tea can be enjoyed on the lawn during summer evenings.
3 shr No smoking CTV in all bedrooms Tea and coffee making facilities No dogs Cen ht CTV No children 4P No coaches
CARDS:

Premier Selected

QQQQQ **Moyness House** 6 Bruce Gardens IV3 5EN (located off A82 Fort William road, almost opposite Highland Regional Council Headquarters) ☎ 01463 233836 FAX 01463 233836
Closed 24 Dec-3 Jan
This elegant Victorian villa is in a quiet residential area just minutes from the town centre. Jenny and Richard Jones run this inviting house with its beautifully decorated bedrooms and well fitted bathrooms. Inviting public rooms overlook the garden to the front. Guests are welcome to use the secluded back garden for an aperitif before enjoying Jenny's cooking.
7 bth/shr No smoking in bedrooms No smoking in dining room CTV in all bedrooms Tea and coffee making facilities Licensed Cen ht 10P No coaches Last d 4pm
ROOMS: s £28-£34; d £56-£68; wkly b&b £181-£220; wkly hlf-bd £310-£349*
CARDS:

QQQ **Ness Bank House** 7 Ness Bank IV2 4SF ☎ 01463 232939 FAX 01463 232939
Closed Mid Dec-Jan
This listed Victorian terraced house has a pretty garden with a climbing rose bush to the front. It overlooks the river and is also very handy for the town centre. The bedrooms are all fresh and offer the usual facilities, and breakfasts are served in an attractive front room with a river view.
5 rms (3 shr) (1 fmly) No smoking CTV in all bedrooms Tea and coffee making facilities No dogs (ex guide dogs) Cen ht No coaches
ROOMS: s fr £27; d £36-£46*

Selected

QQQQ **The Old Rectory** 9 Southside Rd IV2 3BG ☎ 01463 220969
Closed 21 Dec-5 Jan
A comfortable detached home with tastefully decorated bedrooms, complemented by attractive co-ordinated fabrics and furnished in mixed modern styles. The sitting room invites peaceful relaxation and hearty breakfasts are served at individual tables in the smart dining room. Set in a residential area close to the town centre, the hotel also has access from the street to the rear.
4 shr No smoking CTV in all bedrooms Tea and coffee making facilities No dogs (ex guide dogs) Cen ht No children 7yrs 5P
ROOMS: d £40-£44
CARDS:

QQ **Park** 51 Glenurquhart Rd IV3 5PB (on A82 leaving town centre, on W side of river) ☎ 01463 231858
This is a substantial Victorian villa with a distinctive ivy clad frontage and neat front garden, south west of the town on the main road to Loch Ness. The six bedrooms are all located on the first floor and provide attractive decor and good facilities, though not all are en suite. There is a cheerful breakfast room on the ground floor, with comfortable seating available and a well stocked bookcase.
6 rms (3 shr) (3 fmly) No smoking CTV in all bedrooms Tea and coffee making facilities No dogs (ex guide dogs) Cen ht 6P No coaches
ROOMS: s £15-£22.50; d £30-£45; wkly b&b £95-£140*
CARDS:

QQQ **Riverside House Hotel** 8 Ness Bank IV2 4SF (town side of river, past castle) ☎ 01463 231052
Situated beside the River Ness on the opposite bank from the cathedral is this welcoming personally-run guest house, with a small and neat front garden, providing good value accommodation. Bedrooms are decorated in bright cheerful colours and offer mixed, modern furnishings. Public areas include a very comfortable small lounge, a separate smokers lounge and an attractive dining room where enjoyable home cooking is served.
11 rms (5 bth 5 shr) (3 fmly) No smoking in dining room No smoking in 1 lounge CTV in all bedrooms Tea and coffee making facilities No dogs Licensed Cen ht CTV No children 8yrs P No coaches Last d 7pm
ROOMS: s £28-£32*

QQQ **Ryeford** 21 Ardconnel Ter IV2 3AE ☎ 01463 242871 FAX 01463 242871
Guests are warmly welcomed at this friendly guest house which lies in a quiet terrace five minutes walk from the town centre. Boldly decorated throughout, the bedrooms are thoughtfully equipped; several have splendid views across the town towards the Black Isle. Books and a bowl of sweets for the guests can be found in the corridor. There is an inviting lounge and an attractive pine furnished dining room where hearty breakfasts are served.
6 rms (2 shr) (2 fmly) No smoking in bedrooms No smoking in dining room CTV in all bedrooms Tea and coffee making facilities Cen ht CTV
ROOMS: s £18-£22; d £36-£44*

Prices shown in the directory are meant as a guide only and are subject to change. Please check before you book

St Ann's House 37 Harrowden Rd IV3 5QN
(at rdbt junct A82 & A862 at W side of Friars Shott Bridge)
☎ 01463 236157 FAX 01463 236157
Closed Nov-Feb rs Jun-Aug
Graham and Brenda Wilson continue to carry out improvements to their comfortable home on the west side of the river, which is a ten minute walk of central amenities. There is an attractive conservatory extension to the dining room which overlooks the rear garden, and guests can relax with a refreshment in the comfortable lounge. The brightly decorated bedrooms are comfortable with modern appointments.
6 rms (5 bth/shr) (3 fmly) No smoking in bedrooms No smoking in dining room CTV in all bedrooms Tea and coffee making facilities No dogs Licensed Cen ht CTV 4P No coaches :cards, cribbage, chess, draughts.
ROOMS: s £20-£30; d £40-£45; wkly b&b £126-£140*

Sunnyholm 12 Mayfield Rd IV2 4AE ☎ 01463 231336
This friendly and comfortable detached bungalow is situated in a residential area with easy access to the town centre. The compact ground floor bedrooms offer all the expected amenities and are partly pine-furnished. Smoking is not encouraged in the comfortable main lounge though those who do wish to smoke can do so in the sun lounge overlooking the sheltered garden. Hearty breakfasts and, by prior arrangement, evening meals are served at individual pine tables in the attractive dining room.
4 shr No smoking CTV in all bedrooms Tea and coffee making facilities No dogs (ex guide dogs) Cen ht CTV 6P No coaches
ROOMS: s £25-£28; d £36-£38*

Selected

Taransay Lower Muckovie *(NH707436)* IV1 2BB
(off A9 onto B9177 past Drumossie Hotel) ☎ 01463 231880
FAX 01463 231880 Mrs A Munro
Mar-Nov
Mrs Munro looks forward to welcoming guests to her comfortable modern home, which stands adjacent to the family farm on the outskirts of town, offering splendid views over the Moray Firth to the Black Isle and Ross-shire hills beyond. The smartly decorated bedrooms have been cleverly designed to make best use of available space. There is a comfortable lounge, and substantial breakfasts are served around the communal table in the separate dining room which takes full advantage of the wonderful outlook.
2 bth/shr (1 fmly) No smoking CTV in all bedrooms Tea and coffee making facilities No dogs (ex guide dogs) Cen ht CTV 3P
170 acres dairy
ROOMS: s £25-£27; d £38-£40*

Selected

Trafford Bank 96 Fairfield Rd IV3 5LL ☎ 01463 241414
This large detached Victorian house stands in its own gardens in a residential street close to the canal. The house is the home of Peter and Caroline McKenzie and is furnished with many attractive pieces of restored traditional furniture. Dinner, which is available on request, is cooked by Peter and served at a communal table in the elegant dining room. The lounge is spacious and comfortable. Bedrooms offer many thoughtful extras as well as all the expected facilities.
5 bth/shr No smoking CTV in all bedrooms Tea and coffee making facilities Cen ht 8P No coaches Last d 12am
ROOMS: s £40-£50; d £55-£60; wkly b&b £175-£210; wkly hlf-bd £315-£350*
CARDS:

ISLE OF

Placenames incorporating the words 'Isle' or 'Isle of' will be found under the actual name, eg Isle of Arran is under Arran, Isle of.

JEDBURGH Scottish Borders Map 12 NT62

Bridge House 5 Bridge St TD8 6DW
(In Jedburgh, just off A68, by the Jed water & next to Baptist church)
☎ 01835 863405
Ongoing improvements are taking place at this welcoming family run guest house, a former toll house which was recently listed as a place of historic interest. There are two comfortable en suite bedrooms while another room shares the family bathroom. Freshly prepared breakfasts and, by prior arrangement, home cooked evening meals, are served at the communal table in the conservatory, which also doubles as a lounge. This is a non smoking house.
2 bth/shr No smoking CTV in 1 bedroom Tea and coffee making facilities No dogs (ex guide dogs) Cen ht No coaches Last d 4pm
ROOMS: s £16; d £32; wkly b&b £105; wkly hlf-bd £165

Ferniehirst Mill Lodge TD8 6PQ (2.5m S on A68, at the end of a private track directly off A68) ☎ 01835 863279 FAX 863279
This modern purpose-built chalet-style lodge forms part of a riding centre (experienced adult riders only) which has an attractive and secluded riverside setting in 25 acres beside the River Jed. Bedrooms are small and functional, but there is a bright airy lounge with a dispense bar and board games. Meals are taken at shared tables in the dining room.

9 bth/shr No smoking in dining room Tea and coffee making facilities Direct dial from bedrooms Licensed Cen ht CTV 10P No coaches Fishing Riding Last d 6pm
ROOMS: s £23; d £46; wkly b&b £140; wkly hlf-bd £238
CARDS:

Selected

Q Q Q Q **'Froylehurst'** Friars TD8 6BN
(from town centre Market Place leave by Exchange St then 1st right into Friars for 3rd turn on left)
☎ 01835 862477 FAX 01835 862477
Mar-Nov
This imposing Victorian house lies in its own secluded gardens and enjoys fine views over the town. It is adorned with personal pieces including Etta Irvine's own hand-embroidered pictures, as well as featuring original fireplaces, beautiful woodwork and stained glass windows. Bedrooms are mostly well proportioned and although there are no en suites, the two modern bathrooms have double-sized shower cubicles. Guests can relax in the elegant lounge, and breakfast is taken at two sittings around the one large table in the dining room.
5 rms (3 fmly) No smoking in bedrooms No smoking in dining room CTV in all bedrooms Tea and coffee making facilities No dogs Cen ht CTV No children 5yrs 5P No coaches
ROOMS: d £32-£36; wkly b&b fr £100*

Q Q Q **Kenmore Bank Hotel** Oxnam Rd TD8 6JJ
(off A68 entering town from S, take 1st right by church)
☎ 01835 862369
A cosy and relaxing atmosphere prevails at this friendly family-run guest house, which enjoys fine views of the abbey from its elevated position above Jed Water. Bedrooms are individually styled and vary in size, and the public rooms are adorned with the owner's paintings and prints, many of which are for sale.
6 bth/shr (2 fmly) No smoking in dining room CTV in all bedrooms Tea and coffee making facilities Licensed Cen ht 6P No coaches Fishing
ROOMS: s £25-£46; d £37-£46; wkly b&b £175-£322*
CARDS:

Q Q Q ***Meadhon House*** 48 Cadtle Gate TD8 6BB
(on the A68 into Jedburgh, up to the Abbey turn left into the Castle Gate, first B&B on left)
☎ 01835 862504 FAX 01835 862504
Convenient for both the abbey and the castle, this stone building is of 17th century origin. Attractively decorated, it sparkles throughout, from the cheerful dining room to the bright, contemporary en suite bedrooms. There is no lounge, but when the weather permits guests are welcome to enjoy the quiet rear garden with its views across the town.
5 bth/shr (3 fmly) No smoking CTV in all bedrooms Tea and coffee making facilities Cen ht

Premier Selected

Q Q Q Q Q **The Spinney** Langlee TD8 6PB (2m S on A68)
☎ 01835 863525 FAX 01835 864883
Closed mid Nov-Feb
Two roadside cottages have been extended and transformed into an attractive modern home set in landscaped gardens and surrounded by scenic countryside. The spacious bedrooms are highlighted by light colour schemes and contemporary furnishings and Sandra Fry has added all sorts of thoughtful touches to ensure a comfortable stay. The room without en suite has sole use of an adjacent bathroom complete with separate shower cubicle. Downstairs there is a comfortable lounge with Chesterfields, whilst delicious breakfasts are served in the elegant dining room. Two new lodges in a secluded setting in the grounds may be available for bed and breakfast let.
3 shr 2 annexe shr No smoking CTV in all bedrooms Tea and coffee making facilities No dogs (ex guide dogs) Cen ht CTV 8P No coaches
ROOMS: d £40-£42

QQQ **Willow Court** The Friars TD8 6BN (from Market Sq take Exchange St, Friars 50yds along on the right Willow Court is first house on left) ☎ 01835 863702 FAX 01835 864601
This modern house lies in two acres of gardens in an elevated position off the town centre. With the exception of a family room upstairs, all bedrooms are on the ground floor and the twin without en suite has sole use of a shower room nearby. Two comfortable lounges are a feature of the house, and breakfast is taken in the small conservatory overlooking the town.
4 rms (3 bth/shr) (1 fmly) No smoking in bedrooms No smoking in dining room No smoking in 1 lounge CTV in all bedrooms Tea and coffee making facilities Licensed Cen ht CTV ch fac 6P No coaches

JOHN O'GROATS Highland Map **15** ND37

QQQ **Bencorragh House** Upper Gills, Canisbay KW1 4YB (follow sign to Canisbay from A9 - 3m S of John O'Groats - continue for 3.5m. Take 2nd turn on left, 2nd house on left) ☎ 01955 611449 FAX 01955 611449
This working croft of ten acres is home to a variety of animals including Jacob sheep, cattle, chickens, horses and exotic pheasants. The house itself enjoys panoramic views over the Pentland Firth and the island of Stroma, and has a purpose-built guest wing with spacious, well equipped bedrooms, including one family room. There is a large sun lounge which is used as the dining room, while the TV lounge has a cosy atmosphere.
4 shr (1 fmly) No smoking in bedrooms No smoking in dining room No smoking in 1 lounge Tea and coffee making facilities Cen ht CTV 4P No coaches Last d 7pm
ROOMS: s £23-£25; d £37-£38; wkly b&b £120-£125; wkly hlf-bd £180-£185*
CARDS:

QQQ **Post Office House** Canisbay KW1 4YH (3m from town on A836) ☎ 01955 611213 FAX 01955 611213
Easter-October
This 100-year-old stone-built house, with views over the Pentland Firth, is the home of Charlie and Jean Manson, and guests are extended a genuine welcome and instantly made to feel at ease. Jean goes out of her way to ensure that her guests are well cared for. Many thoughtful extras are provided in the comfortable, well kept bedrooms, all of which have showers with one fully en suite. There is a cosy sitting room, where tea and suppers are served, while the breakfast menu is notably extensive; salmon, smoked haddock and plenty of fresh fruit just a sample of the dishes available.
3 rms (1 shr) No smoking in bedrooms No smoking in dining room CTV in all bedrooms No dogs Cen ht CTV No children 12yrs 5P No coaches

KEITH Moray Map **15** NJ45

Selected

QQQQ ✔ **The Haughs** *(NJ416515)* AB55 6QN (½m from Keith off A96, signed Inverness) ☎ 01542 882238 Mrs J Jackson
Apr-Oct
For more than 35 years, Mrs Jackson has been welcoming guests to her comfortable home, a traditional farmhouse on the outskirts of town.
This is an ideal base for those wishing to explore the surrounding countryside and the Whisky Trail. The bedrooms are spacious with solid furnishings and offer a good range of amenities. There is an inviting lounge and enjoyable farmhouse fare is served at individual tables in the sunny dining room.
4 rms (3 bth/shr) (1 fmly) No smoking in bedrooms No smoking in dining room CTV in all bedrooms Tea and coffee making facilities No dogs (ex guide dogs) Cen ht CTV 10P 165 acres beef mixed sheep Last d 3pm
ROOMS: d £33-£37*

KENTALLEN Highland Map **14** NN05

QQQ ✔ ***Ardsheal Home Farm*** *(NN006574)* PA38 4BZ (off A828, 3m S of Ballachulish Bridge)
☎ 01631 740229 FAX 01631 740 229 Mrs D A MacArthur
Apr-Oct
A warm welcome is assured at Mrs MacArthur's comfortable cottage-style farmhouse which is peacefully set close to the shore of Loch Linnhe. There are two upstairs bedrooms which are comfortably traditional, while the ground floor room is furnished in the modern style and has exclusive use of a private bathroom.
3 rms (1 fmly) No smoking Tea and coffee making facilities No dogs (ex guide dogs) Cen ht CTV 5P 1000 acres beef sheep

Premier Selected

QQQQQ **Ardsheal House** PA38 4BX (4m S of Ballachulish Bridge and A82 on A828 between Glencoe and Appin, 1m private road from A828)
☎ 01631 740227 FAX 01631 740342
Closed 21-27 December rs November-February
This splendid house within its own estate on the shore of Loch Linnhe is home to Neil and Philippa Sutherland, who take great pleasure in welcoming guests to their home. Whilst the number of guests they can accommodate is small, there is quite a degree of flexibility in the range of rooms available, all of which are spacious and furnished in period style with attractive decor. Philippa cooks a set dinner by arrangement and it is served either in the conservatory or in the more traditional dining room where family portraits hang. There are two comfortable sitting rooms, both with log fires and one contains the only TV in the house. There is also a full-size snooker table available for guests.
6 bth/shr No smoking in dining room No smoking in 1 lounge Tea and coffee making facilities Direct dial from bedrooms Licensed Cen ht ch fac 12P No coaches Snooker
ROOMS: s £39-£40; d £78-£80*
CARDS:

KILBARCHAN Renfrewshire Map 10 NS46

Q Q ***Ashburn*** Milliken Park Rd PA10 2DB
(follow signs for Johnstone onto B787 and turn right opposite bus garage)
☎ 01505 705477 FAX 01505 705477
This family-run guest house remains a popular stop-over for travellers using the nearby Glasgow Airport and is best accessed from the Howwood Road at the south end of the village. Bedrooms are mixed in size and in style. There is an honesty bar in the spacious lounge, and on occasions, there may be a need to share your table in the dining room with other guests.
6 rms (2 shr) (3 fmly) CTV in all bedrooms Tea and coffee making facilities Licensed Cen ht CTV 8P No coaches Last d 11am
CARDS:

KILLIECRANKIE Perth & Kinross Map 14 NN96

Q Q **Dalnasgadh House** PH16 5LN (located off A9 N of Pitlochry 2m along road signposted Killiecrankie B8079 on the right. House is clearly signposted and can be seen from road) ☎ 01796 473237
Apr-Sep
Mrs McPherson-McDougall looks forward to welcoming guests old and new to her comfortable detached home which stands in carefully tended gardens to the north of the village. Public areas include an inviting TV lounge and a smartly appointed dining room where hearty breakfasts provide a good start to the day. This is a non-smoking house.
5 rms No smoking TV available Tea and coffee making facilities No dogs (ex guide dogs) Cen ht CTV 10P No coaches
ROOMS: s £20-£21; d £37-£38*

KILMARNOCK East Ayrshire Map 10 NS43

Q Q Q **Aulton Farm** *(NS386422)* Kilmaurs KA3 2PQ
(Irvine to Stewerton road A769.First turn right past Cunningham Head crossroads,first farm on the left)
☎ 01563 538208 0378 530564 Mrs A Hawkshaw
A well maintained farm house, which offers comfortable, nicely furnished bedrooms and an attractive lounge. It's the hospitality extended by Ena and Archie and the home-from-home atmosphere, however, that most guests remember.
4 rms (1 fmly) No smoking CTV in all bedrooms Tea and coffee making facilities No dogs Cen ht CTV ch fac 6P Riding 22 acres beef
ROOMS: s fr £18; d £32-£36*

Selected

Q Q Q Q **Burnside Hotel** 18 London Rd KA3 7AQ
(on main road opposite Dick Institute, Library and Museum)
☎ 01563 522952 FAX 01563 573381
Enthusiastic owners David and Judith Dye have worked hard to create this civilised small hotel, a detached sandstone Victorian house, in a west-end conservation area. The inviting lounge is spacious and comfortable, and a separate dining room is a pleasant setting in which to enjoy the good home cooking and hearty breakfasts. All the bedrooms are individually furnished and decorated, and range from appealing single rooms to good-sized family rooms.
10 rms (5 bth/shr) (4 fmly) No smoking in dining room CTV in all bedrooms Tea and coffee making facilities Cen ht CTV 10P No coaches Last d noon
ROOMS: s £20-£27.50; d £40-£42
CARDS:

Q Q **Eriskay** 2 Dean Ter KA3 1RJ (from town centre follow one-way system and right at Railway station and follow Glasgow signs)
☎ 01563 532061 FAX 532157
Situated on the Glasgow Road north of the town centre, this guest house offers good value accommodation. Bedrooms, some of which are of limited size, offer mixed modern appointments together with all the expected amenities. Smoking is not encouraged in the breakfast room which includes a TV.
7 rms (4 bth/shr) (3 fmly) No smoking in dining room No smoking in lounges CTV in all bedrooms Tea and coffee making facilities Cen ht CTV 12P Last d 8pm
ROOMS: s £16-£24; d £32-£38; wkly b&b £125-£145; wkly hlf-bd £181-£201*
CARDS:

KINGUSSIE Highland Map 14 NH70

Selected

Q Q Q Q **Avondale House** Newtonmore Rd PH21 1HF
☎ 01540 661731 FAX 01540 661731
Avondale is a welcoming detached Victorian house which stands in its own well tended garden on the main road at the south end of the village. Bedrooms in pastel colour schemes also feature attractive co-ordinated fabrics which complement the new dark wood, modern furnishings. Books and board games are provided in the relaxing lounge overlooking the front garden and enjoyable home cooking is served at individual tables in the spacious dining room.
7 rms (1 bth 4 shr) (1 fmly) No smoking CTV in all bedrooms Tea and coffee making facilities Cen ht No children 8yrs 8P No coaches Last d 5pm
ROOMS: s £18-£21; d £36-£42; wkly b&b £120-£140; wkly hlf-bd £183-£203

Selected

Q Q Q Q **Columba House Hotel & Restaurant** Manse Rd PH21 1JF (leave A9 at Kincraig/Kingussie and take B9152 towards Kingussie, telephone box on corner of Manse Rd, Hotel drive second on left) (Minotel) ☎ 01540 661402 FAX 01540 661652
A former manse has been converted to create this comfortable and welcoming small hotel which is run by enthusiastic owner Myra Shearer.
See advertisement on p.563. *contd.*

The house stands in its own grounds at the north end of town and offers views of the surrounding countryside from some of the rooms. Bedrooms are furnished in the modern style and offer a good range of amenities. Two four-poster rooms are available. Public areas include a cosy lounge where refreshments are served on request, and an elegant dining room offering enjoyable home cooked fare.
8 bth/shr (3 fmly) No smoking in 2 bedrooms No smoking in dining room No smoking in 1 lounge CTV in all bedrooms Tea and coffee making facilities Direct dial from bedrooms Licensed Cen ht ch fac 24P No coaches Croquet on lawn Last d 8.45pm
ROOMS: s £35-£47; d £60-£90; wkly b&b £160-£200; wkly hlf-bd £210-£265*
CARDS:

Q Q **Sonnhalde** East Ter PH21 1JS (exit A9 and turn left into village. Turn right at traffic lights and then first right. Third house on left)
☎ 01540 661266 FAX 01540 661266
Closed Nov-27 Dec
Bernie and Janis Jones look forward to welcoming you to their comfortable Victorian home which occupies an elevated position above the town beside the clock tower. Many guests are attracted by the range of interesting activity packages offered. This includes Natural History Tours, Hill Walking and Mountaineering, Photography and Fishing. Bedrooms are smartly decorated and offer both modern and traditional furnishings. Public areas include a relaxing lounge and a smart dining room where enjoyable home cooking is the order of the day.
7 rms (4 shr) (2 fmly) No smoking in bedrooms No smoking in dining room Tea and coffee making facilities Cen ht CTV 10P No coaches Last d 4pm
ROOMS: d £37-£44; wkly b&b £123-£146; wkly hlf-bd £193-£216

KINLOCHBERVIE Highland Map 14 NC25

Q Q Q **Old School Restaurant & Guest House** Inshegra IV27 4RH (from the A838 at Rhiconich take the B801 to Kinlochbervie, 2m on the left)
☎ 01971 521383 FAX 01971 521383
Closed 25 Dec & 1 Jan
This former schoolhouse, built in 1879, retains some of its original character in what is now a pleasant restaurant. The accommodation is in a modern house just behind the original house and offers well equipped and pleasantly decorated rooms; some have lovely views. A cosy single room is available in a small building beside the main house.
6 annexe rms (4 shr) (1 fmly) No smoking in dining room No smoking in 1 lounge CTV in all bedrooms Tea and coffee making facilities Direct dial from bedrooms Licensed Cen ht 10P No coaches Last d 8pm
ROOMS: s £29; d £48-£58; wkly b&b £168-£203*
CARDS:

KINROSS Perth & Kinross Map 11 NO10

Q Q Q **The Muirs Inn Kinross** 49 Muirs KY13 7AU (off M90 junct 6 and follow signs for A922 at T-junct, the Inn is diagonally opposite on right) ☎ 01577 862270 FAX 01577 862270
This ever popular cottage-style pub and restaurant is situated beside the main road on the north side of town. Bedrooms, which are attractively decorated and comfortably furnished in pine, are above the bar and accessed externally. Three other bedrooms are located in a house across the road. Public areas are brimming with character and include a choice of contrasting bars where you will find an impressive range of real ales together with an extensive selection of malt whiskies.
5 bth/shr CTV in all bedrooms Tea and coffee making facilities No dogs (ex guide dogs) Cen ht No children 11yrs 8P Last d 9pm
ROOMS: s £39.50; d £55-£59; wkly b&b £165-£177; wkly hlf-bd £240-£312
MEALS: Lunch £14.50&alc Dinner £14.50&alc
CARDS:

KIRKBEAN Dumfries & Galloway Map 11 NX95

Selected

Q Q Q Q **Cavens House** DG2 8AA (on A710) ☎ 01387 880234 FAX 01387 880234
Lying close to the Solway coast, this large country mansion is set in its own mature grounds with a long drive that is lined with daffodils in the spring. The house has a peaceful and relaxing atmosphere, with large, comfortable bedrooms, one having its own sun lounge and two located on the ground floor. The well proportioned, inviting lounge has an honesty bar and is the focal point of the house. Mrs Jeffries home-cooked dinners and hearty breakfasts earn regular praise and are one of the reasons that guests return time and again to this well established house.
6 bth/shr (1 fmly) No smoking in bedrooms No smoking in dining room CTV in all bedrooms Tea and coffee making facilities Licensed Cen ht CTV 10P No coaches Last d 7pm
ROOMS: s £35-£38; d £40-£58
CARDS:

KIRKCUDBRIGHT Dumfries & Galloway Map 11 NX65

Selected

Q Q Q Q **Baytree House** 110 High St DG6 4JQ (from A75 take A711 into town and turn right 200yds past St Cuthberts church into High St. House at junction of Castle St and High Street)
☎ 01557 330824 FAX 330824
Hospitality is clearly evident at this sympathetically refurbished 18th-century town house. The well equipped bedrooms are attractively furnished, and public areas are particularly luxurious, especially the drawing room. The dining room provides a venue for the impressive cuisine. This is a strictly non-smoking establishment.
3 bth/shr No smoking CTV in all bedrooms Tea and coffee making facilities Cen ht 5P No coaches Bikes to explore countryside Last d 5pm
ROOMS: s £39-£58; d fr £58*

Q Q Q **Emahroo** 109A High St DG6 4JG
(turn off A75 onto A711 to Kirkcudbright, drive through past shops, church & museum on right, turn 1st right onto High St, estab is 150yds on right)
☎ 01557 331279
Mar-Sep
This friendly family house lies quietly secluded in its own garden at the end of narrow alley just five minutes walk from the town centre. Attractively maintained it offers thoughtfully equipped bedrooms, one with modern shower room and the other with its own bathroom right outside.
2 bth/shr No smoking CTV in all bedrooms Tea and coffee making facilities No dogs (ex guide dogs) Cen ht No children 10yrs No coaches
ROOMS: s £20; d £34-£36*

Selected

Q Q Q Q **Gladstone House** 48 High St DG6 4JX
(in quiet conservation area of the town situated 5 minutes walk from Harbour, Maclellans Castle & Historic Tollbooth)
☎ 01557 331734 FAX 01557 331734
Susan and James Westbrook's Georgian terraced house has a charming and relaxed atmosphere. Breakfast is served in the cosy and attractive dining room. Upstairs the comfortable lounge runs along the entire width of the building and offers views of the garden to the rear. Bedrooms have a bright country style, with crisp white decor and bed coverings that contrast with cleverly crafted pine furniture.
3 bth/shr No smoking CTV in all bedrooms Tea and coffee making facilities No dogs Cen ht No children 14yrs No coaches
ROOMS: s £29-£35; d £50-£58*
CARDS:

KIRKMUIRHILL South Lanarkshire Map **11** NS74

Q Q **Dykecroft** *(NS776419)* ML11 0JQ
(from S-exit M74 at junc 9, take B7078 for 2m, then B7086 to Strathaven for 1.5m, past village Boghead, first bungalow on left)
☎ 01555 892226 Mrs I H McInally
Closed 25 Dec
A friendly modern farmhouse that continues to offer good value bed and breakfast accommodation. The bedrooms, though small, are tastefully decorated and offer both modern and traditional furnishings. There is an attractive lounge/dining room with views of the countryside.
3 rms No smoking in bedrooms No smoking in dining room Tea and coffee making facilities Cen ht CTV 4P 60 acres sheep
ROOMS: s £20-£1; d £35-£36; wkly b&b £120-£125*

KIRKWALL See **ORKNEY**

KYLESKU Highland Map **14** NC23

Selected

Q Q Q Q **Newton Lodge** IV27 4HW (1.5m S on A894)
☎ 01971 502070 FAX 502070
Etr-mid Oct
This welcoming family run private hotel enjoys spectacular views over Loch Glencoul to the Mountains of Assynt beyond. Public areas include an inviting lounge with beamed ceiling and comfortable leather seating, while in the attractive dining room, local seafood freshly caught by Mr Brauer in his own fishing boat is often featured. Bedrooms are nicely furnished in the modern style and offer a wide range of amenities. Throughout the atmosphere is relaxed and friendly, and many guests return time and time again to this quality establishment.
7 bth/shr No smoking CTV in all bedrooms Tea and coffee making facilities Licensed Cen ht CTV No children 13yrs 10P No coaches Last d 7.30pm
ROOMS: d £52-£60
CARDS:

LADYBANK Fife Map **11** NO30

Selected

Q Q Q Q **Redlands Country Lodge** KY15 7SH (turn off A92 into Ladybank. Go under bridge to right of railway station, turn left and continue for 0.5m) ☎ 01337 831091 FAX 01337 831091
Mar-Nov
Enthusiastic owners Jim and Dorothy McGregor look forward to welcoming guests old and new to their delightful country guest house.

contd.

The house, a former gamekeeper's home, is situated half a mile east of the village and is surrounded by pleasant countryside.The inviting lounge, with plenty of books and board games, can be found in the Norwegian pine lodge adjacent to the main house, which also houses the bedrooms, all fully timber lined and appropriately furnished. The attractive dining room is situated in the main house. Smoking is not permitted.
4 shr No smoking CTV in all bedrooms Tea and coffee making facilities Cen ht 4P No coaches Last d 5pm
ROOMS: d £44-£48; wkly b&b £150-£160; wkly hlf-bd £200-£215*
CARDS:

LAIDE Highland Map **14** NG89

Selected

QQQQ **Old Smiddy** The Old Smiddy IV22 2NB
(from Inverness follow signs for Ullapool, the West A835. At Braemore Junction take A832. In Laide, Old Smiddy is last house on left opposite church) ☎ 01445 731425 FAX 01445 731425
Etr-Oct
Set in a small hamlet south of Gruinard Bay, this charming country cottage has been attractively modernised to provide two pretty bedrooms. One is on the first floor and has a private shower room at the foot of the access staircase. The comfortable lounge leads to the dining room where Kate Macdonald serves dinner and breakfast. There is also a patio area for guests to enjoy the inland views.
2 bth/shr No smoking Tea and coffee making facilities No dogs (ex guide dogs) Cen ht CTV No children 12yrs 2P No coaches Last d 24hrs
ROOMS: s £25; d £36-£52*
CARDS:

See advertisement under GAIRLOCH

LAMLASH See **ARRAN, ISLE OF**

LANGHOLM Dumfries & Galloway Map **11** NY38

QQQ **Reivers Rest** 81 High St DG13 0DJ (adjacent to Town Hall on A7) ☎ 01387 381343 FAX 013873 81343
More than 200 years old, this family-run establishment provides a cosy lounge and bar with real ale, plus a restaurant serving a variety of food to suite all tastes. Upstairs the attractive bedrooms are thoughtfully equipped to include clock radios, mineral water and home-made shortbread.
4 bth/shr (1 fmly) No smoking in bedrooms No smoking in dining room CTV in all bedrooms Tea and coffee making facilities Licensed Cen ht 6P Golf 9 Tennis (hard) Last d 9pm
ROOMS: s £30; d fr £50*
CARDS:

LARGS North Ayrshire Map **10** NS25

Selected

QQQQ **Lea-Mar** 20 Douglas St KA30 8PS
(take A78, on reaching town turn left at sign for Brisbane Glen/Inverclyde Sports Centre. Lea-Mar 100yds on right)
☎ 01475 672447 FAX 672447
Spotlessly maintained to a high standard, Margo and Ron Muir's detached house stands in a quiet residential area at the north end of town, just a short walk from the seafront. The attractively decorated bedrooms have been cleverly designed to make best use of available space, are furnished in pine and, in keeping with the rest of the house, are adorned with lots of personal touches and ornaments. In the lounge, Chesterfields invite relaxation, and enjoyable breakfasts are served at individual tables in the separate dining room which features a collection of crested teaspoons.
4 shr No smoking CTV in all bedrooms Tea and coffee making facilities No dogs (ex guide dogs) Cen ht CTV No children 12yrs 4P No coaches
ROOMS: d fr £48*
CARDS:

Selected

QQQQ **South Whittlieburn** *(NS218632)* Brisbane Glen KA30 8SN (2m NE of Largs town centre off the road signed Brisbane Glen) ☎ 01475 675881 FAX 01475 675881 & 675080 Mrs M Watson
rs Xmas & New Year
This comfortable and welcoming farmhouse is two miles from the town on the Brisbane Glen Road and is surrounded by gently rolling countryside. Bedrooms are bright and cheerful, come in variety of sizes, and are thoughtfully furnished in contemporary style to make effective use of available space. One two-room suite makes an ideal family unit. There is an attractive sitting room, and freshly prepared breakfasts are served around shared tables in the owner's personal lounge.
3 bth/shr (1 fmly) No smoking in bedrooms No smoking in dining room CTV in all bedrooms Tea and coffee making facilities No dogs (ex guide dogs) Cen ht CTV 10P 155 acres sheep/pigs
ROOMS: s fr £19.50; d fr £39*

Selected

QQQQ **Whin Park** 16 Douglas St KA30 8PS
(off A78 at Brisbane Glen sign) ☎ 01475 673437
Closed Feb
Whin Park takes its name from the gorse on the hills that can be seen from the front rooms of this very comfortable bungalow which is situated close to the seafront. Bedrooms are well appointed and attractively decorated. Mr & Mrs Henderson are attentive hosts and breakfast is an added attraction.
5 shr (1 fmly) No smoking in bedrooms No smoking in dining room CTV in all bedrooms Tea and coffee making facilities No dogs (ex guide dogs) 4P No coaches
ROOMS: s fr £25; d fr £50*
CARDS:

The AA's professional Inspectors make regular and anonymous visits to all the establishments listed in the Guide. They accept no gifts or favours from proprietors

LATHERON Highland Map 15 ND13

Q Q Q **Upper Latheron** *(ND195352)* KW5 6DT (2m N of Dunbeath off A9, and 2m S of Latheron) ☎ 01593 741224 Mrs C B Sinclair
Closed Oct-Apr
From its elevated position just south of the village off the A9, this pretty farmhouse enjoys panoramic views over the North Sea. The comfortable and well maintained family bedrooms, one of which is on the ground floor, offer both modern and traditional furnishings. Farmhouse breakfasts are served around the communal table in the cosy combined lounge/dining room.
3 rms (1 fmly) No smoking CTV in all bedrooms No dogs (ex guide dogs) Cen ht CTV 6P 200 acres Cattle Ponies Sheep
ROOMS: s fr £18; d £34-£36*

LAUDER Scottish Borders Map 12 NT54

Q Q **The Grange** 6 Edinburgh Rd TD2 6TW
(on A68, between war memorial and petrol station if heading north)
☎ 01578 722649 FAX 01578 722649
Closed 24-26 Dec
A welcoming cuppa greets guests on arrival at this substantial detached house which lies in its own sheltered garden on the main road on the north side of town. Its spacious bedrooms are a feature and there is also a guests lounge and separate dining room.
3 rms (2 fmly) No smoking Tea and coffee making facilities No dogs (ex guide dogs) Cen ht CTV 4P No coaches
ROOMS: s £16-£20; d £32-£32; wkly b&b £100-£112*

LERWICK See SHETLAND

LEWIS, ISLE OF Western Isles Map 13

SOUTH GALSON Map 13 NB45

Selected

Q Q Q Q **Galson Farm** HS2 0SH (off A857, 20m N of Stornoway) ☎ 01851 850492 FAX 01851 850492
This restored croft house on the northwest coast, enjoying glorious views of the Atlantic, has been lovingly restored by dedicated owners John and Dorothy Russell to provide high standards of comfort. Bedrooms have been carefully designed to make best use of available space and are modern in style - TVs are only available on request. Refreshments are served in the two inviting lounges - one has well filled book shelves and the other gives access to the garden. The kitchen is Dorothy's domain and her carefully prepared 5-course dinners, served around the communal table, remain a highlight of a visit here. By prior arrangement, meals are also available to non-residents.
3 shr No smoking CTV in all bedrooms Tea and coffee making facilities Licensed Cen ht CTV 5P No coaches Clay Pigeon Shooting Last d 6.30pm
ROOMS: s fr £35; d fr £58; wkly b&b £203-£245; wkly hlf-bd £315-£329*
CARDS:

LINLITHGOW West Lothian Map 11 NS97

Q Q Q ***Belsyde House*** *(NS976755)* Lanark Rd EH49 6QE
(1.5m SW on A706, first left after crossing Union Canal)
☎ 01506 842098 FAX 01506 842098 Mrs A Hay
Closed Xmas
Many guests return regularly to this welcoming farmhouse which is peacefully situated above the Union Canal off the Lanark Road about 1.5 miles south of town. Though variable in size, the bright airy bedrooms are comfortably furnished in mixed styles. Hearty farmhouse breakfasts are served at individual tables in the smart dining room which is adjacent to the inviting sitting room. This is a non smoking house.
4 rms (1 shr) (1 fmly) No smoking CTV in all bedrooms Tea and coffee making facilities No dogs (ex guide dogs) Cen ht CTV 10P
106 acres sheep Last d noon
CARDS:

LIVINGSTON West Lothian Map 11 NT06

Selected

Q Q Q Q **Whitecroft** 7 Raw Holdings, East Calder EH53 0ET
(turn off A71 onto B7015, establishment on right hand side)
☎ 01506 882494 FAX 01506 882598
A relaxed and friendly atmosphere is created by the Scott family who are constantly improving this delightful property. The bedrooms, located on the ground floor, are attractively colour co-ordinated, well equipped and contain many thoughtful extras. Guests can enjoy a delicious breakfast freshly prepared from local produce in the attractive dining room.
3 shr No smoking CTV in all bedrooms Tea and coffee making facilities No dogs (ex guide dogs) Cen ht 5P No coaches
ROOMS: s £32-£44; d £44-£46*
CARDS:

LOANHEAD Midlothian Map 11 NT26

Q Q Q **Aaron Glen** 7 Nivensknowe Rd EH20 9AU
(on A768-just off A701 1m south from City bypass)
☎ 0131 440 1293 FAX 0131 440 2155
This welcoming guest house is situated at the western edge of the village with easy access to the City Bypass. The well equipped bedrooms are nicely decorated and attractive fabrics have been used to good effect; and a disabled room is available on the ground floor. Individual tables are offered in the combined lounge/dining room which also boasts a dispense bar.
5 shr (3 fmly) No smoking CTV in all bedrooms Tea and coffee making facilities Licensed Cen ht CTV ch fac 15P
ROOMS: s £25-£50; d £40-£60*
CARDS:

LOCHEARNHEAD Stirling Map 11 NN52

Selected

Q Q Q Q ***Mansewood Country House*** FK19 8NS
(turn onto A84 at Stirling. Travel through Callender and Strathyre to Lochearnhead. First building on the left) ☎ 01567 830213
The Watson family look forward to welcoming you to their delightful home, a detached stone built house standing in its own garden on the south side of the village. Bedrooms have been cleverly designed to offer comfortable accommodation, while enjoyable fare, carefully prepared from local and home grown produce, is offered in the attractive licensed restaurant. A separate inviting lounge with a log stove is also available.
6 bth/shr No smoking in bedrooms No smoking in dining room No smoking in lounges CTV in all bedrooms Tea and coffee making facilities No dogs (ex guide dogs) Licensed Cen ht No children 15yrs 10P No coaches Last d 8pm
CARDS:

LOCHGILPHEAD Argyll & Bute Map 10 NR88

See Crinan

Q **Horseshoe** Kilmichael Glassary PA31 8QA (village is on A816, four miles N of Lochgilphead on Oban Rd. Hotel in centre of the village of Bridgend) ☎ 01546 606369 FAX 01546 602305
rs Oct-Apr (open weekdays only except Xmas)
A traditional inn which has been renovated to include three pleasantly cosy rooms in the house, with four more planned for the annexe behind the hotel. The pretty bistro-style dining room offers a popular range of dishes from the carte menu.
4 shr 3 annexe shr (1 fmly) No smoking in bedrooms No smoking in dining room No smoking in 1 lounge CTV in all bedrooms Tea and coffee making facilities Cen ht CTV ch fac 8P Sauna Last d 9.00pm
ROOMS: s £20-£25; d £40-£50; wkly b&b £120-£150*
MEALS: Lunch £1-£12.95alc Dinner £1-£12.95alc*
CARDS:

LOCHRANZA See ARRAN, ISLE OF

LOCHWINNOCH Renfrewshire Map 10 NS35

Premier Selected

Q Q Q Q Q **East Lochhead** Largs Rd PA12 4DX (from Glasgow take M8 junct 28a for A737 Irvine. At Roadhead rdbt turn right on A760 and premises are located 2m on the right hand side) ☎ 01505 842610 FAX 01505 842610
Enthusiastic owner Janet Anderson has made a superb job of renovating this attractive 100 year-old former farmhouse located in the Clyde Muirshiel Country Park. Janet's enjoyable home cooking is served around the communal table in a combined lounge/dining room. Accommodation is a spacious en suite ground floor double bedroom and an upstairs twin room with its own private bathroom.
2 bth/shr (1 fmly) No smoking CTV in all bedrooms Tea and coffee making facilities Cen ht CTV ch fac 14P No coaches Cycle track Last d 2pm
ROOMS: s £35-£40; d £60-£65; wkly b&b £200-£210; wkly hlf-bd £300-£330*
CARDS:

Q Q **High Belltrees** *(NS377584)* PA12 4JN
(situated 1m off the A737 Glasgow to Largs road)
☎ 01505 842376 Mrs A Mackie
A narrow single track road leads from the south end of the Howwood bypass to this welcoming traditional farmhouse which overlooks surrounding countryside towards Castle Semple Loch. The good sized bedrooms are comfortably furnished and substantial breakfasts are served at shared tables in the cosy combined lounge/dining room. There is also a separate sun lounge overlooking the fields to the rear.
4 rms (2 fmly) No smoking in bedrooms No smoking in area of dining room CTV in all bedrooms Tea and coffee making facilities No dogs (ex guide dogs) Cen ht CTV 6P 220 acres dairy mixed sheep + poultry

Selected

Q Q Q Q ***Woodlands*** Newton-of-Barr PA12 4AP
(from airport follow signs for Lochwinnoch on A737. 'Woodlands' on left past Indoor Bowling Alley)
☎ 01505 843237 FAX 01505 843237
Woodlands, as the name suggests, is set within 16 acres of wooded grounds, where guests are invited to stroll. The two bedrooms, both on the ground floor, are very individual and offer all the expected facilities as well as a host of extras. There is also a sauna that guests can use. The brightly decorated breakfast room overlooks the garden, and there is a comfortable lounge with attractive leather sofas and chairs, books, magazines, and a TV and video.

2 shr (1 fmly) No smoking CTV in all bedrooms Tea and coffee making facilities No dogs Cen ht 8P No coaches Sauna Solarium Gymnasium Last d 8pm

LOCKERBIE Dumfries & Galloway Map **11** NY18

Q Q Q **Rosehill** Carlisle Rd DG11 2DR (south end of town)
☎ 01576 202378
A warm welcome to this splendid Victorian sandstone house is provided by proprietors Gwyneth and Ronnie Callander who have been greeting travellers for over 25 years. Bedrooms are generally spacious and offer modern facilities. The lounge and the dining room are very elegant and comfortable with deep sofas.
5 rms (2 shr) (2 fmly) CTV in all bedrooms Tea and coffee making facilities Cen ht CTV 5P No coaches
ROOMS: s £18-£20; d £32-£40*

LOSSIEMOUTH Moray Map **15** NJ27

Q Q Q **Carmania** 45 St Gerardines Rd IV31 6JX
(on entering town from Elgin A941, branch left uphill. House on left just over brow) ☎ 01343 812276
Closed Nov-Mar
Situated on the west side of town and occupying an elevated position, this smart detached bungalow offers a relaxed and friendly atmosphere. Both the carefully maintained and comfortable modern bedrooms are at ground level, and one room is now en suite. Hearty breakfasts are served at the communal table in the combined lounge/dining room.
2 bth/shr No smoking CTV in all bedrooms Tea and coffee making facilities No dogs (ex guide dogs) Cen ht CTV No children 12yrs 2P No coaches
ROOMS: s £19-£21; d £35-£38; wkly b&b fr £119

Q Q Q **Lossiemouth House** 33 Clifton Rd IV31 6DP
(entering town from Elgin on A941, house is on right before police station)
☎ 01343 813397
A welcoming atmosphere prevails at this 16th-century dower house which stands in its own walled garden close to the beach. The comfortable bedrooms are quite individual in style. There is a relaxing lounge with a wide range of tourist information including interesting tours compiled by the friendly owner. Breakfast is served in the separate dining room.
4 rms (2 shr) (2 fmly) No smoking in 2 bedrooms No smoking in dining room No smoking in lounges CTV in all bedrooms Tea and coffee making facilities Cen ht CTV 6P No coaches Last d noon
ROOMS: s £18-£20; d £30-£36; wkly b&b £110-£120*

MARKINCH Fife Map **11** NO20

Q Q Q **Town House Hotel** 1 High St KY7 6DQ
(opposite railway station in Markinch)
☎ 01592 758459 FAX 01592 755039
The welcoming atmosphere together with hearty wholesome fare are all part of the Town House's appeal, which is personally run by Harry and Lesley Bain. The four bedrooms are comfortably furnished in mixed modern styles and offer a good range of amenities. The attractive restaurant/bar has a convivial atmosphere and the menus offer excellent value for money. A range of private rooms are available for meetings and small dinner parties.
4 rms (3 bth/shr) (1 fmly) No smoking in area of dining room No smoking in 1 lounge CTV in all bedrooms Tea and coffee making facilities Cen ht No coaches Last d 9pm
ROOMS: s £25-£35; d £50-£60*
MEALS: Lunch £11.95-£14.95alc Dinner £12.95-£15.95alc*
CARDS:

MELROSE Scottish Borders Map **12** NT53

Q Q Q **Dunfermline House** Buccleuch St TD6 9LB
(opposite Abbey car park - Melrose is 2m from both A7 and A68)
☎ 01896 822148 FAX 01896 822148
Susan and Ian Graham's charming Victorian house sits in the centre of town close to the abbey. Bedrooms are attractive and some have pine furniture. Four have spacious en suites, whilst the single has sole use of a bathroom close by. Rooms at the front have glimpses of the Abbey, whilst those at the rear overlook the house's terraced gardens. There is a cosy little lounge and a cheery dining room where praiseworthy breakfasts are served.
5 shr No smoking CTV in all bedrooms Tea and coffee making facilities No dogs Cen ht CTV No coaches
ROOMS: s £24-£24; d £48-£48 *

MELVICH Highland Map **14** NC86

Selected

Q Q Q Q **Sheiling** KW14 7YS
(situated 18m W of Thurso, 1m left of A897 coastal junction)
☎ 01641 531256 FAX 531256
Mar-Oct
Occupying a lovely elevated position just east of the village and having unobstructed sea views, this small guest house is the home of Joan and Hugh Campbell. Guests have the use of two lounges, which abound in games and books, with a television and video in one. The elegant dining room with its attractive reproduction furniture and long, shared table is a delightful setting for Joan's extensive breakfast selection.
3 shr No smoking Tea and coffee making facilities No dogs (ex guide dogs) Cen ht CTV No children 5P Fishing
ROOMS: d £44-£48; wkly b&b fr £168*

Q Q Q **Tigh-na-Clash** Tigh-na-Clash KW14 7YJ
(on A836 Thurso/Tongue opposite the Halladale Inn)
☎ 01641 531262 FAX 01641 531262
Closed Nov-Jan
A comfortable detached modern house which stands in its own well tended garden at the eastern edge of the village. The bedrooms vary in size and offer both modern and traditional furnishings. There is a small guests' lounge and carefully prepared breakfasts are served at shared tables in the owner's personal lounge.
8 shr (1 fmly) No smoking in bedrooms No smoking in dining room CTV in all bedrooms Tea and coffee making facilities No dogs (ex guide dogs) Cen ht No children 8yrs 8P No coaches
ROOMS: s £21.50-£23; d £43-£46
CARDS:

MOFFAT Dumfries & Galloway Map **11** NT00

Q Q ***Barnhill Springs Country*** DG10 9QS
(0.5m E of A74 - access at Moffat junction) ☎ 01683 220580
This Victorian country house enjoys fine views of the Annan Valley. It is reached from the southbound carriageway of the A74 by taking the small unmarked road immediately after the junction for Moffat. Bedrooms are well proportioned and although none have en suite bathrooms, one room on the ground floor has the use of its own private shower room. Both the lounge and dining room are comfortable, and dinner is available by prior arrangement.
5 rms (1 shr) (1 fmly) No smoking in dining room Tea and coffee making facilities Licensed Cen ht CTV 10P No coaches Last d 9am

This symbol indicates a 'Child Friendly' establishment - see page 25 for details

Selected

Boleskine 4 Well Rd DG10 9AS
(leave M74 at junction for Moffat, in town cntre turn into Well Street and at end of street right into Well Road, Boleskine on right)
☎ 01683 220601
This Victorian house has been lovingly restored by friendly owners Andy and Sheila Armstrong, whose affection for their house is demonstrated by its period furnishings and all the extras they provide for their guests. Bedrooms are well equipped, two have sitting areas with comfortable chairs and a table. The dining room is cosy, and the breakfast menu offers a great selection - indeed, it is a great feature here.
4 rms (2 shr) No smoking CTV in all bedrooms Tea and coffee making facilities Cen ht No children 12YRS 2P No coaches
ROOMS: s £16-£18; d £32-£36; wkly b&b £96-£108

Selected

Gilbert House Beechgrove DG10 9RS
(from A74 go through town & turn right after school, for 3rd house on left) ☎ 01683 220050 FAX 01683 220050
Situated in a quiet road on the north side of the town, this large Victorian house is within walking distance of the town centre. Bedrooms are mostly well proportioned, beautifully decorated and furnished in a modern manner. Public rooms reflect the elegance of the house, with a stylish dining room where freshly prepared home-cooked meals are served. Mr and Mrs Poynton take great pride in their wine list.
6 rms (5 bth/shr) (2 fmly) No smoking Tea and coffee making facilities Licensed Cen ht CTV 6P No coaches Last d 4pm
CARDS:

Selected

Hartfell House Hartfell Crescent DG10 9AL
(exit A74 at A701 to town centre. At clock tower turn right up Well Street. Cross into Old Well Road. First right is Hartfell Crescent)
☎ 01683 220153
Apr-Oct rs Nov-Mar
Enjoying superb views across the surrounding countryside, this large Victorian house is set in a quiet location high above the town, yet within a five minute walk of the centre. Bedrooms are mostly spacious and offer a high degree of comfort and a host of thoughtful touches. There is a large residents' lounge on the first floor, while delicious home-cooked meals are served in the elegant dining room where guests are also offered a well chosen wine list.
8 rms (7 shr) (2 fmly) No smoking in dining room CTV in all bedrooms Tea and coffee making facilities Licensed Cen ht 8P No coaches Last d 6pm
ROOMS: s £23.50-£25; d £36-£45; wkly b&b £126-£157.50; wkly hlf-bd £197.40-£225.75*

St Olaf Eastgate, off Dickson St DG10 9AE
(turn off A74 2m to town centre. Turn right at War Memorial proceed up Well Street. Turn left at Semple & Ferguson. St Olaf 50yds along on left)
☎ 01683 220001
Apr-Oct
This well maintained guesthouse is quietly situated off the main high street and is reached by turning into Dickson Street (a narrow street) between the Balmoral Hotel and Moffat Weavers Tweed shop. Bedrooms include spacious family rooms and the two which are en suite are all freshly decorated and equipped with tea and coffee-making facilities, and radio-alarm clocks. There is a comfortable first floor lounge with TV and a good breakfast is served in the neatly furnished dining room on the ground floor. Hospitality provided is typically Scottish.
6 rms (2 shr) (1 fmly) No smoking in dining room No smoking in lounges Tea and coffee making facilities Cen ht CTV No children none 7P No coaches
ROOMS: s £18; d £33-£34; wkly b&b £115.50-£119*

MONTROSE Angus Map 15 NO75

Murray Lodge 2-8 Murray St DD10 8LB (on main A92 situated opposite swimming pool towards the north end of Montrose Town Centre)
☎ 01674 678880 FAX 01674 678877
Situated at the north end of town, this comfortable family run establishment has particular appeal to the visiting businessman. The smart modern bedrooms have been carefully designed to make best use of available space and offer a good range of amenities. Public areas include a popular all day coffee shop as well as a separate lounge for house guests. The latter is comfortable and boasts a dispense bar.
12 shr No smoking in 9 bedrooms No smoking in dining room CTV in all bedrooms Tea and coffee making facilities Direct dial from bedrooms No dogs (ex guide dogs) Licensed Cen ht CTV 2P No coaches
Last d 6.30pm
CARDS:

Oaklands 10 Rossie Island Rd DD10 9NN (on A92 - south end of town) ☎ 01674 672018 FAX 01674 672018
Elizabeth and Sandy Crowe look forward to welcoming guests to their comfortable detached guest house which stands beside the main southern approach road into town. The comfortable modern bedrooms are maintained to a high standard and offer a good range of amenities. Hearty breakfasts are served at shared tables in the attractive dining room. Vegetarian and special diets can be catered for.
7 shr (1 fmly) No smoking in dining room CTV in all bedrooms Tea and coffee making facilities Cen ht CTV ch fac 8P No coaches
CARDS:

MOUNT STUART See BUTE, ISLE OF

MUIR OF ORD Highland Map 14 NH55

Sealladh Coille Highfield IV6 7UL (1.5m NW on A832)
☎ 01463 871755
This modern house, opposite The Clash Wood and just one and a half miles north west of the village, is the home of Margo and Jim Anderson where vegans and vegetarians will be particularly welcome. The two bedrooms on the first floor are individually and comfortably furnished and share the spacious bathroom. Breakfast is served in the cosy Regency styled dining room overlooking the rear garden and guests may see Buzzards and Red Kites.
2 rms (1 fmly) No smoking CTV in all bedrooms Tea and coffee making facilities Cen ht 4P No coaches
ROOMS: s fr £18; d fr £32*

MULL, ISLE OF Argyll & Bute Map 10

DERVAIG Map 13 NM45

Q Q **Ardbeg House** PA75 6QJ
(Dervaig through village past pink house, large house on ring)
☎ 01688 400254 FAX 01688 400254
A large white country house standing in its own grounds. The owners have collected a range of Dickensian memorabilia that adds appeal to the house. Public areas include a choice of bars, a comfortable lounge and conservatory-style restaurant. Bedrooms, two with four-posters, vary in size and style
7 rms (5 bth/shr) (1 fmly) No smoking in 1 bedrooms No smoking in dining room Tea and coffee making facilities Licensed Cen ht 12P Fishing Last d 6pm
CARDS:

TOBERMORY Map 13 NM55

Premier Selected

Q Q Q Q Q **Fairways Lodge** PA75 6PS
(in Tobermory Follow signposts for golf course)
☎ 01688 302238 FAX 01688 302238
Derek and Kathy McAdam provide a high level of hospitality at their home, which overlooks the third and fourth fairways of the island's popular nine hole course. The house also offers stunning views of the Sound of Mull. The five attractive bedrooms with quality furnishings are all on the ground floor and four have the magnificent view, whilst the larger room, overlooks the newly landscaped garden. There is a small sun lounge leading off the bright breakfast room and guests are also invited to use the owners' first-floor sitting room. The McAdams can recommend suitable dining venues in the picturesque town.
5 bth/shr (1 fmly) No smoking in bedrooms No smoking in dining room CTV in all bedrooms Tea and coffee making facilities Cen ht CTV 8P No coaches Golf 9
ROOMS: s £28-£35; d £56-£72; wkly b&b £175-£217

NAIRN Highland Map 14 NH85

Q Q Q **Covenanters** High St, Auldearn IV12 5TG
(1m E of Nairn off the A96 in village of Auldearn)
☎ 01667 452456 FAX 01667 453583
This charming country inn is situated in the small village of Auldearn just east of Nairn. Enthusiastic owners Douglas and Louise Harrison have re-established the restaurant, which complements the large, oak beamed Kiln Bar where a good range of freshly prepared meals are served. The bedrooms have been extended, and all are situated on the ground floor with pleasant decor and furnishings.
14 bth/shr (5 fmly) No smoking in dining room No smoking in 1 lounge CTV in all bedrooms Tea and coffee making facilities Direct dial from bedrooms Cen ht 60P Last d 9pm
ROOMS: s £35-£50; d £45-£70*
MEALS: Lunch fr £8 Dinner fr £14.50*
CARDS:

Selected

Q Q Q Q **Greenlawns** 13 Seafield St IV12 4HG
(from A96 Inverness to Aberdeen Road, turn left into Albert Street just before traffic lights,turn 2nd left into Sleaford Street, Greenlawns on right ☎ 01667 452738 FAX 01667 452738
This comfortable Victorian house is owned and run with great enthusiasm by Dave and Sheelagh Southwell, who have made many improvements, including many personalised touches. The bright breakfast room has a host of reading and tourist related material and overlooks the well maintained garden. The comfortable lounge has a television and video as well as a small dispense bar. Bedrooms are well equipped and all have individual character.
8 rms (7 bth/shr) (2 fmly) No smoking in 2 bedrooms No smoking in dining room CTV in all bedrooms Tea and coffee making facilities Licensed Cen ht CTV 6P No coaches Last d 2pm
ROOMS: s £20-£50; d £32-£50*
CARDS:

Q Q Q **Lothian House Hotel** 10 Crescent Rd IV12 4NB (located just off A96 close to centre of town. Turn left before church onto Crescent Rd)
☎ 01667 453555 FAX 455454
Overlooking the Links and close to the town centre, this former doctor's house and surgery is now a private hotel personally run by Marilyn Newbould. Bedrooms vary in style and have all the expected facilities. A good range of dishes are available at dinner in the attractive dining room, which also has a small bar.
6 bth/shr (2 fmly) No smoking in 2 bedrooms No smoking in dining room CTV in all bedrooms Tea and coffee making facilities Licensed Cen ht CTV 9P Last d 8pm
ROOMS: s £28-£35; d £40-£60; wkly b&b £120-£200; wkly hlf-bd £190-£350*
CARDS:

NETHY BRIDGE Highland Map 14 NJ02

Selected

Q Q Q Q **Aultmore House** PH25 3ED (turn right 0.5m N of Nethybridge, off the B970 and then 1st left)
☎ 01479 821473 FAX 01479 821709
Etr-1 Nov rs 26 Dec-5 Jan
Built in 1914, this impressive manor house enjoys fine views of the Cairngorms from a setting in 25 acres of secluded, wooded and landscaped grounds about one mile northeast of the village (follow the signs for Abernethy Outdoor Centre). Spacious day rooms include a sun lounge overlooking the garden with its ornamental pond, a drawing

contd.

room with grand piano, a billiard room and a further quiet lounge on the first floor. Hearty home cooking is served at a communal table in the dining room. The atmosphere is that of a family country house rather than a hotel, making this a relaxing base from which to explore the Spey Valley.

Aultmore House

3 bth No smoking in bedrooms No smoking in dining room No smoking in 1 lounge Tea and coffee making facilities Cen ht CTV No children 12yrs 23P Fishing Snooker Croquet Last d 9pm
ROOMS: s £26; d £52-£60; wkly b&b £156-£180

NEWTON STEWART Dumfries & Galloway Map **10** NX46

Selected

Q Q Q Q **Oakbank** Corsbie Rd DG8 6JB (from A75 rdbt, turn left then right at square, pass church & bowling green then turn left up Corsbie Road, last house on right)
☎ 01671 402822 FAX 01671 403050
Mar-Nov
Built in 1870, this spacious Victorian house sits quietly within an acre of gardens, a few minutes walk from the town centre. Two of the comfortable bedrooms are en suite whilst the other enjoys exclusive use of its own bathroom across the landing. A hearty Scottish breakfast relies on regional delicacies including kippers and haggis whilst the accomplished dinner invariably centres around local fish or game. The dining room boasts a large polished table where all meals are taken. A beautifully decorated lounge is also available.
3 bth/shr No smoking CTV in all bedrooms Tea and coffee making facilities Cen ht CTV No children 2yrs 4P No coaches Croquet
ROOMS: s fr £20; d fr £38; wkly b&b fr £123*

NORTH BERWICK East Lothian Map **12** NT58

Q Q **Craigview** 5 Beach Rd EH39 4AB
(take A198 to North Berwick off A1. Overlooking the West Beach and putting green on Beach Road in centre of North Berwick)
☎ 01620 892257
A house with an interesting history, this 1920 building overlooks the West Beach, close to the putting green, harbour and town centre. Margaret Mitchell is a cheery and enthusiastic hostess and her healthy options and vegetarian breakfasts are popular. Do remember to give your order for the latter the night before.
3 rms (1 shr) No smoking CTV in all bedrooms Tea and coffee making facilities No dogs Cen ht No coaches
ROOMS: s £20-£30; d £32-£42*

Prices shown in the directory are meant as a guide only and are subject to change. Please check before you book

OBAN Argyll & Bute Map **10** NM83

Selected

Q Q Q Q **Ard Struan Guest House** Croft Rd PA34 5JN
(on coming down hill into Oban left into Croft Rd, Ard Struan on left at end of Croft Rd) ☎ 01631 563689
Christine McQuade looks forward to welcoming guests old and new to her immaculately maintained detached modern home, which is situated in a quiet residential area on the edge of town. The attractive bedrooms, one of which has a four-poster bed, are decorated to a high standard and comfortably furnished in the modern style. All the expected amenities plus some thoughtful extras are provided. There is an open-plan lounge/dining room where Christine's enjoyable home cooked fare is served at shared tables. French windows lead to the garden and patio, a very popular area with guests. Entering town from the A85, turn left at the Kings Knoll Hotel then sharp left at the next junction into Croft Road.
4 shr No smoking in dining room CTV in all bedrooms Tea and coffee making facilities CTV 5P Last d 10am

Q Q Q **Braeside** Kilmore PA34 4QR (travel S from Oban on A816 for 3m. On left on entering village of Kilmore) ☎ 01631 770243
Etr-Oct
Situated in lovely gardens and enjoying views towards Loch Feochan, John and Maureen Simons charming home offers bright and airy bedrooms, decorated in soft colours and furnished in mixed modern styles. Public areas include a combined lounge/dining room which also contains a dispense bar. Here guests can relax with an aperitif before sampling Maureen's home cooked fare which is carefully prepared from fresh local produce. Smoking is not permitted.
5 shr (1 fmly) No smoking CTV in all bedrooms Tea and coffee making facilities Direct dial from bedrooms No dogs Licensed Cen ht No children 10yrs 10P Last d 5pm
ROOMS: s £20-£35; d £40-£50; wkly b&b fr £140; wkly hlf-bd fr £225*

Selected

Q Q Q Q ***Briarbank*** Glencruitten Rd PA34 4DN ☎ 01631 566549
This detached house sits on a hillside site just a short walk from the town centre. Access is only by a steep flight of external steps from the street car park and the house would appeal best to the young and fit. A lot of care has been put into the bold decor of the bedrooms and lounge, all of which reflect a historical and Scottish Clan theme with the appropriate artefacts. Guests can choose from an extensive dinner menu earlier in the day and for breakfast there is a very hearty "Lairds" option which includes a wee dram.
3 shr No smoking CTV in all bedrooms Tea and coffee making facilities No dogs (ex guide dogs) Cen ht CTV No children 12yrs 3P No coaches Last d 4pm

Selected

QQQQ **Glenbervie House** Dalriach Rd PA34 5NL
☎ 01631 564770 FAX 01631 566723
Joan and Iain Auld welcome guests to their comfortable home, a sturdy Victorian house close to the swimming pool. The variable-sized bedrooms are decorated and furnished in both modern and traditional styles, and offer all the expected amenities. Joan serves hearty breakfasts and enjoyable home cooked evening meals in the lively dining room.
8 rms (5 shr) (2 fmly) No smoking in dining room CTV in all bedrooms Tea and coffee making facilities No dogs (ex guide dogs) Licensed Cen ht CTV 8P No coaches Last d 4pm
ROOMS: s £20-£25; d £40-£50*

Selected

QQQQ **Glenburnie Private Hotel** The Esplanade PA34 5AQ
(directly on Oban seafront, follow signs for Ganavan)
☎ 01631 562089 FAX 562089
Apr-Oct
Situated on the sea front with beautiful views over the bay to the Isle of Mull beyond, this splendid Victorian house has been lovingly restored by the dedicated owners. Bedrooms include a superior four-poster room and mini suite, while others are generously proportioned. Designer soft furnishings together with extra large beds combine to create an atmosphere of luxury. There is also an inviting small sitting room while freshly prepared breakfasts are served in the dining room.
14 shr No smoking CTV in all bedrooms Tea and coffee making facilities No dogs (ex guide dogs) Cen ht No children 12yrs 12P No coaches
ROOMS: s £25-£35; d £50-£70; wkly b&b £160-£230
CARDS:

QQ **Glenroy** Rockfield Rd PA34 5DQ (at the S end of Gorge Stret, turn into Stevenson Street, keep left of Rockfield School, go behind school onto Rockfield Road) ☎ 01631 562585
Local owners Mr and Mrs Boyd extend a warm Highland welcome at their comfortable semi-detached Victorian home, which stands on the hill above the town. Offering good value tourist accommodation, the variable sized bedrooms are bright and comfortable with mixed modern appointments. Views over the bay are enjoyed from some bedrooms and the first-floor lounge with freshly prepared breakfasts being served at individual tables in the dining room.
7 rms (5 shr) No smoking in dining room No smoking in lounges CTV in all bedrooms Tea and coffee making facilities No dogs (ex guide dogs) Cen ht CTV 7P No coaches
ROOMS: s £18-£19; d £38-£40*
CARDS:

QQQ **High Cliff** Glencruitten Rd PA34 4EW
(from town square take A83 for Campbeltown at the Parish Church and bear left signposted Glencruitten/Rare Breeds Park. Granite house on right)
☎ 01631 565809
This detached Victorian villa is personally run by Maureen Robertson who has recently completed a total refurbishment of the accommodation. High Cliff is quietly located in a residential area just a few minutes walk from the town centre and close to the golf course.
3 rms (2 bth/shr) (1 fmly) No smoking in bedrooms No smoking in dining room CTV in all bedrooms Tea and coffee making facilities No dogs (ex guide dogs) Cen ht CTV 6P No coaches Last d 6pm
ROOMS: d £36-£44; wkly b&b £110-£135; wkly hlf-bd £170-£195*

Selected

QQQQ **Old Manse** Dalriach Rd PA34 5JE
(from A85 follow signs for swimming pool & bowling green)
☎ 01631 564886
Closed Dec-Feb
Anna and Walter Johnston have created a charming atmosphere at this substantial house that occupies an elevated position within it own attractive garden and provides lovely views of the bay from its front rooms. The bedrooms all provide the expected facilities along with some interesting personal touches. The decor throughout is very fresh, in particular the lime/yellow scheme in the breakfast room. The blue lounge is comfortable and homely with a good range of audio/video equipment.
4 shr (1 fmly) No smoking in bedrooms No smoking in dining room No smoking in 1 lounge CTV in all bedrooms Tea and coffee making facilities Cen ht CTV 5P No coaches
ROOMS: d £40-£50; wkly b&b £126-£157.50
CARDS:

Selected

Q Q Q Q **Rhumor** Drummore Rd PA34 4JL (Enter town from A85 to town centre, down George St to roundabout. Left A816 100yrds after BP left into Drummore Rd.) ☎ 01631 563544 FAX 01631 563544
Closed Dec
Visitors are warmly welcomed to Ann Edwards' comfortable detached bungalow which is situated in a cul-de-sac off the A816 at the south end of town. Bedrooms, with tasteful décor and attractive co-ordinated fabrics, are comfortably furnished in the modern style and offer all the expected amenities. There is also a comfortable lounge and separate dining room where carefully prepared breakfasts are served around the communal table.
3 bth/shr (1 fmly) No smoking CTV in all bedrooms Tea and coffee making facilities Cen ht CTV 4P
ROOMS: d £36-£40*

Q Q Q **Roseneath** Dalriach Rd PA34 5EQ
(turn left off A85 beyond Kings Knoll Hotel and follow signs for swimming pool, pass pool and go straight on for 300metres) ☎ 01631 562929
Feb-Oct
This comfortable terraced Victorian house stands on the hill above town and combines a welcoming atmosphere with good value accommodation. Smartly decorated bedrooms have been designed to make best use of available space and offer mixed modern appointments. The relaxing first-floor lounge enjoys views of the bay and is well stocked with books and useful tourist information. This is a no-smoking establishment.
8 bth/shr No smoking CTV in all bedrooms Tea and coffee making facilities No dogs (ex guide dogs) Cen ht No children 8P No coaches
ROOMS: d £40-£50*

Q Q Q **Sgeir Mhaol** Soroba Rd PA34 4JF
(on A816 - opposite Oban High School)
☎ 01631 562650 FAX 01631 562650
A friendly welcome is assured at this comfortable detached bungalow on the south side of town. The redecorated and well maintained bedrooms are designed to make the best use of available space and offer the expected amenities. There is also a comfortable lounge where guests can relax and a separate dining room where breakfast, and by arrangement, evening meals are served at individual tables.
7 rms (5 shr) (1 fmly) No smoking in dining room CTV in all bedrooms Tea and coffee making facilities No dogs (ex guide dogs) Cen ht CTV 10P No coaches Last d 4pm
ROOMS: s £18-£26; d £36-£42

Q Q Q ***Thornloe*** Albert Rd PA34 5JD
(from A85, turn left at King's Knoll Hotel and pass swimming pool, last house on right hand side) ☎ 01631 562879
Closed Nov
Situated on the hill above the town, enjoying views over the bay, Thornloe is a substantial Victorian house with a welcoming atmosphere. Bedrooms, two of which have four-poster beds, are comfortably appointed, though they do vary in size. There is a cosy lounge and attractive dining room where well prepared breakfasts are served, though at peak times, it may be necessary to share a table.
8 shr (2 fmly) No smoking in 4 bedrooms No smoking in dining room No smoking in lounges CTV in all bedrooms Tea and coffee making facilities No dogs (ex guide dogs) Cen ht CTV 5P

Q Q Q **Wellpark Hotel** Esplanade PA34 5AQ
(A55 to sea front of Oban, turn right 200 yards to Wellpark Hotel)
☎ 01631 562948 FAX 01631 565808
Closed Nov-end May rs Etr
From its position on the Esplanade this semi-detached Victorian house enjoys fine views over the bay and offers good value accommodation. Bedrooms are variable in size and offer mixed modern furnishings together with a good range of amenities. Lovely views of the bay can be enjoyed from the first floor lounge and there is a separate breakfast room.
17 shr No smoking in 8 bedrooms No smoking in dining room No smoking in lounges CTV in all bedrooms Tea and coffee making facilities Direct dial from bedrooms Cen ht 16P No coaches
ROOMS: s £26-£37; d £52-£62; wkly b&b £132.30-£195.30*
CARDS:

ORKNEY Map 16

KIRKWALL Map 16 HY41

Q Q Q ***Sanderlay*** 2 Viewfield Dr KW15 1RB ☎ 01856 872343
FAX 01856 876350
This modern house occupies a corner site in a quiet residential area about a mile south east of the town centre. The bedrooms are all attractively decorated and well equipped, with three large family rooms on the first floor having the advantage of small kitchen units. Breakfast is served in a spacious room that also provides some comfortable seating.
6 rms (4 shr) (2 fmly) No smoking in 3 bedrooms No smoking in dining room No smoking in lounges CTV in all bedrooms Tea and coffee making facilities No dogs (ex guide dogs) Cen ht 5P
CARDS:

PAISLEY Renfrewshore Map 11 NS46

See **Glasgow Airport**

PEEBLES Scottish Borders Map 11 NT24

Selected

Q Q Q Q **Venlaw Farm** *(NT254416)* EH45 8QG (turn off A703 opposite David Harrisons Garage) ☎ 01721 722040 Mrs S Goldstraw
Apr-Oct
Reached by a single track off the Edinburgh road, this modern farm bungalow enjoys an attractive setting on a hillside amidst peaceful and secluded farmland. There is a large double and a smaller double both with smart en suites, whilst the twin has use of its own private bathroom with bath and separate shower. The well proportioned lounge is comfortable and inviting and has French windows looking out onto the gardens, whilst breakfast is taken round the one table in the traditional dining room.
3 rms (2 bth/shr) (1 fmly) No smoking CTV in all bedrooms Tea and coffee making facilities No dogs Cen ht CTV 7P
100 acres beef sheep
ROOMS: s £20-£25; d £36-£40; wkly b&b £70-£140

Q Q **Whitestone House** Innerleithen Rd EH45 8BD
(on A72, 100yds E of junct with A703) ☎ 01721 720337
This former manse lies in its own gardens on the eastern approach to the town and enjoys fine views across the local park to distant hills. Carefully maintained and traditionally furnished throughout it offers well proportioned bedrooms and a combined lounge and dining room where breakfast is taken.

3 rms (1 fmly) No smoking in dining room Tea and coffee making facilities No dogs (ex guide dogs) Cen ht CTV 5P No coaches
ROOMS: d £33*

Q Q Q **Winkston** *(NT244433)* Edinburgh Rd EH45 8PH
(1.5m from Peebles on the A703 on the right)
☎ 01721 721264 Mrs J M Haydock
Etr-Oct
This fine Georgian farm house lies in attractive gardens off the Edinburgh road. Bedrooms are bright and cheery, the family room having an en suite shower room whilst the other two share a shower room. Downstairs there is comfortable lounge with a log fire on colder days where an evening cup of tea is served at 9.30pm and also a separate dining room. Guests can buy home-made preserves and baking.
3 rms (1 shr) No smoking Tea and coffee making facilities No dogs (ex guide dogs) Cen ht CTV 4P 40 acres sheep
ROOMS: d £34-£38*

PENPONT Dumfries & Galloway Map 11 NX89

Q Q **The Volunteer Arms** Main St DG3 4BP
(2m W of Thornhill on the A702, inn is on the north west side of the main street crossroads through Penpont) ☎ 01848 330381
Recognised by its salmon pink facade and colourful plants and window boxes in summer, this friendly village inn provides a cosy bar and a pretty little wood panelled dining room where breakfasts are served. Bedrooms are modestly furnished, but two have modern shower rooms.
4 rms (2 shr) No smoking in bedrooms No smoking in dining room CTV in all bedrooms Tea and coffee making facilities No dogs (ex guide dogs) Cen ht 4P Last d 8.30pm
ROOMS: s £22.50-£25; d £35-£40; wkly b&b £157.50-£175
MEALS: Bar Lunch £4.50-£12.50alc

PERTH Perth & Kinross Map 11 NO12

Q Q Q **Adam** 6 Pitcullen Crescent PH2 7HT
(from town centre, over bridge onto A94 Coupar/Angus road, after a few minutes drive guesthouse is on left)
☎ 01738 627179
The Wilson family extend a warm welcome to all visitors at their comfortable home which is situated beside the Coupar Angus Road. The spacious bedrooms offer mixed modern furnishings, and public areas include a relaxing sitting room and a smart redecorated dining room where, by prior arrangement, enjoyable home cooked evening meals are served.
4 shr (1 fmly) No smoking in 2 bedrooms No smoking in dining room CTV in all bedrooms Tea and coffee making facilities Cen ht 6P Last d mid-day
ROOMS: s £22-£25; d £38-£42; wkly b&b £120-£140; wkly hlf-bd £190-£210*
CARDS:

Q Q Q **Anglers Inn** Main Rd, Guildtown PH2 6BS
(4.5m N of Perth on A93) ☎ 01821 640329 FAX 01821 640329
The Brodie family look forward to welcoming you to their comfortable village inn which combines excellent value for money with a friendly atmosphere. Though not large, the brightly decorated bedrooms are enhanced with pretty co-ordinated fabrics and comfortable pine furnishings.
4 bth/shr (1 fmly) CTV in all bedrooms Tea and coffee making facilities Licensed Cen ht 30P Last d 9pm
ROOMS: s £25-£28.50; d £44-£49*
CARDS:

The AA's professional Inspectors make regular and anonymous visits to all the establishments listed in the Guide. They accept no gifts or favours from proprietors

Selected

Q Q Q Q **Ardfern House** 15 Pitcullen Crescent PH2 7HT (situated on the A94 Perth-Forfar Road, 0.25m from Old Perth Bridge) ☎ 01738 637031
Situated on the north side of Perth, this terraced house is convenient for touring the local area, and for the town centre. Mrs Murray offers a delightfully warm welcome to her guests, and is also steadily improving the accommodation. Breakfast, which is selected in the evening, is well cooked, and fresh juice is a real bonus.
3 rms (2 shr) (1 fmly) No smoking CTV in all bedrooms Tea and coffee making facilities No dogs (ex guide dogs) Cen ht CTV 3P No coaches Last d 4pm
ROOMS: s £20-£30; d £36-£42; wkly b&b £112-£126; wkly hlf-bd £182-£196*

Q Q Q ***The Bridgehouse*** 86 Main St, Methven PH1 3PS
(take A85 Perth/Crieff road, village approx 5m from Perth, the Bridgehouse is opposite post office) ☎ 01738 840006
Colourful flowering baskets adorn the front of Elaine Whitehead's comfortable home which is situated at the west end of the village of Methven. The attractively decorated bedrooms are comfortably furnished in mixed modern styles. Hearty breakfasts and, by prior arrangement, home cooked evening meals are served at individual tables in the open plan lounge/dining room. Children are especially welcome at The Bridgehouse.
3 rms (1 shr) (1 fmly) No smoking in bedrooms No smoking in dining room CTV in all bedrooms Tea and coffee making facilities No dogs (ex guide dogs) Cen ht CTV ch fac No coaches Last d 7.30pm
CARDS:

Q Q Q **Castleview** 166 Glasgow Rd PH2 0LY ☎ 01738 626415
Closed 25th Dec-Feb
The Dawson family welcome guests to their comfortable home, a detached Victorian villa set in its own well tended garden beside the Glasgow Road on the south side. The en suite bedrooms are well maintained and offer mixed modern appointments. Hearty breakfasts and, by prior arrangement, evening meals are served at the communal table in the attractive dining room.
3 bth/shr (1 fmly) No smoking in 2 bedrooms No smoking in dining room No smoking in lounges CTV in all bedrooms Tea and coffee making facilities No dogs (ex guide dogs) Cen ht 6P No coaches Last d 5pm
ROOMS: s £24-£30; d £40-£42*
CARDS:

Q Q Q **Clark Kimberley** 57-59 Dunkeld Rd PH1 5RP (0.5m N on A912) ☎ 01738 637406 FAX 01738 643983
The Sayers take great delight in welcoming guests to their comfortable home, situated on the west side of town. All bedrooms are tastefully decorated and guests have the use of a spacious lounge. Hearty breakfasts are a speciality of the house.
7 rms (6 shr) (3 fmly) No smoking CTV in all bedrooms Tea and coffee making facilities No dogs Cen ht CTV 10P No coaches
ROOMS: s £22-£28; d £40-£46
CARDS:

Q Q Q Clunie 12 Pitcullen Crescent PH2 7HT
(on A94 opposite side of river from town) ☎ 01738 623625 FAX 623625
Situated on the north side of town, this family run guest house has a welcoming atmosphere. The well maintained bedrooms are bright and airy and offer mixed modern appointments. Public areas include a relaxing lounge and separate dining room where home cooked fare is offered at both breakfast and in the evening.
7 bth/shr (3 fmly) No smoking in dining room CTV in all bedrooms Tea and coffee making facilities Cen ht CTV 8P No coaches Last d noon
ROOMS: s £16-£25; d £32-£40; wkly b&b £116-£140; wkly hlf-bd £189-£203*
CARDS:

Q Q Q ***The Gables*** 24 Dunkeld Rd PH1 5RW
(take A912 towards Perth. Guesthouse approx 1.5m on right just beyond 4th rdbt) ☎ 01738 624717 FAX 01738 624717
Ongoing improvements continue at this welcoming family run guest house which stands beside the Dunkeld Road on the west side of the city. Several of the non smoking bedrooms have been completely refurbished and others are gradually being enhanced. Smoking is permitted only in the relaxing lounge while hearty breakfasts and evening meals are offered in the upgraded dining room.
8 rms (4 bth/shr) (2 fmly) No smoking in bedrooms No smoking in dining room CTV in all bedrooms Tea and coffee making facilities Licensed Cen ht CTV 7P No coaches Last d midday
CARDS:

Selected

Q Q Q Q Kinnaird 5 Marshall Place PH2 8AH ☎ 01738 628021 FAX 01738 444056
Closed Xmas & New Year
This welcoming guest house forms part of a Georgian terrace and looks out over South Inch park. The cosy bedrooms are tastefully decorated and feature attractive co-ordinated fabrics with comfortable pine furniture. The first floor lounge is a peaceful retreat and the dining room offers a varied well cooked breakfast at separate tables.
7 bth/shr No smoking CTV in all bedrooms Tea and coffee making facilities No dogs Cen ht No children 12yrs 7P No coaches Last d 4pm
ROOMS: s fr £28; d fr £45*
CARDS:

Selected

Q Q Q Q Park Lane Guest House 17 Marshall Place PH2 8AG
(from M90 enter town on A912 and turn left at first set of lights. Park Lane on right hand side opposite park)
☎ 01738 637218 FAX 01738 643519
Closed 7 Dec-20 Jan
This imposing Georgian terrace house, close to town, overlooks a spacious park which complements the lovely floral display that Mrs

Davison has created at the front and back of this well-proportioned, immaculately kept house. All bedrooms are individually styled, well equipped and comfortable. Breakfast is served in the attractive period-style lounge-dining room and the fresh fruit salads are a feature.
6 bth/shr (1 fmly) No smoking in 3 bedrooms No smoking in dining room No smoking in lounges CTV in all bedrooms Tea and coffee making facilities No dogs (ex guide dogs) Cen ht CTV 8P
ROOMS: s £24-£30; d £46-£50; wkly b&b £161-£175*
CARDS:

Q Q Q Pitcullen 17 Pitcullen Crescent PH2 7HT (on A94)
☎ 01738 626506 FAX 01738 628265
Situated on the northern edge of town, this family run guest house offers a welcoming atmosphere together with good value accommodation. Bedrooms, though variable in size, are tastefully decorated and furnishings are steadily being upgraded. There is an inviting and comfortable lounge on the first floor, and freshly prepared breakfasts are served in the attractive dining room.
6 rms (5 shr) (1 fmly) No smoking in 2 bedrooms No smoking in dining room CTV in all bedrooms Tea and coffee making facilities No dogs (ex guide dogs) Cen ht 6P No coaches
ROOMS: s £26-£32; d £44-£50
CARDS:

PITLOCHRY Perth & Kinross Map 14 NN95

Q Q Q ***Arrandale House*** Knockfarrie Rd PH16 5DN ☎ 01796 472987 FAX 472987
Nov-Mar
Enthusiastic owners Atholl and Pat Irvine are constantly improving standards at their delightful detached Victorian villa which enjoys views of the Tummel Valley. All the comfortable bedrooms are decorated to a high standard and pretty fabrics complement smart traditional furnishings.
7 rms (5 shr) (2 fmly) No smoking CTV in all bedrooms Tea and coffee making facilities No dogs Cen ht 9P No coaches

Selected

Q Q Q Q Comar House Strathview Ter PH16 5AT (turn off A9 to Pitlochry, last street on right going north signed to Golf Course, right at top of hill second house on left) ☎ 01796 473531 FAX 01796 473811
Etr-Oct
From its elevated position above the town this substantial detached house, set in its own landscaped grounds, enjoys lovely views over the town to the hills beyond. Bedrooms are mostly spacious with attractive decor and comfortable furnishings while public areas include an inviting lounge and attractive dining room. Throughout, the atmosphere is relaxed and warmly welcoming. A non smoking establishment.
6 rms (4 bth/shr) No smoking CTV in all bedrooms Tea and coffee making facilities Cen ht CTV 6P
ROOMS: s £18-£25; d £40-£48*
CARDS:

Selected

Q Q Q Q **Craigroyston House** 2 Lower Oakfield PH16 5HQ
(in town centre just above Information Centre car park)
☎ 01796 472053 FAX 01796 472053
Douglas and Gretta Maxwell look forward to welcoming you to their charming Victorian home which is conveniently positioned close to central amenities. The tastefully decorated bedrooms are comfortably furnished in period style and all rooms enjoy lovely views over the town to the hills beyond. Public areas include an inviting sitting room where a log fire burns on cooler evenings, and freshly prepared breakfasts are served in the attractive dining room.
8 bth/shr (1 fmly) No smoking in bedrooms No smoking in dining room CTV in all bedrooms Tea and coffee making facilities No dogs (ex guide dogs) Cen ht 9P No coaches
ROOMS: d £40-£56; wkly b&b £140-£196*

Selected

Q Q Q Q **Dundarave House** Strathview Ter PH16 5AT
(from Pitlochry main street turn into West Moulin Rd second left into Strathview Terrace) ☎ 01796 473109 FAX 01796 473109
Mar-Nov
A warm personal welcome is assured at this substantial detached Victorian house which stands in formal gardens above the town and is efficiently run by Bob and Mae Collier. The well maintained bedrooms are bright and airy, with mixed furnishings. There is also a cosy and inviting lounge, and an attractive dining room where freshly prepared breakfasts and, by prior arrangement, enjoyable home cooked evening meals are served.
7 rms (5 bth/shr) (1 fmly) No smoking in dining room CTV in all bedrooms Tea and coffee making facilities Cen ht 8P No coaches Last d 5pm
ROOMS: s £24-£28; d £48-£56; wkly b&b £168-£196; wkly hlf-bd £270-£300*

Selected

Torrdarach Hotel Golf Course Rd PH16 5AU (turn off Athol Road to Golf Course, Torrdarach is last hotel before Golf Course (Red House)) ☎ 01796 472136
Closed Mid Oct-Easter
Richard and Vivienne Cale's substantial detached Victorian home is peacefully set in wooded grounds close to the golf course and enjoys views over the Tummel Valley. Attractive fabrics have been used to good effect in the comfortable bedrooms most of which are furnished in pine. The spacious lounge invites peaceful relaxation while enjoyable home cooked fare is offered in the smart dining room. This is a non smoking establishment.
7 shr No smoking CTV in all bedrooms Tea and coffee making facilities No dogs (ex guide dogs) Licensed Cen ht No children 12yrs 8P No coaches
ROOMS: s £25-£30; d £40-£52; wkly b&b £140-£175*

Well House Private Hotel 11 Toberargan Rd PH16 5HG (Well House Hotel is close to the town centre on a road running parallel to the main street) ☎ 01796 472239
Closed mid Nov - early Mar
A warm welcome is assured at this friendly family run private hotel which is located in a residential area close to central amenities. Colourful flowering baskets and tubs enhance the exterior and good parking is available. Public areas include an inviting lounge where refreshments are served and enjoyable home cooked fare is the order of the day in the attractive dining room.
6 shr (1 fmly) No smoking in bedrooms No smoking in dining room CTV in all bedrooms Tea and coffee making facilities No dogs (ex guide dogs) Licensed Cen ht 6P No coaches Last d 5.30pm
CARDS:

PORTNANCON Highland Map 14 NC46

Port-Na-Con House Loch Eribol, by Sutherland IV27 4UN (0.25m off A838, on shore of loch, 6 miles SE of Durness)
☎ 01971 511367 FAX 01971 511367
Mar-Oct rs Nov-Feb
A comfortable house, peacefully set beside the picturesque shore of Loch Eriboll. The well maintained bedrooms are smartly presented with modern appointments and enjoy views over the loch. Views of Ben Loyal and Ben Hope can be enjoyed from the small first floor lounge where you will find well stocked bookshelves. Local crafts are displayed in the attractive dining room where the emphasis is on local seafood which can, on request, include lobster.
3 bth/shr (1 fmly) No smoking Tea and coffee making facilities Licensed Cen ht 6P No coaches Air available for divers Last d 5pm
ROOMS: d £36-£40; wkly b&b £114-£126; wkly hlf-bd £189-£202*
CARDS:

PORTPATRICK Dumfries & Galloway Map 10 NX05

Blinkbonnie School Brae DG9 8LG ☎ 01776 810282
Closed Dec
This detached villa stands in pretty, well kept gardens in an elevated position overlooking the town and harbour. It is extremely well maintained and has a welcoming atmosphere. Accommodation is all on the ground floor and thoughtfully equipped. Fine views can be had from the delightful lounge and cosy dining room.
6 rms (4 shr) No smoking CTV in all bedrooms Tea and coffee making facilities No dogs Cen ht CTV 10P No coaches Last d 6.30pm
ROOMS: s £19-£22; d £36-£38 *

PORTREE See SKYE, ISLE OF

PRESTWICK South Ayrshire Map 10 NS32

Selected

Fairways Hotel 19 Links Rd KA9 1QG (turn west off A79 at Prestwick Cross, after 800yds, the hotel is on the left overlooking Prestwick Golf Course) ☎ 01292 470396 FAX 01292 470396
This attractive semi-detached Victorian house is opposite the entrance to the golf club, as well as being convenient for the seafront and the station. The modern, comfortable bedrooms are brightly decorated and have all the expected facilities with several thoughtful extras. The first-floor lounge enjoys lovely views over the golf course, as does the spacious ground floor breakfast room which offers individual tables and freshly cooked breakfast.
5 bth/shr No smoking in bedrooms No smoking in dining room CTV in all bedrooms Tea and coffee making facilities No dogs (ex guide dogs) Licensed Cen ht CTV 8P No coaches
ROOMS: s fr £27; d fr £50; wkly b&b £150-£162*
CARDS:

Fernbank 213 Main St KA9 1LH (travelling into Prestwick from airport, house lies on left beyond St Nicholas church (large tower) at 4th set of traffic lights) ☎ 01292 475027 FAX 01292 475027
This well maintained house is situated close to the town centre and the airport. The bed and breakfast operation is as strong as ever, but there is no longer a separate guest lounge. Bedrooms offer the expected facilities, most with timber effect decor and double glazing. The breakfast room with its pine tables and individual lights is most attractive.
7 rms (4 shr) (1 fmly) No smoking CTV in all bedrooms Tea and coffee making facilities No dogs (ex guide dogs) Cen ht No children 2yrs 8P
ROOMS: s £15.50-£18; d £36-£40; wkly b&b £100-£130

Selected

Golf View Hotel 17 Links Rd KA9 1QG (take A77 to Prestwick Airport, turn at Prestwick Cross, opposite Prestwick Golf Course) ☎ 01292 671234 FAX 01292 671244
The Golf View is aptly named, situated as it is overlooking Old Prestwick Golf Club where the very first 'Open' Championship was played in 1860. It is only 200 yards from the beach and Esplanade, with fine views over The Firth of Clyde to the Isle of Arran. Hostess Christine Heslop provides friendly hospitality and the modern bedrooms are thoughtfully equipped. There is a comfortable lounge upstairs where drinks can be dispensed, whilst breakfasts are served at immaculately set tables in the attractive dining room.
6 bth/shr (1 fmly) No smoking in bedrooms No smoking in dining room CTV in all bedrooms Tea and coffee making facilities Licensed Cen ht CTV 10P
ROOMS: s fr £27; d fr £54; wkly b&b fr £175
CARDS:

Kincraig Private Hotel 39 Ayr Rd KA9 1SY (follow A77 onto A79 and continue for 1m past Prestwick Airport)
☎ 01292 479480 FAX 01292 479480
Lying midway between Prestwick and Ayr, this substantial red sandstone house offers a variety of bedrooms styles, all being well equipped. A small bungalow at the rear provides an apartment of two single rooms, ideal for two golfers sharing.
6 rms (5 bth/shr) 2 annexe shr (1 fmly) No smoking in dining room CTV in all bedrooms Tea and coffee making facilities No dogs (ex guide dogs) Licensed Cen ht CTV 7P No coaches Last d prior arrangement
ROOMS: s £20-£30; d £40-£50*
CARDS:

ROSLIN Midlothian Map 11 NT26

Q Q Q ***Olde Original Rosslyn*** 4 Main St EH25 9LD
☎ 0131 440 2384 FAX 0131 4402514
This welcoming family run inn is situated at the south end of the village main street and offers a choice of contrasting well-stocked bars. There is also an attractive Victorian restaurant which offers a range of prime Scottish steaks as well as other tempting dishes. Bedrooms, four of which have four-poster beds, have benefited from refurbishment and are equipped with all the expected amenities.
6 bth/shr CTV in all bedrooms Tea and coffee making facilities Cen ht 14P Last d 10pm
CARDS:

ST ANDREWS Fife Map 12 NO51

See also Leuchars

Q Q Q **Amberside** 4 Murray Pk KY16 9AW
(On entering St Andrews you pass Golf courses on the left at the 117 roundabout go straight & 50m past the next roundabout turn left towards the R&A) ☎ 01334 474644 FAX 01334 850640
This comfortable family run guest house forms part of a terraced row and is situated in a residential area close to the sea front. The enthusiastic owner Mr Wood is making good progress with his improvement programme and the comfortable bedrooms are looking very fresh and inviting. A good choice breakfast menu is offered in the combined lounge/dining room.
6 rms (5 shr) (2 fmly) No smoking CTV in all bedrooms Tea and coffee making facilities No dogs (ex guide dogs) Cen ht CTV
ROOMS: s £22-£29; d £44-£58; wkly b&b fr £150*
CARDS:

Q Q Q **Annandale** 23 Murray Park KA16 9AW ☎ 01334 475310
FAX 01334 475310
Florence McAndie looks forward to welcoming you to her comfortable and well maintained home which stands in a residential area close to the sea front and central amenities. The tastefully decorated bedrooms offer mixed modern furnishings. Public areas include a combined lounge/dining room where freshly prepared breakfasts are served. At peak times it may be necessary to share tables. This is a non smoking establishment.
5 shr (3 fmly) No smoking CTV in all bedrooms Tea and coffee making facilities Cen ht No children 2yrs
ROOMS: d £38-£56*

Q Q Q **Arran House** 5 Murray Park KY16 9AW ☎ 01334 474724
FAX 01334 474724
A warm welcome is assured at this comfortable family run guest house which forms part of a terraced row close to the town centre. The attractively decorated bedrooms are variable in size and offer mixed modern appointments. Freshly prepared breakfasts are served at individual tables in the smart first floor dining room.
5 rms (3 shr) (2 fmly) No smoking CTV in all bedrooms Tea and coffee making facilities No dogs Cen ht CTV
ROOMS: s £19-£40; d £38-£54; wkly b&b £133-£189*
CARDS:

Q Q ***Beachway House*** 6 Murray Park KY16 9AW ☎ 01334 473319
Closed Jan
Forming part of a terraced row, convenient to the seafront and central amenities, this personally run guest house offers good value for money. Bedrooms are brightly decorated and offer mixed styles of furnishings while hearty breakfasts are served in the combined lounge/dining room.
6 rms (5 shr) (2 fmly) CTV in all bedrooms Tea and coffee making facilities Cen ht

Selected

Q Q Q Q **Bell Craig** 8 Murray Park KY16 9AW ☎ 01334 472962
FAX 01334 472962
A family-run guest house which enjoys a prime location, positioned very near the sea front, golf course and all the local amenities. Though varying in size, the bedrooms have been smartly decorated and offer a host of accessories and comfortable pine furnishings. Delicious breakfasts are served at individual tables in the elegant combined dining room and lounge.
5 shr (3 fmly) No smoking in 3 bedrooms No smoking in dining room CTV in all bedrooms Tea and coffee making facilities No dogs Cen ht CTV No coaches
ROOMS: s £30-£50; d £36-£50*
CARDS:

Q Q Q ***Burness House*** Murray Park KY16 9AW ☎ 01334 474314
FAX 01334 474314
Many guests return time and time again to Heather McQueen's welcoming terraced home which is situated within easy reach of both central amenities and the sea front. Heather is a genial host and personal attention is assured. Though some of the well decorated bedrooms are small, all are en suite and offer the expected amenities. The attractive combined lounge/dining room is spacious and offers a selection of books and videos, and the freshly prepared breakfasts provide a good start to the day.
6 shr (2 fmly) No smoking in 3 bedrooms No smoking in dining room No smoking in lounges CTV in all bedrooms Tea and coffee making facilities No dogs (ex guide dogs) Cen ht CTV No coaches

Q Q ***Cleveden House*** 3 Murray Place KY16 9AP
(coming into St.Andrews on A91 go straight on at 2 rdbts into North Street. Turn left into Murray Place after traffic lights)
☎ 01334 474212 FAX 01344 474212
Good value bed and breakfast accommodation is offered at this friendly family run establishment, part of a terraced row which is convenient to central amenities and the sea front. Bedrooms are well maintained and offer mixed modern furnishings. There is a comfortable lounge on the first floor with beverage making facilities and a good range of books and magazines, while breakfast is served at shared tables in the cosy dining room.
6 rms (4 shr) (1 fmly) No smoking in bedrooms No smoking in dining room CTV in all bedrooms Tea and coffee making facilities No dogs (ex guide dogs) Cen ht CTV

Selected

Q Q Q Q **Craigmore** 3 Murray Park KY16 9AW
(on A91 from Cupar direction, straight across 2 mini-rdbts, 1st left down Golf Place, 1st right then 1st right again, to top of street)
☎ 01334 472142 FAX 01334 477963
Closed Dec-Feb
This immaculately maintained guest house, which forms part of a terraced row between central amenities and the seafront, is home to Tilda Carruthers who takes great pride in providing high standards and a warm welcome to all her guests. The bedrooms are spacious and pretty decor and fabrics combine to complement the smart pine

contd.

furnishings. The tempting breakfast menu offers a range of both hot and cold items which are served at individual tables in the combined lounge/dining room. For the comfort of all, smoking is not permitted.
6 bth/shr (4 fmly) No smoking CTV in all bedrooms Tea and coffee making facilities No dogs Cen ht CTV
ROOMS: s £20-£40; d £40-£50; wkly b&b £130-£165*
CARDS:

Selected

QQQQ **Edenside House** Edenside KY16 9SQ (clearly visible from A91, 2m W of St Andrews directly on estuary shore) ☎ 01334 838108 FAX 01334 838493
Closed Nov-Mar
This modernised 18th century house enjoys a fine outlook over the Eden Estuary and nature reserve. Guests can expect a warm welcome and comfortable, pine furnished rooms from this friendly family-run establishment. Most of the bedrooms are accessed externally but all offer the same amenities. An inviting lounge is available and delicious breakfasts are served in the cheerful dining room.
3 shr 6 annexe shr No smoking CTV in all bedrooms Tea and coffee making facilities Cen ht No children 10yrs 12P No coaches
Located on bird sanctuary Stables adjacent
ROOMS: d £40-£52*
CARDS:

Selected

QQQQ ***Fossil House*** 12-14 Main St, Strathkinness KY16 9RU (Strathkinness signposted, Fossil House at top end of village close to pub) ☎ 01334 850639 FAX 01334 850639
Many guests now return on a regular basis to Alistair and Kornelia Inverarity's charming home in the picturesque village of Strathkinnes two miles from St Andrews. Two bedrooms are contained in the converted cottage to the rear of the house whilst two are located in the main building. Each room has been carefully designed to make best use of available space and all are comfortably modern in style and offer a wide range of amenities and thoughtful extra touches. You will find a choice of comfortable lounges in the cottage, one a conservatory and both with ample provision of books, board games and videos. A delicious breakfast menu is on offer which is deservedly winning praise. Those with a big appetite are invited to tackle the 'Fossil Feast'.
2 bth/shr 2 annexe shr (1 fmly) No smoking CTV in all bedrooms Tea and coffee making facilities No dogs (ex guide dogs) Cen ht CTV ch fac 4P No coaches
Croquet lawn Bar-B-Q patio
CARDS:

Selected

QQQQ **Glenderran** 9 Murray Park KY16 9AW (enter St Andrews on A91 straight over rdbt 2nd left into Murray Place right into Murray Park Glenderran on left)
☎ 01334 477951 FAX 01334 477908
Oriental pictures, ornaments and rugs provide added interest at this welcoming guest house which is just a short walk from the Old Course and sea front. Bedrooms, although varied in size, are nicely decorated, contain many thoughtful extras, and offer either en suite or private facilities. A wide range of books, magazines and music are features of the inviting combined living/dining room. Breakfast is served at individual tables.
5 shr No smoking CTV in all bedrooms Tea and coffee making facilities No dogs Cen ht No children 12yrs No coaches
ROOMS: s £23-£29; d £46-£58*
CARDS:

QQQ **Hazlebank Private Hotel** 28 The Scores KY16 9AS
☎ 01334 472466 FAX 01334 472466
Closed 16 Dec-6 Jan
This friendly family run private hotel forms part of a terraced row which overlooks the bay and is within a short walk of the famous Old Course. The attractive bedrooms are comfortably modern in style and several rooms enjoy views over the bay. Hearty breakfasts and, by prior arrangement, enjoyable evening meals are served in the tastefully appointed dining room.
10 bth/shr (4 fmly) No smoking in bedrooms No smoking in dining room CTV in all bedrooms Tea and coffee making facilities Direct dial from bedrooms No dogs (ex guide dogs) Licensed Cen ht CTV No coaches
Last d 6.45pm
ROOMS: s £45-£75; d £60-£96*
CARDS:

Selected

QQQQ **Lorimer House** 19 Murray Park KY16 9AW (A91 to St Andrews, turn left into Golf Place, turn right into The Scores, turn right into Murray Park)
☎ 01334 476599 FAX 01334 476599
Conveniently situated between the town centre and the seafront, this attractively decorated house offers well equipped and comfortable bedrooms, including one on the ground floor. Public areas include a combined lounge and dining room with lovely cornices.
6 bth/shr (2 fmly) No smoking CTV in all bedrooms Tea and coffee making facilities Cen ht CTV No children 12yrs No coaches
ROOMS: s £18-£28; d £36-£56*
CARDS:

QQQ ***Riverview*** Edenside KY16 9SQ (on A91 3m N of St Andrews)
☎ 01334 838009 FAX 01334 839944
Enthusiastic new owner Marion Paton looks forward to welcoming guests old and new, to her comfortable detached home which is located beside the A91 about three miles west of town overlooking the River Eden estuary. All the spacious modern bedrooms are accessed externally through individual patio doors, from either a terrace or balcony. All are en suite and offer comfortable pine furnishings. Hearty breakfasts and, by prior arrangement, home cooked evening meals are served at individual tables in the attractive dining room. For the comfort of all, this is a non smoking house.
7 shr (2 fmly) No smoking CTV in all bedrooms Tea and coffee making facilities No dogs (ex guide dogs) Cen ht 8P No coaches
CARDS:

Selected

QQQQ **Spinkstown Farmhouse** *(NO541144)* KY16 8PN (2m E of St Andrews on A917 Coast Road to Crail, third farmhouse on right hand side) ☎ 01334 473475 FAX 01334 473475 Mrs A E Duncan

A modern farmhouse standing in gardens amid beautiful rolling Fife countryside. The spacious bedrooms are comfortable, tastefully decorated and equipped with period furnishings and some lovely personal touches. The spacious lounge has a baby grand, and breakfast is served around a communal table in the dining room.

3 bth/shr No smoking CTV in all bedrooms Tea and coffee making facilities No dogs Cen ht CTV 3P 250 acres arable cattle

ROOMS: s fr £20; d £40-£42*

QQQ **West Park House** 5 St Mary's Place KY16 9UY (to the W end of Market St, just beyond Hope Park Church) ☎ 01334 475933

Closed Jan

This attractive Georgian house is conveniently situated for central amenities and offers good value accommodation. The well maintained bedrooms, two of which are on the ground floor, are smartly decorated and offer both modern and traditional furnishings. Public areas include a cosy sitting room overlooking the back garden and a tastefully appointed dining room where hearty breakfasts are served. A non smoking house.

4 rms (1 bth 2 shr) (1 fmly) No smoking CTV in all bedrooms Tea and coffee making facilities No dogs (ex guide dogs) Cen ht CTV No coaches

ROOMS: d £42-£52

CARDS:

QQQ **Yorkston House** 68 & 70 Argyle St KY16 9BU (400 yards from petrol station and West Port going in a westerly direction) ☎ 01334 472019 FAX 01334 472019

Closed Xmas & New Year

This long established, family run guest house is conveniently situated close to the West Port and central amenities. The mostly spacious bedrooms are tastefully decorated and offer mixed furnishings together with a good range of amenities.

10 rms (1 bth 5 shr) (2 fmly) No smoking in 2 bedrooms No smoking in dining room No smoking in lounges CTV in all bedrooms Tea and coffee making facilities No dogs Licensed Cen ht No coaches

ROOMS: s £20-£26; d £38-£60

ST CATHERINE'S Argyll & Bute Map 10 NN10

Selected

QQQQ **Thistle House** PA25 8AZ (turn off the A83 onto A815 (Dunoon) at Cairndow and travel for 5m to St.Catherines where Thistle House is on the left beyond the village) ☎ 01499 302209 FAX 01499 302531

Closed Nov-Mar

Standing in its own attractive grounds beside the A815 and overlooking Loch Fyne towards Inverary, this well proportioned house offers spacious and comfortable bedrooms furnished along traditional lines. A very pleasant and comfortable lounge is provided whilst hearty breakfasts are served in the neat dining room. Hospitality by Sandra and Donald Cameron is first class and guests will be assured of a pleasant stay.

4 shr (1 fmly) No smoking in dining room CTV in all bedrooms Tea and coffee making facilities No dogs (ex guide dogs) Cen ht 10P No coaches

ROOMS: s £23.50-£25; d £47-£50; wkly b&b fr £154*

CARDS:

ST MARY'S LOCH Scottish Borders Map 11 NT22

QQQ **Tibbie Shiels** TD7 5LH (just off A708 between Moffat/Selkirk) ☎ 01750 42231

rs Mon & Tue Nov-Feb

Standing on the edge of St Mary's Loch, this historic drovers inn has played host to many famous people such as Robert Louis Stevenson and Walter Scott. Today, the stunning views and great facilities attract visitors from all round the world. Original parts of the inn have been carefully designed to retain much of the character, and modernised bedrooms and resident's lounge ensure a comfortable stay.

5 bth/shr (2 fmly) No smoking in area of dining room No smoking in 1 lounge Tea and coffee making facilities No dogs (ex guide dogs) Cen ht CTV 30P Fishing Last d 8.30pm

ROOMS: s £27; d £48*

MEALS: Lunch £7.85-£9.10alc Dinner £11.75-£15.50alc*

CARDS:

SHETLAND Map 16

LERWICK Map 16 HU44

Selected

QQQQ ***Glen Orchy House*** 20 Knab Rd ZE1 0AX (adjct to coastguard station) ☎ 01595 692031 FAX 01595 692031

Enthusiastic owners Trevor and Joan Howarth have completely transformed this former convent into a welcoming small hotel on the south side of the town, which is close to a practice golf course. Bedrooms, apart from one room, are all contained in the smart new extension and offer comfortable modern standards together with a wide range of amenities. The inviting lounge, with a range of board games,

contd.

now boasts an honesty bar while the extended dining room is the appropriate setting for Joan's enjoyable home-cooked three course dinners and hearty breakfasts.
14 bth/shr (3 fmly) No smoking in dining room CTV in all bedrooms Tea and coffee making facilities Licensed Cen ht No coaches Golf 9 Last d 2pm

SKYE, ISLE OF Highland Map **13**

DUNVEGAN Map **13** NG24

Selected

QQQQ **Roskhill** Roskhill IV55 8ZD (2m S A863, turn off at River Rosgill,100 yrds on left) ☎ 01470 521317 FAX 01470 521761
Situated two miles south of the village beside the burbling River Rosgill is this cottage-style former croft, which has been upgraded to an attractive standard by owners Kevin Brown and Gillian Griffith. An enjoyable set dinner is served at 7.30pm in the cosy dining room and guests will find the small lounge comfortable. Bedrooms, of which one is on the ground floor, are decorated with Laura Ashley fabrics and papers.
5 rms (3 bth/shr) (1 fmly) No smoking Tea and coffee making facilities Licensed Cen ht CTV No children 10yrs 6P No coaches Last d 4pm
ROOMS: d fr £49
CARDS:

PORTREE Map **13** NG44

QQQ **Craiglockhart** Beaumont Crescent IV51 9DF ☎ 01478 612233
Closed Dec
A warm Island welcome is assured at this friendly family run guest house, which is in two adjacent houses on the waterfront overlooking Portree Bay and the harbour. Bedrooms with attractive decor and pretty fabrics are well maintained and comfortably furnished. Family photographs adorn the comfortable lounge and hearty breakfasts are served at shared tables in the smart dining room.
10 rms (3 shr) CTV in 9 bedrooms Tea and coffee making facilities No dogs Cen ht CTV 4P No coaches
ROOMS: s £16-£18; d £36-£46*

Selected

QQQQ **Quiraing** Viewfield Rd IV51 9ES
(on A87 - coming from South - Bridge End - pass BP filling station and guest house 400m on right hand side)
☎ 01478 612870 FAX 01478 612870
This comfortable family run bungalow-style guest house which stands in its own garden, on the southern approach, is only a four minute walk from the town. The bedrooms are bright and airy and offer mixed modern furnishings along with the expected range of amenities. Freshly prepared breakfasts are served at individual tables in the smart dining room.
6 shr (2 fmly) No smoking in bedrooms No smoking in dining room No smoking in 1 lounge CTV in all bedrooms Tea and coffee making facilities No dogs (ex guide dogs) Cen ht CTV 8P No coaches
ROOMS: d £40-£44

SOUTH GALSON See **LEWIS, ISLE OF**

SOUTH QUEENSFERRY City of Edinburgh Map **11** NT17

Selected

QQQQ **Priory Lodge** The Loan EH30 9NS
(just off the High St in the village of South Queensferry)
☎ 0131 331 4345 FAX 0131 331 4345
Friendly owners Calmyn and Gordon Lamb look forward to welcoming you to their delightful purpose built guest house. It is located just off the quaint cobbled High Street in the picturesque village of South Queensferry which sits between the two famous bridges on the south side of the River Forth. The attractive bedrooms are maintained to a high standard and are comfortably furnished in antique pine. There is also a small lounge and guests are welcome to use the kitchen facilities. Tartan has been used to good effect in the attractive dining room where hearty Scottish breakfasts are served at individual tables. Smoking is not permitted in the house.
5 shr (3 fmly) No smoking CTV in all bedrooms Tea and coffee making facilities No dogs Cen ht CTV 5P No coaches
CARDS:

SPEAN BRIDGE Highland Map **14** NN28

QQ **Coire Glas** Roy Bridge Rd PH34 4EU
(on A86, 0.5m from junct of A82, OS:NN 227819)
☎ 01397 712272 FAX 712272
Jan-Oct
This friendly family-run guesthouse stands in its own grounds at the east end of the village with panoramic views of the surrounding mountains. The bedrooms are fresh, bright and vary in size. Public areas include a comfortable lounge with a small bar and an attractive dining room offering a range of well prepared dishes from the á la carte menu.
11 rms (8 shr) (2 fmly) No smoking in bedrooms No smoking in dining room Tea and coffee making facilities No dogs (ex guide dogs) Licensed CTV 20P All above facilities available within 10miles Last d 8.30pm
ROOMS: s £14.50-£25; d £29-£38; wkly hlf-bd £133-£203
CARDS:

Selected

QQQQ **Corriechoille Lodge** PH34 4EY
(off A82, signed Corriechoille, proceed for 2.25 miles keeping left where road forks at 10mph sign. At end of tarmac road, right up hill and left) ☎ 01397 712002 FAX 01397 712002
Mar-Nov
Quietly set within Glen Spean and in an elevated position above the River Spean, this fine house is a short distance from the village along a picturesque road. Magnificent views towards Ben Nevis and surrounding mountains can be enjoyed from the lounge and some of the spacious and well appointed bedrooms. Justin and Lucy Swabey provide friendly and attentive service with well prepared dinners being available if booked in advance.
5 bth/shr (2 fmly) No smoking CTV in all bedrooms Tea and coffee making facilities No dogs (ex guide dogs) Licensed Cen ht 7P No coaches Last d noon
ROOMS: s £20-£30; d £40-£50; wkly b&b £126-£154; wkly hlf-bd £224-£252
CARDS:

Selected

QQQQ **Distant Hills** PH34 4EU (on A86) ☎ 01397 712452
Enthusiastic owners Meg and Ian McLuskey extend a warm personal welcome to guests at their attractive detached modern home on the eastern edge of the village. Bedrooms, though variable in size, are maintained to a high standard and offer tasteful modern appointments. Inviting public areas include a spacious and relaxing split-level lounge with access to the rear patio and garden and a smart dining room that provides an appropriate setting for Meg's enjoyable home-cooking.
7 shr No smoking in bedrooms No smoking in dining room CTV in all bedrooms Tea and coffee making facilities Cen ht CTV 10P No coaches Last d 5pm
ROOMS: s £23; d £36; wkly b&b £126; wkly hlf-bd £203*

QQQ **Inverour** PH34 4EU (10m NE of Fort William, turn on to A86, first turning on right, 10yds from junct) ☎ 01397 712218
Closed 23-27 Dec rs Jan
At this friendly, well-maintained guest house bedrooms have been cleverly designed to make best use of available space and offer comfortable modern appointments. There is an attractive, homely lounge with a conservatory extension overlooking the neat garden. There is also a beamed dining room.
7 rms (3 shr) No smoking in bedrooms No smoking in dining room CTV in all bedrooms Tea and coffee making facilities No dogs (ex guide dogs) Cen ht CTV No children 3yrs 8P No coaches Last d 2pm
ROOMS: s £20-£25; d £36-£45*

Selected

QQQQ **The Smiddy House** Roy Bridge Rd PH34 4EU
(At junct of A82 Inverness & A86 Newtonmore)
☎ 01397 712335 FAX 01397 712043
Dedicated owners Amanda and Kirk Richardson have refurbished this fine detached house to a pleasant standard. The atmosphere throughout is relaxed and friendly and the attractive lounge offers good levels of comfort. Food is available all day in the adjacent Bistro. Upstairs, the attractive bedrooms are tastefully decorated and comfortably furnished in pine.
4 shr (1 fmly) No smoking in dining room CTV in all bedrooms Tea and coffee making facilities Licensed Cen ht 20P No coaches Last d 9.30pm
ROOMS: s £24; d £38*
CARDS:

STEWARTON East Ayrshire

See **Dunlop**

STIRLING Stirling Map 11 NS79

See also **Denny**

QQ **Carseview** 16 Ladysneuk Rd, Cambuskenneth FK9 5NF
(M8/9 junct 9.A91 through 4 roundabouts,at 5th left to A907.2nd left into Ladysneuk Rd,follow rd into village.Carseview on left opp Abbey Inn)
☎ 01786 462235
Alison and David Seaton's comfortable home stands in its own well stocked garden in the small conservation village of Cambuskenneth, and offers a homely welcoming atmosphere. It has two attractive bedrooms on the first floor which share a general shower and toilet on the same level. Public areas include an open-plan lounge/dining room and from the lounge area, French doors open onto the patio. Hearty breakfasts and, by prior arrangement, home cooked evening meals are served around the communal table. This is a non smoking establishment.
3 rms No smoking CTV in all bedrooms Tea and coffee making facilities Cen ht CTV 3P No coaches
ROOMS: s £17; d £34*

QQQ **Castlecroft** Ballengeich Rd FK8 1TN (leave M9 junct10 toward Stirling, 1st right into Raploch Rd. To fire station, turn left at Back'O'Hill then right) ☎ 01786 474933 FAX 01786 466716
Closed Xmas & New Year
Glorious views over the surrounding countryside are enjoyed from this detached modern house which nestles under the shadow of the castle walls. Bedrooms are modern and spacious and offer good facilities, while public areas include a comfortable and spacious lounge with panoramic views and a separate dining room where breakfasts are served at shared tables. The atmosphere is welcoming.
6 shr (1 fmly) No smoking in bedrooms No smoking in dining room CTV in all bedrooms Tea and coffee making facilities Lift Cen ht 9P No coaches
ROOMS: s £30-£42; d £40-£47*
CARDS:

Selected

QQQQ **Lynedoch** 100 Causewayhead Rd FK9 5HJ
(leave M9 Junct 10 to Stirling via Drip Road left at Clocktower roundabout over river,through traffic lights onto Causeway Head road 300m on left) ☎ 01786 473877
A welcoming cup of tea is offered to every new arrival to Sylvia and Ian Wilson's comfortable home which is situated at the north side of town near the Wallace Monument. The well cared for and spacious bedrooms are comfortably furnished and offer all the expected amenities. Public areas include an inviting lounge with well filled book shelves. A good selection is offered at the communal breakfast table in the separate dining room.
2 shr No smoking CTV in all bedrooms Tea and coffee making facilities No dogs Cen ht CTV No children none 2P No coaches
ROOMS: s £25-£40; d £36-£44

STONEHAVEN Aberdeenshire Map **15** NO88

Selected

Q Q Q Q **Arduthie House** Ann St AB39 2DA
(A90 from S, turn into Stonehavenat traffic lights, turn left, take second right (Ann St). house 100yds on left. A90 from N, turn right at lights)
☎ 01569 762381 FAX 01569 766366
Brain and Mary Marr look forward to welcoming you to their comfortable detached home which stands in its own landscaped garden in a residential area close to central amenities. The bedrooms are comfortably furnished in the modern style and offer a range of thoughtful extras. Public areas include a choice of inviting lounges, one with well filled bookshelves, and guests are invited to help themselves to a complimentary glass of sherry. There is also a sun lounge adjacent to the dining room where breakfast, and by prior arrangement, home cooked evening meals, are served at individual tables.
5 rms (1 bth 3 shr) (1 fmly) No smoking in bedrooms No smoking in dining room No smoking in 1 lounge CTV in all bedrooms Tea and coffee making facilities No dogs (ex guide dogs) Cen ht CTV No coaches Last d 6pm
ROOMS: d £36-£44*

Selected

Q Q Q Q **Woodside Of Glasslaw** AB39 3XQ ☎ 01569 763799 FAX 01569 763799
rs Xmas
Aileen Paton looks forward to welcoming you to her delightful home, a modern purpose built bungalow style house set in carefully tended gardens some two miles south of town off the A92. The non smoking bedrooms offer attractive colour schemes and are comfortably furnished in the modern style. Public areas include combined lounge/dining room where hearty breakfasts are served at individual tables.
5 shr (1 fmly) No smoking in bedrooms No smoking in dining room CTV in all bedrooms Tea and coffee making facilities Cen ht CTV 5P
ROOMS: s fr £22; d fr £37

STRANRAER Dumfries & Galloway Map **10** NX06

Selected

Q Q Q Q **Windyridge Villa** 5 Royal Crescent DG9 8HB
(approaching town on A75, follow ferry terminal signs to bottom of Stair Drive. Turn left and immediately left again into Royal Crescent)
☎ 01776 889900 FAX 889900
Situated close to the ferry terminal, this guest house overlooks the seafront, affording spectacular views across the Irish Sea. Olive and Bryce Kelly welcome guests with a tray of tea and home baking. Bedrooms are comfortable and well equipped, and all en suites contain many thoughtful extras. The residents' lounge adjoins the hall and breakfast is offered in the bright conservatory dining room, round a communal table.
3 bth/shr No smoking CTV in all bedrooms Tea and coffee making facilities Cen ht CTV 3P No coaches
ROOMS: s £22-£25; d £38-£42

STRATHAVEN South Lanarkshire Map **11** NS74

Q Q **Avonlea** 46 Millar St, Glassford ML10 6TD
(from Strathaven turn into Commercial Road, continue for approx 2m and 'Avonlea' is third terraced house on left) ☎ 01357 521748 & 521369
Closed Dec
Glassford is a pretty conservation village 1.5 miles east of Strathaven and some four miles from Junction 8 of the M74. Avonlea stands in the centre of the village and enthusiastic owner Miss Rankin looks forward to welcoming you to her terraced home. There are two comfortable bedrooms on the first floor which offer all the expected amenities as well as some thoughtful extras. Hearty breakfasts and, by prior arrangement, home cooked evening meals, are served at individual tables in the attractive dining which overlooks the well tended rear garden and offers access to the patio.
2 rms No smoking in bedrooms CTV in all bedrooms Tea and coffee making facilities No dogs Cen ht No children 7yrs No coaches Last d 4pm
ROOMS: s £22-£25; d £36-£38; wkly b&b £120-£130 *

Q Q **Springvale Hotel** 18 Letham Rd ML10 6AD
(from M74 junct 8 take Kilmarnock (A71) for 5m bypassing Stonehouse)
☎ 01357 521131 FAX 01357 521131
Closed 26-27 Dec & 1-3 Jan
Situated in a residential area close to the town centre, this family-run guest house has a friendly relaxed atmosphere. Bedrooms, though mostly compact, offer mixed practical appointments together with the expected amenities. The lounge is traditional, whilst the dining room, part of which is a conservatory extension, overlooks the well tended garden, and is open to both residents and non-residents for its popular, good value high teas.
14 rms (12 bth/shr) (2 fmly) CTV in all bedrooms Tea and coffee making facilities Licensed Cen ht CTV 8P Last d 6.45pm
ROOMS: s £27-£29; d fr £40*

STRATHPEFFER Highland Map **14** NH45

Premier Selected

Q Q Q Q Q **Craigvar** The Square IV14 9DL ☎ 01997 421622 FAX 01997 421796
This fine detached Georgian house overlooks The Square of this highland spa town and has been lovingly restored by dedicated and enthusiastic owner Margaret Scott. Two of the en suite bedrooms are on the first floor, one of which has a four-poster and is appropriately furnished in period style; the other has twin beds and a private dressing room. The ground floor double room has been carefully planned to make best use of the limited space and is best suited for single occupancy. All the rooms contain the usual amenities. The inviting lounge overlooks the square, with a modern dolls house being a feature. The spacious breakfast room has a large central table with elegant appointments; the local black pudding must be sampled at breakfast.
3 bth/shr No smoking CTV in all bedrooms Tea and coffee making facilities Direct dial from bedrooms No dogs (ex guide dogs) Cen ht 7P No coaches
ROOMS: s £27-£30; d £40-£54; wkly b&b £133-£182
CARDS:

QQQ **Inver Lodge** IV14 9DL (from A834 through Strathpeffer Centre, turn beside Spa Pavilion signposted Bowling Green, Inver Lodge on right hand side) ☎ 01997 421392
Mar-mid Dec
Sound standards of accommodation together with a welcoming atmosphere and delicious food are all part of the appeal of this fine Victorian Lodge, which is very much a family home and is set in a quiet residential area. The two bedrooms are brightly decorated and comfortably furnished, and are equipped with many thoughtful touches. Imaginative breakfasts, and by prior arrangement, enjoyable home cooked dinners based on fresh local ingredients are served at a communal table in the pleasant combined lounge/dining room.
2 rms (1 fmly) No smoking CTV in all bedrooms Tea and coffee making facilities No dogs Cen ht ch fac 2P No coaches Fishing and riding can be arranged Last d 4pm
ROOMS: s £21-£23; d £32-£34; wkly b&b £110-£115; wkly hlf-bd £151-£189
CARDS:

STRATHY Highland Map **14** NC86

Selected

QQQQ **Catalina** *(NC 817679)* Aultivullin KW14 7RY (turn off A836 at Strathy onto Strathy Point Road, 1.5m then left and follow 1m to the end, ☎ 01641 541279 FAX 01641 541314
Jane and Pete Salisbury offer a unique and relaxing experience at their comfortable home which is located about 2.5 miles north of the village on Strathy Point. The former croft house has been extended and modernised with the only guest bedroom being in a self contained wing that also includes a dining room and a cosy lounge with TV and lots of reading material; the whole wing is for exclusive use of the guests. Meal times are not set in advance, as Jane and Pete believe in providing dinner and breakfast at times that suit their guests – a flexible approach that earns much praise.
1 shr No smoking Tea and coffee making facilities No dogs Cen ht CTV No children none 2P No coaches walking Last d any time
ROOMS: s £30; d £38

SWINTON Scottish Borders Map **12** NT84

Selected

QQQQ **Wheatsheaf Hotel** TD11 3JJ (6m N of Duns on A6112) ☎ 01890 860257 FAX 01890 860688
Closed last wk Oct & last 2 wks Feb rs Mon
Overlooking the village green and with spacious gardens to the rear, this country inn could equally be considered a restaurant with rooms, as it has built its reputation on the standard of its food. Bedrooms are pleasantly furnished, most having smart en suite facilities. A magnificent new bedroom has been created from the old lounge, and is well worth requesting. Downstairs is the cosy bar and conservatory style restaurant, with attractive lofted pine ceiling, where delicious Scottish breakfasts are enjoyed.
5 rms (4 bth/shr) (1 fmly) No smoking in bedrooms No smoking in dining room CTV in all bedrooms Tea and coffee making facilities Cen ht 4P No coaches Can arrange golf, fishing & shooting Last d 9.30pm
ROOMS: s £35-£65; d £58-£98
MEALS: Lunch £8-£18alc Dinner £18-£25alc
CARDS:

TAIN Highland Map **14** NH78

Selected

QQQQ **Aldie House** IV19 1LZ (from Inverness, 500yds before Tain on A9, turn left and follow private road)
☎ 01862 893787 FAX 01892 893787
Set in 4 acres of well tended and secluded grounds, just off the A9 south of the town bypass, is this traditional country dwelling house that has been attractively restored by Chris and Charles De Decker. The house has been filled with antiques from their home in Belgium, which helps to create the homely atmosphere in the spacious and comfortable lounge. The dining room is in two sections, and guests will enjoy using the sunlounge extension overlooking the gardens. The bedrooms are all individually furnished and decorated and have many thoughtful touches.
3 bth/shr (2 fmly) No smoking CTV in all bedrooms Tea and coffee making facilities No dogs (ex guide dogs) Cen ht 7P
ROOMS: s £24-£28; d £44-£48; wkly b&b £140-£150*
CARDS:

Selected

QQQQ **Golf View House** 13 Knockbreck Rd IV19 1BN (first right off A9 at Tain (B9174), follow this road for 0.5m, house signposted on right) ☎ 01862 892856 FAX 01862 892856
Closed 16 Dec-15 Jan
A warm welcome is assured at Ian and Ray Ross's charming Victorian home, formerly the Manse, which stands in two acres of secluded gardens, where hens and ducks are kept. There are splendid views across the golf course to the Dornoch Firth. The attractively decorated non-smoking bedrooms are comfortably appointed in both modern and traditional styles. The inviting sitting room overlooks the golf course and hearty breakfasts are served in the pine-furnished dining room.
5 rms (3 shr) (1 fmly) No smoking CTV in all bedrooms Tea and coffee making facilities No dogs (ex guide dogs) Cen ht CTV 7P No coaches
ROOMS: s £28-£38; d £40-£45*
CARDS:

THORNHILL Stirling Map 11 NN60

Selected

Q Q Q Q ❥ **Easter Tarr Farmhouse** *(NS636007)* FK8 3LD
(Off A84 onto A873 just past safari park. Go through Thornhill village.Est. is 2m on left)
☎ 01786 850225 FAX 01786 850225 Mr & Mrs D Lubiewski
Enthusiastic owners Trudi and Danny Lubiewski have lovingly and sympathetically restored their charming home, a sturdy farmhouse which dates back to 1825 and stands beside the A873 about two miles west of the village. On arrival, Trudy will has a pot of tea ready to welcome you and her hearty breakfasts will provide you with an excellent start to the day. The three recently refurbished bedrooms with matching pine are equipped with useful extras. There is a comfortable lounge which invites relaxation while breakfast can be served here or round the communal table in the partly pine-clad breakfast room.
3 shr (2 fmly) No smoking CTV in all bedrooms Tea and coffee making facilities No dogs (ex guide dogs) Cen ht CTV 10P
10 acres poultry sheep horses
ROOMS: s £30; d £36-£48✻

TOBERMORY See MULL, ISLE OF

TOMATIN Highland Map 14 NH82

Q Q Q **Millcroft** Old Mill Rd IV13 7YW
(Leave A9 at the Little Chef, follow the road past the filling station for 1m to Tomatin Inn, turn right into Old Mill Rd, house 50yds on left)
☎ 01808 511405
This charming former croft has been converted to provide self-contained guest accommodation. On the first floor is an adaptable family suite, and the double-bedded room on the ground floor leads off the comfortable and homely lounge/breakfast room.
2 shr (1 fmly) CTV in all bedrooms Cen ht 3P No coaches
ROOMS: s fr £20; d £36; wkly b&b £120✻

TWYNHOLM Dumfries & Galloway Map 11 NX65

Selected

Q Q Q Q **Fresh Fields** Arden Rd DG6 4PB
(turn off A75 into Twynholm, continue past church, turn right into Arden Road - then 0.5m on left)
☎ 01557 860221
Mar-Oct
This three-gabled white house lies on the edge of the village, surrounded by an attractive garden and pretty meadows. The house is adorned with pretty mementoes and has a relaxing atmosphere. There are no TVs or radios in the cheery, pine-furnished bedrooms, but there is plenty to read throughout the house, and a TV lounge.
5 shr No smoking in 2 bedrooms No smoking in dining room No smoking in lounges Tea and coffee making facilities Licensed Cen ht CTV No children 10P No coaches Last d 5.30pm
ROOMS: s £26-£28; d £52-£56; wkly b&b fr £182; wkly hlf-bd fr £273

ULLAPOOL Highland Map 14 NH19

Selected

Q Q Q Q **Ardvreck** Morefield Brae IV26 2TH
(N out of Ullapool on A835, 1.5m to top of hill turn left at sign to Ardvreck) ☎ 01854 612028 FAX 01854 613000
Closed 1 Dec-28 Feb
Spectacular views over Loch Broom towards Ullapool are enjoyed from this friendly family-run guest house – a modern detached house which stands on a hillside to the north of town. Rooms are mostly spacious, offer en suite showers, and are freshly decorated and comfortably furnished in pine. Public areas include a comfortable open-plan lounge/dining room.
10 shr (2 fmly) No smoking CTV in all bedrooms Tea and coffee making facilities No dogs (ex guide dogs) Cen ht 14P No coaches
ROOMS: s £25-£27; d £50-£54; wkly b&b £175-£189✻
CARDS:

Selected

Q Q Q Q **Dromnan** Garve Rd IV26 2SX
(turn left at 30mph sign as you enter town from A835 S)
☎ 01854 6123333 FAX 01854 613364
This family home with its own garden, overlooking Loch Broom, has been extended to provide comfortable tourist accommodation. It has a welcoming atmosphere and offers an open-plan lounge and dining room where substantial breakfasts are served. Bedrooms, though variable in size, are well equipped; all have en suite showers and are tastefully decorated and comfortably furnished.
7 bth/shr (2 fmly) No smoking CTV in all bedrooms Tea and coffee making facilities No dogs (ex guide dogs) Cen ht CTV 7P
ROOMS: s £20-£30; d £40-£48; wkly b&b £140-£160✻
CARDS:

Q Q Q **Eilean Donan** 14 Market St IV26 2XE ☎ 01854 612524
In a quiet residential area set back from the picturesque Highland village seafront is this pleasant bed and breakfast guest house. Mark and Judith Hall are gradually carrying out improvements to the bedrooms, breakfast room and lounge. All expected facilities are provided.
5 bth/shr No smoking CTV in all bedrooms Tea and coffee making facilities Cen ht No children 11yrs 5P No coaches
ROOMS: s £18-£28; d £36-£44✻

Q Q ***Ladysmith House & Scottish Larder*** 24 Pulteney St IV26 2UP
(entering village from E, continue on North Road which turns right after Royal Hotel, take 2nd on left) ☎ 01854 612185
rs New Year-Etr (restaurant closed)
Situated one street away from the waterfront this friendly corner establishment trades as both a bed and breakfast house and a restaurant. Lauri Chilton offers freshly prepared local food, with special theme nights on occasions. The accommodation is mixed with some rooms being attractively decorated and well appointed whilst others are simpler.
6 rms (4 bth/shr) (1 fmly) No smoking in dining room CTV in all bedrooms Tea and coffee making facilities Licensed Cen ht 5P
Last d 9pm

Selected

QQQQ The Sheiling Garve Rd IV26 2SX
(on A835, at S end of village) ☎ 01854 612947 FAX 01854 612947
Closed Xmas & New Year
A comfortable family home overlooking Loch Broom which has been extended to provide comfortable tourist accommodation. It has a welcoming atmosphere and offers an open-plan lounge and dining room where substantial breakfasts are served. Bedrooms, though varying in size, are well equipped; all have en suite showers and are tastefully decorated.
7 bth/shr No smoking Tea and coffee making facilities No dogs (ex guide dogs) Cen ht CTV 7P Fishing Sauna
ROOMS: s £21-£30; d £42-£50; wkly b&b £147-£168

WHITING BAY See **ARRAN, ISLE OF**

WICK Highland Map **15** ND35

Selected

QQQQ The Clachan South Rd KW1 5NH
(situated on A9 first house on right on S side of Wick)
☎ 01955 605384
Enthusiastic owner Elspeth Bremner maintains high standards at her welcoming detached home which stands in its own garden at the south end of town. The bright bedrooms, all on the ground floor, are tastefully decorated, comfortably modern in style, and offer a wide range of amenities. Breakfasts are served at individual tables in the attractive combined lounge/dining room.
3 shr No smoking CTV in all bedrooms Tea and coffee making facilities No dogs Cen ht CTV No children 3P
ROOMS: s £25-£30; d £40-£45*

WIGTOWN Dumfries & Galloway Map **10** NX45

QQQ Jacobs Ladder *(NX372517)* Whauphill, Newton Stewart DG8 9BD (leave Wigtown on A714, after passing through Bladnoch turn onto B7005 for approx 3m, then left onto B7052 & in 0.5m take unclass road, farm on right) ☎ 01988 860227 Mrs M McMuldroch
This period house is located close to the village of Mochrum. Mary McMuldroch provides comfortable, modern accommodation and has recently converted a self contained cottage especially for family use. Two of the bedrooms in the main house have en suite facilities whilst the other has full use of a modern bathroom. This is a popular base for golfers with seven courses located within a half hour drive. Local fishing can also be arranged. Dinner is served daily and makes use of a tried and tested range of home-made cheeses.
3 rms (2 shr) (1 fmly) No smoking in dining room CTV in all bedrooms Tea and coffee making facilities Cen ht 8P 8 acres beef & sheep Last d 3pm

Remember to return your Prize Draw card for a chance to win an action-packed family weekend at one of the eleven Family Fun Hotels in the Hilton Hotels Directory. See inside the front cover for the card and competition details. Don't forget to fill in your name and address before posting!

WALES

Inspectors selected bed & breakfast of the year:

Bryn Derwen Hotel, Llandudno, Conwy

ABERAERON Carmarthenshire Map **02** SN46

Q Q Q **Arosfa** 8 Cadwgan Place SA46 0BU
(turn towards harbour opposite shoeshop (Estate Agents on the corner) 150m approx-next to yellow house on corner overlooking harbour & car park)
☎ 01545 570120
Arosfa overlooks the very pretty harbour of this seaside town. Dating back over 200 years it is run by the friendly Griffiths family who offer their guests a warm welcome. Bedrooms are cosy and well furnished and many contain original fireplaces. Three are located in a nearby cottage that has its own lounge facility. A small bar is provided and the dining room is attractively pine-furnished.
3 bth/shr 3 annexe bth/shr (1 fmly) No smoking CTV in all bedrooms Tea and coffee making facilities No dogs (ex guide dogs) Cen ht 5P No coaches
ROOMS: s £18-£30; d £36-£48; wkly b&b £123-£152✻

ABERGAVENNY Monmouthshire Map **03** SO21

Selected

Q Q Q Q **Llanwenarth House** Govilon NP7 9SF
(E of Abergavenny follow A465 to Merthyr Tydfil for 3.5m to next rdbt.Take 1st exit to Govilon and 1/2m drive is 150yrds on right) ☎ 01873 830289 FAX 01873 832199
rs Jan
Built by the ancestors of Sir Henry Morgan, the infamous privateer and Lieutenant Governor of Jamaica, this beautifully preserved manor house dates back to the 16th century. Personally run by Bruce and Amanda Weatherill, it provides elegantly appointed accommodation with period furnishings and modern equipment. Bedrooms are large and include a room on the ground floor. During cold weather, welcoming log fires burn in the drawing room and dinner can be taken in the attractive dining room. The house is set in its own mature grounds with the Brecon Beacons National Park as a stunning backdrop.
5 bth/shr (1 fmly) No smoking in bedrooms No smoking in dining room CTV in all bedrooms Tea and coffee making facilities Licensed Cen ht No children 10yrs 6P No coaches Last d 6.30pm
ROOMS: s fr £48; d £72-£78✻

Selected

Q Q Q Q **Newcourt** *(SO317165)* Mardy NP7 8AU
(2m N, on edge of village of Mardy)
☎ 01873 852300 FAX 01873 852300 Mrs J Nicholls
Parts of this large stone-built house date back to 1643. It is quietly located near the village of Mardy, which is just north of Abergavenny via the A465. The attractive dining room has been refurbished to a high standard; all guests share one large antique table, and there is an adjacent lounge area. Recently created facilities include a craft shop and a tea room, both located in a former farm building.
3 bth/shr No smoking CTV in all bedrooms Tea and coffee making facilities No dogs (ex guide dogs) Cen ht CTV No children 10yrs 10P Snooker 160 acres arable beef
ROOMS: s £30-£35; d £50-£55; wkly b&b £175✻

Q Q Q **Penyclawdd** *(SO291173)* Llanvihangel Crucorney NP7 7LB
(take the road signed Pantygelli from the A465, Hereford/Abergavenny)
☎ 01873 890591 Mrs A Davies
Peacefully located in a beautiful valley five miles north of Abergavenny, this detached house offers modern accommodation in 2 family bedded rooms. There is a spacious and comfortable lounge where log fires burn in a stove during colder weather, and a traditionally furnished dining room with separate tables. Children are welcomed here.
2 rms (2 fmly) No smoking CTV in 1 bedroom Tea and coffee making facilities Cen ht CTV 6P 160 acres sheep beef, working farm
ROOMS: s fr £16; d fr £32; wkly b&b £97✻

Q Q Q **The Wenallt** *(SO245138)* Gilwern NP7 0HP
(From Abergavenny on A465 go to rdbt approx. 3m stay on A465, turn 1st left and continue to top of country lane) ☎ 01873 830694 Mr B L Harris
This stone-built, 16th-century Welsh longhouse is quietly and remotely located on a 50-acre farm on a hillside, where it commands magnificent views of the Usk Valley. The bedrooms are quite spacious and comfortable; half are located on the ground floor of converted cow sheds. Facilities include a spacious lounge, where welcoming real fires burn in the inglenook fireplace during cold weather. There is also a small lounge bar and a traditionally-furnished dining room, where separate tables can be provided.
4 rms (1 bth) 4 annexe shr No smoking in bedrooms No smoking in dining room No smoking in 1 lounge Tea and coffee making facilities Licensed Cen ht CTV 18P 50 acres sheep Last d 6pm
ROOMS: s £22-£26; d £37-£44; wkly b&b £122-£146; wkly hlf-bd £198-£224✻

ABERPORTH Ceredigion Map **02** SN25

Q Q Q **Ffynonwen Country** SA43 2HT (turn off A487 at Gogerddan Arms towards Aberporth, sign to Ffynonwen 1m on left) ☎ 01239 810312
This friendly and family-run country guest house stands in several acres of farmland that includes two trout lakes where guests can fish. Accommodation is modern and includes several suites of rooms which are suitable for families and less mobile visitors. There is a very cosy lounge bar and a small conservatory sitting area.
5 bth/shr (3 fmly) CTV in all bedrooms Tea and coffee making facilities Licensed Cen ht 30P No coaches Fishing Games Room
ROOMS: s £22; d £44; wkly b&b £138.60; wkly hlf-bd £189✻

ABERYSTWYTH Ceredigion Map **06** SN58

Selected

Q Q Q Q **Glyn-Garth** South Rd SY23 1JS
(from A487 in Aberystwyth and take first left into South Road, Glyn-Garth is on right close to the South Promenade)
☎ 01970 615050 FAX 01970 636835
Closed 1 wk Xmas
The friendly Evans family have welcomed guests to this delightful house for over 40 years. It lies just a few yards from the seafront of this University town and is completely non-smoking. Bedrooms are fresh and well maintained and modern facilities are provided. Family rooms are available and one is located at ground floor level. A lounge is provided for guests.
11 rms (6 bth/shr) (2 fmly) No smoking CTV in all bedrooms Tea and coffee making facilities No dogs Cen ht CTV 2P No coaches
ROOMS: s £19-£20; d £38-£50

Q Q **Llety Gwyn Hotel** Llanbadarn Fawr SY23 3SR (1m E A44)
☎ 01970 623965
rs 25-26 Dec
Run by the friendly Jones family for many years, this hotel lies in the village of Llanbadarn Fawr, just off the A44 and close to Aberystwyth. Bedrooms are equipped with modern facilities, some are suitable for families and many are located in a nearby building. A public bar is available as well as a gymnasium and function suite. This is popular for local meetings and parties.
8 rms (4 shr) 6 annexe rms (1 bth 3 shr) CTV in all bedrooms Tea and coffee making facilities Licensed Cen ht CTV 40P Pool table
Last d 12.30pm
ROOMS: s £22-£27; d £42-£56*
CARDS:

Q Q Q **Queensbridge Hotel** Promenade, Victoria Ter SY23 2DH
(N end of promenade, near Constitution Hill Cliff Railway)
☎ 01970 612343 615025 FAX 01970 617452
Closed 1 wk Xmas
This private bed & breakfast hotel lies on the promenade of this university town. Bedrooms are well equipped with modern facilities and many have fine sea views. Several are suitable for families. A comfortable lounge bar is available for residents and a lift serves all floors. The hotel has been owned and run by the friendly Francis family for many years.
15 bth/shr (6 fmly) No smoking in 6 bedrooms No smoking in dining room CTV in all bedrooms Tea and coffee making facilities Direct dial from bedrooms No dogs (ex guide dogs) Licensed Lift Cen ht CTV
ROOMS: s £34-£40; d £50-£60*
CARDS:

Q Q Q ***Yr Hafod*** 1 South Marine Ter SY23 1JX
(situated on south promenade between harbour and castle)
☎ 01970 617579
Yr Hafod lies on the promenade of this University town. It is a small and friendly guest house and provides well equipped modern bedrooms and cosy public areas. Family rooms are available and many have seafront views. The friendly Evans family offer a warm welcome to their guests and provide good hearty breakfasts.
7 rms (1 bth 1 shr) (2 fmly) No smoking in bedrooms No smoking in dining room No smoking in lounges CTV in all bedrooms Tea and coffee making facilities No dogs Cen ht CTV 1P No coaches

ANGLESEY, ISLE OF Isle of Anglesey Map **06**

BRYNSIENCYN Map **06** SH46

Selected

Q Q Q Q **Ty Coch Country Guest House** LL61 6SZ
(turn off A4080 at Groeslon Inn,Brynsiencyn on sharp bend,follow signs for sea zoo,Ty Cochis 0.5m from Groeslon on the right after tall pine trees) ☎ 01248 430227 FAX 01248 430227
Closed Dec & Jan
This delightful country house is located in beautiful countryside on the south-western corner of Anglesey. There are superb views across the Menai Straits to Snowdonia from many areas. Three spacious bedrooms are provided and are all well decorated and equipped with modern en suite facilities. A very comfortable lounge is available that has a cheery log fire for the colder weather.
3 bth/shr (1 fmly) No smoking Tea and coffee making facilities
No dogs (ex guide dogs) Cen ht CTV 5P No coaches Last d 10am
ROOMS: s £24-£27.50; d £36-£42; wkly b&b £108-£126

CEMAES BAY Map **06** SH39

Selected

Q Q Q Q **Hafod Country House** LL67 0DS (off A5025, turning for Llanfechell, opposite renovated windmill) ☎ 01407 710500
Mar-Oct
This fine Edwardian house lies in an acre of pretty lawns and gardens where tennis and croquet can be played in the summer months. Three smart and modern bedrooms are available that are attractively decorated and well equipped. An elegant lounge is provided and hospitality from owners, Gina and Tony Hirst, is warm and welcoming. Gina is an accomplished cook and much of the produce used comes from her own garden. The house lies on the outskirts of a pretty fishing village where beaches and other amenities are within easy driving distance.
3 shr No smoking CTV in all bedrooms Tea and coffee making facilities No dogs (ex guide dogs) Licensed Cen ht No children 7yrs 5P No coaches Croquet Last d 4pm
ROOMS: d £40-£45; wkly b&b £147*

HOLYHEAD Map 06 SH28

Q Q Q **Rhiwlas** 35 Walthew Av LL65 1AG (on approaching Holyhead main lights, take left lane over bridge, pass turn for town centre, after 0.75m turn left for beach and rdbt turn left) ☎ 01407 760595
A comfortable, friendly Bed and Breakfast located a short distance away from the sea front and convenient for the Irish ferry or for touring the area. Rooms are prettily decorated and have televisions as well as tea/coffee facilities.
4 shr (1 fmly) No smoking CTV in all bedrooms Tea and coffee making facilities No dogs (ex guide dogs) Cen ht 4P No coaches
ROOMS: s £20; d £35*

Q Q **Wavecrest** 93 Newry St LL65 1HU (at end of A5 turn left, after 600 yards turn left by railings, premises 100 yards up hill on right)
☎ 01407 763637 FAX 01407 764862
This brightly decorated guest house is conveniently situated near the Irish ferry and is popular as an overnight staging post as a result. Pretty bedrooms are equipped with satellite television and other modern facilities. There is a comfortable lounge and evening meals are available if booked in advance.
4 rms (2 shr) (3 fmly) No smoking in 2 bedrooms No smoking in dining room No smoking in lounges CTV in all bedrooms Tea and coffee making facilities Cen ht CTV 1P No coaches Last d 3pm
ROOMS: s £16-£20; d £30-£36; wkly b&b £100-£120; wkly hlf-bd £150-£180*

Selected

Q Q Q Q **Yr Hendre** Porth-y-Felin Rd LL65 1AH (from A5 in town centre turn left at War Memorial. Take next left, over crossroads, house on right facing park) ☎ 01407 762929 FAX 01407 762929
Hendre is located a short walk from the promenade in a quiet area of the town. It stands in its own grounds and is convenient for travellers on the Irish Ferries. Rita Lipman has been the friendly owner for 15 years and she offers natural Welsh hospitality in a homely and relaxing atmosphere. Bedrooms are colourful, and fresh and rich wallpapers and fabrics are used to good effect. Several beds have pretty canopies and all rooms are equipped with trouser presses and other modern facilities. Rita uses fresh local produce when possible and her cooking has a distinctly Welsh flavour.
3 bth/shr No smoking in bedrooms No smoking in dining room CTV in all bedrooms Tea and coffee making facilities No dogs (ex guide dogs) Cen ht CTV 6P No coaches Last d 3pm
ROOMS: s £25; d £40; wkly b&b £140; wkly hlf-bd £210*

RHOSCOLYN Map 06 SH27

Selected

Q Q Q Q **The Old Rectory** LL65 2SQ (take B4545 from Valley then follow signs left to Rhoscolyn just after Four Mile Bridge. Continue for 2m then take road alongside church) ☎ 01407 860214
Closed 21 Dec-19 Jan rs 1 wk Oct & last 2 wks of Sep
The Old Rectory is a fine country house dating back to 1850 and there are fine views of the sea and over the surrounding countryside from many rooms. The sandy beaches of Holy Island are nearby and a wide variety of bird life can be viewed in the area. Bedrooms are furnished with period pieces in keeping with the house, all are well equipped with modern facilities and one is located at ground floor level. A warm welcome awaits guests from the very friendly Wyatt family.
5 bth/shr (2 fmly) No smoking in 3 bedrooms No smoking in dining room No smoking in lounges CTV in all bedrooms Tea and coffee making facilities Licensed Cen ht CTV 8P No coaches
ROOMS: s £23-£35; d £56; wkly b&b £170
CARDS:

TREARDDUR BAY Map 06 SH27

Q Q **Moranedd** Trearddur Rd LL65 2UE
(off A5 in valley onto B4545 and take 2nd right after Beach Hotel)
☎ 01407 860324
This pretty guest house lies in a slightly elevated position, is surrounded by well tended gardens and is a good base for enjoying the area. It has been run by Sheila Wathan for many years and she is naturally welcoming and friendly. Bedrooms are fresh and bright and some are suitable for families. A relaxing lounge is provided and there is also a small sun terrace that looks out over the gardens.
6 rms (2 fmly) No smoking in dining room Tea and coffee making facilities No dogs (ex guide dogs) Licensed Cen ht CTV 10P No coaches
ROOMS: s £17-£27; d £34*

BALA Gwynedd Map 06 SH93

Selected

Q Q Q Q *Abercelyn Country House* Llanycil LL23 7YF (0.5m from outskirts of town on A494 towards Dolgellau opposite village church) ☎ 01678 521109 FAX 01678 520556
Closed 21 Dec-4 Jan
Once the local rectory, this fine house dates back to 1729 and lies in wooded grounds, complete with a tumbling mountain stream. Some bedrooms have views of Bala Lake and the hills beyond. A comfortable sitting room is provided and a roaring log fire burns in cooler weather. Bedrooms are smartly decorated and the one room without en suite facilities has its own private bathroom.
3 rms (1 bth 1 shr) No smoking Tea and coffee making facilities No dogs (ex guide dogs) Cen ht CTV 5P No coaches
CARDS:

Selected

Q Q Q Q **Bronwylfa Country House** Llandderfel LL23 7HG (A494, 2m S on B4402 at a right junct; or onB4401 2m then left through village and at a left junct)
☎ 01678 530207 FAX 01678 530207
This fine Victorian house lies in the peaceful village of Llandderfel which is just four miles from Bala. It lies in an elevated position with pleasant lawns and gardens and there are lovely rural views. Bedrooms are smart and modern, many extra items of equipment are provided and one is suitable for families. Guests have use of a comfortable conservatory sitting room and hearty breakfasts are served.
3 bth/shr 1 annexe shr (3 fmly) No smoking CTV in all bedrooms Tea and coffee making facilities Cen ht CTV 8P No coaches
ROOMS: s £20-£30; d £38-£48*

Q Q Q **Erw Feurig** Cefnddwysarn LL23 7LL
(2nd turning on the left after the telephone kiosk at Cefnddwysarn)
☎ 01678 530262
Closed 15 Feb-15 Mar
This attractive, extended and modernised farm cottage enjoys an elevated position, providing fine views over the Berwyn Mountains and surrounding countryside. Two of the bedrooms are en suite with the other two, including one on the ground floor, having adjacent private bathrooms. There is also a cosy lounge to relax in.
4 rms (2 shr) (2 fmly) No smoking in 2 bedrooms No smoking in dining room No smoking in lounges TV available Tea and coffee making facilities No dogs Cen ht CTV No children 6P Fishing Pool table
ROOMS: s £15-£20; d £33-£38*

Q Q **Frondderw** Stryd-y-Fron LL23 7YD (down main street north to south, pass cinema on left then take 1st road on right, up hill 0.25m signposted to Bala golf course and take right fork) ☎ 01678 520301
Mar-Nov
This country guest house is located above the town with lovely views over the lake towards the Berwyn Mountains beyond. Bedrooms are decorated with pretty wallpapers and all have traditional Welsh woollen bedcovers. Two comfortable lounges are provided and a warm welcome is assured from the friendly Jones family. Mrs Jones is a keen lacemaker and regular courses are held with expert tuition provided.
8 rms (1 bth 3 shr) (3 fmly) No smoking in 4 bedrooms No smoking in dining room No smoking in 1 lounge Tea and coffee making facilities No dogs (ex guide dogs) Licensed Cen ht CTV 10P No coaches Golf & Horse riding nearby, windsurfing, rafting Last d 5pm
ROOMS: s £21-£22; d £32-£44; wkly b&b £108.50-£143.50; wkly hlf-bd £175-£217*

Q Q Q **Pen-Y-Bryn** *(SH928363)* Sarnau LL23 7LH (3m NE of Bala on A494. Pass red telephone box on left at Cefnddmysarn, 2nd left, green B&B sign, second Farm) ☎ 01678 530389 FAX 01678 521262 Mrs E Jones
Guests at this 19th-century farmhouse receive a warm welcome from Mrs Jones and her family. Pen-Y-Bryn lies above the Corwen to Bala road and there are lovely views from many rooms towards the Berwyn Mountains. Bedrooms are cosy, very pretty and have en suite or private facilities. There is a conservatory dining room and a choice of two comfortable sitting rooms.
3 annexe bth/shr No smoking TV available Tea and coffee making facilities No dogs Cen ht CTV No children 6P Fishing 200 acres mixed
ROOMS: d £37-£40*

Q Q Q **Trem-Y-Wawr** Cae Groes LL23 7AQ (A494 Corwen-Bala, in town pass police station on right then turn first right signposted "to golf club". Last house on left with parking on side) ☎ 01678 520994
This modern house lies in an elevated position above the town and lake and a warm welcome is extended to her guests by owner, Marjorie Griffiths and family. Three modern bedrooms are provided and these are equipped with televisions and other modern amenities. There is a delightful breakfast room and guests have use of the family lounge if required.
3 rms (1 shr) No smoking CTV in all bedrooms Tea and coffee making facilities No dogs Cen ht No children 4P Golf Walking Watersports nearby
ROOMS: d £32-£40; wkly b&b £112-£140*

BANGOR Gwynedd Map 06 SH57

Selected

Q Q Q Q ***Country Bumpkin*** Cefn Coed, Llandegai LL57 4BG (Bangor side of A5/A55 junct, signposted off A522)
☎ 01248 370477 FAX 01248 354166
Closed Xmas & Jan
Originally an 18th-century farmhouse, this immaculately maintained house offers high quality accommodation. There are just three bedrooms and these are spacious, comfortably furnished and well equipped. A pretty breakfast room is provided for guests as well as a pleasant lounge. There are fine views over Penrhyn Castle and the Menai Straits.
3 bth/shr No smoking in dining room CTV in all bedrooms Tea and coffee making facilities Licensed Cen ht CTV No children 16yrs 20P No coaches
CARDS:

Q Q Q **Goetre Isaf Farmhouse** *(SH557697)* Caernarfon Rd LL57 4DB (2m W on the A4087) ☎ 01248 364541 FAX 01248 364541 Mr & Mrs Whowell
Goetre Isaf lies in several acres where sheep and horses peacefully graze. It dates back to the 18th century and there are superb views over the surrounding countryside. Bedrooms are nicely decorated and one is suitable for families. There is a choice of lounges and also a conservatory that opens out onto the gardens. Exposed timbers abound and the main lounge features an impressive inglenook fireplace. Guests dine family style and much of the produce used comes from the kitchen garden.
3 rms (1 bth/shr) (1 fmly) No smoking in area of dining room No smoking in 1 lounge Direct dial from bedrooms Cen ht CTV P Large garden 10 acres sheep horses bees Last d whenever
ROOMS: s £16.50-£39; d £29-£39

Selected

Q Q Q Q **Nant y Fedw** Trefelin, Llanedgai LL57 4LH (take A5122 to Bangor, turn onto road marked for Llandegai/Tal-y-Bont at Penrhyn castle, down hill for 100mtrs, turn right to large gates, turn right) ☎ 01248 351683
Nant y Fedw was built over 150 years ago to house the artisans working at nearby Penrhyn Castle and has been carefully modernised over recent years. It has a lovely garden, and many exposed beams and timbers still feature throughout the house. Two bedrooms are available and one of these is located at ground floor level. The one without an en suite bathroom has its own private facility. A log fire burns when needed in the comfortable sitting room, and guests dine family style.
2 bth/shr No smoking in bedrooms No smoking in dining room CTV in all bedrooms Tea and coffee making facilities Cen ht CTV 4P No coaches Last d 5.30pm
ROOMS: s £23; d £38*

BARMOUTH Gwynedd Map **06** SH61

Selected

Llwyndu Farmhouse *(SH599185)* Llwyndu, Llanaber LL42 1RR (A496 from Barmouth to Harlech when street lights finish out of Barmouth next turning on the right)
☎ 01341 280144 FAX 01341 281236 Mr P Thompson
This 16th-century farmhouse has been carefully restored and converted and is just two miles north of Barmouth. Bedrooms are modern and well equipped and several have four-poster beds. Many are located in nearby buildings and some are suitable for families. Original features have been retained with thick stone walls, inglenook fireplaces and exposed beams and timbers. There is a cosy lounge for residents.
3 bth/shr 4 annexe bth/shr (2 fmly) No smoking CTV in all bedrooms Tea and coffee making facilities Licensed Cen ht CTV 10P
4 acres non-working Last d 7.30pm
ROOMS: d £58-£68; wkly hlf-bd £280-£349*
CARDS:

BEDDGELERT Gwynedd Map **06** SH54

Selected

Sygun Fawr Country House Hotel LL55 4NE (singposted from A498 on Capel Curig side of village, turn off road over river at sign and track road leads to hotel)
☎ 01766 890258
A 17th-century manor house which lies in beautiful countryside within Snowdonia. Bedrooms are small but pretty and many have superb views. Stone walls and exposed timbers abound and a cosy bar is provided in addition to several comfortable sitting rooms.
10 bth/shr (1 fmly) Tea and coffee making facilities Licensed CTV 20P Sauna Last d 8pm
ROOMS: s £33-£46.50; d £57*
CARDS:

BETWS-Y-COED Conwy Map **06** SH75

Selected

Aberconwy House Llanwrst Rd LL24 0HD (on A470, half a mile north from A5/A470 junct)
☎ 01690 710202 FAX 01690 710800
rs Jan-Mar
There are superb views over the village and the Llugwy and Conwy valleys from this immaculately maintained house. Four of the comfortably furnished bedrooms enjoy these views, and these like the other rooms have many extra facilities. Trouser presses and ironing facilities are included and thoughtful touches such as fresh fruit and electric blankets are also provided. A relaxing lounge is available for residents.

8 bth/shr (2 fmly) No smoking CTV in all bedrooms Tea and coffee making facilities Licensed Cen ht CTV 10P No coaches
ROOMS: d £40-£50*
CARDS:

Bryn Bella Lon Muriau, Llanrwst Rd LL24 0HD (0.5m N of A5 on A470)
☎ 01690 710627 FAX 01690 710627
Bryn Bella is a small but very well appointed Victorian Guest house overlooking the picturesque village of Bets-y-coed and is an excellent location for touring Snowdonia or other local attractions. Bedrooms are comfortable, well equipped, tastefully decorated and most are en suite. There is also an attractive guests lounge with good views over the valley.
5 rms (3 shr) No smoking CTV in all bedrooms Tea and coffee making facilities No dogs (ex guide dogs) No children none 6P No coaches
ROOMS: s £19; d £40-£46; wkly b&b £126-£145

Bryn Llewelyn Holyhead Rd LL24 0BN (travelling west on A5, turn sharp left 100yds beyond "Climber & Rambler" shop) ☎ 01690 710601 FAX 710601
This friendly little guest house is run by Steve and Naomi Parker and provides good-value accommodation which is popular with walkers and climbers. Rooms are well decorated, equipped with TV and some are suitable for families.
7 rms (4 shr) (3 fmly) No smoking CTV in all bedrooms Tea and coffee making facilities Cen ht CTV 9P
ROOMS: s £16.50-£27.50; d £30-£47; wkly b&b £105-£160*

Bryn-y-Gwynt Holyhead Rd LL24 0BN (on A5, approx 100yds W of Spar shop)
☎ 01690 710502 FAX 01690 710502
Located just a few minutes' walk from the village centre and between the River Llugwy and the wooded hillside this small, friendly establishment of Victorian origins is run by Peter and Joyce Melling. Bedrooms are attractively decorated and all have TVs and courtesy trays. There is a

separate guests lounge and a cosy pine-furnished breakfast room where hearty Welsh breakfasts are provided.
4 rms (2 shr) No smoking CTV in all bedrooms Tea and coffee making facilities Cen ht No children 10 4P No coaches
ROOMS: s £20-£22; d £33-£41; wkly b&b £115.50-£136.50

Q Q **Coed-y-Fron** Vicarage Rd LL24 0AD
(enter Betws-y-Coed on A5 (Bangor), pass traffic lights, look for P.O. then St Mary's Church immediately after church turn into Vicarage Rd)
☎ 01690 710365
Coed-y-Fron is a large Victorian house and lies in an elevated and very peaceful location above the church. It is surrounded by mature trees and there are fine views over the village. Modern and well equipped bedrooms are provided and some of these are suitable for families. Mike and Beth Mills are the friendly owners and hospitality is warm and welcoming.
7 rms (3 bth/shr) (1 fmly) No smoking in dining room No smoking in lounges CTV in all bedrooms Tea and coffee making facilities Cen ht No children 2yrs
ROOMS: s £16-£18; d £32-£42; wkly b&b £105-£133*

Q Q Q **Ferns Non Smokers Guest House** Holyhead Rd LL24 0AN
(on A5 close to Waterloo Bridge) ☎ 01690 710587 FAX 01690 710587
The Ferns is a friendly, well established, family run guest house situated near the centre of the village and lies between wooded slopes and the River Conwy. Bedrooms are decorated with pretty papers and rich fabrics and one is now suitable for families. All are well equipped with modern facilities and some beds have attractive canopies. There is also a comfortable lounge for residents.
9 bth/shr (2 fmly) No smoking CTV in all bedrooms Tea and coffee making facilities No dogs Licensed Cen ht CTV No children 4yrs 10P
ROOMS: s £20-£25; d £40-£44

Q Q Q ***Mairlys*** Holyhead Rd LL24 0AN
(On the A5, over the Waterloo Bridge, approx 0.25m past Little Chef next to The Cotswold Outdoor Shop)
☎ 01690 710190 FAX 01690 710190
Feb-Nov
An imposing Victorian building located in the centre of the village and a good base for touring the Snowdonia National Park and surrounding areas

contd. on p.594.

and also popular with golfers. Bedrooms have been refurbished to a high standard and are well equipped with TVs and courtesy trays. There is also a comfortable lounge and guests can enjoy the attractive gardens.
5 rms (3 shr) No smoking CTV in all bedrooms Tea and coffee making facilities No dogs Cen ht CTV No children 14yrs 7P

Q Q Summer Hill Non Smokers Guesthouse Coedcynhelier Rd LL24 0BL (turn off A5 opposite "Climber & Rambler" shop, cross bridge, turn left go through car park, Summer Hill is 70yds up hill on right) ☎ 01690 710306
This friendly guest house is situated above the village and is surrounded by wooded slopes leading down to the River Llugwy. The village and its amenities are just a short walk away. It has been run for over twenty years by Wendy and Alan Hughes and provides neat and well decorated accommodation.
7 rms (4 shr) (1 fmly) No smoking CTV in 1 bedroom Tea and coffee making facilities Licensed Cen ht CTV No children 3yrs 6P No coaches Forest and River walks Last d 5pm
ROOMS: s £18.50-£23; d £37-£40; wkly b&b £104-£145; wkly hlf-bd £170-£212✻

Selected

Q Q Q Q White Horse Inn Capel Garmon LL26 0RW (from Llanwrst to Betws main road turn left at Snowdonia and Chapel Garmon sign) ☎ 01690 710271 FAX 01690 710271
This 16th century inn has retained much of its original character including exposed timbers, stone walls and log fires. The bar features an interesting collection of Victorian pottery and chinaware and a large range of food is always available there. The cottage-style restaurant is a delightful venue for romantic dinners. Bedrooms are on the small side but are nicely furnished and well equipped with modern amenities.
6 bth/shr No smoking in bedrooms No smoking in dining room CTV in all bedrooms Tea and coffee making facilities Cen ht No children 7yrs 30P Last d 9pm
ROOMS: s £30; d £56✻
CARDS:

BONTDDU Gwynedd Map 06 SH61

Premier Selected

Q Q Q Q Q *Borthwnog Hall Hotel* LL40 2TT (on A496)
☎ 01341 430271 FAX 01341 430682
Closed Xmas
This fine 17th-century country house occupies an enviable position on the edge of the Mawddach Estuary. There are quite superb views over this towards Cader Idris and the Arran Mountains from bedrooms and from the public areas. An elegant sitting room opens out onto the gardens during warmer weather and a real fire keeps away the chill during winter months. Bedrooms are spacious and comfortable and one has its own private sitting room. The Library Art Gallery contains many original water-colours, oils and also some examples of pottery and sculpture which can be purchased. The beautiful Garth Gell nature reserve adjoins the property.
3 bth/shr No smoking in dining room No smoking in lounges CTV in all bedrooms Tea and coffee making facilities Direct dial from bedrooms Licensed Cen ht 6P No coaches Last d 8.15pm
CARDS:

BORTH Ceredigion Map 06 SN69

Q Q Q Glanmor Hotel Princess St SY24 5JP
(turn off A487 onto B4353 signposted Borth, Glanmor is situated at N end of sea front) ☎ 01970 871689
Glanmor lies on the promenade with miles of sandy beach nearby. It is also quite near to the local golf course and is therefore a popular venue for visiting golfers. Bedrooms include some suitable for families and all are equipped with televisions and other modern amenities. Residents have use of a cosy lounge/bar.
7 rms (2 shr) (3 fmly) CTV in 4 bedrooms Tea and coffee making facilities Licensed CTV 12P No coaches Last d 5pm
ROOMS: s £21; d £42; wkly b&b £147; wkly hlf-bd £220.50

BRECHFA Carmarthenshire Map 02 SN53

Selected

Q Q Q Q Glasfryn SA32 7QY (leave M4 junct 49 onto A48 to Cross Hands, towards Carmarthen for approx 1m, turn left onto B4310 cross over A40 continue on B4310) ☎ 01267 202306 FAX 01267 202306
This bright and well maintained guest house lies in the centre of a pretty village which itself lies in lovely countryside. The television lounge is cosy and inviting and there is a smart conservatory restaurant which also opens to the public. Joyce and Derek Hart offer a warm welcome and there is a relaxing atmosphere throughout.
3 bth/shr No smoking in bedrooms No smoking in area of dining room CTV in all bedrooms Tea and coffee making facilities No dogs (ex guide dogs) Licensed Cen ht CTV 12P Mountian Bike Cycle hire Last d 9pm
ROOMS: s £30; d £45; wkly b&b £150; wkly hlf-bd £238✻
CARDS:

BRECON Powys Map 03 SO02

See also Bronllys & Sennybridge

Q Q Q Beacons 16 Bridge St LD3 8AH (W side of town centre, just across the river100mtrs on right) ☎ 01874 623339 FAX 01874 623339
rs 24-26 Dec
This 18th-century property has a wealth of charm and character, and is located just west of the town centre across the River Usk. At the time of our

last inspection, the new owners were making many improvements to the accommodation. The bedrooms vary in both size and style, but all are similarly equipped. Separate tables are provided in the pleasant dining room, and other facilities include a comfortably furnished lounge and a cosy bar.
12 rms (9 bth/shr) (4 fmly) No smoking CTV in all bedrooms Tea and coffee making facilities Licensed Cen ht CTV 16P Last d 9pm
ROOMS: s £20-£25; d £36-£55*
CARDS:

Q Q Q **Borderers** 47 The Watton LD3 7EG
(E on A40, on the right 200mtrs past the pedestrian crossing opposite the church) ☎ 01874 623559 FAX 01874 623559
This 17th-century drover's inn still features the original courtyard that now provides access to many of the bedrooms. Bedecked with pretty hanging baskets, the Borderers is a previous winner of Brecon in Bloom. Bedrooms are decorated with matching floral fabrics; family rooms are available and there is a room specially designed for the less able. Breakfast is taken in the attractively decorated dining room.
4 rms (2 shr) 5 annexe bth/shr (3 fmly) No smoking in 4 bedrooms No smoking in dining room CTV in all bedrooms Tea and coffee making facilities Cen ht 6P No coaches
ROOMS: s £22-£40; d £32-£46*

Selected

Q Q Q Q **The Coach** Orchard St, Llanfaes LD3 8AN (town one way system, turn left at traffic lights, over bridge then 300yds on right)
☎ 01874 623803
Closed 22 Dec-7 Jan
This former roadside inn dates back to the 19th century. Owners Val and Paul Ashton have converted the building to provide extremely comfortable, modern accommodation. The pretty bedrooms are particularly well equipped and all have canopied beds and matching fabrics. An attractive lounge is provided for the guests and home cooked meals are available.
6 bth/shr (2 fmly) No smoking CTV in all bedrooms Tea and coffee making facilities Direct dial from bedrooms No dogs Licensed Cen ht No children 5P No coaches Last d 7pm
ROOMS: d £40-£42*

Selected

Q Q Q Q **Llanddetty Hall** *(SO124205)* Talybont-on-Usk LD3 7YR (7m SE off B4558) ☎ 01874 676415 FAX 01874 676415
Mrs H E Atkins
This pretty 16th-century farmhouse is located in the rural tranquility of the Usk Valley. A wealth of original features have been retained with exposed timbers and polished floorboards in many rooms. The lounge is dominated by an impressive inglenook fireplace where fires burn in colder weather. This is a working farm with sheep grazing the surrounding fields and a flock of white doves adding to the pastoral charm.
3 bth/shr No smoking Tea and coffee making facilities No dogs (ex guide dogs) Cen ht CTV No children 12yrs 6P 48 acres sheep Last d day before
ROOMS: s £24; d £38-£42; wkly b&b fr £126*

Selected

Q Q Q Q **Ty Newydd** Cambrian Cruisers Marina, Pencelli LD3 7LJ (Off A40, on B4558, 3m from Brecon)
☎ 01874 665315 FAX 01874 665315
Closed Nov-Mar
This early 18th-century farmhouse is situated beside the Brecon Canal and lovely views of the surrounding countryside can be enjoyed from the conservatory lounge.The friendly owners Ruth and Peter Griffiths also run a canal cruising service. The bedrooms are furnished in an appropriate country style, with pretty co-ordinated fabrics and benefit from modern facilities.
4 bth/shr (1 fmly) No smoking CTV in all bedrooms Tea and coffee making facilities No dogs (ex guide dogs) Cen ht No children 11yrs 4P No coaches Narrowboat hire
ROOMS: s fr £25; d fr £40*
CARDS:

BRONLLYS Powys Map 03 SO13

Q Q Q **The Laurels** Church St, Bronllys LD3 0HS
(after passing the Bronllys sign on the A470 from Brecon or the A438 from Hay-on-Wye look for large yellow house in centre of village)
☎ 01874 712188 FAX 01874 712187
Closed 24 Dec-2 Jan
This large house lies at the A438/A479 junction in the village of Bronllys. It is run by John and Marie Gray and her artistic skills are evident in the rich decorative colours used throughout the house. Just three bedrooms are available and these are fitted with period furniture. There is an elegant sitting room for guests and a pretty breakfast room.
3 bth/shr (1 fmly) No smoking CTV in 2 bedrooms Tea and coffee making facilities No dogs (ex guide dogs) Cen ht CTV No children 7yrs 18P No coaches
ROOMS: s £16-£22; d £36-£40; wkly b&b £105-£140*
CARDS:

BRYNSIENCYN See ANGLESEY, ISLE OF

BUILTH WELLS Powys Map 03 SO05

Selected

Q Q Q Q **Woodlands** Hay Rd LD2 3YL
(just S of Builth Wells on the side of the A470, entrance by lay-by)
☎ 01982 552354 FAX 01982 552354
Located just on the outskirts of the town this lovely period farmhouse is set in its own pretty grounds well back from the road. Ideal for visitors to the mid-Wales countryside or for those stopping off from a longer journey, guests will find a warm welcome from the Nicholls family. Well maintained throughout, the bedrooms are spacious, bright and comfortable whilst the public areas include a traditional style dining room with an impressive staircase dominating the centre of the house. The good, home-cooked breakfasts are generous.
6 shr No smoking CTV in all bedrooms Tea and coffee making facilities Cen ht 6P No coaches
ROOMS: s £20-£25; d £36-£40

BURRY PORT Carmarthenshire Map **02** SN40

Selected

QQQQ **The George** Stepney Rd SA16 0BH (turn off A484 at traffic lights, at Achddu Post Office look for town centre sign, near railway station at lower end of Stepney Road) ☎ 01554 832211
Situated in the centre of this historic port, famous as the landing place of Amelia Earhart, the first woman to fly across the Atlantic 60 years ago. The public areas are spacious and comfortable with two separate dining areas, where a wide range of dishes are available, including daily specials. The attractive 'Friendship' bar is filled with memorabilia of the historic flight and a wide range of local and popular beers are offered. Bedrooms are very well equipped and comfortable with facilities which include sitting areas and modern en suite or private facilities. Les George is a very friendly and caring host, justifiably proud of his homely inn.
5 rms (4 bth/shr) 4 annexe rms (2 bth/shr) (2 fmly) CTV in all bedrooms Tea and coffee making facilities No dogs (ex guide dogs) Cen ht No children 6yrs No coaches Last d 9.45pm
ROOMS: s £18.50-£35; d £35-£45*
MEALS: Lunch £5.50-£18.50alc Dinner £8.35-£19.50alc*

CAERNARFON Gwynedd Map **06** SH46

See also Penygroes

Selected

QQQQ **Caer Menai** 15 Church St LL55 1SW
(within Old Town Walls) ☎ 01286 672612 FAX 672612
Mar-Dec
The town walls form the boundary of the back garden at this friendly guesthouse which has been run by Keith and Hilary Lardner for almost a quarter of a century. An attractive breakfast room is provided and there is also a comfortable lounge for residents. Bedrooms are bright and fresh and all are equipped with modern facilities.
7 rms (3 shr) (2 fmly) No smoking CTV in all bedrooms Tea and coffee making facilities No dogs (ex guide dogs) CTV No coaches
ROOMS: s £20-£25; d £34-£44*

Selected

QQQQ **Hafoty** *(SH504584)* Rhostryfan LL54 7PH (off A487 Caernarfon/Porthmadog road, 2.5m from Caernarfon follow B road signposted Rhostryfan. First left after 30 sign in village, pass school) ☎ 01286 830144 & 0402 371170 FAX 01286 830441 Mrs M Davies
Mar-Nov
Nestling just outside a pretty Welsh village and in the foothills of Snowdonia, Hafoty enjoys fine views over the Menai Straits and Caernarfon Castle. It has been created over several years from converted farm buildings and now provides well equipped modern accommodation. Spacious bedrooms are provided and children are especially welcome. The main house has comfortably furnished and attractively decorated public areas where cheery log fires burn when needed. One bedroom is located in nearby outbuildings and several self catering cottages are also available. Mari and Wil Davies are the very friendly owners and they create a peaceful and relaxing atmosphere.
3 shr 2 annexe bth/shr (1 fmly) No smoking in bedrooms No smoking in dining room CTV in all bedrooms Tea and coffee making facilities No dogs (ex guide dogs) Licensed Cen ht CTV 22P 17 acres sheep Last d 9am
ROOMS: s £28; d £48-£52; wkly b&b £150-£170; wkly hlf-bd £215-£235
CARDS:

QQ **Menai View Hotel** North Rd LL55 1BD
(N on A487. Main Rd into Caernarfon from Bangor overlooking Menai Straight) ☎ 01286 674602 FAX 01492 876661
Located on the approach to the town centre from Bangor, there are fine views over the Menai Straits from many bedrooms and from the first floor lounge. Family bedrooms are provided, one is located at ground floor level and all have televisions.
8 rms (4 shr) (5 fmly) CTV in all bedrooms Tea and coffee making facilities Licensed Cen ht CTV
ROOMS: s £20-£30; d £25-£39*
CARDS:

Premier Selected

QQQQQ **Pengwern** *(SH459587)* Saron LL54 5UH (from Caernarfon take A487 S passing supermarket on right, take 1st right turn after bridge 2m to Saron, through X-roads, farm is 1st drive on right) ☎ 01286 831500 FAX 01286 831500 Mr & Mrs G Rowlands
Closed Dec & Jan
This delightful farmhouse is surrounded by 130 acres of farmland that runs down to Foryd Bay which is noted for its bird life. There are fine views from many bedrooms over to Anglesey and the top of Snowdon can also be seen on clear days. Bedrooms are generally spacious and all are well equipped with modern facilities. A comfortable lounge is provided for guests and good home cooking is served.
3 bth/shr No smoking CTV in all bedrooms Tea and coffee making facilities No dogs Cen ht 4P 130 acres beef sheep
ROOMS: s £30; d £44-£50*

CARDIFF Cardiff Map **03** ST17

QQQ *Albany* 191-193 Albany Rd, Roath CF2 3NU
(exit M4 at junc29, exit M48 at A4161, follow city centre signs, turn right at traffic lights, at Roath Court Funeral Home bear left at rdbt)
☎ 01222 494121
Closed Xmas wk
Conveniently situated for Cardiff city centre, this personally-run guest house is located in the suburb of Roath. Bedrooms benefit from modern facilities, are comfortably furnished and one is on the ground floor. There is a cosy resident lounge and a bright dining room with separate tables.
11 rms (9 bth/shr) (4 fmly) No smoking in dining room CTV in all bedrooms Tea and coffee making facilities No dogs (ex guide dogs) Cen ht

QQQ **Clare Court Hotel** 46/48 Clare Rd CF1 7RS
(800 yards from general railway station)
☎ 01222 344839 FAX 01222 251511
This personally run hotel is situated within easy reach of the city centre and the National Stadium. The bedrooms include family rooms and all are well equipped. There is a pleasant dining room with separate tables and a bar lounge which is adorned with sporting memorabilia belonging to the owner, former Welsh football international Gil Reece.
8 bth/shr (2 fmly) No smoking in dining room CTV in all bedrooms Tea and coffee making facilities Direct dial from bedrooms No dogs Licensed Cen ht CTV
ROOMS: s £25-£28; d £36-£40*
CARDS:

QQQ **Courtfield Hotel** 101 Cathedral Rd CF1 9PH
(from city centre cross bridge over River Taff and turn 1st right into Cathedral Road) ☎ 01222 227701 FAX 01222 227701
Closed 24-31 Dec
Set in a tree lined conservation area within minutes of the city centre and Cardiff Castle, Courtfield Hotel, an attractive Victorian property, has a relaxed atmosphere and the resident proprietors Norman and Keith are welcoming hosts. Bedrooms, equipped with modern facilities, are

comfortable and have been brightly decorated and furnished. Downstairs there is an elegant reception lounge and, adjacent to the dining room, there is a licensed bar.

12 rms (1 bth 4 shr) (1 fmly) No smoking CTV in all bedrooms Tea and coffee making facilities Direct dial from bedrooms No dogs (ex guide dogs) Licensed Cen ht CTV No children 7yrs No coaches
ROOMS: s fr £25; d fr £55*
CARDS:

Q Q Q ***Ferrier's (Alva) Hotel*** 130-132 Cathedral Rd CF1 9LQ
☎ 01222 383413 FAX 01222 383413
Closed 2wks Xmas & New Year
Just a few minutes walk from the city centre, this large Victorian house provides comfortable and soundly maintained accommodation to suit both commercial visitors and tourists. Ground floor and family rooms are both available and there is a lounge bar supplemented by a TV lounge and a dining room with modern furnishings.
26 rms (6 bth/shr) (4 fmly) CTV in all bedrooms Tea and coffee making facilities Direct dial from bedrooms Licensed Cen ht CTV 10P No coaches Last d 7.45pm
CARDS:

Selected

Q Q Q Q ***Marlborough*** 98 Newport Rd CF2 1DG
☎ 01222 492385 FAX 01222 492385
A little oasis of comfort just 5 minutes walk from the city centre, this exceedingly friendly, family run guest house offers well cared for accommodation suitable for both the business traveller and the tourist. On the ground floor there is both a lounge and an attractive restaurant where good, imaginative home-cooking is available both at breakfast and dinner. The bedrooms are generally of generous proportions, all are individually decorated with great care and well equipped with many thoughtful little extras. Secure car parking is also available.
8 rms (5 bth/shr) (2 fmly) No smoking in bedrooms No smoking in dining room CTV in all bedrooms Tea and coffee making facilities No dogs Licensed Cen ht CTV ch fac 8P Last d 7pm

Q Q Q ***Tanglewood*** 4 Tygwyn Rd, Penylan CF2 5JE ☎ 01222 473447
This large detached house is the home of the Griffiths family who offer a warm welcome to both business and leisure visitors. There is an attractive dining room in which breakfast is taken, a spacious lobby area and bedrooms which have been thoughtfully decorated and furnished with care. There is also a large rear garden where guests are welcome to relax.
4 rms

CARDIGAN Ceredigion Map 02 SN14

Q Q Q **Brynhyfryd** Gwbert Rd SA43 1AE (on the B4548 in Cardigan town signposted Gwbert) ☎ 01239 612861 FAX 01239 612861
Real Welsh hospitality is the order of the day at this immaculately maintained guest house. It has been run by Nesta and Ieuan Davies for nearly twenty years and many of their guests return year after year to enjoy the warm welcome. Well equipped modern bedrooms are provided and some of these are suitable for families. Nesta is well known for her home cooking and there is comfortable lounge for residents. Street parking is unrestricted.
7 rms (3 shr) (1 fmly) No smoking in 2 bedrooms No smoking in dining room CTV in all bedrooms Tea and coffee making facilities No dogs (ex guide dogs) Cen ht No children 3yrs No coaches Last d noon
ROOMS: s £17; d £34-£38*

Q Q ***Webley Hotel*** Poppit Sands, St Dogmaels SA43 3LN
☎ 01239 612085
rs 24-27 Dec (b&b only)
This is a family run riverside inn located in a popular tourist area. It lies overlooking the Teifi Estuary at Poppit Sands and enjoys fine views. Four bedrooms have recently been modernised and en suite facilities have been added. The remaining rooms are to be similarly improved over the next year or so. There is a popular public bar, a function room and a small residents lounge. A full range of meals is served.
8 rms (4 bth/shr) (1 fmly) No smoking in dining room CTV in 4 bedrooms Tea and coffee making facilities No dogs Cen ht CTV 53P Last d 9pm

CARMARTHEN Carmarthenshire Map 02 SN42

See also Brechfa & Cwmduad

Selected

Q Q Q Q **Capel Dewi Uchaf Farm** *(SN485203)* Capel Dewi SA32 8AY (4m E of Carmarthen on B4300, from Carmarthenthrough village. Est. on left hand side) ☎ 01267 290799 FAX 01267 290003
Mrs F Burns
Closed Xmas
Fronted by a colourful cottage garden, and with a neatly tended vegetable garden to the rear, this house, reputed to be 500 years old, enjoys a peaceful location with open fields leading to the River Towy. The house has been carefully restored by the present owners, retaining many of the original features, including exposed timbers, feature stone walls and numerous large fireplaces. Bedrooms, including a family

contd.

suite in the adjacent cottage, are richly furnished, in sympathy with the style of the building, and thoughtfully equipped. Good home cooking is a feature of Farm Retreats both at dinner and breakfast.
4 bth/shr (1 fmly) No smoking CTV in all bedrooms Tea and coffee making facilities No dogs Licensed Cen ht CTV 10P Fishing 34 acres non-working Last d 10am
ROOMS: s £37; d £50; wkly b&b £157.53; wkly hlf-bd £314.90*

Selected

Q Q Q Q Cwmtwrch Hotel & Four Seasons Restaurant *(SN497220)* Nantgaredig SA32 7NY
(5m E of Carmarthen, take B4310 at Nantgaredig crossroads towards Brechfa, premises 0.25m N off A40 on the right)
☎ 01267 290238 FAX 01267 290808 Mrs J Willmott
Closed 23 Dec-28 Dec
This very pleasant, personally run small hotel is part of a complex which has been developed from a 200 year old farmhouse and buildings. The 30 acres of landscaped grounds also contain The Four Seasons Restaurant, where dinner is served, and a well equipped leisure centre. The bedrooms, three of which are located on the ground floor of a converted Georgian stone-built barn, are tastefully furnished in a style befitting the age and character of the house. All have modern facilities and equipment. Family bedded accommodation is available. There is a comfortable and homely lounge and a very pleasant breakfast room which retains a lot of original charm and character.
5 bth/shr (2 fmly) No smoking in dining room CTV in all bedrooms Tea and coffee making facilities Licensed Cen ht CTV 20P Indoor swimming pool (heated) Gymnasium Jacuzzi in swimming pool 30 acres sheep Last d 9pm
ROOMS: s £40-£42; d £54-£58; wkly b&b £200-£225*
CARDS:

Q Q Q Glôg Farm *(SN371154)* Llangain SA33 5AY
(leave Carmarthen on the A40 W, turn left onto B4312 signposted Llanstephan, through Llangain turn right signed Llangynog/Glôg, farm 0.75m on right) ☎ 01267 241271 Mrs H E Rodenhurst
This is a small beef farm that lies in lovely Dylan Thomas country. The sandy beaches of South Carmarthenshire are a few miles away and the farmhouse is a good base for the many attractions in this part of Wales. Bedrooms are well decorated and some are suitable for families. There is an attractive rustic dining room and the comfortable lounge has a wood burning stove for the colder weather. The farm is run by the Rodenhurst family who are friendly and welcoming.
4 bth/shr (2 fmly) No smoking in dining room Tea and coffee making facilities No dogs (ex guide dogs) Cen ht CTV 10P Golf 9 Golf 1m 40 acres beef Last d 4pm
ROOMS: s £20; d £40; wkly b&b £120; wkly hlf-bd fr £190*

Selected

Q Q Q Q *Pantgwyn* *(SN460228)* SA32 7ES
(turn off A40 4m E af Carmarthen at Whitemill and follow sign to Pantgwyn Farm) (The Circle)
☎ 01267 290247 FAX 01267 290880 Mr T Giles
Closed Xmas
Located in the heart of Merlin country where Merlin was said to live with his sister, Pantgwyn dates back to the 17th-century. The area is a haven for wildlife and the farm also has a number of pet animals. Bedrooms are furnished in keeping with the house, modern equipment is provided and some are suitable for families. An elegant lounge is provided and this has an inglenook fireplace where logs burn during the colder months. Good home cooking is provided with local farm produce used whenever possible.
3 bth/shr (2 fmly) No smoking CTV in all bedrooms Tea and coffee making facilities No dogs (ex guide dogs) Licensed Cen ht 20P Pool table 12 acres sheep Last d 5pm
CARDS:

CEMAES BAY See ANGLESEY, ISLE OF

CHEPSTOW Monmouthshire

See Tintern

CHURCH STOKE Powys Map 07 SO29

Selected

Q Q Q Q The Drewin *(SO261905)* SY15 6TW
☎ 01588 620325 FAX 01588 620325 Mrs C Richards
Apr-Oct rs Etr (if in Mar)
This delightful 17th-century farmhouse has a wealth of charm and character. It lies close to Offa's Dyke and attracts many walkers as a result. Very much a working farm, it is in an elevated location and commands superb views over the surrounding countryside. Many original features remain with an abundance of exposed timbers and inglenook fireplaces. Two sitting rooms are provided and bedrooms are well equipped and comfortable. Ceinwen and Robert Richards are the very friendly owners and they go out of their way to make their guests feel welcome and at home. Ceinwen is responsible for hearty Welsh breakfasts that set you up for the day.
2 shr (1 fmly) No smoking CTV in all bedrooms Tea and coffee making facilities Cen ht CTV 6P Games room 102 acres mixed Last d 7pm
ROOMS: s £20-£22; d £38-£40; wkly b&b £130-£140; wkly hlf-bd £200-£210*

COLWYN BAY Conwy Map 06 SH87

Q Q Q Cabin Hill Private Hotel College Av, Rhos-on-Sea LL28 4NT (exit A55 at Rhos-on-Sea, follow signs for promenade through Rhos village, turn left at Rhos Fynach public house, College Ave third road on right) ☎ 01492 544568
Cabin Hill lies in a quiet residential area of Rhos-on-Sea and the seafront and local shops are within easy walking distance. Bedrooms are neat and well decorated and some are suitable for families. There is a foyer bar for residents and a separate lounge which is comfortably furnished. Meals are available in the spacious lounge.
10 rms (7 shr) (2 fmly) No smoking in dining room CTV in all bedrooms Tea and coffee making facilities Licensed Cen ht CTV 2P Last d 4.30pm
ROOMS: s £18-£18; d £36-£36; wkly b&b £119-£119; wkly hlf-bd £170-£170

Q Q Crossroads 15 Coed Pella Rd LL29 7AT
☎ 01492 530736 FAX 01492 530736
Closed 24 Dec-2 Jan
Ideally situated for touring North Wales, Crossroads offers both comfort and value. Tucked away in a quiet residential street it is just a short walk from the town centre and shops. Owner Margaret Owens extends a warm welcome to guests and takes pride in the attractively decorated bedrooms, two of which are family rooms. A well appointed and spacious lounge is also available for residents use.
5 rms (2 shr) (2 fmly) No smoking in dining room CTV in all bedrooms Tea and coffee making facilities No dogs (ex guide dogs) Cen ht CTV No children 3yrs 3P No coaches
ROOMS: s £14-£16; d £28-£38*

Q **Grosvenor Hotel** 106-108 Abergele Rd LL29 7PS (on main road through town) ☎ 01492 530798 & 531586 FAX 01492 531586
This private hotel located near the town centre, is also within easy walking distance of the sea front. It provides a choice of comfortable lounges and a cosy bar and games room. The hotel is run by the very friendly Wood family. Meals are available.
18 rms (2 shr) (8 fmly) CTV in 15 bedrooms Tea and coffee making facilities Licensed CTV 16P Pool table Last d 7pm
ROOMS: s £18.50-£21; wkly b&b £116.50-£130*

Q Q Q **Northwood Hotel** 47 Rhos Rd, Rhos-on-Sea LL28 4RS (turn up Rhos Rd which is opposite the building with clock on top, premises 200 yards on the left before methodist church) ☎ 01492 549931
Closed 1 Nov-28 Feb
Located in Rhos on Sea, the Northwood Hotel has been professionally run by Gordon & Agnes Palliser for many years. The seafront and local shops are just a short walk away. Bedrooms are neatly decorated and well equipped. As well as a cosy bar, there is a traditional lounge and a warm and friendly atmosphere prevails with many guests returning year after year.
12 rms (11 bth/shr) (3 fmly) No smoking in dining room No smoking in lounges CTV in all bedrooms Tea and coffee making facilities Licensed Cen ht CTV No children 2yrs 12P No coaches Last d 6.15pm
ROOMS: s £22; d £44; wkly hlf-bd £160-£170*
CARDS:

Selected

Q Q Q Q **Plas Rhos Hotel** Cayley Promenade, Rhos-on-Sea LL28 4EP ☎ 01492 543698 FAX 01492 540088
This imposing property built in 1909 is situated on the promenade at Rhos-on-Sea where it commands panoramic views of the bay, beach and coast, and many guests return frequently. It has been extensively and tastefully renovated by Gillian Ponton, to provide good quality, well equipped, modern accommodation which includes bedrooms with sea views and one bedroom for guests who smoke. The attractively appointed public areas include a traditionally furnished dining room where dinner is available by arrangement and two comfortable lounges, one of which contains a small bar and the other has lovely views over the bay
11 bth/shr (2 fmly) No smoking in 9 bedrooms No smoking in dining room No smoking in 1 lounge CTV in all bedrooms Tea and coffee making facilities No dogs (ex guide dogs) Licensed Cen ht CTV 5P No coaches Last d 7pm
ROOMS: s £28.50-£33.50; d £53-£67*

CONWY Conwy Map 06 SH77

Q Q Q **Bryn Derwen** Woodlands LL32 8LT (on B5106, approx 800yds from castle) ☎ 01492 596134
Bryn Derwen is set in an elevated position which commands views of Conwy. Mr and Mrs Smith extend a warm and friendly welcome. All bedrooms are en suite and offer modern facilities. The property has been sympathetically restored to highlight many of the original Victorian features. Breakfast is served in a delightful room and guests are welcome to use the lounge.
5 bth/shr (1 fmly) No smoking in dining room CTV in all bedrooms Tea and coffee making facilities No dogs (ex guide dogs) Cen ht 6P
ROOMS: d fr £34*

Q Q Q **Glan Heulog** Llanrwst Rd, Woodlands LL32 8LT (from Conwy Castle take B5106, house approx 0.25m on left side) ☎ 01492 593845
There are good views of the town and castle from many rooms in this late 19th-century house which is a useful base for touring Snowdonia and North Wales. It lies in an elevated position and has been greatly improved over recent years. Bedrooms are decorated with pretty wallpapers and are well equipped. One has a four-poster bed and some are suitable for families.
6 rms (1 bth 4 shr) (1 fmly) No smoking in 1 bedrooms No smoking in dining room No smoking in lounges CTV in all bedrooms Tea and coffee making facilities No dogs (ex guide dogs) Licensed Cen ht 7P No coaches Last d 9.30am
ROOMS: d £28-£36; wkly b&b £88-£114*
CARDS:

Selected

Q Q Q Q **Gwern Borter Country Manor** Barkers Ln LL32 8YL (from Conwy take B5106 for 2.25m, turn right onto unclass road towards Rowen for 0.5m then turn right Gwern Borter approx 0.5m on left) ☎ 01492 650360 FAX 01492 650360
This delightful creeper-clad mansion house lies in several acres of attractive lawns and gardens. Horse-riding and cycling are available Children are especially welcome and there is a rustic play area, games room and many farmyard pets within the grounds. Bedrooms are furnished with fine period and antique pieces, all are equipped with modern facilities and one has an Edwardian four-poster bed. An elegant lounge is provided and the dining room is attractively furnished in Victorian style. Freshly cooked evening meals are available and hearty breakfasts satisfy the largest appetites. The atmosphere is peaceful and relaxing and the Powell family are friendly and welcoming.
3 bth/shr (1 fmly) No smoking in dining room CTV in all bedrooms Tea and coffee making facilities Licensed Cen ht CTV 20P No coaches Riding Sauna Gymnasium Cycle hire Last d 4pm
ROOMS: d £42-£56; wkly b&b £135-£170; wkly hlf-bd £185-£225*
CARDS:

Q Q Q **Pen-y-bryn Tearooms** Lancaster Square LL32 8DE (situated in main town square) ☎ 01492 596445
Located in the centre of this famous walled town, Pen-y-Bryn is one of its oldest buildings and dates back to 1575. Many original features have been carefully preserved. It operates as a tea shop during the day and serves a full range of snacks, coffees and more substantial meals. Two cosy bedrooms are provided and these are equipped with modern facilities.
3 rms (2 shr) (1 fmly) No smoking CTV in all bedrooms Tea and coffee making facilities Cen ht 3P No coaches
ROOMS: s £22-£27; d £34-£42*

CORWEN Denbighshire Map 06 SJ04

Q Q *Coleg-y-Groes* The College LL21 0AU (exit A5 at Corwen between Corwen Manor and the White House, turn sharp right past Rapitest) ☎ 01490 412169
Closed 24-27 Dec
Dating back to approximately 1750, the property was originally designed as almshouses for retired clergy, but has now been converted into a peaceful Christian retreat, flanked by the church on one side and pretty gardens leading to a wooded hillside at the rear. Cosy bedrooms are reached via a narrow staircase. There is a choice of lounges, one with an open fire, and dinner is available in the beamed dining room.
6 rms (2 fmly) No smoking Tea and coffee making facilities No dogs (ex guide dogs) Cen ht CTV 6P No coaches Last d previous evening

Selected

Q Q Q Q **Powys House Estate** Bonwm, Holyhead Rd LL21 9EG (from A5 Corwen to Llangollen Road premises approx 1m on left after leaving Corwen) ☎ 01490 412367
Guests are assured of a warm and friendly welcome by the Waite and Quinn families. The house is set in 3 acres of well maintained gardens and woodland, which includes a swimming pool and a tennis court. The entrance hall is wood-panelled and there is a relaxing lounge with a

contd.

wood burning stove. The bedrooms are attractively decorated and include a four-poster bed. Dinner is available by arrangement.
3 shr (1 fmly) No smoking in bedrooms No smoking in dining room CTV in all bedrooms Tea and coffee making facilities No dogs (ex guide dogs) Cen ht CTV No children 2yrs 4P No coaches Outdoor swimming pool Tennis (grass) Last d 6pm
ROOMS: s fr £23; d £38-£40; wkly b&b £133-£140

CRICCIETH Gwynedd Map 06 SH43

Selected

QQQQ Glyn-Y-Coed Private Hotel Portmadoc Rd LL52 0HL (on A497 on right hand side facing the sea)
☎ 01766 522870 FAX 01766 523341
Closed Xmas & New Year
This friendly private hotel overlooks the esplanade with lovely views from many rooms of Criccieth Castle, Cardigan Bay and the Berwyn Mountains beyond. Bedrooms are attractively decorated, several have canopied beds and some are suitable for families. One bedroom is situated in a nearby building and can be used by less mobile visitors. Ann Reynolds and her family have offered a warm welcome to their guests for many years and she specialises in good home cooking.
10 bth/shr (5 fmly) No smoking in 6 bedrooms No smoking in dining room No smoking in lounges CTV in all bedrooms Tea and coffee making facilities Direct dial from bedrooms Licensed Cen ht CTV ch fac 14P Last d 4pm
ROOMS: s £21-£26; d £42-£52; wkly b&b £145-£180; wkly hlf-bd £215-£250
CARDS:

QQQ Min y Gaer Porthmadog Rd LL52 0HP (on A497 400yds E of junct with B4411) ☎ 01766 522151 FAX 01766 523540
Closed Nov-28 Feb
This family-run private hotel lies on the eastern approach to the town and there are superb views from many rooms of the castle and over Cardigan Bay. Bedrooms are smart and modern, all are attractively pine furnished and some are suitable for families. A bar is provided for residents and there is a traditionally furnished lounge. The Murray family are friendly and welcoming and food is wholesome and enjoyable.
10 shr (3 fmly) No smoking in bedrooms No smoking in dining room CTV in all bedrooms Tea and coffee making facilities Licensed Cen ht CTV 12P No coaches Last d 4pm
ROOMS: s £20.50-£23.50; d £41-£47; wkly b&b £143.50-£150.50; wkly hlf-bd £213.50-£220.50
CARDS:

This symbol indicates a 'Child Friendly' establishment - see page 25 for details

CWMDUAD Carmarthenshire Map 02 SN33

QQQ Neuadd-Wen SA33 6XJ
(alongside A484, 9m N of Carmarthen) ☎ 01267 281438
This pretty guest house lies in the centre of a sleepy rural hamlet which itself lies in the wooded Duad Valley. The Duad River runs alongside its pretty gardens and the atmosphere is peaceful and relaxing. Well equipped modern bedrooms include several family suites and some are also located at ground floor level. There is a choice of two comfortable lounges for residents and a liquor licence is held. It has been run by Geoff and Liz Goodbourn for many years and they extend a warm welcome to their guests.
6 rms (4 bth/shr) (1 fmly) No smoking in dining room No smoking in 1 lounge CTV in all bedrooms Tea and coffee making facilities Direct dial from bedrooms Licensed Cen ht CTV 12P Last d 7.30pm
ROOMS: s £17-£19; d £34-£38; wkly b&b £100-£114; wkly hlf-bd £154-£168
CARDS:

DENBIGH Denbighshire Map 06 SJ06

Selected

QQQQ Bach-Y-Graig *(SJ075713)* Tremeirchion LL17 0UH (from A55 take A525 to Trefnant and at traffic lights turn left A541 to x-rds with white railings where turn left)
☎ 01745 730627 FAX 01745 730627 Mrs A Roberts
Closed Xmas & New Year
Dating from the 16th century this Grade II Listed building was the first house in Wales to be constructed with bricks. Owned and run by the very friendly Roberts family, hospitality is warm and welcoming. Bedrooms are furnished with fine antique and period pieces, and modern facilities are provided. Two lounges are available. The largest has exposed beams and timbers as well as an inglenook fireplace and also contains a magnificent 200-year old dining table where breakfast is served. The farm extends to 200 acres and contains a woodland trail.
3 bth/shr (1 fmly) No smoking CTV in all bedrooms Tea and coffee making facilities No dogs Cen ht CTV 3P Fishing Woodland trail Games room 200 acres dairy
ROOMS: s £25; d £40; wkly b&b fr £140*

QQ Cayo 74 Vale St LL16 3BW
(turn off A525 into town at lights, turn up hill supermarket on right, Guest House located up the hill on the left hand side) ☎ 01745 812686
Closed Xmas
The MacCormack family have been running this small and friendly guest house for many years now. This creeper-clad building is situated on the main street, just a short walk from the town centre. Good home cooking is provided in a Victorian themed dining room and there is a cosy lounge with television.
6 rms (1 bth 3 shr) No smoking in bedrooms No smoking in dining room CTV in 2 bedrooms Tea and coffee making facilities Licensed Cen ht CTV No coaches Last d 2pm
ROOMS: s £17-£17.50; d £34-£35*
CARDS:

DOLGELLAU Gwynedd Map 06 SH71

Q Q Q Clifton House Hotel Smithfield Square LL40 1ES (in Dolgellau join one way system. Follow round until coming up the street directly facing hotel)
☎ 01341 422554 FAX 01341 423580
For many years this building served as the Meirionnydd County Gaol, but it now provides much more comfortable, en suite bedrooms! The friendly owner is Pauline Dix and a limited choice menu is available in the character dining room.
6 rms (4 bth/shr) No smoking in dining room CTV in all bedrooms Tea and coffee making facilities Licensed Cen ht 2P No coaches Last d 6.30pm
ROOMS: s £25-£35; d £35-£45; wkly b&b £108.50-£143.50; wkly hlf-bd £210-£245*
CARDS:

Q Q Glyn *(SH704178)* LL40 1YA (1m W of Eldon Square on old Penmaenpool Rd, premises signposted between A493 exit and Dolgellau) ☎ 01341 422286 FAX 01341 422286 Mrs E W Price
Mar-Nov
This 17th-century hill farm lies under the Cader Idris range of mountains on the outskirts of this old market town. The Price family have worked here for many years and offer a warm welcome. Bedrooms are cosy and a comfortable sitting room is provided for guests.
4 rms (1 shr) No smoking in dining room CTV in all bedrooms Tea and coffee making facilities Cen ht TV 6P Fishing 150 acres mixed
ROOMS: s fr £18; d £30-£38; wkly b&b £100-£130

Premier Selected

Q Q Q Q Q Tyddynmawr Farmhouse *(SH704159)*
Islawrdref LL40 1TL (from town centre branch left at top of square and then turn left at garage into Cader Rd for approx 3m. First farm on left after Gwernan Lake) ☎ 01341 422331 Mr & Mrs Evans
Closed Nov-17 Mar
This 18th-century farmhouse has been carefully restored and extended by Alun and Olwen Evans over recent years. It lies at the foot of Cader Idris, some three miles above Dolgellau, and the scenery can only be described as breathtaking. Both the residents lounge and the dining room are comfortable and the latter features an impressive inglenook fireplace. Olwen Evans does much of her own baking and her hearty farmhouse breakfasts are most enjoyable. Just two bedrooms are available and these are spacious and fitted with high quality furnishings. Two self-catering cottages are also available in the grounds.
2 bth/shr No smoking Tea and coffee making facilities No dogs Cen ht CTV No children P Fishing 800 acres beef sheep
ROOMS: s £30; d £44*

DYLIFE Powys Map 06 SN89

Q Q ***Star*** SY19 7BW (off B4518, 9m NW of Llanidloes)
☎ 01650 521345
The Star Inn is situated in wild and rugged countryside in the heart of Mid Wales and is a favourite watering hole for walkers, cyclists and bird watchers. The bars serve a wide range of food and the choice of fresh fish available is worth sampling. Bedrooms are modestly furnished and there is a television lounge available for residents.
7 rms (2 bth/shr) (1 fmly) No smoking in dining room No smoking in 1 lounge Tea and coffee making facilities Cen ht CTV 30P Boat hire Pony trekking Last d 10.30pm
CARDS:

ERWOOD Powys Map 03 SO04

Q Q Q Orchard Cottage LD2 3EZ (on A470 in Erwood village centre, opposite Wheelwrights Inn) ☎ 01982 560600
Located in the small village of Erwood, this is a Welsh stone cottage that dates back over 200 years. It lies in very pretty lawns and gardens that run down to the River Wye. Three well equipped and furnished bedrooms are provided and exposed oak beams still feature. There is a comfortable lounge for residents and a separate breakfast room. Fishing is also available.
3 rms (1 bth/shr) (1 fmly) No smoking in dining room No smoking in lounges CTV in all bedrooms Tea and coffee making facilities No dogs (ex guide dogs) Cen ht CTV 6P No coaches Fishing Last d 9.30pm
ROOMS: d £33-£38*

FELINDRE (NEAR SWANSEA) Swansea Map 03 SN60

Q Q Q ***Coynant & Ganol Farm*** *(SN648070)* SA5 7PU (4m N of Felindre off unclass rd linking M4 junct 46 and Ammanford)
☎ 01269 595640 & 592064 Mr F Jones
This 200 acre holding is remotely and quietly located in a valley some 9 miles from Swansea. From Felindre follow signs for Garswllt. The private road leading to the farm can be found next to the signs for Garswllt. The private road leading to the farm can be found next to the sign for Cwmcerdinen. The modern furnished and equipped accommodation, which includes family bedded rooms and rooms on ground floor level, is divided between two separate houses at different ends of the farm. Both houses have lounge, bar and dining room facilities.
5 rms (3 bth/shr) (2 fmly) No smoking in bedrooms No smoking in dining room CTV in all bedrooms Tea and coffee making facilities No dogs (ex guide dogs) Licensed Cen ht 10P Fishing Riding Games room 200 acres mixed Last d 7pm

FFESTINIOG Gwynedd Map 06 SH74

Q Q Q ***Ty Clwb*** The Square LL41 4LS ☎ 01766 762658
Ty Clwd (Club House) dates back to the time when drovers used to meet in the village square and is a good base for touring Snowdonia and the surrounding countryside. The house has been fully modernised but still retains its character. Bedrooms are tastefully decorated and are very well equipped. There is a spacious comfortable lounge with a South facing balcony which overlooks the Maentwrog Hills.
3 rms

FISHGUARD Pembrokeshire Map **02** SM93

See also Narberth

Selected

Q Q Q Q ✿ **Erw-Lon** *(SN028325)* Pontfaen SA65 9TS (on B4313 between Fishguard and Maenclochog)
☎ 01348 881297 Mrs L McAllister
Mar-Nov
Traditional Welsh hospitality is offered by the very friendly McAllister family to guests visiting their home. A beef farm, it lies above the lovely Gwaun Valley and there are superb rural views to be enjoyed. Three smart modern bedrooms are provided and there is a comfortable lounge for residents. Maintenance standards are high throughout and there is a relaxing and homely atmosphere.
3 rms (2 shr) No smoking CTV in all bedrooms Tea and coffee making facilities No dogs (ex guide dogs) Cen ht CTV No children 10yrs 5P 128 acres beef sheep
ROOMS: s £20-£25; d £40-£45; wkly b&b £140; wkly hlf-bd £210*

GLASBURY Powys Map **03** SO13

Selected

Q Q Q Q ✿ **Fforddfawr** *(SO192398)* HR3 5PT
(from Hay-on-Wye take B4350 Road towards Brecon, farm 3m on the right) ☎ 01497 847332 FAX 01497 847332 Mrs B Eckley
Mar-Nov
This large stone-built house, dating from the late 17th century, is fronted by a neat and attractive garden. The 240-acre mixed farm is bordered by the River Wye, and riverside walks are rich in wildlife, birds and flowers. There is a lovely lounge, with period furniture and an inglenook fireplace. A second lounge area containing a TV is adjacent to the dining room, where guests share two tables.
3 rms (2 shr) (1 fmly) No smoking CTV in all bedrooms Tea and coffee making facilities No dogs Cen ht CTV No children 8yrs 4P Fishing 280 acres mixed
ROOMS: d £36-£42; wkly b&b £126-£135*

HARLECH Gwynedd Map **06** SH53

Selected

Q Q Q Q **Castle Cottage Hotel** Pen Llech LL46 2YL
(exit B4573 to Harlech castle) ☎ 01766 780479 FAX 01766 780479
Closed 3 weeks Feb
This delightful small hotel dates back to the 16th century and still features exposed timbers and low ceilings. It is owned and run by Glyn and Jacqueline Roberts who are both very friendly and welcoming. Glyn is an accomplished chef and the restaurant is understandably very popular as a result. Bedrooms tend to be on the small side but good use is made of the space available and all are attractively pine-furnished and cosy. Comfortable lounge and bar areas are provided and cheery log fires burn during colder weather.
6 rms (4 bth/shr) No smoking in bedrooms No smoking in dining room Tea and coffee making facilities Licensed Cen ht CTV No coaches Last d 9pm
ROOMS: s fr £27; d fr £58
CARDS:

Selected

Q Q Q Q **Gwrach Ynys Country** Ynys, Talsarnau LL47 6TS (2m N of Harlech on the A496) ☎ 01766 780742 FAX 01766 781199
Apr-Oct
Deborah and Gwynfor Williams are the very friendly and welcoming owners of this Edwardian house which is located in the lowland area between Harlech Castle and Cardigan Bay. Bedrooms are decorated with pretty wallpapers and all are fully equipped with modern facilities. Some are suitable for families and children are especially welcome. There is a paddock where the family's pet ponies are kept and well maintained lawns and gardens surround the house. Good home cooking is provided and there is a choice of comfortable sitting rooms for guests.
7 rms (1 bth 5 shr) (2 fmly) No smoking CTV in all bedrooms Tea and coffee making facilities Direct dial from bedrooms No dogs (ex guide dogs) Cen ht CTV No children 3yrs 10P No coaches Last d noon
ROOMS: s £23; d £46; wkly b&b £150; wkly hlf-bd fr £220*

HAY-ON-WYE Powys Map **03** SO24

See also Bredwardine and Glasbury

Selected

Q Q Q Q **Tinto House** Broad St HR3 5DB (centre of Hay-on-Wye opposite clock tower on B4350) ☎ 01497 820590
Closed 24-25 Dec
Tinto House is a charming Grade II listed Georgian town house, built in 1780. To the rear is a large and delightful garden, which extends down to the River Wye. It contains a cobbled courtyard area, which doubles as a secure car park. The bedrooms are traditionally furnished with antique pieces, but have modern facilities and equipment. Family bedded rooms are available, including a ground floor suite with its own lounge, which is located in a former stable block. Welcoming real fires burn in cold weather in the breakfast room, where separate tables are provided.

3 bth/shr 1 annexe bth/shr (2 fmly) No smoking CTV in all bedrooms Tea and coffee making facilities No dogs (ex guide dogs) Cen ht CTV 2P
ROOMS: s £25; d £40-£50*
CARDS:

Selected

Q Q Q Q **York House** Hardwick Rd, Cusop HR3 5QX (on B4348 0.5m from main car park in Hay-on-Wye)
☎ 01497 820705
rs Xmas
Set in its own extensive garden, this late Victorian house is quietly located on the B4348, near Cusop, just half a mile from the town centre. Friendly proprietors Olwen and Peter Roberts have extensively upgraded the accommodation over the last few years. The tastefully appointed bedrooms have modern equipment and facilities. Family bedded rooms are available. Separate tables are provided in the recently refurbished dining room. There is also a pleasant and comfortable lounge.
4 bth/shr (1 fmly) No smoking CTV in all bedrooms Tea and coffee making facilities Cen ht No children 8yrs 8P No coaches Last d 5pm
ROOMS: s £25-£34; d £46-£50; wkly b&b £145.25-£159.25; wkly hlf-bd £233.45-£247.45
CARDS:

HOLYHEAD See **ANGLESEY, ISLE OF**

HOLYWELL Flintshire Map **07** SJ17

Q Q **Bodawel** The Village, Rhewl, Mostyn CH8 9QF (turn off A548 coast road, up hill at lights opposite Mostyn Port, 0.25m on right before post office) ☎ 01745 561624
This bright and fresh little guest house is run by the very friendly Riley family and lies in the village of Rhewl. Two neat and well decorated bedrooms are provided and there is a further room for children which even has its own television set. A cosy lounge is provided for residents and a further cane furnished conservatory looks out over the gardens.
3 rms (1 fmly) No smoking in bedrooms CTV in all bedrooms Tea and coffee making facilities No dogs (ex guide dogs) Cen ht CTV ch fac 4P No coaches Last d 8pm
ROOMS: s £15; d £30*

Q Q Q **Greenhill Farm** *(SJ186776)* CH8 7QF (from Holywell follow sign to St Winefrid's Well. 200yds beyond the well, turn left opposite the Royal Oak and follow road uphill to end)
☎ 01352 713270 Mrs M Jones
Mar-Nov
There are lovely views over the Dee Estuary from this 16th-century farmhouse run by Mary and John Jones. Guests are free to roam around the 120 acres of farm land. Exposed timbers are a feature and there is an unusual window, only visible from inside the property. A comfortable sitting room and panelled dining room are provided, and there is also a games room.
4 rms (2 bth) (1 fmly) No smoking in 1 bedrooms CTV in all bedrooms Tea and coffee making facilities No dogs (ex guide dogs) Cen ht CTV ch fac 6P Snooker Childrens play area, indoor games,darts 120 acres dairy mixed Last d 9am
ROOMS: s £17.50-£19.50; d £35-£39*

ISLE OF

Placenames incorporating the words 'Isle' or 'Isle of' will be found under the actual name, eg Isle of Anglesey is under Anglesey, Isle of.

LAMPETER Ceredigion Map **02** SN54

Selected

Q Q Q Q ***Dremddu Fawr*** *(SN554529)* Creuddyn Bridge SA48 8BL (take A482 towards Aberaeron then 2nd right opposite Creuddyn Bridge petrol station over bridge. Turn sharp left follow road for approx 300yds)
☎ 01570 470394 Mrs M A Williams Jones
Dating back to the beginning of the century this farmhouse lies amongst the trees in what is very much a working farm. Two pretty pine-furnished bedrooms are provided and these are equipped with hair dryers, televisions and other modern amenities. A cosy lounge with a welcoming open fire is available for guests and a warm and friendly atmosphere prevails.
2 shr No smoking CTV in all bedrooms Tea and coffee making facilities No dogs (ex guide dogs) Cen ht ch fac 2P
163 acres beef/sheep Last d 8pm
CARDS:

See page 14-20 for a list of Premier Selected establishments

LITTLE HAVEN Pembrokeshire Map 02 SM81

Selected

White Gates Settlelands Hill SA62 3LA (A40 to Haverfordwest, follow signs for Broad Haven and uphill to Little Haven, past bus stop and first on left) ☎ 01437 781552 FAX 01437 781386

Parts of this former farmhouse date back some 300 years; it is situated on an ostrich-rearing holding and from its elevated position it commands spectacular views of St Brides Bay and the islands of Skomer and Skokholm. The soundly maintained, traditionally furnished bedrooms have modern equipment with extra thoughtful and welcoming touches. The one room without an en suite facility has its own private bathroom nearby. A family-bedded room is available and most of the bedrooms enjoy sea views. Separate tables are provided in the dining room and there is a comfortably furnished lounge. Other facilities include an outdoor heated swimming pool.

5 bth/shr Tea and coffee making facilities Cen ht CTV ch fac 6P No coaches Outdoor swimming pool (heated) Fishing Riding Last d 6.30pm

ROOMS: s £25-£30; d £40-£48; wkly b&b £140-£168; wkly hlf-bd £245-£266*

CARDS:

LLANBEDR Gwynedd Map 06 SH52

Selected

Victoria LL45 2LD (Frederic Robinson) ☎ 01341 241213 FAX 01341 241644

This fine old coaching inn lies on the banks of the River Artro in the centre of a pretty village. Many original features remain and the most impressive of these is the Settle bar with its flagged floor, black polished fireplace and unusual circular wooden settle. Food options are extensive with the regular offerings supplemented with blackboard specials. Bedrooms are attractively pine furnished and all are equipped with modern facilities.

5 bth/shr No smoking in dining room CTV in all bedrooms Tea and coffee making facilities Cen ht CTV 75P Last d 9.30pm

ROOMS: s £30-£35; d £54-£60; wkly b&b £162-£180

MEALS: Lunch £3.50-£7.50&alc Dinner £6.50-£8.50&alc

CARDS:

LLANBERIS Gwynedd Map 06 SH56

Plas Coch High St LL55 4HB (off A4086, turn into village of Llanberis, guest house is on main street near Spa shop) ☎ 01286 872122 FAX 01286 872188

This fine stone built house lies in attractive lawns and gardens in the centre of the village. The Snowdon train service starts just a short walk away. Smart bedrooms are provided and these are decorated with pretty papers and equipped with period furniture. A comfortable lounge is provided for residents and many authentic Welsh dishes are served by friendly owner, Tracey Rogers.

7 rms (4 bth/shr) (3 fmly) No smoking Tea and coffee making facilities No dogs (ex guide dogs) Cen ht CTV 7P No coaches Private Garden Last d 6pm

ROOMS: s £25-£40; d £32-£40

All AA listed accommodation can also be found at the AA's Internet site, whose address is: http://www.theaa.co.uk/hotels

LLANDOGO Monmouthshire Map 03 SO50

The Sloop NP5 4TW (on A466 between Monmouth and Chepstow in the centre of village) ☎ 01594 530291 FAX 01594 530935

Standing in the village of Llandogo, just north of Tintern, this personally run hostelry offers soundly maintained accommodation, including one room with a four-poster bed and a balcony. The inn offers a choice of two bars, where a wide range of wholesome meals is served. Other facilities include a beer garden and a play area for children.

4 bth/shr (1 fmly) CTV in all bedrooms Tea and coffee making facilities Cen ht 30P Last d 9pm

ROOMS: s £25-£30; d £50-£55*

MEALS: Lunch £9.25-£12 Dinner £10-£20*

CARDS:

LLANDOVERY Carmarthenshire Map 03 SN73

Llwyncelyn SA20 0EP (From Llandeilo A40 to Llandovery. Look for Llandovery Rugby Club sign. GH approx. 500yds on right before bend & river bridge) ☎ 01550 720566

Closed Xmas

This Victorian house has been run by the very friendly Griffiths family for almost 30 years. It lies west of the town alongside the A40 and in several acres of well maintained gardens that reach down to the River Tywi. Private fishing is available. Bedrooms are traditionally furnished and include one at ground floor level and others suitable for families. A comfortable sitting room is provided for guests.

5 rms (1 fmly) No smoking in dining room Tea and coffee making facilities No dogs (ex guide dogs) Licensed Cen ht CTV 12P No coaches Fishing Last d 7.00pm

ROOMS: s £20-£24; d fr £35; wkly b&b £112-£140; wkly hlf-bd £185.50-£227.50*

LLANDRINDOD WELLS Powys Map 03 SO06

See also Penybont

Selected

***Brynhir Farm** (SJ067586)* Chapel Rd, Howey LD1 5PB (1m S on A483) ☎ 01597 822425 FAX 01597 822425 Mrs C M E Nixon

Mar-Nov

This working farm has been run by the friendly Nixon family for several generations. It lies in a sheltered valley and parts of it date back over 300 years. Five smart bedrooms are provided and these are attractively furnished and decorated. Family rooms are available and one room is located at ground-floor level. There is a choice of elegant sitting rooms for guests where wood-burning stoves cheer the colder evenings. Evening dinners come in generous portions and provide good value for money.

6 bth/shr (3 fmly) No smoking in area of dining room CTV in all bedrooms Tea and coffee making facilities Direct dial from bedrooms Licensed Cen ht 10P 150 acres Mixed

Griffin Lodge Hotel Temple St LD1 5HF (on A483 in town centre) ☎ 01597 822432 FAX 01597 825196

Closed 23 Dec-2 Jan

Close to the town centre, this detached Victorian house provides modern, comfortable accommodation in a convenient location. The rooms are all well equipped and include family bedded rooms. Separate table are provided in the traditionally furnished dining room. There is handy off-street parking at the rear.

8 rms (5 shr) (2 fmly) No smoking in dining room CTV in all bedrooms Tea and coffee making facilities No dogs (ex guide dogs) Licensed Cen ht CTV No children 3yrs 8P No coaches Last d 9pm

ROOMS: s £22-£28; d £38-£50; wkly b&b £135-£172; wkly hlf-bd £225-£262*

CARDS:

Selected

Q Q Q Q **Guidfa House** Crossgates LD1 6RF (3m N, at junct of A483/A44) ☎ 01597 851241 FAX 01597 851875
Guidfa house is the lovely home of Anne and Tony Millan. The bedrooms are spacious, thoughtfully decorated and with welcome extras such as mineral water and reading material. The cooking is another attraction with Cordon Bleu trained Ann offering a combination of healthy eating with naughty puddings. An attractive lounge is the ideal lace to relax, and small business meetings can be catered for.
7 rms (5 bth/shr) No smoking in bedrooms No smoking in dining room CTV in all bedrooms Tea and coffee making facilities No dogs (ex guide dogs) Licensed Cen ht No children 10yrs 10P Last d 7pm
ROOMS: s £25-£36; d £50; wkly b&b £155-£215; wkly hlf-bd £245-£305
CARDS:

Q Q Q **Holly** *(SO045593)* Holly Farm, Howey LD1 5PP (2m S on A483 near the village of Howey) ☎ 01597 822402 Mrs R Jones
Apr-Nov
Parts of this stone-built farmhouse date back to Tudor times. It is situated south of Llandrindod Wells, at Howey, about 300 yards from the A483, from which it is signposted. The soundly maintained accommodation includes a family room. Separate tables are provided in the traditionally furnished dining room and welcoming fires burn in the comfortable lounge.
3 bth/shr (1 fmly) CTV in all bedrooms Tea and coffee making facilities No dogs Cen ht CTV 4P Walking and Bird watching 70 acres beef sheep Last d 5pm
ROOMS: s £22-£25; d £36-£44; wkly b&b £125-£150; wkly hlf-bd £180-£200*
CARDS:

Q Q *Kincoed Hotel* Temple St LD1 5HF (on A483 50yds beyond the hospital) ☎ 01597 822656 FAX 01597 824660
Situated close to the town centre, this privately owned guest house provides well equipped accommodation. There are a number of family rooms together with a small lounge and a dining room in which hearty breakfasts and home-cooked evening meals are served.
10 rms (5 bth/shr) (3 fmly) No smoking in 2 bedrooms CTV in all bedrooms Tea and coffee making facilities Direct dial from bedrooms Licensed Cen ht No children 2yrs 10P No coaches Last d 9.30pm
CARDS:

Selected

Q Q Q Q **Three Wells** *(SO062586)* Chapel Rd, Howey LD1 5PB (Howey 2m S A483 then unclass rd, E 1m)
☎ 01597 824427 FAX 01597 822484 Mrs Palmer
This old farmhouse has been extended over the years and now provides sound modern accommodation. It lies on a working farm near Howey

village and is just south of Llandrindod Wells. Family suites are provided, there are bedrooms with private lounges and two rooms have four-poster beds. The restaurant is attractively furnished and decorated and there is a choice of lounges, including one for non-smokers and a sun lounge, which overlooks the fishing lake. Staff and owners are friendly and welcoming and a peaceful and relaxing atmosphere prevails.
14 bth/shr No smoking in dining room No smoking in 1 lounge CTV in all bedrooms Tea and coffee making facilities Direct dial from bedrooms Licensed Lift Cen ht CTV 20P Fishing Last d 7pm
ROOMS: wkly hlf-bd £205-£255

LLANDUDNO Conwy Map 06 SH78

Q Q Q **Beach Cove** 8 Church Walks LL30 2HD (last road on left before pier) ☎ 01492 879638
Closed Xmas
Nestling beneath the Great Orme, just a few sandy steps from the shore, Beach Cove offers a combination of comfort, convenience and hospitality. Attentive and amiable owners Bob and Karen Carroll welcome you to this distinctive black and white fronted establishment complete with movie themed dining room. Attractively decorated bedrooms are well equipped and include both a four poster and ground floor room.
7 rms (5 shr) No smoking in 2 bedrooms No smoking in dining room No smoking in lounges CTV in all bedrooms Tea and coffee making facilities No dogs (ex guide dogs) Cen ht CTV No children 12yrs No coaches Solarium Last d 5.30pm
ROOMS: s £16; d £36; wkly b&b £100-£125

We endeavour to be as accurate as possible but changes in personnel and data can occur in establishments after the Guide has gone to press

QQQ *Bodnant* 39 St Marys Rd LL30 2UE
☎ 01492 876936
This pleasant little guest house lies in a quiet residential area of the town and is within easy walking distance of the main shopping centre and promenade. Bedrooms are immaculately maintained and well equipped. The lounge is bright and colourful.
5 bth/shr No smoking CTV in all bedrooms Tea and coffee making facilities No dogs Licensed Cen ht No children 12yrs 3P No coaches Last d 5pm

QQQ **Britannia Hotel** Promenade, 15 Craig-y-Don Pde LL30 1BG (close to North Wales Theatre & 100yds from Texaco garage and Llandudno Conference Centre) ☎ 01492 877185
This long established private hotel is located on the Craig-y-Don promenade with the theatre and other amenities within easy walking distance. Everywhere is bright and freshly decorated and maintenance standards are high. Bedrooms are prettily decorated, family and ground floor rooms are available and most have good sea views.
10 rms (8 bth/shr) (5 fmly) No smoking in dining room CTV in all bedrooms Tea and coffee making facilities No dogs (ex guide dogs) Cen ht No coaches Last d 5pm
ROOMS: s £15.25-£25; d £30.50-£44*

Premier Selected

QQQQQ **Bryn Derwen Hotel** 34 Abbey Rd LL30 2EE (turn off A55 onto A470, turn left at promenade to cenotaph, turn left, straight on at rdbt, turn right into York Road,which is 4th right after rdbt) ☎ 01492 876804 FAX 01492 876804
Closed Nov-Feb
Built as a gentleman's residence in 1878, this grand house has been sympathetically converted by Stuart and Valerie Langfield into a hotel of impeccable taste. Stuart was, until recently, a senior catering lecturer and his flair and intuitive cooking has gained a fine reputation throughout the area. Bedrooms are individually designed and imaginative use is made of rich colours and matching fabrics. Public rooms are elegantly furnished and a warm and relaxing atmosphere prevails. The hotel is located in a residential area of the resort, under the Great Orme and within a short walk of the main shopping areas and beach. A comprehensive beauty salon and sauna is also available on the premises.
10 bth/shr No smoking CTV in all bedrooms Tea and coffee making facilities No dogs Licensed Cen ht CTV No children 12yrs 9P No coaches Sauna Solarium fully equipped beauty salon, aromatherapy Last d noon
ROOMS: s £33.50-£43; d £57-£76; wkly b&b £199.50-£234.50; wkly hlf-bd £308-£343
CARDS:

QQQ **Carmel Private Hotel** 17 Craig-y-Don Pde, Promenade LL30 1BG (on main promenade between the Great and Little Ormes) ☎ 01492 877643
Etr-Oct
There are superb views over the bay towards the Great Orme from many rooms at this immaculately maintained private hotel. It lies on the Craig-y-Don promenade and is within easy walking distance of the resort's many attractions. There is a comfortable lounge for residents and the well equipped bedrooms include several suitable for families. The establishment is now non-smoking.
9 rms (6 shr) (2 fmly) No smoking CTV in all bedrooms Tea and coffee making facilities No dogs (ex guide dogs) Cen ht CTV No children 4yrs 6P No coaches Last d noon
ROOMS: s £15-£18; d £30-£36; wkly b&b £105-£126; wkly hlf-bd £147-£168*

QQQ *Hotel Carmen* Carmen Sylva Rd, Craig-y-Don LL30 1LZ
☎ 01492 876361
May-Oct rs Xmas
This large family-run hotel is located a few yards away from the Craig-y-Don promenade. It provides sound modern bedrooms some of which are suitable for families. A comfortable and spacious lounge is available for residents dinner can be arranged and there is a separate bar.
18 bth/shr (2 fmly) No smoking in 15 bedrooms No smoking in dining room No smoking in 1 lounge CTV in all bedrooms Tea and coffee making facilities No dogs (ex guide dogs) Licensed Cen ht CTV No children 5yrs Last d 5.30pm

Selected

QQQQ *Cornerways Hotel* 2 St Davids Place LL30 2UG
☎ 01492 877334
Mar-1 Nov
This small private hotel has been run for many years by Jeff and Sheila Rumbold. It lies in a quiet residential area of the resort with the main shopping centre and both beaches just a short walk away. Bedrooms are all attractively decorated and many extra facilities are provided, including trouser presses and hair dryers. Good home cooking is served and there is a choice of comfortable lounges.
7 bth/shr No smoking CTV in all bedrooms Tea and coffee making facilities No dogs (ex guide dogs) Licensed Cen ht No children 5P No coaches Last d 2pm

Selected

QQQQ *Craiglands Private Hotel* 7 Carmen Sylva Rd, Craig-y-Don LL30 1LZ ☎ 01492 875090
Mar-Nov
This small private hotel lies just off the Craig-y-Don promenade. It has been owned and run for over twenty five years by Blodwen and Colin Mullin and guests return year after year to enjoy the warm hospitality. Blodwen loves cooking and offers hearty meals using only fresh produce. A comfortable lounge is provided and bedrooms are decorated with pretty papers and fabrics.
6 bth/shr (1 fmly) No smoking in dining room No smoking in lounges CTV in all bedrooms Tea and coffee making facilities Cen ht CTV No children 4yrs No coaches Last d 4pm

Prices shown in the directory are meant as a guide only and are subject to change. Please check before you book

Selected

QQQQ Cranberry House 12 Abbey Rd LL30 2EA (from A470, down Conway Road to Mostyn Street, turn left at bottom rdbt, first right up Arvon Avenue, first left, 5th house on right)
☎ 01492 879760 FAX 01492 879760
Closed Dec-Jan
Louise and Harold Aldridge have welcomed guests to their impeccably maintained Victorian guest house for over 20 years. It lies in a quiet residential area under the Great Orme and there are pretty lawns and gardens at the front and rear. The main shopping centre and seafront are both just a short walk away. Pretty bedrooms are equipped with fine period furnishings and many extra modern amenities are provided. A comfortable sitting room is available for residents and hospitality is warm and welcoming. Louise was a finalist in the 1998 Landlady of the Year award and this is well deserved.
5 bth/shr No smoking CTV in all bedrooms Tea and coffee making facilities No dogs (ex guide dogs) Cen ht CTV No children 5P No coaches Last d noon
ROOMS: d fr £38
CARDS:

Premier Selected

QQQQQ The Lighthouse Marine Dr, Great Ormes Head LL30 2XD (from promenade travel towards the pier, pass it on right and enter Marine Drive just past The Grand Hotel and The Lighthouse is 2m on the right)
☎ 01492 876819 FAX 01492 876819
Built in the style of a small fortress by the Mersey Docks and Harbour Board in 1862, the Lighthouse proudly stands at the northern edge of the famous Great Ormes Head, Llandudno's spectacular headland. It was fully operational until 1985. Many of the original features, such as the panelling in the impressive entrance hall, have been carefully preserved. Bedrooms are comfortable and furnished with quality period and antique pieces. Two have their own lounge areas, one of which is the actual glazed dome which contained the optic. Needless to say, all the bedrooms enjoy stunning views of the Irish Sea and Liverpool Bay and each is equipped with a pair of binoculars. On the ground floor is a spacious and comfortable lounge, where a welcoming solid fuel stove burns during cold weather. Sumptuous breakfasts are served in the beautifully furnished breakfast room. John Callin and family are very hospitable. The Lighthouse won the Bed and Breakfast of the Year Award for Wales in 1997.
3 shr (1 fmly) No smoking CTV in all bedrooms No dogs (ex guide dogs) Cen ht CTV 6P No coaches
ROOMS: s £44.50; d £89-£95; wkly b&b £280.35-£299.25

Selected

QQQQ Lynton House Hotel 80 Church Walks LL30 2HD (proceed along the promenade until you reach the pier then turn left immediately, hotel on right) ☎ 01492 875057 & 875009 FAX 01492 875057
A popular hotel located in an elevated position at the Great Orme end of town, close to the seafront and all the town amenities. The attractive bedrooms, two of which have four-poster beds, are all well equipped with many extras. There is a comfortable lounge on the ground floor.
14 bth/shr (4 fmly) No smoking in dining room CTV in all bedrooms Tea and coffee making facilities Direct dial from bedrooms Licensed Cen ht CTV 7P No coaches
ROOMS: s £22-£28; d £44-£56; wkly b&b £145-£175*
CARDS:

Selected

QQQQ Martins Hotel & Award-winning Restaurant 11 Mostyn Av, Craig-y-Don LL30 1YS (exit A5 at Colwyn Bay or Conwy for Llandudno. Craig-y-Don is around the corner from the North Wales Theatre on the promenade)
☎ 01492 870070 FAX 01492 876661
This is a Victorian town house which used to be the home of the Arch Druid of Wales. It has been tastefully converted into an award winning restaurant with rooms. Located in the Craig y Don area of town, it is close to the seafront and the North Wales Theatre. Rooms are well equipped, and furnished in character with extras such as fresh fruit and home made biscuits supplied.
4 bth/shr No smoking in 3 bedrooms No smoking in area of dining room No smoking in 1 lounge CTV in all bedrooms Tea and coffee making facilities No dogs (ex guide dogs) Licensed Cen ht CTV Last d 9.30pm
ROOMS: s £30-£35; d £40-£54*
CARDS:

Selected

Hotel Messina Hill Ter LL30 2LS ☎ 01492 875260
FAX 01492 875260
Closed Nov-Feb
This family run hotel lies in an elevated position, under the Great Orme, but above the promenade and bay. There are superb views over the seafront from the restaurant and from many bedrooms. Pretty bedrooms are well equipped with modern facilities and several are suitable for family use. There is a cosy bar and this features a large collection of old pop records.
10 rms (4 bth 3 shr) (5 fmly) No smoking in dining room CTV in all bedrooms Tea and coffee making facilities Licensed Cen ht 4P No coaches Last d 6.30pm
ROOMS: d £40-£46; wkly b&b £135-£145; wkly hlf-bd £180-£190*
CARDS:

Minion Private Hotel 21-23 Carmen Sylva Rd, Craig-y-Don LL30 1EQ ☎ 01492 877740
1 Apr-20 Oct
The friendly Buet family have been welcoming visitors here for almost 50 years. It is a private hotel and lies behind the shops and promenade at Craig-y-Don. Bedrooms are smart and modern and two are located at ground floor level. There is a cosy bar and spacious restaurant for residents and also a separate lounge.
12 bth/shr (1 fmly) No smoking in dining room Tea and coffee making facilities Licensed CTV No children 2yrs 8P No coaches Last d 4pm
ROOMS: s £16-£17.50; d £32-£35; wkly hlf-bd £161-£185.50

Montclare Hotel North Pde LL30 2LP ☎ 01492 877061
Mar-Oct
Montclare is located on the North Parade with the main shopping centre and the beach just a short walk away. Pretty modern bedrooms are provided, many with sea views and several suitable for families. Many also have king sized beds that can also be converted for twin occupancy. Public rooms include a cosy bar and cane-furnished lounge.
15 bth/shr (6 fmly) No smoking in 6 bedrooms No smoking in dining room CTV in all bedrooms Tea and coffee making facilities No dogs (ex guide dogs) Licensed Cen ht Last d 3pm
ROOMS: s £26; d £52; wkly b&b £120; wkly hlf-bd £165*

Orotava Private Hotel 105 Glan-y-Mor Rd, Penrhyn Bay LL30 3PH (follow coast road from Llandudno to Rhos-on-Sea, premises are on the left approx 0.5m past rdbt at the bottom of Penrhyn Hill)
☎ 01492 549780
This family run private hotel is right on the sea front and has a well kept garden to the rear with steps leading to the beach. The modern bedrooms are well equipped and most enjoy sea views. There is an impressive panelled lounge which is comfortably furnished and, as well as a residents' dining room, there is a further restaurant which has a good reputation for its fine lunches.
6 bth/shr No smoking CTV in all bedrooms Tea and coffee making facilities No dogs Licensed Cen ht CTV No children 15yrs 10P No coaches Last d 6pm
CARDS:

Rosaire Private Hotel 2 St Seiriols Rd LL30 2YY ☎ 01492 877677
Mar-Oct
Many improvements have taken place in this family-run private hotel in the last couple of years. The lounge has been completely refurbished and is now very comfortable and relaxing. Bedrooms are bright and fresh with new furniture and soft furnishings fitted. The hotel is located in a quiet area of the resort but local amenities are within easy walking distance.
10 rms (2 bth 6 shr) No smoking in dining room CTV in 9 bedrooms Tea and coffee making facilities Licensed Cen ht No children 3yrs 6P No coaches Last d 4pm

---

Sunnycroft Private Hotel 4 Claremont Rd LL30 2UF (from Mostyn St turn into Lloyd St, past the town hall, take second turning on left into St Marys Rd, then first right)
☎ 01492 876882 FAX 01492 876882
Closed 28 Dec-1 Feb
This is a small private hotel located in a quiet residential area of the town, yet with all local amenities within easy walking distance. It is continually being improved and many bedrooms are now attractively pine-furnished. Ground floor rooms are provided and some have pretty canopied beds. Family rooms are also available and one has a four-poster bed. The lounge has also been altered and is now comfortably furnished with cane. The hotel is run by the friendly Elliott family.
9 shr (2 fmly) No smoking in dining room CTV in all bedrooms Tea and coffee making facilities Licensed Cen ht CTV No children 4yrs 4P Last d noon
ROOMS: s £19-£23; d £36-£40; wkly b&b £126-£135; wkly hlf-bd £154-£170*

Sunnyside Private Hotel Llewelyn Av LL30 2ER
☎ 01492 877150
Etr-Oct & Xmas
Sunnyside is located in a residential area of the resort but the promenade and main shopping centre is within easy walking distance. Bedrooms are smart and modern and all have full central heating and are equipped with televisions and other modern facilities. Bar and restaurant meals are available, there is a comfortable lounge and live entertainment is provided during the season.
25 bth/shr (4 fmly) No smoking in 1 bedrooms No smoking in dining room CTV in all bedrooms Tea and coffee making facilities Licensed Cen ht CTV Last d 6.30pm
ROOMS: s £17-£20; d £32-£40; wkly b&b £115; wkly hlf-bd £150*

Wedgwood Hotel 6 Deganwy Av LL30 2YB
☎ 01492 878016 FAX 01492 878016
Closed Dec-Etr
This busy, family run guest house continues to be improved and all rooms now have en suite facilities. It lies in a quiet part of the resort but the main shopping centre and the seafront are both within easy walking distance. Pretty bedrooms have televisions and hairdryers fitted and many rooms are suitable for families. A cosy bar is provided and there is a comfortable lounge.
10 bth/shr (2 fmly) No smoking in bedrooms No smoking in dining room CTV in all bedrooms Tea and coffee making facilities Licensed Cen ht CTV 7P Last d 3pm
ROOMS: s £19-£25; d £38-£50; wkly b&b £133; wkly hlf-bd £175*

Winston 5 Church Walks LL30 2HD (at the bottom of Church Walks which is opposite the pier on the North Shore approx 80yds up left hand side)
☎ 01492 876144
Run by the very friendly Healey family for over twenty years, this well maintained guest house is situated under the Great Orme and near the promenade. Elaine Healey is an accomplished cook and provides wholesome meals for her residents. Bedrooms are attractively decorated, many having pretty canopied beds and all equipped with modern facilities. A spacious lounge is available for residents.
6 shr (1 fmly) No smoking in dining room CTV in all bedrooms Tea and coffee making facilities No dogs Cen ht CTV 3P No coaches Last d 4pm
ROOMS: s £18.50-£19; d £35-£36; wkly b&b £117-£119; wkly hlf-bd £175-£180*
CARDS:

LLANDYBIE Carmarthenshire Map 02 SN61

Selected

Q Q Q Q ***Glynhir Mansion** (SN635152)* SA18 2TD
☎ 01269 850438 Mrs C H J Jenkins
Nestling at the foot of the Black Mountains in a designated Area of Outstanding Natural Beauty, Glynhir Mansion dates from 1708. A clock-tower and stonework, mellowed with age, greet the visitor on entering the cobbled courtyard. The dining room and lounge with their open fires boast many attractive period furnishings along with a baby grand piano. In the summer meals can be taken at the farmhouse tables in the bright and spacious conservatory. On the first floor large bedrooms are furnished in a style appropriate to the age of the building. The 200 acres of grounds include some lovely walks alongside the River Loughor where a stunning thirty foot waterfall is a spectacle not to be missed. The farmyard is full of free running pot-bellied pigs, ducks, peacocks and pigeons. Self-catering cottages are also available.
4 rms

LLANELLI Carmarthenshire Map 02 SN50

Q **Awel Y Mor** 86 Queen Victoria Rd SA15 2TH
(follow A484 town centre signs until traffic lights, straight through lights 500yds on right) ☎ 01554 755357 FAX 01554 755357
This is a family run guest house providing bright bedrooms that are equipped with televisions and other modern amenities. Family bedrooms are provided and all rooms are gradually being improved. The lounge and dining room are open-plan, a table licence is held and there is an enclosed rear car park.
12 rms (4 bth 4 shr) (2 fmly) No smoking in dining room CTV in all bedrooms No dogs (ex guide dogs) Licensed Cen ht CTV 13P Last d 4.30pm
ROOMS: s £17; d £30; wkly b&b £105; wkly hlf-bd £125*

LLANFACHRETH Gwynedd Map 06 SH72

Selected

Q Q Q Q ***Ty Isaf*** LL40 2EA (from Dolgellau, cross river and turn right onto A494 towards Bala, pass Kwiksave store on right then next left signed LLanfachreth & up hill) ☎ 01341 423261
This delightful 16th-century long house was a working farm until recently, but still boasts fresh chickens eggs every morning. Three bedrooms are provided and these are fitted with stripped pine furniture and comfortable beds. There is a television lounge and a separate reading room for guests. The house lies in pretty grounds that contain pet llamas and there are lovely views over the surrounding countryside.
3 bth/shr No smoking Tea and coffee making facilities Cen ht CTV No children 13yrs 5P No coaches Last d 5pm

LLANFAIR CAEREINION Powys Map 06 SJ10

Selected

Q Q Q Q **Cwmllwynog** *(SJ071065)* SY21 0HF
(turn left off A458 into village, pass the church through Milin y Ddol for farm sign 1m on left)
☎ 01938 810791 FAX 01938 810791 Mrs J Cornes
Jan-Nov
This is a fine 17th-century farmhouse surrounded by beautiful countryside. It is very much a working dairy farm and is signposted from the tiny hamlet of Melin-y-Ddol. An impressive lounge is available for residents which has a wealth of exposed timbers and an inglenook fireplace. Pretty gardens run down to a small mountain stream. The farm is owned by Joyce and Roger Cornes who are friendly and welcoming.
3 rms (2 shr) No smoking CTV in 2 bedrooms Tea and coffee making facilities No dogs Cen ht CTV 3P 127 acres dairy Last d 4pm
ROOMS: s fr £20; d fr £40; wkly hlf-bd fr £200*

Q Q **Goat Hotel** High St SY21 0QS
(leave A458 just after light railway station through town hotel opposite church) ☎ 01938 810428
Dating back at least to 1704 and maybe further, this fine old inn lies in the centre of the village near the church and shops. It provides character bars, a pretty restaurant and a pool room. Original timbers and an inglenook fireplace still feature and it is a popular local watering hole. Bedrooms are equipped with modern facilities and one is accessed from the car park.
6 rms (4 bth/shr) (1 fmly) Tea and coffee making facilities Direct dial from bedrooms Cen ht CTV 10P No coaches Last d 9pm
ROOMS: s £22-£27; d £34-£44
MEALS: Lunch £8-£8&alc Dinner £7.25-£14alc
CARDS:

LLANGOLLEN Denbighshire Map 07 SJ24

Q Q Q **Hillcrest** Hill St LL20 8EU
(from Shrewsbury turn left and up the hill by the Grapes Hotel just before the second set of traffic lights sign posted Plas Newydd)
☎ 01978 860208 FAX 01978 860208
Closed 25 Dec
This deceptively large red brick house lies in a quiet part of the town and offers attractively furnished and decorated bedrooms, including one on the ground floor. The cosy lounge has a real fire during cooler months, and evening meals are served in the dining room. Guests are welcome to use the patio and large garden to the rear of the house.
7 shr (2 fmly) No smoking CTV in all bedrooms Tea and coffee making facilities No dogs (ex guide dogs) Licensed Cen ht CTV 10P Last d noon
ROOMS: s £35-£42; d £42-£45; wkly b&b £148-£161; wkly hlf-bd £224-£245*

Q Q Q Oakmere Regent St LL20 8HS (300yds on right hand side from A5 traffic lights in town, towards Shrewsbury/Oswestry) ☎ 01978 861126
Oakmere is a large, faithfully restored Victorian house, in its own grounds with views across the valley to Dinas Bran Castle and the mountains beyond and is a just a few minutes from the centre of Llangollen. Bedrooms are spacious well equipped, tastefully furnished in character and are either en-suite or with private facilities. There is a comfortable guests lounge to linger in or a tennis court is available for the more energetic.
6 bth/shr (2 fmly) No smoking CTV in all bedrooms Tea and coffee making facilities No dogs Cen ht 10P Tennis (hard)
ROOMS: d £38-£40*

Selected

Q Q Q Q Plas Offa *(SJ282406)* Pentre LL14 5AN (3.5m S of Llangollen set back off the A5) ☎ 01691 773760 Mr & Mrs S Mullen
Dating back to the 18th century this house was once the home farm of nearby Chirk Castle. It provides three pretty bedrooms equipped with four-poster or canopied brass beds. Exposed timbers feature throughout the house and there is an impressive inglenook fireplace in the dining room. The house is surrounded by twelve acres of pasture land that is home to several horses. Offa's Dyke runs through the nearby fields.
4 rms (2 bth/shr) (2 fmly) No smoking No dogs (ex guide dogs) Cen ht CTV 20P 12 acres non-working with race horses
Last d 5.00pm
ROOMS: s £30; d £40*

LLANIDLOES Powys Map 06 SN98

Q Q Q *Mount* China St SY18 6AB (off A470) ☎ 01686 412247
The Mount Inn dates back to the 14th century when it started life as a coaching inn. It is also believed to occupy the site of a previous motte and bailey castle and is located near the centre of this pretty market town. Traditional bars have much character with exposed beams and timbers as well as cobbled flooring and log fires. A full range of restaurant and bar food is available and a games room and children's play area are also provided. Bedrooms include one suitable for families.
3 shr (1 fmly) CTV in all bedrooms Tea and coffee making facilities No dogs (ex guide dogs) Cen ht CTV 10P Snooker Play area for children
Last d 8.45pm

LLANRHAEADR-YM-MOCHNANT Powys Map 06 SJ12

Selected

Q Q Q Q Bron Heulog Waterfall St SY10 0JX
☎ 01691 780521 FAX 01691 780630
This impressive Victorian house has been completely renovated by the present owners, Karon and Ken Raines. Original features have been retained with a magnificent curved oak staircase and fine fireplaces. Two of the three bedrooms are particularly spacious and all are attractively decorated and furnished. Period furniture is fitted in keeping with the building and one room has a four-poster bed. Guests dine family style and the atmosphere is warm and relaxing. A self catering cottage is also available.
3 shr (1 fmly) No smoking CTV in all bedrooms Tea and coffee making facilities No dogs (ex guide dogs) Cen ht No children 5yrs 6P
ROOMS: d £40-£46*
CARDS:

LLANSILIN Powys Map 07 SJ22

Q Q Q Old Vicarage Llansilin SY10 7PX (centre of village, follow B4580 from Oswestry) ☎ 01691 791345 FAX 01691 791345
This large former vicarage dates back to 1792 and is surrounded by an acre of garden which contains a croquet lawn. It is quietly located in the small village of Llansilin, which is located amidst picturesque countryside, west of Oswestry via the B4580. The house, which is no smoking throughout, provides spacious bedrooms, and a traditionally furnished, combined breakfast room/lounge, but by the end of 1998 it is expected that separate rooms will be provided.
2 rms No smoking Tea and coffee making facilities No dogs (ex guide dogs) Cen ht CTV No children 12yrs 4P No coaches
ROOMS: s £19-£22; d £38-£44*

LLYSWEN Powys Map 03 SO13

Q Q Q Oakfield Llyswen LD3 0UR (off A470) ☎ 01874 754301
Mar-Oct
Dating back to 1914 this fine house lies in pleasant lawns and gardens near the village centre. Two bedrooms are provided, one has its own en suite bathroom and the other has sole use of nearby facilities. A cosy lounge is provided and this also serves as a dining room. Only non smokers are accommodated.
2 rms (1 bth/shr) No smoking Tea and coffee making facilities No dogs (ex guide dogs) Cen ht CTV 6P No coaches
ROOMS: s £16-£18; d £32-£36

MACHYNLLETH Powys Map 06 SH70

Q Q Q *Maenllwyd* Newtown Rd SY20 8EY (on A489 opposite the hospital) ☎ 01654 702928 FAX 01654 702928
Closed 25 & 26 Dec
This Victorian house lies on the outskirts of the historic town of Machynlleth and is surrounded by pretty lawns and gardens. Margaret and Nigel Vince have welcomed their guests for many years and are friendly and attentive. Bedrooms are attractively decorated and modern facilities are provided. Some are suitable for families. There is a comfortable lounge for residents and a large rear car park. The local golf course and the town centre are both just a short walk away.
8 bth/shr (1 fmly) No smoking in bedrooms No smoking in dining room CTV in all bedrooms Tea and coffee making facilities Cen ht CTV 10P No coaches Last d 1pm
CARDS:

Selected

Q Q Q Q Yr-Hen-Felin Abercegir SY20 8NR (turn off A489 approx 4m E of Machynlleth signed Abercegir. On entering village turn right onto unmade road after telephone kiosk, cross bridge) ☎ 01650 511868
Closed Xmas/New Year
This lovely house started life as a water mill, and is on the banks of the River Gwydol. Two bedrooms overlook the stream and trout and herons can often be seen. The mill has been restored but exposed beams and timbers remain. There is a very comfortable lounge and bedrooms, although not particularly large, are attractively furnished and decorated.
3 shr No smoking Tea and coffee making facilities No dogs Cen ht CTV No children 12yrs 3P
ROOMS: s £25; d £40; wkly b&b £126

MARFORD Wrexham Map 07 SJ35

Q Q Q Brackenwood 67 Wynnstay Ln LL12 8LH
(turn off B5445 by Red Lion pub) ☎ 01978 852866 FAX 01978 852065
Enjoying a peaceful outlook over the attractive gardens and woodland beyond, this is a well cared for guest house, offering pretty bedrooms, some of which are on the ground floor. The lounge is very comfortable and dinner is available by arrangement, in the conservatory dining room.
7 rms (1 bth 3 shr) (1 fmly) No smoking CTV in all bedrooms Tea and coffee making facilities Cen ht CTV 6P No coaches Last d at breakfast time
ROOMS: s £20-£23; d £33-£37; wkly b&b £110-£135; wkly hlf-bd £215-£240

MERTHYR TYDFIL Merthyr Tydfil Map 03 SO00

Selected

Q Q Q Q Llwyn Onn Cwmtaf CF48 2HT
(off A470 overlooking Llwyn-Onn reservoir) ☎ 01685 384384
From its elevated position, this carefully maintained and thoughtfully decorated house looks out over Llwyn-Onn reservoir and the wooded hills beyond. Located some 4 miles to the north of Merthyr, the guest house is convenient for the valleys yet situated within the Brecon Beacons National Park. The bedrooms are well equipped with modern facilities and the public areas comprise a pleasant dining room which overlooks the water together with a spacious lounge.
4 rms (2 bth/shr) No smoking in bedrooms No smoking in dining room CTV in all bedrooms Tea and coffee making facilities No dogs Cen ht CTV 4P
ROOMS: s fr £20; d £40-£44*
CARDS:

MOLD Flintshire Map 07 SJ26

Q Q Q *Druid* Lanferres CH7 5SN (leave Mold on A494 Mold (Ruthin Road), Llanferres is 6m along this road, establisment situated on right hand side midway through village)
☎ 01352 810225
rs 25 Dec
Located south west of Mold at Llanferres, this 17th-century roadside inn has been completely refurbished over recent years. The character bar features a log fire during the colder months and a large blackboard selection of meals is always available, together with a number of real ales. A further restaurant is also available and the inn has built up a good local following. Just four bedrooms are provided and these are well equipped.
4 rms (2 fmly) No smoking in area of dining room CTV in all bedrooms Tea and coffee making facilities Cen ht CTV ch fac 30P games room, pool table, darts, bar billiards Last d 10pm
CARDS:

Q Q Q Heulwen Maes Bodlonfa CH7 1DR
(follow road which crosses Mold high street at the traffic lights situated at top of Kings St, down Earl Rd past Post Office, turn left at bottom)
☎ 01352 758785
Heulwen lies in a quiet part of the town with pretty gardens and green fields to the rear. Two sitting rooms are available and guests dine family-style. Bedrooms, which are smart and modern, have private bathrooms and televisions and tea trays are provided. It is very much a family home and a warm welcome is extended to all.
2 rms (1 fmly) No smoking CTV in all bedrooms Tea and coffee making facilities No dogs (ex guide dogs) Cen ht 3P No coaches
ROOMS: s £18-£21; d £36; wkly b&b £115-£135*

MONMOUTH Monmouthshire Map 03 SO51

Q Q Q Church Farm Mitchel Troy NP5 4HZ
(from A40 S-left onto B4293 for Trelleck before tunnel, 150yds on turn left and follow signs to Mitchel Troy, GH on main road at junct with Commom Rd) ☎ 01600 712176
Situated in the village of Mitchel Troy, with easy access to the A40 and just two miles south-west of Monmout, this lovely 16th-century farmhouse stands in an acre of mature gardens. The house has a wealth of character, with original oak ceiling beams and impressive inglenook fireplaces in both the cosy lounge and the traditionally furnished dining room.
8 rms (6 shr) (2 fmly) No smoking Tea and coffee making facilities Cen ht CTV 12P No coaches Last d noon
ROOMS: s £19-£22; d £38-£44; wkly b&b £126-£147; wkly hlf-bd £210-£231

MONTGOMERY Powys Map 07 SO29

Selected

Q Q Q Q Little Brompton *(SO244941)* SY15 6HY
(2m E on B4385, 0.5m W off A489)
☎ 01686 668371 FAX 688371 Mrs G M Bright
This 17th-century farmhouse lies on a working farm of sheep and cattle. Exposed beams and timbers abound and the cosy lounge features the original inglenook fireplace. Bedrooms are decorated with pretty wallpapers and fabrics and these also have exposed timbers.
3 bth/shr (1 fmly) No smoking CTV in all bedrooms Tea and coffee making facilities Cen ht CTV 4P Shooting in season walking 100 acres arable beef mixed sheep Last d 5pm
ROOMS: s £22-£26; d £40-£48*

NARBERTH Pembrokeshire Map 02 SN11

Q Q Q Highland Grange Robeston Wathen SA67 8EP
(23m W of Carmarthen. Village on A40, property last on right. Do not turn for Narberth)
☎ 01834 860952 FAX 860952
This modern bungalow is the home of Naomi Jones and her family who offer a warm and friendly welcome to their guests. It lies on a working farm just off the A40 road at Robeston Wathen and the family pony grazes peacefully in the paddock. Pretty bedrooms include one suitable for families and there is a comfortable lounge with a wood burning stove for the colder weather. A full licence has now been obtained and Naomi provides good home cooking using vegetables from her own kitchen garden and eggs from her own chickens. Near to the Pembrokeshire ferry ports of Fishguard and Pembroke.
4 rms (1 bth 1 shr) No smoking in bedrooms No smoking in dining room CTV in all bedrooms Tea and coffee making facilities No dogs (ex guide dogs) Licensed Cen ht CTV ch fac 6P No coaches Last d 8pm
ROOMS: s £18-£21; d £35-£42; wkly b&b £126-£140; wkly hlf-bd £189-£206*

NEATH Neath Port Talbot Map **03** SS79

Selected

Q Q Q Q ***Cwmbach Cottages*** Cwmbach Rd, Cadoxton SA10 8AH (from A465 to Neath take third exit off A465 to Tonna Aberdauis, at rdbt take turning for Cadoxton, 0.75m turn right opposite church)
☎ 01639 639825 & 641436
Set on a wooded hillside, high above the village of Cadoxton, this row of former miners' cottages has been sympathetically converted to provide good quality accommodation in a peaceful location. On the ground floor is a bedroom specifically designed for disabled guests. There is a comfortable lounge and an attractive dining room with separate tables. The buildings are surrounded by extensive gardens and this season will see the addition of some self catering accommodation.
5 rms (4 bth/shr) (1 fmly) No smoking in bedrooms No smoking in dining room CTV in all bedrooms Tea and coffee making facilities No dogs (ex guide dogs) Cen ht CTV 7P No coaches Golf 18 walking & biking Last d 6.30pm

Premier Selected

Q Q Q Q Q **Green Lanterns** Hawdref Ganol Farm, Cimla SA12 9SL (exit M4 at junct 43 in direction of Neath. Take B4287 signposted Cimla and turn right at crossroads 300yds past comprehensive school, AA signposted)
☎ 01639 631884
Peacefully located in open countryside, this beautifully restored 18th century farmhouse is part of a 46 acre equestrian and pony trekking centre. On the ground floor guests can relax in the welcoming lounge where fires burn in the enormous inglenook fireplace and meals are taken in the attractive dining room. The bedrooms are well equipped with modern facilities, but furnished and decorated in a style appropriate to the house. Margaret Brown provides a warm welcome for her guests and the family tradition is continued by daughter Karen who runs the equestrian side.
4 rms (2 bth/shr) (2 fmly) No smoking in bedrooms No smoking in dining room CTV in all bedrooms Tea and coffee making facilities Cen ht CTV 6P Riding Last d 7pm
ROOMS: s £20-£23; d £40-£46*

NEWPORT Newport Map **03** ST38

Q Q Q **Kepe Lodge** 46a Caerau Rd NP9 4HH (exit M4 at junc 27, follow town centre signs, at second set of traffic lights turn left, premises on the right) ☎ 01633 262351 FAX 01633 262351
Situated in a quiet residential area, but close to the Civic Centre, this attractive guest house is set well back off the road with ample parking available. The bedrooms are well maintained with good levels of equipment and many personal touches. Separate tables are provided in an attractive dining room and this is supplemented by a cosy lounge which overlooks the garden and orchard.
8 rms (3 shr) No smoking CTV in all bedrooms Tea and coffee making facilities No dogs (ex guide dogs) Cen ht No children 10yrs P No coaches Last d before noon
ROOMS: s £23-£29; d fr £46*

Selected

Q Q Q Q **Rising Sun Hotel** 1 Cefn Rd, Rogerstone NP1 9AQ (M4 junct 27, turn right towards high cross on B4581 3/4 mile from motorway junct on left) ☎ 01633 895126 FAX 01633 891020
Closed 25 Dec rs Closed 3.30pm-5.30pm daily
This friendly, popular inn is situated on the outskirts of Newport and is well located for the South Wales valleys and the route to the Brecon Beacons. The spacious lounge and bar areas include a sunny conservatory restaurant where a good range of food is available. The bedrooms are modern, attractively decorated and well maintained. Outside there are extensive children's play facilities, garden seating and ample car parking.
6 bth/shr (1 fmly) No smoking in area of dining room No smoking in 1 lounge CTV in all bedrooms Tea and coffee making facilities No dogs (ex guide dogs) Cen ht 200P Children's play area Last d 9.30pm
ROOMS: s £35; d £45; wkly b&b £140-£157.50*
MEALS: Lunch £5-£5.25 Dinner £8-£16alc*
CARDS:

NEW QUAY Ceredigion Map **02** SN35

Q Q Q **Brynarfor Hotel** New Rd SA45 9SB (exit A487 at Llanina junct, head for New Quay on B4342, premises 2m on left)
☎ 01545 560358 FAX 01545 561204
Mar-Oct
This fine Victorian house is located on the northern outskirts of the resort. It lies in an elevated position over the harbour, where basking dolphins can been seen, and many rooms enjoy the lovely views. Two bedrooms are

located at ground-floor level in an adjoining building and are suitable for less mobile guests. There is a cosy lounge bar and a separate sitting room.
5 bth/shr 2 annexe bth (3 fmly) No smoking in dining room No smoking in 1 lounge CTV in all bedrooms Tea and coffee making facilities No dogs (ex guide dogs) Licensed Cen ht CTV ch fac 11P No coaches Games room Last d 8pm
ROOMS: s £28-£32; d £46-£60; wkly hlf-bd £205-£260*
CARDS:

NEWTOWN Powys Map **06** SO19

Premier Selected

QQQQQ ❦ **Dyffryn** *(SO052954)* Dyffryn, Aberhafesp SY16 3JD (take B4568 to Aberhafesp, turn right to Bwlchyffridd, bear left at next junct, then left twice. Right at X-roads and farm is down hill)
☎ 01686 688817 & 0585 206412 FAX 01686 688324
Mr & Mrs D Jones
Dave and Sue Jones have lovingly restored this 17th-century half-timbered barn over the last few years. It is surrounded by pretty gardens, including a rushing mountain stream and is part of a fully working farm. Children are especially welcome and there is a play area and many country walks in the surrounding farmland. Exposed timbers abound throughout the house and three well equipped bedrooms are provided. Residents have use of a comfortable sitting room and dining is in the family style. Dave and Sue, together with their young family are exceptionally friendly and hospitable and a peaceful and relaxing atmosphere prevails.
3 bth (2 fmly) No smoking CTV in all bedrooms Tea and coffee making facilities No dogs (ex guide dogs) Cen ht CTV 3P Country walks 100 acres beef sheep Last d 5pm
ROOMS: s £22-£24; d £44-£48; wkly b&b £154-£168; wkly hlf-bd £238-£252*

QQQ **Yesterdays** Severn Square SY16 2AG
(from the junct of Broad St and High St proceed from Barclays Bank along Severn Street for 80yds into Severn Square) ☎ 01686 622644
Closed 2/3 wks in Jan
Yesterdays is a delightful town centre restaurant with the benefit of four guest bedrooms. Dating back to the late 17th-century, it has been carefully converted over recent years by the friendly Aston family. The restaurant with its adjoining bar offers a wide range of good-value food and is open every day. Bedrooms are comfortably furnished. Trouser presses, irons and hair dryers are included in the many facilities provided and each room has an armchair or settee.
4 bth/shr 1 annexe shr (1 fmly) No smoking CTV in all bedrooms Tea and coffee making facilities No dogs Licensed Cen ht No coaches Last d 9.30
ROOMS: s £27.50; d £37*
CARDS:

OXWICH Swansea Map **02** SS48

QQQ **Woodside** SA3 1LS
(from A4118 from Penmaen after 1m turn left for Oxwich and Slade, premises situated at x-roads) ☎ 01792 390791
Closed Dec-Jan rs Nov & Feb
This charming old cottage and adjoining former barn have been cleverly converted to provide well equipped accommodation, which includes bedrooms on ground floor level, a room with its own small lounge and a family suite comprising of two bedrooms. Separate tables are provided in the conservatory dining room, which also contains a lounge area. Welcoming fires burn the original inglenook fireplace in the quaint bar during cold weather. The guest house is situated close to the beach.
5 bth/shr (1 fmly) No smoking in dining room No smoking in lounges CTV in all bedrooms Tea and coffee making facilities No dogs Licensed Cen ht 8P No coaches Last d noon
ROOMS: d £36-£52*

PARKMILL (NEAR SWANSEA) Swansea Map **02** SS58

QQ ❦ ***Parc-le-Breos House*** *(SS529896)* SA3 2HA
(at village turn right 300yds after Shepherds shop, then next left, signposted. Follow private road to end) ☎ 01792 371636 Mrs O Edwards
Surrounded by about 70 acres of its own mature grounds, this imposing country house dates back to the early 19th century. Inside, many original features have been retained, including a remarkable fireplace in the dining room and a most impressive stairway. The bedrooms have a mixture of furnishings with attractive period pieces being gradually acquired over the years. Some rooms are particularly suitable for family occupancy. A riding centre is part of the operation.
10 rms (8 shr) (7 fmly) No dogs (ex guide dogs) Cen ht CTV 12P Riding Games room 65 acres arable horses pigs chickens Last d 3pm

PEMBROKE Pembrokeshire Map 02 SM90

See also Narberth

Selected

QQQQ **Poyerston** *(SM027025)* Cosheston SA72 4SJ
(from Carmarthen take A477 Pembroke road, approx 0.5m past sign for Milton, farm is on the left just before Vauxhall garage on right)
☎ 01646 651347 FAX 01646 651347 Mrs S Lewis
Closed 20 Dec-10 Jan

Poyerston is very much a working farm and is surrounded by lovely countryside. Victorian by origin, it has been extended and modernised over the years and now provides comfortable accommodation. Bedrooms are decorated with pretty wall papers and fabrics. There is a choice of comfortable lounges for residents and Sheila Lewis and her family are friendly and welcoming.

5 bth/shr (2 fmly) No smoking CTV in all bedrooms Tea and coffee making facilities No dogs (ex guide dogs) Cen ht CTV No children 3yrs 12P 350 acres arable beef dairy Last d by arrangement
ROOMS: s £19-£21; d £38-£42; wkly b&b £130-£145; wkly hlf-bd £200-£220*

PENMACHNO Conwy Map 06 SH75

Selected

QQQQ **Penmachno Hall** LL24 0PU
(turn off A5 2m S of Betws-y-Coed on to B4406. Proceed through village and turn right at Eagles Public House signposted Ty Mawr)
☎ 01690 760207 FAX 01690 760207
Closed 21 Dec-14 Jan

A rushing mountain stream flows through the grounds of this 19th-century house that was once the rectory. Several elegantly furnished sitting rooms are available for guests including a gallery featuring local artists and a modern conservatory. Bedrooms are fresh and bright and furnished with appropriate period furnishings. Owner, Modwena Cutler is an accomplished chef and guests dine in the house-party style, looked after by her husband, Ian. There is a relaxing and peaceful atmosphere throughout.

4 bth/shr No smoking in bedrooms No smoking in dining room No smoking in 1 lounge No dogs Licensed Cen ht CTV 30P No coaches Last d 24 hrs prior
ROOMS: s £33; d £56; wkly b&b £182; wkly hlf-bd £285
CARDS:

PENRHYNDEUDRAETH Gwynedd Map 06 SH63

QQQ **Y Wern** Llanfrothen LL48 6LX
(2m N of Penrhyndeudraeth off B4410 between Garreg and Rhyd)
☎ 01766 770556 FAX 01766 770556

This fine 17th-century farmhouse lies in an area of outstanding beauty. Exposed oak beams and timbers abound and the dining room has an original flagstone floor. A very comfortable lounge is provided for guests and a wood burning stove is lit during the colder weather. Bedrooms are spacious and some are suitable for families. Food is fresh and wholesome and often served in house party style.

5 rms (1 bth 2 shr) (4 fmly) No smoking Tea and coffee making facilities No dogs Cen ht CTV 6P
ROOMS: d £38-£42; wkly b&b £114-£133; wkly hlf-bd £194-£213*

PENYBONT Powys Map 03 SO16

Premier Selected

QQQQQ **Ffaldau Country House & Restaurant**
Llandegley LD1 5UD (in the village of Llandegley on the A44 1.5m E of Penybont) ☎ 01597 851421 FAX 01597 851421

This beautifully preserved early 16th-century house is surrounded by lovely gardens and stands on the A44 between Penybont and Llandegley. It has a wealth of charm and character, enhanced by original features such as the low beamed ceiling and stone flagged floor of the traditionally furnished dining room. The bedrooms include a room on the ground floor of an extension to the main house, which has its own separate entrance. This house has a well deserved reputation for the friendly hospitality provided by proprietors Leslie and Sylvia Knott.

4 bth/shr No smoking in bedrooms No smoking in dining room No smoking in 1 lounge CTV in 2 bedrooms Tea and coffee making facilities No dogs (ex guide dogs) Licensed Cen ht CTV No children 10yrs 25P No coaches Last d 6pm
CARDS:

PENYGROES Gwynedd Map **06** SH45

Q Q **Llwyndu Mawr** *(SH475536)* Carmel Rd LL54 6PU
(A467 to Penygroes, in middle of village turn onto B4418. After 500yds left for Carmel, 500yds up hill after cemetery, first left)
☎ 01286 880419 Mr E Williams
Closed 23 Dec-4 Jan
This 19th-century farmhouse tucked away under the trees is part of a small sheep farm and is surrounded by pretty lawns and gardens. There are pleasant views over the sea towards Anglesey and to the mountains of Snowdonia. Pretty bedrooms are provided and owners, Elwyn and Naomi Williams create a friendly and homely atmosphere.
4 rms (1 shr) (4 fmly) No smoking in bedrooms No smoking in dining room No smoking in 1 lounge Tea and coffee making facilities Cen ht CTV 6P 78 acres sheep Last d 4pm
ROOMS: s £13-£18; d £26-£36; wkly b&b £101-£114

PONTYPOOL Torfaen Map **03** SO20

Q Q Q **Ty-Cooke** *(SO310052)* Mamhilad NP4 8QZ
(turn off A4042 to Mamhilad at the Du Pont factory and follow road for 2m, first farm on left past Horseshoe Inn)
☎ 01873 880382 Mrs M Price
This large farmhouse is reputed to date back to at least 1700. It is a working farm, quietly located to the north of Mamhilad village, which is itself north of Pontypool, via the A4042. It provides traditionally furnished farmhouse accommodation, which includes a family bedded room, furnished with antique pieces. Other facilities include an attractively furnished dining room and a lounge where fires burn in cold weather.
3 rms (1 fmly) No smoking Tea and coffee making facilities No dogs (ex guide dogs) CTV P 135 acres beef sheep
ROOMS: s £20-£25; d £36-£40*

PORTHCAWL Bridgend Map **03** SS87

Q Q Q **Minerva Hotel** 52 Esplanade Av CF36 3YU
(from M4 junct 37 take 4229 road to seafront. Hotel is 2.5m further on next to Grand Pavilion Theatre)
☎ 01656 782428
Closed 19 Dec-4 Jan rs weekends (no evening meals)
Situated within a few yards of the seafront and a short walk from the town, this friendly and lovingly maintained establishment offers comfortable, well maintained accommodation. Meals are served in an attractive dining room and there is a guests lounge in which to relax.
9 rms (8 bth/shr) (2 fmly) No smoking in dining room CTV in all bedrooms Tea and coffee making facilities No dogs (ex guide dogs) Licensed Cen ht CTV No coaches Last d 6.30pm
ROOMS: s £20-£25; d £38-£45; wkly b&b £170; wkly hlf-bd £220*
CARDS:

PORTHMADOG Gwynedd Map **06** SH53

Q Q ***Owen's Hotel*** 71 High St LL49 9EU (on A487)
☎ 01766 512098
This small guest house is located in the centre of a busy market and tourist town and also operates a busy cafè and confectionery business. Bedrooms were being upgraded at the time of our last visit and include several suitable for families.
10 rms (3 bth 4 shr) (3 fmly) No smoking in dining room No smoking in lounges CTV in all bedrooms Tea and coffee making facilities Licensed Cen ht CTV 9P
CARDS:

Selected

Q Q Q Q **Tyddyn Du** *(SH691398)* Gellilydan, Ffestiniog LL41 4RB (1st farmhouse on left after junct of A487/A470 near village of Gellilydan) ☎ 01766 590281 FAX 01766 590281 Mrs P Williams
Closed 24-26 Dec
This stone built 16th-century farmhouse lies in an area of spectacular scenery. The main house has two small and cosy bedrooms and also a lounge, which is comfortably furnished and warmed by a cheery log fire when needed. Two larger family suites have been created from converted outbuildings and feature a whirlpool, patio windows and gardens. A further two similar units are currently nearing completion. These have two bedrooms each and private sitting rooms. Paula Williams is the very friendly owner and she and her family create a warm and welcoming atmosphere. Paula is also responsible for the delicious, traditional farmhouse dinners and wholesome breakfasts.
3 rms (1 shr) 3 annexe bth/shr (3 fmly) No smoking CTV in all bedrooms Tea and coffee making facilities Cen ht 10P Large garden suitable for outdoor games 250 acres sheep Last d 5pm
ROOMS: wkly b&b £130-£180; wkly hlf-bd £185-£235

See advertisement on p.617.

PRESTATYN Denbighshire Map **06** SJ08

Q Q **Roughsedge House** 26-28 Marine Rd LL19 7HD
(on A548, coast road, opposite fire station & Llys Nant Day Care Centre)
☎ 01745 887359 FAX 01745 852883
Closed Xmas
This little guest house is located on the eastern end of the town not too far from the golf course. Bedrooms are very well equipped with modern facilities and telephones are the latest addition. Family and ground floor

contd.

rooms are also available. There is a cosy lounge for residents and the attractive pine-furnished dining room also has a small dispense bar.
10 rms (2 bth 1 shr) (2 fmly) No smoking in bedrooms No smoking in dining room CTV in all bedrooms Tea and coffee making facilities Direct dial from bedrooms No dogs Licensed Cen ht CTV 3P No coaches Last d 2pm
ROOMS: s £16-£25; d £32-£40; wkly b&b £95-£125
CARDS:

REDWICK Newport Map **03** ST48

Selected

Brickhouse North Row NP6 3DX
(from junct 23A on M4 follow Euro-Park road for 1.5m. Turn left after sign for Redwick and continue for 1.5m to Brickhouse on left)
☎ 01633 880230 FAX 01633 882441
Situated in a rural community on the outskirts of the village, this impressive three storey Georgian house has been carefully restored and refurbished to provide good standards for the modern traveller whilst retaining original charm and character. Bedrooms are mostly modern in style. Public areas include a choice of lounges and a cosy dining room with impressive furniture and a fine display of china. Mrs Park is a friendly host, justifiably proud of her food and service standards.
7 rms (5 bth/shr) (1 fmly) No smoking CTV in all bedrooms No dogs Licensed Cen ht CTV No children 10yrs 7P Last d Noon
ROOMS: s £30; d £45

RHANDIRMWYN Carmarthenshire Map **03** SN74

The Royal Oak SA20 0NY
(follow signs to Rhandirmwyn from A40 at Llandovery)
☎ 01550 760201 FAX 01550 760332
Situated in a beautiful rural location overlooking the majestic hills north of Llandovery, this village inn dates back to the 17th century and many original features are retained within the bar areas, including a blazing log fire for the cooler months. Bedroom accommodation is well equipped and comfortable and three rooms have the benefit of modern en-suite facilities. A good range of dishes is available both at lunchtime and evening which can be taken within the bar or in the spacious dining room. Friendly and attentive services are provided by the resident proprietors.
5 rms (2 bth 1 shr) (1 fmly) CTV in 3 bedrooms Tea and coffee making facilities 20P Pool table Clay pigeon wknds Last d 9.30pm
CARDS:

RHOSCOLYN See **ANGLESEY, ISLE OF**

RHOS-ON-SEA Conwy

See Colwyn Bay

RHYL Denbighshire Map **06** SJ08

Links 20 Beechwood Rd LL18 3EU
(turn of East Parade opp Suncenter) ☎ 01745 344381 FAX 01745 344381
This family-run guest house lies just off the promenade near to the Sun Centre and other local amenities. Bedrooms are all well decorated and maintained and all have pretty canopied beds. One room is located at ground-floor level and is suitable for less mobile guests and others are suitable for families. There is a small bar in the dining room and a smart and modern lounge is provided.
6 rms (5 shr) (3 fmly) No smoking in bedrooms No smoking in dining room Tea and coffee making facilities No dogs Licensed Cen ht CTV No children 2yrs Last d 3pm
ROOMS: s £18-£22; d £30-£32
CARDS:

Pier Hotel 23 East Pde LL18 3AL
(on promenade between Sea Life and bowling greens)
☎ 01745 350280
Closed 22-31 Dec
Gill and Robert Herndlhofer have been the friendly owners here for over 26 years and offer a warm welcome to their guests. The Pier is located near the town centre, the Sun Centre and other amenities. It is also a useful base for touring the local countryside. Bedrooms, including some family rooms, are decorated with pretty papers and many have good sea views. There is a cosy bar and separate lounge for residents.
8 rms (3 bth 4 shr) (3 fmly) CTV in all bedrooms Tea and coffee making facilities Licensed Cen ht CTV 2P No coaches Last d 3pm
ROOMS: s £16-£19; d £32-£38; wkly b&b £100-£115; wkly hlf-bd £130-£150
CARDS:

Romsley 8 Butterton Rd LL18 1RF ☎ 01745 330300
Closed 15 Dec-6 Jan
This pretty and well maintained guest house lies just off the promenade at its western end. It is family-run and provides well equipped bedrooms where rich fabrics and colourful wallpapers are used to good effect. One room has a four-poster bed and others are suitable for families. There is a comfortably furnished lounge for residents and the Bill family are friendly and welcoming.
7 rms (4 fmly) No smoking in dining room CTV in all bedrooms Tea and coffee making facilities No dogs Licensed CTV Last d Noon
ROOMS: s £14; d £28-£32; wkly b&b £98-£112; wkly hlf-bd £140-£154*

RUTHIN Denbighshire Map **06** SJ15

Premier Selected

Eyarth Station Llanfair Dyffryn Clwyd LL15 2EE
(off A525) ☎ 01824 703643 FAX 01824 707464
Until 1964 and the Beeching cuts, this was a sleepy country railway station. The tranquil location remains but the trains have gone, and a comfortable lounge and outdoor swimming pool occupy the space once taken up by the railway and platforms. Bedrooms are tastefully decorated and are full of personal touches and thoughtful extras. Family rooms are available and two rooms are located in the old station master's house adjoining the main building.
6 bth/shr 1 annexe shr (2 fmly) No smoking in bedrooms No smoking in dining room No smoking in 1 lounge CTV in 1 bedroom Tea and coffee making facilities Licensed Cen ht CTV 6P No coaches Outdoor swimming pool (heated) Golf 9 walking & rambling Last d 7pm
CARDS:

ST DAVID'S Pembrokeshire Map **02** SM72

Selected

Ramsey House Lower Moor SA62 6RP
(from A487 in centre of St David's bear left in front of Midland Bank signposted Porthclais, establishment 0.5m on left)
☎ 01437 720321 & 720332 FAX 01437 720025
This immaculately maintained guest house has been run by Sandra and Mac Thompson for many years. They are naturally friendly and hospitable and guests receive a genuinely warm welcome. Well equipped bedrooms include several located at ground floor level and the lounge, bar and dining room are comfortably furnished and open-plan by style. Sandra is an accomplished chef and most guests dine in as a result. Please note that children and smokers are not accommodated.

7 bth/shr No smoking CTV in all bedrooms Tea and coffee making facilities Licensed Cen ht CTV No children 14yrs 9P No coaches Last d 7pm
ROOMS: (incl. dinner) d £82-£90; wkly hlf-bd £246-£270✱
CARDS:

Q Q Q Y Glennydd 51 Nun St SA62 6NU
(on one-way system next to the fire station)
☎ 01437 720576 FAX 01437 720184
Closed at certain times between Nov & Jan
Run by the friendly Foster family, this is a well maintained guest house, providing bright bedrooms that are equipped with modern facilities. One room is located at ground floor level and other rooms enjoy lovely rural views that include the nearby cathedral. A cosy bar and separate lounge is provided and there is a popular bistro that also opens to the public.
10 rms (8 bth/shr) (4 fmly) No smoking in dining room CTV in all bedrooms Tea and coffee making facilities No dogs (ex guide dogs) Licensed Cen ht CTV Last d 9pm
ROOMS: s £17.50-£26; d £35-£42✱
CARDS:

Selected

Q Q Q Q Y-Gorlan 77 Nun St SA62 6NU (located in the centre of St Davids) ☎ 01437 720837 FAX 01437 720837
Situated just a short walk from the city centre and cathedral, Y-Gorlan provides attractively appointed, well equipped modern bedrooms, several of which enjoy lovely rural views towards Whitesands Bay. The comfortable sitting room also overlooks the same views. Separate tables are provided in the cottage style dining room, which also contains a small bar. Dinner is available on request.
5 shr (1 fmly) No smoking in bedrooms No smoking in dining room CTV in all bedrooms Tea and coffee making facilities No dogs (ex guide dogs) Licensed Cen ht CTV 2P Last d 6pm
ROOMS: s £25-£27; d £45-£50; wkly b&b £135-£150✱
CARDS:

SAUNDERSFOOT Pembrokeshire Map 02 SN10

Q Q Q The Sandy Hill Sandy Hill Road/Tenby Rd SA69 9DR
(on A478 next to nursery) ☎ 01834 813165
Mar-Sep
This former farmhouse dates back to the 18th Century and has its own pretty grounds, including a swimming pool, at the rear. The bedrooms, one located on the ground floor, are all well maintained and benefit from modern equipment. Home cooking can be sampled in the cosy dining room and in addition there is an attractive bar and lounge.
4 rms (3 shr) (1 fmly) No smoking in bedrooms No smoking in dining room No smoking in lounges CTV in all bedrooms Tea and coffee making facilities Licensed Cen ht No children 5yrs 7P No coaches Outdoor swimming pool (heated)
ROOMS: s £22-£27; d £34-£40; wkly b&b £119-140; wkly hlf-bd £175-£198

Q Q Q Vine Farm The Ridgeway SA69 9LA ☎ 01834 813543
Apr-Oct
Located on the outskirts of the town, this 200-year-old farmhouse is the home of the Maxwell family who offer friendly accommodation and carefully prepared home cooking. Vegetables and herbs come from their own mature garden. A spacious and comfortable lounge, where a cheerful fire burns in the winter months, is available for guests to relax in. The bedrooms, one on the ground floor, are pretty and well maintained.
5 bth/shr (1 fmly) CTV in all bedrooms Tea and coffee making facilities Licensed Cen ht 10P No coaches Last d 6pm
ROOMS: s £23; d £46-£50; wkly hlf-bd £206.50-£224✱

SENNYBRIDGE Powys Map 03 SN92

Selected

Q Q Q Q ❦ Bryn y Fedwen *(SN963297)* Trallong Common LD3 8HW (from Brecon take A40 west towards Llandovery, after 7m take second right signposted Trallong, straight over at top of hill onto farm road) ☎ 01874 636505 FAX 01874 636505 Mrs M C Adams
Superb views of the Brecon Beacons and the Usk Valley characterise this family-run working farm. Children are welcome and can assist in bottle-feeding the lambs in the spring. The three bedrooms are comfortably furnished and have modern facilities. One of the rooms is located in a nearby building and this is suitable for disabled visitors and can also be used as self-catering accommodation. Owner Mary Adams provides hearty breakfasts and good home-cooked evening meals on request.
2 bth/shr 1 annexe shr No smoking CTV in 1 bedroom Tea and coffee making facilities No dogs (ex guide dogs) Cen ht CTV 3P 300 acres mixed Last d 7pm
ROOMS: s fr £22; d fr £40; wkly b&b fr £140; wkly hlf-bd fr £210✱

Q Q Q ❦ Maeswalter *(SN932237)* Heol Senni LD3 8SU
(exit A470 onto the A4215, after 2.5m turn left for Heol Senni. Farm 1.5m on right over the cattle grid) ☎ 01874 636629 Mr & Mrs H F Mayo
Surrounded by fields of sheep, this 300-year-old farmhouse is located in the peaceful Senni Valley. All the bedrooms are brightly decorated with modern amenities and there is a room suitable for families. The lounge and dining room occupy what was once the old farm dairy.
3 rms (1 shr) No smoking CTV in all bedrooms Tea and coffee making facilities No dogs (ex guide dogs) Cen ht CTV No children 5yrs 11P 1 acres Non-working Last d day before
ROOMS: s £22-£27; d £35-£38

STEPASIDE Pembrokeshire Map 02 SN10

Q Q ***Bay View Hotel*** Pleasant Valley SA67 8LR (off A477 through village and left by flats then left again down valley for 0.5m for hotel behind chapel)
☎ 01834 813417
Apr-Sep
A private hotel, located in a peaceful wooded valley between Stepaside and Wisemans Bridge. Family bedrooms are provided and there are also some located at ground-floor level. A cosy lounge is available and the bar and dining room, which enjoys lovely views of the valley, is spacious and welcoming.
11 rms (8 shr) (5 fmly) Tea and coffee making facilities No dogs (ex guide dogs) Licensed Cen ht CTV 14P Outdoor swimming pool (heated) Last d 5pm

SWANSEA Swansea Map 03 SS69

Q Q Q **Alexander Hotel** 3 Sketty Rd, Uplands, Sketty SA2 0EU (on A4118, 1m from city centre on road to Gower Peninsula)
☎ 01792 470045 & 476012 FAX 01792 476012
Closed 24 Dec-1 Jan
This friendly, family run hotel is located just 1 mile from the City centre and is well located for the Gower Peninsula and The Mumbles. Bedrooms are brightly decorated and all have televisions and radios. In addition to the lounge and bar there is a games room for guests use.
7 rms (6 bth/shr) (4 fmly) No smoking in 2 bedrooms No smoking in dining room CTV in all bedrooms Tea and coffee making facilities Direct dial from bedrooms No dogs (ex guide dogs) Licensed Cen ht No children 2yrs No coaches Pool table Weights Exercise bike
ROOMS: s £32-£33; d £45-£46; wkly b&b £135-£160*
CARDS:

Selected

Q Q Q Q **Cefn Bryn** 6 Uplands Crescent SA2 0PB (on A4118, 1m from Swansea Railway Station) ☎ 01792 466687
Closed 22-31 Dec & 1-2 Jan
This fine Victorian house is located near the Uplands shopping area and is conveniently located both for central Swansea and the Gower. Bedrooms are spacious, well equipped and some are suitable for families. A comfortable lounge is provided and there is a pretty dining room where breakfast is served.
7 bth/shr (2 fmly) No smoking in 4 bedrooms No smoking in dining room No smoking in lounges CTV in all bedrooms Tea and coffee making facilities No dogs CTV
ROOMS: s £25-£35; d £45*

Q Q Q **Crescent** 132 Eaton Crescent, Uplands SA1 4QR (1st left off A4118 after St James Church travelling W)
☎ 01792 466814 FAX 01792 466814
Closed 24 Dec-1 Jan
Situated in a quiet residential area, this impeccably maintained guest house has many rooms that enjoy fine views over Swansea and the bay. Decoration is fresh and bright and the bedrooms are all equipped with modern facilities. There is a comfortable and attractively furnished lounge and a dining room with separate tables. This is a family run establishment and a warm welcome is extended to guests.
6 shr (1 fmly) No smoking in 2 bedrooms No smoking in dining room CTV in all bedrooms Tea and coffee making facilities Cen ht CTV 5P No coaches
ROOMS: s £27-£30; d £42-£45; wkly b&b £140-£154*
CARDS:

Q Q Q **Grosvenor House Hotel** Mirador Crescent, Uplands SA2 0QX (off A4118 in the uplands area of Swansea)
☎ 01792 461522 FAX 01792 461522
Conveniently situated for the city centre, this carefully maintained guest house is also well located for access to Mumbles and the Gower. The bedrooms are particularly well equipped and the comfortable accommodation includes family rooms. Separate tables are provided in the dining room and there is a spacious lounge. There is a small secure car park at the rear.
7 bth/shr (3 fmly) No smoking in dining room CTV in all bedrooms Tea and coffee making facilities No dogs (ex guide dogs) Cen ht CTV 4P No coaches
ROOMS: s £27-£29; d £42-£45*
CARDS:

TALGARTH Powys Map 03 SO13

Q Q Q **Castle Inn** Pengenffordd LD3 0EP (4m S, alongside A479)
☎ 01874 711353 FAX 01874 711353
A cheerful roadside inn located in the heart of the Black Mountains, the Castle offers smart modern accommodation. The hub of the operation is the traditionally furnished bars which offer a good range of meals in a welcoming atmosphere. Particularly well suited for those who intend to do some walking, a recent addition is a block of "bunkhouse" rooms offering simpler accommodation for ramblers.
5 rms (2 bth/shr) (1 fmly) No smoking in bedrooms CTV in all bedrooms Tea and coffee making facilities No dogs (ex guide dogs) Cen ht 50P Last d 9.30pm
ROOMS: s £19-£30; d £38-£44*
MEALS: Lunch £3.50-£6.50alc Dinner £4.95-£12alc*
CARDS:

Selected

Q Q Q Q **Upper Genffordd** *(SO171304)* LD3 0EN (located on A479 7m from junct with A40. On this A479 Abergavenny to Builth Wells road, turn right 0.25m after sign for Pergerffordd) ☎ 01874 711360 Mrs B Prosser
Mrs Bronwen Prosser has been welcoming guests to her home for over 30 years. Her charming cottage is surrounded by flowers and gardens and lies in the unspoilt countryside of Mid Wales. Two small but pretty bedrooms are available and the sitting room has a wealth of personal bric-a-brac. Brasses and chinaware adorn the walls and ceiling. Guests dine together farmhouse style and Mrs Prosser provides traditional home cooking and her Welsh cakes and bara brith are not to be missed.
2 bth/shr (1 fmly) No smoking in bedrooms No smoking in lounges CTV in all bedrooms Tea and coffee making facilities Cen ht CTV 4P 200 acres Dairy Mixed Sheep
ROOMS: s £20; d £40; wkly b&b £140*

TAL-Y-LLYN Gwynedd Map 06 SH70

Selected

Q Q Q Q ***Dolffanog Fawr*** LL36 9AJ (A487 midway between Machynlleth & Dolgellau, turn left onto B4405, establishment 1m on right) ☎ 01654 761247
Closed 22 Dec-3 Jan
This delightful small guest house was originally a 17th-century farmhouse, lovingly restored by Pam and Alan Coulter. It lies at the foot of Cader Idris and there are superb views across Tal-y-Llyn Lake. Bedrooms are attractively decorated and furnished and the comfortable lounge has patio doors leading out to the garden. A welcoming glass of sherry is offered before dinner which is served party style.
4 bth/shr No smoking CTV in all bedrooms Tea and coffee making facilities No dogs (ex guide dogs) Licensed Cen ht No children 10yrs 6P No coaches Last d 5pm

TENBY Pembrokeshire Map 02 SN10

Q Q **Castle View Private Hotel** The Norton SA70 8AA
(First left after 'Welcome to Tenby' sign pass Coach Park hotel on right before zebra crossing) ☎ 01834 842666
With its elevated position over the North Beach just across the road, the friendly Mardon family welcome you warmly to their pleasant private hotel, ideally located for a gentle walk to the town or down to the sea. Indeed many bedrooms and the relaxing first floor lounge have good views over the seafront. Family rooms are. Upon arrival the Mardons will give you directions to their car park.
12 rms (7 bth 3 shr) (4 fmly) No smoking in dining room CTV in all bedrooms Tea and coffee making facilities CTV 7P
ROOMS: s £16-£23; d £32-£46; wkly b&b £112-£160*
CARDS:

Q Q Q **Clarence House Hotel** Esplanade SA70 7DU
(follow South Parade by old town walls to Esplanade and turn right)
☎ 01834 844371 FAX 01834 844372
Apr-Sep
Owned by the same family for over 50 years, this is large hotel overlooking the resort's South Beach and Caldey Island. All rooms have en suite showers and many enjoy the sea views. Several lounges are available as well as a bar and entertainment is provided during the season.
68 bth/shr No smoking in 30 bedrooms No smoking in dining room No smoking in 1 lounge CTV in all bedrooms Tea and coffee making facilities Licensed Lift Cen ht CTV No children 3yrs In house entertainment, live music Last d 7.30pm
ROOMS: s £17-£36; d £28-£78; wkly b&b £98-£196; wkly hlf-bd £217-£273 *
CARDS:

Q Q Q ***Gumfreston Private Hotel*** Culver Park SA70 7ED
(50yds from Rectory car park, 150yds from 'South Beach')
☎ 01834 842871
This small private hotel is situated just a short walk from the South Beach and is now run by the very friendly Moreland family. The well equipped bedrooms are all individual in size and style and striking colour schemes are used. Many beds have attractive canopies and some rooms are suitable for families. Public rooms include a spacious and comfortable lounge, a pleasant dining room and a cosy bar.
9 bth/shr (2 fmly) No smoking in dining room CTV in all bedrooms Tea and coffee making facilities No dogs (ex guide dogs) Licensed Cen ht CTV No coaches Last d 4pm
CARDS:

Q Q Q **Hildebrand Hotel** Victoria St SA70 7DY
(A477 to Tenby at Kilgetty, approx 5m, follow signs to South Beach from the outskirts of Tenby, Victoria Street is the last street off sea front)
☎ 01834 842403 FAX 01834 844748
Apr-Oct rs Jan-Mar & Nov
Veronica and Jim Martin have been welcoming visitors to their friendly small hotel for around 25 years. Situated just off the seafront esplanade, it is just a short work from both the South Beach and the town centre. The spacious dining room has separate tables and there is a well presented lounge on the first floor. The bedrooms are generally spacious and all are equipped with modern facilities.
7 bth/shr (4 fmly) No smoking in 4 bedrooms No smoking in dining room CTV in all bedrooms Tea and coffee making facilities No dogs Licensed Cen ht CTV No children 3yrs No coaches Last d 11am
ROOMS: s £20-£30; d £33-£48; wkly b&b £110-£145*
CARDS:

This symbol indicates a 'Child Friendly' establishment - see page 25 for details

Q Q Q **Ripley St Marys Hotel** St Mary's St SA70 7HN
(take 1st left on entering town signed Harbour/North Beach and turn right at St Marys Church then 2nd left) ☎ 01834 842837 FAX 01834 842837
Apr-Sep rs Feb-Mar & Oct-Nov (B&B only)
This friendly private hotel is located in a quiet street just inside the old town walls and close to the harbour and beaches. Alan and Kath Mace have been here for more than 25 years and continue to welcome back many guests. There is a comfortable lounge, stone-walled dining room and cosy bar area. The bedrooms are equipped with modern facilities and include rooms suitable for families.
12 rms (8 bth/shr) (6 fmly) No smoking in bedrooms No smoking in dining room CTV in all bedrooms Tea and coffee making facilities Licensed Cen ht CTV 14P
ROOMS: s £22-£25; d £42-£50; wkly b&b £135-£155
CARDS:

TINTERN Monmouthshire Map 03 SO50

Q Q **Fountain** Trellech Grange NP6 6QW
(off A466 at Royal George Hotel and in 1m bear right over bridge round pond and right again up hill for 0.5m) ☎ 01291 689303
Situated in a peaceful valley a couple of miles from historic Tintern, this 300 year old inn offers a wealth of charm and character. The bar and restaurant are in keeping with the character of the building. The well stocked bar includes a collection of more than 50 single malt whiskies.
5 rms (3 shr) No smoking in bedrooms No smoking in area of dining room CTV in all bedrooms Tea and coffee making facilities Cen ht 40P Last d 10.30pm
ROOMS: s £20-£25; d £36-£46; wkly hlf-bd fr £170*
MEALS: Dinner fr £11&alc*
CARDS:

Selected

Q Q Q Q **Highfield House** Chapel Hill NP6 6TF
(after passing Tintern Abbey, take next left at Royal George Hotel, bear left at road fork and uphill for quarter mile into forest. Signed on left)
☎ 01291 689286 FAX 01291 689286
Perched on a hillside far above Tintern this remarkable and stylish stone built house offers wondrous views of the surrounding countryside. The building itself was once no more than a tiny cottage, but has been extended with great care and a good deal of flair. Both the bedrooms and public areas are decorated with imagination. Dinner is lovingly prepared with an emphasis on a Mediterranean style cuisine. The six acres of land around the house include woodland areas with lovely walks.
3 bth/shr (1 fmly) No smoking in bedrooms No smoking in area of dining room No smoking in 1 lounge CTV in all bedrooms Tea and coffee making facilities No dogs (ex guide dogs) Cen ht CTV 14P No coaches Mountain biking canoeing badminton Last d 8.30pm
ROOMS: s £29.50; d £45-£49.50; wkly b&b £195-£295; wkly hlf-bd £295-£345*

Q Q Q **Valley House** Raglan Rd NP6 6TH
(take A466 from Chepstow and turn left at Raglan Road, passing Cherry Tree Inn after 800yds and Valley House after another 200yds)
☎ 01291 689652 FAX 01291 689805
Nestling in a quiet valley, this largely 18th-century house provides comfortable, traditionally furnished accommodation. The breakfast room has exposed stone walls and ceiling. Separate tables are provided. Just to the east of Tintern, the house can be reached by following the sign for Llanishen.
3 bth/shr No smoking CTV in all bedrooms Tea and coffee making facilities Direct dial from bedrooms Cen ht 7P No coaches
ROOMS: s £30; d £40
CARDS:

TREARDDUR BAY See ANGLESEY, ISLE OF

WELSHPOOL Powys Map 07 SJ20

Selected

Q Q Q Q *Gungrog House (SJ235089)* Rhallt SY21 9HS
(1m NE off A458) ☎ 01938 553381 FAX 01938 554612 Mrs E Jones
Apr-Oct
Located two miles above the town, this 16th-century house enjoys lovely views over the Severn Valley area and Powis Castle. It provides two pretty bedrooms and an elegantly furnished sitting room which features an open fire when needed. Holiday cottages are also available within the grounds and the Jones family offer a warm welcome to their guests.
3 rms (2 shr) No smoking Tea and coffee making facilities No dogs Cen ht CTV 6P 21 acres mixed Last d 5pm

Q Q Q **Heath Cottage** *(SJ239023)* Kingswood, Forden SY21 8LX
(behind Forden P.O. off the A490 Welshpool/Churchstoke road)
☎ 01938 580453 FAX 01938 580453 Mr & Mrs M C Payne
Etr-Oct
This 18th-century creeper-clad country cottage lies on a smallholding in the village of Forden. Bedrooms are cosy and modern en suite facilities are provided. Guests have use of a comfortable lounge complete with an inglenook fireplace where cheery log fires burn when needed. Another small sitting room, which is full of tourist literature, is also available. There are fine views over the surrounding countryside and Mary Payne and her family are friendly and welcoming.
3 bth/shr (1 fmly) No smoking Tea and coffee making facilities No dogs Cen ht CTV 4P 6 acres poultry sheep
ROOMS: s £19-£25; d £38; wkly b&b £114*

Selected

Q Q Q Q **Lower Trelydan** *(SJ225105)* Lower Trelydan, Guilsfield SY21 9PH (access via A490 and B4392)
☎ 01938 553105 FAX 01938 553105 Mr & Mrs G Jones
Closed Xmas/New Year
This 16th-century farmhouse is located at the edge of the village of Guilsfield. Original beams and exposed timbers abound and the house is furnished with many fine antique and period pieces. A spacious and elegantly furnished lounge is provided and there is a small honesty bar for residents. Bedrooms are equipped with modern facilities and include one family suite of two rooms. Self-catering cottages are also available.
3 bth/shr (1 fmly) No smoking in bedrooms No smoking in dining room CTV in all bedrooms Tea and coffee making facilities No dogs Licensed Cen ht CTV 10P Children's play area 308 acres beef dairy sheep Last d 5pm
ROOMS: s £27; d £46; wkly b&b £161; wkly hlf-bd £252

Selected

Q Q Q Q Moat *(SJ214042)* SY21 8SE
(on A483, 0.5m from junct with A490)
☎ 01938 553179 FAX 553179 Mr & Mrs W Jones
Apr-Oct rs Feb, Mar & Nov
This is a working farm and has been owned and run by the friendly Jones family for many years. It provides three pretty bedrooms and these are equipped with modern facilities and furnished in keeping with the age of the house. One has an extra children's room. The farmhouse is over 400 years old so exposed timbers and ceiling beams still feature.
3 bth/shr (1 fmly) CTV in all bedrooms Tea and coffee making facilities No dogs Cen ht 3P Tennis (grass) Pool table
260 acres dairy Last d 2pm
ROOMS: s £23-£25; d £40; wkly b&b £133-£140; wkly hlf-bd £210-£217✻

Q Q Q ***Tynllwyn*** *(SJ215085)* SY21 9BW
(in Welshpool follow signs for the Steam Railway, at rdbt take A490 N, after 1m on left, farm at top of the drive)
☎ 01938 553175 Mrs F Emberton
This impressive Victorian house is very much a working farm and it lies just off the Guilsfield road, north of the town. Spacious bedrooms are decorated with pretty wallpapers and fabrics and enjoy lovely views over the surrounding countryside. Family rooms are also available. The sitting room is again spacious and comfortably furnished and there is an attractive dining room and a small bar.
6 rms (1 shr) (3 fmly) No smoking in dining room CTV in all bedrooms Tea and coffee making facilities No dogs Licensed Cen ht CTV 20P
150 acres mixed Last d 6.30pm

WHITLAND Carmarthenshire Map **02** SN21

Q Q Q Cilpost *(SN191184)* SA34 0RP (in Whitland turn into North Road at the Spar Shop, establishment 2nd farm on the left at about 1.5m)
☎ 01994 240280 Mrs Ann Lewis
Apr-Sep rs Oct-Mar
The Lewis family have been welcoming guests to this 200 acre dairy farm for almost 25 years and many return visitors testify to the comfort of the accommodation. Good home cooking is offered in the large dining room, adjacent to a homely and comfortable lounge, whilst the bedrooms, including family rooms, are nicely furnished. There is a heated swimming pool in the conservatory and a full size snooker table is also available for guests' use.
7 rms (3 bth 3 shr) (3 fmly) CTV in all bedrooms No dogs Licensed Cen ht 12P Indoor swimming pool (heated) Fishing Snooker Sauna Extensive lawns & gardens 160 acres dairy mixed
ROOMS: s £17-£23; d £34-£46; wkly b&b £120-£140✻

The AA's professional Inspectors make regular and anonymous visits to all the establishments listed in the Guide. They accept no gifts or favours from proprietors

IRELAND

Inspectors selected bed & breakfast of the year:

Churchtown House, Rosslane Harbour, Co Wexford

Republic of Ireland -
TELEPHONE NUMBER CHANGES

Some telephone codes will change during the currency of this guide. From August 1998, both old and new telephone numbers can be dialled. From December 1998, calls to the old numbers will be connected to a recorded announcement which will advise the caller of the new number, which the caller will then have to redial. From August 1999, only the new number can be dialled.

National Dialling Code (NDC)	Numbering Area	Leading Digits of Current Numbers	New Prefix
41	Drogheda	2, 3, 4, 7, 8	98
41	Ardee	5, 6	68
42	Dundalk	2, 3, 5, 7, 8	93
42	Carrickmoss	6, 90, 91, 92, 94, 98	96
42	Castleblayney	4, 95	97
49	Cavan	3, 6, 7	43
49	Cootehill	5	55
49	Oldcastle	4	85
49	Belturbet	2	95
65	Ennis	2, 3, 4, 6	68
65	Ennistymon	7, 8	70
65	Kilrush	5	90
66	Tralee	2, 3, 4, 8	71
66	Dingle	5	91
66	Cahirciveen	7	94
66	Killorglin	6, 9	97

NUMBER CHANGES IN THE CORK AREA

In the Cork area there will be a two-phase process. Local numbers beginning with 40, 43 or 33 will be prefixed with a 2 or a 7 (see Phase 1 below). In phase two, these new 2 or 7 numbers will be prefixed with a 4 (see Phase 2 below), as will the other first digits.

National Dialling Code (NDC)	Numbering Area	Leading Digits of Current Numbers	New Prefix
PHASE 1			
21	Cork	40	2
21	Coachford	43, 33	7
PHASE 2			
21	Cork	2, 3, 5, 8, 9	4
21	Midleton	6	4
21	Kinsale	7	4

IN CASE OF DIFFICULTIES, PLEASE CONSULT DIRECTORY ENQUIRIES

ACHILL ISLAND Co Mayo Map **01** A4

Selected

Q Q Q Q **GH Achill Cliff House** Keel
(off N59 onto R319 to Achill Island, 15km to Keel)
☎ 098 43400 FAX 098 43007
A new house with panoramic views of mountains, Keel Bay and the beach. Teresa McNamara is the vivacious hostess who has a tremendous wealth of local knowledge. Bedrooms are very comfortable and all are en suite. There are residents lounges on each floor, and the restaurant is open for lunch and dinner. The island has a school of traditional music and many opportunities for climbing and sea angling.
11 bth/shr (6 fmly) No smoking in bedrooms No smoking in dining room No smoking in 1 lounge CTV in all bedrooms Tea and coffee making facilities Direct dial from bedrooms No dogs (ex guide dogs) Cen ht CTV 30P Sauna Last d 8.30pm
ROOMS: s IR£25-IR£50; d IR£50-IR£60; wkly b&b IR£170-IR£185; wkly hlf-bd IR£275-IR£295*
CARDS:

Selected

Q Q Q Q **T&C Finncorry House** Breanascill Bay, Atlantic Dr
(N59 onto R319 into Achill. Pass through Achill Sound village then left for Atlantic Drive. House 1.5m, right turn after shop with petrol pump)
☎ 098 45755 & 086 8252998 FAX 098 45755
Mar-Oct
Located in a peaceful area overlooking Breanaskill Bay, this pleasant house has been purpose built to a high standard with wood floors throughout. The sun lounge is most inviting and there is a dining room and TV lounge. The area with it's marvellously clear light was made famous by the painter Paul Henry. There are also good beaches and a deserted village. Achill is the most westerly inhabited island in Europe and is joined to the mainland by a bridge.
6 shr (2 fmly) No smoking in bedrooms No smoking in dining room No smoking in 1 lounge CTV in all bedrooms No dogs (ex guide dogs) Cen ht CTV ch fac 6P Jacuzzi bath available Last d 2pm
ROOMS: s IR£18-IR£20; d IR£32-IR£36; wkly b&b IR£99-IR£105; wkly hlf-bd IR£169-IR£175*
CARDS:

Selected

Q Q Q Q **GH Gray's** Dugort
(head towards Castlebar, Newport, Mulrany Achill Sound and then Dugort) ☎ 098 43244 & 43315
Closed 25 Dec
Gray's guest house is located in Dugort, one of Achill Island's many villages which sits on the northern shore at the foot of the Slievemore Mountains. Mrs Vi McDowell and her team are very welcoming and offer genuine hospitality to guests. There are ample places to relax, including a smart new conservatory and various lounges. Dinner is served nightly in the cheerful dining room, and the cosy bedrooms all have orthopaedic beds. A self-contained villa, ideal for families, is also available.
5 bth/shr 10 annexe shr (4 fmly) No smoking in dining room No smoking in 1 lounge CTV in all bedrooms Tea and coffee making facilities Licensed Cen ht CTV 30P Table tennis Croquet Pool table Last d 6pm
ROOMS: s IR£25; d IR£50; wkly b&b fr IR£175; wkly hlf-bd fr IR£280

Q Q Q **T&C West Coast House** School Rd, Dooagh
(turn off N59 onto R319 onto Achill Island continue to Keel & then Dooagh, West Coast House signed)
☎ 098 43317 FAX 098 43317
This smart new house is in an elevated position giving superb views over Dooagh to the sea. Recent renovations have resulted in en suite facilities to all bedrooms, and furnishing is to a high standard. Guests can take full advantage of the panoramic views from the comfortable sitting room and adjacent dining room. Achill is Ireland's largest island, now connected to the mainland by a bridge, and offers magnificent scenery and long sandy beaches.
5 shr (1 fmly) No smoking CTV in all bedrooms Tea and coffee making facilities No dogs (ex guide dogs) Cen ht CTV No children 12yrs 10P Last d 6pm
ROOMS: s IR£20-IR£25; d IR£34-IR£36; wkly b&b IR£109-IR£119; wkly hlf-bd IR£119-IR£224*

ADARE Co Limerick Map **01** B3

Selected

Q Q Q Q **T&C Adare Lodge** Kildimo Rd
(in village turn right at bank)
☎ 061 396629 FAX 061 395060
A charming modern house, recently extended and suitable for wheelchair users, stands on a quiet street off the main N21 in a picturesque village famous for its thatched cottages. Its comfortable en suite bedrooms are well equipped with TV, tea/coffee trays and hairdryers. Guests also have the use of a spacious guest lounge.
6 shr (3 fmly) No smoking in bedrooms No smoking in dining room No smoking in 1 lounge CTV in all bedrooms Tea and coffee making facilities No dogs Cen ht CTV 6P
ROOMS: s IR£35-IR£40; d IR£40-IR£45*
CARDS:

Q Q Q **T&C Avona** Kildimo Rd (exit N21 at rdbt in village, premises located 150mtrs on left) ☎ 061 396323 FAX 061 396323
Mar-Nov
This well appointed modern house stands just 100 yards from the main street of a pretty village. Attractive en suite bedrooms, all with colour TV, reflect the owners' careful attention to detail. A courtesy tray for guests to help themselves to tea and coffee is provided in the lounge and there is a separate breakfast room.
4 shr (1 fmly) No smoking in bedrooms No smoking in dining room CTV in all bedrooms No dogs (ex guide dogs) Cen ht CTV 5P
ROOMS: d IR£36-IR£40✻
CARDS:

Selected

Q Q Q Q **T&C Coatesland House** Tralee/Killarney Rd, Graigue (from Adare village follow Killarney road N21 for less than 0.5m, Coatesland House is on left beside W W Doherty's Garage) ☎ 061 396372 FAX 061 396833
Closed 24 & 25 Dec
Coatesland House, situated on the main Killarney road (N21) five minutes from Adare village, is a very well appointed house featuring attractive bedrooms, all with en suite facilities. Proprietors Florence and Donal Hogan are welcoming and friendly and give superb attention to detail. Dinner is available. Nearby activities include hunting, fishing, golf and there is also an equestrian centre.
6 shr (2 fmly) No smoking in 2 bedrooms No smoking in dining room CTV in all bedrooms Tea and coffee making facilities Direct dial from bedrooms Cen ht CTV ch fac 20P Health walker
ROOMS: s IR£22-IR£28; d IR£37✻
CARDS:

ANNESTOWN Co Waterford Map 01 C2

Selected

Q Q Q Q **T&C Annestown House** (6m W of Tramore on R675 coast Road) ☎ 051 396160 FAX 051 396474
Closed 24 Dec-1 Jan rs 1 Dec-1 Mar
This period house stands in an elevated position overlooking a sandy cove with private access to the beach. The en suite bedrooms are well equipped and successfully combine period furnishings and contemporary bathrooms. Public areas comprise a spacious sitting room, a library, a billiards room and a dining room serving dinner by arrangement only. The house has pleasant gardens and is situated 1 hour 20 minutes' drive from Rosslare.
5 bth/shr No smoking in bedrooms Tea and coffee making facilities Direct dial from bedrooms No dogs (ex guide dogs) Licensed Cen ht CTV 10P No coaches Tennis (grass) Snooker Croquet lawn Private beach Last d noon
ROOMS: s IR£40-IR£45; d IR£60-IR£65✻
CARDS:

ARDARA Co Donegal Map 01 B5

Q Q Q **T&C Bay View Country House** Portnoo Rd (half a mile outside Ardara, on the Portnoo road) ☎ 075 41145 FAX 075 41858
Feb-Nov and 3 Dec-2 Jan
This large, modern bungalow on the outskirts of a small town, overlooks the sea.
6 shr (2 fmly) No smoking in bedrooms No smoking in dining room CTV in 3 bedrooms Tea and coffee making facilities No dogs Cen ht CTV 20P Last d noon
ROOMS: s IR£24.50; d IR£36
CARDS:

ARDMORE Co Waterford Map 01 C2

Q Q Q **Newtown View** *(X 182818)* Grange (on N25 Dungarvan to Youghal road, turn left at Flemings public house) ☎ 024 94143 & 086 600799 FAX 024 94143 Mrs T O'Connor
Closed Xmas
This comfortable guest house stands in 100 acres of farmland near the seaside village of Ardmore. The well decorated en suite bedrooms all have TVs and tea/coffee trays; public areas include a guest lounge and snooker room. A tennis court, a secure play area and good car parking are also available.
6 annexe bth/shr (3 fmly) No smoking in bedrooms No smoking in dining room CTV in all bedrooms Tea and coffee making facilities Direct dial from bedrooms No dogs (ex guide dogs) Cen ht CTV 12P Tennis (hard) Snooker 110 acres dairy beef Last d 6pm
ROOMS: s IR£25; d IR£36-IR£40✻
CARDS:

ARKLOW Co Wicklow Map 01 D3

Q Q ***Killinskyduff Farmhouse** (T 254731)* (1m N, off N11) ☎ 0402 32185 Mr M T Bourke
Jun-Sep
A homely modern farmhouse which enjoys a quiet location on the outskirts of Arklow near the sea. Just 10 minutes away from the location of the television series Ballykissangel. Mrs Burke is dedicated to her guests well being and provides comfortable bedrooms and a sitting room with TV where guests can relax.
3 rms (3 fmly) No smoking in bedrooms No smoking in dining room No dogs Cen ht CTV No children 12yrs 22P 165 acres hens tillage Last d 4pm
CARDS:

ARTHURSTOWN Co Wexford Map 01 C2

Q Q Q **T&C Glendine Country House** (from Rosslare-N25 for 5m, 1st & 2nd rdbts turn left, R733 20m towards Wellingtonbridge) ☎ 051 389258 FAX 051 389258
Closed 15 Dec-15 Jan
A Georgian house in its own grounds overlooking the estuary in Arthurstown, and next to the village of Ballyhack where the local ferry crosses to and from Passage East in Waterford. Glendine is a well-maintained house with attractive gardens, a play area for children, and plenty of car parking space. Inside there is a spacious sitting room with TV, a separate dining room, and comfortable en suite bedrooms, one of which has a second bedroom attached which is useful for families.
4 bth/shr (4 fmly) No smoking in bedrooms No smoking in dining room No smoking in 1 lounge CTV in 2 bedrooms Tea and coffee making facilities Cen ht CTV ch fac 20P Working farm Ponies Garden Walks
ROOMS: s IR£25-IR£30; d IR£35-IR£40; wkly b&b IR£120-IR£135✻
CARDS:

ATHLONE Co Westmeath Map 01 C4

Selected

Q Q Q Q **T&C Riverview House** Galway Rd, Summerhill (on N6 2km from Athlone town centre) ☎ 0902 94532
Closed 19 Dec-1 Feb
Three curved red-brick archways distinguish this pleasant house which is well positioned close to the town centre. Carmel Corbett is a friendly owner who offers modern en suite accommodation in attractively decorated and comfortable bedrooms. Other facilities include a cosy lounge, and a breakfast room that opens on to the gardens. Nearby Lough Ree attracts anglers, who are well catered for with a bait and tackle shop, and there is ample off-street parking.

5 bth/shr (3 fmly) No smoking in 1 bedrooms No smoking in dining room CTV in all bedrooms Tea and coffee making facilities No dogs (ex guide dogs) Cen ht CTV 10P
ROOMS: s IR£22-IR£25; d IR£36-IR£40; wkly b&b fr IR£125*
CARDS:

ATHY Co Kildare Map **01** C3

Premier Selected

Q Q Q Q Q **T&C Coursetown House** Stradbally Rd
(turn off N78 at Athy or N80 at Stradbally on to R428)
☎ 0507 31101 FAX 0507 32740
rs Nov-Feb (prior booking only)
This charming Victorian country house is set on a 250-acre tillage farm and bird sanctuary 2 miles from Athy on the Stradbally Road. It has been recently extensively refurbished, and all bedrooms are furnished to the highest standards. Convalescent or disabled guests are especially welcome, and Iris and Jim Fox are happy to share their knowledge of the Irish countryside and wildlife.
5 shr No smoking CTV in all bedrooms Tea and coffee making facilities Direct dial from bedrooms No dogs (ex guide dogs) Cen ht CTV No children 8yrs 22P No coaches
ROOMS: s IR£25; d IR£50*

AVOCA Co Wicklow Map **01** D3

Q Q Q **T&C Ashdene** Knockanree Lower (turn off R752 into village. House 1m on right beyond Avoca Handweavers on Avoca/Redcross road)
☎ 0402 35327 FAX 0402 35327
15 Mar-31 Oct
Set two miles from Avoca, Ashdene represents an ideal centre for touring Co Wicklow. Mrs Burne is very enthusiastic in her care of guests, and takes pride in her breakfast menu.
5 rms (4 shr) (2 fmly) No smoking in bedrooms No smoking in dining room No dogs (ex guide dogs) Cen ht CTV 5P Tennis (grass)
ROOMS: s IR£22.50-IR£25; d IR£35-IR£37; wkly b&b IR£112-IR£119
CARDS:

Q Q Q **T&C Old Coach House** The Meeting of the Waters, Vale of Avoca (take road from Rathdrum follow signs for Avoca, Meetings of the Waters 500yds beyond on right)
☎ 0402 35408 FAX 0402 35720
This black and white coaching inn is in the picturesque Vale of Avoca, where the popular BBC TV programme 'Ballykissangel' is filmed. It has been tastefully restored by friendly Susan and Aidan Dempsey. A warm and inviting atmosphere pervades the restful lounge and smart restaurant. Charming en suite bedrooms feature stripped pine furnishings, pretty decor and tea and coffee-making facilities.
6 shr (2 fmly) No smoking in 2 bedrooms No smoking in area of dining room CTV in all bedrooms Tea and coffee making facilities Direct dial from bedrooms No dogs (ex guide dogs) Licensed Cen ht CTV 8P
ROOMS: s IR£27-IR£31; d IR£44-IR£50*
CARDS:

Selected

Q Q Q Q **GH Sheepwalk House** Beech Rd
(W off N11, Beech Road to Avoca 2m from Arklow, 2m from Avoca)
☎ 0402 35189 FAX 0402 35789
Feb-Nov
A historic 18th-century Georgian house, 2 miles from Avoca and with lovely views across Arklow Bay. The cosy, comfortably furnished bedrooms are equipped with every thoughtful extra. Guests can breakfast in the informal sun lounge which commands sea views, and owner Jim McCabe is a mine of information on golfing, shooting and fishing holidays.
8 shr (2 fmly) CTV in all bedrooms Tea and coffee making facilities Cen ht CTV 12P No coaches
ROOMS: s IR£28; d IR£44-IR£50; wkly b&b IR£154-IR£164*
CARDS:

BALLACOLLA Co Laois Map **01** C3

Selected

Q Q Q Q **T&C Ballygogue Country House** Ballygogue (off N8)
☎ 0502 34025
rs 2 Oct-Feb (by arrangement only)
This lovely old country house has been tastefully furnished and decorated to a high standard with top of the range beds and luxury quality en suite bedrooms. Mrs Bailey loves to cook and her breakfasts reflect this with freshly baked breads and home made muesli being particular features.
3 rms (2 shr) (2 fmly) No smoking CTV in all bedrooms Tea and coffee making facilities No dogs Cen ht CTV 5P No coaches
ROOMS: s fr IR£25; d fr IR£45

BALLAGHMORE Co Laois Map **01** C3

Q Q Q **Ballaghmore House** *(S 183899)* (situated on the N7 between Roscrea & Borris-in-Ossory, halfway between Limerick and Dublin) ☎ 0505 21366 Mrs C England
4 shr (3 fmly) No smoking in bedrooms No smoking in dining room No smoking in 1 lounge CTV in all bedrooms Tea and coffee making facilities No dogs Cen ht CTV No children 3yrs ch fac 8P Golf 18 Fishing Coarse fishing 75 acres mixed Last d 5pm
ROOMS: s IR£20-IR£25; d IR£34; wkly b&b fr IR£107; wkly hlf-bd fr IR£177*
CARDS:

BALLINCOLLIG Co Cork Map **01** B2

QQQ **T&C The Milestone** (on Cork to Killarney Rd N22. 7m from Cork city, 2m W of Ballincollig on N22)
☎ 021 872562 FAX 021 872562
Well maintained house on main Cork - Killanney road, convenient to Blarney and ferries. There are five pleasant, en suite bedrooms, and secure car parking to the rear of the building. Golf, pitch and putt and lake fishing are all available close by.
5 bth/shr (1 fmly) No smoking in 2 bedrooms No smoking in dining room No smoking in lounges Tea and coffee making facilities No dogs (ex guide dogs) Cen ht CTV ch fac 8P
ROOMS: s IR£23-IR£25; d IR£36-IR£40; wkly b&b IR£115-IR£125*

BALLINHASSIG Co Cork Map **01** B2

QQ **T&C Blanchfield House** Rigsdale (main Cork/Bandon Rd N71 between Innishannon Village and Halfway Village)
☎ 021 885167 FAX 021 885305
Closed 24 Dec-1 Jan rs Nov-Mar (restaurant may be closed)
This guesthouse is in a quiet, but convenient location within easy reach of the airport and ferry. Proprietor Patricia Blanchfield offers good home cooking, and private salmon and trout fishing are available.
6 rms (2 bth/shr) (2 fmly) No smoking in bedrooms No smoking in area of dining room No dogs (ex guide dogs) Licensed Cen ht CTV 20P
Last d noon
ROOMS: s IR£22.50-IR£24.50; d IR£32-IR£36; wkly b&b IR£105-IR£140; wkly hlf-bd IR£210-IR£245
CARDS:

BALLISODARE Co Sligo Map **01** B5

QQQ **T&C Seashore House** Lisduff
(turn off N4 into Ballisodare Village, take N59 from village 4km W the Seashore sign is visable, turn right 600m to house)
☎ 071 67827 FAX 071 67827
Attractive dormer bungalow in a quiet seashore location, just 2.5 miles from the village. Comfortable lounge with open turf fire and sunny conservatory dining room looking out over attractive gardens to sea and mountain scenery.
4 bth/shr (2 fmly) No smoking in bedrooms CTV in all bedrooms Tea and coffee making facilities No dogs (ex guide dogs) Cen ht CTV No children 10yrs 6P Solarium
ROOMS: s IR£20-IR£23; d IR£32; wkly b&b IR£96-IR£112*
CARDS:

BALLYHACK Co Wexford Map **01** C2

Selected

QQQQ **T&C Marsh Mere Lodge**
(from Rosslare Harbour take N25 to Wexford then take R733 to Ballyhack) ☎ 051 389186
This charming shell-pink house is situated a few minutes' walk from the Ballyhack ferry overlooking Waterford harbour. Mrs Mcnamara is a friendly host and the house is full of her personal touches. Bedrooms are delightful and a fine tea is served on the verandah.
5 bth/shr No dogs (ex guide dogs) Cen ht CTV 5P No coaches Pony trap rides
ROOMS: s IR£25-IR£30; d IR£35-IR£40; wkly b&b IR£105-IR£140*

All AA listed accommodation can also be found at the AA's Internet site, whose address is: http://www.theaa.co.uk/hotels

BALLYLIFFEN Co Donegal Map **01** C6

Selected

QQQQ **T&C Rossaor House** (from Derry City take A2 towards Moville, turning off at Quigleys Point) ☎ 077 76498 FAX 077 76498
Set in lovely mature gardens in a peaceful location on the Inishowen peninsula, Rossaor is a delightful house in every sense of the word. From the elegant sitting room with marvellous panoramic views of Pollen Bay and Malin Head to the luxurious bedrooms where comfort and good taste are happily married. The friendly warmth of Anne and Brian Harkin makes a visit here a memorable one.
4 bth/shr (2 fmly) No smoking in dining room CTV in all bedrooms Tea and coffee making facilities Direct dial from bedrooms No dogs (ex guide dogs) Cen ht 10P No coaches
ROOMS: s IR£27; d IR£45*
CARDS:

BALLYMACARBRY Co Waterford Map **01** C2

Selected

QQQQ *Glasha (S1104106)* Four Mile Water, Glasha (8m from Clonmel on T27, turn right at Glasha Accommodation sign and drive for 1km) ☎ 052 36108 FAX 052 36108 Mr & Mrs P O'Gorman
Closed 20 Dec-31 Dec
This comfortable country house, set in its own grounds, has recently been refurbished, and has a large sitting room and sun lounge. The en suite accommodation is all very well equipped, and home baking is a speciality. Trout fishing is available on the river which runs through the grounds.
4 shr (5 fmly) No smoking in bedrooms CTV in all bedrooms Tea and coffee making facilities No dogs Cen ht CTV 7P Fishing 150 acres dairy Last d 7pm

See advertisement under CLONMEL

BALLYMONEY Co Antrim Map **01** C6

Selected

QQQQ **GH *Heagles Lodge*** 3 Heagles Rd, Ballybogey BT53 6NZ ☎ 012657 41122 FAX 012657 41001

The Sharkey family look forward to welcoming you to their immaculately maintained detached home which is situated some 4 miles east of Ballymoney off the B62. The charming bedrooms are decorated to a high standard and pretty fabrics have been used to complement the comfortable modern furnishings. The lovely public rooms include a relaxing lounge and separate dining area where the hearty breakfasts provide a good start to the day. This is a non smoking house.

3 shr (3 fmly) No smoking CTV in all bedrooms Tea and coffee making facilities No dogs Cen ht CTV P

CARDS:

BALLYMOTE Co Sligo Map **01** B4

QQQ **T&C Corran House** Sligo Rd (last house on right leaving Ballymote on R293 to Collooney) ☎ 071 83074

A comfortable, well-maintained house stands in attractive gardens just around the corner from the village. En suite bedrooms have attractive decor and are equipped with televisions and tea/coffee making facilities. The area is well-known as an angling centre.

4 shr (2 fmly) No smoking in 2 bedrooms No smoking in dining room CTV in all bedrooms Tea and coffee making facilities No dogs (ex guide dogs) Cen ht CTV 5P No coaches Last d 5pm

ROOMS: s IR£25; d IR£36; wkly b&b IR£95✳

CARDS:

BALLYVAUGHAN Co Clare Map **01** B3

Selected

QQQQ **GH Rusheen Lodge** (on N67 0.75m from Ballyvavghan village) ☎ 065 77092 FAX 065 77152

Closed 17 Dec-Jan

A charming house nestles in the valley of the Burren Limestone mountains, an area famous for its Arctic and Alpine plants in spring and summer. The McGann family were founders of the famous Aillwee Caves and have a fund of local folklore. The bedrooms are excellent, large and well equipped with attractive decor and extras that ensure a comfortable visit. The cosy dining room has patio gardens leading from it. Car parking is available.

8 bth/shr (3 fmly) No smoking in bedrooms No smoking in dining room CTV in all bedrooms Tea and coffee making facilities Direct dial from bedrooms No dogs (ex guide dogs) Cen ht CTV 12P

ROOMS: s IR£25-IR£40; d IR£40-IR£60

CARDS:

BALLYVOURNEY Co Cork Map **01** B2

Selected

QQQQ **GH The Mills Inn** (on main Cork/Killarney Rd N22 15 minutes from Killarney Lake District)

☎ 026 45237 FAX 026 45454

Closed 24-25 Dec

This charming inn dates back to the mid 18th century and stands in extensive gardens including a vintage car and folk museum as well as a shop. Bedrooms are comfortable and Donal and Mary Seannell are welcoming hosts. The bar offers hot food all day and there is also a cosy restaurant.

9 bth/shr 1 annexe bth/shr (4 fmly) No smoking in dining room CTV in all bedrooms Tea and coffee making facilities Direct dial from bedrooms Licensed Cen ht CTV ch fac 24P Last d 9pm

ROOMS: s IR£27-IR£35; d IR£56-IR£64✳

CARDS:

BANDON Co Cork Map **01** B2

Selected

QQQQ **T&C Glebe Country House** Ballinadee (exit N71 at Innishannon Bridge signposted Ballinadee, travel 5m along river bank, left after sign for village)

☎ 021 778294 FAX 021 778456

Closed 21 Dec-3 Jan

This lovely old guest house stands in well kept gardens, and is run with great attention to detail by its vivacious owner Gillian Bracken. Antique furnishings predominate throughout this comfortable house which has both a guest lounge and an elegant dining room. An interesting breakfast menu offers unusual options, and a country house style dinner is available by reservation.

4 bth/shr (2 fmly) No smoking in bedrooms No smoking in dining room Tea and coffee making facilities Direct dial from bedrooms Cen ht CTV 30P Tennis (grass) Croquet Last d noon

ROOMS: s IR£35-IR£45; d IR£50-IR£60; wkly b&b IR£175-IR£210; wkly hlf-bd IR£290.50-IR£325.50

CARDS:

BANSHA Co Tipperary Map **01** C3

Selected

QQQQ **Bansha House** *(R 962320)* (turn off N24 in village of Bansha opposite Esso filling station)

☎ 062 54194 FAX 062 54215 Mr & Mrs J Marnane

Closed 21-31 Dec

Situated in a very scenic area, this Georgian house is approached along an avenue of beech trees, and has 100 acres of land where visitors can roam. It is comfortable, well furnished and noted for the home baking.

8 rms (5 shr) (1 fmly) No smoking No dogs (ex guide dogs) Licensed Cen ht CTV 10P Fishing Riding Registered Equestrian centre 100 acres mixed Last d 7pm

ROOMS: s IR£30-IR£35; d IR£48-IR£54; wkly b&b IR£160; wkly hlf-bd IR£250-IR£260✳

CARDS:

BANTEER Co Cork Map 01 B2

Selected

Q Q Q Q **T&C Clonmeen Lodge** Nr Mallow
(follow N72 to Killarney from the rdbt in Mallows for 7m, at petrol station take next left, premises signposted at junct)
☎ 029 56238 & 56277 FAX 029 56294
This neatly furnished and comfortable house stands a short distance off the N72, beside the River Blackwater and within easy reach of a variety of recreational options which include fishing, walking, pony trekking, and golf. Bedrooms are attractively decorated, and a peaceful, hospitable atmosphere pervades the public areas. Cork Airport is within an hour's drive.
6 bth/shr (4 fmly) CTV in 4 bedrooms Licensed Cen ht CTV 20P Fishing Riding Bicycle hire Last d 9.15pm
ROOMS: s IR£35-IR£40; d IR£50-IR£60*
CARDS:

BANTRY Co Cork Map 01 B2

Q Q Q **T&C *Donemark Rise*** Droumacoppil
(1 mile on N71 frm Bantry/Gengarriff) ☎ 027 51099
Apr-Oct
A dormer bungalow in a scenic location 3 kms from the town centre, where the hospitable Theresa Mullins offers a place to unwind. Bedrooms are en suite and offer versatile accommodation, and there is a TV lounge and dining room for guests' use. Dinner is available on request, and there are private gardens and car parking. Fluent French and conversational German are spoken here.
3 shr 1 annexe shr (2 fmly) No smoking in bedrooms No smoking in dining room CTV in 1 bedroom Tea and coffee making facilities No dogs (ex guide dogs) Cen ht CTV 7P Last d before noon
CARDS:

Q Q Q **T&C *Shangri-La*** Glengarriff Rd ☎ 027 50244 FAX 027 50244
Mid Mar-Mid Nov
Standing in a spacious one-acre garden, this bungalow is within walking distance of Bantry where there are plenty of pubs and restaurants. Breakfast may be taken in the conservatory overlooking Bantry Bay and is a charming spot to enjoy the views; there is also a comfortable lounge and a dining room.
6 rms (4 bth/shr) (1 fmly) No smoking in area of dining room No smoking in 1 lounge Tea and coffee making facilities No dogs Cen ht CTV 12P golf nearby
CARDS:

The AA's professional Inspectors make regular and anonymous visits to all the establishments listed in the Guide. They accept no gifts or favours from proprietors

BELFAST Map 01 D5

Q Q **GH Camera** 44 Wellington Park BT9 6DP
(located off Malone Rd, 5m from Queens University, right at Wellington Park Hotel onto Wellington Park, house half way down on left)
☎ 01232 660026 FAX 01232 667856
Situated in a leafy avenue close to the university, this end-terraced Victorian house offers good value bed and breakfast accommodation. At the time of our visit, plans were in hand to completely refurbish all the bedrooms and to provide all rooms with en suite facilities. The attractive public areas have already been smartly upgraded.
9 bth/shr (2 fmly) No smoking CTV in all bedrooms Tea and coffee making facilities Direct dial from bedrooms No dogs (ex guide dogs) Cen ht No coaches Last d 9am
ROOMS: s fr £50; d fr £70
CARDS:

Q Q Q **GH *Lisdara House*** 23 Derryvolgie Av, Malone Rd BT9 6FN
(Turn off M1 & M2 at Balmoral exit, continue towards centre of Belfast along Lisburn Rd. Derryvolgie Av is on right, 1.5m along Lisburn Rd)
☎ 01232 681549 FAX 01232 681549
Closed 23 Dec-2 Jan
A substantial detached house which is situated in a desirable south-side residential area close to the university. The individually furnished bedrooms make good use of bold colour schemes. Public areas include an inviting lounge with the dining room adjacent. Freshly prepared breakfasts and, with prior arrangement, evening meals are served at individual tables.
4 bth/shr No smoking CTV in all bedrooms Tea and coffee making facilities Cen ht CTV No children 10yrs 6P Last d by arrangement
CARDS:

Q Q Q **GH Malone** 79 Malone Rd BT9 6SH
(exit M1 at Balmoral, enter Stockmans Lane, turn left after fifth set of traffic lights, hotel after third set of traffic lights)
☎ 01232 669565
Closed 24 Dec-6 Jan
There is a welcoming atmosphere at this family-run detached red-brick Victorian house close to the university. The building is undergoing a major improvement programme starting with refurbishment of the bedrooms. Public areas include an inviting lounge and separate dining room where breakfast is served. At peak times, tables may be shared.
8 shr No smoking in dining room CTV in all bedrooms Tea and coffee making facilities No dogs Cen ht No children 12yrs 9P No coaches
ROOMS: s fr £35; d fr £50; wkly b&b fr £245*

Premier Selected

Q Q Q Q Q GH Rayanne Country House & Restaurant 60 Desmesne Rd BT18 9EX
(A2 Belfast-Bangor, past airport and turn off for Holywood/Palace Barracks. Opposite Esso garage turn right up Jacksons Rd, 0.75m past golf club)
☎ 01232 425859 FAX 01232 423364
Genuine Irish hospitality from the McClelland family, and excellent food at both dinner and breakfast, are all part of the appeal of this Victorian house located in Holywood. Public rooms include two charming lounges where the guests can relax. However, the focal point is the elegant restaurant where the innovative menu, combined with Raymond McClelland's technical skills in the kitchen, have deservedly earned wide acclaim, including the award of two Rosettes from the AA. Breakfast is also a memorable experience. The lovely bedrooms, each of which is quite individual in style, have been equipped with a wide range of thoughtful extras.
9 bth/shr (1 fmly) No smoking in bedrooms No smoking in dining room No smoking in 1 lounge CTV in all bedrooms Tea and coffee making facilities No dogs (ex guide dogs) Licensed Cen ht 14P Last d 8.30pm
ROOMS: s £50-£67.50; d £70-£90; wkly b&b £245-£300; wkly hlf-bd £390-£495*
CARDS:

BIRR Co Offaly Map **01** C3

Q Q Q GH *The Maltings* Castle St ☎ 0509 21345 FAX 0509 21345
This one-time brewery and grain store on the River Camcor has been interestingly converted into the Maltings Guesthouse. Facilities include en suite bedrooms, a public bar and restaurant, and a fitness room. Work is continuing on the development of craft shops, and hostel and self-catering accommodation in other buildings on the complex.
52 rms (12 bth/shr) (12 fmly) No smoking in 40 bedrooms No smoking in dining room No smoking in 1 lounge CTV in all bedrooms Direct dial from bedrooms No dogs (ex guide dogs) Licensed Cen ht CTV 70P Fishing Sauna Solarium Gymnasium Last d 9pm
CARDS:

BLARNEY Co Cork Map **01** B2

Q Q Q T&C Ashlee Lodge Tower (4kms from Blarney on R617)
☎ 021 385346 FAX 021 385726
5 Jan-20 Dec
Flower filled baskets adorn this bungalow lodge set in its own landscaped gardens and run by Anne and John O'Leary. A good breakfast menu is offered in the dining room, and most of the bedrooms are en suite.
6 rms (5 bth/shr) (3 fmly) No smoking CTV in all bedrooms Tea and coffee making facilities Direct dial from bedrooms No dogs (ex guide dogs) Cen ht CTV 8P Last d noon
ROOMS: s IR£25; d IR£32-IR£36; wkly b&b IR£108; wkly hlf-bd IR£195*
CARDS:

Q Q Q T&C Blarney Vale House Cork Rd
(on R617 adjacent to golf driving range on approach to town)
☎ 021 381511
Apr-Oct
A new dormer bungalow on an elevated site above the Cork Road and surrounded by landscaped gardens. Everything is very new and of an excellent standard. Ann and Ray Hennessy are enthusiastic hosts. A nice lounge offers guests a chance to relax in the evening.
4 shr (2 fmly) No smoking CTV in all bedrooms Tea and coffee making facilities No dogs Cen ht 9P
ROOMS: s IR£25-IR£32; d IR£36-IR£38*

Q Q Q T&C Buena Vista Station Rd (from village, take third turning on left into Station Rd, house 0.5km on right) ☎ 021 385035
Closed 21 Dec-9 Feb
5 shr (2 fmly) No smoking in dining room CTV in all bedrooms Tea and coffee making facilities No dogs Cen ht 7P
ROOMS: s fr IR£23.50; d fr IR£34*

Q Q Q T&C White House Shean Lower (on R617, Cork/Blarney road)
☎ 021 385338
Conveniently situated close to town in an elevated position with views of Blarney Castle, this attractive well appointed house is dedicated to guests' comfort. There is a lounge, a separate breakfast room and six en suite bedrooms with TVs, hair dryers and clock radios. Spacious shower rooms have power showers.
6 shr (1 fmly) No smoking CTV in all bedrooms Tea and coffee making facilities No dogs Cen ht 7P
ROOMS: s IR£25-IR£32; d IR£36-IR£38*

BORRISOKANE Co Tipperary Map **01** C3

Q Q Q T&C Ballycormac House Aglish
(from Nenagh North on N52 to Borrisokane, then N65, right at signs to Ballycormac House) ☎ 067 21129 FAX 067 21200
An ideal place to relax and leave the cares of the world behind, this lovely 300 year old farmhouse is the dream home of American couple Herbert and Christine Quigley. Fruit and vegetables from their organic gardens play a major part in meals here. An ideal location from which to explore the area.
5 bth/shr No smoking Tea and coffee making facilities No dogs (ex guide dogs) Licensed Cen ht No children 6yrs 8P No coaches Last d 8.30pm
ROOMS: s IR£35-IR£45; d IR£70-IR£80*
CARDS:

BRUREE Co Limerick Map **01** B3

Q Q Q *Ballyteigue House (R 524313)* Rockhill
(travelling S on N20 pass O'Roukes and take next right, pass Rockhill Church, 1m from turnoff premises are signposted)
☎ 063 90575 FAX 063 90575 Mr & Mrs R Johnson
Closed 20 Dec-10 Jan
This country house, surrounded by gardens and fields, stands in a rural area not far from Charleville Golf Course. Margaret and Richard Johnson are welcoming hosts who have created a very pleasant atmosphere for guests, with period furnishings, comfortable accommodation and a relaxing sitting room and dining room where evening meals can be served by prior request. Horse riding, hunting and fishing can all be arranged in the neighbourhood.
No smoking in dining room No smoking in lounges Tea and coffee making facilities No dogs (ex guide dogs) Cen ht CTV P 30 acres cattle horses Last d 12am
CARDS:

BUNBEG Co Donegal Map **01** B6

Q Q Q **GH *Teac Campbell***
☎ 075 31545 & 32270 FAX 075 31545
Closed 24-26 Dec
The Campbell family's guest house is on Main Street, near to the centre of the town, set back behind its private car park. The atmosphere is welcoming and the well equipped en suite bedrooms include some large enough to contain 3 beds and some on the ground floor. There is also a spacious TV lounge and a breakfast room where an evening meal can be served by arrangement. Bunbeg is close to the sea, with a safe, sandy beach and there is also a golf club.
20 shr (17 fmly) No smoking in dining room No smoking in 1 lounge Tea and coffee making facilities Direct dial from bedrooms No dogs (ex guide dogs) Cen ht CTV ch fac 18P Last d 4pm

BUNRATTY Co Clare Map **01** B3

Selected

Q Q Q Q **T&C Clover Hill Lodge**
(take road between pub and Bunratty castle, pass through Folk Park, continue up this road for approx 1.25m)
☎ 061 369039 FAX 061 360520
Apr-Oct
A modern dormer bungalow, not far from Bunratty Castle. Mrs Anne Nash is your charming host and takes pride in the comfort of her accommodation which is of a high standard.
4 shr (2 fmly) No smoking CTV in all bedrooms No dogs (ex guide dogs) Cen ht CTV 10P No coaches
ROOMS: s IR£30; d IR£36*
CARDS:

BUSHMILLS Co Antrim Map **01** C6

Selected

Q Q Q Q **GH *Craig Park*** 24 Carnbore Rd BT57 8YF
☎ 012657 32496 FAX 012657 32479
Closed Xmas & New Year
Craig Park is a delightful late 18th-century farmhouse which has been sympathetically extended. From its tranquil setting some 2 miles south east of town, distant views of the Donegal mountains and the Islands of Islay and Jury can be enjoyed. The house has three comfortable en suite bedrooms, and guests are invited to share the owners' spacious sitting room. Breakfast are served around the communal table in the attractive dining room. This is a no-smoking house.
3 shr (3 fmly) No smoking CTV in all bedrooms Tea and coffee making facilities No dogs Cen ht CTV 10P No coaches
CARDS:

BUTLERBRIDGE Co Cavan Map **01** C4

Q Q Q **GH Olde Post Inn** Cloverhill (on N54, N of Cavan)
☎ 047 55555 & 55266 FAX 047 55111
Closed 25-27 Dec rs Mon (restaurant closed)
A charming red brick house situated beside a church in the tiny village of Cloverhill. Owner Frank Cassidy is a welcoming, attentive host. There is a spacious lounge for relaxation as well as a breakfast room. Bedrooms are all en suite, comfortable and well appointed. Gardens surround the house.
7 bth/shr (1 fmly) No smoking in bedrooms No smoking in area of dining room CTV in all bedrooms Tea and coffee making facilities Direct dial from bedrooms No dogs (ex guide dogs) Licensed Cen ht 30P Last d 9.45pm
ROOMS: s IR£25; d IR£50*
CARDS:

CAHERDANIEL Co Kerry Map **01** A2

Q Q Q **T&C Derrynane Bay House** (1km on Waterville side of village on N70 overlooking Derrynane Bay) ☎ 066 75404 FAX 066 75436
Closed Feb
Set back from the main road, this meticulously maintained house is in an elevated position with scenic views over Derrynane Bay. Tastefully furnished throughout, there is a comfortable sitting and dining room and attractive bedrooms. The owner is very welcoming and provides a good breakfast menu. Walking, watersports, good beaches, fishing and golf are all nearby.
6 bth/shr (2 fmly) No smoking in bedrooms No smoking in dining room CTV in all bedrooms Tea and coffee making facilities Direct dial from bedrooms No dogs (ex guide dogs) Cen ht CTV 10P Last d noon
ROOMS: s IR£25; d IR£35-IR£40*
CARDS:

CAHIRCIVEEN Co Kerry Map **01** A2

Q Q Q **Ocean View Farmhouse** *(V 453778)* Renard Rd
☎ 066 72261 Mrs C O'Donaghue
Closed 3 Jan-19 Dec
A modern bungalow in the middle of spectacular touring country. Bedrooms all enjoy sea views, en suite facilities and comfortable beds. Guests have use of a large comfortable lounge with an open fire and coffee bar. A well organised equestrian centre caters for riders at every level.
6 shr (2 fmly) No smoking in 2 bedrooms No smoking in dining room Cen ht CTV ch fac 7P Riding 45 acres non-working Last d 2pm
ROOMS: s IR£23.50; d IR£34 *

Q Q Q **Valentia View** *(V 457773)* (on N70 2m on the Waterville side of Cahirciveen)
☎ 066 72227 FAX 066 73122 Mr T Sugrue
Mar-Oct
This fine old country farmhouse on The Ring of Kerry has a warm and hospitable atmosphere. Rooms overlook Valentia Island and bay.
6 shr (2 fmly) No smoking Tea and coffee making facilities Cen ht CTV No children 2mths ch fac 20P 38 acres beef Last d 3pm
ROOMS: s fr IR£23; d fr IR£36; wkly b&b fr IR£126*
CARDS:

CAMP Co Kerry Map 01 A2

Selected

QQQQ **T&C Barnagh Bridge Country House** (leave N86 Tralee/Dingle road at Camp and follow Conor Pass road for 1 Km)
☎ 066 30145 FAX 066 30299
Mar-Oct
Barnagh Bridge is in a perfect position to enjoy the northern side of the rugged Dingle peninsula with its unspoilt beaches, ancient sites and powerful natural beauty. It is an eye catching, cream coloured house, cleverly designed to take full advantage of the views of Tralee Bay. Each comfortable bedroom is named after flowers of the area: fuschia, bluebell etc, and their colours are reflected in the decor. Mrs Williams is happy to recommend good local restaurants. Local amenities include golf, hill walking, fresh water and deep sea angling and beaches.
5 shr (2 fmly) No smoking in bedrooms No smoking in dining room CTV in all bedrooms Tea and coffee making facilities Direct dial from bedrooms No dogs (ex guide dogs) Cen ht CTV 7P
ROOMS: s IR£28-IR£35; d IR£36-IR£50*
CARDS: MasterCard, Barclaycard/Visa

CAPPOQUIN Co Waterford Map 01 C2

Selected

QQQQ **GH Richmond House** (on N72, 0.5m from Cappoquin on Dungarvan road) ☎ 058 54278 FAX 058 54988
Closed 23 Dec-1 Feb
This eighteenth-century Georgian house stands in timbered parkland, about half a mile from the picturesque town of Cappoquin. It is family run and offers tastefully decorated en suite bedrooms with direct dial telephones and central heating. There is also a fully licensed restaurant serving a good standard of food. Located in an area of mountains, woodlands and rivers, the hotel is an obvious base for walkers and anglers, but three golf courses are also within easy reach and there are sandy beaches only half an hour's drive away.
9 bth/shr (2 fmly) No smoking in area of dining room CTV in all bedrooms Tea and coffee making facilities Direct dial from bedrooms No dogs Licensed Cen ht No children 20P Last d 8pm
ROOMS: s IR£45-IR£60; d IR£80-IR£120
CARDS: MasterCard, American Express, Barclaycard/Visa, Diners Club

CARAGH LAKE Co Kerry Map 01 A2

Premier Selected

QQQQQ **GH Caragh Lodge**
CARAGH LAKE
(N70, from Killorglin towards Glenbeigh, signed. Turn left at lake, lodge on right) ☎ 066 69115 FAX 69316
15 bth/shr No smoking in dining room Direct dial from bedrooms No dogs (ex guide dogs) Cen ht No children 7yrs 22P No coaches Tennis (hard) Fishing Sauna Last d 8.30pm
ROOMS: s fr IR£66; d IR£99-IR£198*
CARDS: MasterCard, American Express, Barclaycard/Visa, Diners Club

This symbol indicates a 'Child Friendly' establishment - see page 25 for details

CARLINGFORD Co Louth Map 01 D4

Premier Selected

QQQQQ **T&C Jordans Townhouse & Restaurant** Newry St
(centre of Carlingford Village overlooking harbour)
☎ 042 73223 FAX 042 73827
Closed 6-25 Jan
5 bth/shr (1 fmly) No smoking CTV in all bedrooms Tea and coffee making facilities Direct dial from bedrooms No dogs (ex guide dogs) Licensed Cen ht CTV 4P No coaches Tennis (hard) Last d 9.30pm
ROOMS: s fr IR£47.50; d IR£85*
CARDS: MasterCard, American Express, Barclaycard/Visa

CARLOW Co Carlow Map 01 C3

Premier Selected

QQQQQ **GH Barrowville Town House** Kilkenny Rd
(on N9 southside of town, 200mtrs S of N80 junc)
☎ 0503 43324 FAX 0503 41953
rs 25 Dec
This 18th-century town house stands in its own grounds just a short stroll from the town centre. There is a car park at the front, and a semi-formal garden at the back where guests are welcome to sit and relax. A good choice of breakfast dishes is served in the dining room overlooking the gardens and there is also a cosy lounge, furnished in period style, with a grand piano for those with the talent to play.
7 bth/shr (2 fmly) No smoking in bedrooms No smoking in dining room CTV in all bedrooms Tea and coffee making facilities Direct dial from bedrooms No dogs (ex guide dogs) Cen ht CTV No children 15yrs 11P No coaches
ROOMS: s IR£25-IR£30; d IR£40-IR£50
CARDS: MasterCard, American Express, Barclaycard/Visa

Selected

QQQQ **T&C *Fanad House*** Kilkenny Rd
(2km from Carlow Town on the Kilkenny Road) ☎ 0503 43417
Apr-Oct
An eye-catching white house of distinctive architectural design set back from the main road in attractive gardens with plenty of parking space. All the good features of contemporary design have been incorporated into the building, and there is a sense of space and light. The lounge runs the length of the house, and the breakfast area has a marble

contd.

fireplace. Bedrooms are pleasant with good facilities. Mrs McCanon creates a friendly atmosphere, and her home baking is a speciality which her guests enjoy.
4 rms (3 shr) No smoking in bedrooms No smoking in area of dining room No smoking in 1 lounge CTV in 3 bedrooms No dogs Cen ht CTV 10P No coaches Jacuzzi

Q Q Q **T&C Greenlane House** Dublin Rd
(from Dublin take N7 for Nass and follow Carlow sign (N9), at 1st rdbt in Carlow follow town centre signs, estab on right next to St Marys cemetary)
☎ 0503 42670 FAX 30903
rs 25-26 Dec
A very well kept, spacious house in a quiet area on the north side of town. Accommodation is very comfortable, with a big lounge and breakfast room overlooking the patio and garden, and bedrooms are well equipped and versatile. Mrs Dunne is very willing to help plan itineraries for visiting this interesting area. Good car parking facilities are available.
7 bth/shr (2 fmly) No smoking CTV in all bedrooms Tea and coffee making facilities No dogs (ex guide dogs) Cen ht CTV 35P
ROOMS: d IR£42-IR£50*
CARDS:

CARRIGALINE Co Cork Map 01 B2

Q Q **T&C *Beaver Lodge*** (centre of village) ☎ 021 372595
FAX 021 372245
Closed Xmas
An old ivy-clad house standing in its own grounds off the main street.
6 rms (2 bth 2 shr) (5 fmly) No smoking in bedrooms No smoking in dining room CTV in all bedrooms Tea and coffee making facilities Direct dial from bedrooms No dogs (ex guide dogs) Cen ht CTV 14P No coaches
CARDS:

Selected

Q Q Q Q **T&C *Glenwood House*** Ballinrea Rd
(follow signs to Ringaskiddy ferry port, at roundabout follow signs for Carrigaline, on approaching village turn right signposted to Glenwood)
☎ 021 373878 FAX 021 373878
Closed 22-31 Dec
8 bth/shr No smoking in area of dining room No smoking in 1 lounge CTV in all bedrooms Tea and coffee making facilities Direct dial from bedrooms No dogs (ex guide dogs) Cen ht CTV 12P No coaches
CARDS:

CARRIGANS Co Donegal Map 01 C5

Selected

Q Q Q Q **T&C Mount Royd Country Home** (off N13 & N14 on road 236, from Derry city take A40) ☎ 074 40163 FAX 074 40163
Set in mature gardens, Mount Royd is an attractive creeper-clad house with the River Foyle running along the back boundary. The friendly Martins have brought hospitality to new heights - nothing is too much trouble for them. Breakfast is a feast of choices, and an eye-catching display of fresh fruits entices guests to healthy options before succumbing to other temptations. Bedrooms are very comfortable with lots of personal touches.
4 shr (3 fmly) No smoking in 2 bedrooms No smoking in dining room CTV in all bedrooms Tea and coffee making facilities No dogs (ex guide dogs) Cen ht CTV 7P Last d noon
ROOMS: s IR£20; d IR£36*

CASHEL Co Tipperary Map 01 C3

Q Q Q ❦ ***Ardmayle House*** *(S 055452)* (NW on road to Gooldscross)
☎ 0504 42399 FAX 0504 42420 Mrs A De Vere Hunt
Apr-Oct
A fine Georgian house set in 300 acres of farmlands, surrounded by mature trees and home to Annette de Vere Hunt, proprietor and cook. There is plenty of room to rest in this tranquil, rural location where the atmosphere is relaxed and very friendly.
5 rms (4 shr) (1 fmly) No smoking in bedrooms No smoking in dining room No dogs (ex guide dogs) Cen ht CTV 6P Fishing 300 acres dairy Last d noon

Selected

Q Q Q Q ❦ **Dualla House** *(S 120430)*
(from Kilkenny on R691, 1m from Dualla village on right. From Cashel, travelling up main street from Cork, turn right at traffic lights)
☎ 062 61487 & 62285 FAX 062 61487 Mrs M Power
Closed 21 Dec-21 Jan rs 22 Nov-21 Dec & 21 Jan-14 Feb
Located in the Golden Vale of Tipperary, this 200-year-old house is on a 300-acre sheep farm. Period furniture graces the spacious rooms which include a sitting room with turf fire, dining room and comfortable en suite bedrooms. Big breakfasts are a speciality.
4 bth/shr (4 fmly) No smoking CTV in all bedrooms Tea and coffee making facilities No dogs (ex guide dogs) Cen ht CTV 6P 300 acres sheep arable
ROOMS: s IR£23-IR£30; d IR£36-IR£40; wkly b&b IR£110-IR£120
CARDS:

Q Q Q ❦ ***Knock-Saint-Lour House*** *(S 074390)* ☎ 062 61172
Mr E O'Brien
Apr-Oct
7 shr (2 fmly) Tea and coffee making facilities No dogs (ex guide dogs) Cen ht CTV 20P 30 acres mixed

Selected

Q Q Q Q **GH *Legend's*** The Kiln ☎ 062 61292
This distinctive house has been purpose built to blend in with its dramatic location beneath the Rock of Cashel. The restaurant enjoys mystical floodlit views and diners will experience an atmosphere of almost eerie magic in the evening. A guests' lounge and very comfortable bedrooms complete the picture of this smart house on the edge of the town centre.
5 shr (1 fmly) No smoking in area of dining room No smoking in 1 lounge CTV in all bedrooms Tea and coffee making facilities Direct dial from bedrooms No dogs Licensed Cen ht No children 10yrs 7P Last d 9.30pm
CARDS:

CASTLECONNELL Co Limerick Map **01** B3

Q Q **T&C Rivergrove House** (10kms from Limerick turn off N7 for Castle Connell at Daly's Cross. Take second left after 1km and first right. Road turns sharply left, 2nd on left) ☎ 061 377107 FAX 061 377229
Modern creeper-clad two-storey house in an idyllic location on a broad sweep of the River Shannon. Nicely appointed bedrooms with some fine antique furnishings and lovely river views. There is a comfortable lounge/sitting room, and a communal dining room where guests can enjoy delicious home-cooked meals.
4 bth/shr (1 fmly) Cen ht CTV No children 7yrs 6P No coaches
ROOMS: s IR£20; d IR£32-IR£34*

CASTLEGREGORY Co Kerry Map **01** A2

Q Q ❦ ***Griffin's Tip-Top Country Farmhouse*** *(Q 525085)* Goulane (1m from Stradbally village) ☎ 066 39147 Mrs C Griffin
1 Mar-1 Nov
Situated only a short distance from a golf club and a Blue Flag beach, one of the many unspoilt beaches along the coastline of the Dingle peninsula. Mrs Griffin believes in a warm welcome, good beds and home baking to keep her guests happy. The dining room offers a panorama of Tralee Bay.
7 rms (5 shr) (3 fmly) No smoking Tea and coffee making facilities Cen ht CTV 10P 150 acres dairy sheep Last d noon
CARDS:

Selected

Q Q Q Q **T&C Shores Country House** Cappatigue
(on Connor Pass Rd, 1.5m W of Stradbally)
☎ 066 39196 FAX 066 39196
Mar-Nov
An attractive yellow painted house overlooking Brandon Bay. The accommodation is tastefully furnished and comfortable. Planned developments will enhance the accommodation further. Mrs O'Mahony will provide dinner on request.
4 rms (3 shr) (1 fmly) No smoking CTV in all bedrooms Tea and coffee making facilities No dogs Cen ht CTV 5P Last d 5pm
ROOMS: s IR£21.50-IR£26.50; d IR£30-IR£40;
wkly b&b IR£105-IR£140; wkly hlf-bd IR£195-IR£225*
CARDS:

Selected

Q Q Q Q **T&C Strand View House** Kilcummin, Conor Pass Rd (20m from Tralee on the Dingle, Conor Pass Road 1.5m W of Stradbally) ☎ 066 38131 FAX 066 38131
Feb-Oct
A superb brick house 2 miles west of Stradbally on the Castlegregory to Conor Pass Road. Luxury bedrooms enjoy panoramic sea views over Kilcummin Beach, and there is a terraced rock garden to the rear in which to relax. Mrs Lynch is a charming hostess who loves to entertain her guests.

5 shr 5 annexe shr (2 fmly) No smoking in 4 bedrooms No smoking in dining room No smoking in lounges CTV in 5 bedrooms Tea and coffee making facilities No dogs (ex guide dogs) Cen ht CTV 12P No coaches
ROOMS: d IR£36-IR£40*
CARDS:

CASTLEROCK Co Londonderry Map **01** C6

Q Q Q **GH *Cranford House*** 11 Circular Rd BT51 4XA
(on entering Castlerock (Sea Road) turn right after railway crossing into circular road) ☎ 01265 848669
This delightful detached home is located close to central amenities and the golf course. The smart modern bedrooms are decorated to a high standard and offer mixed comfortable furnishings. Public areas include an inviting lounge and a dining room, where breakfast is served at individual tables.
3 rms (1 bth/shr) (1 fmly) No smoking in bedrooms CTV in all bedrooms Tea and coffee making facilities No dogs (ex guide dogs) Cen ht CTV 12P No coaches

CAVAN Co Cavan Map **01** C4

Q Q Q **T&C Halcyon** Drumalee
(turn right off N3 immediately after the cathedral, signposted 'Cootehill'. Turn right at X-roads, 'Halcyon' 100yds on left)
☎ 049 31809 FAX 049 62531
9 Mar-9 Nov
This lovely modern bungalow on the north side of town offers peace and quiet in attractive, comfortable accommodation. Four of the five bedrooms are en suite, and a sun lounge and cosy sitting room overlooking the patio and gardens are relaxing areas for guests. Brid and Walter Myles are the hospitable owners, and their guest house is very popular with anglers as there is good coarse fishing in the many local lakes.
5 rms (4 shr) (4 fmly) No smoking in dining room No dogs (ex guide dogs) Cen ht CTV No children 2yrs 6P Last d noon
ROOMS: s IR£22.50-IR£24.50; d IR£32-IR£36
CARDS:

CHEEKPOINT Co Waterford Map **01** C2

Selected

Q Q Q Q **GH *Three Rivers*** (from Waterford follow R684 towards Dunmore East then follow signs for Cheekpoint)
☎ 051 382520 FAX 051 382542
Closed Dec-1 Feb
This charming house is superbly located overlooking the Rivers Barrow, Noire and Suir, within sight of the twinkling lights of Passage East
contd.

where a ferry provides quick access to Rosslare port. There are well appointed bedrooms, attractive gardens and a sunny balcony. The lounge and dining room are sited to take full advantage of the magnificent views. The house stands within five minutes of Faithlegg Golf Course.
14 shr (4 fmly) No smoking in bedrooms No smoking in dining room Tea and coffee making facilities Direct dial from bedrooms Cen ht CTV ch fac 20P Golf 18 Golf Fishing and riding all close by
CARDS:

CLADDAGHDUFF Co Galway Map **01** A4

Selected

GH Acton's Restaurant & Guest House Leegaun (N59 from Galway to Clifden. N59 from Clifden towards Westport for 2m, left (see our sign) for 4m; house not visible from the road) ☎ 095 44339 & 44308 FAX 095 44309
12 Mar-1 Oct
This secluded guest house and restaurant is located on the seashore overlooking its own private sandy beach. The luxury modern bungalow at the end of a long driveway offers excellent en suite accommodation and comfortable lounges where guests can relax and enjoy superb views of the sea and islands. A licensed restaurant is also available offering the best of local seafood.
7 bth/shr No smoking in dining room CTV in all bedrooms Tea and coffee making facilities Direct dial from bedrooms No dogs (ex guide dogs) Licensed Cen ht CTV 30P No coaches
Last d 8.30pm
ROOMS: s IR£30-IR£35; d IR£50-IR£60*
CARDS:

CLANE Co Kildare Map **01** C4

T&C *Ashley* Richardstown ☎ 045 868533
This charming bungalow is set in a quiet wooded area about half a mile from the main Celbridge/Clane road (R403). Colm and Evelyn Ryan have earned an enviable reputation for their hospitality which brings them many repeat visitors. A complimentary car service can be provided for guests attending local weddings and functions.
4 rms (2 shr) (1 fmly) No smoking in bedrooms CTV in 1 bedroom No dogs (ex guide dogs) Cen ht CTV 9P Last d 5pm

Silverspring House *(N 863272)* Firmount
☎ 045 868481 FAX 045 892246 Mr & Mrs J Phelan
Mar-Nov
A modern farmhouse situated in its own grounds, one mile from Clane. There is a TV lounge and separate dining room for the guests to use. Peaceful gardens surround the house, complete with free range chickens that providing the eggs for breakfast. Nearby are a model racing circuit, race courses, canoeing and fishing.
4 bth/shr (2 fmly) No smoking in bedrooms No smoking in dining room CTV in all bedrooms Tea and coffee making facilities No dogs Cen ht CTV 12P 25 acres beef sheep

CLARENBRIDGE Co Galway Map **01** B3

T&C Karaun House Stradbally (after the village, take first turn right, 0.5m off main road) ☎ 091 796182
Mar-Oct
Teresa and Denis O'Dea's well maintained house is adorned with flowers, both inside and out. It is located in a rural area two kilometres south of Clarenbridge, a village right in the heart of 'Oyster County', well known for its seafood restaurants. The house is comfortable and meticulously cared for with a TV lounge and breakfast room.

3 bth/shr No smoking in bedrooms No smoking in dining room Tea and coffee making facilities No dogs (ex guide dogs) Cen ht CTV 12P Last d 2pm
ROOMS: s IR£23; d IR£34; wkly b&b IR£100*
CARDS:

CLIFDEN Co Galway Map **01** A4

GH ***Ben View House*** Bridge St (entering town on N59, opposite Esso petrol station) ☎ 095 21256 FAX 095 21226
This town centre house offers good quality accommodation at a moderate cost making it an ideal touring base.
10 rms (9 shr) (3 fmly) No smoking in 2 bedrooms No smoking in dining room No dogs (ex guide dogs) Cen ht CTV

Selected

GH Buttermilk Lodge Westport Rd (located on N59 400m after junction with Westport Rd at entrance to Clifden) ☎ 095 21951 FAX 095 21953
Tastefully decorated and appointed bedrooms, all with luxury bath and shower en suite, along with many personal touches can be expected at this large luxury house on the edge of town. Cathriona and Patrick O'Toole are welcoming hosts who offer fresh baking, tea and coffee when you arrive.
11 bth/shr (2 fmly) No smoking in 5 bedrooms No smoking in dining room No smoking in 1 lounge CTV in all bedrooms Direct dial from bedrooms No dogs (ex guide dogs) Cen ht 14P farmland available for walking and hill-climbing
ROOMS: s IR£25-IR£35; d IR£36-IR£50*
CARDS:

Dan O'Hara's Farmhouse *(L 730495)* Lettershea (well signposted on N59 main Galway/Ceifaew road 45m from Galway & 5m from Ceifaew beside the Connemara Heritage History Centre)
☎ 095 21246 & 21808 FAX 095 22098 Mr & Mrs M Walsh
16 Mar-30 Oct
Set back from the road, this smart yellow-painted house is set on a 50 acre farm in the foothills of the Twelve Pins Mountains and is part of Connemara's Heritage and History Centre. Attractively decorated and furnished en suite bedrooms offer a good range of facilities and the building also houses a comfortable sitting room, a tea room, and a craft room.
4 shr (6 fmly) No smoking in bedrooms No smoking in dining room CTV in all bedrooms Tea and coffee making facilities Direct dial from bedrooms No dogs Cen ht 30P 200 acres mixed
ROOMS: s IR£24.50-IR£25.50; d IR£36-IR£38; wkly b&b IR£126*

GH Dun Ri (on entering Clifden via N59 turn left before Statoil service station, signed) ☎ 095 21625 FAX 095 21635
1 Mar-2 Nov
This large, recently estalished guest house stands in a quiet street close to the town centre. All the rooms are furnished to the same high standard and are equipped with modern comforts. Guests enjoy the amenity of a comfortable lounge and a separate dining room.
10 bth/shr (2 fmly) No smoking in bedrooms No smoking in dining room CTV in all bedrooms Direct dial from bedrooms No dogs (ex guide dogs) Cen ht CTV No children 4yrs 10P
ROOMS: s IR£25-IR£35; d IR£36-IR£50; wkly b&b IR£126-IR£175*
CARDS:

T&C Failte Ardbear, Ballyconneely Rd (from Clifden town take Ballyconneely Rd, 1m from Clifden take first turning on the right, hotel 400mtrs from Pottery) ☎ 095 21159 FAX 095 21159
Apr-Sep
A modern bungalow in scenic location on edge of Clifden features excellent standards of comfort and welcoming hosts and is an ideal touring centre.

5 rms (2 shr) (2 fmly) No smoking in dining room No smoking in 1 lounge No dogs (ex guide dogs) Cen ht CTV 15P
ROOMS: s IR£22.50-IR£24.50; d IR£32-IR£36; wkly b&b IR£98-IR£112
CARDS:

Selected

Q Q Q Q ❦ ***Faul House** (L 650475)* Ballyconneely Rd
(1m from town, turn right at Connemara Pottery and follow signs)
☎ 095 21239 FAX 095 21998 Mrs K Conneely
15 Mar-Oct
A fine modern farmhouse stands on a quiet and secluded road overlooking Clifden Bay. It is smart and comfortable with large en suite bedrooms, all well furnished and with good views on all sides.
6 shr (3 fmly) No smoking in 3 bedrooms No smoking in dining room No smoking in 1 lounge No dogs (ex guide dogs) Cen ht CTV 10P 28 acres sheep, ponies

Q Q Q **T&C Kingstown House** Bridge St
(enter Clifden on N59(W) on to one way traffic, 2nd house on right hand side) ☎ 095 21470 FAX 095 21530
rs 23-25 Dec
Situated just off Clifden's main street and centrally located close to all amenities, this pleasant guesthouse offers a warm welcome from the friendly proprietors Mary and Joe King, who provide comfortable accommodation.
8 rms (6 shr) (3 fmly) No smoking in area of dining room CTV in all bedrooms Tea and coffee making facilities No dogs (ex guide dogs) Cen ht CTV
ROOMS: s IR£20-IR£25; d IR£32-IR£38*
CARDS:

Premier Selected

Q Q Q Q Q **GH Maldua** Galway Rd (on N59)
☎ 095 21171 & 21739 FAX 095 21739
Closed Nov-Jan
This large and luxurious house in its own grounds has been recently enlarged and upgraded, and offers spacious bedrooms with quality bathrooms and showers. Facilities include a lobby lounge and relaxing sitting room as well as an attractive breakfast room, and there is a cleverly-built sun trap in the gardens, beside a stream, which guests can enjoy. There is ample car parking.
14 shr (2 fmly) No smoking in bedrooms CTV in all bedrooms Tea and coffee making facilities Direct dial from bedrooms No dogs (ex guide dogs) Cen ht CTV 20P
ROOMS: s fr IR£23; d IR£46-IR£70*
CARDS:

Selected

Q Q Q Q **T&C Mallmore House** Ballyconneely Rd
(1m from Clifden towards Ballyconneely, turn right at Connemara Pottery) ☎ 095 21460
1 Mar-1 Nov
A charming Georgian-style house set in 35 acres of woodland overlooking Clifden Bay, is situated one mile from Clifden on the Ballyconneely road, close to the Rock Glen Hotel. Alan and Kathy Hardman have tastefully restored the house, with parquet flooring and some favourite antiques, together with turf fires providing warmth and atmosphere.
6 shr (2 fmly) No smoking in bedrooms No smoking in dining room No smoking in lounges Tea and coffee making facilities No dogs (ex guide dogs) Cen ht CTV 15P No coaches 35 acres of mature woodland
ROOMS: d IR£36-IR£40

Selected

Q Q Q Q **GH O'Grady's Sunnybank House** Church Hill (from Galway-N59, turn right at Esso station & first left pass R C Church)
☎ 095 21437 FAX 095 21976
Mar-Nov
This comfortable period house stands in an elevated position on the N59 a few minutes' walk from town and O'Gradys Restaurant. Spacious en suite bedrooms have attractive decor and are equipped with TVs and telephones; some enjoy fine views of the surrounding countryside. Public areas include a gracious drawing room and breakfast room, while the mature gardens contain a swimming pool (heated from June 1), a sauna and sunbed, tennis courts and a car park.
8 bth/shr (4 fmly) No smoking in 1 bedrooms No smoking in dining room No smoking in 1 lounge CTV in all bedrooms Direct dial from bedrooms No dogs Cen ht CTV No children 7yrs 12P Outdoor swimming pool (heated) Tennis (hard) Sauna Solarium
ROOMS: s IR£35-IR£45; d IR£48-IR£60
CARDS:

Q Q Q **T&C Waterloo House** Galway Rd (on the Galway road on left 0.5km past Statoil station, 1km from Clifden town centre. From Galway, 1st right after Clifden Glen Holiday Village)
☎ 095 21688 FAX 095 22044
Closed 16 Dec-9 Jan
The inviting home of P K and Patricia Joyce is an easily recognisable yellow painted house, set back from road and within walking distance of Clifden. Patricia is an accomplished cook and in addtion to breakfast, dinner is available by prior arrangement. P K is a keen hill climber and angler who has a wealth of local knowledge, and there is the possibility of salmon and trout fishing just across the road. Guests share the Joyce' sitting room and the immaculate and well equipped bedrooms are en suite. Bicycles are available for the guests to use.
8 rms (6 shr) (2 fmly) No smoking CTV in all bedrooms Tea and coffee making facilities Direct dial from bedrooms No dogs (ex guide dogs) Cen ht CTV ch fac 12P Last d 1pm
ROOMS: s IR£20-IR£25; d IR£40-IR£50; wkly b&b IR£126-IR£168.50; wkly hlf-bd IR£218-IR£260*
CARDS:

See page 14-20 for a list of Premier Selected establishments

CLIFFONY Co Sligo Map **01** B5

Q Q Q **T&C Villa Rosa** Donegal Rd, Bunduff (1m past Cliffony village on the main road N15 to Donegal) ☎ 071 66173 FAX 071 66173
Closed 15 Dec-15 Jan rs Nov & Mar-Apr
This comfortable house is situated on the main Sligo/Donegal route and has good parking facilities to the rear. The surrounding area is famous for its historic folklore, walks and beautiful scenery.
6 rms (4 shr) (2 fmly) No smoking No dogs (ex guide dogs) Cen ht CTV 16P Walking Bird-watching Last d noon
ROOMS: s fr IR£16*
CARDS:

CLONAKILTY Co Cork Map **01** B2

Q Q Q **An Garran Coir** *(W 332358)* Castlefreke (signposted at Maxol Service Station in Clonakilty, 4m W of town, off N71 1m on right) ☎ 023 48236 FAX 023 48236 Mr & Mrs M Calnan
Situated in a scenic rural area, this modern farmhouse is especially welcoming to children, with a play area, pony rides and a large garden. For adults there is a comfortable sitting room and dining room. An extensive range is available at breakfast, and dinner is available by prior arrangement. There is also a tennis court and the opportunity to see the cows being milked.
5 bth/shr (2 fmly) No smoking CTV in all bedrooms No dogs Cen ht 5P Tennis (hard) Last d 3pm
ROOMS: s IR£23-IR£25; d IR£35-IR£38*
CARDS:

Q **Desert House** *(W 390411)* Ring Rd (signposted on N71, 1km E of Clonakilty) ☎ 023 33331 & 34490 FAX 023 33048 Mrs D Jennings
This Georgian farmhouse, overlooking Clonakilty Bay, is an ideal centre for touring West Cork and Kerry.
5 rms (4 shr) CTV in all bedrooms Tea and coffee making facilities Cen ht CTV 10P 100 acres dairy mixed Last d midday
ROOMS: s IR£22; d IR£34*
CARDS:

Selected

Q Q Q Q ***Duvane*** *(W 349405)* Ballyduvane (2km SW on N71)
☎ 023 33129 Mrs N McCarthy
Closed Nov-Mar
About a mile from Clonakilty stands this well kept house decorated in cheerful colours. Comfortable throughout, it offers three fully en suite bedrooms and one adjacent to a bathroom. Guests have their own sitting room, and the dining room serves a breakfast which has won awards. Dinner is available by arrangement. Local amenities include beaches, riding and golf.
4 rms (2 shr) (1 fmly) No smoking in bedrooms No smoking in dining room CTV in 3 bedrooms Tea and coffee making facilities No dogs (ex guide dogs) Cen ht CTV P Fishing 100 acres beef Last d 7pm

CLONMEL Co Tipperary Map **01** C2

Q Q Q **GH *Brighton House*** 1 Brighton Place ☎ 052 23665
A fine 3 storey listed building close to the town centre. The spacious bedrooms are fully equipped and contain some fine antique furniture.

Q Q Q **T&C Farrenwick Country House** Poulmucka, Curranstown (from N24, Clonmel-Cahir road turn right onto R687, signposted to guesthouse) ☎ 052 35130 FAX 052 35377
A modern house on the R687 with good parking and an attractive garden to the front. The bedrooms are fully equipped with TVs, phones, courtesy trays and new orthopoedic beds. There are many local beauty spots and the historic towns of Cashel, Clonmel and Kilkeny are all close by.

4 rms (3 shr) (4 fmly) No smoking CTV in all bedrooms Tea and coffee making facilities Direct dial from bedrooms No dogs (ex guide dogs) Cen ht CTV 11P Last d previous day
ROOMS: s IR£16-IR£23.50; d IR£32-IR£34; wkly b&b fr IR£75*
CARDS:

Q Q Q ***Woodrooffe House*** *(S 122253)* Cahir Rd (0.5m off N24 between Cahir/Clonmel) ☎ 052 35243 Mrs A O'Donnell
15 Mar-15 Oct
A spacious farmhouse set in a peaceful location, off the main road, where guests can enjoy a stroll through the surrounding farmlands. The bedrooms are comfortable with attractive decor, as are the two reception rooms. A good range of leisure activities is available locally and afternoon tea is provided.
3 rms (2 shr) (3 fmly) No smoking in bedrooms No smoking in dining room Cen ht CTV 6P 270 acres mixed Last d 4pm

COBH Co Cork Map **01** B2

Q Q Q **T&C *Elmville*** Lower Rd, Rushbrook
☎ 021 813206
A period house sitting in its own grounds at the junction of Lower Road overlooking the harbour. Friendly hosts Helen and Aidan Gleeson seem to instinctively care for their guests, and offer cheerful, bright bedrooms which can be accessed from the gardens. Breakfast is served in the fine dining room where generous helpings of croissants, fruits, cheeses, cereals and any combination of the 'full Irish' can be enjoyed. There is a comfortable TV lounge, and a baby-sitting service is available.
5 rms (2 shr) (1 fmly) No smoking in bedrooms No smoking in area of dining room Tea and coffee making facilities No dogs (ex guide dogs) Cen ht CTV 8P
CARDS:

COLERAINE Co Londonderry Map **01** C6

Premier Selected

Q Q Q Q Q **GH Greenhill House** 24 Greenhill Rd, Aghadowey BT51 4EU (from Coleraine take A29 for 7m turn left onto B66 for approx 300yds house on right)
☎ 01265 868241 FAX 01265 868365
Mar-Oct
Situated in the Bann Valley overlooking the Antrim Hills, this lovely Georgian house stands in its own well-tended gardens; the daffodil display in spring is stunning. A warm welcome is assured from the friendly owners Elizabeth and James Hegarty. Public rooms are comfortably traditional and include a relaxing lounge (with a real fire in winter), together with a tastefully appointed dining room, where enjoyable home cooking is offered. The bright, airy bedrooms are furnished with a mixture of fitted units and elegant period pieces. All the rooms are equipped with many thoughtful extras.

6 bth/shr (2 fmly) CTV in all bedrooms Tea and coffee making facilities Direct dial from bedrooms No dogs (ex guide dogs) Cen ht CTV 10P Last d noon
ROOMS: s fr £30; d fr £49*
CARDS:

CORK Co Cork Map **01** B2

Q Q Q GH *Antoine House* Western Rd
(1m from city centre on the Cork-Macroom-Killarney road)
☎ 021 273494 FAX 021 273092
This converted four-storey house is close to the University and caters for both tourist and commercial clientele.
7 shr CTV in all bedrooms Tea and coffee making facilities No dogs (ex guide dogs) Cen ht CTV 8P
CARDS:

Q Q Q GH Garnish House 1 Aldergrove, Western Rd
☎ 021 275111 FAX 021 273872
This is a three-storey house opposite the University on the main Cork/Killarney road.
13 bth/shr (1 fmly) No smoking in 5 bedrooms CTV in all bedrooms Tea and coffee making facilities Direct dial from bedrooms No dogs (ex guide dogs) Cen ht CTV 10P
ROOMS: s IR£35-IR£55; d IR£45-IR£70 *
CARDS:

Q Q Q GH *Killarney* Western Rd
(from Cork city to Killarney road N22, premises just opposite University College) ☎ 353-21 270290 & 270179 FAX 353-21 271010
Closed 25-26 Dec
Mrs O'Leary is the welcoming owner of this well equipped guest house which stands near Cork University on the N22 road. The bedrooms all have TVs, telephones and tea/coffee making facilities. A lounge is available to guests and there is a large car park behind the house.
19 bth/shr (3 fmly) No smoking in 10 bedrooms CTV in all bedrooms Tea and coffee making facilities Direct dial from bedrooms No dogs (ex guide dogs) Cen ht CTV 15P
CARDS:

Q Q GH *Redclyffe* Western Rd (take N22 from city centre, through traffic lights at University gates, premises situated on right before next traffic lights, at Gaol Cross) ☎ 021 273220 FAX 021 278382
Closed 24-25 Dec
Period red brick residence conveniently placed for the town centre, with front and rear car parking. Six of the bedrooms are en suite and all are well equipped. Pleasant dining room adjoins the family sitting room which is available for guests' use.
13 rms (6 bth/shr) (3 fmly) CTV in all bedrooms Tea and coffee making facilities Direct dial from bedrooms No dogs (ex guide dogs) Cen ht CTV 20P
CARDS:

Q Q Q **GH Roserie Villa** Mardyke Walk, off Western Rd (take N22 from city centre, pass Jury's Hotel on left, turn right at University College gates, right again for hotel on right)
☎ 021 272958 FAX 021 274087
This family-run guest house stands just ten minutes' walk from the city centre. The en suite bedrooms are well appointed and equipped with TVs, telephones and tea/coffee making facilities. Off-street parking is available.
16 shr (4 fmly) No smoking in dining room CTV in all bedrooms Tea and coffee making facilities Direct dial from bedrooms No dogs (ex guide dogs) Cen ht CTV No children 5yrs 8P
CARDS:

COROFIN Co Clare Map **01** B3

Q Q Q **T&C Fergus View** Kilnaboy (2m N of Corofin en route to Kilfenora, past the ruins of Kilnaboy Church)
☎ 065 6837606 FAX 065 6837192
Etr-Sep
Sensitively renovated to provide an excellent standard of comfort, this fourth generation family home is an attractive farmhouse, centrally located for touring the Burren area. Mary Kelleher enjoys cooking and wherever possible uses all home-grown vegetables to prepare the meals.
6 rms (5 shr) (4 fmly) No smoking in bedrooms No smoking in dining room No dogs Licensed Cen ht CTV 8P Last d noon
ROOMS: s IR£25-IR£29; d IR£36-IR£40*

CORRANDULLA Co Galway Map **01** B4

Q Q Q **T&C Cregg Castle** (9 miles N of Galway, and signposted to the left off the Galway/Tuam Road (N17), just N of Claregalway village)
☎ 091 791434 FAX 091 791434
(daytime only)
7 Mar-1 Nov rs Nov-7 Mar (group & 1wk+ bookings only)
This lovely old castle dates from 1648, and offers historic interest, tranquil country living, and animated conversations around the dinner table. Breakfast is served to suit guests, who are encouraged to feel at home and walk in the grounds of this sanctuary for wildlife.
7 bth/shr (2 fmly) No smoking in bedrooms No smoking in area of dining room No dogs (ex guide dogs) Licensed Cen ht CTV ch fac 25P Sauna Last d noon
ROOMS: s fr IR£40; d IR£60; wkly b&b IR£210-IR£290; wkly hlf-bd IR£322-IR£392*
CARDS:

COURTOWN HARBOUR Co Wexford Map **01** D3

Q Q Q **GH *Harbour House*** ☎ 055 25117
This imposing house stands at the junction by the harbour and only three minutes away from a sandy beach. Many of its rooms have sea views and all are furnished to a high standard. There is also a pleasant lounge and separate dining room. The house is run in conjunction with the owners' self-catering mobile home park.

CRUSHEEN Co Clare Map **01** B3

Q Q Q ***Lahardan House** (R 397889)* Lahardan (take N18, at railway bridge beside Crusheen village follow signs for Lahardan, hotel 1.5m from here in the middle of the Clare Lakelands)
☎ 065 27128 FAX 065 27319 Mrs D Griffey
rs Nov-Apr
This sensitively restored farmhouse stands on 300 acres of land off the Galway to Limerick road near Ennis. It is a charming old building with spacious rooms that invite relaxation. Guests will experience true hospitality from the welcoming Griffey family, and evening meals are served.
8 bth/shr (4 fmly) No smoking in bedrooms CTV in all bedrooms Direct dial from bedrooms No dogs Licensed Cen ht CTV P 230 acres beef Last d 3pm
CARDS:

CUSHENDALL Co Antrim Map **01** D6

Selected

Q Q Q Q **GH Caireal Manor** 90 Glenravel Rd, Glen's of Antrim, Martinstown BT43 6QQ (on A43, 6m N of Ballymena)
☎ 012667 58465 FAX 012667 58465
Caireal Manor is located in Martinstown, between Cushendall and Ballymena, and is ideally located for exploring the spectacular Glens of Antrim and, indeed, the coast. Offering on-site parking, this newly built guest house provides smartly appointed, decorative accommodation that is extremely well equipped. There are two ground floor bedrooms, one of which is fully designed for disabled use. Breakfast and dinner are served in a separate dining room, and a chauffeur service (in limousines) is provided to the proprietor's restaurant in the stunning Glenariffe Glen.
5 bth/shr (4 fmly) No smoking in 2 bedrooms No smoking in area of dining room No smoking in lounges CTV in all bedrooms Tea and coffee making facilities Licensed Cen ht CTV ch fac 7P No coaches Last d 9pm
ROOMS: s fr £25; d fr £50; wkly b&b fr £165*
CARDS:

DINGLE Co Kerry Map **01** A2

Selected

Q Q Q Q **T&C Alpine** Mail Rd (on right on route N86 on entrance to town) ☎ 066 51250 FAX 066 51966
On the edge of Dingle, this large, three-storey guest house is run by the O'Shea family, who maintain excellent standards.
10 bth/shr (3 fmly) No smoking in dining room CTV in all bedrooms Tea and coffee making facilities Direct dial from bedrooms No dogs (ex guide dogs) Cen ht CTV No children 5yrs 20P
ROOMS: s IR£20-IR£35; d IR£35-IR£50*
CARDS:

Selected

Q Q Q Q **T&C Ard-na-Greine House** Spa Rd
☎ 066 51113 & 51898 FAX 066 51898
This modern bungalow is situated on the edge of town towards Connor Pass. All the rooms are en suite and offer an unrivalled range of facilities.
4 bth/shr (2 fmly) No smoking CTV in all bedrooms Tea and coffee making facilities Direct dial from bedrooms No dogs (ex guide dogs) Cen ht CTV No children 7yrs 5P
ROOMS: d IR£36-IR£40*
CARDS:

Q Q **T&C Ballyegan House** Upper John St
(on entering Dingle from the Killarney Tralee Rd turn right at rdbt, at next junct turn right, premises at the top of John St on left) ☎ 066 51702
This large, two-storey house enjoys a quiet position within a short walk of the town centre, and enjoys spectacular views to the front over Dingle Bay. Bedrooms and public areas are comfortable, and there is a large private car park. This is an excellent base for local touring.
6 shr (4 fmly) No smoking No dogs Cen ht CTV 8P No coaches
ROOMS: d IR£36-IR£38; wkly b&b IR£126-IR£133*

Selected

Q Q Q Q **T&C Bambury's** Mail Rd (located on the left hand side as you enter Dingle town by the N86 past the Shell Station)
☎ 066 51244 FAX 066 51786
Set on the edge of Dingle, this pink house is eyecatching on the outside and attractive on the inside with pretty decor and comfortable appointments. There is a cosy lounge and a spacious dining room. En suite bedrooms are excellent with pine furnishings, pottery lamps, tea/coffee trays and big showers. Mrs Bambury is very friendly and helpful.
12 shr (1 fmly) No smoking in 3 bedrooms CTV in all bedrooms Direct dial from bedrooms Cen ht CTV 12P
ROOMS: s IR£20-IR£40; d IR£30-IR£50*
CARDS:

Q Q Q **T&C *Bolands*** Goat St ☎ 066 51426
Closed 25 Dec
Situated on a continuation of the main street in this lively town, the centre point of the Dingle peninsula, Bolands is easily found because of its lilac-coloured extension. The inside is equally smart with a TV lounge and conservatory where breakfast is served. The bedrooms are bright and cheerful and there is a hospitality trolley on this floor where guests may help themselves to tea and coffee. Pubs and restaurants are nearby and it is just a short walk to the harbour area.
6 shr (1 fmly) No smoking in dining room CTV in all bedrooms Tea and coffee making facilities No dogs (ex guide dogs) Cen ht CTV
CARDS:

Selected

Q Q Q Q **T&C *Cleevaun*** Lady's Cross, Milltown
(R559 from Tralee to Dingle follow sign for Slea Head scenic route)
☎ 066 51108 FAX 066 51108
mid Jan-mid Dec
Overlooking Dingle Bay, this luxurious bungalow offers attractive bedrooms with pine furniture, and the opportunity of enjoying Mrs Cluskey's breakfast menu which caters for a wide range of tastes. The house is about 7 minutes drive from town.
9 bth/shr (2 fmly) No smoking in bedrooms CTV in all bedrooms Tea and coffee making facilities Direct dial from bedrooms No dogs (ex guide dogs) Cen ht CTV No children 3yrs 9P
CARDS:

Q Q Q **T&C Cloosmore House** (2km from rdbt on Dingle/Sleahead road, on waters edge) ☎ 066 51117
Mar-Oct
A long modern bungalow on high ground two miles West of Dingle and with fine views over Dingle Bay. All bedrooms are very nicely appointed with polished wooden floors and are fully equipped and comfortable.
3 annexe shr No smoking in 2 bedrooms No smoking in area of dining room No smoking in 1 lounge CTV in all bedrooms Tea and coffee making facilities Direct dial from bedrooms No dogs Cen ht No children 14yrs 6P No coaches

Q Q **T&C *Dingle Heights*** Ballinaboola
(proceed up Main Street for 0.5m until hospital, house 4th on right after further 200yds) ☎ 066 51543
Set high overlooking Dingle Bay, this house features comfortable, well-appointed accommodation and the hospitality of owner Mrs Fitzgerald.
4 rms (3 bth/shr) (4 fmly) No dogs Cen ht CTV 10P

Selected

Q Q Q Q **GH *Doyles Town House*** 4 John St
(in the heart of Dingle town) ☎ 066 51174
FAX 066 51816
mid Mar-mid Nov
Stella and John Doyle are the warm and friendly owners of this charming town house. Bedrooms are spacious, well equipped and tasteful, with period furnishings and marble tiled bathrooms. Adjoining the house is their award-winning and very popular seafood restaurant, where the guests make selections from the lobster tank or try the catch of the day specials.
8 bth/shr No smoking in area of dining room CTV in all bedrooms Direct dial from bedrooms No dogs (ex guide dogs) Licensed Cen ht
Last d 9.30pm
CARDS:

Selected

Q Q Q Q **GH Greenmount House**
(on entering town turn right at rdbt & next right at T-junct)
☎ 066 51414 FAX 066 51974
Closed 21-26 Dec
Greenmount has a reputation for comfort and hospitality, and offers a splendid, recently built extension containing six mini-suites, all overlooking Dingle Harbour. These bedrooms are all spacious with split level lounge areas, and quality furnishings and decor. The original bedrooms are equally as comfortable. A conservatory-style dining room and two sitting rooms provide plenty of relaxation space. The town centre is only a 5 minute walk.
12 bth/shr No smoking in bedrooms No smoking in dining room CTV in all bedrooms Tea and coffee making facilities Direct dial from bedrooms No dogs (ex guide dogs) Cen ht CTV No children 8yrs 12P No coaches
ROOMS: s IR£25-IR£40; d IR£50-IR£70;
wkly b&b IR£160-IR£225*
CARDS:

Q Q Q **Hurleys** *(Q 392080)* An Dooneen, Kilcooley
☎ 066 55112 Mr M Hurley
Etr-Oct
Hurleys Farm is tucked away behind the church in Kilcooley, a mile from the beach and sheltered by Mount Brandon, a popular place for hill walkers. Accommodation includes a cosy TV room, dining room and comfortable en suite bedrooms, graced by some special pieces of high quality furniture. The whole area is rich in early historic and prehistoric relics: ogham stones, ring forts and the famous dry-stone masonry 'beehive' huts. Dingle and Tralee are within walking distance.
4 shr No smoking in 1 lounge No dogs (ex guide dogs) Cen ht CTV 6P
32 acres mixed
ROOMS: s IR£18-IR£23; d IR£32-IR£36*

Selected

GH Milltown House Milltown
(1m W of Dingle on Slea Head road, cross Milltown Bridge and turn left) ☎ 066 51372 FAX 066 51095
Situated on a sea channel to the west of town, the house has been elegantly refurbished and has a warm inviting atmosphere, Mr and Mrs Gill making guests feel really welcome. Bedrooms are all en suite, have attractive decor and are well equipped. There is also a cosy sitting room leading to a conservatory.
10 bth/shr (3 fmly) No smoking in dining room No smoking in lounges CTV in all bedrooms Tea and coffee making facilities Direct dial from bedrooms No dogs (ex guide dogs) Cen ht No children 5yrs 10P No coaches Last d 4pm
ROOMS: s IR£25-IR£60; d IR£46-IR£70*
CARDS:

Selected

T&C Mount Eagle Lodge Ventry
(3.5m W of Dingle on Slea Head Drive) ☎ 066 59754
Etr-Sep
A lovely new house which has a commanding position overlooking Ventry Bay. The Mount Eagle Lodge provides an excellent breakfast buffet for its guests.
4 bth/shr (3 fmly) No smoking in bedrooms No smoking in dining room No smoking in 1 lounge CTV in all bedrooms Tea and coffee making facilities No dogs (ex guide dogs) Cen ht CTV 10P
ROOMS: wkly b&b IR£125-IR£140

Selected

GH Pax House Upper John St
(turn right off N86 at Pax House finger sign, establishment 0.75 mile on left) ☎ 066 51518 & 51650 FAX 066 51518
1 Mar-5 Nov
Pax House is a peaceful detached house in a acre of ground with stunning views of Dingle Bay. The patio off the sitting room is very popular with guests, with a hospitality trolley nearby and fine garden views. Bedrooms are very comfortable and the bathrooms are excellent. Above all, the hospitality and generosity of Joan and Ron Brosnan-Wright will make guests wish to return.
7 bth/shr (2 fmly) No smoking in bedrooms No smoking in dining room No smoking in 1 lounge CTV in all bedrooms Direct dial from bedrooms No dogs Cen ht 10P
ROOMS: s IR£30-IR£40; d IR£47-IR£50*
CARDS:

DONEGAL Co Donegal Map 01 B5

T&C Ardeevin Lough Eske, Barnesmore
(take N15 from Donegal Town (Derry Road) for 5km, turn left at fork for Lough Eske and follow signs for 'Ardeevin')
☎ 073 21790 FAX 073 21790
Apr-Oct
This comfortable homely house enjoys a lovely location high above Lough Eske and with superb views of lake and mountain. Well appointed bedrooms have en suite facilities.
6 bth/shr (2 fmly) No smoking CTV in all bedrooms Tea and coffee making facilities No dogs Cen ht CTV No children 9yrs 10P No coaches Last d noon
ROOMS: s IR£23-IR£27; d IR£36-IR£40*

DOOLIN Co Clare Map 01 B3

GH Cullinan's
(centre of Doolin at crossroads between McGann's Pub & O'Connors Pub)
☎ 065 74183 FAX 065 74239
Charming pine-furnished bedrooms with attractive decorations are a feature of this detached house, whose grounds run down to the River Aille. Chef patron James features locally caught fresh fish on his dinner menu along with steaks, lamb and vegetarian dishes. Other facilities include a residents' lounge, and a patio and gardens with plenty of parking space.
6 bth/shr (2 fmly) No smoking in bedrooms Tea and coffee making facilities Direct dial from bedrooms No dogs (ex guide dogs) Cen ht CTV 15P
ROOMS: s IR£25-IR£35; d IR£34-IR£45
CARDS:

T&C Doonmacfelim House
☎ 065 74503 FAX 065 74129
In a village well known for its traditional Irish music sessions and close proximity to the Aran Islands, Doonmacfelin is a spacious new house offering comfortable accommodation, a pleasant TV lounge, a tennis court, a large car park and friendly hospitality from owners Majella and Frank Maloney.
6 shr Direct dial from bedrooms No dogs (ex guide dogs) Cen ht CTV 20P No coaches Last d 2pm
ROOMS: s IR£20-IR£28; d IR£34-IR£40*
CARDS:

DOWNPATRICK Co Down Map 01 D5

Selected

GH Drumgooland House & Equestrian Centre
29 Dunnanew Rd, Seaforde BT30 8PJ
(5.5m from Ballynahinch on main A24 Belfast/Newcastle road. Take second left past Esso Service Station before village of Seaforde)
☎ 01396 811956 FAX 01396 811265
Almost a century old, this large country house is set in 60 cares of its own grounds which include a well stocked trout lake and equestrian centre. The latter provides the opportunity for guests to join a ride or trek. Nearby, the beautiful Mourne Mountains offer the opportunity to walk or go climbing and the seaside resort of Newcastle a 10 minute drive away. The public areas include an attractively furnished lounge and a separate dining room. The bedrooms are all very large with en-suite facilities and modern equipment.
3 bth/shr (1 fmly) No smoking in bedrooms No smoking in dining room No smoking in 1 lounge CTV in all bedrooms Tea and coffee making facilities No dogs (ex guide dogs) Cen ht CTV 20P No coaches Fishing Riding
ROOMS: s £24.50; d £39; wkly b&b £155*
CARDS:

Q Q **Havine** *(J 457384)* 51 Bally Donnel Rd, Ballykilbeg BT30 8EP
☎ 01396 851242 Mrs Macauley
Closed Xmas wk
For more than 18 years Myrtle Macauley has been welcoming guests to her home and provides Irish hospitality and enjoyable home cooking. Though not large, the well maintained bedrooms are comfortably furnished in both modern and traditional style. One room has an adjacent room for children. Public areas include a choice of homely lounges, one with a piano, the other with the communal dining table.
3 rms No smoking in bedrooms No smoking in dining room
No smoking in 1 lounge Tea and coffee making facilities No dogs P
125 acres beef sheep

DROGHEDA Co Louth Map 01 D4

Selected

Q Q Q Q **T&C Boynehaven House** Dublin Rd
(2km south of Drogheda on the N1 opp Europa Hotel)
☎ 041 36700
A modern bungalow off the Dublin Road, well-screened from noise and view of the road outside. This recently extended house offers excellent standards of comfort, with fully-equipped en-suite bedrooms. Hospitality is also guaranteed, and there is a cosy lounge and interesting breakfast menu. Ample private car parking is available.
4 bth/shr (3 fmly) No smoking in bedrooms No smoking in dining room CTV in all bedrooms Tea and coffee making facilities No dogs (ex guide dogs) Cen ht CTV No children 7yrs 20P
ROOMS: s IR£35; d IR£40-IR£50; wkly b&b IR£140-IR£175*
CARDS:

Selected

Q Q Q Q **T&C Tullyesker Country House** Tullyesker, Monasterboice (3m N on Drogheda/Belfast road N1 on right just past Papal Cross) ☎ 041 9830430 & 9832624 FAX 041 9832624
1 Feb-30 Nov Closed 1 Dec-31 Jan
This large family-run house occupies a spectacular site on Tullyesker Hill, overlooking the Boyne Valley and Drogheda. Many of the well equipped and beautifully decorated rooms look out over the lovely gardens and wooded grounds. Historic and archaeological sites abound in the area.
5 shr (2 fmly) No smoking in bedrooms No smoking in dining room CTV in all bedrooms Tea and coffee making facilities No dogs (ex guide dogs) Cen ht CTV No children 10yrs 20P No coaches
ROOMS: s IR£30-IR£35; d IR£38-IR£48*

DRUMCLIFFE Co Sligo Map 01 B5

Q Q Q **Mountain View Farmhouse** *(G 675422)* Carney
(take N15 from Sligo to Drumcliffe, turn left after Yeats Tavern for 1m)
☎ 071 63290 Mrs M Murphy
Apr-Oct
A modern farmhouse on the edge of Drumcliffe in Yeats Country and close to the site of Yeats' memorial and burial site. Most rooms enjoy spectacular views of nearby Ben Bullin mountain, popular with walking/mountain climbing groups.
5 rms (3 shr) No smoking in bedrooms No smoking in dining room
No dogs (ex guide dogs) Cen ht CTV 6P 45 acres mixed
ROOMS: s IR£23; d IR£36; wkly b&b IR£110

DUBLIN Co Dublin Map 01 D4

See also Howth

Q Q Q **T&C** ***Aarona*** 150 Clonkeen Rd, Deansgrange, Blackrock
(Close to N11 and Deansgarage cemetary)
☎ 01 2893972 FAX 01 2898622
Situated in the residential suburb of Deansgrange, two miles SW of Dun Laoghaire ferry port on the road leading to the N11. This is a semi-detached house with a comfortable TV lounge and dining room overlooking attractive flower-filled back gardens which boast a pair of iron gates. There are four bedrooms, one on the ground floor, all with comfortable beds, good linen and smartly tiled en-suite showers; one is a three bedded room. The house is near to restaurants and pubs as well as the Irish Traditional Music Centre.
4 annexe shr (1 fmly) No smoking CTV in all bedrooms Tea and coffee making facilities No dogs (ex guide dogs) 4P
CARDS:

Selected

Q Q Q Q **T&C Aaron House** 152 Merrion Rd, Ballsbridge
(2.5 miles south of City Centre, 600yds past the R.D.S)
☎ 01 2601644 & 2601650 FAX 01 2601651
Closed 24-26 Dec
Located near the city centre in the residential suburb of Ballsbridge this comfortable house is well equipped and tastefully decorated. The Dunn family have been involved in the business for many years and guests return frequently to experience their hospitality and friendliness.
6 shr (1 fmly) No smoking in 1 bedrooms No smoking in dining room No smoking in lounges Tea and coffee making facilities Direct dial from bedrooms No dogs Cen ht CTV 6P
ROOMS: s IR£30-IR£50; d IR£50-IR£90*
CARDS:

Selected

Q Q Q Q **GH** ***Aaronmor House*** 1c Sandymount Av, Ballsbridge
☎ 01 6687972 FAX 01 6682377
This family run house is comfortably furnished and decorated and is situated close to the Royal Dublin Society Showgrounds and Lansdowne rugby ground.
6 bth/shr (2 fmly) No smoking in 4 bedrooms No smoking in dining room No smoking in lounges Tea and coffee making facilities Direct dial from bedrooms No dogs (ex guide dogs) Cen ht CTV 8P
CARDS:

Premier Selected

Q Q Q Q Q **GH** ***Aberdeen Lodge*** 53/55 Park Av
☎ 01 2838155 FAX 01 2837877
This particularly fine early Edwardian house stands on one of Dublin's most prestigious roads near to the main hotel and embassy suburb in Dublin. Bedrooms are fully equipped and there are suites with air spa baths. It has its own car park and is only minutes away from the centre by DART or bus, as well as being easily accessible from the airport and car ferries. Dinner is served and a Christmas Programme is available.
16 bth/shr (8 fmly) CTV in all bedrooms Direct dial from bedrooms No dogs Licensed Cen ht CTV 16P Last d 9pm
CARDS:

Q Q Q **T&C Aileach** 3 Rossmore Grove, off Wellington Ln, Templeogue (turn left off M50 South onto N81, at next rdbt left for Wellington Lane signposted Crumlin, first right Rossmore Rd first right again Rossmore Grove) ☎ 01 4902939 FAX 01 4929416
This is a comfortable house with TV lounge and a separate dining room for guests to use. The bedrooms are freshly decorated, two of them being en-suite and a third with shower and wash basin. The nearby sports complex has pitch and putt, tennis, badminton, snooker and squash on offer. There are also restaurants and pubs close by.
4 rms (2 shr) No smoking CTV in all bedrooms Tea and coffee making facilities No dogs Cen ht CTV 2P No coaches
ROOMS: s IR£25-IR£30; d fr IR£40✳

Q Q Q **GH *Ardagh House*** 1 Highfield Rd, Rathgar
☎ 01 4977068 FAX 01 4973991
This large former hotel has been greatly refurbished and upgraded by new owners Mary and Willie Doyle. Some of the airy, comfortable en suite rooms look out over the attractive rear garden.
19 bth/shr (4 fmly) No smoking in 10 bedrooms No smoking in dining room CTV in all bedrooms Tea and coffee making facilities Direct dial from bedrooms No dogs (ex guide dogs) Cen ht CTV 20P
CARDS:

Premier Selected

Q Q Q Q Q **GH *Ariel House*** 52 Lansdowne Rd
(turn off at Allied Irish Bank Ballsbridge on left before Lansdowne Rugby Stadium) ☎ 01 6685512 FAX 01 6685845
Closed 23 Dec-14 Jan
A luxurious Victorian mansion built in 1850 is situated in a suburb of Ballsbridge and conveniently close to the city rapid rail service, the RDS showgrounds and Lansdowne Rugby grounds. The house is beautifully maintained, and furnished with fine antique pieces throughout. There is a choice of standard and premier bedrooms, all well equipped, and there are also an elegant drawing room and dining room.
28 bth/shr No smoking in bedrooms No smoking in dining room No smoking in 1 lounge CTV in all bedrooms Tea and coffee making facilities Direct dial from bedrooms No dogs Licensed Cen ht CTV No children 9yrs 30P
CARDS:

Q Q Q **T&C Askill** 86 Stillorgan Grove, Stillorgan
(S from Dublin on N11, pass Stillorgan Park Hotel and after 0.5m take left turn for Stillorgan Park. Right turn before roundabout, house on right)
☎ 01 2884514 FAX 2780426
Tucked away on a quiet residential road off the N11, Askill is near the Smurfit Business School and Dun Laoghaire. The house has a car park and there are good bus services. The attractively decorated en suite bedrooms are equipped with good modern amenities. Lounge and dining room are combined in one large room, and the cooked breakfasts are a speciality of the house. Mr and Mrs Harraghy are friendly hosts.
5 shr (3 fmly) No smoking in bedrooms No smoking in 1 lounge CTV in all bedrooms Tea and coffee making facilities Direct dial from bedrooms No dogs Cen ht 5P
ROOMS: s IR£35-IR£40; d IR£48-IR£52✳
CARDS:

Selected

Q Q Q Q **T&C Beaufort House** 25 Pembroke Park, Ballsbridge
☎ 01 6689080 FAX 01 6609963
Hospitality is a key point with hosts Kay Mullally and Robert Lyne, and a warm welcome is guaranteed to arriving guests. All rooms are en suite and very fully equipped, and public rooms include a comfortable lounge and a conservatory dining room. There is off-street parking, and barbecues are sometimes organised.
7 bth/shr (3 fmly) No smoking in 2 bedrooms No smoking in dining room CTV in all bedrooms Tea and coffee making facilities Direct dial from bedrooms No dogs Cen ht CTV 5P Tennis Comp. membership of leisure club Last d 10.15pm
ROOMS: s IR£35-IR£120; d IR£40-IR£149;
wkly b&b IR£210-IR£695✳
CARDS:

Q Q **GH *Beddington*** 181 Rathgar Rd (on route from M50 into city centre) ☎ 01 4978047 FAX 01 4978275
At the city end of Rathgar Road, near Rathinines, this comfortable, well maintained house offers a good standard of en-suite bedrooms. The spacious lounge is equipped with a wide TV screen, and there is a separate wine bar and a breakfast room. Mr and Mrs Cunningham run their house with friendly dedication, and there is secure car parking at the rear. The hotel stands on a direct bus route to the city centre, three kilometres away.
15 shr (1 fmly) No smoking in dining room No smoking in lounges CTV in all bedrooms Tea and coffee making facilities Direct dial from bedrooms Licensed Cen ht CTV No children 7yrs 10P
CARDS:

Q Q Q **T&C Beechwood** 6 Butterfield Av, Rathfarnham
(turn off N81 at Templeogue Bridge, cross bridge & take first turn left onto Butterfield Ave, establishment is 3 houses along from junction)
☎ 01 4943526 & 4943526
Closed 24-26 Dec
An attractively furnished home just around the corner from Rathfarnham Shopping Centre. The soft coloured furnishings complement the decor throughout the house which has a TV lounge, breakfast room and comfortable en suite bedrooms, all immaculately appointed. Off street parking is available.
4 bth/shr No smoking CTV in all bedrooms Tea and coffee making facilities No dogs Cen ht CTV No children 4yrs 6P No coaches
ROOMS: s IR£25-IR£35; d IR£40-IR£46✳
CARDS:

Q Q Q **GH *Belgrave*** 8-10 Belgrave Square, Rathmines
(from canal up main Rathmines Rd to Swan Shopping Centre, turn left and go to next traffic lights. Turn right for Belgrave Square)
☎ 01 4963760 & 4962549 FAX 01 4979243
Closed 23-31 Dec
Interlinked early Victorian houses in a residential suburb on the south side of the city and on direct bus routes. Restored and modernised to a high standard

with plenty of lounge space, a well appointed dining room and pleasant gardens. The en suite bedrooms are all well equipped and some are on the ground floor. The resident proprietors are very helpful and friendly.
24 bth/shr (2 fmly) No smoking in area of dining room CTV in all bedrooms Tea and coffee making facilities Direct dial from bedrooms No dogs (ex guide dogs) Cen ht CTV 7P No coaches
CARDS:

Premier Selected

GH Butlers Town House 44 Lansdowne Rd, Ballsbridge (On junct of Lansdowne and Shelbon)
☎ 01 6674022 FAX 01 6673960
Closed 23-27 Dec
This fine Victorian house, set in the heart of Dublin's Embassy belt, has been beautifully restored yet still retains the charm of a gracious family home. Accommodation is air-conditioned and all of the bedrooms are individually furnished to the highest standard. Richly coloured fabrics in tones of russet and gold create a restful ambience in the drawing room, where afternoon tea is served. There is also a charming conservatory breakfast room, where a tempting selection of hot and cold dishes is offered. For those who do not wish to dine out, the room service menu includes some local specialities such as Irish Stew. The combination of the ambience of the Victorian era and the friendliness and professionalism of the management and staff make Butlers a very special place to stay.
19 bth/shr No smoking in area of dining room CTV in all bedrooms Direct dial from bedrooms No dogs (ex guide dogs) Cen ht 9P
Last d 10.30pm
CARDS:

Premier Selected

GH Cedar Lodge 98 Merrion Rd, Ballsbridge (opposite the British Embassy)
☎ 01 6684410 FAX 01 6684533
A lovely old house with a modern extension is set back from the Dunlaoghaire Road opposite the new British Embassy and offers comfortable, fully equipped bedrooms. There is ample parking with a secure area to the rear and full access for the disabled.
15 bth/shr (3 fmly) No smoking in 4 bedrooms No smoking in dining room No smoking in lounges CTV in all bedrooms Tea and coffee making facilities Direct dial from bedrooms No dogs
Cen ht CTV 18P
ROOMS: s IR£38-IR£75; d IR£58-IR£110*
CARDS:

Selected

GH Charleville Lodge 268/272 North Circular Rd, Phibsborough (300 yards from St Peters Church)
☎ 01 8386633 FAX 01 8385854
Closed 21-26 Dec
Situated close to the city centre near Phoenix Park, this elegant terrace of Victorian houses has been tastefully restored to a high standard. The two interconnecting lounges are welcoming and the smart dining room offers a choice of breakfasts. Bedrooms are very comfortable with pleasant decor and there is a secure car park for guests' use.
30 rms (28 bth/shr) (2 fmly) CTV in all bedrooms Direct dial from bedrooms No dogs (ex guide dogs) Cen ht CTV 18P
ROOMS: s IR£32.50-IR£55; d IR£55-IR£100;
wkly b&b IR£157.50-IR£315*
CARDS:

Q Q Q **T&C Charlston Manor** 15/16 Charleston Rd, Ranelagh (on main road between Ranelagh & Rathmines) ☎ 01 4910262 FAX 01 4966052
Conveniently situated ten minutes from the city centre, two red-brick houses have been restored to give Charlston Manor five bedrooms at ground floor level. They are attractively decorated and well equipped with TVs, clock radios, tea and coffee-making facilities and all have modern en suite shower rooms. The dining room has individual tables where full Irish breakfast is served. There is secure car parking.
5 shr No smoking in dining room CTV in all bedrooms Tea and coffee making facilities Direct dial from bedrooms No dogs Cen ht CTV 8P
ROOMS: s IR£30-IR£35; d IR£50-IR£60*
CARDS:

Q Q Q **T&C *Cherrytree Lodge*** 19 Parkview, Castleknock
(from N2 turn right at Halfway House Pub, pass Garden Centre, turn right)
☎ 01 8203356 FAX 8203356
Closed Xmas
A beautifully maintained house in a quiet part of Castleknock near Luttrellstown Golf Course, the lodge offers high quality accommodation. The well equipped en suite bedrooms are bright and fresh with quality furnishings. Interconnecting reception rooms enjoy a view of the gardens and off-street parking is available.
3 shr CTV in all bedrooms Tea and coffee making facilities No dogs CTV 4P

Q Q Q **T&C *Clifden*** 32 Gardiner Place (city centre)
☎ 01 8746364 FAX 01 8746122
10 shr (4 fmly) No smoking in dining room No smoking in lounges CTV in all bedrooms Tea and coffee making facilities Direct dial from bedrooms No dogs Cen ht CTV 12P No coaches
CARDS:

Selected

Q Q Q Q **GH *Copper Beech Court*** 16 Hollybrook Park, Clontarf
☎ 01 8333390 FAX 01 8531808
This fine, late Victorian house stands in its own grounds, with ample off-street parking. Spacious bedrooms are all en suite and equipped with modern comforts, and there is also a sitting room and a dining room. The house can be reached either from Howth Road or from the suburb of Clontarf on the sea front, and it is just 2.5 miles from the city centre with easy access to air and ferry ports.

Q Q Q **GH Egan's** 7/9 Iona Park, Glasnevin
☎ 01 8303611 & 8305283 FAX 01 8303312
Situated in a quiet suburb on the north side of the city, conveniently located for the National Botanic Gardens and the airport. Owner Sinead Egan is refurbishing this fine Victorian house and half of the bedrooms have now been completed to offer a high standard of accommodation.There is a comfortable lounge and breakfast room. French, Italian and German are spoken.
25 shr (4 fmly) No smoking in dining room No smoking in 1 lounge CTV in all bedrooms Tea and coffee making facilities Direct dial from bedrooms Licensed Cen ht 8P Last d 8pm
ROOMS: s IR£27-IR£32; d IR£44-IR£51; (room only) *
CARDS:

Selected

Q Q Q Q **GH *Eglinton Manor*** 83 Eglinton Rd, Donnybrook
☎ 01 2693273
A fine Victorian town house set in its own grounds close to the city centre, with off-street parking and attractive gardens. The accommodation has been totally refurbished, with the best of the original features retained, and now offers elegant decor, antique furnishings and beautiful objets d'art in the charming reception rooms. Very comfortable bedrooms are all individually styled with attractive colour schemes, large armchairs, and smart new bathrooms.

Q Q Q **T&C Ferryview House** 96 Clontarf Rd, Clontarf
☎ 01 8335893 FAX 01 8532141
This comfortable modern house, home of the Stafford family, overlooks the sea front promenade, not far from the Yacht Public House. Bright, cheerful bedrooms are well equipped and tea and coffee facilities are available on request. There are two lounges, one for smokers, and an attractive breakfast room leading into the gardens. There is secure car parking and a good bus service to the city centre.
6 rms (4 bth/shr) (4 fmly) No smoking in bedrooms No smoking in dining room No smoking in 1 lounge CTV in 4 bedrooms Tea and coffee making facilities No dogs (ex guide dogs) Cen ht CTV 8P No coaches
ROOMS: s IR£20-IR£25; d IR£36-IR£40*
CARDS:

Q Q Q **GH The Fitzwilliam** 41 Upper Fitzwilliam St ☎ 01 6600448
FAX 01 6767488
5 Jan-15 Dec
Situated on a fine Georgian street near the city centre, this house offers very well equipped bedrooms. Those on the top floor are particularly quiet, although they are quite a climb. There is a TV lounge, and guests have the option of dining in the popular Peacock Alley Restaurant.
12 bth/shr (1 fmly) CTV in all bedrooms Direct dial from bedrooms Licensed Cen ht CTV 4P Last d 10.30pm
ROOMS: s IR£40-IR£45; d IR£64-IR£80*
CARDS:

Premier Selected

Q Q Q Q Q **GH *Fitzwilliam Park*** 5 Fitzwilliam Square
☎ 01 6628280
This beautifully restored Georgian townhouse has been fitted to exacting and luxurious standards. Rooms come complete with soft furnishings and paintings, while the bathrooms are modern and elegant.

Premier Selected

QQQQQ **GH Glenogra** 64 Merrion Rd, Ballsbridge (opposite Royal Dublin's Showgrounds) ☎ 01 6683661 FAX 01 6683698
Closed 24 Dec-6 Jan & 2wks in Spring
This fine gabled house run by Cherry and Seamus McNamee is only 2.5 miles from the centre of Dublin and stands in a pleasant suburb opposite the RDS Centre. The house offers comfort with more than a touch of elegance, and the atmosphere is exceptionally welcoming.
9 bth/shr (1 fmly) No smoking in bedrooms No smoking in dining room No smoking in 1 lounge CTV in all bedrooms Tea and coffee making facilities Direct dial from bedrooms No dogs (ex guide dogs) Cen ht CTV 10P
ROOMS: s IR£45-IR£75; d IR£65-IR£85*
CARDS:

Selected

QQQQ **GH Glenveagh Townhouse** 31 Northumberland Rd, Ballsbridge (N11 towards the city centre turn right at Donnybrook Church, continue to the end of Anglesea Road, turn left pass Jurys Hotel, 200 metres on left) ☎ 01 6684612 FAX 01 6684559
Closed 22-29 Dec
An attractive Georgian house immediately south of Mount Street Bridge on the main bus route to Dun Laoghaire. Bedrooms are comfortable and uniformly well equipped, and there is off street parking.
10 bth/shr (3 fmly) No smoking in 4 bedrooms No smoking in dining room CTV in all bedrooms Tea and coffee making facilities Direct dial from bedrooms No dogs (ex guide dogs) Cen ht CTV 18P
ROOMS: s IR£40-IR£90; d IR£60-IR£120*
CARDS:

Premier Selected

QQQQQ **GH The Grey Door** 22/23 Upper Pembroke St (city centre, close to St Stephens Green and Grafton Street)
☎ 01 6763286 FAX 01 6763287
Closed 25-28 Dec rs Bank Hols
Situated a few minutes from the city centre, this tastefully restored town house is a jewel in the heart of Georgian Dublin. En suite bedrooms are very comfortable with rich fabrics enhancing the gracious atmosphere. Public areas include a charming first-floor sitting room, a spacious private dining room and a choice of two restaurants, the well known 'Grey Door' and the less formal 'Pier 32' with bar adjoining.
7 bth/shr (2 fmly) No smoking in 1 bedrooms No smoking in area of dining room No smoking in lounges CTV in all bedrooms Tea and coffee making facilities Direct dial from bedrooms No dogs (ex guide dogs) Licensed Cen ht Last d 11.30pm
ROOMS: s IR£75; d IR£95; (room only) *
CARDS:

Selected

QQQQ **GH Hedigan's** Tullyallan House, 14 Hollybrook Park, Clontarf (1st right off Howth Rd, from city centre 2nd left off Clontarf Rd, after Clontarf Dart Station)
☎ 01 8531663 & 8531665 FAX 01 8333337

contd. on p.648.

Hedigan's is a fine Edwardiard red brick residence on the north side of the city. The two elegant reception rooms are very comfortable. Bedrooms are luxurious and come with en suite facilities, including some with showers.
9 bth/shr (4 fmly) No smoking in 3 bedrooms No smoking in dining room CTV in all bedrooms Tea and coffee making facilities Direct dial from bedrooms No dogs (ex guide dogs) Cen ht CTV 10P
ROOMS: s IR£35-IR£40; d IR£56-IR£70; wkly b&b IR£175-IR£210*
CARDS:

Q Q Q **T&C *Herbert Lodge*** 65 Morehampton Rd, Donnybrook (1.25m from city centre on N11) ☎ 01 6603403 FAX 01 4730919
Closed 22 Dec-6 Jan
6 shr (3 fmly) No smoking in 3 bedrooms No smoking in dining room CTV in all bedrooms Tea and coffee making facilities Direct dial from bedrooms No dogs (ex guide dogs) Cen ht CTV 2P
CARDS:

Q Q Q **GH Iona House** 5 Iona Park ☎ 01 8306217 & 8306855 FAX 01 8306732
Closed Dec-Jan
Situated in a quiet residential suburb on the north side of the city, this family-run Victorian red-brick house has large modern bedrooms, a comfortable lounge and a small garden for exclusive use of guests. It is conveniently located for National Botanic Gardens and airport.
12 shr (4 fmly) No smoking in area of dining room CTV in 11 bedrooms Direct dial from bedrooms Cen ht No children 3yrs
ROOMS: s IR£32; d IR£64*
CARDS:

Selected

Q Q Q Q **GH Kingswood Country House** Old Kingswood, Naas Rd, Clondalkin D22 (turn left off M50 heading south, premises 1m on left past Green Isle Hotel) ☎ 01 4592428 & 4592207 FAX 01 4592428
Closed 25-28 Dec & Good Fri
Situated off the N7, turn left past Newlands Cross en route from Dublin. This Georgian house offers attractive en suite bedrooms, a cosy sitting room and an intimate restaurant specialising in good home cooking. The proprietors make guests feel very welcome here, and there are also well maintained gardens and ample car parking facilities.
7 bth/shr (2 fmly) No smoking in area of dining room CTV in all bedrooms Direct dial from bedrooms No dogs (ex guide dogs) Licensed Cen ht 60P No coaches Last d 10.30pm
CARDS:

Selected

Q Q Q Q **GH Lansdowne Manor** 46/48 Lansdowne Rd, Ballsbridge (turn left at Trinity College continue down Raussa St, Mount St and Northumberland Rd, turn left at traffic lights, premises on left) ☎ 01 6688848 FAX 01 6688873
Closed 22-27 Dec
Two early Victorian residences carefully combined and luxuriously refurbished in the style of that era. The drawing room has gold decor, very comfortable sofas and easy chairs. Breakfast is served in two further reception rooms, one of which can be used for meetings. Bedrooms are well appointed and contain reproduction French style beds and matching furnishings of a particularly high quality. The staff are helpful and hospitable.
22 bth/shr (9 fmly) No smoking in dining room No smoking in lounges CTV in all bedrooms Tea and coffee making facilities Direct dial from bedrooms No dogs (ex guide dogs) Cen ht CTV 20P
ROOMS: s IR£45-IR£50; d IR£75-IR£85*
CARDS:

Q Q Q **GH Lyndon** 26 Gardiner Place ☎ 01 8786950 FAX 01 8787420
Closed 23-27 Dec
A fine old Georgian townhouse, close to the city centre, in an area enjoying a renaissance. The house has recently been completely restored in tasteful style with rich modern colours throughout. Bedrooms are all en suite and uniformly furnished to a high standard. Guests are assured of secure car parking with 24 hour access.
9 shr (4 fmly) No smoking in dining room No smoking in lounges CTV in all bedrooms Tea and coffee making facilities No dogs Cen ht CTV P No coaches
ROOMS: s IR£35-IR£60; d IR£50-IR£60; wkly b&b IR£175-IR£210*
CARDS:

Q Q Q **T&C Marelle** 92 Rathfarnham Rd, Terenure ☎ 01 4904690 FAX 01 4904690
This attractive house, recently refurbished, is set back from the road in its own gardens. It has good parking facilities.
6 rms (5 shr) No smoking in dining room CTV in all bedrooms No dogs Cen ht CTV No children 5yrs 8P No coaches Last d 10am
ROOMS: s IR£35-IR£40; d IR£52-IR£60*
CARDS:

Premier Selected

Q Q Q Q Q **GH Merrion Hall** 54-56 Merrion Rd, Ballsbridge D4 (Ballsbridge is approx 2m along main route from Dublin city centre to Dun Laoghaire Port. Establishment situated between British & US Embassies) ☎ 01 6681426 FAX 01 6684280
Closed 20 Dec-1 Jan
This elegant town house stands right opposite the RDS showgrounds in Ballsbridge. The friendly owners provide a warm welcome and excellent attention to detail. There is a fine sitting room and a separate breakfast room overlooking the attractive gardens; a good choice is available at breakfast. The en suite bedrooms are comfortable and offer a range of facilities.
23 bth/shr (4 fmly) No smoking in 10 bedrooms CTV in all bedrooms Tea and coffee making facilities Direct dial from bedrooms No dogs Cen ht CTV 10P
ROOMS: s IR£50-IR£100; d IR£60-IR£120
CARDS:

Selected

Q Q Q Q **T&C Merrion Lodge** 148 Merrion Rd, Ballsbridge D4 (2m S of Dublin City Centre on the main road between Dublin/Dun Laoghaire) ☎ 2691565 FAX 2839998
Closed 24-25 Dec
6 bth/shr (2 fmly) No smoking in dining room CTV in all bedrooms Tea and coffee making facilities Direct dial from bedrooms No dogs Cen ht CTV 10P No coaches
ROOMS: s IR£45-IR£60; d IR£70-IR£90*
CARDS:

Selected

Q Q Q Q **GH Merrion Square Manor** 31 Merrion Square ☎ 01 6628551 FAX 01 6628556
24-28 Dec
Ideally situated in the heart of the city, close to the National Gallery and Trinity College, this Georgian house has been tastefully restored, and the two reception rooms have retained their original plaster work. Bedrooms are all en suite and vary in size. Breakfast is a highlight, with a wide-ranging menu on offer.
20 bth/shr (4 fmly) No smoking in bedrooms No smoking in dining room CTV in all bedrooms Tea and coffee making facilities Direct dial from bedrooms No dogs (ex guide dogs) Cen ht CTV 5P No coaches
ROOMS: s IR£45-IR£50; d IR£75-IR£85 *
CARDS:

Premier Selected

Q Q Q Q Q **T&C Morehampton Lodge** 113 Morehampton Rd, Donnybrook (situated on N11 in the residential area of Donnybrook) ☎ 01 2837499 FAX 01 2837595
Closed 24-25 Dec
Totally restored to a high standard, this Victorian house is very conveniently situated near the city centre and bus routes. Excellent bedrooms are provided, and off-street parking is available.
12 bth/shr (2 fmly) No smoking in 6 bedrooms No smoking in dining room No smoking in lounges CTV in all bedrooms Tea and coffee making facilities Direct dial from bedrooms No dogs Cen ht 7P
ROOMS: s IR£55-IR£75; d IR£75-IR£130*
CARDS:

Selected

Q Q Q Q GH ***Mount Herbert Ltd*** 7 Herbert Rd ☎ 01 6684321 FAX 01 6607077

Mount Herbert is a group of linked Victorian residences cleverly adapted and extended to present a fine range of modern amenities, including excellent conference facilities, secure car parking and private gardens.

140 bth/shr (9 fmly) No smoking in area of dining room CTV in all bedrooms Direct dial from bedrooms No dogs (ex guide dogs) Licensed Lift Cen ht CTV 120P Sauna Solarium Badminton court Children's playground Last d 9.30pm

CARDS:

Selected

Q Q Q Q **T&C Northumberland Lodge** 68 Northumberland Rd, Ballsbridge (located on the main route into town, beside the Jurys Hotel) ☎ 01 6605270 FAX 01 6688679

Closed 23-27 Dec

This gracious Georgian house stands in a convenient location, close to the city centre and the Lansdowne Road rugby ground and a few minutes from the public transport systems. Bridget and Tony Brady enjoy welcoming guests to their charming home. The large, well equipped bedrooms are all en suite and there are attractive gardens.

6 bth/shr No smoking in dining room CTV in all bedrooms Tea and coffee making facilities Direct dial from bedrooms No dogs (ex guide dogs) Cen ht CTV 12P

ROOMS: d IR£50-IR£80*

CARDS:

Selected

Q Q Q Q **T&C No 66** Northumberland Rd, Ballsbridge ☎ 01 6600333 & 6600471 FAX 01 6601051

This imposing house has six comfortable bedrooms all fully equipped to a very high standard. Attractive public areas include a dining room and two comfortable lounges, one in a lovely conservatory. It is very convenient for the city, Landsdowne Road and the RDS showgrounds.

6 shr (2 fmly) No smoking in dining room No smoking in lounges CTV in all bedrooms Tea and coffee making facilities Direct dial from bedrooms No dogs (ex guide dogs) Cen ht CTV No coaches

ROOMS: s IR£50-IR£75; d IR£70-IR£120; wkly b&b fr IR£300

CARDS:

Selected

Q Q Q Q GH ***Number Eighty Eight*** 88 Pembroke Rd, Ballsbridge (centrally located in Ballsbridge close to the Royal Dublin Society, Sansdowne Road and approximately 10 mins walk from the city centre) ☎ 01 6600277 FAX 01 6600291

Closed 22 Dec-30 Dec

Near the city centre, 3 Georgian houses have been carefully restored and interlinked to a very high standard to produce this luxurious guest house. A marble tiled reception foyer and a luxurious lounge with big, comfortable chairs create a great first impression, enhanced by the attentive staff. The bedrooms are varied and interesting, some containing a mezzanine floor above the main bedroom where guests can relax with that extra bit of privacy. Good facilities are close at hand including Landsdowne Rugby Grounds.

50 bth/shr (4 fmly) No smoking in 8 bedrooms No smoking in dining room CTV in all bedrooms Tea and coffee making facilities Direct dial from bedrooms No dogs (ex guide dogs) Lift Cen ht CTV 20P

CARDS:

Q Q Q **T&C Pairc na Bhfuiseog** 55 Lorcan Crescent, Santry ☎ 01 8421318 FAX 01 8423671

Closed 16 Dec-5 Jan

An extended modern terrace house, very nicely appointed throughout, with excellent en suite facilities. Convenient for Dublin Airport, ferries and city centre. The owners Ronald and Colette Downey provide a homely atmosphere and lots of local information. Can be hard to locate so ring for directions.

4 rms (3 shr) (1 fmly) No smoking CTV in all bedrooms No dogs (ex guide dogs) Cen ht 4P

ROOMS: s fr IR£30; d IR£46-IR£50

CARDS:

Selected

Q Q Q Q **T&C Park Lodge** 19 Deerpark Dr, Castleknock (from city centre follow alongside Liffey to Phoenix Park and exit at Castleknock gates. Take 1st right after 200m into Deerpark Rd) ☎ 01 8212887 FAX 01 8212887

March-1 Nov

Situated in a secluded residential area, close to the north side of Phoenix Park and the N2, it is just a short drive through the park for direct access to the city centre. Mrs Eileen Kehoe is a perfectionist and this shows in the running of this luxuriously appointed house. Rich fabrics enhance the spacious sitting room overlooking the lovely gardens where guests may take breakfast in the summer months. There is a separate TV lounge where smoking is permitted, but not elsewhere in the house. Two of the comfortably appointed bedrooms are en suite and the third has sole use of the bathroom opposite.

3 shr (1 fmly) No smoking in bedrooms No smoking in dining room No smoking in lounges CTV in all bedrooms Tea and coffee making facilities No dogs Cen ht CTV No children 12yrs 6P No coaches
ROOMS: s fr IR£40; d fr IR£70✳

Selected

GH Raglan Lodge 10 Raglan Rd, Ballsbridge (from city centre when you reach the American Embassy turn left into Elgin Rd, left at rdbt into Raglan Rd) ☎ 01 6606697 FAX 01 6606781
Closed 23 Dec-6 Jan
A charming Victorian lodge, situated on a tree-lined residential road in the suburb of Ballsbridge, close to the US embassy, the RDS showground and with easy access to the city centre. Owner Helen Moran puts great effort into ensuring guests' comfort. The elegant drawing room invites relaxation around the fire, while breakfast is served in the cosy dining room. The bedrooms are all en suite, some are very spacious, and all are well equipped. Guests have use of the garden, and there is secure private parking in the grounds.
7 bth/shr (4 fmly) No smoking in 4 bedrooms No smoking in dining room CTV in all bedrooms Tea and coffee making facilities Direct dial from bedrooms Cen ht CTV 12P No coaches
ROOMS: s IR£50-IR£65; d IR£80-IR£110✳
CARDS:

GH St Aiden's 32 Brighton Rd, Rathgar (turn off M50 junct 9 towards city centre. Premises are located on 3rd turn left after traffic lights in Rathgar village) ☎ 01 4902011 FAX 01 4920234
A fine Victorian house situated in a residential tree-lined road just 15 minutes from the city centre. The well-proportioned reception rooms are comfortable and relaxing, and a hospitality trolley is available for guests. Bedrooms vary in size from spacious family rooms to snug singles, but all offer modern comforts. St Aiden's has a wine licence, and secure parking at the rear of the house.
8 bth/shr (3 fmly) No smoking in 3 bedrooms No smoking in dining room CTV in all bedrooms Direct dial from bedrooms No dogs Cen ht 8P No coaches
ROOMS: s IR£35-IR£45; d IR£55-IR£80✳
CARDS:

GH St Andrews 1 Lambay Rd, Drumcondre ☎ 01 8374684 FAX 01 8570446
Linked semi-detached houses in a quiet residential area. All rooms are en suite and guests are offered refreshment on arrival. Guests can also help themselves to the hospitality table in the lounge. The house is convenient for the city, the ferries and Dublin Airport.
13 shr (2 fmly) No smoking in 2 bedrooms No smoking in dining room CTV in all bedrooms Direct dial from bedrooms Cen ht CTV No children 5yrs 2P
ROOMS: s IR£34; d IR£56-IR£60; wkly b&b IR£140-IR£210✳

T&C Tavistock House 64 Ranelagh Rd, Ranelagh (on the main Ranelagh rd, near the Barge PH) ☎ 01 4967377 FAX 01 4967377
A neat red brick house on Ranelagh Road next to Norfolk Road, very convenient for the City Centre whilst remaining on the outskirts. All bedrooms are en-suite and well equipped, and there is private parking for three or four cars.
7 bth/shr (1 fmly) No smoking in 3 bedrooms No smoking in dining room CTV in all bedrooms Tea and coffee making facilities Direct dial from bedrooms Cen ht CTV 5P No coaches
ROOMS: s IR£30-IR£50; d IR£50-IR£80✳
CARDS:

Selected

GH Trinity Lodge 12 South Frederick St (From N end of Grafton St go along Nassau St past Dawson St. South Frederick St is the next right turn)
☎ 01 6795044 & 6795182 FAX 01 6795223
This listed Georgian townhouse has been recently restored and converted to provide excellent accommodation right in the heart of the city centre. Accommodation consists of en suite quality bedrooms and three luxury suites in annexe accommodation across the street, all beautifully appointed and fully equipped. The many facilities include air conditioning and a personal safe. Most of the city's attractions are within walking distance.
13 shr (5 fmly) No smoking in 8 bedrooms No smoking in dining room CTV in all bedrooms Tea and coffee making facilities Direct dial from bedrooms No dogs (ex guide dogs) Cen ht
ROOMS: s fr IR£60; d IR£95-IR£160
CARDS:

Q **T&C The White House** 125 Clontarf Rd
(facing sea on Dublin Bay between castle & road) ☎ 01 8333196
Closed 24-25 Dec
South facing accommodation on Dublin Bay, approximately 15-20 minutes drive away from airport, ferry and the city centre, and also on a bus route. Tea and coffee making facilities are available on request. The beach and golf, horseriding and swimming facilities are available nearby along with local pubs and restaurants.
6 rms (1 shr) No smoking in dining room No dogs Cen ht CTV No children 8yrs 5P No coaches
ROOMS: s IR£22-IR£28; d IR£38-IR£46*

DULEEK Co Meath Map 01 D4

Q Q Q **T&C Annesbrook Country House** Annesbrook
(N2 from Dublin, 7kms from Ashbourne take R152, house signposted)
☎ 041 23293 FAX 041 23024
May-Sep Closed Xmas & Etr rs Oct-Apr (open for 6+ bookings)
Set in 10 acres of gardens and woodland in the Boyne Valley, Annesbrook is an 18th-century country house which has had many distinguished visitors, including King George IV. The gothic dining room was built for his visit, and owner Kate Sweetman is happy to show guests the lovely plasterwork created for this event. Big bedrooms, all with en suite facilities, are furnished in period style, and there are two spacious reception rooms. Dinner, by prior arrangement, is served at 7pm, and guests dine together. The orchards and walled gardens supply the fruit and vegetables used in the cooking.
5 bth/shr (1 fmly) No smoking in bedrooms No smoking in dining room Tea and coffee making facilities No dogs (ex guide dogs) Licensed Cen ht P No coaches Last d 11am
CARDS:

DUNDALK Co Louth Map 01 D4

Q Q Q **T&C *Rosemount*** Dublin Rd (on N1, 2kms S of Dundalk)
☎ 042 35878
This handsome bungalow stands in beautiful gardens north of the Belfast by-pass with attractive views over surrounding farmland. The nicely furnished bedrooms all have en suite showers and there is a comfortable lounge available for guests.
6 annexe shr (4 fmly) No smoking in bedrooms No smoking in dining room No smoking in 1 lounge CTV in 2 bedrooms No dogs (ex guide dogs) Cen ht CTV 8P

DUNFANAGHY Co Donegal Map 01 C6

Selected

Q Q Q Q **T&C *Sandhill House*** Port-na-Blagh (from Letterway take the N56 and follow the signs for Dunfanaghy, Sandhill House is approximately one mile from Dunfanaghy) ☎ 074 36602 FAX 074 36603
1 Feb-30 Nov
This distinctive, cream-coloured, detached house stands in a prominent position close to the Golf Club and a sandy beach. Appealing colour schemes and high quality furnishings characterise the ground-floor public rooms. Bedrooms are full of charm and have all the expected modern facilities, and one on the ground floor with a shower room is adapted for use by those with disabilities.
7 bth/shr (4 fmly) No smoking in bedrooms No smoking in dining room CTV in all bedrooms Tea and coffee making facilities No dogs Cen ht CTV 12P No coaches

DUNGANNON Co Tyrone Map 01 C5

Premier Selected

Q Q Q Q Q **GH Grange Lodge** 7 Grange Rd BT71 7EJ
(1m from M1 junct 15 on A29 Armagh, take sign for "Grange" then first right & first house on right) ☎ 01868 784212 FAX 01868 723891
Closed 21 Dec-9 Jan
You are assured of a warm welcome at this delightful country house, which sits in 20 acres of grounds and boasts a well tended garden. Norah and Ralph Brown are enthusiastic and sincere hosts, who maintain their charming home, brimming with fresh flowers, in an immaculate condition. The splendid drawing room, with its period pieces and paintings, together with the comfortable lounge, are ideal for relaxation. There are two dining rooms and in summer guests can dine in the bright and airy extension overlooking the gardens, a perfect setting to enjoy Norah's award-winning cooking. Her imaginative and fresh dishes have earned her a reputation as a talented cook with an eye for detail - fine glassware, crisp linen, and even wild flowers to decorate plates. The bedrooms are all individually styled and decoratively furnished; each room has a range of thoughtful extras. This is a fine guest house where you will enjoy hospitality and food at its best.
5 bth/shr No smoking in bedrooms No smoking in dining room No smoking in 1 lounge CTV in all bedrooms Tea and coffee making facilities Direct dial from bedrooms No dogs (ex guide dogs) Licensed Cen ht CTV No children 12yrs 12P No coaches Snooker table Last d 1pm
ROOMS: s £49-£55; d £69-£69
CARDS:

DUNGARVAN Co Waterford Map **01** C2

Selected

Q Q Q Q *Castle Farm (S 192016)* Millstreet, Cappash (from N72 take R671 for 3.5m, turn right at Millstreet establishment 200yds on the right) ☎ 058 68049 FAX 058 68049 Mrs J Nugent
Mar-Oct
This comfortable house is to be found in the west wing of a 15th century castle. Guests are spoilt by their host Joan Nugent who loves to cook and hunt out antiques for her visitors to enjoy. She is helped by her husband Emmett who enjoys showing off his high-tech dairy farm and is a fount of local knowledge. The house is very intriguing with many hidden delights for visitors to savour, including having a glass of wine in the cellar.
5 shr (2 fmly) No smoking Licensed Cen ht CTV 7P Tennis (hard) Fishing 120 acres dairy Last d 4pm
CARDS:

Q Q Q **Hideway Farmhouse** *(X 270876)* Rusheens, Old Parish (take 3rd turning on left of N25 after Marine Bar (5m from Dungarvan). House signposted and just over 1m on right)
☎ 058 46466 FAX 058 46466 Mr & Mrs B Power
Mar-Oct
A modern farmhouse on a working farm, near a sandy beach and ideal for coastal and hill walking and riding. Bedrooms are comfortable and well appointed. The pub holds evenings of traditional Irish music.
3 shr (1 fmly) No smoking in 2 bedrooms No smoking in dining room No smoking in lounges CTV in all bedrooms Tea and coffee making facilities No dogs (ex guide dogs) Cen ht CTV 5P 28 acres beef
ROOMS: s IR£17-IR£22; d IR£34; wkly b&b IR£119*
CARDS:

Q Q *Killineen House (X 302963)* Waterford Rd (off N25, 4.5m E)
☎ 051 291294 Miss B Lynch
Closed Xmas
This attractive house with well-tended gardens and views of Comeragh mountains is situated four miles east of town on Waterford road.
5 rms (3 shr) (3 fmly) No smoking in bedrooms Tea and coffee making facilities No dogs Cen ht CTV 10P 50 acres grass

Q Q Q **Sliabh gCua Farmhouse** *(S 191057)* Touraneena (from Dungarvan take R672 off N25 towards Clonmel for 15km, Farmhouse is signposted on left hand side and is 1km off main road beside Touraneena) ☎ 058 47120 Mrs B Cullinan
Apr-1 Nov
This comfortable farmhouse offers a home from home on a dairy farm in the shadow of the Knockmealdown and Comeragh Mountains. There are lovely views and splendid gardens in which to sit and relax. A popular feature is the well equipped play room provided for young children.
3 shr (1 fmly) No smoking No dogs (ex guide dogs) Cen ht CTV ch fac 6P Fishing private woodland nature walks,playground,treehouse 200 acres dairy beef arable forrestry Last d 12pm
ROOMS: s IR£25; d IR£40; wkly b&b IR£130-IR£165; wkly hlf-bd IR£220*

DUN LAOGHAIRE Co Dublin Map **01** D4

Premier Selected

Q Q Q Q Q **T&C Chestnut Lodge** 2 Vesey Place, Monkstown (off main Monkstown-Dun Laoghaire road. From ferry port, take right turn to Vesey Place from York rd) ☎ 01 2807860 FAX 2801466
Closed 23 Dec-27 Dec
A fine regency double fronted residence tucked away in a terrace of listed houses near the ferry port and the Dart rail system. A very elegant house which has luxurious decor and antique furnishings throughout, run by the charming and friendly owner Nancy Malone. Spacious reception provide a beautiful setting, overlooking the gardens, to be served with an award winning breakfast. Many fine touches, including fresh flowers from the garden, make a stay here that little bit more special.
4 shr (3 fmly) No smoking in bedrooms No smoking in dining room No smoking in 1 lounge CTV in all bedrooms Direct dial from bedrooms No dogs (ex guide dogs) Cen ht CTV P No coaches
ROOMS: d IR£60-IR£70*
CARDS:

Selected

Q Q Q Q **T&C Cumberland Lodge** 54 York Rd (going S from city centre follow Dun Laoghaire car ferry signs, on approaching Georges St turn right at Cumberland Inn into York Rd)
☎ 01 2809665 FAX 01 2843227
Closed 1-22 Nov
Convenient to the ferryport and DART rapid railway, and only 15 minutes from Dublin Central, this charming Regency house has been beautifully restored. Elegant reception rooms are furnished and decorated in keeping with the period, with richly coloured fabrics and rugs, and polished wooden floors. Comfortable bedrooms include two on the ground floor and there is a very large enclosed garage which can accommodate a mini-coach as well as cars.
4 shr (1 fmly) No smoking in bedrooms No smoking in area of dining room No smoking in 1 lounge CTV in all bedrooms Tea and coffee making facilities No dogs (ex guide dogs) Cen ht CTV No children 6yrs 10P
ROOMS: s IR£30-IR£35; d IR£50-IR£55*
CARDS:

Q Q Q T&C *Glenview House* 5 Glenview, Rochestown Av (opposite Killiney shopping centre. From People's Park, up Glenageary Hill, over rndbt to Rochestown Ave, then left.) ☎ 353 2855043
A detached modern house two miles from Dun Laoghaire and conveniently situated for restaurants, pubs, the car ferry port and the N11. Bedrooms are all freshly decorated and there is one on the ground floor. Guests have a comfortable lounge and a separate breakfast room.
6 bth/shr (3 fmly) No smoking in bedrooms No smoking in area of dining room CTV in 4 bedrooms Tea and coffee making facilities No dogs (ex guide dogs) 10P
CARDS:

Q Q Q **T&C Lisadell** 212 Glenageary Rd Upper (from Dun Laoghaire take right up Glenageary Rd Lower, premises located at top of hill on the left past Rathdown School towards Dalkey)
☎ 01 2350609 FAX 01 2350454
A modern detached house in a pleasant residential area, a mile from Dun Laoghaire and close to Dublin. Charmaine and John Goldrick are most welcoming hosts and their visitors' book, provided by an appreciative guest, bears witness to this. Two comfortable interconnecting reception rooms overlook the patio and gardens and all the pleasant bedrooms are en suite, one on the ground floor. Off street parking is available
5 bth/shr No smoking in bedrooms No smoking in dining room CTV in all bedrooms Tea and coffee making facilities Direct dial from bedrooms No dogs (ex guide dogs) Cen ht 5P
ROOMS: s IR£30-IR£40; d IR£40-IR£60; wkly b&b IR£100-IR£185*
CARDS:

DUNLAVIN Co Wicklow Map **01** C3

Selected

Q Q Q Q **Tynte House** *(N 870015)* (from N81 at Hollywood Cross turn right at Dunlavin and follow finger signs for Tynte House, premises past market house in the centre of the town)
☎ 045 401561 FAX 045 401586 Mr & Mrs J Lawler
Closed 23 Dec-2 Jan
A gracious 19th-century farmhouse standing in the square of this quiet country village, just one hour from Dublin on the Kildare-Wicklow border. The friendly hosts, Caroline and John Lawler have recently carried out a lot of restoration and facilities now include en suite bedrooms, self-catering apartments in an adjoining courtyard, a laundry, tennis courts, children's play area and indooor games room. Caroline speaks French, Italian and Spanish, arranges golf and riding holidays and provides evening meals on request.
7 bth/shr (2 fmly) No smoking in 2 bedrooms No smoking in area of dining room Tea and coffee making facilities Direct dial from bedrooms No dogs (ex guide dogs) Cen ht CTV ch fac 16P Golf 18 Tennis (hard) Playground games room with table tennis 200 acres arable beef Last d in advance
ROOMS: s IR£22.50; d IR£34; wkly b&b IR£110; wkly hlf-bd IR£200
CARDS:

DUNMORE EAST Co Waterford Map **01** C2

Selected

Q Q Q Q **Foxmount** *(S 659091)* Passage East Rd, Dunmore Rd (from Waterford take Dunmore East road, after 3.5m take left fork towards Passage East for 0.5m. Right at next Y junct)
☎ 051 874308 FAX 051 854906 Mrs M Kent
10 Mar-4 Nov
This charming 17th-century country house is set on a busy dairy farm amidst beautiful lawns and gardens with screening trees and a hard tennis court. Tastefully modernised, it offers four en suite bedrooms and attentive service from the charming hostess. The farm and gardens provide most of the raw materials for the carefully prepared evening meals.
6 bth/shr (2 fmly) No smoking in dining room No dogs (ex guide dogs) Cen ht CTV 6P Tennis (hard) 200 acres dairy Last d 6pm
ROOMS: wkly b&b fr IR£170; wkly hlf-bd fr IR£284

We endeavour to be as accurate as possible but changes in personnel and data can occur in establishments after the Guide has gone to press

DUNSHAUGHLIN Co Meath Map **01** D4

Selected

Q Q Q Q **T&C *Old Workhouse*** Ballinlough
(on N3 road 1m E of Dunshaughlin village) ☎ 01 8259251
This striking cut-stone listed building (c1841) was indeed once a workhouse and has now been tastefully restored. There are four attractive bedrooms (two en suite and two on the ground floor sharing a bathroom), and the cosy TV lounge and the drawing room (formerly the governor's board room) are filled with antiques. The atmosphere is welcoming and the cooking is excellent - please reserve dinner. Local tours can be arranged and fishing, riding and shooting are all available nearby. Dublin airport is within 45 minutes' drive.
4 bth/shr (1 fmly) No smoking in bedrooms CTV in all bedrooms Tea and coffee making facilities Cen ht CTV 50P Last d noon
CARDS:

ENNIS Co Clare Map **01** B3

Selected

Q Q Q Q **T&C *Aisling Gheal*** St Flannans Cross, Limerick Rd
☎ 065 23810 & 20631 FAX 065 23810
To reach this large modern house, turn off the Ennis-Limerick road, N18, at St Flannan's Cross roundabout. Spacious en suite rooms are equipped with all the expected comforts and furnished to a high standard. The owner prides herself on her baking.
6 shr (3 fmly) No smoking CTV in all bedrooms Tea and coffee making facilities Direct dial from bedrooms No dogs Cen ht 8P
CARDS:

Q Q Q **T&C Carraig Mhuire** Barefield (Located on N18-Ennis to Galway road) ☎ 065 27106 FAX 065 27375
This attractive and comfortable bungalow is set back from the main Galway road in well-tended gardens. Well-equipped bedrooms are welcoming and nothing is too much trouble for charming hosts Mr and Mrs Morris.
5 rms (3 shr) (1 fmly) No smoking in bedrooms No smoking in dining room CTV in all bedrooms Tea and coffee making facilities No dogs (ex guide dogs) Cen ht CTV 6P Last d noon
ROOMS: s IR£18-IR£20; d IR£36; wkly b&b fr IR£105; wkly hlf-bd fr IR£160*
CARDS:

Selected

Q Q Q Q **GH Cill Eoin House** Killadysert Cross, Clare Rd (located 100yds off N18 on the R473 Killadysert road) ☎ 065 6841668 & 6828311 FAX 065 6841669
Closed 22 Dec-9 Jan

This smart purpose-built house stands a short distance from the town centre. It is attractively furnished and comfortable with well-equipped en suite bedrooms. A hospitable owner is always available to attend to guests needs.

14 shr (2 fmly) No smoking CTV in all bedrooms Tea and coffee making facilities Direct dial from bedrooms Cen ht CTV 14P Tennis (hard) Last d 5pm

ROOMS: s IR£25; d IR£44; wkly b&b IR£126-IR£136*

CARDS:

ENNISCORTHY Co Wexford Map **01** D3

Selected

Q Q Q Q **Ballinkeele House** *(T 030334)* Ballymurn

(from Wexford N11 N to Oilgate, right at sign post & follow signs. From Enniscorthy take N11 S to Oilgate, left at signpost & follow signs) ☎ 053 38105 FAX 053 38468 Mr & Mrs J Maher

Mar-12 Nov rs 13 Nov-Feb

Set amid 350 acres of farmland, this classical house - built in 1840 and a good example of the work of Daniel Robertson - has successfully retained its original features while adding modern comforts like central heating and en suite bathrooms. Its fine portico leads to the entrance hall, where a blazing fire helps to create the warm, hospitable atmosphere that pervades throughout. Carefully cooked dinners are served round an elegant table in the fine dining room, and particularly inviting bedrooms welcome guests with a decanter of sherry. Facilities include a billiards room, hard tennis court and easy parking.

5 bth/shr No smoking in bedrooms No smoking in dining room No dogs (ex guide dogs) Licensed Cen ht 20P Croquet 350 acres arable beef Last d noon

CARDS:

Q Q Q **T&C Lemongrove House** Blackstoops

(1km N of Enniscorthy at rdbt on Dublin to Rosslare road (N11))

☎ 054 36115

Closed 20-31 Dec

A large house in its own grounds on an elevated site surrounded by gardens and plenty of parking space. Bedrooms are all individually decorated in warm, cheerful colour schemes, and there is a comfortable sitting room and breakfast room. Ann McGibney keeps her house in perfect order, and its proximity to Rosslare Ferry makes it handy for visitors to and from Britain.

5 shr (3 fmly) No smoking in bedrooms No smoking in dining room CTV in all bedrooms Tea and coffee making facilities No dogs (ex guide dogs) Cen ht CTV 8P

ENNISKILLEN Co Fermanagh Map **01** C5

Q Q Q **GH Achnacarra House** Carrybridge, Lisbellaw BT94 5HX

(Turn off A4 Belfast/Enniskillen onto B514 to Carrybridge. Turn left at Carrybridge. 500yrds on right. Sign at bridge)

☎ 01365 387077

Apr-Oct Closed Nov-Mar

Dave and Norma Ensor look forward to welcoming guests, old and new, to their delightful purpose built home which stands peacefully in 2.75 acres of well tended grounds overlooking a tranquil small lake. Many guests return time and time again, especially angling enthusiasts for whom separate bait, tackle, and drying rooms are available. The attractive lounge has French windows leading to the patio, and enjoyable home cooking is offered in the attractive dining room. A games room is also available. Bedrooms, many of which have triple beds, are compact but offer comfortable modern appointments.

7 shr (2 fmly) No smoking in 2 bedrooms No smoking in 1 lounge Tea and coffee making facilities No dogs Cen ht CTV No children 12yrs 8P No coaches Games room-Pool Darts TV Video Last d 10.00am

ROOMS: s £24-£25; d £36-£38; wkly b&b £120-£127; wkly hlf-bd £175-£180*

Selected

Q Q Q Q **GH Dromard House** Tamlaght BT74 4HR

(2m from Enniskillen, on A4 (Belfast Rd))

☎ 01365 387250

The stately Dromard House, dating back to the last century, is located just outside Enniskillen, on a 180-acre conservation award-winning farm. The estate has its own woodland trail down to the shores of Lough Erne. Sharon Weir offers a warm welcome and traditional hospitality in her immaculate guest-house. The modern accommodation is provided in a converted stable block, which offers guests separate access, although breakfast is taken in the Victorian-style dining-room in the main part of the house. The bedrooms, all en suite, are fresh in appearance and attractively decorated; a number of appealing patchwork quilts and some thoughtful extra touches contribute to a comfortable stay at Dromard.

4 annexe shr No smoking CTV in all bedrooms Tea and coffee making facilities Cen ht 4P No coaches Fishing Woodland trail to Lough shore

ROOMS: s £20; d £35

Q Q Q **GH Tat-Na-Mallaght Farm** Carrybridge Rd, Lisbellaw BT94 5DY ☎ 01365 387174
Apr-Oct
Irene Dunlop looks forward to welcoming you to her comfortable home, a traditional farmhouse which has been carefully modernised whilst retaining a warm relaxed atmosphere. Peacefully set just outside the village on the Carry Bridge Road, the house enjoys views over the surrounding countryside. Irene takes great pride in keeping the house spotlessly clean. Bedrooms are comfortable with pastel colour schemes and modern fitted units. The lounge is tastefully appointed and invites peaceful relaxation while hearty breakfasts and, by prior arrangement, home cooked evening meals are served at individual tables in the attractive dining room. No smoking in bedrooms.
4 rms (2 shr) (1 fmly) CTV in all bedrooms Tea and coffee making facilities Cen ht CTV 10P Last d 6pm
ROOMS: s £18-£20; d £32-£36; wkly b&b £105-£119; wkly hlf-bd £175-£189*

Q Q Q **GH Tullyhona Farm** Marble Arch Rd, Florencecourt BT92 1DE (through Enniskillen follow A4, Sligo road for 2.5 miles then take A32 following signs for Marble Arch Caves. Turn right at NT sign for Florencecourt) ☎ 01365 348452
Tullyhona House is located in a peaceful, verdant setting a few miles outside Enniskillen, very close to the Marble Arch Caves and the National Trust property at Florencecourt. It offers ideal holiday accommodation for families (children will enjoy the range of activities on offer), and yet can offer the business guest easy access to the town. A feature of Tullyhona is its restaurant, open for all-day breakfasts as well as a range of evening meals. The bedrooms, all en suite, are cheerfully decorated and offer comfort and useful amenities.
4 shr (4 fmly) No smoking in bedrooms No smoking in dining room No smoking in 1 lounge CTV in all bedrooms Cen ht CTV ch fac 8P Darts Walks Play area Calving tours Last d 5.30pm
ROOMS: s £18-£22.50; d £32-£38; wkly b&b £112-£133; wkly hlf-bd £152-£168*

ENNISTYMON Co Clare Map 01 B3

Selected

Q Q Q Q **GH *Grovemount House*** Lahinch Rd
(on outskirts of town on the Lahinch rd, on right about 100 yds from the Ungin rd on an elevated site)
☎ 065 71431 & 71038 FAX 065 71823
Apr-Oct
A smart purpose-built house enjoys an elevated site on the outskirts of Ennistymon near The Burren and ideally located for touring County Clare. The bedrooms are en suite and well equipped and the atmosphere is hopitable. Friendly owners will recommend local restaurants and traditional pubs, or arrange golf and lake fishing for guests.
8 shr (1 fmly) No smoking in bedrooms No smoking in dining room CTV in all bedrooms Tea and coffee making facilities Direct dial from bedrooms No dogs (ex guide dogs) Cen ht CTV 20P
CARDS:

FERMOY Co Cork Map 01 B2

Premier Selected

Q Q Q Q Q **T&C Ballyvolane House** Castlelyons
(from N8, turn off onto L188 and follow signs)
☎ 025 36349 FAX 025 36781
This Italianate country house enjoys a magnificent setting in trees, woods and formal gardens which are open to the public in May. The comfortable bedroom all have TVs, tea/coffee making facilities and good bathrooms. Public rooms are filled with antiques and include a pillared reception hall with a baby grand piano and an elegant dining room serving dinner around a fine table. Croquet and private salmon/trout fishing are available and personal attention and a friendly atmosphere are assured.

6 bth No smoking in dining room No smoking in lounges CTV in all bedrooms Tea and coffee making facilities No dogs (ex guide dogs) Licensed Cen ht 25P Fishing Croquet Last d noon
ROOMS: s IR£45-IR£55; d IR£70-IR£90; wkly b&b IR£245-IR£315; wkly hlf-bd IR£406-IR£476
CARDS:

Q Q **T&C Ghillie Cottage** Kilbarry Stud
(take the N72 E towards Tallow/Lismore, then first left out of Fermoy signposted to Clondulane. Establishment 4m on right hand side)
☎ 025 32720 FAX 025 33000
This modernised farmhouse - set on a stud that specialises in crossbreeding traditional Irish cobs with thoroughbred mares - stands in the heart of Munster, near the River Blackwater. Accommodation is provided in cosy pine-furnished bedrooms and the sitting room is comfortable and relaxing. Dinner is available but must be booked in advance. Fishing can be enjoyed on uncrowded beats and the area also offers the chance to walk the Munster Way as well as golf, hunting and riding.
3 rms Tea and coffee making facilities No dogs (ex guide dogs) Cen ht CTV No children 6yrs 6P No coaches Approved fly fishing instructor & guide Last d 4pm
ROOMS: s IR£25; d IR£50; wkly b&b IR£175; wkly hlf-bd IR£287
CARDS:

FERNS Co Wexford Map 01 D3

Selected

Q Q Q Q ❥ *Clone House (T022484)* (2m SE off N11)
☎ 054 66113 FAX 054 66225 Mrs B Breen
Mar-Nov
The hospitable Mrs Breen takes great pride in her farmhouse. Fine furniture from past generations enhances the modern day comforts and the prize-winning gardens are a delight.
5 rms (4 bth/shr) (4 fmly) No smoking in bedrooms No smoking in dining room CTV in 3 bedrooms No dogs (ex guide dogs) Licensed Cen ht CTV 37P Fishing pool table 280 acres mixed working Last d 4pm
CARDS:

This symbol indicates a 'Child Friendly' establishment - see page 25 for details

FOULKESMILL Co Wexford Map 01 C2

QQQ **Horetown House** *(S 870189)* (take right fork at end of village for approx. 1.5km. Pass pub and sharp bend to establishment on left)
☎ 051 565771 FAX 051 565633 Mr I Young
Closed 24-26 Dec
This 18th-century manor house stands in 200 acres of parkland 40 minutes' drive from Rosslane. Ongoing refurbishment has added some en suite bedrooms; other facilities include a drawing room with a huge log fire, the Cellar Restaurant serving country house cuisine, and an on-site equestrian centre.
12 rms (7 shr) (10 fmly) No smoking in dining room Licensed Cen ht CTV 20P Riding All weather indoor riding arena Outdoor riding
214 acres beef dairy mixed Last d 9pm
ROOMS: s IR£27.50-IR£30.50; d IR£45.50-IR£53.50; wkly b&b IR£154-IR£182; wkly hlf-bd IR£255-IR£270.50*
CARDS:

GALWAY Co Galway Map 01 B4

QQQ **T&C** ***Acatalia Lake Shore House*** 134 College Rd
☎ 091 561519 & 561920 FAX 091 561519
A large two-storey house with fine views to the rear over the tidal Lough Atalia. New owners Jerrard and Anne Nestor are currently upgrading the accommodation, and a hospitality tray in the comfortable lounge greets guests on arrival. Bedrooms are equipped to a high standard.
8 bth/shr (4 fmly) No smoking in 4 bedrooms No smoking in dining room No smoking in 1 lounge CTV in all bedrooms Tea and coffee making facilities Direct dial from bedrooms No dogs (ex guide dogs) Cen ht CTV 20P
CARDS:

QQQ **GH Acorn** 19 Dublin Rd (N6 Dublin Road opp Ryans Hotel)
☎ 091 770990 FAX 091 770173
A fine modern house on Dublin Road, with private parking to the front. Plain but comfortable bedrooms, well furnished, and most with en suite facilities. Convenient for the city.
7 rms (6 shr) (2 fmly) No smoking in area of dining room CTV in all bedrooms Direct dial from bedrooms Cen ht CTV No children 10yrs 10P
ROOMS: s IR£20-IR£60; d IR£40-IR£60; wkly b&b IR£140-IR£210
CARDS:

Selected

QQQQ **GH Ardawn House** 31 College Rd
(take Galway East exit off dual carriageway near Galway, follow signs for city centre, first guesthouse on right after Galway Greyhound track)
☎ 091 568833 & 564551 FAX 091 563454
Closed 21-29 Dec
This friendly and hospitable hotel is conveniently situated for the city centre. Breakfasts are a feature here, offering a wide spread of home baked breads, fruit yogurt, cheese and cereal. Bedrooms are all en suite, with colour co-ordinated furnishings. From the N6 follow the route to the City Centre via College Road, and Ardawn House is the first T & C on the right after the Galway Greyhound Track.
8 shr (2 fmly) No smoking in bedrooms No smoking in dining room CTV in all bedrooms Direct dial from bedrooms No dogs (ex guide dogs) Cen ht No children 12yrs 8P
ROOMS: s IR£30-IR£60; d IR£50-IR£80*
CARDS:

The AA's professional Inspectors make regular and anonymous visits to all the establishments listed in the Guide. They accept no gifts or favours from proprietors

Selected

QQQQ **T&C** ***Ashford Manor*** 7 College Rd
☎ 091 563941 FAX 091 563941
4 bth/shr (2 fmly) No smoking in 2 bedrooms No smoking in dining room No smoking in 1 lounge CTV in all bedrooms Tea and coffee making facilities Direct dial from bedrooms No dogs (ex guide dogs) Cen ht CTV ch fac 6P
CARDS:

Selected

QQQQ **T&C Atlantic Heights** 2 Cashelmara, Knocknacarra Cross, Salthill (1Km from Salthill Promenade on coast road to Barna & Spiddal - R336)
☎ 091 529466 & 528830 FAX 091 529466
Closed 22-26 Dec
This fine balconied house overlooks Galway Bay, where enthusiastic hosts, Robbie and Madeline Mitchell, take great pride in their home and pay much attention to detail. All the bedrooms, some with sea views, have TV, tea and coffee making facilities, telephone, hairdryer and many thoughful extras. An extensive breakfast menu, served late if required, features home baking. Laundry service available.
6 shr (3 fmly) No smoking in 4 bedrooms No smoking in dining room No smoking in 1 lounge CTV in all bedrooms Tea and coffee making facilities Direct dial from bedrooms Cen ht CTV 6P
ROOMS: s IR£20-IR£27; d IR£36-IR£50; wkly b&b IR£120-IR£160*
CARDS:

QQ **T&C Bay View** Gentian Hill, Upper Salthill (follow coast road in direction of Connemara take 3rd left after Salthill, signed from main road)
☎ 091 522116 & 526140
17 Mar-Nov
Modern house situated on edge of Salthill. Ideal touring centre.
6 rms (5 shr) (2 fmly) No smoking CTV in all bedrooms Tea and coffee making facilities Direct dial from bedrooms No dogs Cen ht CTV No children 5yrs 6P
ROOMS: s IR£21; d IR£34*

QQQ **T&C** ***Clare Hills*** 4 Threadneedle Rd, Salthill
☎ 091 522653
Stunning views over the ocean can be enjoyed from some of the en suite bedrooms at this seaside house, which has been cleverly adapted to offer the maximum use of space. Good quality fittings and furnishings can be found in all the rooms.
6 shr (2 fmly) No smoking in bedrooms No smoking in dining room CTV in all bedrooms Tea and coffee making facilities No dogs Cen ht CTV 15P
CARDS:

Q Q Q T&C Corrib Fairways Bushy Park
(Take N59 Oughterard/Clifden road from Galway. Situated 2.5m from city on left opposite Glenlo Abbey Hotel)
☎ 091 520510 FAX 091 520511
Closed 21 Dec-4 Jan
A new house on a raised site overlooking Glenlo Abbey and Lough Corrib beyond. All rooms are en suite with luxury shower rooms and furniture in exotic woods specially imported. There is a comfortable TV lounge and the property is within easy reach of the city centre and the Connemara countryside.
7 shr (3 fmly) No smoking in bedrooms No smoking in dining room CTV in 1 bedroom Tea and coffee making facilities No dogs (ex guide dogs) Cen ht CTV P Fishing & Golf nearby
ROOMS: s IR£25-IR£30; d IR£36-IR£50; wkly b&b fr IR£120*
CARDS:

Selected

Q Q Q Q GH Corrib Haven 107 Upper Newcastle
(on N59, at Galway follow the signs for Clifden until Westwood House Hotel and a T-junct, turn right at T-junct and Corrib Haven is on the right) ☎ 091 524171 & 524711 FAX 091 524171
A new, purpose-built guest house stands on the N9 to Connemara, close to the university. The excellent bedrooms all have private bathrooms, and ample car parking is provided.
9 shr No smoking CTV in all bedrooms Direct dial from bedrooms No dogs Cen ht CTV No children 12yrs 13P
ROOMS: s IR£25-IR£60; d IR£36-IR£60*
CARDS:

Q Q Q T&C Eureka Bushy Park (opposite Glenlo Abbey Hotel)
☎ 091 523555 FAX 091 523229
May-Sep
Set back from the main road in landscaped gardens, this modern house has a first floor sitting room overlooking the lough. There is another lounge with adjoining conservatory where breakfast is served. Home baking is a feature, and hostess Mary Connell is more than willing to help guests plan a tour of Connemara or Galway. Bedrooms are comfortable and well appointed.
3 bth/shr (4 fmly) No smoking CTV in all bedrooms Tea and coffee making facilities No dogs Cen ht CTV No children 7yrs P No coaches
ROOMS: s IR£25-IR£30; d IR£36-IR£38; wkly b&b IR£126-IR£133*
CARDS:

Q Q Q T&C *Flannery's* 54 Dalysfort Rd, Salthill
(follow Salthill signs and look for Leisureland on seafront. Dalysfort Rd is across park, parallel with road into Leisureland.)
☎ 091 522048 FAX 091 522048
A spacious house set in attractive gardens, with comfortable public areas. The hospitable Mrs Flannery offers tea on arrival and is a welcoming hostess.
4 rms (3 shr) (2 fmly) Cen ht CTV 4P
CARDS:

Q Q Q T&C Four Seasons 23 College Rd
(from east or south take left turn off motorway following sign for Galway East/city centre. 5th house on right after sports ground/greyhound track)
☎ 091 564078 FAX 091 569765
This comfortable house adjacent to the city centre is the family home of Eddie and Helen Fitzgerald who will immediately make you feel at home and help you with itineraries, site seeing and recommend restaurants for evening meals.
5 shr 2 annexe shr (3 fmly) No smoking in 3 bedrooms No smoking in dining room CTV in all bedrooms Tea and coffee making facilities No dogs (ex guide dogs) Cen ht CTV 7P
ROOMS: s IR£25-IR£35; d IR£36-IR£56; wkly b&b IR£112-IR£175
CARDS:

Q Q Q T&C Four Winds Lodge Gentian Hill, Salthill
(Galway golf club on right, pass petrol station on right, next turning right next to Gentian Villas apartments)
☎ 091 526026
A large old world home set in a wild garden with pond and paving where guests can stroll and relax. Most of the nicely decorated en suite bedrooms have sea views. Situated between Salthill's amenities and the quiet Connemara countryside.
4 shr (3 fmly) No smoking CTV in all bedrooms Tea and coffee making facilities No dogs (ex guide dogs) Cen ht CTV 5P Golf 18
Tennis, squash, fishing ,riding all nearby
ROOMS: s IR£18-IR£25; d IR£30-IR£50 *
CARDS:

Premier Selected

Q Q Q Q Q T&C *Killeen House* Killeen, Bushypark
(on N59 midway between the city and Moycullen village)
☎ 091 524179 FAX 091 528065
Closed 23-28 Dec
This charming 19th-century house stands in 25 acres of grounds stretching down to the shores of the loch. The interior is beautifully appointed with antique furnishings, hand-woven carpets, fine linen and exquisite crystal. En suite bedrooms reflect the character of the house

and are well equipped with TVs, hairdryers and tea/coffee making facilities. Guests have use of two reception rooms and a breakfast room overlooking the garden. The hosts are genuinely hospitable.
5 bth/shr (1 fmly) No smoking in dining room CTV in all bedrooms Tea and coffee making facilities Direct dial from bedrooms No dogs Lift Cen ht No children 12yrs 6P No coaches
CARDS:

Q Q Q **GH Marian Lodge** Knocknacarra Rd, Salthill Upper (from Galway procees to Salthill R336 through Salthill, take 1st right after Spinnaker Hotel into Knocknacarra Rd. Marian Lodge 1st on left)
☎ 091 521678 FAX 091 528103
A large modern house only 50 yards from the seafront on Knocknacarra Road in Upper Salthill. The fully equipped bedrooms have orthopedic beds and en suite facilities. There are a lounge and separate breakfast room also available.
6 bth/shr (4 fmly) No smoking CTV in all bedrooms Tea and coffee making facilities Direct dial from bedrooms No dogs Cen ht CTV 10P Golf
ROOMS: s IR£30-IR£40; d IR£38-IR£44; wkly b&b IR£133-IR£140*
CARDS:

Q Q Q **T&C *Ocean Wave*** 1 Cashel Mara, Knocknarra Cross, Salthill (from direction of city, pass through Salthill along coast, house a mile on right at T-junction)
☎ 091 520620 FAX 091 520620
6 bth/shr (3 fmly) CTV in all bedrooms Tea and coffee making facilities Direct dial from bedrooms No dogs Cen ht CTV ch fac 12P
CARDS:

Q Q Q **T&C *Rhondda*** Barna Rd (from Salthill Promenade travel 0.25m to T-junct and turn left, house 250mtrs on right) ☎ 091 526561
This handsome, yellow-painted house is set back from the Barna road, near the Salthill road. A recently built extension houses bedrooms with modern shower rooms, and most have sea views. The dining room, with separate tables, is adjacent to a comfortable lounge.
4 shr (1 fmly) No smoking in 2 bedrooms No smoking in dining room No smoking in lounges CTV in all bedrooms No dogs (ex guide dogs) Cen ht CTV 8P

Q Q Q **T&C Roncalli House** 24 Whitestrand Av, Lower Salthill (off R336, house on corner close by Ocean Wave Apartment Complex) ☎ 091 584159 589013 FAX 091 584159
Mr and Mrs O'Halloran are the hospitable owners of this modern corner house near the beach and in walking distance of the city centre. Bedrooms are all equipped with TV and shower rooms, there is good lounge space and, outside, a patio and well tended garden.
6 shr (1 fmly) No smoking in bedrooms No smoking in dining room No smoking in 1 lounge CTV in all bedrooms Tea and coffee making facilities No dogs Cen ht CTV 5P No coaches
ROOMS: s IR£18; d IR£36
CARDS:

Q Q Q **GH Silverseas** Cappagh Rd, Barna (coast road to Barna/Spiddal after passing Rusheen Riding Centre on left, next turn right Cappagh Rd)
☎ 091 590575 FAX 091 590575
An imposing modern house in a residential area, overlooking Galway Bay and 1 mile from Salthill. All bedrooms are furnished to a uniformly high standard, but all have different colour schemes. There is a small but comfortable lounge and a separate breakfast room. Mrs McGrath is a caring hostess, and offers a good buffet breakfast.
8 shr (3 fmly) No smoking in bedrooms No smoking in dining room CTV in all bedrooms No dogs Cen ht CTV 12P
ROOMS: s IR£19-IR£25; d IR£34-IR£46*
CARDS:

Q Q Q **T&C *Southern Hills*** Knocknacarra, Salthill (from Salthill town, 1m W adjacent to Galway Golf Club and opposite Spinnaker House Hotel) ☎ 091 528224
Closed 23-26 Dec
A white house distinguished by red bench seats in front, that has been completely renovated, providing attractive decor throughout with large sitting and dining rooms and newly-added conservatory. The smart bedrooms have all the facilities required for complete comfort, and some overlook the 4th tee of the adjacent golf course. There is plenty of car parking space.
6 shr (2 fmly) No smoking CTV in all bedrooms Tea and coffee making facilities No dogs (ex guide dogs) Cen ht ch fac 7P
CARDS:

Selected

Q Q Q Q **T&C Sunrise Lodge** 3 Ocean Wave, Dr Colohan Rd, Salthill (entrance beside Cois Cuan apartments before Seapoint)
☎ 091 525566
A luxurious new house looking out over Galway Bay and the eastern end of the promenade at Salthill. All rooms are en suite and decorated and furnished to a very high standard, and some have front balconies where guests can sit and enjoy the sea views.
6 annexe shr (2 fmly) No smoking in bedrooms No smoking in dining room No smoking in 1 lounge CTV in all bedrooms Tea and coffee making facilities Direct dial from bedrooms No dogs (ex guide dogs) Cen ht CTV 8P
ROOMS: wkly b&b fr IR£126
CARDS:

Q Q Q **T&C *Swallow*** 98 Fr Griffin Rd
☎ 091 589073 FAX 091 589175
rs Xmas
A large modern house with annexe to the rear, in a quiet residential area close to the city centre. Comfortable en suite rooms. The breakfast room opens onto a patio, where guests can eat outdoors on fine summer mornings.
6 shr 4 annexe shr (2 fmly) No smoking in area of dining room CTV in all bedrooms Tea and coffee making facilities No dogs (ex guide dogs) Cen ht 7P
CARDS:

Q Q Q **T&C *Villa Maria*** 94 Fr Griffin Rd, Lower Salthill
☎ 091 589033
3 shr (2 fmly) No smoking in bedrooms No smoking in dining room CTV in all bedrooms Tea and coffee making facilities No dogs Cen ht CTV 6P
CARDS:

Q Q Q **T&C West Winds** 5 Ocean Wave, Salthill ☎ 091 520223 FAX 091 757646
Closed 20-31 Dec
Facing the seafront near the Salthill promenade, this new house is sparklingly fresh. There is a big breakfast room with a conservatory and a lounge area. Bedrooms are attractively furnished, and Rita Joyce is the friendly proprietor.
6 shr (5 fmly) CTV in all bedrooms Tea and coffee making facilities No dogs Cen ht 6P
ROOMS: d IR£34-IR£50; wkly b&b IR£119-IR£140*
CARDS:

Selected

◘ ◘ ◘ ◘ T&C ***Woodhaven Lodge*** Merlin Park, Dublin Rd (off N6, located between Corrib Great Southern Hotel and Merlin Park Hospital) ☎ 091 753806
Closed 22-28 Dec
A large modern redbrick building offering comfortable en suite accommodation with a pleasing outlook. Guests can relax in one of the two inviting lounges.
4 shr (1 fmly) No smoking CTV in all bedrooms Tea and coffee making facilities No dogs Cen ht CTV No children 12yrs
CARDS:

GLENBEIGH Co Kerry Map **01** A2

Selected

◘ ◘ ◘ ◘ **T&C Ocean Wave** (on N70, 1km before Glenbeigh travelling from Killorglin, on left) ☎ 066 68249 FAX 066 68412
Mar-Oct
An impressive dormer bungalow set in landscaped gardens overlooking Dingle Bay. Bedrooms are comfortable and well appointed, and the large first floor lounge enjoys delightful panoramic views across the bay.
6 bth/shr No smoking in bedrooms No smoking in dining room CTV in all bedrooms Tea and coffee making facilities No dogs Cen ht CTV 6P
ROOMS: s IR£25-IR£30; d IR£36-IR£45
CARDS:

GLENCAR Co Kerry Map **01** A2

◘ ◘ ◘ **Blackstones House** *(V 732881)*
☎ 066 60164 FAX 066 60164 Mrs B Breen
Feb-Nov
Blackstones is in a wooded location beside the Caragh River, at the foot of Ireland's highest mountain. New bedrooms have recently been added, most are en suite, and guests have use of a TV lounge and dining room overlooking the river. Dinner is available by prior arrangement.
6 rms (5 bth/shr) (1 fmly) No smoking CTV in 1 bedroom Tea and coffee making facilities No dogs Cen ht CTV 12P Fishing permits can be arranged 360 acres sheep cows Last d noon
ROOMS: s IR£24; d IR£35*
CARDS:

◘ ◘ **T&C Climbers Inn** (from Killarney take the Ring of Kerry to Killorglin, coming over the bridge off the N72 1st right for Glencar, 10 miles from Killorglin) ☎ 066 60101 FAX 066 60104
2 Mar-10 Nov, 27 Dec-5 Jan
Climbers, walkers and cyclists looking for a peaceful retreat in the highlands of Kerry should make for this glen near Ireland's highest mountain range. The inn has a convivial atmosphere and well designed bedrooms. Good food, ranging from bar snacks to fixed-price evening meals, is a welcome feature, and landlord Johnny Walsh has a fund of knowledge about the area. Facilities include a drying room, breakfast room, shop and car park.
1 rms 7 annexe shr (3 fmly) No smoking in bedrooms No smoking in area of dining room No smoking in 1 lounge Tea and coffee making facilities No dogs (ex guide dogs) Licensed Cen ht CTV No children 7yrs 20P Walking and rambeling centre Last d 9pm
ROOMS: s IR£23-IR£29; d IR£36-IR£50*
CARDS:

GLENDALOUGH Co Wicklow Map **01** D3

See also Laragh

◘ ◘ ◘ T&C ***Gleann Ailbhe*** (Glendelough main road beside post office) ☎ 0404 45236
Set in the quaint village of Laragh, right beside the Post Office and near to all the local activities. Hospitality and good humour are high on the list of priorities for Betty and John Kenny who run this pleasant house with dedication and enthusiasm. Wicklow is nearby and this is an ideal place for walkers.
5 bth/shr (1 fmly) No smoking in bedrooms No smoking in dining room CTV in 2 bedrooms No dogs Cen ht CTV 5P
CARDS:

GLENEALY Co Wicklow Map **01** D3

◘ ◘ ◘ **Ballyknocken House** *(T 246925)*
(turn right after Statoil garage in Ashford (N11) house 3 miles from Ashford) ☎ 0404 44627 & 44614 FAX 0404 44696 Mrs M Byrne
Closed 14 Nov-1 Apr
This comfortable farmhouse stands one mile from Glenealy offering pleasant en suite accommodation. Its hospitable owner Mrs Byrne organizes walking and cycling tours. Dinner is also provided.
7 bth/shr (1 fmly) No smoking in bedrooms No smoking in dining room Tea and coffee making facilities No dogs Licensed Cen ht CTV 8P Tennis (hard) 270 acres beef sheep Last d 6pm
ROOMS: s IR£27-IR£29; d IR£40-IR£44; wkly hlf-bd IR£210-IR£220*

GOLEEN Co Cork Map **01** A1

Selected

◘ ◘ ◘ ◘ **T&C Fortview House** Gurtyowen
(6m E of Goleen on R591) ☎ 028 35324 FAX 028 35324
Mar-Nov
Reading the praise of previous guests in the visitors' book leads to great expectations which are more than met. Charming lounge, traditional en suite bedrooms with country pine furnishings, superb breakfasts, and the attention of a dedicated hostess. Evening meals will be served by arrangement.
5 annexe bth/shr (1 fmly) No smoking in bedrooms No smoking in dining room No dogs (ex guide dogs) Cen ht CTV 5P Last d noon
ROOMS: s fr IR£25; d fr IR£50

Selected

◘ ◘ ◘ ◘ **T&C Heron's Cove** The Harbour
(turn left down to the harbour in the middle of Goleen village)
☎ 028 35225 FAX 028 35422
Closed Xmas
This big white house lies in a sheltered cove on Ireland's most southwesterly point near Mizen Head. A warm, friendly atmosphere is created by glowing fires at either end of the lounge in which there is a

wine bar. The restaurant is run by award-winning chef/patron Sue Hill. The bedrooms are comfortable, with some enjoying a view over the harbour from balconies.

5 bth/shr (2 fmly) CTV in all bedrooms Tea and coffee making facilities Direct dial from bedrooms No dogs (ex guide dogs) Licensed Cen ht No children 10yrs 10P No coaches
ROOMS: s IR£25-IR£31.50; d IR£37-IR£50✻
CARDS:

GOREY Co Wexford Map **01** D3

Selected

Q Q Q Q **T&C Hillside House** Tubberduff (turn off N11, 1m after passing Toss Byrnes pub, signposted Hillside House)
☎ 055 21726 22036 FAX 055 22567
Closed 20-28 Dec
A pristine house with pretty gardens, set in a lovely rural location commanding panoramic views of mountains and the sea - only three km from Ballymoney beach. Ann Sutherland is a good cook, providing guests with a variety of home baking for the evening meal. Both reception rooms are big with large windows to take advantage of the beautiful setting. Bedrooms are very comfortable, decorated in attractive colours and have good beds.
6 shr (4 fmly) No smoking in bedrooms No smoking in dining room CTV in 8 bedrooms Tea and coffee making facilities No dogs (ex guide dogs) Licensed Cen ht CTV ch fac 6P Last d 6pm
ROOMS: s IR£20-IR£25; d IR£39-IR£40; wkly b&b IR£125-IR£130; wkly hlf-bd IR£185-IR£200✻
CARDS:

The AA's professional Inspectors make regular and anonymous visits to all the establishments listed in the Guide. They accept no gifts or favours from proprietors

Selected

Q Q Q Q *Woodlands (T 163648)* Killinierin (signposted from N11)
☎ 0402 37125 FAX 0402 37133 P O'Sullivan
Closed Nov-Feb
This Georgian-style residence is tucked back from the main road in a wooded area of farmland. En suite bedrooms are well appointed; three have balconies and all are equipped with TVs. A garden patio stands between the guest lounge and a dining room which serves a good set dinner. Leisure facilities include a tennis court and a games room. Smoking is only allowed in the sitting room.
6 shr (3 fmly) No smoking in bedrooms No smoking in dining room CTV in all bedrooms No dogs (ex guide dogs) Licensed Cen ht CTV 10P Tennis (hard) Snooker Pony rides Walking Chlidren's play room 8 acres mixed Last d 7pm
CARDS:

GRAIGUENAMANAGH Co Kilkenny Map **01** C3

Selected

QQQQ **GH *Waterside*** The Quay (from Dublin-N7 to N9 to R705) ☎ 0503 24246 & 24737 FAX 0503 24733
11 Mar-1 Dec
This fine, early 19th century granary on the banks of the river Barrow has been painstakingly converted to a fourteen room guest house, restaurant and bar. Simply but comfortably furnished, the house offers excellent value for money, personal service and a fine restaurant.
9 shr No smoking in area of dining room CTV in all bedrooms Direct dial from bedrooms No dogs Licensed Cen ht Fishing Snooker Last d 9pm
CARDS:

GRANARD Co Longford Map **01** C4

QQQ **Toberphelim House** *(N 356810)* (from Belfast-take the N55 from Cavan, left at Statoil, right at next junction, house on left)
☎ 043 86568 FAX 043 86568 Mr & Mrs Smyth
10 May-20 Sep rs 23 Sep-9 Apr
A large Georgian country house stands at the end of a long driveway. Children are well catered for with a private playground and a chance to see the various farmyard animals and activities. A separate lounge is also available.
3 rms (2 shr) (3 fmly) No smoking in 2 bedrooms No smoking in dining room No smoking in lounges No dogs (ex guide dogs) Licensed Cen ht CTV 10P Children's playground Stables for guests horses 200 acres beef sheep Last d previous day
ROOMS: s IR£23-IR£35; d IR£40-IR£50*
CARDS:

HOLYWOOD Co Down Map **01** D5

Premier Selected

QQQQQ **GH Beech Hill** 23 Ballymoney Rd, Craigantlet BT23 4TG (leave Belfast for Bangor on A2 bypassing Holywood, 1.5m from bridge at Ulster Folk Museum turn right up Ballymoney Road. House on left) ☎ 01232 425892 FAX 01232 425892
This stunning property sits high in the Holywood hills, yet offers easy access to the town, Newtownards, Bangor and Belfast. Victoria Brann invites guests to enjoy her charming Georgian style home, a first class guest house brimming with style. The tastefully decorated and well equipped bedrooms have some period pieces, and a plethora of facilities and little luxuries welcome the guest. One is treated to tea on arrival and breakfast is served in the elegant dining room; Mrs Brann is happy to recommend one of the many good local restaurants or pubs for dinner. A richly appointed lounge is provided and also a spacious conservatory, with pretty hanging baskets; this is a perfect haven in which to relax and enjoy the panoramic views across the quiet countryside.
3 bth/shr No smoking in bedrooms No smoking in dining room CTV in all bedrooms Tea and coffee making facilities Direct dial from bedrooms No dogs (ex guide dogs) Cen ht CTV No children 10yrs 6P No coaches croquet boules
ROOMS: s fr £35; d fr £60*
CARDS:

HOWTH Co Dublin Map **01** D4

QQQ **T&C Inisradharc** Balkill Rd ☎ 01 8322306
Closed 21 Dec-2 Jan
Set in a charming fishing village with lovely views of the harbour and Dublin Bay which can be seen to advantage from a big outdoor balcony. The breakfast room also has fine views and there is a spacious television lounge. Two of the very pleasing bedrooms are en-suite and the third room has sole use of a bathroom opposite. Well kept gardens surround the property and Dublin and the airport are easily reached by road or rail.
3 bth/shr (2 fmly) No smoking CTV in all bedrooms Tea and coffee making facilities No dogs Cen ht CTV No children 8yrs 3P Golf Cliff walks, restaurants, night ent. all nearby
ROOMS: d IR£40-IR£48*
CARDS:

INISTIOGE Co Kilkenny Map **01** C3

Selected

QQQQ **T&C Berryhill** ☎ 056 58434 FAX 056 58434
High up on the side of a valley, set in 250 acres of farmland and surrounded by pretty gardens, this 18th-century country house was built by ancestors of the current owners George and Belinda Dyer. Reception rooms are limited to a delightful drawing room. Breakfast is a speciality with a wide range available, and light evening meals are available by prior arrangement.

KANTURK Co Cork Map **01** B2

Premier Selected

QQQQQ **GH Assolas Country House** (3.5m NE, off N72) ☎ 029 50015 FAX 029 50795
26 Mar-1 Nov
This 17th-century manor house enjoys a sylvan setting on a tributary of the River Blackwater, surrounded by prize-winning gardens, parkland and rolling country. Magnificent public rooms have log fires and fresh garden and local produce is creatively presented in the restaurant.
6 bth/shr 3 annexe bth/shr (3 fmly) Direct dial from bedrooms No dogs (ex guide dogs) Licensed Cen ht 20P No coaches Tennis (grass) Fishing Croquet Boating Gardens Last d 8.30pm
ROOMS: s IR£65-IR£78; d IR£110-IR£168
CARDS:

KENMARE Co Kerry Map **01** B2

QQQ **T&C Harbour View** Castletownbere Rd, Dauros (leave Kenmare for Glengurriffe take Castletownbere Haven Rd 571, 1st right after bridge, Harbour View is 4m on left on seashore) ☎ 064 41755
Mar-Oct
A dormer-style house on the sea shore, with lovely views of Kenmare Bay and the mountains beyond which can be enjoyed from the picture windows

in the sitting room. Mrs Maureen McCarthy is a cheerful, caring hostess with infectious enthusiasm, and her attention to detail is evident throughout this well-maintained house. Bedrooms are attractively decorated, and are either en suite or have sole use of a bathroom. Dinner is available when pre-booked, and the home-baking is excellent.

4 bth/shr (3 fmly) No smoking in 1 bedrooms No smoking in dining room CTV in all bedrooms Tea and coffee making facilities No dogs Cen ht CTV 6P Snooker Last d 8pm
ROOMS: s IR£28; d IR£39*

Premier Selected

Q Q Q Q Q **T&C Sallyport House** Glengarriff Rd (0.25m S on N71) ☎ 064 42066 FAX 064 42067
Apr-Oct
This superbly refurbished house - set in its own grounds and luxuriously appointed - stands on the left, near the bridge, as you leave Kenmare for Glengarrif/Castletownbere. The Arthur family offer caring, attentive and well-judged hospitality in their elegant country house, and guests will be soothed by the tranquil ambience of a house that overlooks lawns and an orchard, and where fires blaze. Bedrooms invite relaxation, with attractive decor, good-sized bathrooms, and all the facilities are of quality.
5 bth/shr (2 fmly) No smoking CTV in all bedrooms Direct dial from bedrooms No dogs (ex guide dogs) Cen ht No children 10yrs 10P
ROOMS: s fr IR£65; d IR£70-IR£90

Q Q ♈ ***Sea Shore Farm*** *(V 899705)* Tubrid (situated off N71 Killarney Road, signposted just out of town by O'Sullivans Antiques)
☎ 064 41270 M P O'Sullivan
10 Mar-10 Nov
A modern bungalow standing in its own grounds on the edge of town overlooking Kenmare Bay.
6 bth/shr No smoking Tea and coffee making facilities No dogs (ex guide dogs) Cen ht CTV 8P Tennis Sauna Private shore 32 acres

KILCULLEN Co Kildare Map 01 C3

Q Q Q **T&C *Chapel View Country Home*** Gormanstown (take N7 to Naas then N9 to Kilcullen, turn left at traffic lights, at crossroads follow signs) ☎ 045 481325
Mar-1 Dec
This large modern house is set in stud-farm country and run in friendly style by Daniel and Breda O'Sullivan who offer their guests good company as well as good cooking. Soda bread is often on the breakfast menu and dinners can be pre-booked. There is a spacious TV lounge, large dining room overlooking the gardens and plenty of room for parking.
6 shr (2 fmly) No smoking in bedrooms No smoking in dining room Licensed Cen ht CTV 20P Last d 4pm
CARDS:

KILGARVAN Co Kerry Map 01 B2

Q Q Q **T&C Birchwood** Church Ground (500 mtrs E of Kilgarvon village on R569) ☎ 064 85473 FAX 064 85570
Situated on an elevated site facing a natural forest and backed by the Mangerton Mountains in an area ideal for hill walking and touring. The McDonnells are caring hosts in this tranquil location in an acre of gardens, and their bedrooms are comfortable and attractively decorated. Dinner is available, and the nearby Rivers Roughty and Slaheny provide good salmon and trout fishing.
4 shr (2 fmly) No smoking CTV in 2 bedrooms Tea and coffee making facilities No dogs (ex guide dogs) Cen ht CTV 6P Fishing Last d 6.30pm
ROOMS: d IR£36; wkly b&b IR£116; wkly hlf-bd IR£190*

KILKENNY Co Kilkenny Map 01 C3

Q Q Q **T&C Alcantra** Maidenhill, Kells Rd (on R697, 400 metres from its junction with R910 (N10)) ☎ 056 61058 FAX 056 61058
An impressive new house close to the City Centre. Public rooms include a pleasant lounge and conservatory with a separate dining room, all well decorated.
4 bth/shr (1 fmly) No smoking in bedrooms No smoking in dining room No smoking in 1 lounge CTV in 1 bedroom Tea and coffee making facilities No dogs Cen ht CTV 4P No coaches
ROOMS: s IR£22-IR£25; d IR£32-IR£36*
CARDS:

Selected

Q Q Q Q **GH Butler House** Patrick St (follow signs for city centre, is situated on Patrick Street.) ☎ 056 65707 & 22828 FAX 056 65626
Closed 24-29 Dec
Once the dower house of Kilkenny Castle, this fine Georgian building is both elegant and distinctive. It fronts onto Main Street, with secluded gardens to the rear, which are part of the castle estates. Built in 1770, many of the original features remain, including the ornate plasterwork and marble fireplaces. The bedrooms feature contemporary decor, and there are some spacious suites which overlook the gardens and castle. Public areas include a foyer lounge and a rustic breakfast room.
13 bth/shr (4 fmly) No smoking in 5 bedrooms No smoking in area of dining room CTV in all bedrooms Tea and coffee making facilities Direct dial from bedrooms No dogs (ex guide dogs) Cen ht 24P No coaches
ROOMS: s IR£64-IR£69; d IR£89-IR£149
CARDS:

Q Q Q **T&C Mount Danville** Bennetsbridge Rd (less than 1km from Kilkenny Castle. 1st B&B on left past the Castle) ☎ 056 21521
Apr-Sep
Set in secluded gardens four minutes from the town centre - the first bed and breakfast establishment on the left-hand side past Kilkenny Castle - Mount

contd.

Danville has a sitting room and sun lounge in addition to the attractive dining room where breakfast is served round a communal table; three of the four bedrooms have en suite facilities.
4 rms (3 bth/shr) (1 fmly) No smoking in bedrooms No smoking in dining room No dogs (ex guide dogs) Cen ht CTV 15P No coaches
ROOMS: d fr IR£40*

Premier Selected

Q Q Q Q Q **T&C Newlands Country House** Sevenhouses (turn right off N10 Waterford road 4 miles S of Ring road and follow Danesford church sign to reach house in approximately a half mile)
☎ 056 29111 & 29171 FAX 056 29171
Closed Xmas
Set in a quiet rural location, this luxury purpose-built house offers a standard of quality and comfort normally associated with top ranking hotels. Aileen and Seamus Kennedy aim to provide a relaxing atmosphere where guests can relax in superb comfort and enjoy excellent home cooking. Bedrooms are beautifully appointed, equipped with extras like electric blankets and a fridge, and the two junior suites have whirlpool baths.
4 bth/shr (3 fmly) No smoking CTV in all bedrooms Tea and coffee making facilities Direct dial from bedrooms No dogs (ex guide dogs) Cen ht No children 12yrs 8P Whirlpool baths in some rooms Last d noon
ROOMS: s IR£20-IR£30; d IR£40-IR£70*
CARDS:

Selected

Q Q Q Q **T&C Shillogher House** Callan Rd (on N76 Callan/Clonmel/Cork Road, approx 1km south of Kilkenny)
☎ 056 63249 & 64865 FAX 056 64865
A lovely new house stands in its own gardens on the road to Clonmel. It is tastefully furnished and decorated and Mrs Morgan has a keen eye to her guests' comfort.
5 shr (1 fmly) No smoking CTV in all bedrooms Tea and coffee making facilities Direct dial from bedrooms No dogs (ex guide dogs) Cen ht 10P
ROOMS: d IR£36-IR£39
CARDS:

KILLARNEY Co Kerry Map 01 B2

Q Q Q **GH Ashville** Rock Rd (on N22) ☎ 064 36405 FAX 064 36778
Closed 18-30 Dec
Two minutes walk from the town centre, this inviting house is conveniently situated for all amenities and easy to find near the approach to the N22 Tralee road. Accommodation is new and purpose-built, offering all the comforts to make for a pleasant stay, with a relaxing sitting room furnished with deep sofas. There is a private car park behind the house. Tours can be arranged on request.
10 shr (7 fmly) No smoking in 6 bedrooms No smoking in dining room CTV in all bedrooms Tea and coffee making facilities Direct dial from bedrooms No dogs Cen ht CTV 13P
ROOMS: s IR£25-IR£35; d IR£32-IR£50
CARDS:

Q Q Q **T&C Avondale House** Tralee Rd (3km from roundabout on N22) ☎ 064 35579 FAX 064 35579
Xmas
This is a distinctive pink house surrounded by attractive gardens five minutes' drive from Killarney. There is a comfortable lounge and en suite bedrooms equipped with TVs and tea/coffee making facilities. A golf course and riding stables are available nearby.
5 shr (4 fmly) No smoking in dining room No smoking in lounges CTV in all bedrooms Tea and coffee making facilities No dogs (ex guide dogs) Cen ht CTV No children 4yrs 8P Last d 3pm
ROOMS: s IR£22-IR£28; d IR£35-IR£36; wkly b&b IR£120-IR£125*

Q Q Q **T&C *Briens Tara*** Fossa ☎ 064 44355
Set in pretty gardens on an approach road to the Gap of Dunloe, this pink-painted bungalow is run by Carmel O'Brien. Guests have use of a TV lounge. Four of the bedrooms have en suite facilities, and the fifth has sole use of a bathroom. Breakfast is generous and self-catering is also available.

Q Q Q **GH Coffey's Loch Lein** Golf Course Rd, Fossa (N72 pass Prince of Peace church, Fossa, take 1st left)
☎ 064 31260 FAX 064 36151
11 Mar-3 Nov
A comfortable, well kept bungalow set in its own peaceful grounds and overlooking Killarney's Lower Lake. Mrs Coffey has a keen interest in interior decorating and has used this skill successfully in a recent refurbishment of the sitting and dining rooms, both of which have panoramic views of the lake.
12 bth/shr (7 fmly) No smoking in 8 bedrooms No smoking in dining room No smoking in lounges CTV in all bedrooms Direct dial from bedrooms No dogs (ex guide dogs) Cen ht CTV 12P
ROOMS: s IR£25-IR£35; d IR£40-IR£50
CARDS:

Q Q Q **T&C Crab Tree Cottage** Mangerton Rd, Muckross (N71 to Muckross Park Hotel, turn left and continue for 1km)
☎ 064 33169
Apr-Oct
Set in the midst of Killarney National Park and encircled by award winning gardens whose lovely flowers and shrubs can be enjoyed while having breakfast in the conservatory. The owners are very easy going and the atmosphere is friendly and relaxed.
4 rms (3 shr) (2 fmly) No smoking in dining room No dogs Cen ht CTV 6P No coaches Gardens available to guests Last d noon
ROOMS: s IR£22.50; d IR£36

Selected

Q Q Q Q **T&C Crystal Springs** Ballycasheen
(from Killarney Town right off Cork Rd at 1st lights and Texaco. Left into Rookery Rd go to end and Crystal Springs is accross the rd at T junct) ☎ 064 33272 & 35518 FAX 064 31188
This luxurious purpose built house stands on the bank of the River Flesk. It overlooks an old historic mill, and is surrounded by the mountains and lakes of Killarney's National Park. All en suite bedrooms are attractively decorated and very well equipped. Guests can enjoy fishing and there are three golf courses in Killarney to choose from.
6 bth/shr (3 fmly) No smoking in bedrooms No smoking in dining room No smoking in 1 lounge CTV in all bedrooms Tea and coffee making facilities Cen ht CTV 10P Fishing
ROOMS: s IR£25-IR£28; d IR£36-IR£39*
CARDS:

Premier Selected

Q Q Q Q Q **GH Earls Court House** Woodlawn Junction, Muckross Rd (on Muckross Road turn off after Shell petrol station) (The Circle) ☎ 064 34009 FAX 064 34366
Mar-5 Nov rs 6 Nov-28 Feb (group bookings 8+ only)
A distinctive yellow building, contemporary in design and purpose built with the added facility of balconies adjoining most bedrooms. Elegance and luxury can be seen in the decor and the antique furnishings which appear throughout the house. There is a comfortable lounge where rich upholstery fabrics have been used to create an inviting setting for relaxation. Mrs Moynihan and husband Ray are to be congratulated on a very special house, one which can offer that little something extra.
11 bth/shr (3 fmly) No smoking in bedrooms No smoking in dining room CTV in all bedrooms Direct dial from bedrooms No dogs (ex guide dogs) Licensed Cen ht CTV 11P
ROOMS: s IR£38.50-IR£62.50; d IR£60-IR£85*
CARDS:

Selected

Q Q Q Q **GH Foleys Town House** 22/23 High St (Town Centre location, on right of street. Midway between main St and traffic lights, going N towards Tralee) ☎ 064 31217 FAX 064 34683
Apr-Oct
Charming bedrooms with stripped pine furniture and co-ordinated colour schemes are a feature of this delightful town house, which also offers a cosy lounge, a bar and private car park. It is run by Carol Hartnett who is also head chef at her popular adjoining seafood restaurant.
28 bth/shr No smoking in 5 bedrooms No smoking in area of dining room CTV in all bedrooms Tea and coffee making facilities Direct dial from bedrooms No dogs Licensed Cen ht CTV 60P Last d 10.30pm
ROOMS: s IR£49.50; d IR£82.50
CARDS:

Q Q Q **T&C Friars Glen** Mangerton Rd, Muckross
(from Killarney take N71 towards Kenmare and turn left immediately after Muckross Park Hotel. Entrance 300mtrs on right next to garden centre)
☎ 064 34044 FAX 064 34044
Mar-Oct
A beautiful and spacious modern house in a woodland setting, located in the heart of Killarney National Park. The bedrooms are large and comfortable, public rooms are attractive, and all have pleasant views of woods and pastureland.
4 bth/shr (1 fmly) No smoking in bedrooms No smoking in dining room Tea and coffee making facilities No dogs (ex guide dogs) Cen ht CTV 6P
ROOMS: s IR£22-IR£28; d IR£35-IR£45*
CARDS:

Selected

Q Q Q Q **GH Glena House** Muckross Rd
(at Friary church on N22 left and Left again at cinema and Glena House 600yds on right) ☎ 064 32705 & 34284 FAX 064 35611
Only a few minutes from the town centre, this comfortable guest house offers attractively decorated bedrooms, with pine furnishings and modern facilities. There is a big dining room with an adjoining Wine Bar, and a separate lounge for relaxation.
26 bth/shr (6 fmly) No smoking in 10 bedrooms No smoking in area of dining room CTV in all bedrooms Tea and coffee making facilities Direct dial from bedrooms No dogs (ex guide dogs) Licensed Cen ht CTV 26P Library Last d 9pm
ROOMS: s IR£25-IR£40; d IR£46-IR£60*
CARDS:

Q Q Q **T&C Gorman's** Tralee Rd
(on N22 Tralee Rd straight up main st onto Tralee Rd on the left side 3.5 miles out) ☎ 064 33149 FAX 064 33149
A large and attractive bungalow, set in well cultivated gardens. It offers magnificent views from comfortable en suite bedrooms. Open fire in lounge and satellite TV is available. Separate breakfast menu. Discount for senior citizens. Special off season rates.
5 bth/shr (2 fmly) No smoking in 3 bedrooms No smoking in dining room CTV in all bedrooms Tea and coffee making facilities Cen ht CTV No children 4yrs 7P Gardens Last d 6pm
ROOMS: s IR£18-IR£23.50; d IR£32-IR£35; wkly hlf-bd IR£108-IR£180*
CARDS:

Q Q **GH *Green Acres*** Fossa (2km on T67 Killorglin road) ☎ 064 31454
Closed Dec-9 Jan
This modern house is situated on the Ring of Kerry 1.5 miles outside town.
8 rms (6 shr) (2 fmly) No smoking in dining room No dogs Cen ht CTV 10P

Q Q Q **GH Hussey's Bar & Townhouse** 43 High St (on Hight Street towards Tralee Rd) ☎ 064 37454 FAX 064 33144
Closed 27 Oct-11 Mar
In a quiet location on the north-west side of town, with its own pub next door, this is a friendly place where guests and locals mingle. There is a separate breakfast room, and also a TV lounge on the first floor. Bedrooms are attractively decorated, comfortable and well maintained. The car park is at the rear of the house. There are some good restaurants in the neighbourhood.
5 shr No smoking in 5 bedrooms No smoking in dining room CTV in all bedrooms Tea and coffee making facilities Direct dial from bedrooms No dogs Licensed Cen ht No children 10yrs 5P No coaches
ROOMS: s IR£25-IR£30; d IR£36-IR£50✻
CARDS:

Premier Selected

Q Q Q Q Q **GH Kathleen's Country House** Tralee Rd (on N22 3km N) ☎ 064 32810 FAX 064 32340
7 Mar-14 Nov
An exclusive, modern, purpose-built guest house is set in its own lovely gardens one mile from the town centre on the Tralee road. Family-run, luxury accommodation in scenic countryside makes this an ideal touring centre.
17 bth/shr (2 fmly) No smoking CTV in all bedrooms Tea and coffee making facilities Direct dial from bedrooms No dogs Licensed Cen ht No children 5yrs 20P Croquet, reflexology Last d 6pm
ROOMS: s IR£40-IR£75; d IR£60-IR£160✻
CARDS:

Selected

Q Q Q Q **T&C Killarney Villa** Cork-Waterford Rd (N72) (N22 out of town, at rdbt continue on N22, at junct bear left on N72 for 200m) ☎ 064 31878 FAX 064 31878
Etr-Oct
A luxurious country home with roof top conservatory offering complimentary tea/coffee/biscuits from 0700 hrs to 2300 hrs daily. Situated in the heart of the beautiful Killarney lake district and within minutes' drive of the town centre. Family run equipped with all modern comforts, making an ideal holiday destination.
6 bth/shr No smoking CTV in all bedrooms Tea and coffee making facilities Cen ht CTV No children 6yrs 20P Last d 6.30pm
ROOMS: d IR£34-IR£36✻
CARDS:

Q Q Q **GH *Lime Court*** Muckross Rd (5km from town centre) ☎ 064 34547 FAX 064 34121
A very well maintained modern house with spacious sitting room and sun lounge, and well equipped bedrooms with private bathrooms. Many of the rooms have fine views, and some are located on the ground floor. The house is a short walk from the town centre, and there is car parking in front.
12 bth/shr (4 fmly) No smoking in 6 bedrooms No smoking in dining room No smoking in 1 lounge CTV in all bedrooms Tea and coffee making facilities Direct dial from bedrooms No dogs (ex guide dogs) Licensed Cen ht CTV 20P
CARDS:

Selected

Q Q Q Q **T&C Lohan's Lodge** Tralee Rd (3 min drive from Killarney town on N22 towards Tralee) ☎ 064 33871 FAX 064 33871
1 Mar-5 Nov
This luxurious modern bungalow is set in its own landscaped gardens in scenic countryside, 4 minutes drive from the town centre. The proprietors Cathy and Mike Lohan are hospitable and caring hosts. There is a spacious guest lounge and dining room and the breakfast menu is extensive.
5 shr (1 fmly) No smoking CTV in all bedrooms Tea and coffee making facilities No dogs Cen ht CTV No children 7yrs 12P Last d noon
ROOMS: d IR£35-IR£36; wkly b&b IR£120-IR£123✻

Q Q **GH McCarthy's Town House** 19 High St (McCarthy's Townhouse is located in high street (Town Centre)) ☎ 064 35655 FAX 064 35745
Town centre accommodation next door to the Crock of Gold bar and restaurant, and run by the same owners. Comfortable new en-suite bedrooms are available on the first and second floors - the latter with large roof windows but no views, and guests can relax in the TV lounge. A rear car park offers off-street parking.
8 shr (2 fmly) CTV in all bedrooms Direct dial from bedrooms No dogs Licensed Cen ht CTV 10P Last d 9.30pm
ROOMS: s IR£25-IR£30; d IR£45-IR£50; wkly b&b IR£155-IR£160✻
CARDS:

Q Q Q T&C *Nashville* Tralee Rd
(2m from Killarney on main Dublin/Limerick road, N22) ☎ 064 32924
March-November
This white, double-fronted house on the main N22 road is about two miles from Killarney and very easy to find. The large bedrooms are bright, cheerful, and well equipped. Anne and David Nash and their family are very welcoming hosts.
6 shr (2 fmly) No smoking in 3 bedrooms CTV in all bedrooms Tea and coffee making facilities No dogs Cen ht CTV 10P Golf Fishing Horse riding available within 3km

Selected

Q Q Q Q **GH Old Weir Lodge** Muckross Rd
(on main Muckross Rd, 500m from Killarney Town)
☎ 064 35593 FAX 064 35583
Maureen and Dermot O'Donoghue are the welcoming owners of this purpose-built, Tudor-style lodge which is set in attractive gardens and within walking distance of the centre. Maureen O'Donoghue loves to cook, and home-baking is a feature of the breakfasts, with evening meals by arrangement. Her husband will help guests with leisure activities such as boat trips on the Killarney Lakes, or golf and fishing. The comfortable bedrooms are equipped to a high standard, and there is a delightful sitting room overlooking the gardens. There is a drying room, and ample off-street parking.
15 bth/shr No smoking in 10 bedrooms No smoking in dining room No smoking in lounges CTV in all bedrooms Tea and coffee making facilities Direct dial from bedrooms No dogs Cen ht CTV ch fac 15P
ROOMS: s IR£25-IR£35; d IR£40-IR£56*
CARDS:

Q Q Q **GH *Park Lodge*** Cork Rd (premises situated on Park Rd off roundabout on N22 Cork/Mallow entrance road to town)
☎ 064 31539 FAX 064 34892
Closed 23-26 Dec & 4 Jan-1 Feb
A large purpose-built double-fronted guest house with good parking set on the Cork road beside the Killarney Ryan Hotel. The spacious, well equipped bedrooms overlook the front and rear gardens. Park Lodge is just a short walk from the town centre.
20 shr (1 fmly) No smoking in 4 bedrooms No smoking in dining room CTV in all bedrooms Tea and coffee making facilities Direct dial from bedrooms No dogs Cen ht CTV 24P
CARDS:

Selected

Q Q Q Q **T&C Shraheen House** Ballycasheen
(on the Ballycasheen/Woodlawn Rd 1m off N71 turn off at the Shell station. 0.25m off N22 Cork Rd at the white bridge sign)
☎ 064 37959 FAX 064 37959
Closed Xmas & New Year
Located on a quiet road, this large modern house is set in two acres. The bedrooms are all well equipped and have attractive soft furnishings. The quiet gardens and the pleasant sun lounge are very relaxing. Within easy reach of three golf courses or local fishing.
6 bth/shr (2 fmly) No smoking CTV in all bedrooms Tea and coffee making facilities No dogs Cen ht CTV 8P
ROOMS: s IR£25-IR£32; d IR£36-IR£38

Q Q **T&C Sliabh Luachra House** Loretto Rd ☎ 064 32012
Apr-Sep
A fine modern house in delightful gardens on a quiet residential road off Muckross Road, and about 1.5 miles from the town centre. Rooms vary in size, but all are furnished to the same degree of comfort. Private parking is available.
6 shr (1 fmly) No smoking in bedrooms No smoking in dining room No smoking in 1 lounge Tea and coffee making facilities No dogs (ex guide dogs) Cen ht CTV No children 12yrs 6P
ROOMS: d IR£36-IR£38*

KILLEAGH Co Cork Map 01 C2

Selected

Q Q Q Q ❦ **Ballymakeigh House** *(X 006776)*
(located 6 miles west of Youghal on N25 signposted Killeagh Village at 'Old Thatch')
☎ 024 95184 FAX 024 95370 Mrs Browne
12 Feb-1 Nov
Hospitable Margaret Browne, winner of many awards, makes guests feel very much at home in her delightful, 250-year-old farmhouse. The cheerful bedrooms are attractively decorated and an elegant dining room provides the setting for a five-course dinner served every evening.
6 bth/shr (6 fmly) No smoking in dining room TV available No dogs (ex guide dogs) Licensed Cen ht CTV ch fac 10P Tennis (hard) Riding Snooker Games room 180 acres dairy Last d 6pm
ROOMS: s IR£35-IR£40; d IR£60; wkly b&b fr IR£200; wkly hlf-bd fr IR£320*
CARDS:

See advertisement under Youghal

Q Q Q **T&C *Tattans*** (on N25, between Midleton and Youghal on Cork Rosslare route) ☎ 024 95173 FAX 024 95173
Mar-Oct
A town house with its own car park stands on the main N25 Cork-Rosslare road. It offers comfortable bedrooms, a TV room, large attractive gardens and a hard tennis court. Bar snacks are served throughout the day and evening meals are available to residents.
5 rms (4 shr) (3 fmly) No dogs Licensed Cen ht CTV 8P Tennis Last d 10pm
CARDS:

KILLORGLIN Co Kerry Map 01 A2

Q Q Q ❦ **Dromin Farmhouse** *(V806902)*
(3km from Killorglin. Turn off N70 about 1km from Killroglin after the factory then straight for 2km to house) ☎ 066 61867 Mrs M Foley
17 Mar-Oct
Set on a sheep and cattle farm with fantastic mountain views, this elevated bungalow is conveniently near to local beaches, golf, fishing and horse-riding. A private TV lounge is available for guests, and babysitting can be arranged. Evening meals are served, but reservations are appreciated.
4 rms (3 shr) (2 fmly) No smoking in dining room No smoking in lounges Tea and coffee making facilities Cen ht CTV 10P 42 acres dairy sheep Last d mid-day
ROOMS: s IR£20-IR£23; d IR£30-IR£35; wkly b&b IR£105-IR£120*
CARDS:

Selected

Q Q Q Q **T&C Grove Lodge** Killarney Rd (0.5 mile from Killorglin Bridge on Killarney road-N72) ☎ 066 61157 FAX 066 62330
Closed Dec
A lovely riverside house recently extended and developed to a high standard, with all the rooms en suite and fully equipped. Mrs Foley is an enthusiastic host who likes to please her guests and for those who just want to relax there is a patio seating area in the garden by the river.
contd.

10 bth/shr (4 fmly) No smoking in bedrooms No smoking in dining room CTV in all bedrooms Tea and coffee making facilities Direct dial from bedrooms No dogs (ex guide dogs) Cen ht 15P
ROOMS: s IR£25-IR£35; d IR£50-IR£64*
CARDS:

KILMACTHOMAS Co Waterford Map **01** C2

Q Q Q T&C Coumshingaun Lodge Kilclooney
(turn N from N25 onto R676 at Leamybrien, house is 6m on right)
☎ 051 646238
1 Apr-30 Sept
A two-storey house at the bottom of Comeragh Mountains and ideal for exploring them on foot. Well furnished bedrooms all enjoy spectacular mountain views. A pleasant relaxed atmosphere prevails, a hospitality tray is available all afternoon, and there is a wide range of tourist literature. Evening meals are provided.
5 shr (3 fmly) No smoking in 3 bedrooms No smoking in dining room No smoking in lounges Tea and coffee making facilities No dogs (ex guide dogs) Licensed Cen ht CTV 6P No coaches Last d 12pm
ROOMS: d IR£40; wkly b&b IR£130; wkly hlf-bd IR£230
CARDS:

KILMALLOCK Co Limerick Map **01** B3

Selected

Q Q Q Q Flemingstown House *(R 629255)*
(on Kilmallock/Fermoy R512 road, establishment 2m from Kilmallock)
☎ 063 98093 FAX 063 98546 Mrs I Sheedy-King
Mar-Oct
A lovely 18th-century farmhouse which has been modernised to provide stylish en-suite facilities throughout. Public rooms include a comfortably furnished sitting room with antiques, and a two-part dining room with beautiful stained glass windows. Imelda Sheedy-King produces an award-winning breakfast, and much of the produce comes from her own farm. She will provide dinner for her guests by arrangement. The farm is on the Limerick/Mitchelstown road, has good car parking and the countryside is excellent for walkers, riders, anglers and golfers.
5 shr (2 fmly) No smoking CTV in 3 bedrooms Tea and coffee making facilities No dogs (ex guide dogs) Cen ht CTV 40P Riding 102 acres dairy Last d 3pm
ROOMS: s IR£30; d IR£40; wkly b&b IR£135; wkly hlf-bd IR£270*
CARDS:

KILMORE QUAY Co Wexford Map **01** D2

Q Q Q GH Quay House Kilmore Quay (turn off N25 onto R739 following sign to Kilmore Quay, house on left after Hotel Saltees)
☎ 053 29988 FAX 053 29808
6 bth/shr (6 fmly) No smoking in bedrooms No smoking in dining room CTV in all bedrooms Tea and coffee making facilities Direct dial from bedrooms No dogs (ex guide dogs) Licensed Cen ht 16P Angling and diving facilities
ROOMS: s IR£22-IR£29; d IR£36-IR£50; wkly b&b IR£126-IR£175*
CARDS:

KILRUSH Co Clare Map **01** B3

Q Q Q T&C ***Bruach-na-Coille*** Killimer Rd (on Kilrush to Killimere Rd, 1km from Kilrush) ☎ 065 9052250 FAX 065 9052250
Closed 25 Dec
An impressive modern house set back from the road on half a mile for the centre of Kilrush. The bedrooms are comfortable and well equipped and the house is set in attractive gardens facing Kilrush Wood where guests can enjoy an evening stroll.
4 rms (2 shr) No smoking in bedrooms No smoking in dining room No smoking in 1 lounge CTV in all bedrooms Tea and coffee making facilities No dogs (ex guide dogs) Cen ht CTV 8P

KILTEGAN Co Wicklow Map **01** D3

Selected

Q Q Q Q T&C Barraderry House ☎ 0508 73209
FAX 0508 73209
Closed 15 Dec-15 Jan
A granite stone gateway is the entrance to this restored Georgian house half a mile from Kiltegan. The drawing room is adjacent to the TV study, and breakfast is served in the dining room. Light evening meals are available if booked in advance. The bedrooms are all furnished in keeping with the period of the house and have new en suite bathrooms.
4 shr (2 fmly) No smoking CTV in 2 bedrooms Tea and coffee making facilities No dogs Cen ht CTV 12P
ROOMS: s IR£22.50-IR£25; d IR£45-IR£50*

KINSALE Co Cork Map **01** B2

Selected

Q Q Q Q GH Long Quay House Long Quay
(on right immediately after entering town centre from R600, before Super Valu supermarket. House covered in Virginia Creeper)
☎ 021 774563 & 773201
Closed 1-26 Dec
Centrally located overlooking the inner harbour and yacht marina, Long Quay House is a restored Georgian town house with very comfortable bedrooms and a large conservatory lounge. Local amenities include sailing, fishing, golf and sandy beaches.
7 bth/shr (2 fmly) No smoking in area of dining room CTV in all bedrooms Tea and coffee making facilities Direct dial from bedrooms No dogs (ex guide dogs) Cen ht CTV No coaches
ROOMS: s IR£30-IR£45; d IR£45-IR£60; wkly b&b IR£140-IR£180*
CARDS:

Selected

Q Q Q Q GH Old Bank House 11 Pearse St
(main road between Cork City and Cork Airport, we are located on the right hand side at the start of Kinsale Town next door to Post Office)
☎ 021 774075 FAX 021 774296
Closed 23-26 Dec rs Nov-mid Dec 98
Under the personal supervision of Marie and Michael Riese, this delightful Georgian house - once a bank house - has been restored to its former elegance. The en suite bedrooms, with period furniture and attractive decor, combine charm with modern comforts. Dinner is offered in the owners' restaurant. Tee-off times, sailing, deep sea fishing and horse riding can be arranged. Irish, French and German spoken.
9 bth/shr (2 fmly) No smoking in dining room No smoking in lounges CTV in all bedrooms Direct dial from bedrooms Licensed Lift Cen ht No children 7yrs P No coaches
ROOMS: s IR£40-IR£70; d IR£80-IR£140; wkly b&b IR£245-IR£385
CARDS:

Selected

Q Q Q Q **T&C Old Presbytery** 43 Cork St
(from Cork Rd go to the end of Pearce St, turn left, first right and first right again, establishment is on right hand side opposite Parish Church)
☎ 021 772166 FAX 021 772166
Closed 24-28 Dec
This charming period house in the centre of town is on a quiet street. The comfortable lounge is elegant, and there is a delightful breakfast room. The en suite bedrooms are traditional, with stripped pine furnishings, brass beds and interesting memorabilia. One bedroom has external access via a staircase and is very peaceful. Philip and Noreen McEvoy offer warm hospitality, and sailing and sea fishing are available in this Mediterranean-style sea port, which has plenty of excellent restaurants. Reservations are advised.
6 bth/shr No smoking CTV in 5 bedrooms Tea and coffee making facilities No dogs (ex guide dogs) CTV 6P No coaches
ROOMS: s IR£35-IR£50; d IR£50-IR£70

Selected

Q Q Q Q **T&C Old Rectory** Rampart Ln
(drive past St Multose church on left, where rd veers sharp right fro Branden go straight through narrow gap, Rampart Ln is on left after estate) ☎ 021 772678 FAX 021 772678
Closed 21 Dec-1 Jan rs Jan-Feb & Nov-Dec
A former rectory stands in an acre of sunny gardens away from the bustle of the nearby town centre. It has been lovingly restored to provide luxury guest accommodation with the emphasis on comfort and relaxation.
3 bth/shr No smoking in bedrooms No smoking in dining room CTV in 1 bedroom No dogs Licensed Cen ht CTV No children 10yrs 4P No coaches
ROOMS: s IR£50-IR£75; d IR£80-IR£120*
CARDS:

Q Q Q **T&C Orchard Cottage** Farrangalway
(off R607 at sign for Orchard Cottage) ☎ 021 772693
4 bth/shr (2 fmly) No smoking in bedrooms No smoking in dining room CTV in all bedrooms Tea and coffee making facilities No dogs (ex guide dogs) 10P Golf 18
ROOMS: s IR£25; d IR£36*
CARDS:

Premier Selected

Q Q Q Q Q **GH *Perryville House*** ☎ 021 772731 FAX 021 772298
Perryville House is a Georgian house in the centre of town which has been completely restored to a luxurious standard. Afternoon tea is taken in the elegant drawing room and breakfast is served buffet style. Bedrooms are spacious and furnished with antique pieces, and all have new en suite facilities.

Selected

Q Q Q Q **T&C Rivermount House** Knocknabinny, Barrells Cross
(take R600 west towards Old Head of Kinsale, turn right at Barrelscross (2 miles from Kinsale)) ☎ 021 778033 & 778225 FAX 021 778225
1 Feb-1 Dec
This charming house is immaculately kept and surrounded by lovely gardens, a patio and a children's play area. Attractive bedrooms are well equipped and furnished to a high standard and there is a fine, big sitting room with a sun lounge. Evening meals and packed lunches can be provided on request. The house is 4 km from Kinsale, overlooking the River Bandon near a superbly sited new golf course, the Old Head Golf Links. Sea angling and bicycle hire can be arranged.
6 shr (3 fmly) No smoking in bedrooms No smoking in dining room No smoking in 1 lounge CTV in all bedrooms Tea and coffee making facilities Direct dial from bedrooms No dogs (ex guide dogs) Cen ht CTV 10P
ROOMS: s IR£25-IR£35; d IR£38-IR£45;
wkly b&b IR£145-IR£155*
CARDS:

Q Q Q **T&C Waterlands** Cork Rd (follow R600 Road to Kinsale, turn off at 'Welcome to Kinsale' sign, Waterlands sign at this junct, turn right)
☎ 021 772318 & 087 276 7917 FAX 021 774873
Feb-Oct
A house on an elevated site, providing luxury accommodation. A south-facing conservatory breakfast room overlooks the picturesque gardens and serves an extensive breakfast menu. The comfortable, well decorated en suite bedrooms have electric blankets, hair dryers and clock radios. The airport and ferry are a short drive.
4 shr (2 fmly) No smoking CTV in all bedrooms Tea and coffee making facilities No dogs Cen ht CTV 10P No coaches
ROOMS: s IR£26-IR£30; d IR£36-IR£44*
CARDS:

KNOCK Co Mayo Map 01 B4

Q Q **T&C *Aishling House*** Ballyhaunis Rd ☎ 094 88558
A white house standing in its own grounds with good street parking and attractive gardens. Four of the bedrooms are en suite and the fifth is on the ground floor; all are equipped with TVs. Guests have use of two cosy sitting rooms and a separate breakfast room. The friendly owner has information about visits to the famous Knock Shrine, and lake fishing, archaeological sites, golf and riding can all be found locally. Dinner and high tea are available if reserved.
5 rms (4 shr) (2 fmly) CTV in all bedrooms No dogs (ex guide dogs) Cen ht CTV 10P Last d 5pm

See page 14-20 for a list of Premier Selected establishments

KNOCKTOPHER Co Kilkenny Map **01** C3

Selected

Q Q Q Q **T&C *Knocktopher Hall*** ☎ 056 68626 FAX 056 68626
Closed 15 Dec-2 Jan
Built in 1740, this fine example of Georgian country house has been lovingly decorated and furnished by its new owners John and Carmel Wilson who bought the house in late 1996. Many of the fine period furnishings have come from their previous old country house. The four en-suite bedrooms boast antique French beds and other period pieces of note. John and Carmel share their enthusiasm for cooking when their guests order dinner.
4 shr (1 fmly) No smoking Tea and coffee making facilities No dogs (ex guide dogs) Licensed Cen ht 14P No coaches Membership of leisure club Last d noon

KYLEMORE Co Galway Map **01** C3

Q Q Q **T&C Kylemore House** (turn off N59 from Galway at Recess onto R344) ☎ 095 41143 FAX 095 41143
May-Oct
Standing on the shores of Lake Kylemore, protected by the Twelve Pins Mountains, this comfortable house has fishing rights on three lakes in the scenic area of Connemara. Owner Mrs Naughton takes pride in her cooking and serves evening meals by prior arrangement.
6 bth/shr (1 fmly) No smoking in 1 lounge Tea and coffee making facilities No dogs (ex guide dogs) Licensed Cen ht CTV No children 10yrs 8P No coaches Fishing Boat hire Last d 4pm
ROOMS: s IR£25; d IR£36-IR£38 ✻

LARAGH Co Wicklow Map **01** D3

Q Q Q **T&C Carmel's** Annamoe ☎ 0404 45297 FAX 45297
Etr-Oct
A well kept bungalow near Laragh and Glendalough which has recently been refurbished. Mrs Hawkins ensures that guests are well prepared for a days touring in this lovely area. The personal touches in this house create a warm feeling of care of attention.
4 shr (2 fmly) No dogs Cen ht CTV 4P No coaches Last d noon
ROOMS: d IR£36✻

LARNE Co Antrim Map **01** D5

Q Q Q **GH Derrin** 2 Prince's Gardens BT40 1RQ (access via A2) ☎ 01574 273269 & 273762 FAX 01574 273269
Closed 25 & 26 Dec
Enthusiastic owner Eileen Mills looks forward to welcoming you to her comfortable detached home which is located on the north side of town within easy reach of the Ferry Terminal. The well maintained bedrooms are smartly decorated and comfortably furnished in modern style and offer a wide range of amenities. The spacious lounge invites peaceful relaxation while a good choice of breakfast dishes are offered in the attractive dining room.
6 rms (4 shr) (2 fmly) No smoking in dining room CTV in all bedrooms Tea and coffee making facilities Cen ht CTV 5P No coaches
ROOMS: s £20-£25; d £32-£36✻
CARDS:

Selected

Q Q Q Q **GH Manor** 23 Older Fleet Rd, Harbour Highway BT40 1AS (2 minutes walk from Larne Ferry Terminal & Harbour Train Station) ☎ 01574 273305 FAX 01574 260505
Manor Guest House is conveniently located just a few minutes walk from the Larne Ferries and the Harbour station, and has the added bonus of secure car parking to the rear. Guests will enjoy the elegance and charm of the splendid lounge. Breakfast is served in a separate dining room, and is available by prior arrangement. The immaculately maintained bedrooms are very decorative, many boast period pieces, and all have good facilities. One spacious room has an attractive four poster bed.
8 bth/shr (2 fmly) No smoking CTV in all bedrooms Tea and coffee making facilities Cen ht 6P
ROOMS: s £20; d £35-£36✻
CARDS:

LEENANE Co Galway Map **01** A4

Selected

Q Q Q Q **GH Killary Lodge** ☎ 095 42276 & 42245 FAX 095 42314
Mar-Oct rs Nov-Feb
11 bth/shr 9 annexe bth/shr (8 fmly) No smoking in dining room Direct dial from bedrooms No dogs (ex guide dogs) Licensed Cen ht 30P Tennis (hard) Sauna Mountain biking Rock climbing sailing kayaking Last d 8pm
ROOMS: s IR£29-IR£37; d IR£58-IR£64; wkly b&b IR£193-IR£243; wkly hlf-bd IR£323-IR£379
CARDS:

LETTERKENNY Co Donegal Map **01** C5

Premier Selected

Q Q Q Q Q **GH *Castle Grove Country House & Restaurant*** Castle Grove, Ballymaleel ☎ 074 51118 FAX 074 51384
Closed 8-30 Jan rs Feb-1 Apr/Nov-8 Dec (Rest closedSun/Mon)
Dating from the late 17th century, this magnificent country house is at the end of a mile-long drive and surrounded by lovely grounds. A major extension in matching dimensions has enhanced facilities without loss of atmosphere or charm. Luxuriously furnished throughout with fine antiques, the fine public rooms have blazing log fires in winter, while a notable restaurant offers menus to tempt the palate. This is gracious country living at its best, with services to match, in a happy blend of old-world style with the best modern facilities.
8 bth/shr (3 fmly) No smoking in 5 bedrooms No smoking in dining room Direct dial from bedrooms No dogs Licensed Cen ht CTV No children 8yrs 30P No coaches Fishing Last d 9.15pm
CARDS:

Q Q Q T&C Hill Crest House Lurgybrack, Sligo Rd
(take N14 to Derry, at Dryarch roundabout turn right onto N13 to Sligo & proceed for 1m, house at top of hill on right)
☎ 074 22300 & 25137 FAX 074 25137
rs Xmas wk
Set on the outskirts of Letterkenny, this modern bungalow has a pleasant sitting room and a breakfast room. All the bedrooms have en suite facilities, except one which has sole use of an adjacent bathroom. A good base for touring north Donegal and the Giant's Causeway.
6 rms (5 shr) (3 fmly) No smoking in bedrooms No smoking in dining room CTV in all bedrooms Tea and coffee making facilities No dogs (ex guide dogs) Cen ht CTV 12P
ROOMS: s IR£22-IR£30; d IR£32-IR£36*
CARDS:

Selected

Q Q Q Q T&C *Pennsylvania House* Curraghleas, Mountain Top
☎ 074 26808 FAX 074 28905
Closed Xmas
The panoramic Donegal hills make a stunning setting for this distinctive purpose-built guest house, two miles from Letterkenny. A sense of space, warm colours and personal touches contribute to the inviting feel of this house, and accommodation includes a fine sitting room and dining room, and five bedrooms. The Duddys, recently returned from running a B & B in the US, are welcoming hosts. Smoking only in the garden.
5 shr No smoking CTV in all bedrooms Direct dial from bedrooms No dogs Cen ht No children 12yrs 10P Many facilities are available nearby
CARDS:

LIMERICK Co Limerick Map 01 B3

Q Q Q GH Clifton House Ennis Rd
(on direct route to Shannon airport N18, opposite Woodfield House Hotel)
☎ 061 451166 FAX 061 451224
Closed 18 Dec-4 Jan
Providing well equipped, attractive and very comfortable bedrooms has been the aim of the refurbishment of Michael and Mary Powell's guest house. Complimentary tea and coffee are available in the spacious, relaxing lounge and there is an excellent car park.
16 bth/shr CTV in all bedrooms Direct dial from bedrooms No dogs (ex guide dogs) Cen ht 22P
ROOMS: s IR£25-IR£28; d IR£40-IR£45*
CARDS:

Selected

Q Q Q Q T&C *Cloneen House* Ennis Rd ☎ 061 454461
FAX 061 455545
Closed 22 Dec-7 Jan
Attractive, comfortable three storey terrace house only ten minutes from the city centre. Secure parking at rear. Excellent information on local restaurants and entertainment.
6 bth/shr No smoking in dining room CTV in all bedrooms Tea and coffee making facilities No dogs (ex guide dogs) Cen ht 5P
No coaches
CARDS:

Q Q Q GH Clonmacken House Clonmacken, off Ennis Rd
(on N18, turn left at Ivan's shop) ☎ 061 327007 FAX 061 3327007
Closed 24 Dec-4 Jan
Clonmacken House is located close to the city centre, with good car parking in the gardens. The accommodation is comfortable throughout, and facilities include a TV lounge, breakfast room, and en-suite bedrooms which are all attractively decorated and very comfortable.
10 shr (6 fmly) No smoking in 4 bedrooms No smoking in dining room CTV in all bedrooms Tea and coffee making facilities Direct dial from bedrooms No dogs (ex guide dogs) Cen ht CTV 25P
ROOMS: s IR£25-IR£28; d IR£36-IR£45; wkly b&b IR£126-IR£140*
CARDS:

LISBURN Co Antrim Map 01 D5

Selected

Q Q Q Q ❦ Brook Lodge *(J3315608)* 79 Old Ballynahinch Rd, Cargacroy BT27 6TH (M1 exit 6, Ballynahich A49, 3.5m)
☎ 01846 638454 Mrs D Moore
Just off the A49 some three mile south of the M1 is where you will find Mrs Dulcibel Moore's delightful modern bungalow. Surrounded by pleasant countryside, the house offers a welcoming atmosphere and personal attention is assured. Bedrooms, though variable in size, are bright and airy with comfortable modern furnishings, and one room is suitable for disabled use. Public areas include an inviting lounge and smart dining room.
6 rms (4 shr) No smoking in dining room No smoking in lounges CTV in 4 bedrooms No dogs (ex guide dogs) Cen ht CTV 10P
65 acres mixed

LISDOONVARNA Co Clare Map 01 B3

Q Q Q T&C Ore' A Tava House
(1km from town on N67, turn left at water pump, 3rd house on left)
☎ 065 74086 FAX 065 74547
20 Mar-30 Oct

contd.

Situated half a mile from Lisdoonvarna, in a quiet area off the Ballyvaughan road, Ore' A Tava House offers attractive public rooms which include a new conservatory lounge; some bedrooms are located on the ground floor and good car parking facilities are available.
6 bth/shr (2 fmly) No smoking in dining room No smoking in lounges CTV in 4 bedrooms Direct dial from bedrooms No dogs (ex guide dogs) Cen ht CTV 6P
ROOMS: d IR£34-IR£36*
CARDS:

LISMORE Co Waterford Map **01** C2

T&C ***Beechcroft*** Deerpark
(opposite Presentation Convent School) ☎ 058 54273
Closed 15 Dec-1 Jan
Guests experience truly warm hospitality at this pleasant guest house in the heritage town of Lismore, where stately Lismore Castle is the Irish residence of the Duke of Devonshire. Bedrooms are prettily decorated in appealing colours, and all are en suite. Down-filled sofa and armchairs encourage relaxation in the sitting room, and there are loungers in the lovely gardens. Secure parking is available.
3 shr No smoking in bedrooms No smoking in area of dining room Tea and coffee making facilities Cen ht CTV 8P No coaches

LISNASKEA Co Fermanagh Map **01** C5

GH Colorado 102 Lisnagole Rd BT92 0QF
(turn off main Belfast Rd at Maguires bridge on A34 1m on left before Lisnaskea) ☎ 013657 21486 FAX 013657 21486
Closed Xmas day
Eileen Scott's comfortable detached home stands between Maguiresbridge and Lisnaskea. The variable sized bedrooms are bright and airy with comfortable modern appointments. Public areas include a small TV lounge and a more spacious lounge adjacent to the dining room. Here you can enjoy a hearty Ulster breakfast and, by prior arrangement, a home cooked evening meal. Table sharing may be necessary at peak times.
8 rms (1 shr) (2 fmly) No smoking CTV in 1 bedroom Tea and coffee making facilities No dogs (ex guide dogs) Licensed Cen ht CTV 20P
ROOMS: s fr £18; d fr £32*

MALLOW Co Cork Map **01** B2

Selected

GH ***Cortigan House***
(from town centre pass Mallow tourist office, straight through traffic lights turn left, house signposted 300 mtrs on left)
☎ 022 22770 FAX 022 22770
Closed 23 Dec-2 Jan
A period residence set in its own peaceful grounds adjacent to the golf club, and within a few minutes walk of the town centre and all the amenities. The proprietors Sheila and Lionel Buckley are friendly and have the gift of making their guests feel immediately welcome and at home. Bedrooms are attractively decorated and furnished, and all are en suite. The gardens overlook a river where salmon and trout fishing is available.
6 shr (3 fmly) No smoking in 2 bedrooms No smoking in dining room No smoking in 1 lounge CTV in all bedrooms Tea and coffee making facilities Direct dial from bedrooms No dogs Cen ht CTV 10P
CARDS:

Selected

T&C Greenfield House Navigation Rd
(turn off N20 at Mallow rdbt onto N72 Killarney Rd, establishment 300m last house on left) ☎ 022 50231
6 shr (3 fmly) CTV in all bedrooms Tea and coffee making facilities No dogs Cen ht CTV Golf
ROOMS: s IR£20; d IR£40*

T&C Oaklands House Springwood, (off N72)
(turn off Killarney road (N72) at railway bridge (signposted))
☎ 022 21127 FAX 022 21127
Mar-Oct
Situated in a quiet residential area on the edge of town near the fast new N20 Winifred O'Donovan's home is inviting and attractively decorated throughout. The atmosphere is particularly tranquil, with a dining room that overlooks the lovley gardens where guests can sit and enjoy the fruits of Winifred's dedicated work.
4 shr (1 fmly) No smoking in bedrooms Tea and coffee making facilities No dogs (ex guide dogs) Cen ht CTV 6P
ROOMS: s fr IR£25; d fr IR£36
CARDS:

MIDLETON Co Cork Map **01** C2

Selected

GH ***Barnabrow Country House*** Cloyne
☎ 021 652534 FAX 021 652534
Burnabrow has been completely restored by its new owners and is an eclectic mix of old world charm and modern standards. There is also an African influence in some of the striking furniture. There are five bedrooms in the main house and more in the coach house and stone house. There is also a bar, patio gardens and a restaurant where there is an emphasis on organic produce.

The AA's professional Inspectors make regular and anonymous visits to all the establishments listed in the Guide. They accept no gifts or favours from proprietors

Selected

T&C Old Parochial House Castlemartyr
(at Castlemartyr on N25 take turn for Garryvoe/Ballycotton, first on left) ☎ 021 667454 FAX 021 667429
3 Jan-20 Dec
Kathy and Frank Sheehy are welcoming hosts that make guests feel instantly at ease in this lovely recently restored Georgian house. The drawing and dining rooms are furnished with antiques and have open fires. Two of the attractive bedrooms have four-poster beds, and all have good facilities.
3 bth/shr (3 fmly) No smoking in bedrooms No smoking in dining room CTV in all bedrooms Tea and coffee making facilities No dogs (ex guide dogs) Cen ht
ROOMS: d IR£30-IR£40*
CARDS:

MOATE Co Westmeath Map **01** C4

Selected

Temple *(N 267395)* Horseleap
(0.5m off N6, signposted)
☎ 0506 35118 FAX 0506 35118
Mr & Mrs D Fagan
Mar-1 Nov
A Georgian house with 100 acres, built on the site of an early monastery, this sympathetically refurbished farmhouse near the village of Horseleap (midway between Kilbeggan and Moate and half a mile from the N6) offers accommodation in very comfortable en suite bedrooms. Dinner - which must be reserved in advance - is taken round a fine hunting table, then guests can relax by the sitting room fire and join in the chat. Activity packages (golf, riding, cycling or walking) can be arranged here.
4 bth/shr (2 fmly) No smoking in dining room CTV in all bedrooms Tea and coffee making facilities No dogs (ex guide dogs) Licensed Cen ht ch fac Yoga room Massage therapy Children's play room 96 acres cattle sheep Last d 10am
CARDS:

MOUNTRATH Co Laois Map **01** C3

GH ***Roundwood House*** (from Mountrath continue on R440 towards Slieve Bloom Mountains house is 3m from Mountrath) ☎ 0502 32120 FAX 0502 32711
Closed 24-25 Dec
This Palladian villa, in a secluded woodland setting, transports one back in time to an era of grace and leisure. Excellent hospitality and good food are offered by hosts Frank and Rosemarie Keenan.
6 bth 4 annexe bth/shr (2 fmly) No smoking in bedrooms No dogs (ex guide dogs) Licensed Cen ht ch fac 20P No coaches Croquet Boule Last d 5pm
CARDS:

MOYARD Co Galway Map **01** A4

Rose Cottage *(L 673565)* Rockfield
(N59 from Galway to Clifden, 6m from Clifden on the Westport Rd)
☎ 095 41082 FAX 095 41112 Mrs M O'Toole
Apr-Oct
A lovely old style family run farmhouse in one of the most scenic area of Connemara, surrounded by the Twelve Bens Mountains range. A warm welcome awaits the arriving guest who can enjoy tea or coffee and home baking by the open turf fire. Evening meals are available. All bedrooms are en suite, recently upgraded and comfortable. Fishing, sandy beaches and local attractions within easy reach.
6 shr (2 fmly) No smoking in bedrooms Tea and coffee making facilities No dogs (ex guide dogs) Cen ht CTV 10P 36 acres mixed
CARDS:

MULLINGAR Co Westmeath Map **01** C4

Premier Selected

GH **Crookedwood House**
Crookedwood (from Dublin take second exit off Mullingar Bypass, continue to Crookedwood village, at Wood Pub turn right, and continue for 2km)
☎ 044 72165 FAX 044 72166
Closed 2 wks Jan
As charming as its name, this beautifully restored old rectory overlooks Lake Derravaragh and offers exceptionally comfortable bedrooms. There is also an inviting lounge where tea is served, and a bar for drinks before dinner. The evening meals are the highlight of a stay here, and have earned great praise for chef/patron Niall Kenny.
8 bth/shr No smoking in 4 bedrooms No smoking in dining room CTV in all bedrooms Direct dial from bedrooms Licensed Cen ht P Tennis (hard) Last d 9.30pm
ROOMS: s IR£45-IR£55; d IR£90-IR£110*
CARDS:

Selected

T&C Hilltop House Delvin Rd (N52 off N4), Rathconnell (take 2nd exit off Mullingar by-pass road (N4) and follow N52 sign for Delvin, Hilltop sign is 1km from exit rdbt)
☎ 044 48958 FAX 044 48013
Closed 20 Dec-7 Jan
A charming country house in glorious gardens, where flowers and shrubs fill every available space – the creative artwork of the unassuming owner, Sean Casey. This south facing house is well designed and elevated reception rooms have an attractive patio garden adjacent to them. The bedrooms are very comfortable with good en-suite showers. There is a hospitality buffet for tea/coffee lovers in the bedroom corridor. The breakfast menu is excellent with an extensive range of choice, dinner is by advance reservation only. Dympna and Sean Casey will do everything posible to ensure happy visits to their home.
5 shr No smoking CTV in all bedrooms No dogs (ex guide dogs) Cen ht CTV 6P No coaches Last d 24hrs prior
ROOMS: s IR£25; d IR£40*

Selected

QQQQ ♥ **Lough Owel Lodge** *(N 431535)* Cullion
(N4 from Dublin towards Sligo, after third exit for Mullingar, lodge is signposted on left after 1km at lake and a further 1km to house.)
☎ 044 48714 FAX 044 48771 Mr & Mrs M Ginnell
At the end of a short wooded driveway, this secluded farm house has five en suite bedrooms, two with four-poster beds and all with views of farmland and the lake. Leisure facilities include a games room, tennis court, and a boating centre at the lough. Evening meals are served round a large communal table. There is also a lounge for guest use.
5 bth/shr (1 fmly) No smoking in bedrooms No smoking in dining room No dogs (ex guide dogs) Cen ht CTV Tennis (hard) Fishing Games room 52 acres sheep cows Last d 3pm
ROOMS: s IR£22.50-IR£24.50; d IR£35-IR£38✳
CARDS:

NAVAN Co Meath Map **01** C4

Selected

QQQQ **T&C Killyon** Dublin Rd (on N3, River Boyne side, opposite Ardboyne Hotel) ☎ 046 71224 FAX 046 72766
This luxurious house enjoys fine views over the River Boyne from its balcony, and is located on the Dublin Road opposite the Ardboyne Hotel. Comfortable, well-appointed bedrooms and an invitingly attractive lounge make this a popular place to stay, and owner Mrs Fogarty offers a wide range of home cooking.
4 bth/shr (1 fmly) No smoking in 2 bedrooms No smoking in dining room No smoking in lounges CTV in all bedrooms Direct dial from bedrooms No dogs (ex guide dogs) Cen ht CTV 12P Last d noon
ROOMS: s IR£25; d IR£40-IR£50✳
CARDS:

NEWBRIDGE Co Kildare Map **01** C3

Selected

QQQQ **GH** ***Gables*** Ryston, Kilcullen Rd
(from Dublin exit M7 at junc 8), ☎ 045 435330 FAX 045 435355
Closed 23 Dec-2 Jan
The River Liffey curves gently by this well appointed house. Lovely views can be had from the dining room, and the pool, sauna and jacuzzi all make for a very relaxing stay.
9 bth/shr CTV in all bedrooms Tea and coffee making facilities Direct dial from bedrooms No dogs (ex guide dogs) Cen ht 40P Indoor swimming pool (heated) Fishing Sauna Gymnasium Jacuzzi, steam bath
CARDS:

NEW ROSS Co Wexford Map **01** C3

QQQ **T&C** ***Carbery*** Mountgarrett ☎ 051 422742
May-Sep
Set in a pleasant residential area in large gardens, Carbery offers high standards of comfort in attractively decorated, en suite bedrooms. There is also a spacious sitting room and a dining room overlooking the patio and gardens. Mrs Casey is a friendly hostess and the house is ideally placed for touring Killarney and Wexford, just one mile north of New Ross. There are golf courses and many places of historic interest in the area.
3 rms (1 fmly) No dogs (ex guide dogs) Cen ht CTV

NEWTOWNARDS Co Down Map **01** D5

Premier Selected

QQQQQ **GH Edenvale House** 130 Portaferry Rd BT22 2AH
(between Newtownards and Greyabbey, 2 miles from Newtownards on A20) ☎ 01247 814881 FAX 01247 826192
Edenvale is an attractive Georgian property, sitting high off the road in 7 acres of garden and paddock; it is ideally located for Newtownards, the historic Greyabbey, the National Trust estate of Mount Stewart and local sailing and wildfowl attractions. Bedrooms are tastefully furnished and decorated, and offer a high standard of comfort. Diane Whyte's warm hospitality is apparent from the moment one is welcomed into her lovely home with the offer of a delicious afternoon tea. A good breakfast choice is served in the elegant dining room. Guests have exclusive use of the bright, comfortable sunroom to the front of the house, overlooking the croquet lawn and views across Strangford Lough to the Mourne Mountains beyond.
3 bth/shr (2 fmly) No smoking in bedrooms No smoking in dining room No smoking in 1 lounge CTV in all bedrooms Tea and coffee making facilities No dogs (ex guide dogs) Cen ht CTV 15P No coaches Riding
ROOMS: s £30; d £55
CARDS:

NINE MILE HOUSE Co Tipperary Map **01** C3

QQ **T&C** ***Grand Inn*** (situated on the main Clomnel/Kilkenny rd, N76)
☎ 051 647035
This historic, 17th-century historic inn is situated in the scenic Valley of Slievenamon, on the N76.
5 rms (3 shr) (3 fmly) Cen ht CTV 5P Last d 7pm
CARDS:

Prices shown in the directory are meant as a guide only and are subject to change. Please check before you book

OGONNELLOE Co Clare Map **01** B3

QQQ **GH Lantern House** (on R436) ☎ 061 923034 & 923123 FAX 061 923139
mid Feb-Oct
Situated overlooking Lough Derg, in a very scenic setting on the R436 route, this comfortable house offers nicely furnished and decorated bedrooms, together with a popular restaurant. The well tended gardens provide a marvellous view of the lake.
6 shr (2 fmly) No smoking CTV in all bedrooms Direct dial from bedrooms No dogs (ex guide dogs) Licensed Cen ht CTV 25P No coaches Last d 9pm
ROOMS: s IR£24-IR£28; d IR£40-IR£44; wkly b&b IR£126-IR£140; wkly hlf-bd IR£231-IR£245
CARDS:

OUGHTERARD Co Galway Map **01** B4

QQQ **GH The Boat Inn** The Square
(on N59 Galway to Clifden road in centre of Oughterard)
☎ 091 552196 FAX 091 552694
Closed 25 Dec
This popular guesthouse, bar and bistro is located in the centre of the village close to the famous Loch Corrib. Excellent sea, lake and river fishing are available in the area, which also offers a choice of golf courses and other outdoor pursuits. In season, live Irish music is provided most evenings.
11 bth/shr (4 fmly) CTV in all bedrooms Tea and coffee making facilities Direct dial from bedrooms No dogs (ex guide dogs) Licensed Cen ht CTV Last d 10pm
ROOMS: s IR£25-IR£30; d IR£40-IR£50 *
CARDS:

QQQ **T&C *Lakeland Country House*** Portacarron
(through Oughterard, pass Gateway Hotel, house on lake shore)
☎ 091 552121 552146
Closed 20 Dec-3 Jan
9 rms (8 bth/shr) (3 fmly) No smoking in bedrooms No smoking in dining room Tea and coffee making facilities No dogs Licensed Cen ht CTV 20P Fishing
CARDS:

Premier Selected

QQQQQ **GH River Run Lodge** Glann Rd
(N59 from Galway-turn right in Oughterard Square into Camp St, 250yds on turn left across Owenriff bridge, Lodge is 2nd house on right after 250yds)
☎ 091 552697 FAX 091 552669
15 Mar-21 Oct
The accommodation at this newly-built lodge is luxuriously appointed with a lot of nice touches, as well as luxury bath/shower rooms and comfortable armchairs. An intimate restaurant offers a range of interesting dishes, and the lovely landscaped gardens are bounded by the river.
6 bth/shr (2 fmly) No smoking in 2 bedrooms No smoking in area of dining room No smoking in 1 lounge CTV in all bedrooms Tea and coffee making facilities Direct dial from bedrooms Licensed Cen ht CTV 20P No coaches Last d 9.30pm
ROOMS: s IR£30-IR£40; d IR£50-IR£70; wkly b&b IR£155-IR£215; wkly hlf-bd IR£260-IR£320*
CARDS:

Selected

QQQQ **T&C Waterfall Lodge**
(on N59, first house on the left after Sweeneys Hotel)
☎ 091 552168
An elegant period residence beside a river and waterfall, with private fishing. Set in an idyllic location, yet close to the village, the house has antique furnishings, wooden floors, and log fires, all of which contribute to the comfortable and welcoming atmosphere. The en suite bedrooms are all well appointed and equipped, and the owner, Mrs Dolly, ensures a warm welcome. Activities available nearby include pony trekking, mountain climbing, golf and fishing, and there are plenty of pubs and restaurants.
6 shr (2 fmly) No smoking CTV in all bedrooms No dogs Cen ht CTV 8P No coaches Fishing
ROOMS: d IR£40*

PORTAFERRY Co Down Map **01** D5

QQQ **GH *The Narrows*** 8 Shore Rd BT22 1JY
(follow A20 & continue to shore & turn left, The Narrows is then on the left)
☎ 012477 28148 FAX 012477 28105
The Brown brothers have converted the family home into a guest house which is just that little bit different. Built around an 18th-century courtyard, the house enjoys a lovely outlook over Strangford Lough. The bedrooms are spacious and offer fresh decor and sturdy pine furnishings. Public areas include a comfortable first floor sitting room adjacent to which is a small kitchen for use by guests. On the ground floor, the restaurant overlooking the Lough offers wholesome fare prepared from local ingredients.
13 bth/shr (3 fmly) No smoking in bedrooms No smoking in area of dining room No smoking in lounges CTV in 4 bedrooms No dogs (ex guide dogs) Lift Cen ht CTV 5P No coaches Last d 7pm
CARDS:

PORTLAOISE Co Laoise Map **01** C3

QQ **T&C O'Sullivan** 8 Kelly Ville Park COLAOIS
(in town centre 60yds from Tourist Office beside town car park)
☎ 0502 22774
Situated on the outskirts of town, this family-run, two-storey, semi-detached house has a homely atmosphere.
6 shr (1 fmly) CTV in all bedrooms No dogs (ex guide dogs) Cen ht CTV 6P
ROOMS: s IR£25; d IR£38*

PORTSTEWART Co Londonderry Map **01** C6

Selected

QQQQ **GH *Strandeen*** 63 Strand Rd BT55 7LU ☎ 01265 833159 FAX 01265 833159
Apr-Oct
Elizabeth Caskey has created a non smoking environment in her delightful detached home which stands in a desirable residential area enjoying views over the bay to Donegal beyond. The variable sized bedrooms are bright and airy with comfortable modern appointments and there is an elegant combined lounge/dining room. Here hearty Irish breakfasts are complemented by freshly baked bread and fresh fruit.
3 bth/shr (1 fmly) No smoking CTV in all bedrooms Tea and coffee making facilities No dogs (ex guide dogs) Cen ht CTV 6P Fishing Last d breakfast time

RATHDRUM Co Wicklow Map **01** D3

Q Q Q **T&C** ***Abhainn Mor House*** Corballis
(at crossroads on R752, Rathdrum/Avoca road 2k south of Rathdrum)
☎ 0404 46330
Set in the peaceful surroundings of the Wicklow Hills, Therese and Ted Kyriacou run this comfortable house in a way that makes their guests feel immediately welcome. The spacious lounge has satellite TV and adjoins the breakfast room which leads on to the conservatory, overlooking grass tennis courts. Children can play safely in the play area and there is a good car park.
6 bth/shr (2 fmly) No smoking in bedrooms No smoking in dining room Tea and coffee making facilities No dogs (ex guide dogs) Cen ht CTV 10P No coaches Tennis (grass) Last d 11am
CARDS:

Q Q Q **GH Avonbrae** (200yds on Laragh Road after leaving village)
☎ 0404 46198 FAX 0404 46198
Mar-Nov
Lovely rose gardens surround this peaceful rural retreat in the Wicklow Hills. Owner Paddy Geoghegan has spent the last few years refurbishing the house to a very high standard. Bedrooms, with pine furniture, are attractively decorated and residents can enjoy the comfort of a charming sitting room and spacious dining room. An indoor heated swimming pool and good parking complete the attractions.
7 rms (6 shr) (2 fmly) No smoking in dining room Tea and coffee making facilities Direct dial from bedrooms Licensed Cen ht CTV 7P No coaches Indoor swimming pool (heated) Tennis (grass) Games room, table tennis Last d noon
ROOMS: s IR£30; d IR£48; wkly b&b IR£157; wkly hlf-bd IR£255
CARDS:

RATHVILLY Co Carlow Map **01** D3

Q Q Q ***Baile Ricead*** *(S 845836)*
☎ 0503 61120 & 087 440622(mobile) Mrs M Corrigan
Closed Nov-16 Mar
4 rms (1 shr) (2 fmly) No smoking No dogs Cen ht CTV 4P
66 acres mixed

RECESS Co Galway Map **01** A4

Q Q Q **Glendalough House** *(L 835468)*
(signposted 400mtrs off N59, 1km past Recess on Clifden side)
☎ 095 34669 Mr & Mrs T Joyce
May-Sep
This spacious, comfortable bungalow decorated in contemporary style enjoys superb views of mountains and Glendalough Lake from its setting beside the N59, 20kms from Clifden. Two of the cosy bedrooms now have en suite facilities and all are provided with tea/coffee making facilities; guests have a choice of lounges, one of them with TV. Leisure pursuits include an 18-hole pitch and putt course in excellent condition and access to mountain climbing and hill walking.
5 rms (3 shr) (2 fmly) No smoking in bedrooms No smoking in dining room No smoking in 1 lounge Tea and coffee making facilities No dogs Cen ht CTV 10P Golf 18 100 acres beef sheep poultry
ROOMS: d IR£34*

ROSCREA Co Tipperary Map **01** C3

See also Ballaghmore

Q Q Q **T&C Tower Guest House & Restaurant** Church St
(on N7 Dublin to Limerick road alongside Round Tower)
☎ 0505 21774 & 21189 FAX 0505 22425
Closed 25-26 Dec
This comfortable guest house, restaurant and bar is fronted by a smart yellow and green façade. The en suite bedrooms feature locally crafted furniture, attractive decor and a high standard of equipment. The Refectory Restaurant is open for breakfast, lunch and dinner; bar lunches and snacks are available in the West Gable Bar.
10 bth/shr (2 fmly) No smoking in area of dining room CTV in all bedrooms Direct dial from bedrooms No dogs (ex guide dogs) Licensed Cen ht 30P Last d 8.45pm
ROOMS: s IR£25-IR£28; d IR£45-IR£50
CARDS:

ROSSLARE HARBOUR Co Wexford Map **01** D2

Q Q Q **T&C Ailesbury** 5 The Moorings ☎ 053 33185 FAX 053 33185
Mar-10 Nov
A new house close to the church, Ailesbury is run by its friendly owner, Ann O'Dwyer. There is a comfortable lounge and dining room, 4 en suite bedrooms with good facilities. Early breakfast is available for sunrise departures.
4 rms (3 shr) (1 fmly) CTV in all bedrooms Tea and coffee making facilities No dogs
ROOMS: s IR£23-IR£26; d IR£32-IR£36

Premier Selected

Q Q Q Q Q **GH** ***Churchtown House*** Tagoat
(take R736 from N25 at Tagoat, turn between Cushens pub and church house 0.5m on the left) ☎ 053 32555 FAX 053 32555
11 Mar-5 Nov
Churchtown House is a charming period house, set in mature grounds on a link road between Rosslare Harbour and Rosslare Strand, just a short distance from the ferry port. Patricia and Austin Cody are excellent hosts who have spent a lot of time and energy restoring and extending their home. Bedrooms are varied, attractive and comfortable and the reception rooms are spacious and elegant. There is a drawing room, a dining room and a breakfast room which adjoins the conservatory. The Codys love to help guests plan their itinery, and visits to the Viking town of Wexford, the local wildlife preserve, and golf courses, are recommended.
12 bth/shr (1 fmly) No smoking in bedrooms No smoking in dining room No smoking in 1 lounge CTV in all bedrooms Direct dial from bedrooms No dogs (ex guide dogs) Licensed Cen ht CTV No children 20P No coaches Last d noon
CARDS:

Q Q Q **T&C** ***Kilrane House*** (on N25 opposite Cullens Pub)
☎ 053 33135 FAX 053 33739
This period house situated a short distance from Rosslare Harbour in the village of Kilrane, has been restored and all bedrooms now have private bathrooms. There are many original features, open fires and a superb guest lounge. Ample car parking is provided and early breakfasts can be served if required.
6 shr (2 fmly) No smoking in dining room CTV in 2 bedrooms Tea and coffee making facilities No dogs (ex guide dogs) Cen ht CTV 10P
CARDS:

QQQ T&C *The Light House* Main Rd ☎ 053 33214 FAX 053 33214
Mar-Oct
On the main road near the ferry port, easily distinguished by the replica light house in the front garden. A contemporary styled bungalow set in its own grounds with off-street parking. An ideal stopover for ferry users or for those who want to relax for a few days near a beach and golf club. The house has recently been completed so everything is bright and clean. There is a TV lounge and breakfast room in addition to the bedrooms, all of which have excellent en-suite shower rooms. Mr and Mrs Ormsby are a friendly couple and will be delighted to help guests plan trips in the area.
4 bth/shr No smoking in dining room No smoking in lounges CTV in all bedrooms Tea and coffee making facilities No dogs Cen ht CTV 6P
CARDS:

Selected

QQQQ T&C *Oldcourt House* ☎ 053 33895 & 086 8178873
Closed 23-30 Dec
An impressively large, modern house on the quiet shoreside road overlooking Rosslare Bay, just 200 yards beyond Hotel Rosslare,and convenient for the car ferry, beaches and golf courses. The en suite bedrooms are large, airy and furnished to a high standard. There is a comfortable lounge and separate dining room. An ideal base for small golfing parties.
6 bth/shr No smoking in bedrooms No smoking in dining room CTV in all bedrooms No dogs (ex guide dogs) Cen ht CTV 10P
CARDS:

QQ **O'Leary's** *(T 132101)* Killilane
(exit N25 in Kilrane between the two pubs, left at crossroads, right at junction for 1m) ☎ 053 33134 Ms P & K O'Leary
Closed 24-26 Dec
This farmhouse is located in a quiet and peaceful setting overlooking St George's Channel.
10 rms (7 shr) (2 fmly) No smoking Cen ht CTV 14P 100 acres arable Last d noon

QQQ **Orchard Park** *(T 101120)* Rosslare Rd
(turn off N25 at Cushens public house in Tagoat village onto the R736, premises 0.75m on the left)
☎ 053 32182 FAX 053 32759 Mrs E Doyle
This enlarged farm bungalow is in a quiet location on the road between Rosslare Harbour and Rosslare strand. Mrs Doyle, the owner, is currently having the house refurbished. There is a spacious lounge, dining room and play area, and in the grounds there is a tennis court.
6 rms (5 shr) (1 fmly) No smoking in bedrooms No smoking in dining room No smoking in 1 lounge CTV in all bedrooms No dogs (ex guide dogs) Cen ht CTV 10P Tennis (hard) 80 acres arable Last d noon
CARDS:

ROSSNOWLAGH Co Donegal Map 01 B5

Selected

QQQQ T&C *Smugglers Creek* ☎ 072 52366
Closed 18 Nov-26 Dec rs Oct-Etr (closed Mon & Tue)
Perched on a hilltop overlooking Donegal Bay with one of the best views in Ireland, Smugglers has a timeless atmosphere of warmth and conviviality. A splendid inn that is a combination of cosy en suite bedrooms, award winning bar and intimate restaurant. Personally run by the owner, Conor Britton, whose welcome, hospitality and attention to detail are simply excellent. The bar has lots of atmosphere, with stripped pine furnishings, turf fire, and big tables. Whether one dines here or in the restaurant, the freshest of produce is served. Flavours are robust and portions are large. There is a magnificent panorama of miles of sandy beaches and coves, this is a well known surfing area.
5 bth/shr No smoking in dining room Direct dial from bedrooms Licensed Cen ht CTV 25P No coaches Stabling for own horses Last d 9.30pm
CARDS:

ROUNDSTONE Co Galway Map 01 A4

Selected

QQQQ T&C **Ivy Rock House** Letterdyfe ☎ 095 35872
FAX 095 35872
Apr-Sep
Overlooking Bertragh Bay this new, yellow-painted house has been nicely decorated, and provides comfortable accommodation. Public rooms include two adjoining reception rooms and a first floor sitting room. Bedrooms are a good size, five are en suite and the sixth has the use of an adjacent bathroom.
6 bth/shr (4 fmly) No smoking No dogs (ex guide dogs) Cen ht CTV 10P Last d 3pm
ROOMS: s IR£20-IR£28; d IR£34-IR£40*

SCHULL Co Cork Map 01 B2

QQQ T&C **Old Bank House**
(drive through main street, first left after A.I.B. bank, house first on left)
☎ 028 28306 FAX 028 28306
Etr-Sep
This turn of the century house set in its own grounds, adjacent to all amenities in this popular seaside village. Guests receive a warm welcome from Mrs Donovan, and there is a comfortable TV lounge and breakfast room as well as the bedrooms, three of which are en suite whilst the other has a private bathroom. There is off-street parking.
4 rms (3 shr) No smoking CTV in all bedrooms Tea and coffee making facilities No dogs (ex guide dogs) Cen ht 4P No coaches
ROOMS: d IR£36*
CARDS:

QQQ T&C *Stanley House* Colla Rd ☎ 028 28425 FAX 028 28649
Mar- Oct
A visitors' book full of compliments testifies to the popularity of this house which is owned and run by the friendly and hospitable Nancy Brosnan. A combination of comfort, tranquility and spectacular sea views from the sun lounge contribute to the success of Stanley House, guests can explore the harbour and islands from the ferry boat. The house is 1 km from Schull, a lively town where good restaurants and pubs create a happy 'buzz' at this popular port of call for visiting yachts. A sailing school opened in 1997, and other amenities include tennis, hill walking, golf and wind surfing.
4 shr (1 fmly) No smoking in bedrooms No smoking in dining room No smoking in 1 lounge No dogs Cen ht CTV 10P No coaches
CARDS:

SHANAGARRY Co Cork Map 01 C2

Selected

QQQQ GH *Ballymaloe House*
(Ballymaloe is on the L35 from Midleton, 2miles beyond Cloyne on the Ballycotton Road)
☎ 021 652531 FAX 021 652021
Closed 24-26 Dec rs 27 Dec
This charming country house stands on a 400-acre farm, part of the old Geraldine Castle estate. Bedrooms are split between the main house and

contd.

adjacent courtyard buildings such as the 16th-century gatehouse. All of them are comfortable, well furnished and equipped with hairdryers; other facilities include a craft shop and a fine restaurant which uses produce from the farm as the raw material for its dishes.
22 bth/shr 10 annexe bth/shr (1 fmly) No smoking in area of dining room Direct dial from bedrooms No dogs (ex guide dogs) Licensed Cen ht CTV 30P Outdoor swimming pool (heated) Golf 7 Tennis (hard) Craft & Kitchen shop Last d 9pm
CARDS:

SKERRIES Co Dublin Map **01** D4

Q Q Q GH Red Bank Lodge 12 Convent Ln
☎ 01 8491005 & 8490439 FAX 01 8491598
Closed 24-25 Dec
A comfortable period townhouse adjacent to the well known restaurant of the same name and under the same ownership, that of amiable chef/patron Terry McCoy and his wife Margaret. There are two reception rooms, comfortable en suite bedrooms, a secluded garden and secure parking. Terry makes skilled use of the abundant supply of fresh seafood and eating here is an enjoyable experience. A special dinner/bed and breakfast rate is available.
5 shr 7 annexe bth/shr CTV in all bedrooms Tea and coffee making facilities Direct dial from bedrooms No dogs (ex guide dogs) Licensed Cen ht CTV 5P Last d 9.45pm
ROOMS: s IR£35-IR£45; d IR£50-IR£60; wkly b&b fr IR£175; wkly hlf-bd fr IR£350*
CARDS:

Q Q Woodview *(O 220598)* Margaretstown
(5km from Skerries and 0.5km from entrance to Argillan Castle and park)
☎ (01) 8491528 Mrs M Clinton
This large 1930s farmhouse stands in a quiet location near Ardgillan Park. Most of the rooms have en suite facilities and guests are welcome to join the family in the main lounge.
3 rms (1 shr) (2 fmly) No smoking in dining room No smoking in lounges CTV in 6 bedrooms Tea and coffee making facilities Cen ht CTV 8P
5 acres market garden Last d 3pm
ROOMS: s IR£17-IR£20; d IR£30-IR£34*
CARDS:

SKIBBEREEN Co Cork Map **01** B2

Q Q Q T&C Ilenroy House 10 North St
(100 yards from the main street on the N71 Clonakilty Road)
☎ 028 22751 & 22193 FAX 028 22193
A three-storey streetside house stands one hundred yards from the main street on the N74 Clonaklity Road. All bedrooms are en suite and equipped to a high standard. This is an excellent base from which to tour South West Cork and the Sherkin Islands.
6 rms (5 bth/shr) (1 fmly) CTV in all bedrooms Tea and coffee making facilities Direct dial from bedrooms No dogs (ex guide dogs) Cen ht P
ROOMS: s IR£15-IR£17.50; d IR£30-IR£35;
wkly b&b IR£105-IR£122.50*
CARDS:

Q Q Q T&C ***Whispering Trees*** Baltimore Rd
(take N71 from Cork and continue on R595 in direction of Baltimore. House on left) ☎ 028 21376
Feb-Nov
In a quiet location, this well maintained house has an attractive sun lounge, TV lounge and breakfast room. There is a tea/coffee trolley available, and the bedrooms are all well decorated, and have hair dryers and electric blankets. There is a private car park and golf, fishing, tennis and beaches are all available close by.
6 rms (5 shr) (1 fmly) No smoking in bedrooms No smoking in dining room CTV in all bedrooms No dogs Cen ht CTV 8P
CARDS:

SLIGO Co Sligo Map **01** B5

See also Drumcliff

Q Q Q T&C ***Aisling*** Cairns Hill
(approach Sligo on N4 right at 1st set of traffic lights, travelling south from Sligo pass Esso S/Sta turn left at traffic lights)
☎ 071 60704
Closed 24-28 Dec
This well cared for modern bungalow stands on a slight rise off Pearse Road only a short distance from the town centre. Bedrooms offer all modern comforts and there is also a pleasant sitting room with a dining area where at breakfast time guests can enjoy mountain views. This is an ideal place for non-smokers.
6 rms (3 shr) (2 fmly) No smoking CTV in all bedrooms No dogs Cen ht CTV No children 6yrs 6P

Selected

Q Q Q Q T&C ***Realt Na Mara*** Sea Rd, (off Strandhill Road)
(take turn off N4/N15 at junction of Lord Edward St/Strandhill Rd,drive past bus/train station and take 2nd road on right after railway bridge) ☎ 071 70838 FAX 071 50900
Mar-Oct
A superbly designed contemporary house off the Strandhill Road on the edge of Sligo. Offers luxury ensuite bedrooms and public rooms featuring grained pitch-fire woodwork. Mary and Christy Lynch are charming hosts and Mary's home baking adds a welcoming touch.
4 shr (1 fmly) No smoking CTV in all bedrooms No dogs (ex guide dogs) Cen ht CTV 6P No coaches
CARDS:

Q Q Q T&C ***Red Cottage*** Donegal Rd ☎ 071 44283 FAX 071 43417
A friendly establishment with a distinctive red roof stands on the main N15 Donegal road. En suite bedrooms all have TVs and tea/coffee making facilities; public areas include a spacious dining room and a split-level lounge with a sunken TV area. Tennis, squash, golf and hill-walking provide an alternative to the local beach.
6 shr 6 annexe shr (2 fmly) CTV in all bedrooms Tea and coffee making facilities No dogs (ex guide dogs) Cen ht CTV 50P

Q Q Q T&C Stradbrook Cornageeha, Pearse Rd
(enter Sligo on N4, on left past Texaco filling station, 100mtrs from Sligo Park Hotel) ☎ 071 69674 & 50663 FAX 071 69933
Friendly owners, Kathleen and Mel Noonan have recently refurbished their house to a high standard, giving a sitting room, breakfast room and four attractively decorated en-suite bedrooms. Off street car parking is available. French is spoken.
4 bth/shr (2 fmly) No smoking in bedrooms No smoking in dining room CTV in all bedrooms Tea and coffee making facilities Direct dial from bedrooms No dogs (ex guide dogs) Cen ht CTV 6P
ROOMS: s IR£20-IR£23.50; d IR£30-IR£34*
CARDS:

SPIDDAL Co Galway Map **01** B3

Q Q Q T&C Ard Aoibhinn Cnocan-Glas
(1km west of Spiddal village on R336 coast road)
☎ 091 553179 FAX 091 553179
Modern bungalow set back from road in lovely garden. Fine views over Galway Bay and Aran Islands.
6 rms (5 shr) (3 fmly) No smoking in 3 bedrooms No smoking in dining room No smoking in lounges CTV in all bedrooms Tea and coffee making facilities Cen ht CTV 6P Last d noon
ROOMS: s IR£16-IR£18; d IR£32-IR£35*
CARDS:

Selected

Q Q Q Q **T&C Ardmor Country House** Greenhill
(on route R336 coast road out of Galway 1km west of Spiddal Village)
☎ 091 553145 FAX 091 553596
A luxury, split-level bungalow standing a kilometre from the village, with superb views of Galway Bay and the Aran Islands. The en-suite bedrooms are spacious, and have recently been refurbished and newly equipped. There are two fine lounges and a well-stocked library which guests may use, and a pleasant gardens. Mrs Feeney has won awards for her breakfasts.
7 bth/shr (4 fmly) No smoking in bedrooms No smoking in dining room No smoking in lounges CTV in all bedrooms Tea and coffee making facilities No dogs Cen ht CTV 20P
ROOMS: s IR£25; d IR£40*
CARDS:

Selected

Q Q Q Q **T&C Suan Na Mara** Stripe, Furbo
(take R336 coastal route from Salthill via Barna village, turn right at Furbo church, 200mtrs on left) ☎ 091 591512 FAX 091 524168
Closed 23-31 Dec
This modern house stands on a side road beside a church between the villages of Furbo and Spiddal. Chef-patron Brian Clancy and his wife, Carmel, offer the spontaneous hospitality that makes guests feel immediately at home at the end of a long journey. There are two comfortable ground-floor rooms, with family rooms occupying the first floor. The adjoining sitting and dining rooms look out towards Galway Bay in the distance; booking in advance for dinner is appreciated. There are beaches and golf courses nearby, and ferries to Aran Island.
4 bth/shr (1 fmly) No smoking in bedrooms No smoking in dining room CTV in all bedrooms Tea and coffee making facilities No dogs (ex guide dogs) Cen ht 10P Last d 2pm
ROOMS: s IR£25-IR£26; d IR£36-IR£40*
CARDS:

Q Q Q **T&C *Tuar Beag*** Tuar Beag (on R337 0.5m W of village)
☎ 091 553422 FAX 091 553010
A large prominent house a half mile west of Spiddal and incorporating as a feature the walls of the thatched cottage in which four generations of the proprietor's family grew up - now much extended to give excellent accommodation. All rooms are ensuite with fine views over Galway Bay and the Aran Islands. Breakfast is a notable feature.
6 shr (5 fmly) No smoking in bedrooms No smoking in dining room CTV in all bedrooms No dogs Cen ht CTV 20P

STRADBALLY Co Waterford Map **01** C2

Selected

Q Q Q Q **T&C *Carrigahilla House and Gardens*** Carrighilla
(exit N25 at Stradbally turn off by Griffins Garage, premises located behind Stradbally village parish church)
☎ 051 293127 FAX 051 293127
Closed 31 Dec-31 Jan
This unusual building was once a convent and many fine original features remain including heavy wooden doors and wide corridors. These have been renovated and enhanced by modern facilities that have been subtly introduced. The old chapel with its stained glass windows and secret garden is popular with visitors as are the other magnificent gardens. There is also the cheerful Willow Room where guests dine (booking is requested), and an elegant sitting room for relaxation. Bedrooms are en suite and are all very comfortable. There is good parking and a sandy beach, a golf course, horse riding and walks are all to be found nearby.
4 shr (2 fmly) No smoking in bedrooms No smoking in dining room No smoking in lounges CTV in 2 bedrooms No dogs (ex guide dogs) Licensed Cen ht CTV 15P Over 3 acres of ornamental gardens Last d 7.30pm
CARDS:

STRAFFAN Co Kildare Map **01** D4

Selected

Q Q Q Q **T&C *Barberstown House*** Barberstown Cross
☎ 01 6274007 & 6274018
Closed 21 Dec-5 Jan
This completely refurbished Georgian dwelling standing in three and a half acres of gardens is furnished with antiques throughout; it features tastefully appointed en suite bedrooms complete with power showers, and spacious sitting and dining rooms overlooking the gardens. The house is located 15 miles from Dublin and conveniently near to Geoff's Bloodstock Sales, equestrian centres and a golf course.
5 shr (2 fmly) No smoking in dining room CTV in all bedrooms Tea and coffee making facilities No dogs Cen ht CTV 15P Tennis (grass)
CARDS:

STREAMSTOWN Co Westmeath Map **01** C4

Q Q ♥ ***Woodlands** (N 286426)* Horseleap (from Dublin take N6 and continue through Kilbeggan to Horseleap, turn right at filling station. Farm 2.5m signposted) ☎ 044 26414 Mrs M Maxwell
Mar-Oct
Large, attractive house in a sylvan setting off Mullingar/Athlone road.
6 rms (3 bth/shr) (2 fmly) No smoking in 1 lounge Cen ht CTV P 120 acres mixed Last d 5pm

SUTTON Co Dublin Map **01** D4

Selected

Q Q Q Q **T&C Three Coins** 6 Carrickbrack Rd
☎ 01 8322967 & 8725816 FAX 01 8322967
Proprietors, Joan and Raymond Maguire, ensure their guests receive a warm welcome to their charming home situated on the coastal road near Sutton Cross in a quiet residential area that has easy access to Dublin city centre and the airport by both rapid rail and bus services. The comfortable reception rooms have large bay windows that look out onto the gardens. The pine furnished, en suite bedrooms are pristine. Nearby is the fishing village of Howth with its many restaurants, there are well known golf courses and it is an ideal area for hill walking.
4 bth/shr (2 fmly) No smoking in 2 bedrooms No smoking in dining room No smoking in lounges CTV in all bedrooms Tea and coffee making facilities Direct dial from bedrooms Cen ht CTV 5P
ROOMS: s IR£30-IR£35; d IR£44-IR£48; wkly b&b IR£154-IR£168*
CARDS:

All AA listed accommodation can also be found at the AA's Internet site, whose address is: http://www.theaa.co.uk/hotels

TAHILLA Co Kerry Map **01** A2

Selected

Q Q Q Q **GH Tahilla Cove** (just off Ring of Kerry road N70)
☎ 064 45204 FAX 064 45104
Etr-Oct rs Tuesday evenings
Set on 13 acres of quiet and scenic seashore estate overlooking Kenmare Bay, with lawns and terraces sweeping down to the water's edge where there is a private pier. The comfortable and well appointed bedrooms are located in two houses and most have views of the bay. The Waterhouse family take pride in cooking with fresh local produce and dinner is available to residents. An ideal base for golfing, hill walking, fishing and bathing from the pebbled beach.
3 bth/shr 6 annexe bth/shr (4 fmly) No smoking in dining room CTV in all bedrooms Direct dial from bedrooms Licensed Cen ht CTV 20P No coaches Last d 9.30am
ROOMS: s IR£50-IR£60; d IR£70-IR£80; wkly hlf-bd IR£320-IR£340*
CARDS:

TERRYGLASS Co Tipperary Map **01** B3

Q Q Q **T&C** ***Riverrun House*** (turn off N7 at Nenagh drive through Borrisokane for Portumna, turn left at Carrigahorrig for Terryglass)
☎ 067 22125 FAX 067 22187
A charming pink house in a prize winning village and a popular port of call for cruisers on the River Shannon. Tom and Lucy Saunders are a couple with varied interests including gardening and cooking, all of which are of benefit to their guests. The bedrooms are big and comfortable and some of those on the ground floor have access to pretty gardens and a patio area.
6 bth/shr (2 fmly) Tea and coffee making facilities Direct dial from bedrooms Cen ht CTV 8P No coaches Tennis (hard) boats to hire, bicycles free of charge to guests
CARDS:

THOMASTOWN Co Kilkenny Map **01** C3

Selected

Q Q Q Q **T&C Abbey House** Jerpoint Abbey
(on the N9 from Dublin directly opposite Jerpoint Abbey)
☎ 056 24166 FAX 056 24192
Closed 21-30 Dec
Standing on the banks of the Little Argile River, this historic house was once part of the Jerpoint Abbey estates. The bedrooms are well equipped and tea trays and TVs are available on request. A comfortable sitting room overlooks the river banks, and dinner can be taken by arrangement in a separate dining room. There is trout fishing on the river and golf can be played nearby; the area is also known for its local crafts.
7 rms (6 bth/shr) (2 fmly) No smoking in dining room No smoking in 1 lounge CTV in 3 bedrooms Direct dial from bedrooms Cen ht CTV ch fac 30P Fishing Last d 12 noon
ROOMS: s IR£20-IR£30; d IR£36-IR£50*
CARDS:

Q Q **T&C** ***Burley*** Maudlin St (on N9) ☎ 056 24297
A smart modern bungalow set in well-tended grounds on the Carlow Road (N9) approach to the town centre. Pleasantly secluded behind a high wall, this house offers modern bedrooms, a cosy lounge, and secure car parking.
3 shr (2 fmly) No dogs (ex guide dogs) Cen ht CTV 10P No coaches

Q Q Q **T&C Carrickmourne House** New Ross Rd
(from Thomastown follow signposts to New Ross/Inistioge, after 1.5kms turn left, house is signed and is a mile up hill on left)
☎ 056 24124 FAX 056 24124
On an elevated site not far from Thomastown is this split-level house run by Julie Doyle. There is a comfortable TV lounge and the accommodation is provided in five en suite attractively decorated bedrooms. This is a non-smoking establishment.
5 shr (2 fmly) No smoking CTV in all bedrooms Tea and coffee making facilities No dogs Cen ht CTV No children 10yrs 9P
ROOMS: s IR£23-IR£28; d IR£34-IR£40
CARDS:

THURLES Co Tipperary Map **01** C3

Selected

Q Q Q Q **GH** ***Inch House***
(turn off N8 at Turnpike for Thurles, straight through town, turn right at top of square for Nenagh Rd and drive 4m)
☎ 0504 51348 & 51261 FAX 0504 51348
This lovely Georgian house was built in 1720 by John Ryan, a landed Catholic gentleman, whose descendants lived there until the current owners bought it in 1985. The property has been greatly restored and decorated throughout. The elegant drawing room ceiling is particularly outstanding. Relaxation and comfort of guests is the aim here and everything confirms that attitude.
5 bth/shr (3 fmly) Tea and coffee making facilities Direct dial from bedrooms No dogs (ex guide dogs) Licensed Cen ht CTV ch fac 40P Last d 6pm
CARDS:

TIPPERARY Co Tipperary Map **01** C3

Q Q **GH** ***Ach-na-Sheen*** Clonmel Rd ☎ 062 51298
Closed 23-31 Dec
This large, modern bungalow, stands only five minutes' walk from main street of Tipperary and offers sound, comfortable accommodation.
10 rms (7 bth/shr) (2 fmly) No smoking in 8 bedrooms No smoking in dining room No smoking in 1 lounge Cen ht CTV 10P
CARDS:

TOBERCURRY Co Sligo Map **01** B4

Q Q Q **T&C Cruckawn House** Ballymote/Boyle Rd
(signposted on town square) ☎ 071 85188 FAX 071 85188
1 Mar-31 Oct
Cruckawn House offers friendly hospitality and is attractively situated next to a golf club, which visitors may use, on the outskirts of town. The comfortable bedrooms are pleasant, as are the welcoming guest lounge and dining room.

5 bth/shr (2 fmly) No smoking in 3 bedrooms No smoking in dining room No smoking in 1 lounge CTV in all bedrooms Cen ht CTV 8P Golf 9 Tennis (hard) Squash Snooker Sauna Gymnasium Game & course fishing Last d 6pm
ROOMS: s IR£23.50-IR£25; d IR£35-IR£36; wkly b&b IR£120-IR£125*
CARDS:

TRALEE Co Kerry Map **01** A2

QQQ **T&C Ballingowan House** Mileheight, Killarney Rd (approach Tralee on N21/N22, premises on left before McDonalds restaurant) ☎ 066 27150 FAX 066 20325
Mar-Nov
4 shr (3 fmly) No smoking CTV in all bedrooms Tea and coffee making facilities No dogs Cen ht CTV No children 6yrs 8P
ROOMS: s IR£24.50; d IR£36*
CARDS:

QQQ **Heatherville** *(Q 816118)* Blennerville
(exit main Dingle Rd N86 at Blennerville village, premises 0.5m on left)
☎ 066 21054 FAX 066 21054 Mrs H Kerins
Mar-Oct
A luxury modern farmhouse just off the Tralee to Dingle road. Mrs Hanna Kerins and her daughter, Ann, extend a warm welcome to their guests and ensure their comfort. Close to the restored Blennerville Windmill and steam railway.
6 shr (2 fmly) No smoking CTV in all bedrooms Direct dial from bedrooms No dogs Cen ht CTV 8P 40 acres dairy
ROOMS: s IR£24-IR£26; d IR£35-IR£39*
CARDS:

TRAMORE Co Waterford Map **01** C2

QQQ **T&C The Anner** 33 Newtown Hill
(follow R675 through town for approx 1m, through Cove Cross, up hill and turn left opposite golf club and take 2nd right in new housing development)
☎ 051 381628
Closed Xmas
Situated in a quiet location opposite the Tramore Golf Club and near lovely coastal walks, the beaches are within walking distance of the town centre. There is a comfortable lounge with a hospitality trolley, and the bedrooms are all attractively decorated.
3 bth/shr (2 fmly) No smoking in bedrooms No smoking in dining room CTV in all bedrooms Tea and coffee making facilities No dogs (ex guide dogs) Cen ht CTV 3P No coaches
ROOMS: d IR£34-IR£36; wkly b&b IR£112-IR£119*
CARDS:

Selected

QQQQ **T&C *Cliff House*** Cliff Rd ☎ 051 381497
FAX 051 381497
Feb-Nov
Set in its own landscaped gardens with a panoramic view over Tramore Bay, this attractive guest house has a spacious dining room where breakfast is served from an imaginative menu. There is also a charming conservatory lounge. En suite bedrooms are inviting, and include a family room. The golf course is just a few minutes walk away.
6 shr No smoking CTV in all bedrooms Tea and coffee making facilities No dogs Cen ht CTV No children 6yrs P
CARDS:

This symbol indicates a 'Child Friendly' establishment - see page 25 for details

Selected

QQQQ **T&C Glenorney** Newtown (on R675 opposite the Tramore Golf Club) ☎ 051 381056 FAX 051 381103
Feb-Nov
A beautiful, spacious and luxurious home with a spectacular view of Tramore Bay, located opposite a championship golf course. Great attention has been paid to detail and there is an extensive breakfast menu. All the bedrooms are tastefully decorated and the lounge is spacious and luxuriously furnished, making any stay here feel like a "home from home".
6 shr (2 fmly) No smoking CTV in all bedrooms Tea and coffee making facilities Direct dial from bedrooms No dogs (ex guide dogs) Cen ht CTV 6P
ROOMS: s IR£23-IR£27; d IR£36-IR£40*
CARDS:

QQ **T&C Rushmere House** Branch Rd
(on main Waterford Rd beside Majestic Hotel) ☎ 051 381041
Closed Xmas & New Year
Three-storey, 100-year-old semi-detached house situated on main road overlooking sea, with well-tended gardens.
6 rms (3 shr) (2 fmly) No smoking in dining room CTV in all bedrooms Tea and coffee making facilities No dogs (ex guide dogs) Cen ht CTV
ROOMS: s IR£20-IR£23; d IR£32-IR£36*
CARDS:

QQQ **T&C *Sea View Lodge*** Seaview Park ☎ 051 381122 FAX 381122
Closed Nov-16 Mar
A large bungalow with panoramic sea views of Tramore Bay from the dining room and a sun lounge overlooking the garden. Bedrooms are attractively decorated and a pleasant conservatory has been built at the front of the house. An extensive breakfast menu is on offer. Close to the golf course, the beach and horse riding is available nearby.
5 shr (2 fmly) No smoking CTV in all bedrooms Tea and coffee making facilities No dogs Cen ht CTV No children 5yrs 6P
CARDS:

QQQ **T&C Turret House** 2 Church Rd (off R675, signed)
☎ 051 386342
7 Dec-Nov
In an elevated position overlooking Tramore Bay, Turret House has four cheerfully decorated en suite bedrooms, some on the ground floor. There is a separate breakfast room.
4 bth/shr (2 fmly) No smoking in bedrooms No smoking in dining room CTV in all bedrooms Tea and coffee making facilities Cen ht CTV 3P No coaches
ROOMS: s IR£18-IR£25; d IR£32-IR£36; wkly b&b IR£100-IR£110*
CARDS:

WATERFORD Co Waterford Map **01** C2

See also Cheekpoint

QQQ **Ashbourne House** *(S6631140)* Slieverue
(2.5m E of Waterford, off N25 Waterford/Wexford Rd, signposted)
☎ 051 832037 Mrs A Forrest
Mar-Nov Closed 1 Dec-15 Mar
A comfortable ivy-clad house in a quiet residential area where the charming owner serves tea and fresh home-made scones on arrival. There is a hospitality tray in the first-floor sitting room and the welcoming bedrooms are all en suite, one being on the ground floor.
7 shr (6 fmly) Tea and coffee making facilities Cen ht CTV 7P 25 acres beef
ROOMS: s IR£23; d IR£36; wkly b&b IR£98*
CARDS:

Selected

Q Q Q Q **T&C Brown's Town House** 29 South Pde (off N25 at the mall and turn into Catherine St, South Parade is a continuation, Brown's is 800m on right) ☎ 051 870594 FAX 051 871923
Closed 20 Dec-29 Jan
This late Victorian house in the centre of Waterford offers a convivial atmosphere engendered by the friendliness of Leslie and Barbara Brown. Impeccable bedrooms feature big power showers with plenty of hot water, while the comfortable sitting room invites relaxation. Home-made breads and jams are part of the generous breakfasts served around the dining table. Local golf courses, beaches and the Waterford Glass complex are nearby.
6 bth/shr (2 fmly) No smoking in dining room CTV in all bedrooms Tea and coffee making facilities Direct dial from bedrooms No dogs Cen ht CTV No coaches
ROOMS: s fr IR£30; d IR£50-IR£60*
CARDS:

Selected

Q Q Q Q **GH *Coach House*** Butlerstown Castle, Butlerstown (3km from Waterford off N25 towards Cork, signposted on left)
☎ 051 384656 FAX 051 384751
Closed 20 Dec-20 Jan rs 1-25 Oct
Built in 1870 as the coach house to Butlerstown Castle and restored by owner Des O'Keeffe, this comfortable house has been skilfully refurbished, blending the old with contemporary facilities. There is a fine lounge and restaurant and the bedrooms are well equipped and furnished in traditional pine; a sauna is available. The famous Waterford Glass factory, and golfing and fishing opportunities are all nearby.
7 shr No smoking in bedrooms No smoking in dining room CTV in all bedrooms Tea and coffee making facilities Direct dial from bedrooms Licensed Cen ht 15P No coaches Sauna Last d noon
CARDS:

Q Q Q **GH Diamond Hill** Diamond Hill, Slieverue (situated 1.2km from Waterford City off Rosslare/Waterford Road N25)
☎ 051 832855 FAX 051 832254
Diamond Hill is surrounded by superb gardens, lovingly tended by the friendly owners. Their interests in decor and cooking are especially evident, with evening meals available by arrangement. The bedrooms are decorated in warm colours and the public areas are spacious, including a reception lobby, lounge and dining room.
10 bth/shr (2 fmly) No smoking in 4 bedrooms No smoking in dining room CTV in all bedrooms Tea and coffee making facilities Direct dial from bedrooms No dogs (ex guide dogs) Cen ht CTV 20P
ROOMS: s IR£27-IR£32; d IR£44-IR£54
CARDS:

Q Q Q **T&C *Marsuci Country Home*** Oliver's Hill, Butlerstown (take N25 towards Cork for 2m to Holy Cross public house and turn right, signposted. At T junct turn right and house 0.5m on right hand side)
☎ 051 370429 & 350982 FAX 051 350983
Set in a rural location, this attractive stone-built house stands in attractive gardens and offers comfortable, relaxing accommodation. The pleasant bedrooms all have telephones and TVs can be suppplied on request. There is a guest lounge and a separate licensed dining room, which serves dinner on request. Country pubs, restaurants, golf and an equestrian centre are nearby.
6 bth/shr (2 fmly) No smoking in 2 bedrooms No smoking in dining room CTV in 2 bedrooms Tea and coffee making facilities Direct dial from bedrooms No dogs Licensed Cen ht CTV 10P No coaches
Last d 8.30pm
CARDS:

Selected

Q Q Q Q **T&C Sion Hill House & Gardens** Sion Hill, Ferry Bank (take Rosslare road from Waterford over bridge, bus/rail station on left, next entrance after Jury's Hotel on N25)
☎ 051 851558 & 851880 FAX 051 851678
Closed Xmas
Although close to the city this 18th-century residence is situated in extensive and peaceful gardens, that are gradually being restored to their original 1870 design. Rare plants, a walled garden, a meadow and woodlands are to found. Flanked by two pavillions the house has also undergone major refurbishment resulting in two fine reception rooms and comfortable en suite bedrooms. This is a gracious house where the friendly owners like to mix with their guests and as the visitors book shows their hospitality is much appreciated.
4 bth/shr (4 fmly) No smoking CTV in all bedrooms Tea and coffee making facilities No dogs (ex guide dogs) Cen ht CTV ch fac 16P No coaches
ROOMS: s IR£27.50-IR£40; d IR£42-IR£60*
CARDS:

Q Q Q **T&C Villa Eildon** Belmont Rd, Rosslare Rd, Ferrybank (situated on Waterford to Rosslare Rd N25 2km from Waterford City)
☎ 051 832174
May-Oct
A dormer bungalow on the Rosslare/Waterford road, with off street parking, that is conveniently situated for the Waterford Glass Factory, golf clubs and the city centre. Guests can make use of tea and coffee making facilities in the sitting room and from the dining room they can enjoy views of the garden to the countryside beyond. Bedrooms are comfortably furnished. This is a no-smoking establishment.
4 rms (3 shr) No smoking No dogs Cen ht CTV No children 7yrs 6P No coaches
ROOMS: s IR£26.50-IR£28.50; d IR£33-IR£37

WATERVILLE Co Kerry Map 01 A2

Q Q Q **T&C Golf Links View** Murreigh (1km on N side of Waterville village on N70)
☎ 066 74623 FAX 066 74623
Apr-Oct
A new house standing in developing gardens outside the town. Bedrooms are well appointed and have good views.
6 bth/shr (1 fmly) No smoking in bedrooms No smoking in dining room CTV in all bedrooms Tea and coffee making facilities No dogs (ex guide dogs) Cen ht CTV P Putting green Pitch & put
ROOMS: s IR£18-IR£23.50; d IR£32-IR£36*
CARDS:

Q Q Q T&C *Klondyke House* New Line Rd (on N70, beside Waterville craft market) ☎ 066 74119 FAX 066 74666
An attractive house at the western end of the village. Recently extended and refurbished to high standards. A nice sun lounge to the front has views over Waterville Bay. Bedrooms are comfortable with semi-orthopaedic beds and large showers en suite. Breakfast features an excellent choice including an attractive fruit plate, fresh fruit yoghurts and homebaked breads.
6 shr (1 fmly) Tea and coffee making facilities No dogs (ex guide dogs) Cen ht CTV 10P Tennis (hard)
CARDS:

Q Q Q T&C O'Gradys Spunkane (parallel to N70 on northern approach keep straight ahead at church crossing. Southern approach through village and keep right at junct) ☎ 066 74350 FAX 066 74730
Mar-Oct
This smart, new, yellow house stands at the north end of town, close to all amenities. The attractively decorated bedrooms have good sized en-suite facilities and there is a television lounge and dining-room. The grounds provide plenty of private parking and locally there are good eating facilities as well as beaches, fishing and golf.
6 bth/shr (2 fmly) No smoking in dining room CTV in all bedrooms Tea and coffee making facilities No dogs (ex guide dogs) Cen ht CTV No children 4yrs 7P
ROOMS: s IR£18-IR£23; d IR£32-IR£34
CARDS:

WESTPORT Co Mayo Map 01 B4

Q Q Q Rath-a-Rosa Farmhouse *(L 953822)* Rossbeg (on R335 Westport to Louisburgh road) ☎ 098 25348 Mrs M O'Brien
18 Mar-1 Nov
Rath-a-Rosa is a spacious and luxurious bungalow on the shores of Clew Bay. Bedrooms are of varying sizes with a jacuzzi bath available. It is set on 20-acre hill farm with magnificent views, within walking distance of restaurants and pubs. Golf, sailing, hill walking, horse riding, and swimming are all available nearby.
5 rms (4 bth/shr) (2 fmly) No smoking in bedrooms No smoking in dining room No dogs (ex guide dogs) Cen ht CTV 6P 20 acres mixed cattle sheep
ROOMS: s IR£20-IR£27; d IR£38-IR£42*
CARDS:

Q Q Q T&C Riverbank House Rosbeg, Westport Harbour (on R335) ☎ 098 25719
Apr-Oct
6 rms (4 bth/shr) (1 fmly) No smoking in dining room Tea and coffee making facilities No dogs Cen ht CTV 8P
ROOMS: s IR£22-IR£24.50; d IR£36*
CARDS:

Q Q Q *Seapoint House* *(L 972897)* Kilmeena (signposted on main Westport/Newport road N59, 6km N of Westport turn left and continue straight for 2.5km) ☎ 098 41254 M O'Malley
Apr-Oct
Large and luxurious modern, two-storey farmhouse set in 40 acres on Clew Bay.
6 bth/shr (4 fmly) No smoking in bedrooms No smoking in dining room No smoking in lounges CTV in 2 bedrooms Tea and coffee making facilities No dogs Cen ht CTV 8P Sea angling walking 40 acres mixed
CARDS:

Selected

Q Q Q Q T&C Wilmaur Rosbeg
(take N74 from town centre and turn right 0.5m after Asgard public house, signposted) ☎ 098 25784 FAX 098 26224
Apr-Sep
This very comfortable country house, signposted N59 to Louisberg, is three kilometres from the town centre near the Quay. It stands of the shore of Clew Bay within walking distance of many pubs and restaurants. High quality parquet floors and antique furniture create a warm and stylish atmosphere, the perfect setting for Mrs Printer's genuine hospitality. Bedrooms have attractive colour schemes, big shower rooms and hospitality trays. Boats for hire, sailing, golf and horse riding are all available in the neighbourhood.
5 shr (3 fmly) No smoking in 3 bedrooms No smoking in dining room Tea and coffee making facilities Cen ht CTV 10P
ROOMS: s IR£27.50; d IR£35*

WEXFORD Co Wexford Map 01 D3

Selected

Q Q Q Q T&C Ard Ruadh Manor Spawell Rd (opposite County Hall on N25 in 'Westgate' area of town) ☎ 053 23194 FAX 053 23194
Closed 24-29 Dec
A former Vicarage, this magnificent house on the edge of Wexford looks out over the roofs of houses to the estuary in Wexford. The bedrooms and public rooms are spacious and luxurious and the Cahill family take a particular pride in looking after their guests.
6 bth/shr (2 fmly) No smoking in dining room CTV in all bedrooms Tea and coffee making facilities No dogs (ex guide dogs) Cen ht No children 3yrs 12P
ROOMS: s IR£24-IR£32; d IR£40-IR£50; wkly b&b IR£140-IR£175*
CARDS:

Q Q Q T&C The Blue Door 18 Lower George St (on entering Wexford town take exit on rdbt for town centre, George St is third on the right and the Blue Door is opposite Whites Hotel) ☎ 053 21047
A restored town house located off the main street, within walking distance of all amenities including the Theatre Royal, home of the famous Opera Festival. Bedrooms are pristine, with crisp blue and white decor and comfortable pine furniture. The sitting and dining rooms combine to make an inviting spot to relax, or play tapes, and to dip into the bookshelves. Imelda Scallan is a hospitable owner, and supplies tea/coffee facilities for guests to help themselves. Nearby are good beaches, golf, fishing, a swimming pool and fine walking areas.
4 shr (3 fmly) No smoking in dining room No smoking in lounges CTV in all bedrooms No dogs (ex guide dogs) Cen ht 3P
ROOMS: s fr IR£25; d fr IR£40*
CARDS:

Selected

Q Q Q Q *Clonard House* *(T 021199)* Clonard Great (signposted on R733/N25 roundabout. Take R733 S for 500mtrs, first road on left and first entrance on left)
☎ 053 43141 & 47337 FAX 053 43141 Mr & Mrs J Hayes
Closed Etr-mid Nov *contd.*

This lovely old farmhouse is an outstanding example of a well maintained Georgian house over 200 years old. Public rooms include an attractive and comfortable lounge with a large open fire, and some of the bedrooms have four poster beds with beautiful antique lace. Furnishings include many antiques and all the bedrooms enjoy views of gardens and farmlands.
9 shr (4 fmly) No smoking in bedrooms No smoking in dining room No smoking in 1 lounge CTV in all bedrooms No dogs (ex guide dogs) Licensed Cen ht CTV No children 5yrs 10P 120 acres dairy Last d 6pm
CARDS:

Selected

QQQQ **T&C *Darral House*** Spalwell Rd ☎ 053 24264
Closed 20 Dec-1 Jan
A period town house which has been completely refurbished to a very high standard by friendly owners Kathleen and Sean Nolan. Fine high ceilings are a feature of the elegant sitting and dining room, and comfort is the keynote in the en-suite bedrooms which are attractively decorated. Guests are offered a wide range of choices at breakfast, including fresh fruit, fish and other tempting dishes. This popular house has a private car park.
4 bth/shr No smoking in bedrooms No smoking in dining room CTV in all bedrooms Tea and coffee making facilities No dogs Cen ht 6P
CARDS:

QQQ ***Killiane Castle*** *(T 058168)* Drinagh (located off N25 between Wexford and Rosslare) ☎ 053 58885 & 58898 FAX 053 58885 Mr & Mrs J Mernagh
Closed Mar-Nov
8 bth/shr (2 fmly) No smoking CTV in all bedrooms No dogs Licensed Cen ht CTV P Tennis (hard) 230 acres dairy
CARDS:

Selected

QQQQ **T&C McMenamin's Town House** 3 Auburn Ter, Redmond Rd (situated at the west end of town opposite the railway and bus station) ☎ 053 46442 FAX 053 46442
Closed 20-30 Dec
This charming late Victorian residence is within easy walking distance of all amenities, and is 15 minutes' drive to Rosslare ferryport. Owners Seamus and Kay McMenamin offer warm and caring hospitality. The en suite bedrooms have some fine antique beds and are well equipped. A wide choice of breakfast dishes is served in the attractively furnished dining room, and there is a pleasant guests' sitting room. There is secure private car parking and nearby attractions include golf, swimming, beaches, a heritage centre, and an opera house.
6 bth/shr (1 fmly) No smoking in 3 bedrooms No smoking in dining room No smoking in 1 lounge CTV in all bedrooms Tea and coffee making facilities No dogs Cen ht 9P No coaches
CARDS:

Selected

QQQQ **T&C Mount Auburn** 1 Auburn Ter, Redmond Rd (from direction of Dublin on N11, turn left at Ferrycarrig Bridge. House 2 miles on right) ☎ 053 24609 & 21470
Closed Xmas & New Year
Conveniently placed for the station and city centre, Auburn Lodge offers attractive and comfortable bedrooms with all modern facilities, a residents' lounge and a dining room where evening meals are served by arrangement. Access to the car park is via the supermarket car park.
6 bth/shr (3 fmly) No smoking in 2 bedrooms No smoking in dining room No smoking in lounges CTV in all bedrooms Tea and coffee making facilities No dogs (ex guide dogs) Cen ht CTV 6P No coaches
ROOMS: s IR£20-IR£25; d IR£38-IR£44; wkly b&b IR£130-IR£150*
CARDS:

QQQ **T&C O'Briens Auburn House** 2 Auburn Ter, Redmond Rd (opposite railway station and Savoy Cinema and adjactent to Dunnes Stores) ☎ 053 23605 FAX 053 23605
Closed 23 Dec-02 Jan
Centrally placed opposite the railway and bus station, this attractive brick house has been extensively and tastefully renovated. Bedrooms are well equipped and spacious, and guests can relax in the evening in a large and comfortable lounge. Auburn House is the second in a terrace of three houses and should not be confused with the similarly named house next-door.
5 rms (4 shr) (2 fmly) No smoking in bedrooms No smoking in dining room CTV in all bedrooms Tea and coffee making facilities No dogs (ex guide dogs) Cen ht CTV 5P
ROOMS: s IR£25; d IR£36-IR£45*
CARDS:

QQQ **T&C Rathaspeck Manor** Rathaspeck (signposted on N25, near Johnstone castle) ☎ 053 42661 & 45148
May-7 Nov
Standing in its own grounds, which feature an 18-hole par-3 golf course, this 300-year-old restored Georgian country house is situated half a mile from Johnstone Castle. The comfortable, spacious bedrooms are en suite and the public rooms are appointed with period furnishings. Hospitable Mrs Cuddihy will provide dinner by arrangement and the guest house holds a wine licence. Good parking is available.
6 shr (3 fmly) CTV in all bedrooms Tea and coffee making facilities No dogs CTV No children 10yrs 8P Golf 18 Tennis (hard) Last d noon
ROOMS: s IR£25; d IR£40-IR£44

QQQ **T&C *Shanora Lodge*** Newtown Rd (1m outside town on N11/N25, 100mtrs from Esso Service Station) ☎ 053 41414
Closed 23 Dec-8 Jan
This modern house overlooks the River Slaney Valley, enjoying scenic views from the spacious lounge. There are three en suite bedrooms, one of which is a family suite, and two standard rooms on the ground floor which share an adjacent bathroom. There is safe car parking and flower-filled gardens.
5 rms (3 shr) (3 fmly) No smoking in dining room CTV in all bedrooms Tea and coffee making facilities No dogs (ex guide dogs) Cen ht CTV 10P
CARDS:

Selected

QQQQ **GH Slaney Manor** Ferrycarrig (on N25 0.5 mile west of N11 junction) ☎ 053 20051 & 20144 FAX 053 20510
Closed Dec-Jan
This attractive period manor house stands in 60 acres of woodland overlooking the River Slaney and adjacent to a heritage park. The house has been completely restored by the owners, who have retained many fine features while adding modern facilities where appropriate. The elegant, high-ceilinged drawing room and dining room have views

of the river, and a new conservatory offers further seating. Four-poster beds feature in all bedrooms, and there are some rooms with wheelchair access and others for families. The house operates a no-smoking policy, and good car parking facilities are available.
8 bth/shr (2 fmly) No smoking CTV in all bedrooms Tea and coffee making facilities Direct dial from bedrooms No dogs (ex guide dogs) Licensed Lift Cen ht CTV 30P No coaches Last d 3pm
ROOMS: s IR£45-IR£50; d IR£50-IR£75; wkly hlf-bd IR£215-IR£245*
CARDS:

WICKLOW Co Wicklow Map **01** D3

QQQ **GH Gormanstown Manor** Farm Guest House
(just off the main Dublin Rosslare motorway N11 at Lie Doyles or Beehive pub) ☎ 0404 69432 FAX 0404 61832
Set in a peaceful area within easy reach of fifteen golf courses, this farm-style guest house is run by the hospitable Murphy family. All bedrooms are en suite and are attractively furnished. Dinner is provided if pre-booked and Margaret Murphy makes a delicious fruit cake.
9 shr (7 fmly) No smoking in bedrooms No smoking in dining room No smoking in 1 lounge CTV in all bedrooms Direct dial from bedrooms No dogs (ex guide dogs) Cen ht CTV P Golf 18 Large landscaped gardens Golf practice
ROOMS: s IR£25-IR£35; d IR£50-IR£70; wkly b&b fr IR£140
CARDS:

QQQ *Lissadell House (T302925)* Ashtown Ln
(1m from town on main Wicklow/Wexford road, first turn off Marlton Road (L29A), signposted) ☎ 0404 67458 Mrs P Klaue
Mar-Nov
A comfortable two-storey house stands in its own grounds on the outskirts of Wicklow. Bedrooms are neat and well kept; two have en suite facilities and two share a shower room and bathroom. Other attractions include a guest lounge, a breakfast room and ample parking.
4 rms (1 bth 1 shr) (1 fmly) No smoking in bedrooms No smoking in dining room No smoking in 1 lounge No dogs (ex guide dogs) Cen ht CTV 12P Last d 2pm

Selected

QQQQ **GH The Old Rectory Country House & Restaurant** (from Dublin-take N11 to Rathnew then R750 to Wicklow (1m), Old Rectory is on left, 100mtrs after Statoil Garage, entrance has stone walls)
☎ 0404 67048 FAX 0404 69181
Mar-Dec
This charming Victorian residence on the edge of Wicklow town where Linda and Paul Saunders, the friendly owners, have restored this old Rectory to pristine condition. Sample some of Linda's expert cuisine, which makes good use of organic vegetables and fresh local produce. Vegetarians are welcome, there is a peaceful atmosphere, pretty en suite bedrooms and easy parking.

7 bth/shr No smoking in dining room No smoking in 1 lounge CTV in all bedrooms Tea and coffee making facilities Direct dial from bedrooms No dogs Licensed Cen ht 10P No coaches Sauna Gymnasium Last d 6pm
ROOMS: s IR£78; d IR£104*
CARDS:

YOUGHAL Co Cork Map **01** C2

See also Killeagh

Premier Selected

QQQQQ **GH Ahernes** 163 North Main St
(on N25 in town centre) ☎ 024 92424 FAX 024 93633
Closed 21-31 Dec
Offering accommodation in spacious bedrooms, furnished to the highest standard with antiques and modern facilities, this pleasant guest house boasts an award-winning restaurant, well known for its seafood specialities. There is a cosy drawing room provided for guests and parking is available.
10 bth/shr No smoking in area of dining room CTV in 12 bedrooms Direct dial from bedrooms No dogs (ex guide dogs) Licensed Cen ht 12P Last d 9.30pm
ROOMS: s IR£75-IR£80; d IR£100-IR£120*
CARDS:

Q *Cherrymount (X0071723)* (turn north off N25 at the Blackwater Bridge, follow signs to Cherrymount Farmhouse) ☎ 024 97110 Mrs E Long
This 500-year-old farmhouse is situated on high ground off the main N25 road near Youghal. Genuine in style, and its owner, Mrs Long, offers a friendly welcome.
3 rms (1 fmly) Cen ht CTV 6P 70 acres dairy

Hall of Fame
1994-95

PAST AA LANDLADIES OF THE YEAR

Finalists 1994- 95

Christine Moodie, Rovie Farm, Rogart, Sutherland - ***winner***

Muriel Orme, Bank House, Oakamoor, Staffordshire - ***runner up***

Sylvia Knott, Ffaldau Country House, Penybont, Powys - ***runner-up***

Sîan Bisdee, Ashcombe Court, Weston-super-Mare, Avon

Norah Brown, Grange Lodge, Dungannon, Co Tyrone

Fredena Burns, Farm Retreats, Chapel Uchaf Farm, Carmarthen, Dyfed

Sylvia Dobbs, Kenmore Guest House, Littlehampton, West Sussex

Joyce Fielder, Old Stable Cottage, Carew, Dyfed

Jenny Hadfield, Jeakes House, Rye, East Sussex

Jill Jenkins, Thanington Hotel, Canterbury, Kent

Ria Johnston, White Gables, Bushmills, Co Antrim

Elsie Moore, Maes-y-Gwernen, Abercraf, Swansea

Mollie Rees, Dormy House Hotel, Sarisbury Green, Hants

Anwen Roberts, Bach-y-Graig, St Asaph, Clwyd

Jen Spencer, Eyarth Station, Ruthin, Clwyd

Eileen Spray, Grasmead House, York, North Yorkshire

Ivy Stanley, Fresh Fields, Twynholm, Kirkcudbright, Dumfries & Galloway

Muriel White, Chadstone Guest House, Craven Arms, Shropshire

Sue White, Ennys Farm, Penzance, Cornwall

PAST GUEST HOUSE OF THE YEAR AWARD WINNERS 1994 - 95

England Goldhill Mill, Tonbridge, Kent

Scotland Culdearn House, Grantown-on-Spey, Morayshire, Highland

Wales Tan-y-Foel, Betws-y-Coed, Gwynedd

Ireland The Old Rectory Hotel & Restaurant, Wicklow, Co Wicklow

SOME ESTABLISHMENTS MAY NO LONGER BE IN THE AA SCHEME AND SOME MAY HAVE CHANGED HANDS.

Hall of Fame
1995-96

PAST AA LANDLADIES OF THE YEAR
Finalists 1995 - 96

Kathie Ritchie, Tilston Lodge, Malpas, Cheshire - ***winner***
Sue Jones, Dyffryn Farm, Newtown, Powys - ***runner-up***
Judith Clegg, Redacre Mill, Hebden Bridge, West Yorks - ***runner-up***
Ann Addison, Old Parsonage Farm, Hanley Castle, Hereford
Anne Birbeck, Greenhead Hotel, Crook, Co. Durham
Bernie Clarke, Twelve Angel Hill, Bury St Edmunds, Suffolk
Enid Davies, Low Hall, Cockermouth, Cumbria
Gillian Hingston, Piggot's Mill, Thaxted, Essex
Ria Johnston, White Gables, Bushmills, County Antrim
Isobel Little, Culdearn House, Grantown-on-Spey, Morayshire
Andrea Londors, Boswell House Hotel, Chelmsford, Essex
Sally MacDonell, Mardella Farmhouse, Gartocharn, Dumbartonshire
Muriel Orme, Bank House, Oakamoor, Staffordshire
Dorota Perruzza, Green Gables, Chester, Cheshire
Theresa Quinn and Anne Waite, Powys House Estate, Corwen, Clwyd
Sandra Ridden, Westcott Hotel, Falmouth, Cornwall
Marie Rathmell, Hilltop Country Guesthouse, Skipton, North Yorks
Yvonne Thompson, Kingsdown Country Hotel, Deal, Kent
Vicky Umbers, Parrock Head Farmhouse, Clitheroe, Lancs
Jean Wilson, Manuel's Farm, Newquay, Cornwall

PAST GUEST HOUSE OF THE YEAR AWARD WINNERS 1995 - 96

England Channel Islands, Hotel Petit Champ, Sark
Scotland Mardella Farmhouse, Gartocharn, Strathclyde
Wales Ffaldau Country House, Penybont, Powys
Ireland Assolas Country House, Kanturk, Co Cork

SOME ESTABLISHMENTS MAY NO LONGER BE IN THE AA SCHEME AND SOME MAY HAVE CHANGED HANDS.

Hall of Fame 1996-97

TOP TWENTY LANDLADIES

Finalists 1996- 97

Muriel Orme, Bank House, Oakamoor - ***winner***

Barbara Barbour, Beehive Manor, Maidenhead - ***runner-up***

Nicky Davies, Nant Y Fedw, Trefelin, Llanedgai - ***runner-up***

Daphne Burgoine, Fairway Lodge, Okehampton

Jane Conolly, Hills Farm, Leysters, Leominster

Pam Coulter, Dolffanog Fawr, Tal-Y-Lyn, Tywyn

Derek Davies, Alpine Lodge, Llanberis

Linda Harrison, Ashfield House Hotel, Grassington

Alice Jennings, The Jays Guest House, Aberdeen

Peta Lloyd, Fallowfields Country House, Kingston Bagpuize

Julia Masters, The Old Vicarage, Rye

Lilwen Mc Allister, Erw-Lan Farm, Pontfaen, Fishguard

Hazel Michael, Plas Bach Country House, Plas Bach

Sandie Pike, Vulcan Lodge, Horley

Bronwen Prosser, Upper Genffordd Farm Guest House, Talgarth

Olwen Roberts, York House Guest House, Hay-On-Wye

Caroline Robins, Hotel Petit Champ, Sark

Anita Sexon, Kingston House, Torquay

Annette Tofts, The Toll Barn, North Walsham

Gladys Whyte, Torbeag House, Muirshearlich, Banavie

BED & BREAKFAST OF THE YEAR 1996 - 97

England Grey Friar Lodge, Ambleside, Cumbria

Scotland The Grange, Fort William, Highland

Wales The Lighthouse, Llandudno, Conwy

Ireland Ballyvolane House, Fermoy, Co Cork

SOME ESTABLISHMENTS MAY NO LONGER BE IN THE AA SCHEME AND SOME MAY HAVE CHANGED HANDS.

BUDGET ACCOMMODATION

ENGLAND

BUCKINGHAMSHIRE

GAYHURST, Mill

CORNWALL & ISLES OF SCILLY

BOSCASTLE, Old Coach House
BUDE, Pencarrol
FALMOUTH, Harbour House
LOOE, Gulls Hotel
NEWQUAY, Aloha Hotel
PENZANCE, Camilla House Hotel
PENZANCE, Dunedin
PENZANCE, Tremont
PENZANCE, Trevelyan Hotel
PENZANCE, Treventon
PENZANCE, Trewella
ST IVES, The Hollies Hotel
SENNEN, The Old Manor Hotel

CUMBRIA

APPLEBY-IN-WESTMORLAND, Bongate House
EMBLETON, Lambfoot House
NEWBIGGIN-ON-LUNE, Low Lane House
PENRITH, Voreda View
SILLOTH, Nith View
WINDERMERE, Ivy Bank
WINDERMERE. Kenilworth

DERBYSHIRE

HATHERSAGE, Moorgate

DEVON

NORTHLEW, East Worth Farmhouse
SIDMOUTH, Ryton House
TORQUAY, Braddon Hall Hotel
TORQUAY, Grosvenor House Hotel
TORQUAY, Lindum Hotel
TORQUAY, Shirley Hotel
WITHERIDGE, Marchweeke

DORSET

BOURNEMOUTH. Amitie
SWANAGE, Firswood Hotel
WEYMOUTH, Warwick Court Hotel

ISLE OF WIGHT

SANDOWN, Bertram Lodge
SANDOWN, Chester Lodge Hotel

EAST RIDING OF YORKSHIRE

HULL, Earlesmere Hotel

EAST SUSSEX

BURWASH, Woodlands
CROWBOROUGH, The Cottage
EASTBOURNE, Mowbray Hotel

ESSEX

FELSTED, Potash Farmhouse

GLOUCESTERSHIRE

ULEY, Hodgecombe Farm

HAMPSHIRE,

PORTSMOUTH & SOUTHSEA, Fairlea
PORTSMOUTH & SOUTHSEA, The Festing Grove

HEREFORDSHIRE

HOARWITHY, The Old Mill

ROSS-ON-WYE, Brookfield House

KENT

DOVER, Linden
DYMCHURCH, Waterside

LANCASHIRE

BLACKPOOL, Claytons
BLACKPOOL, Lynwood
BLACKPOOL, The Colby Hotel
LYTHAM ST ANNES, Strathmore Hotel
MORECAMBE, Wimslow Private Hotel

NORFOLK

KING'S LYNN, Fairlight Lodge
KING'S LYNN, Havana
THURNING, Rookery

NORTH YORKSHIRE

CLAPHAM, Arbutus House
SCARBOROUGH, Argo Hotel
SCARBOROUGH, West Lodge Private Hotel
YORK, City
YORK, Cornmill Lodge
YORK, Hillcrest
YORK, Minster View
YORK, Sycamore

SHROPSHIRE

SHREWSBURY, Stiperstones

SOMERSET

BATH, Cairngorm
WESTON-SUPER-MARE, Conifers
WESTON-SUPER-MARE, Goodrington

STAFFORDSHIRE

STAFFORD, Old School

WARWICKSHIRE

STRATFORD-UPON-AVON, Curtain Call

WEST MIDLANDS

BIRMINGHAM, Rollason Wood Hotel

WORCESTERSHIRE

MALVERN, Four Hedges

ISLE OF MAN

DOUGLAS, Rosslyn Guest House

CHANNEL ISLANDS

JERSEY

ST MARY, Roc Annick

GUERNSEY

ST PETER PORT, Marine Hotel

REPUBLIC OF IRELAND

CO GALWAY

GALWAY, Roncalli House

CO KERRY

WATERVILLE, O'Gradys

SCOTLAND

ARGYLL & BUTE

CONNEL, Ronebhal
OBAN, Sgeir Mhaol

CITY OF EDINBURGH

EDINBURGH, An Fuaran
EDINBURGH, Ivy House

DUMFRIES & GALLOWAY

CASTLE DOUGLAS, Rose Cottage
MOFFAT, Boleskine

EAST LOTHIAN

DUNBAR, Springfield

FIFE

CRAIL, Selcraig House
ST ANDREWS, Cleveden House

HIGHLAND

DINGWALL, Millcraig
GARVE, Old Manse
KINGUSSIE, Avondale House
SPEAN BRIDGE, Coire Glas

MORAY

ELGIN, Belleville

PERTH & KINROSS

ABERFELDY, West Park Farm
AUCHTERARDER, Allandale House
BLAIR ATHOLL, Dalgreine
BLAIRGOWRIE, Gilmore House

SCOTTISH BORDERS

JEDBURGH, Bridge House

SOUTH AYRSHIRE

AYR, Dargill
BALLANTRAE, Cafe Ballantrae
PRESTWICK, Fernbank

WALES

CARMARTHENSHIRE

CWMDUAD, Neuadd-Wen

CONWY

COLWYN BAY, Cabin Hill Private Hotel
LLANDUDNO, Beach Cove
LLANDUDNO, Minion Private Hotel

DENBIGHSHIRE

PRESTATYN, Roughsedge House
RHYL, Links
RHYL, Pier Hotel

GWYNEDD

BANGOR, Goetre Isaf Farmhouse
DOLGELLAU, Glyn
PENYGROES, Llwyndu Mawr

PEMBROKESHIRE

STEPASIDE, Bay View Hotel

POWYS

LLYSWEN, Oakfield

Child-Free Zone

Of the establishments listed below, most will have a Child-Free symbol against their entry, but some did not want to be highlighted

ENGLAND

Arlington, East Sussex, **Bates Green**

Ashburton, Devon, **Rosary Mount**

Aylesbury, Buckinghamshire, **The Hamlet**

Bakewell, Derbyshire, **Everton**

Bantham, Devon, **Widcombe House**

Barnard Castle, County Durham, **Fox & Hounds**

Bath, Somerset, Badminton Villa

Bere Alston, Devon, **Treyard**

Bowness-on-Windermere, Cumbria, **Langthwaite**

Bratton Fleming, Devon, **Bracken House** - *No children under 12*

Brighton, East Sussex, **New Steine Hotel**

Brighton, East Sussex, **The Twenty One**

Bromsgrove, Worcestershire, **Rosa Lodge** - *No children under 12*

Burford, Oxfordshire, **Elm House**

Bury St Edmunds, Suffolk, **Twelve Angel Hill**

Buxton, Derbyshire, **Coningsby**

Buxton, Derbyshire, **Grendon**

Canterbury, Kent, **The Old Rectory**

Carlisle, Cumbria, **Cambro House**

Carlisle, Cumbria, East **View Guest House** - *No children under 5*

Castle Carrock, Cumbria, **Gelt Hall Farm**

Chard, Somerset, **Hawthorne House**

Cheltenham, Gloucestershire, **Malvern View**

Chillaton, Devon, **Tor Cottage**

Chipping Norton, Oxfordshire, **Falkland Arms**

Cirencester, Gloucestershire, **Smerrill Barns** - *No children under 10*

Crackington Haven, Cornwall, **Trevigue Farm**

Dartmouth, Devon, **Broome Court**

Dartmouth, Devon, **Hedley House**

Deal, Kent, **Sondes Lodge**

Dunster, Somerset, **Dollons House**

Fressingfield, Suffolk, **Chippenhall Hall**

Frinton-on-Sea, Essex, **Forde Guest House**

Grassington, N Yorks, **Ashfield House** - *No children under 5*

Great Yarmouth, Norfolk, **Winchester Private Hotel**

Hathersage, Derbyshire, **Scotsman's Pack Inn**

Hathersage, Derbyshire, **The Old Barn**

Hebden Bridge, West Yorkshire, **Redacre Mill Guest House**

Henley-in-Arden, Warwickshire, **Ashleigh House**

Higham, Suffolk, **The Bauble** - *No children under 12*

Hope, Derbyshire, **Underleigh House**

Ilfracombe, Devon, **Waterloo House Hotel**

Kendal, Cumbria, Higher **House Farm**

Keswick, Cumbria, **Brunholme Country House**
Keswick, Cumbria, **Derwent Cottage**
Lancaster, Lancashire, **Malt House**
Lewes, East Sussex, **Nightingales**
Lichfield, Staffs, Stone **House Farm** - *No children under 5*
Looe, Cornwall, **Harescombe Lodge**
Lowestoft, Suffolk, **Rockville House**
Lymington, Hampshire, **Efford Cottage**
Macclesfield, Cheshire, **Hardingland Farm**
Maidenhead, Berkshire, **Beehive Manor**
Malmesbury, Wiltshire, **The Horse & Groom**
Malvern, Worcestershire, **The Dell House**
Malvern, Worcestershire, **The Mill House**
Matlock, Derbyshire, **Manor House**
Miller's Dale, Derbyshire, **Dale Cottage**
Molesworth, Cambridgeshire, **Cross Keys**
Nettlecombe, Dorset, The **Marquis of Lorne**
Newquay, Cornwall, **Bon-Ami Hotel**
North Wootton, Somerset, **Greenacres**
Moretonhampstead, Devon, **Gate House**
Northleach, Gloucestershire, **Cotteswold House**
Norton St Philip, Somerset, **The Bath Lodge Hotel** - *No children under 10*
Nottingham, Nottinghamshire, Hall **Farm House**
Oakford, Devon, **Newhouse Farm**
Oxhill, Warwick, **Nolands Farm** - *No children under 7*
Padstow, Cornwall, **The Old Cabbage Patch**
Penzance, Cornwall, **Woodstock House**
Perranuthnoe, Cornwall, **Ednovean Farm**
Plymouth, Devon, **Devonshire Guest House**
Porthcurno, Cornwall, **Porthcurno Hotel**
Ravenstone, Leics, **Church Lane Farm**
Reeth, N Yorks, **Arkleside Hotel**
Rushlake Green, East Sussex, **Great Crouch's**
Rye, East Sussex, **Jeake's House**
Rye, East Sussex, **King Charles II Guest House**
St Ives, Cornwall, **Dean Court Hotel**
Salisbury, Wiltshire, **Cricket Field Cottage**
Salisbury, Wilts, **Edwardian Lodge Guest House**
Salisbury, Wiltshire, **Glen Lyn House**
Salisbury, Wiltshire, **Rokeby Guest House**
Salisbury, Wiltshire, **Victoria Lodge**
Shipston on Stour, Warwickshire, **The Manor**
Sidmouth, Devon, **Southcombe Guest House**
Southampton, Hampshire, **Landguard Lodge** - *No children under 5*
Stratford-Upon-Avon, Warwickshire, **Brook Lodge** - *No children under 5*
Stratford-on-Avon, Warwickshire, **Eversley Bears**
Stoke on Trent, Staffordshire, The **White House Hotel**
Stow-on-the-Wold, Gloucestershire, **College House**
Sutton Coldfield, West Midlands, **Windrush**
Sway, Hants, **The Nurse's Cottage**
Tamworth, Staffordshire, **The Sleepy Owl**
Thirsk, North Yorkshire, **Spital Hill**
Tiverton, Devon, Lower **Collipriest Farm**
Torquay, Devon, **Crown Lodge**
Torquay, Devon, **Hotel Fleurie**

Torquay, Devon, **Shirley Hotel**
Truro, Cornwall, **Arrallas**
Truro, Cornwall, **Bissick Old Mill**
Truro, Cornwall, **Rock Cottage**
Tunbridge Wells, Kent, **Danehurst Hotel**
West Drayton, Greater London, **Longford Guest House**
Whitchurch, Shropshire, **Dearnford Hall**
Wight, Isle of, Newport, **Elizabeth House**
Wight, Isle of, Shanklin, **Culham Lodge Hotel**
Wight, Isle of, Shanklin, **Osborne House Hotel** - *No children under 13*
Windermere, Cumbria, **The Beaumont** - *No children under 10*
Winsford, Somerset, **Savery's at Karslake House Hotel**
Wisbech, Cambridgeshire, **Stratton Farm**
Yealand Conyers, Lancashire, **The Bower**
York, **The Heathers Guest House** - *No children under 10*

CHANNEL ISLANDS

Greve de Lecq Bay, **Jersey, Hotel des Pierres**

SCOTLAND

Castle Douglas, Dumfries & Galloway, **Barrington House**
Connel, Argyll & Bute, **Ards House**
Connel, Argyll & Bute, **Ronebhal Guest House** - *No children under 7*
Dingwall, Highland, **Millcraig**
Dornoch, Highland, **Highfield**
Drumnadrochit, Highland, **Enrick Cottage**
Eaglesham, East Renfrewshire, **New Borland**
Elgin, Moray, **Non Smokers Haven**
Gairloch, Highland, **Birchwood Guest House**
Grantown-on-Spey, Highland, **Rossmor Guest House**
Inverness, Highland, **Ballifeary House Hotel**
Inverness, Highland, **Inchberry House**
Nethybridge, Highland, **Aultmore House**
St Andrews, Fife, **Edenside House**
St Andrews, Fife, **Glenderran**
Twynholm, Dumfries & Galloway, **Fresh Fields Guest House**
Ullapool, Highland, **Dromnan Guest House**
Wick, Highland, **The Clachan**

WALES

Abergavenny, Gwent, **Llanwenarth House** - *No children under 10*
Betws-y-Coed, Conwy, **Bryn Bella**
Betws-y-Coed, Conwy, **Bryn-y-Gwynt**
Llandrindod Wells, Powys, **Guidfa House**
Llandudno, Conwy, **Beach Cove**
Penybont, Powys, **Ffaldau Country House**
Talgarth, Brecon, **Upper Genffordd Farm**

IRELAND

Achill Island, Co Mayo, **Gray's Guest House**
Achill Island, Co Mayo, **West Coast House**
Adare, Co Limerick, **Adare Lodge**
Arthurstown, Co Wexford, **Glendine Country House**
Drogheda, Co Louth, **Boynehaven House**
Galway, Co Galway, **Silverseas Guest House**
Kylemore, Co Galway, **Kylemore House**
Mullingar, Co Westmeath, **Hilltop House**
Oughterard, Co Galway, **The Boat Inn**

Readers' Report form

Please write to: Editor, AA Bed & Breakfast Guide,
Publishing Division,
The Automobile Association, Fanum House,
Basingstoke RG21 4EA

Please use this form to recommend any hotel where you have stayed which is not already in our guide.

If you have any comments about your stay at a hotel listed in the guide, we shall be grateful if you will let us know, as feedback from readers helps us to keep our guide accurate and up to date. Please note, however, that if you have a complaint to make during a stay, we do recommend that you discuss the matter with the hotel management there and then so that they have a chance to put things right before your stay is spoilt.

Please note that the AA does not undertake to arbitrate between you and the hotel management, or to obtain compensation or engage in protracted correspondence.

Your name (block capitals) ....

....

....

Your address (block capitals) ....

....

....

....

....

....

Comments ....

....

....

....

....

....

Readers' Report form

. . . .

. . . .

. . . .

. . . .

. . . .

. . . .

. . . .

. . . .

. . . .

. . . .

. . . .

. . . .

. . . .

. . . .

. . . .

. . . .

. . . .

. . . .

. . . .

. . . .

. . . .

. . . .

. . . .

. . . .

. . . .

BED &
BREAKFAST
1999

Please post to: The Editor, AA B&B Guide, Editorial Department, The Automobile Association, Fanum House, Basingstoke, Hampshire RG21 2EA

Please write to: Editor, AA Bed & Breakfast Guide,
Publishing Division,
The Automobile Association, Fanum House,
Basingstoke RG21 4EA

Readers' Report form

Please use this form to recommend any hotel where you have stayed which is not already in our guide.

If you have any comments about your stay at a hotel listed in the guide, we shall be grateful if you will let us know, as feedback from readers helps us to keep our guide accurate and up to date. Please note, however, that if you have a complaint to make during a stay, we do recommend that you discuss the matter with the hotel management there and then so that they have a chance to put things right before your stay is spoilt.

Please note that the AA does not undertake to arbitrate between you and the hotel management, or to obtain compensation or engage in protracted correspondence.

Your name (block capitals) ....

....

....

Your address (block capitals) ....

....

....

....

....

....

Comments ....

....

....

....

....

....

BED &
BREAKFAST
1999

Please post to: The Editor, AA B&B Guide, Editorial Department, The Automobile Association, Fanum House, Basingstoke, Hampshire RG21 2EA

Readers' Report form

Please write to: Editor, AA Bed & Breakfast Guide,
Publishing Division,
The Automobile Association, Fanum House,
Basingstoke RG21 4EA

Please use this form to recommend any hotel where you have stayed which is not already in our guide.

If you have any comments about your stay at a hotel listed in the guide, we shall be grateful if you will let us know, as feedback from readers helps us to keep our guide accurate and up to date. Please note, however, that if you have a complaint to make during a stay, we do recommend that you discuss the matter with the hotel management there and then so that they have a chance to put things right before your stay is spoilt.

Please note that the AA does not undertake to arbitrate between you and the hotel management, or to obtain compensation or engage in protracted correspondence.

Your name (block capitals) ....

....

....

Your address (block capitals) ....

....

....

....

....

....

Comments ....

....

....

....

....

....

. . . .

BED & BREAKFAST 1999

Please post to: The Editor, AA B&B Guide, Editorial Department, The Automobile Association, Fanum House, Basingstoke, Hampshire RG21 2EA

Readers' Report form

Please write to: Editor, AA Bed & Breakfast Guide,
Publishing Division,
The Automobile Association, Fanum House,
Basingstoke RG21 4EA

Please use this form to recommend any hotel where you have stayed which is not already in our guide.

If you have any comments about your stay at a hotel listed in the guide, we shall be grateful if you will let us know, as feedback from readers helps us to keep our guide accurate and up to date. Please note, however, that if you have a complaint to make during a stay, we do recommend that you discuss the matter with the hotel management there and then so that they have a chance to put things right before your stay is spoilt.

Please note that the AA does not undertake to arbitrate between you and the hotel management, or to obtain compensation or engage in protracted correspondence.

Your name (block capitals) ....

....

....

Your address (block capitals) ....

....

....

....

....

....

Comments ....

....

....

....

....

....

. . . .

. . . .

. . . .

BED & BREAKFAST 1999

Please post to: The Editor, AA B&B Guide, Editorial Department, The Automobile Association, Fanum House, Basingstoke, Hampshire RG21 2EA

KEY TO ATLAS

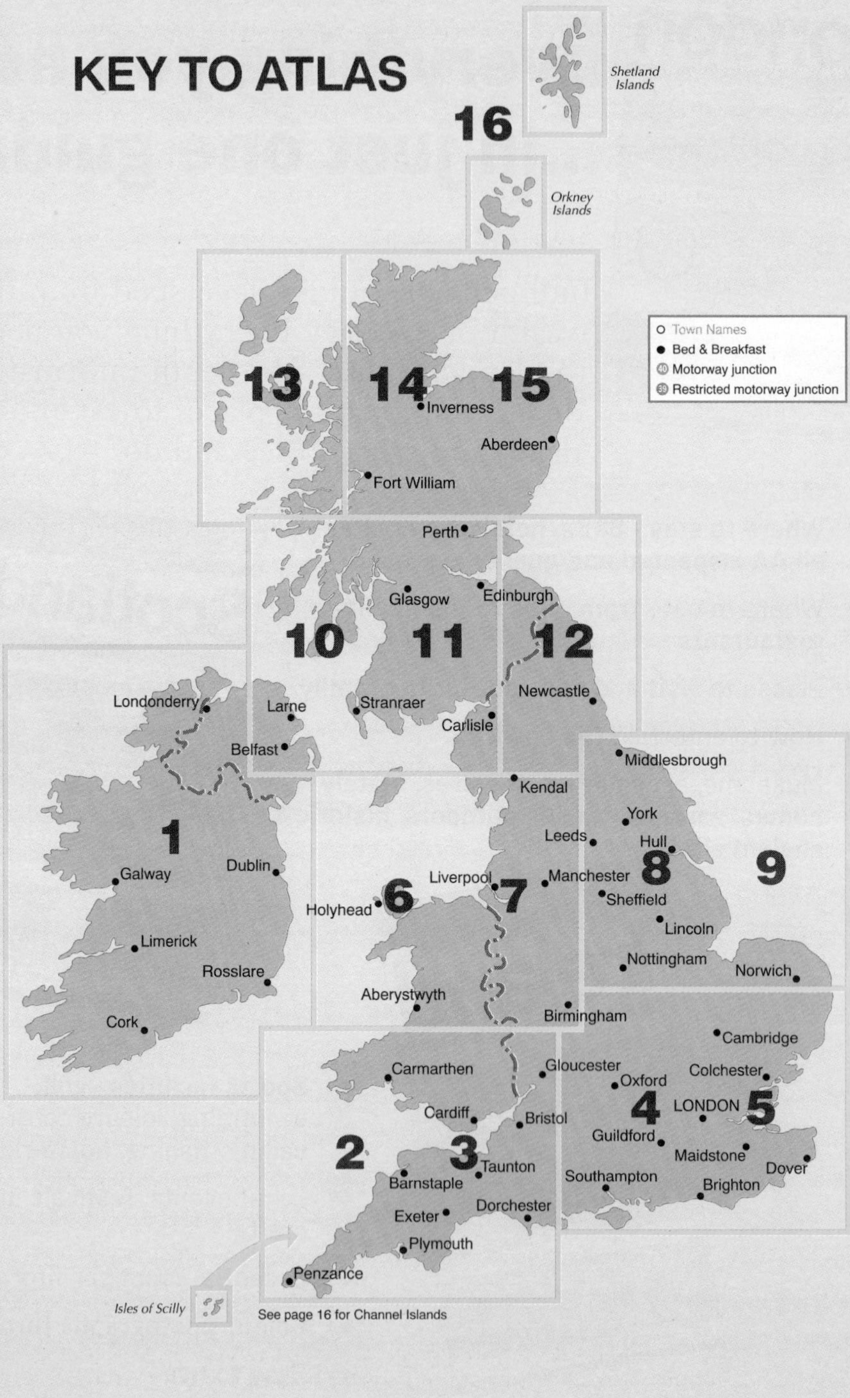

See page 16 for Channel Islands

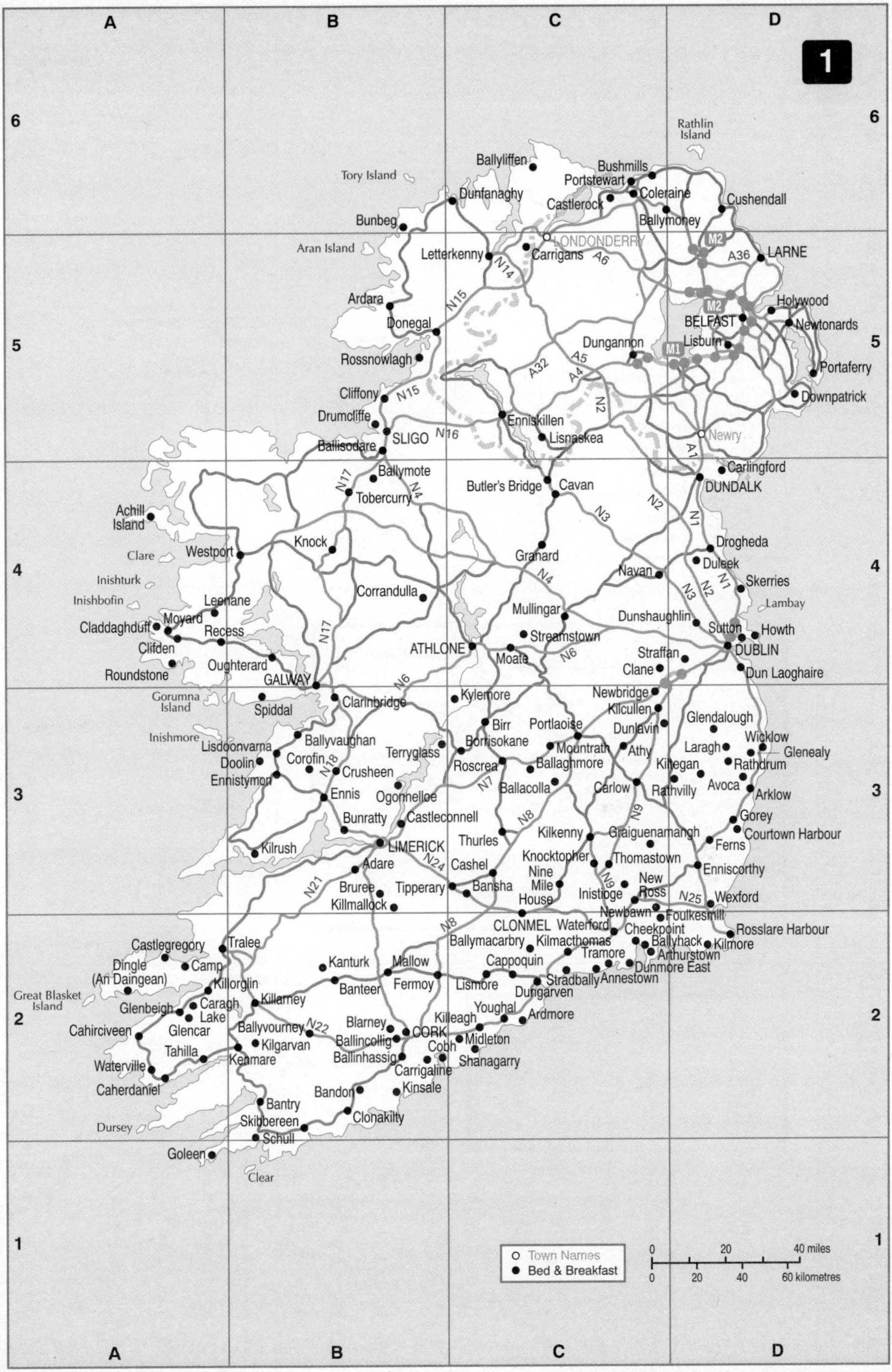

A
B
C
D
1
6
Rathlin Island
Ballyliffen
Bushmills
Tory Island
Portstewart
Coleraine
Dunfanaghy
Castlerock
Cushendall
Ballymoney
Bunbeg
LONDONDERRY
Aran Island
Letterkenny
Carrigans
M2
A6
A36
LARNE
N14
Ardara
N15
M2
Holywood
BELFAST
Newtonards
Donegal
5
Dungannon
Lisburn
M1
Rossnowlagh
A5
A32
A4
Portaferry
Cliffony
N15
N2
Downpatrick
Drumcliffe
Enniskillen
SLIGO
N16
Lisnaskea
Newry
Ballisodare
A1
Carlingford
Ballymote
N17
N4
Butler's Bridge
Cavan
DUNDALK
Tobercurry
Achill Island
N3
N2
N1
Knock
Drogheda
Clare
Westport
Granard
Duleek
Inishturk
N4
Navan
N1
Skerries
4
Corrandulla
N3
N2
Inishbofin
Leenane
Mullingar
Lambay
Moyard
Dunshaughlin
Claddaghduff
Recess
N17
Streamstown
Sutton
Howth
Clifden
ATHLONE
N6
DUBLIN
Moate
Straffan
Roundstone
Oughterard
Clane
Dun Laoghaire
GALWAY
N6
Gorumna Island
Spiddal
Clarinbridge
Kylemore
Newbridge
Kilcullen
Birr
Portlaoise
Glendalough
Inishmore
Lisdoonvarna
Ballyvaughan
Borrisokane
Dunlavin
Wicklow
Doolin
Corofin
Terryglass
Mountrath
Athy
Laragh
Glenealy
N18
Crusheen
Roscrea
Ballaghmore
Kiltegan
Rathdrum
Ennistymon
N7
Carlow
Avoca
3
Ennis
Ogonnelloe
Ballacolla
Rathvilly
Arklow
N9
Gorey
Bunratty
Castleconnell
N8
Kilkenny
Graiguenamanagh
Courtown Harbour
Thurles
Ferns
Kilrush
LIMERICK
Adare
N24
Cashel
Knocktopher
Thomastown
Enniscorthy
Nine Mile House
New Ross
N21
Bruree
Tipperary
Bansha
N9
Inistioge
N25
Wexford
Killmallock
Newbawn
Foulkesmill
CLONMEL
Waterford
N8
Cheekpoint
Rosslare Harbour
Castlegregory
Tralee
Ballymacarbry
Kilmacthomas
Ballyhack
Kilmore
Arthurstown
Tramore
Dingle (An Daingean)
Camp
Kanturk
Mallow
Cappoquin
Dunmore East
Great Blasket Island
Killorglin
Banteer
Fermoy
Lismore
Stradbally
Annestown
Dungarven
Glenbeigh
Caragh Lake
Killarney
Youghal
2
Ballyvourney
N22
Blarney
Killeagh
Ardmore
Cahirciveen
Glencar
Kilgarvan
CORK
Ballincollig
Midleton
Cobh
Tahilla
Kenmare
Ballinhassig
Shanagarry
Waterville
Carrigaline
Caherdaniel
Bandon
Kinsale
Bantry
Clonakilty
Dursey
Skibbereen
Schull
Goleen
Clear
Town Names
Bed & Breakfast
0
20
40 miles
0
20
40
60 kilometres

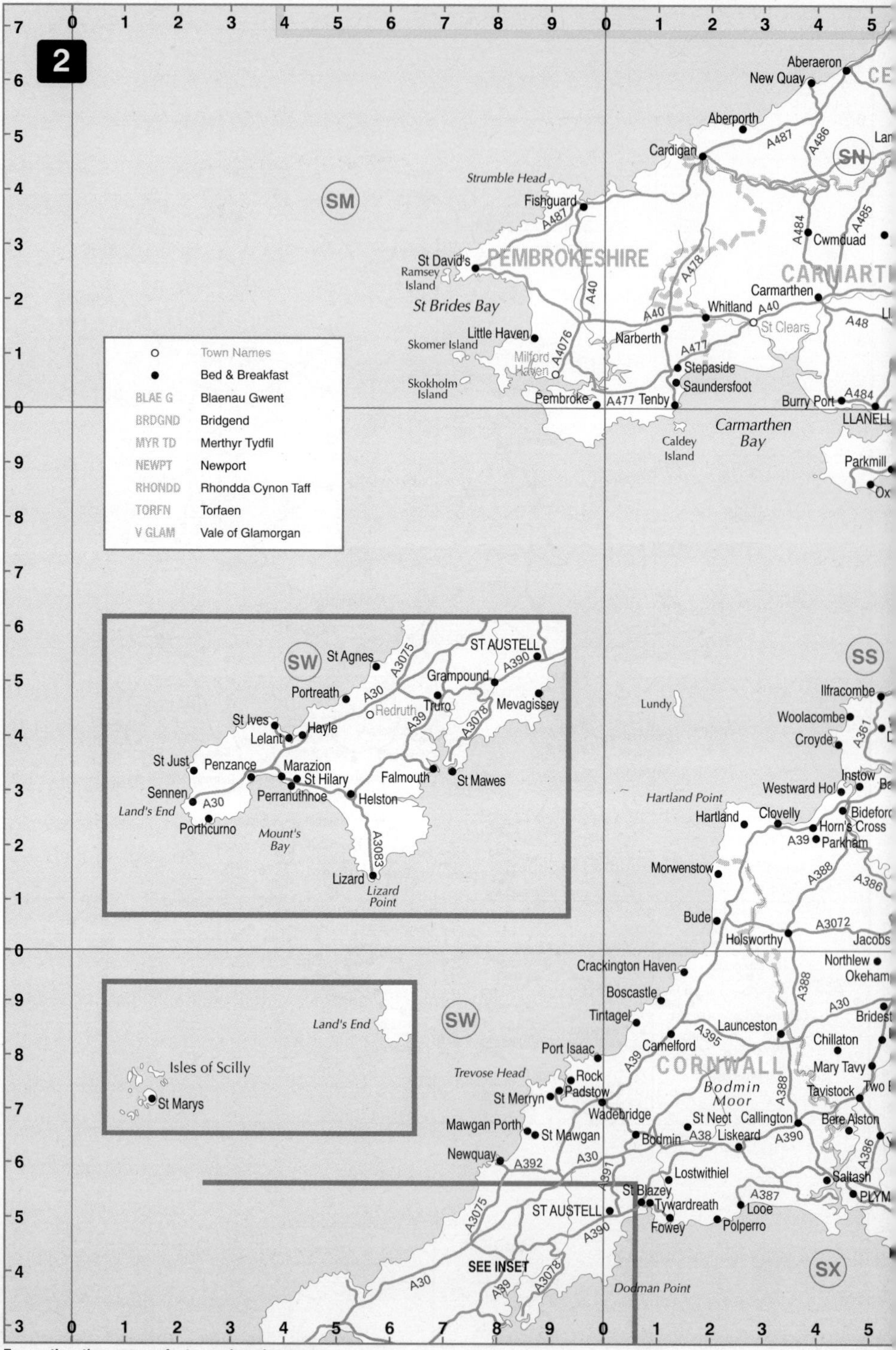

For continuation pages refer to numbered arrows

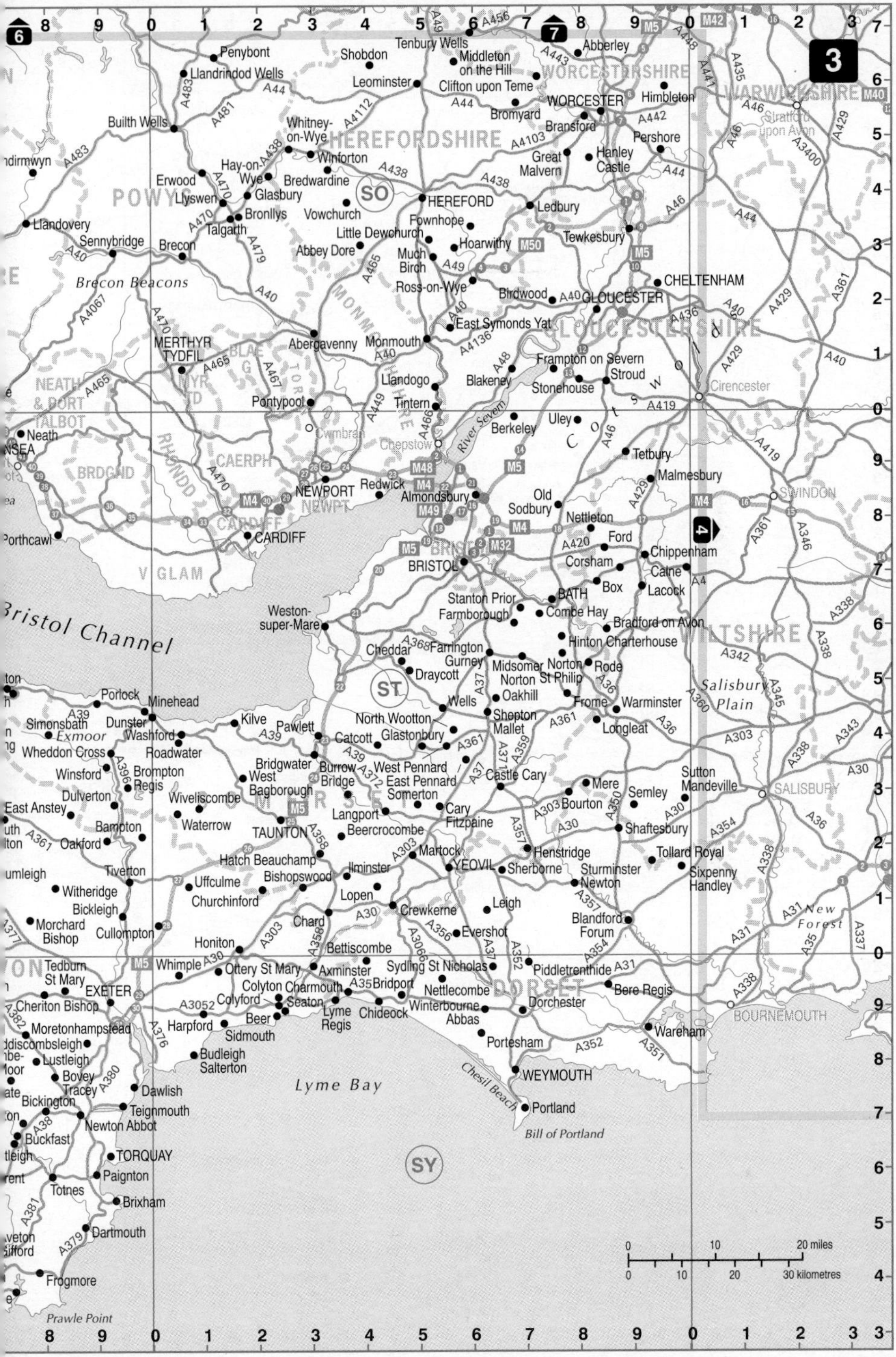
3
HEREFORDSHIRE
WORCESTERSHIRE
WARWICKSHIRE
GLOUCESTERSHIRE
POWYS
WILTSHIRE
DORSET
SO
ST
SY
Bristol Channel
Lyme Bay
Brecon Beacons
Cotswold
Salisbury Plain
New Forest
Exmoor
Chesil Beach
Bill of Portland
Prawle Point
River Severn
Worcester
Hereford
Gloucester
Cheltenham
Tewkesbury
Leominster
Ledbury
Ross-on-Wye
Monmouth
Abergavenny
Brecon
Builth Wells
Llandrindod Wells
Llandovery
Merthyr Tydfil
Pontypool
Cwmbran
Newport
Cardiff
Chepstow
Tintern
Bristol
Bath
Chippenham
Swindon
Cirencester
Stroud
Tetbury
Malmesbury
Weston-super-Mare
Wells
Glastonbury
Frome
Warminster
Salisbury
Bridgwater
Taunton
Yeovil
Sherborne
Shaftesbury
Blandford Forum
Dorchester
Weymouth
Portland
Bridport
Lyme Regis
Axminster
Honiton
Exeter
Sidmouth
Exmouth
Dawlish
Teignmouth
Newton Abbot
Torquay
Paignton
Brixham
Dartmouth
Totnes
Kingsbridge
Minehead
Dunster
Porlock
Tiverton
Wareham
Bournemouth
Swansea
Neath
Porthcawl
Stratford upon Avon
Malvern
Pershore
Bromyard
Tenbury Wells
20 miles
30 kilometres

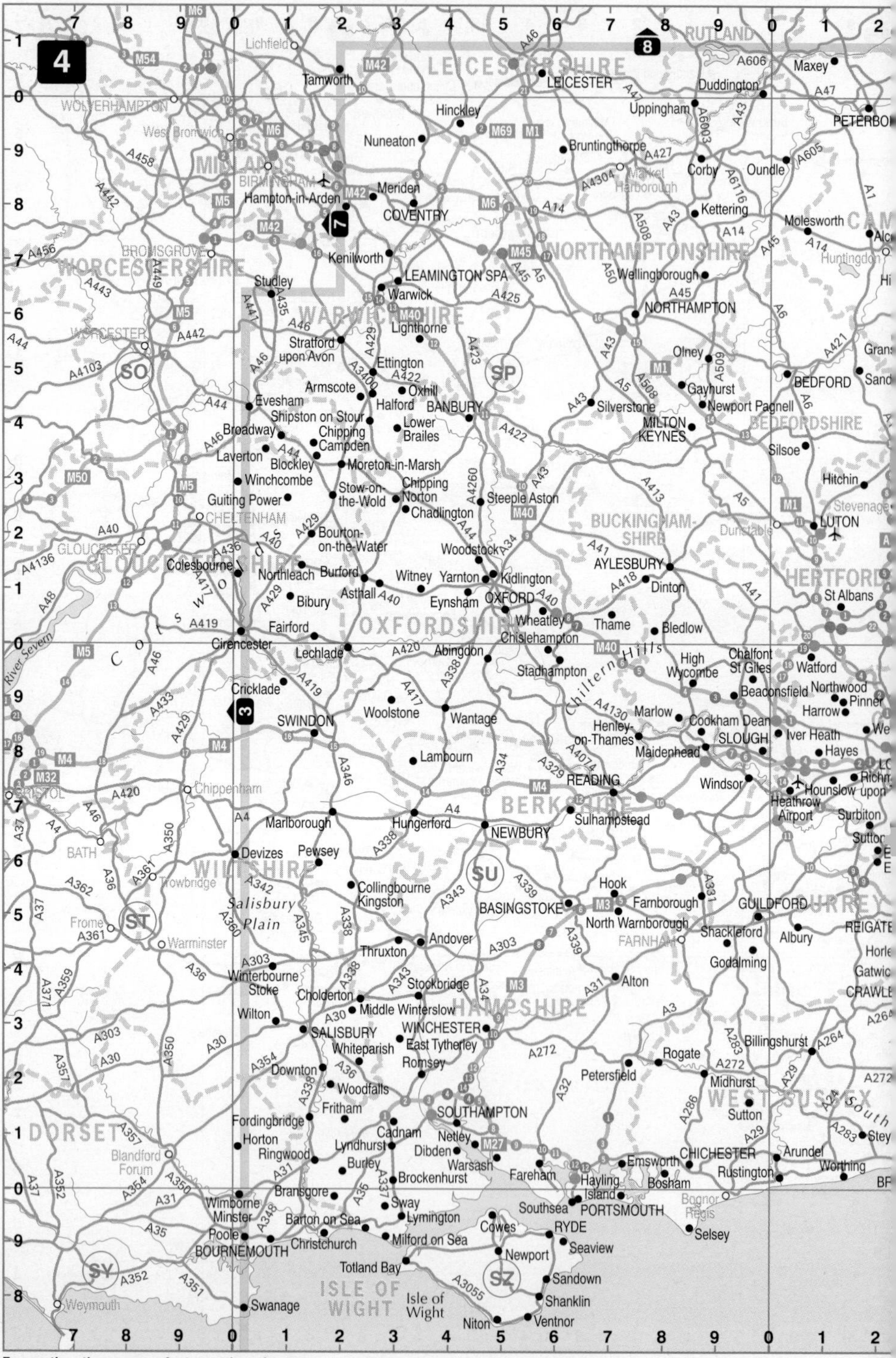

For continuation pages refer to numbered arrows

5
NORFOLK
Swaffham
NORWICH
GREAT YARMOUTH
Downham Market
Stoke Holy Cross
Reedham
March
LOWESTOFT
Tivetshall St Mary
Bungay
Beccles
Brandon
Thetford
Garboldisham
Mendham
Harleston
Ely
Fressingfield
Southwold
SHIRE
Eye
Gislingham
SUFFOLK
Beyton
BURY ST EDMUNDS
Framlingham
CAMBRIDGE
Kirtling
Needham Market
Hartest
Lavenham
Woodbridge
Orford Ness
TM
TL
Boxford
IPSWICH
Sudbury
Saffron Walden
Stoke-by-Nayland
Felixstowe
Nayland
Higham
Manningtree
Bradfield
Mistley
Harwich
Wix
Earls Colne
The Naze
Great Dunmow
Braintree
COLCHESTER
Felsted
Frinton-on-Sea
CLACTON-ON-SEA
Margaret Roding
ESSEX
CHELMSFORD
Maldon
Foulness Island
Romford
Ilford
Basildon
SOUTHEND-ON-SEA
R Thames
Tilbury
Sheerness
Isle of Sheppey
MARGATE
Broadstairs
Whitstable
Herne Bay
Ramsgate
Sittingbourne
Faversham
Wrotham
Aylesford
CANTERBURY
West Malling
North Downs
Sevenoaks
Mereworth
MAIDSTONE
Warren Street
Chilham
Littlebourne
Deal
Tonbridge
Shipbourne
Charing
TR
Penshurst
Pluckley
KENT
ASHFORD
CHANNEL TUNNEL TERMINAL
Dover
TQ
TUNBRIDGE WELLS
Lamberhurst
Cranbrook
Folkestone
Hartfield
Wadhurst
Tenterden
Hythe
Hawkhurst
Dymchurch
Strait of Dover
Crowborough
Appledore
Burwash
Sandhurst
Uckfield
Heathfield
Rye
Rushlake Green
Winchelsea
Dungeness
Battle
SUSSEX
St Leonards
Herstmonceux
HASTINGS
Arlington
Bexhill
Wilmington
Pevensey
Seaford
EASTBOURNE
Beachy Head
TV
Town Names
Bed & Breakfast
20 miles
30 kilometres

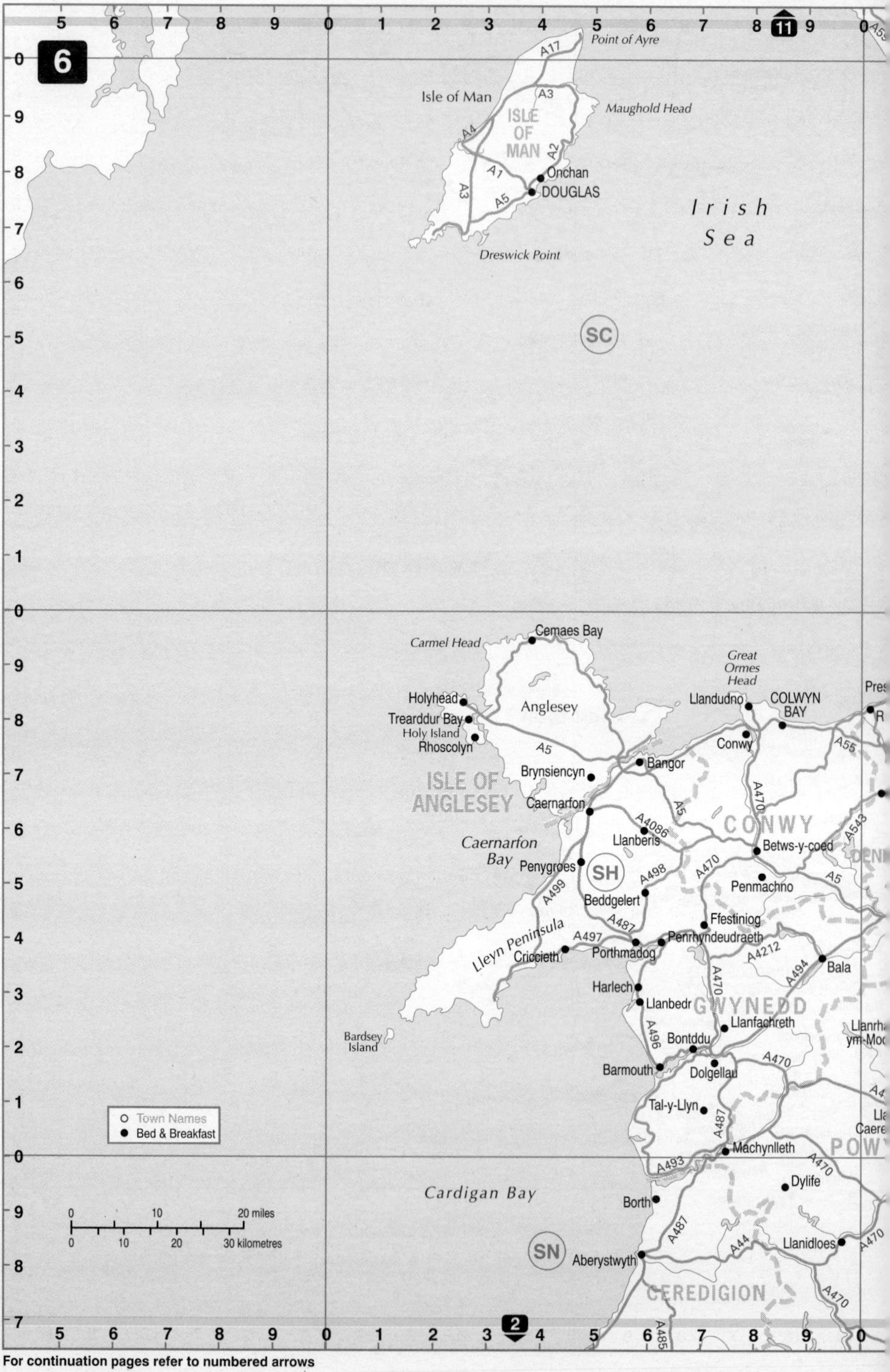

For continuation pages refer to numbered arrows

7
12
8
4
3
North York Moors
Yorkshire Dales
NORTH YORKSHIRE
THE PENNINES
LANCASHIRE
WEST YORKSHIRE
SOUTH YORKSHIRE
GREATER MANCHESTER
CHESHIRE
DERBYSHIRE
NOTTINGHAMSHIRE
STAFFORDSHIRE
SHROPSHIRE
LEICESTERSHIRE
WEST MIDLANDS
Peak District
SD
SE
SK
SJ
SO
SP
Ambleside
Troutbeck
Hawkshead
Windermere
Bowness-on-Windermere
Kendal
Tebay
Sedbergh
Crosthwaite
Brigsteer
Levens
Newby Bridge
Arnside
Cartmel
Kirkby Lonsdale
Yealand Conyers
Ingleton
Carnforth
Clapham
MORECAMBE
LANCASTER
Horton in Ribblesdale
Settle
Giggleswick
Kettlewell
Threshfield
Grassington
Burnsall
Malham
Thwaite
Muker
Reeth
Richmond
Scotch Corner
Hawes
Leyburn
Hunton
Middleham
Northallerton
Thirsk
Ripon
Malton
Harrogate
YORK
Skipton
Ilkley
Slaidburn
Whitewell
Bolton by Bowland
Guiseley
Clitheroe
Keighley
Bingley
Colne
Haworth
Longridge
Weeton
BRADFORD
LEEDS
Selby
Burnley
Hebden Bridge
Halifax
PRESTON
Blackburn
St Anne's
Goole
Dewsbury
Wakefield
Pontefract
Eccleston
Chorley
Rochdale
Huddersfield
Bury
Bolton
Delph
Holmfirth
Barnsley
DONCASTER
Salford
MANCHESTER
Newton-le-Willows
LIVERPOOL
Bootle
St Helens
Glossop
Hyde
Stockport
Sale
Altrincham
Warrington
Manchester Airport
SHEFFIELD
Edale
Hope
Castleton
Chapel-en-le-Frith
Wilmslow
Knutsford
Runcorn
Mersey
Northwich
Kingsley
Tideswell
Buxton
Millar's Dale
MACCLESFIELD
Ashford in the Water
CHESTER
Middlewich
Sandbach
Congleton
CREWE
Alsager
Leek
Marford
Cholmondeley
Nantwich
Audley
Cheddleton
Grindon
Tissington
Ilam
WREXHAM
Malpas
Wybunbury
Betley
Waterhouses
Stanton
Ashbourne
Newcastle-under-Lyme
STOKE-ON-TRENT
Oakamoor
Cheadle
Alton
Alkmonton
NOTTINGHAM
Whitchurch
Uttoxeter
DERBY
Market Drayton
Stone
Doveridge
Wem
Eccleshall
Adbaston
Burton upon Trent
Ruyton-XI-Towns
STAFFORD
Abbots Bromley
LOUGHBOROUGH
Knockin
Newport
SHREWSBURY
TELFORD
Ironbridge
Lichfield
Oakham
Minsterley
Dorrington
LEICESTER
Cressage
Codsall
Longnor
Much Wenlock
Sutton Coldfield
Church Stoke
Church Stretton
Bridgnorth
West Bromwich
Nuneaton
Bishop's Castle
Aston Munslow
Blackheath
BIRMINGHAM
Kinver
Clun
Craven Arms
COVENTRY
Solihull
Kidderminster
Ludlow
Wigmore
Brimfield
Bromsgrove
Henley-in-Arden
M6
M55
M61
M65
M66
M62
M58
M63
M56
M53
M1
M621
M18
M180
M181
M54
M5
M42
M69
M45
A1(M)
A685
A683
A684
A6108
A167
A172
A19
A168
A170
A169
A590
A65
A68
A6068
A59
A64
A658
A61
A58
A163
A614
A63
A6
A570
A565
A640
A638
A629
A628
A635
A161
A159
A616
A57
A631
A620
A156
A621
A623
A619
A1
A556
A533
A50
A54
A53
A515
A60
A617
A534
A483
A41
A500
A523
A6097
A46
A49
A525
A52
A495
A516
A564
A453
A606
A607
A51
A518
A519
A528
A5
A444
A42
A458
A442
A447
A47
A488
A489
A4117
A4113
A449
A448
A4304
A427
A6003
A45
A452
A14
A508
A34
A38

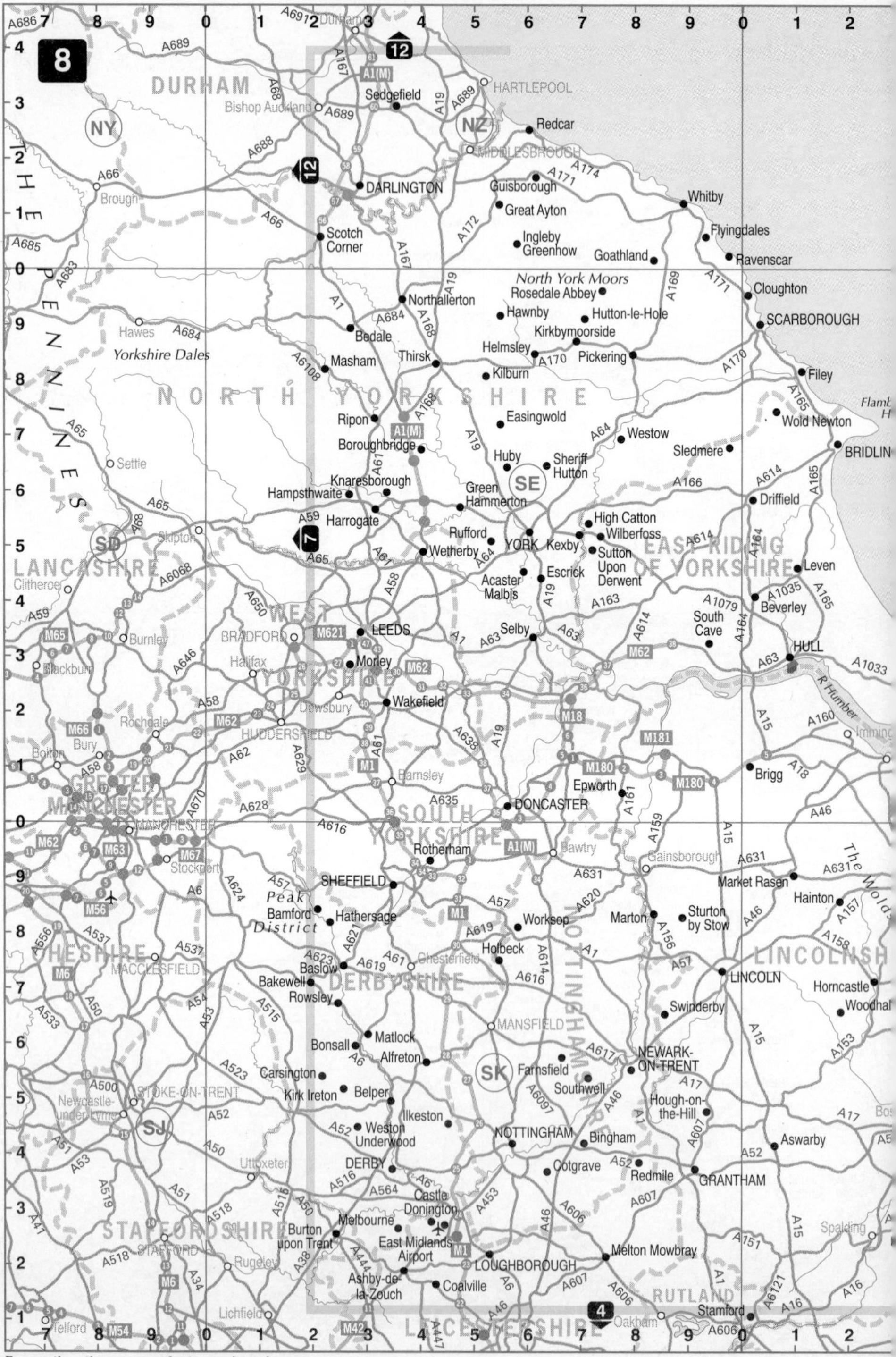

For continuation pages refer to numbered arrows

9
TA
TF
TG
n Head
Skegness
A52
The Wash
Hunstanton
Cley next the Sea
Blakeney
Sheringham
Cromer
Holt
A149
A148
Fakenham
Barney
Thurning
NORFOLK
KING'S LYNN
A17
A47
A10
Wisbech
Castle Acre
A1065
Swaffham
Downham Market
5
Horsford
A140
A1067
Coltishall
A1151
Horsham St Faith
Neatishead
A149
A47
The Broads
GREAT YARMOUTH
0 10 20 miles
0 10 20 30 kilometres
Town Names
Bed & Breakfast

For continuation pages refer to numbered arrows

11
PERTH AND KINROSS
DUNDEE CITY
FIFE
CLACKS
STIRLING
FALKIRK
WEST LOTHIAN
C EDIN
MIDLOTHIAN
N LANS
SOUTH LANARKSHIRE
EAST LOTHIAN
BORDERS (SCOTTISH)
DUMFRIES AND GALLOWAY
NORTHUMBERLAND
DURHAM
CUMBRIA
NORTH SEA
Firth of Tay
Firth of Forth
Solway Firth
St Andrews Bay
Fife Ness
Isle of May
St Abb's Head
Holy Island
Lammermuir Hills
Southern Uplands
The Cheviot Hills
Lake District
Abbey Head
North Head
NO
NT
NS
NY
Dunkeld
DUNDEE
Arbroath
Lochearnhead
Comrie
Crieff
PERTH
Forgandenny
Auchterarder
Auchtermuchty
Cupar
St Andrews
Stathmiglo
Ladybank
Callander
Kinross
Markinch
Thornhill
Dunblane
STIRLING
Cowdenbeath
Dalgety Bay
Dunfermline
Aberdour
Inverkeithing
Denny
Falkirk
Bo'ness
South Queensferry
Linlithgow
Livingston
EDINBURGH
Dunbar
Glenmavis
Airdrie
GLASGOW
Coatbridge
East Calder
Loanhead
Roslin
East Kilbride
Berwick-upon-Tweed
Strathaven
Kirkmuirhill
Peebles
Coldstream
Innerleithen
Galashiels
Biggar
St Mary's Loch
Jedburgh
Hawick
Alnwick
Moffat
Penpont
Otterburn
Morpeth
Langholm
Lockerbie
Dumfries
Gretna Green
Gretna
Longtown
Corbridge
Hexham
Castle Douglas
Dalbeattie
Kirkbean
CARLISLE
Twynholm
Kirkcudbright
Silloth
Wigton
Consett
Caldbeck
Bassenthwaite
Cockermouth
Mungrisdale
Embleton
Penrith
Lorton
Keswick
Troutbeck
Braithwaite
Whitehaven
Thirlmere
Borrowdale
Matterdale End
Grasmere
M90
M9
M80
M73
M8
M77
M74
A74(M)
M6
A827
A826
A822
A9
A94
A90
A92
A914
A91
A915
A917
A85
A84
A823
A811
A1
A198
A1107
A6105
A697
A6112
A698
A68
A7
A8
A71
A70
A702
A703
A701
A706
A73
A726
A721
A72
A8089
A708
A6088
A74
A696
A709
A712
A713
A711
A75
A710
A69
A689
A695
A6
A596
A595
A686
A66
A591
A5086
A688
A691
6 7 8 9 0 1 2 3 4 5 6 7 8 9 0 1
4 3 2 1 0 9 8 7 6 5 4 3 2 1 0 9 8 7 6 5 4 3 2 1
15
12
7

For continuation pages refer to numbered arrows

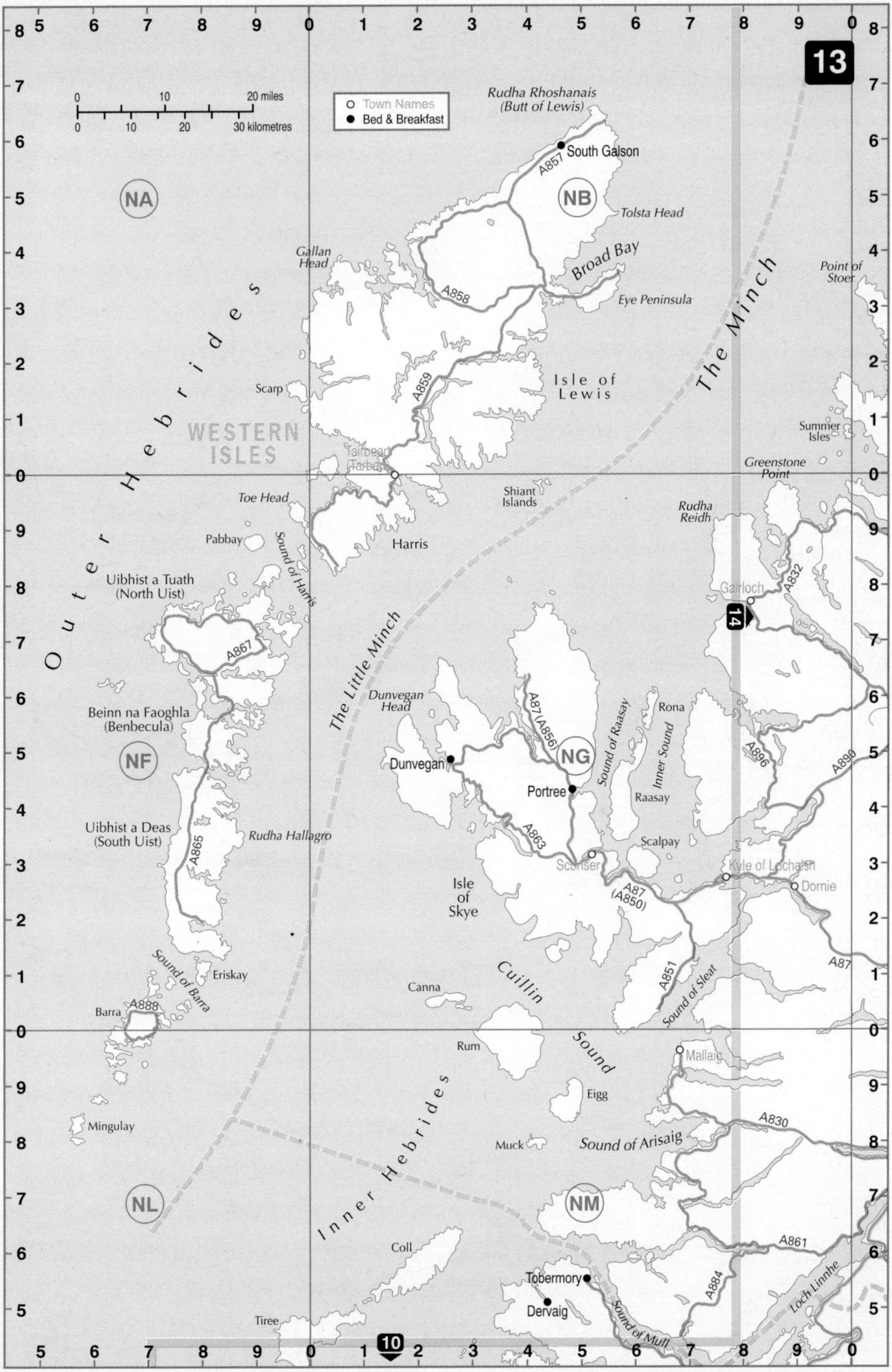

13
0 10 20 miles
0 10 20 30 kilometres
Town Names
Bed & Breakfast
Rudha Rhoshanais
(Butt of Lewis)
South Galson
A857
NA
NB
NF
NG
NL
NM
Tolsta Head
Broad Bay
Eye Peninsula
Gallan Head
A858
A859
Isle of Lewis
The Minch
Point of Stoer
Outer Hebrides
Scarp
WESTERN ISLES
Tairbeart (Tarbert)
Summer Isles
Greenstone Point
Toe Head
Shiant Islands
Rudha Reidh
Pabbay
Sound of Harris
Harris
Uibhist a Tuath
(North Uist)
Gairloch
A832
14
A867
The Little Minch
Dunvegan Head
A87 (A856)
Sound of Raasay
Rona
Inner Sound
Beinn na Faoghla
(Benbecula)
A896
A890
Dunvegan
Portree
Raasay
Uibhist a Deas
(South Uist)
Rudha Hallagro
A865
A863
Scalpay
Sconser
Kyle of Lochalsh
Dornie
Isle of Skye
A87 (A850)
Cuillin
A87
Sound of Barra
Eriskay
Canna
A851
Sound of Sleat
Barra
A888
Rum
Sound
Mallaig
Eigg
Inner Hebrides
A830
Mingulay
Muck
Sound of Arisaig
A861
Coll
Loch Linnhe
Tobermory
A884
Dervaig
Sound of Mull
Tiree
10

For continuation pages refer to numbered arrows

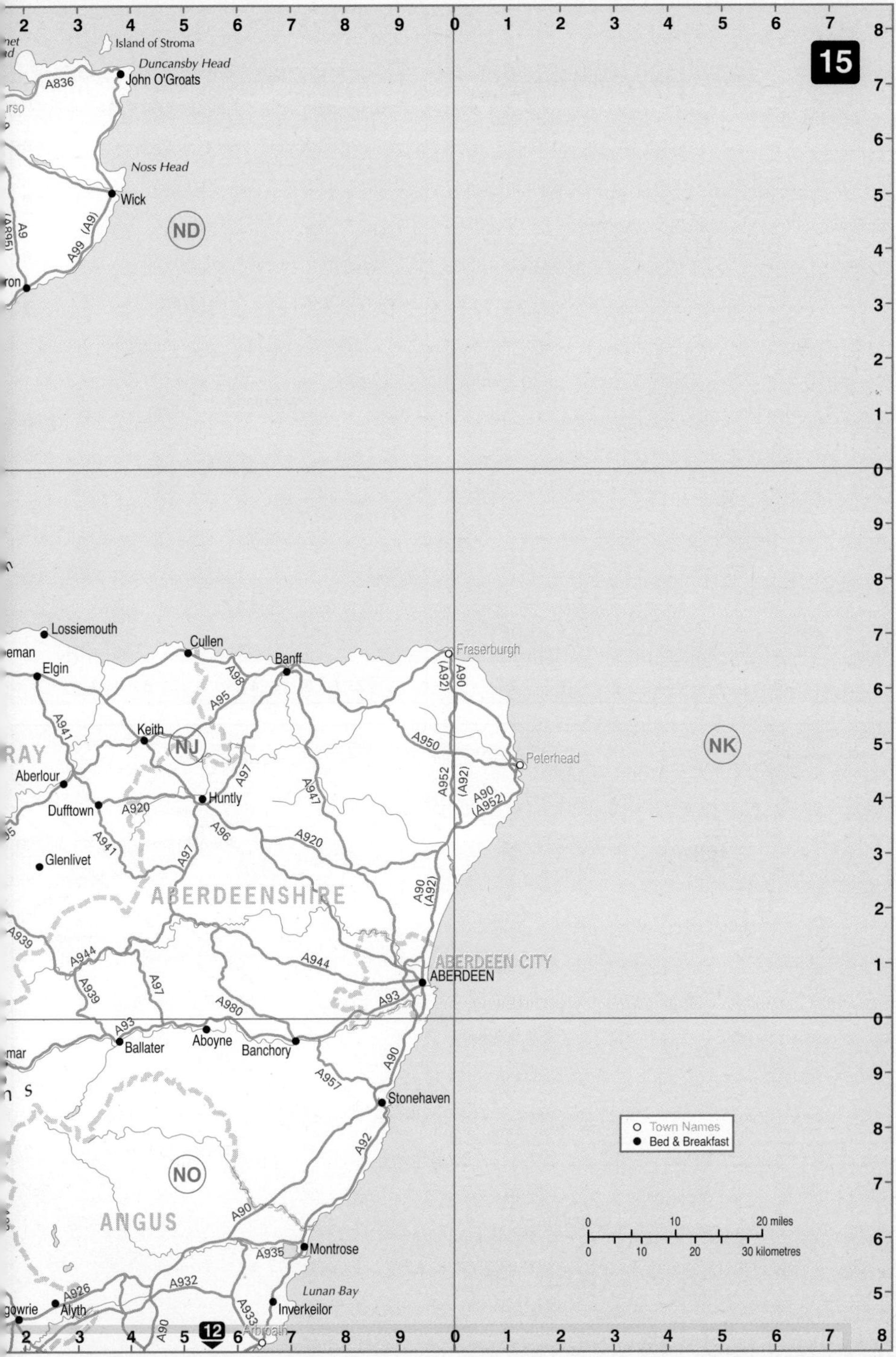

15
Island of Stroma
Duncansby Head
John O'Groats
A836
Noss Head
Wick
A9
A99
(A9)
ND
NK
NJ
NO
Lossiemouth
Elgin
Cullen
Banff
Fraserburgh
Peterhead
Keith
Aberlour
Dufftown
Huntly
Glenlivet
ABERDEENSHIRE
ABERDEEN CITY
ABERDEEN
Ballater
Aboyne
Banchory
Stonehaven
ANGUS
Montrose
Lunan Bay
Inverkeilor
Alyth
Arbroath
A98
A95
A97
A941
A920
A96
A947
A950
A952
A90
(A92)
(A952)
A939
A944
A93
A980
A957
A92
A935
A926
A932
A933
12
Town Names
Bed & Breakfast
20 miles
30 kilometres

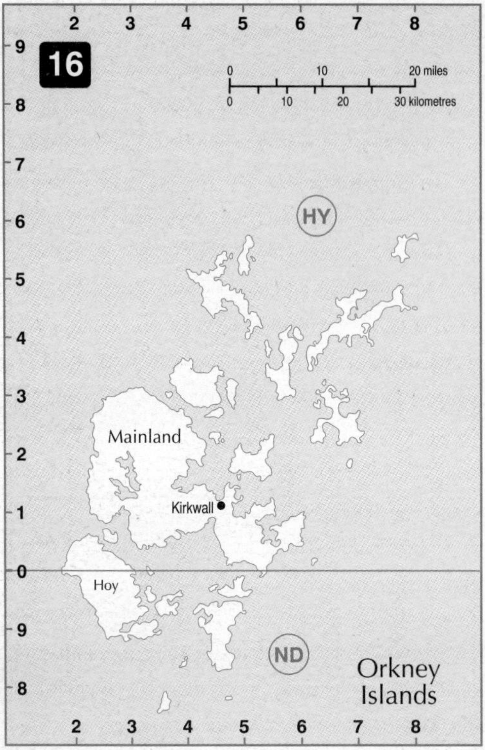
16
0 10 20 miles
0 10 20 30 kilometres
HY
ND
Mainland
Kirkwall
Hoy
Orkney Islands
2 3 4 5 6 7 8
9 8 7 6 5 4 3 2 1 0 9 8

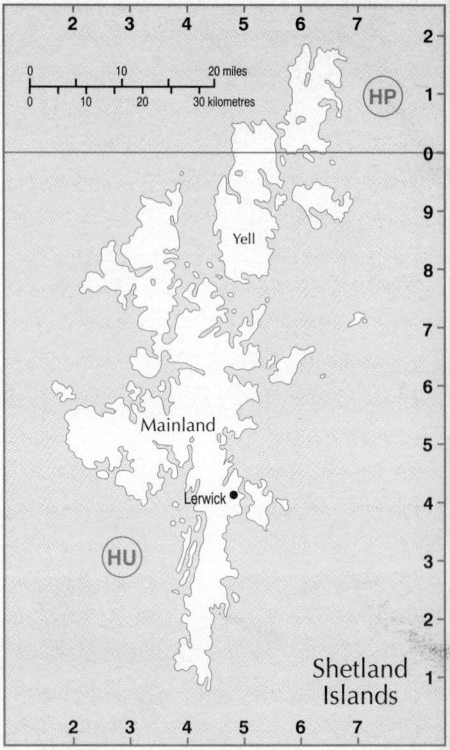
0 10 20 miles
0 10 20 30 kilometres
HP
HU
Yell
Mainland
Lerwick
Shetland Islands
2 3 4 5 6 7
2 1 0 9 8 7 6 5 4 3 2 1

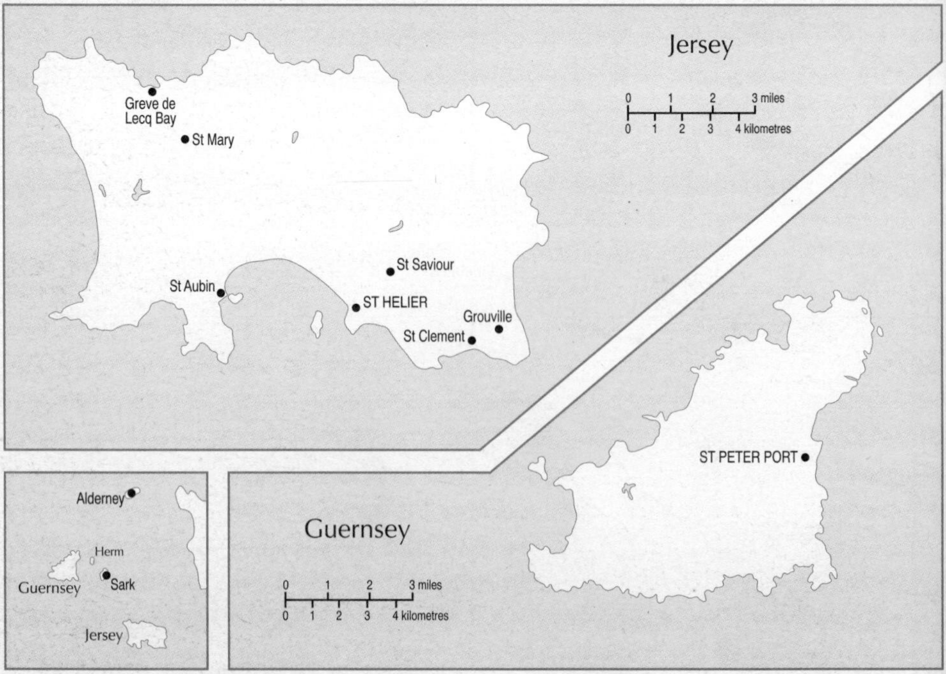
Jersey
0 1 2 3 miles
0 1 2 3 4 kilometres
Greve de Lecq Bay
St Mary
St Aubin
St Saviour
ST HELIER
Grouville
St Clement
ST PETER PORT
Guernsey
0 1 2 3 miles
0 1 2 3 4 kilometres
Alderney
Herm
Guernsey
Sark
Jersey